AS I SEE IT

To: Her Majesty The Queen
Buckingham Palace
London.
With Best wishes

[signature]

AUTHOR
26th April 2001.

AS I SEE IT

*How Cayman Became a Leading
Financial Centre*

Sir Vassel Johnson, Kt,, CBE

The Book Guild Ltd
Sussex, England

First published in Great Britain in 2001 by
The Book Guild Ltd
25 High Street
Lewes, Sussex
BN7 2LU

Typesetting in Times by
Keyboard Services, Luton, Bedfordshire

Printed in Great Britain by
Bookcraft (Bath) Ltd, Avon

A catalogue record for this book is
available from The British Library

ISBN 1 85776 596 6

CONTENTS

PART IV A CHANGE IN FOCUS

FOREWORD

Tom Russell, CMG, CBE

An autobiography makes a unique approach to history, and a failsafe interpretation of events. Sir Vassel's story combines personal memories, accounts written at the time and the deep research of a scholar. Its contribution to the chronicles of the Cayman Islands is invaluable.

What will fascinate the reader is the parallel development of the Cayman Islands and the author. His early days in Jamaica and Cuba, in conditions of hardship and uncertainty, mirror the Cayman Islands after World War I as the 'Islands that Time Forgot'. His steady ascent through the Civil Service to the post of Financial Secretary, and his canny management of the country's economy, are a metaphor for the astonishing economic development of the Cayman Islands and of the prosperity of its hardworking people. That the man epitomizes his country was acknowledged by the accolade of knighthood granted by the Queen before a throng of the people he had served so well, and to such advantage.

I commend this book to all Caymanians and to all whom the magic of these three islands has touched.

Tom Russell

Surrey, 2000

SIR VASSEL GODFREY JOHNSON:
AN APPRECIATION

The Cayman Islands Bankers Association

Sir Vassel, now in his 79th year, was the Cayman Islands' first financial secretary, who steered his country through a maze of legislation and attendant regulations that were required to establish an offshore financial industry. Who would have thought that 25 years later the Cayman Islands would be recognized as a world leader in this industry?

All of us in Cayman today have more than a debt of gratitude to pay for Sir Vassel's insight, courage and determination, which have carried us forward on a journey of exciting development as a leading world financial centre. His career details and list of achievements are too numerous to list here, but suffice it to say that his award from Her Majesty says it all. In the early days, he was prepared to take on officials in London whose educational background, expertise and formal exposure to the activities of the financial world were far greater than his own, and his quote on this was very simple: 'The fact that I hadn't gone to university was a drawback with certain professionals who looked down on me, but it didn't matter whether they looked down on me or looked up to me, I knew what I wanted to say and they had to fall in line.'

In closing, Sir Vassel would readily accept that 'behind every successful man, there is a very good woman'. Lady Johnson – thank you.

ACKNOWLEDGEMENTS

Most of the stories recorded in this book originated from events and developments during the earlier period of my life, at the time when I was privileged in one way or another to become involved with the development of the Cayman Islands. I wrote on page 1 of my first publication in 1982, *The Cayman Islands Economic and Financial Review*, the following: 'If one wishes to achieve a goal and toils diligently and awaits patiently the results he will succeed.' I hope that statement can also be equally applied to this autobiographical account of Cayman's rise, written 17 years later, as a leading international financial centre.

I will now record my thanks to those special persons who so kindly contributed to the work of this book, entitled *As I See It – How Cayman Became a Leading Financial Centre*. I am indeed indebted and very thankful to all of them, knowing that without their valuable input my task would have been very difficult. When I was encouraged by a foreign press reporter to write the story of how Cayman became a leading financial centre, I took for granted that he knew it was a story through which I lived, for he said, 'There is no one else to write it.'

Following the challenge to write this story, John Redman of the *Caymanian Compass* newspaper very kindly offered to assist me with the work. I spoke on tapes that were passed to John; he typed and edited each one at the same time. However, his time with me eventually proved very limited and so I decided to rearrange the basic work myself, for which I had to use a computer.

At the time, in mid-1994, I worked at Montpelier Properties (Cayman) Ltd as Managing Director (1983–97). I discussed the plan with my assistant, Jürgen Gerhardt, who is quite knowledgeable with computers and who also appeared very interested in my private project. I therefore requested his assistance in purchasing a computer and printer. Jurgen's help in this respect and in taking me through a course of training on the computer was invaluable. His wife Bridgette, who also worked at Montpelier as secretary, was of much assistance to me as well for she was using a computer at her desk. I must therefore extend grateful thanks to both Jurgen and Bridgette, for without their initial help with the computer it would have been difficult for me to start the work.

I also had valuable assistance on the computer both in the office and at home from my daughter-in-law, Sheila, Bud's wife, who is a trained computer technologist. My time in the office on the computer was of course limited to after-office hours and therefore explains the length of time spent on the project. After my retirement from Montpelier in June 1997, I was able to make better progress.

Two important subjects I discovered in the early days of my position as Financial Secretary were lack of basic economic infrastructure on which to build and cushion what appeared as oncoming development, and secondly, an urgent need to reorganize the Civil Service. Technical assistance was therefore requested from the British Government to investigate those two areas of need. London sent the request to British Development Division in the Caribbean in Barbados to the Head of the Division, William L. Bell, CMG (Bill). In mid-April 1969, Bill came to Cayman with a strong team of experts from his office. The story regarding how he dealt with both subjects is found in Chapter 9, 'Economic Infrastructure', written also with his input. I will long remember the assistance that came from Bill and his team: my grateful thanks to them.

In 1965, after the collapse of the seamen's trade, an industry that provided the larger part of the country's economy, it became quite clear that a new source of income must be found. I thought that because the Territory had no form of direct taxes, such as income tax, banking and trust associated with tourism would be an ideal alternative. The financial industry moved on quite well; however, in 1970, London discouraged its use by referring to it as 'tax haven business', which name did not go across very well among other countries with their direct tax systems. The call to replace our new financial industry undoubtedly upset me. However, in May 1971, I attended the British Treasury to deal with an exchange control application and took the opportunity while there to discuss Cayman's offshore operation. The Chairman of the meeting, Geoffrey Littler (now Sir Geoffrey Littler, KCB), was Treasury Assistant Secretary in charge of the Exchange Control Division. After the exchange control application was approved I went on to explain the proposal to abolish Cayman's offshore industry and the ill effects such a move could have on the Territory. Sir Geoffrey kindly gave the authority for the Cayman Islands to continue developing its offshore business. I was certainly delighted with that ruling for it allowed the Cayman Islands to become eventually a world-class financial centre. Thank you very kindly, Sir Geoffrey, for that important decision.

Thanks also to the late The Honourable Ernest W.P. Vesey, MP, of Bermuda, who in 1985 assisted me tremendously in preparation for negotiation of the US Treaty.

An individual to whom I must also give special thanks is the person who so very kindly agreed to write the Foreword to my book, Thomas Russell, CMG, CBE (Tom). Tom served as Governor of these islands for a period of seven years from 1974 and is considered the longest-serving Chief Executive among Governors and, previously, Administrators and Commissioners. Apart from coming to Cayman as Governor, Tom was also a past Financial Secretary and was therefore in a position to assist me in my official duties: my grateful thanks to you, Tom.

In dealing with the subjects of banks and trust companies under Chapter 10, 'Finance and Tourism', I had the valuable help of a good friend, Ronald E. Tompkins, TEP, ACIB (Trustee Diploma), while he was Managing Director of the local branch of the Bank of Nova Scotia Trust. In fact Ron and I have also been bridge partners at the Cayman Bridge Club for many years and held the Club's Cup for three years in succession, 1997–99. I wish to thank Ron for his valuable assistance to me with regard to my book.

Others to whom I must acknowledge indebtedness for assisting me are my wife Rita and our children. Thanks must also go to Ms Carol Winker for preliminary manuscript assistance and Mr Ramon D. Alberga, QC, and his son Michael, who is also an attorney, for graciously serving as my legal readers of the manuscript and contract with the publishers. I want also to mention that I had the benefit of a book-writer's opinion on the manuscript from a long-term friend and writer, Ian Paget-Brown of the United States.

Through the lapse of time and memory it has not always been possible to determine who took the various photographs which appear in this book. Some are from local media, *Cayman Free Press* and *Northwester*. To the anonymous other photographers, I can only express a general but heartfelt thanks.

A quotation I am fond of repeating is one written by the English philosopher, essayist and statesman, Sir Francis Bacon. This is what Sir Francis wrote: 'Out of monuments, names, words, proverbs, tradition, private records and evidences, fragments of stories, passages of books and the like, we do save and recover somewhat from the deluge of time.' Maybe I can apply these words partly to this publication on the Cayman Islands.

Sir Vassel Johnson
Cayman, May 2000

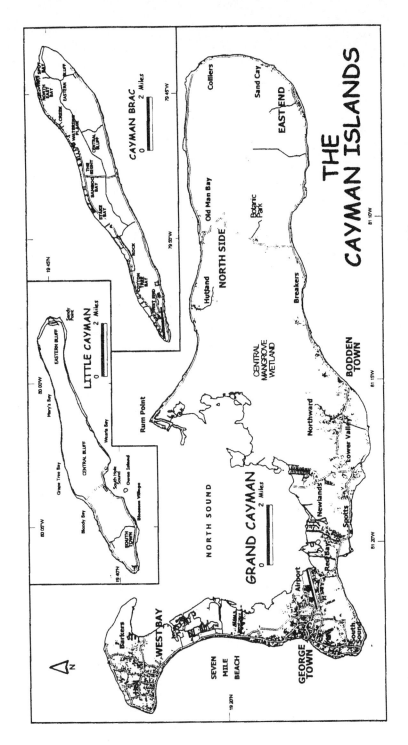

THE
CAYMAN ISLANDS

John Bebb, Land Information System, Cayman Islands, 1999

XV

PART I

MY YOUTHFUL JOURNEYS

1

Jamaica

Jamaica has a long and colourful history and in this first chapter I take pleasure in mentioning a few salient points for two reasons: first, because Jamaica is the land of my birth and second, because of Cayman's early political and economic connections with the larger island nation.

My own personal history began on 18th January 1922. I was born in Jamaica at a place known as Bath in Golden Grove, St Thomas. Before my birth, my mother suffered a leg problem for many weeks. Friends and neighbours advised her to go and make use of the mineral spring at Bath: she was then living at Vere in Clarendon, Jamaica. She took their advice and moved to Golden Grove, where she also prepared to be confined. According to my mother in later years, the leg did improve tremendously after bathing in the mineral spring (I forgot to inquire from her at the time if she also dipped me in the spring water for my legs have been in excellent condition ever since I was born). My mother also told me that when I grew older, probably at age six months, she had me christened at the Kingston Parish Church (Anglican) in Jamaica. When we came to Cayman in 1934 the Anglican denomination had not yet established here, so the family attended Elmslie Presbyterian Church in George Town. All the family and their children are still connected with the Presbyterian Church that has over the years united with the Congregational and Disciples of Christ denominations and is now known as The United Church in Jamaica and the Cayman Islands.

As we begin the 21st century, I still have some cherished recollections of events at the home where I lived in Jamaica; this was between the years 1925 and 1926. I was then three and a half years of age. I lived at the time with my mother and father in the humble surroundings of my mother's parents' home at Portland Cottage in Clarendon. I recall having a younger brother named Ivan: I understood when I grew older that he was born in 1924. My mother's eldest sister, Adella Megoo, and her four children also lived there. We children would have a wonderful time playing together. The house was an ordinary one-storey structure made of wood and roofed with zinc. It was divided into bedrooms, kitchen, dining room and a utility and storage area. The grounds surrounding the house had a few fruit trees like mango and pear and a little distance behind the house my grandfather cultivated a little garden, growing cassava, pumpkin and sweet potato. There was a grassed space in front of the house for the children to play.

An incident I have not forgotten happened one day when we children were playing the game hide-and-seek in the house. I ran into a hot iron sitting on an ironing board and cried out because the palm of one of my hands touched it. Cousin Mattie, Adella's daughter, who was ironing clothes but at the time standing with her back to the iron, rushed to the kitchen, fetched a bottle of molasses and smeared the burned area with the syrup. Molasses in those days was also used as a first aid home remedy for fresh burns. I walked around looking at the burn and feeling sorry for myself while licking the syrup dripping from my hand; its sweetness was a bit comforting to me. Other events were minor as is usual with small children. One day my mother carried me in the yard on the left-hand side of the house and showed me an area where, as a big boy, her brother Tommy would occasionally have a problem with something they called a spirit. It would move Tommy in a circling motion and eventually throw him to the ground. She went on to say that my grandparents reported the incidents to the police and other friends around but no one could help that situation. Eventually they had to stop Tommy going to that particular side of the house.

I must now take some time to mention my parents and grandparents. My father, Charles McKintha Johnson, was born at Four Paths in Clarendon, Jamaica on 28th March 1897 and died in Grand Cayman on 9th April 1947 at the young age of 50. The name given to Charles by his parents was Behari Johan Singh (an Indian name) but when he first attended school in Jamaica his teacher changed his name to Charles McKintha Johnson on the grounds that the Indian name was difficult to pronounce. The schoolchildren complained similarly about the name. The changed name went unchallenged for neither my father nor his parents objected. His parents were Harrigon Behari and Maria Singh, both of whom were born in the Punjab area of Northern India. Harrigon, who was a merchant in India, came to Jamaica with his wife and they both became involved in business in May Pen. They purchased a large property in that town which stretched across the Rio Mino, a river running through the district.

4

There they built their home and shops. They specialized in the grocery business, which included a large bakery. They had three sons – my father, Ramsingh and another I knew only as 'Papa'. They also had one daughter who unfortunately died at four years of age and in very tragic circumstances. My grandfather was working on his wagon at a weekend as usual and took off a wheel, leaning it against a tree so as to have it properly greased. The little girl came around unknown to her father and started jumping on the wheel. It fell on her, across the chest. She was rushed to the hospital, but there was nothing the doctor could do except confirm her death. Harrigon and Maria lived in Jamaica for the rest of their lives. They both died before I had the opportunity of returning to Jamaica: I did return, but afterwards in 1944, as a Cayman Home Guard soldier attached to the Military Hospital, Up Park Camp, Kingston, on a first aid course.

My father had his primary and secondary schooling in Jamaica and thereafter was employed in his father's grocery business. He told me how he liked working especially in the bakery section of the shop, for when his school friends came around he would take baking stones or tins filled with buns or bread and throw them through the window for the boys. His father often wondered why the bakery was not more profitable. Daddy was very kind-hearted to others, especially friends. He was also quite a reader and his choice of books was largely technically and educationally oriented. When he found a subject he liked, such as bees and honey, painting and agriculture, he would not only read the subjects but put what he read into practice to gain the actual art of applying himself to the work. He studied his parents' language, Hindustani, and eventually was able to speak it fluently. I found him a very interesting person because in conversation he was able to hold his own on any subject. The only art he didn't succeed in was that of teaching, for as my early teacher he made me scared of books and reading.

My mother, Theresa Virginia Johnson, née McDoom, was born on 16th July 1896 at Portland Cottage, Clarendon, in Jamaica and died at her Sussex Cottage home on Elgin Avenue, George Town, Grand Cayman, on 31st May 1995. She had attained the grand age of 98 years, 10 months, 2 weeks and 1 day. Her parents were John Baccas and Susan née Francis McDoom: both were born in Madras, South India. Baccas was particularly interested in travelling west because his trade was commercial business and he was in search of better living conditions. He met Susan when he lived at Portland Cottage in the parish of Clarendon and was doing business not far away at Alley. They got married and went to live in Mitchell Town in the same parish. The union produced ten children: five sons, James, Tommy,

Charley, Percy and Albert; and five daughters, Adella, Theresa (my mother), Maud, Mattie and Gwen. The last of both the daughters and sons, Gwen and Albert, died at the same time in August 1998.

Theresa was the kind of mother her children will always remember because of her care and love for all of us. She was also a special friend to the people she came in contact with day by day. For one thing, their cooking attracted many who would visit the home either along with their children or with friends who would come around to see us; they were usually offered a meal. Theresa did possess all the fine qualities of a mother and a friend.

In mid-1926, I travelled on a sailing vessel with my mother Theresa and younger brother, Ivan. My parents were obliged to leave Jamaica owing to the difficult living conditions at the time, brought about by a terrible world economic depression. After investigating other countries in the region, where hopefully life could be more pleasant financially, my father decided that Cuba offered the best possibilities of any. My mother and her two children travelled on a sailing vessel from Jamaica to Grand Cayman in transit and then after a few days in Cayman sailed on another vessel to the Isle of Pines. In later years my mother told us that we had sailed from Jamaica to Grand Cayman on the schooner *Fulmar*, captained by Gerald Coe, and then from Grand Cayman to the Isle of Pines on the schooner *Tuecoy*, captained by Charlie Farrington. (In the early 1990s, both Captain Carl Bush of South Sound and my good friend Louise Llewellyn of George Town confirmed the names of both vessels.)

My mother and younger brother became seasick on both legs of the journey from Jamaica to the Isle of Pines. As a result of their illness they had to remain lying in their bunks below deck all the way across on the boat. That was the first time I recall from memory being on a journey by sea. At four years of age I was strong on my feet and felt no illness while travelling. I was therefore able to move about and help my mother and brother by keeping them supplied with biscuits and soda water: this was the only food they could take on a seasick stomach. I will always remember the 'Uneeda' biscuits we carried, for they are certainly very delicious eating and good for seasick stomachs as well.

We landed first at George Town in Grand Cayman in transit to secure transport for the onward journey directly to the Isle of Pines. My mother found suitable accommodation for the few days we spent in Grand Cayman. We lodged at a house owned by William Anderson, situated on Elgin Avenue in George Town. The foundation of the building was erected on tall pillars that raised the floor level high off the ground. Because of the danger this posed to small children falling

6

out of the doorway on to the ground and getting badly hurt, my mother gave me the specific task each day of ensuring that my two-year-old brother did not fall from the doorway. I too was scared even to look out of the door owing to its height from the ground. During the time we spent in Grand Cayman my mother became very friendly with the late Mrs Gifford Anderson, our landlord's wife, and their daughter Louise, who was then 15 years of age and who in later years married and was known as Louise Llewellyn. Mrs Gifford and Louise would frequently visit us in 1926 in George Town. In 1995, Louise, then aged 85, took pleasure in telling me of her experiences when she had visited us nearly 70 years before and helped my mother with her two boys, I being one, of course.

I cannot remember leaving Grand Cayman for the Isle of Pines but do recall being on the boat as I had to repeat my job of helping my mother and brother, who were again on the sick list. The journey provided little or no experience for me. The first thing I remember from the trip, apart from attending to my seasick patients, is arriving at the mouth of the river that led on to the capital, Nueva Gerona, usually just called Gerona, where we were destined. The boat's speed reduced on the river because of the mangrove trees growing on both sides which prevented the full force of wind filling its sails. The short run on the river was somewhat interesting because of the birds of all colours and sizes and a few small land clearings. My patients remained below deck until we reached our destination at about 10 a.m.

As we arrived and the vessel was in the process of docking, my mother, Ivan and I were standing on the deck of the boat holding hands. My mother suddenly cried out, pointing at the crowd on the wharf and said, 'There is Daddy.' Yes, my father was on hand to take care of us, first through Immigration and then Customs. That was the first time I recognized my father and what he looked like. He was undoubtedly a very handsome man; I loved him very much.

According to a history written by Clinton V. Black in 1958, the Jamaican story dates back to its earliest inhabitants, the Arawak Indians, and moves on to the island's discovery by Christopher Columbus, who was born in Genoa, Italy in 1450. In 1492 Columbus informed the Spanish sovereigns, Ferdinand and Isabella, of an expedition he was planning to discover islands and mainland on the way to reaching Asia by sailing westward. Such a voyage carried three motives. One was the need to discover a new route to the Far East to replace the old one through the Middle East. The second was the desire to spread the Christian faith to distant lands. The third reason was his eagerness for geographical knowledge, finding gold and

7

adventure. The cost of the voyage would be mainly at the Crown's expense. Columbus sailed from Palos de la Frontera in Spain on 3rd August 1492 on his flagship *Santa Maria*. On 12th October he landed on an island in the Bahamas, which Columbus named San Salvador.

It was during Columbus' second voyage that he discovered Jamaica on 5th May 1494. He described Jamaica as 'the fairest island that eyes have beheld; mountainous and the land seems to touch the sky ... all full of valleys and fields and plains.' Jamaica's main attraction to Spain was for the island to be used as a supply base. In the early days of Spanish occupation, men, horses, arms and food from Jamaica helped the conquest of Cuba and much of the American mainland, but afterwards the island's importance grew less. Almost nothing was done to develop the country's natural resources. The chief trade was the supply of fresh provisions to passing ships travelling in both directions between Cartagena, Colombia and Havana, Cuba. The ships that touched in Jamaica brought supplies of clothes, wine, oil and a few luxury items. Vast herds of swine roamed the rich grazing areas of St Ann and the western parishes. A great number of these animals were killed each year just for the fat. There was an annual slaughter of cattle as well, but only for the hides and fat. From the skins of goats that ran wild in the mountains, excellent leather was made.

The country owes much gratitude to the Spaniards who introduced to Jamaica a number of fruit trees and plants in order to increase their food supply. Among those were the banana, plantain and all familiar varieties of citrus except grapefruit. They also grew sugar cane for local use, grinding it by horse-drawn mills. They cultivated cotton, cocoa, tobacco and grapes, from which liquor and brandy were brewed. In spite of those activities, settlers were poor and they were harassed by the high cost of living. At that particular point in time much activity took place not only in Jamaica, but also the rest of the Caribbean. Then came the end of the Spanish occupation of Jamaica, when on 10th May 1655 an English fleet appeared in Kingston Harbour sent out by Oliver Cromwell, Lord Protector of England after the execution of King Charles I. The English fleet was under the command of Admiral William Penn: it also carried an army of 2,500 men commanded by General Robert Venables. Cromwell also appointed a council of three commissioners to accompany the expedition, Edward Winslow, Captain Gregory Butler and Daniel Searle, Governor of Barbados. The action by the British Government was called the 'Western Design'. Its general object was that Britain had decided to take over all the vast territories in the Caribbean held by Spain.

8

Jamaica's long history, from the end of the Spanish military rule over the country and the establishment of a civil government during the 1670s, saw much change and development in the Territory. A 'new Jamaica' emerged in 1865, known as the turning point of the country's history. It had wide powers under a Crown Colony system of constitution. The Governor at the time, Sir John Peter Grant, one of the most capable and forceful Jamaica has ever had, promised that he would change conditions so that if the dead returned they would not recognize the island. To start off, the former 22 parishes were reduced to 14 and the government vestries which formerly ran local affairs were replaced by parochial boards in all parishes. An up-to-date police force was established throughout the island, together with district courts. The Anglican Church, as the recognized denomination, was until then financed by government. That was changed and the money given instead to education. The Institute of Jamaica was founded to encourage literature, science and art. A botanical garden (Hope Gardens) was developed along with many other public institutions and services. The administration under Sir John truly justified the name he gave to the country, a 'New Jamaica'.

The pace of progress under the Crown Colony system of government depended to a great extent on the type of governor appointed to the colony. For instance, Sir Henry Blake, who arrived in 1889, had his term of office extended at the people's request. He built roads and bridges and arranged the successful 1891 exhibition in Kingston from January to May, held in a large building erected for the purpose, which is now the site of the Wolmer's School. The exhibition was opened by Britain's Prince of Wales: he was later to become Edward VII. Sir Henry's relations with the Legislative Council were good. Those of his successor, Sir Augustus Hemming, were not as popular; however, with all his faults, he achieved much under the Crown Colony system. The political life of the country at the time seemed almost stagnant owing to the policy of government that imposed from the top a system under which no people would ever learn to govern in any areas of administration. Nevertheless, even under those circumstances, lying below the surface were changes at work. One that came to light fairly early was the part the Negro section of the community was beginning to play in public affairs. It was certainly encouraged and it grew until by the 1920s there were more Negro members than white elected to Council. By the 1930s, membership was almost entirely Negro. A similar change was also taking place in the Civil Service, where several Negro officers started careers which were to take them to top posts in their departments.

9

The country went through many experiences and changes in the years to follow. One was the economic and industrial depression of the 1920s. Another was a labour rebellion in early 1938, part of which was witnessed by my father, who visited Jamaica at the time. On his return home to Cayman, he told us some of the things that happened while he was standing at a corner of East Queen Street in Kingston and watching some of the events. We asked him if he was not afraid of the arms and other dangerous weapons used by the mob. He said, 'No, the organized armed resistance group were after bigger people than me.'

The result of the rebellion, which took place mainly in the Kingston area, was that two trade unions grew out of it, the Bustamante's Industrial Trade Union and the other run by a cousin of Busta, Norman Manley, whose union was known as the People's National Party. Emerging from that situation, Jamaica moved into a new constitution in 1944, based on a system of partial internal self-government headed by a chief minister. A few years later a slight constitutional reform replaced the partial system into full internal self-government headed by a prime minister. From that juncture, Jamaica opted out of a proposed Federation of the West Indies and moved into independence on 6th August 1962. Before independence, thoughts were given to Jamaica's national symbols, the national anthem and the flag. It was agreed to retain the 300-year-old coat-of-arms, but to change the original Latin motto for one of greater relevance in English. Recommended was 'Out of Many, One People'. This would serve as a constant reminder of the fact that the Jamaican nation is comprised of people of many races who have long lived and worked together in harmony.

At midnight on 5th August, at the superb newly built National Stadium in Kingston, the Union Jack, the flag of Great Britain, was lowered and the island's black, gold and green standard raised for the first time in its place. That symbolized the end of British rule and the birth of the Dominion of Jamaica. The next two days were declared holidays. Her Royal Highness Princess Margaret, accompanied by her husband Lord Snowdon, had arrived on the island four days before to officiate as the Queen's representative. She opened the first session of the first parliament, read a personal message to the people of Jamaica from Her Majesty and presented to the Prime Minister the Independence Constitutional Instruments. Those presentations are all preserved in the Jamaica Archives.

Four months before independence a similar break with the past had been ceremonially played out at the Queen's birthday parade at Up Park Camp. The men of the Royal Hampshire Regiment, the last of a long line of British troops which had served the country for more than three centuries, marched symbolically through the ranks of the newly formed Jamaica Regiment and the police, and then took their departure from the island.

At Jamaica's independence on 6th August 1962, which I attended, my own thought as a son of the soil was that the country then had much to offer its people by way of a strong economy developed under its Crown Colony system of government. Now, of course, politics strongly supported the movement to independence. I was afraid that after independence the economic situation could start to decline. This thought of mine emerged from a statement which was made at a rally of one of its political parties after independence. It suggested that Jamaica should have a look at introducing sometime in the future what they termed 'social democracy', which to my thinking could have meant a mild form of communism. Indeed ten years after that grand occasion of independence, and following the general election of 1972, the new administration became plagued with economic and social problems. That situation I should say continues to torment Jamaica as the country moves nearer the beginning of the twenty-first century.

It is a great pity that Jamaica, the island that was once the pride and joy of its people, fell in that manner. The world in fact looked upon Jamaica at that time as an island that had led the way among successful Caribbean territories. It was a country that had so much to offer, such as encouraging and attracting foreign investment and promoting local industry, thereby providing a bright future for its people. However, in time, a change in the ranks of Jamaican politics led the ship of state off course.

As one born in Jamaica, I followed its political trend for a number of years before and after its independence and therefore had a fair idea that disaster was lurking ahead for that island nation in its quest for political advancement. Jamaica is a country that could have developed to become the financial centre of the Caribbean. However, when it failed in that respect, Cayman grasped the opportunity to build its financial industry to the stage of claiming, in due course, not only first place among Caribbean offshore centres but indeed top global position.

Much of the above Jamaican history I learned from teachers and textbooks. Some of it I was privileged to live through and be a part of.

I recall that 19 years after the Jamaican 1972 general election, the Prime Minister of Jamaica, the Honourable Michael Manley, made a public announcement in the Jamaican *Daily Gleaner* in September

11

1991 advising that he intended completely to liberalize Jamaica's foreign exchange system. Because of a very run-down economy, Jamaica suffered for years from currency and foreign exchange problems. In our economic growth, we struggled from 1975 to abolish Cayman's exchange control system and so the subject of foreign exchange was very dear and important to me as Financial Secretary. Fortunately, five years later in 1980 we succeeded in abolishing the system: that certainly had quite an impact in assisting the successful development of Cayman's financial industry.

I wrote to Mr Manley on 27th September 1991 and congratulated him on the brilliant move he made in his attempt to relieve Jamaica's years of suffering from its weakened foreign exchange situation. In the concluding paragraph of the letter I said, 'Good luck to Jamaica. I am confident you have now put the country on the right course regarding its foreign exchange problems. With the right public co-operation, success is bound to come your way sooner or later.' Mr Manley replied on 24th October 1991 and thanked me for my letter. He was particularly delighted, he said, by my comments on the Cayman experience.

2

A Cuban Experience

The economic depression experienced in Jamaica by 1926 caused my father to consider moving elsewhere in search of better living conditions. His inquiries pointed to Cuba as an island that offered far better prospects than any other in the region.

Cuba is situated in the Caribbean, north-west of Jamaica and 135 miles south of the tip of Florida, USA. It has a land area of 44,000 square miles (more than one-half of the total land area of the West Indies and nine times the size of Jamaica). The capital is Havana. The country consists of the main island of Cuba, the Isle of Pines and other small keys along the north and south coasts. The main island extends approximately 780 miles in length, east to west, and is 19 miles in width in the north-west, and 119 miles in the south-east. The population in 1920 was just under 3 million. The Indian inhabitants were the aborigines of Cuba until the Spanish conquest brought them to near extinction. Since then the population became mixed, with three-quarters being white (mostly Spanish) and the remainder being descendants from the 800,000 slaves imported by the Spanish from Africa.

The climate of Cuba is semi-tropical, with two main seasons, dry (November to April) and wet (May to October). Annual rainfall averages 54 inches. The country's main economy has traditionally depended heavily on the production and export of sugar and tobacco. The fertile soil also supports the raising of cattle and the growing of coffee as well as a wide range of fruits and vegetables on a smaller scale.

Spanish is the official language of Cuba. Christopher Columbus claimed Cuba for Spain in 1492 during his first voyage to the Americas. The country's independence was eventually won in 1899 but was accompanied by a period of American occupation, during which time a number of schools, roads and bridges were built. During

13

World Wars I and II, Cuba was on the side of the Allies. In 1959, following a prolonged period of exile and guerrilla warfare against the Cuban government, Fidel Castro eventually won victory over dictator Fulgencio Batista and soon converted Cuba into the communist state we see today.

The part of Cuba where my father chose to live and work in 1926 was the Isle of Pines, a small island approximately 1,460 square miles in size, lying about 35 miles to the south of mainland Cuba. His reason for selecting this small island was because of its success in agricultural production (vegetables and fruits) which found a ready market in south Florida. My father went there alone to see if conditions were suitable. He was satisfied with what he saw of the island and therefore invited his wife and family to join him, after securing adequate accommodation.

Our first home on the Isle of Pines was just about 300 yards away from the same side of the dock where the *Tuecoy* landed us and the same side of the river on which the capital is built. The house, made of lumber with a zinc roof, was a beautiful little two-bedroom building. Another thing I remember about living there was the lovely aroma from the kitchen, especially when my mother made cocoa while preparing either breakfast or supper. Also I remember the yard with beautiful hibiscus plants blossoming in different colours, as well as periwinkles lining both sides of the walkway in front of the house as far as the gate that faced the river about 100 feet away. There was a road between the gate and the river.

The river, used by boats travelling to Gerona and beyond, is an inlet on the west of the island. It accommodated daily services by large flat-bottomed ships running passengers, mail and cargo between Gerona and other Cuban ports. The house we lived in had a verandah facing the river where the family could sit and enjoy the view of passing boats and other activities across the river, where Cuban gunboats and other craft docked. A few hundred yards away from the river a large sawmill produced lumber from the logs of pine trees grown on the island: the large number of such trees provided the name Isle of Pines. Near our home, to the east, was a large bridge which accommodated traffic to and from the eastern and northern parts of the island. To the east, the road went to Santa Fe, the first capital of the island, ten miles from Gerona. A few miles beyond Santa Fe was the island's third largest town, Santa Barbara. North of the bridge, the road led to the Presidio, Cuba's largest prison.

In 1931, while we still lived on the island, the Presidio was remodelled into a circular building under President Gerardo Machado's administration, thus increasing its size to accommodate up to 5,000 inmates. In 1953, the present communist dictator Fidel Castro was sent to the Presidio along with 23 of his insurgent companions after their unsuccessful assault on President Batista's troops in Santiago, Cuba. It is said that the Presidio is the birthplace of Castro's rebel army's plans for the conquest of Cuba, which finally happened in 1959 when Bastita was defeated. It is also said that Castro liked showing his guests the Presidio and boasting about the tasty plate of spaghetti he once cooked there as an inmate. In fact all the meals produced at the Presidio were usually very tasty: surplus from lunch was sent to the city in the afternoons and given to the poor, who made good use of it. While living there I heard it said that a few people who could well afford to provide their own meals would take advantage of the prison's food.

In the latter part of the 1920s, I knew Gerona as a neat and attractive little city, built on the bank of a river that to my knowledge had no particular name. To the south and beyond the city limits, about a mile away, was a range of mountains that produced good quality marble. A quarry with a large processing plant and other machinery stood at the foot of the mountain directly in front of Gerona. In later years we lived behind that mountain. I very often walked the road to the city, passing the quarry. I would occasionally stop, either going to or coming from town, to look at the operation, at the same time taking a rest from the heat of the sun.

The rocks at the lower parts of the hill were extracted by means of dynamite and conveyed to the nearby quarry for processing into sheets or slabs of beautiful marble. Near the quarry on the right-hand side of the road to Gerona lived a Russian sculptor, Belinki, who had a workshop built onto his dwelling house and there, from the sheets of marble, he made tombstones and other finished products. Occasionally while passing by I would stop at Belinki's to greet him and watch him working, sometimes in his workshop and other times at cooking his meals: of course he never offered me anything to eat or drink. One thing I admired about him was that he was always neatly dressed, as well as being a clean worker in whatever he did.

The streets of Gerona were usually clean and had very little dust. In 1926 there were just a few motor vehicles in the city for transportation purposes: wagons and buggies were still the main means of road transport and could also be hired. Many of the large grocery stores were operated, and perhaps owned, by Chinese. The people of the island were friendly and kind, always ready to assist or give a helping hand. As a boy of six I would go by myself into Gerona to shop. Occasionally it was dangerous travelling around, especially at night, if high-security prisoners escaped confinement and remained at large. In such instances the government would declare martial law and impose a curfew after 6 p.m., meaning that search parties would have the legal right to shoot on sight anyone who did not halt for identification when challenged.

After his arrival, my father was eager to get started with his farming project. That was in fact his main aim in going to the Isle of Pines, for he had been told that the markets in south Florida would buy all the Cuban vegetable products available. He planned to grow watermelons and vegetables such as sweet peppers, onions and tomatoes principally for the American market. He leased a plot of land across the river about a mile from the bridge where we lived. He had a fair amount of cash because of selling all his property in Jamaica before leaving. The first thing he did on the leased property was to build a house. It was made of lumber with a thatched roof. The size was slightly larger than the first one he rented by the bridge. He found that living in his own house was economically to his advantage as the lease was less expensive than rent. Secondly, by living on his own farm he was able to choose his working hours by starting and finishing at his convenience. Also, being on the farm would help to protect his crops from people who might stray in to help themselves. We moved to the new house in August 1926 and our first experience on the property was the severe 1926 hurricane the following month which caused much damage to homes and crops throughout the island.

I was four and a half years old, but I still remember quite well all about the hurricane. The skies did look suspicious during the previous few days but nobody paid attention to it, not being accustomed to watching weather reports. The hurricane struck at about 6 p.m. and blew from the south-east directly onto the front of our house. The wind was fierce and the rain heavy. Within a few hours two houses near ours blew down and the families came crawling on their hands and knees to take shelter with us. Daddy was very glad to see them for the reason – apart from being happy to assist the families with shelter – that our front door, which was facing the wind, began showing signs of weakening and the three men from the other homes could assist him if necessary. A short while after our visitors came, four men including my father began having to take turns, two at a time, to hold the door. My father had not had the presence of mind earlier in the evening to provide battens and nails to secure windows and doors should the need arise.

At midnight a dead calm came and everybody, thinking the hurricane was over, gathered in the out-kitchen to make coffee and tea and to fry johnnycakes to relieve hungry stomachs. After the midnight snack, just when everybody thought they were relieved for the rest of

16

the night, down came the hurricane again, this time heavier than before. The centre of the hurricane had in fact passed over the island, causing the one-hour calm. That is the case with all hurricanes: they create from the circling wind an area in the centre of perfect calmness. When the wind shifted after midnight it began blowing from the opposite direction. In short order the back door revealed the same weakness as the front door had, and the four men had to resume their turns, this time holding the back door. My father had not realized that the hurricane was not yet over when the calm at midnight came, and so he failed again to provide battens and nails for weak doors and windows. By that time I was dropping with sleep. My mother tucked me into bed at about 2 a.m. When I woke at 7 a.m. the hurricane had passed, leaving the island with a vast amount of damaged buildings, property and farms. That was really weather to always remember. The streets and roadways had to be cleared and repaired so as to get traffic moving again.

Daddy made good progress with his farm. In the meantime my first sister, Mary, was born on the morning of 29th January 1927; she died on 8th November 1996. I remember the morning Mary was born in our home: the nurse in attendance invited Ivan and me into the room to see the baby. I quickly discovered that she had a twin small toe on her right foot.

By late 1927 the crops were ready for reaping. Daddy began investigating market conditions in the United States and also shipping arrangements from the island. He visited the government's Agricultural Department, the Chamber of Commerce and shipping agents to get an idea what would be necessary to start the shipping process moving. To his amazement he discovered that after he had spent so much time and money building a house and growing acres of vegetables, the markets in Florida had been closed for most foreign agricultural products including those from Cuba and those we had grown. The reason for the closure of the American markets, as explained to my father by Cuban government officials, was the economic depression of the region just starting to affect living standards in the United States. Our vegetables, including the melons, rotted in the field because only small amounts were in demand in the Cuban market. Another problem was that there were too many big farmers producing the same crops: many had therefore to give up farming and turn to other occupations. While Daddy worried, I had a wonderful time on the farm helping Mother to take care of my baby sister. Whenever I felt the need for a drink of water I would run to the melon field, find a good big ripe melon, burst it on the ground and eat its red mellow centre to quench my thirst.

17

Like other farmers, Daddy began looking around for a job to support his family. He was promised one by an American developer about 10 miles from home. However, going to work that distance on horseback meant him starting out early on Monday morning and not getting back home before weekend. He therefore decided to look for a plot of land nearer the workplace, buy or lease it, and there build a second house. He found a plot to lease about 6 miles from where we lived in town, across the river. It was along the Santa Fe road and a short distance to the north at a place known as Mal Pie; it was actually 7 miles from Gerona. Mal Pie was about 3 miles from my father's workplace and suited him well. That distance would allow him to ride to work in the mornings and be back home in the evenings. He therefore built his second house there. It was about the same size of the first one he had rented in town by the river and very comfortable. We moved to Mal Pie in early 1928; it was there that Noel, the third son, was born in June of that year.

Daddy could only get to Gerona on weekends to do shopping and other business, since he got home from work late in the evenings. In the meantime, when my mother ran short of groceries at home during the week, she would send me to do shopping in town. I had to walk the 7 miles to Gerona and 7 miles back. At six years of age that was quite a challenge and an experience. However, I had no fear of walking alone because most people in those days were kind and helpful and there were no dangerous animals on the island to fear. Sometimes I would walk the full distance to and from town and sometimes I would be fortunate enough to catch a ride. One morning my mother walked me to the main road. At that time a truck came by; it stopped and offered me a lift. While we were travelling along my hat blew off my head and out through the window it went. Without saying anything to the driver, I opened the door and jumped out to retrieve the hat. I fell and hurt my head, but fortunately not seriously. After the driver washed the bleeding area of my head in a pool of water by the roadside and tied the wound with a bandage torn from his shirt, the bleeding fortunately stopped. On reaching Gerona the driver examined the wound again and, after the bleeding was found to be under control, he removed the bandage and put me out at the Chinese store where I was going to shop, which was very kind of him. After completing my errand I left for home and just after crossing the bridge a car came along and offered me a lift home. That was a real blessing considering what it meant for me to walk 7 miles back home in the heat of the day and with a bruised head. This bears out what I said before – that the people of the island were very kind and helpful, especially to strangers.

18

The experience at Mal Pie was not very pleasant for my parents. But I recall one incident especially that touched me about their love for their children. This was in early 1929 when my younger brother Ivan was lost. A quarter of a mile from our home lived another family, the Millers. Their house could not be seen from ours because of a slight rise in the ground between the two houses. My mother arranged to get milk each morning from the Millers, who had quite a few head of cattle. She would take Ivan to the hill, show him the Millers' house, then send him from there to get the milk. On his return home one of the Miller boys would accompany Ivan back to the hill where he could see our home and he would make his way there safely. One day Ivan did not return as expected. Instead of keeping his eyes on the house, he kept them on the trail and soon got on the wrong one, which led him 5 miles to Gerona and back to the house where we lived previously, a mile out of Gerona. The house was locked but the out-kitchen was open. Ivan later explained that when he reached there he was hungry and decided to walk another half-mile towards Gerona to the home of a friend, a Jamaican named McKenzie, for some food. However, nobody was home. He then walked back the half-mile to the old home, picking guavas on the way to eat for supper. He made his bed on the ground inside the kitchen with dried banana leaves and there went to sleep.

At home when night fell and the other three children were being put to bed, it was difficult for me to sleep listening to my mother walking around the house outside, crying and calling for Ivan. My father was working that day not far from where we lived. Someone notified him early in the day that Ivan was missing. He gathered a number of friends in the neighbourhood and started a search. He went to Gerona and reported the missing boy to the police, who also joined in the search. Night came on and, with no luck, he notified the police that the search would be called off for the night. On the way home he decided to go across to the old house although he had been there twice that afternoon and had seen no one. Entering the old kitchen he turned on his flashlight, looked carefully and to his great surprise and amazement his eyes lit on the little boy he was looking for whom he was so longing to see again. One can imagine the joy that stirred within him. He picked Ivan up, mounted his horse, and rushed back to town to report the finding to the police. He then took Ivan to a restaurant for supper and then hurried home. On the approach to the house at Mal Pie my father could not contain his joy and so when he called my mother she knew he had found Ivan. She rushed to the horse and, still crying, grabbed her little boy. I knew nothing about this until next morning when we all joined together at the breakfast table. One thing was missing from the table that morning: milk from the Millers. I find this story very fascinating and worthy of being told because of its mixture of human sadness and grief with enormous joy in the end.

Another incident at Mal Pie had longer lasting consequences. My mother unfortunately sprained her ankle while attempting to mount a horse during a riding lesson. Her sprained ankle required Daddy to leave work for a little while in order to care for the home until she recovered.

By late 1929 Daddy, becoming fed up with Mal Pie, decided to quit his job and move back to Gerona. He found a nice apartment in the city; it was there where my second sister, Beulah, was born in 1930. After living a short while in Gerona, Daddy found a job at a sponge house in the city: this is a factory where sponges taken from the sea are cured and made ready for the market. He liked the work because of the opportunity it provided for him to learn the trade while earning an income to support the family; at the same time he would be home at nights with his wife and family. However, by the end of 1930 the depression had so adversely affected the foreign sponge market that the local company was obliged to cut its labour force. Unfortunately those discharged were the most recent appointees, including my father. After losing that job Daddy decided to move back to the country and engage in farming once more. He found suitable property just 2 miles from the part of Gerona where we lived: it was immediately behind the famous marble mountain with the quarry that faced Gerona. There my father built his third house and the one in which my third sister, Louise, was born in September 1932: she was the last of his four children born on the island.

This is perhaps an appropriate time to mention my early education, much of which I received from my father.

In later years he and I enjoyed each other's company very much and we would often engage in discussions about interesting events and news. However, there was an unfortunate period at the beginning of my school days on the Isle of Pines when things did not work out quite well between us. English schools were not available in Gerona, where we lived at the time, and therefore my father elected to be teacher for Ivan and myself. He was rough with us, but the more so with me. He expected us to read fluently and to know lessons we were looking at perhaps for the first time. This made me nervous to the point where I could hardly concentrate on the work. The drilling went on day after day and week after week until fortunately an English school opened not far from where we lived and I was sent to it.

The teacher, Ms Turcell, was a truly nice lady. She came from an English Caribbean island. Of course she never moved in the classroom without her strap. She did not fail to use it either, when it was necessary to do so. However, she did not scare the children; instead she always had an encouraging word for each one. But after three months in that private school where I had made very good progress, we moved away from the city and my father assumed his old role of being our teacher again. He continued his stern and rough attitude, together with trying to get the lessons across in a hurry and things just did not work out. Gradually it drove me to dislike books. From that time I read what was necessary and important in school or at work; occasionally I would read other books but in the majority of cases I never reached the end.

Two books I did read from cover to cover were *Peter the Whaler*, given to me in 1935 by my minister, the Rev. James Moon of Elmslie Presbyterian Church, and *Mutiny on the Bounty*, presented to me in 1936 by the minister who succeeded Rev. Moon, the Rev. George Hicks. I loved those two books and, in the case of the latter, I promised myself after reading it through a second time that if ever I had the opportunity to do so, I would visit Tahiti to see the place where the mutiny took place.[1]

We had great fun living at the foot of the mountain in the third home we built and the fifth in which we had lived since arriving in the Isle of Pines six years earlier. By then I was over ten years of age and a frequent traveller on foot over the 2 miles to town, selling vegetables, chickens and eggs and shopping for the home. One evening I went to town, caught up with friends and, not watching the time, night caught me there. It was dark and, moreover, a dangerous inmate had escaped prison just a couple days earlier. Martial law was declared and curfew began at 6 p.m. However, I had to get home that night by some means. After reaching the outskirts of the city I decided to walk faster, sing loudly and make a lot of noise the whole of those 2 miles home on the dark roadway; it worked well for I never heard or saw anyone on the road.

Another afternoon when Daddy was away from home my mother sent me to town to get my hair trimmed. When I sat in the chair the barber asked me what kind of trim I wanted, *rapar* (clean cut) or *coca-pelar* (the sides and back). My father was always my barber and he just trimmed the sides, the back and thinned the top a bit. I tried to get this across to the barber; however, when he got through with

---

[1] I eventually made that visit to Tahiti in 1988 in circumstances I would never have dreamt of 50 years earlier.

me he had given me the *rapar*, leaving no hair on my head. As I was approaching home, my mother could see me from a little distance away. She ran to meet me and said, 'Vassel, what did you do with your head?' When I got into the house the two elder children, Ivan and Mary, had a wonderful time chasing me all around to get a feel of my bald head, for that kind of trim was strange in our home. (In early 1996, my younger son Bradley went on a student exchange programme to the University of Queensland in Australia. Returning home in August the same year, he presented us with a *rapar*, a bald head looking similar to his daddy's back in 1932.)

Because of insufficient rainfall, farming behind the mountain was not very successful and so Daddy decided to move away to a site 1 mile further to the south and by a river that had running water all year. There he built his fourth and last house on the Isle of Pines. It is interesting that my parents had four children born on the Isle of Pines and they built four homes there as well. Farming by the river was quite encouraging. Daddy planted rice, ground provisions and vegetables; he also raised rabbits and chickens. All those supplied the home the year round. It was on this property in 1932, while my father and I were working in the rice field one afternoon at about 3 p.m., that we saw in the sky above us a big dirigible craft or airship. Days later my father told me that it was reported in the Gerona press that its name was the *Akron* and that it was the world's largest airship, built by the United States. Unfortunately it was destroyed the same year during a heavy thunderstorm.

Adverse American market conditions brought about by the economic depression in 1927 continued in the early 1930s to affect the export of Cuban products to the United States. At home on the Isle of Pines only small proportions of even small crops moved in the local market; the balance had to be disposed of by using some in the home and sharing the rest with friends. Farmers continued to search for alternative employment in other areas such as construction and/or jobs in hotels. Others gave thought to moving away from home in search of better living conditions.

In July 1933, when Louise was just ten months old, another hurricane struck at about 5 p.m., which reminded us of the one in 1926. A friend of Daddy's from Gerona, Allen, came to our house that evening to encourage my father to move with his wife and family to town for the night. He invited us to his home; fortunately it was the nearest point in the journey to Gerona. Allen was afraid that if we remained at home, the nearby river might overflow its banks in the event of extra heavy rains that night and our chances of surviving the flood would be questionable. Soon we were on the

22

rough 2-miles-plus journey to Gerona, walking in the rain and with the storm's heavy breeze tossing us about. Allen had a tarpaulin he used to spread over my mother to protect her and the young baby, while the other five children and our father held each other's hands. After a rough journey we reached our destination tired, bruised, hungry and wet. Soon Allen's wife, Marie, had us dried, comfortable, fed and put to bed. My mother worked during the night to have our clothes dried and ready for the journey back home next morning. We got home only to find that everything was in the same order as the evening before. Although the 1932 hurricane provided some excitement different from the previous one, it was nothing to compare with that of 1926 in terms of damage to homes, property and crops.

Towards the end of 1933, three Americans, Jennings, Dan and Charles, came to the Isle of Pines. Their story was that, as American ex-servicemen of World War I, they had approached their government with requests for some form of relief job or other assistance to help their difficult living conditions brought about by the terrible depression at the time. Instead of sympathy, their government threatened them violently and this was the reason they fled the country to seek refuge. Of course my father and I, who listened to their story, sympathized with them on the basis of what they told us, for at the time we had no way of proving their story. As a result, Daddy invited the three men to stay with him and the family. They were very helpful I must say, assisting around the house and on the farm. The youngest of the three, Charles, moved around with me to learn something of Gerona. Soon he discovered that in the evenings, from a depot just across the bridge, the prison distributed its surplus cooked food to poor families. Charles went for this food and he and his other two companions enjoyed it very much, but just for a while until they could afford their own meals. After the Americans thoroughly enjoyed their stay on the Isle of Pines, they returned home to the United States in early April 1934.

About the middle of April my father decided to leave the island in search of employment or at least to find something better to do than what was available on the Isle of Pines at the time; it was a similar situation to that he experienced in Jamaica in 1926. His departure from the Isle of Pines was also due to the disappointing experiences that had continually plagued him ever since arriving on the island. It was a place he was once very excited about, but a place where, in a streak of hard luck, he had spent all his money without the pleasure of a return on his investment; an island he was never to see again. Now he was going to try his luck in Panama, another

23

Spanish-speaking country, where in those days the joke was, 'In Panama money grows on trees.' Well, my father certainly did not find any of those money trees, for again his streak of hard luck followed him.

Months went by and my mother heard nothing from Daddy. In the meantime tragedy struck the family. It had started in the latter part of 1933 while my father was home. Ivan, the second boy, was unfortunately struck in the right eye with barbed wire late one evening when he was returning home from gathering firewood. As he passed over the lower strand of wire it suddenly came loose and struck him in the eye. My mother, with good medical advice, treated the eye to near recovery – or so she thought. Sometime in July 1934 the eye became badly inflamed and my mother consulted doctors at Gerona's General Hospital and Medical Centre. Their diagnosis was that Ivan should be taken immediately to Havana for specialist assessment and treatment. My mother had little money and my father was away. However, through the goodness of friends and other kind people, she gathered sufficient funds for the journey.

At home the remaining five children were cared for by very dear friends who were also our neighbours, Mr Williams and his wife and family. They lived near to our home behind the marble mountain; we remained with the Williams until our departure from the Isle of Pines. After about 14 days my mother and Ivan returned from Havana with sad news. Ivan's affected eye and his central nervous system, the spinal cord, were poisoned with meningitis: the eye had had to be removed. Ivan was sent back home to Gerona to be near to the doctors at the hospital for treatment during his last days. Fortunately for us, a Caymanian family, Captain Anderson Watler (known to all as Capie Watler), his wife Clara and their children, who lived not far from the hospital, offered my mother a room for herself and Ivan. In fact it was Capie Watler's daughter China, then engaged to Donolly Yates, who gave up her room to my mother. Donolly unfortunately passed away on 17th March 1997, aged 87. His wife China lives in their home in Miami, Florida. She and all her family will always be our dear friends.

Ivan did not live long after returning from Havana. About ten days after, on 22nd August 1934, his neck and head began contracting or bending backward. My mother was advised to consult a lady medical specialist, living some distance out of Gerona, about Ivan's case and his neck contractions, and to ask whether she could recommend treatment or offer other forms of medical assistance. My mother hired a taxi and sent me with a note to the lady. She wrote a prescription and asked me to take it to the pharmacy. It was a special salve to use on his neck as directed. In a few days the spinal cord broke and his head fell forward, yet, in spite of that critical condition, Ivan lived for a couple days longer and died on Sunday morning 28th August 1934. He was buried that evening. It was a truly sad event, especially for my mother and myself as we three had journeyed together from Jamaica eight and a half years earlier.

Meanwhile we had received no letters from my father, nor heard anything about him since he left home in April. In fact it was not until we all met in Grand Cayman that he knew of the sad passing of his second child and son. This came about because Ivan's illness and death, plus the worsening living conditions for the rest of the family, had made my mother decide to return to her home in Jamaica by reversing the route she had taken in 1926. Just after Ivan's funeral service, my mother heard that the *Nunoca* would arrive in Gerona on 1st September from Tampa, leaving for Grand Cayman the same day. Having made up her mind, on her own initiative, she hurried to pack her luggage and make ready to leave. Captain Charlie Farrington, the same captain whom we travelled with to the Isle of Pines from Grand Cayman in 1926 on the vessel *Tuecoy*, was now in 1934 captain of the *Nunoca*. He would take us back to Grand Cayman. However, he would not agree to take us for what money my mother had accumulated in the two days after her decision to leave the Isle of Pines. She was therefore obliged to sell a cherished pressure cooker given to her by the three American friends who stayed at our home earlier that year. I carried the pressure cooker to our special Chinese shop near to the dock where the boat was making ready to depart. Although the sale fetched only 5 US dollars, Captain Charlie was then satisfied to carry us for the total amount of money we had.

As we steamed away from the dock in Gerona that evening and looked back at the place where we had landed eight and a half years earlier, all of us were in a state of sadness, grief and tears. Those thoughts would haunt us for many years to come, for we were leaving behind one of our loved ones buried in the earth of the Cuban Republic. However, as the boat reached the mouth of the river and faced the open sea heading south to Grand Cayman, the excitement of a new experience began to dominate our minds. As for me, I was somewhat concerned that, aged twelve years and eight months, my future in Jamaica, where we were ultimately bound, looked dim with all my schooling yet ahead.

I was soon back to my old job of caring for my seasick patients, headed by my mother. I could not help but reflect that, since my first voyage, I had lost one of my patients but gained four new ones. In

25

reconciling us to our unfortunate experiences on the beautiful Isle of Pines, that couple of days spent crossing the ocean to Grand Cayman did us much good. Here ends my Cuban experience.

PART II

A CHANGE OF NATIONALITY

3

Cayman – The Early Years

On 3rd September 1934 at about 5.30 p.m. the MS *Nunoca* steamed into George Town harbour and dropped anchor. Among the passengers on board were my mother and her five children. Soon the immigration launch was alongside and the Immigration Officer, Albert Panton, who was also the Clerk of Courts, stepped aboard. The passengers were processed in the ship's dining room. When it was my mother's turn, the Immigration Officer looked at her passport, then at her, and asked if she knew a Charles Johnson, 'Yes,' she replied, 'he is my husband.' Panton went on to explain that her husband had come to Cayman two days before from Colon and was now awaiting a boat to the Isle of Pines to rejoin his wife and family. He then promised that he would try to locate Charles Johnson by next morning and let him know that his wife and family were on this boat. He advised my mother that she and her children should remain on board the boat until tomorrow as it would be quite difficult at that hour of the day to find adequate accommodation ashore. The captain and crew of the *Nunoca* lived in West Bay and so the boat went there to anchor for the night; it would return to George Town next morning.

The night's rest on the boat at anchor was quite an improvement over the previous two nights on the open sea. The next morning the *Nunoca* steamed back to George Town and tied up at the dock located immediately behind the government's warehouse, known in those days as Mr Mallie's Wharf. Sure enough the Immigration Officer had found my father, for by the next morning he was there on the wharf waiting to greet his wife and family and to take us over. Later in the day after passing through Immigration and Customs, he hired transport and carried us to a house he rented on North Church Street at a place known as White Hall. The house was the property of Mrs Akie Ann Rivers, who coincidentally was the mother of Lumie, whom we travelled with on the *Nunoca* to Grand Cayman. Lumie had lived in the United States and was returning home on retirement. The house in which he lived in Grand Cayman was his parents' family home; we settled into a smaller one on the south side of the same property and were quite surprised when we saw our friend Lumie as our next-door neighbour. His mother lived with her eldest daughter, husband and family.

My first experience of Grand Cayman was that the area in George Town where my father took us was nice; we really liked it. I knew little or nothing about Jamaica, having lived there from birth to only four years of age. The Isle of Pines, where we went in 1926 and remained for eight and a half years, was more exciting although it ended with a death in the family. At that time my mother was determined to leave the Republic and return home to Jamaica. In fact, we reached Grand Cayman for the second time but have not moved on any further as yet. My father decided we should remain on the island for at least a little while to see the prospects of yet another, even smaller country than the Isle of Pines. His first impression was that Cayman seemed an ideal choice because immediately he could send his children to English schools, something he had hoped for in the past years. Over 60 years have come and gone and that little while in Cayman still lingers on, but only for six of the children. My parents (now deceased) had a family of eight children: four sons – Ivan (deceased), Noel, Patrick and myself – and four daughters – Mary (deceased), Beulah, Louise and Iva. The six surviving children are all married.

A few brief remarks regarding the Cayman Islands may be appropriate. At first George Town, the capital of the Cayman Islands, was strange to us, with the ocean nearly in the backyard of our first home. The property had a nice beach where we could enjoy sea bathing as opposed to a river bath as on the Isle of Pines. I gradually became better acquainted with the people and things around. Health was good, largely because inhabited areas were gifted with fresh sea breezes because of the small land areas. The men worked on fishing vessels at Mosquito Quays and took jobs in the merchant marine. Earnings by seamen helped to support the economy. The remaining few men at home worked largely in the shipbuilding industry, repairing roads and doing local farming. Apart from shipbuilding at home, the government was the largest employer and paid unskilled workers 3 shillings per day. Skilled wages were 8 shillings to 12 shillings per day with the cost of living correspondingly low. Staple foods included fish and, of course, turtle when available. Other meats like beef and pork were also available according to what families liked and what they could afford.

Sir Allen W. Cardinall was the Commissioner. I remember passing him on the streets many times. He was fond of taking his evening stroll in company with his three senior officials, Bertie Panton, the Dormant Commissioner, Ernest Panton, Clerk of the Legislative Assembly, and Roddy Watler, Chief of Police. On many occasions they walked onto the shore on the south side of Fort George in George Town. They apparently liked that site, the Parsons property, for it had a wooden bench bolted to the rocks on which they would sit, talk and watch the beautiful setting sun to the west. After the outbreak of war in 1939, Cardinall was transferred to the Falkland Islands on his promotion as Governor. He was an able Commissioner, largely responsible for organizing the 1936 Regatta involving 20 local schooners. Smaller craft, including 120 cat boats engaged in local fishing throughout the year, had their own racing competition during the Regatta. Tub races and shore-based games were also part of the week's activities. The event went on from Monday to Friday in January each year until 1939, when the war brought an end to it.

It is interesting to note that the Commissioner was the top-paid Civil Servant: in 1938 his salary was £550 per annum, increasing to £600 the following year. Casual labour was 4 shillings per day.

Local money in circulation as legal tender from the beginning of the twentieth century was the English currency, sterling (pounds, shillings and pence), although the US dollar circulated as well but was not accepted in government offices. In later years the English currency was replaced in Cayman by the Jamaican currency which was in 1968 decimalized (dollars and cents) and also adopted by Cayman. In 1972 the Jamaican currency was replaced by the Cayman dollar carrying the same value. There were no commercial banks on the islands other than a Post Office Savings Bank established in 1908. The bank paid two and a half per cent interest on deposits. Each depositor was allowed a maximum of up to £400 in the account but was not permitted to deposit more than £200 each year. In 1934 there were 78 depositors with a total of £1,993.50 in the bank. The estimated amount of legal tender currency in circulation was £3,000.

The law in force in the 1930s was the English Common Law, although in fact the Cayman Islands were discovered by Christopher Columbus of Spain on 10th May 1503. The three islands of Grand Cayman, Cayman Brac and Little Cayman have a total area of approximately 100 square miles. Grand Cayman is situated 178 miles west-north-west of Jamaica and 480 miles south of Miami. The three islands are said to be projecting peaks of subterranean mountains continuous with the Sierra Maestra range in Cuba. The largest island of the three is Grand Cayman, with an area of about 80 square miles.

The other two islands are 10 square miles each. Little Cayman lies about 60 miles north-east of Grand Cayman and Cayman Brac 7 miles further east.

It is thought that Cayman had been associated with Jamaica from the English occupation of Jamaica in 1655. From that time British ships would often visit Cayman to obtain supplies of turtle for the troops in Jamaica. Also, ships clearing in Jamaica for the United Kingdom would travel via Cayman for ship stores such as supplies of turtle and water. History records that at the signing of the Treaty of Madrid in 1670, by which Jamaica was ceded to the British Crown, Cayman was also included with Jamaica in that grant. There is no evidence of Spanish occupation of Cayman although Spanish coins have been found on the islands. Those coins could have been dropped around during the residency of pirates and buccaneers before they moved on elsewhere allowing other people to settle on these islands.

The administration of affairs began somewhere between the eighteenth and nineteenth centuries when Britain recognized the existence of Cayman and conducted its administrative affairs by way of Justices of the Peace commissioned by the Governor of Jamaica. The Justices functioned under the direction of one of their number, selected from among themselves, and referred to as 'Governor'. In 1831–32, however, the Cayman Islands, which had hitherto been under the control of the Governor of Jamaica, were given a local representative legislature known as the Assembly of Justices and Vestrymen. It virtually set the pattern for the future representative government of the islands. There were equal numbers of Justices and Vestrymen (24–30 in all). The Justices were appointed under a Grand Commission of the Peace, while the Vestrymen were elected from among the local population. From 22nd June 1863 the islands became a Dependency of Jamaica under an Act of the British Parliament, known as the Imperial Act. This meant that the Constitution of Jamaica also applied to Cayman. Under that authority the Legislature of Jamaica could make laws for the peace, order and good government of the Cayman Islands. Jamaica could also amend any of the laws passed by Cayman under the provisions of the Imperial Act. Those powers were closely defined. Since that time various laws were passed, both in Cayman and in Jamaica, until 1959, when Cayman under its new constitution ceased to be a Dependency of Jamaica.

In early times Cayman was completely isolated from the outside world and even from its own parent colony of Jamaica owing to lack of steamship communication services. This situation existed as late as

1916, when it was brought forcefully to the attention of the Governor of Jamaica during his official visit to Cayman. At that time the population of the three islands was 5,564 and the budget CI$8,000.

The administration of Cayman during the period 1898 to 1959 was under a Commissioner selected by London at the request of Jamaica. He was appointed under the Cayman Islands Commissioner's Law (Revised Laws of Jamaica 1938). The law authorized the Commissioner to perform all the duties, and have all the rights, privileges and jurisdiction previously vested in a Custos, followed by a Collector General and then by a Public Treasurer. The Commissioner was President of the Legislative Assembly of Justices and Vestrymen and was responsible for the preparation of the Budget and other business submitted to the Legislative Assembly for consideration. He was also Manager of the Government Savings Bank with its office at Government House in George Town, Grand Cayman, the office and residence of the Commissioner. The Commissioner's Office included in its staff an Assistant Commissioner and a Deputy Treasurer. The Assistant Commissioner was also Collector of Customs, Collector of Taxes and Postmaster, while the Deputy Treasurer was also Assistant Manager of the Government Savings Bank, Clerk of the Vestry and Immigration and Quarantine Officer. Cayman Brac and Little Cayman were under the administration of a District Commissioner. He also held the offices in the Lesser islands of Collector of Taxes, Postmaster and Foreman of Works.

In 1958, while the Cayman Islands continued to be administered by Commissioner Alan H. Donald, the Territory moved away from its near century-old constitutional status as a Dependency of Jamaica. The islands obtained a new constitution approved by London on 20th February 1958: it became effective in the Cayman Islands on 4th July 1959. With the new Constitution came changes. One of importance was regarding the title of 'Administrator', which replaced 'Commissioner'. Ten years later the title of Governor replaced Administrator. Alan H. Donald, OBE (1956–60), was the last Commissioner and the first Administrator and Athelstan C.E. Long, CMG, CBE (1968–71), the last Administrator and first Governor.

Under the new 1959 Constitution the Governor of Jamaica was also Governor of the Cayman Islands. Any official contact the islands wished to make with London continued constitutionally to be channelled through the Governor of Jamaica. A new Legislative Assembly was established under the new Constitution. Instead of 27 Justices of the Peace and 27 Vestrymen as were constituted in 1863, the new composition was 12 Elected Members and 3 Officials. The Assembly was presided over by a President who was the Administrator.

33

Referring to the 27 Justices of the Peace and 27 Vestrymen who constituted the 1863 Cayman Islands Government, brings me to where and how that early local government operated. The first capital of the islands, Bodden Town, had not yet been established. I had the opportunity on 25th November 1998 to visit Pedro Castle, a name well known to all residents (recently it was renamed Pedro St James). I toured the rebuilt three floors of that building. While I was on the second floor looking at what seemed a beautiful office, the security guard for the premises came in and volunteered that what I had been looking at was the meeting place of Cayman's first government. Later on the tour, I spoke to the lady in charge, exhibits manager Ms Mary P. Peever, and she confirmed its significance as the first meeting place of Cayman's earliest government.

The 7.65 acres of the old Pedro Castle property[2] was scheduled to be preserved as a National Historic Site and also to be promoted as a leading tourist attraction. To coordinate such an ambitious project, and ensure Caymanian involvement, a committee of local persons was appointed to conduct a comprehensive search for a group of experts to lead and direct the specialized research required for the restoration project. Canada-based Commonwealth Historic Resource Management Ltd (CHRM) was chosen for its professionalism and experience in key Caribbean restoration projects. CHRM and the Cayman National Historic Sites Committee joined together in the work, which was completed in three years. The grand opening took place on 5th December 1998. The Minister with Portfolio responsible for the project, the Honourable Thomas C. Jefferson, OBE, JP, in his opening presentation stated:

> This is a uniquely historic occasion, since it also marks the 167th anniversary of the birth of democracy in Cayman. Findings in the historical research confirmed that the original structure was built in approximately 1780 by William Eden, a native of England, as a large family dwelling or a plantation great house. Research further revealed that the original Pedro St James structure is the oldest in the Cayman Islands. It is a remarkable building for that period, when the population of Grand Cayman was only 500, of which 250 were slaves. It survived the devastating hurricane of 1785, which destroyed all other houses in Grand Cayman.
>
> In addition to its role as the birthplace of democracy, Pedro St James was one of the buildings from which the proclamation ending slavery was read in May 1835.

[2] Purchased by the government in 1991.

An interesting presentation at the grand opening was read by Mr Harwell McCoy, OBE, BEM, JP, from a historic text prepared by Dr Philip Pedley, head of the Cayman Islands National Archive. Among other important data reported, Mr McCoy read:

To visit Pedro St James is to step back in time to a Cayman that existed 150 to 200 years ago. The most important event to take place at Pedro St James is the one we celebrate today: the meeting of 5th December 1831. Those present at that meeting 'resolved that representatives should be elected for the different districts throughout the island for the purpose of framing Local Laws for its better government.' Who were the men that made this decision? We do not know their names, but probably many of them were the magistrates and lawmakers who called themselves 'principal inhabitants'. Prior to that time lawmakers in Cayman were self-appointed; there is no record of them ever being elected. What makes December 5th 1831 so important is that for the first time in Cayman's history those who made the laws acknowledged that they needed some mandate beyond their own collective wisdom and mutual approval. Their decision changed Cayman's government from being an unelected 'rule by the few' to an infant form of democracy.

Whatever the purposes and motives of those men who assembled there 167 years ago, and however limited the form of democracy to which they gave birth, their decision was a vital step. Five days after the December 5th meeting, the first elections were held. Electors chose a total of ten men to represent five districts. At the end of that month, on December 31st, the new legislature met for the first time and passed its laws [they indeed met on the second floor of Pedro St James].

Pedro St James was a small scale 'Great House' built by William Eden in approximately 1780. Eden came to Cayman from England fifteen years before and married a local lady, Dorothy Bodden, daughter of William Bodden, the most prominent Caymanian at the time. Eden then moved on to build Pedro Castle [Pedro is the District where the Great House was built]. For residents of Cayman, Pedro St James stands as a worthy celebration of the local democratic way of life and a living testimony to the rich history and unique heritage of these islands.

With its first Constitution Cayman also obtained in 1959 a coat of arms ordered by Her Majesty the Queen. It is used as the Official Seal of Government and continues to this day to be used as such. The Coat

35

of Arms was made into a shield with the insignia of the three islands. The design includes three stars representing the three islands. Above the stars is the lion, the symbol of Great Britain, denoting Cayman's close connection with the mother country. The lion also indicates that Cayman is a member country of the British Commonwealth. Above the lion is the turtle, Cayman's emblem. On the turtle is a pineapple (Jamaica's emblem), signifying Cayman's long and close association with Jamaica. The motto 'He hath founded it upon the seas' is taken from Psalms 24:2.

By 1962 Jamaica decided to abandon a proposed Federation of the British West Indian Territories and opt for independence within the British Commonwealth. As Cayman still maintained a connection with Jamaica in that the Governor of Jamaica was also Governor of the Cayman Islands, and also because Jamaica provided other essential services for these islands such as medical and prison facilities, the question arose concerning Cayman's future constitutional position following Jamaica's independence. The matter was discussed locally at great length between government, political and residential factions. There were two sides to the debate. One argued for Cayman to remain associated with Jamaica, but the opposition pointed out that in such an eventuality Cayman could face a dim future, because through such association the islands would likely lose their coveted identity. It therefore advocated a clean break with Jamaica and a move to British Crown Colony status directly with the United Kingdom government. The opposition, led by staunch politicians like Dr Roy McTaggart, William Farrington, CBE, and E.D. Merren, moved and passed in the Legislative Assembly a Resolution for the islands to become a British Crown Colony.

Jamaica's independence was celebrated on 6th August 1962. London simultaneously approved Cayman's Crown Colony status under a new Constitution also effective on 6th August 1962. With new changes, the Administrator became the Head of State in the Cayman Islands and external communications were forwarded directly to London instead of through the Governor of Jamaica as was previously the case. Cayman's move in that direction was eventually proven to be the right course.

Growing up in Grand Cayman

I had reached the age of 12 years 8 months when the family settled in Grand Cayman. I know my father's main concerns had to be providing a house for his wife and children, then finding the means to support them. One of my main concerns was my education, but there was time for some good adventures also as I met more people and made new friends.

The first house we lived in was owned by the Rivers family and was directly in front of the home of Cyril Borden, on the other side of the road where he, his wife Kathleen and their two sons and three daughters lived. As we arrived there straight off the *Nunoca*, Cyril's two eldest daughters, Ivylee and Margie, were our first visitors: of course they stood up in the yard outside the house looking through a window at their strange neighbours and not saying a word. However, weeks later, after everybody became better acquainted, we found both the parents and children of that family to be really nice people: in fact we found all the neighbours the same. The youngest son James, pet named 'Sonny Boy', lived with his grandparents, Jim and Minnie Borden, at the end of North Church Street in a place known as Dixie. The house is still there; its western boundary adjoins the property of the Wharf Restaurant, which was formerly the home of Gradson Parsons and his family. The Borden son-in-law, Esterley Tibbetts, lived in Jim's house until recently when because of illness he was moved to his daughter's home next door. Pete, as we knew him, was married to Jim's youngest daughter, Melba. He and my family were acquainted from back in 1928 when we all lived on the Isle of Pines. Pete worked for an American company and its restaurant in central Gerona, the capital. Some years after coming to Cayman and marrying Melba, Pete joined the Public Works Department and was at one time Acting Head of Department just before he retired in 1977.

Our rented house on North Church Street was on the sea side of the road, with a nearby outdoor kitchen further towards the beach. The beach at White Hall was very attractive and excellent for bathing. Also its south ironshore point was a famous place where sailing vessels would go and have their bottoms cleaned and painted. The ballast would first be taken out, followed by the pulling down of the boat by the masts over to one side for the job to be done, then repeated on the other side. A young lad could learn a lot, just by watching.

We lived at the Rivers' property until mid-1935 when my mother was expecting an increase in the family (Iva). We were obliged therefore to find more suitable housing accommodation so that my mother could be confined at home, as was customary. My father was fortunate enough to find another more suitable house not far away, owned by Jim (Cyril's father) and near to Jim's family's home at Dixie. At the time Jim was building the schooner *Jemson* immediately behind his house and not far from the sea. Besides being our landlord, Jim became a very good friend of the family; in fact his family became special friends to all of us. Jim could not ride a bicycle and would at times walk to town. I rode my father's German gent's bicycle and so I offered to teach Jim to ride so that when he could master the bike he would get one for his convenience. His answer was that 'a man seventy years of age has no business on a bicycle.' However, I insisted and eventually he consented to try bicycle riding. After my school adjournment at 4 p.m. during weekdays, and on Saturday evenings, I would give Jim his lessons, taking him on the sides of the main road. We had one thing in our favour in those days, the small amount of vehicular traffic on the roads. Eventually after a number of weeks Jim began riding by himself. When he gained sufficient self-confidence, he bought himself a bicycle and began cycling to town. As people saw him on the bike they stood in amazement asking others, 'Is that really Jim riding a bicycle?' Yes, it was, and Jim also became very proud of his achievement at the age of 70.

An incident I will always remember involved Cyril and myself. He and I would occasionally arrange to go shooting Cayman rabbits (agoutis) on my father's farm at White Hall. These little reddish-haired animals, known in Spanish-speaking countries as *jutia*, were very destructive to plantations, digging up and eating things like sweet potatoes and cassava. For this reason the government went as far as to pay a bounty for each head produced, as a measure to encourage farmers. The meat of the agouti was a good table dish, and for this and other reasons men were encouraged to go hunting these little animals. A well-known story confirmed by the former Minister of Tourism, Mr Norman Bodden, MBE, JP, was that his grandfather, Levi Bodden of North Church Street, brought a pair of these agoutis, male and female, in a cage to Cayman from Honduras many years before. Some time after they were on the island, both these animals escaped their confinement and took to the bush. They started producing young ones and increasing the wild stocks rapidly; this is of course one of the agouti's breeding characteristics. In a few years there were so many of them on this island, they became a menace to farmers.

Cyril and I would go hunting late in the evenings. On one occasion he elected to climb a tall mahogany tree in the middle of the field and I went to the eastern end and climbed another tree. We had to keep to the lee side of the agoutis (we recognised their tracks into the field); otherwise, if their sense of smell told them that people were in the field, they would not be likely to come out to feed. Both of us had our 12-bore shotguns. Unfortunately the rabbits must have suspected we were there for they did not feed in the field that evening.

38

When it was nearly dark I walked over to look for Cyril and found him sitting on the ground; he could scarcely talk. I inquired what was wrong with him. He explained that as he had climbed the tree he had tied his loaded gun with a thatch string, which is quite strong, onto his waist. When he was seated in the tree and was pulling up the gun, the string broke just as he tried to grab its muzzle and the gun dropped on the butt, muzzle up, but still did not discharge: that seemed nothing short of a miracle. He told me, 'I was frightened out of my wits and felt so silly to have pulled up the gun by the wrong end and with it loaded at that. I truly could not understand why I was so fortunate to escape being shot.' A few years later, during World War II, Cyril joined the merchant marine and went to sea. His ship was torpedoed and he lost his life. I am a great believer that God has a plan for each life and if someone is destined to die at sea, it is not likely he will lose his life on land.

We liked living at Dixie for it was also convenient for my father to get to his farm about a mile to the north in the White Hall lands, which were a part of the Parsons Estate. It was in the house at Dixie that my parents' fourth and last daughter, Iva, was born in August 1935.

Also in 1935, a building was constructed in George Town and opened on 23rd November. It was a joint effort by the Cayman Islands government and the Cuban government to accommodate a combined wireless telecommunication system for the local government and a meteorological weather bureau for the Cuban authorities. The equipment and staff were the responsibility of the two governments' respective offices. The wireless section of the building was seen as Cayman's first step towards establishing a cornerstone for its future international telecommunication system. The other section used by the Cubans for a meteorological office was very important to these islands and the surrounding area. It gathered weather information during the hurricane season especially for distribution in the region. The wireless equipment cost the Cayman government CI$1,392, of which $664 was raised by public subscription. The installation of the equipment, which was undertaken by Cable and Wireless Limited, Jamaica, included one type S100 short wave telegraph transmitter of 100 watts aerial power capable of operating on a range of 30–60 metres.

The opening of the station was attended by a very large crowd, including me and, by coincidence, a little five-year-old girl (Rita Hinds) from South Sound who was to become, 17 years later, my bride. Among the officials attending the opening was the Jamaican Superintendent of Telegraph, Mr T.J. Guilfoyle. He represented the

Governor of Jamaica. Also attending were Señor Castro, Sub-Secretary of Agriculture at Havana; Dr Jose Carlos Millas, Director of the National Observatory at Havana; T.I. Rees, British Consul-General at Havana; and W.H. Stephens of Cable and Wireless, Jamaica. During the opening ceremony the Governor of Jamaica sent a message to the people of these islands via the Cayman Station. The reception was very clear and could be heard via a loudspeaker by all attending the function. Following this a telegram of loyal greetings was sent to His Majesty the King, who graciously replied. Other messages were exchanged with the British Secretary of State in London, with Ceylon, the Falkland Islands, Sydney, Vancouver and Cape Town. Messages were also exchanged with the British Caribbean Islands. Caymanians at the ceremony were very delighted that at last they could communicate with the outside world. That was indeed quite an achievement and the reason we should pay special tribute to the Chief Radio Officer, Arthur Bodden, and his Assistant, Clarence Thompson, who as Caymanians led the way, as they were indeed the master radio operators at that ceremony.

In the following year on 20th January, King George V died. Just a couple days before the royal death, a large limb from a breadfruit tree near our house snapped and fell to the ground on a night that was quite calm though the tree and limbs were in very healthy condition. My father thought that the breaking of the limb represented a token of some death of distinction, and so it was.

Perhaps this is now an opportune time to mention the disappearance of the *Nunoca*, the motor ship that was to leave Grand Cayman and never be seen or heard of again. It became a sad story and certainly Cayman's most mysterious case to this day of a missing boat in the absence of a hurricane or any other form of bad weather. In April 1995 I spoke with Captain Charles Kirkconnell, who lives in George Town but is formerly of the sister island of Cayman Brac, about the missing *Nunoca* as his family owned the ship. He recalled that the *Nunoca* was built by a partnership involving the Farringtons of West Bay and others in the same district towards the end of the 1920s to replace the sailing vessel *Noca*, which had replaced the schooner *Tuecoy*. In 1935, after we arrived in Grand Cayman on the *Nunoca*, its West Bay owners wished to terminate the partnership but the owners could not come to an agreement on terms and conditions, and so they placed the matter before the Grand Court for a resolution. The Grand Court had the boat put up for auction and R.B. Kirkconnell & Brothers of Cayman Brac, Captain Charles's father and uncles, won the bid and became the new owners. Captain Charles also said that H.O. Merren & Co., then the leading merchant in

George Town and in fact the Cayman Islands, offered to take 25 per cent of the shares in the *Nunoca* but not until the Grand Court's auction was settled. However, the events below prevented Merren's equity participation in the *Nunoca*.

Before the auction, the *Nunoca* plied between Grand Cayman, the Isle of Pines and Tampa. After the purchase by Kirkconnell Bros. the boat was captained by Moses Kirkconnell, one of the new owners: the scheduled service then changed to Grand Cayman, Cayman Brac, Kingston, Cayman Brac, Grand Cayman and Tampa. On 4th July 1936, the *Nunoca* departed Grand Cayman for Tampa via the Isle of Pines and has never been heard of since. The *Nunoca* carried empty petrol and kerosene oil drums on deck for refilling in Tampa as was customary in those days before oil storage facilities came to Cayman. She also carried other items on board that could have floated had the boat encountered bad weather like a hurricane or been destroyed by fire and sunk: yet no traces of the *Nunoca* were ever reported in spite of the widespread publicity about her disappearance. Weeks after she departed for Tampa, many speculations and wild rumours hit the streets, even reports that people in the United States had seen and talked with two of the *Nunoca*'s crew members: however, none of it was ever acknowledged or confirmed. The disappearance of the *Nunoca* on that voyage in mid-1936 continues to this day to be Cayman's only such unresolved sea mystery. Of course in those days nobody knew or heard anything about the mysterious and, according to reports, disastrous 'Bermuda Triangle'.

Towards the end of 1937 my mother was again expecting another increase in the family: this time it was the last boy, Patrick. Again the house at Dixie was not too convenient to accommodate the in-house delivery as the family was outgrowing the premises. My father therefore decided to search for another house. He found one owned by Euphemia Nixon on Edward Avenue (formerly known as Rock Hole) and moved there at the end of the year: Patrick was born in that house in April 1938.

On the Isle of Pines my father was first engaged in farming and when that failed due to adverse economic conditions he worked in a sponge establishment. In Cayman he tried his hand at farming, painting and the processing of sponge for foreign markets. The sponge business was owned and organized by Dr Roy McTaggart, who became aware that my father knew the trade well. Sponge was fished at Mosquito Quays, brought to Grand Cayman, processed here and then shipped to Germany, where demand was great as the product was used for various purposes but mainly (as was the strong opinion) for cleaning guns. (Of course a few years later in 1939 when

41

Germany went to war, that confirmed the Germans' urgent need for sponge.) The first few shipments of the finished product fetched such excellent returns that Dr Roy decided to expand the business. He built new premises with improved facilities for processing the sponge. However, shortly after moving to the new facility, problems arose that eventually led to the folding of the business. A German new-comer to the island named Dagon, who married the sister of Ainsley Bodden of a George Town family, applied to Dr Roy for a job at his sponge house on the grounds of references he obtained elsewhere and was given employment.

My father knew Dagon from the Isle of Pines, where they had both worked at the same sponge house, but Dagon was a cook for the establishment and would scarcely have known much about sponge processing, especially for foreign markets. I remember while living on the Isle of Pines going to the sponge house selling chickens and eggs and Dagon was the cook who bought my goods. Dr Roy paid Dagon 20 shillings sterling per day and continued paying my father less than half of Dagon's wage, 8 shillings per day. That resulted in disaster for the business. My father applied to Dr Roy for an increase in his wage on the grounds that he had built the business, which was still developing successfully. Dr Roy made promises to my father, who after a few weeks lost faith in Dr Roy and quit the job. After the second shipment under Dagon, with a lower-quality finished product, the sponge business folded. The wooden sponge house, built on the site of the present Paradise Reef Restaurant, deteriorated in later years and was finally washed away by storms and north-westerly winds.

After the experience at the sponge house, my father did painting of private homes in George Town. One of the employers, Ainsley Bodden, once told me that my father was the cleanest and best painter he had ever come across. He also said, 'Brother, after your dad painted the inside and outside of my two homes, not a drop of paint could be found anywhere in the houses or on the ground outside.' My father was also known for his more artistic painting. This he did on the reverse side of glass which was afterwards framed. By that process the painting could last for an indefinite period of time. Two special verses of scripture that he did in this manner on separate sheets of glass specially for his home were, 'God is Love', taken from I John, chapter 4, verse 8. The second was, 'I will never leave thee, nor forsake thee', found in Hebrews, chapter 13, verse 5. Those two framed verses my father hung on the walls of his living room on the Isle of Pines when my brother Noel was born. The paintings dis-appeared about ten years after, while we were living here in Grand

Cayman: perhaps it happened when we moved from one home to another.

My Formal Education

My most noted experience in Grand Cayman at an early age was entering the government primary school in George Town in January 1935. The school was located on the sea side of North Church Street, in front of Elmslie Presbyterian Church. The school building was demolished in 1974 during construction of the present government dock. All of that area was developed into a fine modern docking facility that officially opened on 16th July 1977 and was operated by a port authority. After the new $4 million development was completed, that section of the street was renamed Harbour Drive.

Also entering the school in January 1935 for the first time was the headmaster, Thomas F. Hill. The only other staff member of the school was the assistant teacher, Miss Una Bush. After my enrolment, Mr Hill did the usual assessment of my academic background, as was the case with all other new students, before placing me at what he thought was an appropriate starting point. I was sent to read in standard two. The school used the *Royal Star Readers* from standard one to standard six. A student would end his primary education at standard six or when he attained age 14, whichever was first. However, after primary school age, opportunity was afforded to students who wished to continue in school and were able to qualify by completing at least standard five: they could enrol for evening studies that started at 4 p.m., after primary classes. The evening studies enabled students to sit each July for the first, second and third year Pupil Teacher Examination (PTE) set by the government of Jamaica. In 1942 the PTE was replaced by the Jamaica Local Examination. This occurred because both teachers and students complained about the difficult level at which the PTE papers were set. The failures just kept increasing each year. Students were not allowed to skip a year of the PTE studies and move up another year.

The third year PTE was the only form of secondary education available in the islands at the time. Many successful third-year students availed themselves of the opportunity to enter the Teacher Training College in Jamaica. Others would find the certificate useful in other respects, such as applying for office positions. In 1949, the Presbyterian Church of Grand Cayman established the Cayman High School, which included primary education. The high school section offered education up to Senior Cambridge level examinations, which

43

could admit students directly into English, Canadian and American universities. The Church of God (Chapel) also established in 1941 a primary and secondary school, Triple C, and qualified its students to enter foreign institutions of higher learning.

Before classes began that first morning in January 1935, the boys in standard three, sitting at their desk behind standard two where Mr Hill sent me, pulled me into their higher class. This went unnoticed by the teachers and so I started school with a sudden promotion to standard three. The push was in fact to my great advantage for at age 13, reading in standard two would have placed me at the age of leaving school in standard four, just short by one year to study for the PTE. I certainly did not let down the standard three boys. School was much fun at times and I enjoyed every day of it. While I was in standard four, the Governor of Jamaica visited Grand Cayman. The children in all government schools were invited to be at the public wharf at Hogsty Bay to greet the Governor when he landed from the warship on which he travelled. That morning we were all there from our school, boys and girls, all well dressed. What provided me with a big smile was seeing a boy from our school well dressed in necktie and jacket but with no shoes. As the Governor landed we cheered him and after he departed for Government House we also went home, having a school holiday for the occasion.

Commissioner Cardinall would each year stop by the school and through a window at the roadside call and speak to the teacher, Mr Hill, requesting that the children in the upper classes write essays. The first one was on St George, the patron saint of England. The timing for the essay-writing exercises was about two weeks before the day on which the occasion was observed: St George's Day was observed on 23rd April. In fact the same essay was repeated the following year. Quite possibly the Commissioner read through all the essays and, not being altogether satisfied with the first year's effort, requested the rewriting. The other essay to write, and the last one for me while in primary class, was on the Battle of Zeebrugge in Holland. Zeebrugge was a seaport facing the North Sea. In World War I, after the Germans captured the port, it was the scene of a daring British raid in 1918. Cardinall was a member of the British forces which fought in that battle, hence his interest. Teachers and students had quite a time finding anything on Zeebrugge but eventually and with the help of Cardinall the records of World War I on the battle were found and the essay written.

The George Town Primary School had a floor built on hardwood stilts raising it high off the ground because the building was so near to the sea. Under the floor the space was used to accommodate storage of items like ship's masts etc. At recess time boys would stoop and get underneath the floor, sit on the masts, talk and eat their snacks. There were two little stores not far from the school where snacks could be bought, one by the Town Hall, owned by William Nixon which sold very nice ripe bananas, candies etc. The other store was on North Church Street, owned by Mrs Cissy Bryan: she was then known to make the best patties in town. Little boys could run to these two shops and get back in sufficient time to enjoy their snacks before school recess ended.

One day under the floor, Norberg Thompson and I were talking and eating, he enjoying a ripe banana for no one else liked ripe bananas as much as he did. I was munching a nice hot patty. Our discussion was centred on money and wealth and what pleasure it must be for those people with lots of money. At that point I looked at Norberg and said to him, 'Norberg, you are going to be Cayman's first millionaire.' He replied with a smile, 'Not me, you.' Well, as it turned out I can confirm that my first million has not yet appeared anywhere near the horizon or even in my dreams, whereas my friend cannot say the same of himself. However, this I can say of him: he is very ambitious and never tired of putting to use his economic multiplier.

Another school memory is that a few of us boys in the upper classes were excellent writers, specializing in copy writing. The Inspector of Schools, the Rev. George Hicks, would occasionally pay courtesy calls on the school to say hello to the teachers and students. On these occasions three or four of the good writers including myself would get together and write a line of something like, 'Our inspector is a good man' and pass it to Rev. Hicks for grading. The group was always satisfied with the result and of course the inspector also enjoyed the fun of it.

The name George Hicks is well respected and cherished in the schools, in the church and among individuals in these islands. This is undoubtedly the reason that the government's Middle High School was in recent years renamed the George Hicks High School and the South Sound Branch of the Elmslie Church was renamed the George Hicks United Church, both in his honour. The same can also be said of Rev. John Gray, a Scotsman. He came to Grand Cayman in 1949 with his wife and family from Jamaica, where he was then working. He was employed specially to take on the Ministry of the West Bay (Presbyterian) United Church. He also at the same time became headmaster of the Cayman High School, which was then established by the United (Presbyterian) Church of Grand Cayman and put in operation with Rev. George Hicks acting as headmaster. Rev. Gray dedicated the rest of his life to the church and the school. This is why he too was honoured in recent years when the West Bay Church was given the new name the John Gray United Church and the Cayman Islands High School was renamed the John Gray High School. This school was taken over by the government from the church in 1964 under the government's 1961–64 Capital Development Programme. Rev. Gray also moved with the school to its new site on Walkers Road under the government's ownership and administration.

After I entered school in early 1935, realizing that I had only two years in which to complete my primary education, which ended at age 14, I paid very special attention to my lessons and always made sure that I kept ahead of the work. I also had to remember the promise I made regarding the favour from the standard three boys. The headmaster on the other hand was very sympathetic and considerate towards me for he kindly allowed me to remain in primary classes to the age of 15. This was so that I could at least read through standard five and be accepted to start studying for the PTE. The first year examination was scheduled for July 1938 and I passed it. I then sat the second year in 1939 but failed the exam. I was sick on the day of the exam in the following year, 1940, but I passed it in July 1941. At the age of 19 I had no fancy to go for the third year so I took a job in August 1941 in the Courts Office as an orderly. After six months, the Clerk of Courts, Mr Eddie Parsons, reminded me that unless I joined the police force I could not continue in the job because the salary was paid from a provision within the police department. I had no intention of becoming a policeman and therefore quit the job.

Coincidentally on my last day in the office my father came to see me and said that he did not see me studying for the third year PTE and wondered what was happening. He spoke in time, for it was then the end of January 1942 and the exam was scheduled for July the same year; studies had already been going on at the school since September 1941. I told my father that in my opinion attempting to pass the third year at that late stage would be an even worse experience than passing the second year after three years of trying. Furthermore, the syllabus for the third year carried seven subjects, one more (teaching) than the other two years; even worse, I had none of the books for the seven subjects. However, my father encouraged me to go and see the headmaster that very evening and ask him to enrol me for the exam in July. I did that and got Mr Hill's strong support. I then became quite serious about studying. The problem was to find books locally, for to order them from overseas would be too late for July.

I started asking around for books and was told that an Everard

Myles had recently done his third year; he was working abroad so I went to his mother, Helena, but she would not let me have the books. The following evening my father, who knew Mrs Myles well, went with me to her home again. Immediately we reached her front gate she saw us and went to a trunk, opened it, and let me select what books I wanted. (Over a period of 14-plus years to June 1997 when I worked at Montpelier Properties (Cayman) Ltd., I could look at Helena's house where I got the third year schoolbooks in 1942. It bordered on the eastern side of my office. Her house was demolished in mid-1997 by the new owner, Mr Jan Wilborg of Norway, and replaced by a beautiful office building.)

I started studying in earnest at the end of February and after four and a half months sat the exam and passed the seven subjects, with distinction in arithmetic. In 1945 when I re-entered the government, I enrolled for a correspondence course in accounting from the Bennett College in England. In later years in the position of Financial Secretary I also enrolled for another correspondence course in English from Wolsey Hall, also in England; I failed to complete both courses due to illness. In October 1969 I attended a six-week seminar at the University of Sussex in Brighton, England, for special studies dealing with Development Planning and Implementation. The seminar was very useful because of Cayman's proposed economic development at the time. In fact studies and recommendations for building the infrastructure for that development were completed shortly before the seminar. More details covering this will follow in Chapter 9, 'Economic Infrastructure'.

This ends the story of my early years in the Cayman Islands. Perhaps my ill health together with employment hardships I experienced at the time are the reasons I took such a keen interest in and, when in a position to do so, pursued, the local economic development to the stage at which we see it today.

4

World War II

The declaration of war by the Prime Minister of England, Sir Neville Chamberlain, on Sunday 3rd September 1939 stirred the entire world, although it was not surprising. The problem came about when Germany, in its plan for world domination, invaded Poland. That night at 7 p.m. my father and I went to the home of Ainsley Bodden to listen to the British Broadcasting Corporation's programme from London with His Majesty King George VI of England addressing the people of the British Empire, now the British Commonwealth. I imagine that people from all English-speaking countries of the world listened to those stirring words spoken by a monarch who up until the end of the war literally ruled the five oceans with the world's most formidable fleet. The King explained the events leading to the war while encouraging everyone to be steadfast and remain calm in what he described as 'difficult days ahead'. In those days there were two friendly homes in George Town with good radio facilities where we could go and listen to special broadcasts like this one; those were the homes of Ainsley Bodden and George Merren.

In 1940, some months after the outbreak of war, Commissioner Cardinall was transferred on promotion to the Falkland Islands as Governor. The Dormant Commissioner, Albert Panton Sr, a Caymanian, became Acting Commissioner until 1941, when Cardinall's replacement, J.P. Jones took over as Cayman's wartime Chief. (While Governor of the Falkland Islands, Cardinall received a knighthood from His Majesty King George VI. Governors in those earlier times almost without exception were knighted.)

All countries within the British Empire became involved in the war in one way or another. The Cayman Islands certainly made its contribution, starting off with Caymanian seamen's involvement in the Allies' Merchant Marine. From the start of the war local seamen were exposed to much danger as German submarines or U-boats infested the waters of the Atlantic Ocean and the Caribbean Sea in search of Allied ships. Many with Caymanians making up their crew complement were torpedoed and sunk, resulting in many Caymanians losing their lives at sea.

From the declaration of war in 1939 the Commissioner practised blackouts or 'lights out' representing preparation for an enemy attack. The practice was to get the message across to young and old alike that a war was on and that it carried with it very strict and sometimes unpleasant obligations. Also there were practices associated with war that had to be recognized, rehearsed and kept in mind at all times. One evening at about 7 p.m., as darkness slowly crept on, the MS *Lady Slater* arrived from Jamaica with passengers, mail and cargo and slowly made its way to 'Mr Mallie's wharf'. People gathered at the waterfront in the vicinity of the dock as was customary in those days when a boat arrived with passengers and mail. Many were out there to greet loved ones or friends or just to pick up mail from the Post Office. Then the Commissioner drove out on the waterfront with a loudspeaker shouting these words, 'Lights out, a blackout is on,' as the car moved slowly along, driven by Ira Thompson. He drove up and down two or three times along the waterfront and through the crowd, shouting the same message and not easing up on the volume of his voice. He even had me scared thinking real enemies were near at hand. Cardinall noticed that the *Lady Slater* was still steaming in slowly to the dock with all its lights on. Perhaps the captain did not hear the orders, or perhaps he did but for the safety of the ship had to take precautions in accordance with marine rules. Suddenly the Commissioner jumped out of his car and walked to the edge of the government's landing at Hogsty Bay not far from where the *Lady Slater* had reached. With an even louder voice he shouted, '*Lady Slater*, turn off those — lights.' The captain, Larry Bodden, must have heard the order that time if he had not before, for immediately the ship was in total darkness. One thought was that the captain's delay putting the lights out was due to a danger this might have posed to the ship, its passengers and crew to dock in what was a very dark night. The captain would have had certain obligations under his Master's Licence for the safety of passengers, crew and the ship. He therefore slowly reversed the *Lady Slater* back into the harbour and anchored there for the night. This was an indication that the captain would not breach the rules of his ship at sea. It was also an indication that Cardinall could enforce the formalities of war in getting his message across. As mentioned earlier, he was in fact a war veteran himself, having fought in many battles in World War I. Perhaps it is worth mentioning too that the following year the *Lady Slater* caught fire in Kingston harbour and was destroyed.

Some months after the start of war, most Caymanian able-bodied men were thinking of the part they could play in the war and the opportunity to make some money at the same time. At that time the local shipbuilding industry, which in previous years had gained a tremendous reputation and provided many local jobs, came to the end of its usefulness and men were looking elsewhere for employment. There were two industries still in operation, turtle fishing at Mosquito Quays and thatch rope making. The men were largely employed in turtle fishing while the women made rope. The rope was sold mainly in Jamaica to fishermen. In 1940 men took to the sea to join friendly ships, while others went to Allied countries to join their armed services. The then industrial activities together with income from seamen working on ships provided financial support for families at home while keeping the economy fairly active.

In 1941 recruits were sent to a British Naval Training Camp in Trinidad known as the Trinidad Royal Naval Volunteer Reserve (TRNVR). The men were taken to Trinidad on the MV *Cimboco*, the local mail ship that plied between Grand Cayman, Cayman Brac and Kingston, Jamaica. On this long journey to Trinidad, Eugene Thompson, a George Town sea captain, was the skipper. Captain Rayal Bodden, a master shipbuilder and civil engineer constructing commercial and government buildings in Cayman, was the chief engineer. Malcolm Coe, although crippled in both legs, was a brilliant telegraphist: he went as the wireless operator, and Rev. George Hicks of Elmslie Presbyterian Church volunteered to go along as chaplain. In spite of travelling the long journey to Trinidad in enemy submarine infested waters, the *Cimboco* made the journey to and from Trinidad safely. Perhaps the enemy would not have suspected the mission of the *Cimboco*. The recruited Caymanians were trained in Trinidad for active duty. According to a story told and confirmed by a former Caymanian Senior Officer of the TRNVR, Mr Harwell McCoy, OBE, BEM, JP, the total number of Caymanian men eventually counted at the camp was 201, and not the 200 listed. He also told the story that the Cayman group had so many men with the family name Ebanks (68), that the name posed problems at the camp and elsewhere in terms of identifying one Ebanks from the other, for when 'Ebanks' alone was called, no one turned up or answered. However, like the British all over, it was not long before a solution was found to the problem, as was the case when they looked for a quick answer to counter the deadly German magnetic naval mines launched against Allied ships in November 1939. Those mines were designed to explode when the metal hull of a ship forming a magnetic field, passed near it and caused a deflection of a magnetic needle in the mine, closing an electric circuit and thus detonating the charge. As soon as the principles were known, the British equipped ships with electric cables that neutralized the ships' magnetic field. The answer to the Ebanks problem was also resolved. Each Ebanks was given a number starting with 1 and ending with 68. The name of each person when called was followed with his respective number, for example, 'Ebanks No. 10'. Such calls were certainly answered without delay.

All the men who went to the TRNVR returned home in 1945 after the war except three who died while still attached to the Navy: they were James Johnson, Ulin Eden and Harvey Smith. There were also those who remained behind because of their involvement in marriages or in special jobs but who made it back home after a while. Most of the men remitted part of their wage to families at home, providing much needed income and at the same time boosting the Cayman economy. It should not be overlooked either that the men who served in the TRNVR played an important role in the war. They did not go to the camp to work for the Trinidadian government or just to be stationed in Trinidad. After training they were all given various assignments such as postings to anti-submarine patrols and to minesweeping and other naval unit duties.

During the war Trinidad was undoubtedly a most important and valuable colony in the British Empire because it produced oil. It was therefore a major bunkering and refuelling station. It was also a routing station where ships would gather, refuel and then be dispatched under sealed orders. One of the ships that went there during the war was the *Queen Mary*, destined for North Africa with troops. Trinidad has a very large harbour at Port-of-Spain with four main channels or *bocas*, three on the west of the port and one on the east. The harbour during the war was considered safe from enemy infiltration and attack. However, as was also told by Mr McCoy, about 2 p.m. one day a German submarine entered through a channel undetected; it was following close behind a big ship. Although Intelligence suspected something unusual taking place at the time of the ship's entry through the channel, no one at the controls could support the suspicion. During the same night a big flash and explosion took place in the harbour. The submarine torpedoed and sank the same ship it followed in, then surfaced and escaped through one of the channels. When it was challenged at the exit, the submarine pretended to be a friendly craft and continued on. Soon Hitler was on the air telling the world about this daring German infiltration and attack in what was then termed 'the impregnable Port-of-Spain harbour'.

51

What the enemies would have very much liked to do in Trinidad was block those four important channels. However, the security and defence systems organized there by the Allies were efficient, reliable and strong and worked well, except of course for the one German infiltration, superbly planned. In all the security and defence systems established at Port-of-Spain, Caymanians certainly played a vital part, and this manpower was considered a most important contribution by the Cayman Islands to the war efforts, especially at this strategic point of operation.

During 1941, the American government introduced the Lend Lease Act to promote the defence of the United States and to provide aid on a more or less reciprocal basis to all nations resisting Axis (German, Italian and Japanese) aggression. Under the Act the Americans negotiated with Great Britain a lease to establish naval bases in various countries of the British Empire, the Cayman Islands being one. In 1941 the United States moved into Grand Cayman and built a naval base, codenamed 'Baldpate', behind the government public library in George Town. During my school summer holidays that year I took a job to work at the base during its construction. I enjoyed the time spent there and the money earned as it became useful in supplementing income for the home.

The Americans were privileged to use any port in the Cayman Islands suitable and handy to their operation. Their principal duty or plan was to protect shipping of the Allies (United States, Great Britain, France and about 48 other nations) by patrolling, attacking the enemy and eventually gaining control of the seas and oceans of the world from German submarine warfare. It is recorded that in the first quarter of 1942 Germany opened its full offensive against Allied shipping and sank 90 ships along America's east coast. However, German submarine warfare against British shipping was active from the outbreak of war. After the United States entered the war at the end of 1941 following Japan's air attack on the American Naval Base at Pearl Harbor in Hawaii, it appeared to have been their plan to control the seas in preparation for the eventual invasion of France and Germany. France was overrun by the Germans in June 1940.

The base in Cayman became very important to Allied defence: it was also very popular with the Cayman Islands. For one thing it made a valuable contribution to the local economy, and secondly, it provided a good programme of social entertainment for the base personnel and their local friends and guests. The government's Town Hall just across the road from the base was used for special USO (United Service Organisation) and other shows, while at other times it would be used as a cinema for nightly shows. As a member of the

Cayman Home Guard I was always welcome to attend the shows. I had joined the Home Guard after completing my secondary education (Third Year Pupil Teacher Examination) in July 1942.

The Cayman Home Guard was established as a local military defence force. Its purpose was to be mainly engaged in training and in performing a 24-hour coastal service watching for enemy craft or any strange movements around the coastline. The latter service was considered quite complementary to the American naval presence in their struggle against German submarine attack on Allied shipping in the area. The Home Guard was a Cayman Company of the Jamaica Home Guard consisting of two officers and 40 men. The Commanding Officer was a Caymanian, Joseph R. Watler, who was seconded from the Cayman Police Force where he was the Chief of Police. The other officer, a lieutenant who was second in command, had been seconded from the Home Guard headquarters in Jamaica. The 40 men were all recruited locally.

To start training the men, a Sergeant Ernie Highfield of the Canadian Army was seconded here for a few months. The training was in flat foot drill and then Highfield would hand over to Sergeant Carley Nixon, who was also transferred from the local police force on secondment along with Commander Watler. The Home Guard built coast watching stations in all the districts. Two were in West Bay at Palmetto Point and North West Point, and there was one each in George Town, Pedro Bluff (near to Pedro Castle off Savannah) and Gauldin Bluff in East End (deemed to be the highest land point from sea level in Grand Cayman). The sixth station was built in the district of North Side. The stations were each staffed with four men, a lance corporal in charge and three privates. In the case of the George Town Station, the balcony of the old Court's House (now the National Museum) served for over a year as a lookout station for the harbour area. In early 1944 a new lookout post was built high up in a silk cotton tree that grew at the south-east corner of old Fort George in George Town. It was erected by Captain Benny Bodden and Fred McTaggart in the crutches of the tree and shaped like a little hip top house (a building with two plain roof surfaces from ridge to eaves). It was connected from the ground by a ladder with 42 rungs or steps. The post was staffed by one person at a time.

One morning a Home Guard, Nathan Ebanks, ventured to climb onto the roof of this little house instead of going inside where he could sit in a chair and enjoy the view in the harbour and around from Pedro Castle to North West Point. He suddenly slipped off the roof and landed on the ground between two of the tree's large roots that rose above the ground. It seemed as though a guardian angel had put

Nathan in that safe little spot on the ground. The Army rushed him off to Cuba for medical attention. Many Caymanians in those days went to Cuba for medical aid. On Nathan's return from Cuba on a sailing vessel a few weeks later, many of us Home Guards and other people went to see if he had really survived the crash; indeed he did. He walked off the boat all by himself. In fact he lived and prospered another 54 years, passing away in December 1998. Years after the fall he got married and raised a family of two daughters. The elder is presently the Director of the National Museum in George Town.

These six lookout posts provided a continuous monitoring of most of the coastline of Grand Cayman. All the posts were required to report by field telephones at half-hour intervals to army headquarters through its Central Reporting Office in George Town, at which Corporal Arthur Ebanks was the officer in charge for a while. Any information of importance was passed to the Government Security Officer, Albert C. Panton Sr, who would in turn dispatch it to the Security Office at the US Naval Base in George Town. This procedure established a useful coordination of efforts between the local American naval base and the Home Guard. The local coast watching stations reported suspicious movements and objects at sea or along the coastline and the Americans carried out the investigations.

Between 1939 and 1942 the waters around these islands became infested with German submarines; ships were torpedoed and sunk daily. At about 10 o'clock on the morning of 14th May 1942, a ship was torpedoed south-west of George Town and left sinking, with a huge stack of smoke rising from the horizon. I heard the news where I lived inland of George Town and rushed to the waterfront to virtually look at the war that had drifted into George Town. Many people on the western shores of Grand Cayman could also see the smoke rising from the hull of the sinking ship. Hours later the *Cimboco* went to the scene in search of survivors. That evening the boat returned to George Town with a number of men recovered from the disaster area. A couple had been severely burnt and as I looked at them chills ran through me. I had doubts that all of them would live. The worst cases were sent to Miami next morning and the others hospitalized in Cayman. The doctors in Miami did not succeed in saving the lives of those severely burnt. The ship was an Allied freighter, the SS *Comayagua* flying the Honduran flag.[3]

[3] In commemorating the 50th anniversary of the end of World War II in 1995, four stamps were chosen for the purpose, 10, 25, 40 cents and $1. The first had the design of Sir Vassel Johnson and Mr Clifton Bodden, the second a United Fruit Freighter, *Comayagua*, which was sunk in sight of George Town by a submarine, the third a submarine and the fourth a blimp.

There was an incident involving a German submarine hanging around Grand Cayman's North West Point shoreline that may be of interest. One morning an American freighter with supplies for the base steamed into George Town harbour and was scheduled to leave port the following evening. However, the base was apparently advised by the American Intelligence Services shortly after the ship's arrival to delay its departure 24 hours: no explanation was given for the order. On the evening of the original scheduled departure of the delayed freighter, the Cayman Home Guard Coast Watching Post No. 2 at North West Point reported, just before darkness fell, an object that resembled the periscope and bridge of a submarine. It was approaching from the ocean directly towards North West Point in the area of the post where the freighter would have travelled on its departure. A report was instantly dispatched to the Home Guard Headquarters through its Central Reporting Office and from there rushed to the US base. Personnel from both the base and the Home Guard immediately visited Post 2. They actually saw the submarine on its second approach to the land. The Americans advised that it was an enemy craft apparently awaiting the ship still tied up at the George Town docks. It was also their opinion that the enemy's visit was connected with the American Intelligence advisory signal the day before.

The next morning all the non-commissioned officers of the Home Guard, including me, were dispatched early in the day to Post 2 with orders to search the area thoroughly and submit a report to the Home Guard's Headquarters. The mission was on a Sunday morning: we went there in the Home Guard army lorry. Having seen nothing unusual around Post 2, we stated exactly that in the report to headquarters. After the exercise was completed we hired a private car, owned and driven by Rayburn Farrington, to take us back to George Town. I had never driven so fast in a car. Rayburn held the record as the fastest driver between the West Bay and George Town cemeteries. Of course no speed cops were around in those days.

In November 1942 I was promoted to lance corporal and put in charge of Post 3, on Pedro Bluff. In early 1943 I received a signal from the Home Guard Headquarters advising that on a certain afternoon before dark, a submarine's periscope and part of its bridge would be surfacing somewhere on the south side of the island off South Sound and in the view of Post 3. I was asked to report the sighting immediately. That afternoon two men were posted on duty instead of one and sure enough at a few minutes past 4 p.m. we reported the submarine. We understood later from headquarters that the craft was an American submarine on its way from Panama to the United States.

55

All the coast watching stations were connected to headquarters by magneto hand-cranked field telephones which were kept in good repair and working condition by the government's Public Works Department. A Spaniard named Theodore Mendez, who was very well known locally as he was married to a Caymanian, Perlina (formerly Bodden), performed the job of telephone service technician; he certainly knew his job well. Occasionally when the telephone rang a voice from the other end would be heard asking, 'You hearie me good?' That was Theodore. One day in 1946 after the war ended and while I was working in the Post Office, a clerk answered the telephone and reported that it was Theodore: he was still the telephone service technician and still asking the same question, 'You hearie me good?' On this occasion he was calling with the same question to test the Government House phone. A short time after the first ring, the phone rang again; that time I quickly answered it myself. Thinking it was Theodore calling, I asked the question, 'You hearie me good?' Well, this time the joke was on me, for it was Commissioner Ivor O. Smith calling from his office to speak with Desmond Watler. With a smile in his voice he replied, for he too knew Theodore's question quite well, 'Yes, I hear you very well indeed. Now may I please speak with Mr Desmond Watler.' Desmond was in charge of the office at the time. That incident, while it made a good joke, was also a good lesson for office staff and others, that nobody should misjudge who may be speaking on the other end of the telephone line.

In April 1943 while at Post 3, I went out to Savannah one morning to have breakfast as usual and to pick up some groceries for the post. Another member, Colin Bodden, went to his home in Newlands at the same time to get his laundered clothes and some ground provisions such as sweet potato, cassava and bananas, as the men cooked most of the time at the post. It was not unusual for two men to be away from the post at the same time. A little while after reaching Savannah I saw a jeep coming from the direction of George Town. It parked by the bluff road and three uniformed men got out and walked in the direction of the bluff. I telephoned the post to alert the men that visitors may drop in, but there was no answer. I walked from Savannah to the post only to find the three uniformed men inside and no one else. They asked me who was in charge: I told them I was. They asked if I knew the seriousness of an abandoned post: I told them yes. They then advised that the matter would be reported to my commanding officer. Shortly after they departed the two missing Home Guard soldiers returned. They had gone down to sea level, about 60 feet below the top of the bluff. They were there trying to catch some fish for lunch; they had been accustomed to doing that, but not to abandon the post for the sake of a fish meal. That afternoon the four of us were replaced and taken to the orderly room before the commanding officer and his second-in-command, Lieutenant Sidley, an Irishman. I was demoted back to a private, Colin lost his leave privileges for a month and the two fishermen, Ellsworth Terry and Herbert Kelly were confined for two weeks. Next morning on parade conducted by Lieutenant Sidley, he told me that it would be a long time before I could be reconsidered again for promotion. However, he remained in Cayman for another three months and the day he was leaving he called me to his office and replaced the lance corporal stripe on my shirt and said, 'Vassel, you have earned it, good luck for the future.' At the end of 1943 I was promoted to full corporal and in June 1944 to sergeant together with two other Home Guard colleagues, Clifton Bodden and Lindo DaCosta.

In 1944 a colleague in the Home Guard, Doren Miller, and I were sent to Jamaica on training. In Jamaica we were separated; he became involved in artillery and I in medical first aid. I went to the military hospital at Up Park Camp in Kingston, where I did my three-month course. It was suspected that our training had something to do with our eventually being included in the Second Caribbean Regiment, which was then in the process of selection and training. The First Regiment saw action in North Africa and Europe. The month after we arrived in Jamaica, August, a hurricane struck and caused extensive damage to the Port Antonio area. The disaster drew excursion tours to the area for weeks so that people could see the extent of damage caused by the hurricane. I completed my course successfully with top marks in the class of 26. By mid-October I was on standby to return home. In the meantime a severe hurricane hit Grand Cayman. I reached home three days after on the *Cimboco*; that was quite an experience for me, especially when we entered the very rough waters off Jamaica's Negril Point and headed for Cayman Brac. The next morning we were surprised to see many large ocean-going ships dodging the weather around Cayman Brac while the small *Cimboco* waded safely through it all. Grand Cayman withstood the heavy hurricane quite well except that afterwards there was an epidemic of dysentery. It resulted in seven deaths in Grand Cayman out of 216 cases reported in the three islands.

By mid-1944 the Allies had invaded Europe. The New Year 1945 therefore began with the excitement of peace filling the air. In August 1945 the war finally came to an end with the fall of Japan, the last of the Axis powers to surrender. Thus ended what has been described by historians as the most widespread, complex and deadly war in the

57

annals of human history. It was a war involving nearly all the countries of the world and causing as much destruction of civilians as of armed forces, a war with a terrible aftermath. That war involved brutalities on a scale never before known to civilized man. One of those was the holocaust, an attempt by Germany's Adolf Hitler's National Socialist Party, or Nazis, to execute by mass destruction in specially built gas chambers the entire Jewish population of Europe. This aspect of the war saddened the entire world, except of course for those people who were involved in that onslaught of outright criminal acts. In thinking about World War II with its massive property destruction and heavy toll of human lives, my deeper thoughts often recalled those beautiful and comforting words of the English poet, Laurence Binyon. In the fourth verse of his poem entitled 'For the Fallen' he wrote,

'They shall grow not old, as we that are left grow old,
Age shall not weary them, nor the years condemn.
At the going down of the sun and in the morning,
We will remember them.'

This is a seven-verse poem written in 1914 which was not given due recognition at publication because little was known then about the author and his work. However, in the period following the cruel World War II, the heartaches and chills from memories of loved ones lost became a constant source of grief and sorrow. At that stage the words of Binyon provided comfort and strength to all those who mourned their war dead. The poem has now certainly earned a well-deserved place in literature for its comforting words that are repeated each year around the world on Remembrance Day. In Cayman as in other Allied countries, there was a mixture of joy and sorrow at the signing of surrender by the Axis Powers, joy that the sting of a vicious six-year war had ended, and sorrow for those who had lost their loved ones.

Many Caymanian ladies during the war married men from the American naval base here in Cayman. As husbands and wives are bound together by their marriage vows and love for each other, it meant that those married women were obliged to follow their husbands on transfer or at the end of the war when the base ended its operation here.

When the base was closed in 1945 the Americans made a proposal to the Cayman government that in taking back their leased land they also took the buildings. Under Caymanian law the land would in any case own the buildings. However, the government accepted the offer

58

with much pleasure. The sale price was a peppercorn of US$10. The property was in 1949, with the government's permission, used by the Presbyterian Church to develop their Cayman High School, which included a preparatory section.

The war having ended, leaving behind its massive destruction, Cayman at once began concentrating on its post-war future as many men were returning home from various theatres of war, men who had to look for a fresh start in life. These were men who had to find new jobs so as to build a new income structure for themselves and their families, income that would also keep the economy of these three small islands fairly buoyant. As we look back over the years of the war, we can recall Cayman's many local activities. These were in the form of the Americans' construction of their naval base here, Cayman's volunteers going to Trinidad, the establishment of the Cayman Home Guard and seamen moving out to join the Merchant Marine. We see that much income was generated by those activities that assisted cashflow and the economy. It also gave many families a small nest egg of savings from which to continue maintaining themselves and their homes for the immediate future until new sources of income were found.

5

The Economy Before and After World War II

In 1935, the year after I came to Cayman from the Isle of Pines, the government began reviewing the islands' financial and economic situation to decide what progress if any could be made to improve things. That year began with the planning of a regatta, which took place in early January 1936 before the schooners departed for the turtle fishing grounds at Mosquito Quays. All of the islands' sailing vessels and smaller crafts were involved in the week's activities from Monday to Friday: there were also other forms of entertainment such as water sports and land-based games. The success of the first year's event was most gratifying and therefore encouraged the promoters to declare the regatta an annual national event. Each of the following regattas saw greater success until 1939, when World War II was declared. This sudden new crisis brought the gala sporting event to an end after January that year. Included in one year's programme was a pageant depicting the landing of pirates in Grand Cayman during its earlier days; the event was staged on the Dixie Beach at the end of North Church Street, thus its name Pageant Beach.

Each of the regattas from 1936 to 1939 was honoured with visits from British warships specifically requested for the occasions. Two sailors from the ships would accompany each schooner taking part in the race; this was largely to put a bit of prestige into the regatta's sporting affairs but also to ensure that rules and instructions regarding the races were maintained. The regatta was held under the auspices of the Cayman Islands Yacht and Sailing Club, founded in 1934, of which His Excellency the Governor of Jamaica was Commodore. The club was presented with 11 challenge cups as well as several cups to be won outright. The publicity given to the islands by the regatta was undoubtedly of great value to the efforts of promoting different forms of development. It resulted in several inquiries from many countries, including a few from South America regarding the islands' shipbuilding industry.

Among the warships that visited Cayman during the regattas, special mention must be made of HMS *Orion*, which came here in January 1938. She was a new ship of the cruiser class. During the war the *Orion* was one of the four British ships (the other three were the *Exeter*, *Ajax* and *Achilles*) that challenged the German pocket battleship *Admiral Graf Spee* in the Battle of the River Plate outside Montevideo harbour in Uruguay. As I remembered the story, the battle with the *Graf Spee* began when it was attacked by the *Exeter*, *Ajax* and *Archilles*, causing the German ship to run and take shelter in Montevideo harbour. The *Orion* then joined forces with the other British ships outside the harbour limits to await the return of the *Graf Spee*. This created much interest in Cayman. Pocket battleships, according to records, are somewhat like the battle cruisers of World War I – large, fast and heavily armed. In spite of this the British bulldogs were not afraid of the *Graf Spee*. Caymanians enjoyed listening to the battle in South America, not only because of knowing the *Orion* when she attended Cayman's 1938 regatta but also because we had great faith in the mother country's naval fleet, the most formidable in the world.

At the end of the 1938 regatta, the *Orion* departed Grand Cayman for Montego Bay, Jamaica. On the evening of the *Orion*'s departure, the captain of the schooner *Goldfield*, Reginald Parsons, mentioned to the owners he had a feeling that bad weather was brewing around the island and suggested taking the *Goldfield* into the North Sound for safety. It would normally in good weather anchor at West Bay, where all the crew members lived. However, the owners instructed that the vessel should be taken to West Bay instead. In the early hours of next morning, a cyclone moved down a short distance to the southeast of Grand Cayman and struck the island at about 5 a.m. The vessel *Goldfield* was at anchor in West Bay with a watchman on board, Gradson Parsons, whose home was in George Town at Dixie, the site of the present Wharf Restaurant. The *Goldfield* was loaded with cargo from Tampa, Florida at the time the cyclone struck: she came in from Tampa over the previous weekend before the regatta started on the Monday morning and therefore had no time to unload her cargo. The heavy winds from the cyclone caused the *Goldfield* to part her anchor and drift out to sea. The vessel rode on with the heavy winds. The day after the cyclone passed Grand Cayman, a request was made to HMS *Orion* through the Cayman Government Wireless Station for assistance to search for the missing *Goldfield*. Next day, Monday, a week after the start of the regatta, the *Orion* was back in Cayman and in the meantime it sent its patrol aircraft to scout around for the missing boat. For the search mission, the Commanding Officer of the *Orion* invited on board his ship Commissioner Cardinall, Captain Parsons of the *Goldfield* and his crew, including the Super Cargo Captain Charlie Farrington, to give some direction as to where they thought the *Goldfield* might have drifted.

The patrol aircraft and the ship searched the areas north of Grand Cayman for quite some time, until later in the afternoon the aircraft radioed the ship to say that the *Goldfield* had been sighted some 75 miles to the north-east of Grand Cayman. The *Orion* hurried to the scene, transferred the crew aboard the *Goldfield* and took the watchman aboard the *Orion*. Both the ship and the schooner sped back to George Town. Cayman will always be most grateful to the *Orion* for the assistance. Happily the Germans decided to scuttle their powerful ship, the *Graf Spee*, outside the harbour limits of Montevideo rather than face battle with the four British cruisers.

Coincidentally, my father visited Jamaica in 1938, travelling on one of Cayman's slowest vessels, the schooner *Amarant*. The sailing regatta had just completed its third year and at each one the *Amarant* was marked to be the last vessel to reach home base, sometimes hours after all the other vessels were at anchor. Yet she went on to establish a record return trip to Jamaica that no other sailing vessel had been able to accomplish. The reason for that record voyage was that the *Amarant* departed Grand Cayman on a Saturday, sailing south-east to Jamaica; she had a heavy north-west gale force wind, coming out of the Gulf of Mexico, behind her. After spending four days in Jamaica she returned home on Saturday, a week later, driven by a very strong south-easterly wind. Her schedule was for a two-week trip, but she was back in one.

The regatta greatly improved the social and economic climate in these islands over the four-year period of the national event, to the extent that the government's revenue doubled. However, in the first two years of the war (1939 and 1940) income fell due to a drop in postal revenue: the shortfall was made good by a subvention from local reserves. The bright financial position up to 1938 enabled funds to be provided for essential capital development such as construction of George Town Post Office and the George Town Public Library Buildings in 1939. They were followed by construction of town halls in West Bay, Bodden Town, East End and North Side. Those six buildings can 60 years later be regarded as the start of strong and reliable structures that have set the pace for what the country represents today: a little city with buildings no taller than four storeys. Before those buildings were completed, the war began and all able-bodied men not employed locally or elsewhere volunteered for services in the Merchant Marine, the Royal Navy like the Trinidad Royal Naval Volunteer Reserve (TRNVR) or the Army. Many Caymanians were at the time employed as skilled workmen in the Panama Canal Zone, Colon, by contractors of the United States Navy and Army. All those activities provided increased remittances to families at home, resulting in a sharp rise in the local spending power and reflecting increases in imports. The period of ten years from the start of the regatta to the end of the war certainly became the starting point for these islands to move on to greater prosperity in the post-war era and beyond.

The era following World War II began with sad thoughts of past cruel experiences. However, on the positive side was that the risks and dangers associated with war were behind and ex-servicemen, in whatever capacity they had served, were happily returning home to be once again with loved ones and friends. As stated earlier, all the men did not return home just as the war ended for one reason or another; a few remained either employed or with their new families elsewhere.

After the war and until the end of the 1960s, the economy depended largely on earnings from seamen, as there was little else for Caymanian men to do at home. The men either worked on ships or moved to other countries like the United States in search of shore-based jobs. The islands did have a few small industries in the pre-war days but they began disappearing during and early after the war. In fact, local shore-based industries employed only a small portion of the available labour force.

Agriculture as an industry had very little local appeal, although the government stressed the need to promote and encourage farming development in Cayman. This was based on the opinion that agriculture in any country must have a link to its economy, for no country should be satisfied to remain completely dependent on other countries' food. However, Cayman's chances of success in this respect were not very hopeful or encouraging in the early days. This was because the islands lacked what other agriculture-oriented countries have: good arable lands, mountains to attract rainfalls, rivers to provide good and sufficient water for irrigation, and a large population that traditionally depended on a certain amount of agricultural products. However, to develop agriculture successfully would be economically beneficial as locally grown food could reduce the cost of living compared to more expensive imported food.

It was always the opinion of Caymanians that their local rocky terrain could not, to any degree of success, assist large-scale farming or the economy. In fact, the lack of incentives from early times to promote agriculture was the reason that Caymanian men specialized in steamship and sailing boat occupations, which also in due time provided them with a worldwide reputation for the sea. Nevertheless, in spite of all the drawbacks to developing agriculture, a few local residents in the early 1970s and 1980s ventured seriously into big commercial farming. Perhaps the risk was just for experimental purposes in terms of using improved techniques for preparing the soil and thereafter producing crops and livestock for local consumption. The efforts certainly produced fair results. The government also began to assist farmers in the battle against insects and blight and in the obtaining of water for irrigation. It also later assisted in building a market for farmers so that their local farm products could be made available directly to consumers at competitive prices. Today agriculture, mainly crops and livestock products, has made fair strides in providing for the local population a proportion of the food they once imported.

Set out below are schedules of the local pre-war industries divided into what would be regarded in these small islands as major and minor economic activities. These industries were the main support of the natives from early years until the end of the war. At that time these home industries faded away and were replaced by income from men working on ships at sea which served the country well until the mid-1960s, when earnings of seamen fell drastically owing to a western hemisphere shipping slump. It was at that point that the present industries of finance and tourism began their building process.

Major Industries

Boat-building: For generations, Caymanians excelled as fine boat-builders and their products were looked upon as being without equal in this part of the world. The boats were built with such a high degree of workmanship that their lifespan measured twice that of similar vessels built elsewhere. Unfortunately the local boat-building trade did not attract foreign interest before the war except for a few orders from the United States and England. Because of lack of better-equipped shipyards, vessels built here were limited to sizes not exceeding 300 tons. Portions of the mahogany frames came from timber grown in Cayman; it is termite-free, unlike the Central American mahogany. The last boats built here were during the war when the builder Captain Rayal Bodden was given a contract by the British Admiralty to construct two trawlers. Captain Rayal hired all available shipbuilders on the islands at the time to work on these two boats so as to achieve a record completion and delivery time. This he succeeded in. However, by that time the war had ended and carried with it the fine boat-building tradition of Cayman. The advanced age of those possessing the shipbuilding expertise and skills also played an important part in the passing of the industry. The younger generation looked further afield to become involved in the growing technology of the era which would equip them for their future careers, especially after passing through an historic war that had given them a wider horizon of opportunities than that which they had known before.

Turtling: Another very well known industry in the history of these islands was fishing for green sea turtle and hawksbill turtle at Mosquito Quays off the east coast of Nicaragua in Central America. The green turtle caught at Mosquito Quays had two fishing seasons, January to March and July to September. Vessels would leave for the quays with turtle nets, equipment and general supplies of food to last for at least three months. They were required to obtain fishing permission from the Nicaraguan government on arrival there and when clearing for the return journey home to report their catch and pay an export royalty of 50 cents per head. The weight of a single turtle caught at the quays ranged from 80 to 200 pounds. The number of vessels involved in turtle fishing ranged between 12 and 18. When the vessels returned to Grand Cayman, the turtles would be crawled in the North Sound near to the George Town Barcadere. The turtles remained in the small confined area for a period of up to one month to allow sufficient time for exporting the larger portion to markets in Key West, Tampa, Panama, Jamaica and other Caribbean islands. The remainder would be butchered and put in the local markets for home consumption. Consumers thought that when turtles remained crawled too long, the meat, and especially the fat that flavours the stew that is so well liked by the natives, would change its taste. The same thought applied when turtles were caught at the quays in the off-season. I confess it was difficult for me to tell the difference in taste until I had lived here a while.

Canning: In 1952 a turtle soup canning factory was established here in Grand Cayman on the North Sound Road. Some of the products were sold in Europe. The cannery was operated on the basis of a monopoly of the luxury soup used even at royal banquets. However, the industry was doomed to failure shortly after it began production due to marketing difficulties in the United States. In a few years the factory closed its operation. The property, including land and buildings, was taken over by Caribbean Utilities Co. Ltd. It is the site of their present electricity production operation.

Local Green Turtle Farm: Since 1968 the green sea turtle had been reared in captivity in Grand Cayman and a few years later the effort developed into a local industry reaching commercial level. Green turtles were from the early days the larger of the two species caught in these islands, green and hawksbill. The green turtle was used in Grand Cayman both for commercial purposes and as a local food. Hawksbill fishing and trading on the other hand was a Cayman Brac activity. The turtle fishing industry was quite popular up to the war days but thereafter very few turtles were caught until 23 years later when a green turtle farm was established here in Grand Cayman. The industry was then revived and became a purely local activity confined to Grand Cayman. The farm was moved from the North Sound area many years ago to Goat Rock, North West Point in West Bay for better quality water for the turtles. After the establishment of the farm, a programme was put into effect whereby each year a certain number of young greens were released into the open seas in an effort to replenish and increase stocks in local waters. Today as we near the end of the century, many green turtles of various sizes can be seen in the waters around the islands.

The Hawksbill Turtle: The hawksbill turtle was once found in local waters but not any longer. Prior to World War II the hawksbill was caught at Mosquito Quays and other nearby locations like the Seranna Quays and Rosalind Bank. Its shell was marketed in England. It was very valuable and used for making jewellery and other items like cigarette cases, belt buckles and combs. Hawksbill meat was not of commercial value but the people of Cayman Brac preferred it to that of the green turtle, whereas in Grand Cayman the choice was just the opposite. Hawksbill fishing and trading was also confined to Cayman Brac, while the green turtle is a Grand Cayman industry. Fishing for turtle at Mosquito Quays ended during the war. Years later, foreign interests revived the industry in Grand Cayman so that today local residents can still enjoy regular meals of green turtle. More will be told about this industry at a later stage by stating its early problems and eventual success.

Thatch Rope: This was a well-known local cottage industry that should not escape mention. It was a Grand Cayman household activity engaged in largely by women with the help of children during their spare time from school. In time of economic need some men

66

with no other source of income would get involved with rope making as well, if only to assist their wives. The rope was made from a silver thatch grown in Grand Cayman and known originally as *thrinax argentea*. However, botanist Dr George Proctor later identified characteristics which made Cayman's silver thatch distinctly different from the one in the Turks and Caicos. The local silver thatch is now named *coccothrinax proctorii* and is our national tree. The shoot of the special silver thatch was cut from the tree before it opened into a broad leaf. It was then dried and worked into round straws; three pieces of the appropriate length were twisted together to make rope. The process was carried out by a local manual contraption that had worked well over the long period of the industry. Rope production peaked in 1921 when 1.2 million fathoms valued at $5,700, or $3 per 1,000 fathoms, were produced and sold. By 1946 the value of rope increased by 100 per cent. The industry remained active until the early 1960s when other cheaper products entered the market. The Cayman rope was in demand by local vessels and smaller fishing boats but the bulk of the production was sold in Jamaica to fishermen because of the rope's durability in seawater and its relative cheapness. A small amount is still being produced here for local use as souvenirs.

Minor Industries

Shark Hides: Shark fishing (for the hides) was a very small industry. The product was sold in England; it fetched a small and low price. The hides were used for making special leather goods such as shoes and belts. Shark fishing was only a late development and a sideline connected to turtle fishing as sharks were caught on the same turtle grounds at Mosquito Quays with worn-out turtle nets and chain lines. The species caught were the nurse and tiger sharks. The industry, along with turtle fishing, faded away during the war.

Lobster (Crayfish) Fishing: The lobster grounds were far away from these islands. The most noted were those around Mosquito Quays and on the reefs off the coast of British Honduras. Just a couple of vessels were engaged in the fishing and the lobsters were taken to chosen markets in 'live wells' in the vessels. The last markets known were those in Panama and the Canal Zone. After the 1938 lobster season in September, the two schooners involved, the *Hustler* and the *Radium*, were on their way home when they were struck by a severe hurricane. The larger of the two, the *Hustler*, did not survive: she was lost with all on board including many prominent Caymanian passengers returning home from the Canal Zone. The master was Captain Larry Bodden of George Town. The other schooner, the *Radium*, did survive the hurricane after her masts were removed and she was left to drift. The crew eventually reached home. The schooner was later passed on to the owners. That hurricane disaster certainly ended Cayman's lobster trade.

Red Mangrove Bark: The bark from red mangrove trees produced an excellent dye that was used during the process of tanning cowhides into leather. Locally the removal of bark from the trees became a small industry for those who were in need of the small income it produced. The trade, however, never produced more than a few hundred dollars per annum. The material from the red mangrove trees was shipped to the market in Jamaica, where tanning factories operated.

Cattle Hides: In the days before the war, Grand Cayman reared about 1,500 head of cattle and as they were butchered, and of course replaced by young heifers, the hides would be cured and sold in Jamaica for tanning into leather. The price was nothing to brag about, but, like the red mangrove bark, it helped a few needy families.

Handicrafts: This small cottage industry provided useful items just for local use and did not reach a level lucrative enough for the export market. Weaved thatch straw was used for making hats, handbags, fans and baskets; they were used by Caymanians and by the occasional visitor. A few of those items are still being made today.

The income of these islands during and after the war steadily improved. Shipping, due to the risk in war, earned vastly more than before. Men engaged abroad during the war also earned much higher wages than before, as would be expected. The savings of Caymanians therefore increased. Nevertheless, many of the men returning from overseas services, and those who served at home, had to find new jobs after the war for they could not live for any length of time on their wartime savings. Traditionally, working on ships at sea was the main source of livelihood for Cayman's men and so they began moving out to sea again in search of jobs in the Merchant Marine. In fact Caymanian seamen had for a long time held an excellent reputation for their seamanship and so they had little problem obtaining a job at sea once they could get to it. In the meantime, Owen Roberts

International Airport was built and a small air service established. One travelling to the United States would need to obtain an immigration visa from the American Embassy in Kingston, Jamaica. However, very few seaman going in search of jobs in the United States Merchant Marine had a good case to apply for a visa; most of them therefore just 'signed on' to the crew lists of boats plying between Cayman and American ports. If during the limited time in US ports a job was not found, then the job seekers would return home.

The struggle to get employment on ships or on shore in the United States at the time was quite frustrating and discouraging and there were few alternatives for those hunting jobs. Even if other countries were able to assist, the fact was that none offered such job opportunities as the United States. However, Providence provided a way that was to be a true blessing. During the early 1950s, the government was successful in negotiating with the United States government permission to grant non-immigrant waivers which would permit local residents to enter the United States. Those who wished to obtain a visa could of course continue to apply to the American Embassy in Jamaica or elsewhere for the facility. The waiver was issued in Cayman by the Commissioner and was valid for one entry into the United States. Once a traveller entered the United States by waiver, American Immigration could extend his stay if necessary. Such a facility was a tremendous breakthrough for seamen as well as residents seeking medical aid and those pursuing other urgent business. Shortly after the waiver facility was established, its effects reflected on the rising economic activities of these islands.

Credit for obtaining the US waiver facilities was claimed by Ormond Panton. In his autobiography *A Special Son*, Panton gives the details of how it all happened. As a young politician in the early 1950s he was eager to start making his mark in Caymanian politics as did his older colleagues in the Legislative Assembly. According to Panton, he was conscious of, and also concerned about, the difficulties encountered especially by seamen and the sick in obtaining visas to enter the United States. He therefore introduced in the Legislative Assembly a motion recommending that the government pursue negotiations with the American government for the establishment of a US Consulate Office in these islands. This would allow visas to be issued here at home and was more expeditious than having to travel overseas to obtain them. When the proposal was presented to the American government in Washington, it was rejected on the grounds of the size of the Cayman Islands.

However, the story went on to relate how a gentleman sent here from the American Embassy in Kingston (a Mr Wilson) to look at the Cayman case was received by local politicians on arrival and treated with true Caymanian-style hospitality. The upshot was that Mr Wilson recommended to the State Department in Washington that the Cayman Islands be allowed to issue through its Commissioner (now Governor) a non-immigrant waiver to any person with a clean criminal record wishing to enter the United States. The recommendation was ratified by a Senate Resolution. Such a facility granted through such a process, if not unique, was certainly unusual. In the early 1950s as a junior civil servant, I was not permitted under Staff Orders to get involved in politics. Therefore, while I was not aware of the full official ramifications of the waiver issue, I nevertheless can confirm the rush and excitement of seamen and others to obtain US immigration waivers here in the Cayman Islands at the time this came into effect. In a short span of time after the waiver breakthrough, the number of men going to sea began to grow and so did the income to families at home. The proceeds of wages from seamen certainly went to good use. A portion went to support the families and the balance was used to repair old homes and build new ones that in time gave all the districts of the three islands an improved and attractive appearance.

In the early 1950s a shipping company in New York, National Bulk Carriers Inc. (NBC), began employing Caymanians on their ships. NBC was in fact the single largest employer of Caymanians at that time. At one count it had over 1,000 men on its payroll. In June 1959, as Acting Registrar of Trade Unions, I processed the application, signed by a group of Caymanian seamen, requesting the registration of Global Seaman Union (GSU). It was the first such union to be registered in the Cayman Islands. The union was organized and owned by Caymanian seamen employed largely by NBC. The local union was looked upon by some outside individuals and institutions as a company's union, meaning it was created and controlled by NBC. However, GSU functioned well as its main concern from the very outset had been to foster good relationships between members, together with keeping a good watch on their employment conditions and level of earnings regardless of the nationality of the membership. Shortly after GSU was registered, Graham Watler of Pedro, Grand Cayman, was selected as its first chief executive with a head office here in Grand Cayman. Isaac Tatum of Cayman Brac succeeded Watler in 1961 as the union's boss; he retired from the position in 1997.

In 1961 the International Maritime Workers Union (IMWU) of the United States picketed the NBC's ship *Ore Monarch* in Philadelphia, accusing its owners, NBC, of operating with non-American crews drawn from their own union, GSU, which was according to IMWU a violation of state law. The matter ended in the Philadelphia court, where IMWU had to present good grounds to prove their case against NBC. At the time I was no longer Acting Registrar of Trade Unions but, being the one who registered GSU on 1st June 1959, I was summonsed by NBC to appear in the Philadelphia court to give evidence on their behalf. My involvement was to prove that GSU was genuinely and legally a Cayman Islands entity organized and owned by Caymanian seamen. The court hearing was quite interesting, with the American lawyers for IMWU trying to manoeuvre the case in an attempt to prove that GSU was in fact an entity organized and run by NBC. However, the end result was that IMWU did not succeed in their efforts. Since then neither NBC nor GSU has been bothered by offshore unions or any other troublemakers regarding the legal status of GSU as a true Cayman Islands seaman union.

Seamen's earnings were certainly the bulk of Cayman's economy for a decade and a half to 1965. Walking around these islands one could see the marvellous improvement to private property as mentioned before. Families with homes made good savings as well from their monthly allowances. With living conditions so well improved and commercial business very prosperous, everybody felt quite happy not to be burdened with financial problems. Mosquitoes, however, still plagued everyone. An old Cayman gentleman, Lishman Godfrey, always made this remark about the mosquitoes while brushing them from behind his ears, 'Oh these mosquitoes, the only good thing I can say about them is that they are no respecter of persons.'

By early 1965 I received the appointment from the government to the position of Treasurer. A couple of years later the title Treasurer was changed to that of Financial Secretary. When I assumed the new position of Treasurer in early 1965, the first thing that came to my notice was that seamen were returning home and hanging about street corners looking for something to keep them occupied. As weeks went by it become quite clear that disaster had struck the seamen's economy. First, an economic recession was affecting most of the western hemisphere, which reduced much of the activity in the shipping industry: ships were being tied up and crew members sent home with no prospect of returning to their jobs. A second problem was that the Merchant Marine was upgrading its tanker fleet with larger automated supertankers that required fewer men to operate in comparison to the need of conventional tankers. Also, container cargo appeared on the scene at the same time and joined ranks with new supertankers for the reduction of crew requirements. All those rather unfortunate factors were clearly an indication that Caymanian seamen must turn their attention away from the sea to perhaps shore-based activities. The loss of seamen's earnings was quite a disaster for the local economy for a while, but the situation presented a most interesting beginning of a new economic era for Cayman.

6

The Civil Service, 1945–65

As related earlier, I took my first job with the government in August 1941 as an orderly in the Courts Office under Mr Eddie Parsons, the Clerk of Courts. I worked there for six months and then went off to study and sit the Third Year Pupil Teacher Examination in July 1942 to complete my secondary education, after which I joined the Cayman Islands Company of the Jamaica Home Guard in August 1942.

In June 1945, shortly before the end of the war in Europe, the Cayman Home Guard was disbanded. Returning to civilian life, I began thinking of new plans for my post-war future. At the time because of a health problem I was admitted to hospital under the care of the Government Medical Officer, Dr William A.C. Hortor. The doctor came from England to Cayman via Jamaica on the MV *Cimboco* in December 1936: he died here 24 years later and was interred at the West Bay burial ground. Hortor's nurse was Miss Annie Bush of South Sound. The hospital, bequeathed to the people of these islands by Miss Helen Lambert, was a little government-operated institution opened back in 1937: it had four beds, an operating theatre, a dispensary and a consulting room. The hospital was constructed on what is now the site of the Immigration Office.

In 1948 I was tempted with taking a 20-year endowment insurance policy with Manufacturer's Life Insurance Company of Canada through a local representative, my boss and good friend Desmond Watler. After some persuasion I decided to go for it. I was sent to a local Adventist doctor for the medical test. My health was in fair condition. After the doctor took my pulse a few times, he looked at me and said, 'I must tell you, young man, according to your heart performance, you haven't very long to live.' Believe me, I did not sleep all that night and spent several other nights worrying over what the doctor told me. After the results of the medical test reached

73

Manufacturer's Life in Canada, they sent back a request that I retake the pulse: however, after the frightening experience from the doctor's test a few days earlier, I refused to do so and advised Desmond accordingly. A few days later the company replied and notified the local agent that they had accepted the medical report and issued my policy; 20 years later I cashed in on that policy. Unfortunately the doctor died a couple of years after he did my medical test.

In December 1945, after partly finalizing arrangements to attend and study accountancy at the Jamaican branch of the Bennett College, England, I was offered a job by Cayman's Postmaster General, Mr A.C. Panton, for a position of temporary clerical officer in the Government Post Office. This involved assisting with philatelic orders, that is, filling and dispatching stamp collectors' orders. I discussed the job offer with my father, who advised that I should sleep on it and by the next day I would probably be better prepared to make the right decision. He wanted me to decide issues of that nature myself. The next morning as we were both having our usual early cup of coffee, and when we usually discussed matters of importance, my father asked if I had yet made a decision regarding the job at the Post Office. I told him yes, I would take it and that the decision was based on a dream I had during the night. Of course I was a great believer in dreams. My father asked what was the dream. I told him it went like this: 'I found myself riding a red horse and came to an embankment with a deep and very wide valley. Suddenly the horse flew through the air while I was still on its back and landed on the other side of the valley. I rode on into an office, dismounted, and began looking around.' That is all I can remember of the dream. Furthermore, riding the red horse into an office after the flying expedition represented that the offer made to me by Mr Panton was a good one and in fact one to my advantage which I should take. And it certainly was so for I remained with the government over the next 37 years and finally retired from the Civil Service on 31st March 1983 after a one-year pre-retirement leave.

After I told my father the dream he smiled and said to me, 'It is quite a good dream and in favour of you taking the job.' I thought afterwards that the dream was only reflecting what I had decided in my heart before going to sleep that night.

I went to work at the Post Office on 16th December 1945. The office reminded me of the job I took there in the school holidays in summer 1938 to work on the construction of the building. My new job and its environment were very pleasant, especially after being there for a few years when other staff members were appointed. Among them were Jim Bodden, followed by his two sisters, Elita and

Carolyn. Also on the staff were Mary Lee Hislop (now Rowlandson), Rita Hinds, who was to become my wife some years later, Sarah Lee Thompson (now Gynell), who succeeded Rita when she took maternity leave, and Wilfred Parchment the messenger. One day I asked Wilfred to bring me a pencil eraser from the mail sorting desk close to where he was at the time; he handed me large pliers used to depress seals used on mailbags and packages. After that we nicknamed him 'the eraser'. Desmond Watler, who was Assistant Postmaster at the time, would sign all collectors' invoices accompanying orders of stamps I prepared. Many collectors acknowledged their orders with very favourable comments. One from the California area wrote back to congratulate us for the very beautiful Cayman stamps but remarked, 'However, the signature on the invoice was most illegible.' For that matter very few signatures are written so that others can read them.

My temporary appointment to the Department of Treasury, Customs and Post Office was confirmed to the Permanent and Pensionable Establishment of the Civil Service on 1st April 1947 by the new Commissioner, Major Ivor O. Smith. My father in his kind and considerate way expressed to me his feelings of delight at my confirmation to the Civil Service. However, eight days later pleasure turned to sorrow. On 9th April 1947 my father died suddenly of a heart condition while travelling to his farm in the White Hall lands. Fortunately, two of the elder children were with him at the time so that one could return home to alert the family.

Although we had lived there ten years, after my father's death my mother was determined to move away from Edward Avenue and find another home. By late 1947 she was fortunate to rent a third house on Mary Street in George Town, owned by Mrs Bride Arch. That area was called Maryland. Before my brother Noel moved from there in the latter part of the following year, he decided he would join other Caymanians working in the Merchant Marine with shipping companies based in the United States. A little while after Noel departed to sea, the family moved again to White Hall, near to the property where we first lived. We loved the house (now Whitehall Bay Restaurant) for the reason that it was just the right sized building and was on the same beautiful white sand beach we remembered so well from when we first came to Grand Cayman. While living in this fourth rented house my eldest sister, Mary, decided in 1948, at age 21, to move to New York to start her working career. She took a job at Columbia University working in the Atomic Research Section of the Department of Physics. Five years later she was, by special invitation, offered a similar job at Cornell University in Ithaca, New York, which she accepted. After working at Columbia for five years and Cornell for seventeen years, Mary eventually retired and settled down with her husband and family. She died on 8th November 1996 at her home at Lansing, New York, leaving behind her husband, Al Curry, and her two children, Tracy and Charles.

By late 1949 we moved for the last time to our own family home on Elgin Avenue, previously owned by Mr Joseph Forbes. The home was originally named Sussex Cottage and was popularly known as the private home of Commissioner George S. Hirst who came to Grand Cayman in 1907 and died here in 1912. He is buried in the Dixie Cemetery immediately in front of the entrance gate.

Throughout the 1940s I continued to gain experience in the Civil Service. I became involved in the work of all three sections of the department – Treasury, Customs and Post Office – as did most of the other staff.

At the start of the 1950s, at age 28, I thought the time had come for me to seriously think of marriage. I remembered back at age 25 I was asked by a girlfriend one evening to make a secret wish as we both watched a beautiful setting sun. My wish was this: 'If I were still single at age thirty, I would not bother with marriage.' Three years after the wish my growing fancy pointed to a petite young lady with ponytail and spectacles whom I had met in 1935 at the opening of the Wireless and Meteorological Offices in George Town. It was also the same young lady who about five years later bought from me one evening roasted peanuts that had upset her stomach that night. In my latter school days I sold roasted peanuts after school in the evenings. I had a pushcart on wheels with a galvanized container made into two sections. One was for the bagged roasted peanuts and the other was equipped with a tank of water heated by fire from burning coals below. A whistle was attached to the top of the tank and as the water boiled, the steam blew the whistle. The noise alerted customers that the peanut vendor was around again. The heat from the boiling water also kept the roasted peanuts warm and crisp.

After her commercial training, the same little lady to whom I sold the peanuts came to work at the Post Office, where I was also employed at the time. As events would have it, we became great friends. This young lady was eventually my choice for a wife although I am eight and a half years older than her. Rita Joanna is the younger daughter of Bradley and Elizabeth Hinds of South Sound. They had one son, John, and two daughters, Jen the elder and Rita. Rita and I were married on 7th February 1952 and have already celebrated our 47th wedding anniversary. The night of our wedding, before retiring, the wish of five years earlier suddenly flashed across my mind and I discovered then that the day of my marriage was only 20 days beyond my thirtieth birthday; that was not bad at all. The day before the wedding King George VI of England died and, because the sad event placed the entire British Commonwealth in state mourning and both Rita and I were Civil Servants, our wedding reception had to be cancelled.

Our first child, born in February 1953, was named after her two grandmothers, Theresa Elizabeth (Tessa). The last child, a boy born in October 1972, was named after his two grandfathers, Bradley Charles. Rita and I lost one son, Julian, in March 1962, aged one. He died during an epidemic of gastroenteritis.

For the first six years of our marriage, Rita and I lived with my mother on Elgin Avenue in George Town. Before our second child, a daughter, was born in September 1954, my wife quit her job at the Post Office to start taking care of the first child and preparing for her second confinement.

For the coronation of Her Majesty Queen Elizabeth II in 1953, many contests were arranged for the celebration, one being for Miss Baby Cayman. Tessa, then four months old, was one of the contestants and she was the one chosen. The first royal visit to Cayman was on 22nd March 1960, when Her Royal Highness The Princess Royal, daughter of King George V, came to Grand Cayman on the Royal Yacht *Britannia*. Tessa was selected from among her school group to present the bouquet to Her Royal Highness at the official welcoming ceremony. As Acting Clerk of Courts at the time, I was privileged along with Rita to be among heads of departments and their spouses invited to the welcoming ceremony and to a reception on the Royal Yacht given by Her Royal Highness.

Over the years as I continued to work in the public sector, our six children grew up and they too took their place in the community. I will name them in chronological order.

For her secondary education Tessa was sent to Bishop's High School in Mandeville, Jamaica, and then to Reading University in England to study for a Bachelor of Arts degree in English. She did not complete her studies as she chose an early marriage instead. Her husband, Robert C. Bodden, is a local realtor and the son of Haig Bodden (a popular politician) and his wife Lurline. Robert became a senior Grand Cayman Rotary Club member and was appointed District Governor for the year 1999–2000. Robert and Tessa have a family of three children, two daughters, Joannah and Jessica, and a son, Justin, who was born between the two girls. Joannah, the eldest daughter, is now a qualified attorney, having in 1998 been called to the Bar at Lincoln's Inn in London. She is employed at one of

Cayman's leading law firms, Maples and Calder. Tessa is actively involved in community work and serves as Chairman of the National Drug Council. Tessa was awarded the Certificate and Badge of Honour by Her Majesty The Queen during the royal visit here in February 1994.

Ronette, my second daughter, is married to Daniel Jurn from the United States; they have one daughter, Katrina. Ronette attended Florida Atlantic University in Boca Raton, Florida, where she majored in Business (Bachelor of Arts). She is employed at the Cayman Islands Monetary Authority.

Zillah, our third daughter, is married to Thomas Isaacs from Jamaica; they have two children, a daughter and a son, Michelle and Richard. Tom also has two other daughters by a previous marriage, Shelly and Sally. After earning her diploma in physiotherapy at the University of the West Indies in Jamaica, Zillah was appointed to the Department of Physiotherapy at the Cayman Government General Hospital and Medical Centre: she is now head of the department. Zillah also holds the Certificate of Health Services Management and was elected a member of the Institute of Health Services Management (UK). Tom is a real estate developer.

Vassel Jr (Bud) is our first son and follows the third daughter, Zillah. He is married to Sheila, the only daughter of Dr Paul Magnus and his wife Cynthia, from Jamaica. Paul first visited Cayman in 1951 as the government's Chief Medical Officer. He returned to Cayman 25 years later (with his wife) to take up permanent residence and private practice. Cynthia unfortunately died in 1989. Bud and Sheila have three sons, Vassel (the Third) (Godfrey), Julian and Maxwell. Bud is General Manager of Atlantis Submarine, having majored in Engineering at Stevens Institute of Technology in Hoboken, New Jersey, USA.

Juliet, the youngest girl, studied Hotel Administration at Cornell University in Ithaca, New York. Juliet was Director of Human Resources at the Hyatt Regency Grand Cayman but then accepted a position at the Government Community College as Head of the Department of Hospitality Studies. After two years at the college Juliet moved to the national airline, Cayman Airways Ltd., as Vice President of Human Resources.

Bradley, our youngest child, attended the University of South Florida in Tampa, Florida, and Eckerd College in St Petersburg, Florida, USA, where he graduated in Marine Science. He is employed by the Cayman Islands government as a Research Officer at its Department of the Environment. Bradley was married to Anna Pereira from George Town at the end of May 1999.

Rita and I are of course very proud of all our children and we continue to cherish our time with them as our various activities allow.

The people and government of these islands were saddened when, on 1st April 1965, an announcement of the Princess Royal's death was made here in the Legislative Assembly. A message to members by the President, the Honourable J.A. Cumber, stated that a telegram received from the Secretary of State for the Colonies in London to the government and people of these islands on 28th March 1965 advised of the royal death. The Members of the House stood for a one-minute silence as a mark of respect to Princess Royal. All of us in the Cayman Islands had fond memories of the Princess's first visit on the Royal Yacht *Britannia* in 1960.

In late 1954, J.C. Lazzari, then Assistant District Commissioner of Cayman Brac and Little Cayman, was about to retire. The Commissioner, Mr Andrew M. Gerrard, CMG, called me to his office and suggested that I take on the acting appointment for Mr Lazzari. The Commissioner was prepared to pay me my current salary plus an allowance equivalent to the salary my wife had received when employed by the government. The offer seemed attractive but it carried one condition which I could not accept and that was that I should go to the Brac in advance to find suitable accommodation. I knew very little about Cayman Brac and less about finding a home there for my wife, children and myself. After considering the offer and thinking of my young wife and family, whom I would have to start moving around, I found the Brac position extremely difficult to accept, though I was aware that it could eventually mean a promotion. I made my feelings known to the Commissioner, who did not take my decision too kindly. We parted, but not on very friendly terms. However, by the end of his tour of duty here in 1956 we became friends again. In later years when he visited here, we became even better friends. He was fond of telling me on his return visits what he knew I meant to Cayman. The last time I heard from Andrew was in 1986 when he sent me a personal message by a friend saying that his wife Ann had died and after some years he had decided to remarry. He and his new bride were then off to Australia on honeymoon. I have never heard from him since. May God richly bless them.

Twice after 1954 I had similar offers to upgrade my official position in the government: I did not accept either of them. In 1955, under Commissioner Gerrard, the three sections of the Department of the Treasury, Customs and Post Office were separated into three independent entities and known as the Treasury Department, the Customs Department and the Post Office Department. The Commissioner in office at Government House also held the position of

Treasurer, while Desmond Watler was given the appointment of Deputy Treasurer and put in charge of the department's physical daily operation. I was appointed Assistant to the Deputy Treasurer. Lee A. Ebanks, a former teacher in government primary schools, became Collector of Customs under this new separation of departments. During the war Lee had been appointed Acting Head of the Police Department, a position known as Inspector of Police. By virtue of that position Lee was also appointed Warehouse Keeper. The substantive holder of the position of Inspector of Police, Major R.J. Watler, known as Roddy, was seconded to the Cayman Islands Home Guard as its Commanding Officer. After the war in 1945, Lee was transferred to the Treasury, Customs and Post Office Department while Roddy resumed his original position of Inspector of Police. In 1955 Lee became the first Collector of Customs for the Cayman Islands.

Heading the Post Office Department was Clarence V. Thompson. During the war while Clarence was attached to the Department of the Treasury, Customs and Post Office, he also held the post of Assistant Radio Officer, while Arthur D. Bodden was Chief Radio Officer.

In early 1955, three years after my marriage and with a family of two daughters, it became quite clear that the level of salary I earned from the government had become inadequate for the upkeep of my home. I thought about alternative employment or activities outside of government. One was to go to sea, as had my younger brother Noel, but he quickly discouraged me from such a move. Another was to obtain the permission of Commissioner Gerrard to take on in my spare time a sideline in jewellery and watch repairing, the things which had a special appeal to me. The Commissioner was also very much aware of the poor salary in the service against the rising cost of living, which he himself complained about. He mentioned to us that he tried to get the message across to members of the Legislative Assembly and even went as far as to propose a salaries review. However, the politicians would not agree to the scheme. He then said to us, 'Listen, boys, your service to the government ends at four p.m. each day; if there is anything you can do in your own spare time to supplement your income, try it, for I certainly cannot help you.'

Happily by then I had become so interested in watch repairing that in early 1955 I enrolled for a course at the Illinois School of Watch Repairing in Chicago and obtained their Certificate of Proficiency on 10th April 1956. In the meantime I applied for a few watch agencies including that for the Mido (Swiss), known to be one of the world's leading waterproof watches. I received the Mido agency and placed it in the name of a new company with the trade name Capital Traders, jointly owned by Glidden & Co. and myself. Two other friends, one from the government service and the other from the private sector, also used Capital Traders for their part of the trade, although each member dealt independently with his firm's lines of merchandise. The four of us also got together and rented a shop from Dr Roy McTaggart on Cardinal Avenue and named it Capital Traders. On 9th July 1956 the first shipment of 12 Mido watches was received and by December of the same year I had ordered a total of 40 pieces. I also had other watch agencies: the Benrus (American with Swiss movement), the Venus and the Enicar (both Swiss). In jewellery and watch bracelets I had agencies like Spiedel and Jacoby-Bend. The store carried each partner's products, such as watches and jewellery, stoves and sewing machines, motor vehicle accessories and Philips radios and record players.

By November 1957 when I was starting to build my house in South Sound, my side of the business made a valuable contribution in cash towards the construction cost. Unfortunately, soon afterwards Capital Traders suffered a burglary and most of my watches were stolen. The police investigation led to the discovery that the store was broken into and the watches taken by a male prisoner serving a sentence in the George Town jail. The prisoner had an intelligent scheme against the police for escaping jail at nights, roaming around town and doing his dirty jobs, including stealing my watches, before returning unde-tected to the lock-up. His scheme was to pull a few iron bars from a window in his cell above ground. Two wooden three-by-fours had been installed as the base of the windowsill in which the bars were put; one piece was splintered in the centre so that a small strip of wood could be taken off. Three or four of the bars were then forced out from the bottom in a circular motion. After escaping, the prisoner would replace the bars so neatly that even if the police visited and looked at the particular window, they would not detect that anything was wrong with it. He would select a convenient time at night after supper to escape and make his rounds.

Members of the public had reported to the police on a few occasions that they saw that particular prisoner at large in town at nights. The police were baffled and decided to move the inmate into an under-ground cell. During the move the prisoner asked the police for the mat-tress he was using in the cell above ground. They became suspicious and in the prisoner's presence the mattress was opened. In it a Mido ladies' watch was found. Thus the clue to the stolen watches came to light. The rest of the watches, about 18 pieces, he had no doubt left with his associates in town. The prisoner was sentenced to serve a longer jail term. The court in its judgement ordered restitution of the stolen watches if ever any were found. Besides the one retrieved from the mattress I recovered another of the stolen Mido watches when it came to me for servicing. After the burglary I made a fresh start to re-build the business and in a short time it was back to normal.

In 1959, under the new Constitution, the title Commissioner was changed to Administrator. The Commissioner's second position of Treasurer was shifted to the Treasury Department and Desmond Watler then became the Treasurer and I the Assistant Treasurer.

Just before the end of May 1959 the local Stipendiary Magistrate, Mr James Astwood, requested the Administrator, Mr Donald, to consider the possibility of allowing me to act as Clerk of the Courts. The substantive holder of the post of Clerk of the Courts, E.S. Parsons, was unfortunately ill at the time and the opening of Grand Court was to take place the following month on 3rd June. The Clerk of Courts was Registrar of the Grand Court in addition to his other duties. For sessions of the Grand Court held twice each year, June and December, a magistrate from Jamaica was requested to preside as Judge of the Court; also requested from Jamaica was a Crown Counsel to prosecute criminal cases (indictments and vagrancy charges).

The Stipendiary Magistrate was a native of Bermuda attached to the Jamaican Judiciary and seconded to the position in Cayman. Those assignments were usually for a period of two years but could be extended or renewed. After Mr Astwood returned to Bermuda, he was in later years knighted by Her Majesty The Queen.

Having held my new title of Assistant Treasurer for such a short time, I was then given the appointment of Acting Clerk of the Courts. I had been in the Courts Office for six months during 1941 but was employed as an orderly or messenger and knew nothing about the legal and administrative duties or the functions and procedures of the office. Nevertheless, I accepted the position and received the appointment from the Commissioner effective 1st June 1959. In later years when I looked back on positions I held in government I could scarcely believe that I was capable of holding them for even a few days. However, I am reminded of the words spoken by Lynn Russell, a CNN announcer on 'Headline News', during an interview with the *Saturday Evening Post* in June 1995. On page 34 of the issue, she remarked, 'If you're afraid of everything, you won't accomplish anything.' Those words in fact expressed my earlier attitude of not being afraid of any task.

As I entered the Courts Office on the morning of 1st June I met my secretary, Mrs Glennis Smith, a very lovely and efficient young lady from the district of West Bay. She presented me first of all with an urgent application for the registration of the Global Seamen Union.

By virtue of my new acting appointment as Clerk of the Courts, I was also Acting Registrar of Trade Unions and Acting Coroner. I spent some time that morning with the Stipendiary Magistrate looking at the work in the office. After going through normal procedures we dealt with the Global Seamen Union application, which was the first such request to the government for registration of a union. It was completed and registered during my first day in office. The next day I concentrated on the Grand Court procedures, meeting the Judge and the Crown Counsel and practising my parts in opening the court and performing the normal duties of a registrar. I also had both the criminal and civil cases put in order. So 3rd June was quite eventful for me: fortunately it ended without mishaps or regrets; all participants seemed to have been in rather good spirits.

I worked in the Courts Office for 15 months and prepared three sessions of the Grand Court as Acting Registrar. At the last Grand Court in June 1960, Mr Parsons, the former Clerk of Courts who was by that time retired from the Civil Service, was sitting in court and listening to proceedings of cases on trial. At lunch break he stopped me outside the court (the Town Hall) and said, 'Johnson, I have been listening to you and watching your performance today. Can I encourage you to study law? You would make a darn good lawyer.' I thanked him for the compliment and the advice but told him I was satisfied with my job at the Treasury and that my intention was to pursue finance. Among my duties at the Courts Office was the prosecution of preliminaries of all indictable offences, petty session cases and conduct of Coroner's Court. I rather enjoyed the time spent there. One thing I will always remember about the Courts Office: in mid-1960 after I had stopped smoking cigarettes for 13 years, I went back again to that filthy habit. Excuse my term, 'filthy habit', but those were the most appropriate words I could think of using at the time of writing. I was aware that smoking was not healthy for anyone, however, once the habit gripped me I could not resist smoking. On the last occasion that I smoked, 31st December 1983, I decided then to enter politics in the November 1984 General Election. In order to imbue myself with the charisma and enthusiasm necessary in order to become a successful politician, which the opposition accused me of not having, I decided to surprise them by quitting the smoking habit. I think running around without a cigarette in my mouth did work wonders for me and certainly did surprise my opposition. Fifteen years have now gone by since I last smoked; I feel well and I can certainly encourage anyone who smokes to try and lay down that filthy habit: mind you, it is not a simple task to undertake but with a bit of willpower it is worth trying.

I had quite a successful tour of duty at the Courts Office. At my last Grand Court in June 1960, I presented a list of criminal cases consisting of 15 indictments and 2 vagrancy charges. Although the Crown Counsel, Karl Brandon, told me on arrival from Jamaica that the cases were 'no good', he was later taken through each of them and shown the strong *prima facie* evidence. The result was that Karl won 16 out of the 17 cases. One indictment ended with a split jury decision and was deferred to the next Grand Court in December of the same year. The case was Regina vs Vance Frederick for assaulting the Chief of Police, Sands Sherwood, when the latter attempted to arrest Frederick. However, my successor in office offered no evidence in the case and withdrew it before the start of the next Grand Court.

Another case of interest related to a young man from Pedro, Trevor Watler, reported missing. The case was passed to the police for investigation. Trevor had apparently gone on a fishing trip early one morning in the vicinity of Pedro Bluff and was never seen or heard of again. After weeks of police investigation and still no clue to the case, a lady relative of Trevor consulted me as Acting Coroner regarding the possibility of registering the death of the missing man, as he was by then presumed dead. The request was in order so a death certificate could be issued. Unfortunately I had no previous experience of the procedure in such instances; neither could the Stipendiary Magistrate assist me. I therefore wrote to the Judiciary in Jamaica for advice on the matter. Jamaica replied to say that the case could be put before the Coroner's Court after the lapse of a period of not less than six months. If by that time the police still had no clue or traces of evidence leading to the whereabouts or cause of disappearance of the missing person, the case might be put to the Coroner's Jury for a decision. After the reply was received from Jamaica and six months had expired since the case was first reported, I presented the matter to the Coroner's Court for authority to register the death. After the court examined the evidence from relatives and the police regarding the missing man, the panel of jurors accepted the application for registration of the case on the grounds of 'presumption of death in the matter of Trevor Watler'. The decision of the court was sent to the Registrar of Births, Deaths and Marriages for registration as a 'missing male person presumed dead'. Following the procedure a death certificate could be issued to the family. Trevor was nephew to my boss, Desmond Watler.

My days at the Courts Office passed quietly, leaving me with a sense of satisfaction that I had done fairly well with the job. I often wondered, however, how I could have succeeded without any qualification to hold the position. I was conscious too that the knowledge gained in my 15 months in office would be invaluable to my future career in whatever sphere of employment I entered. On my return to the Treasury my boss Desmond Watler asked me how I made out in the Courts Office without any previous legal experience or knowledge of the work. He asked me too what was the most cherished principle I applied to the work. My answer was that from day one I adopted my most respected attribute, and that was to be cautious about doing favours in public office procedures, especially where family and friends were involved. That principle certainly shone brightly on the occasion when a member of the family appeared before me to give evidence on behalf of an accused in a case I was prosecuting. Another principle came from the old adage, 'Look before you leap', as there were a few difficult and embarrassing cases involving friends that I had to deal with personally. Rules and principles were certainly the abiding factors.

The court system to my recollection during the 1960s consisted of Mr Horsfall as the first local Grand Court judge while Mr Tyson was the magistrate and also the registrar of companies. I also recall that at the end of the decade if it was urgent to get a company incorporated the applicant would have to walk over to the old court building (now the National Museum) and wait downstairs for a convenient break in the magistrate's proceedings. He would then sign the certificate of incorporation. The question of a separate companies registry at that time became a very important consideration in the development of the tax haven business. The government therefore proceeded to build the Government Administration Building, where the new companies registry was established, thus providing a quick turnaround for incorporations – one of the reasons Cayman started to become a popular place to incorporate companies. At the same time a new Courts Office was built. I therefore have no doubt that our courts and our registrar of companies, trusts and limited partnerships contributed much to the Cayman success story. I should mention that the Government Administration Building is the only glass building erected here so far. Because Cayman is in the tropical hurricane zone, we asked the architects to obtain an assurance from the manufacturers of the plate glass for the walls of the building that it could withstand wind strength of 140 miles per hour. By 1988 when Hurricane Gilbert struck here, the Seismic Research Unit of the University of the West Indies had (in 1985) established the first seismograph station in Grand Cayman. We were therefore able to measure the wind strength of 'Gilbert': it was 134 miles per hour at the Administration Building.

I left the Courts Office in the latter part of 1960 and returned to my substantive position at the Treasury Department. Caribbean politics at the time were no doubt the interest of the day. The larger British West Indian islands were busily examining their constitutional future and the possibility of merging into a West Indies Federation. The Cayman delegation to those meetings was also busily looking at options for their own Territory with its then constitutional link with Jamaica. Much water had already passed under the bridge with respect to those studies and efforts, and much more was to follow. The full political story was told, describing how federation failed, how the larger territories within the region moved to independence as opposed to federation, and how Cayman became a Crown Colony under Britain, by Ormond Panton in his biography *A Special Son*, pages 102–50. Panton of course was a shrewd and devoted politician who studied the interest of the people he represented until the period before his death.

By mid-1961 Cayman's Political Delegation, consisting of Administrator Jack Rose, Ormond Panton and William Farrington was off to London to attend the discussions on the West Indies Federation. Also on the agenda was Cayman's own case for future constitutional consideration. People here were not satisfied with the proposal that Cayman be classed with the group of dependent territories within the Federation of the larger countries. Before the Cayman Delegation departed for London, William Farrington, who was always my very good friend, came to see me in my office, which was then in the Post Office Building still shared by three departments – Treasury, Customs and Post Office. Farrington and I talked for a little while on a few important subjects and then he said to me, 'Vassel, I am going to London this weekend to discuss our political future. I would like while there to discuss with the Foreign and Commonwealth Office the possibility of a project or a scheme that would be very important and beneficial to Cayman and one that would tie in with any future social and economic development. I thought too that it should also fit, at this stage, our present proposed constitutional thinking. I also thought that you would be the ideal person to advise me on an appropriate subject.'

Of course while Willie was talking my thoughts were moving swiftly in many directions. When he was finished presenting his request, I replied immediately and said to him, 'Willie, I recommend that you discuss with London the possibility of a ten-year education plan under their aid programme for Cayman.'

He looked at me thoughtfully and then said, 'That is an excellent suggestion.'

On Willie's return from London he came back to see me, just to

86

say that the British government was very impressed and receptive to his interest in education. They promised to do something about it in their 'Forward Planning' under the Colonial Development and Welfare Scheme (CD&W). This plan included grants to British Dependent Territories within the British Commonwealth, like Cayman, for projects which would fit into the social and economic advancement of the territories.

Not long after Farrington's discussions in London on the education scheme, both this government and London agreed to a five-year CD&W Scheme for the Cayman Islands that included education assistance costing the British government CI$1.578 million. The scheme would include development of a comprehensive education system: Cayman's contribution to the five-year scheme, which was later extended to a seven-year plan and thereafter to ten years, was $285,000. There was also a British Government loan element of $323,000, bringing the total provision including the CD&W grant to $2.186 million. The Education Plan was implemented in 1964, when the government negotiated with the Presbyterian Church, now the United Church of Jamaica and the Cayman Islands, the takeover of its Cayman High School. The school at the time operated on government property behind the George Town Public Library, formerly the site of the American naval base during the war. The preparatory section of the Cayman High School remained with the Church on the same site behind the Library, while the government moved the high school section with its headmaster, the Rev. John Gray, to its present site on the east side of Walkers Road.

The high school was developed into a comprehensive high school and later divided to create two schools, a high school for the senior classes and a middle school for the early age high school students so as to separate the two age groups. That was an excellent move for which full credit must go to the Minister of Education at the time, the Honourable Truman Bodden, OBE.

But it is undoubtedly true to state that William Farrington deserves credit for the part he played in the promotion of education in these islands, starting in the 1960s. The high school has expanded over a vast area along the east side of Walkers Road in George Town. It is a development that has been vital to the successful growth of the local economy and the social system we see today. The success of education, its growth and development, also played a vital role especially in the financial welfare of young Caymanians who once laboured for a livelihood on ships at sea. After those jobs were no longer available, men who had hitherto looked to the sea for their livelihood focused their attention on training programmes in schools

87

specializing in home-based industries. After academic training, those men were able to find appropriate long-term employment at home with incomes comparable to those formerly found at sea. Fifteen years after the collapse of the seamen's industry, Caymanian men and women, as predicted earlier, were moving up into senior positions in banks, trust companies and hotels and also qualifying in law, accounting and many other disciplines in the professional and technical fields.

Many other facilities which these islands needed to help keep up with the rest of the world were initiated or improved upon in the 1950s and 1960s. These included an airport, electricity and telecommunications.

Communication must without a doubt be considered a key factor in all areas of development, especially in small countries like the Cayman Islands that are in many cases considerable distances away from other lands. In this regard and of paramount importance was the construction of Owen Roberts International Airport in Grand Cayman, opened in November 1952. The field had a length of 5,500 feet and the construction cost was in the amount of £95,000 sterling or CI$190,000. The project was financed from three sources: local revenue of $29,000; a British government free grant of $50,000 made under its Colonial Development and Welfare Scheme; and a loan of $111,000 at 5 per cent interest payable over 20 years from the Colonial Development Corporation, a British government lending organization.

At the time few Caymanians had confidence that the investment in an airfield was economically feasible or of practical interest to these islands; they also wondered how the government would pay the debt. No doubt they had lost sight of the fact that the Cayman Islands had at that stage of an increasingly active world to think positively about its future social, economic and political development. It was also necessary for them to think positively of the need to establish air communication links with the outside world, a service that was of paramount importance to these tiny islands especially in developing the tourist industry. Instantly after the opening of the airport, a seaplane service was established to Jamaica and the tourist industry began moving, even if a few of the visitors could not tolerate the mosquitoes for more than a night. A new prospect for the seamen and tourism blossomed. In fact a few years after the airport was opened, the country's prosperity was on a steady rise, as reflected in the government's annual budget; also in due time the airport loan was completely paid.

Many visitors to Grand Cayman, when looking at the name Owen

Roberts International Airport, ask the question, 'Who was Owen Roberts?' Wing Commander Owen Roberts served in the Royal Air Force during World War II. He came to Grand Cayman in November 1952, piloting the first plane to land at Grand Cayman's new airport. While in Grand Cayman he organized his own airline and named it Caribbean International Airways Ltd. On 10th April 1953 his new two-engine aircraft, a Lodestar, with which he planned the next step of developing a local air service, crashed after take-off at Palisadoes Airport in Kingston, Jamaica, on its inaugural flight to Grand Cayman. The port engine of the Lodestar failed and the plane crashed into the sea about 50 feet from the shore at Palisadoes and sank rapidly in about 30 feet of water. There were 14 persons on the aircraft and all died in the crash, except one. Those who died included the pilot, Owen Roberts, and his sister Sue; her husband Lieutenant-Colonel Edward Remington-Hobbs, was the one survivor. Deaths also included co-pilot Banting and six Caymanians, Kathleen DaCosta of George Town and a West Bay family of five members – Dawson Ebanks' wife, their son and daughter and two grandchildren. Owen Roberts left to mourn, in London, his wife Patricia and two daughters. The Grand Cayman Airport was aptly named after Owen Roberts in memory of his efforts for air services in Cayman at a time when the need for such facility was seen by him to be urgent.

When the Grand Cayman airport was completed, attention was diverted to Cayman Brac and their need for an airfield as well. However, in the meantime the people of the lesser islands, Cayman Brac and Little Cayman, under their own voluntary organization and self-help efforts, moved on to develop their own airport. It was built between the administrations of Commissioners Ivor O. Smith and Andrew M. Gerrard and thus named the Gerrard/Smith Airport.

In those early days the people of the lesser islands (as they were officially called then) saw no use in sitting and waiting for central government to provide out of its scarce financial resources even essential services for the two smaller islands. The people of the lesser islands therefore forged ahead to provide for their own urgent need on a sort of priority basis. Before the airport project began, the people of Cayman Brac were also instrumental in providing a public electricity generating system for the island, known as Cayman Brac Power & Light Co. Ltd. A third project was the building of their own hospital: on completion it was taken over and operated by the government on the same basis as the Grand Cayman Hospital. Following the completion of the Cayman Brac airfield, Cayman Brac Airways Ltd. was established by Lineas Aereas Costarricenses SA (LACSA), the national airline of Costa Rica in Central America, which was at the time affiliated with Pan American World Airways Inc. An air service between Grand Cayman and Cayman Brac was established in 1954 by CBA using a Cessna T50 aircraft.

In 1964, twelve years after construction of Owen Roberts Airport, it became obvious that its runway, taxiway and apron were showing signs of rapid deterioration as a result of continual use of the facilities by propeller-driven aircraft. By then, the civil aviation authorities were also notified by one of the two airlines serving these islands, British West Indian Airways Ltd., of its intention to introduce the Boeing 727 aircraft on this route in early 1965 as a replacement for the obsolescent equipment then in use. The need to strengthen the airfield to cope with this new situation became an urgent matter and one of paramount importance. There were no alternatives to the services provided by the two carriers serving these islands at the time, BWIA and LACSA, and if one airline converted to jet equipment, sure enough the other would follow sooner or later. Indeed, improved air services were needed not only for the transportation of local seamen and businessmen, and for the safe carriage of tourists, but also for the general development of the economy.

In response to the Cayman government's urgent request, the British Ministry of Aviation surveyed the runway, followed by tests, and confirmed that the airfield was in need of reconstruction in order to cope safely with especially the Boeing 727 and similar jet-transport. The cost of this work, including the provision of proper night-lighting and other visual aids, was estimated at CI$700,000. The British government generously offered a free grant of $400,000 provided the Cayman government could accept, and service in the form of a loan, the balance of $300,000. The offer was graciously accepted. Repayment of the loan was at the rate of $24,000 per annum. Revenue for the purpose was raised from new revenues. On recommendation of the British government, Hadsphaltic International Ltd. of the United Kingdom was contracted to do the resurfacing of the runway, taxiway and apron and to instal the new lighting system.

In 1954 the experience of heavy hurricanes in this region had prompted the United States to build about 16 weather bureau stations throughout the Caribbean and South America, including a new station here at Owen Roberts International Airport intended to replace the first one built by the Cubans in 1935. By 1964 the increase in air traffic also indicated that the time had come for the exchange of up-to-date information on weather conditions in the region. Accordingly this government applied for and received membership of the Caribbean Meteorological Service on the understanding that the weather information would be provided by the United States Weather

Bureau in Grand Cayman if Cayman paid the salaries of the additional staff required to provide hourly synoptic reports. The Cuban Weather Bureau operated here until January 1968, when it closed its service. At that time the operation was fully taken over by the Americans, who provided their own manager, Frank Roulstone Jr, an American who was a permanent resident here at the time. Frank operated the station until 1988, when this government through its Civil Aviation Department assumed responsibility for the Weather Bureau operation.

Government Wireless Operation, which sent messages overseas in morse code via short-wave radio transmission, closed its services in 1967. In a decade which had seen the introduction of telecommunication satellites, it would have been somewhat unusual for even small countries like the Cayman Islands to be without a modern internal and external communication system to keep in contact with the outside world. In fact it was seen then that the future development of these islands would depend on the installation of a modern and efficient telecommunications system. Of course this was not the only service on which development depended. The provision of a jet-age airfield, good roads, adequate supplies of fresh water, electric power, the control of mosquitoes and sand flies, and eventually the establishment of a deep-water harbour were considered fairly important requirements for successful development.

The government had decided in 1964 that the island's telephone and telegraph system should be improved, and proceeded to invite tenders from firms interested in securing a 25-year franchise to provide such services. The firm Cable & Wireless in the United Kingdom must have had some good reason to suspect that Cayman would soon be improving its telecommunications system. They made contact with the Assistant Administrator, Ernest O. Panton, to provide them with statistical information on the likely telephone need in Cayman in the near future. Mr Panton engaged my brother Noel, who worked in his office at the time, to undertake a survey in the George Town area on a house-to-house basis to ascertain residents' telephone requirements. The result of the test indicated that 340 homes would apply for the facility. It is well known that in a community of people anything new a neighbour has acquired, the others are likely sooner or later to have too. Two years after Cable & Wireless began operating in Cayman they discovered that the telephone system established under a careful five-year projection had been outstripped in just over two years. When they mentioned the discovery of telephone shortage to me, I advised the company that the local economic and social growth rate at the particular time was unlike any other I was aware

91

of. Our growth, at the time, had to be at least double that of any other country I knew about.

The applications to provide a modern telecommunications system were examined by a government-sponsored Telecommunications' Adviser, following which the Legislative Assembly awarded the franchise to Cable & Wireless (West Indies) Ltd., now Cable and Wireless (Cayman Islands) Ltd. (C&W). C&W began immediately to prepare engineering plans and to present a tariff rate proposal that was accepted by the government. C&W opened its new operation in Grand Cayman at the end of 1966, when their domestic and international telephone and telecommunication services were put into effect. The internal system included telephone exchanges in George Town, West Bay and Cayman Brac and radio/telephone links between George Town, Bodden Town, East End, North Side, Little Cayman, and between Grand Cayman and the rest of the world. The main attraction of the new system was that it provided subscribers with an efficient and inexpensive telephone service at virtually no cost to the government. However, the franchise required that the government's only financial commitment was the purchase of sites for the telephone exchanges and aerial masts where no Crown lands were available for the purpose. If the government were committed to buying the property, then the minor expenditure would be recovered in the form of annual rent paid by C&W for these small plots of land.

Before the new C&W system was introduced, about a dozen hand-cranked magneto phones were in the three islands. Initially the C&W domestic telephone system carried approximately 450 lines. By 28th February 1999 the present General Manager of C&W, Timothy Adams, advised that there were at that time in the Cayman Islands' system 26,558 'fixed' telephone lines (i.e. regular direct exchange lines), 5,039 cellular telephone connections and 5,231 internet connections. Assuming a population of 36,000, the penetration factors for each 100 of population would be 74 telephone lines, 14 cellular telephones and 15 internet connections. Those figures meant that the Cayman Islands currently rank quite high in the world for penetration of the three catagories of communication – fixed telephone, cellular and internet connections. In an update given to me by the previous manager, Tony Hart, in July 1996, he reported that at the time there were 2,251 cellular customers, which meant that the Cayman Islands were positioned twelfth in the world for penetration of mobile phones per 100 of population. Their telex service was established in 1969 and that too grew quickly in response to the economic development growth of the Cayman Islands. Internet connections are quite a recent popular development. The internal and external communication systems of C&W are undoubtedly considered one of the services that led the Cayman Islands to successfully build its economy in finance, tourism and all the other associated industries such as insurance, construction and real estate.

Another local service considered of vital importance in shaping not only economic growth but physical development as well and in contributing to social welfare, was a good and reliable system of generating and distributing electricity. What existed at the time was a service providing electricity for just a few hours in the early evenings to residents of George Town. That service was begun in the pre-war days by two brothers, Ed and Charles Hislop, who also operated an ice cream parlour from a front street building near to the breakwater at Hog Sty Bay; the generating plant was to the rear of the parlour. However, moving on to the 1960s when all essential services were being carefully examined to ensure that each one could cope and provide the services necessary to meet demands of oncoming development, electricity was linked in priority with telecommunications.

A company providing electric power until late 1961, Cayman Islands Public Service Co. Ltd., had in earlier years taken over the service from the Hislop Brothers. But they failed to maintain a reliable operation as required by the franchise. Electricity for George Town, the capital, became quite expensive because of the cost of maintaining the old second-hand generators in running condition. The company therefore went into receivership and the government, with no alternative, was obliged to take over what was left of the old system and continue operating the facility under what was then known as Cayman Islands Government Electricity Undertaking (CIGEU).

After the government assumed responsibility for providing electricity, it continued employing Bernard Julier, the former general manager of the company in receivership. At that stage the government purchased two new generators, which enabled CIGEU to supply consumers with an improved and more reliable supply of electricity, especially in those areas where there was no urgent demand to repair lines or replace poles, cables and transformers. By 1964, after CIGEU had operated the system successfully and on quite an economical basis, the government gave thought to the possibility of purchasing the assets and running the concern itself as an electrical utility. However, early the following year, the government rejected this thought as it could ill afford to purchase the assets and at the same time undertake the necessary rehabilitation and expansion of the system which was then seen as necessary and important. The decision was therefore to find a competent and dependable operator to take over electricity under a government franchise and operate the facility on a commercial and economic basis. Action was then taken by requesting the liquidator, James D. Macdonald, a local Canadian attorney, to advertise the company's assets here and in Britain, Canada, the United States and the West Indies, inviting tenders for a Cayman Islands government electrical franchise to cover the capital, George Town.

In the meantime, the government secured the services of Mr Bier, an electrical advisor from the Crown Agents in London, to assist in advising on the choice among applicants for this very important franchise. Four bids were received: one from a group of investors from Lexington, Kentucky, USA, headed by well-known individuals like Robert M. Odear, James S. Shropshire and Evangelos Levas. Those persons visited Grand Cayman at the time of their application so that they could personally see the island and discuss the subject with the government. Another bid came from an investor with an address at Miami Beach, Florida, Robert F. Bell and Company Incorporated. A third bid came from Allan and Company of 30 Broad Street, New York. The last bid was from Dr Roy McTaggart and Norberg Thompson, but this one fell by the wayside before the bids were examined. The two bids from Miami Beach and New York were unaccompanied by the companies' representatives.

Because of the urgency to move on with the study, it was decided that Mr Bier, the advisor, and I would travel to Miami Beach and New York to interview the other two overseas applicants. In August 1965 we visited Miami Beach and New York and conducted the interviews. The impression we gathered after the lengthy talks with representatives of the two companies was that they were not very impressed with the Cayman proposal as a cash investment. They probably thought we were searching at random for someone to salvage a service which to them could be an investment risk, or perhaps they had their eyes on more lucrative and attractive deals elsewhere. We therefore returned home, reported to the government, and recommended that the franchise be granted to the Kentucky group. In September 1965, the government accepted the decision of the Legislative Assembly to award the electrical franchise to the Kentucky group, whose local company was, and is still, named Caribbean Utilities Company Ltd. (CUC).

Both applications for electricity and telecommunication franchises were granted in 1965. The two new local entities, CUC and C&W have certainly performed well since their inception. They put much effort into the planning of those two developments, which resulted in excellent and reliable services all the way through to the present time. The two companies were also known to keep a step ahead of demand:

94

their systems have indeed been giants in the development process of these islands since the franchises were first awarded.

Statistical information provided by C&W has been recorded above. The President and CEO of CUC, Peter A. Thomson, also kindly on request submitted data on his company's operation. He has compared CUC's statistics for the first year of operation in 1966 with the latest figures for 1998 in four categories as follows:

Customers	1966	–	758
	1998	–	17,033
Peak Load	1966	–	0.70 MW
	1998	–	60.40 MW
Installed Capacity	1966	–	1.35 MW
	1998	–	95 MW
Employees	1966	–	52
	1998	–	218

The two companies, C&W and CUC, can be assured that both the public and private sectors appreciate and value their excellent work and efforts to deal immediately with urgent cases, something for which the Cayman Islands have become well known. As we review the excellent work locally of those two giant foreign companies, I should also mention that many other foreign and local individual developers, too many to mention by name, have also performed nobly. They too must be included in the accolade to those who have contributed much to the success of Cayman's economic development.

It may be appropriate at this point to mention the new Government House, residence of the Governor, built on the Seven Mile Beach and completed in 1962. Its first occupant was Administrator Jack Rose. The land on which it is built was part of the government's 99-year lease to Benson Greenall of the United Kingdom. The first substantial development on the leased property was Greenall's own Galleon Beach Lodge, followed shortly after by his Galleon Beach Hotel. The latter remained very popular and the centre of popular nightlife along with, a few years later, the new Beach Club Colony.[4]

Benson Greenall's leased property consisted of hundreds of acres of land stretching from the central Seven Mile Beach area to the North Sound and measuring in width 1,070 feet. It is registered as West Bay Beach South, Block 12C, Parcels 1 and 2. The property was leased to Benson Greenall on 14th April 1950 and signed by His

---

[4] Since then other well-known properties such as the Hyatt Regency Hotel, the Westin Casuarina Resort and others have joined the popular Seven Mile Beach hotels.

Excellency Sir John Huggins, KGC, Governor of Jamaica and its Dependencies. The leased property comprised beautiful beaches, dry lands and swamps. Portions of it were sub-leased to other private investors who developed projects like Safe Haven, with its very professional and popular 18-hole golf course that has already attracted a regional championship. There is also the original Jack Nicklaus 9-hole Britannia Golf Course adjoining the Hyatt Regency Hotel property. Another sub-lease involved the development of the Yacht Club with its yacht basin and marina attracting a large number of yachts each year, especially during the annual fishing tournament. A notable sub-lease is also the site of the Holiday Inn Hotel, which became, along with many other developments on the leased property, a popular spot on the beach. The Holiday Inn, opened in 1974, was demolished in 1998 and the site is scheduled for redevelopment under new ownership.

The Cayman government was able to renegotiate with Benson Greenall in early 1960 the release from the head lease of that portion of beach land on which the present Government House is located. Comments by one or two governors indicated that because the present site of this important residence is on a beach crowded most of the year with tourists and local residents, it was rather too public for the purpose. They thought that a more private location away from especially the tourist traffic might be more appropriate. A case in point in support of that argument was during the administration of Sir John Cumber. One morning during his term of office, a tourist couple, thinking that Government House was a restaurant, walked in from the beach, sat around the Administrator's (now Governor's) dining room table and ordered breakfast. Of course John Cumber, besides being a good Administrator, was also a good comedian. He took on the role of both chef and waiter and soon had the couple well fed. They tried to pay for the breakfast but the chef would not accept the money. After a while John Cumber said to them, 'Listen, this is the Governor's residence and I am the Governor.' (They understood 'Governor' more readily than 'Administrator'.) The couple were awfully shocked and began making apologies; they even offered without success to make a special contribution to Government House. John Cumber was well known for his witty remarks and actions that were amusing to people.

One evening I attended a reception at Government House and entering the front door John Cumber greeted me with the words, 'Good evening, Mr Wassel.'

After smiling as I knew him so well, I said to him, 'Listen, sir, you very well know that my name is Vassel.'

'Yes,' he said, 'but you see, I am living in the West Bay section of the Seven Mile Beach, and down here a "V" is pronounced "W".' He was no doubt quite right. I suspect that the pronunciation of words by Caymanians came from their early ancestors.

Regarding the siting of Government House on the Seven Mile Beach as a governor's residence, other governors and their wives have loved it there. I suspect that the property will no doubt remain a permanent residence for all future official occupants.

At the end of 1964, before the departure of Administrator Jack Rose at the end of his tour of duty, I had occasion to go and see him at Government House on a private personal matter and to say good-bye to him at the same time. In the course of our discussion he told me that I would be promoted from my current position of Assistant Treasurer to succeed Desmond Watler, the Treasurer. He revealed that Desmond would be elevated to Deputy Administrator (later Chief Secretary) to succeed Ernest Panton, who would be retiring at the end of the year. Speculations ran wild for months among both Caymanians and foreign citizens living here over these two pending promotions. However, it was not until December 1964 that the announcement 112 was made by the new Administrator, John A. Cumber, CMG, MBE, TD.

During the discussions with Administrator Jack Rose, he told me that it could be a mighty long time before promotion senior to Treasurer came my way again. He pointed out that the next step up the ladder would be that of Deputy Administrator but that Desmond was still a fairly young man for retirement. With that in mind he was leaving with a recommendation that after serving five years as Treasurer I be moved out of Cayman into the Colonial Service, where chances for promotion were far greater than at home. I thanked him for his thoughtfulness and kindness in planning my future so well and indicated that I was presently delighted to accept the promotion to Treasurer. I said nothing about the transfer overseas after five years but from then on the thought of it began to bother me, since leaving home in those days was not yet a very pleasant thing for me. However, in my own thinking I hoped for an alternative to the Colonial Service and sure enough it presented itself early the following year: the story will be told in the next important chapter 'A Crucial Period'.

Before going on, however, I should wrap up the personal narrative I began earlier in this chapter concerning my watch business.

In 1963 two brothers from Cayman Brac, Captain Charles and Captain Eldon Kirkconnell, moved to Grand Cayman to develop further their family's commercial business under the Cayman Brac trade

97

name Kirkconnell Brothers Ltd. In 1965 they acquired property on Shedden Road across the street from what is now Elizabethan Square and there built Kirk Plaza, a supermarket. The site was in later years sold to Barclays Bank after the Kirkconnells built their new supermarket on Eastern Avenue. In 1996 Barclays Bank built and opened their large and beautiful new bank building on this former Kirk Plaza site. The Kirkconnells' business at Kirk Plaza included general merchandise, jewellery and watches etc. By the middle of the 1960s, Captain Eldon and I agreed to enter jointly on a personal basis into the watch business, maintaining a bank account in our joint names. We started with the popular Omega and Tissot watches and by 1972 we organized quite a scheme to obtain the Rolex agency, the leader in the watch business. The agency in Cayman for Rolex was at the time held by Swiss Stores Ltd. of Kingston, Jamaica; in other words their agency covered both Jamaica and the Cayman Islands. Eldon made two visits to Jamaica to convince Swiss Stores that they should release the Cayman portion of the agency. They would not agree. I encouraged Eldon to go back and sit in the store until they got tired of him and released the agency. That worked beautifully.

Eldon and I had our separate turns visiting the Rolex head office in Geneva to convince them, as we had Swiss Stores, that Cayman should have a Rolex agency separate from Jamaica's joint arrangement. Eldon went first in July 1972 and Rolex promised to visit Cayman the following year in September to look at the island before making a decision. I thought this was not good enough for us. I had to take my daughter Theresa to Reading University in early September 1972 and after completing that mission I slipped over to Geneva in an attempt to convince Rolex that they should look at the Cayman case as a matter of urgency. I had a wonderful time there with them after a standard meeting and discussion. They first took me to the top floor of the Rolex Building to show me the Rolex watch which was tied outside the submarine *Trieste*, which had made a dive to a depth of a few miles at Bartlett Deep in the Caribbean sea south-east of Grand Cayman. I had heard of the famous watch before visiting Rolex and was therefore very delighted to see the timepiece. The case of the watch was not constructed in the conventional commercial or regular design. Next I was taken to the Spare Parts Department, where I placed an order for parts most commonly needed. Lastly I was assured that the firm would visit Cayman before the end of the year. They certainly did and we had Rolex watches in the Kirk's showcase by early 1973.

Seeing that the joint-venture watch business was rapidly developing, in 1975 Eldon and I decided to incorporate a company, Kirkjon

Traders Ltd., owned by Eldon and myself: my 50 per cent share was put in my wife's name. All our watch business and financial transactions were processed through Kirkjon. By 1979 we had accumulated about nine different watch agencies, which included Patek Philippe and Audemar Piguet. In our joint business arrangements I did the ordering, pricing and servicing of the watches and Eldon the sales and finances. I serviced in the late 1970s an average of 25 watches per week for Kirk Freeport Plaza; most of the work was done on weekends.

In July 1979 I took eight weeks' vacation from the Civil Service and spent seven weeks of it at the Rolex watch factory in Geneva doing a special course in the servicing of Rolex watches. While there, many things came to mind. I finally decided that although the watch business with Eldon had developed quite successfully, the pressure of work in my official capacity of Financial Secretary had also increased enormously. At that stage it became quite clear to me that a decision was necessary to determine my future role in the watch business with Eldon: I had to withdraw from the partnership or quit government and certainly it would not be the latter. I therefore discussed the matter with Rolex's senior officials together with the possibility of their providing Eldon with a good service technician at Kirk Freeport Plaza so that I could quietly leave the watch business. They too wondered how in the world I could do the government's important job and also run a watch business involving the servicing of so many watches. They assured me that a good man would be selected for the Cayman assignment; in fact they had one at the time for the job who was sent to Cayman within a few months. That man, Henry Grunenfelder, is very well known at Kirk Freeport Plaza; he heads the watch servicing section. He arrived here in May 1980 and after 20 years he is still in the job there. Henry and I worked in adjoining rooms at Rolex in Geneva in 1979 but I only became acquainted with him when we first met here in Grand Cayman: he recalls, however, seeing me several times at Rolex in 1979.

When I returned home from Geneva, I discussed with Eldon the ending of our partnership in the watch business; that was really sad news for him. However, he agreed with my proposals including financial settlement. Since our parting in business, whenever I walked into his jewellery store Eldon would say to me, 'Vas, I told you that you should not have quit the business.' Eldon and I got along exceedingly well and never had a moment's disagreement in any of our business affairs. Our families also have always enjoyed a very close and cordial relationship.

PART III

THE BUILDING PROCESS

7

A Crucial Period

The current prosperity and wealth of the Cayman Islands, stemming from the strong economic background for which the country is well known today, began in earnest during the 1960s. Its true starting point, however, could be seen as dating back to the days even beyond the start of World War II. In this instance I am thinking of the successful four annual local regattas beginning in January 1936 and ending with the outbreak of the war. It is the hope that the bright economic and financial outlook brought about largely by the existing growth of the twin industries, tourism and finance and their offspring activities such as insurance, real estate and construction, will continue to increase and strengthen. Of course it has been my prediction that as we move on into the 21st century, the excitement of the new millennium will tend to encourage entrepreneurs, local and foreign alike, to maintain the current level of economic excellence.

Looking back quickly at the period from the end of World War II, we have seen major and important milestones growing out of the economic infrastructure built in these islands to encourage and promote development. First was the building and opening in 1952 of Owen Roberts International Airport. Secondly, the smart move of Cayman's Legislative Assembly in obtaining from the United States government, during construction of the airfield, permission for Cayman's Governor to issue a non-immigrant waiver facility to residents wishing to enter the United States (details are in Chapter 6). Thirdly, the move of Cayman in the early 1960s to opt for a Crown Colony system of government. The new status provided a direct constitutional link with Great Britain that grew out of a majority local vote for the change as opposed to a minority vote to continue the association with Jamaica as provided by Cayman's first Constitution of 1959. Prior to 1959 Cayman and the Turks and Caicos islands operated as dependencies of Jamaica, meaning they were administrated under the Jamaican

Constitution. Under Cayman's new 1959 Constitution, while Jamaica's Governor was also Cayman's Governor, an English Administrator appointed through London was responsible for the country's daily affairs.

The fourth important milestone was the abandoning in 1969 of all foreign countries' tax treaties with the Cayman Islands brought about in the first instance when Cayman became a Dependency of Jamaica, thereby sharing in Jamaica's Constitution. Those milestones just mentioned were followed by two other very important developments. First, a team from the British Development Division in the Caribbean, with headquarters in Barbados, visited Grand Cayman in 1969 at this government's invitation, to examine the local Civil Service and at the same time have a look at economic infrastructure needs. Second was the government's move to control the awful mosquito and sandfly problems, which undermined the quality of life for Caymanians as well as visitors and immigrants. These last two achievements certainly set the pace for what Cayman was to become in the years to follow.

Air transport services have no bounds in importance in any country's physical, social and economic development. Also, the United States non-immigrant waiver facility to the Cayman Islands played an important role in building the seamen's economy even if only to serve the period to the mid-1960s. These and all the other developments above constituted a part of the basic foundation that supported the growth of economic activities, leading to the replacing of the seamen's trade with tourism and finance. Such foundation was very ably commented on by Father Charles Judah of the St Ignatius Catholic Church of Grand Cayman when he said, 'Only a fool thinks that what one man accomplishes does not depend wholly and entirely upon the foundation laid by others.' Father Judah was delivering the main address at the Elmslie Memorial United Church in George Town on Friday 19th November 1982 at the Thanksgiving Service celebrating the 150th anniversary of parliamentary government in the Cayman Islands. His words can, of course, fit into every crevice and corner of continuing developments in any country.

Certainly in Cayman's case, any record of progress from the time I headed the Portfolio of Finance and Development in 1965 would be lacking substantially without taking into account those efforts of previous governments and private individuals to support and begin building the economic, physical and social infrastructure. It therefore required that careful research was made into the depth of past activities to record the foundation so ably laid by others, without which there would not be a base to continue the building exercise in 1965.

104

If Cayman's progress must therefore move on to its logical conclusion, there is the need to slip back into yesteryear and there
recount the efforts and the foundations laid by past Commissioners,
Administrators, Governors, Civil Servants, politicians and the private
sector. They have all certainly contributed much to essential services
such as administration and infrastructure, air transportation, telecommunication, electricity and so much more.

On 1st January 1965 the Administrator, Mr Cumber, appointed me
to the position of Treasurer in succession to Desmond Watler, who
was promoted at the same time to Deputy Administrator. In 1968,
after serving four years in these islands, Mr Cumber moved on to
other jobs.[5] Also in 1968 the Cayman Islands inched up the ladder in
its new strides toward economic development. The Governor in
Council at the time decided that as a matter of prestige, recognition
and image building, those heads of departments largely involved in
international affairs and representation should be given new position
titles authorized by law. These changes were effected. The
Administrator's new title became 'Governor', Deputy Administrator
– 'Chief Secretary', Treasurer – 'Financial Secretary', Head of
Mosquito Research and Control Department – 'Director of Mosquito
Research and Control Unit', Head of Civil Aviation Department –
'Director of Civil Aviation', Chief Education Officer – 'Director of
Education', Postmaster – 'Postmaster General', and others.

Simultaneously with the government's newly redesignated titles, it
was also my opinion that branch managers of large international
banks operating in Cayman lacked sufficient head office delegated
authority. This was especially true when they dealt with certain minor
local business matters, urgent in nature yet which had to be referred
to head office for a decision. Of course it is understood that even
today certain transactions of branch banks must continue to be
referred to head office. However, the view in government was that
even with strong head office policies, local managers' administrative
status could be improved to give them more authority when dealing
with ordinary and urgent transactions. I had a very good friend who
was a senior banker in a European bank with a branch established
here in the early 1970s. I discussed with him my views concerning
local bank managers lack of sufficient authority and the possibility of
his contacting the head offices of these foreign institutions and delivering the message. He appeared quite interested in the discussion and
the suggestion and so he went off with the proposal. I did not hear

[5] He served in London during the period 1976–85 as Director General of the Save the
Children Fund, after which he received a knighthood from Her Majesty The Queen.

from him about this particular request, but I am satisfied that the message reached a few banks' head offices. Shortly after my friend went off with the message, an international bank with a local branch office here was provided with a senior manager directly from head office. At the end of that manager's tour of duty in Cayman, he became area manager for this region. All the other local banks operating here were in time also staffed with able and senior managers and eventually with local staff promoted to senior positions. Thus Cayman's banking industry began moving in the right direction. In 1982 when I retired from government after holding the position of Financial Secretary for 17 years, I was satisfied that the local banking community had become highly specialized in local and international business operations and that the Cayman banking fraternity could be considered very disciplined. A few banks collapsed but that was the norm in all banking communities around the world, and Cayman's record was particularly good in this regard.

When I entered my new office as Treasurer in 1965, I had to devise a plan to bring about the settlement of a 12-year-old debt of $20,000 from the Jamaican Government. The debt occurred because of the need for the Jamaican Treasury to effect a number of credits to Cayman's account which fell short by one. As previous Assistant Treasurer responsible for accounts, I had known about that discrepancy for quite some time and had in fact brought the matter to the attention of my boss, the Treasurer, when it occurred. He wrote to the Accountant General of Jamaica about it at the time but received no encouraging response. The error occurred over a British Colonial Development Corporation loan of $110,000 to assist with the construction of the Grand Cayman Owen Roberts International Airport, completed in 1952. Because the loan was not readily available at the start of construction, the Jamaican Government very kindly advanced funds in moieties of $20,000 each to meet contractors' claims and other expenses in the meantime.

When CDC released the loan funds, Jamaica claimed its advances from the proceeds. Unfortunately, however, they claimed one extra advance of $20,000. In 1964, twelve years later, two additional errors of $4,000 each were also discovered in Cayman's accounts with Jamaica. Those latter two errors were with respect to charges for medical supplies debited twice to the Cayman account. By that time Jamaica was in debt to Cayman in a total amount of $28,000. The outstanding debt was certainly worth a trip to Jamaica for the amount was big money to Cayman in those days. In April 1965 I brought those errors to the attention of the Administrator, Mr Cumber, who encouraged me to go to Jamaica at once and argue the case. I did exactly that and after a hard-fought battle with the Accountant General, his deputy and three assistants, they found the two medical supplies duplications amounting to $8,000, but not the $20,000. I therefore went to see the Financial Secretary, G. Arthur Brown in an endeavour to clear the $20,000 error. We spent a few minutes in a friendly discussion for I knew Arthur very well. Shortly after I mentioned my mission to Jamaica and gave some details of the case. He looked briefly at the Jamaica Treasury statements I carried with me, and in short order he discovered the error and gave immediate approval for the credit to Cayman's Treasury accounts. I returned home with the credit statements for the $28,000 feeling that I had accomplished successfully my first important mission.

As Treasurer, later Financial Secretary, I adopted two adages. One is, 'Courage in a good cause brings its own reward.' The other is by John Wesley, founder of the Methodist denomination, who said, 'Gain all you can, save all you can, give all you can.' These were my guiding principles over seventeen years as Financial Secretary and four years as Minister of Development and Natural Resources (1984–88).

Cayman's seaman's economy served the country well during the period leading up to the mid-1960s, a time when the islands' economy certainly strengthened. That period demonstrated what was mentioned earlier, a 'foundation laid by others'. Local seamen were endowed with the tradition of the sea and seamanship from the days of early settlers in Cayman. Many of the locals were themselves descendants of shipwrecked survivors. Those men knew the art of manning ships of any size and class and made their livelihood as sailors. They developed an international reputation for being world-class seamen. They had sailed the seas of the world and undergone many hardships at times.

A genuine hero among seamen was Captain Tom Diaz. I was reminded of his feat in 1962, when His Royal Highness, The Duke of Edinburgh visited Grand Cayman for four days in April, the first guest in the newly completed Government House.

At a state reception at the Old Galleon Beach Hotel, the Duke was delighted to meet Tom Diaz, who had saved his uncle's life some 26 years earlier. He had an interesting chat with Captain Tom, who told him that in 1936 the Duke's uncle, Earl Mountbatten, was in Jamaica with his auxiliary yacht the *Lost Horizon*, and having lost his captain, requested J.S. Webster & Sons of Jamaica to recommend a replacement. 'I was selected by the Websters,' he told the Duke. Tom Diaz was well known in Cayman and by the Websters, who migrated from here to Jamaica and established large business interests there. I also

107

knew Tom Diaz quite well. He was at one time my navigation teacher and was greatly admired by all who knew him in Cayman for his ability as a master sea captain and as a carpenter.

Tom told the Duke that he sailed with his uncle the Earl aboard his yacht in early 1937 but the boat met with tragedy as it approached the Bay of Biscay on the western coast of France. A fire broke out in the engine room of the vessel and it sank to the bottom almost immediately. Due to the skill of the captain they took to a lifeboat with Mountbatten on board and reached Portsmouth safely. On the social side of his English experience, Captain Tom was invited to St James's Palace to dine with members of the Royal Family including the Duke of Edinburgh. He reminded the Duke too of his (Tom's) dress in a full uniform of white with a captain's white hat. Tom said that everything he touched on the table at St James's Palace was golden, and he certainly enjoyed the occasion. Earl Mountbatten was indeed very thankful to Tom Diaz and had recommended to the Marine Board of England that Diaz receive some public recognition. Diaz was therefore granted an open Master's Licence, valid anywhere in the world: it was the only such licence in the Cayman Islands. The story of Tom Diaz goes beyond being just a sea captain. He was also a skilled carpenter and operated a grocery store here in George Town. Many days in my younger years I had to assist him as clerk in his store. Tom's association with Earl Mountbatten and his dining at St James's Palace with the Royal Family is an experience he told to me personally at the time he was giving me lessons in navigation. The history of such individuals should be recorded.

In the mid-1960s when the sea-going industry faced a slump and when the seamen would undoubtedly miss the sea, they had no alternative but to seek employment elsewhere. Few opportunities were in sight either at home or abroad. Returning home, with no prospects of going back to their jobs at sea, would be a near disaster to them.

Another sad situation was that under no circumstances could these men revert at that stage to their time-honoured economic traditions of the pre-war days, such as shipbuilding, thatch rope making and fishing at Mosquito Quays. Those industries were no longer in existence; they had passed away during and after World War II. Many of the men, on the other hand, had during the war acquired skills and much experience in other fields that could serve them well in the post-war period. Their ambition was to continue working either at sea or take shore-based jobs that could lead them to make contacts and acquire improved working conditions, good standards of living and increased opportunities. Now, whatever activities they chose at home, it would certainly take them quite some time to remove the sea from their blood and be entirely satisfied with a home-based life: this on the other hand was not a matter of choice, rather it was one of expediency and need. An alternative activity to sea life was for them to go for academic training to specialize in technical and professional fields, whereby they could in time qualify for senior positions in local industries like finance and tourism, if and when those industries developed. It was the thinking then too that, even if technical training was developed, it would likely take at least 15 years for the government and the private sector to organize and develop the training infrastructure to produce qualified people for the local industries. Of course 15 years later it all happened when Caymanians were holding senior positions in local institutions like banks, trust companies, the tourist industry and other related activities. At the same time a number of qualified Caymanian lawyers, accountants and other professionals were also entering the local job market.

Going back a step into the past prior to 1965, it may be worthwhile to have a look at the local economy which provided the islands' income. Before going to Jamaica in April 1965 on the money chase, I had been watching seamen who returned home from jobs at sea hanging around at street corners in George Town. When I spoke to a few of them to get an idea of what the situation at sea was, they explained that their ships were tied up at the docks in the United States and they were sent home without any return instructions or schedules. It was the thinking then that the situation could be the start of a recession or a slump in the shipping industry. It was an industry that had served the Cayman economy so well ever since the end of the war. Of course the situation was later confirmed to be an economic recession in western-hemisphere shipping. Along with that problem was the fact that shipping was also being effectively revitalized by modern advanced technology in crewing, cargo transportation and other efficiencies. These involved large automated supertankers and containerized cargo ships. Both required fewer crew for their operation. That situation naturally placed a surplus of local seamen on the market. The surplus could not be effectively reduced in Cayman's case because of another new problem coming to light: shipping companies began recruiting cheaper labour from other countries including a few in the Far East. One could therefore see that local seamen were faced with huge tasks if they were to find alternative employment in the Merchant Marine or at home. It must have been quite a feeling of despair to those men who over the previous ten years enjoyed steady employment with National Bulk Carriers, a company that became the largest employer of Cayman's seamen. Now with no job prospects for those men, the 1965 near-disaster certainly led the government to think seriously of alternative activities that would provide job opportunities. It also ran across my mind at the time that the situation might present a golden opportunity for me to become involved in the promotion of some form of local economic activity. That would certainly provide a valid excuse to forget Administrator Rose's offer to send me into the Colonial Service after serving a few years in the local position of Treasurer.

Assessing the overall situation at that point, I termed it 'a crossroads of uncertainties pointing in all directions'. One thing could be seen clearly ahead: unless the mosquito and sandfly problems were promptly and properly addressed to attain the desired level of control, efforts to move economic development forward could not succeed. 'Mosquito control' are therefore two words without which a story of Cayman's success could never have been written. Details of this landmark achievement are set out in the next chapter.

With the successful breakthrough in mosquito and sandfly control, the country went forward with positive indicators that the seamen's industry was being replaced by finance and tourism. The financial industry was coupled with Cayman's rise to become an attractive and well-liked tourist destination, with its exceptional diving facilities considered second only to the world's leader, the Great Barrier Reef of Australia. Such a reputation made the local diving quite popular. In fact the popularity of Cayman as a diving destination was followed in 1986 with the creation of the Marine Parks by statutory provisions: this further helped to set the stage for rapid economic growth. It was recorded at that time that approximately 40 per cent of visitors to Grand Cayman were business people who came with their families on a short vacation as tourists when in fact their main mission was in connection with planned business interests to be based in Cayman.

In the early stages of Cayman's rise to international prominence as an offshore centre, it became necessary to study and to grasp quite fully the basic needs and requirements to achieve and maintain that position. Those fundamental ingredients were political stability, excellent telecommunication, reliable air services, relative freedom in the movement of international currencies, dependable financial services, flexible laws and no form of direct taxes such as income tax, corporation tax, estate tax and inheritance tax. All those requirements also demanded the exercise of technical skills, political acumen and patience. In the process it was necessary to get the message across that the advantages of the Cayman tax haven facilities were not merely 'tax avoidance' as such. It also included peace of mind on the safety of investments based here and the assurance that one was dealing in an offshore situation that offered advantages beyond many

110

other destinations with their burdensome monetary systems and exchange control regulations.

Another point of interest is that no genuine business coming this way had to wait days and weeks to be given satisfactory answers to its inquiries. In addition, the government went as far as to examine its companies' incorporation time factor in an endeavour to make it possible for a company to be completely registered and delivered in 24 hours. This of course was in case of genuine need and urgency; no extra charge would be made for this special service. It should be mentioned too that by the end of the 1970s, these islands were able to provide top professional services to the industries. These included legal, accounting and auditing, trust and banking, insurance and finance, together with services that were also advisory and extended to most areas of business. Even though business operated under a tax-free system, we here viewed this as being very advantageous to the investors' own countries as it maximized the incidence of profits at convenient stages. It was also made quite clear from the very out-set that Cayman would not be used as a harbour for questionable institutions or questionable business deals.

The question that has repeatedly been asked is: 'Why is Cayman a natural tax haven?' The answer is that from the country's early existence, its government's total income was derived only from in-direct taxes. In fact there had never been any thoughts or suggestions that local revenue be mixed with income from direct sources. Government's indirect revenues have until the present time been derived from customs import duty, which provides approximately 40 per cent of total recurrent income. Other significant indirect revenues are sale of stamps, company registration and annual fees, banks and trust companies licensing fees, tourist accommodation tax and many smaller measures. Cayman has developed well without the need to introduce any form of direct taxes such as income tax, corporation tax, capital gains tax, sales tax, inheritance tax, death dues etc. It is also the current policy of this and hopefully successive governments to maintain the present revenue base. If on the other hand the local offshore financial industry and tourism operations were affected by the introduction of any form of direct taxes, it is very likely that those institutions and persons involved locally would quickly assess the situation to determine whether to remain or leave. If the operators did eventually leave, the situation thus created would certainly be a sad one for the country. Of course, income-wise, the same situation was experienced here in 1965 when the seamen's economy collapsed. Thus Cayman has a strong vested inter-est in continuing to support and maintain its current position in spite

111

of adverse remarks being made from time to time about offshore tax havens.

The tax haven operation developed from the outset without hindrance. However, there was one problem in the way which had to be dealt with and removed. During the period that the Cayman Islands were a Dependency of Jamaica, starting in 1863 and ending in 1959, Jamaica negotiated tax treaties with other countries operating the direct tax system, including the United States. Under those tax treaties the free exchange of confidential tax information was a condition. Those treaties held by Jamaica automatically included the Cayman Islands because of our subordinate position as a Dependency. Of course no one paid attention to the commitment even after Cayman's Dependency status with Jamaica was abolished in 1959 or even after Jamaica's independence in 1962 when the Cayman Islands also gained Crown Colony status, meaning a complete separation from Jamaica. I should state that Cayman did not at any time operate any form of direct taxes such as income tax.

After the mid-1960s when Cayman became serious about promoting its tax haven business, it suddenly came to my attention that Cayman was still associated with Jamaica's foreign tax treaties. Instantly Jamaica was advised through the British High Commissioner's Office in Kingston that the Cayman Islands no longer wished to be associated with Jamaica's tax treaties with other countries. Shortly after the request was made, Cayman was notified that effective 1st January 1969 the United States Treasury would withdraw its income tax treaty between the United States and the United Kingdom as extended to Jamaica, including in 1959 the Cayman Islands. This in reality meant that the US tax treaties would no longer apply to Cayman. The decision of the United States Treasury was reported in the *Caymanian Weekly* newspaper of 14th November 1968, page 9. What was most important as well, after the action of the United States to remove the Cayman Islands from its tax treaties, was that Cayman could then establish complete confidentiality in its financial operation and be termed a tax haven.

It was also assumed at the time that since no countries other than the United States had replied to the Jamaica tax treaties' inclusion of the Cayman Islands, these islands could then be considered an established tax haven. This was wonderful news to investors as the new situation provided a real boost to Cayman's offshore business. Had the treaty remained in force, the United States tax authorities, and any others for that matter who may have been similarly associated, might conceivably have demanded certain tax information from these islands. This would have had serious consequences for confidentiality legislation as applied within the legal jurisdiction of these islands. However, it was made specifically and abundantly clear by the United States Treasury in January 1969, which was all important, that from then they had no legal right to request any tax information from the Cayman Islands. As far as Cayman is concerned the same ruling of the United States would apply in cases of any other countries that might have had similar tax treaties with Jamaica which included the Cayman Islands. Since the decision of the United States 30 years ago to exclude Cayman from their tax treaty we have not had any further communications on the subject.

8

Mosquito and Sandfly Control

In the early days of attempted control of mosquitoes and sandflies it was unwise to take a walk after sunset if you were not doused with insect repellent or did not have a 'smoke pot' for company. Until the early 1970s mosquitoes remained one of the major barriers to the development of the Cayman economy. However, eventual control of the nuisance was due to nine years of effort by a remarkable and gifted individual, Dr Marco Giglioli. Throughout that period he fought the war against mosquitoes and sandflies, on many fronts, pioneering new methods of attack.

It was understood that sandflies were not as difficult to control as mosquitoes because the former breed largely in sand, where effective control was much simpler. In the case of mosquitoes, however, anywhere water settled during rains, whether in swamps, marshy lands or rock holes, would be ideal breeding places for them, making them very difficult to control after the rains.

Another difficult situation in Grand Cayman at that time was that more than 50 per cent of the 80 square miles of land area was swampy and ideal for mosquito breeding. In the season April to September, or after heavy rains, mosquitoes were simply awful. Sometimes they would annoy visiting tourists to the extent that a few were known to arrive one evening and depart next day to some more peaceful destination like Jamaica's north coast. To describe the mosquito and sandfly problems in Grand Cayman, the prime development area of the three islands, was quite fascinating from a social point of view and especially among the low-income segments of the society. The mosquitoes certainly caused social and home life during the season between April and September to be quite miserable and unpleasant. Of course Little Cayman, with its 10 square miles of land area and with a large proportion of swamps, still has its attendant mosquito problems as well during the rainy season. Also its small

114

population suffers unpleasantness during the season just like people in Grand Cayman. As Little Cayman develops and the population grows, similar physical control measures as adopted in Grand Cayman may need to be considered and extended there as well.

Not one of the 28 species of mosquito found on Grand Cayman is native to the islands, as reported by the Mosquito Research and Control Unit (MRCU) through John Warren, a member of the editorial staff of the local *Northwester* magazine in its June 1975 issue. Apparently, according to the article, there is no record or mention of mosquitoes in any of the old writings and it is not likely that the mariners would have failed to report their presence. It was the thinking that mosquitoes were brought to the island by turtle fishermen visiting Cuba or Mosquito Quays between 1839 and 1850, for it is recorded that in 1897 two missionaries who landed here from Brazil died of yellow fever. Also in a report to the Bureau of Health and Education in Kingston, Jamaica in 1934, Commissioner Cardinall mentioned that the mosquitoes in Cayman during the rains were thicker than in Alaska or Lapland and nearly as bad in the daytime as at night. At such time no one would think of going out without a portable smoke fire. The plague began without variation in late April and increased to an incredible intensity between June and September. It is local history that animals like cows, pigs and goats have been smothered to death by mosquitoes and that poultry pine and die. These are facts I can personally confirm as well because it was in 1934 at the age of 12 when I came to Grand Cayman and witnessed these awful mosquito problems.

An early attempt to battle the mosquito problem began in 1938 by an officer from the Health Department of Jamaica, Mr Frank Somers. He made the first serious attempt to control mosquitoes by organizing a great public meeting in the George Town Town Hall on Thursday 5th May 1938 with the Commissioner, Mr Allen Cardinall, as Chairman. The subject of the meeting was written in big bold letters: 'WAR has been DECLARED ... Cayman invaded: Ultimatum issued. Flies and mosquitoes to be exterminated' on a public notice board. The meeting created some interest but the programme of control was not very successful as many local residents failed to fully cooperate. Of course Mr Somers had to first gain support of the populace to undertake programmes like bush cleaning and oil spreading in sections of the swamp. Despite some resistance from the local public, the measures seemed to have had some success and the support also grew. On 13th August 1938 heavy rains fell and continued for several days, flooding the swamps and many residential areas. A few days after, swarms of mosquitoes darkened the sky over George

115

Town. They grew so dense that millions of the tiny black objects, looking like dark clouds, took flight and disappeared over the horizon, migrating to their death. Although millions vanished for ever in the great migration, many were left, which continued to make life unpleasant for residents. Mr Somers was discredited for this awful mosquito experience, which was clearly not his fault. He returned to Jamaica shortly after.

In 1942 the government appointed Mr Bertie Ebanks of West Bay to be Public Health Inspector and sent him to Jamaica on a nine-month public health course. In 1948 it was discovered that 99 per cent of houses here in George Town were infected with *aedes aegypti*, the mosquitoes that carry dengue and yellow fever; fortunately neither of those two diseases was present on the island at the time. Later that year a Dr George Giglioli was sent here by World Health Organization (WHO) to advise on the eradication of the yellow fever mosquito and to examine the mosquito population. Dr Giglioli was an internationally known physician and malariologist. He warned of the dangerous situation existing with the presence of the *aedes aegypti* and suggested a properly run campaign to eliminate them.

Shortly after receiving his advice, Mr Ebanks was sent to Guyana to study the method used by Dr Giglioli to treat and eliminate the *aedes aegypti*. On Mr Ebanks' return he began the first large-scale spraying in the island's history. All houses were sprayed inside and outside and under the floor with DDT mixed with kerosene oil in a simple procedure. Before spraying in a house could take place, Mr Ebanks would enter and ensure that anything that could be harmed by the spray was covered. Mr Ebanks laboured intently on the eradication programme until 1950, when after further tests carried out by WHO it was confirmed that no further traces of the *aedes aegypti* mosquito were found. Mr Ebanks must be commended for his masterly and excellent job. In 1955, the year before he retired from the government, Mr Ebanks began the first fogging (ejecting a thick mist by machine to kill insects) to be seen in Cayman. The only difference between then and now is that Mr Ebanks used DDT, a very persistent chemical that would linger in the environment indefinitely. Now all insecticides used in fogging and aerial spraying are strongly non-persistent and break down within 24 hours into a harmless solution. Another of Mr Ebanks' difficult tasks was to ensure that his small budget of $200 per annum would take care of the entire needs of his Public Health Department, which included spraying and fogging. On Mr Ebanks' retirement, he was succeeded by Mr McNee McLaughlin, who also found the tight budget difficult to work with.

People who lived in mosquito-infested areas prior to the introduction of physical control had to cope with the pests as best they could. In those days, homes without screens in the windows and doors had to make use of a smoke pan outside the house, as smoke chased the nuisances away. On the inside, for sleeping at nights, windows and doors had to be closed early in the evenings and the bedrooms sprayed, or smoked with black-flag, a powder that burns slowly while the smoke kills all insects including the mosquitoes and sandflies. Lamps could not be lit at nights in poorly constructed houses as mosquitoes, and in the early mornings sandflies, would crawl through any visible openings in the walls and find their way into the bedrooms. Those homes that had bathrooms with screened windows facing the outside of the house could survive the sandfly problem through a simple device for trapping the tiny flies. As sandflies could get through the screen meshes, a kerosene lamp would be left burning in the bathroom at nights. When the sandflies made their way into the bathroom through the screen, they would immediately be attracted to the lamp. That control made sleeping at nights, and especially in the early mornings, much more peaceful and pleasant for the household.

In 1964 the government was conscious of the need to control mosquitoes so as to get on with economic development. It was therefore decided that a sustained scientific effort should be made to determine the different species of mosquito and their habits so as to obtain advice and assistance from the British government towards a control programme. The assistance came with firm plans for the establishment of a Mosquito Research and Control Unit operation in Grand Cayman. The unit was built and equipped with a new laboratory the same year. The public was warned that the preparation and building of the unit should not be taken as an indication that the mosquito and sandfly problem would be solved in the near future. On the contrary, a thorough investigation and assessment of the problem would take time, and only when the work was completed would the unit be able to determine the most effective and inexpensive methods of controlling the nuisances.

In early 1965 the government went through London and applied for an entomologist to head the MRCU. In fact before construction of the unit began in 1964, the application was placed through London for a director. Dr Raymond Lewthwaite, Medical Advisor to the Ministry of Overseas Development, approached Dr Marco E.C. Giglioli, DSc, FIB 101, PhD, BSc (Hons), regarding the MRCU job in the Cayman Islands. Marco was the son of Dr George Giglioli, who had earlier advised the government through WHO. When first approached, Marco declined the invitation as he had yet another year

117

to go on his contract with the Medical Research Council (MRC) of the United Kingdom: this involved an assignment in Gambia as an entomologist dealing with swamps and mosquitoes. The offer was renewed following the end of his contract with the MRC and this time he accepted the position. He arrived in Grand Cayman in December 1965 with his wife Jean and their two children, George and Maria. However, Marco's first visit to Grand Cayman had been six months earlier. At that time he came in the company of Martin Brunt from the Land Resources Division of the Ministry of Overseas Development in London. The rains were late on Marco's first visit and so he found it very pleasant here with very few mosquitoes; that was really not Cayman's standard for July. However, just as he returned to England to make his final arrangements to move here, the rains descended and the mosquitoes followed. Even after physical control of mosquitoes came into effect, the thought by many people was that when Dr Giglioli left the mosquitoes would return. The interesting part of that legend is that Marco Giglioli will always be with us, as he was buried here after his death in 1984.

Marco's academic achievements were obtained after a very extensive period of studies. This included his higher education at McGill University in Canada in 1946, then at McDonald College, Canada in 1949. Thereafter he moved to London to attend the London School of Hygiene and Tropical Medicine in 1953, then the Institute of Biologists in the United Kingdom in 1964, the University of London in 1974 and again the Institute of Biologists in 1977. At the University of London in 1974 he gained the DSc degree, which is usually given in a single field but in Marco's case it was simultaneously given for medical entomology, zoology and ecology, in recognition of his broad-spectrum approach to scientific problems. From these academic institutions he gained the qualifications he wanted in order to meet the challenges which countries like Cayman posed for him.

His experience began in 1947 in Canada with the Department of Agriculture and Fisheries Research Board. In 1954 he joined WHO and took an assignment in Liberia as an entomologist. From that job he went back to London and worked with the MRC; he was sent on another job to Gambia, where he gained valuable experience from the Gambian swamps and from their mosquito problems. He left Gambia in 1963 and spent two years with the MRC in London writing up his report and the results for publication. Before Marco came to Cayman he wrote to his father, Dr George Giglioli, about the job offer in Cayman and asked his advice since his father had been sent here in 1948 by WHO. In reply, apart from complimentary remarks about the people of Cayman and their homes in comparison to other West

Indian islands, George said this: 'On the question of control, let alone eradication of the Cayman mosquitoes, I could only advise you in one word – Nuts.' Marco nevertheless accepted the job here in 1965 when he was well equipped academically and with the necessary experience and skill to take up the Cayman challenge. In later years, when Marco was satisfied that mosquitoes were effectively under control, he brought his father back to Cayman so he could see for himself that the mosquito problem in Grand Cayman was in fact not really insurmountable. Advanced technology and experience in scientific research had no doubt given Marco the edge over his father.

At Marco's interment in March 1984, His Excellency the Governor, Mr Peter Lloyd, spoke in his tribute of Marco's contribution to the social and economic development of these islands. He went on to say that the formidable task which Marco undertook to control Cayman's mosquitoes and the gratifying results of his efforts deserve the highest recognition. Those words were very appropriate. However, there are few local residents, apart from visitors and the younger generation, who do not fully appreciate the extent to which mosquitoes in Grand Cayman have been controlled and the resulting benefits as reflected in the wealth and prosperity of the Cayman of today. Indeed, without Marco's concerted and venturesome efforts, technical ability and determination to achieve his mosquito control goal, Cayman would not have succeeded in eventually becoming one of the leaders in the world of offshore financial centres. Dr Marco Giglioli was honoured in 1971 by Her Majesty The Queen with the OBE (Officer of the Most Excellent Order of the British Empire).

Marco's study of the local common mosquito problems led him to consider various approaches. The most successful method of physical control is to fill or reclaim swamps where mosquitoes breed. A good example of this is Miami Beach back in the early 1900s. To look at the area today few people would believe that it was once dense swamp. Locally, portions of Grand Cayman's swamps on the north coast from West Bay to Newlands have also been reclaimed. However, it will take a long time for the islands of Grand Cayman and Little Cayman to be converted into dry land, largely because there is a fairly strong local resistance, among the conservation group especially, to reclamation of all swamp lands. This is due to the swamps' connecting support to marine life, particularly in the North Sound area.

A study of Grand Cayman's swamps indicated that the black mangrove, unlike the red and white mangroves, grows generally in areas subject to infrequent periodic flooding by either rains or high tides. It thus provides an ideal breeding environment for the local mosquito.

119

The female lays her eggs on damp mud in the black mangrove forest rather than in water; the eggs are hatched only when the water level rises and the eggs are covered. Laying eggs to hatch as the water level rises explains why five or six days after heavy rains or high tides, clouds of mosquitoes rise from the swamp. This also explains why the black mangrove generally provides the most desired breeding areas for the local mosquito.

The first approach to physical control by MRCU was in March 1968 in an 85-acre swamp area north of Owen Roberts Airport. It was based on the exact system successfully used in Florida, that is, to construct impoundment areas where the water level could be raised and kept constant in order to deny the mosquito a place to lay her eggs. This method was not effective in Grand Cayman. Following the formula used in Florida, the area was completely surrounded by a dyke so it could be flooded by the use of pressure pumps; after flooding, the pumps would be moved on to other areas also to be flooded, returning only to top off water lost by evaporation. Unfortunately the base rock on the island proved to be so porous that as soon as the pumps stopped, the water level would begin instantly to fall; permanent pumps were not financially practical. The rationale behind this method was that, by covering the mud in constant layers of water, mosquitoes would be denied their favourite breeding grounds. But the results of the Grand Cayman experiment were not encouraging. In addition to the problem of leaking dykes was environmental damage when the excess salt water killed the black mangrove trees. At that stage the large amount of water remaining in the dyke area provided ideal breeding grounds for a different kind of mosquito, the *culex nigripalpus*, which can act as a disease carrier. Fortunately the disease *culex nigripalpus* was not present on the island although the mosquitoes were; also, maintaining their favourite breeding grounds would pose a future health danger to Cayman. The overall results indicated that another approach to physical control was necessary.

During this same year, 1968, a port disinfecting officer was appointed and arrangements made for him to spray any ships or aircraft arriving in Grand Cayman. This was particularly important because Cayman Brac, Little Cayman and many nearby islands were still infected with the yellow fever mosquitoes. Grand Cayman, on the other hand, was declared free of *aedes aegypti* from 1950 when the last eradication programme, undertaken by S.O. Ebanks the local Sanitary Officer, and followed by tests by WHO, confirmed that no further traces of the insects were found on the island.

A second experiment to find an acceptable method of physical control was one called 'Hatch-and-Strand', which also failed because it was again centred on the life cycle of the mosquito. The explanation given for this system was that when the eggs hatch, the larvae emerging are water creatures and there is a period of from five to seven days before they can escape as adult mosquitoes. The plan was to produce, by pumping, a flash flood in any given area and stimulate all the eggs to hatch during the dry season. Before the larvae could become adults, the swamp would drain and strand the larvae; they would die as the sun evaporated the remaining surface water. This plan did not succeed due to high tides in the dry season.

The emphasis on physical control shifted a third time and became the final and successful attempt; it is the method presently in use. Briefly, it is to alter the water level favoured by the black mangrove and also the mosquitoes to one preferred by the red mangrove and therefore disliked by the mosquitoes. This was accomplished by building dykes in the swamps and linking them to a series of canals. The system allowed the tide to rise and fall and to move readily and penetrate into the swamps, thus making the more remote black mangrove grounds wetter and therefore less attractive to mosquitoes for the purpose of laying their eggs. This technique also has the advantage that since no pumps are needed to move the water level, there is no continuing cost. In addition the canals provide living space and reservoirs for fish that prey on mosquito larvae, thus assisting in the control programme. Following this marvellous and exciting breakthrough, commented Marco that, 'This physical control is not a one hundred per cent effective cure, for some mosquitoes will always be breeding outside the control areas. However, the point is, if physical control can reduce them by fifty per cent, then with aircraft or with foggers we are bound to further reduce those remaining numbers and thus achieve a higher measure of control.' And by faith, skill, hard work and determination, so it was.

In mobilizing for the massive third attempt, to achieve early success in physical control, Marco made strong pleas to the government for financial support to provide adequate staff, equipment and material for the job. Of course, as Financial Secretary, I understood the programme quite well and the need for the required funds so as to wage an all-out campaign. Therefore, Marco did not have to convince me of his financial need for he would be preaching to the converted. The government, too, was very well convinced that to move forward with economic development in an island infested with mosquitoes and sandflies would be quite impossible unless control of the nuisances came first. However, people in certain areas of politics had some reservations regarding MRCU's fund requirements even though a large part of the MRCU's capital budget came from British aid funds. Marco, in discussing his financial requirements with me, indicated his understanding that funds have always been a sensitive area in any government programme, and rightly so, as it is the people's money which is being spent.

MRCU had a very good record for both improvising needed equipment and for making the most efficient use of funds available to the department. An example was that when Marco decided the fairly expensive British Hy-Mac was the heavy-construction machinery required to cut through Cayman's hard limestone terrain to create the canal network by the dyke system, he wrote to the company in England and obtained the local agency. This saved him 15 per cent on the cost of equipment and spare parts. As a result he ordered several hydraulic excavators from Hy-Mac in 1968 to undertake dyke building. Simultaneous to the order, he sent Tom Jackson, a member of staff, to England to receive training in the use of the Hy-Mac excavating machines. Tom's mechanical skills stood him in good stead in his job as MRCU's leading heavy-equipment operator. Marco also requested a small helicopter to aid his work in the thick swamp areas but the government thought this a big joke. Soon afterwards the Finance Officer of British Development Division in Barbados visited Grand Cayman and over lunch I mentioned to him the helicopter story. He asked what the estimated cost was; I said approximately $72,000. Surprisingly, some weeks later this government was notified that British aid funds of approximately $60,000 were approved for the helicopter project. A number of years later when MRCU decided to review its control programme, the government suggested that the helicopter be sold and the funds invested in an aircraft for aerial spraying. The proposal was finally agreed and when sale of the helicopter was negotiated and accepted, the machine flew away to its second destination.

In 1968, as funds became available, all the major areas of Grand Cayman were fogged. This aspect of control was most effective in areas like West Bay and George Town where the network of roads allowed excellent penetration – unlike the Bodden Town, East End and North Side areas, where the results were not as effective. Although fogging brought reasonable relief in certain residential areas, it was still inadequate for the desired control required over the remaining 50 per cent of mosquitoes not eliminated by the effective dyke system in the black mangrove swamps. The next step was therefore aerial spraying, which has been used with much success in many parts of the world, especially in countries with a perennial problem of access to the interior of the heavily forested swamps. With the aerial spraying scheme came one more problem. Since most of MRCU's capital expenditure funds came through British Overseas Aid, it was a requirement that purchase of the desired aircraft should be within the sterling area. However, agreement was eventually reached for the purchase of an American aircraft, a Cessna Ag Wagon B, which was an ideal and well known machine in this part of the world for this particular job. It arrived in Grand Cayman at the end of 1970. In addition to the desired aircraft, MRCU also recruited an excellent pilot, François Lesieur, who had extensive experience in crop dusting and spraying operations. François at the time held both helicopter and fixed-wing licences as well as being a qualified aircraft engineer. He was in fact a very valuable person to the aerial spraying operation.

Aerial spraying went into effect in mid-1971. It is a highly complex combination of science and art. It also requires the solving of many problems before it can be really effective. Formulas that have worked in other parts of the world may point the way but many tests are required before a combination of solutions that is right for the area in question can be found. Because many of these tests have their roots in the area of physical science rather than biology, a physicist, Cliff Lee, was recruited for the unit.

The George Town and West Bay swamp areas contained the first dykes linked with canals for the physical control programme. The choice of those areas from the Seven Mile Beach was simply because they formed the hub of Cayman's tourist industry, which at the end of the 1960s was being seriously promoted and developed.

By combining the canal network and the successful dyke system with ground fogging and aerial spraying, MRCU by 1974 finally came to the hour of triumph for its successful physical control of mosquitoes. This was indeed the long-awaited moment to start planning the new economy made up of the twin industries of tourism and finance. Nor did the government hesitate to announce its intention to move forward with those plans. It further stated that these islands were being pressured by sheer need to build and reflect, by Cayman's political goodwill, honesty and integrity, the country's ambition to move up the ladder into the world of the offshore industry. Those activities in finance and tourism were in fact the only areas in which Cayman could move to develop its economic potential with any degree of success.

In ending this story on how mosquitoes were effectively brought under control in these islands, we should all say a big 'thank you' to Marco Giglioli for his tremendous efforts as Director of the programme in ensuring that the enormous task would indeed result in a great success. We must also not forget to give due credit and our grateful thanks to all his staff members who worked so diligently with him and whom he left behind to carry on the task of physical control. They all formed a giant team and have certainly done a wonderful job so far.

9

Economic Infrastructure

Looking at Cayman's economic situation early after taking over responsibility for finance and development in early 1965, I had real concern for what I saw. First was the collapse of the seaman's industry and secondly the terrible mosquito and sandfly problem that prevented any attempt to build or establish new industries like finance and tourism, both of which, but especially the financial industry, were in my thoughts for the whole of 1965. By early December of that year Dr Marco Giglioli arrived to take up his position as Cayman's mosquito and sandfly control chief. The news of Dr Giglioli's arrival was most gratifying to a large segment of the population as it brought to them new hope for the economy and also hope for an improved social life once the mosquitoes and sandflies were brought under control. To me it was like a new day dawning, for the news of Marco's arrival also brought to me renewed vigour and encouragement to move on with development of the two industries. We had faith that Marco was the right choice for Cayman. Indeed he was, for eventually control of the pests was achieved, to the good fortune of the country.

Early on the morning of Boxing Day 1965 while I was still lying in bed, my thoughts went into action. First was the most important and crucial decision to be settled: 'Should the government move on with the building of a financial industry?' The answer was positively 'yes'. The other thought that came to mind quickly afterwards was: 'How long would the building process likely take in order that the industry develop successfully and become a prominent part of the economy?' At that moment I began looking through an imaginary tunnel to estimate the time frame. I saw at the other end a light and, in between, a beautiful bright hue. The estimated distance through the tunnel in terms of time representing the growth period to maturity was 20 years. The building of this industry depended too on government's full cooperation, support and action.

By May 1966, government did move forward with a package of three pieces of legislation in support of the financial industry. They were the Banks and Trust Companies Regulations Law, a Trust Law and a new Exchange Control Regulations Law. The latter was to replace the English Exchange Control Law that had been extended to most British Commonwealth countries including the Cayman Islands.

The new Exchange Control Regulations Law (EC) was another of my dreams. I saw from the start that such a local piece of legislation could play a vital role in developing the financial industry. In fact there was on the local statute book at the time the English EC Law extended many years before to all sterling area countries within the British Commonwealth, including Jamaica. During Cayman's constitutional dependency status with Jamaica prior to 1959, Jamaica extended in 1954 the English EC Law to the Cayman Islands. The English law was somewhat restrictive in its foreign investment provisions, which offshore investors complained about. I therefore wrote to the Administrator, Mr Cumber (later honoured by Her Majesty The Queen and known as Sir John Cumber), and requested that he approach the government's legal draughtsman, the Stipendiary Magistrate, Mr Horsfall, to inquire if he would be so kind as to prepare the proposed law. I provided part of the basic information for the draft. However, Mr Horsfall confessed that he was unable to assist without more drafting details. I then suggested to the Administrator that he write to London regarding the request for a new exchange control law. London replied to say that the British government many years ago produced an exchange control law that was extended to all British Territories including the Cayman Islands. Therefore, if Cayman now wished to have a new law it would have to produce one through local efforts. Following London's reply, the Administrator sent me the EC file with a note suggesting that I try my hand at producing the draft legislation.

I immediately appointed a small committee of five persons from the government and the private sector, including me as chairman. About four weeks later I presented the draft law with its accompanying regulations, orders and notices to the Administrator. He replied in these very encouraging words:

Thank you very much for your report No. T/E4 of the 15th September 1965, containing the recommendations of the committee which sat under your Chairmanship to consider a matter of Exchange Control in the Cayman Islands. I am most grateful for your report and I agree entirely with its recommendations which are now to be pursued with a view to implementation as soon as possible. I am particularly impressed with the concise and clear manner in which you have presented a report on this complicated and difficult subject and I commend you for an excellent piece of work.

The draft EC Law and its accompanying Regulations, Orders and Notices were all put to the Executive Council and thereafter to the Legislative Assembly. It gave the Members of the Assembly some difficulties in following the techniques of applying the four pieces of legislation. However, they declared that the new law to them, after appropriate explanation, was far simpler to understand than the English law. Furthermore the members declared that they had confidence that the new measures being recommended would enhance growth in the financial industry. The recommendations were approved and became law in May 1966.

Cayman's new Exchange Control Law did prove very helpful in assisting offshore businesses to plan their investment strategies. Further details on the subject of exchange control and the eventual decision to abolish the system can be found in Chapter 12 'Economic Diversification'. The three new laws just mentioned were to become companions to the Companies Law that came into effect in early 1961 and which was by 1966 making a valuable contribution to the building of the financial industry.

In early 1968 two British parliamentarians, one a Labour Party member and the other a Conservative, visited Grand Cayman. I cannot remember the names of those two gentlemen, but the *Cayman Islands Colonial Report* covering the period 1966–70 on page 8 named the following nine members of the United Kingdom parliament who visited Grand Cayman during that five year period. They were: C.R. Morris, T. Taylor, H. Neil, S. Silverman, R. Pounder, R. Dodds-Parker, J.B. Hynd, J.J. Dunnett and Sir Frederick Bennett. The Administrator, Mr Cumber, arranged and chaired a meeting of all the government's Civil Service heads of departments. The venue was his Government House residence on the Seven Mile Beach. He also invited the two Members of Parliament (MPs) to attend. It was no doubt the intention of the Administrator that for the benefit of the MPs he would have views on the economy expressed by both the officials and the elected members of the government at separate meetings. The purpose of our meeting from a Civil Service perspective was to summarize for the benefit of the visitors the past and present economic performance of the islands in terms of growth or sustainable development. Such development would provide for the present without compromising the ability of future generations to meet their particular needs. Another purpose for the meeting was to advise on any perceived change of direction that development or growth might have been moving in.

The Chairman, after presenting his opening remarks, requested a contribution from each of the local officials around the table. When it was my turn to speak, having assumed the position of the government's economic and financial advisor, I began by stating that it was my view that these islands were definitely moving from the slow pace of the past into a situation that could start triggering an era of vast economic, physical and social development. In fact it was my candid opinion that from what I saw at the time of local business activities, Cayman might already have been moving into what could ultimately be a busy and no doubt, eventful future. I went on to say, 'I am a keen believer that progress or growth is the exchange of one problem for another. We need therefore, to spare no time to decide what, if anything needs to be done presently to build or to lay a sound infrastructure in order to safeguard the islands' position in the event of rapid growth. Perhaps this could be achieved by engaging in an orderly reorganization covering all areas of the public sector so as to set the stage for people to cope with any workload that may perchance emanate from the wake of rapid growth and progress.'

It was also my opinion, I continued, that 'the private sector unlike the public sector of these islands is quite capable of taking care of itself as all its institutions whether commercial or otherwise are much advanced in economic, professional and technical infrastructure. This is a complete reversal of the situation found in many other countries where government progress is sometimes hampered by the need to halt activities and assist private sector development.'

I further stated, 'As there is much to be done in preparation for any future outburst in progress or development in Cayman, it is important that the right approach be made to strengthen all weak areas. This is in order that problems or difficulties may be quickly resolved. Most important as well is the fact that we must pledge whole-hearted support to the task ahead, remembering that it is only through unity and cooperation that strength and success can be achieved. We must also not become complacent over any past achievement, or be careless about what good things the future may hold in store for us. We need indeed to be ever cautious about the path we take while bearing in mind that no country is rich enough to buy back its past. Looking around today at many countries, both large and small, we do see those that have suffered economic and social disaster largely by their own designs, countries that would no doubt now love to buy back their past. But as the old adage puts it, "It is easy to destroy but very difficult to rebuild." Cayman does have a rich heritage. These qualities could certainly place it in an ideal position to start an economic journey with good potential for prosperity.'

I mentioned that control was essential in the case of anyone presenting applications to the government for licences and other development proposals. This was of course based on observations in recent time regarding businessmen presenting applications to Executive Council (the Cabinet) one day and returning the following day knocking on the Administrator's office door as he was chairman of the Cabinet, asking for the replies. This sort of behaviour definitely pointed to the need for control over the manner in which official business procedures were conducted. It would also be true especially when control related to foreign entrepreneurs who were not familiar with such procedures and requirements in a British Colony. Cayman's size and uniqueness perhaps led some people to believe that business arrangements here move rapidly.

A personal experience I had that indicated the urgent need for some form of control over the manner that private sector business was presented to the government occurred one evening when I was standing on the tarmac at Owen Roberts International Airport in Grand Cayman talking with the Administrator. He was awaiting the arrival of his children from school in England and I was meeting a friend. Over the previous few days we had both been in Cayman Brac, along with other members of the Legislative Assembly, on official business. On this particular evening in Grand Cayman Mr Cumber and I were discussing our experiences in the Brac. Suddenly, up came a Texan entrepreneur. Reaching out and giving the Administrator a really big handshake, he then said to him, 'I am so glad to see you, Mr Governor. I have been looking for you over the past few days to present you with a ready-mix concrete proposal from my company. We want to establish such a plant here in Cayman to produce excellent quality concrete for all your future big buildings. If you will give me just a minute, sir, I will run to my car and bring you the proposal.'

John Cumber looked at me, winked, and then in a sort of comical tone, but yet with much gratitude on his face, said, 'That's the way the Yankees do it.'

The gentleman returned and handed the Administrator a bundle of documents along with the designs and drawings and said, 'I will see you tomorrow, Mr Governor.' John Cumber, of course, walked all around the terminal building clutching the bundle of papers in his arms, even when he was greeting his children. This proved my point that control over procedures in dealing with private sector development proposals was of the essence. At the meeting I suggested that it should take the form of written guidelines for the benefit of the business public. I also mentioned the need for a team to be requested from London to investigate and advise on economic and physical infrastructure needs, based on the growth pattern being experienced at the time.

Before I finished my remarks at the meeting at Government House, it became quite obvious around the table that the Administrator was not pleased with certain aspects of what I had said. I thought it was the mention of 'control' since he was in fact an ardent believer in an 'open arms policy' whereby potential investors like the Texan gentleman should not be offended for fear that he may go and not return. The chairman's reaction to my remarks did upset me, to the extent that I became nervous and had to end my presentation. At a later stage before leaving Government House that day and while having a drink, the two MPs, one after the other, came and spoke to me. They suggested that my advice was good and that it should be followed; it was the only course by which the Cayman Islands could succeed in its bid for an acceptable economic development.

In November 1968 a new Administrator, Mr Athelstan C.E. Long, CMG, CBE, took the oath of office. He was the last Administrator and the first Governor. The new official title of Governor was confirmed by law and later by the new 1972 Constitution. The new Constitution made provision as well for one more official member in Executive Council. The Financial Secretary was clearly the official to be considered and I was therefore given the seat as Third Official Member of Executive Council. That appointment also followed on from the recommendations of the team from British Development Division in Barbados who visited here in April 1969 and whose members were amazed to discover that in Cayman the Financial Secretary or Minister of Finance and Development was not a member of the Cabinet.

A few days after Mr Long assumed office in November 1968, I took the opportunity of paying him a courtesy call. We talked generally until I touched on subjects under my portfolio, finance and development, for which I had certain concerns and reservations. However, before dealing with those subjects I mentioned my concern as well for one of the Administrator's own subjects, the Civil Service, and emphasized the urgent need to examine its situation. Secondly I told Mr Long that in my opinion there was a need as well to have an assessment done professionally of the islands' economic infrastructure requirements and if that need were in fact pursued it could lay a foundation for the growth pattern of the islands ahead. I therefore suggested the urgent need to apply for two teams of advisors through the British government. One would study the problems of the Civil Service that had developed early in 1968 and which had resulted in a mass exodus of employees from the government to the private sector. The other team would study and recommend methods for strengthening the economic infrastructure so as to lay a foundation on which all future growth and development of finance and tourism could be based. I spoke too of the need to strengthen controls with respect to development applications by the private sector to the government, explaining what I meant as I had earlier in the year at the special heads of department meeting.

Mr Long was not disturbed by what I said to him. However, since he had just arrived on the island and not yet even settled into Government House, his response was that 'all those things would need to be studied and tackled in good time.' I left the Governor's office somewhat uncertain of the position and where we would go next from there.

Although I was not a member of the Executive Council at the time, I had the Administrator's authority to attend council meetings whenever I had business papers on subjects from my portfolio to present. In January 1969 I had a few papers dealing with bank licence applications and other subjects for presentation to council and therefore attended the first meeting. I decided that since no words had yet been received from the Administrator on my proposals to him at the courtesy meeting the previous year in November, I would mention orally and briefly to council my two subjects of concern, the Civil Service and economic infrastructure needs. At the appropriate time during the meeting and after I had presented my portfolio papers, I requested of the chairman permission to address the council on the two new subjects considered very important and urgent. The chairman ruled me out of order and said that as a senior officer I should have known the procedure in presenting a subject to council. However, the elected members must have sensed the urgent need to present the subjects and therefore requested the chairman to allow me to make the presentation; he then kindly gave his consent for me to speak.

In the submission I began first by mentioning to the council the near crisis facing the Civil Service because employees were moving into the private sector and successfully obtaining jobs: in fact civil servants had no problems obtaining jobs in the private sector. I told the council that in the previous year, 1968, the government had received 20 resignations in nine months from members of the service. It was suspected that the cause was a salaries adjustment effective in January 1968, although there could have been other reasons as well,

131

since a few of those leaving the government accepted lower salaries from the private sector. If the exodus of staff continued, the drain could bring about a staff crisis in the government. Furthermore, as departments were understaffed and at the same time operating partly with new recruits, the situation could be viewed as requiring immediate attention. Following my presentation it was the unanimous view of council that the matter was critically urgent and should immediately be addressed. The appointment of a Civil Service Review Team to examine the problem and find solutions that would halt the crisis was authorized; action was to follow immediately.

The other area of concern mentioned to the council was that assessments of the country's growth indicated that the local economic activities were on the rise. Such a possibility posed a danger that, if indeed sudden and rapid growth took place, the local situation could be adversely affected in the absence of proper basic infrastructure on which to build development. This suggested that an urgent need existed to appoint another team to study and recommend economic infrastructure requirements. Before I departed the council that evening a firm decision on the two matters, the Civil Service and economic infrastructure issues, was reached: it stated that the two subjects should be treated with the greatest urgency. Members requested the chairman to prepare two telegrams to London requesting the two teams to assist these urgent needs. They also expressed the wish to have the text of the two telegrams approved before adjournment so as to ensure their early dispatch next morning. I thanked the chairman and members for their kind consideration and urgent action in dealing with what were viewed as very important issues. I then took my leave. I thought after the meeting that even if I had breached the procedure of council, not being even a member, hopefully my eager and anxious bid to get that urgent message across to all of the government would have its redeeming effects. It was therefore my personal view that the action was not a breach as much as a genuine and sincere effort to do a good deed for the government, the people and the country. In fact my moving quickly to institute appropriate action did resolve what otherwise could have been in due course serious problems and consequences.

Responding to those telegrams, the Ministry of Overseas Development in London advised that our requests had been referred to its outpost, the Barbados-based British Development Division in the Caribbean (BDDC). The division then proposed an initial team visit in April 1969 – a proposal promptly accepted by the Cayman Islands government.

The team, led by the head of BDDC, William Bell, MBE (later

CMG), included his engineering and financial advisors – K.L. Hardaker, OBE, MICE, and A.W. Jackson, OBE. Also included was W.H. Young, MBE, FRICS, from the Overseas Surveys Directorate. The team was to be followed by visits in May by the education and technical education advisors, S.C. Wood, OBE, and Dr J.G. Lavender. Should the team find it appropriate, as in the event it did, it would be joined by the Civil Service and economic development Advisors, J.H.R. Davis, MBE (later CBE), and J.H. Bryden.

The main visit took place between 14th and 17th April. The team sought first to establish priority areas for aid and to identify specific needs.

It was apparent to them that the main problems facing the Cayman government were lack of professional and technical expertise. The other observation was that lack of expertise was not as a result of shortage of funds as the government enjoyed a healthy financial position with minimal public debt. They also recognized that the effort to raise additional funds, whether for recurrent or capital use, appeared to present no real problems either in raising the money or in servicing the debts. They warned, however, that such action to raise money should be based on real needs without jeopardizing the Caymanian tax-free system. It was thought that the identification and preparation of projects for loan financing and for British development aid was quite urgent and should be put into effect at once. Also in the field of finance, the need emerged for the services of a fiscal expert, carefully selected and with carefully written terms of reference, to advise the government through a fiscal committee which the team considered should be established. The fiscal committee's terms of reference would be based on ways and means to maximize revenue without impairing the indirect tax structure. Also, the leader saw the urgent need for an expert, or experts, able to concentrate on project identification, preparation, evaluation and financing, which should be done within the framework of a development plan for the public sector while taking into account private development.

The report of the Bell team sent from Barbados on 28th April 1969 was set out in a document consisting of 14 pages and 3 appendices. It covered all priority areas in economic infrastructure and Civil Service needs, subject in certain instances to the already planned subsequent visits of the education and development sub-teams. Shortly after receiving the report, the Cayman government accepted the recommendations, but with the reservation that modifications and additions which arose from discussions and would form the basis of a technical assistance programme should be taken into consideration. The government also requested the development division

133

to assist it in certain of the follow-ups to their recommendations.

After completing their various studies and disposing of those straightforward financial problems which they had found in other territories the most insoluble, the team turned their attention to the glaring absence of certain types of expertise which weighed heavily against most of the major issues confronting the government. They found that technical assistance was undoubtedly the area for urgent attention. It was discovered too that among the British Caribbean territories covered by the division, Cayman had not received any British technical assistance over the previous four years. This was no fault of London; it was just that Cayman did not apply for the aid except for a salaries commission and an airfield study. The critical need for help, at a high cost as seen at the time, was supported by the team, an indication that Cayman would be regarded as a sort of special project to the division. William Bell and his team probably saw the potential then for what Cayman was to become in the years to follow.

In fact, 25 years after the BDDC team's report on the studies had been received by the Cayman government, Bell wrote to congratulate me on my knighthood. His letter, dated 9th May 1994, provided his home address so I could conveniently correspond with him. At that time unfortunately Jackson and Young had passed away but other team members were still around. I wrote then to Bill Bell to request a copy of his report from the team visit on 14th April 1969. Unfortunately he did not have one so I began doing a research into this government's files through the Financial Secretary, the Honourable George McCarthy, OBE, JP, and the Director of the Cayman Islands National Archive, Dr Philip Pedley. I was fortunate that Dr Pedley eventually tracked down the report. He found it in a file that came from my former Financial Secretary's office, which was destroyed by fire in 1972. The file had survived the fire although its outer edges were marked and stained with burns; however, the inside pages were still in good condition. (The burnt building was the old Government House and former residence and office of the Administrator. After the new Government House was built in 1962 on an attractive site in the middle of the famous Seven Mile Beach for residential purposes only, the old building was converted into offices for the Administrator and members of Executive Council: of course it included my office.) I sent a copy of the report to Bill Bell. He replied to say how delighted he was to see the report again, and as he read it, he felt more than a little sentiment for the work of 25 years ago. He wanted, with permission, to send copies to the surviving members of the team, Wood, Hardaker, John Davis, John Bryden and Gordon Lavender.

I have no doubt that the government's full acceptance and implementation of the Bell team's proposals and Dr Marco Giglioli's tremendous efforts to control mosquitoes and sandflies must stand out as remarkable and important contributions to the tremendous economic growth of these islands. The economic infrastructure developments, supported by the advent of advanced technology in the 1970s and beyond, surely demonstrated a positive tendency to promote growth and development. An offshore business director visited me in office in 1972 to discuss his companies' plans to move their operations to the Cayman Islands. While in my office he made these comments: 'The most important factor in our decision to expand our overseas operations into your area is the political stability afforded by your existing system of government, which has engendered our confidence and faith in the future of the Cayman Islands. Cayman's favourable environment provides an important incentive that has led us to establish business here: hopefully it will be a successful operation.' The remarks of course made me feel quite optimistic that we were on the right track, even politically, to move the islands forward and for them to become a favoured offshore financial centre and tourist destination. In fact few other countries, if any, have seen progress as dramatic and rapid as did Cayman. Some have regarded it as a Cayman that has transformed beyond its natives' wildest dreams, while other residents have not yet realized their envious position of living in a leading international offshore financial centre.

The Bell team during the few days spent here in April 1969 made many observations. It was stated in their reports that between 1967 and 1969 the Cayman economy grew at the phenomenal rate of 29 per cent per annum in current prices. The growth was assisted through the expansion of tourism and offshore finance, out of which also developed other local activities such as construction and a speculative real estate market. Activities of the past such as subsistence agriculture and fishing began declining while new and modern developments such as dairy farming, sport fishing, water sports and diving began to contribute to the economy as well. Those economic activities began to flourish because mosquito and sandfly control was becoming a success story. Other attractions were the excellent local beaches and watersports facilities that supported tourism, while finance grew because of Cayman's tax haven history; that is, it had never been known to introduce any form of direct taxes such as income tax. Added to those attractions was the freedom of the Cayman Islands since January 1969 from tax treaty exchange of information between foreign countries and Cayman because of our constitutional association and obligations previously with Jamaica

135

(see details in Chapter 7, pages 112–3). The local atmosphere began improving and becoming quite pleasant as the country grew into an attractive international business centre. Cayman was also known for its political stability, attractive laws and the natural friendliness of both the people and the government, who greeted visitors and encouraged those who were interested in becoming involved in business ventures here: in fact we regarded them as our business partners.

The Bell team also emphasized that the overwhelming need was not to stimulate the economy or to protect its growth, but to control it in the face of a multiplicity of proposals by developers, not all of whose motives were above suspicion. Mistakes had been made but had not proved irreparable. The Territory's budget was found healthily in balance. The remarks stated that Cayman really lacked only two things to make it a model in the economic field: one was expertise and the other a workable system of land tenure. Of course those two missing ingredients made their appearance on the local scene shortly afterwards.

The report stated as well that the results of the growth seen by the team had been the elimination of any trace of unemployment, tremendous speculation in land, rapidly rising wages and the demand for workers and skills in all areas of economic activities. It appeared, however, that the government had been caught lagging, though this had one major benefit: until 1969 revenues were rising faster than recurrent expenditures, enabling much development to be paid for from budget surpluses. The boom, not surprisingly, brought about very rapid price increases that caused economic and social difficulties. The task ahead was therefore a need for the public sector to match the progress of private development; that called for further improvement of the administrative machine, including provision of adequate public buildings. It was seen too that heavy expenditure must of necessity be committed to new projects like a harbour, airports, roads, water supplies and a much higher level of social services, especially in the important area of education. But most importantly, a decision was required to give an indication of the growth rate, since the prospects seemed, in the medium term, unlimited. The strains in the form of rising prices and wages, shortage of labour and an over-burdened Civil Service were already apparent and would get worse if nothing was done to moderate the pace of development.

The team identified a number of specific areas requiring technical assistance. First was a need to reorganize, restructure and provide improved office accommodation for the Civil Service, together with a revision of its salaries. Secondly, within a reorganized Civil Service there should be the establishment of a Development Unit, a Lands and Survey Department, the urgent examination of the feasibility of establishing, as a statutory body, a Land and Development Board and the reorganization and expansion of the Public Works Department. Other technical needs considered urgent were the drafting of certain land and survey legislation to regulate the innumerable dealings with real estate developers and others, and to end the confusion over land ownership.

Government was at that time in the impossible position of having to negotiate dealings involving the country's most important and valuable asset – land – without ever being really sure who owned it. A most important issue at the time was the preparation of a land-use map, together with the establishment of a comprehensive and efficient system for land titles registration. In the years to follow, those facilities were established and today Cayman has a fine land registration department that confirms title to an individual's property. The land legislation system was presented in the form of three laws. First was the Land Adjudication Law (20 of 1971). It provided a modern system of land registration whereby titles of all lands in the islands became certain and held the government's guarantee. Transfers and other dealings in individuals', companies' or the government's property could also be accomplished expeditiously and without difficulty. The law also provided for the demarcation and survey of boundaries of all lands. Any disputes over boundaries and ownership went to a land tribunal for settlement. The second piece of legislation was the Registered Land Law (21 of 1971). This law made provision for the registration of land and for dealings in land so registered and purposes connected therewith. The other law, the Land Surveyors' Law (22 of 1971), provided for the licensing, regulating and exercise of control over the professional conduct of all land surveyors working in these islands.

The department administering the three laws was headed by a Director of Lands and Survey: he also filled the statutory post of Registrar of Lands and was assisted by a Deputy Registrar, a Lands Officer and a Chief Surveyor. This latter post was also a statutory appointment with responsibility for the operation of the Land Surveyors' Law and Regulations. The Land Registry was responsible for the registration of all land transactions and for the maintenance of all land records and registry maps. It also collected, on behalf of the Commissioner of Stamp Duty (the Financial Secretary) stamp duty payable on all land dealings as well as on various other instruments and agreements. From early 1987, a Senior Surveyor was posted on Cayman Brac to provide a local service to the public of the sister islands so as to assist them with land dealings and attendant problems, give advice and accept land documents with stamp duty paid for processing and registration. The move resulted in a full-time government survey crew resident in the Brac for the first time.

The Bell team, in summarizing its findings, saw Cayman's most glaring problem to be the lack of expertise in its important and specialized areas of progress. One remedy for this seemed to be a massive but appropriate restructuring of the Civil Service. The advice for that exercise would fall on the follow-up team of John Davis and John Bryden, who, I can say with confidence, did an excellent job of improving the service.

Throughout its visit the team was acutely aware of activities of private developers that were not necessarily conducive to the benefit of the Cayman Islands or its people, and which were rarely under control. It consequently recommended that a study be commissioned to investigate the problems arising from private development, and to advise on how they might best be resolved. The team added that the establishment of a Development Corporation might be a solution, but that that would depend on the commission's findings.

Dealing further with the Civil Service and the thoughts about accommodation, the team went on to state that unrealistic salaries were not the only reason why the government was unable either to attract or to retain adequate staff. It was the view that this situation would continue regardless of any salary revision and for as long as the staff remained so shoddily accommodated. They saw no reason for this situation to exist or to continue as the economy was booming, together with the government being in a financial position to make changes. The recommendation, therefore, to deal with this problem, was that consultants be appointed to prepare sketch plans with definite proposals for a new administration building. However, members of the government saw the Legislative Assembly and Law Courts buildings as deserving top priority in the government's accommodation construction schedule for they provided vital services for the country's political and judicial administration. The two buildings were therefore considered special among the plans for new accommodation and became the subject of a Caribbean region, including South Florida, architectural competition. The firm of Rutkowski Bradford and Partners of Jamaica won first prize for the Legislative Assembly building and second prize for the Courts building. The government decided to accept those two designs as they would certainly carry a continuity of architectural flavour from the top designers. Both buildings were constructed in the centre of George Town near to the city's Town Hall and on a site where they faced each other, with a main road intervening. They were completed in 1972 and 1973 respectively. The third building was a central police headquarters completed and opened in 1974 under the then Commissioner of Police, Andrew Greiff. The new police headquarters was on the same site as the original police station built in 1907: it adjoins the government's administration building. The last project on the schedule of new government offices to be constructed was the administration building: it was also completed and opened in October 1975.

In dealing with the financing of the administration building and road construction and improvement as well of other smaller projects, I began lobbying six of the large international banks with local presence concerning the possibility that they might wish to come together and consider a consortium loan to the government. Involved were Barclays Bank International, chosen as the 'lead bank', the Bank of Montreal, the Bank of Nova Scotia and the Canadian Imperial Bank of Commerce, First National City Bank and the Royal Bank of Canada. The banks were requested to give reasonable consideration to the terms and rates of the loan as it was at the time the government's largest single borrowing. Secondly, they were reminded that the financial facility being requested was not a commercial loan *per se* but funds needed to improve public facilities that would be beneficial to the country on a national basis. They came twice with figures that were not quite acceptable: they were sent back each time to try again. On the third occasion the government accepted the offer and signed the loan agreement on 25th October 1974 for an amount of up to US$3.750 million and with a repayment term of 12 years.

At the opening of the new buildings, His Excellency the Governor, Mr Russell, called them 'the pride of the Caribbean' and said the Cayman Islands now boasted some of the finest buildings in the region. He also said that the new administration building especially crowned the country's position and expressed the hope that it would be an example to the rest of the area as well as to some developed countries further afield. He also expressed confidence that the new atmosphere would engender greater output and greater efficiency. That was no criticism of the Civil Service, he said, as the changeover had been accomplished without a hitch and without any disruption of service to the public. Indeed, for the size of Cayman, there was no doubt that we did have at the time some of the most modern and most magnificent structures. Visitors from many countries were lavish in their praise of those four buildings, the Legislative Assembly, Law Courts, Administration and Police Headquarters, and also of the new, beautifully paved main roads throughout the islands. We were proud of them too – and the fact that the BDDC team during their visit in April 1969 saw the urgent need for new office accommodation and improved highways and accordingly made the recommendations for those developments.

The BDDC team also gave thought to a new hospital. The 35-bed facility built in George Town was opened in 1950. It continued to be in use with many expansions and improvements over the years. A new facility constructed on the same site was completed and opened on 27th March 1999.

The present 1950 hospital site and buildings are on the approaches to Owen Roberts International Airport and thus there is a threat to the hospital compound in the event of any possible plane crash disaster either on landing from the west or on take-off over George Town. Apart from the disturbing noise of aircraft passing overhead, the old hospital structure was also becoming inadequate in size, design and equipment. The Bell team in 1969 saw those weaknesses in the facility and therefore recommended that medical consultants be appointed to conduct a survey of hospital requirements and, in the light of their findings, to prepare sketch plans for a new hospital to be constructed at a new and acceptable site. The work was delayed due to other priority projects scheduled for implementation in 1970. To follow up on the Bell report and recommendation, an English team of health consultants was appointed in 1973 to do the survey and to include in their recommendations a carefully selected site for the proposed new facility. The site selected by the consultants, after examining many others, was one at Spotts' north side of the road leading to the eastern districts. The selection was based on the site's position between the eastern and western districts together with its good, level terrain. Unfortunately, due to financial constraint regarding other major projects costing nearly CI$10 million, the government was obliged to delay the hospital project at that stage.

The alternative to accepting and implementing the consultants' recommendation for a new hospital, estimated to cost CI$3 million, was to completely renovate the in-patient section of the old hospital with new facilities and equipment. This included air-conditioning to provide a bit more comfort for both patients and staff, while serving another useful purpose of eliminating most of the external noises caused from passing aircraft. The cost of the renovation project in 1974 covering construction and specialized equipment, was CI$855,000. Many more improvements have been carried out to the old institution over the ensuing years. Twenty-two years after the major renovation, the construction of a new hospital was again considered, but this time its siting did not change from the old 1950 location: as new buildings were erected and commissioned, counterpart sections of the old hospital disappeared.

Before the present hospital project began, the government of 1988–92 attempted to build a new hospital and named it the Dr Hortor Hospital. Dr William Alfred Conrad Hortor, a World War I medical veteran, came here in December 1936 as Government Medical Officer and served in Grand Cayman for many years. The site of the Hortor Hospital was in George Town not far from the old facility; however, the terrain left much to be desired according to many people and especially the government's political opposition. One of the objections to the new building was that the design made it a split-system facility whereby the outpatient or casualty section would remain at the old site. Construction began in late 1992, before the November General Election. The results of the election saw the former opposition of the old House becoming the new government of 1992–96. Following the election the construction contract for the new Dr Hortor Hospital was cancelled and another contract awarded for the facility to be built on the old 1950 site on a planned phasing-in arrangement.

During 1969, a Five-Year (1970–75) Capital Expenditure Programme (CEP) was prepared with the assistance of BDDC. It was revised in 1972 and converted to a Seven-Year (1970–77) Programme. The estimated cost of the capital projects was CI$31.338 million allocated to three financing areas: local revenue $6.584 million, British aid funds $14.418 million and loans $10.336 million. The projections covered 29 items including roads, schools, legislative and courts buildings, mosquito research and control programme, radio station, harbour development, Police Headquarters, Government Administration Building (the Glass House), hospital, water, sewage, farmers' market and an abattoir for slaughtering animals. At the conclusion of the seven-year period, a summary of actual completed projects and their cost was prepared. Unfinished projects numbered four: water, sewage, farmers' market and the abattoir. The cost of finished projects was $17.223 million, financed as follows: local revenue $7.062 million, British aid $3.342 million and loans $6.819 million.

During the 1984–88 political administration, the four remaining projects fell under my portfolio, Development and Natural Resources. Three were completed during those four years, water for George Town, sewage for the Seven Mile Beach and the farmers' market. The abattoir's design and estimated cost were completed but my term of office ended before implementation could begin. It was then a subject carried forward for the attention of the succeeding government. However, ten years later the facility remained in its original design

141

and estimated cost stage with no indication of the completion date. The sanitary conditions of a properly designed abattoir are most important both for the animals and the consumers.

The actual implementation and costs of the Civil Service reorganization and the Seven-Year CEP indicated that the urge for the studies from early in 1968 was justified. There was every indication that over the years to follow the pace of activities being experienced then would continue in the Cayman Islands. Now, following the dawn of a new millennium, it is well recognized that economic growth is still performing quite well and in an acceptable manner. If that trend continues with success, and hopefully it will, the name Cayman Islands will continue as at present to enjoy the excellent reputation of being a world-class offshore financial destination.

In BDDC's concluding remarks, a statement that earned first place among others in their report was that the exclusion of the Financial Secretary from the Executive Council was unique in the team's experience. This, they said, must make the efficient conduct of government business almost impossible. The situation, of course, owes its origin to the constitution that came into effect ten years earlier. In those days the post of Financial Secretary was not yet created. In fact the post of Treasurer, redesignated Financial Secretary, was held by the Commissioner, who was Chairman of the Council. Only two other officials of government in those days were eligible for appointment to council. The government's choice for the two was the Deputy Administrator and the Stipendiary Magistrate, who was the Legal Advisor. The position of Financial Secretary had only been created in 1968 on the re-designation of the position of Treasurer. The Financial Secretary could not therefore be given an official seat on the council until the Constitution was either amended or replaced. The latter took place in 1972 and the number of officials on the council was accordingly increased to three, including the Financial Secretary.

On the question of the 1972 Constitution, there were definitely reasons for its replacement apart from the need to include the Financial Secretary on the Executive Council. In support of a new Constitution, the Governor, Mr Long, in his Throne Speech on 1st May 1970 spoke of its need. He said, 'We have a democratic constitution but one which may have certain shortcomings for dealing with the problems of today and I know the Constitutional Committee set up by this Assembly has been seeking ways and means to improve it.' Indeed, changes brought about by the passage of time gave good grounds for a new Constitution. Examples were the new titles of Governor, Financial Secretary and others, together with the developments being carried out as a result of recommendations by the Bell team. The committee's support of a new Constitution was agreed in early 1971 and the government proceeded to apply through the Secretary of State, London, for a Constitutional Commissioner. In response to the request, Lord Oxford and Asquith, KCMG, arrived in Grand Cayman later in 1971 to begin the work. He conducted meetings and held discussions with the government, officials, politicians and members of the public. Those discussions were followed with the drafting of a constitutional document. After its final touches, the draft document was presented to the government and eventually received the acceptance of the Cayman Legislative Assembly. Thereafter it was forwarded to London, where it received formal approval in August 1972. The approval was followed in Cayman by a General Election in November 1972.

The new Constitution introduced on 22nd August 1972 continued to enshrine the islands' position as a British Crown Colony that had come into effect ten years earlier. Both the Crown Colony status and the 1972 Constitution are still in existence because of their proven popularity in the Caymanians' way of life. The Constitution had a few minor amendments over the years but those did not affect its substance in any way or its general appreciation by the political faction.

In 1986 and 1990 attempts were made to replace the 1972 Constitution but the efforts ended without success (see details in Chapter 13). Now the Cayman Islands are still riding with success the crest of the wave with its 1962 Crown Colony status and 1972 Constitution. The choice by the country's political leaders to continue with the present Crown Colony form of government and constitution gave a greater boost and attraction to Cayman's offshore business.

People in the Cayman Islands were from some time previously under the impression that to move from the Crown Colony status to a more advanced system of government would induce London to take the view that there should be no further devolution of power without setting the date for independence. As a matter of fact I remembered the Governor, Mr Crook, in August 1972 delivering his Throne Speech to the Legislative Assembly and making specific remarks on constitutional changes. On page 4 of his speech he said:

I should perhaps add, for the avoidance of doubt, that it is not normal to grant full internal self-government without at the same time setting an approximate date for independence. But there should be plenty of room for further advance before we reach that stage. In short – if I were a Caymanian I would feel well content with what this Constitution represents, and would want to take time to think very carefully about the next step.

I should think that the Governor's remarks were words of wisdom: they were certainly excellent advice to the people of these islands. In fact the local population had no desire then or now to move from Crown Colony government, for with it Cayman enjoys the best of both worlds. First, offshore investors find the present form of government and the services provided ideal for doing business here. Secondly, investors are delighted with Cayman's close link with the United Kingdom's Whitehall system of government, which provides confidence and stability. It was quite clear to investors that in these islands they would find political stability in addition to the attractive business environment. All these qualities and attractions stemmed of course from the country's early commitment to promoting environmental improvement and sustainable development for the benefit of all who live here.

At that stage and in anticipation of a strengthening economy, it was seen that the Cayman Islands might have been entering a new era that would bring about the enthusiasm which normally greets the dawning of a new year. It was the hope too that although Cayman faced new challenges, the ship of state would nevertheless continue to sail on, endeavouring always to remain in the calmer waters of stability and progress so that the policies and principles it adopted would remain intact. Our hope for success did come to pass: we need only to look around to see the amazing development of the country today.

On 21st October 1969, following the BDDC's exercise in Cayman five months earlier, I departed for London and then to Brighton on the southern shores of England to attend a five-week study seminar at the Institute of Development Studies at the University of Sussex. I was accommodated at the Old Ship Hotel. The seminar was arranged and financed by British Technical Assistance for training through the British Council offices in London. The purpose of the seminar was to give the attending 29 participants from British Commonwealth countries around the world a brief course on Implementing Development Plans, with examples and illustrations given by qualified lecturers and instructors. Development planning was strange to me and, while I gained much insight on the subject, the seminar also included finance and budgeting, two of my favourite subjects.

I arrived in Brighton on Sunday 26th October and just before dinner that evening a welcome reception and introductory gathering took place where all participants and seminar staff presented themselves, naming their countries of residence. A world map was hung on a tripod for the convenience of those who were from small territories and islands to point out their exact location if necessary. When it came to my turn I mentioned that my home was in the Cayman Islands; a number of persons asked me to identify the islands' location. I walked boldly to the map and searched the area in the Caribbean south of Cuba and west of Jamaica but those three little Cayman Islands were not on the map. Perhaps the map was very old and made before the discovery of the islands. However, I pointed with a big smile to the exact spot where they should be located. When a second map was produced the three islands were on it. Mr Bernard Schaffer was the Director of Studies at the seminar. Messrs Richard Stern and Ronald British were Seminar Assistants, Ms Elizabeth Thompson the Administrator, and Ms Diana Badger the Secretary. The seminar taught many principles of development planning and implementation. Three that I made special note of were: (1) The private sector should be controlled by (a) licence (b) quotas and (c) price fixing. (2) The purposes of development planning are to bring order, priority and foresight into government expenditure. (3) With effective development planning, exports can become the engine of economic growth. Referring to (c) of (1) above, price control in Cayman was abolished early after World War II and since then there has been no successful vote for its reintroduction.

The seminar ended on a successful, interesting and pleasant note followed by a grand farewell reception. I departed for London on 1st December 1969 with a friend who attended the seminar, Savy Maurice of Seychelles. The journey to London started in a blitz of heavy early snow, the earliest for England in many moons. I returned home on 3rd December. While on the journey across the Atlantic, I started to draft my Budget Address. The date for its delivery was scheduled in the Legislative Assembly for 5th December. Of course my office in Grand Cayman had sent me a package of material relating to the budget, which I received before leaving Brighton. Also before leaving Brighton I had had a call from the Foreign and Commonwealth Office in London advising that it was the intention to recommend me for the Queen's honour of Officer of the Most Excellent Order of the British Empire (OBE), and inquired if I would accept the honour. I graciously accepted it: the award was announced on 1st January 1970.

At the start of the 1970s it was felt that I was slightly better prepared, after attending the seminar at Sussex University, to move on with Cayman's development programmes. I knew too that it was easy to begin such a job but mighty difficult to complete it. However, I was quite prepared to face the challenge. The work on my schedule at that time related largely to the studies and recommendations of the Bell report in April 1969. In fact implementation of those recommendations made excellent progress which later in the decade brought about dramatic and improved changes to the economic environment of the Cayman Islands. Of course, one advantage that also encouraged offshore traffic to Cayman was the growing uncertainty regarding economic stability in nearby financial centres.

10

Finance and Tourism

Finance and tourism are referred to as Cayman's twin industries. From those two activities developed the building of a new economy during the 1960s. Its main purpose was to find a replacement for the income from seamen, an industry that had ended its usefulness by then. The two new industries eventually made this country famous as one of the leading world offshore financial centres and tourist destinations. The two industries do make counterpart contributions to each other in that the tourist traffic includes many individuals with business interests who travel quite often with their family and friends and register here as tourists. It has been estimated that approximately 40 per cent of tourist traffic to Cayman is in fact shared with the financial industry. The two industries are also regarded as the streams from which other activities originate, such as construction and a real estate speculative market. At a later stage finance would also be seen to include domestic and offshore insurance.

In launching the twin industries in the mid-1960s, the government saw then that reasonably established social and environmental services, even if these were achieved a few years down the line, would be required to get Cayman off to a good start with its new activities. One thing was certain on the social side, unless mosquitoes and sandflies were controlled, many potential business individuals, tourists and other visitors would certainly not risk coming to these shores. If on the other hand those pests were controlled, it would still require that proper economic and public sector infra- structure be put in place to facilitate development. Another important thought at the time was that the financial industry and tourism would need to succeed in order to build a new source of income to replace the almost defunct seaman's economy. The proposed new industries would of necessity need to serve these islands over the foreseeable future as there are no other forms of activity

147

that could provide a substantial enough income to sustain the population.

Finance consists largely of banking and trust services. Bank and trust legislation is backed by a separate trust law, a company law and a new exchange control law. The latter law is to control the flow of sterling (the British currency) outside British Commonwealth countries. In examining the concept of the financial industry as a pillar of the Cayman economy, it was seen to be an activity that should develop and operate largely offshore. Such trend of thought could be easily understood taking into consideration Cayman's significant political stability, excellent telecommunication and electric power, relative freedom in foreign exchange movement of international currencies, reliable financial services and flexible laws. Most important too was the absence of any form of direct taxation such as income tax, corporation tax, capital gains tax, sales tax, property tax, estate tax, inheritance tax or death dues. This appealing situation attracted outside business interests and investors to use Cayman's tax-free facilities. Of course there were also many other advantages offered here in support of the financial industry which will be commented upon later.

Roderick Donaldson, a former government legal draftsman, wrote and published in 1981 an article entitled 'The Economic Stability of Cayman – Its Progress By Design'. The article stated:

> The progress of the Cayman Islands as an international business forum has been such that books and articles on the subject tend to be out-dated even before publication. The progress and economic stability of Cayman was actually created by design and did not all happen by sheer coincidence.

The statement, written by one who had occupied an important government position for ten years, was indeed very factual and to the point.

In order to promote the financial industry, four basic laws were needed at that stage. The first, a Companies' Law, had already been passed by the Legislative Assembly in December 1960 and brought into effect in early 1961. The law was then, in fact, making its good mark on the offshore business. Only the other three laws were therefore needed in order to move things along, a bank and trust companies law, a separate trust law and a new exchange control law.

The English EC Law existed following World War II. It was a measure to prevent heavy drainage of funds from the general Sterling area pool of the British Commonwealth countries so that the reserves of its members could be safeguarded to meet commitments such as war debts. For further comments on this subject see Chapter 11 'Economic Diversification' (Repeal of Exchange Control).

The existing 1961 Companies Law and the other three new laws, the Banks and Trust Companies Regulation Law, the Trust Law and the Exchange Control Regulations Law, were seen as the basic statutory vehicles needed then to move the financial industry along and hopefully in the right direction. The industry would also need to be developed with professionals in the field of legal, accounting and auditing expertise to give it the prestige and reliability necessary to draw the attention quickly of outside interests. The four pieces of legislation mentioned above would be administered under my portfolio, Finance and Development. On the assumption that the four laws would succeed in an attempt to build the new financial industry, early action was taken in May 1966 to introduce the other three pieces of legislation.

Banks and trust companies are provided with a domestic or Class A licence which allows them to conduct their business within the Cayman Islands, and an offshore or Class B licence to be engaged in activities outside the Cayman Islands or offshore. It was usual under the law for applicants requesting a bank licence also to apply for a trust licence. In fact under the 1966 law it would cost no more for the two licences than it would for one. In any case the large banks especially operated within the confines of their counterpart trust companies.

Before banks came to Cayman, residents exchanged money for goods and services. When banks appeared on the scene their purpose was to make money work. They borrowed money, paying the lender interest. In turn the banks would on-lend the money to whomever needed it. By doing so, the banks made a profit, which was the difference between the borrowing and the lending rates. The larger the banks' cashflow and their corresponding lending, the larger their profits. Banks, however, provide a large number of other services, all of which must fall under the definition of 'banking' and all of which are designed with the intention of putting money to work whether locally in the islands or internationally in the offshore markets.

One of the principal activities of banks in these islands is dealing offshore in the Eurodollar market. Eurodollars are generally any US dollars outside the United States. These dollars in the external markets represent the American balance of payments deficit. That situation is caused by any American imbalance in trade, investment abroad, American tourists travelling outside their own country and other ventures based abroad, like the conflict in Kuwait and Iraq where the United States, in terms of resources, was thus extensively committed. United States dollars are only redeemable in the US but, as US trade constitutes such a large part of world trade, merchants and governments outside the US are quite willing to be paid in US dollars at the official trading rate. In fact the US dollar has been for a long time the leading acceptable currency in international trade, followed by the British pound Sterling, the Deutschmark and the Swiss franc. Eurodollar loans can sometimes amount to hundreds of millions of dollars. The banks in Cayman, for instance, spend much time splitting up Eurodollar loans into manageable sizes and borrowing the money from other banks around the world who may, in any case, and for their own interest, wish to share the risk. The local banks also lend US dollar deposits held by them in the Eurodollar market. Therefore in principle, a large part of the offshore business is taken up in the Eurodollar market deals.

As stated above, the purpose of banking is to borrow and on-lend money at a profit. In other words, a bank can only lend what it has. In these islands, banks lend in Cayman dollars or what they have in Cayman dollar deposits, as the Cayman dollar is the local legal tender. Because of the widespread use of US dollars in the Cayman economy (facilitated by the Cayman dollar fixed exchange rate to the US dollar) banks also lend in US dollars.

In the early days of Cayman's tax haven banking operation, the principle behind introducing the offshore system was to afford international investors a legitimate expectation of a level of privacy in their financial affairs. Offshore accounts allowed individuals to invest as they wished, for instance, trading in precious metals and other assets. Investors were also able to use the accounts to profit from currency fluctuations and purchase of foreign real estate and to take advantage of higher interest rates available in foreign countries. Also the income from those accounts would be void of tax deductions in the Cayman Islands, while the account holder might still be responsible for the payment of taxes to his government.

In addition to the provision of a full range of banking services, a sophisticated offshore financial centre also needs to offer an array of other services, particularly trust, company management, captive insurance services and mutual fund administration.

Any jurisdiction that intends to promote itself as an offshore financial centre needs to attract quality trust companies, which for the most part tend to be subsidiaries or affiliates of major international banks. The Cayman Islands was no exception in this regard in the 1960s when the potential of the islands was recognized by the

150

Bank of Nova Scotia Trust Company, which at the time had one offshore centre in the Bahamas. In consequence they established a Cayman subsidiary in 1965. I very well remember the time Scotiatrust was admitted here with its first General Manager, Mr John A. Collins, who in later years received from Her Majesty The Queen the honour to be an Officer of the Most Excellent Order of the British Empire (OBE). The year 1965 was also the time I was promoted in the government to the position of Treasurer. Following the Scotiatrust initiative to establish in Cayman, other banks and trust companies followed suit with the 1966 Trust Laws enacted and brought into effect.

As stated earlier, a Companies Law was enacted and brought into effect in early 1961. In addition lawyers, accountants and specialists in company and insurance management were also beginning to arrive in Cayman.

The modern day trust world has been aptly described as a sophisticated amalgam of lawyers, advisors and trust companies dedicated to the protection of wealth. There is nothing modern about trusts, however; the idea has been around since the twelfth century. It was developed in England in Anglo-Saxon times as a method whereby asset disposal in a predetermined manner could be effected on behalf of English noblemen who set off on Crusades to the Holy Land leaving their castles and estates to family trustees. While trustees are no longer expected to fight off the marauding barbarian, in other respects the trustee's role has changed little since the Crusades. From those early days grew the concept that a legal arrangement charging a third party with the responsibility for certain actions within prescribed rules and within certain legal boundaries would be useful. In modern times that concept has been refined and developed through the process of laws into a flexible planning tool extensively used to great advantage and particularly so in offshore jurisdictions where rules of common law apply.

The trustee relationship as recognized and enforced by equity (a common law concept) has proved immensely useful for international tax planning and asset holding. As a result, civil law jurisdictions without equity have been seeking to introduce the concepts into their legal systems. Unfortunately, many have misunderstood, and seem to believe that trust law, in some way, 'creates' the trust, and that the trust can therefore be 'modified' by statute. This is not so; trusts are unique to British common law and the concept should always be confined to those jurisdictions governed by it.

To help understand the basics, a brief look at the principal components is necessary. When a person decides to create means whereby his accumulated wealth can be protected, invested and managed, both during and after his lifetime, he will probably be advised to establish a trust. A trust is a unique legal institution and established by means of a deed whereby trustees are appointed to give effect to the settlor's or grantor's wishes. It is neither a contract nor an agency and it exists in law through the legal personality of its trustee. From the start the trustees are the principals and legal owners responsible for the assets and all actions under their stewardship.

The trustee offers a settlor full independence from the trust and once the assets have been transferred, the settlor's rights and liabilities should cease. This can give important benefits from a taxation viewpoint and so tax avoidance is not the only reason why people choose offshore trusts.

It is generally considered that the development of the trust concept has been driven by tax laws and this factor does not cause the Cayman Islands to be popular with the taxing authorities of the high-tax countries like the United States, Canada and the United Kingdom. There are, however, a number of major non-tax reasons which those authorities often seems to overlook, such as:

Confidentiality: Since the essence of the trust concept is that legal title to the trust assets is in the name of the trustee, the names of the beneficial interests are automatically hidden. Thus the settlor, who may be a beneficiary himself, can retain a large measure of control whilst the world at large will see the assets as belonging to the trustee.

Exchange Control: The offshore trust is a legitimate vehicle to be used by those who fear the imposition of exchange controls which would effectively impede the movement of their assets. In 1980 the Cayman Islands abolished exchange control and was free to allow movements in both directions of foreign exchange transactions. In fact the year before (1979), the United Kingdom government, which first introduced exchange control, was first to abolish control on their own currency, Sterling.

Protection Against Inflation: This is fairly simple to achieve, with non-resident accounts established under an offshore entity with conversions into hard currency assets.

Forced Heirship: Many civil law countries restrict testamentary freedom under domestic forced heirship laws. If a potential settlor wishes to circumvent such rules he should select an offshore jurisdiction that has expressed trust legislation designated to uphold the trust and thus defeat any forced heirship claims.

Asset/Creditor Protection Trusts: This description refers to the intent of individuals who consider themselves potentially vulnerable to litigation (from a medical malpractice suit or a divorce suit). Trustees are generally very wary over the acceptance of such trusts: however, in the event of a claim against the trust assets, they need only to prove that the act was not done in bad faith. At a tax planning conference Milton Grundy, who is an authority on trust laws, suggested that 'the meeting ground between the offshore trust and personal insolvency is a world without maps'.

Succession Planning: Many individuals do not wish their property to pass absolutely to their heirs under a will and may prefer to establish a more long-term arrangement. For example, a husband married to a young second wife may wish to make provision for children of his first marriage. In such circumstances it is fairly common for the second wife merely to receive a life interest in the income, with the capital passing to the children of the first marriage on her death or remarriage.

As with other jurisdictions (both offshore and onshore) there have been occasions in Cayman when trustees have abused their positions and have fraudulently converted the assets under their control. However, the location of a trust is not really relevant to the frequency or whereabouts of fraud. Trustees' business is highly confidential and some unorthodox activity is bound to occur whatever the location. Nevertheless, it is worth mentioning two distinct differences between offshore and onshore trustees:

i) offshore trustees normally enjoy less regulation by government bodies;
ii) onshore trustees avoid jurisdictions which in most cases do not regard tax avoidance or the circumvention of exchange control as crimes.

Other important services offered by trust companies include executorship, pension administration, corporate management, registered office facilities and the provision of all aspects of mutual fund administration.

Thirty years after the establishment of the finance industry, the Cayman Islands ranked as the world's fifth largest financial centre after London, New York, Tokyo and Hong Kong. With more than 500 banks and trust companies, which include nearly all of the world's top 50 banks, Cayman's recognition as a major player in the financial world cannot be disputed. What is even more significant, however, is the fact that of the registered banks and trust companies, nearly 100 have a physical presence in the Cayman Islands. This is a good indication of the prestige that large international banks now derive from such, as opposed to having a mere name plate. The growth in bank deposits has been equally phenomenal and currently stands at in excess of US$500 billion.

Confidentiality of customers' banking and trust accounts was, from the early years of banking and trust legislation, governed solely by the British common law. The authority came from the well-known case in 1924 of Tournier vs. The National Provincial and Union Bank of England, in which the court ruled that there is an implied contractual obligation of financial confidentiality governing the bank's account for a person. The common law provision stood the test of time alone in these islands until 1976 when Cayman introduced a companion piece of legislation known as the Confidential Relationships (Preservation) Law. This and the common law provision have served the local situation well, especially in restricting foreign investigation interventions like the well-known 'fishing expedition' scheme used to circumvent confidentiality while in search of tax offenders in offshore jurisdictions.

The local confidentiality law was brought into effect in September 1976 to counter the misuse of confidential information. What prompted the almost sudden creation of the law was that from early that year much concern was expressed by the local financial community over an incident known as 'the Anthony Field case'. This started at the Miami International Airport when Field arrived there from Grand Cayman. On landing he was served with a subpoena calling on him to testify before a US grand jury concerning his clients' affairs. Field was Managing Director of Castle Bank and Trust (Cayman) Ltd. based in the Cayman Islands. The Cayman government became very concerned over the situation, for the far-reaching effects such an incident could throw across the international financial community. It was understood that the Americans acted from a decision of their Fifth Circuit Court of Appeals on 13th May 1976, which opened up the possibility that any Cayman bank or trust company official who flies into Miami might be served with a subpoena calling on him to testify about his clients' affairs. I personally saw this as a case of foreign governments' investigators snooping into our banking affairs without a showing of reasonable cause. The thought that bothered me most was the effect it could have on the local offshore business.

The case was the subject of an appeal by Castle Bank's legal advisors to the US Supreme Court that resulted in long arguments on both sides. The decision of the court was that Field was ordered to violate the legal commands of the Cayman Islands by appearing before the US grand jury for the investigation. In the decision the judge said, 'In a world where commercial transactions are international in scope, conflicts are inevitable. Courts and legislatures should take every reasonable precaution to avoid placing individuals in the situation Mr Field finds himself. Yet this court simply cannot acquiesce in the proposition that United States criminal investigation must be thwarted whenever there is conflict with the interest of other states.'

While the arguments were taking place in the US court, Cayman had at least to be seen by its financial community as taking some form of action in the matter. On a bright early morning in late July 1976, I rushed into the office of the government legal draftsman, Roderick Donaldson, and discussed with him Cayman's lack of legislation to govern confidentiality and requested that he give the drafting of such a law a trial. Donaldson was always ready with his drafting skill to produce any requested draft legislation. In fact such a request was a pure delight to him and he would simply come alive when such challenges were hurled at him.

In a few weeks the draft was produced and we spent some time mulling through the various sections until a satisfactory text was agreed. It was given the name the Confidential Relationships (Preservation) Law and accepted by Executive Council and thereafter the Legislative Assembly with the usual appropriate amendments. The law came into effect in September 1976. In my budget address delivered to the Legislative Assembly on 2nd March 1977, shortly after this law came into effect, I stated that, 'Under the Confidential Relationships (Preservation) Law recently enacted, no information relating to a customer or client account with any institution within the local financial community can be divulged to anyone. A foreign government investigating a case relating to a crime other than a tax offence may request this government to assist it in providing the relevant information. The law provides that applications for such information be made through the local police to the Governor in Executive Council. Such a request would be examined to ensure that the purported offence would, if committed in the Cayman Islands, be an offence under Cayman statutes.' Thus the stage was set to defend and safeguard confidentiality of customers' financial information in these islands as far as this was possible under the law.

The Confidential Relationships (Preservation) Law was further amended in 1979 to state in more precise terms the circumstances in which it is lawful to seek, obtain and divulge confidential information as defined by the law. The legislation was intended to protect the

155

confidentiality of financial transactions and to prohibit persons from divulging privileged information relating to business matters in the Cayman Islands. The amendments specified two important areas. First is an instance where the law exempts from application 'constables' investigating offences 'committed or alleged to have been committed within the jurisdiction', such constable being 'of the rank of Inspector or above'. Secondly, 'repeal of section 5 of the principal law' which reads, 'Nothing in this Law shall by implication be deemed to derogate from the rule in Tournier vs. The National Provincial and Union Bank of England (1924) 1KB 416. This deals with the civil duty of banks to preserve the confidentiality of the business of their customer which rule is said to have application to the islands.' The repeal of Section 5 suggested there might have been some transgression of Cayman's local law on confidentiality although this was not stated in the object of the Bill.

Legal experts, financial advisors and knowledgeable investors supported the government's amendment of the law forbidding unauthorized divulgence of privileged information or the illegal harassment of individuals who have chosen these islands for legitimate business activities. Anyone tampering with this favourable situation would, they suggested, be working against the best interests, progress and economic image of the islands.

One important case worthy of mention involving confidentiality relates to the refusal by the Bank of Nova Scotia, Cayman Branch, in 1983 to comply with a 'forced consent' judgement of a US court requiring the bank to release privileged information. The case, according to a staff reporter of the *Wall Street Journal*, arose out of the United States Internal Revenue Service (IRS) investigation of a Lawrence Ghidoni of Tallahassee, Florida. According to the report, during the mid-1970s Ghidoni was involved in a booming business in timber and pipes sold in the Middle East and was alleged to have diverted a fair proportion of his profits to an account in the Cayman Islands. Investigation of this case led the IRS to obtain in some illegal manner records of Ghidoni's secret account in Cayman. Ghidoni pleaded guilty to filing a false US income tax return and received a three-month jail sentence. In this case the IRS took a more direct approach, bypassing respect for Cayman's legal jurisdiction requirement relating to confidential information, and requested a US court to order Ghidoni to sign a statement (forced consent) allowing his Cayman bank, the Bank of Nova Scotia, to release records of his account. The IRS contended that the US Constitutional Fifth Amendment right against self-incrimination did not cover bank records.

The Bank of Nova Scotia through its US branch office was cited for contempt of court for its refusal to release the confidential information requested by the United States in Ghidoni's case and fined a sum of approximately US$1.8 million. The local law on confidentiality did not assist the bank's case in this instance.

Roderick Donaldson, early after completing the 1979 amendment legislation to the Confidential Relationships (Preservation) Law, retired from the government aged 74 after serving in the position of Legal Draftsman in Cayman for nine years. He died and was buried at sea on Monday, 16th March 1981. He was well liked, respected and very much missed in the government and in the community. His services in legal drafting of laws are to be remembered as a part of the building of the local economy as we see it today.

Looking back on the Anthony Field case in 1976, I must qualify our strong insistence on defending Cayman's law on confidentiality in a world then buzzing with narcotics and commercial crimes. We in the Cayman Islands declared from the outset of planning the creation of the offshore industry that these islands would not be a harbour for questionable institutions. We were also aware, before the law on confidentiality came into effect, that particularly in this hemisphere commercial crime, drug trafficking and money laundering were on the rise. In that respect we were ready to assist offshore countries' investigation of those offences while keeping strictly in mind our commitment to safeguard clean privileged information. This was of the essence in ensuring the success of the financial industry. Secondly, in the process of investigating cases that would touch on tax offences, this government was not prepared to enter into any form of compromise, and we were greatly concerned about external crime investigators coming here on pretence of friendly visits when in fact they came here to snoop around on what has already been described as 'fishing expeditions'. This was a term used when investigators deliberately and illegally fished out privileged information without seeking formal government approval; this was quickly challenged in order to avoid interference in local tax matters while at the same time defending Cayman's status. A former Governor, Kenneth Roy Crook, CMG, speaking at a tax seminar held here in March 1974 pointed out, 'And when we say "Keep Cayman clean" we don't just mean litter.'

Thirteen years before the introduction of the first Cayman banking legislation in May 1966, Barclays Bank International Ltd., now Barclays Bank PLC, was the first offshore commercial bank to establish an office here – on 2nd March 1953. The bank was a branch operation of its Kingston, Jamaica, office. Back in those days, as big property developers like Benson Greenall began looking seriously at moving to Cayman, the question arose about the absence of large

157

commercial banks. The government of Jamaica was requested by Caymanian interests to encourage banks operating in that country to consider extending their services here. Barclays was the only one at the time to accept the invitation. Its first manager was Cyril Thames. The bank initially conducted business under a local Trades and Business Licence. Following the introduction of the Banks and Trust Companies Regulation Law in May 1966, Barclays Bank on 11th November 1966 applied and obtained its Bank and Trust Licences under the new banking legislation. At the time, and as Treasurer, I was appointed Bank Inspector under the law. This was in addition to three other appointments, Collector of Taxes, Licensing Authority under the Tax Collection Law and Controller of Exchange.

Following Barclays Bank's establishment here, many other such commercial banks and trust companies decided to come along and see what Cayman had to offer. Those following Barclays were The Royal Bank of Canada, The Bank of Nova Scotia Trust Company and its counterpart, Bank of Nova Scotia, Canadian Imperial Bank of Commerce, First National City Bank, Mercantile Bank and Trust Company, and Sterling Bank and Trust Company. The names were not necessarily in order of their arrival. Those institutions, except Sterling Bank, which collapsed and went into liquidation on 15th September 1974, formed the nucleus of what was to be, many years later, the world's third largest banking centre in terms of the number of institutions.

In 1967 Jean Doucet, a 46-year-old French-Canadian, came to Grand Cayman to start a banking operation. The following year he organized Sterling Bank and Trust Company Ltd. (Sterling Bank) and obtained a Class A licence for a domestic operation. He also applied for a Class B (offshore) licence for a second bank, International Bank Ltd., which was also approved. The combined operation was opened along the Seven Mile Beach opposite the main road from the Beach Club Colony, since renamed the Beach Club Hotel and Dive Resort. The bank's offices were named Interbank House, and popularly known as Interbank and sometimes referred to as Doucet's 'kingdom' or 'empire'. Doucet was the President, Chairman and a shareholder of both banks.

From the early days of Interbank's operation, some doubts clouded the minds of a few local individuals both in the private and public sectors with regard to the reliability of Doucet's banking operation. As a matter of strictly adhering to the principles involved in considering an application for especially a Class A bank licence, added efforts were put into the investigation of Sterling Bank. This was largely on the grounds that we were dealing with a small private com-

158

pany and the people involved had been known only for a short period of time. In addition, the government spared no effort to examine and investigate thoroughly public comments about a few doubtful areas relating to Doucet's operation. Yet nothing surfaced in terms of motives or schemes that would throw doubt on the proposed operation or lead to a departure from good banking practices. Executive Council therefore proceeded to grant Sterling Bank a Class A bank and trust licence.

Back in early 1970, the government introduced new planning regulations and a Statistics' Law: the latter was once on the statute book of these islands but for some unknown reason it had been removed during a law review some years earlier. Both pieces of legislation met with strong political opposition. The situation led eventually to a demonstration by political opposition members of the Legislative Assembly and their public support group, joined by a number of 'black power' troublemakers, which immediately began to scare tourists, visitors and local business persons. In spite of the demonstration, the government moved on with the Bills through the Legislative Assembly amid the tension and fury. The demonstrators, while under close police vigilance, ended up at the Beach Club Colony. This was just across the road from Interbank House and where Jean Doucet lived as well. It was reported that Doucet was seen with the demonstrators in Beach Club and that he also had the group to dinner at his home. People around town, including other bankers, called me, in my position as Bank Inspector, to complain about Doucet's involvement with the demonstrators.

I called Doucet to my office, locked the door behind him, and seriously questioned his involvement with the demonstrators, while reminding him of his moral and official obligations in the community as a Class A banker. He certainly did not deny the fact that he was with the demonstrators at the Beach Club Colony treating them to a drink then inviting them to his home for dinner. He tried to justify his action by stating what could have eventually erupted into a catastrophe for the country if he, like other bankers, had crawled into bed and ignored the growing hostility being created by the demonstrators. He said that it was certain that the frame of mind he found among the demonstrators would have led them one night to walk through Cardinall Avenue and smash the windows of banks and shops. This, he said, would have been awful publicity for what was deemed to be a growing and attractive financial centre. He assured me that he was able to convince the boys over a drink and a meal to calm down and call off their mission. His side of the story had merits and I accepted it. However, before unlocking my door for his exit, I impressed on him the fact that if at any time he should slip out of his bounds as a banker and hurt people or the local banking community, I would see him behind bars. He looked at me and asked, 'You mean jail?' I assured him that was exactly what was meant. His reply was, 'I believe you'll darn well do it.' I reminded him that one is usually put in jail as a result of his own conscience and his own design in any illegal or unlawful commitments.

Doucet undoubtedly did much to assist many local residents with loans and mortgage financing to build and repair their homes and improve their little businesses, much of which financing would not normally have been obtainable elsewhere. He also did much in the way of promoting Cayman's offshore business. One opinion of the man was that his main drawback seemed to have been that he knew no limit to his speed in promoting new business. He often remarked that many of his efforts were largely for the benefit of these islands and the people. However, Doucet's empire began crumbling around mid-1974 when false rumours against Sterling Bank hit the streets and triggered a run on the bank's deposits. Up until then the bank maintained an above-average liquidity ratio, as revealed in its audited accounts. It was felt that the false rumour on the streets indicated that somebody wanted Sterling Bank out of the way and that false accusations both against Doucet and his bank were the only recourse available.

In the Sterling Bank issue, I as Bank Inspector knew most of what took place from day to day. Few of the many false and vicious rumours against the bank came directly to me, but common among them was one that advised people likely to have deposits in the bank to withdraw their money, for the bank was broke. A few prominent persons came to me for advice on their deposits in the bank. When they were questioned about the source of their information, it became abundantly clear that the rumours were a deliberate plot against the bank; exactly what I had thought all along. I told those who came to me for advice that if wild and false rumours continued against the bank, it would in fact have no alternative but to close its doors before long: the decision to withdraw their deposits must therefore be their own. Up to that stage the bank's liquidity was not seriously affected. The Executive Council was kept informed of the situation. Indeed, once a run on a bank's deposits begins, it must have strong backing to withstand the drain.

Another false accusation advised the public that the bank was involved in Mafia operations, citing the fact that some people could not determine the bank's source of funds employed in, for instance, the purchase of the Governor's harbour development. A few individuals actually thought that the deal involved Mafia money and that it was the reason for Teamsters Union chief Jimmy Hoffa's visit to Grand Cayman during the Sterling Bank crisis. Another rumour was that Jimmy Hoffa, who visited Cayman after his release from a United States jail sentence, came here to see Doucet, therefore Sterling Bank was a Teamster bank. When questioned about this, Doucet said that he did not see the man, and that he understood that Hoffa had stayed somewhere in South Sound. The statement of where Hoffa lodged was indeed correct; I could confirm that because I also lived in South Sound and knew where the man was accommodated. The sad part about Jimmy Hoffa as reported was that when he returned to the United States he disappeared and was never heard of again. Another name Sterling Bank inherited was 'The Bay Street Boys' Bank'. This came about after a group of Bahamian business-men visited here and held investment discussions with Doucet.

In all the confusion caused by the rumours about the Sterling Bank operation, I kept in close liaison with Doucet and his auditors. In early August when there seemed no ease in the run on the bank's funds, I advised Doucet to solicit from abroad the services of a very competent investigator, associated if possible with a reputable bank, to try and unravel his bank's crisis situation. He hired a retired CIA colonel who came here, as we had agreed, unannounced. I read his report and, to say the least, nothing in it surprised me. In the cir-cumstances, Doucet did not wish the report circulated beyond his board of directors and myself. He told me later that because of the unsurprising contents of the report, he would lodge it where no other eyes would behold it. In any case at that stage the bank's liquidity situation indicated that it was too late for another rescue attempt.

On Sunday night 15th September 1974 at about 8 p.m., two gen-tlemen came to my home at South Church Street and introduced themselves to me as Keith Norman and Robert Landori-Hoffman. I had not seen either of them before. They advised me that at a meet-ing in Montreal that day, arranged by Jean Doucet and his partners, Marcel Dion and Daniel van Dreunen, the shareholders and directors of Sterling Bank and International Bank had taken the decision to close the banks' operations. The two gentlemen reporting to me that night had been appointed the liquidators. Norman and Hoffman advised that the boards of the two banks directed them to inform me at the earliest opportunity of the action of the boards. I heard then what was expected at any time, and as the press termed it, 'Grand Cayman's most flamboyant financial institution, Interbank House, closed its doors.' The following day, Monday 16th September, as the banks displayed on their front door a closure sign that read, 'Closed because of liquidity problems', the government considered two main issues relating to the liquidation of Interbank House. First, that the liquidation should be put under the supervision of the Grand Court; this recommendation was accepted by the court. Secondly, that a third liquidator be appointed by the court who would represent the local interests. The court appointed Michael Austin, manager of the accounting and audit firm of Peat Marwick, Mitchell, as recommended by the government.

In early October 1974 the liquidator Keith Norman reported to me orally that in the examination of Sterling Bank accounts, certain discrepancies were found involving the purchase and distribution of gold bars from Switzerland and these transactions appeared to be lacking proper explanation. He also said that all the liquidators thought the discovery could be a case of fraudulent conversion. In any case, he went on to say, it was a matter in their opinion requiring police investigation. I told Mr Norman that the three liquidators should prepare a joint statement of the facts covering the matter and thereafter submit it to the court for a ruling on whether or not their findings actually constituted a *prima facie* case calling for further investigation by the police. If the court's decision called for further investigation leading to possible prosecution, the government would take the matter from there. About ten days later the liquidators brought me the court's ruling stating that the Interbank gold case did in fact require police investigation.

I discussed this with the Governor, Mr Thomas Russell, and then requested that he contact the Chief of Police, Andrew Greiff, and request him to arrange the investigation of the case through his Criminal Investigation Department. The Chief of Police in a few days reported to the Governor that Superintendent Alan Binney had been selected and placed in charge of the Interbank missing gold case. I was happy about this arrangement. In fact at that point in time I remembered what I told Doucet in 1970 during the political demonstration over new laws, that should he step out of bounds as a banker at any time and hurt people or the banking community, I would see him behind bars.

In preparation for the Doucet case, I got together with Alan Binney and discussed a few details of his involvement so that we both could have a fair understanding of the course of action being taken. In fact we got together quite often to talk about important aspects of the case, and more especially the cost involved, which in the end amounted to about $50,000: that was certainly a tidy sum of money in those days but the issue rose above cost. Alan did do an excellent job on the case, as was confirmed at the end of the more than six weeks' trial before the presiding magistrate, the Honourable James Shaw. He said, 'Superintendent Alan Binney, who led the investigation in this case, must be commended for a tremendous job of work.'

Alan found Doucet in Monaco and immediately began to work on his extradition and the procedure to deliver him to the Cayman Islands. Extradition was very complicated in that part of Europe but with the kind assistance of Scotland Yard the process was completed fairly quickly. Doucet was arrested on 14th August 1975 at Nice Airport in France, which borders Monaco, and brought to Grand Cayman via London and Palisadoes Airport in Kingston, Jamaica. The Cayman government had arranged for an Inter-islands Air Service DC 3 aircraft to be on standby at Palisadoes to connect with the London flight. No chances were taken in transporting Doucet, such as going via the United States. When he landed at Owen Roberts International Airport in Grand Cayman, a few people saw him but could scarcely believe that he was really Jean Doucet; he was rushed off in a police van to the George Town jail. By next morning Doucet's capture was hot news around town and this time it was not a false rumour.

Doucet's popularity in these islands was quite obvious. Many depositors of his Sterling Bank, however, naturally began to grieve over the loss of much of their savings. Others supported him for his kindness to them in many ways. For this reason the government had no choice but to be very cautious about the preparations for his trial. Certainly no local or nearby attorneys would be considered for conducting the prosecution. Instead an eminent London Silk, Victor Durand, QC, was brought in to lead the Crown's case. The other hurdle was a question of whether Doucet's case should be tried as an indictable offence before a jury or summarily before a magistrate. The former would provide the judge with wider scope for considering a lengthier sentence on conviction. However, this route was certainly not the choice of the government. Of paramount importance was to have the process of the trial in the hands of someone in whom the Crown and the country could have confidence. The case was therefore heard by magistrate James Shaw, a Canadian, as was Doucet.

In passing sentence, which was spread over many hours, the magistrate said of the accused, 'I don't believe anybody has expressed this yet – that there is no suggestion in any of the evidence I have heard in this lengthy trial that there was any personal gain to him. Maybe it happened, but certainly there is nothing I have heard on which such a finding could be made. I think it is obvious that these offences were in order to keep the bank going and not to try to divert money into his own pocket. But,' said the magistrate, 'this did not

163

diminish betrayal of the trust reposed in the accused and his banks by the complainants, the world banking community, and by the people of these islands.' Jean Doucet, after a trial that lasted six weeks and charged with 13 counts of fraudulent conversion, was sentenced to nine months' imprisonment on 3rd December 1975. Though he gave notice of appeal, Doucet remained in custody as he could not meet the bail requirements set by the court of personal surety of $100,000 and two others of $250,000 each to be vouched by Caymanians. His sentence was reduced by the usual remission of one-third for good behaviour. No date was fixed for hearing the appeal, as transcription of the taped evidence would likely take many weeks to complete, with the likelihood that the case would be mentioned at the Grand Court sitting in July for the fixing of a date for the hearing. In the meantime Doucet served the sentence and departed these islands. Nothing further was heard of the appeal.

The Interbank collapse eventually cleared the way for the local banking community to get on with its development. Of course Sterling Bank was the first but not the only failure in the Cayman domestic banking system.[6] Sterling Bank fell in the midst of its growing popularity and increasing business; its collapse was actually to the delight of some people. In late 1974, after my involvement ended in the Interbank collapse, I took the opportunity of looking at my portfolio with a view to improving staff numbers and also improving methods and systems in my office to cope more efficiently with the rapidly growing financial industry. At a tax seminar held here in January 1974, and long before the Interbank collapse, Governor Kenneth R. Crook, giving the opening address, referred to me as one who has 'strong but over-burdened hands'. He was alluding in the statement to his upcoming plan to appoint a bank inspector to relieve me of some of my heavy workload. In fact from back in 1971 I did see the need for the establishment of two new posts in my office and wrote then to the Governor for permission to insert them in the estimates of expenditure; they were a Controller of Exchange and an Inspector of Banks. The first post was made obsolete by the abolition of exchange control in 1980. However, it was still necessary in 1975 to establish the post and appoint someone to administer its affairs. Unfortunately, three years after the request was made for the two posts in 1971, neither of them had yet been filled. At that stage the need for additional help became even more acute and demanding. I discussed this, together with all my other responsibilities which

---

[6] Twenty-three years later a second Class A bank, First Cayman Bank, went into liquidation.

were considered very demanding, with the Bank of England representative on the Cayman Currency Board, Mr Gordon Hall; he agreed entirely that it was quite time for some form of assistance to come my way.

The continuing question was, where would the government find a Bank Inspector? It was agreed that the individual should be professionally and administratively trained in banking and trust and with experience in internal controls and field assignments. A request was therefore made to the Bank of England to kindly assist in recruiting a suitable officer and if possible that the bank bear a proportion of the annual salary. The bank agreed to assist in finding a Bank Inspector but suggested that we apply to the United Nations International Monetary Fund (IMF) in Washington for a bursary to cover the entire cost of salary attached to such a post. Very happily the IMF approved the request. The recruiting of the person was coordinated between the IMF, the Bank of England and the Cayman Islands. On 1st June 1975, Mr Gordon Aiton, FIB (Scot), FCIS, arrived to take up the first appointment as the new Bank Inspector. Gordon was born in Glasgow, Scotland, in 1933, educated at the Glasgow High School and began his banking career with the Royal Bank of Scotland. On arrival in Cayman he quickly organized the Bank Inspector's office and took time to introduce himself to the banking community and others before settling in.

In the meantime and since the function of exchange control was not yet suspended by this government, action was also taken to organize an exchange control section in my office and to find a suitable person to perform the duties. In early 1974 Tom Jefferson, who hailed from West Bay but who was then working in New York City, paid me a visit and we discussed the possibility of the Cayman government's offering him a job in my office. Later that year he accepted the invitation to the job dealing with exchange control. Shortly after being appointed he was sent to the Bank of England on a short training assignment to become especially acquainted with the subject of exchange control. He returned to Grand Cayman at the end of the course, established himself in a section of my office and took over responsibility for the day-to-day exchange control functions. Tom was conscious then of the need for him to improve his academic background and therefore attended Vanderbilt University in Nashville, Tennessee. After a one-year course that started in August 1974, Tom attended South Florida University and George Washington University, all of which led him to an MSc degree in National Accounts and Economics. He spent over three years in universities and returned to office to assume the position of Deputy Financial Secretary, a new

165

position occupied initially by Linford Pierson after he graduated as a professional accountant in the United Kingdom. Linford moved to another portfolio on promotion so that the post in my office was available for Tom when he returned home from university. During Tom's absence from office, his nephew, John Jefferson Jr, and also Mrs Catherine Chisholm joined my office to assist principally in the bank inspectorate and exchange control sections. At that stage my office, and the portfolio in general, had a fair complement of staff. All of us worked together in harmony and in a very pleasant and cordial association. Finance and Development soon began to make an impression on the offshore business world. I think it is appropriate too for me to mention that Tom was my successor in the position of Financial Secretary at my retirement on 31st March 1982. Later he entered politics and is presently the Minister for Tourism. He also enjoys the Queen's award of the OBE while at the same time he is a Justice of the Peace.

Tourism

The tourist industry, as I said before, is looked upon as one of the two main pillars of Cayman's economy. The Commissioner, Mr A.M. Gerrard, in delivering his 'swan-song', or last address, to the Legislative Assembly on 15th January 1957 before handing over to the new Commissioner, Major Alan H. Donald, said 'The tourist industry has taken giant strides, and, through the maintenance and organization of employment facilities for seamen, there has spread through every section of the community a quite extraordinary prosperity and well being.' While it is true that the tourist business began expanding from Mr Gerrard's administration, there were yet, however, the mosquitoes and sandflies to overcome before any real growth could be expected or experienced from tourism. On the assumption that control of those pests was in the making, and having regard to the Mosquito Research and Control Programme being fully implemented by the end of the 1960s, the government could very well from then begin to steer the country towards a tourist and finance oriented future. An important development that came into effect on 1st January 1965 was the creation of the Cayman Islands as a 'free port', whereby the government removed or reduced import duties from luxury goods as a means of promoting the tourist traffic. Local merchants involved in the sale of luxury goods to tourists indicated their appreciation of the government's duty-free facilities by building new, beautiful stores with attractive glass showcases to display their stocks. Today Cayman's modern jewellery stores can be classed with the best anywhere.

In late 1967, tourism was developed under a statutory board. However, from early in the decade, sales offices were established in Miami and New York as another step forward in promoting the industry. Although it was a fairly expensive venture in terms of the board's limited financial resources, the government encouraged approval of the cost, fully realizing the potential benefits of such investment and as well bearing in mind the adage, 'It pays to advertise.' In fact offices in those destinations would serve well as an advance base for advertising Cayman. The intention in developing the use of the two United States sales offices was to promote traffic during the summer months or off-season period in order to keep the hotels active all year. To have them opening for just half the year during the tourist season, starting at the end of the year, was very expensive. Another benefit of the two United States offices was to cover the important areas of the North American tourist market that in those days provided about 80 per cent of tourist traffic arriving in these islands.

To follow the progress of tourism, detailed studies and surveys were undertaken in 1972, on behalf of the Cayman government, by Messrs L.B. Greenstead, MBE, FRCS, and John Crayston, BSc, MA, of Transport and Tourism Technicians Limited, London, under assignment by the Overseas Development Administration of the Foreign and Commonwealth Office in London. The terms of reference included a study to determine potential markets and promotional consideration necessary to exploit these markets. The studies also called for an examination of the monthly occupancy rates of hotels and length of stay of different types of visitors and planned to recommend ways of encouraging higher utilization. In the light of the above, the consultants were to examine the organization of the Tourism Board and the offices in Miami and New York to consider whether any changes would be desirable and in particular whether the board should be constituted as a government department. The team was also requested to examine the past growth in tourism with particular reference to locations within the islands and to indicate the likely pattern of development over the next ten years. This exercise allowed the Cayman government to make meaningful decisions about its tourist industry. First, it was recognized that tourism could continue to be a significant and worthwhile contributor to revenue and thus to the local economy. Secondly, and likewise important, it was determined that through a properly organized and administrated department, with clearly defined responsibilities and the ability to implement firm tourism policies, the government could control tourism and its growth.

The decision to create such a department under the provisions of a tourism law, to staff it properly and grant it the powers it needed to conduct its business, and allow adequate financing, would achieve the expected results. Those new policies were announced on 1st August 1973 and became effective on 1st January 1974. The licensing policy provisions under the new Tourism Law drew some adverse comments both here and internationally. Those provisions stated that persons offering sleeping accommodation for more than six tourists would be required to be licensed by a board called the Hotels Licensing Board. The board consisted of a chairman, who was the Director of Tourism or Head of the Department, and two other persons appointed by the Governor in Council. The board had power of inspection of premises, and, where standards appeared likely to cause discredit upon the islands as a tourist resort, the board also had power to withhold, suspend, revoke or refuse to renew any such licence. Persons so aggrieved by a decision of the board had the right of appeal to the Governor in Council. It was also sought to impose a small graduated licence fee to offset the cost of administration.

The authority imposed upon the Hotel Licensing Board was carefully mulled over. However, the board's functions eventually gained approval from a public that saw the provisions of the licensing policy as being sound and right, especially for this part of the world, and assisting in Cayman's tourism development. It was also the view that it is important in operating tourist accommodation facilities here in the Cayman Islands, or anywhere else for that matter, that certain standards be maintained and monitored by a regulatory body, otherwise, who would know whether those standards were being met? In fact tourists coming to these islands had long been complaining about cleanliness of hotel rooms and general appearance of some accommodation. This was why it became necessary for the government through legislation to oversee properties used for such purposes.

The Director of Tourism, Mr Eric Bergstrom, MBE, speaking at a local tax seminar in January 1974, stated that in 1963 tourists arriving in these islands numbered 5,000 and ten years later the number had grown to 40,000. At that time, he said, the industry was short of qualified local personnel but the government was reluctant to import more off-island staff than was absolutely necessary. This was because of fear that importing too many foreign workers would have the tendency of upsetting the social balance and not preserving jobs for the young and upcoming Caymanians. He also stated that after the new Holiday Inn was completed that year, it had been decided by the government to block the approval of any more hotels of that size until there were enough school graduates capable of being employed as staff. In my opinion that was not a sound proposition. In fact five years later the government's political policy was to offer a number of attractive incentives and schemes to potential hotel developers in an attempt to attract a large hotel to these islands, but none came. Ten years after the Holiday Inn was approved, Hyatt Hotels came along with an interest. I remember the occasion of Hyatt's application well, for it was in 1985 when I was a Minister in the government and responsible for development. Every effort was put into that case to ensure that the Hyatt was approved, for its presence on the local scene was like a breath of fresh air and furthermore it placed a completely new perspective on the prestige of the industry. It was also looked upon as a blessing in disguise in generating new efforts in the growth of the tourism economy.

After the substantial control of mosquitoes and sandflies during the first half of the 1970s, it was recorded that between the years 1976 and 1980, tourism grew annually at a phenomenal rate of 136.4 per cent. Growth in the Caribbean region on the other hand, was reported as not being smooth all the way through. The region sometimes met obstacles, like air transportation problems in the form of airline rescheduling, limited tourism infrastructure and major shifts in worldwide tourism trends, much of which were influenced by political changes in the region. Cayman, however, had been most fortunate in promoting its tourism growth during that same period. After studying the most significant five-year growth during the period 1976–80, the Tourism Department employed the American firm of Levethol and Horworth to carry out another tourism study focusing on the future of tourism in the Cayman Islands and covering a ten-year period to 1990. At the presentation of the report to the government by representatives of the study team at the end of their exercise, political interest appeared to have dwindled. As a result, the report, to my knowledge, was never officially processed. One reason for lack of interest on the part of the elected government could have been the absence of proper coordination between the Director of Tourism and the elected ExCo Member responsible for the subject with regard to certain policies injected into the study.

Cruise ships started visiting Grand Cayman from the 1930s when the *Atlantis* and *Arandora Star* between them made three stops here; the war brought to an end those visits. In 1969 at the resumption of cruise ship visits, a total of 1,300 passengers landed during the year. The record of tourist arrivals by air for the year 1964 was 4,834. The growth in tourism from both cruise ships and by air passengers con-

tinued over the years, although growth was restricted until mosquitoes and sandflies were physically under an advanced stage of control by the mid-1970s. Then in the five-year period 1976 to 1980, as
stated in the preceding paragraph, the growth rate exceeded 134 per
cent per annum. Statistics obtained from the information systems of
the Cayman Islands Government Department of Tourism indicated
that 20 years later, in 1995, tourism by cruise ships grew in numbers
per annum to 682,885 and by air to 361,444 for a total of 1,044,329.
The origin of tourists by air began with the largest number coming
from the United States (74%), then Jamaica (5.8%), and smaller numbers from Canada, the United Kingdom and 'the rest of the world',
which included Europe and Japan. Hotel beds available in 1995 were
3,986. Apartments, cottages and guest houses provided another 1,592
rooms.

Visitors from all countries and all walks of life have fallen in love
with Cayman. In early February 1982 Lady Bird Johnson, widow of
United States President Lyndon B. Johnson, paid a brief visit to
Cayman. Lady Bird, along with Texan friends, stayed on the famous
Seven Mile Beach. She spent part of the time snorkelling over some
of the island's celebrated reefs and also travelled around observing
the scenery. She told the Cayman Islands News Bureau, 'Two things
that struck me most about these lovely islands are, one, the charm and
friendliness of the Caymanian people, and the other, the beauty of
your natural treasures – the beach, the water and the reefs with their
enchanting marine life. Those marvellous Caymanian cottages with
their overtones of Victorian architecture are particularly striking.
They obviously represent a valuable part of the Caymanian heritage
and I hope the people here are able to preserve them during the years
ahead.' Lady Bird Johnson went on to say, 'I am particularly struck
by the beauty and abundance of fauna on Cayman. The plants and
trees here are beautiful. You are so fortunate to have so many different plants, shrubs and flowers, each one of which seems as though it
were more beautiful than the last.'

Her comments are significant, especially in light of the fact that she
led many beautification projects in the United States while her husband was in office.

I have briefly set out in this chapter an overview of Cayman's twin
industries, finance and tourism, from the early years of the 1950s.
Having watched their growth over the succeeding 40-plus years, I am
not surprised that their development has progressed so well. The
Cayman Islands became in the 1990s virtually a global spot which
offshore people liked to visit and use for both business and vacation
purposes. The present Cayman economy owes its existence, as in

170

other countries, to the system of government that created it and encouraged it. In our case this began at a time when the country's meagre economy, based largely on seamen's earnings, faltered. From that point in time it became quite obvious that as the years moved on and as controls and infrastructure fell into place, finance and tourism were bound to become the mainstay and cornerstone of Cayman's future economy. It was indeed quite encouraging to see both the public and private sectors sparing no time to support, strengthen and promote these two industries which will hopefully serve not only the present day needs but also provide as well for successive generations. There is no doubt that the Cayman Islands have reached a milestone of great economic success that by good fortune will continue to serve the country in the long term, provided there is no external interference to discourage either segment of the present economy.

If one were permitted to gaze into a crystal ball to look at the immediate future of these islands, it would not be surprising if one saw a signpost with a notice reading, 'Be cautious; avoid complacency for it is easier to build than to rebuild.' I should also quote the warning to both the private and public sectors delivered in my budget address to the Legislative Assembly on 18th November 1981, the last such address before I exited the Civil Service on 31st March 1982. The warning said, 'Much has already been achieved but there is yet a great deal to be done. So let us not criticize or attempt to destroy the work of others; rather let us improve on what has already been done while continuing to build and manage the country's present economy in a manner that will ensure its continued excellent performance.' This advice is still, 18 years later, quite appropriate. In fact both the public and private sectors have maintained a good pace in protecting and expanding the industries, backed of course by the government's improved financial services and effective regulations. Important to mention is the 1996 legislation, the Proceeds of Criminal Conduct Law, which provides measures for detecting, punishing and confiscating the financial proceeds of serious crimes, including narcotics trafficking and money laundering. Those are crimes that, to say the least, have the damaging effect of ravaging the world if left without adequate control.

The Proceeds of Criminal Conduct Law, brought into effect on 10th December 1996, was very well received in London and other foreign countries like the USA. On 1st August 1997, FCO in London stated (*Cayman Compass*, 6th August 1997, front page): 'The British government were pleased that the Cayman Islands were the first to introduce such legislation with the introduction of the Proceeds of Criminal Conduct Law in December 1996. As one of the world's leading banking and offshore financial centres, it is right that the Caymans should want to meet the highest international standards of financial regulations in order to prevent criminal money from entering its financial system. The British government has fully supported the Caymans' action to meet this objective and will continue to do so.'

I should mention in ending this chapter that, as a continuing effort to promote and expand tourism, an application was received by the government in early 1985 for the licensing of a commercial submarine for the purpose of carrying passengers below the surface of the sea. The proposal came from Mr Dennis Herd of Sub Aquatics Development Corp. Ltd. of Vancouver, BC, Canada. Mr Herd was also a design engineer who started work on the sub the *Atlantis* some three years earlier with the assistance of a Mr Whitney and a Mr Roberts. They had all been involved in the commercial submarine business for approximately 15 years. They designed, built and operated many of the world's leading commercial submarines, including the *Taurus*, which achieved a world record dive in the central Caribbean to the south-east of Grand Cayman.

The submarine was built to American Bureau of Shipping standards; this is the world's leading and most respected authority for certification of commercial submersibles. Each design stage was submitted to the Bureau for approval prior to proceeding to the next. The construction proceeded under their daily scrutiny, including both sonar and X-ray of the welds. The pressure test by immersion in 200 feet of water with the Bureau's personnel present was successfully completed in early July 1985. The sub was insured with Lloyd's of London for a minimum of $1 million Hull and Liability. For operation, the owners leased waterfront property on South Church Street in George Town where they still operate. The sub drew 10 feet of water and the location for docking was ideal in terms of depth of water, proximity to cruise ship passengers (their main market) and viewing area and support facilities. Passengers would be taken to a depth of 30 to 50 feet to see popular sites like Eden Rock and shipwrecks. The craft carried 28 passengers plus a crew of 2 for a one-hour underwater dive. All other facilities, including the administration staff of 25 personnel approved by the Bureau, were provided.

On submission of the licensing application to the government, there was lengthy confusion as to who should take on portfolio responsibility for the project. What scared people about the new operation was the safety aspect of it. After a few weeks I eventually requested my Principal Secretary, Mr Kearney Gomez, to try and find the application and if no other portfolio was dealing with the subject, to fetch it to my desk. He did so and after a few days I began preparing the submission to the Executive Council. The safety considerations as outlined in the last paragraph appeared in order to me. However, additional investigations had to be made. I subsequently discovered that the vessel was always buoyant in its operation as it was powered-down by thrusters so that in the event of power failure it would automatically rise to the surface. It also carried 5,000 pounds of lead weight attached that could be released by the pilot hydraulically, enabling the craft to surface extremely swiftly if necessary. Despite those features the sub would carry sufficient life-support systems to enable it to stay fully submerged for up to 72 hours with a full complement of 28 passengers and 2 crew members. Apart from the qualifications and training required by the Bureau and insurers, pilots of *Atlantis* were required to complete at least three years of technical study at a recognized technical institute. Another safety precaution was that at all times the submarine was to be accompanied by a surface boat that carried a minimum of 30 life jackets, fire extinguishers and other safety requirements. The boat would move above the submarine at all times while it was submerged and would be in contact with the captain, advising of surface conditions and traffic by radio-phone. Signs, 'Beware, Submarine Below' would be clearly visible: a megaphone would also be on hand to warn off surface traffic verbally.

After my investigation was completed, I had no problem in recommending the application; it was accepted without reservation. When the *Atlantis* was preparing for its maiden commercial dive, the company invited me, also my family, to go for an initial dive. It was on a Sunday morning after our church service at George Hicks Church in South Sound. I accepted the offer, not so much for the novelty of the underwater experience, but to give confidence to the public and others who would be thinking of the safety aspect of the submarine. It would be somewhat of a relief to the public to know that the Minister, his family and staff had taken the first dive. I had from my home my wife and five children (the sixth being off the island). Also with me on the sub were four of my grandchildren, the eldest son of Minister Anthony Eden, my Principal Secretary and his little son and my secretary and manager from Elizabethan Square. The 16 of us enjoyed the dive: it also gave the *Atlantis* owners confidence in their Cayman operation to have had government staff do the first dive.

Undoubtedly, the submarine operation, as did the Hyatt Regency Hotel that opened a short while after, injected an important dimension into the tourist industry. That boost to tourism was being advocated over the previous five years. It was very fortunate that the new government of 1984–88, made up of members from the new 'Dignity Team' of which I was a member, began its administration with much confidence from the public.

11

The Cayman Currency

The Cayman currency was issued on 1st May 1972: it replaced the Jamaican currency that was hitherto the legal tender of the Cayman Islands. Both currencies, however, remained legal tender for the next four months in order to allow the Bank of Jamaica to completely withdraw its circulating notes and coins in the Cayman Islands. The introduction of the Cayman currency was not only seen as timely, but was also considered at the time a most popular move when everybody was busily promoting the local financial industry and tourism. The new currency was also considered favourably by those involved in general trading, commercial business and domestic financial affairs: in fact it was hailed as being very acceptable by the entire community. In guiding the performance of the new currency, there was also the effort to raise the standard of living and quality of life in the Cayman Islands. This was not only for the benefit of Caymanians but also for the good of entrepreneurs or foreign investors and imported technical staff and their families who would eventually settle here to become partners in the building process of the local industries. The newcomers would also assist in maintaining a lower level of inflation, stabilizing prices and establishing sound business policies and practices while promoting the new local currency.

The background history of currency in these islands is quite interesting for what little can be found on the subject. Going back to the early seventeenth century, records reveal that Jamaica and her associate dependencies, the Turks and Caicos Islands and the Cayman Islands, relied upon a system of barter, i.e. trading by exchanging goods for goods. By the next century the position changed, with the activities of the buccaneers coupled with Jamaica's strategic importance as a military and naval centre. This eventually led to an influx of metallic currency, mainly of Spanish origin, and included the well-known 'piece of eight', valued at five shillings Sterling. The circulation of Spanish currency in the British West Indian islands caused the United Kingdom government to exercise control over the currency situation. In 1825 Britain circulated through all the British islands of the West Indies the British silver shilling, which eventually replaced the Spanish gold doubloon and the Portuguese gold *joanese*. That action left these islands with a currency system based on Sterling for the remainder of the nineteenth century and part of the twentieth century until 28th January 1974, when the Cayman Islands switched the parity of its currency from Sterling to the US dollar.

Looking at the currency situation from the beginning of the twentieth century, the Cayman Islands in the years to follow were traditionally supplied with currency by Jamaica until Cayman issued its own currency. Also to be noted is that from then until today the US dollar also gained a measure of recognition in local trading. After Jamaican became independent in 1962, the Jamaican pound and English coins continued to be the only legal tender in Cayman and remained so until the islands introduced their own currency in 1972. A notable currency development took place in 1968 when the Jamaica currency adopted the decimal system, replacing the traditional Sterling pounds, shillings and pence. This of course followed the devaluation of the English pound in 1967. Cayman was left in 1968 with no alternative but to go along and accept the Jamaican decimal system that continued to be the legal tender in these islands. In fact the period before changeover to the decimal system did not allow Cayman sufficient time to consider other alternatives.

Moving into the modern eras of commerce and trade, Jamaica saw that the lengthy and more difficult system of calculation by the old English pounds, shillings and pence could be made more simple and easier to calculate by moving those units into the decimal system. The English also came to this conclusion years later when they too moved their currency into the decimal system. At the time of decimalization the Cayman government also contemplated the possibility of making it a double effort by also going metric, which is a decimal system relating to weights and measures and using metres, litres and grams as units of measure. This was largely for the benefit of the local schools in the first instance. After completing decimalization of the currency, the Cayman government approached me to take on the job of converting to metric. It was my feeling that as my portfolio responsibilities were rapidly expanding and becoming quite significant, it would be more appropriate for someone from the Education Department to take on that responsibility. In any case the metric system was relevant to the schools as it related to the science of number, quantity and space. The exercise in converting to metric was never officially undertaken by the government. However, over the years, and with the development of the local education system, the metric system automatically found its way onto the curricula of the schools.

By introducing the Jamaican dollars and cents system on 8th September 1969, Cayman moved away from the former British currency units of pounds, shillings and pence. The dollar, however, continued to bear parity, with the pound Sterling equivalent to two Jamaican 10-shilling dollars. Following decimalization, and for the first time, all the coinage was issued by Jamaica. All UK subsidiary coins that had been used both here and in Jamaica until then were gradually withdrawn from circulation.

In order to undertake decimalization of the Cayman currency for the purposes of convertibility and pricing in the business and commercial sectors, the government appointed a decimal currency committee to administer the changeover. The Bank of Jamaica, which was responsible for the changeover programme in Jamaica, very kindly assisted the Cayman government with its conversion programme by sending to Cayman Mr D.R. Clark and two other colleagues to assist the local committee. During this period of decimalization it became increasingly apparent that the Jamaican currency should be replaced at some convenient stage in the near future with a new Cayman currency. In fact the question was made more acute with the Sterling devaluation in 1967, which led a committee of the Chamber of Commerce in early 1968 to recommend that urgent consideration be given to the introduction of a separate Cayman currency.

As a result, Mr Gordon Hall, CBE, and Mr John Howes, both of the Bank of England, visited Grand Cayman. At a meeting with the Administrator, Sir John Cumber, the Bank of England officials and me, we discussed among other financial matters the question of a proposed Cayman currency. Mr Hall looked at the size of the local circulation from an estimated assessment made by the Bank of Jamaica, and then informed us that economically such a small system would be too expensive to be undertaken by the government. However, looking on the proposed growth in economic development about to descend upon these islands, I made a strong plea to Mr Hall that on his return to London he might care to have a second look at the possibility of a Cayman currency. The Administrator also presented a strong case from the political and social angle. He repeated my request and with a big smile said, 'We can afford it.' The upshot of our efforts was that on Mr Hall's return to the bank he did review the matter and gave it his support, which was conveyed without delay to the Administrator. Immediate action to study a new currency was followed by the government.

Following decimalization of the local currency in September 1969, a recommendation was presented to the Executive Council for the establishment of a Currency Committee. The terms of reference were to review the whole subject of a local currency, taking into consideration the new Jamaican decimal system that was then in circulation as legal tender, and make recommendations for the development of a future currency system for the Cayman Islands. The members appointed to the committee were Mr Clifton A. Hunter, MBE, Mr Colin A. Whitelock, FIB, and Mr John A. Collins, AIB, with Mrs Sybil McLaughlin (then Clerk of the Legislative Assembly) secretary to the committee. I was made the chairman by virtue of my position as Financial Secretary with portfolio responsibility for currency.

After careful deliberations and examination of public sentiments in support of a Cayman currency as expressed earlier by the Chamber of Commerce, the Currency Committee strongly recommended to the government that a local currency would be to the economic, political and social advantage of the Cayman Islands. Further, the printing and administrative costs would in a short period of time be absorbed by profits from its rapidly growing circulation. This recommendation was accepted by the Executive Council and followed by the formal approval of Her Majesty's government in view of the rapid economic progress of these islands, especially with regard to increasing revenues from tourism and the financial industry. The Bank of Jamaica, responsible for the circulation of Jamaican currency in the Cayman Islands, raised no objection to the proposed new Cayman currency. In fact the bank gave the newly created statutory Currency Board responsible for the local currency valuable assistance throughout the transition period. Formal United Kingdom approval for a new and independent Cayman currency was obtained in September 1970, following which the Currency Committee was charged with the responsibility of introducing the proposed currency legislation.

I remember taking the draft Currency Bill to the Legislative Assembly and explaining during its introduction, as best as I could, the interpretation of the various sections. Many Members debated the Bill and expressed their delight over the fact that the country had at last seen fit to introduce its own currency. The Legislative Assembly then moved into committee stage to consider the Bill by the usual procedure, clause by clause. A few Members advised the President, who was the Governor, Mr Long, that though they could use or spend money the science and the legal aspects of a currency system and its administration was very complicated for them. They therefore gave consent for the Bill to be accepted in its entirety without the usual detailed scrutiny. They also expressed confidence that the Third

Official Member, the Financial Secretary, had worked out the details of the proposed Bill in association with the Bank of England and International Monetary Fund (IMF) and, therefore, they were quite happy with the draft as presented. Other Members remained silent, which was an indication that they too had agreed to the shortened route of the committee stage procedure of the recommended Currency Bill.

The Currency Committee had in fact consulted the Crown Agents in London on a decimal currency system similar to the Jamaican currency then legal tender in the Cayman Islands. The Crown Agents at the time represented the Cayman government in all its Civil Service and departmental needs in the United Kingdom and elsewhere overseas, together with any need to consult the Bank of England, as they did with the Cayman currency. The unit of currency supported by the Crown Agents, the Bank of England, and the British government was a 'dollar' divided into 100 cents and named the Cayman dollar. It would, however carry a value equivalent to the US dollar or .8333 cents of the Jamaican dollar. For parity purposes, the Cayman dollar would be pegged to the pound Sterling but would still be equivalent to one US dollar. This fixture based on the equivalent value of the US dollar would, however, change before the Cayman currency was issued in May 1972, due to a prior devaluation of the US dollar.

The next important step of the Currency Committee was to consider the number of notes and coins and their denominations, the time of issue and their design. The committee deliberated at some length and eventually decided to recommend four notes and four coins for the local circulation. The relationship of intrinsic value to face value would apply to both notes and coins, i.e., $1, $5, $10 and $25 notes, and 1 cent, 5 cents, 10 cents and 25 cents coins respectively. The reason for notes and coins being of the same denominations was in order that the Cayman currency system would be just a little different from other currency systems. This was also the case regarding the special recommendation of the $25 note as opposed to the $20 note.

Research by the committee indicated that no other countries in this hemisphere had a $25 note. One in the Far East was mentioned. The committee argued too that for spending purposes there was little difference between a $20 note and a $25 note. It was thought too that the $25 note, being unique in these parts, would be attractive as a collector's item and that the wealthier tourists on a visit here would no doubt take one of the notes as a souvenir. Once any local note is removed from the local circulation, it becomes in time a profit to the board because it reduces the board's liability for notes in local circulation. The committee also thought that the $25 note would be very

179

useful to banks, commercial firms and other large establishments for the payment of wages and other purposes. The size of the four notes was a special feature as well. They were made the same size as the US Federal Reserve notes, or 156 x 66 millimetres, largely in order that they would fit in smaller wallets used for US dollars. This had much to do with Caymanians' traditional close association with the United States. In fact many Caymanians had over the years adopted many habits and customs from the Americans.

The government accepted the recommendations of the Currency Committee and gave it the authority to move on freely with putting together the designs of both the notes and the coins and also preparing the programme for the issue. The committee kept a very close liaison with the Bank of Jamaica as they agreed to be responsible for withdrawal of all the Jamaican currency in circulation in the Cayman Islands at the time of issue of the Cayman currency. They would credit the equivalent value of Jamaican currency withdrawn to the account of the new Currency Board through this government's account with the Crown Agents in London. This was because in the withdrawal process, Cayman dollars would replace the Jamaican dollars and the board had to be paid for the supply of Cayman dollars put into circulation, the proceeds of which would become the Cayman currency reserve. This was important so that all currency in circulation is backed by a special reserve that gives the system strength and stability.

The contract for printing the currency notes was awarded to Thomas De La Rue and Company Limited of the United Kingdom, following approval of the designs in late 1971. In the case of all notes, the obverse, or front, design included the portrait of Her Majesty The Queen based on one produced by Anthony Buckley: it also carried the Cayman Islands coat of arms. A turtle watermark was featured and depicted for front face viewing. The most up-to-date security requirements used in banknote printing at the time were adopted. The reverse, or back, of each denomination was given a distinctive design and colour. For instance, the $1 had an underwater scene featured in positive blue; the $5 had a Cayman schooner in green; the $10 a seascape in red; and the $25 a map of the Cayman Islands with a compass rose in brown.

The approved four denomination coins carried the Machin effigy of Her Majesty The Queen on the obverse, with different designs for each on the reverse side. The 1 cent coin carried a Cayman thrush perched on a branch, the 5 cents a crayfish, the 10 cents a hawksbill turtle breaking the surface of the sea and the 25 cents a Cayman schooner. The committee put these designs together and sent them to

180

the Crown Agents for vetting. When the reply was received and the Crown Agents' comments on the designs examined, we discovered that the Cayman lobster sported a pair of large front claws; this was not our intention. We should have requested the design of a crayfish instead referred to locally as 'Cayman lobster'. However, we called in a photographer from the *Compass* newspaper, Mr Budd Gordon, explained to him the crayfish/lobster problem and requested that he look for a true crayfish and let us have a nice photograph of it. The design of the crayfish used on 5 cents coin was indeed produced by Budd Gordon.

The contract for minting the coins was awarded to the Royal Mint. It was agreed that the coins would be designed by the recognized specialist, Stuart Devlin, for the Royal Mint and that minting should begin in late 1971, six months before the issue. However, I was advised that sometimes the Royal Mint can fall behind with their delivery programme. In our case, such delay had to be avoided if we were to meet the 1st May 1972 deadline for the issue. I therefore made an appointment with the Royal Mint through the Crown Agents shortly after the Currency Law was approved by the Governor. The purpose of my visit to the Mint was to settle the delivery date of the coins. I was advised that I would meet at the Mint two gentlemen, Mr Frederick Cornell and a Mr Kitchen. After we discussed the coins programme and progress with the order, I requested to see the head of the Mint. I was told that the Chancellor of the Exchequer is Master of the Mint and that Mr Clover, the Deputy Master, is actually the man in charge at all times, with his office right there in the Mint.

I met Mr Clover later that morning. In the course of discussion he said to me, 'Mr Johnson, this office of mine is the largest and most prestigious in all of London.' After having a look around I could very well believe him. He then opened his bar and offered me a drink. We both had a sherry. Then I mentioned my concern about the delivery of the coins in time for the issue on 1st May 1972. He asked when we would like to have the coins in Cayman. I requested that they arrive in Grand Cayman through the Bank of Jamaica in Kingston in early 1972. Mr Clover's reply was, 'I can assure you, Mr Johnson, that they will arrive in the Cayman Islands in very early 1972.' On 2nd January 1972 we had a call from the Bank of Jamaica saying that our shipment of coins had arrived and they would be forwarded to us in a couple of days by Cayman's mail ship. Thomas De La Rue had by then also shipped the notes.

The Cayman Islands Currency Law 1971, which came into effect in October 1971, was designed to provide the necessary statutory authority for the issue of currency in the islands and at the same time

181

to create a Currency Board to issue and manage the new currency. The law indeed represented a major step forward in the development of currency arrangements in the Cayman Islands and for the first time full responsibility for currency rested with the Cayman Islands government.

A continuation of the link with Sterling was considered to be important for the maintenance of confidence in the new currency and therefore the new law contained a provision that placed an obligation on the board to convert currency into Sterling on demand. The board was also designed to function with a minimum of staff so as to limit the administrative cost. At the same time it was felt that the board should be given the power to hold local assets in the Currency Fund so as to enable it to participate in investments in local securities. As a future act of policy this was to be undertaken in conjunction with a government move to provide an acceptable local liquid asset for the banking system. Although the board has been given certain powers to enable it to perform limited banking functions, it was not intended then that it should extend its functions beyond currency issue and redemption. However, in January 1997 the board developed into a Monetary Authority with greater responsibilities in a wider range of functions involving all financial services.

Following introduction of the Currency Law 1971, Currency Commissioners were appointed to the board by the Governor in accordance with Section 3 (1) of the Currency Law. They were: the Financial Secretary, Mr V.G. Johnson, OBE (*ex officio* Chairman); the Chief Secretary, Mr D.V. Watler, OBE; and Mr Gordon Hall, CBE, of the Bank of England. Other persons appointed as members to the board were Mr John G. Palfrey, Currency Officer, who was seconded from the Bank of England for the position; Mrs Marcia Bodden of the Treasury Department, Deputy Currency Officer. At the end of Mr Palfrey's term of appointment, Mrs Bodden succeeded him as Currency Officer, and Mr Barclay Coe, who was deputy to Mrs Bodden in the Treasury, became Deputy Currency Officer.

An agreement between the Cayman Islands government on behalf of the Currency Board and Barclays Bank DCO was reached at the end of 1970 and became effective in 1971. Under the agreement Barclays Bank was designated as Agent of the Currency Board for the purposes of providing currency storage facilities as well as handling the physical issue and redemption of the Cayman currency. This service was of course intended to be temporary until the Currency Board was properly housed in a good building with a strong vault and other facilities capable of taking over the functions from Barclays Bank. The board assumed these functions after the new government administration building was opened in 1975. At that time the board took the opportunity of putting on record its gratitude to the Bank of Jamaica for the benefits derived in the Cayman Islands from the long use of the Jamaican currency. Also on record was the Bank's invaluable advice over the years with regard to currency matters and for its assistance in the onward shipment of the new currency from Jamaica to the Cayman Islands. The board also thanked Barclays Bank for its advice and services as Agent Bank to the Currency board, the Crown Agents for arranging the production and shipment of the notes and coins, and the Bank of England through Mr Hall and Mr Palfrey for advice and services. On record also was this government's gratitude to the Foreign and Commonwealth Office for supporting and approving the Cayman currency, the Royal Mint and Thomas De La Rue for their timely production of the initial stocks of currency coins and notes, respectively, for the initial issue.

Shortly after enactment of the Cayman Islands Currency Law in October 1971, severe disturbances arose in the international currency markets that resulted in an agreement on realignment of exchange rates, giving rise to a *de facto* devaluation of the US dollar in terms of all other currencies. As a result it became clear that the fixed exchange rate of the Cayman dollar at par with the US dollar enshrined in Section 10 of the Currency Law would no longer remain a statutory fixture. The law was therefore amended in April 1972 to allow the Governor by order under the Currency Law to declare that the Cayman dollar would bear a value to Sterling. This would give the necessary flexibility to meet present requirements without loss of confidence in the Cayman dollar before the issue date on 1st May 1972. Acting in accordance with the provisions of the new Section 10, the Governor declared that the parity of the Cayman dollar should be 2 Cayman dollars equivalent to 1 pound Sterling. Regrettably the fixed exchange rate of the Cayman dollar at par with the US dollar, which everybody so strongly supported, and which would have avoided the American tourists complaining that the Cayman dollar was so much more expensive than the US dollar, had been lost. However, this was through no fault of the Cayman Islands government or its Currency Board: it was the US currency devaluation that crippled the local effort towards a Cayman dollar with a par value to the US dollar.

About ten days before the issue of the Cayman currency and redemption of the Jamaican currency notes and coins then in circulation, a publicity campaign was organized and set in motion by the Government Information Service in consultation with the board. Posters were used to illustrate the new notes and coins and to inform the public of the conversion date. On 1st May 1972 the International Monetary Fund, the United Nations' central bank, was informed that in respect of the Cayman Islands, a new currency named the 'Cayman dollar' had been introduced that day. Also that its units per metropolitan unit were 2 Cayman dollars to 1 pound Sterling, or 1 Cayman dollar was equal to 10 shillings Sterling. Each day the local banks were required to find new exchange rates for all foreign currencies including the US dollar.

On 1st May 1972 the Currency Board issued the new currency. The new Cayman dollars and cents were accepted by the public with much enthusiasm. The bulk of the changeover was successfully completed in a short period of time. By the end of June 1972, J$710,895 notes and coins had been redeemed. The machinery for withdrawal was quite simple. All Jamaican currency held by or returned to the banks was paid over at frequent intervals to Barclays Bank as Agent of the Currency Board, in exchange for an equivalent amount of Cayman currency. The Currency Board would then inform the Bank of Jamaica of the amounts so withdrawn. In a short period of time the Currency Board's account with the Crown Agents in London would be credited with the Sterling equivalent. On advice of the Sterling settlement, sealed parcels of Jamaican currency were handed over to Barclays Bank in their other capacity as Agent for the Bank of Jamaica. The sealed parcels were subsequently returned to Jamaica.

The Bank of Jamaica generously agreed to redeem the Cayman dollar at par with the Jamaica dollar, or dollar for dollar. The Sterling equivalent settled by Jamaica in London went to the board's banking account for the new currency. In order to ensure an adequate supply of currency during the changeover period, Jamaican notes and coins remained legal tender in Cayman until 31st August 1972.

When the pound Sterling floated in June 1972 the Cayman dollar followed suit while continuing to maintain its parity with Sterling at CI$2 to £1. In January 1973 the Jamaican dollar, which had also been floating with Sterling since June 1972, fixed its foreign exchange rates and switched parity from Sterling to the US dollar. This resulted in a devaluation of 6 per cent in terms of the Jamaica dollar's previous market rate and thus established a new central rate of J$1 equivalent to US$1.1. The Jamaican dollar devaluation and fixed exchange rate changed the relationship between that currency and the Cayman dollar after they had both enjoyed par value since 1st May 1972. When the news of the action taken by Jamaica reached Grand Cayman on a Monday morning in January 1973, a group of Cayman bank managers came to my office to inquire what I intended to do about the floating Cayman dollar. I told them that the government had made no decision as yet on the matter, that they should remain calm and when it was time to take necessary steps, the public would be advised accordingly. A month later, in February 1973, the US dollar again devalued, this time by 10 per cent (16 per cent in one month) to a new value. The Jamaican dollar moved downwards with the US dollar, thus further widening the exchange rate difference between the Cayman and Jamaican dollars.

In September 1973 I discussed with the government at some length the subject of the Cayman currency, its floating position with Sterling and the possibility of considering a readjustment some time in the months ahead. I expressed the feeling that it was time for the situation to be examined with the aim and possibility of re-establishing confidence and prestige in the local dollar by considering a new fixed exchange rate. This view was strongly supported by the government and later by the financial industry. Following my discussion in the Executive Council, I also submitted a proposal for the Cayman currency's parity to be switched from Sterling to the US dollar. The grounds for this recommendation were based largely on trade between the Cayman Islands and the United States. It was estimated that about 75 per cent of Cayman's imports came from the United States and it therefore made no economic sense to have the Cayman currency realigned or bearing parity with Sterling. This would mean severing the Cayman currency's long and traditional parity link with Sterling. It was therefore recommended that on the basis of proximity and trade with the United States, the Cayman dollar enter a new arrangement to switch its parity from Sterling to the US dollar. As explained earlier, it had been originally planned that on 1st May 1972 the Cayman dollar would have an equivalent value with the US dollar while still maintaining parity with Sterling. That did not materialize, owing to the devaluation of the US dollar in early 1972, just months before the Cayman currency issue.

A third point regarding the proposed Cayman currency adjustment was the question of the current floating rate and whether consideration should be given to its revaluation or devaluation. In the 15 months since June 1972 when floating began, the dollar lost approximately ten per cent in value, moving downward from its original rate of US$1.20 to US$1.17. My feeling was that the Cayman dollar should be revalued to its original rate established on 1st May 1972 of US$1.20. I also felt that these points should be discussed thoroughly with the Bank of England and the International Monetary Fund (IMF). The latter institution is the United Nations' central bank, established in July 1944 at Bretton Woods in New Hampshire, USA, by its parent organization. On obtaining from the Bank of England

and the IMF their professional and candid opinion on the three points suggested for the Cayman Currency adjustments, together with their support for implementation, the government forwarded the proposals to the Foreign and Commonwealth Office (FCO) in London for final and formal approval. London also approved the measures.

As the subject of the Cayman currency adjustment required top secret status in the government, I requested from the time we received Executive Council and London's final approval, that the matter be dealt with only by my secretary (Mrs Jenny Manderson) and myself. The Chief Secretary, Desmond Watler, was the coding and decoding officer for all telegraphic communications on the subject between Grand Cayman, FCO, the Bank of England and IMF in Washington. I brought the Governor up to date with progress on the programme from time to time and tried to do the same with Desmond, who, however, refused to have any knowledge of what was taking place with the exercise even though he was a member of the Currency Board. That was certainly honesty at its highest level, as in all international currency readjustment exercises there has got to be, without any exception or compromise; otherwise speculation will run rampant.

Working out the details of the adjustment programme fell to the IMF, the Bank of England and myself. In the meantime, the Cayman dollar continued floating while we maintained our top secret plan of action so that the public, and more especially the financial community, would be kept completely out of the picture. The danger was that immediate switching would begin by moving foreign currency holdings into Cayman dollars and awaiting the action of revaluation of the local currency on 28th January 1974, which would then earn speculators a tidy profit on the deal.

To move on to the changeover date, consequential amendments to the Cayman Islands Currency Law 1971 would be necessary. However, since several of the provisions of that law were transitional and considered as no longer serving a practical purpose, it was recommended that the existing currency law be rewritten in a more precise and pertinent form. Due to the highly confidential nature of the proposed currency adjustments, the rewriting could not take place prior to 28th January. In the adjustment programme the new law was scheduled to be effective in March 1974. Therefore, in order that statutory provisions be put in place to meet the 28th January deadline, an order by the Governor under the Currency Law 1971, containing the appropriate provisions, was made to put the adjustments into effect. The temporary arrangements would continue on a day-to-day basis (bank working days) until the new Currency Law was put into effect.

186

Revaluation and switch of parity from Sterling to the US dollar were scheduled to proceed as planned, and as 28th January was a Monday, I called a meeting of all available local managers of clearing banks to my office on Friday 25th January at 6 p.m. That was the closing hour for all public banking business for the weekend. Monday was therefore the beginning of a new business day when bankers would all be ready to implement the currency changes. At the meeting I spoke briefly. After my opening remarks I distributed a statement on the subject that was also sent to the press. In the statement I said:

The government has been aware of the concern felt by the public over the substantial increases in price which have taken place over the past few weeks. In an endeavour to ease the current high level of inflation, which is largely imported, it has been decided to remove one element of uncertainty by fixing the Cayman dollar exchange rate to the US dollar and therefore breaking away from the previously-held traditional links with the pound Sterling. This move has been forced upon the government not through any mistrust of Sterling or for weakening of the ties with the United Kingdom, but simply because the continued devaluation of Sterling during the current period has had a very strong detrimental effect on import prices.

Henceforth, the Cayman dollar will be allowed to float against Sterling and all other currencies except the US dollar and those that are linked to the US dollar. The government has also decided that the measures which have now been adopted to fix the Cayman dollar to the US dollar, would not be complete unless the Cayman dollar was also restored to its former parity with the US dollar. It has therefore been decided to revalue the Cayman dollar by approximately ten per cent and that from the opening of business next Monday morning, January 28th 1974 the rate of exchange for the Cayman dollar shall be CI$1 to £0.54 or US$1.20.

For the time being the Currency Board will continue to quote rates only in Sterling, which will be issued daily and will be based on the London Sterling-dollar cross rate for that day, and will only exchange Cayman currency for Sterling as at present. It is intended, however, to proceed with legislation to amend the Cayman Islands Currency Law to allow it to deal in US dollars and hold reserves in US dollars.

When questioned by the press regarding public understanding of the authority to vary the value of the Cayman dollar, I gave the assurance that such action was ratified by the International Monetary Authority under the Smithsonian Agreement of 1971. I also gave to the press an undertaking against a further alteration in the value of the Cayman dollar in the immediate future; indeed, 25 years later there has been no change in the value.

The programme proceeded well and with much enthusiasm from the public as in the case of the 1st May 1972 changeover from the Jamaican currency. There was slight concern, largely by non-Caymanians, that the Cayman dollar was perhaps the most expensive of any: it was equivalent to US$1.20 (or US$1 = CI$.8333). The concern was based largely on the effect an expensive Cayman dollar would have on the country's growing foreign trade. Nevertheless, the government's reaction was that in a short time everybody, even American tourists, would become accustomed to the value of the Cayman dollar, which was otherwise so very attractive in design and size.

Prior to the currency adjustments in January 1974, the government negotiated a consortium loan of $4 million from the larger of the local international commercial banks. The loan was to assist the financing of a number of capital development projects such as the George Town port, resurfacing of all the islands' main roads with hot mix asphalt and construction of a new Government Administration Building. Eventually the loan was approved at rates and conditions satisfactory to the government. A couple of the banks in the group had apparently brought to Cayman their portion of the loan in US dollars before the necessary procedure and arrangements for finalizing the loan agreement had been completed. Those particular bankers holding US dollars locally decided in the meantime to lay off the funds in London, where interest rates on deposits were most attractive. Shortly afterwards, however, the surprise of the Cayman dollar revaluation and the switching of its parity from Sterling to the US dollar hit the public, with shocking surprises for all those who held long in local US dollars against CI dollars. Two days after revaluation three senior officials of Bahamian international branch banks, also represented in the Cayman Islands and involved in the consortium loan with the proceeds laid off on deposit in London, came to see me over my government's surprising action to revalue its dollar.

The Bahamian bankers were seeking the government's guarantee in some form as a future safeguard or assurance that they would not be taken by surprise in case of currency adjustments; this would avoid the embarrassing experience of 28th January 1974. My reply was that their request had no merits because historically no government had ever dared predict, let alone give a guarantee against, the future outcome of their currency system in the event of either devaluation or revaluation. I went on to say that bankers had certain responsibilities for their business, their customers and for what might be possible regarding the local currency system. For instance, bankers had known that for the past 18 months the Cayman currency was floating with sterling and that it had lost some of its original value against foreign currencies. Certainly there stood the possibility for some form of action by this government to remedy the situation, especially after Jamaica, our close currency associate, had moved a year before to take action against its floating currency position. Jamaica fixed its exchange rate with foreign currencies and since then all eyes had been on Cayman, guessing and predicting what would or could happen to the Cayman dollar. It would therefore have been prudent for the financial community to keep alert to the situation, not raising questions at this stage about a possible government guarantee against future currency adjustments.

The bankers advised that they would take appropriate action to safeguard their own interest. That threat was certainly implemented. The United States dollar selling rate by the local banks was widened from CI$0.84 to CI$0.85 but buying remained unchanged with cash at CI$0.80 and draft CI$0.82. The widened selling rate continued for about six years: there was no doubt about the margin of profits made by all the banks from the widened selling rate, for the figures were revealed in their annual accounts. By late 1980 the public complained bitterly and so did the government about the exorbitant rate of 85 cents at which the banks sold US dollars in draft form or in cash. The clearing banks, those involved in local domestic banking, decided, after strong government intervention, to narrow the rates by 1 cent, split into half a cent on each side of the buying and selling rates, or 81.5 cents and 84.5 cents respectively. I saw the move, however, as a reasonable starting point and decided to present the proposal to the budget meeting of the Legislative Assembly in February 1981 for discussion with Members.

While on the way to the Legislative Assembly I met Berkley Bush, Minister of Government for Communication and Works, before we entered the Chamber. He accused me of collusion with the banks over the proposed change of US dollar rates. This is what he said: 'What kind of rates are you proposing with the bankers for the currency adjustment? The 84.5 cent rate will confuse even the wealthy, much more so the poor.' I told him that the rates were proposed by the bankers, not me, and that he should make his views known inside the Chamber so that I could take immediate action. He certainly

189

advocated in a strong presentation that the .85 cent rate be reduced to 84 cent and that the 82 cent rate remain unadjusted. I went back to the bankers with the message of the Legislative Assembly and, after strong lobbying with them, the proposed 84 cent rate was accepted and put into effect during March 1981. Thus US dollar rates were back to square one, with both the banks and the public happy about the change. In fact 18 years have gone by and the rates have not yet been readjusted.

It is interesting to note a comment by Mr Peter A. Tomkins shortly after the 28th January 1974 currency adjustments. Mr Tomkins was at the time President of Cayman National Bank and Trust Company, his comment, carried in the *Northwester Magazine* in March 1974 on page 16, was headlined: 'Dollar switch means a new ball game for bankers.' He began by saying:

> It is easy for one to criticize when one is gifted with the 20/20 vision of hindsight. Before anyone is too quick to criticize remember that supposedly more financially astute bodies than our government, have not been doing particularly well with the international monetary situation over the last couple of years or so, either. The point is that a sound decision has been made, our currency is where it belongs, and natural economic forces are going to keep it there 'For ever and ever'. Or perhaps (as a prudent banker) I should say for the foreseeable future.

Well, Peter, we are just passing a quarter of a century since the switch on 28th January 1974 and the action then to move the parity of the Cayman dollar from Sterling to the US dollar is as acceptable and firm today as ever before. May the move with its tremendous support by the local population continue to serve Cayman as well in the fore-seeable future as it did in the past. I am sure that all those who live in these islands today have accepted the Cayman currency and its link to the US dollar without reservation.

In April 1975 it became necessary to amend Section 11 of the Currency Law, Law 1 of 1974, that effected permanent changes to the action on 28th January 1974. Section 11 basically stated that any local transactions such as contract, sale, payments etc. done in relation to Jamaican currency would be acceptable as though the trans-action were done in the local legal tender. In fact shortly after the Jamaican currency ceased to be legal tender in these islands on 31st August 1972, it was placed in the same position as any other foreign currency. The Board was therefore free to encourage the local circulation and use of the Cayman currency. The opportunity was

190

also taken to amend Section 12 of the Law to render more explicit the legal tender provision and the fact that the board should continue to have the sole right of issuing legal tender notes and coins in the islands. Also an amendment to Section 16 allowed as legal the permissible value of collectors' pieces.

Further amendments to the 1974 Law were made in July 1976 and April 1978. The 1976 amendment gave the board authority to hold Canadian dollars denominated assets in order to spread the range of its investments. It also gave authority to introduce greater investment flexibility by extending the eligibility of its securities from a limit of five years to maturity to a limit of seven years. A further amendment authorized the board to accept local bank deposits payable otherwise than on demand and carrying interest in the meantime; it was also authorized to accept government deposits upon the same basis. The 1978 amendment gave the board authority to promote the establishment of bank clearing systems and provide facilities for the clearance and settlement of transactions between commercial banks. It also provided for the granting of loans or advances for fixed periods not exceeding one month on such terms and conditions as the board may determine.

The 1978 amendment was proposed after the local clearing banks suggested that the Currency Board look at the possibility of taking over the banks' clearing arrangements. The system apparently had continuing problems with one of their numbers, hence the reason for putting the clearing proposition to the Board. In November 1979 a meeting of the Board was arranged with the clearing banks to evaluate their clearing needs. The banks advised that the clearing arrangements had improved satisfactorily and that there was really no need at the time for the Board to take over this function. They also advised that it would be fairly expensive for the Board to operate the system. At that time there was no cost involved as the bankers paid their own clearing cost. The Board, however, had the legislation in place should there be any future need for it.

After the meeting in November 1979 I found written in my diary the following note: 'Clearing arrangements for local banks are to be tied in with future conversion of the Currency Board into a Monetary Authority.' The board certainly maintained that policy and gradually converted itself into a Monetary Authority 18 years down the line on 1st January 1997. In mid-1997, after my retirement from Montpelier Properties (Cayman) Ltd., where I was employed as Managing Director for over 14 years, the government invited me to become a Director of the Monetary Authority, which position I accepted.

The financial position of the Currency Board as reported on 31st

December 1973, its first twelve-month year of operation, revealed that the board was strong and expected to remain so, particularly in view of the success of its proof coin programmes. The assets of the board at that date increased for the year by 86 per cent. That was partly as a result of a 52 per cent increase in currency in circulation and partly from receipts of CI$123,202 from Currency Board investments and CI$398,389 from the issue of proof coins. The Board repaid the government a loan of CI$81,195 obtained to meet the cost of the currency issued in 1972. Economically the Cayman currency can be looked upon as Cayman's finest investment. In fact all of Cayman's investments and developments of those early years outstripped their initial estimated performance.

The Cayman currency collectors' proof coin programmes of the 1970s have apparently given the Monetary Authority some concern over those coins' redemption over the years. The Board was first approached in mid-1972 by the World Coin Corporation of Panama and their Paramount International Coin Corporation of Englewood, Ohio, responsible for marketing and sales, with proposals for the issue of various sets of collectors' proof coins. The Board and the government examined proposals for the first two issues, an eight-coin proof set and a two-coin set commemorating the silver wedding anniversary of Her Majesty The Queen and Prince Philip. Not having any previous knowledge or experience with regard to numismatic coins, the government decided that I should visit London for discussion with people over there who were more familiar with the subject.

I visited the Crown Agents, the Bank of England and the Foreign and Commonwealth Office in London and had a full round of discussions on the proof coin programme. It was explained to me that coin collectors, or numismatists, were keen on what they included in their collections. Once they bought proof coins the value would escalate and the coins remain locked away in their collections in the long term. It was also my understanding that royalties from the programme would go to a proof coin reserve to meet any unforeseen liabilities; in the meantime, the funds could be invested and the income applied to the reserve for its further strengthening. The proof coins programme was seen to provide other added benefits to the country such as advertising and promotion.

I returned home and submitted a report to the Board and to the government. That was followed by a paper supporting the two issues, the eight-coin proof set to cover a period of five years and a two-coin silver wedding set, for which minting would cease at the end of 1972. The Board's comments in its 1973 *Report* about those two issues were, 'Being legal tender the coins are a liability to the Board, although they are unlikely to be presented for redemption since they are sold as collectors' items at a price considerably higher than their face value.'

One main consideration of the government in going along with the proof coin programme was that at the particular point in time the country was in search of ways and means of promoting the islands' offshore business. Certainly nothing seemed more appropriate for the purpose as using the prestigious Cayman proof coins as a medium for advertising. In fact it did do justice to the Cayman Islands in that respect. Whatever may eventually be the outcome of proof coins, the programmes of the 1970s did a great job in many ways for Cayman, especially when we look around today at the massive build-up of wealth in the country.

On the basis of the information I received in London regarding proof coins, the Cayman government recommended the two coin programmes to the FCO in London, for which approval was given. The Currency Board, before accepting World Coin's proposals, formulated a policy that it was necessary to choose very prestigious designs which should on the front or obverse of all the coins, with only special exceptions, bear the portrait of Her Majesty The Queen, and on the back, or reverse, prominent Caymanian scenery. Exceptions were made for the reverse designs of special issues, including Her Majesty's silver wedding which carried the effigies of Her Majesty and Prince Philip and Her Majesty's Silver Jubilee with the Coronation regalia. Other exceptions were the Kings of England issue with each king's effigy, the Queens of England issue with each queen's effigy and the wedding of His Royal Highness Prince Charles and Lady Diana Spencer with their effigies.

Proof coins were tested in the marketplace beforehand by publication of the designs, prices and other details. Booked orders that were received even before the coins were produced indicated that they were very beautiful and very popular.

The first two programmes introduced in November 1972 were for an eight-coin set with denominations of $5, $2, $1, and 50 cents in silver (.925 fine) and the other four coins were the denominations then in ordinary circulation – 25 cents, 10 cents, 5 cents and 1 cent. This set was issued yearly over five years and the only variation in design was the change of date according to the year of issue. The second programme was a set of $25 gold (18 kt.) and $25 silver (.925 fine). The issue was in honour of the silver wedding anniversary of Her Majesty The Queen and Prince Philip; the two coins were no doubt a very popular set. In June 1973 the President of World Coin Corporation, Robert McGrath, and Vice President David McGrath (his son), along with the President of Paramount Coin Corporation, Max Humbert, visited Grand Cayman. Max presented to Governor Kenneth Crook a cheque for CI$226,564.94 on account of royalties from the first two coins programmes.

When Prince Charles visited Grand Cayman in July 1973 on HMS *Minerva* as a member of its crew, this government pondered over an appropriate gift for the Prince. At the time the Currency Board ordered and received a pair of cuff links made from the gold CI$25 coin, intended to be a display item for the Board's continuing promotion of the beautiful silver wedding coins. The cuff links arrived just in time for the Board to suggest to the government that the gold cuff links be used as a special gift to the Prince; he accepted them with much delight. That further confirmed the popularity of the coins.

In addition to the first two proof coin programmes, the board accepted five other proof coin proposals to be scheduled over the period to the end of March 1982. They were also considered to be very popular amongst numismatists. The first set was produced in 1974 for the centenary of Winston Churchill. The occasion was commemorated with a CI$100 gold coin and a $25 silver coin. There was an exception in design; the obverse side carried the effigy of Sir Winston Churchill instead of the effigy of Her Majesty The Queen. The reverse side had the Cayman Islands coat-of-arms. The second programme was a $100 gold coin and a $50 silver coin honouring each of the six sovereign Queens of England, Mary I, Elizabeth I, Mary II, Anne, Victoria and the present Queen, Elizabeth II. This issue consisted of six gold coins and six silver coins.

In 1977 the third programme was an issue consisting of a $50 gold coin and a $25 silver coin commemorating Her Majesty The Queen's Silver Jubilee. While the obverse carried the effigy of Her Majesty The Queen, the reverse displayed the Coronation regalia of the British monarch – the Coronation chair, St Edward's crown, the orb, the royal sceptre, the ampulla and the spoon. In 1979 the fourth programme, another special issue, portrayed the 37 sovereign Kings of England complementing the Queens of England collection. This unique set consisted of ten individual $50 gold coins and ten individual $25 silver coins. Each coin carried the effigy of Her Majesty The Queen on the obverse and the effigy of one of the 37 Kings on the reverse along with the nine Royal Houses: Norman, Plantagenet, Lancaster, York, Tudor, Stuart, Hanover, Saxe-Coburg-Gotha and Windsor. This collection of kings featured for the first time Queen Elizabeth II, her father King George VI, her uncle Edward VIII and her grandfather George V.

The last programme with which I was involved before leaving the

194

Currency Board as Chairman on 31st March 1982 was one to honour the marriage of His Royal Highness Prince Charles and Lady Diana Spencer in 1981. The issue consisted of a $100 gold coin, a $10 silver proof coin and a $10 cupro-nickel coin. These, as in other issues except the Sir Winston Churchill issue, carried the portrait of the Queen on the obverse and the portraits of Prince Charles and Lady Diana on the reverse with the inscription 'Royal Wedding'.

The Currency Board in 1981 issued two higher-value notes above the $25 bill for ordinary local circulation: a $100 note and a $40 note. The latter was withdrawn from circulation in the early 1990s and replaced by a $50 note. While there was no question about the $100 note, the same could not be said about the $40 note. The first recommendation by the Board to government was in fact to issue a $50 note and not a $40 note. This was in order to continue the normal sequence and progression of the decimal system – 1, 5, 10, 25, 50 and 100 – applied in currency note denominations. However, the Minister in the Executive Council (the Cabinet) responsible for the Pirates' Week Festival argued in favour of the $40 note, saying it could represent the occasion well as the note would carry on the reverse a scene featuring Pirates' Week landing. Many offshore visitors attending the celebration in October each year, said the Minister, would take a $40 note with them as a souvenir and as a reminder of the occasion. This was in fact wishful thinking, for the public did not like the note in the first instance and secondly, the value was beyond the reach of the average visitor to take one as a collector's item. In fact nobody was eager to put the note in his wallet.

The government sent me to the Foreign and Commonwealth Office in London to argue the case for the $40 note as opposed to the $50 note. As stated before, there was definitely never a question about the $100 note. When I presented the letter from the Governor to the FCO official outlining the proposal to introduce the two additional Cayman currency notes, he looked at me, smiled and then asked if I felt well. We both laughed. He then inquired, 'Why not a $50 note instead of the $40?' I decided to tell him my side of the story as currency was my subject in any case. I went on to explain that the present elected side of the government had over the previous few years tried to lobby me into agreeing to remove the exchange rate difference between the Cayman Islands dollar and the US dollar so as to establish an equality in value of the two currency systems. I argued with the politicians against their proposal, indicating that such action would mean a devaluation of the Cayman Islands dollar of approximately 12 per cent. They still were not satisfied; no doubt they thought that I was not qualified to give such an answer. Without any further discussion I requested the Bank of England to write a paper. After the politicians read the Bank's comments, which also warned of devaluation of the Cayman dollar, they never again broached the subject with me. That is why I remained quiet when they requested the $40 note. The FCO's reaction was, 'In that case we approve the proposed $40 note.'

Another incident relating to the $40 note is worth mentioning. The order for the $100 notes printed by Thomas De La Rue and forwarded to the board was received before the $40 notes. The latter would follow on a given date. Accordingly the time was set for the ceremony to introduce the $40 note. On the morning of that date the notes had not yet arrived. The consignment that had been shipped via Jamaica was stored in a security locker at the Norman Manley International Airport in Kingston. All airlines bound for Grand Cayman, despite urgent reminders and appropriate shipping documentation, arrived without the notes. Just hours before the ceremony was to start, a private plane piloted by a Mr Glen Galtere was chartered and sent to the Norman Manley Airport to pick up the shipment of notes. Two senior officers were sent on the flight, Deputy Financial Secretary Mr J. Lemuel Hurlston (later the Honourable J. Lemuel Hurlston, CVO, MBE, JP, Chief Secretary) and my Chief Accountant, Mr Louis Moncrieffe, to ensure that the notes were found, delivered and transported to Grand Cayman in time for the ceremony.

The airline officials at Kingston airport responsible for the consignment did not appear concerned about the many oversights in dispatching the notes nor did they attempt to apologize. Mr Moncrieffe, a Jamaican national, said that while their attitude left much to be desired, it did not disturb him in the least bit for he thoroughly enjoyed the beautiful view of the Jamaican countryside made possible by the low flying of the aircraft. On return to Grand Cayman the aircraft was met by currency, security and customs officers who arranged a quick dispatch of the consignment to its destination at the Currency Office.

This last experience leading to the release into circulation of the $40 notes together with their withdrawal from circulation a few years later will now end this chapter. The currency story and the technical aspects of its administration were undoubtedly quite an experience for me. As a Member of the Legislative Assembly debating the new Currency Bill in the House in 1971 said, 'I like to earn money and spend it, but the science of money as put forward in this Law is too technical and difficult for me to understand.' The currency story also reminds me of the experience I had in 1959–60 when appointed to act as Clerk of Courts without any prior knowledge of law or administration of a courts office. Yet I remained in the acting position for 15 months leaving a very satisfactory record and with no regrets.

12

Economic Diversification

In November 1976 a new government was elected and headed by the Honourable James Manoah Bodden, popularly known as Jim, who organized and became the leader of the local political group known as 'The Unity Team'. Jim, who died in early 1988, was a few years later declared a National Hero. His statue is erected in front of the Legislative Assembly Building across the street in the gardens of the Law Courts Building. In July 1996 a second National Hero was declared: this time it was a living person and a woman, Mrs Sybil Ione McLaughlin, MBE. She was at the time Speaker of the Legislative Assembly.

The new government of 1976–80 was comprised of Jim Bodden, Haig Bodden, Truman Bodden and John McLean. In their administration in early 1977 they suggested the need to strengthen the local economy as it had, according to them, become somewhat sluggish following the worldwide economic recession, the full force and effect of which was felt in these islands from January 1975. As the government's Financial and Economic Advisor, I felt that there was no positive direction in which the country could at the time move to develop an acceptable scheme of activities to build a third industry. Those views were expressed particularly for the attention of the Executive Council Member (in effect, Minister) for Trade, Jim Bodden. I further pointed out to the Minister that these islands were not fortunate enough to have the resources or the potential to start building yet another industry. The government should therefore concentrate its efforts on expanding and improving the present economy from within the ambit of its two existing facets, finance and tourism.

Looking at the country's programmes of development over the almost 25 years since then, I believe the advice given at the time was quite sound as all growth and expansion of the economy has moved within the two industries. A few well-known measures sprang from

198

them, such as the Insurance Law of 1979 with its tremendous impact on both domestic and offshore business. A second measure brought into effect, in 1980, was repeal of the Exchange Control Law so as to declare Cayman 'a centre free of foreign exchange restrictions'. Freedom from exchange control was in fact an added attraction mainly to boost the offshore operation but as well to relieve residents of the necessity to constantly apply for exchange control permission when purchasing or investing in the hard currency markets like those of the United States. A third local business activity that boosted the tourist industry quite well was the cruise ship visits. Those expansions within the existing economy also provided worthwhile domestic boosters such as construction and real estate activities, both of which moved quite rapidly as large buildings were rising everywhere and the buying and selling of land, mainly in the speculative market, was providing valuable contributions to the economy.

The financial position of the government for 1975, the first year of the recession, was not of much harm to the local economy as the budget nearly balanced, thanks to continued prudent administration under the new Governor, Thomas Russell, CMG, CBE, who succeeded Kenneth Crook, CMG, in July 1974. To maintain the 1975 financial position in its fairly stable form required careful management. In 1972, in my official position of Financial Secretary, I had argued a case with the British government at the British Development Division in Barbados pleading that the Cayman Islands be allowed to build a special reserve from a portion of new revenues introduced on 3rd December 1970. The reserve was named the Capital Projects Fund (CPF); it would accumulate to the equivalent of approximately three months' local revenue collections, or an amount of CI$3 million. Those funds would be earmarked as part of the financing for a number of capital projects, including government offices, the port and a road improvement programme. The projects, however, or most of them, had not yet been finally processed or made ready for implementation.

The case for the CPF was also based, to my mind, on the likely event of a recession striking suddenly and disrupting especially capital programmes for which a portion of any new revenues had been intended. At least in such circumstances the special reserve would ease the financial burden while other remedies were being sought or considered. London's ratification of the special reserve was required. Of course we saw one snag against such approval. Any British Dependent Territory like the Cayman Islands receiving British aid for any purpose could not at the same time build or establish a special revenue reserve. Under the policy London could very well have ruled

199

or adopted the attitude that, Cayman being a financially aided territory, had no grounds for being granted special authority to create a capital reserve while at the same time continuing to receive budgetary assistance for capital projects.

This Territory was never grant-aided, meaning that at no time did its recurrent budget require British government funds supplementation as did a few other British Territories of less fortunate financial circumstances. However, even with our favourable position, British capital development aid funds continued to be allocated to the Cayman Islands until June 1980. At that juncture the British Government, through its Secretary of State for Foreign and Commonwealth Affairs, Lord Carrington, advised Cayman's Governor, Mr Russell, of the decision to end British capital aid to the Cayman Islands. The Governor replied saying that the Cayman Islands Legislative Assembly and people sent grateful thanks for the financial aid received by the islands from Britain over the past years. Lord Carrington in reply said, 'I note with great pleasure the sentiments of the Cayman Islands as British capital aid to their territory ceases. I share with them their pride that through their own endeavours the economy of the territory has developed to the point at which this step has been made possible. This achievement speaks highly of the Cayman Islands government and people. I send to all Cayman Islanders my best wishes for the continued development and prosperity of the territory.'

The case for a special reserve was first rejected at the 1972 meeting in Barbados but afterwards referred to the British Ministry of Overseas Development in London. Because of a very strong and convincing case put forward by Cayman, and also the gracious attitude of London to the Territory for its loyalty, devotion and spirit of self-help, the case for the special reserve was finally approved. At the end of 1974 and just before the recession struck, the CPF reached its goal of $3 million. The special reserve was definitely tested by the 1975 recession and found to be an excellent standby facility. The larger portion of the reserve was used to supplement recurrent and capital revenue and as a result the year ended with a very small deficit of only $31,000. That was indeed quite an achievement, thanks to the special reserve. The following year, 1976, the recurrent accounts ended in a surplus of $2 million. The CPF continued to be fed with a portion of the proceeds of the new revenue introduced in 1970. In 1980 when the fund reached over $1 million and there was no further need for the standby arrangement, the CPF balance was transferred to general reserve.

During the economic recession in 1975, the government thought it would be an ideal plan to create a new organization called the

Financial Community Committee (FINCOCO). Such a body would be ideal to maintain a closer relationship between the financial institutions and government for many useful purposes. The committee was established and it was comprised of three members from the government and six from the financial community. From the government were the Bank Inspector, the Economic Advisor and the Deputy Financial Secretary. Representing the other group were a banker for the clearing banks, a trust officer for the trust companies, two bankers for other banks and trust companies not in association with the clearing banks, an accountant for the audit and accounting firms and a lawyer for the legal fraternity. The committee met quarterly. Its usefulness became questionable in due course as each side appeared afraid of divulging privileged information to the other. As a result, about three years later, a similar committee was organized, with myself as Chairman and the managers of four local international banks as members. This second committee met quarterly as in the case of the first committee; no minutes were taken and each member spoke freely and offered useful information to the group. Important information was passed to the Governor and Executive Council. The committee remained active and useful until my retirement from the government at the end of March 1982.

In August 1975 the Chamber of Commerce became somewhat concerned about the recession and its effect on the local financial industry, which was at the time the largest contributor to the economy. I was kindly requested by the chamber to address its members in, as they called it, my 'words of wisdom' to say how Cayman was doing financially. The request was an attempt to allay the fears of many people concerning Cayman's performance during the recession. In the presentation I encouraged the Chamber to strongly support local industries and said that the end of the year should see a more encouraging outlook for all of us as the worst period of the recession should by then have come to an end. In their reply they pointed out that only three weeks earlier they had made a similar plea for support of local industries. They were gratified to see that I had not only endorsed their point of view, but had been meticulous to set out the advantages that would be derived from so doing. Members of the Chamber took the opportunity of arranging a period for question time. In their own words they said that the expert way in which the answers were given should assist the Chamber in its task of formulating a healthy economic climate in the islands.

Back in 1969 during the exercise carried out by the British Development Division's team to examine the Civil Service and economic infrastructure (see the story in Chapter 9), the Regional

Economist, Mr John Bryden, who was a member of the team, undertook to examine the economy over the period 1967–69. The survey was undertaken to provide an economic basis for a five-year plan 1970–75, which was later converted into a 1970–77 plan, and also to provide the framework for future aid and loan requirements. The survey made available a great deal of information; for instance, that the economy had grown by some 29 per cent per annum over the period 1967–69. It also stated that no economy could possibly experience growth rates such as that without undergoing stresses and strains. The growth was due to considerable progress in the sectors of construction, tourism, finance or the tax haven activities and related services.

In spite of the improved financial position, the elected side of the 1976 government decided that there was a good case for economic diversification and that they were prepared to carry out the test. The thought that apparently lingered on in the minds of the Ministers was to encourage, in any case, light industries that were not labour intensive. They discounted the fact that the cost and availability of labour would place the Cayman Islands at a disadvantage to the rest of the Caribbean. To encourage light industries, they thought, would only require careful planning and presentation, which could take a little while to get off to a good start. An attractive brochure entitled *Industrial Development in the Cayman Islands* was prepared for the presentation and published. It carried guidelines with a number of incentives under the Customs Law. Import duty would be waived, exempted or reduced on importation of the raw materials. In the brochure, an invitation was extended to potential investors. It also suggested that propositions from interested developers could be discussed with James M. Bodden, the Minister of Trade, and also with the Chamber of Commerce for further advice and information.

While the thought of light industries occupied the minds of Members of Executive Council, up came a proposal for the establishment of an oil transfer station off the coast of Little Cayman. The investigation of that operation was under discussion from May 1974 between the owner, Captain Harold E. Van der Linde through his company, Cayman Energy Ltd., potential customers who were owners and oil magnates, and the Cayman government. In the proposal the transfer operation would pay to the government a royalty of three-quarters of a cent per barrel of transferred oil with revenue to the government estimated at $300,000 for 1978. In the discussions it was also agreed that following the start of a successful ship-to-ship oil transfer operation, there were plans for a $100 million crude oil storage facility to be built on Little Cayman which would pay a royalty to the government of 1 cent per barrel. It was also the plan that

202

following the crude oil storage facility an oil refinery would also be built on Little Cayman. Those were great plans that unfortunately did not materialize. However, the oil trans-shipment operation went on for a number of years.

The agreement for the ship-to-ship oil transfer operation was signed on 17th February 1978 between Captain Van der Linde and me in the Executive Council Room in the presence of the Governor, Mr Russell. Also present were the Attorney General, Gerald Waddington, and the Attorney for Cayman Energy Ltd., Mr John J. Abberley, and other Members of the Executive Council, and Members of the Legislative Assembly Captain Charles Kirkconnell, Craddock Ebanks and Dalmain Ebanks. The agreement, which took a few years to finalize, was vetted and approved by Mr William John Reeve of the Foreign and Commonwealth Office in London. Mr Reeve was a consultant with Petroleum Studies Ltd. employed by the British government in an advisory capacity. Cayman Energy Ltd., Captain Van der Linde's Cayman Company, was an offshoot of his Transportation Concepts and Techniques Inc. of New York City, characterized as a holding company for worldwide marine operations involving bulk trans-shipment of grain, petroleum and other commodities.

The first ship-to-ship oil transfer operation took place off Cayman Brac. Four miles offshore lying adrift was the Finnish supertanker *Pellos* carrying 965,294 barrels of crude oil from Forcados, Nigeria, and steaming towards her was the Greek supertanker *Lymra*. In a little while both ships, in spite of heavy rains, were joined up for the operation. Among the men who became prominently involved in the ship-to-ship oil transfer at Little Cayman were Mooring Masters Captain Harold Banks, son of District Commissioner Guy Banks, and Captain Elmon Scott, both born in Cayman Brac. Likewise involved and worthy of mention were others from Cayman Brac. Captain Eddylee Martin was in charge of Cayman Energy's tugboat and he had an additional two crew members, Harrison Myrie and Austin Scott. The tugboat involvement continued until the operation at Little Cayman ended. Among the ships taking part in the oil transfer operation was the world's widest and sixth largest, the Norwegian supertanker *Nanny*. She carried a dead weight of 503,000 tons.

Little Cayman is about 1,000 miles from the United States gulf ports refineries and 800 miles nearer than Curaçao, Bonaire and Trinidad. That means that by using Little Cayman the United States would save between 8 and 10 cents per barrel because of the lesser shuttle distance. Another advantage to Cayman Energy Ltd. was the safety aspect of the oil transfer operation at Little Cayman. Those factors made the business move on successfully. In my report to the

203

Legislative Assembly on 15th November 1978 I told the House that the ship-to-ship oil transfer operation at Little Cayman was since the middle of 1978 making good progress in the volume of transferred oil. It was then seen that if the trend of business continued through the year, royalties could very well reach the 1978 estimated figure of CI$300,000 provided the operation was not hampered by delays as a result of inclement weather from north-westers and hurricanes. The royalty paid for 1978 was in fact only short of the target figure by $10,774. In 1978 there were about 40 local persons fully employed in the Little Cayman operation at very attractive salaries.

On 3rd April 1978 Cayman Energy Ltd. was awarded a franchise by the Cayman government to construct and operate a shore terminal on Little Cayman with a total storage capacity of 10 million barrels of crude oil. Construction of the terminal was due to start on 1st October 1978 but because of unavoidable organizational delays that date was moved to 1st April 1979. The contract for construction of the terminal was awarded to a consortium of French companies who gave the assurance that, all being well, the project would start the following year.

In the meantime the people of Cayman Brac and Little Cayman, who for many years had been faced with a stagnant and dwindling economy, were rejoicing at being on the threshold of a bright economic future. In fact 1978 was a bright year for Cayman Brac. Construction of the new Aston Rutty Civic Centre located on the Bluff started early in the year and was completed the middle of 1979. The main auditorium of the building has a seating capacity for 750. To commemorate the opening, the June 1979 session of the Legislative Assembly was held there.

In the Budget Address to the Legislative Assembly in November 1979 I made comments on the oil terminal construction at Little Cayman. I really had nothing of interest to report except to say that Cayman Energy Ltd., then faced with difficult financial problems, had to rely on new partners to join the operation in order to produce better results. Start of construction of the oil terminal was therefore delayed until 1980. On 18th November 1981, when delivering the last Budget Address to the Legislative Assembly, I reported what appeared to be the end of the Little Cayman oil terminal project. I mentioned the fact that the ship-to-ship oil transfer operation had struck a recession and the business had fallen by over 40 per cent of the 1980 volume for the same period, January to June, 1981. That was certainly the end of an exciting period for the two smaller islands and for Captain Van der Linde's genuine efforts to put the Cayman Islands on the map after closing the biggest deal ever made with the

Cayman government for the oil transfer operation. It was also a genuine effort on his part to create a worthwhile business in the Cayman Islands.

The problem with Little Cayman's oil terminal construction and the ship-to-ship operation seemed to have been caused by certain oil developments in the United States. The Louisiana Offshore Oil Port (LOOP) was by then built and in full operation. LOOP was the United States' first supertanker port; it is sited 21 miles off the Louisiana coast in the Gulf of Mexico. LOOP was built at a cost of $500 million by Marathon Oil, Texaco, Esso and other major oil companies. It is linked to the shore installation by 125,000 feet of steel pipeline 56 inches in diameter, with a daily through-put capacity of 1.4 million barrels of imported crude oil representing about 20 per cent of the United States' importation. LOOP would undoubtedly have been attracting some of the business from Little Cayman's operation.

The ship-to-ship crude oil transfer operation at Little Cayman began in August 1977 and by June 1981 the four years of transferred oil provided the government with royalties of CI$1.8 million. The 1980 operation was the biggest. By 1981, however, the end of what had served the people of the lesser islands so well was clearly in sight. One observation at the time was that the economy of these islands had traditionally encouraged free enterprise and fostered the growth of financial and trading institutions. For that reason the government would be on the alert for any new economic activities that might present themselves.

Going back to the government's desire to develop light industries in 1977, after a period of advertisement the first application was received from Robert F. Stack of the United States for a concession under the industrial incentive scheme to establish an assembling plant for mopeds. This vehicle was a mode of transport somewhat like a motor bike, except it could be moved along by either pedalling or by its small motor power. The applicants, Stack Manufacturing Co. Ltd., had succeeded in obtaining an exclusive ten-year contract with National Car Rentals to supply all NCR Caribbean licensees with mopeds trade-named Seagull. NCR would sell or rent mopeds to tourists out of a warehouse in Miami that the company planned to acquire. The operation was seen as a promising industry. The local manager was Glen Henning, formerly of Cayman Brac.

The second application under the industrial incentive scheme was submitted by Mr and Mrs Ray deSouza of Raymar Creations Ltd. They wished to establish a plant to manufacture ceramics, porcelain and stoneware largely for the tourist market. A third concession was

205

awarded to Cayman Miracle Paint Co. Ltd., managed by Lenny Webb, who had a similar plant operating in Florida. The company would mix and package all types of bulk imported paint and paint-related products into smaller containers for sale to the public; they labelled the business 'a manufacturing industry'. When the operation started it brought much adverse reaction from the local hardware merchants and paint vendors. They contended that their firms were required to pay customs duty on imported paint and paint products while Miracle Paint, a small new company, was enjoying duty-free status on its imported finished products under the Customs Law. However, shortly after Miracle Paint went into business, it folded, packed up and quit, as did all the other persons and companies granted concessions under the industrial incentive scheme.

Three other concessions were approved, taking the total to six. The first of these was Precision Tool and Die Limited: the second operation, a companion company, was Cayman Aluminium Products Ltd., better known as Cayprod. These two companies established their factory at the Airport Industrial Park complex and were managed by a John Moore. The companies operated at the same location for quite a few years but eventually folded. The other company and sixth concessionaire, named Cayman Coffee Corporation Limited, hoped to go into full production by early 1978. The company was owned and managed by Robert Markowitz; also involved was Bill Stroup of the local Viking Gallery. Under an exclusive patent, coffee was brought from Nicaragua, Costa Rica and Colombia to be concentrated by a special process to produce what was known as 'coffee tabs'. A tab weighed about 0.7 oz and was about the size of a small cookie. Each unit tab would yield eight cups and was estimated to save about 25 per cent per cup of coffee. Because of the high yield, the company geared production to the export market rather than selling to the local retail dealers. This business also folded in due course.

The ministers of the government of 1976 thought there was potential in building a third industry to strengthen further the local economy. Naturally, a wise and energetic government would think along those lines, especially when they saw cashflow lacking and were not able to finance ambitious development programmes outlined in their political manifesto. Mind you, a vast capital programme of works involving many projects which were perhaps some of their own had just then been implemented by the previous government of 1973–76. Except for the 1975 economic recession, the country was making good progress. However, as politicians, they had a commitment to their constituencies to provide a few new services promised in their election campaign. For that reason politics and reality had to be thawed out, but in any case politicians had the final word. This happened in the case of their attempted light industry programme. When the various schemes failed and the dust settled, like diplomats they rose to the occasion and accepted what the islands could best develop. That is a classic example of the enormous contribution by Cayman's politicians to the successful development of their country.

Although the attempt failed to establish light industries as a third aspect of the Cayman economy, it brought to mind the old maxim: 'Nothing beats a trial but a failure.' That attempt at economic diversification was not really the end of the thinking on the subject. In 1985 while I was a political member of the 1984–88 government in charge of the Portfolio of Development and Natural Resources, another study was undertaken jointly by the government and the Chamber of Commerce. It explored the possibilities of other new areas of development, such as manufacturing, agriculture and other services. The report of the study began by pointing out an overwhelming majority of positive factors as against the negative side: this gave Cayman an edge in finding new sources of activity for diversification. A quick review of the local economy and resources was also done for a comparison with other regional countries to determine potential for Cayman. However, Cayman was in the enviable position of not facing immediate pressure of either unemployment or balance of payments problems. It also had the luxury of continuing to promote its seasoned offshore financial services, tourism activities and related services. The end result was similar to the attempt made at encouraging light industries ten years earlier. In fact Cayman, with its high standard of living, sophisticated economy, high literacy rate and small population, had no need for massive economic activity.

The conclusion of the report on that second and virtually last attempt so far at investigating economic diversification was quite interesting. It stated that Cayman, having a local business community of some size and sophistication, should make its first priority in economic diversification the development and expansion of existing business. The starting of new businesses should be by local entrepreneurs and expatriate Caymanians. A second suggestion was for the establishment of joint ventures between local businesses and foreign companies. The last recommendation was that Cayman should endeavour to attract a large percentage of direct foreign investment. Given those priorities, the report said, there were three sectors that stood out as the most likely areas for development – import substitution, new export and the service sector. Those thoughts were seen as reasonable and in fact a logical conclusion. However, my opinion is

207

that for the foreseeable future, finance and tourism and activities created within those two industries will be the only major contributors to the local economy.

The government was advised that, in the earlier attempt to develop light industries under the Industrial Incentive Scheme as a means of diversifying the economy, the investors were somewhat offended. They contended that part of the reason for their winding up the Cayman ventures so soon after being granted the concessions was because of the lack of prompt and enthusiastic official cooperation. In a small territory like this when two people order the same item from overseas and one pays import duty and the other is exempted, as in the specific case of the paint manufacturer, it becomes difficult to give a satisfactory explanation to the local public for the difference in treatment. Secondly, it takes quite a long time in Cayman to develop struggling infant industries – the reason the incentives package was given; but there was no stipulation as to the term of the concessions. The investors were also troubled with importation problems from delays of ships at times, together with labour shortage and its high cost; those difficulties were not stated by the concessionaires in their public complaints about the lack of support from government officials.

Back in 1970 the British government, through an official from its Foreign and Commonwealth Office (FCO) in London, Derek Matthews, OBE, visited Grand Cayman. In the presence of the Governor and myself, Derek suggested that the Cayman Islands consider replacing its tax haven business with other forms of economic activities. My immediate reaction was: 'What other activity? You mean something like taxing funds passing through Cayman?' Derek thought that my suggestion was a brilliant one: in fact I meant it to be a big joke. However, for two years after his visit we had communications from the FCO reminding us of the proposed measure to tax money passing through the islands and inquiring when the draft bill would be presented to the Legislative Assembly. The last occasion on which the FCO wrote on the subject, the reply was framed in such a way as to give a kind hint that Cayman had no intention then or at any other time in the foreseeable future recommending such a tax measure to the Legislative Assembly. Quite honestly it was out of sheer shock and confusion at the suggestion that we should consider replacing Cayman's tax haven business that I carelessly mentioned as a substitute the tax on external funds passing through Cayman. I knew that such a tax would certainly have an immediate adverse effect on Cayman's tax haven operation: that was perhaps the very thing Derek was looking for. Our last reply to London must have

208

Sitting in Executive Council are (left) the Governor Thomas Russell and Financial Secretary Vassel Johnson signing an agreement on 25th October 1974 for the largest loan ever to government by a consortium of six international Banks. Their local managers and attorneys are standing. Barclays Bank became 'The Lead Bank' acting as agent for the other five banks. See Chapter 9.

The Nova Scotia Bank and Trust Company Building was constructed in the early 1970s in the centre of George Town, capital of the Cayman Islands. It is one of the fine local commercial buildings constructed on a portion of property formerly owned by the Crown. One of the conditions in the sale was that the building should complement the Courts Building and the Legislative Assembly Building on the same block, which were the subjects of special regional architectural competition.

V G Johnson escorts his mother Theresa to the wedding of her daughter Louise to Alan Dibben on 16th May 1981. Theresa was then aged 84.

Opening of the Government Administration Building on 17th November 1975. Standing in front of the building are all Heads of Departments with the Governor, Mr Thomas Russell, in the centre front row with V G Johnson on his left and the late Desmond Watler on his right. See Chapter 9.

A farewell party held in March 1982 on the retirement of V G Johnson from the Civil Service and sponsored by the Commissioner of Police Jim Stowers (standing). On Jim's right is the Governor, Peter Lloyd and on his left Mrs Lloyd, V G Johnson and his wife Rita (partly hidden). See Chapter 13.

From left to right: (back to camera) Dr Marco Giglioli and V G Johnson, (front to camera) Prince Philip Duke of Edinburgh, Her Majesty the Queen and Governor Peter Lloyd. The royal party travelled across the North Sound on the cabin cruiser *Marlin Darlin* to Rum Point (10 miles) to open a new road connecting the districts of North Side and East End along the periphery of the coastline. This was the Queen's first and the Duke's second visit to the Cayman Islands. See Chapter 15.

V G Johnson comtemplating on
31st December 1983 whether or
not that should be his last
cigarette. It certainly was
eighteen years ago.
See Chapter 15.

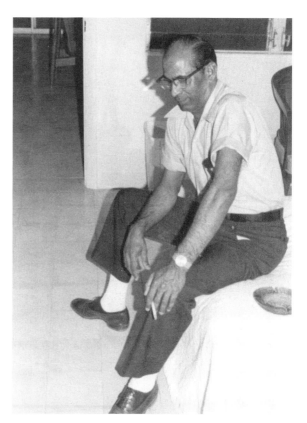

V G Johnson 'in the air' as supporters of the General Election celebrated the results when it was announced on the morning of 14th November 1984 that the Dignity Team, of which Vassel Johnson was a candidate, won the Election. See Chapter 15.

In early June 1985 V G Johnson (left) meets Senator Larry Smith – D Fla – Chairman of the House Task Force on International Narcotics Control. See Chapter 16.

Friday 4th July 1986, in Grand Cayman, the historic signing of the Mutual Legal Assistance Treaty by the Cayman Islands and the United Kingdom with the United States. Seated from l to r: US Under Secretary of State Ronald S Spires, UK Under Secretary of State Timothy J Eggard and HE the Governor of the Cayman Islands G Peter Lloyd. See Chapter 16.

Vassel Johnson, Chairman of the Water Authority, in the presence of members, turns the switch to start, for the first time, the flow of piped desalinated water through George Town, the capital, on 11th February 1988. See Chapter 18.

Cayman's team to the 1988 Commonwealth Parliamentary Association Conference in Canberra, Australia. L to r: Carol Kirkconnell and her husband Charles, the Minister for Communication; Georgette Myrie, Clerk of the Legislative; Vassel Johnson, Minister for Development and Natural Resources, and his wife Rita. See Chapter 20.

Vassel and Rita Johnson touring the Mediterranean, including the Holy Land, on the *SS Renaissance* from 10-21 August 1998. In this scene they are celebrating the birthday of their eldest grand-daughter Joanna Bodden.

V G Johnson, Chairman of the Cayman Turtle Farm Board of Directors, presented to Her Royal Highness Princess Alexandra on 1st November 1988 a certificate stating that the Princess sponsored the release of 500 green sea turtle yearlings from the turtle farm into local waters. Behind them are (from left) the Governor Mr Scott, manager of the farm Jim Wood, Mrs Johnson and members of the Princess's escort. See Chapter 20.

The knighting of Vassel Johnson by Her Majesty the Queen, which took place on a dais immediately in front of the Parliament Building at 10.30 am on 26th February 1994. Prince Philip is seen standing by his chair. See Chapter 21.

Sir Vassel and Lady Johnson with their extended families shortly after the knighting of Vassel Johnson by Her Majesty the Queen. See Chapter 21.

carried our message quite clearly: the file on the subject seems to have been closed since then.

The Cayman Islands were aware all along that metropolitan countries like Britain and the United States, operating their direct tax systems, resented the offshore tax haven operations which offered tax-free facilities covering all forms of external financial services. Cayman had no alternative but to go for the tax haven operation to assist in rebuilding its economy. The previous five years had been spent searching diligently for various forms of activity to provide a new income to replace seamen's earnings which had been the basic economy until the mid-1960s. At that stage, as mentioned previously, adverse conditions at sea sent the men back to their homes in Cayman where there was nothing of consequence for them to do. All the small industries of the past, including shipbuilding and fishing at Mosquito Quays, had been blown away by the winds of World War II: those industries had then become only pleasant memories. The Territory therefore had no choice but to take on and develop the twin industries of offshore financial services and tourism. For all intents and purposes those two activities seemed the only way out to provide a reasonable replacement economy for these islands.

One can imagine that in spite of Cayman's strong case for developing the offshore financial services, Britain would in those days be very concerned over one of its Crown Colonies being so involved. Of course the Cayman Islands had not been the only British Territory attempting to develop offshore finances. It was perhaps not too well understood either that these islands did not produce raw materials from which to develop a manufacturing industry, nor did they have mineral resources as in other countries. The local terrain, being rocky, did not provide good arable land to promote and develop commercial agriculture. Cayman therefore had to remain within its limited economic bounds to offer what it could, purely for the involvement of its working population so that they could maintain their families and provide for the upcoming generations. Fortunately, avenues for the two new industries eventually opened and the opportunity was taken to start the building process which went very well indeed. In the course of time job availability increased until a full employment situation developed, which brought with it a rising inflation, but that too was eventually brought under control.

I was more than convinced that Cayman would suffer unduly by dropping the offshore industry. For one thing, many overseas staff and investors then engaged in the local growing financial institutions would most certainly have had to leave the country and return home or go elsewhere in search of jobs. This bothered me considerably. At

209

the time Cayman had need for special permission from the Bank of England's Exchange Control Section. It had to do with a required provision under the local exchange control regulations to grant to overseas non-resident persons special dispensation to deal in foreign investments. In mid-1970, I visited London on official business. I took the opportunity then of going to see my friends at the Bank of England and in particular its Exchange Control Section to discuss Cayman's special need for the Exchange Control (EC) facility. I knew the Head of Exchange Control, Mr Brian Bennett, and another dear friend and senior officer, Mr Ronald Lusty, now the Reverend Ronald Lusty.

In discussing the matter with Ronald, I recall that he assured me his office would support the application for the special EC facility. However, he advised that formal approval is given by Her Majesty's Treasury and that it would be necessary for me to attend in person to present the application. Early in 1971 Ronald wrote to me and advised that the appointment at the Treasury had been set for 3 p.m. on 25th May, 1971 and that Brian Bennett would accompany me there. I began thinking seriously about that proposed visit and whether in fact I should not, after dealing with the EC matter, broach the subject that had worried me for the past year, the infamous suggestion by Derek Matthews that the Cayman Islands replace its tax haven business. In fact I had broached the subject at the Bank of England but they could not interfere.

At the Treasury I met the person who would be chairman of the meeting, Geoffrey Littler. He held the position at the time of Treasury Assistant Secretary in charge of the Exchange Control Division. Geoffrey was in later years knighted by Her Majesty The Queen. The meeting approved my application under Exchange Control and the chairman requested Brian Bennett to officially convey the decision to the government of the Cayman Islands. Thereafter I sought permission of the chairman to present my other case, on Derek Matthews' proposal, even though the subject was not on the Treasury's agenda. Surprisingly Derek was sitting in the meeting with his economic and financial advisors. The chairman approved my request.

This second issue was a bit dicey as it involved the Foreign and Commonwealth Office and its proposal, through Derek, to replace the Cayman Islands tax haven business with some other form of local activity. It was therefore not surprising that Derek, armed with his two advisors, was in attendance. The chairman asked that I present my case.

I began by stressing certain underlying difficulties associated with the request made by the FCO through Derek Matthew and described them briefly. I mentioned the size of the Cayman Islands, its location and the fact that the islands did not have resources like other countries, such as raw materials and mineral products, to develop a manufacturing industry. Neither, I said, did the islands have arable land to venture into commercial agriculture. I went on to say that in the past the islands' economy had depended on the wages of men going to work with the American Merchant Marine. However, that industry had virtually folded five years earlier owing to a world economic recession and other factors associated with the technical upgrading of shipping. The existing two industries, tourism and offshore finance, were popular choices to replace seamen's earnings; fortunately they were currently making fair progress. In fact the two industries had now taken up much of the slack in employment and everybody seemed quite happy with the progress. It was therefore to the benefit of the working population that the Cayman Islands continued building its financial industry along with tourism. The country had confidence that the two industries would certainly provide a growing economy capable of meeting the demands of the years ahead. Furthermore, if the financial operation were suspended, the staff and investors of the financial institutions and the other activities based offshore would be forced to leave the Territory and move back home, largely to Britain, Canada and the United States. This would create a near disaster for Cayman.

Following my presentation the chairman spoke and said that 'a good, strong and convincing case was put forward by Cayman's Financial Secretary on behalf of his country, the Cayman Islands, to retain its finance industry.' He immediately pledged to support the case and also suggested that the Cayman Islands continue undisturbed to develop its offshore finance. He hoped too that the industry would be based on good principles and policies backed by appropriate legislation. He wished the industry and Cayman in general every success in their efforts. He then asked Derek Matthew if he would like to make comments on Cayman's presentation, to which Derek replied with a smile and a very kind, 'No, thanks.'

The meeting at the British Treasury and the decision of the chairman certainly replaced my fears with much satisfaction and enthusiasm. I was confident too that Sir Geoffrey's kind decision would enable Cayman to successfully build itself into a world-class offshore financial centre. After the meeting I gave the chairman the assurance that the Cayman government had indeed established well thought-out principles, policies and legislation for the building of its industries. Indeed, 18 years later the Cayman Islands moved up the ladder of success to become one of the most stable and attractive centres in the international corridors of offshore finance and certainly one of the leading social and economic systems. These islands gradually became the most desirable global offshore financial haven. Many features provided that rewarding position, one being the genuinely friendly attitude that greets foreign investors. Another is the appropriate legislation designed to streamline the process of investments by which entrepreneurs can operate. It was known too that international investors were a choosy lot who, when conditions did not suit, would jump from one country to the other and move their funds to whatever jurisdiction satisfied their needs best. The Cayman Islands, following the meeting at the Treasury in London, appeared on the map as a desirable offshore jurisdiction and a shift away from other centres. This enormous success must today be shared with Sir Geoffrey Littler of the British Treasury, Derek Matthew of the Foreign and Commonwealth Office (who did not rebut Sir Geoffrey's decision), and Brian Bennett and my good friend the Reverend Ronald Lusty of the Bank of England.

After Britain abolished exchange control in 1979, Ronald retired, went into the Church's ministry and received training to become a minister of religion. Ronald and his wife Marjorie live in Reading. When my eldest daughter, Theresa, attended Reading University in 1972, Ronald and Marjorie kindly agreed to be her guardians. Twenty-five years later Theresa, her husband Robert Bodden and their three children, Joannah, Justin and Jessica together with my wife Rita, and myself, visited England, mainly to attend Joannah's graduation at Exeter University Law School. We seized the opportunity then of visiting Ronald and Marjorie in Reading, so that Theresa's children could see the university their mother attended; Robert knew Reading from 1973 when he visited Theresa. The time spent at Reading in early July 1997 provided a truly wonderful occasion for our reunion.

One of my official misgivings in the case of the meeting at the British Treasury with Sir Geoffrey Littler on the issue of abolishing Cayman's tax haven operation was that on reaching home I kept the matter quiet to await the FCO's report to Cayman's Governor. My home office and the Governor knew that one of my missions to London was in connection with the exchange control matter at the British Treasury: others were the usual visits to the FCO, the Bank of England and the Crown Agents. On return to Cayman I did submit my usual report to the Governor but omitted comments on the tax haven presentation at the British Treasury and the decision. I thought years later that the importance of the tax haven issue and the support given by the British Treasury for its continuation would have made it a prime case for reporting. What baffled me was that in spite of Derek Matthews of the FCO and his two specialists attending the meeting, to my knowledge London did not report the matter to Cayman's Governor. At least, the Governor said nothing to me about the meeting. I had mixed feelings about my action in that it was not passed through official channels after my visit to London. Before I left Cayman, however, there had been no clear indication that the subject would be pursued following the exchange control issue. However, if I took the bull by the horns in that all-important issue, I apologize. At least I was satisfied by not being alone (three FCO representatives were there as well). I decided in any case to maintain a low profile on the subject until questioned about my action. Up to the present time its confidential status remains unchanged, while of course the Cayman Islands have galloped away with a most success-ful offshore business.

Following the failure of the government to promote light industries as a new segment of the local economy, my advice was that Cayman should embark on a programme of expansion within the ambit of its two current industries, finance and tourism. In finance, I thought about an insurance law that would provide for fairly urgent domestic needs while at the same time establishing offshore trading in the vast potential of the captive insurance market. I also had a strong leaning towards abolishing exchange control, which I thought would virtually convert the Cayman Islands into an area free of foreign currency exchange restrictions. Investors from around the world would then feel free to move in and out of the country at will to conduct their financial business. In tourism, there was the possibility too of expand-ing cruise ship business, according to evidence seen from the begin-ning of the 1970s. The government supported those views and gave me authority to proceed accordingly.

The first attempt at producing an insurance law was undertaken in January 1978 by the legal draftsman, Roderick Donaldson. The draft, which had a total of 53 sections divided into 11 parts, was submitted to the Executive Council in mid-November 1978. At that stage, the government decided that there was a need for a professional insur-ance advisor to join forces with the legal draftsman to design and structure a suitable law. The application to recruit such an advisor was sent to London without delay. In early January 1979, David Dunbar Carrow, a retired insurance broker, provided through British Executive Services Overseas (BESO) of the United Kingdom, arrived in Grand Cayman to assume the position of Insurance Advisor to the Government. From early 1978 this government had arranged with BESO's Director, Mr Ted Westnage, who came here on a visit, the possibility of recruiting through his organization executives or advisors who were experienced practical businessmen and who could be employed on a temporary short-term economic basis in developing countries. BESO's policy was to undertake assignments on a three- to four-month basis, for a maximum of six months. During that time the advisors would tackle specific problems and needs and set up systems and generally give the expert advice necessary to build an efficient operation. The executives were recently retired businessmen who were still active and in tune with current techniques. They operated on an expenses-paid basis only and did not receive a fee for their services. This government was most grateful for the opportunity of recruiting from BESO on short notice such expert services so economically.

Mr Carrow, the BESO insurance advisor, was to assist in preparing legislation to cover domestic insurance as well as to expand it to cover offshore operations, with particular emphasis on captive insurance. A committee was then appointed to assist the advisor, the legal draftsman, the Attorney General and me in moving on with the second draft insurance law, hopefully one that would be acceptable. The committee was comprised of 16 members and was made up largely of people from the local insurance industry. The Attorney General, the advisor and the legal draftsman were members, while I chaired the meetings. I had a very good friend, Fred Reiss, known internationally as the architect of the Bermuda captive insurance industry. Fred had a business established here and would visit Cayman occasionally; I therefore took the opportunity of inviting him to serve on my insurance committee. He accepted the invitation on the grounds that he would gladly attend the meetings when in Grand Cayman. It was thought that Fred's presence on the committee, with his vast insurance expertise especially in captive insurance, would be of much value to us. Fred was owner of American Risk Management Company, the oldest and largest of insurance management companies. It had parts of its international chain in Transnational and United Insurance Co. based in Cayman. The local operation was managed by Don Middleton, who resided here in Grand Cayman; their legal advisor and attorney was Sidney Pine of New York, who visited Grand Cayman when his services were required.

At the end of November 1981, Fred built and opened along West Bay Road across from Seven Mile Beach a beautiful office building named Finsbury House. The building, later named Transnational House, was used in February 1983 to provide a stately royal suite for Her Majesty The Queen and the Duke of Edinburgh during their visit. The Governor, Mr Russell, at the opening of the building in 1981

214

called it 'a bold and prestigious announcement to the world that the offshore insurance industry and particularly the Reiss Group of Companies and the companies managed by them, are solidly based in the Cayman Islands.' By then the Insurance Law was seen as a major piece of legislation acceptable to both the government and the industry.

My first insurance committee meeting was held on 22nd January 1979, with all members present. We laid out a programme within which to proceed with the study and eventually to produce a new draft law. However, the advisor had to return home in early February for a few weeks though he would be back on 24th March. When leaving, he secured the authority of this government to stop by Bermuda and Bahamas on the way back to have a look at their insurance legislation. The purpose was to obtain any assistance he thought necessary that would be available to him for the benefit of preparing the Cayman Islands insurance law. Ten days before David Carrow's return, he sent me a draft of a new law based largely on Bermuda's legislation. His reason for choosing the Bermuda law as a guide was because of its provisions dealing with the offshore captive side of the industry. I discussed this latest draft with the insurance committee and Executive Council Members. On 19th April, eleven members of the local industry addressed me on the last draft prepared by David Carrow, as follows: 'As regards domestic business we have no major comments. As regards offshore business we believe that the draft would fail in its objective, as we understand it, and would result in the departure of a substantial portion of the offshore business presently here. To a greater extent we believe that it would discourage new offshore insurance business.'

A local legal firm also wrote me on 18th May and advised as follows: 'Be cautious of over-regulation with Cayman's law based on outside legislation. This would severely prejudice the Cayman Islands' chances of developing into a worthwhile alternative to Bermuda, bearing in mind the extensive expertise and geographical position of Bermuda to New York and London.'

Up to that time matters affecting the insured and insurer in this field had not been subject to any form of regulation or legislation. Now, of course, there was concern in all of Cayman, not regarding big reputable firms, but the many small operators who began establishing themselves in the islands without difficulty. A few of them, as in the case of a number of other commercial businesses, proved in time to be unreliable and collapsed or just simply went out of existence. This is why there was now the urgent need for control of the industry by legislation, bearing in mind at the same time

215

the advice to government to 'be cautious of over-regulation'.

The third draft insurance law prepared by the insurance advisor and the legal draftsman was based on the latest comments presented to the insurance committee from both the local industry and the legal fraternity. The Attorney General, The Honourable David Barwick, and I had a standing arrangement, apart from serving on the committee, to meet each morning during working days with the advisor, Mr Carrow, to discuss any progress made on the latest draft bill. Each morning's results were practically the same: in other words we saw no improvement over the previous day's presentation, and the bill in its existing form was definitely not acceptable to the government: it was a draft modelled on Bermuda's law. One morning during a meeting of the trio, I suddenly found myself tearing away at my draft copy of that latest insurance bill before us and dumping the pieces into the waste paper container. I then said to my two colleagues, 'If you will bear with me for a moment I would like to outline briefly the sort of legislation that might be acceptable to all concerned.' In my layman's language I presented what my thoughts were about a new insurance law: that it could be structured along the same simple lines of the Banks and Trust Companies Regulation Law. I also mentioned that control of the provisions of the new law should be by an insurance inspector provided by the law, in the same manner that the Inspector of Banks performed his duties under banking legislation. Insurance companies, I went on to say, would be licensed like a bank, in two categories, domestic or general and offshore, to cover captives and others. In the final stages of the new insurance law the inspector's revised designation was Superintendent of Insurance.

I asked both my colleagues if they agreed with my presentation and they said yes. I then requested the advisor to move on in association with the legal draftsman and try their hands at preparing another completely new draft. It was out of this draft that eventually, with the work and amendments of the committee, a new proposed draft insurance law was presented to the Executive Council and the Legislative Assembly at its budget session in November 1979. Because of the need for a few amendments, the new law did not come into effect until June 1980. At the time the draft law was presented to the Assembly, the government applied in London for a superintendent of insurance. On 8th April 1980 John E. Darwood, the new Superintendent of Insurance, arrived to take up the position. He started immediately to review licence applications from over 300 insurance companies and by July the same year 330 companies applied for licences, 250 of which were offshore operators. Of those selected, 185 were granted licences; that included 122 offshore operators, 17 domestic insurers and 21 underwriting managers. The others were brokers and agents. The start of the insurance business was very encouraging. The Superintendent, who was very keen, helped to ensure that the islands attracted a complement of genuine insurers. He reported that, after the law was passed, about 200 companies who may not have been 'real' insurance companies 'packed their bags and left'.

The Insurance Law provided four categories of licence: two class As, a domestic and an external or local insurer carrying on business in or from within the islands; and two Class Bs, one exempted insurer carrying on other than domestic business from within the islands, and the other an exempted insurer which accepted insurance business other than domestic business from its shareholders, members or such other persons specifically approved by the Governor. An application could be made by a person, an insurance company, a mutual insurance office, an underwriters' association, an insurance agent, a broker, a sub-agent or an underwriting manager.

The growth of captive insurance companies, so called because they underwrite solely for their parent companies, was most encouraging. In fact two years after the local Insurance Law came into effect, the Cayman Islands were declared the second offshore captive insurance destination after Bermuda, the leader. Eighteen years later Cayman remained in second place after Bermuda, with 432 captive insurance companies on the government's register. Of those there were 14 classes: the largest was medical malpractice, representing 33 per cent. Others were workers' compensation, 19 per cent, and property, 13 per cent. The remaining 35 per cent was divided among 11 other business classes. The statistics also revealed that of the 432 companies, pure captives comprised 60 per cent, with written premiums of $1.295 billion out of a total of $1.962 billion. Also 84 per cent were unrestricted and the others restricted. Locations indicated that 83 per cent were from North America. The two largest local insurance managers, according to the records in 1997, were Johnson & Higgins with 22.5 per cent of the companies, with written premiums of $417 million, and Midland Bank Trust, taking 17.8 per cent, with written premiums of $222 million. Cayman's second place in offshore captive insurance operation at the end of 18 years' existence is considered very attractive. As can be seen from these figures, Cayman did emerge as a centre for serious insurance operation after its new Insurance Law of 1979 forced insurance companies to register and comply with certain conditions under the new law. Before that it was impossible to tell whether an insurance company was genuine or just being used to perpetrate fraud.

For the benefit of the general public who may want to know a bit more about captive insurance, the following is from a report provided by a BankAmerica survey in 1981. It indicated that at the time more than 500 of the largest companies in the world owned and operated subsidiary insurance companies known as captive. That category of insurance was created back in 1970 and since then it has grown to take great prominence in worldwide finance. A captive insurance company is not primarily intended for tax benefits, but that is an added saving and thus the reason for establishing them in offshore centres like Cayman, Bermuda and others. It is said that captives have been so successful that it is estimated that savings of approximately 35 per cent can be made in direct cost to the parent, and premiums paid by parent companies to their captives back in 1981 exceeded $2.5 billion. Other advantages are that, being a member of the multinational's family, a captive has the use and enjoyment of the premium of the parent company generating a cashflow that would not be available if insured through a commercial company. That cashflow could be further enhanced by delay of premiums to its captives, and similarly of course the captives could delay the payment of claims to their companies. A further major advantage is that captives provide full insurance coverage at a reduced cost. They also serve as the central point to simplify, coordinate and control worldwide risk management. Therefore, insurance and reinsurance needs may be finely tuned to the resources and problems of the parent company. It can be seen from the foregoing brief comments that the organization, management and administration of the captive do need expertise and careful attention to a broad range of areas such as loss prevention and investment management.

The abolition of Exchange Control (EC) was the second measure for economic expansion recommended in my portfolio, Finance and Development. Abolishing EC was my own idea following the floating of Sterling on 23rd June 1972 when Britain removed all foreign exchange rates from its standard monetary unit, the pound Sterling. The action meant that on banks' working days Sterling had to find new foreign exchange rates. As the Cayman currency at the time bore parity with Sterling, CI$1 being equal to half of £1 Sterling, the Cayman government followed the action of Britain and floated the Cayman dollar as well. The local banks were responsible for obtaining new foreign exchange rates from London in the early mornings before opening for business. Prior to the day that Britain suspended the foreign exchange rates on Sterling, the Cayman Islands, like many other Commonwealth countries, administered EC for the benefit of controlling Sterling. Commonwealth countries administering

EC and designated under the Exchange Control Law as 'Scheduled Territories or Overseas Sterling Area' (OSA) were tied to Sterling. The question after Sterling floated was what form EC should take in its administration, for at that stage Sterling could be viewed as a foreign currency within the Scheduled Territories including the Cayman Islands. Furthermore, following the 23rd June action by Britain, all OSA countries were excluded from the United Kingdom's EC Law. This was a new situation and a strange one at that, for all OSA countries then had to decide their own policy regarding capital movements by both residents and non-residents alike in the light of what was in their best interest. Here in Cayman, EC was administered very liberally in the first instance and even more so after the floating of Sterling and the Cayman dollar.

I submitted in late 1973 a proposal to the Executive Council recommending repeal of EC in the Cayman Islands. This action followed the disbanding of the Sterling area by Britain in June 1972. My paper was based on the assumption that the absence of EC could inspire greater confidence in the islands as an offshore financial services centre. It would also enable the country's foreign currency earnings to improve. My second assumption was that freedom in the movement of resident and non-resident funds for investment purposes in countries of investors' choice would also foster greater confidence and promote wealth which would add a new lustre to Cayman's offshore business. Freedom for an individual to do with his money as he wishes, to conveniently move it in and out of the country without restrictions, must be very beneficial and attractive. In fact, as stated earlier, in the past EC was administered very liberally in these islands and therefore placed few restrictions upon individuals and businesses; now the position would be further improved by the abolition of EC. However, there were those, both bankers and politicians, who felt that the move would not be healthy for the Cayman dollar as it would encourage even wider use locally of the US currency. I certainly had no fear that the status of the Cayman dollar would be impaired to any extent. Furthermore, the benefit to be derived from the removal of restrictions on foreign exchange would more than offset any losses likely to be suffered from a drop in the Cayman dollar circulation. The Executive Council was not altogether unanimous in its views on removing the restriction; therefore the matter was shelved for the time being.

The United Kingdom was consulted on the matter of EC suspension in early 1975. The Bank of England sent an advisor, Mr A.J.T. (Tony) Williams, to Cayman to investigate the proposal. His report favoured suspension but not complete abolition of the system as I had

219

advocated. It also pointed out that Cayman should always be in a position to reintroduce EC at short notice if that became necessary. There was a general agreement in the financial community and among a few members of the government that EC could be limited to a few regulations, one of which was to continue the restriction on Rhodesian currency or assets situated in Rhodesia. This was in any case a specific request by London: it could of course be accommodated, not necessarily under the Exchange Control Law where it was then in effect, but under other special legislation in case EC were abolished. I still hoped nevertheless to win my battle to abolish EC in the near future.

While awaiting abolition of EC, an amendment to the Companies Law, Section 2, was proposed to the Legislative Assembly and approved. The measure carried a new definition in the law to provide a distinct difference between a resident and a non-resident company, the latter being restricted from dealings in local business and in local currency but permitted to engage in offshore foreign currency dealings. That amendment was in preparation for the abolition of EC. However, another problem under the Companies Law bothered me. Among the categories of company was one termed 'ordinary non-resident company', used for offshore EC activities. That category paid a higher annual fee than did another local entity known as an 'ordinary domestic company'. If and when EC was abolished, it was possible for many offshore operators to re-register as an ordinary domestic company; such action would result in the loss of a good amount of the government's annual revenue. It was therefore incumbent on my part to find an equitable solution to the problem beforehand in order to carry out the intended repeal of the EC Law and at the same time preserve the full income paid by ordinary non-resident companies.

Discussions continued between the local banks, the government and Tony Williams of the Bank of England who was also a member of Cayman's Currency Board at the time. The balance in the future of EC was at the time gradually swaying between retention, suspension and repealing of the law. In August 1978 I was in London on official business. Accompanying me was Desmond Watler, who had at the time just retired from the government as Chief Secretary. On my itinerary was a scheduled meeting with Gordon Hall, Tony Williams and Richard Chalmers at the Bank of England, along with representatives from their Exchange Control Section and the FCO; Desmond accompanied me to the meeting, which was specially to continue our discussions on abolishing EC.

The subject of abolishing EC was a proposal to repeal the Cayman

Islands Exchange Control Law. My main reason for the proposal was that EC had outlived its useful days in Cayman and having the law removed from the statute book was seen as a new dimension supporting the progress of the financial industry and the country in general. Also the English currency had undergone a number of changes since the days prior to its floating in June 1972, and so six years later it had no relationship with the Cayman currency for EC purposes. The meeting at the Bank was rather lively and ended with unanimous support to abolish Cayman's EC system. Little did I know at the time however, that Britain was then in an advanced stage of planning to abolish the English EC and that such action was scheduled to become effective in mid-1979. No wonder all the English members of the meeting at the Bank of England on Thursday 10th August 1978 were so happy to support Cayman's proposal to go the same route then being pursued by the United Kingdom government.

On my return home I reported to the government the outcome of the meeting at the Bank of England in London. All concerned were happy to go along with London's decision. My only remaining problem was to find or devise a solution to preserve the revenue relating to non-resident entities after abolishing EC. Earlier in 1979 I had established a special committee, chaired by my deputy, to study the means by which such a solution could be found. After three months the committee reported that the matter was beyond their ability to resolve, i.e. to find a scheme for what was requested. What kept my ego searching for an answer to the problem was the fact that Britain had forged ahead of the Cayman Islands in abolishing EC in mid-1979. Here we were at the end of the decade, six months later, still searching for a solution to our problem in order to become the second to abolish EC before being overtaken by yet others from within the OSA countries. However, why should anyone feel badly that Britain was first to abolish EC? After all, they introduced the system after World War II. They should most certainly be given credit for having the wisdom to abolish it before any other countries of the British Commonwealth designated OSA, or Overseas Sterling Area.

When I got home in the evenings, and in the mornings before rising out of bed, I would study this worrying subject: just how to abolish EC and retain the annual fees paid by non-resident companies. This went on for quite some time until Christmas and the New Year was over. During early 1980 I was still confident that the way around my most pressing issue would present itself sooner or later. In fact perseverance was one of my finer attributes, prayer being the greatest of them all. I had also been a great believer in the words of Epictetus, the Stoic philosopher, who once said, 'No great thing is

221

created suddenly, any more than a bunch of grapes or a fig. If you tell me that you desire a fig, I answer you that there must be time. Let it first blossom, then bear fruit, then ripen.' I felt that the stage of my ripened fruit which I had waited for for so long was near at hand. Before I celebrated my birthday on 18th January 1981, the important moment I had been awaiting came to me. It happened early one morning at about 5 o'clock. I usually wake at that time if something urgent or pressing is bothering me. That morning, before I started thinking over my problem subject, as usual I said a few words of prayer and then continued the search in my mind. After about ten minutes while in deep thought, I found myself jumping out of bed and hurrying to my study to make notes of what had clarified itself in my thoughts. 'How poor are they that have not patience,' said Shakespeare.

As I reached office later in the morning I immediately made telephone contact with David Barwick. I told him that the answer to the EC problem we had been researching for a long time had suddenly come to me in bed that morning. He hurried over to my office. I followed the notes I made earlier and explained to him as I went over the necessary steps required to be taken. They would be in the form of amendments to the Local Companies (Control) Law in order to preserve the non-resident status of companies after the Exchange Control Law was repealed. As to the annual fees, that was already secured under a 1975 amendment to Section 2 of the Companies Law whereby a new definition of a non-resident company was recommended and approved and which stated that the non-resident entity was a Cayman Islands company. David looked at me and said, 'Very brilliant.' I could see that he was relieved for my sake that I could proceed with my seven years of efforts to repeal the Exchange Control Law. He kindly proceeded with amending the laws himself.

The amendments to the Local Companies (Control) Law, Law 24 of 1971, were effected under Section 2 dealing with definitions and interpretation. The first was 'non-resident company' with the following definition: 'a company in respect of which a currently valid certificate designating it as such has, or is deemed to have, been issued under subsection (3).' Subsection (3) states:

If the Financial Secretary is of the opinion that a company is not a company which does, or intends to, carry on business within the islands he may, on application by or on behalf of such company, issue a certificate designating it to be a non-resident company. Such a certificate shall be *prima facie* proof of the fact that the company to which it relates is not a company that carries on business in the islands. The Financial Secretary may, at any time, cancel a certificate issued under this subsection. Any person aggrieved by any decision given by the Financial Secretary under this subsection may, within seven days of the communication of the decision to him, appeal therefrom to the Governor. That decision shall be final and binding upon the applicant and shall not be the subject of appeal to, or called in question by, any court.

The last amendment to the Local Companies (Control) Law was at subsection (4) of Section 2. It stated as follows: 'A declaration under section 3 (3) of the repealed Exchange Control Law, designating a company a non-resident company and in force immediately prior to the twentieth day of May 1980 shall have effect as if it were a certificate under subsection (3).' Reference to subsection (3) at the end of the last sentence meant the amendment to the Local Companies (Control) Law, at Section 2. The Exchange Control (Repeal) Law, 1980, Law 5 of 1980, was passed unanimously by the Legislative Assembly on 17th March 1980, assented to by the Governor on 9th May 1980 and brought into effect on 20th May 1980. Here ended the long journey of efforts, determination and patience, with victory at long last to abolish exchange control in the Cayman Islands with no loss of revenue.

In presenting the draft Exchange Control (Repeal) Bill to the Legislative Assembly on 17th March 1980, I reported that some bankers, while supporting the proposed Bill, felt this was not the most suitable time to put it forward. This they explained was because of the big difference in interest rates on the CI dollar and the US dollar. They believed this would generate speculation with switching from one currency to the other. They thought too that people enjoying the facility of a Cayman dollar loan would perhaps find their interest rate rising because of such speculation. The government's view was that, regardless of when EC was abolished, it would be bound to affect some individuals in one way or another. My own view was that while the bankers' fear might have merits, the time would come in the very near future when everybody agreed that the action to abolish EC was a very wise one.

It was quite interesting to hear in the Legislative Assembly at that session some of the comments on the EC Repeal Bill made by the three ministers of government. First, the Honourable James M. Bodden said, 'I had been pushing for it for years. I would have liked to see Cayman give the lead, with Britain following.'

The Honourable Truman Bodden in his contribution, while welcoming the Repeal Bill, said, 'It could only have a good effect on the economy: I would discount the fears of presumably only a minority of bankers. The real concern of the public at present is regarding the wide spread of three cents between the selling (CI 85 cents) and buying (CI 82 cents) rates of the US dollar introduced in January 1974 following the revaluation of the Cayman dollar.' The wide-spread rates complained about were dealt with immediately following that meeting and eventually, early during the following year, 1982, the government succeeded in having the banks reduce the selling rate from CI 85 cents to CI 84 cents.

The next minister to speak was the Honourable Haig Bodden. He contrasted Cayman's situation with the rest of the Caribbean territories where the natives going abroad could only take a small amount of currency. Yet such rigid controls had not stopped money flying out of those countries. The Jamaican dollar, he said, was now only worth about a third of the Cayman dollar yet their own stringent exchange controls made investors keep away. In winding up he said, 'Perhaps it is good for us that these countries have not realized the error of their ways. The more they tighten their controls the stronger the Cayman dollar gets. The investor who brings his dollars here knows they are safe, he can invest, and he can take out his profits. But no investor will move his money from the place where he is making the most profit.'

The last speaker was a non-government member, Miss Annie H. Bodden. In her contribution she supported the move, saying that she had implicit faith in the mother country. She stated too that she also trusted the Financial Secretary, 'although I don't have too much trust in too many people these days.'

Replying to the debate, I made the point that the move would have no effect on the Cayman dollar prime rate although bankers might see the wisdom in adjusting the rate because of speculation. On the subject of the wide spread between selling and buying US dollars, I pointed out that bankers felt they must be covered for risks when they sold US dollars. However, I gave the assurance to members that the matter would be dealt with at the earliest opportunity. I went on to tell members that abolition of EC in the Cayman Islands had been proposed over seven years before. The action met with many difficulties arising during that period; however, they had all been overcome. Now abolition of EC would be effected in a package of three Bills before this Assembly and Members had indicated support for the three. Apart from the Exchange Control (Repeal) Law, there were two other Bills for amending the Local Companies (Control) Law and the Companies Law. I went on to mention that after Britain greatly reduced the sterling area in June 1972, no reason was seen locally for retaining EC. The UK agreed with that view after a visit by a Bank of England official, who confided that he wished Britain was also in a position to follow that wise move. The recommendation to abolish EC was not presented here before because the Cayman government and the local financial community were not in accord over the move, which they claimed did not fully justify the proposed action.

Following approval for repeal of EC by the Legislative Assembly on 17th March 1980, I was invited by the Rotary Club of Grand Cayman on Thursday 29th May 1980 to speak on the abolition of EC in the Cayman Islands and its effect generally. In my statement I began by telling the gathering that the end of EC in these islands meant a new dimension in the progress of the financial industry. This, however, did not alter the fact that the Cayman dollar would continue to be the legal tender of the country and that it should therefore be supported by every resident. I went on to say that the abolition was a move to liberate pressure created by currency restrictions on development and would allow residents to take full control of the movement, and ultimate use, of their own currency. The move, I said, was hopefully another example of the islands being steered in the right direction. Assent to the law had been held back for a couple of months owing to some complications in the widening disparity in the prime interest rates of the Cayman and US dollars, which had caused concern over the lending rates of the Cayman dollar in particular. It was a situation where the rapid rise of the US dollar staggered the international money markets with the prime rate spiralling to a cyclical peak of 19.5 per cent and with lending rates reaching 23 per cent. In all of that foreign currency trading, the Cayman dollar prime rate remained at 10 per cent. Fortunately the US dollar began a sharp decline in April 1980 and in a couple of months it fell to a level where little difference existed in the deposit rates of the two currencies. The Governor therefore gave his assent to the repeal of the Exchange Control Law.

At the end of my presentation the Rotary Club members posed a few questions to me. One was whether there was a likelihood that the Cayman dollar be put at par with the US dollar. 'I could not answer for the government,' was my reply. Certainly, I pointed out, such a move would cause a devaluation of the Cayman dollar and would not be in the best interest of the country. Another question was whether the government would be investing in gold. In reply I said that I had in fact been requested to investigate the possibility of the government's investment in gold and silver. However, I was advised by our London financial experts to beware of commodity trading (gold,

225

silver etc.) as such investments involved long-term results. In the case of the Currency Board funds, for instance, I pointed out that there was the need for a steady annual investment income from its surplus and reserve funds and therefore commodity trading in precious metals would be unwise. The last question concerned the determining factor which caused the government to switch the parity of its currency from Sterling to the US dollar. I explained that the main reason was the fact that approximately 70 per cent of our imports came from the United States and it therefore made no economic or monetary sense to continue having the Cayman currency aligned to the pound Sterling.

With both the Insurance Law and repeal of the Exchange Control Law successfully finalized and implemented, the two systems took off at a rapid pace like would-be stars in an athletic race, thereby contributing much to economic development. The local community and domestic business as well as the offshore financial industry were especially pleased and grateful for the action taken by the government. The two systems, insurance and EC repeal, also crowned with delight and pleasure what was seen as the Cayman Islands' most famous and outstanding financial decade, the 1970s: it was a packed ten years of economic activity.

13

My Final Years in the Civil Service

This chapter deals primarily with those projects, institutions and leg-islative cornerstones which had their genesis during my time in the Civil Service, especially that period after 1965 when I was promoted to the official position of Treasurer, which was re-designated Financial Secretary in 1968. In those early years many bright prin-ciples influenced my daily general thinking and performance. The philosophy that deals with ultimate reality was the first to adorn my thoughts. It came from the following words of Shakespeare that I kept repeating frequently, 'This above all: To thine own self be true, and it must follow, as the night the day, thou canst not then be false to any man.' Another thinking was regarding the economy and wealth of the country. The theory I subscribed to was that the government should raise revenue and save during boom periods in order to have the ability to spend in times of economic recession. That theory was in our case to be most helpful between the years 1970 and 1976. In the early part of that decade, at a time when the economy was performing quite well, the government introduced new revenues and placed a part of the proceeds in a special reserve called the Capital Projects Fund. That fund was earmarked specially to assist the financing of capital projects that were then in the planning stage, and as well to meet urgent financial need created by economic stress and strain. The theory served the country very well during the 1975 recession; the details can be found in Chapter 12 'Economic Diversification'. In my economic theory, revenue measures should not be introduced in times of recession because such action would have the effect of deepening the suffering of the poorer persons.

In 1965, when I inherited the Portfolio of Finance and Development, Cayman had just lost its prime segment of the economy, the seamen's industry. It was felt that the islands were then being pressed by sheer need to find a new income, and that this could best be achieved by reflecting on the country's political goodwill, honesty and integrity. It was well known too that to move on with the search for a new income would require technical skills and the acumen of statesmanship, spiced with patience – a God-given virtue, possess it if you can.

In replying to the debate on my budget address presented to the Legislative Assembly on 9th November 1979, I made the following statement:

When I was appointed in 1965 to my present position, much thought came to my mind about the financial future of this country. Those thoughts were placed on record and in reports in those early years. They stated among other things that Cayman should one day become completely independent financially including freedom from British capital aid and should also one day become one of the leading offshore finance centres of the world.

Shortly after that time these islands did begin moving in that direction. They were fortunately blessed with the fact that violence and crime were very well controlled, windows of homes and shops were not required to be burglar-barred and security was found largely in financial institutions, certain government offices and a few upmarket residences. This sense of security, without doubt, gave Cayman the edge in the Caribbean as a very well liked business and tourist destination. The friendly and hospitable attitude of the people, along with the islands' lustre of glory and distinction, also added more attraction to the smooth operation that provided much pleasure for visitors. Few other countries have seen progress as dramatic and rapid as did these islands. Today as the country begins the historic third millennium, all of Cayman can proudly say, 'Thank God, we have reached those goals of enviable levels predicted so long ago. Now we can rejoice over the growth, stability, prosperity and harmony that surround us.'

On the political scene, one could hear varying views expressed about individuals who stood for election to become members of the Legislative Assembly and Executive Council. Among those members were ambitious men and women who vied for position to make their mark on the country's history. I worked very closely with politicians from 1965 when, by virtue of my position as Treasurer, I entered the Legislative Assembly as the third official member appointed by the Governor and authorized by the Constitution. I worked and rubbed shoulders with politicians for a period of 23 years including the four years in 1984–88 when I myself became an elected member of the Legislative Assembly. During that period I could very well state

228

without fear of successful contradiction that all of Cayman's politicians had a sense of purpose for the people they represented and for the government's interest as well. And with it they also had the profound integrity to tell the truth and abide by the ethics of their position. When there was the need to find creative ways to keep the home fires burning, they would all rally to the cause and assist where possible in order to find ways and means of resolving problems. This is one of the fine attributes of Cayman's politicians which led to the great prosperity that the islands enjoy today.

Cayman's politicians also reminded me, in their performance of duties and attitude towards others, of the spoken words of Indira Gandhi, Prime Minister of India, when she said, 'One must take out of the land, sea and air only what he can replace in them.' One example is that if the natural environment of the land is damaged in some respects by, for instance, the reclaiming of swamp by the removal of mangrove, there is a requirement to replace what has been removed. This is achieved by creating facilities to foster required developments such as yacht marinas, golf courses and replanting beautiful gardens and fruit orchards around attractive homes and housing developments. One fact worth remembering is that removing some of Cayman's mangroves in reclaiming swamp lands was most beneficial in ridding the islands of much of their mosquito problem, especially along the Seven Mile Beach, the hub of Cayman's tourist industry.

The local politicians found it a pleasure to operate under a democratic government. Their feelings about it were that democracy should be seen in the light of its ability to give the people freedom in the way they wished to lead their lives. The country on the other hand, should provide everything needed to enable a person of whatever colour, religion or social background to be happy, content, prosperous and energetic.

I was also aware of the role of the press and had occasion to speak about it at a Commonwealth Parliamentary Association Conference in October 1980.

The conference, held in Lusaka, Zambia, was quite interesting. It included for the first time in its history a 'Little Countries Conference' which allowed the smaller territories to discuss their little problems and issues that would not be too relevant to the big nations. At the end of the little countries' first meeting the members declared that it was worth the efforts put into its organization. I selected quite a few subjects to present at both the little and general conferences. The one dealing with big countries had a couple of subjects that drew some public interest. One I participated in dealt with the question of a one party system in government. The Zambian *Daily Mail* carried comments of various speakers on the front page of its Friday 3rd October 1980 issue. The reporter quoted me as saying:

> Since in the one party state there is seldom any form of opposition, the need is seen for a strong press representation to act the part of the public's watchdog. The press should not be muzzled by the government in one party states if there is to be freedom of expression. The press must report freely and with an established board comprised of government and private members to guide and defend the principles of freedom of the press and allow for the smooth operation of the one party system. It is wrong to assume that the multi-party system offers greater stability just as it is wrong to assume that one party is dictatorial.

The speech went on for about ten minutes and at the end of it the chairman of the conference complimented me on my presentation.

I must relate something of a personal nature which occurred during that trip to Lusaka. Before the meeting started, the delegates were treated to social events. They were divided into a few groups and each invited on a different tour of the country. My group included my wife Rita and youngest son Bradley, then eight years of age. Our group went on a safari in Zambia's large international wild game park. On our return to the lodge that evening, I discovered that my wallet was missing. I became very concerned for without it I could face embarrassing financial and other problems. I went to the driver of one of the jeeps and discussed the matter with him. He encouraged me to go back and try to find it. We did. The driver took an armed guard and the three of us were soon on the way. The Speaker of the House, a native of Zambia, who was on the safari with us earlier that day, was not at all happy at the idea of our going back into the park. He explained how dangerous it was to go in wild parks especially at that time of the evening when animals were out feeding. However, I insisted on going, and so did the driver.

We went the full distance of the safari, scanning the roadway carefully, to where we had come upon a pack of lions earlier in the day. On our return the lions were still there, standing on raised ground on the side of the road. They appeared like frozen objects. There was no movement in them at all. The driver spoke to the armed guard, then instructed me to lie flat on my back in the jeep. He slowly turned the jeep around and drove away almost breathless. To this day I think of how foolish I was to go on that mission and to ignore the advice of the Speaker; in fact I shiver when I think of the dangerous expedition and wonder why, just why, those lions did not come out at us, especially at their feeding time. On the journey back to the lodge I found the wallet. It had fallen out of my pocket by a stream in some white sand where we had stopped earlier in the day to transfer from a bus into jeeps for travelling over rough roads. I firmly believe that what saved the three of us that night, because one rifle would have been a joke among all those lions, was that we trusted in divine protection.

The incident made me recall the time over 40 years earlier when I had gone hunting with Cyril Borden in George Town. He had climbed a tree and pulled his shotgun up after him on a piece of thatch string. The string broke and the gun fell, butt muzzle up, yet the cartridge did not explode. Both incidents could have had a dreadful ending.

As I approached the age of 60 on 18th January 1982, I began thinking about the day I would retire from the Civil Service, which is compulsory at 60 under the Pensions Law. On a voluntary basis I could have retired at 55 years of age but this was far from my thoughts as the building of the financial industry, which was my chosen government career and greatest ambition in life, was yet far from completion. Even when I reached 60, although the finishing line of victory was in sight, it had not yet been crossed. However, I spent a further four years in government (1984–88), elected to the Legislative Assembly and given a seat in Executive Council. I became a Council Minister responsible for the Portfolio of Development and Natural Resources. During that period I saw Cayman dashing to the summit and joining forces with other leading offshore financial centres of the world.

When I retired in 1982, a journalist asked me if I wished to describe my achievements and successes during my 17 years in office as Financial Secretary. My answer was this: 'I will try. First, my effort was to create the offshore financial industry. While working strenuously on that subject, I tried, for my own benefit, to build around me as I moved along, a fabric of public trust demonstrated in my performance. And then I helped to create a reservoir and filled it with goodies for the benefit of the present and future generations of Caymanians.' I went on to say that: 'It was my honour and privilege to serve the Cayman Islands, my adopted country, and its government, in the ranks of the Civil Service. This of course demanded a deep sense of devotion to duty, self-respect and the ability to offer a fine service to the public. I watched the country grow and develop following World War II, in the way we see it at this point in time. I am certainly glad to have been a part of it all. The most admirable aspect

231

of the country's progress was to watch the indomitable spirit of the local population in action which created much of the initiative that moved progress and development to its present level.'

At the beginning of the 1970s the main local economic indicators, such as tourist statistics and the government's local income, revealed an inflationary growth rate of approximately 30 per cent per annum. This rapid movement in domestic inflation made even more apparent the urgent need for reorganization and expansion of public services and the provision for improved infrastructure. Had the situation remained unattended it would have led to an embarrassing and unsatisfactory state of affairs while eventually bringing about general economic and social instability. However, the government had already requested assistance from the British government, in the form of a visit to Cayman to have a look at these urgent needs. The work was undertaken by the British Development Division in Barbados, a branch of the Ministry of Overseas Development in London. The Civil Service and economic infrastructure were the two areas covered. As detailed in Chapter 9, the teams found those areas sadly lacking and recommended the reorganization and restructuring of the public service and improvement of infrastructure needs in specific areas. Those recommendations were accepted and implementation began during the 1970s.

The Constitution

There were important developments in 1972. One was the move for a new Constitution originating out of a resolution unanimously resolved by the Legislative Assembly in 1969 to deal with constitutional advancement through a Select Committee of the House. Accordingly, on 23rd June 1970 the House resolved unanimously to refer the reports and minutes of their Select Committee to the United Kingdom Secretary of State and to request his advice, guidance and provision of a constitutional expert. Pursuant to that resolution, the then Secretary of State, Sir Alec Douglas-Home, appointed Lord Oxford and Asquith in late 1971 to be a Constitutional Commissioner for the Cayman Islands. Lord Oxford recommended constitutional advancement. The new Constitution came into operation on 22nd August 1972 although the previous Constitution had been suitably amended in the meantime to facilitate the November 1972 political General Election. A constitution is very important to any country because it is the basis on which all future development, prosperity, peace and harmony will rest. Important steps were put forward in

Cayman's new Constitution. First, the two Nominated (appointed) Members of Executive Council as provided in the previous Constitution were abolished. Secondly, the three elected Members in Council were increased to four and the two official Members increased to three; as a result the number of Members in Executive Council under the new Constitution remained unchanged at seven. In Executive Council elected Members were all charged along with Official Members with portfolio responsibility for running the affairs of the country. This was the first time that elected Members to Executive Council were given such wide responsibilities.

The Governor, Kenneth Crook, in delivering his Throne Speech in the Legislative Assembly on 7th August 1972, said to the members, 'You have achieved a Constitution which will give time for the careful and progressive development of participation by elected representatives of the people. You have not fallen for the popular belief that anything carrying the "colonial" label is bad.' This statement indicated that the new Constitution continued to be based on Cayman's Crown Colony system of government. The Governor went on to say that, 'Further changes will follow. In my recent discussion in London, I gathered that the British government would put no artificial obstacles in the way of that change. I should perhaps add, for the avoidance of doubt, that it is not normal to grant full internal self-government without at the same time setting an approximate date for independence. But there should be plenty of room for further advance before we reach that stage. In short – if I were a Caymanian I would feel well content with what this Constitution represents, and would want to take time to think very carefully about the next step.'

The words of the Governor, that the Cayman Islands should take time to think carefully about the next step in constitutional advance, were well remembered. In fact they were tested on 13th September 1977 when a 24-strong mission from the United Nations Special Committee on Decolonization visited the Cayman Islands. The sub-committee was led by Mr Berenado Vunibobo, Ambassador of Fiji to the United Nations. The team visited to discuss with all of Cayman their views about constitutional advances. The first meeting was held with the Members of the Executive Council. I asked Mr Vunibobo if he could truly advise of any colonial territory, small or large, that has enjoyed complete success after moving to an advanced system of government, either internal self-government or independence. He looked me straight in the eyes and said, 'Mr Johnson, that is an unfair question.' The visitors met with no success on their part to move the local Constitution forward. They were told by the people of the three islands in a loud clear voice, 'Leave us alone.'

In the Ambassador's report back to his full UN committee in New York he said, 'The Caymanians confirmed their contentment with their present political and constitutional status and mentioned that they themselves would seek changes when they felt it desirable to do so.' At the meeting in New York, Cayman was represented by the Governor, Mr Thomas Russell, The Honourable Truman Bodden of the Executive Council and Mr George Smith of the Legislative Assembly. Mr Bodden closed his presentation to the Committee with the following request: 'That the Committee advise the General Assembly that, in accordance with the inalienable right of the Cayman Islands to self-determination, the peoples of the Cayman Islands do not want any change and recommend that they should not be forced to accept any change in their Constitution.' In the meantime, a local petition with many thousands of signatures was addressed to Her Majesty The Queen. It requested that the United Nations Decolonization Committee of 24 (Members) be advised that the people of the Cayman Islands, a British Dependent Territory, be allowed the right of self-determination with respect to any form of proposed constitutional changes. After presentation of the Mission's report to the United Nations, the First Secretary of the United Kingdom's Mission to the United Nations said, 'The Caymanians, for their part, are fully capable of seeking change if and when they think it desirable to do so.'

Another attempt at constitutional reform bobbed up again in November 1990. On this occasion, after continued political discussions on the subject here and in London, the United Kingdom government through its Secretary of State for Foreign and Commonwealth Affairs, The Right Honourable Douglas Hurd, CBE, MP, appointed two Constitutional Commissioners in November 1990 to review the Constitution of the Cayman Islands. They were Sir Frederick Smith and Mr Walter Wallace. The following were the terms of reference:

> To ascertain and evaluate opinion in the Cayman Islands upon possible paths of Constitutional evolution, having regard to political development in the islands and to the social and economic development of the islands since the introduction of the present Constitution in 1972. In conducting the assignment, consult with the Governor, the Members of the Executive Council and the Legislative Assembly, interested organizations and members of the public, and to report.

The Commissioners visited the islands from 6 January to 6 February 1991 in order to hold the required consultations. Their first observations were that 'the Cayman Islanders have a tradition of hardiness and independence of spirit. With few opportunities at home, they have in the past earned a livelihood at sea, either as turtle fishermen or as members of crew on foreign-owned ships sailing around the world or by working in North and Central America. Times have changed and now there is no lack of employment opportunities in the islands' two main industries, tourism and offshore finance.' The team's very well organized discussions involved many political proposals for changes, one of which was to create the post of Chief Minister. This was from a public point of view a very contentious issue. However, during the 1992 campaign for the November General Election, there were clear indications from the people of the islands that they did not wish to have major constitutional changes or a new Constitution. Following discussions with Executive Council and the Legislative Assembly, a few amendments to the existing Constitution were recommended to the Foreign and Commonwealth Office in London while rejecting the recommended draft Constitution by the Commissioners. Amendments to the existing Constitution took into account all forms of minor development changes, a few of which were brought about by the effluxion of time over the previous 20 years. The recommendations of the Constitutional Committee of June 1970, together with the expert input of Lord Oxford, the Constitutional Commissioner, which produced the Constitution of 22nd August 1972, certainly provided one that has withstood the test of time. It is also pleasing to the people, at the beinning of the 21st century, to see their 1972 Constitution still serving as well as the day it was introduced.

Cost of Living Index

I mentioned earlier in this chapter a local concern in the early 1970s over an inflationary situation, the annual rate of which averaged 30 per cent. The situation was frequently a subject of discussion by the public in the form of questions about the government's intended action to find an effective solution to the problem or whether those responsible for the subject were unwilling or unable to take on the task. Quite clearly inflation should be everybody's concern as there is no magic wand to wave it away. In fact, countries far better equipped to control the problem than Cayman have also found that it is usually a difficult one to control or remove. This concern continued until August 1974, when the government decided to invite from the United Kingdom someone experienced in the control of inflation to assist the situation. Dame Elizabeth Ackroyd, Chairman of the Consumers' Council in Britain for five years and considered very qualified in sorting out inflationary problems, was recommended. She began her assignment by organizing public meetings in all the districts of these islands and explaining to the people that to combat inflation would be a very difficult and controversial subject.

The 20,000-word report by Dame Elizabeth on anti-inflation measures was received at the end of September 1974. The Governor immediately sent me a copy. I was very interested in seeing the recommendations as inflation was in fact a subject shared with my portfolio. The Governor also circulated copies to all members of the Executive Council. Later he sent copies to members of the Legislative Assembly accompanied by a letter in which Executive Council Member for Information, the Honourable Trevor Foster, stated that the government was not committed to accept any or all of the recommendations. In her report Dame Elizabeth made the following comments: 'It is not my function to make a political judgement about whether my proposals would be acceptable. I would not think however that any of them is so outlandish as to be out of the question in the present inflationary situation, one which others, rather than I, have warned could lead, if not checked, to a crisis in the islands.'

Once I saw the report, I quickly hid it in my office and told the Governor that I had no interest in presenting the recommendations to the Legislative Assembly. The most critical aspects of the report, which contained 44 recommendations, were two proposals to introduce a modest level of personal taxation and a property tax. Dame Elizabeth's contention was that those two measures were preferable to the customs duties that are more than a third of Cayman's total revenue budget. Whatever her better judgement might have been in presenting the two direct tax proposals, she did not take into consideration the tremendous benefit Cayman derived from its local offshore business and the adverse effects her two direct tax measures would have against it; like a cat among pigeons.

On the matter of income tax, or the personal tax recommended along with property tax, Dame Elizabeth had this to say: 'Not only is income tax a fairer way of raising revenue in social terms, since its burden can be tailored to the victims' financial circumstances, but also by the same token it is a more flexible and efficient instrument for reducing purchasing power.' She claimed that a whiff of personal taxation would not scare away the offshore industry. However, this is a chance nobody in these islands would take. In fact, in later years other tax havens introduced forms of direct tax such as payroll tax that raised much concern among their local and offshore interests.

236

The report, however, did provide the government with a few reasonable proposals which were acceptable, such as establishing a cost of living index and the collation of the statistics essential to keep track of the national economy and rising prices. Following this effort on inflation control, I decided to pursue personally the route of voluntary control rather than control by legislation. The exercise was unannounced while the assistance of Captain Charles Kirkconnell, then a Member of the Legislative Assembly and a general Cayman merchant (Kirk Plaza Supermarket), was solicited. We looked at areas of the shopping basket that were more or less susceptible to general price increases and the occurrences that would trigger such movements. We found that topping the list were increases in the salaries of Civil Servants, followed by taxation on petrol, tobacco, bank and companies' fees etc. introduced to supplement revenue shortage during the budget presentation. Charles took the lead to fix new prices on any freshly taxed items in any areas of his business. This he followed up by advising the public accordingly. In this way other businesses had no choice but to follow suit in fixing their new consumer prices. The joint effort by Charles and me began in late 1976 when inflation of cost of living prices was at a level of between 15 and 18 per cent per annum.

In June 1978 I addressed the Chamber of Commerce on the subject 'Voluntary Control over Inflation is Possible'. I explained how the Cayman economy had recovered so well from the 1975–76 recession and that the trend was expected to continue for the next five or six years. Actually the next recession was not felt until 1984, eight years later, and was one of the reasons the government was replaced: a recession in Cayman is noted for its political changes. I told the Chamber that the offshore financial and tourist industries were well known for their inflationary effects, especially in the areas of labour and imports, which could cause increases in the cost of production, thus taking new prices beyond competitive levels. I went on to say that inflation was then on a rise due to the renewed vigour in the economy and unless some form of control was instituted, rapid growth could lead to bottlenecks. Anti-inflationary measures employed in other countries would not necessarily have the same effects here. I encouraged the Chamber to consider voluntary control over inflation, which to some extent could achieve, through agreements and co-operation, reasonable limits on prices of goods and labour. In my closing remarks I said, 'My hope is that you will not only support this proposition for voluntary control, but perhaps even suggest a programme which you feel could achieve the desired results.' When I was leaving the Civil Service in 1982 the level of inflation had fallen to 8 per cent and in the years to follow it levelled off at 4 per cent.

Land Laws

An important feature of the 1970s was the many important laws produced and brought into effect, legislation that formed the basic legal framework on which these islands functioned and developed. The first law I want to mention is The Land Holding Companies Equity Transfer Stamp Duty Law 1971, which was replaced on 1st January 1977 in an amended form including the title the Land Holding Companies Share Transfer Tax Law. The story behind this law is that during 1971 a good friend told me that he had learned something new that day and then volunteered to tell it to me. He said that to avoid paying stamp duty on land when sold, incorporate a new company and put the land in the name of the new company. When the land in the company is sold, just transfer the shares of the company to the new owners. The transfer would not require the payment of stamp duty under the Companies Law. Telling me the story was actually reporting the evasion of the government's revenue because under the Stamp Duty Law the Financial Secretary is *ex officio* Commissioner for the collection of stamp duty and has care and management of the collection of all stamp duty under that or any other law. I thanked him and decided to move quickly on rectifying that route of tax escape.

I immediately visited the office of the legal draftsman, Roderick Donaldson. I explained to him as best I could my problem with regard to a company holding land and transferring its shares to a new owner without paying government stamp duty: that would be the same as selling the property without paying stamp tax. Roderick was in my opinion a brilliant legal draftsman. He was very good at finding ways on the spur of the moment to resolve every difficult situation. In a few days he produced the draft of a law which was afterwards suitably amended to provide the legal instrument requested. It required that every land-holding corporation or its legal or beneficial owner make a return to government on a prescribed form showing all the landed property held at the time by the corporation. It was an offence under the law if a land-holding company transferred its shares without paying the stamp duty. The law certainly stemmed the tide of tax evasion from that particular avenue. I said nothing to my friend about the plug put into his brilliant scheme to evade stamp duty. Roderick will always be remembered in that decade as the architect of especially difficult legislation like the Land Holding

Companies Share Transfer Tax Law and, later, the Confidential Relationships (Preservations) Law.

At the mid-1972 session of the Legislative Assembly, a package of three land laws was also passed: they were the Land Adjudication Law, The Land Registration Law and the Surveyors Law. Prior to those laws coming into effect, ownership of land in these islands was in many cases uncertain and this had the tendency to retard progress and ultimately prosperity. The laws, however, spurred much doubt and speculation at first but when the adjudication process moved ahead and owners of land began receiving good guaranteed titles for their property, the system was highly praised by all. A few Caribbean territories sent representatives here to look at the system with the hope of adopting it.

Another law that followed the three land laws at the same session of the Legislative Assembly was the Development and Planning Law, together with its regulations. A first set of regulations was previously introduced under the Interim Land Development Bill but these were rescinded and the Assembly appointed a committee to consider and recommend a new law and regulations. These were enacted and the new board, the Central Planning Authority, constituted. Thus ended the struggle with the many pieces of controversial legislation. Yet those measures provided a legal basis under which there could be control in the public's interest. They also aimed at bringing order out of possible land development chaos and frustration that would have the effect of impeding the development of reputable international business. These laws would also ensure that control over those who live and work in Cayman should be in the hands of people who derive their authority from the natives of these islands.

The Stamp Duty Law was also subject to a rushed repeal and replacement in 1973. At the time condominiums were just being constructed on the Seven Mile Beach. When the first units were ready for the market, the owners came to the government to inquire if, as in the case of private dwelling homes built on registered property on which stamp duty had already been paid, the units would be exempted from stamp duty. The advice given was that they are quite different from family homes in that the condo units when sold are considered a commercial transaction subject to stamp duty under the law. The units, including the proportionate part of the land on which they are built, would attract stamp duty on their market value.

The condo owners and their lawyers got together and worked out a scheme to avoid paying the government stamp duty on the market value of the property. The units' cost had already been established before construction began. They eventually agreed that the transfer for temporary possession of the units would be by way of a long-term lease. Stamp duty under the law on this category of lease would be paid at the then maximum 10 per cent of the average annual rent. The lease could be for any number of years: 99 years was a popular figure used. When this was discovered, the government moved quickly to replace the Stamp Duty Law. The item 'Lease or Agreement for a Lease' under the schedule of the law was completely restructured to its present form. The term of a normal lease under the new law was placed at a maximum period of 30 years. Beyond that time the lease would be treated as a normal land transfer or conveyance attracting stamp duty on its market value and not on the average annual rent. Other minor amendments to the law were also effected at the same time. The long lease scheme used for the transfer of condo units was short-lived, as in the case of the land-holding companies selling their shares to avoid paying stamp duty.

The Caymanian Protection Laws, Companies, Trade and Business Licensing

I should also mention other important laws brought into effect by the Legislative Assembly in the 1970s. In mid-1972 three important pieces of legislation came into effect, the Caymanian Protection Law (CPL) and its two companion laws, the Local Companies (Control) Law and the Trades and Business Licensing Law. I recall playing a small part in the early days of planning the CPL. At the beginning of the Legislative Assembly in early 1972, I was on my way home for lunch at the adjournment of the House. Captain Eldon Kirkconnell, OBE and Mr Burns Rutty, members of the Legislative Assembly, called to me and asked if I could stop by Kirk Plaza supermarket. They both wanted to speak to me.

When I entered Eldon's office, with Burns also present, Eldon said to me, 'Vas, we have been giving serious thought to Caymanians' business and other interests in these islands now that development appears to be expanding at a rather rapid pace. In this respect we believe there should be a law to protect local interests so that if outsiders want to participate there are legal steps by which to do so. We would like it if you could assist us to prepare a draft resolution to the Legislative Assembly along those lines so we can move it at this meeting.'

I was happy to assist. Before starting, however, I said quietly to myself, 'Here goes my lunch.' Not really, I did the draft resolution, went home and had lunch and was back to the meeting in good time.

240

The three of us looked at the draft over and over and made appropriate amendments. The product of that resolution brought about the Caymanian Protection Law. It confers Caymanian status on persons of British nationality who fulfil the required stipulations. A person who has Caymanian status is regarded as a person belonging to these islands and having every right to take part freely in the affairs affecting the Cayman Islands. The law was amended several times until 1992, when it served as the basis for the new Immigration Law now in effect.

At the establishment of the board charged with the responsibility of administering the affairs of the CPL, the first chairmanship was offered to me. I declined the offer and stated that in my view a born Caymanian should be given the appointment. Wenthworth Bodden, a Principal Secretary, was selected for the position. All other members of the board were also Caymanians. Hence, more and more, the future of these islands was being vested in the hands of those who really lived in Cayman. Under former laws, confusion existed. For example, persons could be given immigration clearance to come into the islands with no guarantee that a work permit would be issued to them. Nor was there any guarantee that, even if given a work permit, they would obtain a licence to operate a business within these islands. All of these functions were delegated under the new CPL to its board: thus if a person was given permission to enter and work in Cayman, he or she was also assured of being able to get all of the necessary permits.

The Local Companies (Control) Law, also administered by the board of the CPL, made provisions by which any company which had a minimum of 60 per cent of its capital owned by residents of these islands would be able to operate without let or hindrance. This was indeed a good step forward as it helped to ensure the future stability of the Cayman Islands. Persons from outside coming in to set up local companies could be assured that once their entities were declared local companies under the law, they had no need to fear their business might be nationalized, as happened in many other countries. In fact they could consider themselves a part of Cayman working in harmony with the people and the country. Companies that were not local companies would be required to get special permission to operate in Cayman. The Trades and Business Licensing Law was also administered by the board of the CPL. Local business had only to present an acceptable location and attractive building to be used in order to obtain from the board a trades and business licence under the law. Businesses proposed by outside investors had more difficulties obtaining permits.

241

An important law introduced in the 1970s was the Confidential Relationships (Preservation) Law that came into effect on 13th September 1976: details are in Chapter 9, 'Finance and Tourism'. Other laws approved by the Legislative Assembly in the 1970s were the Insurance Law and the repeal of the Exchange Control Law. The Insurance Law was passed by the Legislative Assembly in November 1979 and brought into effect in June 1980. The Exchange Control (Repeal) Law came into effect on 20th May 1980. Its first recommendation for repeal went to the government in early 1973. Details of these last two laws are in Chapter 12, 'Economic Diversification'. To say the least, 1972 was recorded as a year when great laws dominated the sessions of the Legislative Assembly.

Government Records

On another subject, I must mention the awful disaster that struck the government on Sunday 23rd July 1972 shortly after midday, when the old Government House off Elgin Avenue was destroyed by fire. The loss of records was quite serious. It was said that the fire destroyed all but the memory of those who worked there at Government House for a long number of years. Two such persons were Miss Frances Bodden, MBE, JP, who served at Government House for 32 years from 1928 to 1960, and Mr Ernest O. Panton, MBE, ISO, JP, who worked there for 33 years, from 1931 to 1964. Both these persons shared a large fund of memory about the eight commissioners under whom they worked. They were H.H. Hutching (1919–29), Captain G.H. Frith (1929–31), E.A. Weston (1931–34), A.W. Cardinall (1934–40), J.P. Jones (1941–46), I.O. Smith (1946–52), A.M. Gerrard (1952–56) and A.H. Donald (1956–60). The Dormant Commissioner, A.C. Panton, also acted in 1940 while awaiting the arrival of Cardinall's successor, J.P. Jones, who was known as the 'Wartime Chief'. The old Government House, built in 1908 by the Commissioner, Dr George S.S. Hirst, was not lavish of space as it was used for office and home: he had a wife and two children, Marcus and Jane. After a new residence (referred to as Government House) was built in the early 1960s, the original was turned into offices.

The day following the fire, a few minutes after 9 a.m., with the prompt and invaluable support of a member of the business community, Mr Jean Doucet, the government took temporary premises just across the road from the burned building. By the end of the month because of the need for centralized accommodation, space was taken in the West Wind Building near the waterfront. Because of public spirit, the owners of West Wind made substantial concessions to include special arrangements for length of the tenancy together with a moratorium on rent payments. The government moved on with planning and building a new Administration Building on the same site of the old building slightly nearer to the main road, Elgin Avenue. It is a four-storey glass building, known as the 'Glass House'.

At the time of construction in 1974 the new Administration Building was the first building with all-glass walls in the country, and it continued to be the only one at the end of the century. What other people are afraid of is the fact that Cayman is situated in the tropical hurricane belt area, requiring buildings to be made of substantial material. The government had the assurance that the glass used in the Administration Building was guaranteed by the manufacturers to withstand heavy winds. There has been one test so far, from Hurricane Gilbert in 1988 (mentioned earlier), when winds in the area of the building blew at a force reaching 134 m.p.h. The new Administration Building was opened on 17th November 1975 and provides offices for the Governor, all members of the Executive Council and their back-up staff. Of course, a quarter of a century later government staff are housed in at least six quite large buildings.

Early after the destruction of the old Administration Building in 1972, there was concern that many of the government's records accumulated over many decades and lost in the fire would be difficult to replace. It was with that thought and concern in mind that I decided my portfolio would at least make a brave attempt to put together what financial information could be found anywhere in the public or private sectors. The thought of attempting the exercise haunted me until two years before my planned retirement from the Civil Service, when, with no work yet started on the project, I moved on with it right away. I appointed my Deputy Financial Secretary, Mr J. Lemuel Hurlston, as chairman of the special committee to guide that very important project. Other members of the committee were our Financial Advisor, Mr Kenneth Digby, who was in the process of completing the 1980 population census; the Assistant Statistician, Ms Carolyn Cupidon-Ebanks; and Government Information Officer, Mrs Olive Miller. Both Mr Hurlston and Mrs Miller have in recent years been honoured by Her Majesty The Queen.

Knowing the broad terms of reference for the project, the committee went to work searching out as they went along areas where information would be likely to be found and analyzing any records dated beyond 1904. The effort was greatly assisted by portions of the information coming from the private collection of the former Chief

Secretary, Mr Desmond Watler, and from records of the *Annual Colonial Reports* kept by Mrs Olive Miller. The unfolding of 75 years of information in one volume was named *The Cayman Islands Government Economic and Financial Review*. Although the work was rushed in order to meet the deadline coinciding with my retirement on 31st March 1982, and though the book urgently needs reviewing and updating, it provides very valuable financial and other historic data. For instance, it reveals a deficit of £149 in 1904. Yet through the economic depression of the 1920s and 1930s and the activities of World War II, the country emerged to enjoy its current prosperity. My impression was that after such a disaster as the 1972 fire, the task of restoring lost records by a team of five people was certainly a marvellous job. My four team members deserve the praise of the country. I want to record again that we were much indebted to Mr Watler and Mrs Miller for providing a portion of the most valuable data.

The presentation of the *Review* was first made to His Excellency the Governor and thereafter to the Executive Council and the press on 26th March 1982, five days before I exited the Civil Service. In making the presentation I said among other things:

> The progress and economic stability of the Cayman Islands was created by design; it certainly did not all happen by sheer co-incidence. There are basically three grounds for the success and progress experienced by the islands. First is the government's complete freedom from direct taxation; secondly, the long history of political stability; and lastly, the charm of the people. The occasion today reveals yet another success by design, the introduction of the first published edition of *The Cayman Islands Economic and Financial Review*. The book focuses upon the effects of the public sector fiscal policies in respect of the allocation, distribution and utilization of its resources. The publication has seven parts with 25 sections and a total of 45 tables. The information addresses a variety of subjects including Economic Development, Development Planning, Reserve and Investment Funds, Public Debt, Taxation, British Aid, Capital Projects, the Financial Industry, the Civil Service, Statutory Bodies and other relevant information.

I went on to say, 'To build a sound financial administration is a long and painful task. Quick and easy results are not to be expected. Even for advanced countries, the task has not been easy or ever finished. The information contained in this publication gives evidence of some

244

of the painful tasks endured by the local administration.' At the end of the address I quoted the essayist Francis Bacon, who said, 'Out of monuments, names, words, proverbs, tradition, private records and evidences, fragments of stories, passages of books and the like, we do save and recover somewhat from the deluge of time.'

National Events

Looking on the social side of life in Cayman, there are three yearly entertaining activities seen as national events which provide much amusement and excitement for the public. The government either initiated or became involved in all three. They are Pirates Week, the Agricultural Show and Million Dollar Month Fishing Tournament. Pirates Week was first introduced in the last week of October 1977. Its main purpose was to attract visitors to boost the tourist traffic that had lost much of its volume by that time of the year. The first year was planned for experimental purposes. However, it proved such a success that the following year the time was extended from one week to ten days and its programme of events covered all the districts, including Cayman Brac. As well as boosting the incoming traffic, a major aim of Pirates Week was to bring together Caymanians and vacationers so that they could become better acquainted. Apart from the attractions of the festivities, it was also an occasion for visitors to catch a glimpse of Cayman as an increasingly attractive vacation destination, especially for those tourists from North America who would also be interested in other local economic activities. The festivity also brought back home many Caymanians and other residents living abroad.

The second interesting event is the one day Agricultural Show that takes place each year on Ash Wednesday, the first day of Lent, which is usually in February. It is one of the established statutory public holidays. The first show opened in 1962 and it is still popular today. It is a show where a large part of the population gathers as it provides an opportunity for friends and even families who perhaps only saw each other last at the previous gathering to meet again. It is an occasion too when the local people meet and become acquainted with the many visitors who like this form of entertainment. The show provides many attractions from its exhibits of farm products, livestock and handicraft items proudly displayed at the stalls by the producers themselves. The stalls are always attractive and the government makes the effort to emphasize at these shows the need to promote and encourage agriculture in these islands. The point is that agriculture in any country should have a link to its economy.

245

In 1985, government practised what it preached by moving ahead to establish a Farmers' Cooperative with ten founding members, who included the leading farmers in the islands. The government followed that development by the building of a Farmers' Market so as to ensure that the system would grow and thus become a reality. In the years to follow one would need only to attend the Farmers' Market to see its growing size and stocks as evidence of the corresponding expansion of farms in the islands. The Agricultural Show draws a large crowd of residents and visitors who happen to be on the island at that time, which is the thick of the tourist season. Unlike Pirates Week, the Agricultural Show does not attract tourists or Caymanians living abroad.

The third national event is popularly known as Million Dollar Month (MDM) Fishing Tournament, a sporting event that provides an attraction to anglers, those who enjoy fishing with hook and bait. The annual one-month tournament was first held in June 1984, a time considered the best in the year for blue marlin fishing and for other game fish as well.

The main thought behind the anglers' annual one-month event was similar to what brought about the annual Pirates Week celebration at the end of October. The Cayman Islands' heavy tourist traffic traditionally began a downward slide from the end of April, so that by June to November there was a need to boost traffic by some form of economic activities to create a form of public appeal and entertainment. The brilliant thoughts leading to both Pirates Week and MDM came from Jim Bodden.

The appeal of MDM was that a million dollars provided under a special insurance policy would be the prize to any person who landed a blue marlin to break the weight record of the heaviest landed to date. Of course it is understood that the heaviest marlins are caught on the fringes of the Caribbean and the Atlantic; the Cayman Islands are far from those areas. Some heavy marlins are caught off the Caymans' shorelines reaching an average of 400 pounds. But of course these are far from the record-breaking monsters of over 1,300 pounds. MDM generated quite some offshore traffic from yachts and fishing boats attending. It also provided much fun and a great challenge to participants to beat records of the many species and classes of game fish for which prizes are offered. In 1998 the MDM Fishing Tournament folded after the promoter and president, Bill Rewalt, decided to retire. However the Cayman Islands Angling Club organized a replacement to MDM known as the Cayman Islands International Fishing Tournament. The first event took place between 25th April and 3rd May 1998 for just one week instead of the former one-month event. This new tournament also began with much enthusiasm and interest, as did the original MDM.

The Law School

Another government initiative, in a different field, is the Law School. As the local financial industry developed, it was seen that the time would come when, rather than continuing to recruit from external sources all the required lawyers as well as other qualified professionals and technical personnel, Caymanians should be encouraged to qualify in the various disciplines. This came forcefully to me when in early October 1972 I visited Washington, DC, and met with a friend who was working in a law firm in that city. Our first discussion was centred on a complaint by his firm about the poor legal service offered by the Cayman Islands to offshore business interests. On my return home I certainly made the allegation known among the local legal profession. At that stage most qualified lawyers came from outside Cayman, largely England. In early 1973 a local study began in order to determine where Cayman's students, interested in qualifying in the legal profession, could be trained. At the time Caymanian law students usually studied either in the United Kingdom or at the University of the West Indies in Barbados, where its law faculty is established.

Qualifications obtained either in the United Kingdom or from the University of the West Indies automatically entitled a Cayman student to admission as an attorney-at-law in these islands. It was also possible to qualify in other common law countries of the Commonwealth, such as in Canada, and be admitted in the Cayman Islands. In such cases it would only require the Judge of the Grand Court to satisfy himself that the applicant possessed a qualification comparable in standard, law, practice and procedure with persons qualified in Britain or in Jamaica. However, the Cayman Islands Law Society supported in principle a system of local articling to be followed by the writing of suitable local examinations based on the British legal system.

The matter became so interesting and important that at the end of 1975 the local government was requested to decide whether or not it would subscribe to the requirements of a regional governing body known as the Council of Legal Education of the West Indies. If Cayman subscribed to those requirements, it would not be permitted to send law students to study in countries other than the West Indies or to allow persons to practise in these islands not qualified through

247

the Council of Legal Education of the West Indies. The Cayman Islands saw that it was imperative in the circumstances for its students to continue to have the right to receive their legal education in any country of their choice inside or outside the Caribbean region. The islands also wished to retain the right to admit British-qualified lawyers when it was thought desirable to do so; that was of course against the rules of the Council of Legal Education of the West Indies.

From this juncture, the government took a keen interest in continuing its efforts to find the tools to develop a system of legal education in the Cayman Islands. By 1980 a foundation for the system was found and adopted in the Legal Practitioners (Amendment) Law and its regulations that came into operation at the beginning of 1981. The law prescribed that the system of training be a combination of practical experience in legal work under articles served in a local legal office and the successful passing of examinations in legal subjects set and marked by independent external examiners. This was an excellent proposed first step by which to establish the Law School. After the school was established it made wonderful progress in the years to follow.

In August 1981 Professor Paul Fairest, Head of the Law Department of Hull University, England, visited Grand Cayman by special invitation to discuss with the government and legal practitioners what should be done to provide a legal education system in the Cayman Islands. He saw evidence that the need was there for such a system locally; his report, directed to the local Legal Advisory Council, recommended the setting-up of a law school. The proposal was accepted and forwarded to the government. Apart from a few minor changes, the report of Professor Fairest was accepted in full. It provided the blueprint for the present Cayman Islands Law School.

Following acceptance of Professor Fairest's report, a Legal Advisory Council consisting of three members was appointed. The Chief Justice, Sir John Crampton Summerfield, KB, CBE, QC, was appointed chairman. He was formerly recruited in England in late 1979 and became Cayman's first Chief Justice. He was a Bermudan and in that country Sir John moved up in the service of the government to occupy the position of Judge of the High Court. He was the trial judge in Bermuda in early 1979 in the case involving the double murder of the Governor, Sir Richard Sharples, and his aide-de-camp, Hugh Sayers. The accused in these two cases was sentenced to death. A third murder also in Bermuda near the time of these two and in which Sir John was also involved was that of the Commissioner of Police, George Duckett, but there was no conviction in his case.

Continuing with the appointment of members to the Legal Advisory Council, the other two members were the Attorney General Michael Bradley and Ramon Alberga, QC. A school director, Peter Rowe, was appointed along with other staff.

The Cayman Islands Law School was opened in late 1982 in a tiny, unpretentious ante-room in the Law Courts Building with an enrolment of seven students. The Governor, Mr Peter Lloyd, officially opened the school. In attendance were Chief Justice Sir John Summerfield, Law Society President Mr Charles Adams, British MP Mr David Hunt, Mr Peter Rowe and the press. The Governor in his remarks said, 'This seems to be an historic day. I say that advisedly for I do not know of any other country with a population below 20,000 which has its own law school.' He also spoke of the ambition and imagination of those involved in putting together such an institution with its enormous need and value on the island.

President of the Law Society, Mr Charles Adams, said the society fully endorsed the establishment of the Law School. Its ultimate goal, he said, was to be recognized as a good training ground for lawyers, ranking with other established schools, 'as a good place for lawyers to be trained'. He said the pace of growth here in the past few years had made the move a necessary one and that his Law Society recognized the need for the opportunity for Caymanians to qualify legally starting in their own teaching institution. In his ending remarks he said, 'The Cayman Law School is a very well integrated teaching establishment that the islands, considering their size, can be proud of.'

In early January 1983, Professor Fairest returned to the islands, to see how the school was progressing and said he was happy with what he had seen. Morale was very high. The students were finding the course interesting and even those who were new to law had a very clear indication of what an attorney had to do. Moreover, he said, the attorneys who were supporting the scheme by accepting students as articled clerks, and thereby giving them practical experience, seemed to think it was working. He said in particular, 'A very great deal of credit is due to Mr Charles Adams, who first approached me in the United Kingdom about my coming out to report on the need for a law school. Mr Adams' continued support for the Law School from the time it was merely an idea to the present, has been invaluable. Much credit is also due to the Director of Legal Studies, Peter Rowe, who has accomplished so much in such a short time. It is necessary now for the Law School to look to the future. It is clear there is a great deal of interest on the part of Caymanians in law as a profession. We must therefore build on the success already achieved. In particular it must be made known that law in the Cayman Islands offers an opening to people presently in other professions or types of work.'

There was yet further progress required in order to allow local graduates to become better qualified by obtaining a law degree. In early 1985 Peter Rowe, former Director of Legal Studies here, wrote to Cayman's Chief Justice, Sir John Summerfield, on the subject of the law degree. Mr Rowe, who was then a senior lecturer in law at Liverpool University in England, mentioned his earlier position at Cayman's Law School and his strong views that Cayman law students should graduate with a law degree. This he said was the normal method of entry, in most countries, to the legal profession. He advised that he had written a paper on the subject and, if supported by Liverpool University, an external law degree at ordinary level would be conferred on Cayman students. The letter also reported that he had received support from his law faculty suggesting that he should proceed further with the idea.

On 18th December 1985 the local Legal Advisory Council met to consider the proposal from Liverpool University. The council strongly supported the proposal and advised the government accordingly. After official approval, the matter was forwarded to the Faculty Board of the University of Liverpool, where it was finally ratified on 5th February 1986. The Cayman Islands Law School then became an affiliated institution of the University of Liverpool.

Since then many of Cayman's law students have attained impressive distinctions both from the Cayman Law School and from the Liverpool University. The second year of operation of the University of Liverpool's Bachelor of Laws (Honours) degree was marked in 1992 with the Cayman Islands Law School admitting a further eight new students into that full-time programme. Also in 1992, three students graduated from the Attorney-at-Law Course, with a fourth graduate receiving the Bachelor of Laws degree with distinction. In 1993 five students graduated from the Attorney-at-Law Course, bringing to twenty-nine the total number of graduates since the first graduation ceremony in 1987.

The Community College

The Community College of the Cayman Islands is another teaching institution worth mentioning. It is a government-sponsored tertiary education system coming after secondary education, or third in rank before university entrance. The Community College, as it was originally named, was established in 1975 as a part-time schooling system.

For the next five years, from 1976, three other schools were also founded in Grand Cayman, the Trade School, the Hotel School and the Marine School. They were located at different sites and their supervision was the responsibility of the Ministry of Education and the Ministry of Tourism and Labour. In 1985, the government decided to centralize the administration of all public post-secondary educational institutions in the islands. The three schools, together with a secretarial/business studies section of the sixth form comprised of A level students, were amalgamated to form the Community College of the Cayman Islands.

In the mid-1970s, when consideration was being given to establishing a law school in Cayman, the thinking also pointed to the need for a local commercial college. At the time a very strong debate was taking place between governments of the Caribbean contributing to the University of the West Indies and the university itself, on the question 'Why should the university not give more thought to technical training and vocational guidance in its schools' curriculum?' After all, the countries of the Caribbean depended largely on economies requiring specialized knowledge and technical skills in subjects including banking, insurance, tourism, agriculture and manufacturing industries. Yet the university was continuing to concentrate efforts on its academic faculties.

Benson Ebanks, the former Minister of Education, and I represented the Cayman Islands at a meeting in Barbados with the University of the West Indies and the heads of Caribbean governments concerned with the subject matter. Out of those and future discussions, and with the support of the university, grew the urge to promote commercial colleges or technical institutions in the region. One such technical school was established by the university itself at Mona, Jamaica, and known as CAST, College of Arts, Science and Technology. Many Caymanians have graduated from that school, including Mr Heber Arch, Mrs Althea McLaughlin, Mr Ezzard Miller and Mrs Andrea Rankin.

The Community College of the Cayman Islands in 1987 received support from the government through the Legislative Assembly to be established as a semi-autonomous post-secondary educational institution. A mission statement followed indicating that the college would serve the educational needs of the Cayman Islands. Goals were set and the college continued moving forward and expanding into quite a sizeable school. Administration is by a board of governors consisting of ten members, including a chairman and a secretary, and also by an academic and advisory committee. Among the school's array of associate degree programmes, certificate programmes and much

251

more, is also a professional development programme that offers studies designed to allow persons employed in local industries to develop their professional skills. These studies are normally offered on a part-time or day release basis.

Radio and Television

Looking into other areas of local development in the 1970s, one that is of note is the establishment by the government of Radio Cayman Broadcasting System: it was officially opened in March 1976. The advent of the local radio system was the subject of prior discussions before its opening, between the local public and the government. At the time I actually became involved as Financial Secretary in promoting the government's interest in both radio and television. Eighteen years later, as a private citizen, I became involved in Cayman Television Service Ltd. (CTS) as a Director and shareholder; my son-in-law, Robert C. Bodden, is the majority shareholder and Chairman. CTS and CITN (Cayman Islands Television Network), also privately owned, are the only two current commercial television companies licensed by the Cayman government; both are managed by Weststar TV Ltd., owned by United States citizens and Caymanians. The services providing local television are hailed as leaders in the Caribbean. Weststar TV, built the facilities that resulted in a fine service housed in their newly built headquarters offices with very modern and expensive equipment and a full complement of staff. Local residents enjoy the service.

The importance of radio to Cayman was not difficult to understand. In earlier years each residential home in these islands was practically an isolated outpost of a disconnected world. Many families lived and died knowing a world that measured only a few miles in any direction. However, with modern development came improved homes and offices, air travel, electricity, telephone, international telecommunications and so much more. The population advanced through those various stages of development to a standard of living higher than in many other similar territories. By the mid-1970s people thought, 'Well, why not have our own radio broadcasting system as well, which would improve the quality of life by giving us our own facility to listen to world affairs and obtain general international knowledge both in spoken words and music?' In fact the services provided by radio and television have in modern times become much in demand as a social amenity, apart from the quest for local and international news and educational programmes.

The first attempt at establishing radio broadcasting in these islands was in early 1971, when the Bermuda Broadcasting Company was invited to do a feasibility study. Through the British government we were able to obtain the services of Roy Dunlop, MBE, who was at the time managing Radio Anguilla, to advise this government on the Bermuda proposals. The gist of Roy's report was that Cayman should set up its own commercial radio station rather than grant a franchise to an offshore entity, and pointed out that a private company, no matter how good its intention, would not necessarily be keenly concerned with service to local listeners. He also pointed out that television could be prohibitively expensive as well as technically difficult to provide for the three islands and should therefore be put in abeyance. Since Roy was a broadcasting manager and administrator rather than a technical person, this government sought further technical advice from the British government. A broadcasting engineer, Leslie Lester, was sent out by the Crown Agents to do a study. He produced in April 1972 a very extensive report covering all aspects of setting up a station, including architectural drawings of a station and quoting both estimated capital and recurrent costs.

When the Administration Building was lost to fire in 1972, all priorities had to be rearranged: the radio station proposal was therefore put on a back burner for the time being. In the meantime, once the public was aware that the country was interested in radio broadcasting, a number of private individuals and firms approached the government and expressed interest in developing the project. A few applicants also submitted their estimates of cost for the station: the figures ranged as low as $50,000. It was thought that such a system at that cost could be no more than a one-man, hole-in-the-wall operation, which would not be in accord with the developing standards being set here at the time. In spite of the eagerness of the private sector to become involved in local radio, the government decided in September 1973 that, due to the fragile regional political situation, broadcasting must come under strict government control. What many Caymanians were afraid of was that a communist country was sitting almost on our doorstep and therefore caution had to be exercised to avoid the facility falling into the wrong hands.

The government's decision immediately prompted the arrangement for a feasibility study to establish a broadcasting station to serve the three Cayman islands. Roy Dunlop's services were again requested. In February 1974 he arrived and brought along Tom Gutteridge, a Marconi radio engineer who was in the Caribbean on a visit at the time and who helped with much of the initial technical work. The report from that study was basically an update of the previous reports

253

but with particular reference to costs and selection of broadcasting frequencies. Following his report, Roy Dunlop brought to the islands Ray Smith, an experienced Grenadian radio engineer, to provide further technical expertise in the choice of broadcasting frequencies, siting of transmitters, the types of aerials to use and the various transmitter links. His report was submitted in June.

In late 1974 Roy was invited to take a three-year contract with this government first to guide the project through its various phases of construction and thereafter to assume the position of manager. The effective date was 1st January 1975 as he completed at the end of 1974 his five-year contract with the government of Anguilla. At the end of his assignment in Anguilla, Roy received the MBE from Her Majesty The Queen. He had joined the Foreign Office in London in 1961 and served in Nigeria, Guyana and Anguilla in the field of broadcasting.

The local portfolio responsible for radio and television was Communications and Works. After Roy had been here for nearly a week, in early 1975, I met him one morning near to my office on the second floor of the West Wind Building where the government had established headquarters after the burning of its Administration Building in June 1972. I asked him about progress on the broadcasting project. His reply was that for days he had been trying to secure an appointment with the Minister or his Principal Secretary in Communications and Works to get moving on the project; as yet he had not seen either of them. Roy was preparing to leave the island the next day. The problem was that the opposition, led by Jim Bodden, would not support the broadcasting scheme as a government project: they thought that because of cost and other factors, it should be passed to the private sector. This is why the political side of the government was perhaps reluctant to be more active in moving the project along. I invited Roy to see me in my office that afternoon so we could both set up a programme on which to proceed with the work.

At the meeting we identified and established all the necessary procedures by which the project should be pursued and also the estimated capital expenditure of CI$408,860 – far more than the $50,000 cost proposed by the private sector interests. I immediately sent a telegram to British Development Division in Barbados to inquire if they would recommend to the British government financial assistance with respect to the capital cost of the radio project. Two days later a positive reply came back, indicating that $222,700 would be considered in the form of a grant and $186,160 as an interest-free loan, both from the British government. The Cayman government would provide an amount of $100,000 for the first year recurrent cost. The next step was to obtain approval and financing for the project from the Finance Committee of the Legislative Assembly.

I arranged the meeting of the Finance Committee, at which there were five opposition members and five government supporters. As chairman of the committee I did not have a regular vote; however, I had a casting vote, only to be used in the case of a tie in the voting process. We argued the motion for two hours in heated debate with Jim Bodden's opposition team and then the question was put to the vote, but only when the five government supporters were present. Before the voting took place Jim Bodden rose and pleaded with the chair to be fair and give the benefit of the doubt to the opposition, as is sometimes the general practice in cases of equality of votes (for and against). My reply was that if the motion were not my own, maybe I would give some sympathetic consideration to the matter in that respect. In the records of the Legislative Assembly, that was perhaps the first occasion on which the chairman of the Finance Committee was obliged to use his casting vote to break a tie in the voting. I certainly had to use my casting vote to win what was virtually my own motion. (Readers should note that Finance Committee meetings were not open to the public then as they are now.)

In following the progress of the local radio broadcasting development, it suddenly dawned on me to inquire how far afield other countries would be able to hear Radio Cayman. Roy said that Geneva had approved a 2,000-watt transmitter and we would need to wait to judge its performance. I thought that a 2,000-watt station would produce a weak signal and one that could perhaps serve at most the three Cayman islands. I knew at the time that one of our favourite nearby radio stations in Miami operated on a 10,000-watt facility that produced an excellent reception. I therefore requested Roy to reapply for a 10,000-watt transmitter system; it was eventually approved. In the years to follow, Roy told me that he received letters from listeners as far away as Norway and Australia saying they heard Radio Cayman on the air and the reception was quite good.

Before Radio Cayman was opened I inquired about the long-term cost of operating the broadcasting facility and whether it would become self-supporting. Roy said that was not his instruction. I pointed out to him that as a matter of financial policy, and provided there were no particular reasons to consider otherwise, at least the future recurrent cost of operating the station should be covered by the new Broadcasting Department's own ability to produce an income from advertising revenue. I told him too that this was in fact a point we discussed when we first met. He should therefore organize a commercial advertising section in the station, to become permanent and to start operating from day one. He did exactly that and six years later the department became financially self-sufficient in its recurrent and capital cost, and later its revenue exceeded total costs.

Radio Cayman definitely found a niche in the temple of Cayman's social and economic development. The department, as any other in the government, had its problems from time to time but the important thing is that it offered a good and reliable service to the country; it certainly filled all its obligations very well. When Roy was leaving his Cayman position in January 1980 on retirement, he had this to say in describing his and his wife's stay in Grand Cayman: 'Our association with the government and people of Cayman has been a source of great satisfaction, and indeed a pleasure, all along the way. I have also enjoyed working with, and assisting from experience, where possible, the Caymanian staff of Radio Cayman. I think my wife will agree with me that the time spent in Cayman is the happiest of any of our overseas assignments. There is a stability here that is sometimes lacking in other countries.' We in Cayman were indeed happy to have had the invaluable services of Roy to develop and administer Radio Cayman all the way to maturity. Roy Dunlop is a name that will be long remembered in Cayman, not only for his expertise in radio broadcasting but also for his very pleasant and friendly attitude to all.

Computer Service

A government computer system was also developed in the 1970s. In 1974, having carefully observed the start of computerization in the private sector, I made contact with the British Development Division in Barbados to inquire if they would support under their aid programme the cost of a computer system for the Cayman government. I gave details of the grounds for the inquiry. Surprisingly, in a couple of days a positive reply was received. I then submitted the recommendation to Executive Council, only to be told that the government could not support the proposal then. I advised the British Government accordingly and requested that the matter be re-submitted at a later stage.

Four years later, when computers were rapidly overtaking manual tasks everywhere except in the government, I went back to the Executive Council with a strong case to develop a computer system for the government. I advised that in this age of advanced technology, the operation of the government could not continue to be serviced by difficult manual methods which were both time consuming and labour intensive. The tendency must be to aim for minimization of strains and maximization of output. Most of the departments of government, such as Immigration, Treasury, Companies Register and Ship Registration, were growing at a rapid pace and their accounting systems could not continue to be done manually. On that occasion, the council gave unanimous approval for the introduction of a computer service which was implemented in 1979. A small Burrows computer, partly financed by British aid at a cost of $10,000 was purchased: it completed successfully two important programmes, the 1979 Population Census and the 1980 Trade Statistics. However, early after the service was established, it became evident that the equipment did not have sufficient capacity to accommodate the increasing number of requests for its use.

In preparation for the new computer system, the government had recruited through the United Nations Development Programme the former Auditor General of Jamaica, Mr Rudolph V. Irvin ('Son' as we knew him). His main duties were to assist in setting up our computer systems for the production of management information: he also became involved in the Population Census and Trade Statistics exercises. Son was no stranger to Cayman because as Auditor General of Jamaica he was also External Auditor for the Cayman government accounts and had therefore visited here many times. He eventually became our long-term friend. He arrived in Cayman on 29th February 1980 to take up his UN appointment. He served a two-year contract period. The system also employed Cheryl Gorchik, an efficient manager.

In 1981, the government approved the purchase of a larger computer which could meet the various demands. The new digital computer was installed in October 1981 in a newly decorated and properly equipped office in the Administration Building. Steps to ensure its performance and service were taken by recruiting technical staff and establishing a Management Committee, which I chaired. The committee dealt with systems development, monitoring progress and ensuring maximum utilization. A computer consultant from the United Kingdom was also employed for the initial orientation period of the new system. In the years to follow, the system expanded and developed until it became the country's largest computer, servicing the entire government operation.

Population Census

Mention was made earlier that the first programme on the new computer was the Population Census taken in 1979. The regional population census of 1960 and 1970 was sponsored by the United Nations and organized by the Faculty of Social Services of the University of the West Indies. The Cayman Islands participated in both exercises and, although invited again to participate in the 1980 census, the government declined the invitation. The reasons were that there would be advantages if the Cayman government conducted the exercise itself: the time factor for completion would be greatly reduced and the data that would be most appropriate to local needs could be chosen here. In preparation for the census the government appointed through British Executive Services Overseas a Census Advisor, Mr Kenneth Digby.

The questionnaire used in conducting the census sought information on housing, population, employment, immigration, transportation, education, waste disposal and the number of Caymanians living overseas. The head count completed on 8th October 1979 indicated that there was a population of 16,677, including 663 visitors, in the three islands. Those figures revealed that the population of the islands had increased by 65.64 per cent in the past ten years, with the figure for the capital, George Town, actually doubling in that time. The total residents were divided into 8,113 males and 8,564 females.

In the case of the 1980 *Annual Trade Report*, the second programme assigned to the first computer, the exercise was successfully completed and published on 9th July 1981. The prime objectives of establishing government information systems were to develop and maintain comprehensive statistics for the benefit of the government and the public. With the ever-increasing demand for information, especially on imports and exports, it was decided to develop and process by computer trade statistics presented in a detailed manner based on international standards. The 1980 published report was produced from Customs records and revised by the Statistical Commission of the United Nations and modified to meet requirements in the Cayman Islands. Imports and exports for 1980, according to the report, were CI$85.826 million and CI$2.227 million respectively.

In April 1979 a seminar was held here attended by a group of 50 scientists, engineers, sales promoters, bankers and financial advisors. The purpose was to unveil the marvels of a chemical substance which, according to the promoters, when mixed with gas would produce a fuel offering greater mileage and less cost. It carried a slogan that said, 'Easing of the world's energy problems'. I was requested to

258

give the welcome address. One of the speakers for the seminar was a United States Congressman, Mr Guy Vander Jagt, who held a seat on the United States' powerful House Ways and Means Committee. Before the meeting got under way, Mr Jagt took an interest in looking at Cayman's financial operation and budget surpluses. In his opening remarks he paid me tribute when he told delegates that I could be utilized in Washington to balance America's top-heavy budget.

In approaching 31st March 1982 I began feeling a tinge of loneliness for the Civil Service, a government institution in which I had served a period spanning 36 years and which I would shortly vacate. I was leaving a portfolio, Finance and Development, in which I had spent 17 years in a static position. This was no fault of the government's. I had been offered promotion during that period but declined the offer on personal grounds: a commitment not to quit the position until I had completed a special job in my portfolio.

The offer for promotion had come in 1977 from London through Governor Thomas Russell. It was at the time when Desmond Watler, the Chief Secretary, served notice of his retirement from the government; his position was offered to me. I told the Governor I would need at least a week to consider the offer, although I could have told him then what was in my mind. It was quite clear to me from at least 12 years before that I was destined for one purpose in the government, to remain in charge of finance and the economy until the Cayman Islands achieved the goal set in December 1965: for these islands to become one of the leading offshore financial centres of the world. The one-week delay for a reply to the offer of taking over the position of Chief Secretary had scarcely expired when the Governor was back to me for a decision and advised that London was pressing him for a reply. Without hesitation I told him the decision was to deny myself the gracious offer for promotion. This was based on my plans as Financial Secretary to build the Cayman Islands into a world-class offshore financial centre. The process was far from completion; if I walked away from the position at this stage it was my candid opinion that a replacement either locally or from overseas would be difficult to come by in order to continue and finish the building process. In fact other Caribbean islands were also scanning the horizon for people who could assist their economic development largely along the lines of the Cayman offshore financial industry, but to my knowledge they have not yet succeeded.

Refusal of the promotion haunted me for a while. I thought at times, why deny myself the second most senior position in government and in fact the most senior appointment a local Civil Servant could attain then, and now, as long as Cayman remains a Crown Colony? The appointment of a Governor is made by the Secretary of State and ratified by Her Majesty The Queen. Governors by British appointment will continue as Head of State for the foreseeable future unless there are constitutional changes to allow local appointments. I wondered too who else would have refused such a promotion. However, soon after making the decision, my regrets disappeared, as in the cases of the offers in 1954 and 1964. After subsequent events, including service in the elected government, I knew I had achieved what I set out to do. According to popular publications in 1988, Cayman had moved near to the pinnacle of success as a world leader in offshore financial services.

On 20th August 1981 I wrote to the Governor, Mr Thomas Russell, serving notice that because I would reach 60 years of age on 18th January 1982, I was obliged under the Pensions Law to retire from the Civil Service at that age. However, I requested departure from the service on 31st March 1982 since the Governor would be leaving on retirement at the end of December 1981 and the new Governor would take over shortly afterwards. On 24th August 1981 the Governor replied and approved my retirement effective 1st April 1983, with one-year pre-retirement leave starting 1st April 1982. The long leave was awarded to compensate for the amount of vacation leave lost over the previous years because of my heavy workload.

I delivered my last budget address to the Legislative Assembly on 18th November 1981. In it I paid tribute to political leaders, now deceased, with whom I had worked: Clifton Hunter, William Farrington and Ashton Reid. As my tribute to them indicated, they were three fine gentlemen and true representatives of the people, men who possessed rare qualities of humbleness and respect and who were always strong advocates of what they thought was best for the country. I also paid tribute to the staff of my portfolio, the Civil Service, members of the Executive Council and the Legislative Assembly. To my staff I said, 'I am very deeply appreciative of the unfailing loyal support I received from all officers regardless of rank. I am very proud of them all for they are fine people who possess sterling qualities and who have done a wonderful job, many times under adverse circumstances and occasionally with public criticism.'

I went on to thank other members of the Civil Service for their co-operation and assistance over the years. I reminded them that they had been paid a fine tribute in 1962 by Sir Kenneth Blackbourn, the last English Governor-General of Jamaica, who was also, before Jamaica's independence, Governor of the Cayman Islands. Sir Kenneth told civil servants that he had visited many countries in the

260

Caribbean and elsewhere and that there was no doubt in his mind that the Cayman Islands Civil Service was the finest he had seen anywhere. I too would say after my years of experience dealing with other governments, especially in this region of the world, that we do have a fine Civil Service and every care should be taken to preserve it.

I thanked members of the Executive Council and the Legislative Assembly for the support they gave me which brought much ease to my work. Ever since I entered the assembly in 1965 and the Executive Council in 1972, there was a cordial relationship between the members and myself, which resulted in a strong and meaningful financial administration for the government. The country as a result profited enormously, as seen in the years to follow when it developed into a thriving offshore financial centre and tourism destination. In the process of growth and development of the economy, the government ensured that all its business deals and negotiations were transacted with due caution and in a clean atmosphere.

In early 1982 I began my rounds of farewell visits to the public and private sectors which included one to Cayman Brac from Thursday 25th February to Sunday 28th February. My wife accompanied me on the visit. The District Commissioner, Mr James Ryan, kindly prepared the programme. On Friday we travelled to Little Cayman and toured the island before returning to Cayman Brac that evening to attend a reception arranged in my honour by the civil servants of the island. The party, which was attended by past and present politicians as well, was marked by speeches by the District Commissioner and Mr Trevor Foster, a former elected member of the Executive Council, and by the presentation of a beautiful gift to me. In reply I spoke of the progress made by Cayman Brac in recent times. I went on to mention that seven years earlier I made a statement in my budget address that the sister islands were then still struggling for some form of activity to broaden the base of their economy and to activate and pursue social interests.

I made mention of the oil transfer operation off Little Cayman and its activity within the two smaller islands, starting in 1978. Those had in fact reversed the earlier fear of business stagnation, declining economic activity and a dwindling population, many of whom moved to Grand Cayman to seek jobs and become involved in new business. All of that has today turned to enthusiasm over economic and social growth resulting in a booming situation. The year 1980 was described as the most prosperous in the history of the two smaller islands. This improved financial situation was largely due to the products of economic activity from the oil transfer operation together with the fair-sized sums contributed by the government to capital development. However, full credit to progress must go to the people who live here and who made many sacrifices to achieve the glowing position they now enjoy. I also paid special tribute to the public spiritedness of the residents in such admirable endeavours as setting up their electricity supply, starting work on their airport and building their hospital. All those efforts by the people resulted in great achievements that opened the way to later progress and development.

Mention was made of the beautiful gift (an office desk pen set made of caymanite) I received in Cayman Brac. Perhaps I should add that in Grand Cayman, the government, the Civil Service and the private sector presented many gifts to me. Two I want to mention in particular are, first, a bridge table and four chairs specially made in England. The gift came from the Bankers' Association and was chosen because of my interest in the game. The second special gift, a Patek Phillip clock, engineered by the factory in Switzerland, was flown from Geneva via Montreal and Miami to Grand Cayman on 31st March 1982 in time to be presented before I stepped out of office. The gift came from Swiss Bank and Trust Corporation. It was chosen because they called me 'a clock collector'. I have indeed been associated with clocks and watches for a long time.

Before stepping down from my office of Financial Secretary, I thought that some indication should be passed to the Governor, Mr Lloyd, concerning my impression of staff and other matters affecting the Portfolio of Finance and Development. The memorandum, dated 25th March 1982 and written in confidence, contained six pages and covered many subjects. It was copied to my successor designate, Mr Thomas Jefferson. Speaking generally, I said:

> My successor is inheriting a well organized portfolio. While there may be a few weaknesses here and there, which is inevitably the case in any large organization, by and large it does have a group of very dedicated and hard working officers of all ranks especially those in the senior grades. Any success that I might have claimed over my 17 years as Head of the Portfolio is due of course to the very able and strong support I received at all times from my staff.

I then went on to make comments on all important sections of the portfolio, such as Customs, Treasury, Savings Bank, Currency Board, Registrar of Companies, Bank Inspection, Insurance, Audit, Computer, Statistics and, lastly, my own office. The Governor in reply thanked me for being so thoughtful in presenting so clear a picture of what

I was leaving behind for his benefit and that of my successor.

I cannot end this chapter without mentioning one of the delights and pleasures of an experience shared not only by us in the Cayman Islands, but by the entire world. It was in July 1969 as we here in this small part of the globe were poised to enjoy the beginning of what promised to become Cayman's most prosperous financial era. I was standing in front of my home on South Church Street in the South Sound area, looking at a full moon shining brightly in a clear and beautiful sky and imagining I could see what was happening up there. That was the great day when man first landed on the moon during the historic Apollo 11 moon landing. It was Neil Armstrong, leader of the American spaceship team, who was the first man to set foot on the moon. Following him was Dr Edwin E. 'Buzz' Aldrin (Doctor of Science). We in Cayman had the pleasure of Dr Aldrin's visit in June 1980 when he and other associate doctors attended a medical seminar at the Holiday Inn Hotel along the Seven Mile Beach on the Medicine and Physiology of Scuba Diving. Dr Aldrin was a featured speaker at the seminar because of his experience of weightlessness in space, similar to that experienced in diving.

The 1969 moon landing was the beginning of a new era in space exploration: that historic event also coincided with the beginning of a new economic era for the Cayman Islands.

14

Air Services

One subject that created much interest during the 1960s was the growing need for local air support services to assist the growing economic and social development of these islands. Eventually Cayman Airways Ltd. (CAL) was established as a local entity. Since its inception the company has been a subject on which it seems almost every resident and many visitors have expressed some opinion at one time or another. Because of this general interest, and because my own involvement continued from my Civil Service years into my political career, it is appropriate that air services with its basic story, Cayman Airways, be discussed in a chapter of its own.

CAL was incorporated in 1968 with an equity capital allocated in the majority (51 per cent) to the government of the Cayman Islands and the balance (49 per cent) to the Costa Rican Airline, Lineas Aereas Costarricenses SA (LACSA). Expertise and flight equipment for CAL were provided by LACSA. In October 1976 the government increased its shareholding in CAL to 60 per cent while LACSA's was decreased to 40 per cent. The cost of the government's increased shares was charged to the profits of CAL. In fact the airline progressed so well after extending the second arm of its international operation to Miami on 3rd May 1972 (the first was to Jamaica on 15th December 1968) that it declared a dividend. This government's share was CI$68,850. That dividend was virtually the first and last paid by CAL out of the profits of a non-subsidized operation.

The board of CAL was comprised of six members, three selected by the Cayman Islands government and three by LACSA. The first Chairman was Cayman's Director of Civil Aviation, Mr J.V. Verran, and when his term of office ended with the government in 1971, I succeeded him as Chairman and served until mid-1977. The new DCA, Mr John Ellison, continued as a member of the board. The other Cayman government director was the Attorney General, the

Honourable Gerald E. Waddington. The manager of CAL, Mr Norman Bodden, was Secretary of the Board. LACSA's three directors were Captain Otto Escalante, Chief Executive; Roberto Morales, Executive Vice President of Production; and Orlando Ramirez, Executive Vice President of Marketing.

Before the creation of CAL, LACSA was the only airline to offer a service to these islands. It also owned Cayman Brac Airways, which operated an inter-island service between Grand Cayman, Cayman Brac and Little Cayman. As time went on and the islands moved on with their economic development, the need was clearly seen for a local and efficient air service that could expand into the international markets. Again LACSA was the only airline to come forward and propose to the Cayman Islands government that CAL be established in a joint venture partnership with the local government and themselves.

CAL started as a domestic carrier serving the three islands and by the following year, 1969, it had expanded into the international market with flights to Jamaica. In April 1971 British West Indian Airways Ltd. (BWIA) serving these islands on the routes between Kingston, Cayman and Miami, gave this government six months' notice of its intention to suspend operation to Cayman. The grounds were that they planned to convert to larger aircraft that Owen Roberts Airfield could not accommodate at the time. In fact BWIA was converting to the jet age and Grand Cayman's airfield was not yet up to that standard.

CAL, immediately after BWIA's withdrawal notice, began preparation for the Cayman–Miami service. On 3rd May 1972, CAL, a British carrier under the Bermuda II Agreement between the United States and Britain, expanded its operation to Miami, Florida. On CAL's inaugural flight in the early afternoon of 3rd May, an incident occurred which I must mention. As the flight neared Cuba with a full load of passengers, including government and private sector invited guests, it ran into air turbulence and suffered an enormous fall of several hundred feet. Among the invited guests on board were the Governor, Mr Kenneth Crook, and his wife, members of the Executive Council and the Legislative Assembly and their spouses; in fact the only senior official not on board was Mr Dennis Foster, who remained home as Acting Governor. At the time of the air turbulence the cabin staff had just started the arranged reception. Hostesses found themselves struggling about with their trays; glasses flew to the ceiling and across the cabin. Loud shouts came from some of the passengers that caused near panic among others on the flight. Although all those on board became frightened during the fall, no casualties were sustained. In the case of an earlier LACSA flight from San Jose, Costa Rica, to Miami, Florida, via Grand Cayman, however, on reaching a point off the Nicaraguan coast, the aircraft ran into air turbulence and as a result it suffered an enormous fall that caused the death of one person, a Mr Castro, who was editor and one of the owners of the *La Prensa* publication of Costa Rica. A few other persons on the flight also received injuries from the fall. A well-known Cayman sea captain, Allie O. Ebanks, was on the same LACSA flight; he escaped injury.

Six years later, in 1978, CAL established a third scheduled service to Houston, Texas. In 1984 a scheduled service was also established between Miami and the Turks and Caicos Islands but this was discontinued the following year because of economic reasons. By 1985 CAL had expanded into charter operations in order to improve equipment utilization. At the time CAL operated its services with two Boeing 727–200 aircraft. Those were fine machines and well known for their tremendous public appeal. Besides the safety feature of being equipped with three engines, the configuration of the aircraft allowed for a large freight compartment which provided a fine contribution to its revenue-earning capacity.

In 1977 the government became quite ambitious in the airline business and proceeded to purchase LACSA's shares to become full owners of CAL. To say the least, I was not very impressed at the time by this decision. I knew all too well some of the difficult times CAL had experienced in the past nine years of this partnership and on every occasion LACSA did the rescue operation without a charge to CAL. Who else would have performed those services free of charge? I remembered during the economic recession of 1975 that the share capital of CAL was completely diminished on its balance sheet. When the situation was discovered I went to a directors' meeting in San Jose, Costa Rica, and announced that unless the shareholders were prepared to inject fresh capital into CAL the board would need to put the airline into liquidation. LACSA's Chief Executive, Captain Otto Escalante, whom I had always regarded as the essence of a gentleman, told the board, with the strong support of his other two directors, 'CAL will continue to fly regardless of the situation. We will purchase all the vacant seats of CAL for the next year of its scheduled services until the airline's finances improve.' Fortunately, CAL's finances improved within the year. Those were the excellent people that the government had as partners in CAL.

The public was not very convinced that the government should own CAL outright nor that it was a good move in the country's best interest. One could hear views expressed such as, 'The anticipated ending of CAL's agreement with LACSA is looked upon as a reckless, retrograde step.' It was also said that even if the government managed to obtain the services of another plane, it would cost the country more money and the people higher taxation. Indeed, in July 1992 a statement to the press was made by a minister in the Executive Council to the effect that the government's total capital injection into CAL at that point was CI\$45 million. Furthermore, in the early 1970s, while Chairman of CAL, I had discussed on a few occasions with Captain Otto Escalante of LACSA exactly how he saw CAL's future as an international airline. He drew an analogy between Pan American Airways and LACSA. He said that LACSA's operation had begun with Pan Am part-owning LACSA, just as LACSA part-owned CAL. Pan Am provided expertise, technical assistance and guidance to LACSA until the airline grew to become capable of caring for itself. At that stage Pan Am withdrew completely and handed over the operation to LACSA: it then became a truly national airline fully owned and operated by Costa Rica. Otto then said, 'That was exactly the same plan we had in mind for CAL.' I thought that such a plan was just marvellous, for no small territory like Cayman can suddenly own and operate its own airline, because of the very high cost involved.

I resigned from CAL in 1977 when the government purchased LACSA's shares in CAL to become full owners of the local airline. In November 1984, when I was Minister for Development and Natural Resources, the Governor, Mr Lloyd, requested as a special favour that I take over the chairmanship of CAL again. This was because of the airline's serious operating losses and the need to improve its financial operation. In fact when I took over as Chairman in 1984, my first job was to do an assessment of the airline's financial position. Following that examination, a press release was issued, signed by the four elected members of the Executive Council: Norman W. Bodden, Minister for Tourism, Aviation and Trade, whose portfolio included CAL; Captain Charles L. Kirkconnell, Minister for Communication, Works and Development; Benson O. Ebanks, Minister for Health, Education and Social Services; and myself, dealing with the Portfolio of Development and Natural Resources. The release was published in early December 1984. In brief, it stated that according to the uncertified balance sheet as at 30th June 1984, the accounts revealed an accumulated deficit of US\$16,237,553. The accounts for the following year also revealed a further accumulated deficit for the period July to October 1984 of US\$1,271,576, or a total deficit to 31st October of US\$17,509,129. Secondly, although cash in hand at 31st October 1984 was

US$301,995, outstanding bills on the same date amounted to US$4,758,000. Since amounts due to government for landing fees and interest and principal repayments by CAL were not included, the debt was nearer US$6 million.

During my election campaign in late September 1984, I made early contact with Swissair in Zurich, the Swiss national airline, in an endeavour to find a suitable team of consultants to examine CAL. The reason for that early move was to get prepared for the eventuality of my team winning the General Election and having to take over CAL, as it was then known generally that the financial affairs of the airline were in an awful state. We wanted, if successful in the election, an early examination of CAL in the specific areas of financial, technical and administrative weaknesses conducted by consultants who were capable of producing a factual and unbiased report. Swissair was chosen as I had always regarded it a fine, professionally operated and financially successful airline.

The first visit from Swissair in connection with the CAL exercise was by Mr Konrad Lindermann, Vice President of Cooperative Projects, on 24th November 1984. Then in mid-December 1984 the Honourable Norman Bodden, the Executive Council member with portfolio responsibility for CAL, and I met in Miami with two other consultants from Swissair for preliminary discussion on the terms of reference for the study and the cost involved. Those two gentlemen, Mr Willie Gantner, Division Manager of Cooperative Projects, and Mr Erik Zenker, Manager of Methods Economics, arrived in Grand Cayman on 6th January 1985; they formed the Swissair Team for the study of CAL. The work, scheduled for four weeks, was followed by the team's report on 25th March 1985. It was fully implemented except for one recommendation, that for economic reasons the two Boeing 727–200 aircraft be replaced by the B737–217. The report pointed out that the 727 was a medium-to-long range aircraft, while all CAL's routes are short-range, including charters, apart of course from the Houston route, which is medium-range. The report also pointed out that the 737 was the best-selling jet in the world because of its twin engines, considered the most productive, which made the aircraft very economic in its class. Of course, while Jim Bodden and I did not agree on many issues, he had my full support for leasing the two 727s, considered an excellent choice both for safety and public appeal and also for their freight-carrying capacity. What was more, they were practically new equipment when leased from Air Florida in March 1982 when that airline was folding its operation.

My advice to the government was that I could not agree with the change of equipment as recommended by Swissair. The report, I pointed out, stated that the potential loss of revenue from not using the 727 would be more than compensated for by using the smaller aircraft, which would also be more suitable in developing possible new markets. This presentation was not merely the team's own belief, but a result of their computerized tests carried out by experts in Geneva. The reaction from my colleagues in the government was that if changes were not made then, they would have to be undertaken sometime in the near future. My reply was, 'Sufficient unto the day is the evil thereof.' I contacted the team in Zurich and advised them of my problem in accepting the change of equipment recommended. They immediately revisited Cayman and went through the recommendations with me once more. In the end they told me that in my position as political representative for the subject, I had the prerogative to accept or reject any recommendation. They also agreed that the 727 were fine aircraft with much appeal to the travelling public for their safety and other attractive features. They then advised that if Cayman felt comfortable holding on to the 727 and bearing the cost of their operation, by all means to do so. I carried the Swissair report to the board of directors of CAL with the recommendations and the results of my discussion with the team a few days before, and suggested that all the recommendations be approved except the one dealing with change of equipment. The submission won the unanimous approval of the board and also the government's acceptance.

After the report was accepted, I began examining areas of possible cost-cutting in the operation. One that came clearly to the surface was the cost of buying aviation fuel locally as opposed to in Miami, where it was less expensive and where the fleet of aircraft could easily refuel. I called in Mr John A. Davis, Texaco Caribbean Inc. Area Manager, from Kingston, Jamaica, for a discussion of the fuel prices. Texaco supplied at the time all Cayman's aviation fuel. Mr Davis agreed with my concern and I requested him to write back to me in ten days with a decision as to whether or not he was prepared to match the prices in Cayman to Miami's. If the reply were in the negative CAL would certainly move its refuelling to Miami. I somehow had no fear that Texaco would increase Miami's price to match ours. Nine days after our meeting I had a telephone call from the Area Manager advising that the fuel price adjustment in Cayman to match Miami's price was approved with immediate effect.

After the successful Texaco fuel price adjustment, considered a tremendous financial saving to CAL and, for that matter, all aircraft refuelling in Cayman, I proceeded to strengthen CAL's administration. The Swissair study was followed by the employment of two overseas consultants, one in finance and the other in marketing, in order to strengthen those important areas of the operation. Of course, as in the case of the Swissair team, those consultants in finance and marketing were engaged and approved before the General Election in November 1984 through British Executive Services Overseas in London. Following those studies, a new salary grading in the administration was introduced with retroactive effect to 1st January 1985. Three local employees, Ernie Bodden, Mike Adam and Charles Winton, with whom I had previously discussed, on my beach under the trees, my proposed recommendations for their elevation in CAL to replace senior offshore employees, were placed in top positions on three months' probation. It appeared that the subsequent administration had no use for local senior officials in CAL. Mike stuck it out; Ernie, a fine acting head of administration, quit some years later after being embarrassed; and Charles could not find a suitable position. New staff orders and rules were introduced, together with the establishment of guiding principles by which the airline would operate. These indicated CAL's importance as set by its duties, policy and purpose of existence: those principles, after approval by the shareholders, were documented.

In late 1984 our new government discovered that a two-year moratorium against a second United States carrier wishing to serve on the Miami–Cayman route would expire on 31st March 1985. We immediately appealed through the British government for extension of the moratorium under the Bermuda II Agreement. Further extension was extremely important for the survival of CAL. I also followed up this appeal for extension with a visit to Washington via Miami, where on 16th December 1984 Norman Bodden and I met the two Swissair specialists for discussion on the terms of reference and cost of the CAL study. The meeting was successful and the agreed study would begin early in January 1985. At that stage my Principal Secretary met me in Miami, along with Minister Bodden's Director of Civil Aviation, Sheldon Hislop, and Principal Secretary, Harding Watler. The party of five journeyed on to Washington on the evening of 17th December, where we were met by John Angell of the British Embassy; also there to see us were two Washington attorneys associated with our mission, Messrs Steve Boynton and Richard Parsons. The visit to Washington was to deal specifically with two subjects, conservation and aviation.

The visit to Washington covered two days, 17th to 19th December. First on the programme of Tuesday 18th December, after a business breakfast with the two US attorneys and our group of five from the Cayman Islands, was the signing of a conservation agreement, about which more will be said later.

The Cayman team, joined by the Managing Director of CAL, Mr Tino Gonzales, attended the British Embassy in Washington at 11 a.m. for briefing on the Bermuda II moratorium relating to Eastern Airlines' application to fly the Miami–Cayman route. The briefing was followed by lunch at the embassy, after which we proceeded to the State Department and Department of Transportation in company with an embassy official for preliminary discussions. The Americans held tight to what they regarded as their right to support Eastern's application, but we also put forward strong grounds to discourage the granting of the application on 1st April 1985 after the end of the first two-year moratorium. The Americans could not commit themselves on the issue at that early stage, so the matter was left in abeyance for further study and negotiation. The meetings in defence of CAL's survival were quite interesting and we departed Washington leaving behind a very pleasant atmosphere. By Thursday 20th December we were back home. I personally felt that the visits to both Miami and Washington were useful. The continued effort to extend the moratorium beyond 31st March 1985 was left in the hands of the British Embassy in Washington. However, we waited until early March and after receiving no communication on the matter, the Minister, Norman Bodden, and I were excused from an ongoing important meeting of the Legislative Assembly and departed for London on 7th March 1985.

On the afternoon of 8th March we attended a meeting in London at the Ministry of Transport that had been previously arranged by the Foreign and Commonwealth Office. The meeting was an attempt to try and sort out our concern over the delay in receiving a communication with regard to our request for an extension of the moratorium with regard to Eastern Airlines' application to fly the Miami–Cayman route. We requested that a schedule be prepared and sent to the British Embassy in Washington with dates for approaching the State Department in Washington as follow-ups on Cayman's requested extension of the moratorium. In the meantime I had a reliable private contact in Washington who kept checking on the US government each day for possible progress on the subject; of course, he also had a personal interest in our effort to extend the restriction against Eastern joining the other two carriers on the Miami–Cayman route.

Finally the good news came in on Friday 29th March at about 7 p.m. My contact in Washington advised me that the American government had considered the Caymans' case for extension of the moratorium and had granted the request for a further two-year period. On Monday 1st April I mentioned the approval to the Governor, Mr Lloyd, and to the Minister of Aviation, Mr Bodden. I could see that

271

they were of two opinions: one, 'Is it really true, for today, 1st April is known traditionally as "all fools' day": could what the Minister is telling us be a tomfoolery, a joke?' The other could have been: 'Oh well, why not keep the results quiet until the official notification is received.' All the Caymans' airlines and the government's civil aviation anxiously awaited the results: it did not reach Cayman until the second week in April. My information was in fact quite correct. We were very delighted at the efforts of the British government in dealing so expeditiously with the matter. We were also quite pleased at the kind thoughts of the United States government in favourably considering our request, a matter so vitally important to the financial welfare and survival of the national airline and also to our second carrier, Republic Airline of the United States.

I should mention, in closing the story of CAL, an extremely considerate act on my part towards the airline just before I exited the Civil Service on 31st March 1982. As Financial Secretary and Chairman of Finance Committee, I knew Jim had lease-purchased two B727 200 aircraft from Air Florida at a cost of US$20.5 million. He sold the lease on CAL's BAC 1–11 aircraft for US$4 million, thereby leaving a shortfall of US$16.5 million on the B727s deal. In the circumstances, the government lent CAL on 29th March 1982 US$9 million, and the balance of US$7.5 million was the subject of a loan from the Royal Bank of Canada. Jim talked about the need to build an aircraft hangar and an administration building for CAL, but with the airline's debt at the bank he was unable to meet the additional financing. Furthermore the debt at the bank would ultimately be the government's responsibility as the owner of CAL. In mid-March 1982, in the spirit of my former strong support for CAL, and knowing the satisfactory financial position of the government at the time, I moved and obtained approval of the Finance Committee for an advance to CAL of CI$14 million (US$16,800,00). That amount was to settle the balance owing on the lease-purchase of the two B727s. It was assumed that Jim could then find the financial means to build his hangar and administration building. He certainly did move on with those two developments following the windfall cash advance to CAL. As I presented the motion, Jim could not believe his ears and asked me to repeat what I had said.

My last important involvement with CAL before I resigned from its board of directors at the end of 1985 was the inauguration of its Cayman–Tampa, Florida, air route on Monday 16th December. The occasion was marked by a ceremony at the Tampa International Airport. Over 40 local government and business officials and guests attended the function, including our Governor, Mr Peter Lloyd, who performed the act of cutting the celebration cake. The Minister for Tourism, Aviation and Trade, Mr Norman Bodden, and I were also in attendance. The route to Tampa was more or less reopening the long past trading connection between Cayman and Tampa in the days of sailing vessels, which ended when, due to more modern cargo and passenger-carrying facilities, the connection was removed to Miami. However, Tampa to us was always a quiet and attractive seaport that for many decades had become the home of many Caymanians, and therefore the area continued to be a desirable spot in the United States for us. The re-entry of CAL to Tampa in December 1985 was hailed and supported by all in Cayman as an excellent move.

At the end of 1985, I resigned the position of chairman of CAL and was succeeded by Mr Arthur Hunter, OBE. My portfolio was quite loaded with many important projects requiring urgent attention. They had been partly neglected because of my involvement with CAL. However, the airline progressed quite well for the rest of my political administration through to the end of 1988. Sadly, however, shortly after I exited the government the leases of the two 727s were sold by the new government and replaced by the lease of two 737s, just as the Swissair team had suggested in 1985. That move, to say the least, was only to place more of a financial burden on the owners, the Cayman Islands government. As stated earlier, the airline's accounts to mid-November 1984, when I took over as chairman of the board, revealed a total accumulated loss of $14.7 million (US$17.5 million). Seven years later, however, a statement on CAL's financial position by a member of the government indicated that the airline's indebtedness had by then exceeded $40 million.

The story of CAL will be ongoing as long as the government can continue to provide its subsidy. However, the real purpose behind the government's strong support of its national carrier is to guard against the day when, because of national economic disaster, all other foreign carriers might desert their services to these islands. Naturally CAL would be the only guaranteed standby airline to provide the local service in such an eventuality. With this thought in mind, I knew from the time I became a founding director in 1968, followed by many years as the chairman, that the Caymanian public would take much interest in the affairs of their national airline. That was not merely because CAL is locally owned and provides an important service, but also because it is regarded as a national emblem that enhances and projects the image of the Cayman Islands abroad, and especially to the visitors who come to these islands flying the national carrier.

PART IV

A CHANGE IN FOCUS

15

Prelude to Politics

After retiring from the Civil Service and exiting public office on 31st March 1982, I felt rather strange in some respects. It was a feeling I soon appreciated would have been the norm in any such circumstances. Nevertheless, the slight change was not disturbing to the extent of causing me to be unmindful of the nearly 37 years I spent in the government's service. Those years were difficult to forget, especially the mistakes, criticisms and censures which were often the teachers that led the way through strenuous times to provide the crowning of those years with pleasure, delight and satisfaction.

Prior to my retirement and after delivering the last of 14 budget addresses on 18th November 1981, I was quizzed by the press regarding my views on Cayman's financial, economic and social growth. Throughout this stage of the country's development and during the years that I occupied the hot seat of Financial Secretary, there had been undoubtedly enormous changes. I began by stating:

> If anyone is looking for treasure or for a quiet rest he should perhaps visit Cayman, the islands time forgot until a few decades ago when they began transformation into an internationally renowned offshore financial centre. The support services offered here are very prompt, efficient and reliable and provide the attractions to investors to look at Cayman for its clean, healthy and attractive business and social atmosphere. Because of this investment climate, new business is constantly flowing to the Cayman Islands. We have always welcomed investors who proved reliable and even invited them to become our partners in the local activities of their choice. Cayman is known as a centre where business flows unmolested and where well-known hospitality awaits everyone.
>
> Traditionally the islands have always been free of any form of

direct taxes such as income tax, a redeeming position that certainly established the country's status as an offshore business haven. The attraction of investors to Cayman has been phenomenal, especially in the last decade, and this is not due solely to the environment created by the absence of direct taxes. Other attractions were also political stability, friendliness of the people and the government towards everybody, and banking confidentiality instituted by local laws to protect the interests of individuals and institutions admitted to do business here. Political stability relates in part to the constitutional Crown Colony status with Britain introduced 20 years ago. That status was looked upon then, and now as we near the end of the twentieth century, as a heritage of the people of Cayman to safeguard and ensure that self-government or independence does not creep in through the back door and into the system of government. If significant constitutional development did take place, the current strong economy largely supported by the dependable British link providing Cayman's 'Whitehall system' of business would weaken.

In fact I remembered speaking to the public through the *Cayman Times* in early December 1981 and saying that the British link was the key to Cayman's economic success. In the statement I said:

Most countries of the British Commonwealth, small and large alike, have been struck forcefully by the fever of internal self-government and independence, but the Cayman Islands have never even dreamed such a misfortune. What I have always asked is whether any of those countries, especially the small ones, can produce any genuine proof of success in their venture into advanced constitution. The response has quite often been negative. Our Crown Colony status and constitutional link with Great Britain is the key to our political stability and to international confidence in the business offered by the Cayman Islands. We hope to retain the present status quo for many years to come. The present position gives us the assurance of hope for the future. The good performance of the economy of any country will depend on political and social stability, for no business can survive where there is constant change of policies.

Back in December 1964, when the *Tradewinds* newspaper was first published, an editorial was written entitled 'Of The Future'. I quote below a portion of the presentation dealing at that point in time with the islands' future regarding thoughts of constitutional independence:

We believe that the people of these islands should ponder long and carefully before accepting such a change which we believe shows no promise of betterment. We should not think that the Colonial Office would oppose more independence for these islands. We believe, on the contrary, that they would welcome the chance to be able to close their files on the Cayman Islands and be relieved of all responsibility with respect to them. We believe the future will be better served by the politicians devoting selfless effort to the improvement of these islands as a Colony of Her Majesty than by trying to selfishly bring to themselves more pomp and circumstances and power. And to say nothing of money which would of necessity come out of your pockets and mine.

The article also said in the opening paragraphs, 'We are a very small community, both in area and population. We have very limited resources and are seriously handicapped by generations of a woeful inadequacy of education, but we do have wonderful people, charming, polite and industrious. We have magnificent beaches, a beneficial climate and exceptionally fine water.' Although on the subject of education the country has improved enormously in its school system since 1964, nevertheless the editorial just quoted was quite correct and should be remembered even 35 years later.

Cayman's Crown Colony link with Britain has on a few occasions been debated locally to test the people's attitude towards a change of constitutional status to internal self-government, which would normally be the country's next move forward. On every occasion the loud reply has been 'Leave well enough alone, we are happy with our British link.' As a result, those who vie to become elected members of the Legislative Assembly would never stand a chance of winning a seat if constitutional changes were one of their manifesto's presentations. Cayman has done well under the present form of government. Change it and the country will regret the day it happened.

In concluding my last budget address to the Legislative Assembly I had praised members for their exceptionally good leadership, considered very essential in the development of the country's economy. I went on to say:

The prosperity we see in the Cayman Islands today is the result of many years of careful planning and hard work. More than ever before members need to safeguard what has been achieved against undesirable influences of the outside world which could easily destroy the country's economy. Nothing is so essential in the life of a country as good leadership with the right imagination and thinking, leadership that can exercise control in a constructive and balanced manner that will not hesitate to tread the high ground that lies between iron-bound tradition and unbridled dreaming. The Cayman Islands have been blessed up to the present time with good leadership; may this continue. It is my view too that the value to the Cayman Islands of the financial industry is far more than the sum total of its institutions, the services offered and the income to the country. The most valuable asset is the confidence reposed in the Cayman Islands by the international financial community. We must therefore do everything to safeguard and protect our good name and continue to build on it.

In the winding-up I also made reference to the General Election due in November 1984 and said, 'While there could be political manoeuvres by candidates to enhance their own chances of success at the polls, we must hope that there will be no bitterness between individuals. Instead all should aim for a healthy and vigorous contest, one which will create public interest and at the same time promote the many opportunities for progress that lie ahead for these islands.'

I felt after exiting the Civil Service that I had reached 'zero hour' when things could not stand still. For one thing I was much too young to get into a hammock under the trees on my beach and read and sleep, especially when I knew that my pension from the government, as soon as it came into effect in April 1983, could not continue to maintain my home. During the one-year pre-retirement leave I drew full salary and, being a senior government officer on leave, I was not permitted, under official protocol, to accept a private sector job. The reason was obvious in that I was leaving my official position, with many top government secrets. In fact as a continuing Civil Servant on leave, I was still committed to the Official Secrets Act. The year's leave was, on the other hand, quite useful to me for purposes of future planning.

The thing that bothered me most was the fact that the building of the financial industry, which I had committed myself to complete while in the position of Financial Secretary, had not yet reached the pinnacle of its success. How and when the job would be finally completed raised some concern. There was, however, one avenue through which I could re-enter government, and that was via the political arena. That route also depended on whether I was smart enough to win a seat in the Legislative Assembly in the November 1984 General Election, contesting against the powerful Unity Team. If success greeted me at the polls I could perhaps try to engage my influence in some manner through both my official and political friends to continue or to complete the building process of the financial industry.

But first on my agenda was to find an increased income or a new job. I thought about establishing a family business in financial consultancy, with the intention of sharing an office with a friend in the private sector. However, following that thought, I had a surprise visit from the Honourable Sir David Gibbons, KBE, JP, of Bermuda inquiring about the possibility of my representing his family's proposed new business venture in Cayman even if only on a part-time basis. Sir David was looked upon as my counterpart in Bermuda. He was at one time Premier and Minister of Finance. He is credited with being very involved in the building of his country as a leader in the offshore financial industry. I told Sir David about my own plans regarding the establishing of a private business and the progress I had made with it so far. He did not take what I said as very meaningful or as a refusal of his offer and promised to see me again on his next visit to Cayman.

About three months later Sir David was back on the island and came to see me. After rolling his proposal over in my mind again and discussing it with my wife, I accepted the job. It was scheduled to start on 2nd January 1983. One snag was in the way. I could not take on a private sector job until 1st April 1983. However, after discussing the matter with the Governor, Mr Lloyd, he kindly gave me official release to start the new job in January as Managing Director of the Gibbons' new company, Montpelier Properties (Cayman) Ltd. The development is also known as Elizabethan Square. I signed the acceptance letter for the new job on 23rd December 1982. The business, a shopping and office complex in central George Town with a leasing capacity in 1997 of approximately 90,000 square feet, was purchased by the Gibbons from the original owner, Stanley Cook of Canada. The property included the former site of the Catholic church, purchased by Stanley Cook in the 1970s, at which time the church moved and erected its new building off Walkers Road, together with the development of its primary and secondary school complex.

I went on in 1983 to develop my new trading company, V.G. Johnson & Associates Ltd., as well as applying and obtaining from the government the Notary Public commission. I had been appointed a Justice of the Peace on 29th April 1977. Along with my job at Elizabethan Square I also became involved as time went on in small amounts of private business. When the *Caymanian Compass* newspaper discovered that I had accepted a job in the private sector, they came out with a front page article on 12th January 1983 saying

281

'Retired Financial Secretary, the man who has been credited with masterminding the Cayman Islands tax haven, now heads Elizabethan Square.'

While preparing for pre-retirement leave, I saw the need to share my spare time with the Church. I was then a member of the Board of Elders of Elmslie Memorial Presbyterian Church: I had become a communicant member some years after coming to Grand Cayman in 1934. In 1958 after I moved to my new home in South Sound, my family and I attended what is now known as the George Hicks Memorial Church (a branch of Elmslie), which is closer to our home. I knew that Elmslie's Board of Elders had been discussing from 1980 the urgent need to erect a fence to the front of the property facing what is now Harbour Drive. The board also discussed the possibility of a vehicle parking lot to the south of the church. No decisions were apparently forthcoming regarding the design and cost of those two projects. I therefore decided to personally take on the two jobs. I became involved in the building of the vehicle parking lot as the old tombstones in what was the church's former graveyard were crumbling and had to be carefully taken up and placed along the east boundary of the property for preservation. They were all repaired and put in good order. Mr C.L. Flowers, MBE, kindly used his company's equipment to move the tombs and personally supervised the operation. Mr Flowers donated the use of his equipment and his time to the church. As to the building of a car park in the old graveyard, there was definitely a need for the parking facility and with no alternative sites. For one thing, additional land near to the church was not available for the purpose and neither could nearby parking be found to rent. The projects were completed and handed over to the church at no cost.

My next move to become involved in further social work was in South Sound, my wife's district and where we had lived since 1968: I found three projects requiring urgent attention, the public cemetery, the community hall and the church. At a meeting in the South Sound George Hicks Church, I gave notice for a meeting in the community hall of residents of the district to discuss the cemetery and the community hall. About 30 people attended. The two sites and their conditions were discussed. The third project, the church, was of course a subject to be discussed with Elmslie's Board of Elders. At the meeting in the community hall a standing committee, with myself as chairman, was recommended to take over management of both the cemetery and the community hall projects under specific terms of reference. Other members of the committee were Brent Bush, Carl Bush, Valentine Hurlston and Cleaver Bush. A resolution was passed requesting the chairman to write to the Chief Engineer of the Public Works Department, as both properties were owned by the Crown, advising him of the action taken by the people of the district at the special meeting. I was also to request the government's approval of the appointment of a committee to do the necessary improvements to the two projects. Secondly, I should outline the conditions of the two projects and request the government's financial assistance to meet the cost of the improvements. The funds were approved shortly after.

Regarding the cemetery, there was much work necessary to give it an improved appearance in the district. For instance, huge and tall casuarina trees grew along the east boundary of the property and their large roots especially obstructed most of the burial area. It was therefore agreed that the trees be removed, the burial area extended towards the beach, the entire parcel of land cleaned and a new fence erected along the front and east boundaries of the property with the sign 'Cemetery' erected in front. In the case of the community hall, about two years earlier the government had contributed some money to rebuild the hall and through additional community effort the building and grounds were partly completed. In the latest efforts the government provided an added amount of $41,000 to complete the project. Thus the two projects were duly completed and so I turned my attention to the little South Sound Church project. That work involved renovations and new additions to the main structure, together with new furniture and equipment. The work as scheduled was also completed to the satisfaction of the members and the community of the district. Elmslie made a contribution to the cost.

After my retirement from the government in 1982, I was requested to be a member of the organizing committee of the Legislative Assembly, selected to prepare and put together a programme to commemorate the 150th anniversary of parliamentary government in these islands and chaired by Mrs Sybil McLaughlin, Clerk of the Legislative Assembly. The celebration began on 19th November 1982. First was the message by the Governor, Mr Peter Lloyd. It read:

This month the Cayman Islands will celebrate 150 years of parliamentary government. It gives me great pleasure to be associated with this historic event. All Caymanians can justly take pride in so long a period of good government. But they should remember, too, that the stability and the prosperity they now enjoy were built upon this solid foundation which was laid by their forefathers – to whom they should be thankful. It is fitting that a special day has been set aside to mark the occasion. I hope that, when they celebrate it, the young people of these three beautiful islands will honour their heritage and, looking forward, will help build a future even fuller and more colourful than the past. I send greetings to all Caymanians at this time, with the wish that they may continue for another 150 years to follow the example they have been set. God bless you all.

At 9 a.m. a special thanksgiving service at Elmslie Memorial Church in George Town was led by the Minister, the Rev. Ralph D. Pickering. The Rev. Fr. Charles Judah of the Catholic Church delivered the sermon. Also officiating was the Rev. Nicholas Sykes of the Anglican Church. The day continued with a packed programme of activities that included a pageant of school children, a fancy dress competition, an essay competition, a fancy show, quadrille dancing, a firework display at Hogsty Bay and street dancing until midnight. The programme covered five days, from the special opening day on Friday 19th November to Tuesday 23rd November. It included celebration activities at Cayman Brac with a free tour of the island, a boat trip to Little Cayman and a tour of the districts of Grand Cayman. The celebration was considered very well planned: it was most enjoyable throughout the three islands.

Another event occurred around that time which affected many people in Cayman and had significant consequences. Three days after retiring from the Civil Service on 31st March, I was sitting before the radio listening to the latest news. Headlined was Argentina's declaration of war on the Falklands to take possession of those islands from Britain. That Friday the news of the invasion was actually a surprise to the whole world. In the meantime Britain, as a true and devoted mother country, made ready to defend the integrity of the Falklands as a British Territory.

According to historical facts from the *Compass* of Tuesday 8th June 1982, the Falklands conflict with Argentina dated back to 1833, when the two countries began quarrelling over the islands. The Falklands consist of 200 islands totalling 4,697 square miles. All but 1.7 per cent of the land area is on two main islands, West Falkland and East Falkland. The islands at that time had a population, almost all British, of about 1,800. Of these, 1,100 were employed, mostly as sheep herders. The economy is supported predominantly by sheep herding, wool processing, hides and skin. The islands had over 600,000 sheep. About half the land was privately owned by the Falkland Island Company, similar to Britain's old Hudson Bay Company. It employed half the work force. The second biggest landowner was the British Crown. The islands are regarded as valuable for their strategic location at the gateway to Antarctica which puts them within striking distance of shipping traffic plying the Cape Horn route between the Pacific and Atlantic oceans. Moreover, the ocean bed near the Falklands is believed to contain vast amounts of oil and natural gas.

By modern standards the Falklands crisis was seen to be a fairly clean war with few civilian casualties. It actually provided a useful lesson from the interaction of modern ships, aircraft, missiles and improved military technology. It was a clean war due to the 7,500 miles of ocean separating Britain from Argentina. While the flotilla of British ships was on its way to the South Atlantic following a firm pledge by the British government to free the Falklands from the occupation of Argentina, other actions were taken by Britain. Among them was the freezing of Argentine assets in Britain, said to amount to $1.5 billion in gold, securities and currency deposits. Also the British government halted the sale of arms and military equipment to Argentina.

In the meantime sentiment over the Falklands situation ran high in these islands, largely from the thinking that Cayman, as a British Crown Colony with a communist country practically sitting on its doorstep, could perhaps one day meet the same fate as the Falkland Islands. As a result of the local thinking, a Falkland Islands fund-raising drive was organized by Mr Sibert R. Watler (Bert), who was then occupying the position in the Legislative Assembly of Sergeant-at-Arms. The slogan adopted for the drive was 'Mother Needs Your Help' and the proceeds of money raised would in time be handed over to Britain for the South Atlantic Fund, which provided benefits for the Falkland Islands conflict. Several local fundraising drives followed Bert's initiative and in time the interest grew very strong until the government itself decided also to participate in the programme.

In early June 1982 the Chief Secretary, Dennis Foster, visited London on the first of two government missions. The first was the momentous occasion when Denis presented himself at Buckingham Palace to deliver a cheque for half a million pounds Sterling from the people and government of the Cayman Islands to assist in Britain's war efforts in the Falkland Islands. The cheque represented monies from Cayman residents in the several fundraising drives as well as a sizeable contribution from the government. Presenting the cheque at the Palace he said, 'As islanders ourselves we understand the love of the people of the Falklands for their homes and their islands. We stand with the United Kingdom in the fight to protect their fundamental human rights and especially their freedom to live in the way that they themselves choose.'

Seven months after the war with Argentina ended, the British

Prime Minister, Mrs Margaret Thatcher, on 11th January 1983 made a personal visit to Port Stanley, the capital of the Falkland Islands. There she pledged to defend the colony 'for a very long time'. On the third day of her unannounced visit to the South Atlantic colony she was honoured by leading officials for her courageous, steadfast and unyielding leadership.

Denis' second mission to London in 1982 was to attend the opening of the Cayman Islands Offices in London headed by a former Governor of Cayman, Thomas Russell: he has in fact been head of that office since its inception. At the ceremony Denis spoke of Cayman's seafaring traditions and mentioned how in the two world wars, young Caymanian men volunteered to serve in the Royal Navy and in the Merchant Marine, giving their lives because they believed in freedom and the need to resist aggression. Today, said Dennis, the 'law of the jungle cannot be allowed to prevail'. He went on to say that it was admirable to see in the conflict over the Falkland Islands, the United Kingdom's 'resolute example and willingness to defend the rights and principles involved. Even though the effort was at a cost to young lives, it will nevertheless give heart to the small nations and territories who have recently found the world a more menacing and frightening place in which to live.'

A Royal Visit

Shortly after I took over the management position at Montpelier Properties, the Cayman Islands experienced what I would term a most colourful event, one this country had never before witnessed in its entire history. We had the distinguished pleasure of welcoming the royal visit of Her Majesty Queen Elizabeth II and her husband, His Royal Highness the Duke of Edinburgh on 16th February 1983. The royal visitors arrived at Owen Roberts International Airport at 11.30 a.m. on Her Majesty's VC 10 aircraft. The Governor, Mr Peter Lloyd, met the royal couple, followed by Mrs Lloyd and other official dignitaries of the welcoming party. Shortly after the welcome at the airport the royal couple departed for Morgan's Harbour in the district of West Bay where they, the Governor and other special guests embarked on the cabin cruiser *Marlin Darlin* on their journey across the North Sound to Cayman Kai at Rum Point. Lunch was served on the voyage across the North Sound in spite of the heavy south-easterly wind causing the sea to be a bit choppy. The caterers who prepared and served the special lunch were Caribbean Club from the Seven Mile Beach. Four of their kitchen staff, headed by the chief chef John

Buschelbauer, were selected for that assignment. John is now one of the owners of the popular Wharf Restaurant on North Church Street in George Town.

Dining with the Queen and the Duke aboard the boat were the Governor, Captain Charles Kirkconnell, the Commissioner of Police Mr Jim Stowers and me. After lunch was served, three other invitees, Dr Marco Giglioli (the mosquito chief), Mr Kent Eldemire and Ira Thompson (a long-time governor's chauffeur), sat with the royal couple for coffee. I had the pleasure of sitting on the Queen's right at lunch and we both became very involved in much personal and general discussion. At the end of the Royal Visit I wrote to the Governor expressing my grateful thanks for the invitations to the royal events and congratulated him for his excellent performance throughout the 24-hour programme. In reply he said in the last paragraph, 'The Queen told me afterwards how interesting she had found your conversation.'

The Queen and the Duke journeyed on from Cayman Kai to open the new road connecting North Side with Gun Bay; the road is built along the periphery of the coastline. The royal party stopped at a specially built station a short distance from the North Side end of the road to perform the opening ceremony by unveiling a plaque with the appropriate special details of the occasion and naming the road The Queen's Highway. That was followed by speeches from three elected members, the Honourable Haig Bodden, the Honourable John McLean and Mr Craddock Ebanks representing the North Side district. The royal couple continued the journey along the new road driving through Gun Bay, East End, Breakers and on to Bodden Town, where they attended an exhibition of local crafts. From Bodden Town they travelled to Transnational House across from the Seven Mile Beach, where a special exclusive and luxurious suite on the first floor of the stately apartments was placed at their disposal. It was prepared as a private accommodation that would serve their 24-hour stopover in Grand Cayman. The property was then owned by Fred Reiss of Bermuda, who himself put much effort into the remodelling and redesigning of the suite for that special occasion. It is still looked upon today as a 'royal suite'. The property is at present owned by Mr Norberg Thompson of George Town. Unfortunately Government House was not large enough to accommodate the Queen and the Duke and their entourage.

Later in the evening Prince Philip visited the Cayman Turtle Farm. That was his second visit to see the turtles, as he had been to the farm back in 1962 when he, without the Queen, came to Grand Cayman for the first time.

The first day of the 1983 royal visit ended with a reception in the grounds of Government House at 8 p.m., to which 600 guests were invited although it was thought that more like 750 people attended. Following the reception a formal dinner was also given at Government House by the Governor and his wife for the royal couple. A total of 22 guests were invited.

The following day, Wednesday 17th February, after the Queen and Prince Philip had had breakfast, they made their rounds at Transnational House to say farewell. Thereafter they proceeded to the Legislative Assembly, where the Queen at 10.45 a.m., taking the throne and wearing her crown, delivered a speech. It was the first occasion on which a reigning monarch delivered a Throne Speech in the Cayman Islands. In her remarks she acknowledged Cayman's involvement during the Falklands crisis. 'The Cayman Islands are one of the very few territories in the Commonwealth which I have not previously been able to visit during my reign,' she said. 'My husband and I are therefore delighted to be with you here today. It gives me special pleasure to be able to open the Legislative Assembly and to deliver my speech in person.

'Although small in size and population, these islands have forged ahead and are now a progressive and prominent community in the Caribbean region. I was much moved by the message of loyalty and support sent to me by His Excellency the Governor at the time of the Falkland Islands conflict and also by the generous donation of £500,000 Sterling from the government and people of these islands for the South Atlantic Fund. During this year, efforts will continue to maintain the high level of cooperation and confidence between the government and the private sector so that economic development may continue at a steady pace. Further investment in infrastructure in Cayman Brac and Little Cayman will lay a firm foundation for the orderly economic development of the sister islands. During this year new legislation will be enacted and amendments made to existing laws. A committee is at present studying the British Nationality Act 1981 with a view to advising on necessary changes in the Caymanian Protection Law. The newly instituted Legal Studies course will provide the necessary training for capable young people to launch a legal career.'

Her Majesty's speech covered many other subjects and in her closing remarks she said, 'My government are pleased with the friendly relations that exist between the Cayman Islands and surrounding territories, and appreciate the availability of facilities in the USA to the residents of these islands. United Kingdom agencies also provide technical aid and consultant services to projects here.

'Mr President and members of this honourable house: Prince Philip and I have been very touched by the warmth of the welcome given to us by the people of the Cayman Islands. We shall take away with us the happiest memories of our visit. I pray that the blessings of Almighty God will continue to rest on the government and people of these islands.'

After the Throne Speech Her Majesty conducted an investiture of those persons she had named and placed on her New Year's Honours List. That was followed by Prince Philip presenting awards to participants in the Duke of Edinburgh Award scheme. Following the investiture and awards, Her Majesty The Queen and Prince Philip went on an informal walkabout outside the Legislative Assembly, meeting as many people as time permitted. From the Legislative Assembly the royal couple proceeded officially to open The Pines, Cayman's first retirement home. The royal couple were met at The Pines by Mr Richard Arch, Chairman of the National Council of Social Services, responsible for the creation of the home. After the formalities at The Pines and the Queen's last act of awarding the title 'Royal' to the Cayman Islands Police Force, Her Majesty and Prince Philip departed for Owen Roberts International Airport, where at 12.55 p.m. they boarded their aircraft and departed for Mexico. Thus ended the Cayman Islands' most prestigious experience of a visit in the person of the reigning monarch.

As I have already recorded in Chapter 11, 'The Cayman Currency', back in July 1973 His Royal Highness Prince Charles, Prince of Wales, came to Grand Cayman on an unofficial visit as a lieutenant on HMS *Minerva*. The Prince toured the islands with stops at West Bay, Bodden Town, North Side and East End, stopping for lunch at the Tortuga Club.

There was one royal visitor who did not receive much publicity and for obvious reasons. He was Prince Andrew, then 22, the second son of Queen Elizabeth and Prince Philip. On 4th March 1983, HMS *Bristol* visited Grand Cayman en route from Belize, formerly British Honduras, where she maintained a watchdog presence offshore. Later in 1983 the ship would sail south again for the Falklands Islands, an area well known to its 29 officers and 378 crewmen on board, who were in the thick of the Falklands conflict in 1982. The *Bristol*'s companion ship, the 19,500 ton aircraft carrier HMS *Invincible*, was docked in Jamaica at the time. The *Invincible*'s most famous crewman was Prince Andrew, a sub-lieutenant and anti-submarine helicopter pilot: he was given a mission to fly misdirected mail to the HMS *Bristol* in Grand Cayman. The Prince's green Sea King helicopter, carrying the mail, hovered over the main dock, and the sacks of mail were lowered by winch. Visiting government officials on board the *Bristol* were told who was flying the helicopter and, along with members of the ship's crew, waved as the royal pilot manoeuvred his craft above the ship's deck.

The Prince sent a message to His Excellency the Governor, Mr Peter Lloyd. It read, 'What a beautiful island you have – sorry I could not have been there with the Royal party' (meaning his parents' visit the month before). The Governor's reply said, 'The government and people here all hope your Royal Highness may be able to land and see more of these islands some time. That would be a great honour for us and we could promise the warmest of welcomes. Meanwhile, we are delighted by, and grateful for, your Highness' kind message.' HMS *Invincible* had led the flotilla of British warships in early April 1982 to free the Falkland Islands from Argentina's occupation.

In the first two years after my retirement, I had accepted a number of appointments. One was a request by the United Church Council to conduct a casual survey of their Cayman Preparatory School in view of its recent introduction of the first three high school classes or the classes of the middle school, now the George Hicks High School. This was followed by the request that I take on the chairmanship of the school's board of governors. I did the school's report and also accepted the position on the board and remained chairman until April 1984, when I began my preparation for the November 1984 General Election. Other positions I accepted were from the government in early 1983 to become Chairman of the Public Service Commission and appointment to the Board of Parole Commissioners that dealt with the discharge of long-term prisoners. I also remained in both government positions until April 1984. I held as well directorships in the private sector of a bank and of a trust company, and served as a trustee of another bank. Those private sector jobs proved to have had no adverse effect on my political career.

In July 1984 I fully made up my mind to be a candidate in the November 1984 General Election for the George Town constituency. A group of us with the same aim, covering all the political constituencies of the three islands, came together and organized ourselves into what was known as the 'Dignity Team'. We decided to challenge the famous 'Unity Team', whose members apparently were not concerned about their opposition or losing the election, for they had deemed themselves popular enough to win all future general elections, thereby guaranteeing the country a lifetime Unity Team government. Our team members were therefore well aware that they had a fairly tough job ahead to convince the voting public that the Dignity Team had something more appealing to offer the people and the country than did the Unity Team. I was told by supporters of the other side that I did not have the charisma to be a politician; however, I dismissed from my thoughts that discouraging remark and went on with the plan.

Apart from my early life, I had been first a soldier, then a long-term Civil Servant holding for 17 years the position of Financial Secretary, equivalent to Minister of Finance and Development, and since 1965 had been a member of the Legislative Assembly. As an official member of the Assembly I had the opportunity of rubbing shoulders with politicians and learning their *modus operandi*. The 17 years' experience was invaluable to me in many respects, but especially at a time when I was considering becoming involved in politics. For example, I recalled a most interesting occasion when I saw politics and its debate in top form. It was at my first meeting of the Legislative Assembly on 1st April 1965. The President, J.A. Cumber, presented what I would term 'a hot message'. It dealt with an application for a licence to operate casino gambling in the Cayman Islands. Apart from the absurd thought of a casino in Cayman, the President referred to Grand Cayman as 'an island of rumours', meaning the subject of the message had been widely talked around town. Politician Mr Warren Conolly, OBE, JP, voiced his exception to the reference of 'an island of rumours'. After elected members had all thoroughly aired the subject, it was put to a vote. The proposal for legalized casino gambling in these islands was unanimously defeated. From then until now no other such proposal has been put to this government. The presentation of views in what is evil and what is good for Cayman expressed by many prominent and experienced elected members was quite a good lesson to me on the subject of political debate.

I felt in 1984 that my desire to get involved in politics had a special value to me and perhaps to the country. As previously explained, my ambition was to re-enter government through the political arena in an endeavour to complete the job of building the financial industry. Nothing could discourage me then from moving on to arrange my election campaign. Even though threats were made against me should I appear on the political platform (and I still have some of those signed and unsigned letters), those were like throwing water on a duck's back: they had no discouraging effect on me. In fact the threats gave me the urge to move quickly onto the platform, which I did shortly after.

The three George Town Dignity Team candidates were Norman Bodden, who was then a current member of the Legislative Assembly, Arthur Hunter and I. Norman, Linford Pierson and I won the three

George Town seats. Political campaigning seemed great fun in the contest. One thing that came out of it was a sense of *esprit de corps*, a very strong team spirit spiced with pride and honour amongst especially its novice members, like me, at the thought of being political representatives of the people and the country.

The election was very successful for the Dignity Team. We won eight seats of the twelve, Unity Team took three seats and one went to an Independent candidate who was apparently an ardent supporter of the opposition. The Unity Team's dream of always winning a Cayman general election had faded away into frustration and no doubt embarrassment. In late 1984 the team, to boost its election campaign chances, completed a new Terminal Building at Owen Robert's International Airport. That was followed by a very pleasing event when the team arranged the first flight to Cayman of the world's most famous aircraft, the British Airways Concorde. Both events were enjoyed by the public, but apparently had little impact on Election Day.

The Dignity Team formed the new government, using its four most able and deserving members. Benson O. Ebanks became Minister for Health, Education and Social Services; Norman W. Bodden, Minister for Tourism, Aviation and Trade; Captain Charles L. Kirkconnell, Minister for Communication, Works and District Administration; and my portfolio was Development and Natural Resources plus the chairmanship of Cayman Airways (see Chapter 14 'Air Services'). Other Members who formed the team's backbench supporters were McKeeva Bush, Daphne Orrett, Ezzard Miller and Captain Mabry Kirkconnell.

There were seven portfolios in the Cabinet or Executive Council, four headed by elected ministers and three by officials. In each portfolio the Governor had carefully allocated the subjects together with departments, statutory boards and committees for which each Member of Council would be responsible. In the case of my portfolio, the name previously applied to it was 'Agriculture, Planning and Natural Resources'. I requested that Agriculture and Planning be replaced with 'Development'. The reason was that under my portfolio there were four departments, two of which were Agriculture and Planning. It therefore seemed somewhat odd to have only two of the four departments forming a part of the name of the portfolio. The Governor kindly accepted my recommendation. Development in fact meant in that context physical infrastructure, for which the portfolio was responsible under its Planning Department.

At the first meeting of the Legislative Assembly the day following the General Election, called for the selection of four elected members for the Executive Council, we spoke to the people and our supporters. I personally thanked them for the confidence they had reposed in me and went on to say, 'After seventeen years of continuous service in the Legislative Assembly as an official member, I am now returning by the popular choice of the people as an elected politician. The jubilant mood which greeted Cayman when the election results were known gave me inspiration, strength, encouragement and determination to ensure that the future of these islands moves in the right direction. Our Dignity Team has now taken over the people's government at the crossroads of its history and at a point where team members are faced with the great task of reshaping the future of our homeland. We can only now pray for God's guidance and wisdom and ask that He lead us in the right way. The people should also be aware that nothing can be politically right where it is morally wrong.' I gave the reassurance of my intention to fulfil the promises I had made to the electorate. In conclusion I wished the Governor and his family and all the lovely people of these islands my sincere good wishes for the coming festive season.

At that stage the new government was all set to move on to examine in detail its newly inherited political responsibilities and apply any necessary changes that would foster the policies enshrined in its manifesto. We discussed among ourselves the defeat of the Unity Team, who had entered the race with great enthusiasm but at the end of it were faced with the task of opposing a very strong government both in numbers and in its fighting qualities as former opponents. We celebrated our victory with thankfulness and took the opportunity to look forward with anticipation to a successful four-year political administration.

For me, an early example of this occurred in January 1985 when the Minister of Health, Education and Social Services, the Honourable Benson O. Ebanks, OBE, sent me a memorandum indicating that 1985 was 250 years since the first Royal Land Grant had been officially recorded. The Royal Grant deeded land to three individuals in the Cayman Islands. The Proclamation was made on 7th September 1734 in the eighth year of the reign of His Majesty King Charles II. The three persons to whom the grant was made were Daniel Campbell, John Middleton and Mary Campbell and their heirs. The Proclamation went on to state that the Letter of Patent was later officially entered at the Island Record Office, Jamaica, on 28th February 1735. Although the memorandum may be correct in assuming that some sort of occupation had already begun a good number of years earlier, it presented the first real recorded evidence found so far that indicated plans for an official permanent settlement of land grant in the Cayman Islands. The paper on the subject proposed that the

Cayman government form a special committee to look into different cultural events, not necessarily festive, that could be put on throughout the year to celebrate the 250th Anniversary of the Settlement (Royal Land Grant) on a national level. Those events would serve to direct the public's attention to the natural significance of the grant 250 years previously. The celebration could also bring together all Caymanians in an event that was seen to enrich the country's sense of itself. However, rightly or wrongly, as the Minister responsible for the subject, I took the decision that air services, conservation and the turtle farm in my portfolio required all of my attention at the time. In fact we had just recently celebrated the 150th Anniversary of Parliamentary Government. Now at the start of a new government with Ministers' portfolios loaded with high-priority subjects, it would be difficult to become involved at this time again in a new programme to run throughout the year 1985.

After being sworn into government on 20th November 1984, I was interviewed by the *Caymanian Compass* regarding my impression of being an elected Executive Council Member. The interview was quite lengthy and dealt also with Cayman Airways. As to being an elected member of the Executive Council, my reply was:

It is a bit strange to sit in a politician's office after having been a civil servant for so many years. However, we are not here to pull down hills and build mountains, but to aim at improving on what has been built in government. Also for all the elected members in our team to work together in harmony with the officials of the Executive Council, members of the Legislative Assembly and the Civil Service. My own basic principle of being a politician is that emphasis must be laid on the wishes and needs of the people and not necessarily on what is best for the government. Nevertheless, in order to achieve excellence in our work, everyone must cooperate in what we do to promote in the right direction the growth and development of the country.

I believed in that approach throughout my career in public service. My belief is no less strong today.

16

The Mutual Legal Assistance Treaty and its Forerunner, the Narco Agreement

In 1983, shortly after my retirement from the Civil Service, problems began brewing on the horizon of these islands with narcotics trading in this region. As a result the United States declared war on drug dealers and traffickers. The Americans claimed that the Caribbean islands were a well-used refuelling and transfer centre for ships and aircraft carrying marijuana and cocaine into the United States. It was alleged that smugglers were prepared to pay $30,000 per shipment of marijuana and $250,000 per shipment of cocaine for the services. The Americans estimated that the drug trade through the Caribbean area netted annually about $25 billion and that much of the money was being laundered through Cayman, it being a much bigger banking centre than existed in any of the other regional countries. In fact at that particular time these islands, with over 500 banks, emerged as a significant banking centre attracting even undetected criminal funds. This government had no way of confirming or denying any statement on drug movements through Cayman except for traffickers and dealers caught here. The local police, however, sometimes in association with the United States Drug Enforcement Administration (DEA) had by then increased their vigilance over possible drug movements through Cayman. One thing was for sure, the local confidentiality law gave no protection or support to narcotic dealers or to money launderers identified as such. If foreign investigators requested privileged information relating to a criminal offence and a *prima facie* case was not made against those so accused, however, the local authorities, in keeping with the law, could not release the information.

Two years earlier, while I was Financial Secretary, the Americans had approached the Cayman government on a number of occasions for information relating to purported drug and other criminal offences. The government cooperated to the extent of requiring the standard *prima facie* evidence from the investigators. However, many of the requests came from applicants who were merely trying to fish for information from whatever sources. The local authorities could just not support those unauthorized investigations. Our big friends were not very pleased with such an attitude; nevertheless, the statutory requirement of maintaining Cayman's confidentiality had to be preserved. We, however, exerted efforts to keep alerted to smugglers whose intentions were to stash their cash here and later convert it to usable assets in what is known as 'money laundering'.

At that stage shrewd American government prosecutors were finding other ways of peeking behind the curtains of countries like Cayman, who operated strict confidentiality to cover their bank customers' financial affairs. The Americans were also seeking to improve methods in their efforts to combat the growing intensity of international drug trafficking. We had in fact become aware of the drug-related financial scandals buzzing around the region and were not surprised when US prosecutors were obliged to consider more drastic steps to circumvent confidential laws. They were convinced as well that, apart from the narcotic problems, a vast amount of information pointed to ways in which money was being moved out of the United States into tax havens. They therefore introduced a four-pronged-attack system to aid their investigation. Those were subpoenas and summonses directed at banks, civil discovery orders, compelled consent and conspiracy theory.

The first was that banks would be ordered to comply with United States discovery requests even though disclosure would require the banks to violate their country's secrecy laws. The second, civil discovery orders, required civil litigants to produce requested documents even if by doing so they might be subject to criminal prosecution in their country of business. The third and most dangerous of them all was compelled or forced consent. The US authorities saw this as the most effective means of penetrating bank secrecy. All that it required was for banks or persons to 'consent' to disclosure of documents by third parties. The consent waived any secrecy rights in the documents. The last of the quadruple attack system, conspiracy theory, did not really bother Cayman for it related to the United States successfully prosecuting their own taxpayers for conspiring to use foreign secrecy laws to evade US taxes.

The Cayman government did not at any time fail to give due recognition to the seriousness of drug trafficking and money laundering crimes in this hemisphere and was at all times prepared to assist the effort to investigate, bring to justice and control those offences. Cayman had in fact taken significant steps to cooperate with the

United States DEA by assisting them so as to avoid breaching the local confidentiality system to aid the investigation. In 1982 Cayman entered into an informal Letter of Agreement with the United States providing for cooperation in criminal matters.

In mid-June 1983, the local press approached me requesting that I consider doing a press release on my 'concerned look at drugs in the islands'. Certainly the effects of drugs, money laundering and other commercial crime activities mixed in the economic development of these islands bothered me. Although the government's economic policy was no longer my responsibility, the invitation to speak out on drugs nevertheless gave me a golden opportunity to express my long pent-up inner feelings on so critical and important an issue. It was an opportunity as well to get the message across, not only to the Cayman Islands, but the whole world so that people would know our thinking on drugs. This was also a time when a medical doctor in one of our nearby friendly offshore centres was jailed on drug charges. Both the *Caymanian Compass* and the newly established *Cayman Pilot* carried the article in their 24th June 1983 issues.

I chose for my presentation the title, 'Which Way Cayman?' I realized that the article would be based on the question regarding the future well-being of the Cayman Islands, a question that many other countries were also asking themselves, 'Which way are we going?' In my introduction I stated that:

One of those countries which comes to mind is the United States of America. I very well believe there are people in that country asking this question 'Which way are we going?' Those people have expressed in recent years much concern over their serious drug problems, and the fact that the country is spending over $60 billion a year on this one commodity – DRUGS. Imagine all that money going outside the country to buy drugs illegally, to buy something that is detrimental to individuals, to society and to the country in general. The export of that large sum of money is also robbing a big portion of the country's foreign exchange reserve.

The constant abusive use of drugs by individuals causes serious physical and mental health problems. Therefore, all those who are either involved in, or concerned over, the problem, whether they are young or old or rich or poor, should be reminded of the old Arabian proverb that says, 'He who has health has hope, and he who has hope has everything'. Hope is the only good common to all men. Besides the health problem there is the trafficking problem, well known to be the root of many other evils, evils of serious criminal nature; an example is

297

the sudden and unexpected death and disappearance of people, which sooner or later leads to drug connections. Another concern too is the inducement into the illegal drug ring of good, honest and upright citizens who once caught in the net are not likely to escape the trap again.

In September 1980 I represented the Cayman Islands at the Commonwealth Parliamentary Association Conference in Lusaka, Zambia. At that meeting I spoke on a number of subjects, one of which was drugs. The subject was 'International Collaboration in Controlling Drug Addiction and Trafficking'. The research indicated that the drug problems of today [20 years ago] had reached such a great proportion worldwide that it was considered the single major national problem common to most countries around the world. It certainly is a major problem to the police and other law enforcement agencies, because the drug trade is centred deeply in international crime organizations. Those crime organizations control almost the entire drug trade and movement. They control the growers and producers, they control the transporters, the importers, the distributors, the pushers, and even a large percentage of the users. Police have only been successful in trapping a few pushers and users: the big boys, meaning the producers, transporters, importers and distributors go scot-free, except for the occasional arrest. Even then it takes a long time to prove the offence. Rounding up a few pushers and users is like taking an aspirin for a toothache – the pain eases for a short time and then it is back again worse than ever.

It is believed that in many countries prominent people from a cross section of the community are associated in one way or another with this big group. Otherwise, many of the deals, especially big deals, could not be traded successfully: this is mainly the reason too why the problem has reached such great proportions. The problem may not necessarily involve government officers as purported, but it does involve people from all sections of society who are also caught in addiction and trafficking. Most of the countries concerned with drug problems have established a high-powered group of representatives which include the DEA and FBI of the United States, Interpol and top police officers of the many other member countries, large and small. Cayman is also a member of that group and our Commissioner of Police attends the meetings every year. It seems however, that as tough as members of this high-powered group may be, they are up against a brick wall in their attack on the problem. One of the reasons is that drug dealers have access to the best representation the legal profession can offer, which is more than a match for what governments can produce. The result is that law enforcement agencies, after working so hard to put a case together, end up in frustration when the case is either dismissed by the court or the accused gets off lightly. Another reason for this too is that perhaps while the law enforcement chaps are busily marshalling their case, someone might be injecting sabotage into it and thus the end results must again be frustration.

What is of particular concern to us in the Cayman Islands today is the fact that perhaps prominent people here may be connected with big drug deals. If that is really true then nobody really knows where our problems will all end, for the fact is that this type of illegal business offers quick and extremely big dividends and there are many who will queue up for a share. There is no doubt about it: this illicit business can attract and induce many to participate. It would include people from all walks of life, from the poor in the streets to the senior executives trapped in the ring almost innocently by some devious schemes of the underground. They would be obliged to remain locked in the ring and could not afford to dissociate themselves from it for fear of their life. Another of the many concerns relates to the illegal sale of dope to even the very young in schools, children who are induced into the drug habit from a tender age. It is at this point that the fabric of society starts to shred and weaken, for when the young begin to lose a purpose in life, and drugs will do that, hope will decline and chaos appear.

Public opinion has generated much fear and concern in society and so this searching question is posed: 'Which Way Cayman?' Do we want to see crime become the fabric of the society of this country? Someone wrote that fear and concern do not empty tomorrow of its sorrow, they empty today of its strength. It should therefore be our sacred duty to guard, protect and preserve our strength of today by avoiding fear and concern and the source from which they flow. Cayman is small – 100 square miles and 20,000 people. There was a time when the country suffered tremendous financial hardship, a time when its future looked as dim as the twilight hours of the evenings. Many readers can remember those days: I can, for I lived here since 1934. But whatever our circumstances might have been, we were always thankful to God for what we had and what we were. Nobody goes hungry here: there is much generosity among the people who are always willing to assist. A question we could very well ask ourselves is this: can the fall from this exalted position be just as rapid as our progress over the past few years? One thing is sure, with the good comes the evil, for there is good business and there is dirty business: there is clean money and there is dirty money, and there are honest businessmen and there are crooks. We should not then be naïve enough to think that there are not people around who are willing to be involved in unclean things.

Another interesting point is that in recent times we have heard comments from the foreign press that because of Cayman's strict Confidentiality Law, which protects the secret operation of local financial industry institutions, drug traffickers and crooked operators are creating a haven here for themselves. It is a place where they can wash their dirty money and where the crooks can transform into gentlemen. In fact the local police with the assistance of foreign law enforcement officials are carefully planning their attacks on those so criminally involved.

I did not mean to alarm readers in any way, and forgive me if I did, for in spite of all the evils around us, and my earlier comments, Cayman can still boast some good features and attractions which are fast becoming rare commodities in other parts of the world. Also to be noted are our problems here that have not yet reached unmanageable proportions or the stage where they are embarrassing to the country. Nevertheless the situation needs careful watching and skilful management. Are we going to support a haven of crooks and drug traffickers, or are we going to seek God's help to lead us in the right direction? We have always sought divine direction in all our endeavours, for traditionally the Cayman Islands has been a Christian community.

I will thus end here this brief extract from my presentation of the article 'Which Way Cayman?'

On 29th August 1984, one month after I decided to offer myself as a candidate in the General Elections to be held later that year, an Agreement was signed by the governments of the United States and the United Kingdom concerning the Cayman Islands, related to the exchange of information on narcotics offences. Its purpose was to assist in obtaining bank records of suspected narcotics traffickers. Following its signing, the historic Agreement was made into law and known as the Narcotics Drugs Law 1984. The 12-page Agreement included as item 7 a proposal for the Cayman Islands through the United Kingdom to negotiate with the United States a Law Enforcement Treaty (LET) later known as the Mutual Legal Assistance Treaty (MLAT).

Before the actual signing of the Agreement but after discussions had been concluded in London, the United States on 21st June 1984 issued a side letter to the Agreement. It read:

The United States side is pleased with the substantial progress made during the UK/Cayman meeting in London regarding the proposed interim Narcotics Agreement with the United States. The United States side is particularly pleased that the Cayman side has agreed to negotiate a law enforcement treaty that would cover cooperation in a broad area of law enforcement matters. Such a treaty should afford a greater degree of harmony and mutual satisfaction in law enforcement cooperation between Cayman and the US.

As we expressed during our recent meeting with UK and Cayman officials, the US remains sensitive to Cayman concerns regarding the issue of witness subpoenas, and is prepared to discuss these concerns, among other issues, during the contemplated negotiations on a law enforcement treaty. Recognizing Cayman sensitivities regarding witness subpoenas, the United States exercises careful scrutiny and appropriate discretion in enforcing such subpoenas against Cayman residents.

Cayman was certainly pleased with the statement, which strengthened its efforts to move on in due course with the treaty negotiation.

Concerning the Narcotics Executive Agreement, it was interesting to me to see a comment made by the United States Justice Department just a little while after the arrangements were made effective. It said, 'Under that Agreement, the Cayman Islands agreed to provide among other things, bank records within two weeks of being presented with a certification from the Attorney General of the United States establishing that the US needed the records in connection with a case involving drug trafficking. We have sent the Caymans approximately 100 requests and have been delighted with the responsiveness and adherence to the terms of the Agreement shown by the Caymans.'

Following a press conference after the return of a Cayman team visit to Washington in the early part of June 1985 (I was a member of that team), the local newspaper suggested that I had criticized the Narcotics Agreement on my election platform in 1984. It stated: 'Since he [meaning me] has been a Government Member, he has been able to examine the full implications and he has come to the conclusion that it was a reasonable Agreement, considering the difficulties experienced. He now believes the Agreement in its present form is acceptable.'

301

My reply to that statement was that my concern on the platform was not for the Narcotics Agreement and the fact that it provided, by administrative as opposed to judicial process, the release of confidential information relating to investigation of narcotics activities. Rather my concern was from the fact that in spite of the implementation of the Agreement, United States government agents continued probing, on tax charges, the records of Americans doing business here. This I said was undoubtedly of concern to us for there is no doubt that such action resulted in the loss to Cayman of some good and clean business. I went further to say:

> The foreign investigators went as far as to have their courts entertain consent judgement on account holders in Cayman aimed at forcing the individuals and the local banks to surrender the requested confidential information. Since coming to my political office that situation has been closely monitored by the new Executive Council so as to limit the release of information to only genuine cases, and also to restore any confidence that might have been lost prior to this.
>
> Countries of the modern democratic world must practise and honour the old legal principle of 'comity' which is a mutual respect between nations to honour the laws of the other. A breach of tax laws in other jurisdictions is not an offence here so why should a foreign country insist on investigating in the Cayman Islands a breach of their own tax laws?

This was my criticism on the platform. I could not understand the purpose of the Narcotics Agreement when the US, as a party to the Agreement, continued its efforts to investigate purported tax offenders in our jurisdiction. And what was more, this was outside the context of the Agreement, which had the destructive effect of scaring away good business. I went on to say that:

> Although I have accepted the Narcotics Agreement which binds us to cooperate in the investigation of narcotics-related charges, I still remain very vigilant against any interference in our confidentiality system where tax-related charges are concerned. For this reason I have expressed the view that the keynote to the next negotiation (the Mutual Legal Assistance Treaty) must be based on reciprocity, i.e. equal commitment of the parties instituted by the force of law.

When the new government of 1984–88 was sworn in on 20th

302

November 1984, it began to examine the many subjects set out on its agenda, one of which was the Law Enforcement Treaty which Cayman had committed itself to consider. The new government thought that as narcotics trafficking and other commercial crimes were on the rise globally, if the Cayman Islands was to survive the efforts of continuing to build its economy based largely on finance then a clean business atmosphere must of necessity be created locally. The old adage 'Look before you leap' bothered some people in that, for instance, if war were suddenly declared on money laundering and fraudulent transfers, the situation thus created would harm Cayman's most valued asset, financial confidentiality. In considering that delicate issue, it was thought that a safety valve should be devised to protect the country's interest which could be in the form of a state-ment explaining to the international public Cayman's views over the part it would play in maintaining its commitment under the Narcotics Agreement. At the same time and in the same statement we would defend confidentiality in the Cayman Islands. Following that plan, the then Financial Secretary, Mr Jefferson, and I in early 1985 made a statement in *Taxes International* of the United Kingdom entitled 'Cayman Commits itself to Financial Confidentiality'.

The statement was based on the enactment of legislation imple-menting the historic information-exchange Agreement with the United States known as the Narcotic Drugs Law of 1984. The law represented an unprecedented international cooperation in eradicating the worldwide flow of illicit drugs and drug profits. The law oblig-ated the Cayman Attorney General to produce the requested infor-mation swiftly and under strict confidentiality in order to prevent any leakage to targets of the US investigation. The following is the text of our statement.

The Narcotics Agreement reflects the unique economic and geo-graphic status of the Cayman Islands. On the one hand, Cayman is the home of an offshore financial centre of longstanding stability, reflected by the fact that ours is one of the largest euro-dollar markets in the world. More than 400 banks and trust companies are registered to do business in Cayman. Our financial sector employs almost 900 people; three-fourths of them are Cayman citizens. The economic vitality of our islands is grounded in the health of our financial industry and its commitment to con-fidentiality in all legitimate financial affairs. On the other hand, we cannot turn our backs on certain geographic realities that also play a central role in life on the islands. An estimated $80 billion in illegal drug money will flow through financial institutions in

303

the United States and the Caribbean this year. Our waters and shore are tempting targets for drug-smugglers searching for a convenient point of trans-shipment to the North American continent. And our financial institutions are vulnerable to the sophisticated narcotics financier/profiteer who adroitly engineers the 'laundering' of drug-related capital through the international banking system. Caymanians are well aware of the dangers which narcotics-smuggling and narcotics-profiteering pose to a small Caribbean island. We have enacted some of the toughest drug laws in the world, and they are enforced with a vigour that has earned commendations from the United States Drug Enforcement Administration. The Narcotics Agreement is a very special step forward. It is a declaration by Caymanians that our confidential banking legislation will not afford a shield behind which the drug traffickers can threaten the foundation of our financial system, the integrity of our free government, and the fabric of our society. We take great pride in being the first Caribbean Territory to enact such a law. But in some financial circles this bold measure has been mistaken as an 'early sign' that we are about to abandon our commitment to financial confidentiality. This is certainly a misunderstanding of the truth.

The Cayman Islands will continue to welcome, as we have in the past, financial institutions and their clients whose funds originate from a source – and are to be put to a purpose – which is lawful in the Cayman Islands. We understand the desire of US tax and securities authorities to investigate and prosecute all alleged violations of US tax and commercial laws, wherever those violations occur and wherever potential evidence thereof may be found. Conversely, those authorities must appreciate that Cayman will not compromise its sovereignty, as expressed in a fundamental commitment to financial privacy, for the convenience of every US law enforcement effort. Our commitment to retaining full confidentiality for legitimate commercial and tax-planning activities is evidenced by our decision to forego participation in that portion of the United States' 'Caribbean Basin Initiative' which offers attractive convention-business enhancements, but at too high a price (a comprehensive tax-information exchange agreement). As of January 1984, US tax treaties with exchange-of-information provisions were in force with 32 governments including Switzerland, the Netherlands and the Netherlands-Antilles, but not with the Cayman Islands.

We believe that by having a formal inter-governmental agreement which authorizes the sharing of information in certain instances and through certain channels, we have strengthened the health of underlying confidentiality in all legitimate financial affairs, rather than undermining it. The Narcotics Agreement is clear on the point of exclusivity. No US subpoena from a Grand Jury or otherwise, related to documentary information falling within the scope of the Agreement, may be enforced in the United States without prior agreement of the United Kingdom or the Cayman Islands. Thus, the vexing problem of extraterritorial law enforcement, multiple layers of information requests, and gentlemen's agreements subject to conflicting interpretations, have now been replaced with a clearly defined single artery of communication for narcotics-related documentary information to the benefit of all parties involved. In the narcotics area an ounce of diplomacy has been worth many pounds of subpoenas, contempt orders and undercover harassment. Just as comity and compromise were the parents of a successful Narcotics Drugs Law, so must they also be employed to further harmonious law enforcement efforts between our two governments in other areas.

The statement was signed jointly by Thomas Jefferson and Vassel Johnson.

Following the joint statement by the Financial Secretary and myself, our government seriously considered, as a next step in continuing to build a clean local business atmosphere, the selection of the Cayman team that would join the British team in negotiating the Treaty with the United States. The initial first meeting was scheduled to start on 13th November 1985. The British team members had already been selected in the first half of 1985. They were the Honourable Humphrey Maude, CMG, Assistant Under Secretary, Foreign and Commonwealth Office, London, the Leader; the Legal Counsellor, Mr J.D.P. Bickford of the Foreign and Commonwealth Office; and Mr D.R. Snoxell of the Economic Relations Department also from the Foreign and Commonwealth Office. The Cayman team comprised the Attorney General, the Honourable Michael Bradley; the Financial Secretary, the Honourable Thomas Jefferson; the Minister of Government responsible for Health, Education and Social Services, the Honourable Benson O. Ebanks, and me, Minister for Development and Natural Resources. At a later stage, joining the Cayman team was Sir Ian Percival, QC, a former Conservative MP and former Solicitor-General of England during Mrs Margaret Thatcher's first government.

After my appointment to the Cayman team, a friend of mine in Bermuda, the Honourable Ernest W.P. Vesey, MP, called me by telephone to discuss my plans for the meeting with the Americans later in the year. Ernest knew me well to be a person who would endeavour to strengthen my team's position in any way possible for that most important mission. He persuaded me to do two things in preparation for the Americans, whom he described as 'very shrewd and very experienced negotiators who always shoot for the stars, that is, the best deals in their favour'. The first suggestion was that I should contact a Richard Gray of Gray and Company, in Washington, a leading lobbyist, and try to secure his services for the Cayman team: Ernest gave me Gray's address and advised that he was a well-known individual who moved around in the White House, where he was once employed, and at the State Department, where he was also employed after leaving the White House: he commanded much respect within the United States government. Ernest felt that there was insufficient general recognition in the right quarters of the United States of the lengths to which the Cayman Islands had gone to cooperate with the United States in the suppression of trade in narcotics as well as in other crimes excluding tax or fiscal matters. He also said that a firm such as Gray and Company obviously did have contacts within the present United States administration to possibly influence the forthcoming negotiations in favour of the Cayman Islands. Ernest definitely sold me the idea of hiring Gray and Company.

The second recommendation by Ernest was that I should endeavour to appoint to the Cayman team the Rt. Hon. Sir Ian Percival. Ernest said that both the British and Cayman teams did have legal representations in their present membership; however, all members of both teams were Civil Servants, except Benson Ebanks and me, who were politicians. He therefore felt that we should have a political legal advisor in the person of Sir Ian, a very prestigious and brilliant attorney who, apart from serving the team well, would create an excellent image and impression on our side of the table. Again Ernest sold me the proposition of having Sir Ian as a possible member of the Cayman team.

I arranged a special meeting with my other three elected colleagues of the Executive Council to discuss the Ernest Vesey's two proposals to hire Richard Gray and Sir Ian. We agreed Benson Ebanks would accompany me to Washington to see Richard Gray after the appropriate contact and arrangements for the meeting were made with him. Thereafter Norman and I, who would need to visit London in early March on a Cayman Airways issue, would during the same visit see Sir Ian. The next hurdle was to convince the British team of the new additions. We were aware that the British did not believe in lobbying but we did not know how they would react to the proposal to hire Sir Ian. However, we decided to present the two proposals to them, one at a time. Shortly afterwards the British team visited Cayman for discussions with the government and the Cayman team regarding the up-coming negotiations in Washington. The British team also suggested that the Cayman team visit Washington during June 1985. The main purpose was for us to have preparatory discussions with the British Embassy and at the same time clear the air in the United States for the Treaty negotiation by meeting through the assistance of the British Embassy, prominent Senators, Congressmen and the American Press. I then took the opportunity of presenting to Mr Maude and his team our proposal regarding the appointment of a lobbyist in Washington by the name of Richard Gray of Gray and Company who had been specially recommended to us.

As suspected, the British team spoke out against the appointment of a lobbyist. Apparently they regarded lobbying as professionally unethical, especially in cases of top-ranking negotiations like a treaty between two countries. On the one hand their argument did look feasible, but on the other we knew that the going with the United States would in the circumstances be somewhat difficult unless we were properly prepared to defend our side of the discussion. I therefore pressed my case before Executive Council to have a lobbyist on our team and was pleasantly surprised when there was a silence around the table: to me silence indicated consent. I proceeded immediately after the meeting to speak in person with Richard Gray, with whom I had been in contact over the past ten days, and made firm arrangements to see him in Washington on 8th February 1985. As a follow-up I next wrote to the Governor, Mr Lloyd, for the usual official authority for Benson and me to visit Washington in connection with the possible appointment of Gray and Company as lobbyists to the Cayman team. After nearly two hours of discussion in Washington with Richard Gray and a selected few of his top executives, Benson and I were very impressed with the presentation and thought it could be correct that Richard Gray was in fact the leading lobbyist anywhere in the United States. Included among Gray's top executives were William F. Bolger, a former United States Postmaster General and Alejandro Orfila, former Secretary General of the Organization of American States (OAS).

In the discussion with Richard Gray and his team, he pointed out that we must be prepared to give something to the Americans in return for the protection we sought, but after that was agreed, then somebody must ensure that the arrangements were honoured across the board. This, he said, was where they could give much assistance.

307

He pointed out that if his firm were to represent the Cayman Islands effectively, they should be present at important meetings even if not allowed beyond the corridor during proceedings; there were doubts in our minds that the Americans would accept that. The matter of cost to employ a lobbyist and whether the Cayman government could afford it was another area of discussion. Gray's one year charge of US$60,000 retainer fee and a per hour charge for actual work by people earning from $60 to over $200 appeared expensive. However, the point for careful consideration was the value to Cayman of settling at that stage the country's most important issue. If Gray and Company could do the job well, and there was no doubt in our minds that they could, then the charge was not considered altogether exorbitant when compared to what had been and was still being paid by Cayman for legal representation. In fact I did write to Richard Gray on 30th January 1985 advising that the cost of his work would be a sensitive area in the discussion because of Cayman's budget. It occurred to us that it could be wise to consider forgoing other hired legal service at that stage and concentrating our efforts instead on the lobbying side. In any case, Gray and Company had a very eminent attorney amongst its top executives, J. Peter Segall, who would be a part of Gray's Cayman team. We succeeded in convincing the Cayman government that employment of Gray and Company for the Treaty negotiation would be in Cayman's best interest and therefore signed the contract.

Our next project while on a visit to London for discussion with the British, related to the effort to appoint Sir Ian as a member of the Cayman team. Of course they did not support this proposal either. Mr Maude claimed that both the British and Cayman teams had one very able attorney each and therefore he did not see the need for another lawyer. It became necessary again, as in the case of arguing for the lobbyist, to restate my case for having someone with the image and stature of Sir Ian on our team. Indeed, this point was well driven home in the first round of negotiation when we stepped into the Conference Room of the State Department in Washington and were being introduced to the American team. When Sir Ian Percival was introduced as a former Solicitor General of England, a member of the American team asked me, 'How were you able to recruit such an eminent person on your team?' I just smiled.

The last leg of our recruiting journey for the Treaty negotiation was to London to see if we could influence Sir Ian to join our team. The mission to London on 7th March 1985 by Norman Bodden and me involved two specific jobs. One was to deal with the Cayman government's concern over US approval of another airline to fly the Miami–

Cayman route, as dealt with in Chapter 12 'Air Services'. The other purpose of the visit to London was to meet Sir Ian and discuss with him the possibility of retaining his services to assist the Cayman Islands government in the Treaty negotiation with the United States government. As we had thought, Sir Ian was a likeable gentleman and one of very high repute and standing not only in Britain but also internationally. We concluded after the meeting that Sir Ian was well suited to join our team with his level of legal experience and knowledge of the subject and as a politician. He also understood our case and our concern quite well and thought that a small territory like Cayman should not minimize the need for good representation in such delicate issues as defending its confidentiality system and tax haven status. He said that confidentiality in our context was legally and morally very legitimate, and should be defended as such, since it promoted a prime segment of the Cayman's economy.

After a very lengthy discussion, which started at 7.30 p.m., Sir Ian suggested that our first step be to decide whether we wished to retain his services: he would, he said, be delighted to represent the Cayman Islands. If we retained him he suggested we pass the information on to the UK team, especially to the Honourable Humphrey Maude and David Bickford. He would at that stage also like to liaise with Cayman's Attorney General, Michael Bradley, a member of the Cayman team. He thought that a second preliminary meeting should be arranged between him, as representing Cayman, and the UK team to discuss specifics such as timetable and objectives. He said that specifics were necessary so that if the ultimate goal were a treaty, Cayman should decide what were the areas for the most effective control, bearing in mind that it was vital to ensure non-interference in our confidentiality system as it related to tax matters. This, he said, was the focal point for which defence must be marshalled. Sir Ian thought he could take care of this alone quite comfortably without our presence in London: he was thinking of cost saving on our behalf. He requested that our Attorney General provide the liaison with him in this instance. Sir Ian saw no reason why he should not sit with the Cayman team at the negotiating table if he were representing Cayman; he would certainly clear this with Her Majesty's government.

Sir Ian mentioned that he was in association with a large group of top Washington lawyers (Sidley and Austin) who could assist him if necessary from that side. By coincidence Sidley and Austin were at the time also representing Cayman's legal interest in the United States. At this stage of the interview with Sir Ian we took the liberty of mentioning our contact with Gray and Company, the Washington lobbyists. After Richard Gray's background was outlined to him, Sir

309

Ian thought he would be most usefully involved on the political side of the issue both within the State Department and among the American investigating agencies (IRS and DEA) and the public. The Cayman government and the British team agreed that Sir Ian should be appointed to the Cayman team.

Bearing in mind the advice of Mr Maude that the Cayman delegation should visit the United States before the Treaty discussions began in Washington, we started to put together the programme following the appointments of Gray and Company and Sir Ian. The Cayman group departed Grand Cayman on Sunday 2nd June 1985 for New York City and Washington, DC, with a full seven-day programme for the two destinations. We arrived first at La Guardia Airport in New York at 3.34 p.m. After settling into our New York City hotel, the Grand Hyatt, we arranged a working dinner in the hotel with Charles Francis and Peter Segall of Gray and Company, mainly to review the itinerary and matters related thereto. On Monday morning 3rd June the Financial Secretary attended two press interviews, *Marketwatch* at 9.30 and *Business Week Magazine* at 10.30. At 12 noon the team attended luncheon at the Institute of Foreign Bankers, hosted by the Royal Bank of Canada. At 2.30 we had coffee with senior Wall Street attorneys, followed at 4.30 by a press interview with the *Financial Times* of London. On Tuesday 4th June there were three press interviews with *American Banker*, *Caribbean Update* and the *Journal of Commerce*. Lunch intervened at 12.30 hosted by Barclays Bank in honour of the Cayman delegation. At 9 p.m. we departed for Washington and were accommodated at the Watergate Hotel.

On Wednesday at 8.30 a.m. we attended a breakfast briefing session hosted by Larry Smith (Democrat, Florida). He was Chairman of the House Task Force on International Narcotics Control; also at the breakfast was Robert Lagomarsino (Republican, California), a member of the House Task Force. At 10.30 the Attorney-General, Michael Bradley, attended the Justice Department for discussions with Philip White, representing the US Internal Revenue Service. Lunch at 12.30, which was most enjoyable, was hosted by Sir Oliver Wright, GCMG, GCVO, DSC, British Ambassador to Washington. On my return home I wrote to Sir Oliver on 13th June and thanked him for kindly inviting the Cayman delegation to his luncheon party on 5th June. I went on to say in the letter, 'Our visit to Washington was deemed an interesting one. This was simply because the programme was arranged against a somewhat unusual background insofar as it related to the United States government and the Cayman Islands, a small British Crown Colony with Gray and Company, a private United States firm, intervening. However, with your kind assistance, our visit was a most satisfactory one and one to be remembered.'

On Wednesday 5th June at 3.45 p.m., we met with John M. Walker Jr., Assistant Treasury Secretary for Enforcement and Operations. At 5.30 p.m. members of the Cayman delegation were invited to a reception hosted by the vice chairman of Gray and Company, Admiral Daniel J. Murphy, USN (Ret.). On 6th June at 8.45 a.m. Michael Bradley attended a 'newsmaker' breakfast for a press interview with the National Press Club and at 11 a.m. he attended another press interview for CBS's *Nightwatch*: he was accompanied by Senator Warren Rudman (Republican, New Hampshire). At 11.30 a.m. the delegation met with Congressman Bill McCullom (Republican, Florida), ranking minority member, House Judiciary Subcommittee on Crime. After lunch there was a briefing session hosted by Senator Paula Hawkins (Republican, Florida), Chairman of the Senate Subcommittee on Children, Family, Drugs and Alcoholism. At 4.30 p.m. we met with Senator Dennis DeConcini (Democrat, Arizona), a former prosecutor.

Shortly after Christmas 1985 Dennis DeConcini along with his wife and family visited Grand Cayman. My wife and I met them at the Governor's luncheon on New Year's Day. On his return home from Grand Cayman he wrote to me on 8th January 1986 to say how he enjoyed meeting me again, along with my wife, and hoped that he would be able to return the favour in Washington. This is the sort of close association we established in some parts of the US government during our team's visit to New York and Washington in early June 1985.

On 7th June a press interview with *Newsweek* magazine at the Watergate Hotel was followed at 12.30 by lunch at the International Club hosted by Tom Harris, Commercial Counsellor of the British Embassy. During lunch we discussed negotiation strategy relating to the Treaty, after which we departed for home. During the six days in New York and Washington, Gray and Company placed at our disposal six senior members of their staff. They were Admiral Murphy, Stephen Johnson, Peter Segall, Bruce Fein, Charles Francis and Adonis Hoffman. Richard Gray himself was always able to see us at short notice on any questionable points. One that required discussion with him came from the British Embassy. It said that the Americans were concerned that during the Treaty negotiation it might be possible for Richard Gray to participate in some way with the subject matter. We were therefore requested to persuade him to abstain from any comments during the discussions or even being seen in the

311

corridors leading to the negotiating room in the State Department. We immediately went over to Gray and acquainted him with the message from the State Department to the British Embassy and requested that he should maintain a low profile during the discussion stages of the Treaty unless we required his assistance for any specific reason. In fact he was delighted to comply with the request, especially after being told that the Americans were aware of his involvement with the Cayman Islands team.

After the successful tour of New York and Washington in June 1985, we began preparing for the start of the Treaty discussion. My prime concern was regarding strategy in approach, especially after receiving a model copy of a proposed Treaty from the United States government. In early July 1985 I decided to take a vacation without my wife and selected the top of Jack's Hill overlooking Kingston, Jamaica, where my daughter Zillah Isaacs lived with her husband Tom and their daughter Michelle. I spent two days with them, relaxing and playing dominoes with Tom and other friends. For the next two days I selected a convenient place in the home to continue relaxing and just looking at the mountains, the skies and the city of Kingston below; in between I would read the model US Treaty given to us. Soon I was preparing a draft of a position paper I would address to Sir Ian and copy to all other members of the British and Cayman teams, including the Chairman, Mr Maude.

On return home I consulted my good friend, Attorney Michael Alberga of the firm of Myers and Alberga, regarding my draft position paper on the Treaty. He became very interested in the contents and undertook to vet the paper and put it into some shape to become quite a substantial presentation. It was entitled 'United States/Cayman Islands Treaty – Narcotics and Other Offences'. The opening paragraph to Sir Ian read, 'I thought it would perhaps be in our best interests if some of my own thoughts were conveyed to you in writing regarding the upcoming preliminary discussions on the proposed Treaty between the United States and ourselves. I therefore set out below some general points; these are without prejudice to any other thoughts or points that may be expressed by other members of the Cayman and/or United Kingdom teams.' The confidential document carried eleven paragraphs, the last of which had eight sub-paragraphs. Many excellent points were put forward and in conclusion I said, 'The above points are meant to assist in our preliminary work and at the same time give you a fair overview of my political thinking. As you know our offshore financial industry catering to the international market is, as in the case of most offshore financial centres, a very fragile and unstable sector of the economy. When the income derived

312

from offshore activities is a large slice of the economy, as in our case, you can naturally understand our grave concern when a foreign country like the United States becomes exposed to our confidential information. This would in one way or another surely touch on and affect our financial position.' I received no comments from other members of the teams on the contents of my paper. At the conclusion of the Treaty, Michael did a comparison of its final text with our stated position at the start of negotiation and the results were amazing: our policy on confidentiality and tax offences had been strictly maintained.

On 2nd September 1985 Benson Ebanks and I wrote jointly to a Mr Dan Henninger, Assistant Editor of the editorial page of the *Wall Street Journal* in New York. It was about an article appearing in their newspaper of 14th August 1985 by Thomas E. Ricks entitled 'Tax Evaders Find Foreign Banks Aren't Havens of Secrecy Anymore'. The article contained serious misinformation about the nature of financial confidentiality in the Cayman Islands. It concluded that US tax authorities had 'punctured the bank secrecy of the Cayman Islands' and described the 1984 Narcotics Agreement as 'an unprecedented and still-unique information-exchange agreement of considerable help to US narcotics authorities'. The statement suggested that the Agreement had opened a door the US tax authorities were about to pour through.

The new Cayman government was therefore deeply concerned that our ongoing efforts to rid our offshore financial operations of any real or apparent association with illegal money laundering continued to be misunderstood and misrepresented to the American public. We sent Mr Henninger an article for publication headed 'The Cayman Islands' commitment to financial confidentiality does not extend to individuals involved in drug money laundering'. The record was set straight. Our four-page article concluded by stating:

The Cayman Islands will continue to welcome, as in the past, financial institutions and their clients whose funds originate from a source – and are to be put to a purpose – which is lawful in the Cayman Islands. We understand the desire of US tax and securities authorities to investigate and prosecute all alleged violations of US tax and corporate laws, wherever those violations occur and wherever potential evidence thereof may be found. Conversely, American authorities must appreciate that Caymanians cannot and will not compromise their sovereignty as expressed in a fundamental and legal commitment to financial confidentiality for the convenience of every US law enforcement effort. As we have seen, an ounce of diplomacy may be worth

313

many pounds of subpoenas, contempt orders and undercover harassment. However, just as comity and compromise were the parents of the Narcotics Agreement, so must they also be employed to further harmonious law enforcement efforts between our two countries in other areas.

The Letter of Agreement and fee structure from Gray and Company to provide public communications and government affairs counsel and services in the United States was submitted on 24th October and approved by the Cayman Islands government on 29th October. Thus we were all set for the journey to Washington to start the Treaty negotiation. The date set for the first round of talks was 13th to 15th November 1985. The British team of three was accommodated at the Wellington Hotel and our group of five went to the Watergate Hotel. The Cayman Islands delegation arrived in Washington on Sunday 10th November at 2.25 p.m. and the British team on Tuesday 12th November at 3.05 p.m. At 6 p.m. on 12th November a briefing meeting was held at the British Embassy, largely to deal with the opening presentations at the start of the talks the next morning.

On Wednesday 13th November 1985 talks began in the Department of State, Room 1107. Facing our team of eight members headed by the Chairman, Mr Maude, was the American team of five members, with Mr Andre Surena, Legal Adviser at the State Department, as Chairman. The other four members on the American team were Mr Mark Richard, Deputy Assistant United States Attorney-General; Mr Philip White, Director of the Office of International Affairs, Department of Justice; Mr John Harris, Senior Trial Attorney, Department of Justice; and Mr James Springer, Trial Attorney, Department of Justice. After introductions, the meeting started at 10 a.m. with the Chairman's opening remarks followed by remarks from Mr Maude, our leader. Discussion continued until 5 p.m. One thing I remember of the day's proceedings which I wish to mention was my own presentation. Shortly after the meeting began, discussions were centred on the Cayman Islands: it appeared to me that the Americans around the table did not have a clue what they were talking about in addressing issues concerning the Cayman Islands. I asked the Chairman if any of his team members had ever been to Cayman. He checked on each one but all admitted that they had not. I then suggested that it would serve his team well if they took some time off after the meeting to visit the country so that in future they would not need to argue at cross-purposes over Cayman issues. Silence prevailed for a while and there was no commitment.

Talks continued at the State Department on Thursday and Friday

314

from 9 a.m. to 5 p.m. On Friday the meeting was held in Room 1205. At the adjournment on Friday 15th November the Chairman requested suggestions regarding the next venue for the second round of talks. I quickly took part in the discussion and suggested that the Cayman Islands be reserved for the signing of the Treaty. Silence again prevailed until the Chairman inquired, 'Where do we go next?' I suggested London; that was unanimously agreed.

This first round of talks saw intensive negotiations after which representatives of the three countries involved were able to agree upon the terms of a draft Agreement to be known as the Mutual Legal Assistance Treaty (MLAT). The terms were submitted to the respective governments for approval and confirmation. The title of the Treaty differed from that originally proposed in the Narcotics Agreement. This change reflected the new concept of mutuality of assistance on criminal matters between Cayman and the United States. The procedures contained in the draft Treaty for the giving of such assistance also reflected the concept of mutuality. As the terms of the draft Treaty were still at that stage subject to confirmation by the respective countries, it was not possible for them to be announced. However, it was the hope that the governments would be able to conclude a formal signing ceremony in the early summer, at which time the terms of the Treaty would be made public. Even after the signing ceremony, the Treaty would not come into force until instruments of ratification were signed and appropriate legislation enacted. In the United States, before ratification can take place, approval must be obtained from the Senate. In the United Kingdom, a Treaty can be ratified after it has been laid on the table of the House of Commons for at least 21 working days. In the Cayman Islands it is necessary for appropriate enabling legislation to be enacted and given assent by the Governor; thereafter the law needs finally to be approved by London.

Early in 1986 and before the second round of talks began in London, three members of the American team visited Grand Cayman on Sunday 5th January. They were met at the airport by the Governor, Mr Lloyd and his wife and taken to Government House, where they were accommodated. They were the Chairman, Mr Surena, Mark Richard and Philip White. A full programme was prepared for them, with Monday and Tuesday being quite packed. They attended a meeting of the Executive Council (the Cabinet) on Tuesday at 2.15 p.m. This was followed at 3.30 p.m. by a dive on the *Atlantis* submarine and thereafter a farewell reception at Government House at 6.30 p.m. They departed at 7.35 a.m. on Wednesday. I think they enjoyed the visit and learned much about the country, its people, its economic activity and our valuable asset, confidentiality.

In mid-January 1986 the Cayman team was notified by the British team that discussions would take place at the Foreign and Commonwealth Office in London starting Thursday 23rd January and ending on Saturday 1st February 1986. A programme for the visit was given to each member of the Cayman delegation. The discussion would review any progress made during the Treaty's first round of talks in Washington and what could be expected during the second round in London starting on 15th April 1986. On the lighter side of the programme, on Tuesday 28th January we attended a performance of *Me and My Girl* at the Adelphi Theatre and on Friday evening at our hotel, the Inn on the Park, there was a reception for us involving 110 guests, all of whom we knew. The social evenings were quite enjoyable. We returned home on Saturday 1st February.

We were off again on Sunday 13th April 1986 for the second round of talks on the US/UK/Cayman Treaty, to start in London on 15th April. For the flying experience of our life we persuaded the government to allow us to fly the British Airways supersonic aircraft Concorde from Miami via Washington to London and return, which was approved. Also of interest was that each passenger flying Concorde at that time received a flight certificate that related to the Concorde's tenth anniversary celebration. We were delighted with the experience. Two members of our team, because of their size and height, merely fitted comfortably in the slightly smaller seats of the Concorde compared with other commercial passenger-carrying aircraft. The passenger compartment of the Concorde carried a front panel box that revealed as the aircraft rose from the runway its altitude, speed, temperature and other information. On each mission it flies at 1,350 m.p.h. and climbs into the earth's stratosphere, gaining an altitude of 11.4 miles. It is indeed a most impressive aircraft. We took off from Washington at 5 p.m. and arrived in London at 11.30 p.m., in time to have dinner, a good night's rest and breakfast next morning.

The Cayman delegation met with Sir Ian at 10.30 a.m. on Monday 14th April to discuss a few points of interest. Talks with the American team started on Tuesday at the usual time and adjourned at 5 p.m. Meetings continued on Wednesday and adjourned on Thursday 17th April at 4 p.m. as we were scheduled to return home on Concorde that evening. At the adjournment the Chairman inquired about the next meeting's venue as it was quite evident that a third and possibly final round of talks would be necessary to see the end of the negotiations. I quickly spoke up again and reminded the Chairman of the proposal put forward at the adjournment of the first round of talks in Washington that we would like to reserve the Cayman Islands for the signing ceremony of the Treaty. Mr Surena asked again, 'Where do we go from here for the third meeting?' I suggested back to Washington. The suggestion was agreed to and the meeting adjourned.

At home we had scarcely had time for anything not labelled 'very urgent' before we were on our way again to Washington for the third round of talks with the Americans on the Mutual Legal Assistance Treaty scheduled for 28th April to 1st May 1986. Those four days were quite hectic. One of the important issues was to agree on the 'scope of assistance' relating to 'criminal offences'. In the United States criminal offences include tax offences but not so in the Cayman Islands as Cayman is a tax-free country. If the Treaty were to be based on mutuality, then certainly the Treaty's schedule of criminal offences could not in honesty include tax offences. This was difficult for the American team to accept, especially when they had to explain to their masters the strange omission of tax offences in such an important Treaty. However, it was very important to us that tax offences be excluded from the Treaty, otherwise it would mean instant death for Cayman's economy. The issue required the meeting to spend two days arguing the point and continuing the talks until past midnight. What I can say about the American team is that one of their fine attributes is patience. We were happy about that, for eventually we won our argument and by so doing made history in the United States and elsewhere.

In the final analysis we were confident that the agreement reached during the negotiations of the Mutual Legal Assistance Treaty would in no way damage our financial industry. It would instead enhance legitimate business opportunities and demonstrate the government's determination not to allow our Confidential Relationship (Preservation) Law to be used as a shield for criminal activities.

Officials of the United States, the United Kingdom and the Cayman Islands governments on 3rd July 1986 signed an historic Treaty to provide mutual legal assistance on a broad range of criminal activities. The landmark Treaty, signed in the Legislative Assembly in George Town, followed and extended the 1984 Narcotics Agreement between the three countries. Signing the Treaty was – for the United States – Under Secretary of State Mr Ronald I. Spiers; for the United Kingdom – Under Secretary of State Mr Timothy J. Eggar; and for the Cayman Islands – His Excellency the Governor, Mr G. Peter Lloyd.

Mr Spiers described the Treaty as 'A model of cooperation and a tangible and significant manifestation of the commitment of our two countries including the Cayman Islands, to work cooperatively in our respective efforts to combat crime and to find practical means of bridging our differences.' He revealed that a similar agreement, applicable to the Turks and Caicos Islands, would soon conclude in Washington.

Mr Eggar described the Treaty as 'a milestone in mutual legal assistance between our three governments in the war against international crime. I think it is particularly significant because it tries to tackle a problem thrown up by the increasing ability of criminals to move their ill-gotten assets around. The treaty takes our three countries into 'uncharted waters' which will take close cooperation, patience and a willingness to understand the intentions and difficulties of each side in order to make the Treaty work. But I take comfort from the smooth operation of the 1984 Narcotics Agreement which was due in no small part to the determination of the Cayman Islands not to allow their territory to become a refuge for the proceeds of crime. While the Treaty brings the three countries into uncharted waters, such waters need hold no terrors for the people of these islands.'

The Governor hailed the Treaty as a move which would 'help provide a solid foundation for the further development of the Territory's financial industry. The signature of the Narcotics Agreement two years ago made plain that we were determined to deny shelter to drug traffickers. The present Treaty is evidence of our determination to fight serious crime. It commits local and United States law enforcement officials to cooperate in the investigation, prosecution and suppression of criminal offences by honouring each other's requests for financial records and other documentary or physical evidence, immobilizing criminally obtained property, locating fugitives or witnesses and other forms of assistance.'

Specifically excluded from the Treaty were any matters relating directly or indirectly to the regulation, imposition, calculation or collection of taxes, unless this involved the unlawful proceeds of a crime covered by the Treaty. The provisions of the Treaty would be administered in the Cayman Islands by a Judge of the Grand Court sitting alone as an administrative tribunal or central authority as described in the Treaty. The United States would also have its central authority administered by the Attorney General or a person designated by him. The Treaty is quite an interesting document to read with its concluding statement providing that the governments of either the United States or the United Kingdom including the Cayman Islands, may terminate the Treaty by giving three months' notice in writing to the other government at any time.

After the signing ceremony, the Legal Department moved on with the drafting of the Bill to give legal effect to the Mutual Legal

Assistance Treaty. In the meantime and until the Legislative Assembly met on Monday 1st September 1986 to consider, among other business matters, the MLAT, much discussion, speculation and criticism were thrown at the government for accepting the Treaty without the public's consent. Of course those allegations came from the voice of the opposition, formerly the government of 1976–84 who had introduced the Narcotics Agreement during their administration in 1984.

Having accepted the Treaty we were obliged to ensure that the Mutual Legal Assistance (United States of America) Law 1986, would be passed by the Legislative Assembly. On Sunday night 31st August I went to my office at Elizabethan Square and gave serious thought to how I would proceed next morning to address myself to the MLAT legislation, especially with the opposition jumping on our backs for accepting the Treaty without the consent of the public. Eventually I came up with my plan: of course I cleared it with the President of the Legislative Assembly, the Governor, and the Attorney-General, who would guide the Bill through the various stages in the House. As soon as the Attorney-General moved the first and second readings of the Bill and it was put to the members for debate, I would be the first to rise and speak on it. This plan worked beautifully, although the opposition members tried to beat me to the draw.

I told the House I had regard for my long standing in the government, and for my position as a member of the Treaty negotiating team. I also told the members that I regarded the Treaty as 'a magnificent achievement', one for which the country should be ever thankful to the four local members of the negotiating team under the guidance of our English counterparts, long after the malice of politics had been forgotten. The Treaty, I assured them, set the stage for the future economic well-being of the country because it preserved and left intact the offshore financial centre, while giving the US nothing but the right to pursue their criminals in our country and according to our laws.

After the four opposition members of the House failed to upset the overwhelming support for the MLAT Law, they 'walked out' of the Assembly. A few days later they were going around with a petition addressed to the Right Honourable Sir Geoffrey Howe, QC, MP, Secretary of State for Foreign and Commonwealth Affairs of Her Majesty's government, London. The petition carried six questions and answers which, according to them, tended to confuse or mislead the public. The petitioners were therefore requesting Sir Geoffrey to advise on the kind of amendments required to the Treaty and its enabling legislation to render them acceptable to the public. For

319

instance, they inquired whether the Treaty could not be renamed a 'Law Enforcement Treaty' instead of a 'Mutual Legal Assistance Treaty'. Obviously they were thinking of the name they had suggested in the Narcotics Agreement. The petitioners also sought a change of government before the November 1988 General Election: quite a tall order, especially when in most of the voting in the Legislative Assembly in our administration the results were 9–3 or 8–4. They certainly could not win a censure motion against the government. I am not aware that their petition was dispatched to London, or, if it was, that a reply was forthcoming. The fact is that Britain was just then patiently awaiting ratification of the same Treaty by their Parliament. I thought then that a first test for the Caymans' opposition petition would have been to send it for debate at Hyde Park Corner in London.

The Mutual Legal Assistance (United States of America) Law passed the Cayman Legislative Assembly on 12th September 1986, with assent given by the Governor on 5th November 1986. Britain's ratification of the Treaty followed closely behind Cayman's approval of the Law. However, the Americans' ratification was not completed until August 1987. The Letter of Submittal from the Department of State in Washington by the Secretary of State, Mr George P. Shultz, to the President of the United States, Mr Ronald Reagan, with the text of the Treaty attached, was dated 23rd July 1987. In the letter, and among other comments, Mr Shultz's words to the President were:

I have the honour to submit to you the Treaty between the United States of America and the United Kingdom concerning the Cayman Islands. It relates to Mutual Legal Assistance in Criminal Matters with protocol, signed at Grand Cayman, Cayman Islands on July 3, 1986, together with related note exchanged at London the same day. I recommend that the Treaty be transmitted to the Senate for its advice and consent to ratification. The Treaty covers mutual legal assistance in criminal matters. In recent years, similar bilateral treaties have been concluded and have entered into force with Italy, the Netherlands, Switzerland and Turkey, and have been signed with Canada, Colombia, Morocco and Thailand. All those agreements are part of a highly successful effort to modernize the legal tools available to law enforcement authorities in need of foreign evidence for use in criminal cases. This particular treaty represents a major breakthrough in United States efforts to enlist the cooperation of Caribbean 'bank secrecy' jurisdictions in the investigation and prosecution of trans-border crime. The Treaty contains many provisions similar to those in the other treaties as well as some innovations. The Treaty will not require implementing legislation, and will utilize existing authority of the Federal Courts.

On 4th August 1987 President Reagan transmitted the Treaty Documents Nos. 100–08 to the Committee on Foreign Relations and ordered them to be printed for the use of the Senate. In the communication the President addressed the Senate as follows:

> With a view to receiving the advice and consent of the Senate to ratification, I transmit herewith the Treaty between the United States of America and the United Kingdom of Great Britain and Northern Ireland concerning the Cayman Islands. It relates to Mutual Legal Assistance in criminal matters, with protocol, signed at Grand Cayman on July 3, 1986, and related notes. I transmit also, for the information of the Senate, the report of the Department of State with respect to the Treaty.
>
> The Treaty concerning the Cayman Islands provides for a broad range of cooperation in criminal matters. Mutual assistance available under the Treaty includes: (1) executing requests relating to criminal matters by undertaking diligent efforts, including the necessary administrative or judicial action (e.g. for the issuance of subpoenas and search warrants), without cost to the Requesting Party. (2) Taking testimony or statements of persons by non-compulsory or compulsory measures. (3) Effecting the production, preservation, and authentication of documents, records or articles of evidence. (4) Providing assistance to each other in proceedings for forfeiture or restitution of proceeds of an offense or for imposing fines. (5) Serving judicial documents, writs, summonses, records of judicial verdicts and the court judgements or decisions. (6) Effecting the appearance of a witness before a court of the Requesting Party. (7) Locating persons and (8) Providing judicial records, evidences and information. I recommend that the Senate give early and favourable consideration to the Treaty and give its advice and consent to ratification.

Thus ended quite a rewarding exercise for the Cayman Islands. Looking at the Treaty over the past 12 years, I have wondered many times just how the Cayman Islands could have developed economically without such a treaty in place.

17

Conservation: The Turtle Farm and Marine Parks

In my new political office with the 1984–88 government, I conveniently remembered the words of someone who said, 'There is no class of men so difficult to manage in any country as those whose intention is good but whose consciences are bewitched.' This statement also reminded me of what we sometime hear termed as 'paradoxes in politics' – statements that contradict themselves or conflict with common sense but which contain a truth – for example, 'more haste less speed'. With those words in mind I thought that we had to work calmly and confidently especially in dealing with the public and therefore started by arranging an early discussion with my Principal Secretary, Mr Kearney Gomez, and marine biologist, Mr Joe Parsons. The meeting dealt specifically with the need for us in the portfolio to put careful thought into marine conservation. I thought especially of the need to protect certain species of underwater marine life such as turtle, conch and lobster. Those were in any case considered the most sought-after seafood in these islands, which immediately told of the need for their protection. I was also aware that once again the issue of attempting to commercialize the products of green sea turtles farmed at Cayman Turtle Farm (CTF) would be up for negotiation because that species of turtle came under the United Nations' Convention on International Trade in Endangered Species of wild Fauna and Flora (CITES).

Knowing that my first two important subjects would be Cayman Airways and conservation, I made early arrangements on 16th December 1984 to travel to Miami and Washington, DC, with the Minister for Aviation, Norman Bodden. Our meeting on CAL matters was successful, as explained in Chapter 14 'Air Services'.

The visit to Washington covered two days, 17 to 19 December. First on the programme on Tuesday 18th December, after a business breakfast with our two United States Attorneys Messrs. Steve

322

Boynton and Richard Parsons and our group of five from the Cayman Islands, was the signing at 9.30 a.m. of a Memorandum of Understanding (MOU) with the United States government. Present at the ceremony were our two attorneys and party of five from the Cayman Islands. The MOU related to the exchange of scientific information on endangered species, specifically the green sea turtle. The MOU was signed first by myself on behalf of and as authorized by the Cayman Islands government. Others to sign were officials of the United States government, Mr Ray Arnett, Assistant Secretary of the Fish and Wildlife Service, Department of the Interior, and Mr David Winchester, Assistant Secretary of the National Marine Fisheries Service, Department of Commerce. Before signing the MOU I spoke at the well-attended gathering, which included the press; the meeting was considered very friendly and cordial. On his return home Minister Norman Bodden, reporting to Governor Peter Lloyd of Cayman on the signing ceremony of the MOU, said: 'This was a most impressive ceremony, well attended by various senior US government officials and the press. I might add here that Mr Johnson's short and impromptu address was well presented and from comments made after the meeting was also well received.'

The MOU established a system for exchanging relevant, non-confidential and non-privileged information concerning conservation of wildlife and its environment, and particularly relating to sea turtles. Each party to the MOU would designate from time to time a person or office responsible for such communications and would so notify the other parties. The MOU contained four Articles on a three-sheet document. Articles I and II dealt with Cooperative Programmes, Article III with Mechanisms and Article IV established Final Terms which included effective date and termination.

Having successfully completed the Washington mission in signing the MOU, two important projects still awaited my attention. First was the proposed creation of a marine park system throughout the three islands and, secondly, to lead a team to the United Nations in Buenos Aires, Argentina, to deal with Cayman Turtle Farm's green sea turtles issue.

CITES and the Turtle Farm

Capturing wild turtles from the ocean had been a well known industry in Cayman until World War II prioritized other marine activities. With the introduction of Mariculture Ltd. (predecessor of the Cayman Turtle Farm) the green sea turtle industry returned to Grand Cayman

23 years after the war ended. That was at a time when Caymanians had almost forgotten the taste of their once favourite local dish. Having returned to the table the meat then became even more popular than before. The quality of turtle meat depended largely on the feed. In the early stages of the farm's operation there was a problem to provide sufficient of their natural food, which was mainly sea grass grown in certain shallow protected areas around the coastline of Grand Cayman. However, grass was not easily obtained and the supply in any case was also limited to commercial turtle farming. The farm's research into developing a suitable formula for its growing turtle population went on for a long time. Eventually the researchers and the Purina Company came up with a suitable feed, described as 'fish meal' spiced with soya bean as the protein base. This was an acceptable substitute and is apparently still being used successfully.

The green sea turtle is the most sought after species amongst all turtles; its food and other values have attracted it into the net as the world's most valuable reptile. Due to over-exploitation in other parts of the world in the years following the war, a new interest in the Cayman turtle industry was developed when a number of foreign investors established in Grand Cayman in 1968 a green sea turtle farm known as Mariculture Ltd. The operation first began at Salt Creek in the North Sound and later moved to Goat Rock at North West Point in West Bay because of the need for improved sea water supply. The farm started with the purchase of about 15,000 eggs from Costa Rica, where the green sea turtles abound. The young greens from this first lot of eggs became the farm's first turtle population.

The farm made steady progress and by 1972 Mariculture began to be known internationally for its products. Inquiries then started flowing in from around the world. By that time its scientific research programmes enabled it to become largely self-sufficient in the production of eggs for its hatchery. The company became delighted with its progress; it was an indication that the farm was being successfully developed. But that was only a prelude to problems stemming from serious false accusations by conservationists against the farm. They implied that the green sea turtle could face extinction as a result of commercial trading. Their allegation made no mention of the fact that the farm had become self-sufficient in eggs and young turtles for its replenishment needs. In early 1973 the green turtle (*chelonia mydas*) was added to the list of endangered species by the US government. With support from a few other nations, they drew up a petition declaring that there must be established an effective system for regulating international trade in endangered species. The petition was later adopted by the United Nations and known as The Convention on International Trade in Endangered Species of Wild Fauna and Flora (CITES).

As the convention went into effect it banned the green sea turtle and its products from exportation into countries associated with the UN regulating petition. CITES, to say the least, crippled the farm's development efforts. In 1979 the United States went a step further and banned the importation of all turtle products, which were then sold in many countries, including the United States. In fact, sales to the United States made up 70 per cent of the farm's export trade. Now there were only very few, small foreign outlets where the farm could trade. American tourists, who formed the bulk of travellers to Grand Cayman, could no longer buy turtle-shell jewellery from the farm and take it back to the United States, as shells were also included in the US banned turtle products: this was another big blow to the farm. By the mid-1970s the farm went into receivership.

Shortly afterwards, a German entrepreneur, Dr Heinz Mittag, visited Grand Cayman. Before coming here, Dr Mittag had been advised by his local attorney, Marshall Langer, that while he was in Cayman he should see me (the Financial Secretary), as I would per-haps be able to put him on to local investment opportunities. Dr Mittag, who was escorted to my office by another Cayman lawyer, Ian Paget-Brown, made the point that he had sold his business in West Germany and decided to reinvest a portion of the proceeds in Cayman. I immediately suggested to him that he might care to take a look at the turtle farm as it was just then in receivership and up for sale; it could be a good venture and one that might attract his atten-tion. He seemed delighted and I thought his interest was largely because turtle was his favourite hobby. It was understood that his interest in the farm was also as a result of his daughter studying or being interested in marine biology. He nevertheless thanked me and promised he would see the receiver appointed under a court order to liquidate the farm. Dr Mittag did buy the farm in 1977 with a stock of 60,000 green sea turtles. He also bought the company Mariculture Ltd. and renamed it The Cayman Turtle Farm Ltd.

Dr Mittag offered the government 50,000 shares in the new com-pany. The government bought the shares as an indication of the islands' support for the farm and as an encouragement to the new owners. However, the high hopes of success had by 1980 turned into despair because of the CITES restrictions. In 1983 the farm presented a ranching proposal to CITES at a UN meeting in Botswana. The resolution requested again the down-listing of the farm's green turtles to commercial trading. The proposal had very little support, yet at the same meeting CITES approved in principle a far less attractive ranching proposal submitted by Surinam which was clearly a critical political attitude against Cayman's turtle farm. That latest decision of the United Nations placed the farm in a further dilemma. Following the CITES meeting, Dr Mittag accepted his losses in many millions of dollars and sold the farm to the government for a small fraction of its cost. Nobody else apart from Dr Mittag would have invested such a large sum of money in the farm and the doctor was quite conscious of his error by then. However, he still had hopes that under the government's care the farm would one day succeed, and so it did.

When I entered politics in 1984 I was made responsible for the Portfolio of Development and Natural Resources. The farm became one of my portfolio's projects and immediately after the election in November 1984, I took over the chairmanship of the farm's board of directors. By April 1985 I was off to Buenos Aires, Argentina, with my Permanent Secretary, Mr Kearney Gomez, and Dr Jim Wood, manager of the farm, to join the British team also attending the UN meeting. Our mission was to present, on behalf of the Cayman Islands, ranching and other proposals for the farm's improvement, this being another attempt at trying to relieve the awful pressure brought to bear on the farm by the CITES restrictions. We decided to employ every effort possible in an attempt to reverse the farm's status to that of commercial trading which it once enjoyed.

The Cayman members arrived in Buenos Aires on Sunday 21st April 1985 at 1.10 p.m. and met the UK team at 4.30 p.m. We reached our hotel at about 1.50 p.m. I immediately tried to telephone my wife to let her know of my safe arrival. The hotel operator asked for information regarding the location of Grand Cayman: I gave it to him in detail. Every couple of minutes he would be back with the same request for more information. After having enough of it and being tired, sleepy, hungry and what not, I said to the operator, 'Listen to me, chap, Cayman belongs to England and it has not changed its location in the Western Caribbean, it is still about two hundred miles south of Cuba.' 'Thank you, sir,' said the operator in a quiet, gentlemanly and polite manner. It was less than a minute later that the phone rang again; that time it was my wife. Of course that incident was soon after the Falkland Islands War and England was well known and respected, but for our case and at that particular time it was certainly not to our advantage.

The farm's well-prepared papers for the meeting supported its presentation of yet another attempt to have its green sea turtles downlisted to allow them to trade again in the international commercial markets. The proposal was put forward by the UK team as the Cayman Islands, a British Crown Colony, had no membership status at the UN.

326

The resolution with its large bundle of supporting documents was rejected, and so were similar resolutions by other countries.

There was a feeling among the Cayman team that although the atmosphere in Argentina was quite pleasant and friendly generally, nevertheless the recent 1982 Falkland Islands War involving Britain and Argentina had much of Argentina's anguish in defeat reflected in their opposition to our motion. In fact the sympathy for Argentina from most of the Central and South American countries over the outcome of the war was quite evident in the pooling of votes from that area and undoubtedly made a difference in the final decision. Perhaps, had the voting been based on the farm's efforts and successes in its conservation programme, the results of the presentation might have been somewhat more pleasing to the Cayman team.

Both the Cayman and British team members were very disappointed over the decision of the UN against the turtle farm's case. The count of votes indicated that about 27 nations voted in favour of the Cayman resolution out of 68 countries represented. After some deep thinking I said to my two colleagues, Gomez and Wood, 'Don't worry, boys, this may not be a disappointment altogether for Cayman Turtle Farm. When I get back home a proposal will be put to the government for development of the farm purely as a domestic operation and hopefully in a couple of years it will move away from a government-subsidized entity to a viable economic venture.' Both men laughed at me but my prediction actually became a reality in the estimated couple of years. Jim Wood had some bright ideas for certain improvements and between the three of us we prepared a programme and presented it to the government on arrival back home. It was the thinking then as well that it would be futile to continue arguing the turtle farm's case with the UN. In fact this useful and prolific reptile, the green sea turtle, was very ingrained in Cayman culture, the island's name being originally *Las Tortugas* (the turtles). In fact, the turtle appears as a national emblem on the Cayman flag and our coat of arms. We therefore thought it should not be allowed to become extinct and that the farm should be improved commercially to attract more visitors, thereby increasing income from that source, as well as developing other areas of the operation purely for the domestic market.

Another improvement was the idea of building a snack bar at the farm that would serve turtle soup and turtle-burgers, and also a flora and fauna area using Caribbean plants and animals indigenous to these islands. Included in the improvements were three alligators, once also a native of these islands. The last one, according to residents, was seen in 1935 at Little Cayman.

327

The final part of our proposals to the government was the recommendation to increase the turtle stock and to market all the meat locally, the stew including the fat for home dishes and the steak for restaurants. Hitherto, oil extracted from turtle fat was sold in Japan for use in cosmetic preparations. In Cayman the fat would be sold with the stew as the mixture produced a better-tasting dish. Secondly, the fat, if mixed with the stew, could fetch a better local price than if processed into oil and sold in Japan.

It should also be mentioned that the three alligators purchased by the farm in Christmas, Florida, just outside Orlando, became an amusing joke both at the farm and around town. They were given the names of the four elected members of the government, Charles (Kirkconnell), Benson Norman (Benson Ebanks and Norman Bodden) and Vassel (Johnson), split up among the three alligators. Anyhow, the ministers did not mind the joke for the alligators attracted quite a large number of people to the farm, local residents and visitors alike, which helped to increase entrance fee income.

In order to go ahead with our special proposed project for the farm's improvement, a working capital in the amount of CI$100,000 was required in the form of either a grant from the government or a loan to the farm. Although the farm was given a difficult time in obtaining the money, funds in the amount of $100,000 were eventually raised from the government in the form of a loan. The complete project cost amounted to approximately $160,000: the additional money was provided from the farm's own resources. The development project moved on quickly and was completed by mid-1986. On 7th January 1988 I arranged an official opening of the farm's new facilities with the Governor, Mr Alan Scott, in attendance. Also there were members of the Executive Council and other officials and members of the public.

In my opening speech I said, 'I believe the farm is now a truly valuable asset to the Cayman Islands with its new facilities displaying exhibits of Caymanian flora and fauna and a snack bar with an information gallery. The farm was not a "lost cause" when the government's efforts in 1985 to lift the ban on foreign trade, placed on it by the United States, failed. Following that disappointing experience, new avenues were explored which produced what we see here on display today. The green sea turtle is a traditional food of Cayman and for that very reason the farm is useful. The farm raises enough turtle meat, approximately seventy thousand pounds a year, to supply the public. However, it costs much more to raise the turtle than what selling the meat can produce.'

The manager of the farm, Dr Jim Wood, confirmed that the

additional money earned by the farm came from tourism. Turtle souvenirs (gift items made from the shell, oil and turtle logos) made up approximately 80 per cent of the sales, he said, a reversal of the sales trend ten years ago when it was the turtle meat and by-products making up the bulk of the sales. He went on to say that to make money from the turtle all the products had to be sold. Of course one of the products the local market could not absorb was the shell, which made beautiful furniture, but there was so much of it: yet the accounts did reveal that the farm was making money. Another area of money making was the number of tourists visiting the farm each year. By March 1988 the figure was expected to reach nearly 90,000.

I mentioned that the farm was now not exclusively a turtle reserve. Visitors could view other local flora and fauna in new display enclosures that made use of space left by redundant turtle tanks. There were also the Cayman iguanas running around in an enclosure among the indigenous yucca, sea grape and royal palm, and a freshwater hickatee living in a pool. Also there were the Cayman rabbits, the agouti, and an aviary containing Cayman and Honduran parrots and blue and yellow South American macaws.

The official visiting party examined the crocodiles, our namesakes, and also an aquarium at the northern end of the farm containing creatures to be found in the waters surrounding the islands: a shark, a moray eel and tropical fish. After that we toured the snack bar and enjoyed turtle soup and turtle-burgers. Dr Wood told the visitors that the farm sold up to 100 turtle patties a week to curious tourists. He said that the burgers were an inexpensive way to try turtle meat and that after resolving the difficulty of finding suitable staff for the snack bar, it would be opened seven days a week.

The farm made a dramatic start and an earlier recovery than expected. By 1st April 1988 the government's subsidy to the farm, which had at times exceeded $200,000 per annum, was no longer required; the $100,000 loan for the farm's improvements was paid and the company's balance sheet also revealed a profit. Each year since then, for at least ten years, the farm has recorded a profitable and successful operation. The successes of its 1986 development and its dramatic financial recovery by 1988 confirmed the wisdom of Dr Mittag and his own decision to preserve the farm by selling its assets to the government, albeit at a tremendous discount on his actual cash outlay on the project.

In submitting to the Legislative Assembly my annual report and audited accounts of the farm for the fiscal year 1st April 1987 to the 31st March 1988, I stated as follows:

The past year's operation of the farm has been the most financially successful year in the company's history. No government subsidy was required and a profit of CI$75,721 was made. As in recent years the majority of income was derived from tour admission fees and gift shop sales. The gift shop was modified to increase its area by 273 square feet. Sale of edible and non-edible turtle products accounted for only 32.9 per cent of income. The number of tourists visiting the farm increased during the year to 89,539 from 75,653, an increase of 18.4 per cent. Revenue from tours rose 17.5 per cent to CI$287,056. Retail sales from the gift shop increased from $292,570 to $372,619 or 27.4 per cent. Overall income of the farm for the year increased 22.7 per cent to $1,042,939.

During the year 3,179 turtles weighing 175,713 lbs were butchered, producing 65,811 lbs. of turtle stew, 13,260 lbs of steak and 2,342 lbs of fin. Herd weight, excluding breeding stock, increased from 353,682 to 375,907 lbs. During the 1987 reproductive season 55,066 eggs were set, producing 16,779 hatchlings. Of these, 5,603 were released into local waters, 2,560 were shell grafted and held for release as yearlings in October 1988 and the remaining 8,616 held as future farm stock. In October 1987, 501 yearlings were released which brought to 20,562 the green sea turtles released into Cayman waters since 1980. The farm should, under strong management, continue to improve its financial position, become self-sufficient and pay dividends to the government.

It was also the hope that CITES would make a record of the farm's tremendous progress and success following the UN decision in 1985 to reject the farm's request for removal of the restrictions against its foreign commercial trade. The request was seen at the time as the only hope for the farm's survival. However, the testing of patience can sometimes result in wonderful discoveries and developments such as these, for CTF today, according to our records, may be the only such green sea turtle farm in existence. All the others have fallen by the wayside for want of support from CITES and the world of conservation. Fortunately, in 1985 Cayman decided it would no longer hang on to the shirt-tails of CITES, for we had seen, from the time it first came into being many years before, that it persistently tried to deprive CTF of the opportunity to raise the greens in captivity and sell its products offshore. The farm's scientific research and experimental programmes are of much value. Those programmes have been placed at the disposal of a vast number of institutions and individuals around the world who may in time develop an interest in rearing the green sea turtle in captivity to preserve the species and increase the wild stock.

In 1979 CTF was approached by the Mexican government to assist it in the conservation of their endangered Kemp's Ridley sea turtle, known as *lepidochelys kempii*, the smallest of the sea turtles, weighing between 40 and 80 pounds. Those turtles are found only in the Gulf of Mexico. The purpose of the approach was to secure assistance in having the Kemp's breed and lay in captivity as they were a severely endangered species. Secondly, the Cayman turtle farm was seen as the safest haven anywhere for Mexican needs. In April 1979 a group of scientists and businessmen met in the United States, with representatives from CTF; they drew up an agreement for placing the Kemp's Ridley at Cayman Turtle Farm. The proposed ongoing programme was that the Kemp's' eggs would be collected at Rancho Nuevo, Mexico, and sent to the Galveston Laboratory of the National Marine Fisheries Service where the young would be reared until big enough to survive in the wild. The farm took on the programme very successfully.

Five years after the first batch of Kemp's arrived at the farm, the captive-breeding herd laid 877 eggs, producing 266 hatchlings. In August 1987, 160 of these hatchlings were transported to Galveston, Texas, for rearing to one year of age at the United States National Marine Fisheries Laboratory. In 1988 I went out on a boat trip in the Gulf of Mexico, along with other officials and the press, to witness the release into the wild of those hatchlings. One area of the programme Dr Wood and I discussed was the fact that the farm had never been offered financial or any other form of compensation for its efforts in providing labour and the other costs of maintaining and feeding the Kemp's stock. However, the free programme was quite a credit to the farm.

Marine Parks Legislation

The Cayman Islands marine parks were established in 1986 by regulations made under the Marine Conservation Law of 1978. Another companion piece of legislation was an order made under the Customs Law to restrict the importation of spare guns and parts. These regulations and the order were enacted to protect marine fauna and flora, including underwater coral, spiny lobsters, conch and other forms of marine life, such as the different species of turtle that inhabited the waters of these islands. Regarding spear guns, I had wished over the

331

previous few years, while in the position of Financial Secretary, that some form of control could be placed on the use of those dangerous marine weapons. Where I lived on South Church Street, on the beach side of the road, was an area where every Sunday, without exception, a group of young men from the Walkers Road area gathered with their spear guns striking anything underwater coming in sight. After putting up with the annoying destruction of young underwater creatures for some time I approached elected members of the Executive Council on the matter of possible spear guns control. I related to them my own experience of the destruction to sea life being caused by the use of those damaging underwater weapons, especially in the area where I lived. However, they spoke up and said that for political reasons they could not assist in the situation. When I was campaigning in the political race in 1984, I noticed that the spear gun situation had become even worse, and what came up on the weapons was a disgrace. I remained calm, however, by hoping that the opportunity would present itself for me to deal meaningfully with the issue: it certainly came my way and I did make good use of it.

At the presentation in the Legislative Assembly in early 1985 of the proposal to establish marine parks in these islands under the Marine Conservation Law, I included in the motion a recommendation to ban the use of spear guns. The members thought, however, that spear guns should instead be controlled and that their use be confined only to accommodate tour boat operators. Those are people who take visitors out on tours, and one of the novelties on the boat ride would be to spear the controlled number of lobsters for the day's meal. The Assembly's decision was agreed: I did not oppose it because it appeared to me that at least we were getting a foot in the door on the subject of spear gun control. However, the public soon heard about the Assembly's thoughts on the subject and organized a demonstration led by Gilbert McLean, a well-known politician, on the spear gun issue and its proposed use by tour boat operators only. The demonstrators thought the decision of the Assembly was very unfair to local residents by not giving them similar or equal opportunity to use their own spear guns.

Just before Christmas 1985, the Civil Service held its customary annual luncheon, with the venue that year at Faces Night Club, located north of the Cinema Theatre on the West Bay Road. I attended the function and so did Gilbert McLean. We both took the opportunity of getting together during that festive occasion to discuss the spear gun issue; we happily came to an amicable agreement on the subject. The proposal was that I would recommend to the government that control be put on spear guns in the form of licensing. Anyone over the age of 18 years who had lived in these islands for at least five years could apply to the government for a special licence to own and use the instrument underwater outside any declared marine parks and replenishment zones areas in the three islands. Gilbert was quite happy with the compromise and so were his followers.

When the order under the Customs Law was prepared in April 1986 to restrict the importation of spear guns, which was generally agreed in the government, neatly slipped into the order after 'spear guns' were the words 'and spare parts'. Nobody noticed it then until about a year later when the old spear guns were in need of spare parts, and it became a great surprise to owners to discover that they could not purchase them locally or order them from abroad. Fishermen came to me about it. I presented the matter to the chairman of the Marine Conservation Board. However, it appeared that no one in the government was enthused over interfering with the matter. In fact the subject came under my portfolio and I certainly was not prepared to touch it. The Customs order therefore remained in its original form. The disappointment among spear gun owners of not being able to purchase or obtain spare parts continued until the issue died a natural death, and all to the good of Cayman's marine life. Thus also came my long awaited wish to abolish the use of spear guns in the Cayman Islands.

The following year the Marine Conservation Board declared March 1987 an amnesty month for unlicensed spear guns. The Chairman of the Board, Mr Don Foster, in declaring the amnesty, said, 'We feel there are quite a number of spear guns which have not been licensed and we cannot be happy with such a situation. So we have decided to give everyone a last chance to comply with the law and apply for licences for their spear guns. But after the end of March, there will be no leniency toward anyone found with an unlicensed spear gun. Such weapons will be confiscated and the owners and users prosecuted, facing penalties which could be as severe as a five thousand dollar fine and twelve months in prison.' Mr Foster also reminded those persons with the first licences issued the previous year that renewal should be made annually on the anniversary of the issue.

The government first gave consideration to the creation of the marine parks in 1982. My Principal Secretary back at the time under the previous government, Kearney Gomez, made a public statement on the subject. He said, 'We wish to set up marine parks for everyone to enjoy and to benefit from, while protecting the natural environment for the generations who will follow us.' That was quite a factual and appropriate statement as would be seen in the years to follow. The press announcement of the proposed system was made by the leader of the Unity Team, who was Minister for Tourism, Aviation and Trade and not by the Minister responsible for marine conservation under the portfolio of Agriculture, Land and Natural Resources. However, study began early afterwards but for some unknown reason the subject was shelved. I knew the early story behind the parks system. Therefore after being assigned responsibility for the newly named portfolio of Development and Natural Resources, I requested my Private Secretary in early 1985 to let me have the files on the subject. I considered marine parks very important to these islands, and in fact a development that should not be delayed in its preparation and implementation. I therefore started to work on the subject in early 1985.

Marine parks, new to these islands, were to pose problems for the natives. The formula and controls selected for their implementation would certainly disrupt the people's long-standing and traditional form of fishing with hook and line and fish pot in the shoal waters of the three islands. The regulations would designate certain parts of all Cayman's shoreline waters as restricted marine areas for purposes of marine research, development, conservation and replenishment. The system was launched in early 1985 by a team from my portfolio that included Joe Parsons, a marine biologist from my office, and Ms Gina Ebanks (later Mrs William Petrie) from the Natural Resources Laboratory of the Mosquito Research and Control Unit, also within my portfolio. Mrs Ebanks-Petrie became Head of the Department of the Environment during the 1990s. The presentation of the parks proposals to the districts in 1985 did not go down well; they were rejected because the people could not be convinced that the system was good for the country. This was so, even though they acknowledged that lobsters, conchs and whelks, the country's prime seafood which once abounded in local waters, had practically disappeared due to overfishing. Still they rejected control which attempted to repopulate the local waters with those vital foods.

In early 1986 plans were again drawn up and a special team selected for the second attempt at getting across the vital message to residents of the districts concerning the urgent need for marine conservation in the form of a marine parks system. In the plans, careful thought was given to the strategies and approach to be used in presentations to all the districts. The 1986 team was similar to the first one in 1985 except for one addition, an attorney, Mrs Dace Ground, wife of the Honourable Attorney-General, Richard Ground. We thought that the legal aspect joining force with the technical expertise and involving two ladies in the presentation would help in

334

the way of strategies and approach. The team was given orders, using the same time frame as in the 1985 attempt, to move on with the important assignment. I gave the team a special instruction to be used in difficult cases. It was that if in their presentation they ran into difficulties, they should take a break and get back to me in person so I could examine the problem and suggest action.

Maps of the three islands were prepared clearly indicating marine park zones, replenishment zones and environmental zones. Regarding the first zone (marine parks), no taking of any marine life alive or dead was allowed. Line fishing from shore or beyond the drop-off at the edge of the deep, and taking fry, and sprat with fry or cast nets, were permitted. Fish traps, spear guns, pole spears and seine nets were totally prohibited. In the second zone (replenishment) no taking of conch or lobster by any means was permitted. Line fishing and anchoring was permitted. Spear guns, pole spears, fish traps and nets were prohibited. The third zone (environmental) prohibited without exception the taking of any marine life, alive or dead. Also, no anchoring of any boat or in-water activities were permitted. In fact there was only one such area in the three islands declared an environmental zone. It was in the eastern section of the North Sound between Water Quay and Duck Pond. A brochure entitled *Facts about Cayman's Marine Life* was also prepared and circulated locally for the benefit of visitors; it included a summary of Cayman's Marine Conservation Law.

The first problem which the team encountered related to a request in East End for the removal of seaweed or grass from a small area of the sea bottom in a proposed replenishment zone. The work required there was to deepen the area slightly to create a commercial boating facility for the benefit of the district: at the same time it could be used as a public bathing beach. I looked at the request and thought to myself, 'Why allow such a small and practically unimportant issue to foul our attempt to achieve greater things?' On that basis I gave permission for approval of the request. The news of that decision quickly spread not only in East End but throughout the eastern districts and perhaps did more good than harm to the programme: in fact that was the only case coming from the eastern districts for special permission.

The team next visited West Bay, the district thought all along to be the worst of the problem areas. One real issue did surface in West Bay. The marine park zone there in fact covered all of George Town and West Bay. It started from Sand Cay apartments at South West Point in George Town, ran to the edge of the deep and then went all along the George Town waterfront, the Seven Mile Beach and on to Broad Walk at North West Point in West Bay. The people of West

Bay said through their representative team to my team, 'We have for generations used the waters in front of this district for all our fishing needs. Now you are telling us that in a short time the people of West Bay will not be permitted to use their time-honoured fishing area? Certainly there has got to be a compromise or an exception to the rule in this case.' Shortly afterwards I was presented with the West Bay problem. I told my team that the West Bayers were quite right: there had to be a way for them to be accommodated with fishing in their marine parks' area. In fact I thought also that the length of the park on the west of the island was much too long, as it embraced all the shoreline between South West Point and North West Point.

The decision was not long in the making. I sat with my team and worked out the compromise. An area of approximately 100 yards between the West Bay Cemetery and Victoria House to the east, and running parallel (south) to the ocean, would be declared a replenishment zone. In that area line fishing and anchoring would be permitted and also the taking of fry and sprat by a fry or cast net. When the decision was taken back to the West Bay residents they could scarcely believe it. However, they were most appreciative of the decision and since then no other problems appeared in the West Bay area. The team therefore moved on to Cayman Brac and Little Cayman; in a fairly short period of time the entire exercise in the three islands was completed.

The marine parks regulations establishing parks around Grand Cayman, Cayman Brac and Little Cayman were made in May 1986. In December 1986, a full-time Marine Enforcement Officer, Mr Ladner Watler, on loan from the Police Force, was appointed and transferred to my office to serve the Grand Cayman area. I recalled advising the Legislative Assembly early after his appointment, that Ladner was like 'Superman' for one never knew 'whence he cometh'. He was as good as all that; a very dependable enforcer. I have had personal experiences of Ladner's alertness on the job and wondered how he could have moved as rapidly as he did.

In a public statement made through Government Information Services on 23rd December 1986, Ladner said, 'I know that people have stopped doing what they have previously been doing in the North Sound, for instance. I think, however, we are gradually getting the message across and people are realizing that unless we look after what we've got, Cayman will lose its attractiveness and we shall all be worse off.' In another statement in mid-1987, he appealed to the public for cooperation between dive boats and fishermen in their respective uses of the waters around the islands and in conforming to regulations. He also remarked that: 'There are thousands of young conches and turtles throughout the waters around Grand Cayman. A positive change is already evident.' In contributing to this achievement, he prosecuted a number of violators, the aim being to achieve cooperation through an emphasis on education rather than enforcement. Watler was liked generally by the public notwithstanding his action on the job, and this was the reason for the success of his enforcement of the marine parks regulations. There was never an indication that the position for enforcement officers was no longer necessary: there are many in the public that are just sitting and waiting for an opportunity to get out there and do the things they were accustomed to doing long ago.

When I was asked by Government Information Services in November 1986 for my view on the new Enforcement Officer, I said, 'This is the beginning, I hope, of seeing full-time, experienced enforcement officers with the power to arrest offenders and provide consistent and reliable enforcement of the Marine Conservation Law. When we met with the public about establishing the marine parks, better enforcement was an issue raised in every district. We are therefore pleased to have an officer with Ladner Watler's excellent credentials to begin this new phase of giving marine conservation real meaning in Cayman.'

Ladner took up his new duties on 1st December 1986 after 12 years' police service, the last eight of which he was a detective constable in the Special Branch. He was seconded to the new post of Marine Parks Enforcement Officer by arrangement with and cooperation of the Commissioner of Police. In May 1988 another officer formerly associated with the Police Force was also employed to serve in Cayman Brac and Little Cayman. My portfolio went on to include installing necessary markers, moorings and signs in the parks areas. All those actions made the islands fully aware that Cayman's marine parks had eventually become a reality. The country has since rejoiced over this achievement: may enforcement of the regulations continue successfully. I recall moving the marine park recommendations and legislation through the Legislative Assembly in May 1986 when an opposition member making his contribution to the debate said, 'We should not get buried in marine parks and all this sort of nonsense.' Nevertheless, in mid-1986 the public at large was all ready to support marine conservation and they did it willingly for they were by then convinced that it was a good thing for the country.

The North Sound has always been, to my thinking, a crucial area of Grand Cayman for the part it plays in marine conservation. The vast swamps bordering it from the land side, and the nearly 10 miles of reef stretching from North West Point to Rum Point, suggests that its vast body of water does contribute much to the marine life of

Grand Cayman. For that reason, when the North Sound was being considered as a part of the parks system, the large area was divided in two equal parts, the east to be replenishment and environmental zones and the west economic development. The swamp areas running along the Seven Mile Beach, being a large part of Benson Greenall's leased property from the government, were at the time being developed. The larger projects included the Governor's Harbour, the Cayman Islands Yacht Club and Marina, Snug Harbour, Canal Point and Safe Haven. Because of those activities, the western half of the North Sound had to be assigned to economic development. One thing for sure was that the whole of Grand Cayman could not be closed either to conservation or to economic development. There had to be a balance between the two.

In the mid-1960s, the Seven Mile Beach area with its large tracts of swamps was considered the hub of the developing tourist industry. As the swamps were mosquito breeding grounds, it was thought that economic development in the area and the reclaiming of much of the swamp lands would assist the control of mosquitoes. In any case, as mangrove swamps were removed, the areas eventually became developed, with golf courses, yacht basins, residential homes and condominiums. In time the areas were also covered with gardens and fruit trees, an act of afforestation to restore a part of the land's natural environment. Apart from other small developments further east such as the Rum Point, and the Water Quay developments, North Sound Estate (formerly Rackley's Canal), Omega Bay Estates, Prospect Park and Tropical Gardens, the remaining areas were still dense swamps requiring mosquito control.

The Wickstead Report

The North Sound in Grand Cayman is a subject that has been discussed since long before marine parks were developed in 1986. I recall visiting the Foreign and Commonwealth Office in London in late 1960 and while having lunch with the Principal Secretary, West Indian Department, Mr A.J. Fairclough, he asked me what in my opinion was considered Cayman's most potential area for development. I told him the North Sound; he asked me to describe it. After outlining its location, size and usefulness, partly as a marine conservation area, I saw him nod approvingly. A few years later, in May 1973, London approved through the Ministry of Overseas Development an aid programme to finance a Natural Resources Study of the Cayman Islands which would specifically include the North Sound.

338

The team appointed for the study would be led by Dr J.H. Wickstead of the Ministry of Overseas Development, London, and the Marine Biological Association of the United Kingdom. Dr Wickstead was designated the Technical Director of the study and would be responsible for overall coordination and the production of the preliminary, interim and final reports. Dr M.E.C. Giglioli, Director of the Mosquito Research and Control Unit, Cayman Islands, was the Resident Director who would be responsible for the local administration and running of the Natural Resources Study Laboratory and its associated equipment. There was a large staff of UK specialists involved in the study including Dr D. Stoddard of the Department of Geography, Cambridge University, a field expert who gave specialist advice in the study of the coral reefs and mangroves.

The terms of reference for the study were as follows:

1. To determine the nature and extent of the natural marine resources of the Cayman Islands, their current and potential importance to the islands, and the current and foreseeable damage to which those resources might be subjected.
2. To recommend legislation and other measures for the utilization and preservation of those resources.
3. To produce the following reports: a preliminary report by August 1974; an interim report by January 1975; a final report by November 1975. In the preliminary and interim reports particular attention was to be paid to dredging operation.

Part I of the Final Report and Recommendation was completed in December 1975. In it Dr Wickstead said, 'With regard to the manner of presentation of the study, each of the institutions concerned presented its own section. They were not written in isolation as there was a regular interchange of data, opinions and personnel to ensure that everybody had the benefit of the overall data derived from every stage of the investigation.' He went on to say, 'The study would not have been possible without the support of the MRCU and the local direction and organization by Dr Giglioli. To Dr Giglioli, also, with Dr Martin Brunt, must go much of the credit for the initial groundwork and activity that enabled the Natural Resources Study to become an accomplished fact.'

On various occasions it was necessary to get all those concerned with the study together to discuss plans, results, etc. The Royal Society of London very generously allowed Dr Wickstead's team to use their accommodation and facilities. Members of the Natural Resources Study Liaison Committee and the Cayman Islands

Conservation Association were always ready with advice and local knowledge, he said; individual Caymanians were always helpful when approached. Finally the thanks of all concerned were due to the Land Resources Division of the ODM, London, for arranging the production of the final report.

There are a couple of interesting opening paragraphs in the Introduction that I will quote:

> It would appear that the Cayman Islands are at an important crossroad in their development history. As recently as 1946 it was possible for James Billymyer to write: 'Comparatively few visitors come to the islands because of the poor and uncomfortable transportation. The only regular means of communication with the outside is a small motor vessel, carrying mail, passengers and cargo, which runs fortnightly between Georgetown and Kingston, Jamaica, touching at Cayman Brac...' 'There is no air communication.'
>
> This is in strong contrast to what Alexander Melinad was able to write in January 1975: 'As a result, an efficient worldwide telecommunication system has been established. In addition, George Town, the Capital, on Grand Cayman Island, now has two flights a day to Miami and four flights a week each to Kingston, Jamaica, and to San Jose, Costa Rica, connecting with major international air routes.' The rate of development of the islands, particularly Grand Cayman, has been extremely rapid, almost geometrical in its progression. There are those who voiced the opinion that it has been too fast and that it became out of hand.

As the government's Financial Secretary for the period 1965–82 I can voice the opinion and without fear of successful contradiction that the last sentence in this second paragraph referring to 'the rate of development' is without foundation. In fact no growth or development in the Cayman Islands has so far been out of hand.

The final report of the Natural Resources Study was presented for consideration of the Cayman Islands government. As there would be various private sector development proposals put to the government, the report suggested that its recommendations be considered before deciding any future policy regarding development in the islands. It also recommended that any exploitation 'of a limited natural resource' should be under the government's control, either directly or indirectly.

Many recommendations were made in the report on subjects like canal survey, coastal mangroves, sea grass, dredging, sand deposits in the North Sound and elsewhere, artificial reefs and marine parks. The report, which may be found at the National Archive, can provide details of the studies and recommendations. It was indeed considered a very useful exercise and one that as time slips on will become more meaningful to economic development around the shorelines of these islands.

Another subject that has created much interest to tourists and other visitors to Grand Cayman is a trip to Stingray City in the North Sound near to Rum Point. Many readers will know about the stingray. It is one of the many classes of fish that inhabit tropical seas. It grows to about 3 feet wide and has fins radiating from its sides and head. Eyes are located on the upper surface of the body. The clefts of the gills and mouth are on the underside. The tail is very slender, whip-like and long, and armed with sharp, flattened, bony spines, serrated on both sides, capable of inflicting very severe wounds. But after that description I should add that Cayman's stingrays are tame and very entertaining to those who go to visit them, and jump in the conve-nient 4 feet of water among the tropical animals and touch and hold them. For that reason the sport trips to Stingray City have grown very popular, more so than any other such entertaining sport created else-where. In fact, Cayman's Stingray City is naturally created and not man-made.

In 1988 North Sound boat captains and dive operators, headed by Mr Ron Ebanks of Charter Boat HQ, organized a public meeting at the West Bay Town Hall advocating that the group work jointly on a proposal to protect stingrays by declaring them an 'endangered species'. My Principal Secretary told the *Caymanian Compass* (Monday 21st March 1988) that 'endangered' species were governed by international convention. However, he intimated that the govern-ment would consider any proposal to make the stingrays a 'protected' species under Cayman's Animals Law. The message for the need to protect stingrays nevertheless came across to the public very well. The allegation that fishermen had been fishing stingrays for bait was strongly supported by Mr Peter Milburn of the Watersports Operators Association, who declared Stingray City as the 'world's number one diving site'. He felt that Stingray City was unique, that it was some-thing from which the islands benefited and that it should therefore be preserved for generations to come. Now, ten years later, that amenity has become more popular than ever before. With very few excep-tions, everyone planning to come here makes sure that a visit to the famous Stingray City in Grand Cayman is a part of the itinerary.

Back in June 1986 it fell to me to deliver the public message on

Environment Week. It was in any case an opportunity to speak on a subject I described as very important, one that relates to the things which surround us and which affects not only the daily lives of people who live in the Cayman Islands, but the whole world:

It is therefore understandable why a special time is set aside for us to pause and take fresh stock of our surroundings, to appreciate what we have, and to take any steps necessary for the protection of our God-given natural assets. Our environment is undoubtedly more precious than most people realize. The air we breathe, the land on which we live, the sea that surrounds us and feeds us, must be all kept clean and pollution-free if we are to live healthy lives, which is so important.

The environment is not just something that affects a few conservationists, it is something that should be of utmost concern to all of us for our own sake and the sake of our children and of generations to come. Once the environment is polluted it can sometimes take a long time to remedy. One extreme case to bear in mind is certain kinds of nuclear waste that will not be rendered harmless for thousands of years. Although we do not have nuclear waste to worry about in the Cayman Islands, it is nevertheless a good example of an environmental problem in one country that is capable of affecting everyone around the globe. Here in these tiny islands environmental problems are minor in nature and quite capable of being contained and remedied with just a little concern and effort on the part of everyone in the community.

We must therefore ensure proper garbage disposal, adequate water and sewerage facilities, proper building and town planning regulations and a respect for marine life so that over-fishing and the unchecked depletion of stocks do not occur. Also important are the protection of coral and other marine resources and all possible safety precautions and monitoring when dredging permits are issued to ensure a continued buoyant economic development. Although a large part of the land area of these islands is swamps, if we take time to ensure that our environment is protected in the manner stated earlier, it will stay clean, healthy and beautiful. Not only our health and our economy depend on such an attractive atmosphere, but also the large numbers of visitors who come to Cayman to enjoy the amenities we offer.

In ending I said, 'During Environment Week, I would ask everyone to pause, reflect on what I have said, and become an active partner in the community effort to protect our environment.'

342

18

Water and Sewerage Development

Normally these two subjects, a public water system for the capital, George Town, and water and sewerage for the Seven Mile Beach area in Grand Cayman, popularly known as 'the hub of the tourist industry', would be connected to the chapter on 'Economic Infrastructure'. However, the subjects must for obvious reasons appear in this section dealing with my political career and involving the enormous efforts put into the development of both water and sewerage between 1985 and 1987. The importance of the two schemes to Grand Cayman at that particular stage of the country's social and economic development cannot be over-emphasized. The subjects arose with the new government of 1984–88. In fact water and sewerage were looked upon then as 'the creation of a new era', one that would certainly emphasize the need to promote social and economic development in Cayman. For that reason the further delay in the development of water and sewerage would not have been in the best interest of the islands' progress, especially taking into consideration the awful situation existing at the time in the absence of these essential facilities. The capital of these islands and its tourist resorts have their importance and significance in the life of the people living here and the visitors who stream in daily from all over the world. Water, especially a good drinking supply, is the most demanded amenity in life and a sewage facility is next in importance. The Governor, Peter Lloyd, in his Throne Speech in March 1982 said, 'Government has declared its policy on water and sewerage. It will introduce legislation to protect the existing water resources, will create a Water Authority to administer this legislation, and will provide in a phased manner, a public water and sewerage system to Grand Cayman for the operation of which the Water Authority will be responsible.'

The situation that developed here in Grand Cayman in 1985 demanding urgent attention to the production of a new water system,

343

especially for George Town, and also sewerage for the Seven Mile Beach, was caused by two problems. First, water was affected by the absence of rains for nearly six months from January 1985, when cisterns or roof catchment containers went dry. Secondly, wells were also affected due to long periods of very low tide influencing ground water levels. Sewerage did not become a problem requiring urgent action until 1984, when divers reported seeing faeces floating in the waters along the Seven Mile Beach and moving out into the deep. We knew then that in the absence of a proper sewerage system along the Seven Mile Beach area the situation would likely lead to the eventual outbreak of a health-endangering epidemic which would certainly spell disaster for Cayman's tourist industry, quite apart from its potential effect on the resident population. I will deal first with water, the more pressing of the two services.

Due to the absence of proper water facilities in these islands, there came a time dating back to the early 1950s when those areas in need of the facilities began to feel the effects. Tourism activity on the Seven Mile Beach in those earlier days was described by Frank, the eldest of three sons of Mr and Mrs Clarence L. Flowers, as 'still a glimmer on the horizon'. However, with the development of Galleon Beach Hotel, Beach Club Colony and a number of other tourist resorts coming into operation and others in the process of construction, the glimmer became closer and brighter. In those days, apart from storing water from rains in large cisterns, water had to be supplemented by water trucks. There were frequent drought periods, especially in the early parts of the year before the rainy season began in the summer when the tourist activity was still at its peak. That situation eventually led Mr Clarence Flowers, the father of Cayman's block-making industry and the main provider of water to all of Grand Cayman, to give serious thought to the future of hotel operations, especially on the Seven Mile Beach. There was also greater demand by the public in general for more water.

The Flowers' company began tackling the problem by mounting a 500-gallon tank with a gasoline-driven pump on a cargo truck as their basic water delivery system. Some people had large cisterns and could store more than a year's supply of water and so they were kind enough to sell the surplus water to the Flowers' trucking business for the public and hotels' need. As the demand grew, one company sank special wells for an alternative source of water, to be used mainly for bathing, washing clothes, flushing toilets, cleaning floors etc. Well water, however, containing lime and salt, was referred to as 'hard', meaning that it would cause plumbing fixtures to deteriorate rather quickly; however, at that time and because of heavy public demand for water, there were no other alternatives. Yet with all the disadvantages found in the use of well water and in spite of the development of good water in later years, well water is still in demand up to the present time. The 500-gallon tank was eventually replaced with a 1,000-gallon tank. Well water had gradually been replaced to a large extent by 1987 with top-quality piped desalinized city water. The Flowers' company, although it continued to deliver ground water on request, moved over to city water and increased its water carrying capacity to four tankers of 4,550 gallons each. This larger capacity was to supply areas out of reach of the piped city water.

Mr Flowers had seen the growing need for bottled drinking water from dispensers and in 1974 purchased an on-going business of that type from a friend, Mr William Parkhurst. Twenty-five years later the bottled drinking water has become a large and successful business: it is used both in commercial business offices and in private homes. In the early part of the same year, 1974, due to a severe drought and low tides, the Seven Mile Beach area especially suffered a terrible water shortage. In the midst of the crisis, Mr Parkhurst, an American who lived here for some time, pioneered the development of the Cayman Water Company to produce piped drinking water especially for the Seven Mile Beach area. Clarence Flowers and another American, Philip Lustig, who were also members of the Cayman Water Company's board, joined Bill Parkhurst as shareholders and spearheaded the successes of the company. The board in the meantime notified the large commercial users of water, such as hotels, to cut back on the use of their supply as much as possible. That was in order to conserve the vital remaining supply of the company's water for allocation to the hospital, which was given top priority, and secondly to residents according to need and availability. Cayman Water Company was by then producing 50,000 gallons per day and was able over a short period to store 100,000 gallons. In 1978, however, the board undertook major expansion and the company increased its production to 2 million gallons per day.

The water crisis experienced in 1974 was due not only to lack of rains, but also to exceedingly long periods of low tides that prevented the wells reaching their normal levels and thereby requiring the use of some of the scarce cistern supplies. It was in fact brilliant thinking on the part of the trio, Parkhurst, Flowers and Lustig, to develop the Cayman Water Company to provide the Seven Mile Beach with that vital commodity. Their efforts deserve due recognition and award of credit for the part they played in successfully laying the water infrastructure and thus continuing the development of tourism in that area.

Lack of rainfall and low tides pestered Grand Cayman at intervals. In early 1985 another of those water shortages bothered the island. I was then the Minister responsible for water, and also sewerage. Cayman Water Authority, established in 1983 under the Water Authority Law of 1982, was the legal entity under which water and sewerage developed. The Water Authority was managed by a board consisting of a chairman and eight members appointed by the Governor. With the Governor's consent I became chairman of the board. I knew of course that the Authority would be faced with the prospect of endeavouring to establish the two very vital projects: water for George Town and sewerage for the Seven Mile Beach. I wanted to lead the way in this as well as in all the other boards and committees under my portfolio, such as the Housing Development Corporation, Agricultural and Industrial Development and Cayman Turtle Farm. I eventually became chairman of all the boards and committees under my portfolio. Before going to sleep at night I liked to be assured that all my portfolio projects were moving in the right direction.

In dealing with the water problem, the board thought of two sources to examine for establishing a permanent and reliable supply in view of the need to promote economic development – water of course being considered a vital commodity in support of such growth. The two sources were ground water and, secondly, fresh water produced by the process of desalination of salt water. Both sources were looked at almost simultaneously. In the case of ground water, the Director of the Water Authority, Mr Richard Beswick, had many contacts abroad on the subject. During 1985 he recommended to the board a graduate, Mr Kwok-Choi Samuel Ng, doing his PhD thesis at the University of Alberta, Canada, who wished to base his work on the 'Geological Aspect of Ground Water Exploitation in Grand Cayman'. The board accepted the suggestion and awarded him financial support covering the period of the study to the end of 1985.

The study identified three freshwater lenses on Grand Cayman: one in the Lower Valley area, another at East End and a third in North Side. The East End lens was twice the size of the other two. The Lower Valley and East End well fields and reservoirs were officially opened to the public in November 1983. They were both estimated to have abstraction rates of 100,000 and 80,000 US gallons per day respectively. The Lower Valley water was distributed in George Town. The well field at East End was pumped for 31 per cent of the year and only used to meet local demand when sufficient water was not available at Lower Valley. The demand for East End water increased by 600 per cent over its first four years of operation up to

346

1986. Such increase was mainly attributable to the greater demand for water and partly due to the reduced monthly production of Lower Valley well field. The total quantity of water produced since the beginning of the well field operation was 14,595,768 gallons. At that time we were appalled at the rate of deterioration of plumbing fixtures, especially at the George Town Hospital, due to the well water's high content of lime and salt. It was thought too that the cost of piping and other infrastructure to develop a system running from East End to George Town was then economically beyond the reach of the government. Furthermore, unless the water was passed through the process of desalination, the public would not accept it for general use.

Richard Beswick had also recommended that the board look at an Israeli company, Israel Desalination Engineers (IDE), recommended as leaders in the field of good-quality water production. Their process was by evaporation using steam and would therefore produce the purest water. The company was invited to Cayman to look at the possibility of establishing a water system here in George Town. Before IDE visited they must have acquainted their government with Cayman's request, for I was invited to Jamaica to discuss the subject at the Israeli Embassy in Kingston; my wife Rita accompanied me on the mission. Cayman's water problem was explained to the embassy official who met me. He was rather sympathetic with Cayman's need for a good water system and advised that IDE would certainly assist us as best they could.

Shortly after the meeting in Kingston, IDE visited Grand Cayman and discussion with the government began on our water need. Their proposal was in fact quite attractive. The IDE system of desalination of either well or salt water was the most economic method of producing distilled water using waste steam. No problems were foreseen using that system because waste steam was readily available from the generators of Caribbean Utilities Company Ltd. (CUC). The two companies, IDE and CUC, decided to undertake the water system jointly. CUC provided the building and equipment and IDE the staffing and technology. The government entered into a franchise with IDE and CUC's newly incorporated company, Central DeSal Ltd. (CDL), through which water would be produced and delivered to the Water Authority's reservoir built on government property just across the street from CUC at Red Gate. The reservoir adjoined the government's Public Works Department to the west. The normal production capacity of Central DeSal was 450,000 imperial gallons per day, although they could move up to 490,000 gallons per day in the event of greater demand. Under the franchise, the government was not prohibited from negotiating with other water-producing firms if

347

this became necessary when the demand rose beyond CDL's available capacity or after expiration of the agreement. Of course CDL also had the option of increasing their production capacity in the event of greater demand.

When CDL's preparations were under way for construction of the system in CUC's compound near to the steam generators for the connection, I was invited by IDE to visit the opening of their new desalination plant in Bonaire on Saturday 5th April 1986. The system in Bonaire was quite impressive and filled me with enthusiasm over Cayman's new water development, scheduled to come on stream in a couple of years' time. I was next invited by IDE to visit their operation in St Thomas and St Martin in the Virgin Islands on 16th October 1986: they wanted me to see their distillation plant fully in operation at those two locations. They flew me there in a private jet, returning the same day. Again I enjoyed the opportunity, which was good experience for our own up-coming operation.

What pushed research in early 1985 for a new source of fresh water was, as I stated before, a terrible drought from lack of rainfall accompanied by a long period of low tide affecting the water levels in wells. Problems with well water were largely in South George Town where the Flowers' Water Trucking Service was obliged, due to demand, to open a couple of large wells on the Walkers Road which drew heavily on the ground water supply in that area. On 4th January 1985 I received four petitions from the residents in South George Town complaining about the awful state of their ground water supply. They appreciated the urgent need for water in other residential sections, but they saw no need to rob Peter to pay Paul in this instance. The government and the Water Authority could do little about the situation. However, the Director of the Water Authority was asked to investigate. Richard Beswick found that the abstraction from the Walkers Road wells, over a period of seven days, was reaching 225,000 gallons. A portion of the water was used for irrigation at the golf course. In the circumstances, the Water Authority had to insist that abstraction from the two wells be significantly reduced until alternative sources were available.

The George Town water supply project saw good progress by the end of 1987: it placed contractors ahead of their programmes' time schedules. The contract to procure the plant and materials for the initial phase, which went to tender late in 1986, was awarded on 27th February 1987 to Propax Industrial Exports of United Kingdom. The civil engineering contract followed on 1st June 1987: it was awarded to Petroservicios of Colombia in South America. Following strong public support for the project, and after re-evaluating the final con-

348

tract prices, the Authority and the government decided to increase the scope of the project. Extension of the supply area included Walkers Road, South Church Street, Smith Road, Crew Road and Tropical Gardens. The additional funds were sought, negotiated and obtained from the Caribbean Development Bank in Barbados and the local branch of Barclays Bank. The project's distribution increased from about 5 miles of pipeline to approximately 17.5 miles. The number of connections increased from 550 to 1,200. CDL commissioned the plant, and water was produced by 21st January 1988. When I turned on the switch for the public water connections, 150 homes in the George Town area had been connected or were in the final stages of connection. The exercise of connection would continue as pipes were laid.

At the March 1988 session of the Legislative Assembly, I reported that piped water for George Town had become a reality and a most tremendous development for the country. Those homes in the piped water area were to be mindful that besides the water's low price, other tangible savings were in eliminating charges by truckers and the cost of pumping and electricity. New homes could even enjoy further savings in capital cost for building cisterns or other water storage systems. Residents outside the piped water area would also enjoy some benefits as truckers could buy this top quality low-priced water from the Authority for outside delivery at some saving. The price of the water was the main issue in negotiating the franchise with the producers, in order to ensure that while we were obtaining a top quality product we were also obtaining the lowest price possible. This was important from the point of view of the many low-income families who would need to use the water. As finances became available, residential areas around George Town outside the first and second phases of the pipe network were connected. After completion of George Town and availability of fresh financing, the Water Authority continued east to Red Bay and beyond. Ten years later the pipelines were still continuing to East End and North Side. In the same period West Bay was also covered with a piped water system, built and operated by the Cayman Water Company under a government franchise. Thus Grand Cayman's water needs were well taken care of. In Cayman Brac several deep well hand pumps were constructed on the freshwater wells which were drilled on the Bluff during 1986. The pumps were operating and producing a limited quantity of water, largely used by farmers and residents for irrigation, cattle watering and other domestic purposes except drinking. Some years later the Water Authority provided good-quality water for general purposes in Cayman Brac.

Water truckers' services were considered very important and they did provide excellent service with larger trucks, one reaching 9,000 US gallon capacity. There were six trucking services: H.A. Bodden, Dee's Water, Eden's Water, C.L. Flowers & Sons, Wilford Ryan and Thompson Water. Four of the truckers drew water from East End, all six from Lower Valley, the Water Authority and the Cayman Water Company, and one from the two private wells on Walkers Road. The total quantity of water drawn by the truckers in 1987 was 51.4 million gallons or an increase over 1986 of 20 per cent.

In normal circumstances the Authority would have required the services of outside consultants, architects and additional staff to undertake these two major, specialized and complex projects, water and sewerage. However, the staff of the authority, including the head of the operation, Richard Beswick, actually assumed full responsibility for the projects from start to finish. This included designs, architectural and engineering input, together with supervision and financial control of both projects, which involved financial investment of over $15 million. Sewerage was actually until then the government's largest single project, valued at approximately $11 million. The Director himself was also the engineer and consultant in charge of the contracts for both projects. Added to these responsibilities for the two large new capital works programmes, the Authority had many and varied operational functions, including the protection of water resources, supervision of water franchises, operation of well fields and sale of water. In addition to those services, the Authority also began setting up the accounting and financial control system for the administration. This was in order that from the start of the operation the Authority would, as in the case of other statutory corporations, be completely responsible for the financial and administrative affairs of the two new public utilities. During the programme the Authority also established the first plumbing inspectorate under the Water Authority Law for setting of standards for work and licences. The Authority's involvement in all aspects of the construction and supervision of the two projects undoubtedly saved the government quite a tidy sum of money and, what is more, improved the administrative ability of the Authority.

In several ways, sewerage was a more difficult subject to deal with. A development plan was approved in 1984 for a sewerage system with the necessary treatment works to be built along the Seven Mile Beach in an area north of George Town and the public garbage dump. However, when I entered the government in November 1984 I found that the authority had just started research for the project. In fact in the following year, 1985, both water and sewerage were simultaneously

350

programmed. From then the two developments were adopted for implementation: they were completed and commissioned in early 1988.

At the start of the sewerage project along the West Bay Road we found one problem surfaced with regard to the scheme. For economic reasons the designed work at planning stage in 1984 did not recommend the inclusion of the Snug Harbour Development; that scheme nevertheless had of necessity to be considered in 1985. A new 'small bore system' which would be both economical and efficient was contemplated. A feasibility study of the system for George Town had already been completed and recommendations in the report awaited examination on completion of the Authority's works programme. The cost of both studies for George Town and Snug Harbour was a gift from the Canadian government for which Cayman was most grateful. However, 13 years later the small bore system for those two sewerage projects is still pending a decision. I exited politics and the government in November 1988 after completing the other portion of the Seven Mile Beach sewerage project and also the George Town piped water scheme.

The immediate need for a sewerage scheme along the West Bay Road came out of concerns about an epidemic outbreak. The problem was that during heavy rains or very high tides, as water rose between the road and the North Sound swamps, cesspool leakage from buildings along the developed areas of the beach appeared in the swamp waters. Worse than that: divers off the western Seven Mile Beach, as mentioned before, came to my office and reported to me in person that in many of their dives they came into contact with drifting sewage below the surface of the sea. In such circumstances there was no question about the urgency of building the sewerage facility in order to safeguard the tourist industry.

The sewerage project met with difficulties in mid-1987 caused by heavy flooding as trenches were dug for laying the pipes. The question of how to deal with the great volume of water produced by the open trenches did not have an immediate solution. The problem occurred at the George Town end of the West Bay Road at the turn from the main road to the sewage treatment works – a short distance to the east and north of the public garbage dump. However, despite the difficult problems, progress was made and by the end of the year a significant portion of the main line had been laid. The sewage treatment works was completed and five of the pumping stations commissioned.

The water-handling problems caused the contractor to modify the method of construction and a large part of the southern pipeline was

351

laid using a diving technique. This variation in his method resulted in a serious contractual dispute. The contractor claimed that his tender qualification protected him from extra costs associated with the ground water handling problems. The consultant engineer, on the other hand, after seeking legal advice, based his interpretation of that section of the contract on what was originally agreed: he took the view, and held to it, that the contractors were responsible for the cost of carrying out the full works. In fact at the time of tender the contractors, who had been established in Cayman for some 20 years, should have known of water problems and the levels in those parts: they were therefore not entitled to the claim of additional costs.

On Thursday 20th March 1986 I visited the 20-acre site of cleared swampland allotted for the first phase of the sewer treatment works next to the North Sound public dump. Also on a visit to the site were my Principal Secretary, the Director of the Water Authority and two senior staff dealing with the sewerage project. While there I took the opportunity to review the plans for the construction of the treatment plant. First was the preparation of the site, a 114,533-square yard geo-textile membrane which would be filled in with marl and placed on top of the cleared swampland. It would act as a separation layer and tension member to stop the marl fill from being pushed into the ground. It would also allow any swamp gases that might be produced under the works to be drawn off. Building of waste stabilization ponds would follow. The ponds would allow aerobic action to break down raw sewage into effluent to be pumped to the golf course for irrigation purposes. The major civil engineering for this aspect of the project was scheduled for completion by the end of 1986, while the laying of pipes from the West Bay Road to the treatment plant was scheduled for 1987. The sewerage operation was put into effect a short time before the switching on of water on Wednesday 10th February 1988. Thus came to an end the building and commissioning of Cayman's two important projects, water for George Town and sewerage for West Bay Beach. They were undoubtedly important to the country. Without them, continued social and economic development would have suffered.

In ending this chapter, I must on behalf of the government and the people of these islands pay humble respect to all the directors of the Water Authority who became members of its board during my four years as chairman and minister of government responsible for the subject. I consider those directors to be gentlemen who did not shirk their committed responsibilities as members of the board. For that reason their efforts resulted in great successes in developing water and sewerage for Grand Cayman. The nine members, including the secretary (the director of the Authority, Richard Beswick), all displayed a true *esprit de corps*, or team spirit. One director was my political colleague, Captain Charles Kirkconnell, Minister for Communication, Works and District Administration. He gave to my board the same strong support as though he were dealing with a subject under his own portfolio because, as in the case of other members, he knew the true value to the future development of these islands of the projects under consideration. A second director was my former staff colleague at Finance and Development, George McCarthy, who in 1985 was Deputy Financial Secretary and later Financial Secretary. Other directors were Donovan Ebanks, Chief Engineer PWD; Peter Foye, Chief Environmental Health Officer; Harry Chisholm, Manager of the Royal Bank of Canada; Richard Flowers of C.L. Flowers & Sons; Vernon Jackson, JP, former Director of Education; and Brainard Watler, a private sector businessman. To those directors we owe much gratitude and thanks for their work, their special efforts and their achievements on the Water Authority's board.

353

19

The National Trust

The creation of a National Trust was a subject which, with a number of others, dominated my thoughts from the early days of the government of 1984–88, of which I was a part. Earlier in the 1980s Mrs Helen Harquail, originally from Saskatchewan, Canada, and her late husband, Frank J. Harquail, talked about settling down as permanent residents in Grand Cayman. They lived at the time in the White Hall Estate area on the east side of the West Bay Road. However, misfortune followed when Mr Harquail died. His wife then purchased a 12-acre parcel of land to the east of where she lived and proposed to donate it to the people of the Cayman Islands in memory of her husband. In the meantime there were suggestions as to how the property could be developed. Mrs Harquail thought that the first permanent building should be a theatre named the F.J. Harquail Cultural Centre in appreciation of her husband. The name included the words 'Cultural Centre' as opposed to 'theatre' as it was envisaged that a variety of cultural events would also take place in the building. However, the name eventually approved was the F.J. Harquail Theatre. The first production staged in it was *The Farce Scapino*, starring Peter Jackson, Michael Broderick and Corinne Glasgow. Following this first show, the theatre was officially opened in 1986 with the well-known show *The Sound of Music*. The local stars were Gwen Diaz as Maria and Daphne Orrett as Mother Superior.

In the planned development for the 12-acre plot of land it was thought that, in addition to the theatre, theme parks could be created where arts and crafts would flourish to allow the area to eventually become a centre for research into the past. Along with marine exhibits and historical houses, there would be space for a 'town square' with meeting rooms, a market and retail outlets to encourage people to use the facilities and not just to visit them. However, nearly 20 years later, all the proposed concepts of the development plan, except for the theatre, are still dreams holding out hopes for the future.

At the presentation of the proposed development of the 12-acre plot, Mrs Harquail organized a large garden party to introduce the scheme, which she named the Cayman National Cultural Foundation (CNCF). The Governor, Mr Lloyd, and his wife attended. Also attending were my wife and I. In fact I was asked to be Honorary Chairman of CNCF: I accepted the position and was thereafter requested, along with other prominent individuals, to make a public presentation regarding CNCF. The following was my statement:

We do watch from day to day, sometimes with amazement, the rapid growth and development taking place in these islands. Part of the growth no doubt has cultural reflections of foreign societies, more especially the American society, in our lifestyle and habits that may no doubt tend to threaten our own cultural influences. I say this because Caymanians have visited, lived in and long been associated with the United States, it being the source of Cayman's economic dependence for job opportunities. Nevertheless, it may now be time as we grow through development to maturity, to start giving some thought to our own culture and heritage in order to avoid further erosion of native customs and ways of life. In other words we must defend the freedom and integrity we have long enjoyed here in our homeland. Of course I must say, with respect, that American culture, especially in music and movies, is regarded these days as dominant among many other countries and has drawbacks as well as advantages; it is therefore just a matter of which should be chosen.

Cayman does have much to be proud of with regard to its past culture and heritage. The people are intelligent and industrious: they live in comfort and happiness through poverty or wealth and through war or peace. The memories of the past, that is, the good that has been said and thought of past generations, are rapidly fading away. Even now there are only faint recollections of many of the cultures we would still boast and which reflect the peace and stability that are the main foundation to the progress and wealth of these islands which so many enjoy today.

A new proposal is now being presented for the establishment of a Heritage Village to be named 'Cayman National Cultural Foundation'. That development would contain, among other facilities, a theatre, a museum, maritime displays, art, craft and a centre for research into the past. The proposal is to my mind a

355

very ambitious project and certainly a top priority national need if we are to rescue, preserve and reflect in our daily activities, whether in our writing or in our other areas of endeavour, the heritage and culture of the past. I encourage all, government and the people alike, to support this programme to the fullest; you will not at any time regret any of your efforts to contribute your money or your services in building this national cultural centre.

Following Mrs Harquail's garden party introducing CNCF, and her earlier public statement indicating that the 12-acre plot of land in White Hall would be donated to the people of the Cayman Islands, I pondered and wondered for some time about the gift. My concern was really as to what organization in the country, as custodians for the beneficiaries, should take responsibility for the property. If the gift were made to the government, which in this case was likely, without specific stipulations, in years to come the property would not necessarily be used according to the wishes of the people. The thought of custodians of the people's gifts had not arisen before and to me personally it was very important that the matter be settled at the earliest opportunity. Mrs Harquail's gift therefore became another of my 'early morning in bed' problems. It was at that time the idea of a National Trust came to me. The Trust, established under appropriate legislation, would become the custodian of the people's gifts: in any case, the people would themselves be the trustees to administer the provisions of the law. The Trust would take possession of all properties donated for the benefit of the people.

I became satisfied that gifts to the people would be made more effective through a National Trust, as such vehicle provides an ideal guarantee for safe custody of the property and ensures strict adherence to its purpose and use. I went to my office that morning in early 1985 and sat down with my Principal Secretary, Kearney Gomez, and together we discussed the matter. After explaining my thoughts on the subject, I asked if it was possible for him to appoint a committee to research a National Trust and also to recommend a draft law for consideration. Kearney's reply was, 'No problem, sir.' I heard nothing more about the subject and had in fact completely forgotten it when about two years later, Kearney walked into my office early one morning and handed me what appeared to be a report. I looked at it and asked him what it was. He replied with a big smile saying, 'Mr Johnson, you can't remember asking me to do this?' 'This, what?' I asked. He then said, 'The National Trust recommendation, along with the draft law you requested me to have done through a committee.' I then felt great having received the report for the creation of a National

Trust together with the draft law and thought that even if I were exiting office at the end of that political administration in November 1988, I would have had the law put into effect by then. I thanked Kearney for a job well done. The committee he organized to deal with the subject matter was under the chairmanship of Mr Joe Heavener, then a staff member of the Cayman National Bank. Also on the committee was Mrs Dace Ground, a qualified attorney and wife of the Attorney-General, Richard Ground. Dace and attorney Ian Boxall, also on the committee, were responsible for the drafting of the National Trust Law. There were 16 members on the committee providing an excellent cross-section representation for the three islands.

Before receiving the National Trust recommendations from Kearney, I had read reports about national trusts' attitudes in certain regional territories and the difficulties those governments were experiencing with respect to the use and/or proposed development of their own Crown property within the township areas. The problem stemmed from the fact that those trust organizations became quite firm in their objections to the proposed use of the property. Right or wrong, it was my opinion that something was wrong with the spirit of their trust laws. I decided that our trust must abide within properly thought out and acceptable terms of reference drawn from its purpose, its goals and its priorities. I therefore undertook all by myself to review completely the draft law to ensure that, if necessary, it would be put in a suitably amended form to satisfy the purpose intended in its application to the Cayman Islands.

After completing the exercise, I discussed the amended draft version of the law with the Attorney-General, Richard Ground, as he had ultimate responsibility for its preparation even though it was a subject under my portfolio. I had to submit the draft Bill to the Executive Council and also steer it through the Legislative Assembly. Secondly Dace Ground and Ian Boxall, sitting on the National Trust committee as legal advisors, had done an extremely good job on the original draft bill: however, for certain added safeguards I saw as important and necessary, I undertook to do the amendments. In the circumstances I was not sure how Richard would have viewed my tampering with the legal work of the committee and its two qualified lawyers, and worse, one was his wife. After I spoke, Richard said to me, 'Vassel, you have the responsibility for this proposed draft law; I am only here to ensure that it is presented in good and proper legal drafting form; nothing else must take precedence in its construction and presentation. If I am satisfied with your added words and how they fit into the paragraphs, so be it.'

Cayman's heritage has been built largely on its maritime values –

an industry which is now of blessed memory. However, the heritage aspect of the industry must be preserved so that it can tie in with the new values of today to provide a complete history of these tiny islands. The old values bring back to memory the time of the four-year regatta (1936–39) when all of Cayman and its visitors saw in George Town harbour a gathering of the approximately 20 schooners built in these islands and owned locally. They were all taking part in the races. Champion amongst them was the *Goldfield* owned by Cromwell Watler, the father of Desmond Watler, my former boss. The vessel was modelled by Fossie Arch and built in the family's George Town shipyard, where his father, James Arch, and other brothers, Elroy, Jim, Loxley, Raib and Seth worked. The Arch family, Captain Rayal Bodden of George Town and the Tibbetts family of Cayman Brac were considered the leaders in the shipbuilding industry of Cayman.

Out of the mention of maritime values came back to memory the story of the ultimate ending of Cayman's champion sailing vessel *Goldfield*, which was, some years after World War II, sold abroad. In early 1984 an enthusiastic number of persons living here organized the Goldfield Foundation for the purpose of making public appeals for money to repurchase the vessel and bring her back to Cayman. The proposal was that after her return she would be permanently docked in George Town for all to admire as part of the Caymanian heritage. The difficulties of raising donations, of the purchase arrangements and eventually of getting the vessel back to Cayman involved a long drawn-out and difficult process. However, eventually the *Goldfield* was repurchased and brought back to Grand Cayman, but by that time the interest and the efforts for the vessel's preservation project had waned. The vessel's eventual resting-place is in a North Sound *barcadère* with her keel resting on the sea bottom. The programme by the *Goldfield* preservation group was apparently lacking in two areas of planning: (a) putting the boat on local public display after its return and (b) having in place financial arrangements for its on-going care and maintenance.

There is no doubt that it is an excellent idea to preserve Cayman's past heritage as far as possible in order to remind the people of their former lifestyle; this is in fact the norm in all countries. Of course, in this modern age of advanced technology we see developments such as computers and other electrically controlled equipment, and so much more, that does change our lifestyle. They must also remind one and all that, as the hymn writer wrote, 'Change and decay in all around I see.' My own thought regarding the *Goldfield* preservation scheme was that a smaller replica of the vessel should have been arranged. I am sure that an approach to its designers, who would still have the vessel's model, requesting them to do this small job, would have filled the purpose well and at a fraction of the cost spent on the project that was eventually abandoned midway.

The National Trust Bill was presented to the Legislative Assembly on Friday morning 11th September 1987 and given unanimous support by its 15 members in the first and second readings. The basic purpose of the Bill was to preserve Cayman's natural heritage, its culture and its history. It was also envisaged that the trust would hold property and create parks and historic sites. Those would be opened to the public so that people could become engaged in programmes leading to the preservation of the national heritage. The Trust would be independent of the government but responsible to it. Transactions carried out by the Trust would be exempt from stamp duty. There was also provision in the law that annual accounts should meet current commercial standards and be tabled in the Legislative Assembly annually.

In introducing the National Trust Bill I told the Assembly Members that 'National Trusts are an accepted and appealing idea in many countries of the world. Their main purpose is to preserve the historic, natural and maritime heritage of the country. This draft Bill was undertaken from 1985 by a special committee comprised of representatives of the various districts of the islands. The committee members under the new law will become the "Founding Trust Council" and will hold office during the first year of operation, after which new members will be appointed under the statutory provision. The trust will preserve Cayman's heritage in much the same way that the government-sponsored legislation creating Cayman National Cultural Foundation would preserve Cayman's' culture. Both CNCF and the National Trust will form a "complete package" ensuring the preservation of culture and heritage in these islands which is most desirable. The Trust cannot acquire land or property under compulsory act as is the case with the government's purchasing power. This has been carefully arranged to ensure that it does not accumulate "an abundance of power" which would lead it at some stage to challenge even certain government action, as has happened in other countries. The Trust will not be offensive to the society in any way: this is in order to safeguard its usefulness and for it to be of the greatest appeal to everyone. In fact the Trust will be open to gifts of property, money and time as the sources of its existence.' I referred to the Trust as a 'valuable and significant step in ensuring the preservation of what is best in the Caymanian heritage' and reiterated the hope that its tremendous potential would be appreciated and given the support it deserved.

At this presentation of its second reading, the National Trust Bill was opened to the floor in committee stage for the debate. The unanimity which greeted the opening first and second readings did not continue during the committee stage on Friday afternoon. I should explain that while this stage of a Bill in the Assembly is opened to the public, it is generally less formal and not included in Radio Cayman's broadcast of proceedings. Also the Presiding Officer comes down from the President's chair and sits at the Clerk's table as chairman of the committee. Members do not rise to speak and are not limited in the number of times they may speak or put questions as the Bill is discussed and as it moves on section by section.

During the committee stage of the National Trust Bill, a number of points were made and clarifications accepted by the opposition members. One they argued very strongly was their request for the first annual general meeting of the National Trust Council to be moved from October 1988 back to June 1988. Their point was that the October date would practically coincide with the date of the country's General Election in November 1988 so that their suggested earlier date would be more suitable and convenient to all concerned. While the Attorney-General, the second official member, advised that there was no legal difference between the two dates, the Assembly's vote for the date change was defeated 3–10. The Bill therefore passed its second reading without amendment and was set down for the third reading on Monday morning 14th September 1987.

Over the weekend and before presentation of the National Trust Bill for its third reading, I mulled over in my mind the events of the Bill's presentation on Friday 11th September and its end results. I ultimately thought that the Assembly's rejection of the proposed change of date should instead have been accepted. After all, it was a reasonable proposal and the only request made by the small three-member opposition; furthermore, the subject of a National Trust was seen as a measure to benefit the entire population.

On Monday morning 14th September, before presentation of the National Trust Bill for its third reading, an unusual departure in procedure took place and one that perhaps had not been known to happen before. I proposed a motion that the Bill be recommitted to its second reading committee stage for two proposed amendments. One would relate to how members administering the Trust would be chosen; the other would change the date of the Trust's first annual general meeting from October 1988 to April 1988. Those were of course two areas of the Bill that had drawn considerable discussions at the previous Friday's committee stage second reading. But my gesture was apparently misunderstood or my motive mistrusted. After

360

hearing some of the comments of members, I felt obliged to state in my debate on the motion: 'I could have come here today and proposed the final third stage reading without offering these two plums, the proposed amendments before us. However, the reason the changes are being suggested is that we always advocated a unanimous decision in the approval of this very important piece of legislation. It was therefore thought that these two areas where differences of opinion were apparent last Friday would be rectified today to the satisfaction of all concerned. I cannot think what went wrong in the opposition camp on the other side of the House for them to have said the "ridiculous things" they have about us. If that is their attitude, then the Bill can go forward without the amendments. In other words, because of the ungratefulness of the opposition speakers I will no longer support my own proposed changes.'

I then moved to withdraw the motion. The opposition had wanted from the House what they called an 'ironclad guarantee' assuring that no persons from the committee that studied and recommended the proposed National Trust and the accompanying legislation would be appointed 'founding members'. Those were persons who would administer the Trust until the first statutory annual general meeting, when Trust administrators would be elected. In my own thinking, what better persons could there be for the starter job than those who had in the first place sorted out the concept of the Trust and understood it best? At that stage they would certainly be most worthy of selection as the caretakers and managers of the system for the short period of time. Those recommended were also considered very competent for the job as they were closely related to Executive Council and my portfolio of Development and Natural Resources. It would therefore be impossible for business matters by the founding members to be examined impartially. This row reminded me of what is known as a storm in a teacup.

Regarding the original choice that October be the preferred time for the annual general meeting, I explained that the selection was not for political reasons. The committee's report named October because accountants were prepared to give their services in dealing with the Trust accounts throughout October free of charge, as that was a slack time of the year. The reason now for proposing that the change of date be from October to April, and not June as suggested by the opposition the previous Friday, was that either the first of January or the first of April are popular starting dates of new 'financial years'. Those dates also provided an early start in the year to get on with various special budgetary arrangements in order to attract greater public interest in supporting business activities. Executive Council member Benson Ebanks, in his contribution to the proposed change of date motion, said that 'Action taken earlier today in offering to amend the date from October to April is a gesture to meet some of the objections expressed on Friday. It is not an action that had to be taken. The government offered an olive branch to those who seemed to attach a lot of significance to the date; instead of accepting the olive branch, some members seemed to spit on it and bite the hand that offered it. It appears that whatever the government does is misunderstood. It takes considerable determination and conviction to pull back the branch that was offered: the branch is not going to be offered again. If the gesture was mistaken for weakness, members must understand that the government was strong to take a stand and stick to it.'

A few other recognised supporters of the government bench spoke on the motion while blowing hot and cold, although in the final voting they gave their support to the motion, which was passed 9–5. Immediately following this motion another was put forward by the opposition that the Bill be recommitted to second reading: it was defeated 4–9. I then moved on with the third reading and final voting on the Bill to establish the National Trust; it was passed.

Having successfully obtained approval from the Legislative Assembly for the National Trust, and after the law received the Governor's assent and was put into effect, I watched with great pleasure and delight, and without any further involvement, its implementation and administration. The law appeared to have created quite an impact on the people after they understood its true meaning and value to the country. We see many calls upon the community and government from time to time for assistance in very many different social and human needs, and all those appeals have their merit. It is my hope, now that the National Trust has become law, with its main purpose being to preserve Cayman's heritage, that people will rally to its support in every way possible.

After the National Trust Law was passed in the Legislative Assembly, I made a public statement on the subject in the *Compass* newspaper on 25th September 1987. It was headed, 'National Heritage Transcends Politics'. In the statement I said, 'Our National Trust and the marine parks introduced early in 1986 are two pieces of legislation that must be looked upon as vital in our efforts to preserve the national heritage of the Cayman Islands.'

After a somewhat strange and windy procedure in the Legislative Assembly in dealing with the National Trust Law, I added, I would now like to clarify a few points that may not have been clear to the listening public and those who read the press reports. The working committee that dealt with preparation of the legislation was set up in 1985 to recommend to the government the form of legal instrument required to provide for the preservation of Cayman's national heritage. This was an activity pursued by all countries that valued their heritage, and in some cases the work dated back to their early history. The members of the working committee chaired by Mr Joe Heavener were dedicated to the task and were people of integrity who worked hard and in my opinion did a masterful job in their recommendations. It was quite simple for people to talk about community effort, but few are able and willing to give freely of their time and their effort, as was the case with the working committee that prepared the National Trust report and legislation. In my opinion the trust would be well served to have a nucleus of those people who knew exactly what this effort was all about to remain in position to guide its formative period. I continued:

We were mindful of the fact that the Trust could only succeed if it had a broad base of community support. Therefore, it was our intention to approach the various business organizations and ask that they put forward names of proposed founding members for the consideration of the Executive Council in order to set up the Trust. After the debate on the Bill on Friday 11 September, and the concern expressed about the future path of the Trust, I thought that spelling out clearly in the Law itself the procedure for these first appointments would have satisfied Members. At the same time I would also have amended the controversial date, 'October 1988' to 'April 1988' for the first annual general meeting so that fears would be allayed and the Bill passed through its remaining stages with the unreserved approval of the House. I therefore took the unusual step on the following Monday morning, 14th September, of asking that the Bill be recommitted to committee stage to consider the two points.

I was taken by surprise at the subsequent turn of events, and according to the debate it seemed that my motion had erupted into a political football. The more the opposition spoke the more it annoyed other members, not because of new insights put forward, but because of their search for political mileage. It was a regrettable turn of events and I thought that in the best interest of those genuinely concerned over the preservation of Cayman's heritage, the debate should be shortened. I therefore withdrew my motion on the ground that the date October 1988 was in fact well thought out and acceptable to the government. I would like the public to be assured that the appointment of the founder

363

members will follow the original thought. I therefore urge business associations and individuals to respond to our requests for nominations. The Trust will be the custodian of the people's heritage for present and future generations. It must therefore be seen as the people's Trust for the benefit of the entire Cayman Islands and not for just a few. Our national heritage transcends politics; in other words the national heritage should always have first place over politics. The guidance of the National Trust will, I hope, always be in the hands of the entire community, for this is the way it should be.

The audit firm of Deloitte Haskins and Sells kindly provided the first financial statements for the National Trust, covering the period from its inception on 14th September 1987 to 31st July 1988. In a paragraph of their covering letter, the auditors stated: 'The Trust, in common with many charitable entities of similar size and organization, derives a substantial proportion of its income from voluntary donations. These cannot be fully controlled until they are entered in the accounting records, and are not therefore susceptible to independent audit verification.' The statement was approved by the council of the Trust under the signatures of the chairman, Wilbur Thompson, and the treasurer, Naul C. Bodden. Assets amounted to $64,671 in cash and liability $410.

In early November 1987 it came to my knowledge that the government owned a parcel of land in the East End area off the Queen's Highway, known as the Salinas. The land contained 685 acres of wetlands. It was decided to start the Trust's Land Reserve Programme operation by donating to it all the government's 685 acres of land at the Salinas. I therefore recommended to the Executive Council that the property be donated to the Trust. The Executive Council approved the transfer as a gift and exempted the transaction from stamp duty. The Salinas serve as home to many birds and other wildlife. Although detailed surveys, aerial inspection and some bush walking were needed to sort out exactly what was there, the general idea at that point was that the land would be held in trust for conservation purposes. Its development would be dedicated to preserving the flora and fauna in that area of Grand Cayman but would have a wider benefit of preserving the quality of life for present and future generations.

The Governor, Mr Scott, in his Throne Speech on 12th February 1988, spoke of the National Trust. He said, 'The law creating the National Trust was passed in the 1987 session of the Legislative Assembly. This supports the recognition by the government of growing interest and enthusiasm by the community in the preservation of

Cayman's heritage. The founding council of the National Trust has been established and district committees are now being set up. The National Trust is to undertake the reconstruction of the George Town Fort. This property was awarded to the Trust by the court in the matter of the Sterling Bank liquidation with the cooperation of Messrs. Maples and Calder and the Honourable Thomas Jefferson, the Financial Secretary. Pierson, Heldring and Pierson Ltd. have generously donated US$5,000 towards the project. The Trust intends to produce a precise and comprehensive description of the Fort as it was, before deciding how to proceed with the construction.'

The first annual general meeting of the Trust was held in mid-October 1988. It was well attended and described as an enjoyable event. Its council for 1988–89 was elected. It consisted of 13 members, including a Chairman (Kirkland Nixon), Vice-Chairman (Robert C. Bodden), Treasurer (Naul Bodden) and Secretary (Suzan Merren). The members included the Governor's wife, Mrs Joan Scott. The Governor was Patron. Also appointed were district committees. Apart from the officers and members of the Trust appointed at the AGM, the seven district committees' chairmen also sat on the Trust Council.

Of much importance in the framework of the National Trust is the establishment of a National Botanic Park developed by a committee headed by the Chairman of the National Trust. It is located on lands owned between the government and the Trust on the east side of the cross-island road from Frank Sound to North Side. Work on the first phase of the park began in early 1990 and a loop trail, an 8-foot-wide path nearly a mile long which encloses the central woodland of the park, was completed by early 1993. The park, which will take many years to complete, has been open ever since the completion of its first phase, for the enjoyment of local residents and visitors alike. In February 1994 Her Majesty The Queen, on her second visit here, opened the Botanic Park. It continues to be beautifully developed.

The Trust also plays an active role in serving on government programmes, including the historical Pedro Castle restoration, the Blow Holes project along the East End Road and other historic and environmental tourist attractions; this is apart from its own smaller-scale projects and programmes. It also continues to work closely with young people in developing its historic and environmental educational programmes.

20

Mission Accomplished

The title of this chapter will indicate that I am nearing the end of my personal account of Cayman's journey to the summit of world offshore financial centres as well as to its status as a preferred tourist and diving destination in this region of the globe. Whatever name may ultimately be given to this book, the story will not change, for it relates to the development of a new economy to replace the former earnings of the country's outstanding seafaring men which came to an abrupt ending in the mid-1960s. The name given to this chapter came to mind for the first time a year before I ended my political career in late 1988. I explained in 'Prelude to Politics' that I entered the political arena at the end of 1984 mainly for one purpose, to complete the job I started in 1965 to assist in building Cayman into one of the world's leading offshore financial centres. In my four years in the government, 1984–88, much work was accomplished towards that end, until finally in late 1987 the bright hour of that achievement began appearing on the horizon. The first indication came from an article I read in the December 1987 issue of the *Saturday Evening Post* by M. Timothy O'Keefe. In part it read at page 70:

> Even before the current tourist boom, Grand Cayman was one of the Caribbean's most prosperous islands, ranked with Switzerland and Liechtenstein as one of the world's largest international banking centres. Although the island's population numbers only around 20,000 at the last count, it had nearly 500 registered banks and another 17,700 licensed corporations. Most do not actually exist on site; they are instead represented through other banks or trust companies doing business there. Thus, they are discreetly hidden, not evident on every corner like convenience stores.
>
> Despite its enviable financial situation, the government has

followed a policy of carefully controlled growth and development in order to prevent the island from suffering the way some other islands did from over-rapid expansion. This policy has given Caymanians a per capita income among the highest in the Caribbean and defused possible resentments against tourists. On the contrary, the Caymanians are open, friendly people who genuinely like us. To prove it, they've provided a much broader range of accommodations than most islands. Pre-eminent are the condominiums along the Seven Mile Beach, where visitors typically stay a week and sometimes as long as a month. True luxury hotels are only a recent addition, the first having opened in late 1985 – the Grand Pavilion, a small 60-room facility with what many regard as the island's best restaurant. Last winter, the Grand Pavilion had to relinquish its position as Cayman's only luxury hotel when the new $50 million, 236-room Hyatt Regency Grand Cayman opened just a few blocks away. The Hyatt faces the new Jack Nicklaus-designed Cayman Course, the first golf course in the world featuring the use of a Cayman golf ball. This ball, lighter than the traditional golf ball, travels only about half the distance.

After reading that portion of the *Saturday Evening Post* article and especially Mr O'Keefe's statement that Cayman 'ranked with Switzerland and Liechtenstein as one of the world's largest international banking centres', I thought to myself, 'Well, that's it, mission accomplished.' It meant that I had at last succeeded in achieving my aim of 22 years before to move Cayman up into the top offshore financial centres of the world. I could therefore now quit politics and government and move quietly into my second retirement after November 1988. In any case I had taken on a private sector post (Managing Director of Montpelier Properties (Cayman) Ltd.) from January 1983 and was quite happy to continue in it, together with the other directorships in private financial institutions.

I enjoyed the four years of local politics. One of the government members in the 1984 election campaign tagged me a 'Jamaican' during my preparation for politics, meaning I was a foreigner and could not therefore qualify under the Elections Law to be a candidate. However, when the Jamaican nationality status argument did not succeed he quickly changed my nationality to that of a Cuban because I had lived in the Isle of Pines, Cuba, for eight and a half years before coming to Grand Cayman in 1934. That did not help him either for it was like water off a duck's back.

My being born in Jamaica did not, I hope, cause me to be a worse person here in Cayman than its natives. Jamaica in its geography and development is indeed a beautiful country. In writing my first chapter, 'Jamaica', I went into some of its earliest historic and geographic descriptions to accentuate the beauty of the land of my birth. I also made mention of the country's declining social and economic situation beginning ten years after its independence. Toward the end of Chapter 1 'Jamaica' I made the following statement: 'As one born in Jamaica I followed its political trend for a number of years after its independence.'

Thinking of the Jamaican versus Caymanian economic and social affairs starting in the 1960s, reminds me of an article I read on the subject written by Morris Cargill in the Jamaican *Daily Gleaner* newspaper of Sunday 17th January 1988:

The impressive development of the Cayman Islands continues apace. When one considers that this development started only in 1962 the achievement is even more remarkable. Why, one may ask, has Cayman, a tiny trio of islands without natural resources managed to achieve such prosperity and good order while Jamaica flounders in a mire of corruption, lawlessness and comparative poverty? The answer, in detail, is complicated; but if it is to be summed up in a sentence or two it is that Cayman worked on the principle of seeking first to make money, so that all its social benefits were added into it. While Jamaica was bogged down in our usual morass of words, Cayman was getting down to the essential task of earning. Cayman acted. We talked and moralized. The basis of Cayman's prosperity is, of course, tourism. The extent of this can be understood when we consider that about 250,000 tourists visit there on a population of about 18,000 people. Were we in Jamaica to attempt to match this proportion of tourists to population we would have to attract, not the million visitors we are so proud of, but something like 30 million. This obviously, is an absurd figure and out of the question. The figure is given merely to illustrate a point. And to this illustration must be added the observation that the kind of visitor attracted to Cayman is not on the whole the bargain-hunting package-tour variety, but the wealthy tourist who spends a great deal of money of his own volition.

To this solid basis of tourism must be added the number of financial institutions, over 400, attracted by a carefully arranged tax haven. There is no income tax and no property tax in Cayman. Taxes are indirect and on the whole reasonable. Yet the islands can afford an excellent system of fine roads and a first class system of schooling for all, in which all children are bussed free to school in a clean and orderly way. There is no poverty in the Jamaican sense, no slums, no unemployment, and very little crime. The Caymanian dollar is 10% higher than the US dollar, a clever manipulation which itself is a money earner. The medical services are good, and Caymanian attention to the aged is caring and exemplary. The public services work with remarkable efficiency. A small example might be found interesting. A new water supply is being arranged for a residential section of Grand Cayman, entailing the laying of a great deal of new pipes. A pipe had to be brought to the home of a friend under a cut-stone wall around her house. She asked what would happen if the digging collapsed part of her wall. The reply was 'of course the authorities would replace it.' 'But suppose,' she asked, 'you do not replace the wall as it was before.' 'No chance of that,' the engineer replied. 'Before starting we would photograph your wall.' One cannot imagine our own Water Commission paying such careful attention to detail. Yet at this point it should be observed that no paradise is ever free of serpents. Cayman is a wonderful example of skilfully contrived prosperity and good order.

There is an amusing comment made by another Jamaican friend also writing in the *Daily Gleaner* in an article in which he mentioned old friends he met in Cayman. I have no idea of the date of the article but the writer is Thomas Wright in his 'Candidly Yours' column. This is what he said: 'It was quite remarkable how many old friends I met, just walking along a street in George Town one morning. It gives one the feeling of having died and being reunited in an after-life with old chums you never thought you'd see again. All missed Jamaica, but all swore they'd never go back. I don't have it in my heart to blame them.' Mr Wright went on to end his article by saying, 'The Caymans used to be dependencies of Jamaica. I have the disquieting feeling that by the end of this century, if not before, Jamaica will be a dependency of Cayman.'

During my years in the government, especially after 1965, a fear that bothered me very much and which persisted over the next two decades, was the doctrine of communism and the danger it posed to democratic countries like Cayman, especially with these islands being so near to communist Cuba. As I understand it, communism under the Marxism/Leninism theory provides for capitalism to be overthrown and replaced by a society in which economic values are shared or owned in common by the people and the state. However, when the theory goes into practice, the order apparently changes:

369

instead the state takes complete charge under strict discipline. The people must then be responsible for their own welfare. In other words, every man must provide for himself. That is the long and short of why communism is so much feared by other countries.

There is a previously untold story I would like to mention at this time. In 1968 Caymanians living in communist Cuba but wishing to return home, unlike quite recently, met with difficulties through delays through intergovernmental negotiations between Cayman, represented by the British Government, and Cuba.

On 29th September 1968, the Bahamian government organized a celebration on San Salvador to commemorate the landing of the Olympic flame on the island. A plaza or monument built for the Olympic flame by an organizing committee of the Mexican Olympic Games and their architect, Señor Pedro Alvarado, covered an area of about 1,080 square feet. It had a base with five circular concrete rings representing the international Olympic symbol. Attending the commemoration were His Excellency the Acting Governor of the Bahamas, Mr W.H. Sweeting, the Acting Premier, Mr Clement Maynard, and other local and regional dignitaries. I was privileged to be representing the Cayman Islands at the function. When I arrived in the Bahamas the first social function was a lunch at Government House. While having drinks, I saw a gentleman standing by himself in a corner of the reception room. After inquiring about the person, I was told that he was the Cuban Foreign Minister. I walked over and introduced myself and he did the same. We then became friends. After the function at San Salvador we returned to our hotel at Paradise Island in Nassau. Before departing for home I had a little chat with the Cuban Foreign Minister about the difficulties we were experiencing in having our nationals released by the Cuban government to return home. He promised me that on reaching Havana he would look into the matter and have it resolved without delay. Two weeks later planeloads of Caymanians and other Caribbean nationals were released and sent to Cayman. The talk was that a female British ambassador had recently been appointed to the Cuban position and it was she who did the trick. I did not report to the Cayman government my contact with the Cuban Foreign Minister in Bahamas because of my fear at the time that it could be taken as my being associated with communism.

Nearly 20 years later my fear for communism began to disappear after reading in the *Caymanian Compass* newspaper of 21st May 1987 an article written in Rome entitled 'Gorbachev Praises Democracy'. That was followed by an interview with the Soviet Communist Party General Secretary, Mikhail Gorbachev, at the

Kremlin, specially arranged by Gerardo Chiaromonte, editor-in-chief of the Italian communist party newspaper *L'Unita*. Excerpts of the interview, in Italian, were released and carried by the Associated Press. When asked about the concept of democracy in the context of ongoing reforms, Soviet leader Gorbachev replied: 'It is valuable in itself. Without democracy, there isn't direct participation in management of production, there isn't social justice, there isn't the participation of everyone in the problems of society as a whole.'

Following that statement, in 1988 great and rapid changes engulfed the Russian communist idealism when Mikhail Gorbachev engineered in four days sweeping reforms that moved his country into the realm of economic and political transfiguration. The effort to create those new institutional orders he called a 'revolution without bullets'. That major and dramatic victory indicated that the four-day battle in the Communist Party might not have 'shaken the world', but it certainly sent tremors throughout Soviet society. After being so long under communist rule, Russia was forced under Gorbachev's brave and dynamic leadership to throw communism on the dung heap in exchange for economic values and the people's social welfare. Thus ended my fear for communism, along with the fears of millions of other people around the globe who also had great concern at the thought of Russian communist rule. At that stage I found myself in an improved frame of mind. For sure my greatest fear, the doctrine of communism, was demolished in the Soviet Union, where it was first adopted. Secondly, my greatest ambition, to successfully achieve for the Cayman Islands economic revolution, had been accomplished. I was now in fact free to move quietly from government and politics into retirement at the end of November 1988.

Reading the previous last two paragraphs may cause readers to wonder what communism has to do with this chapter of the Cayman story. My answer is simply that in the days when '-isms' bothered people in many societies around the world, no country could expect to attract sufficient business or make satisfactory progress in economic development in an international atmosphere where there was always fear and concern for safety and security. Although Cayman's financial atmosphere and security were considered top-rated, it did not lend itself altogether to people living in troubled countries who found it difficult to travel freely and safely. Today, of course, the situation has changed enormously to the point where people in almost any country are free to travel safely and take advantage of vacation and/or investment opportunities here in Cayman or elsewhere in other international offshore financial centres.

Moving into the last of my four years in political administration,

371

there are a few things in need of mention before my exit from office: the first is of course Cayman's economy and its financial progress. To build a sound financial administration and one of long-term value becomes quite a lengthy and sometimes painful task. Examples of such struggles can no doubt be seen in many offshore centres, and even advanced countries that have made brilliant starts in this respect but never had the privilege and satisfaction of reaching the finishing line. Cayman was undoubtedly very fortunate in this respect. It has long been recognized internationally that the leading offshore centres of the Caribbean are Bermuda, the Bahamas and the Cayman Islands. Speaking for Cayman, we have never hidden from other countries our developed economic and social infrastructure or our basic systems and services needed to promote progress and success. Research and statistical information have always been carefully collected, compiled and published for the benefit of others also involved in offshore activities. These are considered the fundamental needs in a technological age for providing essential information required as a basis for sound planning and decision making. For instance, one of the crucial statements I made publicly in my budget address in November 1981 concerned our financial industry. I said: 'The value to the Cayman Islands of the financial industry is far more than the sum total of its institutions, the services offered and the income to the country. The most valuable asset is the confidence in these islands of the international financial community. We must therefore do everything to protect our good name and build on it.' That was indeed good advice to others as well.

An economic theory we believed in was quoted in my first book, *The Cayman Islands' Government Economic & Financial Review*, published on 26th March 1982. It stated in the opening presentation that if one wants more of something such as works, savings or output, one should tax it less; and if one wants less of something, for example, employment, one should subsidize it less. It went on to state that Cayman has in fact effectively demonstrated the correctness of the former part of the theory. The supply side of economics, as the theory is called, deals with the use of fiscal policy to increase production and aggregate supply by making work more attractive than unemployment and savings more attractive than no savings. In fact the supply side of economics focuses on the effects taxes have on relative prices and hence economic growth. However, in the long term, every country has to solve its administrative and economic problems by applying what is most acceptable to its society. Very fortunately for Cayman, there are basically three reasons for the progress and success experienced by these islands. First is the

372

government's complete freedom from direct taxation; secondly, the long history of Cayman's political stability; and lastly, the charm of its people. These were spiced by the adage that: 'In business you don't get what you deserve; you get what you negotiate.'

During my 20-plus years' involvement in Cayman's economic development, I became aware of the fact that a careful study had to be made between the narrow margin dividing physical development and conservation. What I found in many cases was that environment-based challenges were hurled at physical development without any thought of what might eventually be quite useful in providing job opportunities for the young and upcoming generations. The thought also was that men could no longer find jobs at sea and therefore had to depend on local employment. Areas of my particular concern were those involving useful projects like the Yacht Club, Safehaven and the Vista del Mar developments in the heart of the mosquito-infested Seven Mile Beach, described as the 'hub of the tourist industry'. It was also my own thought that conservation in Cayman should be argued intelligently before attempting to 'kill the goose that would lay the golden egg'. Looking today at the areas extending to the North Sound with its fine developments, one could not disagree that those three projects are undoubtedly of much credit to the country. The attractive Yacht Club and Marina accommodate many high-valued yachts, and also Safehaven has among its other developments a highly-rated golf course already making its mark on regional sporting events. The third project is the first class housing at Vista del Mar. The owners of that project spared no expense in ensuring a commitment to the excellence of the development. It lies in an area behind the Yacht Club within a splendid and imposing entrance which is outlined by a 200-foot-long curved wall supported by eight classical and monumental stone columns embracing a 16-foot-tall Spanish colonial fountain carved out of solid stone. The main boulevard is paved in a red brick cobblestone pattern. The description of Vista del Mar could go on but it would serve a more useful purpose if visitors, with permission, could also go and see its beautiful buildings and gardens. With the progress of those various developments, mosquitoes have dramatically reduced, to the delight of all who reside and are employed in the Seven Mile Beach area.

While the opposition was questioning those swampy project areas under development, other operators were also dredging other swamplands of the North Sound; they were perhaps even supported by those who challenged our accepted three projects. One of the 13 operators given dredging approval prior to November 1984 definitely conducted dredging slightly offshore without the use of silt-screen protection, causing large portions of the North Sound waters to become murky with loose marl falling back into the sea and being scattered by wind and tide. Yet no complaints about that faulty operation were received from the dredging challengers. However, action was taken to rectify the situation and bring the works under appropriate control.

One may believe that my four-year political career was enjoyable and somewhat 'a bed of roses'; that would be the height of exaggeration. However, I must say unreservedly, and on behalf of every member of the 1984–88 government, that the Cayman Islands have never in the past experienced a four-year period with more achievements and greater successes. In addition to those developments already mentioned there was the promotion of agriculture with the building of a Farmers' Market that took patience and time but eventually succeeded.

Another issue of much importance related to both public beach access and seaward boundary of land between the Crown and private ownership. Regarding beach access by the public, hotel and condo owners objected to the public using their backyard, the beach, for social functions, including line fishing, as had traditionally been the custom in Cayman. Of course what is the law and what had formerly been custom were sometimes difficult to sort out and reconcile. However, as these particular problems came to the government's attention, I immediately made a public statement to assure residents that their concerns were being investigated and where appropriate necessary action to ensure their rights would be taken. This subject was my portfolio responsibility and the reason for my involvement. The statement was carried on the front page of the *Compass* newspaper of 18th November 1987 entitled 'Public Beach Access Reaffirmed'.

I advised the public that the 19th-century Prescription Law gave residents an 'absolute and indefeasible' right to use beach-lands seashore for fishing, bathing and recreation. The law is originally Jamaican, dated 25th February 1882. Section 4 of the law was made applicable to the Cayman Islands (local law 65/1955) specifically to protect established rights of access to beaches. Section 4 (1) reads:

> When any beach has been used by the public or any class of the public for fishing, or for purposes incident to fishing, or for bathing or recreation, and any road, track or pathway passing over any land adjoining or adjacent to such beach has been used by the public or any class of the public as a means of access to such beach, without interruption for the full period of 20 years,

374

the public shall, subject to the provisos hereinafter contained, have the absolute and indefeasible right to use such beach, land, road, track or pathway as aforesaid, unless it shall appear that the same was enjoyed by some consent or agreement expressly made or given for that purpose by deed or writing. [Subsection (2) states] No act or other matter, whether submitted to or acquiesced in or not, shall be deemed to be an interruption within the meaning of subsection (1) if the same took place between the 8th day of February 1954 and the 30th day of December 1955.

The law is therefore quite clear insofar as the public's right to beach access is concerned. In addition to the Prescription Law, there is a requirement under the planning regulations that developers of any beachfront site of 200 feet or more must provide a public beach access at least 6 feet wide. That local requirement would be strictly enforced, and the access marked by the distinctive sign bearing the swimmer symbol. Secondly, private owners of beach property had no right to secure boundaries by fencing any areas of the seashore as this would impede public access and besides give an ugly appearance to our beautiful beaches.

Allied to the problem of access was defining the seaward boundary of land between Crown and private landowners. The custom of earlier times was the right of the Crown to own the sea up to 'high water mark'. This is defined as the line of median high tide between ordinary spring tide and neap tide, that is, when the water rises and falls the least, or half-way between spring tides. As land was a most sensitive issue in the Cayman Islands, I decided to take a deep look at the subject in question and endeavour to resolve the matter at the earliest opportunity and in the most amicable manner. The concern of private landowners whose property bounded on the sea, such as hotels and condos, and especially those on the Seven Mile Beach, was the division line between Crown foreshore and landowners. I can confirm that when I first came to Cayman in 1934, high water mark had by custom been accepted here as the division between Crown foreshore and private ownership. Also in those days the division was noted by the growth of vegetation on the beach where high tide reached its highest point. When land registration took place in the 1970s, the Lands and Survey Department continued to rely on 'edge of vegetation' as the boundary in existence from earlier times. However, as construction on beach property took place, that 'edge of vegetation' line began moving further and further away from the sea towards the developments. In some cases the demarcation line reached near the backdoor of hotels and condominiums because developers cleaned their beach property for the enjoyment of guests and others. I thought if at that stage the matter were to remain unresolved, in short order the government could own most of the hotels and condos on the beach. Putting jokes aside, it became quite clear then that the 'edge of vegetation' policy could play no part in settling this worrying and serious problem.

I presented a paper to the Executive Council for authority to research the subject of the demarcation between Crown foreshore and private ownership with the aid of a committee consisting of suitably qualified members who would recommend whatever action was necessary to rectify the situation. Since it was my portfolio subject I chaired the meeting. It consisted of a total of seven members drawn from the government and the private sector. Apart from myself the others were the Minister for Communications and Works and Development, Captain Charles Kirkconnell; Attorney-General Richard Ground; Queen's Counsel, Ramon Alberga; attorney Charles Adams; the Registrar of Lands; and the Chief Surveyor. Both the Registrar of Lands and the Chief Surveyor were championing the 'edge of vegetation' concept. The first meeting of the committee was held on 15th January 1987 at 4 p.m.

Before the first meeting took place I did research on the subject from the appropriate files in my office dating back to the start of the land adjudication system in the early 1970s. I was fortunate to find a very useful file on the subject containing correspondence with the Foreign and Commonwealth Office in London by the portfolio's former Principal Secretary, Brian Lauer, dated 24th March 1976. The person in London who dealt with the subject was attorney David Bickford, who became well known to us ten years later during Cayman's 1984–88 political administration. He was a member of the UK team that dealt with the Cayman/United States Treaty negotiation in 1985–86. In fact since 1997 David has been representing this government in London on special issues.

The advice obtained from London was that Cayman should consider adopting again the 'high water mark' formula used in earlier times and which was then used very successfully in England. The recommendation by London was supported by my committee and accepted by the Executive Council. Following the decision the Land Survey Regulations were amended by the Executive Council on 5th May 1987 redefining the seaward boundary of land. The new regulation provided that where any parcel of land is bounded by the sea its seaward boundary shall be the high water mark defined as the line of median high tide between ordinary spring and neap tides. In the mangrove areas the mark is the edge of the mangrove vegetation. A similar proviso followed in the case of iron shore property which stipulated that if high tide does not rise above the edge of the iron shore, private ownership extends to the end of the iron shore.

Thus ended in a very satisfactory manner the efforts of the government to settle in the long term and by statutory provisions in May 1987 the public's two bothersome issues, beach access rights and the demarcation between Crown foreshore and private ownership. Amendment to the Land Survey Regulations removed all doubts regarding foreshore boundaries, whether on the sandy beach, the iron shore or mangrove swamps.

At this stage in September 1988, on the eve of my exit from office, I must mention the death on 7th May 1988 of James Manoah Bodden, popularly known as 'Jim'. While on the subject of deaths, I must also mention the sad passing on 3rd September 1995 of George Haig Bodden, formerly of Bodden Town. Jim and Haig were two astute politicians and members of the famous political Unity Team, which they created and which formed the government of 1976 to 1984. They were two legislators for whom I had much admiration and respect whether in their role as opposition or as part of the government. They were not people to easily or quickly reject or accept proposals not put forward by their own team. As Financial Secretary during their administration from 1976 to their becoming the opposition at the end of 1984 and beyond, I can say we got along very well. They held respect for my financial policies, which was most important to the country and myself, and also for the part I played in the government of 1984–88. They often amused me in what I thought was purely politics at high speed. They told me on many occasions that their team would dominate the government of the country indefinitely. However, that prediction was good for only eight years until the Dignity Team took over.

Haig's son Robert is married to my eldest daughter, Tessa, and we, parents and children, together with families and friends, would often gather at our private homes on social occasions to eat, drink and play our favourite games of either bridge or dominoes. During my election campaign in 1984, my being Dignity Team and Haig Unity Team posed some difficulties for the children in having parents on both sides of the political fence. However, through our strong family affections, all went well. Also, Jim and I had mutual respect for each other. Our worst days, of course, were in connection with the Cayman Airways issues. Jim also liked the social side of life. One night, as was customary in my case, I went to the Cinema Theatre and the first person I saw there was Jim, a place I had never seen him before. The movie showing that night was *Doctor Zhivago*. I said to him, 'Jim, I have never seen you at a movie before.' His reply was, 'Anywhere *Doctor Zhivago* is showing, you will see me there.' May the political contributions of both Jim and Haig be long remembered in these islands.

On Saturday 10th September 1988 I departed Grand Cayman accompanied by my wife, Rita, and the Honourable Captain Charles Kirkconnell and his wife, Carol, to attend the 34th Commonwealth Parliamentary Association Conference in Canberra, capital of Australia. We travelled to Melbourne, Australia, via Houston and Los Angeles in the USA, Papeete in Tahiti and Sydney, Australia. We took this route because, in the process of preparing for the journey, I suddenly remembered *Mutiny on the Bounty*, the book I had enjoyed so much as a boy, and the promise I had made myself to see Tahiti if ever I could.

I decided to amend the itinerary for Rita and me and persuaded Captain Charles to do the same. The four of us spent 24 hours in Tahiti, touring the entire French island. I saw many things that reminded me of the book, and the movies made from it. I remember one starring Clark Gable and another with Marlon Brando. In fact, while on the tour our guide pointed out the home where Brando lived while the movie was being made.

We arrived in Melbourne one day ahead of schedule. From Melbourne we travelled to Hobart, Tasmania, where the Eighth Commonwealth Parliamentary Association Little Countries' Conference was held from 15th to 18th September. I explained in Chapter 13 that the Little Countries' Conference held for the first time in 1980 in Lusaka, Zambia, allowed the smaller countries to discuss all by themselves their little problems and issues that would not be too relevant to the big nations. The minutes of the meeting are, however, incorporated with those of the general conference.

On the morning of Wednesday 14th September Rita switched on the television to get the latest world news before heading off to the conference. In short order the news was on, with a large headline stating: 'Jamaica and the Cayman Islands destroyed by Hurricane Gilbert.' What a shock. However, after contacting Charles Kirkconnell about the news, which he had also seen, I telephoned directly home to Grand Cayman to get the true report. In less than a minute my youngest daughter, Juliet, was on the line. She was able to comfort us, saying that the news on world television was far from being correct. In fact Cayman was, shortly before my telephoning, able to get telecommunications and the local telephone system back in working order. No loss of lives was reported so far and all buildings were also still standing, some with minor damage.

The Little Countries' Conference opened on Thursday 15th September in the Tasmanian House of Assembly Chamber in Hobart. The agenda for discussion consisted of four items. I selected the first, 'The concept of the Commonwealth exchange of prisoners', and Captain Charles took the third item, 'The need to unite small countries to deal with international communities'. Captain Charles was unavoidably absent when called upon and so I volunteered to speak on the subject without a prepared text. My paper on exchange of prisoners, apart from being a well-researched subject, revealed that the Cayman Islands was the only small country that had yet adopted the only two schemes for the transfer of prisoners available to countries around the world – Commonwealth and others. The two schemes are the Commonwealth Scheme for the Transfer of Convicted Offenders and the Council of Europe Convention on Transfer of Sentenced Persons.

Delegates were given a tremendous welcome in Tasmania: without doubt all enjoyed the friendly atmosphere and hospitality of both the government and the people. The Cayman delegation included Mrs Georgette Myrie, Clerk of Cayman's Legislative Assembly. The General Conference in Canberra was opened on Monday 19th September at 10 a.m. by the Governor General, the Rt. Hon. Sir Ninian Stephen at the capital's new and very prestigious Parliament Building. I participated in two panel discussions: 'Environmental protection in relation to population growth, industrialization and urbanization' and 'The role of parliamentary committees in the control and scrutiny of government expenditure'. I rather liked the last subject. The conference agenda was made up of one plenary and three panel subjects. The farewell, flavoured with Australia's celebration of its bicentennial year, was given in pomp at the close of the conference and ended with a reception and dinner. We departed Australia on 26th September, spending ten days in Hong Kong and travelling via Tokyo to Honolulu. Rita and I spent three days there particularly to see the aftermath and great destruction of Pearl Harbor during World War II, and to spend our time accommodated on the famous Waikiki Beach. We returned home on 3rd October via San Francisco and Houston.

On 31st October, Cayman enjoyed a grand occasion, a visit by a member of the extended Royal Family, Princess Alexandra. A public notice by Governor Scott on 8th June 1988 advised that, according to an announcement made from St James's Palace in London, Her Royal Highness The Princess Alexandra, accompanied by her husband the Honourable Angus Ogilvy, would visit the Cayman Islands. The Princess was born on Christmas Day, 1936. Her parents were Prince

George and Princess Marina, Duke and Duchess of Kent. When Princess Alexandra was aged five her father was killed in a flying accident whilst on active service in World War II. In December 1960 Her Royal Highness was created a Dame Grand Cross of the Royal Victorian Order (GCVO). In November 1962 the Princess became engaged to the Hon. Angus Ogilvy, second son of the Earl of Airlie, and was married in Westminster Abbey on 24th April 1963.

The Princess and her husband arrived in Grand Cayman on a royal aircraft at 4.50 p.m. on 31st October. The visit covered the period 31st October to 4th November. When Her Royal Highness Princess Alexandra landed from the aircraft the Governor and Mrs Scott met her. The party then moved on to the receiving line to meet members of the Executive Council and the Legislative Assembly and their wives. Also included were the Commissioner of Police and Mrs Rowling and the Director of Civil Aviation and Mrs Hislop. Following the presentation of dignitaries at the airport, the Princess drove to the Grand Pavilion Hotel, where the royal suite was once more occupied. That afternoon at 6 p.m. the Princess attended the Welcoming Ceremony at the Legislative Assembly. The ceremony began with a prayer by the Reverend Talmage Ebanks, followed by addresses by the Governor and the Honourable Benson Ebanks. Her Royal Highness replied. Thereafter I spoke, followed by Benson Ebanks. We both presented gifts from the government and people of the Cayman Islands to Her Royal Highness. The Princess returned to the Grand Pavilion at 7 p.m.

The second day, Tuesday 1st November, Princess Alexandra toured West Bay and then the turtle farm. As Chairman of the Board of Directors of Cayman Turtle Farm (1983) Ltd. and the Minister of Development and Natural Resources responsible for the subject, I gave the official welcome to the Princess in the following presentation:

Your Royal Highness, Your Excellency, ladies and gentlemen,

We are delighted to welcome you here today, Your Royal Highness. Most visitors to this island would feel they missed something if a visit to the turtle farm were not on their itinerary. Also a visit to 'Hell' which is just a short distance from here, but we decided, Your Royal Highness to spare you even a glimpse of the old devil, which in Cayman is only sharp cliff rocks with the sound of a bell.

The government purchased this farm in 1983, from a private group of owners, to continue its unique operation, which is a source of pride to Caymanians. It has in fact been operating for 20 years.

The turtle symbolizes our sea-faring and turtling heritage: at one time it was the main economic activity in these islands. In more recent times, however, our concern with the environment has led us to put much effort into conservation of the turtle. The existence of the farm, indeed, guarantees the continuing existence of this endangered species.

It therefore gives me great pleasure to ask Your Royal Highness to accept this certificate as a memento of your visit today. The certificate indicates that so far this year we have placed into the open sea 500 yearling turtles in continuation of our conservation programme begun in 1980. The number released to date is now over 20,000. We hope that the certificate, and the concern of our fellow creatures which it represents, will be a pleasant memento of your visit to us in the Cayman Islands.

I then presented to Her Royal Highness Princess Alexandra the Certificate dated 1st November 1988 and signed by me as Chairman of the Board.

On 5th November 1988 the Personal Assistant to the Princess, Ms Valerie Hampton wrote to me from St James's Palace in London with this message:

Princess Alexandra has asked me to write to you to say how much she enjoyed her visit to the Turtle Farm and hopes that it will continue to be successful.

The Princess also hopes that you will have a very happy retirement and sends you and Mrs Johnson her warmest good wishes.

I, too, would like to say how interesting it was to sit next to you during the Governor's Dinner.

After the visit to the turtle farm, the Princess toured all the districts and important sites and buildings and ended with the Governor's special dinner for the Princess at Government House on Thursday 3rd November at 7.30 p.m. The dress was black tie and decorations, and the guest list named 22 invitees. Princess Alexandra departed Grand Cayman on Friday morning 4th November at 9 a.m.

The General Election was now just days away. While the candidates campaigned I had time for reflection. I had agreed to an interview with Wil Pineau, editor of the local magazine *Newstar*. He began his article with the statement:

Vassel Johnson steps down from elected office in November

1988 after serving four years as Executive Council Minister in charge of the Portfolio of Development and Natural Resources. His decision not to seek re-election concludes the final chapter of 44 years of public service which he began in December 1945 as a clerical officer in the then combined Department of Treasury, Customs and Post Office. He rose to become Cayman's first Financial Secretary in 1965, in which role he was largely responsible for developing the financial community – through timely legislation and insightful policies – into one of the world's most successful and prosperous tax havens. Johnson is leaving behind when he retires a small wonder of accomplishments.

In the exclusive interview, Wil discussed with me the reason I was not seeking re-election to political office. He thought that at this stage I should offer a bit of advice to aspiring national leaders entering the political arena in the forthcoming election. I told him that here in Cayman many people were semi-independent of outside advice and unless approached I would be reluctant to offer my advice to other people. Secondly, my reason for not continuing in politics was because my wife, my family and other relatives did not wish me to continue after the end of this term. The reason was largely, I imagined, because they were aware that I would, at the end of 1988, have given government 44 years of service. At my age, they argued that I should not go through the hassle of dealing with a very busy portfolio and should take it easy and enjoy a bit of life while I could still move around and do so. As for me, I gave the decision very careful thought. After looking back over the period of this administration which I termed 'the country's finest hours', I thought it would be most appropriate to allow other people, especially young politicians, to come forward and contribute to the administration of the country. There was a lot of interest in politics at the time, some of it no doubt due largely to the level of wage paid to elected politicians since January 1983.

Wil Pineau then asked me if I would miss the power of elected office, meaning the ability to change policies in order to better the lives of fellow Caymanians. The answer was this: 'Actually I have always – even as a civil servant – kept the public's interest in mind. When I entered politics in November 1984, the public's need was really not strange to me because I allowed myself before then to become accustomed to that understanding. Because of the length of time I have been involved in the government's civil service and political administration, I feel that I have done my share and that others should now carry on.'

382

I was next asked, 'Was it difficult to adjust to elected office in 1984 after spending your entire career in the civil service?' Not really, I said, because as Financial Secretary and Official Member of the Legislative Assembly since 1965, I had to rub shoulders with politicians so it was not strange to me. When I decided to go into politics it was really because I felt that the country's financial administration and other services generally needed to be strengthened. It was my thought that if I could be of any help, I would address the situation while at the same time continuing to build the financial industry. We formed a group to contest the election in an attempt to take control of the 1984–88 government, which we did.

I was also asked, 'British Journalist Simon Winchester in his book on the Caribbean wrote in a passage about Cayman that Vassel Johnson in the 1960s was the "genius waiting in the wings" in terms of the development of the financial community. Was it actually your idea to develop Cayman as a tax haven?'

In reply I said:

Well, there has got to be somebody who takes the lead. In 1965 I was put in the position of Financial Secretary responsible for finance and economic development. Most services created here since 1965, apart from the promotion of tourism, involved the building of the financial industry so that the financial community came directly under my responsibility. There are many aspects of the financial industry such as the addition of the domestic and offshore insurance system and abolishing of foreign exchange control that were originally my proposals. These and other improvements in the administration moved the industry along so that it eventually became very rewarding for the country. In fact, back in 1965 I did visualize the day that Cayman would become one of the leading offshore financial centres of the world. This was in spite of the fact that in those days the islands were not in a very healthy position financially...

Another question: 'Were you involved in the Mutual Legal Assistance Treaty which awaits ratification by the United States Senate, and what has been its effect?' In reply I said:

The Treaty has been helping Cayman ever since it was signed in early July 1986. Many people were scared that it would force investors to do their business elsewhere. However, what it really did was to force the undesirables to leave town, exactly what we wanted to achieve, and encouraged clean and reliable business operators to come here, people who could add prestige to the industries. When the MLAT Law was being introduced in the Legislative Assembly, private sector lawyers became concerned over losing a lot of business. I assured them that while the law would scare away drug business it would pave the way to encourage good clean business coming here. This was proven to be quite correct for the mere signing of the Treaty in the Cayman Islands encouraged added and new business.

A crucial question also put by Wil Pineau was this: 'Can you predict the future of the financial industry in Cayman?' In my answer I said:

Cayman is now known throughout the world as a clean centre of operation. People who have good and genuine business interest will come to Cayman, for the political situation has always been quite attractive and so has the social and economic well-being of the country: those are quite strong and should remain attractive features for a long time to come. There is a lot of good business around the world today just looking for a clean spot like Cayman to establish; a place that is quiet, attractive and provides all the necessary services required to support the operation. Without doubt we have it all in Cayman. Our telecommunications, electricity and air services are as good as you will find anywhere. Every service, including our legal, accounting, auditing, insurance and banking are top-rated. I see the twin industries, finance and tourism, continuing to grow and expand. Of course the private sector and the government will together need to uphold, guard and improve their policies and never change them because that could be to the detriment of the country. As the politicians would say, 'If something works, why change it?'

Another question put to me was: 'Did you have a good working relationship with Bodden Town MLA Jim Bodden, who passed away this year?' The reply was:

Jim was a very astute politician. I believe that for the foreseeable future and even beyond, there will never be another Jim Bodden in this country. Whatever else anyone might want to say about him in any aspects of his political career, he had a very forceful way of doing things. I think he attracted many people because he knew the art of politics and had with it a kind heart, giving especially to the poor; thus he gained many followers. Jim and I were good friends from the time we worked together

384

in the post office in the latter 1940s. There was one thing about him: he did not say something before your face and another behind your back. We did not see eye-to-eye on all issues but eventually we resolved our differences.

I was also asked: 'What do you see as your most significant contribution to the betterment of Cayman in your 44 years in the public sector?' Answering this question I said:

The financial industry was largely my involvement, and of course, I could not have accomplished so much without the backing of the Legislative Assembly, the Executive Council, the civil service and the private sector. No one man accomplishes anything by himself and neither can any one man be an island unto himself. There are many things within the financial industry that I have been involved with personally – almost too many to mention, but by faith and trust I have fared well with them all.

'Many tourists come to Cayman because of the beautiful beaches, water and coral reefs offshore. Some scientists have suggested that irreparable damage – from cruise ship anchors and waste – is occurring. Is this a concern of yours?' To this last question from Wil Pineau, I bravely replied as follows:

It certainly is, and looking back to 1985 one would definitely see the reason for the urge then to introduce the Marine Parks Regulations which came into effect in May 1986. The thought behind the marine parks was that the system would be very important in preserving the marine environment of the waters around the islands. We have always had much concern for the preservation of marine life in Cayman and largely because the country is known as a leading diving destination in this part of the world. Divers do form a big part of our tourist industry throughout the year.

A question put to me in early 1988 by a visiting businessman was, 'Of the many offshore financial centres, both British oriented and non-British, why is the Cayman Islands held internationally as the choice among them all?' This is a question I have had to answer on many occasions and was quite happy to repeat it. I explained to the gentleman that Cayman's offshore business is based largely on banking. This is a service requiring guaranteed secrecy in its operation.

385

All the British colonies involved in the offshore banking business have relied on financial confidentiality by applying the British Common Law case in Tournier vs. the National Provincial and Union Bank of England. This famous case, invoked widely to safeguard bank secrecy, states that there is a duty upon bank employees not to divulge information about their customers' bank accounts without the customers' expressed or implicit permission.

In 1976 Cayman became aware that the Tournier case was not quite reliable in safeguarding banking confidence. The demand of an increasingly highly taxed world required that personal and business privacy be of the highest standard. We therefore moved forward to devise our own secrecy legislation hoping that it would satisfy the local and international need. The new law was named the Confidential Relationships (Preservation) Law. A writer described the effect of this law as 'transforming the small Cayman Islands into one of the foremost financial centres on earth'. Thus far, with an amendment in 1979, the Law has served its purpose very well. I ended by saying to the gentleman, 'That piece of local legislation makes the difference among offshore centres.' The gentleman seemed pleased with the explanation and decided to move his entire business to the Cayman Islands. That was not the only case of satisfaction expressed by other investors to members of the Cayman financial community. At the beginning of the new century Cayman continues to rank with other leading global financial centres.

Cayman's popularity is also based on many other qualities easily seen by one just moving around and observing social standards like living conditions and per capita income. It is also easy to understand what the local stability means. The country has from the early days of building its present economy enjoyed full employment: also the absence of direct taxes made it a true tax haven. Its telecommunication, electricity and air services are not lacking in quality and neither are its back-up services for the industries, like accounting, auditing, legal and other professional and technical facilities. It was interesting, however, to see a commentary in the *Offshore Investment* issue of October 1986 by the Economist Intelligence Unit. In the report it was pointed out that Britain is the best tax haven in the world and offers incentives at least as good as those of the Cayman Islands or Luxembourg. The unit's report also points out that it is possible to establish a company in the United Kingdom with non-resident tax status through which profits from overseas trading can be channelled. Such a company will pay no UK taxes. The report says the UK has been used to shelter overseas profits in this way for many years and that their tax system is one of the most favourable in the world for business. Well, there we go; very nice that the mother country can compete with us in the tax haven business!

Another eye-catching comment by *Offshore Investment* was this: 'Without the will or the means adequately to compete against the booming offshore sector, and with wealth crossing frontiers with increasing technical ease, high tax jurisdictions not surprisingly regard offshore finance with jaundiced eyes. Onshore politicians have sought to condemn offshore centres as seducers of honest men, and as treasure chests of crime. After all, offshore centres did not produce high taxation, they were born of it.'

In early 1998 the Organization for Economic Cooperation and Development (OECD), with a membership of 29 countries including the United Kingdom and the United States, issued a report in which its policy statement was set out as:

(1) to achieve the highest sustainable economic growth and development and a rising standard of living in member countries, while maintaining financial stability, and thus to contribute to the development of the world economy;
(2) to contribute to sound economic expansion in member as well as non-member countries in the process of economic development; and
(3) to contribute to the expansion of world trade on a multi-lateral, non-discriminatory basis in accordance with international obligations.

The report addressed what member countries considered to be harmful tax competition which had become an emerging global issue. Many offshore financial centres became somewhat concerned over the issue which in fact pointed to measures to counter distorting effects of harmful tax competition and harmful tax practices. However, Cayman did not see this as offending its *modus operandi*, that is, the operating policies of its financial industry, in fact the Cayman Islands' position was made abundantly clear by its Governor, Mr John Owen in his Throne Speech delivered on 19th February 1999: 'Cayman must take advantage of the OECD initiative and send a clear message to the world as well as the OECD that Cayman is committed to maintaining itself as a quality jurisdiction which also acknowledges its responsibilities to the international community.' The statement by the Governor certainly conformed to the principles I accepted at the time of my meeting at the British Treasury in May 1971 when the chairman stated that he hoped the Caymans' financial industry would be based on good principles and policies backed by appropriate legislation. Even before that time I can definitely confirm that the operating principles and policies applied by the Cayman government to the structure of all aspects of its financial industry embraced the high standard later advocated by Her Majesty's Treasury.

Our third Financial Secretary, the Honourable George McCarthy, in his budget address on 4th November 1994, made this statement about the Cayman Islands:

> The Cayman Islands government has repeatedly demonstrated its diligence in preserving its reputation and also in deterring the use of financial institutions for illicit activities, through the joint efforts of the public and the private sectors.
>
> The Cayman Islands supported the work of the *Caribbean Financial Action Task Force* (CFATF) established in 1989 by the G7 summit. CFATF has endorsed the 40 recommendations proposed for implementation by all participating countries. The first of these recommendations was to fully implement and ratify the 1988 Vienna Convention against illicit traffic in narcotic drugs and psychotropic substances. In fact, most of the 40 recommendations made by the CFATF were already in place in the Cayman Islands.

In an address delivered in Barbados in August 1998, Mr Ian Paget Brown, a well-known English barrister who came to the Cayman Islands in 1971, spoke about the Cayman Islands and referred to them as 'the financial centre'. This is what he said about Cayman: 'There can be no doubt that the political and economic stability of the Cayman Islands is the primary reason for the development of Cayman as a jurisdiction of choice of the international financial community.'

Statistics by the Cayman government covering all areas of its financial services as at 30th June 1999 were: Companies 49,473, Mutual Funds (over US$200 billion in assets) 2,079, Mutual Funds (over $120 billion in assets) 170. Captive Insurance Companies and Insurance Managers were 494 and 26 respectively. Exempted Company Managers 53. Banks and Trust Companies (including restricted banks and trusts), and Trust (including restricted trust) 195, 272 and 106 respectively, for a total of 573.

While I was packing my bags to leave my office, my Principal Secretary, Kearney Gomez, said to me, 'So much has been accomplished by this portfolio in the four years, 1984–88; would you agree, sir, if I prepared a summary of major projects undertaken over the period?'

I smiled and replied, 'Try it, Kearney.' He prepared an annotated schedule of 20 subjects. I have elaborated on his notes in the following summary.

Protection of Endangered Species: The portfolio's minister signed in Washington along with officials of the United States Fish and Wildlife Service, Department of the Interior, and the United States National Marine Fisheries Service, Department of Commerce, on 17th December 1984, a Memorandum of Understanding for cooperation in conservation of endangered species.

Agriculture – Farmers' Cooperative, Farmers' Market and Abattoir: In 1985, recognizing the need for the promotion of agriculture, the Executive Council was requested to allow the portfolio to establish an Agricultural Development Committee with terms of reference which would enable it to focus on ways and means of achieving progress in the sector. Farmers were very much behind the effort; their aim was to make a success of agriculture through cooperative efforts in order to fulfil their hopes. In 1986 a Dr Elmer Close of the United States was commissioned to assess the feasibility of establishing a Farmers' Cooperative to market local farm products. The report of Dr Close was positive and as a result a study group from within the Agricultural Development Committee was selected to develop the concept of the Farmers' Cooperative. The Coop was registered in April 1987 following which the approval of the government was obtained to appoint a manager/secretary for the office.

The next step in developing agriculture was to embark upon two major capital projects for the programme. First was a Farmers' Market: this was completed at a cost of approximately CI$250,000. The intention behind the market project was that it be leased to the Farmers' Cooperative as a retail outlet for local produce. The second project was an abattoir. This would be constructed, equipped and operated to USDA standards. A consultant for the project was appointed and became involved in providing design details; architects were appointed for the project and the proposed site prepared. Government approval for the required construction cost was also obtained. The facility is intended to enable local meat producers to compete in the market place. The project should be completed and put into operation during the following year, 1989.

Building Code: In early 1985, a draft building code project was found resting in the office for quite some time. It was then

389

decided to revive the project. A new committee was appointed, together with the engaging of an advisor to produce a new draft code. After extensive consultation both with the professional societies involved in the construction industry and the general public, a final draft for Grand Cayman was produced. At the request of Cayman Brac, a separate code is being prepared for the lesser islands. Both codes for the Cayman Islands should simultaneously be presented to the Legislative Assembly in 1989. This set of draft building codes was reported to the Governor in my letter to him of 18th November 1988. Also reported to him as unfinished projects were the Development Plan Review, Land Ltd.'s request for a dredging licence in Governor's Harbour, planning guidelines on fast food restaurants, increase in George Town water supply and water for West Bay. The Governor was requested to pass these documents and files I was leaving with my Principal Secretary to my successor in office.

Grant of Licences to Caymanian Surveyors: Under the provisions of the Land Surveyors' Law, surveyors' licences may be issued by Executive Council by virtue of an applicant's proven surveying experience. Through the recommendations of the portfolio, two Caymanians were admitted to the ranks of the profession within the years 1987 and 1988.

National Trust: Details of the National Trust have already been written in Chapter 19.

Amendment to the Development Plan (Re-zoning) and the Development and Planning Regulations 1977 (Height Restriction): In order to relax certain height limitations on non-habitable structures regarding construction of the Grand Cayman Hyatt Hotel, an amendment of the Development and Planning Regulations 1977 was made to the Legislative Assembly. This was to enable the hotel to erect an elevator tower above the statutory height, which was regarded by the developers as a key element of their project design. The Hyatt, recently awarded a 4 diamond rating, will prove a valuable addition to tourism in these islands and will in fact give the local industry a new perspective with respect to its future development.

In order to enable major development projects to proceed, re-zoning of the Cayman Islands Yacht Club property, the Safehaven Property and the Land Ltd. property owned by a Caymanian, all on the North Sound side of the Seven Mile Beach were re-zoned for commercial purposes by the Legislative Assembly. Two of the projects were well under way.

Restructuring of HDC and Refinancing Through Banks and Insurance Companies: The Housing Development Corporation, a subject of much importance to low-income residents in need of their own home, overcame a number of initial obstacles including lack of loan funds, personnel problems and relatively high overhead cost. The latter was substantially reduced with the relocation of the HDC office to the Tower Building, where rent and electricity were free. Also, amalgamation of HDC with an Agricultural and Industrial Development Board resulted in equal sharing of the administrative cost. New fundraising through offerings of a 5 per cent debenture stock to local financial institutions from early 1985 produced an additional CI$583,000, bringing the total borrowed money for on-lending purposes to CI$1,218,000.

Development Plan Review: A comprehensive review of the Development Plan began in 1985 and included the Development and Planning Law and Regulations. The drafts of these three planning instruments should be produced by the end of this year and ready for presentation to the public and Legislative Assembly in 1989. Although the process has been time-consuming, the end of the tunnel is now hopefully in sight. Planning guidelines are most essential at this stage of development.

Petroleum Agreement: The portfolio was instrumental in finalizing in July 1985 an agreement for the exploration and production of petroleum in the Cayman Islands. However, with the immediate fall in oil prices following the signing, the agreement was terminated a year later within the terms of the instrument.

Dog Control Programme: In response to the growing nuisance of the stray dog population, along the Seven Mile Beach area especially, a dog control programme was implemented in 1986 to combat the problem. The programme has been very effective over the past two years and will continue with expansion into other areas of the islands if and when necessary.

West Bay Beach Sewerage Project: This project got under way in 1986 and is scheduled for completion in April 1988 although there could be slight delay in the final tidying process. Cost and other details are covered in Chapter 18.

George Town Water Supply: The water supply system also got under way in 1986. The first phase was completed in May 1988 at a cost of CI$3.5 million. Further expansion will continue according to demand and as capital funds become available. (For further details turn to Chapter 18.)

Marine Conservation and Environment: A previous chapter covers the subject of marine conservation and includes the Marine Parks Regulations covering the three islands and made effective in May 1986. The regulations also cover permanent moorings, no-dive sites and the turtle protection. The staff at the Natural Resources Laboratory was increased to meet the on-coming demands for scientific study necessary as development generally expanded. They were involved in the establishment of the marine parks, together with setting up programmes for monitoring the coral reef and other marine areas of Grand Cayman.

The Governor, Mr A.J. Scott, wrote me on 28th November 1988 on the eve of my retirement and had this to say about two of my cherished projects, conservation and establishment of the National Trust. 'These and especially the National Trust are milestones in the social development of the islands as well as being vital in the preservation of the islands as an attractive place for visitors. The resurgence of the many threatened species, throughout the marine parks and the protection zones, is now well known to all, even those who at first disbelieved the possibility of control.'

Dredging Inspection Team: With the continued increase in development involving dredging, my office established in 1986 a Dredging Inspection Team to advise the government on dredging applications and on those approved and to monitor such projects. The terms of reference were later revised to include all coastal works.

Cayman Turtle Farm: The farm was reorganized in 1986 to increase its potential as a tourist attraction and to make available to the local market the steak and stew including the fins. A snack bar and fauna and flora exhibit area was opened in 1987. The farm also leased 7 acres of land to Caribbean Sea Farms for a shrimp farm, thereby divesting itself from producing and trading in shrimp products. (The story of the farm is also contained in Chapter 17.)

Amendment to the Land Survey Regulation: In response to the need for clarifying the means by which foreshore boundaries are defined, previously determined by policy rather than a definition established by law, an amendment to the Land Survey Regulations was put forward and approved in April 1987. As a result of the amendment, the seaward boundary of a parcel was made by the high water mark, which was precisely defined, thereby removing doubt as to foreshore boundaries on the sand beach, iron shore and mangrove areas. The story of seaward boundaries is also contained in earlier paragraphs of this chapter.

Reorganization of the Agricultural Department: The Department of Agriculture was restructured during this period when an agronomist and an extension officer were added to the staff in January 1987 and July 1988 respectively to provide technical assistance to local farmers.

Public Jetties and Boat Ramps: Public jetties were built in South Sound, East End and North Side and the jetties at George Town Barcadere and Batabano were renovated. Boat ramps were built at Water Cay, Old Man Bay and East End. The portfolio was also instrumental in clearing and marking channels in North Side, East End, Frank Sound and South Sound.

Dredging: Three major dredging licences were approved during this four-year period.

(i) The Cayman Islands Yacht Club was involved in dredging an 80-acre site contiguous to Governor's Sound and Salt Creek. The Governor's Sound channel was widened and deepened in the process to allow safe passage of large and expensive yachts especially during the annual fishing tournaments.

(ii) The Safehaven project involved dredging of 1.4 million cubic yards of fill offshore from the Welch Point site in North Sound to reclaim a 280-acre site and create artificial beaches on North Sound. A 10-acre portion of adjoining Crown land was also to be filled for the government, to be used as a public park.

(iii) The third licence involves a native Caymanian whose permit allowed him to dredge 2 million cubic yards of fill for stockpiling and to sell it to the public, and for reclaiming a 176-acre site to the north of George Town Barcadère.

Convention on the Protection of Migratory Species of Wild Animals: In further efforts to support international conservation, this portfolio was instrumental in having this government included in the Bonn Convention on the Protection of Migratory Species of Wild Animals and the Cartagena Convention for the

Protection and Development of the Marine Environment of the wider Caribbean Region. We also participated actively in the Ramsar Convention on the Conservation of Wetlands and Waterfowl. A study was conducted to identify the important wetlands and waterfowl species. These areas are in the process of being designated as Animal Sanctuaries and registered as Ramsar sites (Wetlands of International Importance Especially as Waterfowl Habitat).

The foregoing 20 projects occupied most of my portfolio's four years. A few, about seven, were not finally completed. I passed them on at the end of 1988 through the Governor for others to deal with. I am afraid that ten years later a few of those seven unfinished projects are still outstanding.

Another subject of much interest is road transportation. As a community grows so does its vehicular traffic: this in time can create problems if vehicles are not properly controlled or roadway infrastructure adequately provided especially in small countries like Cayman. Having lived through rapid traffic growth in the 1960s, I decided to approach the elected members of the government about the growing problem. Near to the November 1969 budget and after completing a package of proposed new revenues for the financial year 1970, I broached the subject of vehicle control. I suggested that unless the Legislative Assembly was prepared to place some form of restriction on importation of vehicles, their size, year of manufacture and annual quotas, traffic congestion on the roads would in a few years become a real source of concern. The members looked at me and said, 'Motor vehicles are strictly political. You are a civil servant, so concentrate on your subject, finance.' Their attitude did not bother me in the least bit for I am an ardent believer in the epigram 'Nothing beats a trial but a failure'. At least the government could not pretend at a later stage that they were not forewarned of an inevitable traffic problem.

Fifteen years later when nothing of any consequence had been done to relieve traffic congestion on the roads, especially from the districts into George Town in the mornings and back home in the evenings (peak traffic hours), the indication was that the problem had then reached serious proportions. By this time I had become a politician and a member of the government. My government, through the Minister for Communication and Works, the Honourable Captain Charles Kirkconnell, proposed to the government in 1988 a motion, which was accepted, that a team of consultants and road engineers be hired to examine the deficiencies in Cayman's roads system. The motion went on to state that if their report was approved they should move on to carry out the necessary improvements. The firm of Wilbur Smith Associates, in association with David Lashley and Partners and Robertson Ward Associates (Consultants), undertook the studies. The proposed plan was approved and implementation of the development phases began. The report, known as The Master Ground Transportation Plan (MGTP), recommended a major road construction programme over the next ten-year period; it would provide a network of roads capable of handling the rapidly growing demands upon the transportation system. This would involve amendment to the Roads Law to include compensation for land that the government wished to acquire. The total cost as presented was CI\$18.784 million.

The MGTP 'immediate action projects' included Eastern Avenue/ West Bay Road at a cost of \$70,000. This first starter project began on Eastern Avenue, bypassing the George Town Cemetery and went on to the West Bay Road to the Treasure Island Resort. This portion of improvement on the West Bay Road carried three traffic lanes considered essential for dividing traffic by the cemetery into central and north George Town. It was the beginning of an excellent programme but unfortunately at its completion a new government took over in November 1988 and almost immediately the MGTP was put to rest. Ten years later a subsequent government undertook to continue the three lanes on the West Bay Road to a distance a little beyond Government House: the centre lane is for turning right or left. During this same programme a new road known as the Harquail Bypass was built. It leads traffic from close by the Cinema Theatre on West Bay Road to North Sound Road junction for distribution in that part of the George Town eastern roads network including the airport and eastern districts.

Sometimes it boosts the morale just to hear the nice things one person has said about another. With that in mind and with the hope that no objection will be raised by the individuals, I would like to quote, in closing, the words of the three Governors under whom I served latterly either on their retirement or on my leaving the service. They are Thomas Russell, Peter Lloyd and Alan Scott.

Thomas Russell: 29th December 1981.

'I shall be leaving the Cayman Islands in a few days time and wanted you to know how much I have admired the discharge of your duties, and have appreciated your advice and guidance during my term of office here. You are the only Member of Executive Council and Official Member of the Assembly to have run the full course with me and I cannot recall one occasion in over seven years when you have not measured up to the demanding exigencies of your office with less than 100%. Perhaps because we have done the same job – although compared with your lengthy career as a Financial Secretary I can only count myself as an apprentice – I think that we both realized soon after my arrival that we shared the same philosophies of public administration and this has led to a working relationship of great warmth and closeness.

Your contribution to the country, however, goes far beyond your portfolio responsibilities and the astonishing economic success of the Cayman Islands is due in no small measure to your perspicacity, ability to see a job through, and your relationship with all elements of Caymanian society. Although none of us is irreplaceable, you, in particular, will be very difficult to replace.'

Thomas Russell served a period of seven years from 1974 and he is considered the longest-serving Governor of the Cayman Islands. Shortly after leaving here at the end of 1981 he was selected to replace the Crown Agents of London as the Cayman Islands' government representative in the United Kingdom, which position he occupies at time of writing.

Peter Lloyd: 29th March 1982.

'As you are, after a long and distinguished career, preparing to retire from the Civil Service, I should like to express my appreciation of and gratitude for your over 36 years of service dedicated to the task of building a better community in the Cayman Islands.

Your colleagues in the Legislative Assembly and the Executive Council, together with many other organizations and individuals, have already expressed their congratulations on accomplishments which have brought immense credit to yourself, to your family and to the Cayman Islands. I join them in congratulating and in thanking you.

As the Colony's Financial Secretary for the past seventeen years, you have demonstrated the efficiency, drive and management skills of an outstanding Civil Servant.'

Peter Lloyd's term of administration spanning five and a half years from 14th January 1982 to mid-1987 was considered very successful. He was privileged to welcome to these islands for the first time Her

Majesty The Queen, on 16th February 1983. Peter Lloyd was also priviledged as Governor of these islands to be one of the three signatories to the historic Mutual Legal Assistance Treaty between the United States and the Cayman Islands; the other two signatories were those of officials of the United States and United Kingdom governments. The treaty was signed here in Grand Cayman on 3rd July 1986.

Alan Scott: 28th November 1988.

> 'On your retirement at the end of a second, distinguished career, it is my pleasure to write and thank and congratulate you for what you have achieved during your tenure of the Portfolio of Development and Natural Resources.
> I would especially like to thank you for the wise and constructive advice you have given in Executive Council meetings; and on less formal occasions. I realized very quickly how special this help was going to be, and you have never failed me with it.'

Alan Scott served as Governor of these islands from mid-1987 to 1st September 1992. He was also privileged to welcome to these islands a first visit on 31st October 1988 of Princess Alexandra and her husband the Honourable Angus Ogilvy. Their visit ended on 4th November 1988.

As I reached the end of the course, a period spanning 23 years from 1965, I was greatly relieved that my labour for the country was not in vain. In fact while reviewing the process and progress of development, I could see the efforts that became brighter with each dawning year. I thought that at this stage we should not look at the level which the country reached in 1988, but instead peek at the struggle over many decades to achieve our successes. I recall back in 1952 when Andrew Gerrard came here to take over the office of Commissioner, he landed on the waters of the North Sound in an aircraft that shortly after went to the bottom of the ocean outside Palisadoes Airport. The airline that owned the aircraft, Caribbean International Airways, died with its owner Commander Roberts and its only piece of equipment, a Lodestar aeroplane. The adventurous owner, an Englishman, Commander Owen Roberts, his pilot and many others, including a Caymanian family of five, all died: only one man, Lieutenant-Colonel Edward Remington-Hobbs, of 14 on board, lived to tell the tale. Yet the efforts for an established air service that would be of tremendous benefit to the social and economic development of these islands did not cease. Today, nearly 50 years after the attempted air service that ended in tragedy, we find ourselves living in a different world for we now have air services which, for the size of the community, are unparalleled anywhere in the world.

My instinctive pride sometime becomes faintly hurt by the notion of a few who believe that all Cayman's growth has happened just by accident. Nothing is further from the truth, nothing has happened by accident, any more than you board an aircraft in Grand Cayman today and find yourself a few hours later in New York or London. The development of these islands required a vast amount of planning with a remarkable selection of technical skills to bring the country to where it is today. The progress we have made here is the result of deliberate policies and the result of putting those policies into effect. The result created a climate and an atmosphere in which the chosen policies could grow and could flourish. Yes, all those who have been involved in the building process have done a wonderful job, sometimes in difficult circumstances and often with exacting tasks for which the country will ever be grateful. In these last few words I wish to extend my grateful thanks to many people. First my dear wife and family, who stood by my side in good times as well as on difficult occasions. Then the Commissioners, Administrators, Governors, the Executive Council and the Legislative Assembly, the Civil Service and private sector, for the tremendous assistance given to me in my years when we all worked together with one aim and one purpose: for the good of the country and its coming generations.

21

Postscript

A Singular Royal Award

In September 1993, life took on a different pace with the announcement that Her Majesty Queen Elizabeth II would be returning for her second visit to Cayman. In late November the Governor, Michael Gore, called me to his office to say confidentially that the Queen wanted to confer on me the honour of a knighthood and asked if I would accept it. The public announcement of the Queen's Honours was made at the usual time, the end of the year, on 31st December. The award was to be presented during the Royal Visit, scheduled for 26–28 February 1994.

This second visit of the royal couple was a very prestigious occasion for the Cayman Islands and a time when the people again in a great fashion of enthusiasm proclaimed their loyalty to the British Crown. The visit, part of an eight-country Caribbean tour, provided the occasion for a number of local events. The Royal Yacht sailed from Belize and dropped anchor in George Town Harbour on Saturday morning. First on the programme was Her Majesty's second Throne Speech to the Legislative Assembly of the Cayman Islands at 10 a.m. This was the only Throne Speech delivered by the Queen on the tour, even though she addressed the parliaments of five different countries. The Throne Speech was of much interest. It began with these words.

> Prince Philip and I are delighted to make this return visit to these beautiful islands. I am especially pleased to be present today to open the Legislative Assembly and to deliver my speech in person.
> The Privy Council recently approved an amended Constitution, updating the 1972 Constitution, to take account of developments

399

on the islands. Next week you will elect a fifth member of the Executive Council, thereby easing the burden on other ministers, which has been increasing with the remarkable developments which have taken place in recent years, notably since our last visit in 1983.

The financial sector remains the key to a successful future for these islands. My government is determined to maintain a financial services industry of high quality and integrity, through strict adherence to prudent policies, augmented by the production of the new mutual funds legislation.

This year the public and private sectors will launch a major promotional programme to increase the awareness overseas of the high quality financial services, and company and shipping registration, offered by these islands. Of particular note is the planned hosting of the Red Ensign Shipping Register's Annual Conference in April, for the first time in the islands' history.

In her closing, the Queen commented: 'Prince Philip and I were touched by the welcome we received this morning and we look forward to our visits on the island today and tomorrow.'

The Throne Speech was followed by an investiture on the steps of the Legislative Assembly of those persons named in Her Majesty's New Year Honours List. Of course it was on that occasion that I was chosen by Her Majesty to be the first person in the Cayman Islands to receive the knighthood. On the same occasion my youngest brother Patrick (retired Deputy Director of Civil Aviation) was awarded by the Queen the honour of Member of the Most Excellent Order of the British Empire (MBE). My eldest daughter, Theresa Bodden, also received the Queen's Badge of Honour for her involvement on the Drug Advisory Council. (In January 1998 Theresa was appointed chairman of the newly established National Drug Council launched by the Minister of Health, Drug Abuse Prevention and Rehabilitation, the Honourable Anthony Eden.)

Other items on the programme for the royal visit included a tour of the Cayman Islands National Museum, where the royal couple saw the exhibit commemorating the 200th anniversary of the Wreck of the Ten Sail. Next on the programme was the official opening of phase one of the Ed Bush Sports Centre in West Bay. In the evening it was entertainment time with dinner at 7.30 p.m. on board the Royal Yacht *Britannia* hosted by the Queen and Prince Philip. My wife and I were privileged to be among the invited guests. The next morning at 10 a.m. the royal party attended service at Elmslie Memorial Church in George Town. Thereafter the royal party travelled to Frank Sound to declare open the Queen Elizabeth II Botanic Park. They also visited the site in East End selected to commemorate the Wreck of the Ten Sail. The land-based park, selected to give a view of the reefs where the now-famous wreck occurred, was also dedicated by Her Majesty. At all the functions the Queen took time out of her busy programme for customary 'walkabouts' meeting persons in the vast throngs who wanted just to be a part of the exciting occasion. Her Majesty and Prince Philip departed Grand Cayman on Sunday evening at 4 p.m. on the Royal Yacht.

There was a vast number of articles written and comments made nationally and internationally about the visit, especially the knighhood.

Robert Hardman of the *Daily Telegraph* in London wrote in the *Majesty* royal magazine of April 1994 the story of the Royal Visit to Grand Cayman. In his story he said, 'From Belize the royal party sailed to Grand Cayman, the largest of the Cayman Islands, where the Royal Yacht was moored off the capital, George Town. There the Queen took the rare step of holding a public investiture to salute the man who transformed the Caymans into the world's leading offshore financial centre. Like Sir Francis Drake and Sir Francis Chichester before him, Sir Vassel Johnson, a modest and shy former Financial Secretary, was knighted in the main square in front of hundreds of cheering locals.'

In the British magazine *Business Age*, Tom Rubython, editor and publisher, writing his Cayman story on the knighthood, said: 'Sir Vassel is a man of small stature with a wiry frame. He has the same unmistakable presence as Mahatma Gandhi. He created the Cayman Islands in their current form. In many ways he has done the same job for Cayman as Gandhi did for India.'

Wil Pineau of the *New Caymanian* wrote on Friday 25th February 1994, the day before the royal party arrived, 'Never before in history has a Caymanian received such a high honour. And it is only fitting that Johnson, architect of Cayman's robust offshore financial industry and a public servant for more than 40 years, will have his shoulders touched by Her Majesty the Queen. Johnson's knighthood also seems to signify a greater level of respect shown by the British monarchy towards the Caymanian people. Traditionally, knighthoods are awarded only to citizens of British Dependent Territories that have advanced to a higher level of administrative maturity. It now appears that the Queen considers the Cayman Islands to have crossed that coveted threshold.'

In the *Cayman Executive* magazine, the editor, Ms Ryhaan Shah, wrote: 'Johnson's knighthood places Cayman in the arena of nations

401

across the world proud to have produced persons of sterling character who deserve this great honour.' In describing the ceremony itself
she observed: 'After exchanging a few brief words with the Queen,
Sir Vassel strode off the dais and, acknowledging the cheers from the
crowd who watched the investiture outside the Legislative Assembly
building, he turned and bowed. It was a gesture that was in keeping
with the character of this gentle statesman, his bow proclaiming that
the glory was not his alone but belonged to all of Cayman.'

I could not have articulated my feelings better. I was grateful
because my adopted home has been good to me. At the same time I
trust that I have been good for it.

I considered it an added blessing that the honour came to me while
my mother was still alive. She died the following year, at the grand
age of 99.

Cayman's success is now established. On 7th March 1997 the
Governor, Mr John Owen, MBE (he has since then been honoured by
Her Majesty the Queen with the CMG), said in his Throne Speech.
'These islands have now reached the summit of their success and
graduated from being an offshore financial centre to one of the
world's major international financial centres. It competes for business
with London, New York, Tokyo and Hong Kong. Cayman has also
set an example, not only with the Caribbean region, but to financial
centres worldwide, of being a jurisdiction which is committed to the
fight against dirty money.'

The wealth of Cayman today will hopefully continue to benefit its
people for many generations to come.

Wreck of the Ten Sail

Coincidentally, 1994 was being marked as the 200th anniversary of
the Wreck of the Ten Sail, a topic that had interested me from the
time I first learned about it as a boy. I had visited East End for the
first time in 1937, when I was 15, to attend the district garden party.
The Presbyterian churches in the eastern districts were the first to
hold these events, between Boxing Day and New Year's Day. The all-
day festivities were a time when the church members organized sales
of products mainly from their gardens to assist the church's finances;
thus the name 'garden party'. While in East End on that first visit, I
became interested in the hull of ships lying not far offshore at
Gauldin Bluff, a place on the shoreline in East End's eastern section,
considered the highest point of land from sea level anywhere in
Grand Cayman. The name of the Bluff comes from the bird, the

gauldin (heron). The name 'gauldin' is found at pages 49 and 50 of the book *Birds of the Cayman Islands*, the author of which is Mrs Patricia Bradley, wife of Cayman's former Attorney-General and Turks and Caicos Islands' Governor, Michael Bradley.

On inquiry into the wrecks at East End I was told that those were the remains of the famous and historic 'Wreck of the Ten Sail': people knew little else about the disaster. In later years when development of both tourism and finance began to move, the Wreck of the Ten Sail was popularly used in advertisements. The old legend of the wrecks told visitors that, because of the exceeding assistance given by the people of East End in saving the lives of the ships' crew, the King of England by special decree exempted the Cayman Islands from taxes. However, the true historical factors of the shipwrecks were not recorded in the early history of these islands, due mainly to the fact that the story could not be found in libraries, museums or archives in England or Jamaica. Nevertheless the tale of the wrecks and its popularity continued. As can be imagined, I was intrigued by the story, especially during those years when I was concerned with the country's finances as Financial Secretary.

The growing popularity of the Wreck of the Ten Sail caused the Legislative Assembly in August 1969 through its Member Mr W.W. Conolly, to propose in a motion that the tercentenary of the Treaty of Madrid in 1670 be marked by the preparation of a new history of Cayman. That motion was passed and followed by the commissioning of Dr Neville Williams, MA, DPhil, FSA, FRHistSoc, Deputy Keeper of Public Records in Great Britain, to rewrite the history of the Cayman Islands. Dr Williams was requested to spend some time researching public record offices and the National Maritime Museum in London for the story covering the East End wrecks. Although much effort went into the research, he found nothing of interest.

The government's continuing interest in the East End shipwreck disaster led the more recently established Cayman Islands Museum, headed by Miss Anita Ebanks, and the National Archive, led by Dr Philip Pedley, to take a new interest into the shipwreck research. In 1980 Dr Margaret Leshikar-Denton of Texas, USA, first heard of the Wreck of the Ten Sail when she visited Cayman at the government's invitation and as a participant in an archaeological survey conducted by the Institute of Nautical Archaeology. In 1988 Dr Leshikar-Denton went on to do her PhD and thereafter returned to Cayman to assist with the opening of the National Museum. In 1990 she selected the shipwrecks as the focus of her pending dissertation regarding the subject as a significant event in Cayman's history.

In her research for the pending dissertation, Dr Leshikar-Denton travelled to the Public Record Office and the National Maritime Museum in London, to the Jamaica Archives in Spanish Town and to the National Library of Jamaica in Kingston. She also corresponded with archives in France. In all those places she was generously facilitated in her research work. In her study she focused on the subject of two Royal Navy frigates patrolling off the French colony of Santo Domingo in Haiti, where they captured a French vessel, *L'Inconstante*, between 1789 and 1794. The prize, a fine, swift frigate, armed with 12-pounder guns, was brought to Jamaica, where the hull, sails, rigging, ordnance and stores were provided by the British Admiralty. Since there was already an *Inconstante* in His Majesty's Service, the Commander-in-Chief of the Jamaican squadron renamed the frigate the HMS *Convert*. Its first mission was to escort a homeward-bound convoy of merchant ships, resulting in the famous East End Wreck of the Ten Sail.

In her continued research, Dr Leshikar-Denton finally discovered that on 8th February 1794, when the warship *Convert* was wrecked with nine of her merchant convoy on the East End reefs, Cayman was linked to the mainstream of world events. In her statement she said:

> The historical facts are exciting, while contemporaneous documents provide a glimpse into the lives of the people who experienced the calamitous event 200 years ago. Archaeological investigations have shown that in addition to a valuable archival record and delightful folklore, remains of the shipwrecks also exist. With the help of a team of dedicated volunteers, working within a three-mile zone, 30 underwater sites and eight land sites, dating between the eighteenth and twentieth centuries were found. A number of these represent vestiges of the *Convert*'s convoy. Although the sites have been salvaged in the past, there remains a unique relationship between the Royal Navy frigate, the merchant ships and the shipwreck salvage sites. Thus, the East End reefs represent a significant historical shipwreck zone. Scientific recovery, conservation and analysis of artefacts, now and in the future, will result in a collection of artefacts and information that will enable a wider story of the Wreck of the Ten Sail to be told. These artefacts tell a story of Cayman, the Caribbean, Europe and the world in the late eighteenth century.

Discovery of the age-old story of the Wreck of the Ten Sail was a delightful accomplishment for the Cayman Islands. The 200th Anniversary, 1794–1994, was commemorated by an exhibit on Tuesday 8th February 1994 at the Cayman Islands National Museum, which Dr Leshikar-Denton joined as Marine Archaeologist. The anniversary was also marked by a Philatelic Bureau stamp issue, a Currency Board commemorative coin programme, a National Archive publication, Visual Arts Society art competitions and public lectures. Moreover, the Wreck of the Ten Sail was featured prominently in the itinerary for Her Majesty Queen Elizabeth II and His Royal Highness the Duke of Edinburgh.

Curriculum Vitae

Sir Vassel Godfrey Johnson, Kt., CBE, JP

DATE OF BIRTH 18th January 1922.

PLACE OF BIRTH Jamaica.

RESIDENTIAL STATUS Moved to the Cayman Islands in September 1934 and attained Cayman status as of right.

MARITAL STATUS Married Rita Joanna Hinds of South Sound in 1952 and together we have raised a family of four daughters and two sons.

EDUCATION Attended Primary and Secondary Schools in Grand Cayman and in 1942 attained the Third Year Pupil Teacher's Examination Certificate (secondary education) the highest academic qualification then available in Cayman.

Military and Civil Service

1942 Entered the Cayman Islands Civil Service (Courts Office). After obtaining secondary education, I joined the Cayman Company of the Jamaican Home Guard for two and a half years.

1945 Discharged from the Army at the rank of Sergeant and awarded by His Majesty King George VI the 1939–45 World War II Medal.

Re-entered the Civil Service on 16th December 1945 as Clerical Officer in the Department of the Treasury,

406

Customs and Post Office. (In following years studied accounting and English by correspondence courses from Bennett College and Wolsey Hall respectively, both of the United Kingdom).

1955	Appointed Assistant to the Deputy Treasurer after reorganization of the Treasury, Customs and Post Office departments into three separate entities.
1959–60	Acted as Clerk of the Courts for 15 months (the post being vacant due to illness of the substantive holder).
1962–76	Public Recorder (additional appointment).
1965–82	Treasurer and Collector of Taxes. Also Economic and Financial Advisor to the government. In 1968 the post of Treasurer was re-designated Financial Secretary and the office in 1972 moved from the Post Office Building to the Administration Building, the seat of government, which included the Governor's Office.
	Member of the Legislative Assembly by virtue of the position of Treasurer.
1965–76	Licencing Authority (responsibility transferred to the Police Department after 1976).
1966–80	Controller of Exchange (foreign currency). The system was abolished in 1980.
1966–75	Inspector of Banks and Trust Companies. Growth of the banking industry during this period eventually

	required a full time Inspector as of 1975.
1968–77	Appointed a Director of Cayman Airways and became the Chairman 1971–77.
1969–77	Chairman of Cayman Islands Corporation (a board controlling civil aviation administrative policies).
1969	Attended a study course relating to development planning and implementation at Sussex University in Brighton, England.
1970	Awarded by Her Majesty The Queen the honour to be an Officer of the Most Excellent Order of the British Empire (OBE).
1971–82	Chairman of the Cayman Islands Currency Board. (The first Cayman Currency was issued on 1st May 1972.)
1972–82	Appointed, under the new Constitution, a Member of the Executive Council responsible for the Portfolio of Finance and Development as the former Constitution did not provide a seat for the Treasurer.
1977	Acted for a few weeks as Governor of the islands.
	Appointed a Justice of the Peace for the Cayman Islands.
	On 7th June Her Majesty The Queen forwarded me a medal to be worn in commemoration of her Silver Jubilee: 6th February 1952–6th February 1977.
1977–82	Chairman of Government Vehicles

	Funding Scheme (a board that controlled the government's fleet of vehicles).
1980	Awarded by Her Majesty The Queen the honour to be a Commander of the Most Excellent Order of the British Empire (CBE). In this instance the CBE replace the OBE.
1982	Wrote and published on 26th March the first *Economic and Financial Review of Government* covering the period 1904 to 1981.
	Proceeded 1st April on one year pre-retirement leave.
1982–84	Chairman of the Board of Governors of the United Church's Cayman Preparatory School.
1983	Retired on 1st April from the government's Civil Service.
	Appointed in January as Managing Director of Montpelier Properties (Cayman) Ltd. (Elizabethan Square), a private sector position (retired 30th June 1997).
	Director of three private sector banking institutions.
1983–84	Chairman of Public Service Commission (Govt).
	Member of the Board of Parole Commissioners (Govt).

Politics and Government

1984	Entered politics and won a seat in the George Town constituency. The

Legislative Assembly elected me as one of the four Members of the Executive Council. The Governor allocated to me the Portfolio of Development and Natural Resources.

Chaired four boards in the portfolio: Water Authority, Housing Development Corporation, Cayman Turtle Farm and Agricultural and Industrial Development.

1984–85   Served on a second occasion as Chairman of Cayman Airways from November 1984 to December 1985.

1986   Introduced in May the Marine Parks Regulations, which applied to the three islands.

1988   Completed construction of the George Town Water System and the Seven Mile Beach Sewerage Scheme and opened both facilities to the public.

Completed and introduced legislation establishing the National Trust Law.

Retired from government and politics in November and continued (in a full-time capacity) at Montpelier Properties (Cayman) Ltd.

1992   Director and Partner in Cayman Television Service Ltd.

1992–95   Returned on a second occasion to become Chairman of the Board of Governors of Cayman Preparatory School.

1994   Knighted by Her Majesty The Queen in her New Year Honours.

The foregoing summary of positions

served in the Cayman Islands is also contained in *Who's Who 1995*, the 147th annual edition of a biographical publication produced by A & C Black of London. The summary can also be found in the Cayman Islands' *Who's Who*.

1997	Retired from Montpelier Properties on 30th June.
	Appointed a Director of the Cayman Islands Monetary Authority in July.
RELIGION	Senior Elder of the United Church, formerly Presbyterian.
HOBBY	Bridge.

GOVERNORS AND CHIEF OFFICERS OF THE
CAYMAN ISLANDS[8]
FOR THE PERIOD 1934–99

1934	Allen Wolsey Cardinall, CMG	Commissioner
1940	Albert Colin Panton, Sr, MBE	do. (Acting)
1941	John Penry Jones	do.
1946	Ivor Otterbein Smith	do.
1952	Andrew Morris Gerrard, CMG	do.
1956	Alan Hillard Donald, OBE	do. (and first

Administrator under the new Constitution of 1959)

1960	Jack Rose	Administrator
1964	John Alfred Cumber, CMG, MBE, TD	do.
1968	Athelstan Charles Ethelwulf, CMG, CBE	do. (and first

Governor under the new Constitution of 1972)

1971	Kenneth Roy Crook, CMG	Governor
1974	Thomas Russell, CMG, CBE	do.
1982	Peter Lloyd, CMG	do.
1987	Alan J. Scott, CVO, CBE	do.
1992	Michael J. Gore, CVO, CBE	do.
1996	John Owen, CMG, MBE	do.
1999	Peter J. Smith, CBE	do.

[8] Sources: (1) *The Cayman Islands Annual Colonial Report* (prepared in London)
         (2) *The Cayman Islands Government Economic and Financial Review*, published in 1982 and dating back to 1904

INDEX

413

414

415

416

East End
  bathing beach 335
  town hall 62
  water supply 346
  Wreck of the Ten Sail 400–5
Ebanks, Allie O. 266
Ebanks, Anita 403
Ebanks, Benson O.
  Community College 251
  financial confidentiality 313
  Minister 267, 292–3, 305–6
  National Trust 362
  royal visit 380
Ebanks, Bertie 116
Ebanks, Corporal Arthur 54
Ebanks, Craddock 203, 287
Ebanks, Dalmain 203
Ebanks, Dawson 89
Ebanks, Donovan 353
Ebanks, Lee A. 80
Ebanks, Nathan 53–4
Ebanks, Ron 341
Ebanks, S.O. 120
Ebanks, Talmage 380
Ebanks-Petrie, Gina 334
Ebanks family name 50–1
economic diversification 198–226
Ed Bush Sports Centre 400
Eden, Anthony 400
Eden, Ulin 51
Eden, William 34–5
Eden's Water 350
Edinburgh, Duke of 107–8, 214, 286–9,
  400, 405
education 86–7
Eggar, Timothy J. 317–18
Eldemire, Kent 287
electricity 93–5
Elizabeth, Queen 214, 286–9, 365, 397,
  399–401, 405
Ellison, John 264
Elmslie Presbyterian Church 43, 282, 284
endangered species conservation 322–3,
  389
environment conservation 229, 322–42
Environment Week 342
Escalante, Captain Otto 265–7
Ethelwulf, Athelston Charles 412
Eurodollars 149–50
exchange control 12, 152, 165, 210,
  218–26

Exchange Control Regulations Law
  126–7, 149, 221–4
Exchange Control repeal 219–20, 242
exchange of prisoners 379

Fairclough, A.J. 338
Fairest, Professor Paul 248, 249
Falklands War 284–6, 327
Farmers' Cooperative 246, 289
Farmers' Market 141, 246, 374, 389
Farrington, Captain Charlie 6, 25, 62
Farrington, Rayburn 55
Farrington, William 36, 86–7, 260
Fein, Bruce 311
Field, Anthony 154–5, 157
finance industry 110, 147–66
  confidentiality 152, 154–7, 296, 301–5,
    313, 386
Financial Community Committee 201
financial services statistics 388
First National City Bank 139, 158
fishing 30, 67–8, 335–6, 374–5
C.L. Flowers & Sons 350
Flowers, Clarence L. 282, 344
Flowers, Frank 344
Flowers, Richard 353
Flowers' Water Trucking Service 348
Forbes, Joseph 76
foreshore access 374–5, 392–3
Foster, Dennis 265, 285
Foster, Don 333
Foster, Trevor 236, 261
Foye, Peter 353
Francis, Charles 310, 311
Frederick, Vance 84
free port 166
Frith, Captain G.H. 242

Galleon Beach Hotel 95, 107, 344
Galleon Beach Lodge 95
Galtere, Glen 196
Gandhi, Indira 229
Gantner, Willie 268
Gauldin Bluff 402
General Elections 143, 232, 268, 280,
  290, 381
General Hospital 78, 140
George Hicks High School 45, 290
George Hicks United Church 45, 282–3
George Town 29–31
  Administration building 139, 243

417

turtle fishing 30, 32, 50, 65–6
Tyson, Mr 85

unions 70–1
United Church in Jamaica and the
Cayman Islands 3
United Nations Special Committee on
Decolonization 233–4
United States narcotics treaty 300–18
United States withdraws tax treaties
112–13
Unity Team 198, 280, 290, 292, 293, 377
University of Liverpool law degree 250
University of Sussex 47, 144, 408

Van der Linde, Captain Harold E. 202–3
van Dreunan, Daniel 161
vehicle control 394
Venables, General Robert 8
Verran, J.V. 264
Vesey, Ernest W.P. 305–6
Vista del Mar 373
Vunibobo, Berenado 233

Waddington, Gerald 203, 265
wages 30
Walker Jr, John M. 311
Wallace, Walter 234
Warren, John 115
water 141, 343–53
Water Authority 343, 346, 352–3
Water Authority Law 346, 350
Water Quay developments 338
waterfowl 394
Watler, Bert 285
Watler, Brainard 353
Watler, Captain Anderson 24
Watler, China 24
Watler, Clara 24
Watler, Cromwell 358
Watler, Desmond 56, 73, 80, 84, 358
Assistant Postmaster 75
Chief Secretary 186, 220, 244, 259
Deputy Administrator 97, 105
Treasurer 82, 85
Watler, D.V. 182
Watler, Graham 70
Watler, Harding 270
Watler, Joseph 53
Watler, Ladner 336–7

Watler, Roddy 31, 80
Watler, Trevor 84
weather bureau stations 39–40, 90
J.S. Webster & Sons 107
West Bay
fishing grounds 335–6
mosquito control 122–3
roads 395
sewerage project 351–2, 391
Sports Centre 400
town hall 62
water 390
West Indies Federation 86
West Wind Building 242
Westin Casuarina Resort 95n4
Westnage, Ted 213
Weston, E.A. 242
Weststar TV Ltd 252
wetlands 394
Wharf Restaurant 287
White Hall 29, 37–8, 354, 356
White Hall Restaurant 75
White, Philip 310, 314, 315
Whitelock, Colin A. 178
Wickstead, Dr J.H. 339
Wickstead Report 338–42
Wilborg, Jan 47
wildlife 329, 341, 393–4
Wilford Ryan 350
Williams, Dr Neville 403
Williams, Tony 219–20
Winchester, David 323
Winchester, Simon 383
Winslow, Edward 8
Winton, Charles 270
Wireless and Meteorological Office 76
Wolsey Hall, England 47, 407
Wood, Jim 326–7
Wood, S.C. 133
World War II 48–59
Wreck of the Ten Sail 400–5
Wright, Sir Oliver 310
Wright, Thomas 369

Yacht Club 60, 96, 373
Yates, Donolly 24
Young, W.H. 133

Zambia 229–31
Zenker, Erik 269

DUNCAN GRANT

DUNCAN GRANT

FRANCES SPALDING

Chatto & Windus

LONDON

First published in 1997

1 3 5 7 9 10 8 6 4 2

Copyright © 1997 by Frances Spalding

Frances Spalding has asserted her right under the Copyright,
Designs and Patents Act, 1988 to be
identified as the author of this work

First published in Great Britain in 1997 by
Chatto & Windus Limited
Random House, 20 Vauxhall Bridge Road,
London SW1V 2SA

Random House Australia (Pty) Limited
20 Alfred Street, Milsons Point, Sydney
New South Wales 2061, Australia

Random House New Zealand Limited
18 Poland Road, Glenfield
Auckland 10, New Zealand

Random House South Africa (Pty) Limited
P O Box 337, Bergvlei, South Africa

Random House UK Limited Reg. No. 954009

Papers used by Random House UK Limited are natural, recyclable
products made from wood grown in sustainable forests. The
manufacturing processes conform to the environmental
regulations of the country of origin

A CIP catalogue record for this book
is available from the British Library

ISBN: 0 7011 3409 7

Typeset by Deltatype Ltd, Birkenhead, Merseyside
Printed in Great Britain by Mackays of Chatham. PLC,
Chatham, Kent.

CONTENTS

CONTENTS

ILLUSTRATIONS

INTRODUCTION

'The first merit of a painting is to be a feast for the eye.' So Delacroix wrote in his *Journals* which played a vital role in the formation of Duncan Grant's aesthetic. He read Delacroix on more than one occasion, and himself praised 'the simple representation of beautiful familiar things' in Simon Bussy's pastels, when as a young man he tried his hand at art criticism. In recent years art historians and film critics discussing 'ocular politics' have made us aware that representation is rarely simple and the artist's gaze far from innocent. Duncan Grant's own vision was structured by many things, his eclecticism and his sexuality among them. Often allusions to other works of art appear in his paintings, as in his *Baptism*, which draws upon Piero della Francesca's famous painting in the National Gallery, London. But these allusions, brewed sometimes for many years in his memory and subconscious, reappear subject to a visual logic and wit that transmutes them into a language recognisably his own.

A feast for the eye can take many forms and Duncan Grant's work encompasses a variety of strategies, techniques and methods of representation. At a vital moment in the history of British art, he was at the cutting edge, a bold innovator and the only Bloomsbury painter to exhibit with the Vorticists. He never lost his interest in abstraction, both in design and art, but the main body of his work is representational, inspired by his knowledge of past art and his fascination with appearances; with, for instance, the rhythms that can be detected in the human figure or the dissolution of form into colour under certain effects of light. What bound his life and art together, whether he remained in his studio or made visits abroad, was the delight and curiosity that fed his looking: he loved the rhyming of shapes and colours discoverable in still-lifes; his paintings make discernible the character of a landscape, a town or a building; and his drawings, especially, reveal his knack for catching human idiosyncrasies betrayed by pose, dress or movement. A biography allows us to travel with him through time and to gain some idea of how his many experiences stimulated and enriched his art.

Writing biography is an arduous and at times frustrating, task, but at the same time a fascinating, life-changing experience. One particular delight, when working on a subject within living memory, is the opportunity to meet those who knew the person one is writing about. Many of Duncan's friends and relatives talked of the pleasure he gave. 'One was always happy with him,' Lady Freyberg recalled, of meetings at which they did little more than sit and talk. Richard Shone, who became a young friend in Duncan's later years, would arrive at Charleston with the expectation 'that the fun would begin' the moment he lifted the latch on the studio door. In the course of conversations like these, small and often unexpected details leave behind glimpsed facets of a person who, though departed, increasingly fills the mind.

Duncan Grant was, however, still at Charleston when I first visited it in 1974. He had been indirectly responsible for stirring my interest in Roger Fry: after seeing an exhibition of Duncan Grant portraits, which – hung in chronological order – made vivid the sudden excitement about modern art that erupted in the pre-1914 period, I wanted to learn more about the man who had mounted the two Post-Impressionist exhibitions which had created such a catalytic effect. I began research which eventually led to my book, *Roger Fry: Art and Life*, and in connection with this went to see Professor Quentin Bell. After lunch and a lengthy session of questions and answers, he suggested tea at Charleston. On arrival Quentin gave me a tour of the house which ended in the large downstairs studio and there, seated behind a screen beside the stove, in his ninetieth year, was Duncan.

This was my only real meeting with Duncan Grant, though I was delighted to see him again in September 1976 when he came, in a wheelchair and wearing a straw hat, to the opening of the exhibition 'Portraits by Roger Fry' which I had organised at the Courtauld Institute Galleries, then in Woburn Place. But even with such slight acquaintance, I have never forgotten his voice. If its gentleness was at that time in part due to frailty, it was nevertheless combined with a lilting note of enquiry and habits of pronunciation that communicated a delicacy of thought and feeling. He died in 1978 and two years later I began work on a biography of Vanessa Bell. It was while reading various documents connected with her life that Duncan began to haunt my mind. A decade later his grand-daughter, Henrietta Garnett, asked me to write his life. After some hesitation, for there were other potential candidates who had known him well, I accepted, realising, even then, that because Duncan's life embraced such a panoply of places, people and incident no single account will ever exhaust the richness of his story, which in this instance it is my privilege to tell.

One of Duncan's core beliefs was the need for a rational approach to human nature. Like other members of Bloomsbury, he thought that behaviour, if analysed and weighed up with feeling and intelligence, could respond to logic; and therefore that decisions and actions could be made on a human and not a religious basis.

In October 1916 he wrote to his friend David Garnett that he thought the finest poetry was 'an expression of apparent aloofness from the human feelings involved, by a person who has suffered all feeling ... a state of mind I am most happy in myself when I have the luck to get there, which isn't nearly as often or as frequent as I would wish'. But this capacity to detach himself from his feelings without denying them increased with time. A gain in serenity went hand in hand with his absolute love of painting through which he expressed his exaltation of life. He saw the magic in people and took pleasure in a meal or a party and especially in conversation. Though a deeply compassionate man, he had no wish to get bogged down in the minutiae of melancholy events and during his later years he navigated his way through difficulties with dignity, sympathy, charm and humour.

My single remaining wish is that something of his quietly festive character, which animated his life and the lives of others and still today irradiates his art, will also be found by the reader in the course of this book.

ACKNOWLEDGEMENTS

My thanks go first of all to Henrietta Garnett for giving me the permission and encouragement to write this book, and for granting access to all the papers in Duncan Grant's possession at the time of his death. I am also profoundly indebted to Angelica Garnett, again for access to papers in her possession (many of which have since been given to King's College, Cambridge) and for hospitality, help and openmindedness. Much gratitude goes also to the late Quentin Bell who read chapters of this book while it was in progress and whose comments, together with occasional remarks from his wife, Olivier, were immensely welcome. In the later stages of this book, I was particularly helped by conversations with Richard Shone whose familiarity with Duncan Grant made many descriptions and anecdotes wonderfully vivid. And I am grateful also to Paul Roche for twice putting me up in Mallorca and willingly sharing with me his memories of Duncan and the people he knew.

For generous assistance with the writing of this book, I am indebted to the following: Thos. Agnew's & Sons; Lord Annan; Mr and Mrs Igor Anrep; Mr and Mrs Brian Ashford-Russell; Mr and Mrs Michael Bagenal; Adrian Batchelor-Taylor; Lt. Col. Sir John Baynes; Cressida Bell; Alan Bennett; Helen Bergen; Deidre Bland; Peter Boston; Tony Bradshaw; Mr and Mrs Christopher Bridge; Dr David Brown; Mr and Mrs Martin Brunt; Richard Buckle; Richard Chapman; the Hon. Alan Clark; Colette Clark; Helen Cole-Hamilton; Judith Collins; John Constable; Dennis Creffield; the late Frances Creighton; Caroline Cuthbert; Veronica Demuth; the Duke and Duchess of Devonshire; Lord Drogheda (Derry Moore); Lady Dufferin, the Marchioness of Dufferin and Ava; Ben Duncan; Lady Freyberg; P. N. Furbank; Lord Gage; Fanny Garnett; Nerissa Garnett; Oliver Garnett; Mr and Mrs Richard Garnett; R. A. Gekowski; Adrian Goodman; Elizabeth Grant; Mr and Mrs John Grant of Rothiemurchus; Lady Katherine Grant; Janet Green; the late Sir Roger de Grey; Douglas Hall; the late Christopher Hammersely; John Haylock; the Right Hon. Sir Edward Heath; Mr and Mrs John Higgens; Derek Hill; Sir Howard Hodgkin; the late Diana

Holman Hunt; John Hubbard; Holly Johnson; Stanley Jones; Andras
Kalman; Francis King; Wolfgang Kuhle; Mark Lancaster; Lady Lucinda
Lambton; Deidre Levi; Paul Levy; Oliver Lodge; Nicky Loutit; Dr
Richard Luckett; Sandra Lummis; William McBrien; Clodagh Macken-
zie; Julia Matthews; the late Robert Medley; Mr and Mrs Donald
Mitchell; Isobel Moore; Richard and Sally Morphet; Virginia Nicholson;
Anthony d'Offay; Jane O'Malley; Frances Partridge; Jennifer Langlands
Pearce; Patrick Proctor; Mattie Radev; Christopher Reed; John Richard-
son; Clarissa Roche; Toby Roche; Charles Rodier; Tania Rose; S. P.
Rosenbaum; Dr George Rylands; the late Desmond Shawe-Taylor; Ellen
Sheean; Rupert Sheppard; Dr F. H. W. Sheppard; Herta Simon;
Pandora Smith; the Rev. Peter Smith; Max Stafford-Clark; Maggie
Thornton; Linda Tilbury; Michael Tollemache; Patrick Trevor-Roper;
Simon Watney; Joy Woolley.

To the following I am indebted for permission to quote from
documents in their possession or over which they own copyright:
Henrietta Garnett, for permission to quote from Duncan Grant's
writings, and to her and Paul Roche for permission to reproduce his
pictures; to Angelica Garnett for extracts from her own letters and those
of Vanessa Bell; to the late Quentin Bell for extracts from Clive and
Julian Bell's papers and from his own letters; to the Estate of the late
David Garnett for permission to quote from David Garnett's published
and unpublished writings; to Annabel Cole for permission to quote from
the writings of Roger Fry; to Adrian Goodman for permission to quote
extracts from Lady Ottoline Morrell's diaries; to Ellen Sheean for
permission to quote extracts from Vincent ('Jimmy') Sheean's letters; to
Crispin Rogers for permission to quote a Claude Rogers limerick; to
Frances Partridge for permission to quote published and unpublished
extracts from her diaries; and to the Society of Authors on behalf of the
Strachey Trust for permission to quote from the Strachey papers, and for
permission from the Virginia Woolf Literary Estate and the Hogarth
Press for permission to quote from her published letters and diaries.
Unpublished writings of J.M Keynes are copyright the Provost and
Scholars of King's College, Cambridge, 1997.

I am grateful to the staff of the following institutions for access to
material in their collections and for assistance: Jennifer Booth and her
staff in the Tate Gallery Archives; Jacqueline Cox, Modern Archivist at
King's College, Cambridge; Rosamond Strode and the Britten-Pears
Foundation; the British Library Manuscripts Department; Elizabeth
Inglis in the University of Sussex Library; Stephen Chaplin in the Slade
School of Art archives; the India Office Library; the Fawcett Library;

Francis Mattson, the Berg Collection, New York Public Library; Joyce Crow and the Sussex Archaeological Society; the National Art Library in the Victoria & Albert Museum; the Harry Ransom Humanities Research Center in the University of Texas at Austin; Liverpool University Archives; and the Manuscript Department in Cambridge University Library.

Finally, a great many thanks go to Malcolm Turner and Lucy Gent for their encouraging support; to Daniel, just for being there; to my editor Jenny Uglow for her humane, perceptive advice; to my copy-editor Mandy Greenfield, to Carmen Calill, who commissioned this book, and to Chatto & Windus for accepting a slight delay.

ONE

Of Scottish Descent

'Duncan Grant,' wrote Walter Sickert in 1929, 'like another gentleman in Europe in a somewhat more difficult line of business, was born with a crown on his head.' Just as King Alfonso XIII of Spain enjoyed a long reign, despite several attempts on his life, so Duncan Grant became a long-standing monarch within his own field. Few English artists of his generation brought such colouristic complexity and subtle organisation to their handling of landscape, still-life, portraiture, allegory and myth. 'Duncan conquered,' Sickert wrote, 'he saw, he came.'[1]

Whether any hint of future laurels could be observed when he was born in 1885 has not been recorded. As usual, in a large family, there was a lot going on. The chief event that year was the golden wedding anniversary of his grandparents, Sir John Peter and Lady Grant. The proceedings began at two o'clock in the afternoon, when a large number of people on the Rothiemurchus estate assembled at the farm and, led by a piper, marched on to the lawn in front of the Doune.

This noble house, some three miles from Aviemore, is the ancestral home of the Grants of Rothiemurchus, a branch of the Clan Grant, which still owns extensive land in Inverness-shire. Sir John, like other lairds before and after him, found the Doune a mixed blessing, a financial burden not always mitigated by the income from the estate, which was largely dependent on the uncertain fortunes of the timber industry. Nevertheless, the Grants of Rothiemurchus had traditionally occupied 'rather a high position among the lesser barons of their wild country'.[2]

The original Doune, which takes its name from the Celtic word for fort, had been built on a small mound nearby. From this hill, as times grew less rude, the Grants descended, building the present house, which from the sixteenth century onwards was gradually enlarged, its stern dignity giving way in the Victorian period to rather grandiose accretions (since removed). Nothing, however, could spoil its position, for it faces up the Spey valley, with the hills of Invereshie and Glengeshie in the distance.

Among those gathered in front of the house that day were Duncan's parents, Captain and Mrs Bartle Grant, and his uncle and aunt, General and Mrs Richard Strachey. Sir John, who had suffered a stroke two years before, was conveyed to the scene in a pony carriage and presented with a silver bowl from his tenants. He was a large man, over six foot tall, with a broad, passive face, not unlike a kabuki mask, a snub nose and mild, dreamy blue eyes. He now spent most of the day stretched out on a sofa wrapped in a plaid rug. And in time this is how his grandson came to remember him. It seemed to the four-year-old Duncan that the eighty-two-year-old laird paid less attention to him than to Walter Scott's slow-moving plots, which wove themselves into the pattern of his days through the medium of the female voice, for his wife, daughters and daughter-in-law were his readers.

His habit of lying on sofas had in fact begun many years before his stroke. Because he had more than once almost died in infancy, he had been greatly indulged by his family, who believed that he lacked energy. He abhorred all sport, disliked riding and rarely went out. But he outstripped his colleagues with his vigorous concentration and became one of the ablest public servants of his day.

Soon after entering the East India Company's service in 1827, at the age of twenty, he had shown exceptional powers of judgement and decision-making. By 1854 he had become a member of the Governor-General's Supreme Council, and during the 1857 Mutiny he was also acting as Lieutenant-Governor of the Central Provinces. At this time he was suspected of a bias towards the Indians because of his skilful settlement of land disputes. Two years later he became Lieutenant-Governor of Bengal, receiving the KCB in 1862. He found further outlet for his formidable administrative powers as Governor of Jamaica between 1866 and 1874, earning himself the honour of KCMG and lasting esteem among Jamaicans.

In 1893 his grandson, Duncan, two weeks short of his eighth birthday and staying with his mother at Sir John's London home in Norwood, had a premonition that his grandfather would die the following day. Sure enough, on the night of 6 January Sir John passed away in his sleep. 'I was told,' Duncan Grant later recalled in a memoir, 'that he had been a great and good man but that God had been merciful and taken him at a great age. So all was more or less satisfactory and rather exciting. The only thing was that it was so easy for me to imagine my grandfather as a corpse – he was always white as wax, silent and laid out at full length.'

Duncan was also anxious about his grandmother's state of mind. At half-past eleven she sent for him. He walked into her large, bright bedroom in the Norwood villa and found her sitting up in bed, wearing a very pretty bonnet trimmed with ribbons, drying her eyes, but talking and laughing with his mother. She flung her arms around the small boy and told him not to be unhappy. 'I soon forgot the horrors of death in the company of this vivacious old lady to whom I was devoted and, warmed back to life, I went through my tricks which never failed to make her die of laughing . . .'[3] His tricks involved the impersonation of various characters, conveyed through gesture, facial expression and the tone of voice in which he uttered complete gibberish. Even his mother, though on this occasion she tried to restrain him, found herself laughing.

Sir John's sister, Elizabeth Grant (Duncan's great-aunt), wrote a private memoir for the Grant family, part of which was edited for publication in 1898 by her niece, Lady Strachey, as *Memoirs of a Highland Lady*.[4] In it Elizabeth Grant tells of her childhood and adolescence in Rothiemurchus and elsewhere, and of her father's attempts to pursue his legal and political ambitions and to improve the family fortunes. This man, the first John Peter Grant (1774–1848), spent more money than was wise in becoming Member of Parliament for the 'rotten borough' of Great Grimsby, and still more on alterations and additions to the Doune and the estate. Like other Grants, he was very aware that the family could trace its lineage back to John Grant, Fourth of Freuchie, Chief of Grant and, therefore, through his marriage in 1539 to Lady Marjorie Stewart, to the Scottish throne. With such ancestry it is not surprising that the first John Peter Grant's ambitions exceeded his means, and that at the age of fifty he once again had to work for his living. He resumed his career as advocate at the Scottish Bar and then became a judge in Bombay, eventually becoming Chief Justice of the Supreme Court in Calcutta.[5] He, too, earnt a knighthood and was on his way home to enjoy a well-earned retirement at Rothiemurchus when, catching a chill from a cold bath, he died at sea in 1848, aged seventy-four.

Despite the success that accompanied the careers of father and son, both were financially hard-pressed. In 1887, six years before Duncan's grandfather, the second Sir John Peter Grant, died, a loan had to be raised upon the entailed estate. The Doune had frequently been rented out, Sir John reluctantly taking up residence elsewhere, in Kelvinside Gardens, Glasgow, as well as in London, at Clifton Lodge, Upper Norwood, where he spent his winters.[6]

When the second Sir John died, his estate amounted to over £7,000, but almost one-third of this was claimed by unpaid debts. His widow received many letters of condolence which, in the memories they revived, returned her to better times. Before long Lady Grant moved to Bedford

House, The Mall, Chiswick, where she was able to provide a home for Duncan during the school holidays while his parents were abroad.

She, too, was descended from an eminent Anglo–Indian family, and as Henrietta Isabella Philippa Sophia Chichele Plowden had married the second John Peter Grant in 1835.[7] She was then a tall, dark-eyed beauty, with a love of books, drama, music and painting. Her letters, which are numerous, reveal a lively, intelligent woman, on close terms with artistic and musical figures of the day and able to discuss matters of policy with the governing Lords of India. Her first son, John Peter the third, was born a year after her marriage. Eight more children followed – one, a daughter, being stillborn. By the time her youngest son, Bartle, was born in 1856, Lady Grant, after twenty-six years in India, had returned to live in England. In time, Bartle's son Duncan became one of Lady Grant's thirty-eight grandchildren.

With five boys and three girls, Lady Grant was familiar with the mixed blessings of motherhood. The boys caused her the most trouble, either by performing abysmally at school or by the readiness with which they fell into debt. Their failings were never venal, more the result of weakness and eccentricity. George, the third son, was nicknamed 'Mad Grant' at Eton, a soubriquet shared with his younger brother, Charles, at Rugby. School reports make dispiriting reading. Charles, for example, was described as shiftless, idle, unpunctual and untidy, his failure to excel being linked to his energetic pursuit of amusement. Even the 'Record of Family Faculties', kept for private amusement by their sister Jane Maria, gives a poor account of the boys. Duncan's Uncle Trevor, for instance, emerges as charmingly hopeless:

> Very weak in will; deficient in persistency and self-assertion. Easy going and indifferent, with an over-sensitive shrinking from annoying any one . . . has an active and clear intelligence; but energy so far below [average], that it is impossible to point to any achievement. Hardly ever writes a private letter, and even when doing his administrative work [in the Bengal Civil Service] well, gets into disgrace for neglecting official correspondence.[8]

In the eyes of other Anglo–Indians, he slid from grace when he married a Eurasian girl, who gave him four sons, one of whom died in the embrace of a bear. Uncle Trevor never brought this wife home and the official pedigree of the Grants lists only his second wife, Clementina Gouldsbury, by whom he had three more sons.

Jane Maria was far less censorious about her sisters, Duncan Grant's

4

aunts. The eldest, Frances Elinor, is described as generous, simple, frank and warm-hearted. She inherited her parents' love of music, played the piano well and had a charming voice; she married Sir James Colvile, had no children and enjoyed friendship with artists and musicians, among them Sir Frederic Leighton, President of the Royal Academy. Through his Aunt Elinor, Duncan caught a glimpse as a young man of the late Victorian art world, but he owed more to Aunt Janie and her liberal attitude to education. He also had a special affection for his third aunt, Henrietta, who was mildly demented – allegedly owing to a fall when she was two. But, as this generation of Grants knew, no Highland family was altogether free from the taint of madness.

One recurrent characteristic among the Grants was an undemanding gentleness which, paradoxically, had a powerful effect on others. This quality was apparent in the eldest of Lady Grant's children, the third John Peter Grant, a member of the Bengal Civil Service, who came of age in 1857, the year that the great Sepoy revolt broke out. Trouble had begun in March with the XIXth Bengal Infantry, who mutinied prematurely and were promptly disbanded. In the interval before the general revolt, many of these disbanded men took up service in the police force. With the spread of the mutiny, the small outlying stations in Bengal, lacking any form of defence, were exposed to danger. At the same time considerable sums of public money were stored in their treasuries. An order was therefore issued that all such money should be transferred to Calcutta.

John Peter Grant received an order to collect treasury money from a station about a week's march from Calcutta. He was given a police escort composed entirely of disbanded mutineers from the XIXth Bengal Infantry. These men, still smarting from recent punishment, heard daily how their comrades elsewhere were murdering officers and plundering the treasuries. Now they found themselves protecting a sum of £25–30,000, with no one to withstrain them but a very young, solitary British youth, who marched with them by day, sat and joked with them by their camp fires and slept an untroubled, fearless sleep in their midst every night.

The temptation to rob and murder must have been enormous. The remarkable fact that these soldiers, who had been disloyal in March, became trustworthy in May, can be accounted for, to some degree, by the serenity of their young commander. He gave no sign that any idea of danger had occurred to him and this had its effect on the men. And he must have had some very real and assured sense of security for no sense of fear to have affected his demeanour. Duncan inherited this inner

5

certainty, a capacity to defuse difficult situations, to arouse loyalty in the most unlikely people, and in general to quieten, charm and disarm.

Duncan Grant's father had a small head and hands and very small feet. This would not have been so noticeable were he not also unusually stout. He became so at the age of twenty-four and thereafter did not significantly alter in shape. His love of food made him interested in the recipe book, inscribed 'Rothiemurchus 1770', compiled by his great-grandmother, Elizabeth Raper, mother of the first John Peter Grant. He not only admired it as a model of neatness, with its alphabetical index at the end, but also recognised that the type of cuisine recommended, particularly the marinating of meats and the treatment of vegetables, came closer to French than English cookery.

During the last year of his life Bartle Grant prepared this recipe book for publication by the Nonesuch Press. As his introduction reveals, he was fascinated by his great-grandparents – William Grant, who practised medicine and whose writings on fever were translated into both German and French; and his wife Elizabeth, a plain, short, warm-hearted and quick-tempered woman who, though musical and accomplished, had a touch of coarseness in her nature. She was famous (among other things) for riding pillion from Elgin to the Doune behind her husband's cousin, James Cameron, wearing high-heeled, pointed-toed shoes with large rosettes, a yellow silk quilted petticoat, a chintz farthingale bundled up behind and a little black hat with a feather stuck on one side of her powdered head. Throughout the journey she sang aloud songs from *The Beggar's Opera* with such vigour that they remained lodged in her cousin's memory for ever.

Bartle Grant's admiration for his intrepid great-grandmother, who left behind not only recipes but also fragments of journals and some poetry, emerges clearly in his introduction to her cookery book. Her journals, he claims, display 'the force and directness of her language, her untiring energy and shrewd common sense'. But what he most admires is her keen enjoyment of life and its good things. 'I cannot improve upon her description of herself,' he concludes, 'my great-grandmother must have been indeed . . . "vastly agreeable".'[9]

A readiness to enjoy life was also a part of Bartle's character. 'Rather self-indulgent,' the 'Record of Family Faculties' states, to which is added the tart remark that he was given to brooding over supposed offences. Though his family thought him eccentric, Bartle possessed quiet determination and considerable sensitivity. From an early age he excelled at music, picking up tunes by ear and playing the piano. 'Joachim has arrived,' wrote Lady Grant to her husband of the famous Hungarian violinist in 1868. 'I think I told you in my last he asked immediately after Bartie.'[10] Then twelve years old, Bartle had for some reason started school late, was backward in Latin, had done no Greek and, in his mother's opinion, was unlikely to do well at public school. Despite this, she assured her husband that 'in general and out of the way information he will beat most lads of sixteen'.[11]

He was destined for the army. At Edgeborough School, Guildford, he worked reasonably hard, learnt the piano and organ, and irritated his housemaster with his habit of slinging his slippers across the room. At the age of sixteen he was sent home for idleness and impertinence, and a tutor in mathematics prepared him for the entrance examinations to the army school at Woolwich. Lady Grant was distressed by his insubordination and want of self-control, but eventually Bartle reached Sandhurst and in 1875 became a Sub-Lieutenant with the VIIIth Hussars. After three years in Afghanistan, where he was awarded an Afghan Medal, he spent the next part of his career in India. In 1883 he was made Captain and the following year, while stationed in Meerut, he married Ethel Isabel McNeil at Gurdaspur, where she was living with a cousin, Georgina Willis, wife of Colonel Alfred Harcourt, a civil officer in the Punjab.

Ethel, who had been born in Victoria, Australia, seems to have moved in with the Harcourts after the death of her father, Nathan McNeil, left her and her two sisters orphaned. At the time of her marriage she was just under twenty-one years of age. The McNeils were descended from lairds of Ayrshire,[12] with distant connections through Archibald McNeel and Grizzel Stewart to Banquo (though not accepted by some as an actual historical character) and earlier still to Kenneth I or MacAlpin, King of the Scots, who died in 843. It is an impressive lineage. Certainly, to have even a putative ancestor commemorated by Shakespeare is something about which to boast. Another McNeil family tradition was that a Spaniard wrecked from the Armada had married into the family, and their olive complexions and black hair were supposed to derive from him.

Though descended from Highlanders, Ethel McNeil's immediate forebears came from Ireland, where they had settled after the Battle of the Boyne and whence they had emigrated to Australia. However, in the way of immediate relatives, all that she had were two sisters – Violet and Daisy. Ethel was extremely fond of Colonel Harcourt (Uncle Fred), a man of perfect integrity, an able administrator and a proficient watercolourist, a great many of whose sketchbooks remained in Ethel's (and afterwards Duncan's) possession.[13] Yet she wrote calmly, at the time

7

of her engagement, to Bartle's sister, Jane Strachey, 'I assure you I do not feel at all overwhelmed at the claims of Bartle's numerous relations, for you are all so very kind to me, and welcome me so heartily among you.'[14]

Bartle, meanwhile, was very aware that this young woman would become his better half. He told Jane:

> Ethel's face is even more reassuring to look at in the life than in her photograph, and though she is not extraordinarily beautiful, she is extraordinarily good ... She declares herself quite prepared to love anybody connected with me! You will like her I'm sure: she has plenty of sense (a good deal more than I have), a great sense of humour and she laughs like a child when she's amused.[15]

Ethel was aware of Bartle's need of her, for while telling her future sister-in-law of her certainty that they would be happy together, she added, 'and we will help each other to be economical'.[16]

Though Bartle became a Major in 1886, he could not, even with his wife's help, avoid falling into debt. Whilst in India, a country he loathed, he borrowed £500 from the bank, persuading two brother officers in the VIIIth Hussars to 'back' the bill. These and other loans accumulated, until in 1889 he was obliged to give his list of debts to the Official Receiver. His elder brother George – so Lady Grant's nephew George Plowden (a magistrate in Meerut) informed her – stepped in and saved Bartle in the nick of time, finding £6,000 to settle his pressing debts. Throughout these trying circumstances, Plowden told Lady Grant, Ethel's plucky behaviour showed great strength of character.

Towards the end of his life, on the radio programme *Desert Island Discs*, Duncan Grant told his interviewer that during his childhood his father had changed regiments because the VIIIth Hussars had been 'a bit too smart for him' and he could not afford it. But the actual crisis had been far more dramatic, Bartle having come very close to court martial and possibly imprisonment due to his debts. He appears to have been stripped of his office as Major, for when he entered the Border Regiment in 1890 it was as a Captain. Army life in India aroused in him a certain cynicism. Some years before he had earnt small sums scribbling paragraphs for the front page of the *Civil and Military Gazette*, whilst admitting to his sister Jane that a dissertation on the uselessness of the Viceroy came readily to his facile pen.

Bartle and Ethel Grant's only child was born at ten past three in the afternoon on 21 January 1885 in a large bay-windowed room at the

Doune.[17] Six months later the minister of Rothiemurchus baptised him Duncan James Corrowr Grant. Soon afterwards he was taken to Canterbury, where his father's regiment was stationed, and thence he went with his parents to India. As a small boy he revisited Rothie- murchus every two years, with one or both parents – the Scottish hills, pines and climate, the splendour and remoteness, wildness and silence offering a welcome contrast to hot and noisy India. Like most Highlanders, Duncan remained deeply imbued with a sense of his origins.

During his childhood he moved with his parents around India, from Meerut to Chakrata to Mooltan. Woven into the texture of his life would have been the sound of bugle calls, the clatter of hooves, the jingle of harness and the regimental ceremonies, such as the compulsory Sunday Parade, that gave the British army in India such powerful mystique. Military families in India often led agreeable lives for several years at a time. A way of life had remained unchanged for three generations and the standards that prevailed remained inviolably British. A plethora of servants helped make this possible; it was customary for a married officer to have as many as six servants, each with particular duties concerning lamps, fires, bathwater, cooking or sanitation. Officers' quarters were arranged so that every bedroom had its own bathroom with a tin bath and a thunder-box – an extremely comfortable commode with arms and a bucket. Army wives, with all the drudgery of domestic life taken care of, sat in chintzy drawing-rooms or went down to the Club to get the newest English library books, successfully bringing the ethos of Aldershot, Catterick and Colchester to a country about which they remained largely ignorant. Immured by privilege in a way of life that offered little scope, army wives were often enfeebled by boredom. To the end of her life Duncan Grant's mother never quite lost the manner of a memsahib.

It remains a matter of speculation what effect Bartle Grant's debt crisis had in the long term on his marriage. By 1891 Colonel Young, who gave the six-year-old Duncan two rabbits, had become a close friend of the family. He inspired a lifelong devotion in Ethel. Whether it was because of this or not, Bartle Grant began to have affairs. Duncan did and did not know what was going on. Nothing was said and yet, as he later recollected, when he went as a boy with his father to the opera in the company of one of Bartle's old flames and her child, he found himself wondering if he was seated next to his half-brother.[18] As a child, Duncan even hinted at the possibility of error when he said of a spaniel, 'She's had nine puppies. Isn't it lucky they're all spaniels?'

In the afternoons Duncan played like other army children in the playground at the Club, accompanied by nannies and *ayahs*, who sat apart from each other, the nannies despising the *ayahs*. Duncan was immensely fond of his English nanny, a woman called Alice Bates. She was, he would recollect, a good companion and teacher, so widely read that his father could not mention a book she had not devoured. She took great interest in Duncan's painting and probably helped to preserve the mass of juvenilia by him that still exists. As a boy he developed a passion for weddings and designed wedding dresses and bridal processions in a 'gothic' style. But in everything he drew or painted he expressed a certain wonder at what he saw. Many years later he told a *Daily Herald* reporter that his first painting was of an Indian bazaar, which had fascinated him with its light and movement. His love of creating imaginary worlds found further outlet in model theatres, which occupied him a great deal in early youth.

Duncan's sense of security owed much to Alice Bates. (In later life awareness of this led him to place an advertisement in *The Times*, by which he made contact with her again.) It was whilst in her care that he experienced one moment that he never forgot. Aged six and living in Chakrata in the Himalayas, he was dressed for a party in black satin breeches, a lace ruff and white wig. Unaware of his father's financial difficulties, he sat, dangling a silver-handled cane, confident and reflective:

> A strong feeling overcame me which I can only describe as an aristocratic feeling, suggested I suppose by my get up. But I distinctly remember the certain satisfaction of the feeling of power and direction with which I was filled. At that time of course, no sense of poverty had entered my life. We had many native servants. I had an English nurse. I was devoted to my mother and liked the company of the army officers, friends of my father. With this sense of security and background, it was easy to loll and dream of power, and to believe that to observe life was the way to live.[19]

Most army children were sent back to England for schooling when they reached the age of seven. Duncan stayed with his parents until the age of nine. Separation, when it came in 1894, was hardest for him in relation to Alice. But because he had already travelled a great deal, Duncan was used to exchanging the sun, colour and sounds of India for a very different environment and may not have felt too uprooted. Nevertheless, the attachment which in later life he developed towards Charleston suggests that his peripatetic childhood had left unsatisfied his need for a permanent home. He left for England from Burma, for his father was now stationed at Rangoon, and all his life kept a distinct memory of the entrance to Rangoon harbour in early morning. The vast pagoda covered with gold and the brilliantly coloured silks worn by the natives helped him realise that purely visual experience could amount to a great event.

Ethel Grant had earlier asked her sister-in-law Jane Strachey for advice on Duncan's lesson books. Aunt Janie may also have suggested the preparatory school to which Duncan went, Hillbrow, as she chose it for her own son, James, who was a couple of years younger than Duncan. By 1894 Duncan accorded Aunt Janie a place of importance in his life. 'I cannot write a very long letter today,' reads one letter to his grandmother, Lady Grant, 'because I have to write one to Mother and Aunt Janie. Good-bye from your loving little Duncan.'[20]

In school holidays he lived with his grandmother in Chiswick and benefited much from her company, for she talked without self-consciousness about her past, her love of paintings and her experiences in Italy. While talking with her about pictures, Duncan first encountered the concept of 'composition'. He also became familiar with the ceiling of her summer house, which had been decorated by an Italian painter. He soon discerned that Lady Grant belonged not to the Victorian age but to the Regency period: two of her children had been sired by one of the ruling Lords of India, during the hot weather in a hill town, while her husband was engaged on work elsewhere. He returned to find her with child, and on both occasions either forgave her or decided that the matter could be overlooked. 'She was a beautiful old lady,' her grandson recalled, 'directly a relic of the Byronic age.'[21]

Lady Grant died in January 1896 while Duncan was still at preparatory school. As a consequence, Duncan stayed with various relations, including the Stracheys, until his parents came home from Rangoon. By now Bartle Grant was tiring of the army and in June 1898, five months before his time at Rangoon was due to end, he began applying without success for club secretaryships in India and, with even less hope – as he was unable to present himself to the relevant committee – for a Constableship at Banff in Scotland. Gazetted out of the army in November 1898, he returned to England and took a lease on 10 Cathcart Road in south-west London. By September 1899 he was once again in debt. He had inherited nothing from his mother except some books, divided between him and his brother Charles, and two family photographs showing four generations of men and women. He may have greeted the advent of the Boer War with a certain relief, for it meant that, as an officer of the Reserve, Bartle was called back into the army and entered the Royal Garrison Regiment in Malta.

Bartle Grant leaves the impression that, though he made the best of any circumstances, he was always a man misplaced. In Rangoon he wrote a book on Burmese orchids, having 'found the want of a book of reference at a moderate price, suitable for a beginner's use, a serious obstacle to my progress'. *The Orchids of Burma and the Andaman Islands described* was privately printed in 1898, at a cost of £1,307 4s to Bartle, who, not surprisingly, was the next year unable to pay his rent. Though he stated his aim in modest terms, he had produced a reference book of lasting value and was pleased when, in later years, he found it described in one book catalogue as 'Indispensable to all Orchid Collectors'. He was also an excellent pianist and among his large collection of music were quantities of manuscript sheets copied out in his elegant hand. He brought together an orchestra in Rangoon, selected music by the best composers and conducted with such enthusiasm that his musicians performed well, and their concerts in the Rangoon Theatre were compared with those given at the Queen's Hall in London. Though his time in Malta was brief, he had no sooner arrived than he was busy with matters musical and theatrical, sitting on various committees, ordering instruments for a band, becoming Mess President and, as stage manager to the ADC, working on productions of *Our Boys* and *The Yeomen of the Guard*. Among Duncan's juvenilia is a hand-painted Christmas card showing his father conducting. 'Go it, Impresario Grant,' reads the message.

Hillbrow preparatory school, situated a hundred yards down the road from the public school of Rubgy, was a small, spartan institution with only about forty pupils, run by Mr and Mrs T. J. Eden. Duncan was two years ahead of his cousin James Strachey and the young Rupert Brooke. One of his contemporaries, Carl Hillerus, recollected that Grant was 'impervious to arithmetic, illustrating all his book margins with little drawings, and whose father was in the Indian Army. I remember his parents visiting the school on one occasion and being taken to tea at "Hobley's", the Rugby confectionaries, by a very sweet lady – his mother.'[22] He added that an old school photograph commemorating a Parents v. Boys cricket match includes, as scorer, Duncan Grant.

'Being an only child,' Duncan put on record in 1969, 'I had been indulgent in yielding to my childish dreams without any interference. I went to an English private school. It was only when I got there that the dangers and sorrows of life became apparent.'[23] Solace was to be found in drawing and painting. 'Your little drawing of Walsham Hall,' his mother wrote from Rangoon, 'makes me long more than ever to go and pay a visit there. You seem to have had a splendid time . . .'[24] Duncan's talent for art was spotted by the art master at the senior school, who began setting him exciting, unorthodox tasks, such as the copying of Japanese prints. The headmaster's wife (who read Dickens aloud on Sunday evenings) lent Duncan a large volume of reproductions by Burne-Jones, whose sensuous treatment of the human figure, lingering *sfumato* and highly wrought sense of design made a terrific impact on him. After the cluttered compositions and overdressed figures found in the Royal Academy's yearly picture books, over which Duncan had pored, Burne-Jones seemed thrilling. 'For years I would ask God on my knees at prayers to allow me to become as good a painter as he.'[25] Even at the age of ninety, when interviewed on radio, Duncan said of Burne-Jones, 'Never in a way have I ever forgotten him, though I've had many other influences.'[26]

Although he took away from Hillbrow Ruskin's *The Elements of Drawing* as a prize for art, Duncan had otherwise performed badly. His parents had intended him for Wellington or Charterhouse, but Bartle Grant's financial resources in 1898, together with his son's lack of academic ability, put both schools out of reach. From Burma, Ethel Grant wrote to Jane Strachey:

I was so *very* glad to hear that you thought him [Duncan] looking so improved in health, and that he no longer twitches and fidgets ... It was *very* kind of you dear Janie to take all the trouble you did about Duncan, and I am most grateful. I cannot help feeling disappointed that he has not done better than he has at Hillbrow ... at first they wrote so much about his ability and so forth. I remember Mr Eden saying to me once that Duncan had so many tastes, that he was afraid he would never be good at any one thing. In his reports he always gets two *excellents*, one for music, the other for drawing![27]

At fourteen Duncan entered St Paul's School, West Kensington, a day school that made special provision for army children. There he sat in French classes with a rubber band around his head, gazing at the teacher with a perfectly innocent expression, whilst the rest of the class sat in suspense as the band worked its way up his head and finally flew off with a pop. He achieved some glory on the football field, but in no other subject except art. During his two years at St Paul's he won seven prizes for art, four for landscape painting, two John Watson Drawing Prizes and one Special Art Prize.

Looking back on his schooling, he remarked, 'I luckily had a very clear-headed aunt.'[28] No longer *the* Mrs Richard Strachey, Aunt Janie had become, to her regret – as there were others similarly titled – plain Lady Strachey, her husband having been made Knight Grand Commander of the Star of India in 1897. Legend has it that she went to see Duncan's master at St Paul's with the question, 'Why do you keep him on here in your class, if he's doing no good? Shouldn't he start doing what he wants to do?' With the problem so simply put, the solution was obvious: Duncan should apply to the Royal Academy Schools. This he duly did, having worked hard at all the various categories, but failed to gain acceptance. 'I was disappointed,' he recalled many years later, in a letter to a young woman who had likewise been turned down by the Slade, 'mainly for the sort of reasons you are, that it would have helped my parents to take my painting seriously. But it did not in any way depress me about my own work. I felt so certain that I was doing what I must do.'[29] On turning seventeen Duncan went instead to Westminster School of Art, a place with which he was already familiar, for in order to draw from a life model he had attended evening classes there as a schoolboy.

He had also attended art classes given by the artist and teacher Louise Jopling, a spirited, independent woman. The height of her career had coincided with the glamorous era of the Grosvenor Gallery run by Sir Coutts Lindsay. Louise Jopling had not only exhibited there but, owing to her friendship with Sir Coutts, and also with Millais and Whistler, both of whom painted her portrait, she had moved among the cream of London's society.[30] Her school in Clareville Road, next to the studio of Dudley Hardy – her aide-de-camp each year when she held a fancy-dress dance for her pupils – was run on liberal lines but with the oft-repeated command 'only be diligent'. She also compiled a useful practical manual, *Hints to Students and Amateurs*, which offered advice on materials and methods of drawing and painting, on pastel, anatomy and perspective. After the death of her second husband, the watercolourist Joe Jopling, she married George Rowe, who was related to the Grant family, which may explain how Duncan came to attend her classes. Her most notable quality remained her large-heartedness: she was by all accounts one of the kindest of women.

Though Duncan credited Lady Strachey with his release from formal schooling, the original idea had in fact come from his parents. They gave much thought to his future in November 1901, after which Ethel wrote to Jane Strachey, 'We want your advice about Duncan very much.' The notion that Duncan should follow his father into the army had been dropped, and instead hope had been pinned on him entering a firm of rice merchants, Bulloch Bros, as Ethel's letter reveals:

> If there happens to be a vacancy when he is the right age, 18, I think he
> is pretty certain to be taken, but there may not be a vacancy. Our friend

J. W. Orr, one of the partners, has promised to do what he can . . .
Under the circumstances we think we had better have another iron in
the fire, and are contemplating taking him away from St Paul's at
Christmas and letting him go in for drawing seriously for the next year.
What do you think of that? Bartle would like him to go and study in
Paris as he thinks he would get the best teaching there . . . I want your
opinion very much Janie . . . they are pleased with him at the
Westminster School of Art. He was sent to the Life Class at once . . .
Duncan wrote to his father that he simply loved the drawing there but
that he did not get enough of it . . . I wonder if your friend Mr
[Arthur] Melville would look at some of Duncan's sketches and tell you
what he thinks? Would you mind asking him? Perhaps we think too
highly of him, and yet no less than four people, all men, made the same
remark this summer, that they thought Duncan had more than talent,
that he had genius for drawing.[31]

As the letter shows, Duncan's remark in old age to Quentin Bell that his
determination to paint was 'not very much encouraged by my poverty-
stricken parents'[32] was misleading. It ignored, among other things, the
visits he had made with his father to Old Master exhibitions, Bartle
Grant having an especial fondness for Rembrandt. When Jane Strachey
obtained a further opinion on Duncan's drawings, Ethel Grant, thanking
her, added, 'I *should* be so happy if Duncan could be an artist.'[33] She was
still more rapturous when her sister-in-law told her that three artists had
now admired Duncan's work, but that all were against the idea of sending
him to Paris. 'That I suppose is out of the question,' Ethel replied, 'but
surely if he is to be an artist he ought to be learning all day long and
working hard at it? You must remember now he only gets a few hours a
week.'[34]

Bartle agreed with his sister that Duncan should remain at St Paul's
for one more term, and was grateful to his brother Trevor for offering to
house the boy. Bartle too felt that, as soon as possible, Duncan should
devote all his time to art: 'I think it essential this training should be
constant and exclusive of any other. The greater his talent, the more
necessary it is that it should be properly directed, and that he should
obtain a mastery of the craftsmanship of his profession . . . Now that we
have expert opinion on Duncan's powers, it would be more than a pity if
he were not given every chance of distinguishing himself.'[35] These were
not the words of an obstructive parent.

In the end it was settled that Duncan would leave school at Christmas
and would not live with his Uncle Trevor, but with the Stracheys, Bartle
paying them £2 10s a month for his upkeep. The fees at Westminster

School of Art were moderate, but even so it was hoped that Duncan might get a London County Council scholarship. His housemaster at St Paul's, Robert Cholmely, let him go with somewhat puzzled reluctance. 'I am sorry to lose Duncan both from my form and my house, and wish even apart from that, that he would be a schoolboy a little longer. I have always felt that I only had him by two strands of a rope . . . He is such a pathetically loveable creature, I cannot bear the idea of his not doing the right thing.'[36]

His fears were groundless. From the moment that he finished school, Duncan Grant never deviated in the pursuit of his vocation. All the fidgeting, the tomfoolery, the vagueness and lack of concentration vanished the moment that he stood or sat at an easel. He did not, however, always do the 'right thing'. Many years later, invited to open an exhibition at the Mayor Gallery, he recollected a similar occasion at which Lord Roberts had presided. Bartle Grant, who on retiring from the army had taken up an appointment at the Royal Artillery Mews at Woolwich, had invited Duncan to the ceremony, thinking that he would enjoy seeing this great soldier. After everyone was assembled, and just as Lord Roberts was making his speech, Duncan inadvertently leant against the cord of the flag covering the picture, thereby unveiling it a few moments too soon. Though deeply penitent, he was amused to see how, as in the story of the Emperor's new clothes, everyone behaved with great tact and apparent blindness. Meanwhile a sprightly young officer sprang on to the mantelpiece and nobly held the flag in place until the moment arrived to drop it. At the Mayor Gallery, a few moments before pulling another cord, Duncan admitted that it gave him great satisfaction at last to have been actually asked to perform this act.

TWO

An Inhabitant of the Attics

One port of call for Bartle and Ethel Grant had often been the North
Kensington home of the Stracheys. They spent days there, either on
arrival from, or before returning to, India. In the autumn of 1892 Duncan
and his mother passed several weeks in 'that huge domed Italianate
palace', as he later described it, where there was a noticeable lack of
garden or courtyard, a heavy use of yellow marbled paper and, despite the
many residents, only one lavatory. This was within audible distance of
the drawing-room which, ill-lit by gas-jets, filled almost the whole of the
first floor. Though strange, vast and hideously ugly, this house fascinated
Duncan as a child, with its paved floors, its coloured-glass dome over the
main staircase and the little, hidden servants' staircase creeping to the top
of the house, its endless bedrooms, nurseries and out-of-sight kitchens
and basement rooms of all sorts. Around 1902, after many comings and
goings, Duncan took up permanent residence here, becoming, in his
words, 'an inhabitant of the attics of that vast Caravansari, that was 69
Lancaster Gate'.[1]

In this tall, seven-storey-plus-basement house, Duncan became
translated from a mere cousin into an intimate member of the family.
There were ten children in this bookish, articulate household. Duncan
became especially fond of Philippa – Pippa to her friends – who was
thirteen years his senior. She was lively, intelligent, possessed with a keen
sense of the ridiculous, had a screeching laugh, and was very sweet-
tempered. Duncan found two further allies in James, who had followed
him to St Paul's, and Marjorie, both of whom were close to him in age. It
was James who, shortly after Duncan had been confirmed by the Bishop
of London, undermined his faith by suggesting that they consult the
Encyclopaedia Britannica on the subject of miracles.

At first Duncan knew Lytton, who was five years his senior, much less
well. He had caught glimpses of this cousin only in vacation periods, for
between 1897 and 1899 Lytton had completed his schooling at Liverpool
University College, after which he had gone up to Trinity College,
Cambridge. It seemed to Duncan that the tall, lanky, invalidish

schoolboy, who was 'intensely nervous, easily perplexed . . . timorous and savage by turns',[2] was transformed by Cambridge and the more enlightened attitude of mind he found there, which acknowledged intellectual integrity but also freed Lytton's leaning towards the frivolous and indecent.

His sisters claimed that he giggled fairly continuously from the age of three to nineteen. But his biographer, Michael Holroyd, has observed that laughter and jokes were segregated from the main tide of his feelings and hid darker emotions. Duncan held the same view, insisting in some memoir notes on Bloomsbury that Lytton was *not* always giggling and joking when young, but was often ill or depressed. Combative motives lay behind his reliance on wit which, in his maturity, Lytton used deliberately to puncture pomposity or to remove barriers. His sensitivity and quick mind gave him a feline receptiveness, which at Cambridge began to invite confidences from others; 'always there was this atmosphere,' his fellow student, Clive Bell, wrote, 'that sense of intelligent understanding mingled with affection'.[3] In addition, Lytton's talk – like that of all the Stracheys – was imbued with a literary and historical flavour.

In joining the Stracheys, Duncan found himself part of a vast Victorian household; vital, chaotic and entertaining. As well as the ten children, there were many visitors and visiting relations, much coming and going, laughter, argument, different voices speaking at once. Over it all presided Lady Strachey, always ready to take part in a play-reading, to enter a literary or political discussion, adept at billiards and an old hand at teaching young people how to dance a Highland reel. She was not too busy to keep an eye on Duncan and to report on him to Bartle Grant in February 1902. 'Duncan is very cheerful, and I am sure he likes his work; he is a very nice boy indeed and most pleasant in the house. He and Jem [James] seem to get on very well too and do have similar tastes; the songs in [Heinrich Hoffman's] *Struwelpeter* are now their joy.'[4]

Lady Strachey's sympathy with Duncan drew on a shared interest in art. She was a large woman, who sometimes appeared ungraceful, in part owing to her long arms and the lack of muscular co-ordination that caused her, when writing her autobiography, to devote one entire chapter to accidents. Her blue eyes were very myopic and in 1917, after she had to undergo surgery to have an eye removed, she taught herself braille, knowing that her sight in the other was steadily failing. A large part of her life had been spent in India: both her father and grandfather had played significant roles in its history and she had married one of her father's under-secretaries, Richard Strachey, who took responsibility not only for his own ten children but also for his wife's feckless younger brothers, bailing Trevor Grant out of debt in 1863. He left India in 1872, ostensibly to retire, but in London became a member of the India Council, a Fellow of the Royal Society, Chairman of the Meteorological Society, a member of the Managing Committee of Kew Gardens *and* eventually Chairman of the East India Railway and of the Assam Bengal Line. Up until the age of ninety he attended the office several days a week and abandoned this practice only when deafness obliged him to quit. He died aged ninety-one in 1908.

Richard Strachey had a high opinion of his wife's intelligence and was aware on first meeting her, when she was eighteen and he thirty-one, that she was a creature of uncommon worth. After his retirement she became a prominent figure in mid-Victorian London, her literary taste and his scientific interests bringing her in touch with many distinguished people. She spent much of her time in London studying French and English literature, writing and publishing, and enjoyed a correspondence with George Eliot. The author's husband, George Lewes, told Lady Strachey that she was the closest approximation to Dorothea in *Middlemarch* that he had ever met. But her gift lay not so much in creating literature as in re-creating it, through her enjoyment of reading aloud. She knew much of Milton by heart, adored Jane Austen and had a special love for Elizabethan and Jacobean drama. 'She read with fire and ardour', Virginia Woolf recalled, relishing also Lady Strachey's rich store of bygone stories and scandals.[5]

Lady Strachey had been a feminist ever since reading John Stuart Mill's *On Liberty*. She had helped circulate the first petition to Parliament for women's votes, and was a stalwart member of the National Union of Women's Suffrage Societies (NUWSS), marching regularly in their processions, writing pamphlets and fund-raising. She shared her beliefs with her daughter Pippa, and it was probably Pippa who made Duncan join the NUWSS, for in 1911 she upbraided him for having allowed his membership to lapse for two years. He was also drawn in by the Artists' Suffrage League, founded in 1907 when it held a poster and postcard competition, which Duncan entered. He won no prize, but was asked to submit again in 1909 when a four-pound prize was on offer for a poster 'suitable for use at elections'. One Barbara Forbes sent him the following suggestion: 'A man in a *sailing* boat (the sail represents the Vote). A woman with only *oars* – out in the sea of *Labour*.' Duncan interpreted this earnest idea with humour. In his poster both are heading towards the Houses of Parliament, glimpsed in the distance over the top of a wave, but while the young woman pulls on heavy oars in the trough of the wave, the young man sails effortlessly past on the top of the wave with the wind in his sails. The original caption was 'Britons, why handicap the weaker vessel?' but in the end the pithy 'Handicapped!' proved sufficient.[6] Duncan carried away first prize, shared with W. F. Winter, and his poster remains one of the most striking pieces of suffrage memorabilia.

Nowhere is there any hint that Duncan felt homesick at 69 Lancaster Gate. When later questioned about his time with the Stracheys, he spoke only of his fascination with the family. He looked on Sir Richard as 'the silent symbol of all that was good and wise and dignified and beautiful'.[7] In the evenings the old man sat reading on one side of the fireplace, while his wife busied herself with something on the other, as Duncan recalled:

> I never quite made out how they put up with the hurly burly that went on at the other end of the room where the piano stood, and where James, Marjorie and I, with Pippa playing the accompaniment, shouted songs from 'Patience', 'HMS Pinafore' or the latest Gaiety Comic Opera. Dorothy in those days was dressed very smartly and might come in late from a fashionable dinner party . . . Pippa was perhaps my favourite in the family, always it seemed ready to talk to me of fascinating subjects. Then there was often Pernel, quiet, observant and witty, and Marjorie, high spirited and often shocking, with outrageous views.[8]

Among such a crowd he did not want for company. Moreover, it would have been difficult to pine for others in Lady Strachey's vigorous and indomitable presence. In 1917, shortly after her eye operation, she and other patients had to take refuge in the hospital basement during a Zeppelin attack. As they sat waiting for the All Clear, one doctor remarked that if the Germans could see Lady Strachey at that moment, calmly smoking a cigarette while around them bombs were falling, they would despair of ever achieving victory. Leonard Woolf has left a description of her in the last year of her life: blind and frail, she sat talking about books and poetry with him and Virginia one summer evening in 1927 in the garden of Gordon Square, and at the mention of *Lycidas* recited it from start to finish. On another occasion they walked past her house in Gordon Square when she was seated on the first-floor balcony. Told they were passing, she rose, sightless, and acknowledged their presence by opening her arms wide, in a gesture that seemed to shower munificent blessings from an earlier age.

In January 1902 Duncan began to study full time at Westminster School of Art, which shared a ramshackle building near Westminster Abbey with the Royal Architectural Museum. (Two years later it moved to the Westminster Technical Institute in Vincent Square.) Its Principal was the Slade-trained portrait painter Mouat Loudan, an elegant gentleman whose ability to make children look angelic had made him a success, even if he was dismissed by Duncan as 'of no account whatever'.[9] As often happens, Duncan gained more at art school from his contact with the students than with the staff. Though some of his peers astonished him with their indolence, all joined in the buzz of discussion, which to Duncan seemed continuous. He loved listening to their knockabout arguments and was fascinated by the different characters involved.

One who became a particular friend was the gentle, retiring Marius Forestier. His father, a prolific French draughtsman, had come to London in the 1890s, joined the staff of the *Illustrated London News* and made a home for his family in a large Victorian villa in West Dulwich, which Duncan sometimes visited. As well as being a diligent contributor to illustrated magazines, M. Forestier painted with painstaking detail huge historical scenes in a studio at the back of the house, which opened on to the garden. Owing to his beard and thick, grizzled hair, his children nicknamed him 'la père Zeus'. Apparently, the longer the Forestiers lived in suburban London, the more they became 'distinctly and incorrigibly French'.[10]

Duncan's knowledge of French art at this time was very slight. He did, however, become friendly with another student, Norman Gould, who talked continuously about Degas and Whistler and produced small panel paintings of beach or river scenes in imitation of the latter. Whistler's emphasis on tasteful selection, on the simple but perfect statement, as found in the work of Norman Gould, aroused Duncan's distrust. 'There seemed nothing further to say if one could say it so well,' he commented.[11] In fact at this stage Duncan had seen very little work by either Degas or Whistler, but had surmised a great deal from reproductions and the occasional photograph.

It is possible that something of his second-hand knowledge of Whistler entered Duncan's painting of London Bridge (whereabouts unknown), which one of his relatives, Herbert Rendel, commissioned in 1901. And in the autumn of 1902, while again living temporarily with his parents at Streatley-on-Thames, Duncan tried his hand at an Impressionist painting, though he had only the vaguest understanding of what Impressionism meant. The result was a small autumnal landscape, a view of the main street from his bedroom window, a painting that he kept all his life and which still hangs in the large studio at Charleston. While painting it, he had an experience that he never forgot:

> a sort of visionary experience . . . it had a curiously objective outside of myself sort of character. 'You must go out into the world' my inner voice said – 'to learn all that there is to know and be seen in the world of painting. The Impressionists you must see and learn from and then there are other things going on at this very moment of which you know nothing.' I realised that all this was true and made up my mind to follow the advice of this inner voice. I also remember that I assumed that in order to do this, I must go to France.[12]

Though he took holidays in France, another three years were to pass before Duncan could act on this prompting. In the meantime Westminster School of Art served him well. He became adept at various period styles of illustration, imitating Beardsley, Walter Crane and others, and developing an easy naturalism in his drawing of animals and the human figure. When, some sixty years later, the Tate Gallery bought *The Kitchen*, Duncan told a curator that he had painted it at the age of seventeen. Owing to the subtlety and control displayed in this picture, its date has been questioned;[13] but even if he painted it some three years later, it remains a fine example of his early work and demonstrates his lifelong interest in the effect of light on colour, its gentle, modifying pressure here creating evanescent hues as it falls on copper pans, across wallpaper or over the well-scrubbed surface of a kitchen table. This picture shares with the work of other Edwardians, such as William Nicholson and Gwen John, a tonal acuity and a distillation of feeling that owe much to Whistler.

In the 1960s Duncan admitted to Diana Holman-Hunt, granddaughter of the famous Pre-Raphaelite, that he was indebted to her forebears for the survival of some of his early paintings. In his teens he had been a great friend of her mother, his exact contemporary, whom he had found bewitching. But it was Diana Holman-Hunt's maternal grandmother – 'Grandmother Freeman' – who intrigued Duncan most: 'a *very* frivolous woman, full of ideas, a lively conversationalist, always elegantly dressed,' he recollected.[14] She and her husband were friends of the Stephens and Stracheys and entertained regularly, and in considerable style, in London and at their two country houses, one of which was at Wraysbury, on the river near Windsor, the other at Winchelsea. Duncan was invited for 'a Friday to Monday' and Lady Strachey, knowing that he would have the advantage of meeting Mrs Freeman's close friend, William Padgett, a painter of the Barbizon School, gave her approval.

Padge, as he was affectionately known, had arrived in Winchelsea about ten years earlier with his spinster sisters. Mrs Freeman's interest in him had caused much scandal and speculation, which further increased when, after a ten-year gap in child-bearing, she gave birth to a son. Rumours, which stemmed from the Freemans' butler, told of confession and sensible tolerance. At any rate, Mr Freeman was delighted to have a son and heir at last and invited Padge to be godfather at the christening. A studio was also provided for him in Bedford Gardens, conveniently close to the Freemans' London home, where his paintings hung on the walls between others by Royal Academicians.

Duncan, looking forward to his weekend visit (possibly as much for its social as its artistic interest), boarded a train at Charing Cross, knowing that he had to change at Ashford for Winchelsea. On arriving at the junction he was alarmed to hear his name shouted by the station-master, who strode down the platform in his top hat, ringing a bell to draw attention to the announcement. Duncan was horrified to learn that Mrs Freeman's butler had telephoned: he was expected for dinner not at Winchelsea but at Wraysbury. The station-master merely waved him across the platform to a special train, which had been ordered to return Duncan to Waterloo Junction. Prior to 1914 there was a railway connection between this junction and Waterloo proper, and Duncan soon found himself on another special train, which carried him a further twenty-one miles to Wraysbury. There a carriage was waiting. On reaching the house he met Mrs Freeman, 'an entrancing vision hovering in the drive', who, when Duncan apologised profusely for the trouble and cost he had caused, assured him that the fifty pounds she had spent on each train was inconsequential compared with her need to avoid odd numbers at dinner.

That weekend he paid careful attention to Padgett's paintings, admiring especially his landscapes. Not long afterwards Padge died, aged fifty-two, in the Freemans' house with Mrs Freeman at his side. He left money to his sisters but all his pictures, prints, drawings and artist's materials to his lover. Before many weeks had passed Duncan received an invitation from Mrs Freeman to visit Padge's studio and to remove anything he wanted in the way of artist's paraphernalia – easels, palettes, brushes and paints: her butler would be in attendance. On arriving at 57 Bedford Gardens Duncan was astonished to find a plethora of fine materials – expensive canvases, sable and hogshair brushes, the best-quality paints. He loaded as much as he thought decent into piles and boxes by the front door, watched and waited on by the butler, who finally summoned a hansom cab. Despite Duncan's embarrassment of riches, the

butler remarked as he left that Duncan had been foolish not to order a
carrier to take away the lot: they would, of course, now sell the rest.
Nevertheless, for the next few years Duncan's paintings, in material
terms, were probably some of his best.

One of the educational advantages of living at 69 Lancaster Gate was
good conversation. In addition, although the house exhibited very little
aesthetic appeal (Lady Strachey once told Virginia Woolf that her ideal
would have been to spend her entire life in boarding houses and, as
Michael Holroyd has added, most of the homes she inhabited bore this
appearance),[15] its inhabitants were not uninterested in art. The Scottish
painter Arthur Melville was a friend of the family and occasionally dined;
so did the scholar of Italian art and art critic to the highbrow *Athenaeum*,
Roger Fry, then regarded as something of an old fogey in the art world,
as he found much English Impressionism lacking in design. On these
occasions, as Duncan recalled, there could be 'for me thrilling talk about
painting'.[16] Still more important to Duncan was the arrival of Simon
Bussy.

This French artist first met the Stracheys in Paris, through the
Guieysse family, with whom Pernel had lodged in 1898. Their daughter,
Louise Guieysse, married Auguste Bréal, who had studied with Bussy
and Matisse under Gustave Moreau at the Ecole des Beaux-Arts.[17] Bréal
introduced Bussy to the Guieysse family and he was lodging in their
house when Pernel Strachey arrived in the winter of 1898 to work on her
French doctorate.

Pernel admired Bussy's pictures and drew her parents' attention to
them, Sir Richard agreeing to buy one when they visited Paris. The
following year Bussy gave the Stracheys a portrait of Pernel, a small,
intense pastel and a good likeness. Two years later, in 1901, he visited the
Stracheys at 69 Lancaster Gate. His presence had a noticeable effect on
Dorothy, who thought him charming, amusing and who began dreaming
in French. She was then in her mid-thirties, with no definite attachments,
and had been prone to periods of depression.[18]

Bussy, an unlikely candidate for her affections, was very small and
highly conscious of the fact, self-exacting and solitary. Passionately
interested in nature, in trees and plants as well as animals, birds and fish,
many of which he studied at London Zoo, he also had a penetrating
intelligence and was *au fait* with French and English literature, as
Dorothy soon discerned.[19]

Born and brought up at Dole in the Jura, Bussy had arrived in Paris in
1886, where he entered the Ecole des Art Décoratifs. On his first day he

sat down beside a pale young man who was copying a nude from an engraving – Georges Rouault, who became a lifelong friend. In 1890 Bussy moved to the Ecole des Beaux-Arts, training first under Elie Delaunay and then, after a period of military service, under Moreau. He made a lasting friend of Matisse, his contemporary, and was still closer to Auguste Bréal, who became not only a painter of talent but also an author of books on Rembrandt and Velázquez. Bussy began the habit that Duncan was later to imitate, of working in the studio in the morning and then copying in the Louvre in the afternoon.

In 1896 he had executed a series of landscapes in pastel, their sombre tonalities owing much to Moreau. These were exhibited the following year at Durand-Ruel, a venue of no small importance, for it had come to be regarded as the sanctuary of the Impressionists. Bussy received praise from Degas, Rodin and Pissarro, and for a brief period copied Monet's example, painting the same view under different conditions of light and atmosphere. Such was his success at this time that he bought himself a magnificent fur coat, which made the as-yet-unknown Matisse furiously envious. But the largest and most ambitious paintings that Bussy ever produced were the five works he sent to the Salon d'Automne in 1905, which were a curious throw-back, a mélange of Pre-Raphaelitism, Gustave Moreau and Whistlerian tonalities. He continued also to work with pastel, a medium in which he gradually arrived at a stylisation that overlooked surface detail in the search for a very still presentation of essential forms.[20] There is also an Oriental ingredient in these pastels, which reflects Bussy's admiration for Japanese prints.

In 1901, however, he was hoping for success through portraiture and came to England with an introduction to the artist William Rothenstein. They became close friends, Bussy taking a studio near to Rothenstein in Kensington and there giving lessons in painting to a small number of pupils, among them Dorothy Strachey, Constance Lloyd – a Birmingham girl, whom Duncan was to get to know well a few years later in Paris – and Duncan himself. 'His lessons remain with me as the best I have ever received,' Duncan later recollected. 'He was the most just of masters but at the same time the most severe.'[21] Bussy made him fearful of the dangers of the *à peu près* – the 'good enough' – and gave him, Duncan claimed, an artistic conscience.

Bussy encouraged his pupils to copy in the National Gallery and gave them certain maxims: *La couleur doit être pensée* was one, another being his insistence that a picture should have a *clou* on which the whole composition should hang. In addition, he taught the necessity of working every day, not just when inspiration directed. But nowhere was his integrity more apparent than in his work, where the artist's temperament and personal calligraphy were effaced in the search for an implacable precision. Through Bussy, Duncan learnt an attitude to work that was humble, attentive, scrupulous and self-denying.

In the summer of 1902 a near-tragedy happened, when a spirit lamp exploded in Bussy's face and he feared he might lose his sight. The Stracheys invited 'Little Bussy', as they referred to him, to stay with them again when he came out of hospital. During his convalescence he proposed to Dorothy. Lady Strachey met the news of their engagement with kindness and acceptance, perhaps not unmindful of Dorothy's age, for she was thirty-seven when they married in April 1903. Emma Guieysse gave them land at Roquebrune in the South of France, on which a house had been partly built, on the understanding that the money this represented would be forthcoming in time. (To her agreeable surprise, most of it was repaid in 1918.) The house, when completed, became La Souco, which remained their home, and that of their daughter Janie who was born in 1906, until Simon's death in 1954. However, regular visits were made to Scotland and to Paris, where Bussy sent work to the Salon d'Automne until his failure to obtain critical attention turned him bitterly against large public exhibitions.

Around 1912 his work changed. Some years before he had discovered that by mixing gelatine with his pastels he could obtain the solidity and depth of oils. With this technique perfected, he ceased painting directly from nature. The animals, birds, reptiles and fish that he now portrayed, in a near-monochrome palette, as well as his skies, trees and buildings, were not the product of patient observation but a reassembling of known facts in such a way as to remove the accidental for the sake of sharpness, purity and precision. Though his subject matter is always clearly recognisable, the reality presented is poetic – an invention, a unique decorative statement about the specific nature of an animal or place, expressed with a sense of absolute necessity. Duncan Grant put it well when he said, 'if the eye of M. Ingres had been directed to the contemplation of the Bird of Paradise . . . the character of his discoveries would have had something in common with M. Bussy's.'[22] When some of these pastels were exhibited at Galerie Blot in Paris in 1913, Guillaume Apollinaire compared them with Persian miniatures. Bussy's animal studies were perhaps also an outlet for his misanthropic feelings, for they can hint at states of mind and traits of character more usually ignored in polite human portraiture.

While living with the Stracheys, Duncan was invited by his aunt to accompany her on a round of visits to celebrated artists. It was Picture Sunday, the day on which painters opened their studios to friends and put on view the paintings they were about to send to the Royal Academy. Lady Strachey and Duncan set off in a four-wheeled cab and arrived at a magnificent residence belonging to the animal painter Briton Rivière. The elderly painter chatted delightedly with Lady Strachey, while her nephew, looking past the other guests, caught sight of polar bears at the far end of the room, walking majestically by the light of the midnight sun over immense tracts of ice.[23] In kindly fashion, Rivière turned to Duncan and remarked, 'I expect you only admire Whistler and that sort of thing', to which Duncan immediately replied that though he was indeed an admirer of Whistler, he did not 'damn' everyone else on that account. The word 'damn' seemed to ring painfully clear among the fashionable throng and he blushed in confusion. Once safely in the four-wheeler again and rumbling towards the studio of Holman Hunt, Duncan asked Lady Strachey if he had been wrong to use this word 'damn'. To his relief she replied that in the context it seemed perfectly acceptable.[24]

As a student at the Westminster School of Art, he remained under probation, so far as his career was concerned, until he was twenty. He then had to go to the City of London, where his name had been entered with the rice merchants Bulloch Bros, and either sign on or scratch his name off the list. It gave him, he remembered, 'a sort of horrid pleasure' to score through his name.[25] But if his future was from then on decided, his family's finances remained insecure.

Bartle Grant had returned home from Malta and obtained a job with a travelling theatrical company, which toured Scotland in the spring of 1903. Billed as 'Secretary', his job involved keeping an eye on the box-office staff, checking ticket numbers with returns and doing the artists' salaries on Fridays. He was earning three pounds a week and sending Lady Strachey £2 10s a month for Duncan's upkeep. 'Hope Dunks is going on satisfactorily,' one letter ends. 'Love to all.'[26] In 1904, when Duncan entered a line-drawing competition and had his drawing of a horse reproduced in *The Country Gentleman*, he gave his address as 59 Carlisle Mansions, Victoria, SW, where he was presumably living with his mother. Towards the end of 1904 his father obtained a post as a military instructor at Woolwich and in 1905 set up home in Fellows Road, Hampstead, where Duncan again joined his parents.

One of Duncan's schoolfriends, with whom he had been amorously involved, wrote telling him about the class he was now in. 'Please write again soon,' the letter ends, 'as I always long to hear from you.'[27] As a day-boy at St Paul's, Duncan had enjoyed more freedom than at Rugby to wander the streets. And it was in the streets of London that he had his first sexual encounter. Towards the end of his life, Duncan, at his friend Paul Roche's urging, wrote down his memories of this event. He had noticed in the National Gallery that many people stood a long time in front of Bronzino's *Venus and Cupid*, an extremely sensual if obscure allegory, the precise meaning of which remains the subject of debate. One day, while Duncan was looking at this picture, a man came and stood close to him:

> He had his hands in his pockets and coming very close rubbed his hand against my penis. This rather had the effect of exciting me, and he said something about the picture, did I not find it very fine? He then said let us go downstairs and look at the watercolours – in those days there was a series of small rooms in the basement hung with watercolours. We were alone in a room – he pulled out my cock and very soon I came onto the floor. I rubbed the mess with my foot when the guardian came in and asked what it was on the floor. I quickly said I had a cough and could not help spitting on the floor. He had to be satisfied with my explanation.
>
> I sometimes met my friend again in various places. Once among the crowd of people listening to the sermons in Hyde Park. Here people stood so close to each other that it was easy to have contact without being seen. My friend turned out to be a young Swede, and I liked him. I remember going home one day and wondering if I could produce the same sensation by myself, so masturbated for the first time. About this time my parents thought I looked pale and called in a Dr to examine me. My father stayed in the room while the Dr told me to take down my trousers. He pointed to my genitals and said I hope you don't play about with this, pointing to my parts . . . It will be seen that I received very little sexual education at this time of my life.[28]

His heart was another cause of concern. When he was about fifteen and playing tag, running round and round a table with his cousin Phyllida Ridpath, they both suddenly thought there must be a bird in the room. It turned out to be Duncan's heart, which was cheeping like a sparrow. He thought no more about it until two years later. While staying with his parents at Streatley-on-Thames in the autumn of 1902, Duncan cut his leg one morning while swimming in the river before breakfast. Realising that he needed stitches, he limped to the doctor, had the wound attended to and returned home at around ten in the morning, to find his mother ashen-faced over his disappearance. The next few weeks found him laid up in bed. His parents, who continued to worry that he was pale and delicate, asked a doctor to examine him. After the doctor left, his parents, with a cheerfulness that did not disguise their distress, suggested that Duncan should spend the winter with his Aunt Lell (Lady Colvile) in Menton,[29] for the doctor had discovered something wrong with his heart. Duncan next made a trip to a Harley Street specialist in the company of his father, only to discover that a displaced muscle was causing his heart to squeak. It was not in the least serious, but it was thought, nevertheless, that a winter in Menton would do him no harm, and Lady Colvile had taken the Villa Himalaya, which sits on the easternmost tip of Menton-Garavan, overlooking the Mediterranean.

On a January day early in 1903 Duncan set out on his journey, stopping in Paris *en route*. Looking back on this, his first trip to the French capital, he remembered a slight agitation on his parents' part at one so young being allowed to spend a night in Paris alone. He was told not to get into any trouble but was himself, at that age, vague as to what that might mean. In any case he was too excited by the city, by his visit to the Louvre and, in the evening, to the Théâtre Français to be much tempted by anything that people might offer. What did catch his attention was a display of books with English titles in a shop window in the Palais Royal. One in particular caught his eye – *How We Lost Our Virginities*. It was, he recalled, 'a gay little book dealing with the adventures of a group of young ladies. It certainly was very explicit and amused me during the journey to Menton.'[30] Arriving at his aunt's villa he was delighted, on walking through the garden, to find roses in full bloom, every sort of tree flowering and sprays of mimosa filling the slightly chilly evening air with their scent. He unpacked in a carefree state of mind, but neverthless took the precaution of putting *How We Lost Our Virginities* under the white paper that lined the top drawer in which he put his collars and ties.

Duncan was fond of Aunt Lell, who was never a dull companion. She had many stories concerning people she had known, and together they read French books to teach him the language. Though he was virtually a prisoner at the Villa Himalaya (Aunt Lell, fearing the attractions of the town centre, gave him no pocket money), Duncan was happy enough, painted most of the day, went for walks and returned dutifully in time for meals. Only occasionally did he suffer a nostalgia for a more free-thinking spirit. Lady Colvile, a widow in her mid-sixties, had many virtues and considerable intelligence. But her religious beliefs, far from encouraging an understanding of human failure, made her judgements severe. This sweet, reasonable lady could at a moment's notice strike terror into anyone's heart. She also lacked humour: books that others found amusing struck her as distressing, tedious or horrible, but never funny. 'I simply *cannot* see the point of that joke,' she would say.

Duncan was less happy when Sir William and Lady Thistleton Dyer and their daughter arrived. He found Sir William, who was head of Kew Gardens, a bore, thought him and his wife ill-matched and likened their docile daughter to a hospital nurse. His only bond of sympathy with the young girl was that they both thought their elders talked too much about food at meals. Sir William, apprised of their opinion, announced at the start of one meal that, owing to this criticism, they were going to leave it to the young that day to supply topics of conversation. The result was such a resounding silence that the next day the conversation returned uninhibitedly to comparing the spaghetti of Naples with that of Palermo.

Among the staff at the Villa Himalaya were a squat but dignified Prussian maid called Ida and a butler called Harris, who struck Duncan as lazy, dishonest and overbearing. Ida lived a life apart in her room, where she ate her meals, and was enslaved to Lady Colvile, having acted as her travelling companion since before Duncan was born. The only other person she was ever known to smile upon was Duncan himself. She had spoiled him since childhood, as he admitted. 'I took it for granted she adored me and was fond of her in a sort of way, and anyhow it was a relief to go and gossip with her without restraint and pull her leg and shock her and make her laugh a low guttural German laugh.'[31]

The Thistleton Dyers finally left and Duncan's uncle, Trevor Grant, came out to join his sister. Shortly after his arrival a graveness settled over the villa. The next day, after Aunt Lell had retired to bed and Harris had bolted the shutters, Uncle Trevor informed Duncan that the butler had found the little book in Duncan's drawer. Trevor had read it and shown it to a doctor in Menton, who had told Trevor that 85 per cent of all mental illness could be traced back to the reading of such literature in early life. The doctor had then asked Trevor if there were any oddities in Duncan's behaviour. Trevor thought a little and then commented that he had noticed Duncan seemed unable to *finish* any of his pictures. That, the doctor informed him, was a sure sign of mental decay.

Duncan pluckily suggested that Uncle Trevor was perhaps not the best judge of when a picture was finished. A voice of thunder commanded him to be silent. The mentally unstable, he was told, always found excuses for their conduct. With this, all hopes of reasoning with his uncle vanished. Obliged to listen to a torrent of platitudes, denunciation, heart-rending appeals to his better nature, combined with practical advice on hygiene and diet, Duncan, at the first possible moment, fled into the mountains. During the rest of his stay he moped, barely opened his mouth and hated everything. His elders now perceived him as untidy, careless and vague. When nervous, Duncan blinked a lot and this, in conjunction with everything else, led Trevor to the conclusion that Duncan was, without any doubt, an imbecile. He wrote to his brother Bartle to advise medical consultation. It was a rather dismal figure who finally kissed Aunt Lell and travelled home on a train which, this time, circulated Paris.

On arriving home, Duncan found his father a good deal upset by Trevor's letter. Bartle showed it to his sister, Lady Strachey. Although she suggested that the matter did not merit much importance, Bartle arranged for Duncan to be seen by Dr Hyslop, the head of Bedlam, a genial man and an amateur painter. It was a painless interview. After a few indirect questions, the doctor put his hand on Duncan's shoulder and told him not to worry: there was nothing wrong with him. Moreover, he went on, he himself often began a picture and, for one reason or another, got no further than a sketch. With these reassuring words the whole curious incident was dismissed.

A sense of innocent surprise continued to accompany Duncan's sexual education. After his experience in the National Gallery, however, he readily understood what was wanted when a middle-aged gentleman began talking to him while he drew the *Discobolus* in the British Museum. Duncan accepted an invitation to tea and was taken to a fashionable lodging near Hyde Park Corner. Several return visits were made. 'My sexual life with him,' Duncan recalled, 'was not very exciting but I rather liked the man.'[32] When the gentleman suggested that Duncan might be in need of some money and offered him a hundred pounds, he was astonished. It was very exciting to be offered such a sum, but impossible to accept, as he would never have been able to explain to his relatives how he came by such a princely sum. Looking back on the episode, Duncan recalled, 'As may be imagined my emotions had not been deeply touched but only my sexual feelings.'[33]

While this hidden life continued, his feelings found outlet elsewhere. He was seeing a good deal of some relations at whose house in Kensington he often had tea. There Duncan fell doubly in love, with both a daughter and a son. So obvious was his love for the daughter that his mother commented on it, making Duncan realise that he had somehow managed to conceal his equally strong attraction to the brother. The young man himself was surprised when Duncan gave him some indication of his feelings. At home, Duncan's readiness to flirt found a ready response in his parents' maid, a young woman called Lizzie. On one occasion Bartle Grant walked into the dining-room to find her seated on his son's knee. Duncan had no intention of taking things further, but his father thought the situation less innocent than it appeared and indicated that it should stop.

Though most of his life Duncan was an active homosexual, he did not let his sexual leanings distort his view of the world. No sexual prejudice or bias trammelled his response to those he met, with the result that his friendships with women often went very deep. His openness of mind and readiness to absorb new insights also affected his art. Nevertheless, he was ready for fresh experience when in the winter of 1904 his mother took him to Florence.

They lodged in the Hotel Bachielli near the Ponte Vecchio, with a Colonel Forster and a woman called Naomi. In some rough memoir notes Duncan recollected that Naomi flirted with the Florentine officers and laughed at the Ewbanks. Each year Louisa Ewbank, who was distantly related to Ethel Grant, left the Isle of Wight house that her late husband, the Revd Henry Ewbank, had built, finding it cheaper to winter in Florence. Her daughters, Elinor, Monica and Dorothy (all blue-stockings), visited her there as and when they could. All spoke Italian fluently and were avid Italophiles. They were occasionally visited by their cousin, Florence Ewbank, whose early death enabled Duncan in 1916 to make use of her Suffolk farmhouse at a time when, as a conscientious objector, he needed to work on the land.

The Ewbank sisters were high-spirited and close to Duncan in age. The eldest, Elinor, became the first woman at Oxford to gain a First in Chemistry and also did valuable research work with explosives during the First World War. She was the most interested of the three sisters in art and in her later years lived in a house at Park Town, Oxford, amid quietly elegant surroundings, which contained several of Duncan's pictures, a set of dining-room chairs covered with needlework based on his designs, and tiles decorated by him around two fireplaces and along the back of some open shelves in her bathroom. She and her sisters, as young women, were much given to ragging their mother, who, having taken up sketching in her widowhood, had been nicknamed 'Kodak' in the hope that if she was placed in front of a scene she would automatically produce a view.

In the company of the Ewbanks, Duncan became familiar with their infectious enthusiasm for any site or building that had some connection with Italian history, literature or art, be it Savonarola's birthplace, Tasso's dungeon or a palace that had belonged to the Este family. For Louisa Ewbank there was almost no piece of architecture that did not surrender many layers of association. The Ewbanks were also highly sociable, introducing Duncan to a Mrs Maitland, whom he was to meet again in Paris and whose daughter, Helen, was to remain a lifelong friend. Rupert Brooke's sisters were also in Florence.

On several occasions Duncan accompanied the girls from both families in a hired trap on a picnic outing to some little town near Florence. He enjoyed himself, even though violent, youthful disagreements sometimes punctuated these outings. When Rupert Brooke himself appeared, he and Duncan chatted in cafés, their exchange of ideas adding to Duncan's happy memory of this holiday and the impression that he had been surrounded by lively, cultivated people. He began reading Bernard Berenson and looked at Florentine art under the spell of his views, which seemed so much clearer and more common-sensical than Ruskin's.

Every day he visited the Uffizi. His interest focused chiefly on the early Italians, especially Piero della Francesca and Masaccio. He never forgot his first impression of the Brancacci Chapel, where he experienced Masaccio's grand simplicity of concept and use of emotive gesture. At the request of Harry Strachey, one of Lytton's cousins, Duncan began copying parts of these frescos, keeping for himself a small oil of Adam and Eve being cast out of the Garden of Eden, their grief counterpointed through their contrasting poses. He also made a copy of Piero della Francesca's portrait of the warrior Duke of Urbino, Federigo da Montefeltro, a more or less exact transcription which, neither sold nor given away, always hung at Charleston during his lifetime and is still there today. Duncan's admiration for this artist further increased after he visited Arezzo and saw the great frescos illustrating the Legend of the Holy Cross. On his return to London he sought out Piero in the National Gallery, making a copy of the angel musicians (destroyed in the blitz) and of Mary and Joseph (King's College, Cambridge), in his *Nativity*.[34] He also paid more attention to Piero's *Baptism*, and some fifteen years later painted a variation on it. These and other great icons of the Italian Renaissance helped form his visual and cultural inheritance; they joined a growing cache of imagery on which his imagination was to feed throughout his working life.

THREE

Lytton and Paris

Since his night in Paris on his way to Menton in 1902, Duncan's attention had often turned towards France. He was aware that while he was in Florence during the winter of 1904–5 Durand-Ruel, the Parisian art dealer, had brought to London an exhibition of work by the leading French Impressionists. It was a controversial show, the Edwardians still finding the chromatic brilliance of true French Impressionism hard to accept. When the art critic Frank Rutter, anxious that a work should be acquired for the nation, opened a 'French Impressionist Fund' subscription list in the pages of *The Sunday Times*, the National Gallery announced that Boudin was the most modern artist it was prepared to accept.

Pernel Strachey kept Duncan up to date. 'The picture exhibitions have filled us with excitement,' she wrote towards the end of February 1905. 'The French Impressionists have just closed amid weeping and wailing. Whistler has just opened. Watts reigns at Burlington H[ouse].'[1] At Westminster School of Art the Impressionists were the subject of heated discussion, Marius Forestier told Duncan, in a letter that also reported on the bicycle Duncan had lent him (useless) and on the commotion ('all sorts of scandals have come out')[2] caused by a letter awaiting Duncan in the school's office from a girl they had met at Streatley.

That same year Simon Bussy had his work rejected in London by the International Society. His bitterness, reported by Dorothy, must have made Duncan even more aware that progress and experiment in art had more chance of survival in Paris than in London. Nevertheless, he returned happily enough to London that spring, lived with his parents and began working again at Westminster School of Art. But the notable developments in his life that year concerned not so much his artistic training as affairs of the heart. He now learned that sexual relations did not necessarily exclude love.

Soon after he joined the Strachey household in 1902 Lytton obtained rooms in the south-east corner turret of Trinity's Great Court. Duncan first visited him there in June 1903. He was familiar enough with

Lytton's Cambridge life to notice the excitement caused that autumn by the publication of G. E. Moore's *Principia Ethica*, which remains one of the most significant ethical treatises of the twentieth century, famous also for its celebration, in its final chapter dealing with 'The Ideal', of the value of art and friendship. Lytton rated it so highly that he told G. E. Moore that it had shattered all writers on Ethics from Aristotle and Christ to Herbert Spencer and F. H. Bradley. Duncan, a witness to this enthusiasm, asked his mother that year for a copy of the book as his Christmas present. But whether his understanding of Moore came from reading the book itself or from listening to discussion of it, he probably perceived that Moore's philosophy justified his choice of vocation and upheld his childhood insight – that much happiness lies in observation. Moore's anti-materialist philosophy rated states of consciousness higher than action: the only things valuable in themselves are states of mind, of which the most valuable are 'the pleasures of human intercourse and the enjoyment of beautiful objects'. Taken as a whole, *Principia Ethica* inspired its readers to live a better life, to choose more carefully its ingredients. 'The best ideal we can construct,' Moore wrote, 'will be that state of things which contains the greatest number of things having positive value, and which contains nothing evil or indifferent.'[3] Contrary to the opinion later voiced by Maynard Keynes, that Bloomsbury ignored the moral implications of Moore's philosophy, Leonard Woolf rightly argued that *Principia Ethica* made them more acutely aware of the consequences of their actions; the question – what *ought* one to do – was now always to the fore.[4] It seemed to Woolf as if Moore had removed an obscuring accumulation of scales, cobwebs and curtains, revealing, as if for the first time, the nature of truth and reality, good and evil, character and conduct.

Moore bred in those friends, later to form the core of Bloomsbury, a pronounced rationalism, a desire to employ the tools of reason in order to arrive at a more lucid view of the world. Lytton Strachey, Bertrand Russell and others delighted in Moore's company because his search for transparency gave him a marvellous simplicity of character: he always spoke the truth, it never occurring to him to do otherwise, and did so in the simplest manner, ticking off the points he was making on his fingers and proceeding with the utmost clarity. A similar childlike innocence was betrayed by Moore's habit of sticking his tongue out in delight after he had made a joke.

Through Lytton, Duncan also became familiar with the arcane mysteries of the Apostles, the exclusive Cambridge *conversazione* society, membership of which came by invitation only to the select few. Potential candidates were, unknown to them, labelled 'embryos' and their conversation and character were carefully monitored. The aim of the society was to further a common interest in working out a philosophy of life. In practice it created a hidden network of intellectuals, the rule of secrecy binding its members together with an exceptional degree of loyalty, to such an extent that when Tom Driberg went to see a former member, Guy Burgess, in Moscow in the 1950s, the latter, though he had betrayed his country, refused to reveal any of the Apostles' secrets.

Lytton was not so discreet. He gossiped freely to Duncan about the personalities involved in the Apostles, especially since G. E. Moore's fellowship at Trinity ended with the Michaelmas term of 1904, after which he went to live in Edinburgh until 1908, leaving Strachey and Keynes as the dominant figures within the society. But the pleasure to be had from Strachey's company resulted not only from his love of gossip, but also from his distance from habitual ways of thinking or behaving: everything he did – the way he stood or sat or buttered bread – differentiated him from the crowd. Then, too, the lens that he turned on life exposed the preposterous, the incredible or the absurd in human appearance or behaviour.[5] To listen to Strachey talk, or to be the recipient of his letters, was to share his acute, often slightly hysterical view of the world and to be invited to giggle at it as often as at himself. He hated pretentiousness or any form of cant and was anti-religious, rebelling against a religion that had been the cause of much sexual oppression.

At some point Lytton found himself irresistibly attracted to his dark-haired cousin with the grey-blue eyes, and let him know it. Legend has it that Duncan replied, 'Relations we may be: have them, we may not.'[6] His resistance, however, broke down in the summer of 1905. That year the Strachey family rented Great Oakley Hall, six miles from Kettering, where Lytton continued working at his dissertation on Warren Hastings in the hope that it would earn him a Fellowship. At the start of August Duncan arrived on a visit that lasted two to three days. Lytton, having earlier fantasised about Duncan as an object of lust, suddenly found him in his arms one sunny morning in the orchard, apparently succumbing to similar emotions. In a letter to Maynard Keynes, with whom he gossiped freely about homosexual passions, Lytton likened the experience to a glimpse of heaven: 'Incredible, quite – yet so it's happened . . . Oh dear, dear, dear, how wild, how violent, and how supreme are the things of this earth! – I am cloudy, I fear almost sentimental. But I'll write again. Oh yes, it's Duncan. He's no longer here, though; he went yesterday to France. Fortunate, perhaps, for my dissertation.'[7] The hysteria was intended partly to entertain: when writing for himself alone, Lytton exchanged hyperbole for sober, moral resolutions:

> In the future when we meet, I want to be worthy of what I felt then, of what I am feeling now. I want our intercourse to be unmarred by the weaknesses that I know are mine too often. I want him to love me as I love him, and to deserve his love. Let me stand erect in my own self-consciouness, in that he may find in my strength the splendour that I find in his beauty; and let us be occupied with the cleansing aspirations of our art as much as with each other and with ourselves.[8]

Lytton's idealism, together with his capacity to reflect on his feelings and those of others, drew Duncan into a relationship unlike any he had previously experienced.

There was a disappointing silence from France after Duncan's departure. When a letter did come, it brought descriptions of his holiday at Camiers, as well as the pleasing sentiment that he was thinking often of Lytton. That autumn Lytton was disappointed in his hopes of a Fellowship and resigned himself to poverty, drudgery and life once again at Lancaster Gate. Duncan, meanwhile, after a further holiday in Carmarthenshire, began working on his own in a studio in Upper Baker Street. It was furnished with little more than his drawings and paintings. 'They're superb,' Lytton told Maynard Keynes, 'and I've no doubt of his supremacy qua artist. He made me an omelette in a frying-pan over the fire, and we ate it on the bare wooden table with bread and cheese and beer. After that we drew our kitchen chairs up to the fire, and smoked cigarettes and talked.'[9]

Almost every twist and turn in his affair with Duncan was presented to Keynes by letter. Keynes, who had just embarked on his fourth year at King's College, was undecided whether his main intellectual preoccupation was economics or moral philosophy. He had taken over from Strachey as secretary of the Apostles, and much of his time was spent assessing the virtues and attractions of various 'embryos'. Dark-haired, slim, with a receding chin and sensual lips partly concealed by a trim moustache, he looked at the world through amused eyes, his brilliant, sly mind ceaselessly analysing his every encounter with people or ideas. Some fifteen years later Strachey summed up Keynes: 'An immensely interesting figure – partly because, with his curious typewriter intellect, he's also so oddly and unexpectedly emotional.'[10] In 1905 Keynes was struggling with his feelings for Arthur Hobhouse, the undergraduate with whom Lytton had at one time been besotted. After months of courting, during which Hobhouse had persistently turned a cold cheek, Keynes had suddenly received from him a declaration of love. Lytton's advice, when sought, was not to hold back but to 'rape' him while he had the chance. A bold correspondent, in practice Lytton handled relationships with considerable delicacy. None more so than his involvement with Duncan, as his letters to Maynard make clear.

'Your horrible prophecy has come true – too quickly.' So Lytton told Maynard only two months after his affair with Duncan had begun:

This morning a letter from D. – a regular knock-down one. You know how careful I've been – after past experience – to keep the physical affection in abeyance, and to lay as much stress as possible on the mental. Well, I'm now told that he doesn't care for me as much – in the mental way – as I care for him; and that, though he has a 'passion, a wild thing, I cannot control' for me, that that isn't enough. Isn't fate ingenious?[11]

Two days later, after what he calls an 'interview' with Duncan, Lytton reported to Maynard that everything was all right, and the relationship between himself and Duncan, if still a little lop-sided, had been smoothed over. 'There's distinctly something of the lovee about his affection if not about his lust. And I can't help feeling that the latter is liable to lapse in time. But for the present I'm content to hoist the sails for at any rate a temporary Cythera. We hope to come to King's on Saturday week.'[12]

Maynard's replies to Lytton's letters suggest that, vicariously, he was almost as caught up in this affair as his friend. 'What is amazing,' he told Lytton, 'is this – you are the only person it would be the least good his being in love with, and he is the only person for you to be in love with. I am in love with your being in love with one another.' Maynard went on: 'In the name of all that's good, don't go buggering him for buggering's sake. It would be so damned easy. And don't for the moment at least think every kind of disaster on the brink.'[13]

Lytton welcomed Maynard's advice and encouragement, especially when Duncan's occasionally stand-offish behaviour left him fraught with fearful anxiety. Even after meetings with Duncan that had been happy and relaxed, Lytton sometimes felt the relationship to be a trifle unreal. He was also jealous of the friendship between his younger brother James and Duncan. In Cambridge Duncan lunched with James while Lytton went to see Maynard. When Lytton told Maynard his fears, the latter pointed out that James and Duncan had been schoolboy friends and that

Duncan would surely laugh at the notion of James becoming the object of passionate love.

But the nerviness in Lytton was not easily quelled. If Duncan parted from him, as he did after their visit to Cambridge, without making an appointment for another meeting, Lytton felt cut to the core by what he took to be a lack of affection. At other moments he perceived a brake on Duncan's affection: 'It seemed to me almost as if he was afraid of me and my affection – as if he didn't dare to face something he couldn't reciprocate.'[14] When the reality of their relationship began to clarify, Lytton found it painful but less torturing. In late October 1905 he was writing to Maynard:

> Duncan was here this morning, as abundant as usual, and as charming, and as beautiful, and as good, and as absolutely lost. Lost, I mean, to me; because I now see quite clearly what our relation has settled down into – an affectionate indifference punctuated with week-ends of lust. This is exaggerated, but the truth is nearer to it than the dream I once thought was going to be reality. Alas! And I can't be sure whether I should be thankful or not . . . I'm almost satisfied with what I've got.[15]

Together they went to Windsor to inspect the Holbeins. In the course of this outing they had a 'grand explanatory conversation', as Lytton afterwards told Maynard, during which Duncan proved himself capable of impressive frankness: 'all openness and clearness, and all melancholy goodness and impotent kindness and everything but love'.[16]

Maynard's interest in the affair led him to seek out Duncan one day at the National Gallery, where he was copying a picture. He bore Duncan off to lunch and afterwards had the gall to advise Lytton, sanctimoniously, that he should not regard Duncan's work as an obstacle to their relationship: it was understandable that when in the middle of a painting Duncan should refuse to go on expeditions. Lytton, however, continued to want more of Duncan than he could get.

Maynard, meanwhile, was discovering how easily his mind could handle problems of supply and demand. 'I find Economics increasingly satisfactory,' he told Strachey, 'and I think I am rather good at it. I want to manage a railway or organise a Trust or at least swindle the investing public. It is so easy and fascinating to master the principles of these things.' Human behaviour, however, was much less predictable; in the same letter Maynard admits to feelings of anger towards Duncan ('Why can't he see . . . ?'), owing to his treatment of Lytton.[17] It was a criticism that Lytton instantly rebutted: 'Oh no, you mustn't be enraged with

Duncan. He sees everything, you know; and he's probably better than us. I have a sort of adoration. When I hear other people talking about him, I'm filled with a secret pride. *Il s'élève en mon coeur une secrète joie. Après tout je l'ai possédé* – if only for an hour and a half.'[18] A week later Lytton went to hear the pianist Richard Buhlig. It was a dull concert, brightened by Duncan's presence. 'It's quite true,' he afterwards admitted, ' – when he's there, all one can do is to be in love with him.'[19]

As time went on Lytton began to fear that if he stopped loving his younger cousin, he would never find it in himself to love another. He now felt cut off 'infinitely and eternally' from the innocence and delight of his summer passion:

> Can you imagine a country morning in August, with windows open, and late breakfast on the table, and flannel suits, and low collars round the neck? It was before the flood, when, as no one quite knew that anything would ever happen or even matter, we could all be happy together, and, as there was nobody else in the room, and I found myself standing behind him while he was finishing his sardine, I ventured to let my hand give one stroke to his brushed and charming hair. Oh! I do feel the same affection now, but with what regret, and what bitter shiverings round the fire. The best things come to us before we know they are coming, and vanish before we know they have come.[20]

'Alas! You and Duncan,' Maynard replied. 'I think you'd better go on loving him. Time works both ways. You know I am still in love with the idea of you two together.'[21] Yet to Lytton's surprise, the affair was to turn again – Duncan's affection appearing in such a way as to leave him in no doubt that, as Lytton told Maynard, 'he's absolutely mine'. It was, however, difficult for him to realise fully the joy that this brought, as he felt battered and exhausted by the course of the affair. Perversely he also found that, if anything, he loved Duncan 'a little less for being so absurd as to love me. But,' he concluded, 'this is a momentary contortion. We have reached the reign of Affection – but one can't expatiate; one can only accept.'[22]

The affair, in Lytton's mind at least, continued to seesaw, reaching the heights and then plunging heavily. During the Christmas period a chill seems to have fallen over their friendship, and Duncan kept away from Lancaster Gate. But the first week of January 1906 found both men guests of their aunt, Lady Colvile, at her home, Park Cottage, Ledbury, in Hertfordshire. Lytton had arrived with few expectations, even wondering if a five-day tête-à-tête with Duncan might leave him dissatisfied with Duncan's intellect. To his surprise, conditions were amorous and blissful, and Duncan impressed Lytton more than ever, as he confessed, again to Maynard:

> But how often didn't I feel that it was he who was the great person and that I was a mere ineffectual shade? His mind! – I didn't realise before what it was – the audacity, the strength, the amazing subtilty [*sic*] . . . he never once offended my sense of the good and true and suitable by any single word. But please remember – he's a *genius* – a colossal portent of fire and glory . . . His feelings transcend all – I have looked into his eyes, and the whole universe has swayed and swam and been abolished, and we have melted into one indescribable embrace. His features were moulded by nothing intermediary, but by the hand of God itself; they are plastic like living marble, they clothe a divinity, a quintessential soul. I rave; but I weep too. Looking at his face, I imagined last night the marks of time upon it. I saw the lines and the ruins and the desolation of age, I saw Death too, and the face composed in Death; and I prayed that the whole world might stand still for ever.[23]

This turbulent letter was the product of habit. Lytton frequently adopted an epistolary manner that was high-pitched and slightly camp. Real emotion is translated into heady, near-hysterical prose, partly to excite his audience. In this he did not fail. From Cambridge Maynard wrote:

> I had a very exciting breakfast this morning reading your letter. You have triumphed. You have proved these things possible. But yet, secretly, I was a little sad; partly I suppose envy, but chiefly, I think, because you insist so much he is a genius, I am still afraid that it's all impossible . . . I don't know what sort of state you must be in. Even I in a dull sort of looking glass way have been trembling with nervous excitement. I was totally unaware whether or not I had eaten anything this morning until I examined the plates.[24]

Then suddenly Duncan began talking of Paris. Some years before, his aunt, Lady Colvile, had given him £100 on the understanding that he was to use it as he wished when he came of age. As his twenty-first birthday approached, he conceived the idea of living and working in Paris for as long as this money lasted. (As it turned out, this gift enabled him to pay for his studies and amusements and to live without undue starvation in the French capital for an entire year.)

On his birthday, 21 January 1906, Duncan invited Lytton to lunch with him and his parents at their Hampstead home. Also present was Colonel Young. Duncan told Lytton that the Colonel was the first person he had ever loved. 'He's now a pale, rather nice but quite unbeautiful military man,' Lytton told Maynard, ' – about 43, I suppose. Seventeen years hence I shall be that age, and Duncan 38. How mad and horrible! The middle-aged fill me with frigid despair – they have so little to recommend them . . .'[25] Meanwhile, Lytton, aware that they would soon be parted, continued to regard Duncan with unease and jealousy. 'You know,' Maynard offered sagaciously, 'it will be better for you in many ways when Duncan is definitely across the sea than now when he is more often about to be than seen.'[26]

By now Lytton had no illusions as to his importance in Duncan's eyes. Soon after their week together at Ledbury, both had gone to a dance at their relations, the Ridpaths. It amused Lytton ('champagne, youths and utter absurdity reign so completely'), and he watched as Duncan fell in love with a pink-and-white-faced male cousin called Raper ('Rather a propitious name?'). Writing to Maynard, he threw in the conclusion that there could be no doubt that Duncan's 'amours will be something too extravagant as time goes on'.[27]

The prospect of Duncan living footloose and fancy-free in Paris filled his female relatives with alarm: his mother and Lady Strachey were aware that, in the opinion of many, the Parisian art world was inextricably linked with debauchery. Pippa Strachey confessed to Lytton that she feared Duncan might become 'infected'. Lytton reassured her, stressing her cousin's inherent goodness. Afterwards he told Maynard: 'The conversation with Pippa was particularly curious because it took place in my room – as we were going to bed – in the exact position where, five hours earlier, D and I had had a rather bad fit of the gropes. I shudder to think how fearfully infected she would have found his mind if she'd looked in then – oh no, it was all right, I'd locked the door! But really, if he'd never done that with me, how could I have been so certain that he was free from all chance of infection?'[28]

Duncan had told his benefactor, Lady Colvile, of his plans with considerable nervousness. Her small house at Ledbury sat in the grounds of an Elizabethan manor owned by a rich banker called Biddulph whose wife, Lady Elizabeth, invited Lady Colvile and Duncan to tea. On hearing of Duncan's decision to spend time in Paris, Lady Elizabeth offered to supply him with introductions, to a retired governess and also to some 'old friends of the family', the de Gramonts, neither of which Duncan took up. But later in life, when he learnt of the de Gramonts' connection with Proust, Duncan could not help wondering what his life in Paris would have been like had he entered their world.

Still at Ledbury, he was entranced when Aunt Lell read aloud from

Dickens, an author he did not normally like, and thought her still more wonderful when she played Offenbach on the piano, her contralto voice trilling along in superb Victorian fashion in duet with his mother's. Deep snow lay on the ground and he took his mother tobogganing in a nearby park, excitedly whooshing them both down a precipice at a frightening speed, until his mother was hurled out in hysterics.

It was finally arranged that he would leave for Paris on 18 February. Up to the very last day he was struggling with a portrait of one of his Ridpath cousins. At the same time his relationship with Lytton continued to wax and wane. When Duncan cut short his visits, Lytton was left all too aware of a resistance, a need on Duncan's part to keep himself separate. Then, at the start of February, Lytton was thrown into further turmoil by the news that his younger brother, James, had made a confession of love to Duncan. In a dither, Lytton wrote to Maynard, 'Did James propose? And did Duncan accept him? Or reject him? Or wobble? Lord! I should like to know.'[29]

Amid all this fuss Duncan (who felt almost moved to love by James's stricken state, but did not in fact return his affection) made his first appearance at the Friday Club as Lytton's guest. This exhibiting and discussion society had been founded the previous summer by Vanessa Stephen, who wanted to try and create in London an artistic milieu similar to that she had briefly experienced on a visit to Paris.[30] As such it was sympathetic to Duncan. But as a newcomer and guest Duncan probably did not make his presence conspicuous.

On 18 February he finally departed. Lytton travelled with him to Paris, *en route* to Menton. Paris had already received an exodus of students from the Westminster School of Art, and Duncan had arranged to join Forestier and two others at the Hôtel de l'Univers et du Portugal in the Rue Croix des Petits Champs, a stone's throw from the Palais Royal. It was a curious haunt run by M. and Mme Troulet, the husband a faultlessly dressed shadow, the wife very up-to-the-minute, with her elevated *toupée*, impressive bust and ringed fingers. Just inside the hotel's entrance, in a little glass box, sat Rosalie, an old peasant woman in a white Berrichon cap, who seemed to live in this box, taking her meals alone there and keeping an eye on all who came in and out. She had brutally horrific tales about the behaviour of the Germans in the Franco-Prussian War and would hiss at Duncan, 'You must hate *les Allemands*.' She seemed devoid of affection for any human soul, yet warmed to Duncan, who, she said, had '*un bon coeur*'.

Once past Rosalie, the hotel residents found themselves in a dark hall. Through glass doors could be glimpsed the dining-room, which was also rather dim, though always set in festive fashion with mitred napkins and a great array of glasses, three to each setting. In the evening this room was transformed into a brightly lit spectacle, Mme Troulet presiding at the head of the table, where she ladled out soup for her guests. Duncan and his friends played no part in these occasions, for they belonged to a different tier of clients, who lived at the top of innumerable flights of stairs, in the attic rooms that led into each other without any linking passageway. These charming, light rooms, with their sloping ceilings and dormer windows, had been let, at very reasonable rates, to foreign students.

Duncan shared a room with Marius Forestier, with whom he was on easy terms. The two friends lay awake talking, laughing and arguing, their uncomplicated friendship allowing Duncan to bask in Forestier's devotion without the complications of sexual attraction. Forestier was not clever and when Lytton returned to Paris, Duncan quickly realised there was no point in introducing these two to each other: their approach to life was so different that they would have been incompatible. That Duncan himself enjoyed the company of both tells us much about his appreciation of very different individuals. He lacked neither discernment nor strong tastes of his own; but his approach to people was open, accepting, interested; and he was loved by others for letting them be what they were.

Forestier no doubt helped familiarise Duncan with French customs. On his visits to the Forestier home in West Dulwich, Duncan had experienced the kind of noisy, argumentative family life that seemed to him invincibly French. But released from his father's overpowering presence, Marius retained an unconscious melancholy that was, for Duncan, part of his charm. Many years later, Duncan heard through another friend that Forestier had committed suicide. While the question 'why?' reverberated without answer in his mind, he was at the same time not altogether surprised by the news.

Forestier's name always remained associated in Duncan's mind with 'one of the most inglorious episodes of my stay in Paris'.[31] One of Forestier's French uncles had sent money for him and a friend to spend educatively, in a brothel, a custom perhaps more common then than it is today. Duncan was chosen as Forestier's ally and given his share of the money. Before any plan was hatched, Duncan – having learnt from Michel, the servant who spent hours polishing the floors by skating back and forth with pads attached to his shoes, that the house opposite was a brothel – had one evening bolted through its door alone. Afterwards he was unable to fathom whether it was shyness or pure selfishness that had caused him to act unilaterally. He appears to have been as open to this experience as to any other that came his way, and though embarrassed to find himself, once inside the house, the only male confronting Madame and a circle of ladies sitting on stuffed chairs, he quickly chose the youngest and prettiest and found her charming. 'I had only enough money for a *tournée*, and much too soon Madame's rap tap tap was heard on the door. But I had chosen well.'[32] The young woman begged him to return, but Duncan never saw her again.

On arriving in Paris Duncan had acted on Simon Bussy's advice and enrolled at the Académie Julian under Jean-Paul Laurens. To his mother, he very quickly admitted disappointment with the school, and that Laurens's own painting, which smacked of official Salon art, filled him with horror. He sought further help from Bussy, who supplied him with a letter of recommendation to Jacques-Emile Blanche, who had recently founded an *académie* called 'La Palette'. It was a small, informal school, having only some twenty students and not run for profit, the fees merely covering the cost of models and heat. Blanche brought to his teaching the same *savoir-faire* that made him a successful portraitist, able to adapt his approach and method according to his sitter and making adroit use of pose, setting or background detail to allude to his sitter's interests or character. As a portraitist, Blanche could keep up a flow of talk without affecting his concentration and, being much travelled and a man of the world, was never short of conversation. In William Rothenstein's opinion, there was no person known to him equipped with a more discriminating sense of good painting or good literature. Blanche took pleasure in his academy, visiting it twice a week. Bonnard and Vuillard were also listed as visiting artists, though Duncan never saw either of them. Blanche, on the other hand, appeared to enjoy teaching. Perhaps because his work at this time was very much under the spell of Sargent and had become rather slick, he impressed Duncan less as a painter than as a person.

He was a big, strong man, somewhat blunt-featured but sharp-tongued. He came from a wealthy family; his father, Dr Emile Blanche, a noted pathologist, ran a private lunatic asylum. The family enjoyed a summer villa at Dieppe, where their son made friends with its many visitors, his studio at the Bas Fort Blanc becoming a centre of attraction for Degas, Whistler, Helleu, Boldini, Sargent, Sickert, Beardsley and Charles Conder. He was very much at home with the English, having taken refuge with his mother in London during the Franco-Prussian War and retaining as some of his earliest recollections English people and the English tongue spoken at his father's house in Passy. A pronounced Anglophile, Blanche devoted more space in his book of memoirs, *Portraits of a Lifetime*, to his familiarity with London society than to his life in France.

Towards the end of his life Blanche turned rather bitter, denouncing Matisse, Derain, Picasso and others, whom he felt had detracted from the recognition he himself deserved. But there was no hint of this in 1906 and Duncan found him a stimulating and exciting teacher. Blanche often took his students to the Louvre on Mondays, when it was shut to the public, and there would talk about certain pictures or give a critical appreciation of a copy that a student was making. He had an unexpected passion for an aspect of the Louvre that was far from first-rate – its collection of English eighteenth-century portraits. Standing in front of a Hoppner, he would point to a patch of white in the dress and declare it to be the most brilliant bit of painting in the entire Louvre. This was the only moment when Duncan could not share his teacher's enthusiasm; he looked hard and searchingly for aesthetic significance but could see only a patch of purest Flake White. Mostly, however, he found Blanche's comments very much to the point and never forgot him saying of a Chardin, '*C'est bien émouvant, c'est le drame de la lumière.*' Duncan himself was copying a Chardin at this time but, as he afterwards regretted, was too shy to show it to Blanche.[33]

Bussy had recommended La Palette partly because he and Dorothy thought that Duncan should benefit from the atmosphere of artistic discussion and enthusiasm generated by young male French students. Nearly all the pupils at Blanche's school were French, with the exception of Charles Maresco Pearce, who had earlier studied under Augustus John and William Orpen at their Chelsea School of Art. Many of the French students were far from serious, but there was a core of dedicated pupils to which Duncan belonged.

Though he found it an effort to wake up every morning, Duncan worked hard in Paris. After coffee and a brioche in a nearby *crémerie*, he would arrive at La Palette at eight o'clock. The morning session finished at noon, by which time he was always very hungry and so hurried to a little restaurant nearby in the Boulevard S⁺-Germain, which was patronised by students of all sorts. There, with Forestier and other ex-Westminster pupils, he had a decent meal, a carafe of wine and coffee for less than two francs. Most afternoons he spent in the Louvre. In the evening he sometimes treated himself to a meal at La Mère Duval, a restaurant not far from the hotel, where the clients ate beneath a high, iron roof, its structure plainly visible. Duncan's favourite meal was potato soup, *raie au beurre noir* and *confiture d'orange*. After this he would sometimes study anatomy or copy drawings in the library of the Ecole des

Beaux-Arts, a practice that he gave up when he felt tiredness was affecting his eyesight.

He began to make new friends. One of these was Constance Lloyd, a well-to-do Quaker girl, one of several daughters of a rich Birmingham banker. Though a talented painter, she had been disappointed by the Slade School of Art, where Professor Tonks (who once admitted he was a hurdy-gurdy with only two tunes – construction and proportion) had no conception of her abilities. She had then attended the class in Kensington that Simon Bussy had started on his first visit to England and had fared better, becoming a lasting friend of the Bussy family. She had not coincided with Duncan at Bussy's classes, but in 1906, while living in Paris under the weight of parental disapproval, light of pocket and sharing her small Montparnasse apartment with her friend Aline Bayley, another of Bussy's pupils, she was given Duncan's address by Pippa Strachey. Her first letter to him at the Hôtel de l'Univers et du Portugal must have given him some idea of her character, as she could not resist asking, 'Is Portugal then not included in the Universe?' Once introduced, Duncan frequently went copying in the Louvre with Constance and Aline, or shared a meal with them in the evening. Through Constance, Duncan also met other characters living in the Montparnasse quarter.

His mother's sister, Daisy McNeil, a great traveller and seldom without friends in any country, knew a French family whom she thought Duncan might like to meet. He duly received an invitation that took him one Sunday, in his best clothes, to a distant suburb. Everything – the garden gate, the lilac, the white muslin dresses, the friendly daughters and magisterial father – upheld a perfect image of the French bourgeoisie. But one visit was enough and Duncan did not repeat the experience.

Simon and Dorothy Bussy's contacts were more useful. Their most rewarding introduction brought Duncan the friendship of the erudite painter and art historian Auguste Bréal. 'We are writing to the Bréals about him [Duncan],' Dorothy told Lady Strachey. 'He couldn't have a better pilot and guide than Auguste and they have a very large and interesting circle of friends.'[34]

Bréal had become known to the Stracheys during the period 1899 to 1902 when he and his family had stayed in England, renting cottages in the Limpsfield area to be near Bréal's friend, Ellen Heath, the painter and intimate friend of Edward Garnett, who lived close by with his wife Constance. Owing to Garnett's intervention as a publisher's reader, Duckworth's had been persuaded to publish Bréal's books in English;

Constance Garnett translated his *Rembrandt* (1902) and Dorothy Bussy his *Velàzquez* (1904).

Duncan went to see Bréal soon after arriving in Paris, while he was unhappily attending the Académie Julian. He was relieved to hear Bréal say that Laurens's pictures were ugly and that Blanche was a better alternative. Bréal, with his black pointed beard, bright eyes and bubbling vivacity, was eager to help. It was he who obtained Duncan a ticket to the Beaux-Arts library and offered to introduce the young man to any painter he cared to meet. Duncan appears not to have pursued Bréal's offer of further introductions. However, when in the course of conversation Bréal suggested they should visit Degas, Duncan was on tenterhooks with excitement. But the suggestion, so swiftly made, was equally suddenly dropped, Bréal moving on with the remark that he preferred Renoir's work to that of Degas, who, Bréal thought, hated everything he painted. Duncan offered a defence in faltering French, but Bréal merely replied that his initial remark had been mere opinion, and there the matter ended.

This was not the only opportunity that Duncan missed. The previous autumn Matisse, Derain, Manguin, Marquet and Vlaminck had created a sensation at the Salon d'Automne, their use of pure colour giving rise to the nickname *les fauves* (wild beasts). The following spring, between 19 March and 7 April, the Druet Gallery mounted a large one-artist exhibition of Matisse's work. Coming so soon after the furore of the previous year it would have been essential viewing for anyone wanting to keep abreast of recent developments in art. Duncan, however, did not see it; nor later that year did he visit the seminal Salon d'Automne, where again Matisse's work was the subject of controversy. His friends described to him some of the pictures on show. Duncan felt he understood enough from what they said not to have to go and view the works himself. Even while causing a sensation, Matisse failed to dislodge Chardin in Duncan's pantheon. Undisturbed, the young man happily went on copying in the Louvre.

It was enough, perhaps, in his first few months in Paris to gain familiarity with his surroundings. 'I sometimes think Paris the most lovely place in the world', he told Lytton:

– on a fine afternoon walking up the Tuileries through the Arc du Carousel into the Louvre in my grey suit with its *ligne d'invitation* and my yellow stick. But the ordinary boulevard in one's ordinary clothes on a wet day which it always is, is the most depressing place on earth. On Sunday night I went to see *Le Misanthrope* but as I had read it before I was thoroughly disappointed . . . I had formed very different notions of their characters or rather of their persons.[35]

He was happier listening to the Misanthrope's tirade on the gramophone in the shop where, after dialling a number and putting a coin in the slot, you could hear Sarah Bernhardt make her Phèdre speech or listen to Yvette Guilbert's latest song. These were his discoveries, classic prose and popular songs for the moment catching his attention while one of the most revolutionary periods in the history of art passed him by. Duncan's focus of enquiry remained fixed on the Louvre. He copied not only Chardin but also Terborch, Rubens and Rembrandt, and developed a passion for Poussin, especially his drawings. His nonchalant attitude towards avant-garde fashions left Duncan able to absorb in depth the art of the past so that later, after he had passed through a period of bold experimentation, he could return to traditional themes and reinvent pastoral and bathing scenes, the amorous gambollings of gods, goddesses, mermaids, satyrs and other mythological creatures, landscapes and still-lifes in modern terms.

FOUR

Sic Transit

Ill with a cold and diarrhoea, Duncan took to his bed in early April 1906, depressed and heartily sick of Paris after only two months. His spirits were so low that the sight of a bunch of cowslips, left at the hotel by Constance Lloyd, who had heard he was feeling seedy, caused tears of gratitude.

If physically demoralised, he was also discovering that though Paris might offer a great many distractions, life was no simpler here than elsewhere. In this city Duncan was to witness the emotional complications of others and to suffer his own. He had been aware, shortly before leaving England, that James Strachey's sudden declaration of love had upset another Cambridge undergraduate, Walter Lamb. It was therefore slightly disconcerting to learn that Walter's brother, Henry Lamb, had, with his mistress Euphemia, taken lodgings in the same street as himself. They did not stay long, but the following year they returned, now married, and Lamb enrolled at La Palette, where he and Duncan met daily. By then Lamb's friend, the painter Augustus John, was also in Paris, with his mistress Dorelia. She fell in love with Lamb and, with John's approval, conducted an affair with him while Euphemia was away. Duncan was made uneasy, not by their unorthodox relationships but by the posturing and emotional dishonesty. Lamb's cynicism was foreign to Duncan's temperament. 'That Lamb family sickens me,' he told Lytton in April 1907, 'and that man John.'[1] As John's wife, Ida Nettleship, was a close friend of Constance Lloyd, Duncan learnt more than he wished about the Lamb–John ménage. He felt uncomfortably surrounded by a tangle of relationships and in his 'Paris Memoir' he recollected that drama seemed constantly in the air.

In April 1906, however, the drama was almost entirely of his own making. When Arthur Hobhouse from Trinity College, Cambridge, visited Paris, Duncan fell in love with him and to his surprise found that his love was returned. This complicated his relations with Lytton, whom he felt obliged to inform. It also caused additional reverberations because Hobhouse had been the nominee of both Lytton and Maynard for election to the Apostles; both had fallen in love with him and temporarily out of sympathy with each other when Keynes succeeded in having a mild affair with the young man. It was as if they were all caught up in a Scottish reel, the insistent pulse of the music and its interminable repetitions obliging them to form new partnerships.

Hobhouse was an unlikely partner in this game of passion. He was the nephew of the formidably high-minded Fabian, Beatrice Webb, and the son of a Liberal MP and privy counsellor. He himself had studied medicine at St Andrew's before reading natural sciences at Cambridge. He eventually entered the legal profession, followed his father into politics and remained an active Liberal. He also had religious leanings; by 1910 he was living in a Roman Catholic settlement in Wapping. Even as a young man, though irresistible in appearance, having fair, slightly frizzy hair and aquiline features, Hobhouse already displayed a certain woodenness. Maynard once wrote of him to Lytton, 'He never never *adds* anything. He lives according to rules and . . . is always trying to do what he vaguely thinks ought to be done in such circumstances. He never judges anything individual on its own merits.'[2] Reminiscing about this affair in old age, Duncan likewise complained that Hobhouse had been 'full of unnecessary duties'.[3]

Lytton received the news of Duncan's latest amour during the course of his visit to Menton. He had just turned twenty-six, a fact that left him shuddering with disbelief and which he did his best to disguise. Still worse was the sight of his Aunt Lell, caught not in her usual whirl of Menton tea parties, charity bazaars and mission meetings, but in bed one morning without her wig, while his Uncle Trevor, as was his habit, prowled the seashore in a flapping overcoat, one of life's wrecks, abandoned, solitary, odd and slightly unhinged. 'Whenever I think of old age,' Lytton wrote to Duncan, 'I turn pale with horror – the ruin, the loneliness, the regret.'[4]

Duncan had been much on his mind and figured frequently in conversations during Lytton's visits to Roquebrune to see his sister Dorothy and her husband Bussy. At this time they were radiantly happy and fully settled at La Souco, built on the hillside looking down over the Mediterranean coastline. Although the house contained many exquisite things – Chippendale chairs, a Rodin bronze of Paolo and Francesca, books, paintings and pots – its white walls also created an airy feel that Lytton enjoyed. He relayed to Duncan advice from his sister and brother-in-law. 'Dorothy advises you to pay a visit to Durand-Ruel's private house, which, she says, is crammed with Impressionists and open to the public once a week. Simon says that the pictures he showed in

England were simply the "rebut" of his collection – so it must be pretty superb.'[5]

'I have something to tell you,' Duncan's letter to Lytton began. It told of Hobhouse's visit to Paris and attempted to persuade Lytton of the reality of the situation:

> I know you will think that our feelings aren't strong for one another or that I am amusing myself without knowing it . . . But he was so honest, so humble, so very conscious how unhappy he was because of them [his feelings for Duncan] that I nearly burst with pity for him. He knows about you and hopes that you won't be jealous of him. I honestly believe he is very fond of me. He told me he loved me as much as is possible for him to love anybody. I suppose you will be enraged if I say it seems to make no difference between you and me. But as far as I can judge . . . it does not.[6]

Duncan ended his letter with the remark that there was no embargo on Lytton telling Maynard, because 'Hobby' felt rather proud of his feelings.

Lytton, of course, wrote to Maynard the day that he received Duncan's letter. Maynard reassuringly replied that, being as always 'in love with you and Duncan as a unity', he could not help feeling that Hobhouse was no more than an episode.[7]

Lytton saw clearly, however, the difference that this new relationship would make. 'It's true, I suppose,' he wrote to Duncan, 'that we can like each other as before, and kiss each other, and go through, as before, the whole dreary phantasmagoria of desire: but we can never be alone together.'[8]

It was at this point that Duncan took to his bed, ill and depressed. He had read Lytton's letter in a restaurant and promptly burst into tears. It was intolerable to think that he had made Lytton miserable, this friend to whom he might always want to tell things he could tell no one else. He was wounded by Lytton's reference to 'the whole dreary phantasmagoria of desire', claimed that he felt nothing sensual towards Hobhouse, yet in the same breath admitted a constant desire to embrace him. However, Hobhouse had now left Paris. At one point Duncan had feared he was departing before any real intimacy had been established, but they had travelled together as far as Amiens, where they were so enwrapped in conversation that Hobhouse missed three trains in succession, thereby convincing Duncan of his love. Afterwards unwell and in bed, Duncan longed for Hobhouse's presence and would have got on the next train to London had not his mother's arrival in Paris been imminent. Feeling a selfish brute, he wrote instead to Lytton, begging him to come to Paris for a few days.

Lytton, whose poor health had already begun to turn his thoughts homewards, agreed to spend a week in Paris *en route* to London. Duncan was greatly cheered, and in the meantime accompanied his mother to the races at Auteuil, where he was charmed by the fashionable dresses and fascinated by the jockeys and the horses.

When Lytton arrived at the Hôtel de l'Univers et du Portugal he was cold and feverish, had a raging temperature and went straight to bed. A doctor prescribed large doses of quinine. Duncan was so alarmed by Lytton's state that he wrote to Pippa Strachey, asking her to come to Paris to help look after her brother. She did so, but Lytton's recovery coincided with a railway strike and their departure had to be delayed another week.

Duncan sat on the end of Lytton's bed, gazing at him, so his cousin felt, with loving coldness. James Strachey wrote, telling Lytton of his conviction that Hobhouse had first fallen for Duncan some three months back in Cambridge. Hobhouse also wrote, telling Lytton piously that recent events were for the 'universal good', as he had now learnt for the first time to love. Looking up at Duncan's strong and radiant face, Lytton realised more fully than before that he had irredeemably lost his love and it would be foolish to beg for unwilling kisses. Feeling a complete wreck, he returned home with Pippa in the first week of May.

Maynard was right in his estimation that Hobhouse would be no more than an 'episode' in Duncan's life. Maynard knew, from his own brief fling with this young man, that Hobhouse was disinclined towards physical intimacy; through Lytton, Maynard also knew of Duncan's appetite for sex and guessed that it might quickly exacerbate Hobhouse's need to withdraw. And he was right: when Duncan next saw Hobhouse, in July when he returned home for the summer, their relationship was far from easy. A few days after his arrival, Duncan wrote to his friend:

I am so depressed by the most appalling doubts and fears that I must arrange to come and see you if only for a day/hour at the very shortest interval possible. When can it be? Is Monday next the nearest? My darling if I could only be sure you *really* loved me I should be perfectly happy, but if I am deceiving you into believing you are or you are by any chance deceiving yourself, my dear I believe I should nearly die . . .

Don't be frightened, it's I who am terrified . . . It's only when I think of the awful catastrophes – you and Keynes, Lytton and me – that a shudder of death makes me rigid with fear. Oh my dearest angel do be able to tell me it is different than it was with Keynes.[9]

Whatever Hobhouse's reply, he agreed to accompany Duncan on a visit to Rothiemurchus that summer. But in the autumn, through a desultory exchange of letters, the friendship petered out. It finally ended on 18 December 1906. 'Hobber told Duncan this evening very kindly that he had no feelings at all towards him,' James Strachey told Lytton.[10] 'I feel rather lonely,' Duncan had admitted to James, adding *'Sic transit'*.[11]

In his 'Paris Memoir', a frank account of this period that Duncan wrote for a group of friends, he overlooked this affair completely. Though it caused such trauma at the time, it would seem that the relationship had little lasting significance. What he did choose to mention in his memoir was his mild flirtation with the eccentric Birmingham painter Maxwell Armfield.

Armfield was a curious character, outwardly timid and diffident, but tenaciously wedded to his own beliefs. He had become an artist against the wishes of his engineer father and had studied at Birmingham School of Art, where he had ignored most of the technical teaching on offer, developing a jewel-like style, partly influenced by his love of the Pre-Raphaelites, partly by his friendship with another Birmingham painter, Joseph Southall.

Some four years older than Duncan, Armfield had first approached him in the National Gallery, while Duncan was copying part of Piero della Francesca's *Nativity* under Simon Bussy's supervision. Duncan thought Armfield extremely handsome, if slightly effeminate, shared with him a love of music and did not mind when he began sending letters, written in an elaborate, old-fashioned script, in which he addressed Duncan as 'Piero'. The sentiments in these letters were, like his paintings, somewhat overwrought. Duncan, who could write emotional but never sentimental letters, must have disappointed him with his replies. But undeterred, Armfield argued that the separation caused by Duncan's months in Paris would stimulate the imagination and give to their friendship 'the elusive quality of artistry'.[12] Duncan found these letters equivocal, flattering though it was to be told he had a Gallic fascination, for Armfield admitted that Duncan's 'pagan irresponsibility and exquisite gay airiness' both attracted and troubled his nonconformist conscience.

Armfield admired the Pre-Raphaelites' concern with truthfulness in art and abhorred the loose, painterly effects favoured by French artists. Yet he himself was admired in France, perhaps because certain of his paintings hinted at an erotic romanticism similar to that found in the work of Gustave Moreau. When some of his pictures were accepted by the Salon, he arrived in Paris and stayed in Duncan's hotel. Throughout his short visit, and afterwards in letters, he warned Duncan against French influence in his painting. He feared that Degas's interest in the superficial and accidental would encourage Duncan to take short-cuts in his study of appearances. But his preaching always remained good-humoured and was done partly, as he admitted, to test his own feelings. He also had sufficient self-awareness to know that he was 'congenitally conservative and rather narrow'. Despite all his high-flown phrases and teasing innuendoes, he was thrown into horrified confusion when Duncan, imitating Lytton's farewell gesture on leaving Paris, tried to kiss him goodbye in public.

Alone in Paris, Duncan floated inwardly on a raft of parental love and support. 'Good-bye my precious boy,' his mother had written after his departure, 'I miss you very much but I hope Paris is going to do great things for you and that you are going to be very well and happy there.'[13] His father held the enlightened view that it was only in this city that drawing was thoroughly understood. Yet there were limitations to the relationship. With his father, especially, there was a greater than usual reserve, perhaps because of the silence and compromise that Bartle Grant's affairs imposed. Even with his mother, to whom he was devoted, Duncan came to realise that intimacy could be maintained only if he left much unspoken. Ethel Grant came from a part of society where indelicate matters, although recognised and understood, were not explicitly referred to. We catch a glimpse of her anxieties over Duncan in a letter that she wrote to Lytton, after he had informed her of Duncan's safe arrival in Paris: 'I have confidence in him, but I know that there are temptations for a young man, especially in a town like Paris, and I feel so powerless to help him. He is very reserved but I suppose there are some things that boys cannot speak to their mothers about.'[14] Wisely, she proceeded on these lines, tactfully renouncing any right to information.

Despite his emotional conflicts, Duncan continued to work happily at La Palette. By the end of March 1906 he had been allowed to begin painting from the model. His day now began in the Louvre, where he was still copying Old Masters, and continued after lunch in front of the 'nood', as Constance Lloyd called it. He had also begun to catch Blanche's attention, as he proudly told James Strachey: 'This distinguished portrait painter has been very kind to me, admired my drawings and daubs away a good deal on my tentative efforts to paint. At 4.30 I hurry round to a "croquis" or sketching class where one pays 5d and for two hours can draw from the model who changes poses every twenty-five minutes. After that I recross the river and dine at a little bouillon . . . and sometimes . . . go to a café with some quasi-friends or to the "concert rouge" where one gets excellent music and good coffee for 1/-.'[15]

He was glad that such a packed life left little time for introspection. When he did think about himself, Duncan underwent such doubts and mental contortions that it was agony if no one like Lytton was around to help. He continued to read obsessively, at dinner and at other free moments, and feared ruining himself at one particular bookshop on the Rue de Seine, which had an open-air stall. He was pleased to pick up an exquisitely printed edition of La Fontaine's fables and hoped to find Racine's plays in the same edition.

Towards the end of May he and a thousand others took part in the Quatr'Arts Ball. As the theme that year was Orientalism, the general effect was like some gigantic Eastern bazaar or a slave market by Delacroix, as there was a lot of exposed flesh. Duncan had never experienced anything like it. Though *au fait* with what the French call *le vice Anglais*, he had until now been insulated from blatant displays of sexual attraction. The following morning he felt twenty years older and proudly told Lytton, 'I have seen Lust walking about undisguised, debauchery carried to its limits, drunkenness and frenzy everywhere prevalent.' He himself had gone dressed as a warrior with scarlet spear, silver helmet and green and purple coat, but in the final reckoning the ball only confirmed his belief in 'the beauty of restraint in language, clothes and even actions'. He had, nevertheless, been vastly entertained. 'Everyone was exceedingly good natured and uproarious, the champagne was unlimited so that being fairly drunk I was able to stand shocks I might not otherwise have been able to hold and "comme spectacle" it was unrivalled.'[16]

Immediately before he returned to London at the end of his first stint in Paris, Duncan spent a week at Versailles. It was a favourite haunt and he had gone there often, on day outings, taking picnics and friends. 'It is more full of ghosts than any place I know,' he told Lytton.[17] Back in London he was faced with more fleshly apparitions. With Hobhouse still in the offing, Duncan had to manage his relations with Lytton carefully. When Lytton asked him to collaborate in the writing of an article on the painter Arthur Melville, Duncan declined, with the excuse that he was going to Somerset for two weeks, after which he intended leaving, at the end of July, for Scotland.

Duncan was at this time on good terms with his Scottish relations, a situation that was to alter when in the First World War he became a conscientious objector. The laird of Rothiemurchus was his cousin, the fourth John Peter Grant, who during the course of Duncan's summer visit conceived the idea of commissioning him to copy G. F. Watts's portrait of his grandfather, the second Sir John Peter Grant, which hung in the National Portrait Gallery. By September Watts's widow had granted permission for a copy to be made. Sadly, its whereabouts are unknown.

In the autumn of 1906 Duncan temporarily abandoned Paris and in October enrolled instead at the Slade School of Art.[18] He had not felt entirely at home in Paris and may have wanted an opportunity to see more of Hobhouse. Perhaps too he wanted more freedom. The Slade was run on very flexible lines: students had a choice of paying fees for the full or half-term and could also enroll for a three- or six-day week. Duncan enrolled as a three-day-a-week student for the second half of the autumn term and kept up a pretty regular attendance. It was, nevertheless, a backward step. According to Slade rules, all students on entry had to draw from the antique until judged sufficiently advanced to draw from life, and they were allowed to paint from life only when judged proficient at drawing. The dominant figure at that date was not the Slade professor Fred Brown, but his assistant, Professor Tonks, whose ideas about drawing, combined with his saturnine manner, had earnt him a legendary reputation. Duncan knew all too well the qualities that he admired and felt rather guilty at the ease with which he adapted himself to Slade requirements in order to earn Tonks's approval. 'I executed a drawing perfectly in the manner of Tonks,' he remembered. The bait was taken: Duncan's drawing was held up as an example of what good drawing should be. 'I felt rather mean, and also disillusioned.'[19]

In many ways this autumn was an unsatisfactory period. In October Duncan sat in Leicester Square, waiting for a canvas to be stretched, and wrote to James Strachey. He was glad that James had decided he was no longer in love with him and that a mutually strong affection was retained. But he refused to be angered by James's denigratory remarks about Hobhouse. James was not the only Strachey anxiously concerned about Duncan's love life. Immediately after his return home in December, Lytton wrote to Maynard, 'I saw Duncan yesterday for a little. My feelings fluctuate almost as much as Hobber declares his do – (1) excitement (2) spiritual affection (3) mere lust (4) intellectual interest (5) jealousy (6) boredom (7) despair (8) indifference. As you may imagine (5) was caused by the entrance of Pippa.'[20]

Despite Hobhouse's declared absence of feeling, Duncan remained hopelessly in love and felt shattered every time they met. A bout of influenza added to his depression. The only positive outcome of his abortive relationship with Hobhouse was that it left him with a tenet of belief that was to remain at the centre of his philosophy of life. As he explained to James Strachey:

> I saw Arthur yesterday and it nearly did for me. I suppose I have a wrong conception of life, and so I must be more or less unhappy all my life. I wish I could die in an ecstasy of song like Isolde, it seems such an easy way and delightful one out of difficulty. I went to *Tristan* last night so am rather in a pulp.
> I must say I think the perception of beauty is a good *moral* quality. I used not to think so. It makes no end of difference because with it one can face the truth however ghastly. Without it I couldn't have borne *Tristan*, I should have gone straight to Waterloo Bridge – and over.[21]

He was still very much in need of Lytton's friendship, partly because he could discuss homosexual feelings freely with him, but also because his cousin had an interest in art and went regularly to exhibitions. 'If it weren't for you I am sure I should not be able to bear life now,' Duncan told his friend in January 1907.

Though association with the Stracheys had brought Duncan into contact with the Stephen family, he did not yet attend their Thursday evenings at 46 Gordon Square. These had begun soon after the four Stephen siblings moved from Kensington to Bloomsbury, where these 'at homes' became a regular meeting place for those friends who in time became known as 'Bloomsbury'. At first the evenings comprised an uneasy mix of old and new friends. It took a while for Thoby Stephen's Cambridge friends, with their well-established male camaraderie, to feel at ease with his two sisters. Such was the gap between the sisters and these young men that in November 1906 even Lytton learnt indirectly of Thoby Stephen's untimely death from typhoid, following a visit made by the Stephen family to Greece and Turkey. Soon afterwards came a further piece of news concerning Vanessa: two days after Thoby's death she had accepted, having previously refused it, Clive Bell's proposal. They were married the following spring.

At some point, as 1906 drew to a close, Duncan decided to return to Paris. Early the next year he reappeared at the Hôtel de l'Univers et du Portugal and was rapturously received by Mme Triolet. When he asked if there was a room, Rosalie, on guard as usual in her glass box, replied, 'But for whom would there be a room if there wasn't one for you?' He slipped back easily into his former life. 'I hadn't been in the Louvre two minutes before I felt I had never left it, so soaked am I without knowing it in Paris. I find I had remembered all of the horrors but none of the charms which are many.'[22] So he wrote to Lytton on his twenty-second birthday, grateful, however, for Lytton's promise to visit him should life become unbearable, as Duncan still feared it might.

He was affectionately greeted by his colleagues at La Palette but dismayed to see that women were now admitted as students. It was a relief to learn that he was not expected to speak to them, as they were mostly Russian or Czech. While he had been away, La Palette had acquired an international reputation and Blanche had moved to larger premises, which included a dining-room, library, salon, piano and even a WC, as the students proudly showed Duncan. This fine establishment was situated in the Rue du Val de Grâce in the then fashionable *quartier* of Montparnasse. But a glamorous address did not help Blanche: in his memoirs he admitted feeling unequal to the task of correcting the work of all the 'self-styled geniuses' who now descended on him, many of whom, to the consternation of both Blanche and his assistant, Charles Cottet, had no desire to learn about anything except Fauvism. Duncan found this obsession with the style of the moment meretricious. The row of earnest Swedes he found hard at work at their easels every morning when he arrived at the studio may have further diminished his willingness to see the point of Matisse's work.

He decided to look for lodgings closer to La Palette and found a bright but not large room off the Boulevard Raspail, at 22 Rue Delambre, run by a Mme Lizot. It was close to Constance Lloyd's flat and to the Bréals'. Early in February 1907 he moved in. His window looked out on to an open space where flats were about to be built. The room was heated by a china stove in which he burnt *roulets*. Near the stove was a table at which he wrote and on which he ranged his collection of books – Shakespeare, Molière, Racine, La Fontaine, a guide to Paris, *The Origin of Species* and Blake's poems. Equally important to Duncan were his visits to the Louvre, where once again he began copying. He chose a watercolour by Rubens in which a youth flies through the air with a portrait of the far from dainty Marie de' Medici to show Henri IV. 'It sounds bizarre,' Duncan admitted to Lytton, 'but there are a great many other characters in the sky and on the earth which carry it beyond criticism.'[23]

He showed this picture to Lytton's cousin, St Loe Strachey, and his wife when they visited Paris. St Loe was editor of the *Spectator*, then the most widely read political paper, liberal in tone. When shown the Rubens, St Loe remarked that it was 'very fine official painting', which left Duncan marvelling at his gift for the pre-coined phrase. But he enjoyed the company of these two Stracheys, especially St Loe's historical tales and gossip. In turn, St Loe must have warmed to Duncan, as two years later he commissioned him to write four reviews for the *Spectator*.

For his breakfast cup of coffee, Duncan often went to the Café du Dome on the corner of the Rue Delambre and the Boulevard Raspail. Because it was a small place, it was impossible to ignore another English painter who also made use of this café – Wyndham Lewis, then unknown but later to become a dynamic figure within the Vorticist movement. Duncan's gorge rose at the mere sight of Lewis, though he could not understand why: Lewis always had interesting things to talk about and Duncan found himself drawn in and obliged to reply. Nevertheless, after seeing him, Duncan sank into the depths of despair. Lewis, it seems, had a knack of off-loading bad feelings, as Lady Ottoline Morrell later observed. She once invited Lewis to a tea party and wondered if anyone other than Lewis could manage to cast such gloom over the proceedings simply by the way in which he devoured his bread and honey.

A performance of *Electra* gave Duncan the opportunity to see some superb acting. Thrilled by the play, he told Lytton that he would never forget the shiver that ran through the audience when, in reaction to the false tale that Orestes is dead, Clytemnestra shrieks with mad joy, and Electra with agonised despair. He was equally passionate about Poussin's drawings ('so grand and splendid and at the same time so intimate in a conscientious way')[24] and pleased that Manet's *Olympia* had at last gone on display in the Louvre. His appetite for books had not lessened, and youthful excitement accompanied his every new discovery, whether in literature or art. A Rembrandt he was copying, of a young man in a black cap with stick in hand, seemed to him 'nearly divine'. At the same time he was astounded by *Coriolanus* and *Timon of Athens*, both of which he read for the first time, and took issue with Lytton's opinion that the character of Coriolanus had not been worked out properly. But the book that utterly delighted him this spring was *Tristram Shandy* – 'my constant companion at meals . . . I feel rather lonely without him. It is certainly infinitely the best novel I have ever read, yes better even than Jane [Austen].'[25]

He still showed no inclination to learn about the latest developments in art, though he paid careful attention to the Impressionists, visiting Durand-Ruel's, admiring especially the Renoirs and struggling with Degas, whose stature he recognised but whose intensive research he found oppressive. However, one of Degas's pictures that he saw at Durand-Ruel's stung him into intense admiration. This picture, simply titled *Interior*, but which several writers who knew Degas personally insisted should have been called *The Rape*, has given rise to a variety of interpretations.[26] The positioning of the man, who leans against the door of the bedroom, hands in pockets, and the half-dressed woman turned away from him and slumped on a chair, suggest a sombre sexual drama; Duncan thought it could be a scene straight out of a Maupassant tale. He told Lytton, 'But there wasn't the smallest article in the room from the lady's earrings to the nail scissors on the table that didn't seem quivering with the most vital importance. And it was so full of beauty too . . . '[27] The rich, dark colouring, the use of floral wallpaper to heighten the claustrophobia and the subtle effects of light were ingredients that reappeared a year or two later in Duncan's own psychological drama, *Crime and Punishment*.[28]

More at home in Paris than he had been the previous year, Duncan was pleased to discover that Mrs Maitland and her daughter Helen, whom he had met in Florence in 1904, were living in the Place St Sulpice. Though poor, they were a little richer than Duncan and his student friends, for whom their flat became another home. The two women paid five francs a day to have their meals sent up from Foyot's, a nearby restaurant, whose beef steaks were so generously proportioned that they could easily be shared with casual guests. Duncan, though aggravated by Mrs Maitland's gullibility – she was then studying painting under the instructions of a quack, who insisted that his pupils had to dance on the roof every morning and prepare their canvases with the yolks of ducks' eggs – admired the gallant manner in which she lived. Nor did he ever forget the sweet, piping voice with which Helen sang the songs she was learning at a school for cantors.

Various artists congregated in the Maitlands' flat: Ian Strang, son of the well-known painter William Strang, Henry Lamb and the painter and mosaicist Boris Anrep.[29] Like Constance Lloyd, the Maitlands were close to the Augustus John circle and Duncan soon learnt that John's wife, Ida, was dying in a Paris hospital. But it was a tragedy happening at a considerable remove from himself, for on the few occasions that he did meet John, his mistress Dorelia and Lamb in bars or restaurants, they were often so drunk that he got little out of them. A background figure to all this was another of Constance Lloyd's friends, Gwen John, who lived alone with her cats on the outskirts of Paris.

Used to the exacting intellectual demands of the Strachey family, Duncan was perhaps ill-at-ease amid the laxity of this Bohemian circle. Its emphatic heterosexual emphasis may also have undermined his sense of self. It was James Strachey whom Duncan most wanted to see that March, for he was intrigued to learn that his cousin had formed a sudden passion for Rupert Brooke. At Duncan's invitation, James visited Paris

later that month and was shortly followed by two others: Maynard
Keynes, now working in the India Office, and the mathematician H. T. J.
(Harry) Norton. Duncan, as he often did with visitors, took them to
Versailles, where Keynes ruined its romance by talking unceasingly about
its waterworks and how the management of them compared with the
Unter der Linden in Berlin. Keynes and Norton had been seen off at
Charing Cross by Lytton, who was given an account of their visit
immediately on their return.

Afterwards Lytton wrote to Duncan, expressing the hope that he had
liked Maynard better than before. As Strachey was aware, there was
something in Keynes which, despite his brilliance, did not vibrate; a
spiritual deadness that made him obtuse in some situations or, in
Lytton's words, 'intolerably dim'. This, he thought, would not irritate
Duncan, as he was far too good-natured. But the vagaries of his friends,
Lytton realised, were trivial compared with the dire warning presented
by Duncan's sightings of Augustus John. These left Lytton shuddering
with horror: 'I often feel that the only thing to do is to chuck up
everything, and make a dash for some such safe, secluded office-stool as is
pressed by dear Maynard's happy bottom. The dangers of freedom are
appalling!'[30]

When Lytton learnt that the Bells, together with Virginia and Adrian
Stephen, were planning to visit Paris that spring, he sent Vanessa a note
in one of his letters to Clive. 'My dear Vanessa, will you look up my little
cousin when you're in Paris? He would like it very much, and this is his
address – Duncan Grant, 22 Rue Delambre, Boulevard Raspail.'[31]
Duncan, forewarned of their arrival by Lytton, was told that he might
find their company amusing but that he could easily avoid seeing much of
them, if this went against his wishes. At Clive's invitation ('will you come
and wrangle about pictures with us at the Louvre on Saturday
afternoon?'[32]) Duncan met them in the Louvre's Salon Court and dined
with them that night and on one or two subsequent occasions. 'Clever
and amusing, wonderfully lively and good looking,' ran Clive Bell's
report to Lytton.[33] Duncan was equally smitten. 'What a quartet!' he
wrote. 'I seem to like them all so much, after these frogs and people. I feel
I should rather soon be bored with Bell and he with me, but he's been
very charming. As for Virginia I think she's probably extremely witty and
amazingly beautiful, and then there's old Adrian.'[34] Only Vanessa escaped
comment, which may suggest that Duncan found her difficult to fathom.
At one point in the course of their meetings he had been dismayed to find
himself sharply at odds with her in his opinion that Rembrandt was one
of the greatest painters in the world.

Immediately after the Bells and Stephens left Paris, Duncan moved again, to a large studio room at 9 Rue Campagne Première. In this square room, high up and with a window taking up almost one entire wall and looking out to the sky, he felt cut off from the world and indifferent to each new scandal attached to either Henry Lamb or Augustus John. The former occupant, an American, had left behind all the necessary furniture. The building itself reminded Duncan of a prison, its long, silent corridors leading to entrance doors behind which one remained wholly unaware of any other inhabitants. As far as Duncan could recall, he never spoke to a single person in the block.

Here Pippa Strachey visited him on her way through Paris – a heart-warming presence, 'triumphant', Duncan thought, in her aloofness from gossip. Here, too, he hung up a disembowelled rabbit beside a cabbage and other still-life ingredients, in an attempt to paint a Chardin. In May the weather turned so bitterly wet and cold that the chestnut avenues lay thickly strewn with torn-off buds and fresh green leaves.

That same month Maxwell Armfield wrote, asking Duncan to join him at Chartres. Duncan did so, wanting a break from Paris and hoping also that there might be the chance of a flirtation. He was indeed '*ébloui*' by the beauty of the statues ornamenting the north porch of Chartres Cathedral, thought the glass heavenly and the building itself more impressive than any other Gothic church, including Amiens, that he had ever seen. Armfield, whose memoirs incorrectly suggest that he and Duncan met at Chartres by chance, tells how Duncan's enthusiasm kindled his excited response to the beauties of the cathedral.[35] But Armfield himself was a disappointment: Duncan now found him dreary and depressing. When the time came to say farewell, and Duncan could have pressed for signs of affection, he wanted nothing but escape. Left to himself, he hoped fresh air and the effect of reading Walter Scott would rid him of the morbid depression which had suddenly engulfed him.

FIVE

Maynard

On 9 June 1907 Duncan travelled to Florence, where he joined his old friends, the Ewbanks. Mrs Ewbank was a kind woman, old-fashioned and vague. One morning she looked out and noticed that the boys rummaging for frogs in the Arno immediately below their drawing-room window had no clothes on. She expressed surprise to Duncan, who feared afterwards that he had been a little too eager to verify her observation. He did, however, notice how every evening a crowd gathered to watch the male youths bathing in the Arno, and as each one stepped trembling out of the water, a murmur of approval or disappointment rose from the nearby bridge.

On this second visit to Florence, Duncan spent much of his time at I Tatti, the home of the connoisseur Bernard Berenson, whose collaboration with the art dealer, Joseph Duveen, had made him rich. Duncan's introduction probably came through his eldest Strachey cousin, Elinor Rendel, who was staying with the Berensons, flaunting her best frocks and, to Duncan's amusement, hobnobbing with princesses and countesses. He turned up at I Tatti most afternoons, took part in mixed bathing parties in a lake surrounded by trees and, on a visit to a nearby villa, was smitten by the beauty of the scenery, the fountains, the marble balustrades, cypresses and vistas of blue hills. Aware that Berenson had been the subject of gossip, owing to his liaison with the notorious Duveen, Duncan decided that much of it had been unfairly malignant. 'Monsieur is very amusing and really I believe very kind, rather even perhaps a tragic figure as he believes himself to have wasted his life and to be left in the cold by the coming generation. It's not altogether his fault that perhaps he's rather conceited, if you only saw the sickening adoration of the American females that come and worship!'[1]

The Ewbanks were leaving for England at the end of June, so it was arranged that Duncan would move on to Certaldo, a small Tuscan town where his mother's friend, Mary Robbins, had recently bought a twelfth-century castle, which had belonged to the Strozzi and was built into the walls of the town. On his journey there Duncan visited the quarries of

Settignano, a place inevitably linked in his mind with Michelangelo. He slept under the trees, suffering terribly from mosquitoes and eating black bread and drinking black wine. Despite these hardy conditions, it was a romantic experience, especially when the moon rose over the vast, deserted caves held up by monolithic pillars.

At Certaldo he spent most of the day reading *Alice Through the Looking-Glass* and Macaulay's *History of England*. Then Miss Robbins pressed a generous sum of money into his hand and advised him to visit Siena in order to see the famous *palio*. He did so, spending a happy week there alone. That and his discovery of San Gimignano made this Tuscan holiday memorable, deepening further Duncan's love of Italy, its culture and way of life.

He returned to Paris merely to wind up his affairs and to spend a week with Lytton at Versailles in La Bruyère's house. They lingered in the public gardens, especially those of the Grand Trianon, and it made a fine end to his student life. Though he was to spend another half-term at the Slade in 1908, he was aware that his parents hoped – as a letter from his mother makes clear – that he would return to London 'full of ideas for starting on your own'.[2] One possibility open to him was portraiture. In May his mother had heard from the Laird of Rothiemurchus: he was greatly pleased with Duncan's copy of the Watts portrait, which now hung in the library at the Doune. Would Duncan, for a modest sum, he asked, now paint his own ugly features? If so, he would pay Duncan's railway fare and put him up so that the task could be combined with a holiday. Duncan accepted the commission and spent most of August at Rothiemurchus, not entirely happily, as conversation was often rather stiff. But among the other guests was a schoolboy from Winchester who donned a kilt every night, revealing, Duncan noted, 'divine knees'. There was also an elderly French lady, the Dowager Manvers, mother of the laird's second wife, whose entertaining talk was reminiscent of an earlier, less repressive age. Still more consoling was Loch an Eilan, part of the extensive Rothiemurchus estate, and made romantic by the ruined fortress in the middle of its placid waters. The country leading up to and around this loch surpassed anything that Duncan had experienced in Italy or Burma. He went on praising the scenery at Rothiemurchus until the end of his life.

Back in London, living again with his parents at 143 Fellows Road, on the lower slopes of Hampstead, he began looking for a studio of his own. The Stracheys were nearby, having moved in June to 67 Belsize Park Gardens. As his emotional life lacked focus at this time, Duncan found himself once again entangled with Lytton and left desolate by a meeting in Whitehall with Hobhouse, who treated Duncan severely and asked him to return his letters. After this Duncan cancelled a weekend visit to Cambridge on hearing that Hobhouse had also been invited. Meanwhile, James Strachey was pressing for Rupert Brooke's election to the Apostles against considerable opposition. Even Duncan had doubts about Brooke. 'I was very glad to get your letter,' he told James, '. . . I am really glad to hear that Rupert does care about other people's feelings, it makes the whole thing infinitely less ghastly than I imagined.'[3]

In November, Duncan gave the Bells and Virginia Stephen dinner. Lytton, hearing of this, told Duncan that whereas he could almost conceive of marrying Vanessa, Clive's attractions were, for him, still greater. 'I enjoyed my dinner party very much indeed,' Duncan replied, with guileless simplicity. 'I think I might manage to like being married to Virginia – but not to Clive. I suppose you think this odd?'[4]

The following year Duncan's friendship with Maynard Keynes developed a new twist. Duncan knew that Lytton had talked freely to Maynard about him, and this awareness gave his association with Keynes an implicit intimacy. In February 1908, while painting a portrait in Cambridge, where he stayed five days, Duncan saw a great deal of Maynard. Though Lytton had once observed that Keynes's common sense 'was enough to freeze a volcano',[5] there was something very attractive about the way he put his head on one side and, with his kind, tolerant smile, seemed to caress the speaker with his detached, reflective interest. His speculative mind would search out hidden connections or, with an unexpected frankness, make a sudden parry and thrust that left his listener surprised by an increase in self-knowledge. This power to manipulate others had been satirised by Lytton. 'Keynes sits like a decayed and amorous spider in King's, weaving purely imaginary webs, noticing everything that happens and doesn't happen, and writing to me every other post.'[6] So Lytton had written in January 1906, little realising that before very long the object of his affections would become ensnared by Maynard.

There were changes afoot that spring. Lytton's father, Sir Richard Strachey, had died on 12 February 1908 and his absence left Lytton painfully aware that at home he was now swamped by the female sex. He and Duncan talked of sharing a place together and Duncan went house-hunting in the Inns of Court, only to find that what was available was too expensive, neither he nor Lytton having sufficient funds. At the same time Maynard, still a clerk in the India Office's Military Department, was trying to get back to Cambridge. He suffered initial disappointment that year when he failed to be elected a Fellow of King's College, but a fortnight later was offered a lectureship in economics by the Cambridge economist Alfred Marshall and by the end of July was once again installed at King's. Wisely, Keynes retained his contacts with the India Office and his first publication, in 1913, dealt with India's monetary system. It assured his fame in Whitehall and he was invited to join the Royal Commission on Indian Currency and Finance.

Both Maynard's parents were redoubtable Cambridge figures, and as a child, Maynard had grown up in a Cambridge whose intellectual life was shaped by the aftermath of a crisis in religious belief. Doting parents, a free-thinking mind and an easy familiarity with the highest intellectual standards gave him a 'cocksureness' which, in Clive Bell's opinion, was his one besetting sin, though he later found others. Maynard's self-confidence, however, helped to offset a profound belief that he was ugly. He once told Lytton, 'I have always suffered and I suppose I always will from a most unalterable obsession that I am so physically repulsive that I've no business to hurl my body on anyone else's. The idea is so fixed and constant that I don't think anything – certainly no argument – would ever withstand it.'[7] This discontent, though initially a cause of shyness, may ultimately have exacerbated his pronounced sexual appetite.

Having followed the affair between Lytton and Duncan for some two years, Maynard was aware that it had more or less ended. He had an eye for male beauty and was responsive to a face that Lytton once described as 'outspoken, bold, and just not rough . . . the full aquiline type, with frank grey-blue eyes, and incomparably lascivious lips'.[8] If Maynard was hoping for an opportunity to get closer to Duncan, it came in June, when Lytton disappeared to Cambridge for four weeks. Earlier that month Duncan had written to Maynard denouncing, with uncharacteristic vehemence, a young South African Jewess whom he had had to take in to dinner. The bias of anti-Semitism at this date was like much English snobbery, an unanalysed prejudice, often inherited, which crudely expressed an awareness of difference. But Duncan's description of the 'cretinous, gluttonous Juive' whose childish greed caused her to flatten 'her fat slimy nose against the glass door leading to the food', contains a surprising degree of physical revulsion, partly racial and partly sexual in origin.[9] It might have remained unspoken, had he not also wanted to amuse Maynard with a description of an eighteen-year-old whose whole mind was set on mutton cutlets and strawberries.

This rare but frank admission of racial feeling was not the only aspect of his mind that Duncan exposed to Maynard as to no other. Before the end of June he had fallen in love with Maynard and experienced an immediacy of rapport greater than he had ever known before. Towards the end of his life, when he reminisced about this affair, Duncan gave his friend Paul Roche the impression that Maynard 'was closer to Duncan than anyone except perhaps Vanessa [Bell], and even closer than her in some respects . . . in the uncluttered recognition one male can have of another'.[10] In Maynard, Duncan found not only someone who returned his love but whom he could admire greatly, recognising in him all the things that he himself could not be: clever, worldly and aware of all the main issues; ruthless and effective; a protector of the more fugitive and fragile abilities in others. The significance of Maynard for Duncan went very deep and in old age, long after Maynard had died, Duncan experienced many dreams in which Maynard figured and from which he would wake anxious to be ready for his appearance.

Maynard, to an even greater extent than Lytton, liberated Duncan through his own attraction to the genuine and that which was without pretence. The last weekend in June Maynard took Duncan to his parents' house in Cambridge, where they sat in the garden reading and then bicycled to Clayhithe for tea. Duncan afterwards claimed that it was one of the happiest interludes he had spent since his schooldays. On 25 July Keynes moved back into King's College where, as Duncan was jealously aware, his duties as an Apostle once again involved him in the perusal of potential 'embryos', one of whom, a youth named George Mallory, had an outstanding physique. Maynard was surprised that summer to discover how rampant homosexuality had become at Cambridge: 'The thing has grown with leaps and bounds in my two years of absence and practically everybody in Cambridge, except me, is an open and avowed sodomite.'[11] Meanwhile he found that every time he walked into his room it was in the hope of finding Duncan there, and Duncan, in turn, could not conceive of being apart from Maynard for any length of time. 'I have just received an invitation to go and spend some time in the Orkney Islands with a millionaire who owns Hoy,' he informed Maynard in July, referring to a friend of his mother's, Thomas Middlemore, who in 1898 had bought the island for £32,000. 'Much as I love the Orkneys I love you more and don't know what to do. Do advise me.'[12]

It was quickly agreed that Maynard would join him in the Orkneys for part of this holiday. But before then both had the difficulty of confronting Lytton, who, with his acute sensibility, had observed when Keynes whispered an aside to Duncan, while all three friends were lunching at Simpson's, that a liaison had begun. It was a bitter state of affairs, for Lytton, who placed such importance on relationships, had until recently been convinced that he had occasionally caught glimmerings of real love in Duncan's affectionate gaze. Now he had to realise that he had lost both idol and confidant, a double blow that must have left him horribly alone. He was also extremely sceptical about Maynard's capacity for love and raged against him to his brother James, privately dismissing his rival as 'a safety-bicycle with genitals'.[13]

Whatever the convoluted and contradictory nature of Lytton's feelings, his immediate reaction was magnanimous. Keynes received a letter expressing acceptance of what had happened and a present of some books; Duncan, who had expressed interest in an art teacher called Dr Bach, was invited to take lessons with him at Lytton's expense. It was all too unbearably kind and, having its desired effect, reduced both young men to tears. Of the two, it was Keynes who took more pains to allow for and try to mitigate Lytton's suffering. Duncan, after a short letter acknowledging Lytton's goodness and generosity, lapsed into silence.

Eventually Duncan left for the Orkneys. 'Goodbye,' he wrote to Maynard, ' – whenever I think of you your affection for me seems to me marvellous.'[14]

After twenty-seven hours of continuous travelling he arrived at Stromness, grateful for a bed in a modern hotel, even though his double-bedded room seemed to make a mockery of him in Maynard's absence. He had been alarmed to discover that the sea crossing, instead of lasting one hour as he expected, took five, and he was unable to avoid being sea-sick. The next day a motor boat came to take him to Melsetter, Thomas Middlemore's estate on Hoy. The small boat tossed and dipped in a stormy sea for what seemed like three hours, but Duncan, drenched to the skin, thoroughly enjoyed himself, observing the cormorants, the seals, the spray and the colours in the islands, sea and sky. Even so, he was glad of the champagne given him on arrival.

After only two days Duncan began to groan inwardly at the obtuseness of his fellow guests. 'Dearest,' he wrote to Maynard, 'at this moment I would give my soul to the Devil if I could kiss you and be kissed.'[15] His obsession with Maynard may partly have blinded him to the qualities of others: when playing at seances around a card table on his second evening, he kept pretending to himself that the young woman's hand he had to hold was really Maynard's.

The house itself Duncan admired. Built by W. H. Lethaby in a robust Arts and Crafts style, it seemed to him 'chaste and severe . . . suitable to the country and unaffected and comfortable'.[16] Thomas Middlemore's wife had patronised Burne-Jones, and his pictures as well as some by David Cox and George Morland hung on the walls. Duncan also found a copy of Berenson's book on Florentine drawings, which he re-read before turning to Jane Harrison on Greek art.

The Melsetter estate was a world unto itself, containing four or five gardens, a model farm, a bakery, laundry, museum, theatre, chapel, telegraph office and even its own golf course. Duncan behaved like a model guest, agreed to read the lessons at the Sunday service and joined an expedition to a shooting lodge on the far side of the island, where they ate an enormous lunch. Afterwards they walked to a hut carved out of rock, which had figured in one of Walter Scott's novels. From the hillside the view of the neighbouring islands was breathtaking, the panorama constantly changing under weather conditions that came and went in the twinkling of an eye.

Though taken out of himself by these vistas, Duncan nevertheless began to feel enormous strain at Hoy, owing to the split between his inner thoughts and his outer behaviour. Writing to Maynard provided an outlet for his feelings and he waited eagerly for his replies. 'You are the only person I feel I can speak to,' he told Maynard:

> You cannot imagine how much I want to scream sometimes here for want of being able to say something that I mean. It's not only that one's a sodomite that one has to hide but one's whole philosophy of life; one's feelings even for inanimate things I feel would shock some people. Here I am surrounded by them, not a soul to speak to ... it's so damnable to think that they can only think me a harmless sort of lunatic or a dangerous criminal whom they wouldn't associate with at any price.[17]

A change of environment and new people obliged Duncan to see himself though others' eyes. 'I wonder whether I am really something quite different and not a human being at all,' he wrote unhappily to Maynard, adding, 'I sometimes think so, and if it wasn't for you I think I should think so at this minute.'[18] Maynard's letters were 'like drams of whisky to the frozen explorer', for everyone around him seemed to have a heart of ice. If he embraced anyone, it would have to be a seagull, as they seemed more human than his fellow guests. Meanwhile he read and painted, slept and ate, the last two activities being the more dominant. He had also agreed to take part in a play. In between he was looking for lodgings on the island where he and Keynes could enjoy some time together. In preparation for this, he gave Keynes a list of the books he had with him, so as to avoid duplication – a Shakespeare, Dante's *Inferno*, *Principia Ethica*, Carlyle's history of the French Revolution, *Les Liaisons Dangereuses* and some books on art.

Keynes, too, had found this period of separation so soon after the start of their intimacy difficult to bear. He had moments of despair, needed reassurance of Duncan's love and violently craved his company. Though he had initially hoped to keep their relationship private, he now found himself telling the mathematician Harry Norton of it, finding relief in being able to talk about Duncan. 'I can only call up two visions of you distinctly,' he wrote, ' – one of you standing in the passage at the moment I open the door of 125b [St James's Court], the other of you lying on your back by my side with your eyes closed, all black and white.'[19] Aware that he had a good chance of getting a larger set of rooms at King's, Maynard relayed this news instantly to Duncan, adding, 'if I get them you will be able to come and live with me whenever you want to'.[20]

On 18 August Duncan met Maynard at Stromness. He had disentangled himself from the party at Melsetter but very much wanted to go back to Hoy in Maynard's company. Their first attempts to find rooms in a farmhouse failed, so they stayed instead in the Mason's Arms Hotel at Stromness. There Keynes began work on his 'Theory of Probability' and Duncan painted. Owing to their persistence, and their willingness to transport beds across from the mainland, they eventually found rooms on Hoy at Orgill Farm, in a wild, mountainous district. Everything seemed to conspire to make them happy. Wherever he looked – at the landscape, the vegetation and wildlife, at the farm lads who drove them about in a gig, or at the schoolboys living in the nearby lodge – Maynard found things to delight his eye. They led a peaceful, orderly existence that allowed for several hours' work each day, read Jane Austen aloud and went for tremendous walks. As far as Duncan was concerned, he never wanted to do anything else. By the middle of September he had begun a portrait of Maynard, who sat cross-legged, working on his theory with a board on his knee. In the portrait he looks up, a smile flickering over his face and lighting his eyes, the shared intimacy between painter and sitter making this one of Grant's most vivid likenesses.[21]

Their period at Orgill Farm was broken by a ten-day stay at Melsetter, whence they moved when Maynard became feverish. Even while recuperating, he still managed to do three hours' work a day, beginning an article on Indian prices and currency for the *Economic Journal*. Duncan, meanwhile, began a still-life, the cold weather making painting outdoors impossible, and immersed himself in *Anna Karenina*. The softening effects of luxury at Melsetter did not spoil them for Orgill Farm, but before finally leaving the Orkneys they returned once more to Melsetter, to spend some days at the shooting lodge. It was with considerable reluctance that on 22 October the two friends departed, Maynard heading back to Cambridge, Duncan travelling to Rothie-murchus where he spent a few days at the Doune.

After the wildness of Hoy, Rothiemurchus seemed enchantingly lovely, remote and idyllic, the birch trees gold and green beside the River Ord, the silence broken only by the echoing noise of the deer. It was for Duncan a somewhat dispiriting visit after his time with Maynard, but at a lunch party he met the forty-year-old daughter of the painter Sir Lawrence Alma-Tadema, who insisted that he should visit her family's home in London. He also copied a Raeburn portrait of his great-grandmother, thinking that his father might like it. But he looked forward to seeing Maynard again in Cambridge. 'This place is so gorgeously lovely that the Orkneys have been blotted out of my visual memory,' he admitted to his friend. 'But not you.'[22] Nevertheless, the unalloyed happiness they had experienced in the Orkneys was not to recur. By the time Duncan had settled back into his life in London, autumn had more or less ended and the chill of winter approached.

Laura Alma-Tadema kept her word and in time Duncan found himself invited to one of her father's salons. Soon after arriving in England in the 1860s, this Dutch painter had begun to enjoy huge success with his reconstructions of domestic scenes set in ancient Greece or Rome, works that often relied for their appeal on maidens, marble and the Mediterranean. By the Edwardian era they had begun to acquire a gently titillating eroticism which, owing to the classical setting, was quite acceptable; Alma-Tadema enjoyed a fortune, a grand house, a knighthood and finally the Order of Merit. Small wonder that Duncan's curiosity was aroused.

After pressing a bell in a quiet-looking street in St John's Wood, he found himself ushered into another world. The garden smelled of tropical spices, fountains splashed beside marble pergolas and inside the house – in which every possible material, including jasper, bronze, brass, rare gems and coloured glass had been used to create lavish effects – women floated about in richly coloured tea-gowns. Duncan enjoyed the spectacle that this visit represented, but experienced it through the eyes of an outsider. Alma-Tadema's taste gave him the impression that naked women might be found behind sliding panels. He could not help simultaneously imagining the different ambience that would have been created had the house belonged to a 'sodomite'.

Very different was the bleak workroom in Long Acre that Duncan looked at as a possible studio, where young women spent their days cutting out underwear. He rejected it as being too impossibly large to heat and continued the search. In mid-December he moved into a studio at 19 Belgrave Road, then part of St John's Wood, which he furnished and decorated. Although rather a lot of time was spent admiring his new surroundings, he could now be happy, active and undisturbed. One of the first pictures he painted here was a portrait of Pernel Strachey, viewed from the side, with a picture on the wall behind her, an arrangment made popular by the success of Whistler's portraits of his mother and Thomas Carlyle.

It did, however, take him time to adjust after his Scottish interlude. On his return from Rothiemurchus he had stopped at Cambridge, to see Maynard, and there fell ill with influenza. Perhaps this left him in a weakened state because by mid-November, in London, he was frequently close to tears. He blamed his depression on Maynard's absence, though in fact Maynard had come to London hard on Duncan's heels in order to clear up his affairs at St James's Court. He, too, then caught influenza and spent several days in a Hampstead hospital, after which he recuperated with the Stracheys in Belsize Park Gardens. But it was a difficult time and Duncan, unsettled by their summer intimacy, now had to establish a *modus vivendi* with a person living in a different city from himself.

Meanwhile he went regularly to concerts, plays, galleries and exhibitions, and enjoyed the stimulus that London offered; Keynes, on the other hand, was committed to Cambridge. 'I was miserable to be without you last night,' he had told Duncan on his return from the Orkneys, 'but to-day I am so happy to be in Cambridge that I am as cheerful as anyone could wish. I hope you are. When I have both you and Cambridge, I shall be the most fortunate creature in the world.'[23]

Though Duncan enjoyed hearing talk of 'embryos' and inversion ('the thing is absolutely universal,' Maynard reported on his return; 'nothing else is talked about and everybody considers himself one'[24]), he had no intention of becoming a mere appendage to Maynard's life. Immediately after his return from the Orkneys, there was just a hint that he might. 'The general appearance is *extraordinarily* married,' James Strachey reported to Lytton when Duncan arrived in Cambridge at the end of October. 'If D. comes here to live, however, there'll certainly be flirtations . . . the Machine will be merely amused and exclaim "You always come back to me – to me – to me!" And he always will.'[25] On 28 November Duncan returned for a two-week stay at King's. There he made a drawing of Keynes's sister, his main task, however, being the completion of his portrait of Maynard, begun in the Orkneys, which Maynard's parents wanted to buy. It had now been agreed that Duncan's studio would double as Maynard's London *pied-à-terre*. Even so, arguments had begun – Duncan disappointing Maynard with his failure to write regularly, his muddling of arrangements and the amount of time that he gave to others. Duncan apologised for being 'selfish'; but at other times he resisted the interpretation that Maynard put on his behaviour. 'What a brute you make me out to be! And it's no use my being sorry because it doesn't according to you make me alter my behaviour. So that I must remain a brute and try not to be sorry.'[26]

The problem (as with Lytton) was that Maynard wanted more than Duncan was able to give. When Duncan chattered blithely to Maynard – about his visit to Ledbury, where his aunt, Lady Colvile, was giving a dance; about his attraction to another guest, his cousin Raper Frere, an Apollonian beauty with crimped hair and a taste for women; or the high-church vicar from Gloucestershire whose solemn questions kept Duncan awake until the early hours – the latter could discern in harmless material of this kind some malignity that proved Duncan's hardness of heart. Then, too, if Duncan, for what he thought were entirely justifiable reasons, cancelled a meeting, Maynard would be reduced to tears.

When in January 1909 Maynard learnt that the bedroom under his was unoccupied and that his bedmaker had the right to let it out, he immediately told Duncan there was a place for him at King's whenever he wanted. Behind his offer lay anxiety over Duncan's elusiveness, for his links with others repeatedly drew him elsewhere, while his fidelity to painting remained absolute, returning him always to the studio. There was nothing Maynard could do except try to infiltrate himself into Duncan's life in whatever way he could. Thus when Duncan announced that he wanted to read Delacroix's *Journal*, Maynard obtained a copy for him from Cambridge University Library.

Duncan's interest in Delacroix doubtless began in the Louvre, in front of *The Massacre of Chios*, *The Death of Sardanapalus* or *La Barque de Don Juan*. In 1907 his cousin Dorothy Bussy published a monograph on this artist with Duckworth's. It was the first on Delacroix to appear in England where, until then, he had been granted little more than a passing reference. Dorothy provided a good introduction to this artist's career, offered some spirited analyses of his paintings and quoted from the *Journal* that Delacroix kept for forty years. Though his *Journal* had not yet been translated into English, Duncan read it enthralled, meeting in its pages a character as keenly observant, as natural and unconstrained in manner as himself; an artist whose lively and entertaining reflections on the world of letters, art, theatre, politics and music would have added to his own understanding of human life. But it was Delacroix's constant preoccupation with the technical aspects of painting and with aesthetic values that made the *Journal* such a crucial part of Duncan's artistic education.

74

While reading this book Duncan worked on a large picture of a tea party for which Pernel Strachey, among others, had posed, and also on a portrait of his cousin Phyllida Ridpath. The size of his new studio made possible the use of large canvases. In the evenings, however, he still returned home to his parents and when guests stayed, he slept at the Stracheys'.

He had now begun to work independently, employing his own models and engaging, so he told Maynard, 'an aged American Jew' whom he met in the street.[27] He occasionally returned to Westminster School of Art for classes in drawing and modelling, and found himself copying in clay the eye of Michelangelo's *David* – 'an immense and terrifying object'.[28] Delacroix's *Journal* had left him teeming with ideas, which could find little outlet in portraiture, to which he seemed committed. He was now painting an ex-King's man, Arthur Cole, barrister and music-lover.[29] As a young man Cole had suffered from a stammer and like other Cambridge undergraduates of his generation, had been greatly inspired by G. E. Moore. It was perhaps owing to Moore's liberating effect that he was able to lose his stammer and in Duncan's studio to boast freely of how he and his fiancée had bathed naked on a visit to Cornwall. 'He seems quite at home,' Duncan reported of his studio visits, 'and talks a great deal which is enormously comforting, even about copulation, which he evidently considers a good in itself.'[30] Duncan, having recently obtained a set of tickets for the complete cycle of *The Ring* at Covent Garden, may also have discussed music with Cole, a topic in which Maynard showed little interest.

More and more Duncan realised his need for a circle of friends with whom he could discuss feelings and interests that he could not share with his elders.[31] Unthinking acceptance of convention was no longer possible to a young man educated in part by the conversations of his Cambridge-educated friends. Lytton, who was still hankering after Duncan's affection, insisted that he should now take hold of his experiences:

Duncan, I think you ought to think more. I don't believe you ought to be quite as calm and solid as you are. The world is a difficult and complicated place, and I don't see much point in being in it if one isn't really aware of what's going on, and I don't see how one can be aware unless one reflects and thinks and takes trouble. Don't you agree? . . . Are your feelings really clear? If they're not you ought to try and make them so, though that's generally a difficult job.[32]

Meanwhile, Duncan's friendship with Clive and Vanessa Bell was slowly ripening. He dined at their house in Gordon Square in January 1909, though it was not until November that Vanessa wrote, 'Dear Duncan, May I call you so and will you call me Vanessa?'[33]

At a dinner with Virginia and Adrian Stephen in Fitzroy Square in June 1908 Duncan had first begun to realise how very different Vanessa was from other women that he knew. He heard of the amusement Lytton had caused the Bells when he read aloud three of his indecent poems, one of which – 'Morning Lust' – had especially delighted Vanessa. 'Aren't they a scandalous trio?' Duncan wrote to Maynard,[34] as yet scarcely able to believe that a woman of her class could be other than a paragon of decorum. He subsequently learnt that Vanessa had copies made of Lytton's poems so that one of these could be given to her sister.

Behind Vanessa's glee lay a history of repression. For nine years, between the ages of fifteen and twenty-four, she had lived in circumstances made oppressive by her widowed father's gloom: 'Though we had many carefully guarded passions and excitements and interests, there is no doubt that our youth, Virginia's and mine, was lived in an atmosphere of profound melancholy. One felt it callous to be happy.'[35] After Sir Leslie Stephen's death, it was Vanessa who had decided that the family should move from Kensington to Bloomsbury, where she had deliberately furnished 46 Gordon Square in a very different style from that which had prevailed in their former house at Hyde Park Gardens. Even after her marriage to Clive Bell, the décor of this house seemed strikingly casual for its day. Lytton had reported to Duncan, after a visit to Gordon Square in June 1907, that the drawing-room had no carpets or wallpapers, had curtains some of which were blue, some white, two basket chairs and a Louis XV bed, on which this 'wild sprightly couple'[36] lay side by side. Lytton observed all this with a homosexual's sceptical curiosity about heterosexual life and was relieved to notice after one visit that because the Bells had been less insistent on their love for each other, conversation had been easier. Duncan, too, found the Bells intriguing. After his visit to their house in January 1909 he told Lytton that he had found Clive 'rather chastened and alone'. Vanessa, however, 'came in radiant as usual' from a sitting she had just given Henry Lamb.[37]

Tall and statuesque, her face made slightly heavy by the slow curves shaping her full mouth, eyes and eyelids, she was neither pleasingly attractive nor conventionally pretty, but strikingly beautiful. What made her especially 'radiant' at this date was her realisation that in the company of an intimate circle of friends, established during their 'at homes' at Gordon Square, she need no longer be constrained by polite civilities but had the freedom to say what she thought. This did not come naturally to most women of her class who, unless they came from the enlightened intelligentsia, were taught to suppress any personal interests or instincts that did not match the behaviour and manners expected of a lady. This crippled mentality irritated Maynard Keynes, who found himself in a state of nervous irritation after a two-hour class in which there were women students: 'I seem to hate every movement of their minds. The minds of the men even when they themselves are stupid and ugly, never appear to me so repellent.'[38] In the same week that he made this complaint he entertained Vanessa Bell who, with her husband, paid a weekend visit to Cambridge and took tea in Maynard's rooms. Also present were James Strachey, J. T. Sheppard and Rupert Brooke. Maynard told Duncan:

> That lasted until half-past seven, and got, towards the end, rather amusing. Vanessa explained how interesting it was for her to come up and have a look at us, Lytton having explained every one of our secrets. She was perfectly lovely – I've never seen her more beautiful – and very conversational. Is she always so now? She seemed to hold the floor.[39]

The tea party took place the day after Maynard had moved into a suite of rooms over the gatehouse at King's College, which leads from King's Lane into Webb's Court, rooms he was to occupy until his death. Duncan became very familiar with them and, in the course of time, painted two different mural schemes here, collaborating on one with Vanessa Bell. But even before they gained this distinction, Maynard was convinced that he now occupied the handsomest rooms in college.

His letters to Duncan suggested that a new star had risen in the Cambridge firmament – George Mallory of Magdalene. The son of a rector, he was charming and impulsive, interested in ethics and keen on argumentative discussion. Opinion differed as to his mental gifts, but all were agreed on his beauty. By February 1909 he had become friends with James Strachey, who doted on him.

Duncan was intrigued by the stories surrounding Mallory, but felt that the other-worldliness of Cambridge was far removed from the coarser delights of London. He had gone again to Sir Lawrence Alma-Tadema's house, eaten a terrific supper and drunk too much champagne. 'Vy ees a[n] art critic like an eunuch?' Duncan was asked by his host. 'A what?' he replied. 'A eunuch! Because 'e knowse all about zet but can't do anythink.'[40]

At St Loe Strachey's suggestion, Duncan himself tried his hand at art criticism, writing four pieces for the *Spectator*. The first was on an exhibition of Simon Bussy's pastels at the Goupil Gallery. Duncan, presuming that he could rely on what he already knew about Bussy's art, went along to the show and found the pictures so unexpectedly lovely that his theories fell apart and he was left having to compose 400 words about he knew not what. Lytton suggested that if he had difficulty beginning the article, he should start by writing the main thing he wanted to say. In the final article Duncan stressed the interrelatedness of form, tone and colour in the conception of the whole. Hence, he argued, the intentional suppression of certain natural details, the studied choice and measured effects.[41]

Though the *Spectator*, unlike the *Times Literary Supplement*, was not committed to anonymous reviewing, Duncan signed this piece, as he did all four of his *Spectator* reviews, simply with the initial 'G', which suggests a lack of certainty about his capacities as a critic. His second article looked at an exhibition of paintings by Philip Wilson Steer, in which he found 'wonderful lessons in the use of pure colour' and 'an atmosphere of pure, almost physical pleasure'. 'No great intellectual struggle, we feel, is brought before us, no new conception of existence to be understood ... we bask in the delight of simply seeing. What an exceedingly difficult thing it is to see simply ... Mr Steer [of all modern English painters] comes far the nearest to seeing Nature with a completely unaffected eye.'[42] In June 1909 a visit to the New English Art Club enabled Duncan to praise in print Augustus John's portrait of William Nicholson and to mention in passing Mrs Clive Bell's 'exquisite still-life'.[43]

S. P. Rosenbaum has suggested that Lytton Strachey may have helped in the writing of these reviews.[44] Another possibility is that certain touches of journalistic rhetoric were added by an assistant editor, or that St Loe Strachey himself may have rewritten or added certain remarks. Duncan's longest piece celebrated the opening of the new Victoria and Albert Museum. Critical of the façade ('an ugly collection of shapes'), he nevertheless welcomed the spacious display of objects inside, which in the old building had been kept in closely packed cases lining dim corridors.[45]

This was the last article that he wrote for the *Spectator*, probably because his heart was not in reviewing. At the same time his ambitions as a painter lacked direction. He continued to favour portraiture and in March 1909, during a visit to Cambridge, began painting a rather sombre portrait of J. T. Sheppard's *amour*, Cecil Taylor, a graduate of Emmanuel College who became a highly regarded teacher of classics at Clifton College, Bristol, where this portrait now hangs. Duncan again used the side-view, seated pose that Whistler had made so popular and positioned the Japanese print on the wall behind, so that the upward movement created by Taylor's crossed legs leads the eye to the print, its swaying figure continuing the rising movement and countering the static effect of the horizontals and verticals elsewhere. The dark greens and reds have a rich sonority owing to Duncan's use of layered glazes.

Still more successful was his portrait of Lytton Strachey, begun towards the end of March. Lytton was still in torment with regard to Duncan, still anxious to know that his cousin cared for him. Duncan may have hoped that this portrait would reassure Lytton of his affection and respect. However, whereas in his portrait of Maynard the sitter looks up from his task, engaging the viewer with his smiling gaze, Lytton is shown with his face in shadow, cut off from the spectator by his absorption in his book as he sits, hemmed in by the nearby leather-bound volumes and the chintz-covered armchair, his long, thin hands resting on the pages of his book.

That spring Duncan worked hard at what he called his Royal Academy picture 'which ended in a pitiable condition and left me in one too'.[46] It is not known to which picture he was referring, but he left it and another at the portals of the Royal Academy in the hope of having them accepted for the Summer Exhibition. Both were rejected.

Nothing seemed to go well for Duncan that spring. His relations with Lytton were awkward and even his friendship with Maynard had its difficulties. On a visit to Cambridge, he was delighted when Maynard produced the second volume of Delacroix's *Journal*, but he then left it by mistake in the hansom that took him to the station. His unsettled state caused concern in others and, after a certain amount of string-pulling, he was offered the post of assistant master, to teach Latin, English, drawing and arithmetic at Birmingham Grammar School for a salary of forty pounds a year on the condition, so he informed Maynard, 'that I am a Disciplinarian and Social'.[47] In the same letter he wondered gloomily if he would do better becoming a 'pusher' of stereographs.

On 7 April 1909 Duncan and Maynard left for a fortnight's holiday at Versailles. It was a familiar haunt to Duncan, a place that touched his historical imagination and where he had been happy. On this occasion, however, romance was noticeably absent. The day after he returned he wrote to James Strachey:

Perhaps if you have seen him Maynard will have felt depressed enough to tell you . . . I am no longer in love with him. I don't think you've

79

ever said a word about him to me since last year in June when I
suppose you heard from Lytton what had happened – no doubt
because you knew that I knew that you thought it was impossible. I was
certain at the time that I was in love with him – perhaps I was, perhaps
it was only passion, but anyhow it is not this that now remains but an
affection that is on the whole exceedingly strong . . . But I no longer
believe myself to be *in* love with a person who sometimes bores me and
sometimes irritates me, and from whom I can live apart without being
unhappy, however much I may like to be with him. All this is not very
new to Maynard. We have talked about it honestly enough since the
day after our arrival at Versailles . . .[48]

While writing to James, Duncan was aware of the repercussions that this
news would have on Lytton. The triangular relationship binding him,
Lytton and Maynard together was still strong enough for Duncan to ask
Lytton in May if it was permissible for him to remain fond of Maynard.
However, in freeing himself from Maynard, he had gained an increased
sense of independence and now resisted what he felt to be Lytton's desire
to make him into a second version of himself. Meanwhile Maynard, who
had commissioned a panel decoration in his main room at Cambridge,
sent Duncan the necessary measurements with the glum remark, 'I still
reckon everything here with reference to when I shall see you again. I find
it difficult to remember that anything is changed . . .'[49]

What all three friends still needed, and continued to give each other,
was indecent conversation. It released them from the circumspection and
deceit that their homosexuality, the law and social prejudice imposed on
them. When Duncan found some baths in Whitechapel where young
Jewish boys bathed naked and birches were used, ostensibly to improve
circulation, he sent a salacious description to Maynard. References to his
models also pepper his letters. It was well known at this date that artist's
models, both male and female, were sometimes willing to perform a
variety of services, the profession often being little more than a front for
prostitution. Duncan appreciated male beauty wherever he found it.
Whereas some homosexuals of his class turned to working-class men for
release from inhibitions bred in them by privilege, Duncan, feeling no
such need, took people on their own terms, liking some and not others,
according to their character traits. One model, who had become homeless,
he put up in his studio for a week, admitting to Lytton that at times 'the
appallingly lengthy tête-à-têtes with a cockney accent, the latent
womanising instincts . . . send a sudden chill down the spine'.[50] He and
Maynard, who was still using the studio at 19 Belgrave Road as his
London *pied-à-terre*, became very fond of 'St George', as they nicknamed

one model, an actor called Francis Nelson, who struggled to get work with touring companies.

Yet if Duncan had an ideal, it came close to that glimpsed this year whilst sculling downriver one weekend to Datchet, where he saw a youth alighting from an enormous closed motor car: '. . . a triumph, not of beauty, he had carrot hair, slightly long, and a slightly tilted nose, but of grace of charm, impossible to conceive of, a something, a quality as perfect as the aroma of an infant of three years joined to the shy wit, the fascinating stutter, the twinkling glance, of that miracle of breeding, a well mannered Eton boy of sixteen.'[51]

If passion had evaporated, Duncan's friendship with Maynard had survived, taking its place alongside other friendships in his life. That summer he began to make fairly regular appearances at the home of Adrian and Virginia Stephen in Fitzroy Square. Like the Bells, they too held weekly 'at homes'. These informal gatherings provided occasions at which Virginia and Vanessa, who had been educated at home, could experience the easy companionship, the raggings, slang, jealousies and so on that school or university would have provided. But even in 1909, by which time they had gathered round them an inner core of friends, these evenings could be awkward, lacking in conviviality. After Clive and Vanessa Bell arrived, bringing Duncan in tow, the conversation became more lively, Vanessa sitting on the sofa with Lytton discussing homosexuals but stopping when, to Vanessa's amusement, an abrupt silence in the room drew attention to their gossip. As Adrian observed, she delighted in sailing as close to the wind as she could, bringing out bawdy remarks with glee, like a spoilt child delighting in obstreperousness. Looking back on this period later, in an article for *Horizon* on Virginia Woolf, Duncan recalled: 'Apostolic young men found to their amazement that they could be shocked by the boldness and scepticism of two young women.'[52]

Duncan dined alone with Virginia and Adrian Stephen on 8 July, amusing them with his accounts of recent parties. After dinner a barrister's wife, Mrs Charles Sanger, joined them, together with Lady Ottoline Morrell, who was soon to add Duncan to her guest list for her own Thursday 'at homes'.

That summer Keynes took a house at Burford in the Cotswolds, where he intended to work and entertain friends. Duncan meanwhile had gone to Pensarn, Llanbedr in North Wales to stay with his Ridpath relatives and continue work on the portrait of his cousin Phyllida. Though the garden of the house where he was staying looked out over sea and sands, Duncan was so bored by the company that he invented an interest in the

Fabians, who were gathered nearby, and took himself off to hear Sidney Webb give a series of lectures on Elementary Socialism. The area did, however, have another interest. 'The Fleet is here,' Duncan wrote to Maynard, 'and even *The Times* says it is impossible not to have strong feelings of affection towards the sailors . . .'[53]

He joined Maynard at Burford during the first week in August, arriving two days after J. T. Sheppard and Cecil Taylor. James Strachey, who was also present, told Lytton that the ménage consisted of two couples and himself. In fact, the stay at Burford was fraught with jealousy and suspicion. Duncan, who went on with his portrait of Taylor, could not understand why Sheppard's nerves were so shaky, until it came out that he thought Duncan was flirting with Taylor. As a result Duncan went about scarcely daring to look at or talk to Taylor, not even during the bicycle ride that all of them made to Blenheim. Yet, despite these difficult circumstances, he painted a watercolour of Burford High Street[54] which, with its gentle gradations of tone and delicately stated topography, suggests a mind serenely free from all human complications. Lytton, too, at this time experienced a release from the tension of the last four years. Detached and sympathetic, he commiserated with Maynard over the ending of his affair with Duncan: 'Love's the very devil. But it *is* Time's fool; and my experience is that when it's once flown finally out of the window one's astonished to find one can get on well without it. How shocked James would be by such sentiments! Are you shocked too? But really after all I'm not so very cynical!'[55]

SIX

A Ceremonial Birching

Uncertainty hung over Duncan's life during the autumn and winter of 1909. When his parents moved from 143 to 135 Fellows Road, he momentarily revived the idea of living with Lytton. Nothing came of this, but he did move studio in November, taking two rooms on the second floor of 21 Fitzroy Square, with Maynard paying the rent and using one room as his London *pied-à-terre*. Duncan supervised the furnishing of these rooms and in the intervals added fashionable Augustus John ingredients – a gypsy caravan and a tent – to a landscape that he had begun at Burford. In the evenings he went to the theatre, concerts or the opera; with James Strachey, he heard the first London performance of Elgar's First Symphony.

As an artist, he was now working on his own. Immediately after his return from Paris, during the summer term of 1908, he had re-entered the Slade, signing in as a part-time student two or three days a week during May and June. There exist from this period a few very fine figure drawings that attest to Slade influence. But he gained little from this institution other than the friendship of a fellow student, Vera Wadding-ton. Nine years older than himself, she attended the Slade over a lengthy period, saw Duncan in Paris while he was at La Palette and would work with him and Frederick Etchells in 1912 on a wall painting in Brunswick Square. Though her contribution was whitewashed over, as a result of criticism from the Bells and Maynard,[1] she had sufficient standing as an artist to be included in the survey of twentieth-century art shown at the Whitechapel Art Gallery in 1914. A lively, talkative, contented woman, she continued painting all her life. According to her nephew, Richard Gott, she and Duncan had a mild fling. Whether or not it was sexual remains unclear.

Duncan's allegiance as an artist was now given to the Friday Club. A small but serious concern, it held exhibitions that aspired to be annual and became so from 1910 until 1918. It attracted many able young artists, among them John Nash, Gwen Darwin and Derwent Lees, but also 'a lagging contingent of gentlemen dilettantes and ladies from the Slade'. [2]

Owing to Vanessa Bell's important role in its formation, its lay-members included many Bloomsbury friends and relations. Many of the Club's discussions took place at Gordon Square, although the first meeting Duncan attended was held in Henry Lamb's studio. 'We used to talk about the Impressionists and that sort of thing,' Duncan recalled. 'But not what was going on at the moment, not at all. Nobody went to France. I'd just come back *from* France but I hadn't become acquainted with the Fauves even then.'[3]

The Friday Club held no exhibition in 1909. Duncan, in search of an alternative, sent his work in November to the New English Art Club. Founded in 1886 in opposition to the Royal Academy, it had over the years matured more and more into a nursery for the Academy, many of its original members having changed allegiance or exhibiting at both venues. The jury in 1909 accepted two of Duncan's watercolours, one of which was *Burford High Street*, but rejected his oils. It is hard to understand why: as a portraitist, he had begun to display compositional acuity and an impressive control of tone. He could also handle paint with considerable skill, re-creating surface textures with great sensitivity to the fall of light. These qualities can be found in his portrait of James Strachey and in *Crime and Punishment* (both Tate Gallery), the latter also satisfying the Edwardian love of psychological drama in that it shows a woman, who has just finished reading Dostoevsky's famous novel, sitting, overwhelmed, with her head in her hands.

Duncan's failure to please the New English jury was spotted by William Rothenstein. He later recorded in his memoirs that Grant and Simon Bussy 'were not welcomed as they should have been' by the New English Art Club. He made his opinions known to the jury of the Club and sent Duncan a letter praising the watercolours that were shown, as well as the rejected oils. This encouragement came as a pleasant surprise. It was not just politeness that led Duncan to say in his reply that he placed high value on Rothenstein's opinion – a letter that Rothenstein printed in full in his memoirs.[4] Duncan remained on visiting terms with him until the advent of Post-Impressionism caused an abrupt parting of the ways.

One place where Duncan did now belong was Bloomsbury. In Fitzroy Square he was a neighbour of Adrian and Virginia Stephen, a fact that helped him gradually overcome his shyness. On discovering that he was going to be alone on Christmas Day 1908, they invited him to lunch. Virginia afterwards said that she found him charming but difficult – 'he has too many ideas, and no way to get rid of them'.[5] Duncan was also becoming more familiar with the Bells and with their house at 46 Gordon

Square, where Augustus John's large painting *Pyramus* filled one entire wall.

In their attempt to see things afresh, Bloomsbury cast aside the shibboleths of their elders and tried to accept no standard that did not accord with their own unaided judgement. Truth was sought, and respected. Concomitant with this was a desire for the real, and for a response to life which, though sceptical, was also full: to be incapable of enjoyment was, in the eyes of Bloomsbury, an unforgivable sin. When, towards the end of his life, Duncan was questioned about the characteristics of Bloomsbury, he not only mentioned 'honesty and a love of truth which led to friendships among all members' but also their love of parties. These were, he recalled, 'excellent, delightful, helpful'.[6]

Courageous and free-thinking, Bloomsbury encouraged an anti-establishment attitude of mind, a refusal to accept any authority without questioning the value on which it rested. This helps to explain why, at the last minute, when two other bright sparks fell away, Duncan and Virgina Stephen agreed to take part in the Dreadnought Hoax, which Horace Cole was planning in collaboration with Adrian Stephen, the two men having been friends at Cambridge where they had perpetrated a number of small hoaxes. The object of this new hoax was the largest and most powerful warship in existence – the *Dreadnought* – which made all previous battleships obsolete, its name becoming the generic title of all the battleships and battlecruisers built after it. The ship, which was the same length as Westminster Abbey, was a swaggering, ostentatious symbol of arrogant patriotism. What finally tipped the balance in its favour as the focus of a hoax was the fact that the Stephens' cousin, W. W. Fisher, was stationed on the boat as flag-commander to Admiral Sir William May. In Adrian Stephen's anti-establishment view, 'anyone who took up an attitude of authority over anyone else was necessarily also someone who offered a leg for everyone else to pull'.[7]

Though the scale of this hoax surpassed anything that Cole and Stephen had previously achieved, a precedent had been set when, as undergraduates, hearing that the Sultan of Zanzibar was in England, they had impersonated him making a state visit to Cambridge. Three other friends had been coerced, a trip made to a theatrical costumier in London and a telegram sent warning the authorities of their arrival. They were duly met at the station by the Town Clerk and driven in a carriage to the Guildhall, where they were formally received by the Mayor. There followed a royal tour of the principal colleges and a visit to a charity bazaar. Afterwards Cole supplied the *Daily Mail* with a full account of what had happened. The Mayor asked the Vice-Chancellor to have Cole and Stephen sent down. The Vice-Chancellor agreed to do so if the Mayor insisted, but suggested that for the sake of his reputation he might like to think the matter over. He did so and no retribution followed.

Having got away with this, Cole and Stephen were game for still more outrageous acts. What they were now planning was the most colossal practical joke on the Admiralty. Duncan, Adrian and Virginia Stephen, Cole and two others – Anthony Buxton and Guy Ridley – were to constitute another royal appearance as four Abyssinian princes,[8] accompanied by an interpreter and a Foreign Office official. Preparations began days beforehand, and there were lengthy discussions with the theatrical costumier Willy Clarkson concerning the correct dress and make-up. The princes, one of whom was Virginia Stephen, were provided with short, crisp, curly black beards and artificial lips, and faces, hands and arms had to be dyed before head-dress and flowing robes were donned. Not only was it decided that each prince should wear an early Christian cross on a gold chain, but that their persons should glitter with costly jewels. Cole squandered a small fortune in attaining this end: he regarded imitation jewellery as useless and spent £500 on real gems.

The date fixed for the hoax was 7 February 1910.[9] The night beforehand Duncan slept at the Stephens', in order to be on hand at seven o'clock the next morning when Mr Clarkson's assistants arrived to make them up. Even Adrian, who was acting as the interpreter, had to have a fairly elaborate disguise so that W. W. Fisher would not recognise this six-foot-five-inch gentleman as his cousin. The moustache, false beard, sunburn powder and bowler hat all made him look, so he thought, 'like a seedy commercial traveller'.[10] Duncan, too, thought that in this get-up Adrian looked 'a horrid sort of fellow . . . of German extraction'.[11] In order to reach the *Dreadnought*, then docked in Portland Harbour, they took a train from Paddington to Weymouth. Because of the false lips that the princes were wearing, only Cole and Adrian could lunch on the train, with Cole attempting to teach Adrian Swahili from a grammar book bought from the Society for the Propagation of the Gospel. A telegram, now to be found in an Admiralty Papers file in the Public Record Office, preceded their arrival. It announced that Prince Makalin of Abyssinia and his suite would arrive at Weymouth at 4.20 p.m. 'He wishes to see *Dreadnought*,' the wire read. 'Kindly arrange meet them on arrival regret short notice forgot wire before interpreter accompanies them Harding [*sic*] Foreign Office.'

On Cole's instruction, the telegram was sent mid-afternoon. According to Admiral May, it did not arrive until 3.45 p.m., leaving him no time to wire the Admiralty or do anything other than prepare for the imminent arrival of these royal visitors. The then Under-Secretary of State for Foreign Affairs was Sir Charles Hardinge, and May assumed they were acting on his authority and that the short notice was merely another test of the navy's infallible efficiency and love of ordered display. Duncan, who had always admired the navy from afar, now found himself and his friends the object of their attention. He told Maynard:

> We drew up on Weymouth Harbour Station, where we found a lovely young lieutenant in full clothes drawn up with a detachment of blue jackets, saluting. We then stepped into the Admiral's carriage ... Eventually, moment of moments [we] drew up at the *Dreadnought* where we found a full regiment of marines drawn up on deck playing Yankee Doodle, streaming flags in every direction: the Admiral and full staff drawn up on deck to receive us. Can you believe it? They were perfectly charming and showed us all over the ship.[12]

If Duncan looked on with incredulous delight, Adrian's heart quailed when he learnt that there was a man on board who could speak to Abyssinians in their own language; luckily, the same man was absent on leave that day. This left Adrian free to resort to Virgil's *Aeneid*, large chunks of which he had learnt by heart as a schoolboy. With great fluency he flung slurred passages at the princes, who murmured '*Bunga, bunga*' as their chorus of approval, Virginia offering as a variation on this '*Chuck-a-choi, chuck-a-choi*'. When light rain fell and, simultaneously, Adrian noticed that Duncan's moustache had begun to peel off, he murmured about the hot Abyssinian climate and English drizzle to the Captain who, taking the point, led them below, a diversion that allowed Adrian to dab unnoticed at Duncan's moustache. An offer of tea, for obvious reasons, had to be refused, Adrian informing the authorities that the princes disliked eating in public. On behalf of the princes, he accepted with dignity the Admiral's apology for the fact that there was no Abyssinian flag on board, nor could they discover among the music its National Anthem. The National Anthem for Zanzibar had to be played in its stead. '*Bunga, bunga*,' the princes murmured, the party declining an eighteen-gun salute and making a sharp departure in order to catch the six o'clock express train to London. A carriage had again been booked and, now in their element, the princes played their parts thoroughly, insisting that the waiters wear white gloves when they served food in the private carriage.

Once again Cole could not resist making the affair public. He first told the Foreign Office, causing an investigative flurry at an official level, with letters passing between Admiral May on the *Dreadnought* and the Admiralty, and in Parliament, where questions were asked. A photograph of the participants in the hoax, taken just before they set out, reached the press, no doubt with Cole's help. Meanwhile it was alleged that during the course of the hoax the Royal Abyssinian Order had been conferred on Admiral May, who had applied to the King for permission to wear it, a story that the Admiralty denied. King Edward himself expressed anger at the way in which his navy had been made to look foolish, and the press went to town on the story. Sailors in uniform were mocked in the streets by cries of '*Bunga, bunga*', the same phrase appearing in music-hall songs. Such was the embarrassment caused to the navy that the ship's log, now housed in the Public Record Office, contains no mention of the Abyssinians' visit, the whole event having been expunged from the record.

It was hard for the authorities to know how to act. Sir Charles Hardinge thought the best plan was to do nothing. Adrian learnt through Mrs McKenna, wife of the First Lord of the Admiralty, that an apology would help. As a result he and Duncan went to Whitehall for a meeting with the First Lord in his private rooms. It was an awkward affair. The suggestion on the part of the two young men that they wished, by apologising, to remove the blame that had fallen on the officers in charge led McKenna to reply that such a suggestion was impertinent: no one in the navy was to be blamed and apology was not to be countenanced. They left feeling like errant schoolboys, afterwards hearing indirectly that McKenna had secretly been amused by the hoax but, not wanting a repeat of the same, had treated them harshly.

In fact the only illegal aspect was the sending of a telegram under another person's name, and though action was considered, none was taken. Some kind of justice had to be sought, however, and the navy took it upon themselves to carry it out. Had they discovered at the time of the hoax that one of the party was a woman, they would have thrown her into the sea. As it was, they contented themselves by venting their anger on a couple of the people involved. Duncan was one of these. One Sunday morning while he was breakfasting, a party of officers arrived at his parents' Hampstead house. According to Adrian Stephen, the maid announced that some gentlemen had called to see him, and a moment later his mother saw her son tripped up and pushed into a taxi. The door slammed shut and off it drove. Naturally alarmed, she appealed to her husband for advice as to what they should do. ' "I expect it's his friends from the *Dreadnought*," said Major Grant with his usual beaming smile, and so, of course, it was. Duncan found himself seated on the floor at the feet of three large men who were carrying a bundle of canes.'[13] With these, the officers intended carrying out a ceremonial birching. They drove north and, on reaching a grassy area, told Duncan to get out. Realising there was no use fighting against his fate, Duncan meekly did as he was told, thereby taking the wind out of their sails. 'I can't make this chap out,' said one of the officers, 'he does not put up any fight. You can't cane a chap like that.' In the end two ceremonial taps were administered and the party broke up, the naval officers by then very concerned as to how Duncan was to get home, as he was still wearing his slippers and had no hat. He was pressed to accept a lift, which he declined, feeling it would be less embarrassing to travel home by Tube.

When Duncan moved into Fitzroy Square, it had a derelict air, despite its elegant Robert Adam façades. Most of the terraces no longer housed the well-to-do, but offices, nursing homes and small artisans' workshops. The only relic of the gentility that had once characterised the square was the beadle, who marched round dressed in top hat and a tail-coat piped with red and studded with brass buttons.

The Stephens, also on the west side but eight doors away at no. 29, were the only people in the square, as far as Duncan knew, who had a whole house to themselves, complete with cook, maid and dog. 'A close friendship sprang up between Adrian Stephen and myself,' Duncan recalled, 'and I had only to tap on the window of his room on the ground floor to be let in. The maid told Virginia that "that Mr Grant gets in everywhere". But very irregular as my visits were, they became more and more a habit, and I think they soon became frequent enough to escape notice.'[14]

Their house fascinated Duncan. He was aware that it had been divided so that the habits of both siblings were adequately satisfied: Virginia worked in a room on the second floor, while Adrian took over the front room of the ground floor. His study was book-lined and much lived-in, a comfortable place in which to give friends tea. It was also the room in which their Thursday evening gatherings took place. The main drawing-room occupied the whole of the first floor. It was well proportioned, with long windows overlooking the square, and furnished with a green carpet, red brocade curtains, comfortable furniture and G. F. Watts's portrait of Sir Leslie Stephen hanging on one wall. Yet the room also had, to Duncan's mind, a ghostly feel and he thought the Stephens did not feel very much at home in it. It did, however, house the pianola, Duncan marvelling at the performances of Beethoven and Wagner, the trills and roulades, which Adrian, merely by pumping the machine with his feet, could produce. The effort of doing so caused him to sway like a performer, so that someone coming into the room and seeing him from the back might have mistaken him for a new Paderewski.

Like others, Duncan would turn up at about ten o'clock on Thursday evenings, for whisky, buns, cocoa and conversation. He found Virginia at this time very shy; she never addressed the company as a whole, but would talk to the person nearest to her. He also noticed, 'There was something a little fierce and aloof in her manner to most men. To her women friends especially older women like Miss Pater and Miss Janet Case she seemed to open herself with less reserve.'[15] With hindsight, Duncan felt that many of those who attended the Thursday evenings, among them Desmond MacCarthy, Charles Sanger, Theodore Llewellyn Davies, Charles Tennyson and Hilton Young (later Lord Kennet), had not yet 'come alive' for her. He had the impression that she responded so intensely to new experiences, and was so fascinated by facts she had not come across before, 'that feeding on detail she hardly had time to consider the present'.[16] It was only years afterwards that, having viewed the scene from many angles, she was able to gain a complete picture of what had happened. Nevertheless, in the company of the Stephens, Duncan instinctively felt that they had come through suffering to an independence, which rubbed off on their friends. 'They had enough money to live on. They were in a position to defy the conventions of the world that had produced them and that same world naturally felt aggrieved.'[17]

In January 1910 he persuaded Virginia to sit for him. At least two sittings took place, and after the second Duncan remarked to Maynard that she sat like a rock.[18] All that resulted from this was a drawing, but a year later he had the opportunity to do something more. Virginia visited her sister at Gordon Square when Duncan was painting there. As his painting tools were already spread about the place, she felt no alarm and proceeded to have a long conversation with her sister while Duncan, almost unconsciously, caught her likeness in a vibrant oil.[19] Her dislike of sitting for artists troubled all subsequent attempts at catching her likeness. Duncan himself may have felt a little nervous on both occasions. 'To be intimate with Virginia Stephen,' he later recalled, 'was not to be on easy terms. I do not think that one expected it to be easy. Indeed the greater the intimacy the greater the danger of sudden outbursts of scathing criticism.'[20]

This did not surprise Duncan, as no one in this group of friends received much kindly encouragement of their work. And yet one fundamental link between them was a respect for the seriousness with which vocations were pursued. Complete frankness was expected from every member. As for the notion of success, Duncan was of the opinion that no one ever thought about it at this date, perhaps because it seemed, if not wholly unobtainable, too far off.

He was, however, troubled by his failure to earn money. Sale of his work through the New English Art Club brought him £4 12s in January 1910. The absence of any more regular income left him dependent on the generosity of others. For this reason he turned again to the notion of becoming a schoolmaster and that same month attended an interview with a Dr Barber at the Leys School in Cambridge, after which Maynard's parents gave him dinner and four shillings for his return fare to London. He was informed by letter that he was too young and inexperienced for the post. 'I am disappointed,' he admitted to Maynard, 'as I think I could have borne it, and it would have set the money-waggers silent.'[21] Keynes, who had recommended him for the post, heard the same from Dr Barber: 'If he had been less of a boy in appearance and had had a little experience I should probably have taken him.'[22]

Duncan's dedication to art, meanwhile, never wavered. He finished his portrait of Cecil Taylor and, so he told Maynard, began a self-portrait (one of several painted at around this time) and was also working on 'Marjorie'. This last was probably *Crime and Punishment*, for which Marjorie Strachey sat with her head in her hands. Duncan originally called this work 'Despair', a subject that perhaps came close to his feelings about his own career, for in February he took on a stand-in job for a week at a school in Islington. Though he had only four little boys in his class, he found himself drifting into the behaviour of a regular schoolmaster, reacting over-severely and with irritation at the slightest provocation.

That month he accepted Maynard's invitation to accompany him on a visit to Greece and Asia Minor, an opportunity made possible by Maynard's financial generosity. Duncan felt it his duty to inform Maynard, before they set out, that he had fallen in love with Adrian Stephen.

Adrian, though now in his twenty-seventh year, was still regarded by his siblings as the baby of the family. He had been his mother's favourite and was possibly more devastated by her early death than anyone realised. Virginia was later to remark teasingly that he had been 'squeezed in the womb' by the weight of their father's work on the *Dictionary of National Biography*. It had certainly been noticeable that Leslie Stephen had less time for his younger son than for his much adored elder son, Thoby. Adrian followed Thoby to Trinity College, Cambridge, where again he was made aware that he could never be more than a pale imitation of his more successful and highly popular brother. The bitterness he felt may have fed his interest in hoaxes, which allowed him, if only momentarily, to get the better of those with power and authority. He also had a pronounced sense of humour and a sympathy with outsiders. Saxon Sydney-Turner, the quirkiest, least privileged member of Bloomsbury, was most frequently to be found in Adrian's rooms. At this time it was also becoming apparent that, though he attempted to follow the same path as Thoby, Adrian would never succeed in becoming a barrister. As an alternative he found work as a legal historian.

'I don't suppose for a moment it will ever come even to my saying anything to him,' Duncan wrote to Maynard of Adrian. 'But the fact remains, that although I seem clearly to see his faults (and they are many) I am always extraordinarily happy when I'm in that house, and he's there. I'm not, I suppose, very unhappy when I'm not, though sometimes, faintly. So that you see the whole thing amounts perhaps only to a sort of pleasant friendship.'[23]

One thing Duncan did observe in the Stephens' house in Fitzroy Square was that its peaceful existence was sometimes disrupted by arguments so fierce that on one occasion Adrian sent a pat of butter flying in Virginia's direction. It missed her head and left a permanent stain on the wall. At such moments Duncan knew better than to take sides, as family solidarity was such that both would have turned on him instantly. When, in November 1911, the two Stephens took a house in Brunswick Square, which Duncan and Maynard shared with them, Adrian's lack of self-love could sometimes leave him totally inert and he would sit all day in a chair until something external to himself obliged him to move. A year or two later he was further wounded by unrequited love for Noel Olivier and sat in his chair weeping. Others took him out and walked him round the square, tears still pouring down his face because of Noel's refusal to marry him.

For a few years, however, until he was taken in hand by Karin Costelloe, Adrian could be flattered and warmed by Duncan's interest and affection. It was a fully sexual affair and liberated Adrian, who for a short period went with prostitutes and visited a brothel. Two portraits of him by Duncan remain at Charleston, both of which catch the pallor of his long face and the steadiness of his gaze, which conveys a subdued watchfulness. The impression remains of hidden depths, of a character whose complexities are withdrawn and possibly too deeply entangled to allow for any surface indication of them. Awareness of this may eventually have helped Adrian in his final choice of career: psychoanalysis. This licensed the inward gaze, allowing links to be made between the unconscious and the conscious, between inner and outer, thereby offering the possibility of discovering what sources of animation lay beneath his pale flesh.

With Thoby's death painfully lodged in her memory, Vanessa Bell took it upon herself, before Duncan left for Asia Minor in the spring of 1910, to warn him (apologising as she did so for her 'grandmotherly' behaviour) never to wash his teeth in ordinary water. She also gave him advice on how to cope with diarrhoea.

Shortly before leaving he attended a Friday Club meeting in order to hear Roger Fry give a talk. In January that year Fry and the Bells had met by chance on Cambridge railway station and, in the course of their journey to London, had agreed that an exhibition of modern French art was urgently needed in London. Fry had subsequently been invited to Gordon Square, where his lively mind and fascination not only with art but also with literature had stimulated furious discussion. At the Friday Club he read a paper entitled 'Representation as a means of Expression', in which he pursued ideas that he had first put forward in the *New Quarterly* in April 1909, in 'An Essay in Aesthetics' (reprinted in 1920 in Fry's seminal book *Vision and Design*). In this he acknowledged a debt to Denman Ross's *Theory of Pure Design*, one of the first texts to discuss the role played by forms and colours in art, considered as abstract entities in themselves. Fry pursued this notion further and tried to examine the way in which 'the emotional elements of design', as he now termed line, mass, space, colour, light, shade and the inclination of plane, relate to our physical experience of life – mass, for example, relating to our experience of gravity, rhythm to our awareness of muscular activity, and so on. The effect of Fry's reasoning was to free artists from the tyranny of mimetic representation. His final conclusion became a clarion call to modern art:

> We may, then, dispense once and for all with the idea of likeness to Nature, of correctness or incorrectness as a test, and consider only whether the emotional elements of design inherent in natural form are adequately discovered, unless, indeed, the emotional idea depends at any point upon likeness or completeness of representation.[24]

Fry's ideas would have opened Duncan's mind to the possibility of liberation from the hegemony of the Graeco-Roman and Renaissance traditions, with their emphasis on the close approximation of art to visual appearances, just as he was about to have his first major experience of Byzantine mosaics. Similarly, on his return, Fry's aesthetic reasoning may have helped him to obtain much pleasure from a major exhibition of Japanese art held in London in May.

Duncan and Maynard left London on 17 March 1910 and were away for seven weeks in all. They travelled by boat from Marseilles to Athens, and on arrival found a hotel that faced the Acropolis. They had shared a cabin *en route*, and during this time and throughout the rest of the trip appear to have avoided the unfortunate state of affairs that had marred their trip to Versailles. Duncan did afterwards feel obliged to apologise for behaving badly at times; he had done so, he explained, not out of a desire to be unkind, but owing to a periodic need to emphasise his difference from Keynes.

In Athens they employed a dragoman to accompany them on a journey by horse through the Peloponnese. They travelled through mountain villages to Bassae, carrying food supplies with them. It was a memorable trip. 'I must tell you about Greece when I see you,' Duncan wrote to Lytton. 'It is a divine country . . . but the remains of ancient Greece. Oh! how melancholy they make one.'[25] They moved on to Turkey, travelling on the *Paquebot Senegal*, stopping at Troy, where they stayed for two nights with an English couple, the Calverts, who owned a farm on the banks of the Skamander. At Smyrna they were both much taken with the exotic colours and noises of the bazaar. However, Duncan was disappointed with Constantinople, finding it too large and its narrow streets filthy, though he thought the Hagia Sophia one of the most impressive buildings he had ever seen. He felt much happier at Brusa (sometimes spelt Broussa or Bursa), the ancient Ottoman capital, with its magnificent mosques, tall minarets, cypresses and hot spring baths, situated amid beautiful scenery overlooked by Mount Olympus. One of the most significant experiences of all was the opportunity to familiarise himself with Byzantine mosaics. He was especially impressed by those in the Kariye Djami in Istanbul, though another year was to pass before evidence of this interest appeared in his work.

He looked so healthy on his return to London that people remarked on his appearance. Things were quieter than before, partly because Virginia Stephen, whose state of health ever since her breakdown in 1895–6 had been a cause of concern, had fallen ill before Duncan left for Greece and since then had suffered a relapse. Because of her delicate state, the Stephens' Thursday evenings had ended. Duncan, however, managed to see a great deal of Adrian, in between concentrated bouts of painting, as he was trying to finish what he called his 'Academy' picture – 'Despair' [*Crime and Punishment*], which he knew he would have to retitle. He considered calling it 'Grief', a somewhat topical title, as he had returned to London to find the nation mourning its late King. Shop windows were framed with black bands, everybody seemed dressed in widow's weeds, and even the chocolates on sale had been dyed purple. By chance Duncan witnessed the procession that accompanied the removal of Edward VII's remains to Westminster Abbey. He caught sight of Queen Alexandra, in a bridal veil, bowing to left and right, followed by a band playing a lively air.

In Greece his interest in figure drawing had revived. He himself posed naked at Bassae for some photographs that Maynard took. 'I developed Apollo in his temple at Bassae yesterday and printed him to-day,' Maynard told Duncan. 'He is *lovely* . . . It will be quite unnecessary to take in the *Sportszeitung* anymore.'[26] Though these snaps satisfied an erotic purpose, they also assisted Duncan's interest in the male nude as a vehicle for artistic expression. But it was not yet a subject that he felt able to deal with joyously and openly in his art and, back in London, he returned to *Grief*, which he intended sending to a Friday Club exhibition along with his portrait of James Strachey, which was still in progress. He gave Maynard permission to show the photographs of himself viewed from the back to intimate friends, provided he did not let on who it was – 'you must say that it was a shepherd or something and that no-one wears clothes in Arcadia'.[27]

An interest in homo–eroticism continued to fuel the friendship between Maynard and Duncan. From Cambridge, Maynard sent enticing descriptions of potential 'embryos'. 'Mr Luce sounds lovely,' Duncan replied (of Gordon Hannington Luce, an undergraduate at Emmanuel College, who was to become another of his conquests); 'cannot he be induced to pose in some empty niche – as St Sebastian?'[28] More worrying gossip concerned Virginia Stephen. Vanessa, who had given birth to her first son, Julian, in 1908, was now expecting her second child and simultaneously worrying about her sister, who had agreed to take a 'rest cure' and spend some six weeks in a private nursing home in Twickenham. Duncan went to see her immediately before she left for the home and found her in despair at the thought of not being allowed to see or hear from anyone for a fortnight.

This year Duncan at last experienced a degree of success. After seeing three of his paintings at the Friday Club exhibition in Mill Street in June 1910, William Rothenstein told Duncan that he thought they represented a 'capital' exposure of his 'serious capacity'. That year Vanessa Bell observed to Clive that there was something so fine and grand in Duncan's work that he might turn out to be a great painter. Such praise increased Duncan's confidence in himself and socially he now felt more at ease.

After dining with Henry Lamb one evening in July, he willingly accompanied him to one of Lady Ottoline Morrell's 'at homes'. She looked, Duncan thought, 'superb in a magnificent gown of grey clinging material with a red rose at her bosom' as she sat in a firelit room with incense burning. The conversation gradually decomposed into an admission by Ottoline and her husband Philip of affairs with both sexes, though to Duncan's regret much of this talk happened after he left and he only heard of it at second hand.

With Adrian now living alone at 29 Fitzroy Square, it was perhaps inevitable that Duncan spent much of that summer in his company. This upset Maynard, whose expectations regarding Duncan were still very high. Duncan visited Maynard in Cambridge in July, but afterwards apologised for behaving 'so unbearably'. Back in London he made visits to an army barracks to study horses for a mural he was planning, and missed Adrian, who had disappeared to Skegness. Rather at a loose end, Duncan went down to Brighton to see the exhibition 'Modern French Artists' organised by Robert Dell, where amid large quantities of Impressionist and academic painting were works by Gauguin, Matisse, Cézanne, Degas and Puvis de Chavannes. The impact made by Post-Impressionist artists was muffled by the muddled display, and the two artists most thoroughly represented were the conventional Louis Legrand and the dour Alphonse Legros. Duncan, who thought the show well worth visiting, met James and Pippa Strachey there, together with their mother, Lady Strachey, who readily voiced her fury at some of the pictures. It gave Duncan a foretaste of the critical onslaught that would be aroused later that year by the first of Roger Fry's two Post-Impressionist exhibitions.

If his days were busy, his evenings were often rather empty. 'I get bored with going to music halls,' he admitted to Maynard, 'and so sit and read alone [which] rather adds I find to the silence.'[29] The solution, in Maynard's eyes, was for Duncan to join him at Burford, where he had again rented a house for the summer. But, in the meantime, Adrian had procured a room for Duncan with a Mrs Hawkins at Skegness and as a result he decided to travel north.

First, however, he paid a couple of calls. Tea with Saxon Sydney-Turner in his rooms satisfied Duncan's curiosity concerning the rumour (correct) that he would find hanging in the sitting-room, on hideous mid-Victorian wallpaper, two identical prints. His second visit Duncan described to Maynard:

I went to tea with Vanessa on Monday and saw the new baby. The whole scene was quite a revelation to me of the passionate life that obtains in the early life-surroundings of a human being. To begin with there was Vanessa lying against heaped cushions with the radiant face of a mother of sons. Then her confidante Miss Snowden inventing things to be done for her. But the most important of all the vast and good humoured Gamp who sails into the room at 5.30 o'clock to give the squeaking infant a turn at its mama's nipples. She is an extraordinary character beaming with health, and is so jealous of her charge, that unless one gives it the most fabulous flattery, she is enraged.[30]

Despite his appreciation of others, Duncan still found that he mostly wanted to be with Adrian. He remained close to Maynard, with whom he occasionally made love, though he had to make an effort to satisfy Maynard's needs. But by December Maynard found that even when he was in town, staying at 21 Fitzroy Square, he had no guarantee of seeing Duncan, who was usually at 29 with Adrian. 'You're married to Adrian now,' he grumbled, 'which you weren't before.'[31] In reply, Duncan protested that he was not permanently at Adrian's side, nor did he wish to be. He wanted to go on seeing Maynard, and their relationship – though losing its significance and at times uncomfortably unbalanced – drifted on for some months yet.

That autumn Duncan began copying Michelangelo's *Entombment* in the National Gallery, apparently unaware of the shock and excitement about to be caused by the exhibition 'Manet and the Post-Impressionists', which opened in London on 5 November. He did know that Clive Bell, who assisted Fry in the selection of the show, was in Paris in October, but the implications of this seemed to him marital rather than artistic: 'Vanessa arrives today [from Studland] and is probably by this time a widow as Clive is in Paris,' Duncan gossiped to Maynard, 'and no communications have arrived from him.'[32]

Duncan barely knew Roger Fry at this time. Arrangements were made for him to visit Fry's Guildford home in October, but these had to be cancelled at the last minute. 'I'm so sorry but please don't give me up as no good,' Fry apologised, adding a note to the effect that he had admired one of Duncan's paintings at the Bells'.[33] Within a matter of weeks all this had changed and Duncan was to find himself caught up in the furure caused by Fry's introduction of French Post-Impressionism into Britain.

SEVEN

The Art-Quake of 1910

The exhibition now regarded as a landmark in the evolution of modernism came into existence almost by chance. Roger Fry, hearing that a West End dealer's premises, the Grafton Galleries in Dover Street,[1] had a gap in its programme, persuaded the management that they might do worse than mount a show of modern French art. He himself would select the works for the exhibition and would nominate a secretary to help with the business transactions.

The man he chose had recently entered the Bloomsbury circle. Desmond MacCarthy had begun to make a reputation as a literary and dramatic critic, and had married Molly Warre-Cornish, who was related to the Stephens through her aunt by marriage, Lady Ritchie, the novelist Anny Thackeray. The MacCarthys were always short of money, so when Fry suggested that Desmond, soon to become the father of a third child, should act as secretary, this notoriously unbusiness-like man willingly went along to be interviewed. The gallery director offered him a fee of £100. He added that *if* – and here he threw in a pitying smile – there were profits, Desmond would receive half of them. His attitude implied that few people were likely to be interested in such art, let alone want to buy it. Fry, too, predicted a financial failure and urged MacCarthy to keep all expenses low. He himself took nothing in the way of financial reward and was gambling his reputation as a critic on the hunch he had about the importance of modern French art. MacCarthy, on the other hand, to everyone's surprise, walked off with his share of the profits – £460 – a lump sum larger than any other he ever earnt.

Fry masterminded the show with a mixture of intuition, energy and luck. It was an approach that did not exclude muddle. Many years later MacCarthy claimed that he had got the job as secretary largely because Fry enjoyed his company and would not have felt comfortable with 'anyone implacably efficient'.[2] The unprofessional duo set off for Paris, armed with a bottle of champagne, which they drank on the boat bound for Calais, MacCarthy still suffering from the influenza that Fry had insisted should not deflect them from their purpose. Clive Bell met them in Paris, where their crucial contact was the journalist Robert Dell, who had organised the 'Modern French Artists' exhibition in Brighton earlier that year. Though he was to make his name as French correspondent for the *Manchester Guardian* and the *New Statesman*, Dell had been the founder-editor of the *Burlington Magazine*, was still more interested in painting than in politics and quite undeterred by one of the worst French accents that MacCarthy had ever heard. Dell took them to see dealers. Day after day MacCarthy watched as Fry sat with his hands on his knees, exclaiming aloud with surprised delight at the pictures put in front of him. MacCarthy's reactions were more equivocal: Van Gogh's portrait of Monsieur Rolin, the postman, struck him as 'wonderfully hideous, alive and . . . disconcerting', almost certain to send people back to the turnstile, clamouring for the return of their entrance fee.[3]

One of Fry's gifts was his ability to extemporise in any circumstances. He had intended ending his French visit with a short bicycling tour with his friend Goldsworthy Lowes Dickinson. When Dickinson backed out, Fry simply insisted that MacCarthy should take his place. It proved immensely enjoyable even though, at their final destination, Rheims, MacCarthy, having taken a fall, arrived covered with tar. Thence he took a train to Munich; Fry, whose faith in others was as inexhaustible as his energy, trusted completely in MacCarthy's ability to select more works there on his own. Fry also left it to MacCarthy to build on an introduction from the critic Felix Feneon to Mme Gosschalk-Bonger, through whom they obtained further paintings by her brother-in-law, Van Gogh.

A similar haphazardness affected the choice of title for the show. With artists as diverse as Manet, Gauguin, Cézanne and Matisse, as well as the now relatively forgotten Pierre Laprade, Auguste Herbin and Pierre Girieud, it was difficult to find a suitable umbrella term that would contain them all and signify their difference from the Impressionists. Discussing this problem with MacCarthy and the gallery owners, Fry lost patience. 'Oh,' he is reported as saying, 'let's just call them post-impressionists', a term which, as he went on to point out, was at the very least chronologically accurate.[4]

News that something unusual was afoot brought journalists flocking to the press day on 5 November. MacCarthy, anxious not to provide any easy targets for philistine abuse, had been careful to vet the subject matter of each picture, keeping a wary eye out for glaring nudity, and at the last moment deciding that two pictures would be best left unhung. Even so he was aware, as he watched the press scribbling, tittering and expostulating, that the exhibition would administer a huge shock to the

English public. The press did not fail his expectations. Such were the excitement and rancour conveyed by the reviews that, once the exhibition finally opened on 8 November, the public crowded in.

Much has been written about the reaction to this show and its impact on artists.[5] Though the critical response was mixed, it was mostly reactionary and derisive. The art critic Robert Ross professed 'a certain feeling of sadness that distinguished critics ... should be found to welcome pretension and imposture'.[6] Representatives of the medical profession endorsed a view that the paintings were the work of the mentally deranged.[7] To those whose pictorial diet had been fed by the Edwardian love of tonal gradations, elegance, naturalism, sentimental anecdotalism and mimetic veracity, Post-Impressionism seemed crude, unskilled and unreal. The only source of help lay in MacCarthy's catalogue introduction, written at Fry's behest and based on some of his scribbled notes. In it MacCarthy attempted to direct attention away from notions of correct or incorrect representation and to replace it with an awareness of the artist's attempt to capture 'the emotional significance which lies in things'. It was good advice in relation to the art of Van Gogh or Gauguin but less obviously helpful in relation to the more constructive and analytical work of Cézanne.

What neither Fry, nor MacCarthy, nor anyone else had predicted was that the exhibition would be interpreted as symptomatic, not just of radical new developments in art, but of social and political unrest. Britain might be enjoying a period of 'splendid isolation', but threats and anxieties were accumulating that made for an underlying nervousness. Industrial unrest had erupted in the Welsh coal-miners' strike, which was broken up that month by troops. The Irish were demanding Home Rule and the Suffragettes were gaining in strength. Only a few days after the show opened at the Grafton Galleries, the Suffragettes marched on the House of Commons while Asquith spoke on the question of Women's Rights: 117 arrests were made, the six-hour protest marking a 'Black Friday' that set off a programme of window-smashing, arson and bombs as the Suffragettes, denied political power through the normal democratic procedures, resorted to violence. In certain articles that appeared in the press, Post-Impressionism became linked with Socialism and Women's Suffrage, all three suggesting an impatience with the old order in favour of new ideals. When the critic Frank Rutter published a small pamphlet that year, *Revolution in Art*, in defence of Post-Impressionism, he dedicated it to 'Rebels of either sex all the world over who are in any way fighting for freedom of any kind'. Meanwhile Fry, who was regularly being denounced as an anarchist, was surprised to see how deeply he had offended those aristocrats who had once so eagerly attended his lectures on Italian art. To be cultured, it had been assumed, was an occupation for the leisured, and therefore for the privileged. Fry's suggestion that all one needed to appreciate a Matisse was a certain sensibility had rather terrifying democratic implications. Admiration for the Post-Impressionists, therefore, aligned one with the twentieth century and with change.[8] Quentin Bell has observed that by exhibiting Post-Impressionism in London, Fry overnight 'destroyed the whole tissue of comfortable falsehoods on which that age based its views of beauty, propriety and decorum'.[9]

Duncan left no account of his immediate reactions to Roger Fry's first Post-Impressionist exhibition. We know, however, that between 8 November 1910, when the show opened, and 15 January 1911, when it closed, he made good use of a season ticket.[10] The foremost proof, however, of the significance that this event had for him is to be found in his paintings. Suddenly impatient with the conventions shaping, for example, his elegant portrait of James Strachey,[11] he began to search for alternative styles, which allowed the ingredients in an artist's vocabulary – colour, pattern, line, shape and pictorial space – to have a vibrancy and reality of their own, independent of any representational role.

He did not visit the exhibition until a week after it opened: he was too hard at work getting pictures ready to send to the New English Art Club's winter exhibition. That year he needed an invitation before he could submit entries and one had been supplied by Roger Fry, with certain qualifications. 'As you know,' he warned Duncan, 'I am by no means enthusiastic about the Society but still it is so far the only one that offers much chance and perhaps you should make use of it.'[12] Together they agreed that Duncan should visit 'Manet and the Post-Impressionists', as the exhibition was eventually called, on 15 November, after which he and Fry would travel together to Durbins, Fry's house near Guildford, where Duncan was to stay the night. In the meantime Duncan saw no irony in focusing his attention on the New English, a society that was rapidly becoming a bastion of rearguard action. One of its supporters, Philip Wilson Steer, walked round the Post-Impressionist show in silence, allegedly saying as he left, 'Well, I suppose they all have private incomes.'[13] He and Professor Tonks, in the weeks to come when Cézanne became the subject of endless debate, so wearied of this artist's name that they took to calling him 'Mr Harris'.

Duncan worked hard getting his pictures ready for the New English, and at five in the afternoon on submission day dashed off with them in a cab. One picture, he told Maynard, 'is not really finished in the least'.[14] None probably had the degree of finish expected by the New English jury, as they rejected everything Duncan submitted except a pencil drawing. Shortly afterwards, however, Clive Bell paid ten pounds for one of his oils. This was probably delayed payment for *The Lemon Gatherers*, which Vanessa Bell had bought in June.[15] She informed Clive that she had done so the day afterwards, adding that in her opinion Duncan was 'certainly much the most interesting of the young painters'.[16]

With its frieze-like row of foreground figures, loosely painted in sombre colours, *The Lemon Gatherers* remains a significant work in Duncan Grant's career. It is said to have been inspired by some Sicilian players whom he saw perform tragedies based on peasant life at the Shaftesbury Theatre in London in the spring of 1908. However, the low viewpoint and the scale of the figures in relation to the format admit an important debt to Piero della Francesca's frescos based on the story of the True Cross at Arezzo. The potential drama, between the row of figures and the luminous sky and landscape beyond, is not fully realised, and in 1913 Duncan was to return to this same subject, making the shapes, intervals and tonal contrasts more pronounced. He revived the subject yet again in 1919, when he made a third picture out of the left-hand side of the composition. The dramatic effect of a low viewpoint fascinated him and he adopts it again in *The Dancers*[17] of 1910–11, where it gives a certain grandeur to the dancers silhouetted against the sky. Here the colours, brighter in hue than those used in *The Lemon Gatherers*, and the schematic handling found in the treatment of the grassy knoll, reflect his move towards a Post-Impressionist style.[18] Unlike the wild and extravagant contortions adopted by his later drawings and paintings of dancers and acrobats, under the inspiration of Matisse, Nijinsky and the Ballets Russes, these female dancers remain stately and restrained as they circle gracefully against an evening sky. More sweeping and experimental is the second and larger version[19] that he made of this subject for the Second Post-Impressionist Exhibition of 1912–13. Again the heads of the dancers bump along the top of the canvas, and, though this version is more broadly handled, the lazy rhythms suggest amplitude and space, the picture conveying an impression of being much bigger than it actually is.

The sale of a picture to Clive allowed Duncan to repay Maynard some of the money he owed him. There were days when he simply had no money at all; in order to dine with Adrian and Virginia Stephen and Vanessa Bell in November 1910 at a French restaurant in Leicester Square, he had to borrow 2s 6d. At times like these the cheque from Maynard that arrived the next day came as a godsend. His paintings continued to sell mostly to friends, though his reputation took off rapidly during the next few years. Soon after Adrian Stephen bought the first version of *The Dancers*, completed in 1911, he sold it to Eddie Marsh, then working as a secretary but later to become an eminent civil servant and picture-collector, and it hung for some time in a prominent place in his living-room in Gray's Inn. While it remained in his collection, Marsh arranged for a facsimile reproduction to be made of it, together with one of John Nash's *Cornfield*, by means of colour collotype. Published by the Fine Art Trade Guild in both limited and unlimited editions, this was the first instance of the gradual dissemination of Duncan Grant's work into the popular domain.

His visit to Durbins, Roger Fry's house at Guildford, gave Duncan a glimpse into the older man's tragic personal history. For several years his wife, Helen, had hovered on the brink of permanent insanity and early in 1910, on medical advice, he had given in and agreed to have her certified and committed to an asylum. The pain this caused him, together with a sense of waste, had liberated him from any petty precautions or interest in prestigious positions. Nothing could now deter him from pursuing his own convictions and interests with a certain recklessness and daring energy. There was also a guileless streak in Fry, fostered by his severe Quaker background, which resulted in him never expecting anyone to be anything but completely truthful. It had shocked him to discover, whilst working as European Adviser to New York's Metropolitan Museum of Art, that the Chairman of its Trustees, the fabulously wealthy John Pierpont Morgan, was not averse to putting his own interests as a collector before those of the museum he ostensibly served. Fry was appalled and made his opinions known to Morgan, with the result that Fry's appointment with the museum was abruptly terminated.

On this first visit, Duncan enjoyed meeting Fry's son and daughter, Julian and Pamela. He thought them well brought up and observed how they spent all one morning painting a view from a window with their father. The surrounding countryside was beautiful and Fry's talk of founding some alternative to the New English interested Duncan. As a bond of friendship, they exchanged pictures. Fry, however, was almost twenty years older than Duncan and considerably more experienced. Shared interests and genuine admiration for each other's talents drew them together, but their friendship always retained a vein of reserve, caused in part by Duncan's respect for Fry's intellect. 'I thought Roger Fry extremely nice but rather exhausting,' Duncan afterwards wrote to Maynard, ' – he makes up his mind so extraordinarily quickly.'[20]

Whereas Bloomsbury had so far been predominantly literary, its agenda was now reset by Roger Fry: during the course of his first Post-

Impressionist exhibition, he wrote three essays on Post-Impressionism for the *Nation* and delivered a public lecture in the Grafton Gallery, which was afterwards published in the *Fortnightly Review*.[21] He frequently fell into conversation with visitors to the show and gave lectures on it in the provinces. The public furore that the Post-Impressionists aroused obliged Bloomsbury to abandon the privacy of the drawing-room and engage in public debate.

Duncan must have found the importance suddenly accorded to painting enormously stimulating. The new freedom that gradually began to appear in his work finds a parallel in his handwriting, which changes, becoming larger and more idiosyncratic, the characters betraying those quirks of formation that were from now on so vividly to convey his personality.

In March 1911 the painter Francis Dodd wrote to Duncan offering to propose him for membership of the New English Art Club: he had admired a work by Duncan in a recent Friday Club exhibition and C.J. Holmes was willing to second his proposal. It was an honour that had come too late: Duncan was now more interested in alternative outlets. A member of Sickert's Fitzroy Street Group had mentioned that they were thinking of reforming the group along the lines of a twice-yearly exhibiting society. Would Duncan join it? He did so, becoming a founder member of the Camden Town Group and exhibiting in its December 1911 show *Parrot Tulips*,[22] which was bought by the collector Edward Marsh. He was also aware that Fry had hopes of some kind of advisory position at the Grafton Galleries, where he wanted to mount at least one show a year that would bring together 'the best non-academic forces'.[23] The Contemporary Art Society (CAS) was another vital ingredient within the changing scene. It had been founded in 1910 in an attempt to encourage museums and galleries to acquire modern art. Fry acted as a buyer for the CAS during its first year and in January 1911 asked Duncan if he could have first refusal on his next imaginative work.

There was a feeling in the air that a new era had begun. When the first Post-Impressionist exhibition closed in mid-January, a party was held that seems to have celebrated both an ending and a beginning. It took place at Crosby Hall and many of the guests, including Adrian and Virginia Stephen, went dressed as Gauguinesque savages. Fry had recently bought reams of brightly patterned cloth, made in Manchester for the African market, and draped in this, some of the revellers seemed determined to banish the elegance and restraint associated with the Edwardian period. The party must have been a great success, for when Duncan held another in his studio that spring several guests again wore Gauguinesque costumes. Rumours concerning the earlier party gave one of his guests, Karin Costelloe, daughter of Mary Berenson, the expectation that she would find her host dressed in practically nothing at all. Instead she found 'our bold host amply covered in yellow cotton and buttercups in his hair, with a generous display of jaeger vest at the open neck, clutching firmly a voluminous cloak.' Expecting to see life in a new and shocking way, she found the actual party fairly dull. 'Then the company settled themselves on the floor and by the light of two dim candles and the fire, sustained a weary and wandering discussion on the relative values of belief in true and false propositions, till two fifteen, when the lights were turned on and we dispersed.'[24] Much livelier was the party that her sister Ray gave two years later, to which Duncan came dressed as a whore great with child. In the course of the proceedings he was suddenly seized with labour pains and, after much commotion, during which doctors and midwives were summoned, finally succeeded in giving birth to a pillow.

'Everyone is moving out of town for Easter,' Lytton Strachey informed his brother James towards the end of March 1911. 'Duncan and Pozzo [Maynard] to Italy via Africa, Bloomsbury [Roger Fry and the Bells] to Athens via Austria and Norton to Japan via Moscow.' He added that one of the principal features of the last month had been movement within Bloomsbury – 'chiefly Nessa and dear Clive (who's possibly working up for a grand Reconciliation)'.[25]

Despite Bloomsbury's love of gossip, in which Lytton especially indulged, very little had been said about the Bells' marital difficulties. In the summer of 1908, a few months after the birth of her first child, Vanessa, whilst holidaying in awkward circumstances in lodgings in Cornwall, had felt doubly betrayed by the flirtation that had sprung up between her husband and her sister. The following year Clive had revived an affair with a Mrs Raven-Hill, a married woman who had played no small part in his pre-marital sexual education. At one point Duncan had learnt that Clive was 'in disgrace' but there was never any report of serious trauma or upheaval. It could, however, be inferred that the basis of the Bells' marriage had shifted and that the expectations invested in it had altered.

Duncan was happy that spring to accept Maynard's proposal that they should visit Sicily, but less delighted by the news that Gwen Darwin, granddaughter of the famous scientist, had become engaged to the French painter Jacques Raverat. 'I am going to Firle tomorrow where are to be the newly engaged couple (Jacques and Gwen) and Ka Cox, but [isn't] it queer of those two to get married?'[26] Marriage was an institution that depressed him and which he came to dislike more and more, but in this particular instance Duncan had reason to feel disturbed by the news. The previous year Jacques had proposed to Ka Cox and, although she had refused him, he was still hoping for intimacy with her, claiming that he loved both her and Gwen. All three were 'Neo-Pagans', a group of friends slightly younger than the Bloomsbury group, interested in the simple life, and in Fabianism, and whose figurehead was the gloriously handsome but somewhat unhappy Rupert Brooke.

The visit to Firle took Duncan to Little Talland House, a semi-detached cottage leased by Virginia Stephen and named by her after the house in Cornwall where the Stephen family had spent their summer holidays. His acquaintance with Jacques and Gwen, who were to marry on 27 May 1911, must have solidified there into friendship, for he offered them the use of his studio during his absence in April. Gwen and Jacques shared, and possibly helped stimulate, Duncan's interest in wall painting: later that year they invited him to become part of a group of eight, the number needed for a course of six lessons on the techniques of wall painting at Chelsea Polytechnic.

With Jacques, Duncan felt an immediate sympathy. The son of an intellectual French businessman who had made his fortune as head of the Le Havre docks, Jacques had been sent to school in England, at Bedales. Thence he had gone to the Sorbonne to read mathematics, returning to England for further study at Emmanuel College, Cambridge, where he had met Rupert Brooke. In his early twenties he suffered a sudden mental and physical collapse, a breakdown that may have signalled the onset of the multiple sclerosis (not diagnosed until 1914) that cut short his life. Advised to give up mathematics, he returned to England and, after a short period working for the Ashendene Press, entered the Slade. 'I like to paint flat pictures,' he wrote to Duncan. 'Gwen says a lot of nonsense about tactile values. Do you think one ought to think about them? I think that if you want to say things about solid objects you ought to carve. I am going to start tomorrow. I shall paint God as flat as a pancake and carve him as round as an apple.'[27] Duncan agreed to visit Jacques and Gwen in the summer of 1911 at Jacques's family home, Prunoy, in France, in order to join with them in the making of a wall painting. The plan was abandoned because difficulties arose between Jacques and his family. He and Gwen fled to another part of France for the rest of the summer, hoping that the change of scene would make Jacques feel less tired and nervy.

Duncan's spring travels again proved fruitful to his development as an artist. The trip Maynard had organised took them to Sicily via Morocco.

They spent a few days in Tunis, where they admired the beauty of Arab males and visited the Bardo Museum with its extensive collection of late Roman mosaics. They also visited the holy Muslim city of Kairouan, where Duncan bought two plain vases to which he added painted decorations, and which he kept all his life. Continuing their journey, the two friends crossed to Palermo, visiting also Taormina, Segesta, Monreale and Syracuse. For Duncan, the most significant experience was probably his visit to the great Norman cathedral of S. Maria la Nuova in Monreale, with its famous twelfth-century mosaics, for it was immediately after this trip that the influence of mosaics began to appear in his painting. He was also impressed by the dramatic use of simple geometric patterns in the Romanesque stone-carving in the cathedral's cloister.

On a personal level, the holiday had its complications. Duncan had warned Maynard that he wanted to spend some days with Adrian, who had also planned to visit Italy that April. Maynard, suffering bitterly from a want of Duncan's affection, faced loneliness and misery. There was little Duncan could do to improve matters, so he simply got on with his plans. It was in Adrian's company that he finally left Capri for Naples, whence Adrian caught a boat home. Duncan took a train to Rome, where he spent many hours in the Sistine Chapel, Michelangelo's murals deepening still further his interest in the human figure as a vehicle for expression.

He left Rome for Paris, with the intention of putting into use an introduction from Simon Bussy to Matisse. But his first attempt to meet this artist led to the discovery that Matisse was 'at home' only on Monday afternoons. Duncan therefore resolved to stay on in Paris over the weekend, lodging at his old haunt, the Hotel de l'Univers et du Portugal, where he found many of the characters he had known before ('which is pleasant, but I do not really like Paris'), and was delighted to discover that a fine exhibition of Ingres's work had just opened ('a great piece of luck').[28]

Finally the day came for his visit to Matisse – this artist, some sixteen years older than himself, who in the last seven years had emerged, in competition with Picasso, as one of the most innovative figures within French art. To Duncan's surprise this *fauve* lived with his wife and daughter in a small red-brick house in the suburbs of Paris at Issy-les-Moulineaux. Like many an English suburban villa, the house had a large garden and a greenhouse in which, again to Duncan's surprise, Matisse grew not rare orchids but nasturtiums. There was also a big studio in the garden where Matisse was at work on a large painting of nasturtiums, as well as a very large canvas, which was probably the early version of

Dance, now in the Museum of Modern Art, New York. For some reason Duncan felt unable to engage the painter in discussion. 'He saw I couldn't talk to him about painting,' he recalled many years later, 'and I was very pleased to see him at work. He left me alone in a very understanding way.'[29] If Duncan lacked words, he made good use of his eyes: Matisse's painting, *Nasturtiums*, incorporates part of the large decorative work, *Dance*, into its background, actual space blending with pictorial space as the real flowers merge with the painted figures in an uninterrupted continuum, a visual idea that Duncan adopted for his own purposes, from now on frequently blending still-life objects or flowers with background cloths, pictures or mural decorations.

The impact of Matisse, coming so soon after his experience of North Africa, Sicily and the *terribilità* of the Sistine Chapel, must have left Duncan surfeited with stimuli. It took some months before the French artist's example began to influence his handling of colour. A more immediate impact can be observed in *Man with Greyhound*,[30] which almost certainly post-dates his visit to Matisse's studio. The emphatic outlines created by the leaping dog and crouching man, and the interplay between the positive and negative shapes, echo the formal concerns shaping Matisse's *Dance*. It is as if Duncan had suddenly learnt to diminish the emphasis on materiality, on textures, light and shade, in order to allow for a more vibrant use of line, interval, structure and movement. Matisse helped liberate him from the tyranny of appearances, freeing him also to develop a very personal vein of fancy and wit.

Unmitigated colour and originality of form did not belong only to Matisse at this time. In the summer of 1911 the Russian Ballet came to London. Nijinsky appeared in both Schumann's *Carnaval* and in Weber's *Le Spectre de la Rose*, and in the second of these performed his famous breath-taking leap through open French windows in order to reach the sleeping Karsavina. He was the incarnation of pure sexuality and great art. Duncan was enthralled. Though he did not meet Nijinsky in person until the following year, when the dancer returned to London in Diaghilev's company, he shared fully in the excitement aroused by the daring, yet serious, elegant and exotic *Ballets Russes*.

A desire for the new seemed to be infecting not just art and ballet but also human relationships, and the person most alert to the new freedoms was Vanessa Bell. She appeared to have rejected completely the repressive and the inhibiting. When Duncan visited her in August 1910, soon after the birth of her second son, Quentin, she expressed disappointment that, owing to the presence of her friend Margery Snowden, they could not discuss improper subjects. Writing to her husband, she would allude to

Mrs Raven-Hill as 'your whore', without rancour of any sort; and she could even persuade her taciturn brother Adrian to discuss 'inversion'. Though he did so with reference to an imaginary affair, Vanessa all the time knew that it was an exact mirror of his relations with Duncan. What did shock her was Adrian's apparent coldness towards Duncan. It caused her to remark to Virginia in June 1911, 'I am inclined to be somewhat sceptical about the great passion.'[31]

Her own passion at that moment, had she admitted it to Virginia, was for Roger Fry. During a trip to Turkey that she and Clive had made in Fry's company during April, Vanessa had fallen very seriously ill, undergoing a complete collapse. As Clive was made nervous by illness, Fry had taken charge. He had not only revealed a gift for nursing, but had kept his patient entertained by cluttering her room with the products of his forays into local bazaars or the small paintings that he had done of the surrounding landscape. In her passive state Vanessa was enlivened by his energy, charmed by his unselfconsciousness, attracted by his knowledge, perceptiveness and omnivorous interest in things and ideas. Their affair began soon after they had returned to England. 'You know you have given me something quite new and very large and beautiful,' she told Fry, ' – both you and your character and your whole view of life – and I . . . feel that it has made and will make the most tremendous difference.'[32]

Fry's chequered career had left him a rather isolated and singular figure, but during the four years leading up to the First World War he became a potent catalyst for change. He worked ceaselessly, as a painter, writer, lecturer, critic and impresario, to awaken an English audience to modern art and to the new ways of looking that such art made necessary. A glance at his pocket diaries for these years shows a man who ran a schedule that enabled him to attend meetings connected with the National Art Collections Fund or the Contemporary Art Society or the *Burlington Magazine* on the same day that he returned from visits abroad, to Munich, Paris, Vienna or wherever he had contact with leading dealers and collectors; a man who in 1910 went regularly to Hampton Court to discuss the conservation and repair of the *Triumph of Caesar* cycle by Mantegna, which he supervised; who accepted invitations to lecture up and down the country, as well as giving a series of lectures at the Slade every autumn and spring term between September 1909 and December 1913.

Fry's Slade lectures became the testing ground for his aesthetic ideas. He insisted that his own attempt to formulate an aesthetic theory was provisional and, as in the nature of a scientific hypothesis, was to be held only until such time as some new phenomenon demanded that the theory be revised. At the Slade he tackled specifically the problem of representation in art. It was, he pointed out, almost always essential in pictorial art; yet at the same time he believed that whatever acts as pure representation tends to destroy the unity of a work of art, 'because it stands for another reality' and therefore 'cannot be a functional part of the whole'. For him the painter's problem was how to transmute the representation of natural objects so that they become a functional part of the overall design. This idea became central to the development of a Post-Impressionist style in England.

In another series of Slade lectures, he addressed the history of monumental painting. He argued that when painting expands beyond the easel it has a decorative and communal role, which in the past has been peculiarly adapted to the expression of ideas and emotions associated with the Church. He pursued his thesis using historical examples drawn from many ages. His interest in wall painting encouraged Duncan's interest in this art, though there is no record of him enrolling at the Slade for any of Fry's lectures, as Vanessa did during the academic year 1912–13. But the ideas that Fry explored at the Slade would have spilled over into discussions within Bloomsbury and helped form the climate of ideas in which Vanessa and Duncan worked.

Passionately disinterested in his views on art, Fry was open and responsive to every suggestion that came his way. When a friend he had met at Cambridge, Basil Williams, invited him to organise the decoration of the dining-room at the Borough Polytechnic in South London, where Williams was Chairman of the House Committee, Fry promptly accepted the task. He persuaded Duncan and two other young artists, Frederick Etchells and Bernard Adeney, to submit designs on a given theme. Duncan found himself invited to a meeting with Williams at the Polytechnic on 30 June 1911, at which the scheme was approved. Though Duncan agreed to do two of the designs, there was still more wall space than could be filled in the time available, as the murals were to be painted on-site during the summer vacation, so two more artists – Macdonald Gill, brother of the sculptor Eric Gill, and William Rothenstein's brother, Albert, who later changed his name to Rutherston – were added to the roster.

As with other Fry ventures, the arrangements were *ad hoc*, the artists swiftly gathered, availability probably having much to do with the choice of individuals. Fry, as was later demonstrated by his Omega Workshops, was not interested in rigid homogeneity; he simply arrived at a theme – 'London on Holiday' replacing his earlier idea of 'Getting the Food' –

and allowed each artist to work as he liked within this remit, though it was agreed that colour would graduate towards a dark contour, as in mosaic work, to increase the rhythm of the design. To help unify the scheme it was further decided that each scene would be enclosed in a geometrically patterned border and that bands of colour would go round the doors and under the decorated portions of the wall. Knowing that the funds available were small, Fry kept the total cost down to £100. When deciding who should do what, he showed remarkable trust, giving the largest space to Frederick Etchells, a young man just out of art school who had assisted Fry with his restoration work on the Mantegna cycle at Hampton Court.

Of all the artists involved, it was Etchells who proved to be most in sympathy with Duncan in matters of style. Etchells's *The Fair*, based on that held annually on Hampstead Heath, made use of stylised drawing, rhythmic repetitions and a schematically rendered background, as did Duncan's two pictures, *Bathing* and *Football*. The man bowling in Etchells's *The Fair* finds an echo, in the expressive distortion used in the drawing of the back, in Grant's footballer, who faces the oncoming players with his shoulders similarly hunched. 'They all worked together,' Fry later said of his Borough Polytechnic artists, 'taking their ideas from one another,'[33] a fact that encouraged his interest in anonymous workshop practice. Not surprisingly, this scheme established a friendship between Duncan and Etchells, the two men subsequently collaborating on other ventures and sharing an interest in translating Victorian hunting prints into Post-Impressionist pictures. At some point Duncan became the owner of two paintings by Etchells,[34] while Maynard bought his *The Dead Mole*, which was to feature in the Second Post-Impressionist Exhibition.

The Borough Polytechnic scheme received much attention from the press and this helped advertise Duncan's gift for decorative work on a large scale. In both *Bathing* and *Football* he had drawn on his admiration for Michelangelo and for Byzantine mosaics, yet had interpreted his subjects in startlingly original and modern terms. The repetition of the taut curves in the athletic outlines of his footballers conveys the rhythm and movement of the game. In *Bathing* the seven nudes, diving, swimming and clambering into a dinghy in the upper left corner, can be read as a single figure shown in continuous movement, as in a Muybridge photograph using rapid shutter action.

Most public mural schemes of the late Victorian and Edwardian periods had used historical, symbolic or allegorical content. At the Borough Polytechnic, however, the subject was contemporary life, Duncan's paintings celebrating activities that went on in the Serpentine and Hyde Park. One critic, unprepared for the complete absence of patriotic or moralistic sentiment, feared that the murals would have a degenerative effect on the polytechnic's working-class pupils. Others were less negative in their response, and Duncan was the artist most often singled out for praise. The *Eye-Witness* (9 November 1911) reported that *Bathing*, with its 'streaming wavy lines which symbolise water, shows how near an artist can get to suggesting reality by a convention which makes no attempt to represent it'. The article continued, 'His football players are fine too. They scamper and bound like Frankenstein monsters made of cat-gut and steel.' In the opinion of the *Spectator* critic (11 November 1911), the overall effect was light and bright, the designs enlivening the room and charging it with a curious vitality. In keeping with the mood of these decorations, the walls of the nearby passageways and stairs had been painted sky-blue, orange, white and primrose.

Though Duncan had earlier painted a mural for one of Maynard Keynes's rooms in Cambridge, combining motifs from *The Lemon Gatherers* with a group of dancers, it was the Borough Polytechnic project that confirmed his liking for large-scale decorative schemes and brought him to the attention of the public. Robert Ross, writing for the conservative newspaper, the *Morning Post*, felt that he was the man to watch. 'Mr Duncan Grant will one day be heard of beyond the walls of the Borough Polytechnic,' he opined. 'Perhaps he is the Millais of the New Pre-Raphaelites . . .'[35]

Of all the artists and writers drawn into Lady Ottoline Morrell's orbit, Duncan was unusual in that his relations with this complex, powerful woman were wholly unvexed. She thought him 'an adorable fellow, so simple and full of humour – a lovely character'.[36]

Some of his friends, however, found him mercurial and elusive – not untrustworthy or disloyal, but a person with scattered interests. One of his most pronounced charms – a ready responsiveness – may have had a destabilising effect on his relationships, for it enabled him always to move on, a new interest detaching him as swiftly as he had in the first instance become attached. In the summer of 1911 it was Adrian Stephen's turn to complain that Duncan's attention lay elsewhere. 'I shall arrive at Holborn Viaduct at 7.35 next Tuesday evening the 22nd,' he told Duncan, 'in case you still take any interest in my movements which seems very doubtful as you have not written for such ages.'[37] Duncan swiftly repaired their friendship, inviting Adrian to stay with him at Fellows Road while his parents were away; and in September he spent a week with Adrian at Walberswick in Suffolk. They stayed at the Bell Hotel and rented one of the artists' studios that looked out over the river, a scene that reminded Duncan of certain Dutch artists.

The third person in their relationship, as Adrian was to discover, was no longer Maynard, but James Strachey. It was, however, a short-lived passion: by the summer of 1911 James was writing to Lytton, 'All my old friends have left me. I had a final scene with Duncan the other night in which I accused him of faithlessness. He just got up and left the room. But later I found him in the dining-room staring into infinity. Is it possible that all's not well?'[38]

That summer and autumn the concerns of Duncan's heart remained as mysterious as his finances. Invited by Roger Fry to spend a weekend at Durbins, Duncan turned up a day late, having been unable to lay his hands on enough money for the train fare until he looked in a drawer and found a half-crown. Yet this same summer he not only stayed at Walberswick, but went on a bicycling tour in France with Roger Fry and Clive Bell, in order to look at churches in the region of Poitiers, Bourges and Limoges, including the great Romanesque church at St-Savin with its painted columns and barrel vault. This trip, which finally converted Duncan to France, ended in Paris, where the three friends met Vanessa and went to see the Salon d'Automne. Duncan then went on to Turin and Milan before finally returning home. There is never even an inkling of a suggestion that he behaved liked a sponge, yet somehow his expenses were met, he travelled and enjoyed life on the minimum of funds, with friends whose generosity never became patronising. However, his financial plight must have been very real, as it motivated Fry to think of ways in which artists could earn a living wage and yet still have time to do their own work. Eventually he was to come up with a solution in the Omega Workshops.

At Fry's house that summer Duncan painted a portrait of Roger's daughter, Pamela, seated beside the lily pond. Winifred Gill, a young woman employed to take care of the Fry children, helped keep the young girl still by reading aloud. It was also suggested, during one of Duncan's visits, that the bare walls of the summer house should be ornamented with a mosaic based on badminton players. Sketches were made and work begun, though only a small section of this design was translated into mosaic. Duncan made several trips to Guildford that summer, some to Millmead Cottage, rented by the Bells. Maynard joined him there and afterwards reported to his fellow King's man, Frankie Birrell, 'there's enough bawdy talk [here] I should think to satisfy the most susceptible'.[39] Vanessa Bell had now taken a shine to Duncan and invited him to join them at Studland in September. 'I hope you're coming here either with Adrian or before him,' she wrote, 'and won't mind as usual having a rather doubtful bed.'[40]

Rapid changes of allegiance in his love life may have caused Duncan at this time to question his sexual identity. Soon after he and Maynard moved in November to 38 Brunswick Square, a house near the Foundling Hospital shared with the two Stephens (and later with Leonard Woolf), he conceived of mural decorations and persuaded Vera Waddington to help paint them. Her diary for 1912 records regular visits to 38 Brunswick Square during May and June. 'Went to the studio,' one entry reads, 'and began on the wall. It was most thrilling. Duncan played about most of the time and talked post-impressionism.'[41] It is likely, therefore, that their brief liaison took place at this time. If so, there was reason for confusion in the mind of a young man who knew he was attractive to women and could enjoy their company, yet occasionally saw himself as competing with a woman for the attention of a man. It was precisely this situation that momentarily turned his thoughts back to Adrian.

Duncan had first met Karin Costelloe, the daughter of Berenson's wife Mary by her first marriage, while she was a student in Paris, working at a thesis on Bergson. She had suffered ear problems since the age of seventeen and various operations had been performed in an attempt to preserve her hearing; for some years it fluctuated, her deafness later becoming a serious problem only partially alleviated by the use of an ear trumpet. In 1911 she began seeing a lot of Adrian and Duncan, and at the end of the summer she wrote of Duncan in her diary, 'It doesn't matter what he does or says (fortunately for he puts this constantly to the test!) he is incorruptibly pure. I have a feeling about him which isn't in the least being in love, but makes me perfectly contented when he is there and rather sad when he isn't . . . I think he is fond of me in his remote but childish way. I don't want him to be in love . . . Yesterday I made him have supper with me in the Park and we got on rather well.'[42] Later that year Karin accompanied Duncan and Adrian home one evening to 38 Brunswick Square, where she became the object of their horseplay, Duncan attempting to push her into Maynard's room, as if he were already consciously or unconsciously wanting to get her away from Adrian (whom she was eventually to marry). Karin, unaware of difficulties ahead, concluded in her diary, 'Their ways are odd but I am really fond of them and they are nice to me. It has been a very, very nice season.'[43]

If there was an incorruptible streak in Duncan's character, as Karin believed, it was connected with his unsullied pleasure in art. When Roger

Fry organised the Contemporary Art Society's first touring exhibition in December 1911, he praised Duncan's work in the catalogue for its 'spontaneous lyrical feeling of singular purity and intensity'. Fry was the first to state that Duncan had finally found his voice in art. Though he might go silent and stare into space when questioned by his friends about affairs of the heart, he had much to say in paint – enough to last him for the rest of his days.

EIGHT

'The Coming Genius'

'This is a most ghastly house,'[1] Duncan wrote to Lytton from St John's Vicarage, Birkenhead, in January 1912. He was *en route* to Manchester, to see a Contemporary Art Society exhibition in which both he and Etchells were represented, and was staying with George Mallory. Three years earlier Duncan had been sceptical about the rumours concerning Mallory's beauty. 'I have never heard such a romance as that of Mallory,' he had written to Maynard. 'He looks like, is called and apparently *is* an Arthurian hero . . . It all sounds very far distant from me, and I fear will do so, even when I am in Cambridge.'[2] But in May 1909 Lytton endorsed the legend. 'Mon dieu! – George Mallory! – When that's been written, what more need be said? My hand trembles, my heart palpitates, my whole being swoons away at the words – oh heavens! heavens! . . . he's six foot high, with the body of an athlete by Praxiteles, and a face – of incredible – the mystery of Botticelli, the refinement and delicacy of a Chinese print, the youth and piquancy of an unimaginable English boy.'[3]

During his final year at Magdalene, Mallory wrote an essay on the biographer James Boswell, eventually published in 1912. However, he had no delusions about his literary talent and in 1910 became an assistant master at Charterhouse, Godalming, where he taught history and art. By then Lytton, whose passion for Mallory was mostly vented in letters to others ('His body – vast, pale, unbelievable – is a thing to melt into and die'),[4] had won his friendship. Mallory developed a 'profound respect' for Lytton's intellect and his pursuit of 'the doctrine of freedom'; and, as a result, he 'put up with much in him that I could hardly tolerate in another'.[5] When Lytton and Mallory made a trip to Hampton Court, Duncan went too.

Gossip concerning Mallory included the rumour that he had once declared love to James Strachey and been rejected. During his first term at Charterhouse he wrote to Duncan, 'Lytton encouraged me to think that you might be willing to spend a weekend here. Why not come next Saturday?'[6] Duncan had to decline this invitation, as he was committed to finishing a portrait in Cambridge where, he admitted to Mallory, life always seemed 'very complicated'.[7] They kept in touch, however, and early in 1911 Mallory thought he had obtained for Duncan a commission to paint a portrait of his old tutor, A. C. Benson, whom Mallory had helped through a period of extreme depression. Either the authorities at Magdalene refused to vet the choice or Duncan turned the commission down, because the official college portrait of Benson, painted that year, is by R. E. Fuller-Maitland. But Duncan did paint two pictures for Mallory to hang in his classroom, and in 1913 he designed a poster to advertise *Green Chartreuse*, a school magazine produced by Mallory, Robert Graves and two others. The magazine, which appeared on Old Carthusian Day, created quite a flutter, as did the poster, which, far from upholding public-school proprieties, portrayed a larger-than-life-size green monk quaffing from an uplifted glass. 'The poster was executed by Duncan Grant in his most impressionist style,' one of Mallory's biographers recalls, 'and flaunted on the cricket pavilion throughout the match.'[8]

After one of his visits to Charterhouse, Duncan wrote to Mallory: 'I did not mean to suggest that I was in love with you. I am far too fond of somebody else I think to fall in love. But I cannot help wanting to express my feelings for people to them and mine are so complicated towards you that I was somehow conscious that a kiss would somehow do it. When I say complicated I mean difficult to explain in words ... I think you beautiful for one thing ...'[9] It was easier to put his feelings into paint, especially as Mallory proved a willing model, posing in the nude for paintings and photographs taken by Duncan. When Mallory came to London he sometimes stayed with Duncan at Brunswick Square, and on one occasion dined with him in the company of Rupert Brooke and Edward Marsh.

Mallory had begun climbing as a schoolboy, an interest that Duncan at this stage thought less dangerous than marriage. He was deeply shaken when he received news of Mallory's engagement. Uncertain how to reply to his friend's letter, he complained, 'You might have made your letter a little more interesting if possible by telling me who it is you are going to marry! Anyhow I hope you will be happier than you have ever been before, that would suit you down to the ground.'[10] Duncan continued to write occasionally to Mallory after he married Ruth Turner on 23 May 1914 and during the First World War found at one point that they shared feelings of despair. Even when Mallory showed a lack of understanding in relation to some of Duncan's more experimental paintings, Duncan retained an affection for his friend. After Mallory's tragic death in 1924, on his third expedition to Mount Everest, Duncan's sadness was deepened by information from Clive Bell: the old colonel leading

Mallory's expedition had refused to employ a former conscientious objector, choosing instead a man relatively inexperienced. Had the colonel acted differently, Mallory's life might have been saved.

When Duncan posted Maynard three photographs of Mallory in January 1912, he also sent news of Virginia Stephen's health. After another bout of nervous instability, she agreed to stay in bed for several days and seemed more tractable than was generally the case when she was ill.

His concern for her well-being had taken him in the summer of 1910 to Twickenham, where she had been incarcerated in a nursing home for some weeks. 'Will you tell Duncan,' Virginia afterwards wrote, 'that I was told he had called, and that I am furious they didn't let me see him. Miss T. [Thomas] thought him an extremely nice young man.'[11] Like her sister, Virginia was aware of Duncan's infatuation with her brother and a little amused by it. He was, nevertheless, one of the handful of guests present when Virginia married Leonard Woolf at St Pancras Register Office in August 1912, and at the lunch party afterwards. Her half-brothers, George and Gerald Duckworth, looked at Duncan suspiciously, possibly because he was wearing borrowed clothes which did not fit him.

Virginia's friend, Ka Cox, delighted in Duncan's company. One of the Neo-Pagans, she had graduated from Newnham College, Cambridge and now had rooms in Clifford's Inn, where the Neo-Pagans and Bloomsbury occasionally commingled. It was probably through Ka that Duncan met the Fabian Sir Sydney Olivier's four daughters, with whom he went to a fancy-dress dance at the home of H. G. Wells in March 1912. That same month Ka sat to Duncan for her portrait, telling him 'you're so patient and I'm so tiresome'.[12] Duncan, however, must have enjoyed her solid shape and independent mind, for he painted her portrait twice,[13] and used her as the model for his *Seated Woman* (Courtauld Institute Galleries), which was included in the Second Post-Impressionist Exhibition. In July, when their paths failed to cross, Ka was disappointed: 'I gather I shall miss Duncan – he always cheers me, so I'm sad.'[14] A month later she was happy to find herself 'oddly companioned'[15] with Duncan, Maynard and Etchells in an inn at Everleigh, near Marlborough, which Maynard had rented for himself and his various visitors throughout July and August.

Friendship with Ka kept Duncan up to date with the news of Rupert Brooke, who frequently appeared in Duncan's life but never became a central figure. They had first met at preparatory school, after which Duncan temporarily lost sight of Rupert until he became an undergraduate and they occasionally met at Cambridge. In the summer of 1911 Duncan stayed with Rupert at the Old Vicarage at Grantchester. Here

Brooke liked to lead the simple life, bathing naked in the river, eating his meals out of doors, wandering barefoot, while all the time suffering inwardly from his idealistic passion for the beautiful, virginal, practical Noel Olivier, a long-drawn-out courtship that froze his emotional development and ended with an affair with Ka Cox. At Grantchester Duncan painted, leaving behind some of his canvases in the summer house, (where they were discovered by chance in 1919 by Lance Sieveking who was wandering around the by then deserted house and garden). It seems that Duncan was not quite hardy enough for Rupert's taste: when planning a camp later that summer, Brooke, writing to Maynard Keynes, made a teasing reference to Duncan: 'The company going to Camp is quite select and possible company for such delicate blooms as Virginia and Duncan; and Bryn [Olivier] is white with desire that they should come.'[16] Duncan was not coerced, but he did dine with Rupert and the King's man, Francis Bliss, at the Eiffel Tower restaurant in London in the autumn. On that occasion Duncan found himself for the first time attracted to Brooke. But it was a fleeting emotion and the real thrill of the evening was an after-dinner visit to the cinematograph to see a film called *Caesar Borgia*.

Despite their mutual friends and shared interests, the friendship between Duncan and Rupert was never close. But Brooke's charisma was so strong that once he had captivated others, they remained under his spell. He shuttled between London and Grantchester, pursuing a literary career, gradually entering a more worldly society and allowing the adulation that he received to affect his character. He became belligerent and reactionary. Though in 1912 he wrote a perceptive review of the Second Post-Impressionist Exhibition, he subsequently became aggressively philistine, capable also of anti-Semitic and anti-feminist views. According to Michael Hastings, his head was so turned by the attention he received from Churchill, Duff Cooper, Beaverbrook and others that once, emerging from a party given by Lady Asquith at 10 Downing Street, and seeing Duncan walking in, he crassly exclaimed, 'What! *you* here!'[17]

Another Cambridge graduate who hovered on the periphery of Duncan's life was the slightly eccentric Gordon Hannington Luce, a protégé of Maynard and an Apostle. Duncan met Luce in Cambridge and painted a portrait of him using a loose, spotted touch. (Vanessa Bell referred to this method, which set in around January 1912, as 'Duncan's leopard manner'.)[18] At this time Luce, knowing that he had little likelihood of making a living as a poet, decided to go East and, with help from Maynard's India Office connections, obtained a job teaching

English literature at the Government College, Rangoon. He sailed for Burma in September. Shortly before leaving he had a brief affair with Maynard, though it was Duncan with whom he was besotted. 'Passionate regrets to Duncan,'[19] he wrote to Maynard, enclosing a sonnet in Duncan's praise. Another letter to Maynard ends, 'Love to Duncan – if only he needed it!'[20]

After only seven months in Rangoon, Luce was surprised to find that he wanted to marry a Burmese girl, Teetie Moun Tin, although he wished 'that she were a boy'.[21] Keynes was horrified and warned Luce that such a marriage would be a 'crime'. But it was his parents' concern that caused Luce to delay marriage for two years, during which time he came to think that it would be a crime *not* to marry her. A year after the marriage Teetie produced a daughter, causing Luce to marvel afresh at the female sex.

In 1918 Luce sent Maynard some of his poems, as he was anxious to know if they merited publication. Maynard's affirmative reply delighted him, as did the mention that Duncan was willing to undertake woodcuts for the book. As it turned out, no woodcuts by Duncan appeared in the book of poems by Luce that Macmillan's published in 1920; but a second edition, published in 1923 by the Hogarth Press, contained two abstract decorations by Duncan. Though Luce earnt his reputation chiefly as an authority on Burmese history, this small book of poems gave him much joy. His life had carried him far from Cambridge and the Apostles. But with a praising letter from E. M. Forster, he could once again sign his letters to Maynard 'fraternally yours'.

No definite chronology has yet been arrived at for Duncan's pre-1914 paintings, but it would seem that those produced in his so-called 'leopard manner' were done during the winter of 1911–12. Working with broken touches of colour, he created images that shimmer on the picture surface at the same time as they suggest depth and form. This manner was the first of several attempts he made to find a lively method of handling paint such as Gainsborough achieved in his late style with his calligraphic brushwork. The 'leopard manner', in its lack of fixity, also enabled Duncan to keep his ideas open while the work progressed. As a result the paintings produced in this style have an exploratory feel. He used the 'leopard manner' for a half-length portrait of his mother, with her head in profile;[22] for a large figurative work based on Virginia, Adrian and Leonard seated on the roof at Brunswick Square;[23] for the Brunswick Square street scene mural in Maynard's room, and other paintings. Duncan's pointillism never aspired to the scientific exactitude of his

French counterparts; but where his blue, green and yellow spots mingle in the sky in his *The Queen of Sheba*, they convey a marvellous sensation of heat.

Duncan could not have painted this subject without being aware of the grand precedent set by Piero della Francesca's Arezzo frescos, which show the visit of the Queen to King Solomon. But his picture has a playfulness and wit that are entirely his own. The King, hunched with weighty wisdom, is offset by the Queen's animated gestures, the sinuous movement of her arms finding an echo in the necks of the camels seen through the window. His first attempt at this subject took the form of an oil sketch, which was either given to, or bought by, Maynard.[24] The idea for this work may have come to Duncan from Carl Goldmark's opera *The Queen of Sheba*, premièred in London in the winter of 1911, though there is no proof that he saw it. A more likely source was one of his ancestors, a Mrs Sophia Elizabeth Plowden, who had honour conferred on her by Imperial Firman. In March 1911 Lady Strachey received a letter from a relative reminding her of this event, remarking also that the story echoed the Queen of Sheba's visit to Solomon, as recounted in the Koran.[25] It is almost certainly a story that Lady Strachey would have shared with her children, two of whom, Lytton and Pippa, posed for the figures in Duncan's painting.

But the subject might never have gone further than the oil sketch, had not Jane Harrison, a classics don at Newnham College, Cambridge, taken an interest in Duncan's work. 'Here may arise a question of wall decoration,' she wrote to Maynard early in 1912, 'and from rumour I am inclined to hope Mr Grant is the coming genius.'[26] She regretted not having seen the Borough Polytechnic decorations, but wondered instead if she might view the four-panel mural that Duncan had painted in Maynard's sitting-room in Webb's Court. Soon afterwards she visited Maynard's rooms in the company of another classicist, Francis Cornford. Though the design of this mural, with its group of dancers framed on either side by basket carriers, was somewhat ill-suited to the space, it impressed both onlookers. The central motif of the round dance was reminiscent of Matisse's *Dance*. The low horizon threw the tense, angular silhouettes of the dancers into relief against a mottled sky. After seeing this mural, Harrison and Cornford recommended Duncan to the Newnham authorities for the job of decorating a wall space in the college, although opposition was already afoot and funds were as yet non-existent. Nevertheless, Jane Harrison wrote to Duncan, mentioning that she had been told he had already done 'a wonderful design of the Queen of Sheba'. That, she said, 'is what I should like of all things'.[27]

As a result Duncan embarked on a five-foot-square enlargement of his original oil sketch. The expectation that the finished work would fill a public space brought out a theatrical element in his work, which is reinforced by the stage-like setting suggested by the grey line along the bottom of the picture. But his exuberant, fanciful, humorous imagination failed to please the Newnham authorities, few of whom shared Jane Harrison's interest in contemporary art, and the commission proved abortive. Instead, the painting was bought by Roger Fry, lent by him to the Second Post-Impressionist Exhibition and in 1917 entered the Tate Gallery through the auspices of the Contemporary Art Society.

Further proof of Duncan's growing reputation came in April 1912, when the theatre director Harley Granville-Barker asked him to design costumes for *Macbeth*. Duncan accepted readily, little realising the disappointments that this project would bring. However, owing to various setbacks, he did not begin work on the designs until the following year. A vein of fancy enabled him to empathise with the imaginative world created through dance or drama. He himself may have inspired the ballet *Jeux*, which Nijinsky choreographed and for which Leon Bakst designed the sets. The two men had arrived at Lady Ottoline's in Bedford Square one afternoon in 1912 when Duncan and others were playing tennis in the square. Lady Ottoline recalled, 'They were so entranced by the tall trees against the houses and the figures flitting about and playing tennis that they exclaimed with delight: *"Quel décor!"* '[28] Though in an interview the following year Nijinsky stated that *Jeux* originated from his watching tennis at Deauville, Richard Buckle has pointed out that the house in the background to Bakst's set for this ballet had a severity that was closer to the elegant simplicity of Bedford Square than to any French equivalent.[29]

Nijinksy, who was prone to illness and influenza, was that year under Diaghilev's close surveillance and was allowed few outings into society. But Lady Ottoline had become a warm friend and he went, as arranged, to her house to meet young artists. 'Duncan G[rant] of course became at once their pet,' she afterwards told Lytton. ' – I saw Nijinsky looking him all over!'[30] Duncan was invited again, on two or three occasions, once when Nijinsky was the only other guest. However, communication proved difficult, for though on-stage Nijinsky danced like a man possessed, he was shy in company, squat and plain, and spoke very little English. Even his French was extremely vague.

Conversation flowed easily at Asheham in the summer of 1912. The lease on this Regency house, some seven miles outside Lewes in Sussex, had been taken by Virginia, in agreement with her sister, the year before.

While she and Leonard were on honeymoon in the late summer of 1912, Vanessa Bell and her children took over the house, Vanessa intending to stay until winter set in. The house received a stream of visitors, among them Duncan, who slept on a mattress in the bath, having arrived for a weekend visit but staying almost two weeks. The garden was hopping with toads and newts and the way of life was simple – badminton was the sole form of entertainment – but even the urbane Clive Bell found it delightful and no one wanted to leave. Vanessa thought the house, which faced the Ouse valley, and the surrounding countryside perfect for painters and much work was done at Asheham: Clive was beginning to contemplate his book *Art*, pictures were painted and a poster designed for the forthcoming Second Post-Impressionist Exhibition. Duncan executed the poster after Vanessa had the idea that it should show a fashionable lady looking with horror at the forthcoming event. It was then handed over to Frederick Etchells, who did the lettering.

Much thought and preparation went into the arangements for this second exhibition, partly because Fry had a more specific purpose in mind. The first show, he argued, had introduced the 'Old Masters' of Post-Impressionism. Now his intention was to display its contemporary development, not only in France, its native ground, but also in England, where it was still of very recent growth, and in Russia where, as he believed, Post-Impressionism had liberated and revived an old native tradition. Fry had gone to Paris in July to select the French pictures and this time had access to the Stein collections and help from Picasso's dealer, Kahnweiler. He also brought back photographs taken by Monsieur Druet of Van Gogh's, Cézanne's and Gauguin's work, to hang in the show, so that visitors could be reminded of the older masters. When he, Clive and Vanessa Bell made a brief visit to Cologne in early August to see the Sonderbund exhibition of contemporary art, it was left to Duncan to find 'Cookham', as Stanley Spencer was nicknamed, whom Fry especially wanted to include in the English section. The build-up towards the opening date, on 5 October, put pressure on Duncan, who found himself 'working like hell' to get his paintings finished in time. 'I do nothing but ruin what I have already done which drives me to distraction,' he complained to Maynard.

By then most of the French paintings had arrived. Duncan found them interesting but reserved special praise for the Matisses which, he said, were 'radiantly beautiful'.[31] Then in the last week before the show opened he dashed over to Provence, for a short bicycling tour around Avignon and Nimes with Fry, who also insisted on a brief journey into the Auvergne. It was splendidly hot and on their return journey they stopped in Paris for a hectic, lightning visit. One fleeting but satisfactory aspect of this excursion was that Duncan met Picasso for the first time.

Since the furore he had aroused with 'Manet and the Post-Impressionists', Fry had done much to stimulate the growth of a modern movement in English art. At the Alpine Club Gallery in January 1912 he had held a solo exhibition of his recent paintings, in which emphatic outlines helped signal the new expressive and constructive Post-Impressionist manner. In addition, he had begun painting some of his frames with simple geometric patterns, to enhance the decorative vitality of his work. Duncan and Vanessa likewise began patterning some of their frames – this extension of the picture into the environment finding its logical conclusion in 1913 with the opening of the Omega Workshops. Even before this date Fry had been anxious to strengthen the new movement in art through group, rather than individual, effort. With this aim in mind he had invited Wyndham Lewis to a meeting with himself, Duncan and Etchells at the Bells' house in Gordon Square. This may have been the Mill Street Club, mentioned in an undated note from Fry to Grant, notifying the latter of a meeting. No further mention is heard of this club, though Fry's desire to stimulate communal effort later gave rise to the short-lived Grafton Group, the name under which he, Lewis, Grant, Etchells and Vanessa Bell exhibited in March 1913.

A similarly erratic development attended Fry's attempts to promote a revival of interest in mural painting. After the success of the Borough Polytechnic scheme he had hoped to involve his artists in decorations for London hospitals, but the project never materialised. However, in November 1911 a committee was set up, chaired by the art critic and painter D. S. MacColl, to promote commissions for murals in public institutions. It advertised its aims in *The Times* in January 1912, called for subscriptions to help fund such work and announced that an exhibition of designs for murals would be held in Crosby Hall in May or June. Though it was rumoured that the honorary secretary, Charles Aitken, Director of the National Gallery of British Art (as the Tate Gallery was then called) wanted to get commissions for Grant and Etchells, none of their designs were hung in the Crosby Hall exhibition.[32] Vanessa Bell concluded that Duncan must have delivered the designs to the wrong address.

The show aroused little enthusiasm and proved afresh how difficult it was to gain approval for mural schemes in England. Duncan perhaps hoped for a commission when he attached the word 'decoration' to his painting *The Red Sea*,[33] which he sent to a Friday Club exhibition in 1912. Nothing, however, was forthcoming and his most ambitious wall painting in 1912 remained the huge street accident, involving horses and two hansom cabs, which he and Etchells executed on a curved wall in the main ground-floor room at 38 Brunswick Square.[34] Vanessa Bell, who observed its progress, was surprised how indistinguishable the styles of Grant and Etchells had become. Soon afterwards Duncan began another mural of tennis players in Adrian Stephen's room on the first floor. In the same house he also ornamented a window bay with nude figures in balletic poses.

By the spring of 1912 Duncan had come to the fore as an excitingly innovative artist. Fry, alert to new developments, had already spotted Wyndham Lewis's significance, but it was Duncan whom he singled out in a letter to the French dealer and poet, Charles Vildrac, in April 1912. 'Duncan Grant will exhibit and certainly he has genius, perhaps Etchells also; the others like myself have but a little talent and at least goodwill.'[35] Fry was collaborating with Vildrac on an exhibition that opened the following month at the Galerie Barbazanges in Paris. Vanessa Bell inspected the hanging of this show in Fry's company and afterwards told Duncan, 'Your *Dancers* was a great success and looked very beautiful . . .'[36] What made his art exceptional at this date was not a single-minded pursuit of an identifiable style or theory, but a vision wholly free of the pictorial conventions that had shaped his earlier work. Between his portrait of James Strachey, painted in the winter of 1909–10 and *The Tub* (both Tate Gallery), probably painted after seeing the 'primitive' quality of certain pre-Cubist paintings by Picasso in the Second Post-Impressionist Exhibition, there is a vast conceptual leap. Those skills that make the portrait so convincing are precisely those which in *The Tub* he rejected in favour of a more schematic but expressive handling. He used the same crude, vibrant hatching to delineate a variety of objects – the floor, the curtain on the dresser behind, the screen or curtain to one side, even the nude's ribs.[37] Here and in other of his Post-Impressionist paintings he took what he needed for the moment, preferring experiment to consistency; even the 'leopard manner', which for a while became associated with Duncan's name, never coalesced into a stylistic hallmark and soon gave way to new experimentation.

While on honeymoon with Leonard, Virginia Woolf had sent Duncan a letter (now lost) describing their journey through Spain. He could not reply immediately, Duncan told her in late September, because of 'trying to finish some dozen pictures for this blessed Grafton show', a torment that made him 'almost believe that Uncle Trevor was right and that I shall end my days in the Royal Bethlem Hospital surrounded by hundreds of unfinished works'.[38] Quite how many were finally hung in the Second Post-Impressionist Exhibition, which opened on 5 October 1912, is not known, but there were probably more than the six mentioned in the catalogue. Those listed include *Pamela*, an impressionistic likeness of Roger Fry's daughter; *The Dancers* (second version); the fanciful *The Queen of Sheba*; *The Countess*, an imaginative portrait composed like mosaic out of patches of brilliant colour; a portrait of the French artist, Henri Doucet (now lost); and Ka Cox's monumental figure, as found in *The Seated Woman*.

Amid the outcry caused by the distortion in the treatment of appearances in the work of Matisse, Picasso, Othon Friesz and others, certain critics did now attempt to give the new movement the attention it deserved. One of the most thoughtful critiques was Rupert Brooke's two-part review, which appeared in the *Cambridge Magazine*. 'It is almost unnecessary,' he began, '. . . to say that everybody who is interested in pictures must go to this exhibition.' He regretted 'the air of slight incompetency that hangs over the whole exhibition', for a month after it had opened some of the Russian pictures had still not arrived, and the initial catalogue provided scant information and contained no illustrations other than one Matisse. However, an illustrated and more informative edition of the catalogue was in production and did eventually appear. Brooke noticed that the selection was rather 'hotch-potch', and some pictures sentimental enough to have disgraced the New English Art Club. He perceived that Matisse and Picasso were two leading figures, but he found it difficult to like Picasso and, after analysing his work at some length, dismissed him as a 'minor' artist. Confronted with Matisse (some twenty of his paintings were shown and an equal number of drawings), Brooke praised the 'pure bright and generally light colour . . . the stern simplicity and unity of design'. 'His world is clean, lovely and inhuman as a douche of cold water. He paints dancing; and it is the essential rhythm of dance that, with a careless precision, he gets.'[39]

Though the show seems to have been something of a movable feast, a work by Simon Bussy arriving some five or six weeks after it had opened, it was weighted towards French art. In addition, Fry invited Jacques Copeau and Charles Vildrac to come to London in order to represent the modern movement in French drama and literature. Matisse and Picasso had only just begun to be evaluated by the art world (Clive Bell acquired Picasso's *Cruche, bol et citron*, a still-life contemporaneous with his work towards *Les Demoiselles d'Avignon*, in October 1911 for four pounds); but their significance had been recognised, and critics could not help noticing that the English contribution, by comparison with the French, seemed gauche and uneven. P. G. Konody, in the *Observer*, wrote, 'Every word of their [the English artists'] artistic language is traceable to some French root. There is no eccentricity, no affection, no mannerism in French that does not find a ready echo in English Post-Impressionist art. And, let it be said at once, like every echo, it is feebler than the original sound.'[40] He also noticed that when the English pictures were grouped together, they appeared dull and colourless compared with the primary colours that danced across some of the French canvases. To him, Duncan Grant was the most interesting of what he called 'the Grafton band', if also the most uneven. Rupert Brooke, who found 'crude and moving nobility' in Stanley Spencer's *John Donne arriving in Heaven* and 'an unexpected amount of emotional appeal' in Wyndham Lewis's angular, near-abstract drawings for *Timon of Athens*, was likewise ambivalent in his response to Duncan's unsettled style:

> Mr Grant has painted better things, perhaps, than any he shows here. But several of these are lovely. He is always a trifle disappointing. One always feels there ought to be more body to his work, somehow. Even his best pictures here are rather thin. But there is beauty in *The Seated Woman*, an exquisite wit and invention in the delightful *The Queen of Sheba*, and a grave loveliness in *The Dancers*. His genius is an elusive and faithless sprite. He may do anything or nothing. Also, he is roaming at present between different styles and methods. What an eye for beauty! Why aren't his pictures better? But it's absurd to suppose they won't be when he has 'found himself'. Both he and Mr Etchells are unfortunately fond of a spotty way of laying their paint on ... Mr Etchells' danger also lies in a lack of fervour; but he inclines to stolidity, Mr Grant to prettiness.[41]

One buyer who came to the fore during the course of the Second Post-Impressionist Exhibition (which continued into the new year, in slightly altered form, after the arrival of some Cézanne watercolours) was Hilton Young. The son of a baronet, and a graduate of Trinity College, Cambridge, he was a familiar figure within Bloomsbury, since his father had been a friend of Sir Leslie Stephen. As a child, Hilton had bowled a hoop with the Stephen children in Kensington Gardens. After training as a barrister he had turned to journalism, becoming first assistant-editor of the *Economist* and then in 1910 financial editor of the *Morning Post*. A brave, highly intelligent man, he lost a leg during the First World War and was awarded the DSO for his service to the navy. Later still he became an MP and married the widow of Captain Scott of the Antarctic, Kathleen Bruce, a notable sculptor.

Neither Hilton nor his brother Geoffrey, who advised Maynard and Duncan on their trip to Asia Minor, were ever part of Bloomsbury's inner core, but they were insiders on the outside, as Hilton observes in his unpublished autobiography: 'Bloomsbury, at the start, was very exclusive – it did not suffer fools gladly. They lived in an intellectual enclosure. But they were curious about the outside world, rather, one might say, as a collector of beetles, for instance, is interested in the world of beetles. They were glad that some selected beetles, as it were, should come into the enclosure for them to find out what was going on there outside: that was how I came in ... My own gradual change from orthodox opinion ... was no doubt already in progress: but I have no doubt ... its progress was helped by contact with these fine minds, which had so wholly freed themselves from the burden of tradition.'[42]

At the Grafton Galleries Hilton acquired a handful of works by lesser-known French artists, including two works by Chabaud, whose earnest, clumsy handling upheld Roger Fry's belief in the need for forthright expression and large design. Hilton also became the proud owner of Duncan's *The Dancers*, the larger of the two versions, and never parted with it. In January 1914 he added to his collection a townscape by Jean Marchand, another French painter whom Fry admired. Vanessa Bell approved his choice, assuring him, 'It will be very satisfactory to live with I am sure.'[43]

Duncan enjoyed the company of this man, whose wide interests ranged from politics to ornithology, and endured the discomfort of a motorcycle sidecar in order to travel with him in March 1913 to Pen-y-Pass, a place very popular with George Mallory and other climbers. The two-day journey was arduous, riddled with hailstorms. On the second day the chain on the motorcycle became unhitched, damaging the machine and causing them to career into a stone wall. Things did not improve much when they finally arrived at the hotel in Snowdonia. Some thirty-five people were in the climbing party and though any amount of liberal banter about the Holy Trinity was tolerated, the atmosphere of public-school morals was crushing. Accompanying others on what was said to be a 'walk' rather than a 'climb', Duncan found himself traversing huge mountains covered with snow. He was nevertheless still able to respond to what he saw, for the country all around was astonishingly beautiful. Even amid unsympathetic company and under physical duress, he reacted to his surroundings with a painter's instinct, which seemingly nothing – no internal crisis or external distraction – could diminish.

NINE

Immoral Furniture

The term 'genius', so often bandied about in connection with Duncan Grant's name, with hysterical affection by Lytton, well-meaning serious-ness by Jane Harrison and with a sense of qualitative difference by Roger Fry, left Duncan wholly unaffected. His indifference to fame, his freedom from self-obsession, gave him unconscious strength. Once, while holding a candlestick with a lighted candle in it, he fell down a long flight of stairs. He regained the landing, not only with his candle still alight but without apparently having noticed his tumble for, after the fall, he returned immediately to the discussion that was in progress before he fell. When this story was told, Duncan steadfastly denied that it was true, but Osbert Sitwell, with whom it originated, had at the time been walking at his side.[1]

This absence of self-importance left Duncan open to others and helped bring him many friends. He remained curious about life, perennially intrigued by human behaviour, and entered into the spirit of any party, dressing up, dancing or play-acting as the occasion demanded. He and Adrian gave a party in January 1913, after which Adrian wrote to Ka Cox, 'Duncan and Margery [Marjorie] wound up the entertainment by dancing till they both fell exhausted on the floor and could not move another step.'[2]

As a painter, he welcomed the stimulus provided by new experiences. He readily accompanied Maynard to the Russian Ballet and in February 1913 willingly attended a luncheon given by Roger and Clive in honour of Gertrude Stein, who was in London with Alice B. Toklas. Duncan, in conversation with the art historian Sarah Whitfield, later recollected that both Gertrude and her brother Leo had visited the Second Post-Impressionist Exhibition. 'We saw a good deal of them at that time. I think I had known them in Paris before that and I used to go to Gertrude's Thursday evenings.'[3] His memory, more accurate in spirit than in letter, here muddles Gertrude Stein's Saturday afternoons with the Thursday 'at homes' held by the Stephens at Fitzroy Square. And though his introduction to Picasso in the autumn of 1912 may have come through the Steins, there is no evidence that he attended their 'at homes' that year. He did, however, become familiar with Gertrude and Leo Stein in 1913, the year that Leo decided he could no longer stand his sister's unshakeable belief in her own genius. Her colossal conviction in herself extended to her feelings for Alice B. Toklas, to whom she had become effectively married. Leo, on the other hand, distrusted himself so much that even the passion inspired in him for the street-singer and model Nina Auzias left him perplexed and directionless.

After the situation at the Rue de Fleurus, where the Steins had amassed a remarkable art collection, became frosty, with brother and sister communicating only by letter, Gertrude and Alice began looking for another apartment. In the event they did not move out, as Leo suddenly left Paris for Settignano, near Florence, taking with him the Renoirs and the Matisses. Duncan, who had got to know the Steins just before Leo's departure, remembered the quarrelling and how Leo turned against Picasso as a way of disagreeing with Gertrude. 'I don't think that Gertrude could put up with the things he said about Picasso with ease,' Duncan recalled. 'I remember I met him in a café once and he said Picasso was tremendously gifted but there was no synthesis in his pictures. That apparently was the end of it.'[4]

Conversation with the Steins further stimulated Duncan's interest in the work of Picasso and Matisse. There had been fifteen Picassos in the Second Post-Impressionist Exhibition and some forty Matisse paintings and drawings. The new freedoms that this art represented set a challenge that could not be ignored. By March 1913, in time for the Grafton Group exhibition, Duncan had painted his *Blue Sheep Screen*[5] in which, under the influence of Matisse, he had adopted decorative, non-naturalistic colours. The sheep, mostly painted in three different shades of blue, are faceted into schematic areas of light and shade. The shadows they create are dull pink, while the wicker fencing around the sheepfold echoes the striation used to suggest the ground on which the sheep stand. As in Matisse's *Dance*, which, on the end wall in the end gallery, had been the focal climax of the Second Post-Impressionist Exhibition, Duncan paid careful attention to the relation between figure and ground, between the awkward, idiosyncratic outlines of the sheep and the spaces around and between their legs. The interlocking of all the parts into a rhythmic whole creates a marvellous buoyancy. Still more striking at the Grafton Group exhibition was Duncan's huge painting *Construction* (now lost), in which a green giant hovered over a tiny blue church in what Duncan intended as a homage to Christopher Wren. The bold freedom with which he now painted impressed Vanessa, who wrote to her sister, 'Duncan's art is supposed to be improving, and I think his latest works are very good. There is hope after all that he may be the long looked-for British genius.'[6]

Vanessa had been following Duncan's work with interest for some time, appraising it at regular intervals. In July 1912 she had suddenly worried that he had lost direction and that 'the usual English sweetness was coming in and spoiling all'.[7] But her confidence in him now revived. By January 1914 she was telling Hilton Young, who had balked at the amount of distortion Duncan had used in a picture based on Adam and Eve, that not only was his work getting better, but 'that he will do finer things, far, than any of us ...'[8]

She was six years older than Duncan and in her early thirties. Perhaps because of his close involvement with Adrian, her manner towards Duncan had become as easy and familiar as that towards a younger brother. One evening at Gordon Square in November of 1911 Vanessa, who had been posing for Duncan, decided she wanted a bath at the same time that he needed to shave in preparation for dinner. The solution seemed obvious to Vanessa and, as Clive who was there did not object, she simply had her bath in Duncan's presence. 'I'm afraid he remained quite unmoved,' she wrote teasingly to her lover, Roger, 'and I was really very decent. I felt no embarrassment and I think perhaps it was a useful precedent.'[9]

Finding herself in love with Fry, at a time when she was recuperating from a breakdown in her health, had proved an unexpected, welcome boon. She had pursued the affair with discretion but no guilt, knowing that her marital relations with Clive were already compromised by his promiscuity. If, before the advent of Roger, she had to some extent retreated from sexual relations, he once again unleashed her sensuality with the result that she was, if anything, more beautiful at this time than she had been before. At Asheham she abandoned the proprieties of conventional dress for more gypsy-like costume, its simplicity allowing greater freedom of movement. Duncan sent an admiring description of her to Virginia, mentioning the brightly coloured handkerchiefs that Vanessa wound round her head and her 'blooming health'.[10] Alert to her own sexuality, she also gossiped readily about other people's and saw no reason why her interest in sex should not affect the art they produced. She and Duncan, she announced to Roger, had decided to emulate Eric Gill and take on indecent subjects. 'I suggest a series of copulations in strange attitudes and have offered to pose. Will you join? I mean in the painting. We think there ought to be more indecent pictures painted ...'[11] Though she wrote with more bravado than intent, Duncan had no inhibitions about the erotic content which, as E. M. Forster noticed, surfaced now and then in his work. When one of Duncan's pictures, a *Mars and Venus* (now lost), was sent in 1912 with other English paintings to the Galerie Barbazanges, Paris, the manager, an Englishman called Percy Moore Turner, declared it too indecent to hang.

Though intent on living life to the full, ever since her miscarriage in Turkey, Vanessa had been under medical surveillance. The breakdown that had followed the miscarriage had left her on some days unable to get up, in a state of mental panic, incapable of grasping reality. Nervous disorders, in that they also affected Virginia and Adrian, seem to have been a part of her family inheritance. Even when she had recovered, both bodily and mentally, she envied the Olivier sisters, whose high spirits and rude health at this date made unnecessary the precautions that Vanessa knew were necessary for herself and Virginia. If Roger had stimulated in her a greater openness to experience, she had at an earlier stage in her life been bludgeoned weekly by her twice-widowed father's tirades over the family accounts, which helped vent his grief as well as his exaggerated fear of financial ruin. These had developed in her an ability to bury her feelings, to retreat from emotion; a habit of suppression that had dangerous side-effects, threatening to petrify other of her responses and leaving her susceptible to depression. It was perhaps inevitable that the ingenuous streak in Roger's nature, which left him free and uncluttered in the pursuit of ideas, would ultimately prove incompatible with her more complex make-up.

During 1912 Vanessa suffered occasional setbacks to her health and, as Christmas approached, decided not to go with Clive, as was usual, to his parents' house in Wiltshire. He and the children, accompanied by at least one maid, departed, leaving Vanessa at Gordon Square. On Boxing Day Duncan called, lay on the floor and talked with her about Leslie Stephen's *Mausoleum Book*, which had been written, not for publication, but as a testimony to his grief after the death of his second wife. The book drew Vanessa's ambivalence to the fore, for the mere mention of it could cause her to shudder, yet she kept it always close to her: under her bed at Gordon Square and, in years to come, under the sofa in the large studio at Charleston. Duncan's interest in her relatives may have allowed her to acknowledge some of the difficult and complex feelings which the memory of her parents aroused. She found his talk about the book 'desultory' but also somehow oddly 'cheering'. In the same letter to Clive she describes Duncan's ideas for her studio: 'We are to turn my studio into a tropical forest with great red figures on the walls, a blue ceiling with birds of paradise floating from it (my idea), and curtains each one different. This is all to cheer us through London winters.'[12]

Even while her affection was given to Roger, she was aware of a more than usual sympathy with Duncan. Once, when Roger had some dealings with the classical scholar and Newnhamite, Melian Stawell, who was a little in love with him, Vanessa teased him with the mock protest that whereas he might well be in Melian's arms, she, alas, was not in Duncan's but alone in Sussex. If not consciously, she had at another level begun to recognise the attraction that Duncan held for her. He was, however, still associated in her mind with Adrian: when early in 1913 she invited Duncan to visit her at Asheham, she added that he and Adrian were welcome to come either together or separately. She hoped that Duncan's involvement with Harley Granville-Barker's *Macbeth* would not make a visit impossible, and kept him informed about a forthcoming Italian holiday which, it was planned, would include both Duncan and Adrian. Arrangements for this had to be fitted around Roger's schemes, which kept him busy even when he turned up at Asheham one Sunday. Though Vanessa gave him some crochet to do in an attempt to keep him quiet, he had painted two pictures before the morning was out and had become deeply embroiled with Clive in a discussion about art.

Granville-Barker had originally intended to present *Macbeth* at the Savoy Theatre in 1912 and rehearsals took place, along with those for *The Winter's Tale*, in the summer of that year. *The Winter's Tale* opened on 21 September 1912 and, though considered a landmark in the staging of Shakespeare, was not a financial success. As a result, *Macbeth* was cancelled and replaced by a production of the more popular *Twelfth Night*. However, plans for *Macbeth* were revived and Duncan spent much of April 1913 working on designs for this play. Some of his ideas must have been realised, as the account book for the Savoy productions of 1912 and 1913 contains in its 'Stock in Hand' section a list of scenery constructed for *Macbeth*. Duncan found Barker 'personally the most delightful companion to work with', but felt himself to be temperamentally ill-suited to the various crises that accompany theatre design:

I found the London theatre at that time rather a harassing affair, especially for a young painter eager to get on with his own work . . . The preparations were endless, and the constant visits to dress-makers and scene-painters – at great distances apart in this huge city – and even differences with leading ladies about the cut of their clothes, wore me down. I therefore threw up the job, handed Barker my drawings, and was generously paid for them.[13]

Barker also wrote Duncan a kind letter in which he admitted that designing for the theatre must seem to an artist like 'muddling through all the time'.[14] Those costume drawings that remain show that Duncan made use of strong colour. In Act 2 Scene 1, Duncan's Macbeth would have worn a fur-lined purple coat, grey silk undershirt and red shoes.

Unable to leave for Italy with the Bells and Fry at the appointed time, Duncan, once he had abandoned *Macbeth*, joined them at Venice in the third week of April – alone, however, as Adrian had also abandoned plans to come. What perhaps made this trip possible for Duncan was that, in addition to the money he received from Granville-Barker, Clive had recently bought one of his pictures for forty pounds, the most he had so far received for any work.

The holiday began badly, Duncan suffering a throat infection from which he had recovered by the time the party moved on to Ravenna, where the mosaics intrigued him far more than anything he had seen in Venice. Roger and Clive, in their enthusiasm for art and architecture, had planned a packed itinerary. When they reached Padua an exhausted Vanessa rebelled and refused to sightsee more than one site a day. She admitted to her sister, 'I find that Duncan sympathises with me and if he and I had the conduct of the party in our hands we should settle down somewhere for a month and spend most of our time loafing. Perhaps it's as well we can't.'[15] Instead she agreed to be hustled off to Urbino, where they admired Piero della Francesca's *Flagellation* in the Ducal Palace. The next day they travelled to Spoleto, eventually to Rome, then to Civita Castellana, whence they drove to Viterbo, stopping the night at Nepi, where Duncan painted a picture, the landscape there reminding him of Asia Minor. One of the last places they visited was Arezzo, where Duncan again saw Piero della Francesca's frescos.

The notion had begun to develop in Vanessa's mind that she and Duncan did not belong to the intellectual discussions that often went on around them. The previous spring, when she had travelled in Italy with Clive and Roger, she had imagined Duncan painting on his own, at a time when he was either in Cambridge or London, and wrote to him, 'Are you living in an awful atmosphere! I suspect so. In fact I think I shall really be welcome, shan't I, to keep you company as one of the outsiders.'[16] This teasing remark did in fact touch on an affinity they shared, awareness of which would have brought them closer together. Travelling and painting alongside Duncan in Italy in 1913, Vanessa had the opportunity to become still more familiar with this young painter whose work she admired greatly, whose bold experimentation never obliterated a refreshing delicacy of perception, and who, even at his most crumpled and unshaven, was immensely attractive.

The crystallisation in her feelings towards Duncan that took place in Italy became more apparent to both of them during the next few months, when they spent a great deal of time together working on designs for a new venture, the Omega Workshops. While she had been abroad, Vanessa had received a letter from Virginia with a teasing postscript: 'I am amazed to hear that you have fallen in love at last. I only hope you were smartly repulsed.'[17] Because Vanessa had been extremely circumspect with Virginia over her affair with Roger, knowing how indiscreet her sister could be, it is unlikely that this aside refers to Duncan. It is said that when she did tell Virginia of her feelings towards Duncan, she broke down and wept. But Vanessa's reply to Virginia's letter – 'My love was not repulsed. I fear it was not even noticed'[18] – even if it is part of an ongoing joke, aptly describes the relationship that had developed between her and Duncan.

While so much intimate detail in the history of Bloomsbury is documented, it is curious that this change of affairs in Vanessa's life caused so little written comment. It is as if her friends and relations respected the silence that at certain moments in her life, as when her marriage had lost its direction, she drew round herself, instinctively knowing that patience and reserve were the best course. In this instance repression was made doubly necessary owing to Duncan's homosexuality. The endearments and suggestive teasing that she poured freely into her letters to Roger do not reappear in her letters to Duncan after he had replaced Fry in her affections. What bound him to her instead was her ready acknowledgement of his homosexuality. 'What did Lytton say to you that was so beastly,' she wrote in February 1914. '... Is he making love to you now or what? I suspect him of wanting to have another affair with you, but you'll only snub him.'[19] Fearful perhaps of being snubbed herself, she proceeded cautiously, sharing with her brother's lover no more than the excitement caused by the forthcoming opening of the Omega Workshops. There was a great deal of work to do and experiments to be carried out in new media. Whatever her feelings, and those of Duncan, there was much to distract them and others from the complex state of affairs that had evolved. An alteration had occurred, but some time was to pass before they or anybody else had any notion of how deep and far-reaching it was to be.

Shortly before leaving for Italy in April 1913 Roger Fry found a home for the Omega Workshops. He had taken a lease on 33 Fitzroy Square, a tall Adam corner house on the south side, which, as he foresaw, would provide ample space for both workshops and showrooms. He had persuaded Duncan and Vanessa to become his co-directors and G. B. Shaw, among others, to take shares in the venture, and as a result a handful of artists had already begun to produce decorative pieces of applied art. At the Grafton Group exhibition in March 1913 the critic for the *Daily Express* noticed that as well as paintings on show there were 'firescreens, bed-screens, woolwork chaircovers and tablecovers, all in the most approved of modernist designs'.[20]

The Omega opened to the public in July. With this event on the horizon, the venture inevitably remained to the fore of everyone's mind during the visit to Italy that spring. Fry had left Frederick Etchells in charge as Business Manager during his absence, and in Italy he, Duncan and Vanessa bought, to sell at the Omega, peasant pottery and cloth which, Fry believed, displayed a freshness of decoration often lost through machine production. Alert to every new possibility, Fry encountered a young man whom he judged to be a genius and promptly commissioned him to decorate boxes for the Omega. The others also enthused, Clive buying one of the young man's large oils and Duncan carrying away two large painted wooden totems, fairground-like figures, which still ornament the studio at Charleston. The young man has never been identified. The fact that he went by the name of Dante Paradiso and was very beautiful may help explain his charm.

Certainly the advent of the Omega meant a broadening of outlook in the applied arts, a readiness to look beyond accepted notions concerning craftsmanship and good taste. One of Fry's ambitions was to reintroduce a creative impulse, which he felt had been crushed and atrophied in many manufactured designs by the pressures of commercial life. He was not against machine production, but thought that it should be harnessed to the artist-designer's needs. He battled with the Royal Wilton carpet factory and overcame their initial refusal to reproduce what they thought 'insulting' patterns. He persuaded a French firm to manufacture six printed linens, using wooden blocks covered with felt, in order to retain the softness of touch inherent in the artist's original designs. He made use of, but was not inspired by, the possibilities offered by the machine. Nor, on the other hand, was he a preservationist, wanting to restore a dying or forgotten craft, though he did help revive Victorian cross-stitch and Berlin wool-work, the latter because it was strong and durable. His approach was essentially pragmatic, appropriateness and practicality determining the choice of process. He enjoyed the hand-made, because the tremors of movement visible in the end product betrayed the sensibility of the maker; but when skilled craftsmanship was needed, as in the case of marquetry, he handed over the artist's designs to a skilled cabinet maker, John Joseph Kallenborn, who worked nearby in Marshall's Yard, Seaton Street, off the Hampstead Road.

Fry argued that since Morris and the Arts and Crafts movement there had been no significant development in the decorative arts. Post-Impressionism marked a return to a more architectural and structural basis of design, and therefore was in Fry's view peculiarly adapted to the applied arts. One aim at the Omega was to allow the new movement in art to spill out and animate surfaces of all kinds; another was to create a situation in which artists could earn a living – thirty shillings in return for three half-days' work. The end result was a creative exuberance, a playfulness with colours, patterns and motifs; as an alternative to inert traditionalism, the Omega acted as a protest against oppressive forms of authority and uniformity.

Its greatest challenge lay in its use of strong, clear colour at a time when such hues were generally found only in children's toys, circus decoration and gypsy caravans. Inside both private and public buildings much of the paint used on woodwork that escaped imitation graining was rich red, chocolate or dark green, colours that did not show the dirt as much as lighter tones would. The quantity of soot in the atmosphere quickly blackened outdoor paint, while the taste for heavily lined curtains darkened interiors. In a period when principles of taste were deeply ingrained and strictly adhered to, any alternative to tasteful gloom aroused panic, suspicion and moral condemnation. When in 1914 one of the workers at the Omega asked at Liberty's for some emerald-green silk, the shop assistant replied, 'Emerald, Madam, is a colour we *never* stock.' Soon after the Omega opened, two ladies arrived in the hope of seeing 'immoral' furniture, a term used by the *Morning Post* of some chairs that had been painted scarlet.

Duncan played a leading role at the Omega in its early years. His empty pockets had shown Fry how badly young artists needed part-time work. Now the Omega supplied it and Duncan readily accepted any task that needed doing. Fry, despite objections by his relatives on religious grounds, coined the name Omega, which was, very usefully, both word and sign, the latter becoming the firm's trademark. Duncan painted its signboard[21] with a huge Omega symbol on one side and on the other a blue arum lily precariously poised in a wine goblet. With Vanessa, he worked on designs for printed linens, getting even more muddled than she did with the repeats. He was prepared to turn his hand to anything, large or small – decorating a fan with the heads of two kissing lovers, or the surface of a table or large screen with loose, amorphous patches of colour that took their starting point from his observations of a lily pond.

At Fry's request he designed a doll's house, which was fitted up with electric light. He also turned his mind to jointed wooden toy animals, Kallenborn cutting out the shapes that Duncan drew in plywood, after which workers at the Omega rubbed them down with sandpaper, painted them with features and markings, added celluloid varnish and then put them together with nuts, bolts and washers, which could be tightened to make the animals keep their positions. One or two of these animals always sat on the mantelpiece in the workshops' hallway.

In his work for the Omega, Duncan, seemingly uninhibited by any fear of failure, revealed a vital and instinctive decorative sense. He understood how an interesting design could be made out of the simplest shapes if slight variations were introduced, as in his design for a rug made for the Ideal Home Exhibition in 1914, with its stepped oblongs and rows of hatching.[22] Whether designing a fire-screen with brightly coloured birds and flowers to be embroidered by Lady Ottoline Morrell or Vanessa Bell, painting dancing figures to ornament the first-floor niches on the building's façade or merely drawing an advertisement card, he brought a spirit of gaiety and enjoyment to everything he did. So essential had he become to the Omega during the summer and autumn of 1913 that his disappearance to Cambridge in November, during the run-up to the Christmas exhibition, left Fry desperate for his return. 'Please please come back soon – we're opening early next week and must have the sign up. Also of course there's 100,001 things to be finished. Please come. China to be painted. Roger.'[23]

A workshop caretaker had been found in a Mr Miles, whose wife sat day in, day out in an upstairs room patiently executing cross-stitch to artists' designs. She looked like a slim black cat, with her hair smoothed down on either side of her head, and became as much a feature of the Omega as her cockney husband. His fierce loyalty to the Workshops led him to christen their son Arthur Omega Miles, and once, when manning the room representing the Omega at the Ideal Home Exhibition in 1914, he was so incensed by a rude remark made by a circumambulating critic that he retorted, 'In saying that, you shows your taste and your breedin' in one.'[24]

Equally loyal was Winifred Gill, the young girl who earlier had helped to look after Fry's children and done part-time secretarial work for his sister Joan. She turned her hand to any task that needed doing and, fifty years later, in a series of letters containing her recollections of the Omega, stressed its light-hearted atmosphere – 'the happiest possible climate for inspiration'.[25] After Roger Fry's death she told another of his sisters, Agnes, that it was 'impossible to imagine how much happiness, how much richness and breadth of emotion and sensation would be gone out of my life if I were to eliminate all that came to me through him'. With the Omega in mind, she added, 'He made the utmost a possibility.'[26]

Fry's energy and enthusiam powered the venture, which he ran haphazardly, welcoming all and sundry into the Workshops. He invited the Slade-trained Ursula Tyrwhitt to do work for the Omega, an offer she turned down, but which other young unknowns, such as Cuthbert Hamilton, accepted. Naïve and trusting, Fry left his opened letters on his desk, visible to all, and expressed surprise when Winifred Gill hid them under the lid. When she explained that someone might read them, he replied, 'Good gracious, no one here would do a thing like that.'

In fact anything could happen at the Omega. The clientele was almost as colourful as the work on show. Winnie Gill and other young assistants might look up from their work to see Yeats or H. G. Wells or Arnold Bennett wandering around the showroom, surveying the items for sale. Visitors included Rupert Brooke, the Sitwells, Ezra Pound, the Countess Drogheda and Lady Ottoline Morrell. The jobs to be done varied greatly, partly because of Fry's willingness to respond to any suggestion or request. When Winifred Gill made a necklace out of some Woolworth's beads, Fry said it was like a Picasso and encouraged her to do more. The fashion of the day was for long necklaces, so there was a great deal of scope, and further supplies of beads were bought from a Mrs Bacon, who ran a bead shop lined with tiny chests of drawers in nearby Endell Street. Frederick Etchells's sister, Jessie, arrived to work at the Omega, with hair the colour of pale gold, pink cheeks and large, pale blue eyes. With slow, indolent movements and a voice to match, she wove a bead bracelet for the dancer Karsavina. When one day Duncan brought in a net-like collar made of white African beads and pendants, it inspired yet more Omega necklaces.

Press coverage and word-of-mouth gossip helped spread the Omega's reputation. One person who simply turned up, asking for work, was Nina Hamnett, a young artist who had first exhibited in July 1913 at the Allied Artists' Association in London. Possibly Fry remembered the portraits she had shown in this vast exhibition because, without asking for any proof of her ability, he told her to start work the next day. As Fry never knew when he would need extra labour, the employment procedure was somewhat haphazard and to an extent depended on contacts. When Nina Hamnett married a man called de Bergen, who changed his name to Roald Kristian during the war, he automatically entered the Workshops, contributing woodcuts to certain Omega publications as well as executing some designs based on animals. Nina Hamnett also brought in the sculptor Henri Gaudier-Brzeska, who designed a marquetry tray, made a cat in pottery and two large plaster maquettes for stone vases for Lady Hamilton. He never worked on the premises, but looked in regularly at 33 Fitzroy Square to see if any money was owed to him for the drawings and small pieces of sculpture he had left for sale.

Duncan, too, benefited financially from the Omega, but more important was the opportunity it gave him to experiment with all kinds of decorative problems and thereby stimulate his visual imagination. He, too, worked mostly elsewhere, visiting the Omega only to put his head round the door, ask for Vanessa or Roger and then disappear again. For a fortnight he startled the workers at the Omega by appearing several times in correct morning dress. Word went round that he was courting a doctor's daughter, but later Winifred Gill realised that his smart appearance coincided with the fact that his mother was in town. She arrived at the Omega one day with a friend, introduced herself and charmed all whom she met. Standing in front of one of Duncan's pictures, shaking her head gently, she was overheard saying to her companion, 'And he *can* draw quite well.'[27]

The Omega, Vanessa decided in September 1913, 'is very amusing . . . as long as one isn't there'.[28] Duncan probably shared this view because, though stimulated by its design opportunities, he continued to pursue his own interests. That summer he painted a portrait of Lady Ottoline Morrell, entertaining her with humorous stories while he drew the line of her profile and jaw so that it echoed the brim of her extravagantly decorated hat. Her habit of flaunting her Portland pearls inspired Duncan to attach a string of Woolworth's pearls to the canvas. In the final solution these were replaced by a painted simulation of real pearls, an ironic acknowledgement of the artifice involved in the capturing of likeness. That Duncan worked without any apparent constraint or any need to satisfy the sitter's vanity tells us much about his friendship with Lady Ottoline. She was charmed by his humour and child-like enjoyment of life and her fondness was returned. When early in 1913 she disappeared to Berkshire to look after her daughter Julian, who was ill, Duncan was one of the first to visit.

In August he travelled to Norfolk, clutching camp stool, easel and bottle of champagne, to take part in a camping holiday at Brandon, near Thetford, which was intended by Maynard and Vanessa to repeat the success of a similar holiday held in 1911 at Clifford Bridge. Again Duncan fitted in easily, enjoying the company of three of the Olivier girls, Ka Cox, Adrian, Roger, Maynard and others. He painted the economist Gerald Shove lying reading on the ground and two pictures of the tents, their angular shapes echoed in the foliage of the trees behind, rendered in a Cézannian patchwork of colour.

Though Vanessa slept in a nearby farmhouse, this holiday provided another opportunity for intimacy with Duncan. In September when Maynard invited him to Cambridge to finish a picture, Duncan turned down the offer, saying that he had to visit a relative at Wissett in Suffolk. He may have done so, but in addition he went down to Asheham to stay with Vanessa. After he left, she complained, 'We've been very solitary here since you left and it's very odd having my bath alone.'[29]

If the Omega had momentarily receded, it demanded attention again in October when four of its artists – Wyndham Lewis, C. J. Hamilton, Frederick Etchells and Edward Wadsworth – sent out a round-robin letter accusing Fry of mismanagement and underhand behaviour. It was, in Maynard's opinion, 'simply a piece of disordered egotism masked by a want of power of literary expression',[30] but it was serious enough for Vanessa, Duncan, Clive and others to co-operate in deciding what action to take on Fry's behalf while he remained abroad on a painting holiday in Provence.

The chief figure behind this rumpus was Wyndham Lewis, whose behaviour betrayed deep insecurity. At the Omega he once bragged to Winifred Gill that he got a lot of letters, most of them from women, and to prove his point thrust his hand into his pocket and withdrew a fistful of buff envelopes. Duncan surmised that Lewis had been in the Omega only for what he could get out of it. So he told Roger, in a letter dealing with the issues that the round-robin raised, Fry afterwards thanking him for 'all the bother and worry that you have gone through in fighting my battles'.[31] Lewis's chief complaint concerned a commission to decorate a room for the Ideal Home Exhibition, which, he argued, Fry had kept for the Omega when originally the commissioning body, the *Daily Mail*, had intended it to be shared between the Omega, Wyndham Lewis and the non-Omega artist Spencer Gore. Loose ends in the various accounts dealing with this rumpus suggest that the central dispute resulted from a genuine error, in that two people were responsible for the commission and the instructions given may therefore have differed. But whether or not it was inadvertently mishandled, the Ideal Home room acted as a catalyst for ill-feeling that Fry had aroused in other ways. The round-robin letter sneered at 'this family party of strayed and Dissenting Aesthetes' whose efforts 'would not rise above the level of a pleasant tea party' without the modern talent they had been obliged to gather from other sources.[32] Fry, unwilling to believe that anyone at the Omega would stoop to reading his letters, had to face the fact that he had been nurturing enemies, both mocking and malevolent.

Though the departure of Lewis and his allies lost the Omega a degree of talent, its most distinctive and advanced designs in the pre-1914 period were by Bloomsbury artists and not the proto-Vorticists. In November the marquetry tray based on Duncan's elephant design arrived in the Workshops and was widely admired. That same month the *Daily Sketch* carried a photograph of the nursery painted at the Omega in a style associated with paper cut-outs, with clouds on the ceiling and animals and trees on the walls. 'Would you let your Child Play in this Nursery?' ran the by-line to the article dealing with this 'futurist nursery'.[33] There was also new excitement about pottery, Fry having found a man in Mitcham who was prepared to work with him on ceramics for the Omega. Duncan himself went down to Mitcham in December to try his hand at pottery. Again, he appears to have contributed significantly to the Omega through this medium, for several drawings exist by him for large simple pots. They are similar to the severe, angular pots which he had designed in April 1913 for the banqueting table in *Macbeth*.

In December 1913 work for the Omega had to be fitted in between concentrated bouts of painting. Duncan was finishing *The Ass* (now in a private collection), which he sent to the second Grafton Group exhibition, held in January 1914 at the Alpine Club Gallery. The picture was bought by Roger Fry. Based on a Persian miniature, *The Ass* is massive and tough, the black outline and hatching, like crude stitching, reinforcing the surface of the canvas at the same time as they contribute to the strong, rhythmic movement that animates the whole. It is as if both ass and background have been cut up and reassembled according to a concept more rigorous than any naturalistic interpretation. One cloud slices into the landscape while the chunky background foliage, like the curtain in Picasso's *Les Demoiselles d'Avignon*, helps flatten space. It was one of Grant's most powerful works to date and an image that he returned to in April 1914 in a softer style.[34]

Also included in this show was Duncan's *Adam and Eve*, which the Contemporary Art Society bought, at Clive Bell's instigation. Though Clive had in the summer of 1913 vetoed the proposal to buy Stanley Spencer's *Apple Gatherers*, his loyalty to Duncan and other artists in his circle of acquaintance enlarged his sympathies and he had no difficulty with the free use of distortion in *Adam and Eve*, with Eve's swelling thighs and tapering calves or with Adam's wriggling contours as he stands upside-down on his hands. It was too much, however, for George Mallory who, having enjoyed *The Queen of Sheba* with its portrayal, as he saw it, of 'this intellectual passion for finding out', struck out at *Adam and Eve*, complaining at the violent depiction of Adam. 'It makes me wonder whether you can be aiming at some remote asceticism of the spirit beyond my horizon. And have you forgotten the value of simple enjoyment in life?'[35] Such criticism made Duncan aware of the bitter hostility that the painting aroused. He had begun it, he told Mallory, with the half-conscious intention of making a surreptitious attack on the subject-picture; hence his unserious treatment of a rather pretentious subject. What seemed to him a joyful use of distortion for design purposes appeared to others to be the result of insincerity.

Even before he received Mallory's criticisms, Duncan had begun to despair over this picture. 'I have been busy lately with an [*sic*] large picture which I brought to birth with great labour and pain and I see is likely to be a thankless offering.'[36] So he told Lytton, the day before he left London for Menton, where he was to stay again with his aunt, Lady Colvile, at the Villa Henriette, James and Marjorie acompanying him as far as Paris. He had not misjudged the reception his painting would receive: while he was away he heard from Vanessa that the press notices for the Grafton Group show, though on the whole good, had condemned the distortion in his *Adam and Eve*. One of his harshest critics was Sir Claude Phillips in the *Daily Telegraph*. After noticing that the fracas at the Omega had depleted the Grafton Group of the English Cubists, and that work by French artists (Picasso, Marchand, Doucet, Vilette and Friesz) had been supplemented instead, Phillips went on to deplore Duncan's contribution:

> What shall we say of Mr Duncan Grant, who is here seen wasting a fine talent, deliberately, and sneering at himself, and at art? We should be inclined to leave him to his own devices were it not that in one of the decorations here exhibited he once more asserts his splendid powers as draughtsman and designer. This is styled *The Ass*. Surprising is the force and the beauty of rhythm in this study, almost on the scale of life . . . But what is to be said of such a wilful absurdity as the vast *Adam and Eve* . . . What of *Cyclamens*, and what of *Slops*. They do not even merit mirth.[37]

Two others upset by *Adam and Eve* were Duncan's friends Jacques and Gwen Raverat. 'I believe distortion is like Sodomy,' Vanessa concluded. 'People are simply blindly prejudiced against it . . .'[38]

Preparations for the Grafton Group exhibition may have depleted Duncan's reserves of energy, because in Paris he caught the grippe. He travelled on to Menton in feverish condition and collapsed on arrival.

Low in spirits and health, he reacted negatively to his aunt, whose arid intellectualism, prejudices and selfishness all seemed to the fore. But, as always, she rose to the crisis and bestowed on Duncan such affection that before long he was only able to admire, noticing also that despite her magnificent inner resources his aunt was a profoundly lonely woman. When they celebrated his birthday on 21 January 1914 Duncan was surprised to learn from his mother that he was only twenty-eight. 'I thought I was twenty-nine,' he told Maynard. 'So I have a whole year to spare!'[39] In fact his mother was wrong and he right.

From Menton he went to Roquebrune to see the Bussys. They had taken responsibility for Maynard Keynes, who had fallen ill with diphtheria while staying in an hotel nearby. He was now recovering in a nursing home, though still infectious, and Duncan had to talk to him through a window. Soon afterwards Duncan joined his mother on board a ship heading for Tunis, where they met Aunt Daisy and her charge, a Miss Elwes, who in time was to become his mother's companion. The thought of their destination excited Duncan. 'I'm hoping the Arabs will fill the gap I feel in female society,'[40] he told Lytton, who, he knew, would understand exactly what he meant.

Lytton replied to Duncan in Tunis, admitting his inability to like the *Adam and Eve* painting. 'I fling my arms round your neck and kiss you a million times ... and await the moment when you reach your Watteau period, with the most tranquil expectation. Won't you in the meantime paint me a little Tunisian view that I should really like? With a chocolate-coloured male bum in the foreground? It would be very nice.'[41]

Lytton's teasing still amused, but now held Duncan's attention far less than the description Vanessa sent him of Picasso's studio. Her letter began with thanks for the sprays of oranges and lemons that he had sent. Their strong colour had appealed to her eye and she had immediately begun to paint them. She then went on to describe her experiences on a recent visit to Paris with Clive and Roger. They had, as arranged, met Gertrude Stein, who took them to see Picasso in the Rue Schoelcher. His studio bristled with work, not only paintings, drawings and sculptures but also the Cubist constructions that he had begun to make out of pieces of wood and other debris. He also showed his visitors paintings done as a child, as well as work from his Blue Period. The effect of all this on Vanessa was to convince her that Picasso was 'one of the greatest geniuses that has ever lived'.[42] She had been careful to notice the Picasso that Duncan had admired at Kahnweiler's, reporting her reactions to it and to Matisse's studio, which they also visited along with Michael Stein's collection.

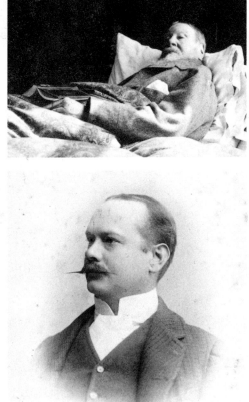

ABOVE: Ethel Grant
ABOVE RIGHT: Sir John Peter Grant,
Duncan's grandfather
RIGHT: Bartle Grant
BELOW: Duncan, scorer for the
Hillbrow cricket team

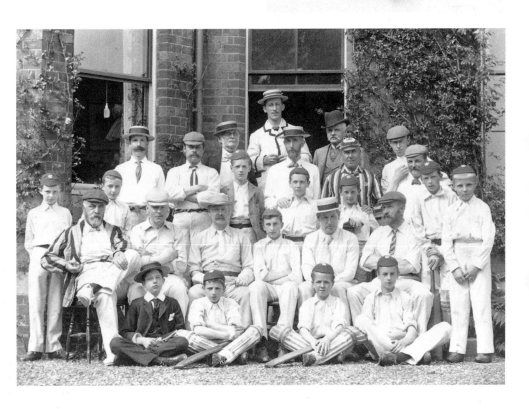

TOP: Lady Strachey
ABOVE LEFT: Duncan as a boy
ABOVE RIGHT: Duncan as a young man

ABOVE: *Crime and Punishment*, 1909, Tate Gallery
BELOW: *James Strachey*, 1909–1910, Tate Gallery

LEFT: Duncan, Virginia and Adrian Stephen
BELOW: *Dancers*, second version, 1912, Private Collection
BOTTOM: *Dancers*, 1910–11, Tate Gallery

ABOVE: *The Queen of Sheba*, 1912, Tate Gallery
RIGHT: *Man with Greyhound*, 1911, Private
Collection
BELOW: *Adrian Stephen*, 1910, Charleston Trust
BELOW RIGHT: *The Tub*, c.1912–13, Tate Gallery

TOP LEFT: Vanessa Bell at Asheham
TOP RIGHT: Vera Waddington
LEFT: Duncan, David Garnett, Saxon
Sydney-Turner and Barbara Bagenal
outside the latter's tent at Charleston,
summer 1917
ABOVE: Roger Fry at Brandon, 1913

ABOVE: *The Birds*, Final Scene, as performed in 1924, in Cambridge with costumes and sets designed by Duncan Grant, assisted by Douglas Davidson
BELOW: Angus Davidson, *c.*1924, Collection Wolfgang Kuhle

LEFT: Duncan Grant overmantel design, c.1924, for Angus Davidson's house at 3 Heathcote Street (destroyed)

ABOVE: The Music Room, with designs and decorations by Vanessa Bell and Duncan Grant, as shown at the Lefevre Gallery in 1932

BELOW: Maynard Keynes's main room at King's College, Cambridge, as it was in his day, with decorations by Duncan and Vanessa, also painted and furnished with their advice.

Vanessa's letter would have stimulated Duncan's eagerness to return to Paris in February 1914. He had been asked by Jacques Copeau to design costumes for a performance of *La Nuit des Rois* (an adaptation from *Twelfth Night* by Theodore Lascaris) at the Théâtre du Vieux Colombier. The theatre had opened the previous October, a group of writers and artists having got together under Copeau's direction with the intention of releasing 'the spirit of the poet from the text of the play'. In order to carry out this idea, scenery was suppressed or simplified to the absolute minimum. So successful were the first few productions that within eight months the theatre had·become known all over France and Europe. *La Nuit des Rois*, which first opened on 19 May 1914 at the Vieux Colombier, became Copeau's most frequently produced classic play. When it was revived in 1917 it was performed not only in Paris but also in New York, whither Copeau transferred his company that year. For the 1917–18 season Duncan's name was listed among the 'Costumiers, Décorateurs, Accessoiristes, Architectes'. In New York the play continued to enjoy success, despite the fact that its relatively bare stage made no concessions to the Broadway ideals of stage art.

Though it was to be one of Duncan's happiest experiences, his association with Copeau began with aggravating delays that kept him hanging around in Paris in February 1914 with little to do. 'It sounds too beastly,' Vanessa wrote, 'your having to wait on in Paris, for most likely the play will only be put off again I suppose . . . Do be strong minded and say you can't stay on indefinitely.'[43] While dithering in Paris, he fell ill again and spent three days in bed reading Clive Bell's *Art*, which argued that the essential quality distinguishing works of art from other objects is 'significant form'. 'I think it is exceedingly good,' he told Clive. 'I read it with the greatest relish from beginning to end – only it is really too short – I mean I should have liked it to go on. Of course the main thesis could not come upon me with any great newness, as you will imagine. But it will no doubt have effects of all sorts . . .'[44]

In Paris he too visited Picasso's studio in the company of Gertrude Stein. Noticing the Spanish artist's involvement with papier-collé, Duncan offered to bring him the rolls of wallpaper that he had found in his cupboard in the Hôtel de l'Univers et du Portugal. Picasso was delighted, as he was having difficulty getting hold of wallpaper and sometimes had to shave small pieces off the wall, but his initial response was to protest that it was stealing. This objection was overlooked and Duncan agreed to return on his own with the wallpaper. It was a thrilling but also daunting prospect, as he admitted to Clive: 'I think I shall find it difficult to know what to say . . . one wants a Roger's tongue or a

Gertrude's bust to fall back onto.'[45] No record exists of this second visit but it enriched their friendship.

Once Duncan recovered from his illness and began working for Copeau ('You seem anyhow to be capable of enjoying Copeau,' Vanessa observed in early March),[46] he entered upon a month of what he afterwards called 'pure enchantment'. He had first met Copeau in London in 1912, when he lectured at the Second Post-Impressionist Exhibition as a drama critic and founder of the *Nouvelle Revue Française*. Duncan did not then think of him as an actor or producer of plays, but Copeau must already have had the project for the Théâtre du Vieux Colombier in mind. When Duncan received a letter from Copeau asking him to undertake costume designs and simple décor for *Twelfth Night*, he was heartened to learn that Copeau, having seen Granville-Barker's *Twelfth Night* in London in 1912, wanted something very different. He did not have Barker's resources and would anyway be working with a small stage; therefore, as he said, much ingenuity was needed to surmount the material difficulties they would face at the Vieux Colombier. He also wanted 'to collaborate with artists of taste' and thought that Duncan's 'charming and fantastic imagination' would find itself very much at home in this marvellous comedy. He asked Duncan to keep the cost of dress-making as cheap as possible and to devise a set that would suffice for the whole comedy, with perhaps one or two supplementary backcloths. 'I imagine surroundings in every respect unobtrusive,' he concluded; 'all the amusement of form and colour being produced by the costumes and gestures of the actors.'[47]

Duncan had found these instructions clear and helpful, had done the necessary drawings and was now anxious to see Copeau's conception come to life. In the turmoil of preparation, working in the small, barn-like theatre with very little money, Copeau, Duncan observed, 'appeared to be everywhere, his blazing eyes aware of all that passed'.[48] Already the reputation of his theatre was such that people used to wander in off the street to see what was going on. Duncan saw André Gide in this spectator rôle. He also observed that however much mockery and laughter went on in the corridors, Copeau's word was law on the stage and even famous actors like Jouvet became obedient and accepted his scolding. 'How this miracle of hard work, wedded to merriment and goodwill, was achieved', Duncan later admitted, was beyond his powers of explanation. Copeau's many-sided character dazzled him, and when, in the heat of the moment, the various aspects of Copeau's character were all brought into play, the real miracle, Duncan thought, was how a mere human machine could take the strain. At other moments he observed Copeau off duty – on a couple of occasions Duncan went home with him for lunch and caught a glimpse of a very different character, a man apparently without preoccupations as he joked with his children and listened to their stories.

When the play finally opened in May Duncan must have returned to Paris, as legend has it that he was still chasing round just before the curtain rose, making final adjustments to the actors' costumes. In his desire to sustain the mood of comedy, Duncan had ignored the kind of details, such as hats or swords, that would have given the play an historical reality. The absence of these accoutrements and the emphasis on the shapes made by the costumes contributed to the fluid, free, almost improvised quality of the staging – the production having, according to Michel Saint-Denis, 'a peculiar floating lightness'.[49] Although the company was exhausted and, to save their voices, ended by rehearsing in whispers, the first night was a success, the play becoming the talk of Paris. Amid the confusion and anxiety of the rehearsals Duncan had been unable to predict what the end product would be. The performance came as a revelation to him, for, more used to hearing Shakespeare read aloud, he realised that even in translation it did not lose its music.

Duncan's pleasure in *La Nuit des Rois* and the collaborative effort involved appears to have matched that of Copeau, who afterwards wrote Duncan a grateful letter, thanking him for devoting himself so wholeheartedly to the play, acknowledging also the artistic camaraderie that had arisen between them. '*J'ai été vraiment charmé de ces quelques jours pendant lesquels nous avons travaillé ensemble et j'ai trouvé en vous ce que j'aime tant et qui est si rare: un homme véritablement épris de son travail.*'[50] He expressed the hope that they would collaborate again the following year on another project. The press had been unanimous in its praise of *La Nuit des Rois* and Duncan would in time receive 2 per cent of the total receipts.

What looked like the start of a promising association was to be cut short by war. It made all subsequent collaboration between the two men difficult, and though Duncan did design costumes for another of Copeau's productions, circumstances prevented him from enjoying the close involvement that had made *La Nuit des Rois* such an inspiring experience. When Duncan had first agreed to work for Copeau, he had certain views of his own about the theatre and, as he recalled, had even sent Copeau 'a very youthful essay on my theories of lighting in the theatre; a subject of which I had no experience, and which he politely ignored'. After four weeks at the Théâtre du Vieux Colombier all his preconceptions had been blown away. 'The month or so that I worked with Copeau,' Duncan claimed, '. . . was a time of pure enchantment for me – I had found the theatre of my dreams.'[51]

TEN

Croquet and Cuckolds

While Duncan worked on *La Nuit des Rois* in Paris throughout most of February and March 1913, he was greatly missed at the Omega. Vanessa kept him up-to-date with news of the latest developments: they were eagerly awaiting the arrival at the Workshops of pots made by her and Roger in the Mitcham pottery, as well as those Duncan had sent from Tunis; and they were deeply embroiled in a commission to decorate Lady Hamilton's hall. Vanessa's design for a stained-glass window had been rejected in favour of one by Roger, but hers had instead formed the basis of a mosaic roundel for the hall floor.

Fry, too, wrote with the welcome news that some of Duncan's pictures had sold at the recent Grafton Group exhibition. One of these, *Cyclamens*, had been rendered entirely in terms of hatching, under the influence of Picasso's *Nude with Drapery* (1907), which Duncan had seen in Gertrude Stein's collection. But though the exhibition had been a success, there was scant demand for the Omega's decorative items and this increased the sense of struggle under which Fry laboured. 'I feel that the hatred we arouse by the Omega and our shows is steadily increasing. I wonder why I inspire such intense dislike. The Lewis group do nothing even now but abuse me ... I often wonder whether we can stick it out, especially as it means for me almost endless small worries about details.'[1]

Vanessa, more able to keep her distance from the Omega, was less affected by its problems. She also had other plans in mind, among them the notion of forming a lending library of pictures. Support was canvassed from Maynard and others, who suggested (to tease the anti-religious Vanessa) that it should be called the Christian Dining Society. Her desire for change and experiment coloured her views of the latest Friday Club exhibition which, with the exception of Bomberg and Nevinson, she dismissed as 'utterly hopeless'. 'Of course,' her letter continues, 'I may have been prejudiced by the fact that nearly every second picture is a biblical scene. The young are reverting to Pre-Raphaelitism really – with all the moral and literary part of it as strong as ever. Do come back soon. It's so depressing to have no good painters about. There's a compliment for you!'[2]

Duncan, meanwhile, had been sending Vanessa descriptions of his travels. After Tunis he had journeyed into the Sahara to an oasis of date palms. 'I do wish we could go to your oasis,' she replied. 'I wonder if you would risk the possible scandal, which after all wouldn't be very probable and might do you more good than harm anyhow, and elope there with me some day – as I believe we should potter very harmoniously with no undue hurry or over strain . . .'[3]

Underneath the teasing lay genuine desire, her suggestion gently hinting at what their relationship could be. She could not risk being openly loving but, as her letters reveal, she could flirt, encourage, amuse, sympathise and in this way steadily deepen their exchange. She drew attention to the fact that they shared an aesthetic standpoint, one that found theoretical justification in Clive's *Art*, a small, polemical book that made a large impact. Vanessa's distrust of moralising and story-telling aligned her, after the appearance of *Art*, with a view that quickly became the new orthodoxy among people of advanced taste. Through her association with Roger and her attendance of his Slade lectures, she had witnessed the evolution of the new aesthetic. It had been formulated, he argued, almost entirely by practising artists with a tendency for speculation: 'Maurice Denis' article on Cézanne was its first adumbration and I must confess to having done something towards its gradual formulation. Its chief point lies it its attempt to explain painting rather by its analogies with the non-representative arts of music and architecture and an insistence on its unlikeness to literature.'[4]

Theory was put into practice after Duncan's return, when he and Vanessa sat down on several occasions in front of the same still-life. They must have discussed Picasso's use of papier collé, because they too began to introduce collage into their work. The most interesting examples of this are the still-lifes that both produced based on a bottle, lamp and soda syphon. In the background to her picture Vanessa incorporated fragments of a map of Germany, as well as newspaper dating from mid-September 1914, which contains reference to the 'Killed, Wounded, Missing'.[5] It is tempting, therefore, to relate the title, *Triple Alliance*, to the international crisis which the following year produced an alliance between England, France and Italy. Duncan, on the other hand, made no use of maps or newspaper, but playfully attached to the neck of his painted bottle a scrap of paper containing the letters 'bulm' which links the bottle in the viewer's mind with Bulmer's cider. However, in both pictures the three objects are arrayed like soldiers, in such a way as to convey an air of confrontation. Another possible source for Vanessa's choice of title was labour unrest: as a consequence of strikes in schools, coal mines and the building trade that spring, there was widespread anxiety in the summer of 1914 that there would be a general strike in the autumn as a result of a 'triple alliance' of railwaymen, transport workers and miners. But even if Vanessa adopted this title after the picture was completed, it still suggests that she and Duncan were unable at times to separate formal concerns from non-pictorial ideas. Though formalism, at its strictest and narrowest, requires us to leave behind connections with politics, morals or literature, the motivation behind Bell's and Grant's painting is often inextricably linked with non-formal ideas.

Duncan's visit to Picasso's studio had coincided with the period of 'synthetic' Cubism. Instead of small facets and a few graphic details to suggest objects in space, Picasso had begun re-combining, in a more concise fashion, select details that re-create both what we see and know. As a result the object becomes a composite of different views. Papier collé had played a crucial part in this development. Though Duncan perceived the inherent playfulness in Picasso's use of this medium, it is doubtful if he understood Cubism well enough to grasp the full potential of papier collé and the way in which it renewed the conceptual complexities of the Cubist language. In his own painting, Duncan always mixed papier collé with paint, often adding coloured paper to his pictures to enrich the colour or create a shape. In the summer of 1914 he began a series of portraits of Vanessa, who posed for them in a long red evening dress. In one full-length portrait of Vanessa in this dress, the papier collé has become so merged with the painted image that its identity is lost and only rediscovered on close inspection of the picture surface.[6] In this instance papier collé appears to have been used primarily as an extension of Duncan's palette, a shorthand method for establishing the colour chords he wanted. Elsewhere, in the one of two half-length portraits of Vanessa,[7] Duncan incorporated two patches of material said to have been taken from the actual evening dress. They act like the statement of a musical theme, the brush elsewhere offering variations upon it in loose imitation of the original pattern.

His enthusiasm for collage, which lasted well into the following year, came at an opportune moment. As he once told a *Daily Herald* reporter,[8] after seeing Matisse he had realised that he no longer wanted to make coloured drawings: instead he wanted a new form of expression in which colour determined the composition. In his still-lifes especially, he had begun to translate objects into patches of rich colour, often accentuated in hue or translated into heightened tonalities. The freedom with which he had begun to analyse his sensations and transmute what he saw into unexpected chromatic harmonies had caused objects to dissolve and backgrounds to merge with foreground detail in a floating tapestry of coloured marks. The introduction of papier collé, often taking the form of crudely cut, large angular shapes, helped strengthen the construction of his pictures. Papier collé allowed him to simplify – a desire held in balance with his natural impulse to elaborate and embellish. He had observed this conflict in himself as a young man, when writing to William Rothenstein, 'I feel very strongly the need for simplicity . . . but objects to me have a most deceptive way of looking simple, and I only realise my mistake when I try to make them.'[9]

Meanwhile a close working relationship between Duncan and Vanessa had become established. Both painted a still-life of boxes and artificial flowers placed on the corner of a mantelpiece which provide an interesting comparison.[10] Vanessa, who must have worked from a seated position as her viewpoint is lower, builds her composition around a spiralling conglomeration of shapes, which climax at the summit. Duncan, on the other hand, uses a much less striking arrangement of forms and instead allows the drama of his composition to develop through his use of colour: working with a series of warm–cool contrasts, he allows the brilliant yellow around the edges of one box, together with a rich vermilion, to charge the picture with sudden intensity. Though the two pictures display very different artistic personalities, both depend for their success on a feeling for the integration of the whole picture at an abstract level.

Vanessa's work over the last three years had revealed an emphatic search for the architecture underlying any scene or subject, and a willingness to strip away all inessentials. She was more rigorously reductive than Duncan in her use of schematic representation and simple interrelated blocks of colour. Inevitably, their interest in papier collé as an entity in its own right, combined with the need to make abstract patterns for the Omega, led to experiments in their painting with a non-figurative language. However, unlike the Vorticists, Bloomsbury artists showed no interest in a machine-age aesthetic that attempted to align art with the economical lines of machinery and the aggressive energy of modern urban life. Instead, as Richard Morphet has argued, Duncan's and Vanessa's abstract art grew naturally out of their concern with the classical values of painting. In Morphet's opinion, some of their products are more uncompromising than any other British abstract art of the period.[11]

Much of the work that Duncan did in Vanessa's company in 1914 took place at Asheham. Though the lease on this house still belonged to

Virginia Woolf, it was used by Vanessa and her children whenever possible and in April 1914 was briefly sub-let to Maynard. Duncan and Vanessa joined his party of young men. Afterwards Vanessa thanked him, her bawdiness conveying her delight in free speech but possibly also providing an outlet for unconscious aggression at a sexuality that excluded her. 'You are rather like a Chinese Buddha as host,' she afterwards told Maynard. 'You sit silent, but not so silent as Saxon, and manage to create an atmosphere in which all is possible . . . Anyhow the result is what I imagine it would be with a Buddha – one can talk of fucking and sodomy and sucking and bushes and all without turning a hair.'[12] Duncan, slightly abashed that the attractions of Asheham had prevented him from being elsewhere, wrote to Lytton, 'Very sorry was away at Asheham. Croquet and cuckolds.'[13]

As Vanessa admitted in one of her memoirs, they had only the haziest idea of political developments in Europe. So involved were they with the optimism and sense of freedom that accompanied what seemed to be a renaissance in the arts, especially painting, that they could take little interest in the motives or ambitions of distant countries and rulers. When reminiscing with Duncan about this period, over fifty years later, Winifred Gill recalled:

> The war crept up on us by degrees, but with increasing speed and horror and utter incredulity as the days went by. Was it only a week from the scarcely noticed assassination of some vague archduke and his wife, to full implication in war? Where was Serbia . . . anyway? There was no radio and the only way to keep up with the news was either to keep an eye open for telegrams posted outside newspaper offices, or to buy each edition of the newspapers as they came out. I think my record was eleven in one day.[14]

Because many holidaymakers were abroad on 4 August, the announcement of war was followed by a three- or four-day moratorium, which allowed people to return home. During this time a German boy appeared at the Omega, wanting to buy a present for his mother. Although everyone present behaved as though nothing was out of the ordinary, there was something hushed and uneasy in the atmosphere.

Shortly before the war began Duncan gave an 'at home' for the musicians, the d'Aranyi sisters, great-nieces of the renowned Hungarian violinist Joachim. Jelly d'Aranyi is said to have been in love with Duncan, but it was another sister, Adila, who afterwards wrote from Ostend, where they were holidaying, 'I wonder if you really mean to come? It would be quite lovely and please let us know when so that we could meet you.'[15] War put an end to any such plan, and to Duncan's hopes of meeting Feri [Ferenc] Békassy, a former King's man and one of the Neo-Pagans, in Vienna at Christmas. His friendship with this Hungarian aristocrat had deepened that summer and Feri had thanked Duncan 'for saying you liked thinking that I exist in the world'.[16] As they walked across Firle Park together, soon after the assassination of Archduke Ferdinand, Békassy said it would lead to a European war. He was soon proved right. In the moratorium that followed the announcement of war, during which the banks remained closed, Maynard Keynes managed to raise enough money to enable Békassy to return to Hungary so that he could fight in the war against Russia. Criticised by others for strengthening the enemy forces and probably sending Békassy to his death, Maynard justified his action by saying that, having failed to dissuade him, he felt obliged to respect his friend's freedom of choice. Duncan must have written to Békassy the night he left. The next day war was declared between Britain and Austria-Hungary and his letter was returned. Earlier, for reasons other than war, Duncan had admitted to Békassy feelings of depression. He now apologised: 'One ought never to be depressed or rather let anyone else know one is depressed.'[17] This maxim, for the time being, helped push aside anxiety and despair. He took further comfort during the first weeks of August from Maynard's conviction that, owing to the limited wealth available for war purposes, peace would have to be made before a year was out. Nevertheless, a process had begun that was profoundly to affect the world as Duncan knew it.

He fled to Asheham, where Vanessa's children jumped about naked, delighted at the freedom that the hot weather allowed them to enjoy. The quiet at Asheham was conducive to work, and while there, Duncan turned his mind to still-life, landscape and to an abstract scroll, which he intended to be viewed through an aperture as it was slowly wound past to musical accompaniment. Nearly fifteen feet long and eleven inches high, it is composed of seventeen sections, in each of which appears a cluster of oblongs that tilt, fall and rise again as the scroll progresses. Most, but not all, of the oblongs are constructed out of pre-painted papier collé, the thin paint and rapid brushwork used to cover their surfaces modifying the harshness of their geometry. Schematic shadows, created by stippling, underline the suggestion of overlap and set up a tension between the emphatic flatness of the papier collé and the illusion of three dimensions. As well as the rising and falling movement of the oblongs, Duncan wanted to convey a change of mood through the use of colour. He scribbled ideas for the scroll on the back of a London Joint Stock Bank receipt: 'Black green white yellow to grey to dark grey to black. Begin again solemnly in grey and green . . . yellow again gayer to red and yellow accompaniment.'[18]

For many decades this scroll, now in the Tate Gallery collection, lay rolled up forgotten in Duncan's studio. Though it is related to his interest in collage and abstraction, it remains a one-off piece, startlingly ambitious and experimental for its day. Both Richard Shone and Simon Watney have related it to the contemporaneous interest in kinaesthesia, Shone recording Grant's interest in the newspaper announcement of a concert in which Scriabin's music was to be accompanied by changing coloured lights.[19] Also significant is the fact that Duncan began working on this scroll after war had been declared, inventing, at least on paper, the vertical armature and winding mechanism that would enable it to move past an aperture. Though he never exhibited this work, a film was made of it in action soon after it had been acquired and restored by the Tate in the 1970s. When viewed as it was intended to be seen, in movement, the work has a solemnity that is rare in Grant's work, an emphasis on change, the rising and falling movement suggestive of the historical process, the experience made additionally moving by the plangent harmonies of the slow movement from one of Bach's Brandenburg Concertos, which Duncan specified as the accompaniment.

Towards the end of August Adrian arrived at Asheham with Karin Costelloe and for the next seven days, as Karin noted in her diary, they 'were hardly apart except for the very few hours which were left for sleep'.[20] She and Adrian were continuing a long and painful discussion about Karin's feelings and whether she should, or should not, marry Adrian. Though it was for them a fraught period, it was evident to all the rest that Adrian and Karin had become a couple. Duncan found it hard to bear.

For some years he had been intimate with Adrian and understood him better than most. A sad character, lethargic and ineffective, with hollow cheeks, a lantern jaw and long limbs, Adrian nevertheless had immense charm, though it was not apparent to all. The Olivier girls and others younger than him perceived it better than Thoby's friends, who tended to regard him as a pale shadow of his dead brother. Duncan, however, loved and trusted Adrian, knowing him to be incapable of insincerity or dishonesty. Adrian had tried in turn to be an actor, a doctor and a barrister, without success, and now, at the age of thirty-one, was still unclear as to what his future would be. At some level he remained unstirred; a misfit, dogged in memory by a remark he had overheard –

that it was 'the wrong son who had died'. He nevertheless enjoyed people, often held 'at homes' and was capable of wild enjoyment. It was at one of his parties that Vanessa danced until she was half-naked and the French painter Henri Doucet came dressed as Christ. On another occasion, at two in the morning, Adrian suggested setting off for the races and a cab was hailed. The idea lost its attraction when they learnt that the only race meeting on offer that day was 200 miles away, at Pontefract.

During the course of their friendship, Duncan and Adrian had been invited to a number of grand parties. One particular occasion Duncan never forgot: 'We went to one ball, a tremendous affair, and about 3.0 a.m. we had breakfast, bacon and eggs with two girls, daughters of the house. Adrian carried on like anything with them; he was very amusing and had no feeling that he mustn't enjoy himself. It was one occasion when he was unconstrained and amusing and a success and made them roar with laughter.'[21]

With memories like this, Duncan felt saddened to see Adrian shackled to Karin Costelloe, a hearty, somewhat gauche young woman with a schoolboy appetite and prickly emotions. Earlier that year, while Duncan was working for Copeau, Karin, who was also in Paris writing a thesis on the philosophy of Henri Bergson, had invited him to a tea party that included Gertrude Stein, Alice B. Toklas, Charles Vildrac, Mme Bergson and her two daughters. In order to avoid any embarrassment, Karin, with a fellow sufferer's sympathy, warned Duncan in advance that one of the Bergson daughters was deaf. But Karin's finer qualities were often obscured by the obtrusively garish colours that she wore, and her clumsy manner so irritated Leonard Woolf that he found it difficult to sit in the same room as her. Virginia, some years later, concluded that one of Karin's positive assets was vitality and that Adrian took 'constant delight in her substantiality'.[22]

But at Asheham, in August 1914, Duncan could not disguise his troubled state. He was made additionally anxious by the fact that Adrian did not seem to be in love with Karin. Karin herself sensed that they had reached a parting of the ways, as her diary records: 'As we left Asheham a fresh trouble came in the shape of Duncan's grief. Everyone assumed that we were either engaged or on the point of it, and Duncan was heartbroken at being left alone. Adrian had tears in his eyes as we got into the cab and I felt miserable because I was sure I was going to bring unhappiness to them both.'[23] The following month Vanessa received a short letter from Adrian telling her nothing except that he was now engaged. A month later they were married. The honeymoon in St Ives was a disaster and, on their return to London, Adrian offered Karin a divorce if she wished it. They decided against it and moved to Cambridge, where Karin had a fellowship at Newnham. There, things did not improve. In fact, as Karin wrote in her diary, no place could have been more ill-chosen. 'Cambridge in wartime was the lowest well of the inferno, a desert of gloom, empty of undergraduates and peopled by soldiers and acrimonious dons. We saw almost no-one and there was nowhere to go and nothing to do. I wept nearly every day and Adrian was in despair.'[24]

'Karin – I was against that from the start.' So said Duncan, fifty years later. 'I couldn't understand it . . . I never really believed in it, I never believed that Adrian was in love with her or she him. I don't think it was a very happy marriage, they had a great many quarrels.'[25] It was, however, a marriage that survived. In January 1916 Karin gave birth to the first of their two daughters, after which her relations with Adrian seemed to improve. Not, however, their circumstances. Adrian had declared himself a conscientious objector and, in order to do work of national importance, took over a dairy farm, with disastrous results. A year later they were allowed to transfer to proper agricultural work until 1917, when Adrian suffered a breakdown that affected his heart. Thereafter, for the rest of the war, he confined himself to clerical work.

To the end of his life, however, Adrian could number Duncan among his most loyal friends. Partly because he valued his friends so highly, Duncan dreaded war. 'I feel sure one ought to give way to depression,' he wrote to Lytton in September; '. . . one ought to plunge into the horror, think all one's friends are killed, that even oneself is killed that everything one cares about is done for, that the Louvre is on fire and all the children one knows butchered and boiled and then one rises to the surface cheerful. I can't think why perhaps it['s] simply a silly belief in the indestructibility of sublimity . . . I am thinking of joining St Loe [Strachey]'s force, the National Reserve – I hear there are not enough muskets for them.'[26]

On all sides Duncan heard talk of people enlisting. His old student-friend Maresco Pearce wrote asking if he would care to join the Artists' Rifles – 'It's really a very good life and for the moment seems to me less futile than painting – though it probably isn't!'[27] Francis Birrell, a young friend of Adrian's, also had designs on Duncan. 'I am sick of this ludicrous war,' he wrote to a friend, 'and the bloody corps I joined disgusts me . . . I am trying at present to get transferred to the Sussex Yeomanry, with perhaps Duncan Grant – a rather unwilling yokefellow – but I daresay the romance of being a gentleman ranker will persuade him.'[28] Having a father who had been in the army, Duncan was all too aware that his family expected him to fight. These thoughts were in the air, if not at this stage openly discussed, when he visited his parents at Dartford.

In October 1914, 38 Brunswick Square was given up and Duncan moved his belongings into a studio on the top floor of 22 Fitzroy Street. Between them, marriage and war were bringing the world he had known to an end. Temporarily he lost his sense of direction. He was a notoriously bad sailor, yet considered following Hilton Young into the navy. Next he decided to offer his services as translator but, as he had no knowledge of German, was told that he would be of little use. Then he heard of a job as a railway guard on the troop trains travelling from Le Havre to the Front. While all these possibilities ran through his mind he wrote to Mallory, 'I don't know . . . whether it is wiser to remain at home and try to work or try to do something useful.'[29]

By November the horror of war began to fill the newspaper reports. Maynard was deeply upset when a fellow King's man Freddie Hardman was killed in action. He wrote to Duncan, 'It is too awful that such things should happen. It makes one bitterly miserable and long that the war should stop quickly on almost any terms. I can't bear that he should have died.'[30] Two weeks later he wrote again, 'I hope you've not even been talking any more of anything warlike. I am sure you ought not to.'[31]

As conscription was not yet on the cards, Duncan was still free to live his life as he wished. Like others, he enjoyed what distractions remained. He went to Covent Garden with George Mallory and regularly appeared at meetings of the Caroline Club, a play-reading society formed by the Olivier daughters, which met at their parents' home in Caroline Place. He joined Bloomsbury's play-reading society, which had last met in January 1909. Clive minuted its revival in October 1914. 'In these days of storm and darkness, it seemed right that at the shrine of civilisation – in Bloomsbury I mean – the lamp should be tended assiduously. It has been decided, therefore, to read plays, ancient or modern, English or foreign, tragic, comic or simply bawdy at 46 Gordon Square, on Thursday evenings, at nine of the clock.' The first reading, on 29 October, proved better than expected. ('The preliminary incompetence and inconsequence of the painters gave ground for apprehension.')[32]

This tendency to regard painters as a race apart was a mythology that Vanessa had encouraged, in part to reinforce her association with Duncan. How comforting to receive amid the self-questioning and uncertainty caused by war a letter from Asheham that began, 'It seems such ages since you went and I have heard nothing of you since. It is horrid not having you here.' In Duncan's place, Harry Norton and James

Strachey were enjoying the ease that Vanessa seemed able to create around her. 'I have been a good deal set upon since you left,' her letter continues:

> ... Norton says I have become a slut and have quite changed all my habits since he has known me. A good deal is put down to your example. One painter alone is simply mobbed I find. Nothing escapes notice – holes in one's stockings, green paint on one's face, shoes down at heel, slowness of mind – all is put down to being a painter. I wonder why non-painters haven't points to lay hold of to the same extent.[33]

While his fondness for Vanessa deepened, Duncan began to notice a young man who had for some time been a regular attender at Adrian Stephen's poker parties. Socially a little awkward, he had appeared at these week after week in evening dress, though no one else wore even a dinner jacket. He was not up-to-date in artistic matters and though he had visited the first Post-Impressionist exhibition in 1910 he had, like most friends of his family, regarded many of the pictures as monstrosities or freaks and had fiercely denounced the Matisses. His appearance on the fringes of Bloomsbury owed much to chance. He had gone to a dance at Crosby Hall in aid of one of the Women's Suffrage societies. There he saw Adrian Stephen, whom he had met only once before but had instantly felt was his friend. Afterwards, he became a regular at Adrian's poker parties and was aware that Duncan, who did not like cards, sometimes managed to break up the game with his conversation. As a result, the young man felt a certain animosity towards Duncan. He later recalled that on occasions he left the house miserably unhappy and jealous. 'For in some way I felt that Adrian's house in Brunswick Square was my spiritual home and his friends – except for Duncan Grant – were the people I should most like to know ... Duncan, in particular, disliked me, mistaking my shy silence for an affectation of superiority and worldliness. But, in spite of protests, Adrian continued to invite me.'[34]

Yet David Garnett's memoirs are not always accurate. The January 1913 invitation, on the back of which Garnett later wrote, 'Earliest letter inviting me to one of Adrian's parties',[35] is in fact in Duncan's and not Adrian's hand. It is possible that Garnett's emotions got the better of his reason and that he failed to notice signs of friendship on Duncan's part. Throughout his life Garnett enjoyed friendships with many talented and intelligent people, having himself a marked independence and a confidence in his own point of view.

He was seven years younger than Duncan and the son of Edward

Garnett, writer and publisher's reader, an absent-minded, eccentric individual whose opinion on literature was so authoritative that Ford Madox Ford called him the Non-Conformist Pope of the literary world. David's mother was Constance Garnett, whose translations had introduced many English readers to Turgenev, Tolstoy, Dostoevsky, Chekhov and Gogol. Stories concerning Constance's first visit to Russia, during which she met Tolstoy and stayed at Yasnaya Polyana, were among her son's earliest childhood memories. He, too, went to Russia with his mother in 1904. While there, he spent most of the time living with shepherds in open country, learning their language and appreciating their communal style of life. He was not unprepared for this experience for he had grown up in the country, at Limpsfield in Surrey, then a small hamlet with cottages clustering around a wooden windmill. A house, called the Cearne, had been built for his parents on the southern edge of the High Chart – a large expanse of open woodlands, mostly beech and pine, which fostered the young boy's independent character, his love of nature and readiness to do things for himself. He could, with no discomfort, sleep out of doors even in wet weather.

One of the reasons Edward and Constance Garnett chose this place to live was so that their son could have the companionship of the four Olivier daughters, whose parents had converted two cottages into a house on Limpsfield Chart. Aside from this connection, the Garnett family did not fit easily into any social hierarchy and never really belonged to the local community. Constance Garnett was a shy woman and the position of their house, situated in a garden encircled by woods and approached by a rough track through magnificent beech trees, helped set them apart. David Garnett later claimed that he grew up 'shy, wild, afraid of people'.[36]

To his friends and family he was known as Bunny. The nickname came into being as the result of a Randolph Caldecott illustration of Baby Bunting crawling on the floor in a rabbit skin. This provoked in the small child such adoration that a rabbit skin was obtained, cured and made into a cap for him to wear, as a result of which the village boys began calling him 'Bunny' and the name stuck.

By the age of twelve, the year he visited Russia with his mother, he combined, as he has written of himself, 'social awkwardness with an imperturbable belief in the value of my opinions'.[37] His youth had been spent in the company of the Olivier sisters, who shared his love of the High Chart woods and swarmed up and down trees at a moment's notice. He admired their proud and aristocratic outlook on life, though he also noticed how vehement their prejudices were. He himself had not fared too well at University College School, then in Gower Street, where he had been much baited and teased, but his early problems with learning turned out to be associated with recurring tonsilitis. Eventually he went on to study botany at the Royal College of Science, under the aegis of Imperial College, becoming an associate in 1913. By then his chief interest had become the mode of reproduction and spore formation in the ascomycete fungi. His discovery of a new species brought him a prize and a recommendation for a scholarship, which enabled him to stay on at Imperial College and begin research. As a student he had been living with his father in Hampstead. Now, in order to be nearer South Kensington, he persuaded Edward Garnett to take a maisonette at 19 Pond Place, off the Fulham Road.

While living at Pond Place his feelings for Duncan underwent a sea-change. He retrieved the impression that Duncan had made on him when they first met. At Limpsfield one afternoon Bunny and the Olivier girls had gone round to the home of some neighbours called Hobson, to play croquet and tennis. Suddenly two young men walked round the corner of the house. 'One of them was Adrian Stephen, the other a dark young man, who gave the impression of being slightly made, though he was really five foot ten and well-proportioned. He had very clear grey-blue eyes and a beautiful expressive mouth and held himself with unconscious pride.' Just at that moment Mrs Hobson, who had recently retired from the croquet lawn in a state of visible anger, came out to see who the visitors might be. 'Duncan saw her coming and turned aside to greet her – with hesitation and shyness I have no doubt – but in three sentences his perfect manners had her tamed.'[38]

Later that afternoon, aware that Adrian wanted to speak alone with Noel Olivier, Duncan took Bunny aside. The good looks and unselfconscious dignity of his companion caused Bunny to feel shy and, as he recalled, 'I found little to talk about.'[39] But by the winter of 1914–15, this shyness had become a thing of the past.

Both Duncan and Bunny went to Lady Ottoline's wartime parties, which during the winter of 1914–15 were held weekly, every Thursday night. No warmongers were admitted and an atmosphere of pure hedonism reigned. The success of the Russian Ballet had encouraged a craze for dressing up and at these parties a large trunk of fantastic costumes would be produced. At some stage in the evening Philip Morrell would sit down at the pianola and the guests would improvise dances according to the tunes that were played. The spectacle this created was bizarre, for an onlooker might catch sight of Augustus John or Arnold Bennett strangely arrayed, Bertrand Russell dancing a hornpipe or Lady Ottoline herself prancing at the head of a troupe of young women from the Slade. She noticed that her guests expressed their personalities as they danced. 'Duncan Grant was almost fierce, but full of humour and grace, as he bounded about like a Russian ballet dancer, or wound in and out in some intricate dance with Vanessa Bell or Bunny Garnett, who looked really fierce and barbaric in bright oranges and reds, a gay-coloured silk handkerchief on his head. Duncan's special dance was one of Brahms's Hungarian Dances.'[40] Equally memorable, though in a different vein, were the delicate and courtly minuets danced by Lytton, James and Marjorie Strachey. Momentarily an old world and the new coexisted, music and dance keeping the bitter reality of war at bay.

ELEVEN

An Intricate Dance

At the age of twenty-two, Bunny Garnett was a tall, well-built, blue-eyed young man, very aware that both men and women found him physically attractive. Travelling home one night in a taxi, he suddenly flung an arm round the shoulder of his close friend Francis Birrell and kissed him. As Birrell was homosexual, Bunny's friends gossiped about this embrace but concluded that nothing further would come of it, as Bunny's interests so clearly lay with the opposite sex. That he had acted similarly with another man only proved his excitable nature and the readiness with which he translated affection into physical acts.

His sentimental education was greatly advanced by Lytton, who in December 1914, invited Garnett and Birrell to join him at Lockeridge, near Marlborough, where he had rented a house. While they were there Lytton read aloud his droll satire 'Ermyntrude and Esmerelda', a correspondence between two young ladies, similar in style to *Les Liaisons Dangereuses*, describing their first sexual adventures. Bunny understood from Lytton's story that the chief virtue in love or lust was sincerity. It liberated his desire to have a love life unclouded by sentimentality and a sex life unfettered by the constraints imposed by religion or conventional morality.[1]

Lytton's other guests included two Olivier sisters, Noel and Daphne, and Duncan. On Boxing Day, while Lytton rested for an hour or two, the others tramped over the Downs. Bunny found himself walking beside Duncan, who seemed not proud and aloof but delightfully entertaining. In turn Duncan was bewitched by Bunny and afterwards warned him by letter that it was dangerous to be kind to people like himself. 'You mustn't go on unless you don't mind my wanting to see you much oftener than you want to see me. Lots of things happened at Lytton's that I didn't quite understand and I am depressed and rather miserable now . . . if you see me again soon you must be VERY KIND but honest as the day. Yours D. Grant.'[2]

Before he had time to reply Bunny found himself once again in Duncan's company. At Maynard Keynes's invitation, he dined at the

Café Royal on 6 January 1915 and was placed between Duncan and Vanessa. Seventeen people in all were present, and when Vanessa returned in advance of the rest to 46 Gordon Square, where a party was being held that same evening, J. T. Sheppard took her place at the table. 'Felt shy and drank a lot of champagne,' Bunny wrote in his diary. It helped him rebut Sheppard's flattery during a taxi ride to Gordon Square, with the clever remark: '*You* can't realise how much more wonderful it is for me in meeting you to find the explanation of so much in my friends that I had admired but not understood,' a compliment that acknowledged Sheppard's luminary role at King's College, Cambridge.[3]

When the party began at 46 Gordon Square the guests listened to music played by the d'Aranyi sisters before moving upstairs to the first floor, where double doors separated the front room from the back, for a performance, with huge marionettes made by Duncan, of Racine's *Bérénice*. Dances and songs followed, the mood of the party becoming carefree and drunken. When Bunny went to thank his host, Maynard replied, 'I would kiss you if there weren't so many people present.'[4] He departed in the company of Duncan, who seemed upset. Bunny badgered him as to what he was feeling, asking him also to explain the letter he had sent. Very nervously Duncan admitted that he was in love with Bunny. Such a thought had not apparently crossed Bunny's mind, for he was so surprised that at first he thought Duncan was lying. Together they walked back to Duncan's studio, where Bunny stayed the night, chastely, Duncan merely holding his hand as it hung out of the bed.

The following morning Clive, who was himself pursuing a liaison with Mary Hutchinson, a married woman with a very stylish appearance, entertained her with a summary of the previous night's events. The complexities and intrigue, he declared, had been enough to send a person back to the nursery in search of sanity and innocence. 'Even Duncan,' Clive commented:

> felt the need of Quentin's society this afternoon though he's spent the night, or such part of it as remained, with Bunny in his studio. It seemed to me that nearly all the love-making was carried on by the males *inter se*. But it was all very promiscuous, and pleasantly civilised I thought. Rather like *Twelfth Night*: it wouldn't have been very surprising if Bunny had turned out to be a girl and Vanessa a boy: and no one seemed quite to know how he or she was going to pair off: to be sure, I've no idea how anyone did.[5]

On the first evening after the party Bunny, as his diary records, returned to Duncan's studio: 'He inspired me suddenly with passion born partly of curiosity about this darling strange creature so like an animal and so full of charm.'⁶ The following morning, feeling rather seedy, Bunny went back to Pond Place and stayed indoors all day. Duncan, thinking that as it was Saturday Bunny had gone to the Cearne, 'rushed down there, blundered about the woods, fell into an elephant trap and called at half past ten. Finding I wasn't there he rushed off wild eyed and got back to London rather shattered.'⁷

The following week Duncan had to assist with a marionette show at the Omega, for which he had designed a stage and four characters, including an *ingénue* with enormous staring eyes in a heart-shaped face and a duenna with a formidable platform bust. He invited Bunny to the performance. He now saw his young friend daily, slept with him often and realised he had fallen head over heels in love. 'Darling, darling Bunny,' one letter begins: 'I adore you because I think you capable of being so splendid and so good . . . All I want to say my angel is that I'm not going to be selfish and spoil your life. I really want you to do what you want. Be happy and love as many people as are worth it, and remember that this is my *real* point of view. I am silly. After all I have my work to which I am passionately devoted, I suppose you had better learn this.'⁸ Duncan soon began painting Bunny, and in one side-view portrait placed his head in close juxtaposition with a picture on the wall behind, showing the lower half of a female nude.

What exactly Bunny felt at this time is hard to gauge. Association with Duncan drew him further into the Bloomsbury circle, where homosexuality was treated lightly, almost as a stylish gloss to friendship, not as something that shocked or displeased. Within Bloomsbury there was no attempt to conceal homosexual affairs and Lytton could not resist openly teasing Duncan about Bunny, which, as Clive observed – possibly because of the short space of time that elapsed between Duncan's affairs – 'made Duncan become suddenly like a widow with a sore reputation'.⁹ Moreover, Bunny was quickly made aware that his alliance with Duncan seriously affected another: before two weeks had passed, Vanessa Bell had arranged to come and take tea with him at Pond Place. Bunny afterwards wrote: 'She was altogether charming and talked to me. I said I had thought the best thing to do would be to be brutal to Duncan but I have found it impossible . . . she said she was glad I had. She was in love with Duncan but couldn't feel jealous of any man. Duncan always had been in love with a man – Adrian for a long time, Maynard at one time . . . She thought we could have nice times together. I said I had been much more falling in love with her than Duncan and that I was a womaniser. I kissed her a great deal. She is the greatest darling in the world. She said incidentally that Clive said he would never live with anyone but her, but of course had his affairs.'[10]

In this way their triangular relationship began. Like all such relationships, it required tact, forbearance and restraint to keep the tangle manageable. If Bunny's absence was prolonged, Duncan began to fret. Vanessa, mindful that jealousy could poison her relationship with Duncan, had to judge when to stand back and when to offer him the assurance he needed. In such a delicate situation, she wisely kept the tone light. When he went to stay with his parents at Dartford, she wrote, 'I imagine you sitting up brushed and shaven and a very well behaved, good beast, instead of the poor little rough creature I have to harbour sometimes. Have you written to Bunny and not to me?'[11]

Whatever the imbalance in Vanessa and Duncan's relationship, it was now deeply rooted. She had become increasingly important and necessary to him as the wartime atmosphere worsened. A revival of nationalism had turned the British public against modernism and when, later that year, Mark Gertler exhibited a distorted picture of Eve, an outraged viewer pasted a label over her belly that read 'Made in Germany'. In such a climate Duncan would have valued highly Vanessa's understanding of his interests. He was also more vulnerable at this time as a homosexual, owing to a trial that had run for weeks as a result of Robert Ross taking Oscar Wilde's erstwhile lover, Lord Alfred Douglas, to court on the charge of defamatory libel. Once again the public had been shocked and enraged by details of Wilde's private life, as his relations with Douglas were raked over, mention also being made of Ross's taste for painted boys. Although the case was eventually dismissed, it had brought homosexuality back into the arena of public discussion and incited a wartime fear of sexual deviance and a desire to suppress any form of culture associated with it.

Still more paralysing was the news that arrived from the Front. In a letter to Duncan, Maynard mourned the killing of two former undergraduates from King's in April. 'And to-day Rupert [Brooke]'s death. In spite of all one has ever said I find myself crying for him. It is too horrible, a nightmare to be stopt [sic] anyhow. May no other generation live under the cloud we have to live under.'[12] Lytton also shared his grief with Duncan: 'The meaninglessness of Fate is intolerable; it is all muddle and futility . . . It is like a confused tale, just beginning, and then broken off for no reason, and for ever . . .'[13] Duncan, though never intimate with Brooke, had known him for many years and was familiar with the smiling, teasing, careless, graceful figure that he had been, before he had become obsessed with certain *idées fixes* and full of warnings about the wickedness in others. His reponse to Rupert's death was to paint a homage to him in abstract terms. The sombre, rich tones of this icon were at one time enhanced by a patch of silver foil, which was attached to the lower part of the picture and would have thrown off reflected light. Towards the top of the picture two lines form an acute angle, which, like a Gothic arch, carries overtones of spiritual ascent.

The Omega made a determined effort to resist the depressing effects of war. It began holding 'Art Circle' evenings, designed to introduce refugee artists and musicians to English hostesses. At one of these the audience listened to Belgian music. On another occasion the famous cellist Mme Suggia performed. While she was playing, a fire broke out on the roof. Mr Robinson, the manager, was informed of this by a passing bicyclist. He called the fire brigade, which in those days wore brass helmets worthy of Roman legionaries. According to Winifred Gill, Mr Robinson asked the men who arrived to hide their helmets under their jackets as they went upstairs, to prevent any panic developing in the audience. They obligingly did so and, in spite of two fire engines, two or three pumps and a large noisy crowd in the square, Mme Suggia was a match for them all: the audience heard and suspected nothing.

Far more frightening, from Duncan's point of view, was the visit that D. H. Lawrence made to his studio. Bunny had known the novelist for some years, as a result of his father's collaboration as editor with Lawrence, and had offered to introduce him to Lady Ottoline. In fact they met before he had time to arrange an introduction, and on 21 January 1915 Bunny found himself dining at her house in company with Lawrence and Frieda. After dinner Duncan, whose thirtieth birthday it was, joined the party. Lawrence, who had a pronounced interest in art and had heard about Duncan's paintings, asked if he might see some and it was arranged that he, Frieda and E. M. Forster would take tea in Duncan's studio the next day.

Silence reigned the following afternoon while Duncan brought out one picture after another, including his portrait of Ottoline with Woolworth's pearls attached, and his huge painting of a green giant overshadowing a tiny St Paul's Cathedral. Suddenly Lawrence rose and began walking up and down the studio, in a state of evident mental agitation. His love of art, practical involvement with painting, his ideas about sexual and artistic wholeness, combined with his missionary zeal, caused a sermon to erupt that was designed to bring Duncan back to the true path. 'It was not simply that the pictures were bad – hopelessly bad – but they were worthless because Duncan was full of the wrong ideas. He was barking up the wrong tree and would have to learn to approach his subjects in a completely different frame of mind if he wanted ever to become an artist.'[14] So David Garnett recollected the tirade. Forster slipped away, murmuring quietly about a train that needed catching, and the Ukrainian, S. S. Koteliansky, arrived to collect Lawrence and Frieda, but had to sit down and listen. Occasionally Frieda interrupted the peroration, insisting that one painting was to be preferred over another, or to admire a portrait. Her remarks appeared to go unnoticed. 'Lawrence would give a wincing glance at the new picture and discover in it new material for his argument. Finally, in despair, Duncan brought out a long band of green cotton on two rollers. I stood and held one roller vertically and unwound while, standing a couple of yards away, Duncan wound up the other, and a series of supposedly related, abstract shapes was displayed before our disgusted visitors. That was the worst of all.'[15]

Duncan spent the whole visit in agony. He sat, rocking gently, with his hands on his knees, saying not a word in his own defence. When Lawrence finally said they had to leave, Duncan rose, showed them down the dimly lit stairs and ushered them politely into the foggy night. Back in the studio he and Bunny re-stacked the canvases against the wall and washed up the cups and saucers in silence.

In 1953, when Edward Nehls was preparing a composite biography of D. H. Lawrence, Duncan stated that the visit to his studio had been painful 'because I felt that Lawrence was quite unsympathetic to what I was trying to do at the moment', but that, aside from this, his personal relations with the writer were always rather pleasant.[16] The accuracy of his second remark can be judged from a letter that Lawrence sent Lady Ottoline less than a week after his visit. 'We liked Duncan Grant very much. I really liked him. Tell him not to make silly experiments in the futuristic line with bits of colour on moving paper. Other Johnnies can do that. Neither to bother making marionettes – even titanic ones. But to seek out the terms in which he shall state his whole. He is after the Absolute . . .'[17] Lawrence later made constructive use of his negative reactions in *Lady Chatterley's Lover*. In this the game-keeper hero, Mellors, is taken to the studio of the artist Duncan Forbes, 'a dark-skinned taciturn Hamlet of a fellow with straight black hair and weird Celtic conceit of himself . . . His art was all tubes and valves and spirals and strange colours, ultra-modern, yet with a certain power, even a certain purity of form and tone: only Mellors thought it cruel and repellent.'

Duncan rightly observed to Nehls that Lawrence's attitude towards him changed after the writer visited Cambridge in March 1915 and began to associate Duncan with Maynard Keynes. Lawrence stayed with

Bertrand Russell at Trinity College, dined in Hall, held forth eloquently on Socialism afterwards in Russell's rooms and the following morning, at eleven o'clock, he and Russell called on Keynes. They walked into his rooms and found no one there. Russell began writing a note for him when Maynard emerged from his bedroom, blinking with sleep and in his pyjamas. The sight of Maynard, *déshabillé*, aroused in Lawrence unbearable feelings: 'And as he stood there gradually a knowledge passed into me, which has been like a little madness to me ever since. And it was carried along with the most dreadful sense of repulsiveness . . . I began to feel mad as I think of it – insane.'[18]

So he told Bunny who, with Birrell, was to aggravate further the repulsion that had suddenly consumed Lawrence. The two young men spent a weekend with Lawrence and Frieda at Pulborough in Sussex shortly after his visit to Cambridge. Lawrence had been appalled by their ceaseless and often irreverent chatter and felt each to be encased in his own hard shell. Afterwards he told Koteliansky that, left with a sense of corruption, he had dreamt of beetles. 'It is this horror of little swarming selves that I can't stand,' he told Lady Ottoline: 'Birrells, D. Grants, and Keynses [*sic*].'[19]

Lawrence subsequently not only told Bunny never to bring Birrell to see him again, but also took him to task, vehemently, over homosexuality. His morality was cut-and-dried, untouched by doubt or ambivalence; he approved, even idolised the young Eleanor Farjeon, but condemned outright her cousins, the four Olivier sisters. 'It is foolish of you to say that it doesn't matter either way – the men loving men,' he told Bunny:

It doesn't matter in the public way. But it matters so much, David, to the man himself . . . that it is like a blow of triumphant decay, when I meet it in Birrell or others . . . It makes a form of inward corruption which truly makes me scarce able to live. Why is there this horrible sense of frowstiness, so repulsive, as if it came from deep inward dirt – a sort of sewer – deep in men like K[eynes] and B[irrell] and D[uncan] G[rant] . . . You must wrench away and start a new life. B. and D.G. are done for, I think – done for for ever. K. I am not sure. But you, my dear, you can be all right. You can come away and grow whole, and love a woman, and marry her, and make life good, and be happy. Now David, in the name of everything that is called love, leave this set and stop this blasphemy against love.[20]

Lawrence's views, as Quentin Bell was the first to suggest and S. P. Rosenbaum has argued conclusively,[21] were stirred by a dread of his own homosexual susceptibilities, which are revealed in his writings, notably the cancelled prologue to *Women in Love*. As a result, though a brave iconoclast in other ways, he adopted a fearful and deeply conventional attitude to homosexuality. His letter represented the kind of opinions which, as Duncan knew, outside of Bloomsbury threatened his relationship with Bunny on all sides.

After a hectic winter of weekly play-readings, parties at Ottoline's and 'Art Circle' evenings at the Omega, there arose a need to get away. Clive and Vanessa, leaving their two boys, now at a small primary school, in the care of a maid, abandoned London for West Wittering, on the Sussex coast. They had agreed to rent St John and Mary Hutchinson's small house 'Eleanor', situated down a rough track about half a mile from the village and in close proximity to the estuary that ran in from the sea up to Bosham, some five miles distant. Nearby was an old boatshed that Professor Tonks used as a studio, leaving his key with the Hutchinsons. This Mary now gave to Duncan, who went down ahead of the Bells and settled into the boatshed, where Bunny visited him at the weekend. Their time together was made idyllic by the weather and the discovery of some of Tonks's wine. Duncan had met Bunny at Chichester station and the two friends had bicycled the six miles to West Wittering. They also walked to Itchenor, whence they took the ferry across to Bosham for lunch. Nothing marred their high spirits and they conceived the idea of writing a novel together. 'We talked the whole time,' Bunny wrote in his diary, 'and were happy and planned the novel. Came back to tea and read *The Idiot* and again to the sweet lassitude of sleeping in each other's arms.'[22]

In March Vanessa arrived and was for a while alone with Duncan. There was clearly no pretence between her and Clive concerning the nature of her relationship with Duncan, because in one letter she remarks, 'No little Grant has yet had a chance to come into existence.'[23] She had also informed Bunny of her wish to have a child by Duncan, which terminated any hopes that the younger man harboured of sleeping with her. Meanwhile Clive's liaison with Mary Hutchinson, whose five-year marriage had proved only a limited success, deepened. It was to become the most significant relationship in Clive's life after his marriage, though Vanessa was as yet unaware of this. 'They treat me rather as though I were a widow – discreet sympathy,' Clive said of Vanessa and Duncan to Mary. 'I find it most engaging.'[24]

By the time Clive arrived in April a way of life had become established at Eleanor that offered a complete contrast with London. Vanessa tried to ignore the few newspapers that reached them, wanting no horrors of any kind to mar the peace or the excitement she felt at reading her sister's first novel, *The Voyage Out*. Apart from the crows, which got on Duncan's nerves and which he mistook for boys riding quickly past the window, there was little to disturb their calm.

He nevertheless fell ill in April and took to his bed. He thought a good deal about Bunny and told him his worries. 'I have had a letter from my mother bothering about my doing nothing for my country. I cannot afford to do anything except to fight and she apparently doesn't much want me to do that. What the devil am I to say?'[25] There were still times when Duncan did not have the money in his pocket for a bus fare. Even when he heard that Aunt Hennie, who had died in March, had left him a small inheritance of about £800 with which, presumably, he could have bought himself a commission, his wartime situation remained unresolved. He continued for the time being to do what he did best – paint. With the benefit of Tonks's studio, he felt rather abashed when, after living there unauthorised for some weeks, he received a kind letter from Tonks inviting him to make use of it rent-free. The boatshed had great rolling doors opening on to the water, which was pleasant except when an east wind blew, and a small bedroom and kitchen on the landward side.

A house party developed one weekend at Eleanor when Lytton and Maynard arrived. Duncan sent Hilton Young news of both: 'Maynard is a very grand personage now as I daresay you know. He goes to the Treasury everyday and works very hard and told me he had saved the government £1,000,000 (a million) in a morning ... Lytton is getting very benign and is writing, I'm told, a very good work consisting of short lives of eminently disagreeable Victorians.'[26]

The only thing that marred Duncan's enjoyment of West Wittering was Bunny's absence. It put things slightly out of kilter, as Vanessa was aware. To keep the Bear, as she called Duncan, happy, she knew that she had to make Bunny feel accepted, even when he was not actually present. She wrote to him:

> You're wrong in saying the Bear has forgotten ... He seems to me to think of you a great deal and we often talk of you. Yesterday we talked of your looks and decided that we liked looking at you and after all what more can one say of anyone? ...The children aren't here yet so we're quiet and grown up except when Duncan and the cow dance together as they did this morning. But Clive and Lytton who are known as the old gentlemen don't think us very grown up. They speak of us as 'they' as doctors do of lunatics and Lytton was very much angered when Duncan drove him with his head into the sea and tried to pee on his hat and drew cocks and cunts in the sand. They have glasses

of hot water every night which just keeps their insides going – it makes Duncan dash to the back of the house ten times a day . . . You see what discord and discomfort really exists in this paradise you have imagined.[27]

At Wittering Duncan began wearing spectacles. Owing to them, he said, he did not feel in the least tired after a long spell of painting. Though they reappear in his 1919 self-portrait (Scottish National Portrait Gallery), his need of them was intermittent, which suggests that the strain at Wittering was psychological rather than optical.

He was now working with impressive boldness and authority. His most significant papier collé works date from 1915 and include *Flower and Vase* and *Interior at Gordon Square* (both in private collections), the latter relating to an oil of the same title in the Tate Gallery collection. When asked to supply information on this painting, Grant told Richard Morphet that it was done soon after he had copied a 1913 Picasso in Roger Fry's possession, which made use of oil and papier collé. Duncan admitted that the experience of copying the Picasso may have influenced *Interior at Gordon Square* in that both are concerned with the overlapping of planes. But of the two works bearing the same title, it is the papier collé one that is the larger and more satisfying work. Large slabs of colour are created by cutting up hand-painted paper and these simple, angular shapes are fitted together, jigsaw-like, in a terse, abrupt composition. The colour transitions are bold, and the large sweeps of the brush used to coat the paper before it was cut up help create textural richness. So confident was Duncan now in his handling of abstraction that he sent two non-figurative works to the Vorticist exhibition held in June 1915. One of these appears to have been a construction, as Vanessa told Clive that Duncan, on visiting the show, had found his work badly hung and had to replace a piece of wood that had fallen off.

He was directed by no theoretical or ideological restraints and painted imaginative, realistic or abstract works as they took his fancy. If his total *oeuvre* suffers from a want of inner cohesion, it nevertheless represents an adventurous, joyful, eclectic vision. At this period, especially, Duncan's work is notable for its audacious handling of pictorial means. There is also a vein of private imaginative wit in his work, visible in those pictures where flowers droop exaggeratedly or limbs extend in elegant distortions. Though he borrowed ideas and motifs from the work of others, translating them for his own purposes, he gave his allegiance to no style, retaining his independence even while he listened to the views of others. 'I have been going on with the still life I began when you were here of pots and pans,' he told Bunny after one of his visits to Eleanor. 'It is much better now I think and rather *solid* (I'm told) . . . so it might please you.'[28]

In the Easter holidays Julian and Quentin Bell arrived, both children in the highest of spirits on seeing the sea. They boated on the estuary, Duncan taking great pleasure in their company, not so much as a surrogate father but as a companion in their adventures. When they returned to London in May, Vanessa moved into the boatshed with Duncan but, aware of the extra dimension to Duncan's life, simultaneously wrote to Bunny inviting him to join them at Whitsuntide, which he did. 'If you have your nights together it seems to me your days can be spent *à trois*,' she remarked airily to Clive after admitting that she ought to feel *de trop*.[29] But to Roger she admitted that it had been a difficult situation and impossible to avoid those aspects that were painful to her.

It was perhaps easier to admit pain to one who had himself been deeply hurt. Falling in love with Vanessa after the grim helplessness he felt in relation to his wife's illness must have seemed to Fry like a miraculous reprieve from the horrors of life. As his letters reveal, his love for her rested upon a profound and clear-sighted appreciation of her character. He admired the way she lived, very intensely but also naturally, with a reasonableness and a practicality that he thought demonstrated great imagination. 'You give me a sense of security,' he told her, 'of something solid and real in a shifting world . . . You have genius in your life as well as in your art and both are rare things.'[30]

Losing Vanessa to Duncan had once again left Roger disconnected, his personal life unfocused, her rejection of him doubling his experience of loss. Unhappiness drove him in the spring of 1915 to leave England and to visit his sister, Margery, then working with the Friends' War Victims' Relief Fund in the districts of the Marne and the Meuse. There he saw evidence of wanton destruction, the Germans having ravaged whole villages and small towns deliberately and for no conceivable purpose. He put up at Sermaize-les-Bains in the Marne and briefly involved himself with the work that the Quakers were doing. He was further depressed at this time by the death of his friend Henri Doucet. 'There's no one else to take his place,' Roger wrote to Duncan, thanking him also for a letter in which he had been glad to learn that Duncan was still fond of him. 'One gets fancies when one's miserable and somehow I thought that you had got to feel I was in the way.' In his depressed state, he concluded his letter to Duncan, 'I don't think suffering is good for anyone.'[31]

During this bleak time Fry's habitual fertility with ideas temporarily waned and he published only one article that year. (Three that he wrote

for the *Nation* on the destroyed districts of France were turned down.)
From Paris in May, he wrote to Clive, 'You know I think that you and
Nessa have managed to make the only breatheable atmosphere in
England, at least for me . . . only I feel a good deal less in the centre of
things than I did. In painting Nessa and Duncan have taken to working
so entirely together and not to want me, and altogether I find it difficult
to take a place on the outside of the circle instead of being, as I once was,
rather central.'[32] Later that month he stayed with the Bussys at
Roquebrune. Pippa Strachey was also there and a temporary liaison arose
between them, which warmed Fry. But by July he was back in England.

'I hope Duncan won't be pestered again,' he had written to Clive from
La Souco,[33] having heard how he and Bunny had been interrogated by
the police at West Wittering on the grounds that they might be spies.
Wartime hysteria was rife at this time, and the notion that England was
infiltrated by spies was fed by fear of German invasion. 'Do you manage
to keep yr. views about the war,' Roger had asked in this same letter, 'and
when'll the pamphlet come out?' When Clive's pamphlet – *Peace at Once*
– appeared that summer, it was seized by the police and forwarded to the
Public Prosecutor. It challenged the shallow optimism of the militarists,
caused his father temporarily to cut his allowance and G. K. Chesterton
to attack him in the pages of the *Nation*. On the instructions of the Lord
Mayor of London all copies were withdrawn and burnt. None of this
altered Clive's views in the least and his second dissenting essay, 'Art and
War', appeared in the *International Journal of Ethics* that October. On
behalf of Duncan and others, he here argued that the artist's only duty to
his country in wartime was to go on being an artist.

On his return to London at the end of May Duncan again helped out at
the Omega. It was struggling on, despite the loss of workers caused by
the war. The manager, Charles Robinson, had left to do war work with
the Quakers in Corsica and Winifred Gill had taken over his responsibilities, assisted in the evenings by a man called Paice, who came in to help
with the books. The Miles family had also gone, a new caretaker having
arrived in the form of Mr Upton, whose wife, also a feature of the
Workshops, was portentously stout and rather surly. The artists no
longer had to gesso the furniture before applying decoration, as this was
now done by a retired professional house painter, who claimed he had
decorated a drawing-room at Buckingham Palace. Germans had overrun
the town where Omega linens had been printed, but an alternative firm
had been found further south. A cargo of hand-dyed silks from the Near
East also arrived, brought by the wandering scholar John Hope-

Johnstone. These led to the suggestion that Omega designs for curtains and bedspreads could be embroidered in India. Duncan did a design with this in mind, involving goldfish and wavy lines, and two months later it came back realised. Omega pottery had also been placed on a better footing after Fry began co-operating with Roger Carter of Poole Potteries.

Everybody was very sad at the Omega when Gaudier-Brzeska died in combat. Still more did Duncan grieve for Feri Békassy, killed in Bukovina on 25 June. 'I can't help thinking a good deal about Feri,' he told Bunny. 'He's the only person I had any real affection for that has been killed so far.'[34] His current affections were divided, for he had found it possible to love two people, but less easy to be, in turn, the object of two people's love. 'I sometimes feel how much I owe to my friends and how bloody I am,' he admitted to Bunny. 'I am so fond of Nessa. I am ashamed she should be so fond of me and you are fonder of me than I deserve and I must just abjectly love both of you and hope not to be too much noticed for it.'[35] One evening Bunny went off with the drug-addicted model, Betty May. 'I am selfish but not so dangerously so as not to want you to be frightfully happy,' Duncan bravely wrote to Bunny,[36] finding it always easier to accept in theory rather than in practice Bunny's need of women.

Vanessa, meanwhile, went to Guildford to help Roger re-establish his life at Durbins. She became anxious for news of Duncan and was as upset as he was when he did not hear from Bunny. At Durbins the absence of servants and the general untidiness created a depressing state of affairs, made worse by Roger's gloomy talks with Vanessa and the fact that his sister Joan was in a contrary mood, making difficulties about finding a servant in order that all should run as badly as possible. Vanessa packed Roger off to a nearby registry office in search of domestic help and, in her habitual way, took the whole situation in hand.

In June 1915 Bunny, having finished his research and seeing no possibility of a job, went to France; having volunteered as a helper with the Friends' War Victims' Relief Fund he joined the Mission Anglaise at Nettancourt, in the Meuse. Duncan, meanwhile, alone in his studio, had found some poems that Bunny had written, which made him dizzy with emotion and determined to love his friend till the end of time. 'Bunny, you don't realise how much I love you,' reads one of his letters. 'My heart aches to see you and to tell you I care for you more than you can possibly imagine . . . It's miserable without you.'[37]

He gave way to depression easily in Bunny's absence and agreed, somewhat unwillingly, to accompany Vanessa and Lytton on a visit in July to Lady Ottoline's Oxfordshire home, Garsington. When they arrived the weather was cold and grey, but nothing could dispel the fantastic atmosphere of the house which, in Vanessa's eyes, was almost too full of small objects, bright colours and strong scents, but still a surprise and pleasure to experience. 'Ottoline sits in ropes of pearls and Turkish cloaks,' she told Bunny, 'and Maria [the governess] wafts about in transparent skirts and Julian dances naked.'[38] Duncan, too, found himself caught up in the fantastic goings-on. 'We danced to the pianola bare foot and fairly bare legged on the lawn after dinner on Saturday,' he reported to Bunny. 'It was rather a wonderful sight as the windows sent out a sort of moth light onto the lawn which lit up people at intervals.' Nevertheless he came away from Garsington miserable and wondered afterwards if the cause had been 'the spectacle of her ladyship, that unhappy woman'.[39]

In August a commission for the Omega took Duncan and Vanessa to Dorchester to see a Mr and Mrs Debenham. A powerful motor car met them at the station, and in this they sailed up to a magnificent stone house situated in a park with a winding river. Mr Debenham welcomed them on the doorstep and gave them tea with his daughters and wife. Vanessa used this occasion to take Duncan to nearby Wareham, which she remembered as a quiet, sleepy, small country town with beautiful houses and a river. But on arriving that evening they found it filled with soldiers and no rooms were to be had. Instead they went on to Corfe Castle, signing themselves in at an inn as Mr and Mrs Grant. Only then did they realise they had insufficient funds to pay the bill and so had to stay another day, awaiting money from Maynard. On the last day they walked to Swanage, where they found no alternative to a very expensive lunch, all other tea shops and restaurants being closed. At moments like this Vanessa came close to sharing Roger's disparagement of England as Bird's Custard Island.

Always keen to leave London in August, she took the rent that summer on a small house at Bosham, not far from West Wittering, for herself, Clive and the children. Called The Grange, it was plain, neat, prim and painted white. 'All is clean and thin and tidy and there is none of the lovely colour of the lodging house,' she complained to Duncan, admitting, however, that tidiness was very soon done away with. She had sat to Duncan for at least one portrait that summer and, as if to complement his love of strong colour, was planning to make herself a bright green blouse or coat out of some Broussa silk. 'You know you mustn't think that you've got to finish your pictures before you come here,' she wrote, 'or you'll never come, as you certainly won't ever think they're finished. Are you gallivanting every night and with whom? I imagine you very happy and independent with very nice letters from Bunny to keep you going by day and I shouldn't like to say what by night but please dear creature write and tell me. I love you so much.'[40]

With Clive now deeply involved in his affair with Mary Hutchinson, which created complications both in London and at Bosham when Mary and her husband St John ('Jack') were down at Eleanor, Vanessa was often left on her own with the children. But she was never alone for long, as she attracted visitors wherever she went. By the time Duncan arrived, in the second week of August, Clive was staying at Eleanor with Mary and others, and Maynard was already at The Grange. He joined Duncan, Vanessa and the boys on a boat trip down the estuary, stopping for tea under an oak tree, with the children in the highest spirits and looking, Duncan thought, beautiful beyond words. This visit was also memorable for a party held at Eleanor for which masks were made. They danced to gramophone music and performed a play entitled 'Euphrosine ou les mystères de sexe', in which the heroine changed into a boy halfway through. Charades followed, based on the words 'sodomy' and 'passion'. These ended with a dramatic bedroom scene in which Duncan and Mary were found in bed together by Jack, Duncan escaping out the back window wearing nothing but a shirt, to the astonishment of a sailor laying his nets outside, and Mary murdering Jack with a knife. Aside from these excitements, Duncan was also aware of moments of sheer beauty, as when he walked over to Eleanor for tea: large herons and a great many sandpipers stood about on the mud outlined against the sky.

Vanessa realised this summer at Bosham that in Duncan's company she was 'extraordinarily selfishly happy'. 'I have known it often lately,' she wrote to Bunny, adding that awareness of happiness was one of the advantages of age.

> It has been hot and sunny and I sit out or in and paint with the animal and he takes me for walks in the evening and he's there when I wake up and when I go to bed and sometimes in between too (which in between can be read either way) and he's been so extraordinarily charming and odd in his ways and speech and so unlike any body or anything else in this world and so amazingly nice that I have been as childishly happy as one can be . . . I must tell you that his complexion has been lovely lately – a kind of wonderful rose tint very evenly spread beneath the brown which has added a great deal to his attractions.[41]

After Duncan left, Roger arrived and though much of the time he was as active as ever, he subjected Vanessa to long and gloomy talks. In the middle of one of these, Blanche, the cook, interrupted to say that Bunny had rung earlier. This news startled Vanessa, as it meant that he was back in England. As she wrote to Duncan: 'It was so tantalising and Roger went on talking and I could hardly keep my attention decently fixed so as to answer even at random. His talk became more and more unreal and more and more of a strain . . . The first few days of his stay were awful . . . But I know I have been behaving rather badly the last day or two partly because I haven't been able to help wanting to hear from you very much and one's intelligence goes to the dogs when one is waiting for the post . . . I have been very silent and according to him quite incomprehensible. He goes tomorrow I think – I had to pretend you might come at the end of the week as I felt I couldn't stand being quite alone with him.'[42]

It was no easier for Duncan on his visits that summer to his parents at Dartford, where he encountered much anxiety over his future. Mrs Grant's gentleman friend, Colonel Young, was of the opinion that Duncan ought to join the artillery, as it would be a disgrace if he had to be conscripted. Ever since May when a coalition government had been formed, with Asquith remaining Prime Minister, the issue of conscription had been to the fore; those in favour of switching to conscription from voluntary enlistment had gained powerful positions within the Cabinet. With a quarter of a million men already wounded or killed – a figure that was to double over the next few months – it was becoming increasingly clear how expensive in terms of casualties the war was going to be. At the same time, volunteers for the army were beginning to diminish. That autumn Duncan had 'awful conversations with my mother about this duty to one's country and being influenced in one's opinions by other people which always enrages me'.[43] They succeeded only in upsetting each other. 'The war is simply undermining my life', he told George Mallory that summer, 'so the less said about it and its horrors the better.'[44] But Duncan could not avoid war talk, especially when Zeppelin bombs began to drop on London, one landing in the middle of Queen's Square in Bloomsbury, breaking every window in the square and causing fires to break out in nearby Great Ormond Street and Lamb's Conduit Street.

Both Vanessa and Duncan had been aware for some time that Bunny wanted to abandon working for the Quakers in France, but dared not return home as he had no job. Vanessa had promised to look out for one and Duncan had written to his Aunt Daisy, then head-nurse at a small hospital at Ceret in the French Pyrenees, asking if work could be found for himself and Bunny. She replied that a driver was needed to help bring the wounded to the hospital and that there was a shed where Duncan could paint in the garden. These and other possibilities were being considered when Bunny unexpectedly arrived in London on a fortnight's leave in October. Duncan was so overcome by this that the following day he took himself off to his parents' home. 'I needed a day alone to get over seeing you all of a sudden,' he explained to Bunny. 'I can hardly believe even now that you are in England. It is only because I feel an extraordinary warmth inside that I know you must be somewhere near.'[45] On his way home Bunny had learnt of a job at the Pasteur Institute in Paris, which he intended to pursue. Meanwhile Duncan had received a letter from Copeau asking if he was free to design costumes and accessories for a production of *Macbeth*. This made Duncan determined to accompany Bunny on his return to Paris. He told George Mallory of his plans, adding, 'I am sorry you have been depressed lately. I have [been too] fearfully at times. It is intolerable.'[46]

In early November he and Bunny crossed the Channel to Dieppe, Duncan having obtained official approval from the Foreign Office to undertake work in Paris and assuming that this took care of all the legalities. At Dieppe, however, he was separated from Bunny, who was obliged to continue journeying alone, while Duncan became the object of intensive questioning. His answers convinced the authorities that he was a pacifist anarchist. He became the butt of some British soldiers, who threw insults his way and asked jeeringly if he was *en route* to the recruiting office. The French officials then offered him two alternatives: immediate deportation or a concentration camp. Returning the next day to Dover, Duncan was again subjected to insolent crowing from the passport officials and it was an injured, dejected creature who arrived the next day at 46 Gordon Square, where his friends, seemingly oblivious to wartime hostilities, were enjoying a play-reading.

Hearing of Duncan's plight, his much-travelled aunt, Daisy McNeil, took up his case with H. C. Wallis, the British Vice Consul in Dieppe, and received the following reply: 'I have seen the Authorities relative to the refusal to permit your nephew to proceed to Paris. It appears that his answers to questions put to him were entirely unsatisfactory ... His manner was so strange and sentiments so unEnglish causing the English Authorities to agree with the French that it would be impossible for him to remain here or to proceed to Paris ... believe me it is better for him to remain at home.'[47]

Duncan, not prepared to give in, wrote to Copeau asking him for a letter of authorisation that would satisfy the French officials and enable him to reach Paris. This took time, as Duncan's first letter appears never to have reached Copeau, who was still waiting for Duncan in mid-November and unaware of any difficulties. Duncan still hoped that he, Bunny and Vanessa, who had suggested letting 46 Gordon Square, might all live together in Paris. In the meantime, he accompanied Vanessa to an exhibition of Roger's pictures, which he found impressive. Having heard also of an offshoot of the Camden Town Group, the newly formed Cumberland Market Group, they attended one of their Saturday afternoon 'at homes'. 'They peg away at quite good pictures,' Duncan told Bunny, 'and somehow it was very consoling to me to be there.'[48] On a visit to a London Group exhibition he was so impressed by Mark Gertler's *The Fruit Sorters*[49] that he afterwards wrote a praising letter to the artist.[50]

He continued with his own work, executing several designs for embroideries for Ottoline, one of which was made into a brilliantly coloured fire screen. But it was a gloomy, unsettled time. He forced himself to look in at 46 Gordon Square after dinner when he knew that D. H. Lawrence and Frieda were there, deciding that he had to face Lawrence, even though he still felt anger towards him. Yet his sympathy was immediately aroused when he heard that, on the grounds of obscenity – though more accurately because it denounced war – Lawrence's *The Rainbow* had been prosecuted and suppressed, its publisher Methuen ordered to hand over all copies in existence. 'It is too sickening about his novel being seized,' he wrote to Bunny. 'Oh! Damn, damn. Why shouldn't Lawrence be friendly when there are so few decent people in the world? and why should I be eternally separated from you? . . . I can't always be telling Nessa how depressed I sometimes am. It isn't fair on anyone and she does make me so much happier.'[51]

One way in which Vanessa cheered him was by talking of alternative ways of living. She suggested starting a colony in Cornwall, where they could live cheaply in lodgings and have a common dining-room and a big studio and need never see any newspapers. In the meantime, much oppressed by the world, Duncan went to see his parents, expecting them to sever relations with him over his attitude to the war, for he had recently received a letter from his mother that struck an hysterical note. In order to prepare himself for the encounter he walked from the station to Wilmington House, where he hid for a little while in the hall coat-cupboard, still feeling unready to speak. When finally he found his parents in the library, all difficulties vanished, as his father's manner was so affable and leisured that any sense of discord melted away. After lunch he walked round and round the garden with his mother, explaining, perfectly calmly, the reasons for his conduct. They were, after all, quite normal as parents – 'such a funny mixture of hysteria about ideas and good sense about other things,' Duncan told Bunny.[52]

He was reading Flaubert's *A Sentimental Education* which, though long, he recommended to Bunny, afterwards turning to Dostoevsky's *The Idiot*. In December he went to Asheham for a few days with Vanessa, Clive, Mary Hutchinson, Lytton and two Slade students – Barbara Hiles and Dora Carrington. As no servants were available, the girls helped Vanessa cook and they all ate their meals in the kitchen and drank rum punch in the evenings. This was the occasion when Carrington, after being kissed by Lytton during a walk on the Downs, crept into his room while he slept, intent on paying him back by cutting off his beard. Just as she was about to do so, he opened his eyes, his gaze turning her animosity into love. Two years later, on a return visit to Asheham, she reminisced with incredulity, 'It is strange living here again when I remember how amazed I was with you all round the fire that evening I first came.'[53]

On 7 December Duncan finally received from Copeau a letter of authorisation, stating that he was coming to France at Copeau's request to design costumes for *Macbeth* and bearing the signature of the Commissionaire of Police in Paris. This, Maynard thought, would get Duncan past all red tape and he offered to show it to the War Office so that they could check its validity with French officials. Aware that Paris had once again become a possibility, Duncan nevertheless admitted to Bunny that he felt so despondent that he hardly dared hope, for fear of being disappointed again.

Whereas in August 1914 a man had to be at least five foot eight inches tall to enlist as a soldier, by the end of that year the acceptable height had dropped to a mere five feet. Even so volunteers, who had previously come forward in large numbers, now held back. Meanwhile a national register had been compiled, which showed that over two million single men of military age could still be recruited. By December the notorious Derby Scheme, which had attempted to pledge men of serviceable age to call-up on moral rather than legal grounds, was abandoned and a Military Service Bill was introduced to enforce recruitment by conscription. It ruled that all single men of military age should be automatically enlisted, entering the Reserve until needed. Even before this Act was passed on its third reading on 23 January 1916, Duncan had informed Copeau that the Bill had put an end to his hopes of returning to France. He hoped that he could work on *Macbeth* at a distance, from England. Copeau disliked this idea but begged Duncan to keep him informed about what was happening to him.

He had, in fact, a couple more months of freedom. When, finally, the Military Service Act was implemented in March, it offered three loopholes: exemption would be granted to those who could satisfy a tribunal that they were medically ineligible, engaged in work of national importance or unable to bear arms on the grounds of conscience. For the rest of the war Duncan had to adjust his existence to these regulations.

TWELVE

From Wissett to Charleston

After his abrupt separation from Duncan at Dieppe, Bunny had gone on to Paris, where he waited hopefully for a while before returning to work with the Quakers at La Fontaine Sommeille, near Verdun. The stiff moral atmosphere, together with his colleagues' habit of watching out for each other's sins, increasingly sickened him. In January 1916 he did a bunk and returned to Paris, where he hoped to attach himself to the Pasteur Institute. 'That at least is preferable,' he told Duncan. 'You will probably not be able to get out of England. I cannot come back until I can earn my living there, so I must live in Paris. Accept it. Forget each other. Damn!'[1] Either no work was available or he suddenly abandoned ship: before January was out he was back in London, living with Duncan at 22 Fitzroy Street.

Both men objected to war, not on religious but on moral grounds. When the war began Bunny had momentarily thought of joining up, in anticipation of the honour and renown such action might bring, but what he had seen of war at Sommeille made him more determined to have no part in it. He decided against joining the armed forces on the principle that he could not delegate responsibility for his own acts to any officer.

Since the war had begun Duncan had sold no pictures and, apart from what he earnt at the Omega, had no source of earned income. Bunny was also now unemployed. Both therefore decided to find an occupation that would earn them a livelihood and would not go against their conviction that it was their duty to take no part in the war.

They were to benefit from circumstances resulting from the death of Mrs Grant's relative, Florence Ewbank, who had owned Wissett Grange, not far from Halesworth in Suffolk, and had rented out the nearby Wissett Lodge to a tenant farmer. He had looked after some six acres of land, including the orchards attached to the Grange. The fruit farm had been kept in excellent condition until the previous autumn, when the tenant farmer had died. Duncan's father, Bartle Grant, who appears to have been managing Miss Ewbank's estate until the lease ran out, had to find a replacement. In the past the farm had been run by two men, a boy and a woman. Now Duncan and Bunny agreed to take it on, in the hope that this kind of employment would help to exempt them from conscription. Before leaving London both men sent in papers requesting exemption to the Local Tribunal of St Pancras; Keynes and Morrell supplied testimonials as to Duncan's character and honesty.

Visitors to Wissett Lodge travelled by train to Halesworth and then telegraphed from the Angel Hotel for an omnibus, or made use of a small trap sent from Wissett to meet them and driven by a gypsy higgler called Cutts. Duncan and Bunny made their first visit to the area in the company of Bartle Grant, who uttered occasional snorts and further released the discomfort he felt at his son's pacifism by referring to Bunny as 'your friend Garbage'. But neither parental disapproval nor the state of the unpruned apple trees and the diseased blackcurrant bushes dismayed Duncan and Bunny. After they had taken their bearings, Duncan left Bunny at Wissett and returned to London in order to complete their move.

He arrived at Gordon Square in time to take part in a reading of Middleton's *The Changeling*. Afterwards he wrote to Bunny, 'Oliver [Strachey] was suspicious of our happiness at Wissett. But I more and more long to begin life there in earnest. I only hope you will like it Bunny. I wouldn't live there without you. This isn't a threat, because after all it could always be given up. Nessa is longing to go and the children are wild with excitement.'[2]

Wherever he alighted, even if it was only for a short period, Duncan took up his brush and made himself at home. In London he continued work on a large picture, probably *The Kitchen*, which he exhibited the following year at the Omega and either sold or gave to Maynard.[3] He had begun the picture a couple of years before, using pure colour and schematic delineation. Now he began to employ a more solid style, with dense, mottled tones modelling the figure of the boy on the far right. This change in style may have been a reaction to a remark about his 'shakiness of handling' in the *Westminster Gazette* on 17 November 1916, but a more likely influence was Sickert, whom Duncan visited with Vanessa shortly before returning to Wissett. Confronted with Sickert's rigorous method of picture-making, Duncan admitted feeling inchoate as an artist.

A couple of days later Duncan called on Wyndham Lewis. His purpose remains unclear, but both made no mention of the rumpus over the Ideal Home commission. Ezra Pound was also present. 'We had a very dull conversation,' Duncan told Bunny, 'about what would happen after the war amid a litter of drawings by Lewis of copulation on copulation.'[4] If

Duncan had forgiven Lewis his attack on Fry and the Omega, he was less tolerant of Will Rothenstein, who appeared one day at 46 Gordon Square. 'He came just as the children and me [*sic*] were going to make an aeroplane and it was a disappointment to all,' he told Bunny:

> Everything he says seems to have a four fold motive. He came partly to explain why he had joined an appalling Lord Mayor's Committee for the furtherance of the arts during wartime . . . and partly because [Bernard] Adeney had told him I would have on no account any dealings with him (Rothenstein) whatever job he might offer me, which was quite untrue. But he took two solid hours to say this among a lot of other transparent lies. That we were *difficult* (Nessa and I) and anti-social and ought to accept some sort of compromise such as doing tombs for dead heroes, rather than go without work. In vain we clamoured for tombs and reredoes [*sic*] but on he went maundering malicious twaddle.[5]

By the end of March Duncan had given up all notion of painting, for he was occupied from morning till night at Wissett with jobs that left little time to paint. He and Bunny had become willing, if somewhat experimental, farmers, finding by trial and error ways of ridding the orchard of bugs; attempting to keep tiny, sickly chicks alive in the oven; persuading Carrington's friend Barbara Hiles, when she visited them, to act the part of a horse while Duncan tried to plough a field; and dyeing the tails of their white leghorn chickens blue to prevent them from being stolen. Bunny, who began keeping bees, was pleased to discover not only Miss Ewbank's Bee Journal, but also her diary of work in the garden and orchard and her notebooks full of household tips and cooking recipes. Domestic help arrived punctually each morning at eight-thirty in the form of a tall, rather grandiose lady, and a very old gardener came as and when he chose to assist in the garden.

Vanessa made a day-visit to Wissett in order to ascertain whether it was possible for her and her sons to join Duncan and Bunny. Maynard had already agreed to guarantee payment of the rent on Wissett Lodge; now it was decided that the liability would be shared between him and Vanessa. Just as she was about to move, she heard from Duncan's mother that there were other tenants wanting to take the remainder of the lease in October. As everything was uncertain until they heard whether or not the tribunal had granted Duncan and Bunny exemption, the likelihood that the house would be theirs for only a limited period of time did not upset her. She arrived with Julian and Quentin, Blanche, her cook, and Flossie, the nursemaid and, once installed at Wissett Lodge, set to work to make the house pleasant and habitable. She removed ornaments and small tables and things left behind by the previous tenant; dyed chair covers; distempered the walls; and reorganised the house along lines that made possible both liveliness and peace.

Before leaving London for Wissett she had written Duncan a 'horrid' letter. She afterwards apologised: she had missed him badly in his absence, yet knew that she had limited claim on his attention. She may also have been aware that his long separation from Bunny during the previous year had allowed his love for this young man to grow in his mind, untested by reality, and that he was now, if anything, more deeply besotted with Bunny than before. 'I shall see you soon I hope,' wrote Vanessa, 'only I daren't hope anything much – life is so upsetting nowadays and things turn up every few minutes which change everything.'[6] Elsewhere, she admitted feeling starved as a result of not being able to talk to him: 'I'm already getting petrified within. I can't conceive what I should have done if you'd really gone to Paris nor how I shall ever get on without you. It's dreadful to depend so much on you. Please tell me if you're happy. Your loving R[odent].'[7] Her letter crossed with one from Bunny urging her to join them, as Duncan was pining in the country without her. Despite this encouragement, it had been a relief to discover on arrival, as she told Maynard, that the house was habitable and the hens productive. Her two boys played freely in the garden and the servants, Flossie and Blanche, were much taken with the soldiers at Halesworth. In general there was an atmosphere of well-being and content. If only the forthcoming tribunals did not menace their future, life at Wissett, she concluded, would be perfect.

The fact that she did not at first hear from Clive did not worry her: it was more likely he was engrossed by Mary Hutchinson than destroyed by a Zeppelin. She continued to look to him, and to Maynard, for worldly news and gossip. However when Clive and Mary visited them at Wissett, their tolerance did not extend to fleas or to Duncan's new puppy, called 'Little Henry' after Ottoline's brother, Lord Henry Cavendish-Bentinck, who, at his sister's suggestion, had recently paid sixty pounds for three of Duncan's paintings. Despite his zest for life, Clive did not have Duncan's fresh and original perspective. It was Duncan who found in the house and read aloud to Vanessa a child's book extolling the effects of a religious education; it was Duncan who encountered an elderly lady in Hampstead who called him 'brother brush', painted like the Douanier Rousseau and had lived in India in a house called Windermere. 'It sounded the oddest adventure,' Clive afterwards commented, 'but then Duncan's adventures always sound odd as most people's sound banal. I wonder why?'[8]

Books and visits to London helped feed Duncan's love of life. During Barbara Hiles's visit he read aloud *Uncle Vanya*. Wanting to re-read *Tristram Shandy*, he was pleased to find a fine edition among the books in the Lodge. On his occasional trips to London he enjoyed every moment, lunching with Maynard and Roger and afterwards accompanying the latter to the National Gallery and the Carfax Gallery. 'Fearfully exhausting for a provincial,' he wrote to Vanessa,[9] confirming what she herself felt, that the effect of full-time life in the country had affected them deeply. 'I feel that all our ways are changing,' she told Lytton. 'We are so much overcome by the country as compared to London that I doubt if I shall ever return to Gordon Square.'[10] In her scheme of things there would be regular jaunts to London, but for the moment the foliage and the flowers, the scents and sounds around them kept her and her companions perpetually happy.

Underneath this idyllic existence lay the unspoken possibility that prison awaited Duncan and Bunny if their pleas for exemption were turned down. In May both their cases were heard before a local tribunal, at Blything, its jury composed largely of Suffolk farmers. Philip Morrell, Keynes and Adrian Stephen made representations on their behalf. Adrian's dry, legalistic arguments left the farmers unmoved, as did Maynard's attempt to allude to the literary figures that had distinguished Bunny's upbringing. Exemption was denied and the only hope of overturning the decision lay with the Appeal Tribunal, which met at Ipswich later that month. At this Maynard adopted a more aggressive approach, announcing at the start that more important work awaited him at the Treasury and that he therefore hoped for an expeditious hearing. This impressed the tribunal and he was afterwards able to telegraph Vanessa with the news that exemption had been granted. Duncan and Bunny could now appeal to the Central Tribunal with regard to alternative employment: if they could prove that they were engaged in work of 'national importance' they would avoid the kind of uncongenial labour imposed on conscientious objectors.

No longer living in fear of sudden arrest, Duncan and Bunny returned to farming in high spirits. Hot weather had set in and Bunny's mother, Constance Garnett, arrived on a visit. 'She is just what you would imagine,' Vanessa told Lady Ottoline, 'and talks away steadily and continuously and sensibly exactly like one of her own translations if it weren't a translation. So she's not very exciting, but very nice, and full of valuable hints about fowls and vegetables.'[11] Saxon Sydney-Turner was also expected and it was thought that he and Mrs Garnett would get on well. After they left, Vanessa travelled alone to Guildford to see Roger, a visit she regretted as Roger's melancholy made it difficult and she herself felt remote from Duncan and as a result depressed.

It was then Duncan and Bunny's turn to take time off from Wissett. They travelled to Garsington, ostensibly to inspect some pigs, but were quickly drawn into the business of painting frescos with Carrington and Dorothy Brett in a nearby building that had been turned into a studio. Duncan felt it was another instance of people and circumstance bending to the force of Lady Ottoline's personality, which seemed to extend far beyond her presence, like her penetrating and lingering scent. Despite her benevolence, a vein of falsity in her manner and a tendency to strain and gush inspired a great deal of malice and mockery. Once, while attending a fitting for a dress at the Omega, she announced in her deep, dragging voice, in a tragic descending scale, 'Is there just a bit of dry bread that I might eat? I am so *hungry*.' Duncan returned from this or another visit with a story of Ottoline on the roof at Garsington that delighted the six-year-old Quentin. She was wearing a magnificent robe reaching to her feet, but fastened only by a jewel at the back of her neck. As she leant forward it fell apart, revealing her posterior, which was adorned with purple powder. Whether or not this story was true, it was entirely characteristic.

Nicknamed Lady Omega Muddle by Lytton Strachey, Ottoline was the subject of stories that suggested conflicting interests. She had done a great deal for the Omega Workshops, buying from it and helping to popularise its wares with others. But when it came to a set of six dining-room chairs, she suddenly cancelled her order. Shortly afterwards Vanessa visited her and found a set of newly acquired antique dining-chairs in use. When asked why she had decided against the Omega chairs, Ottoline claimed that they were far too expensive. Vanessa, finding this excuse unacceptable, pressed Ottoline to name the asking price and the poor woman did so, mentioning a sum double the actual amount, desperate in the face of Vanessa's uncompromising veracity.

Nevertheless it was Ottoline's turn to cause alarm in the summer of 1916 when she announced she was arriving at Wissett on a visit. Vanessa rightly foresaw that her flamboyance would quickly make the Lodge's small rooms, already darkened by the roses and wisteria that smothered the house, feel claustrophobic. Ottoline's unhappy childhood at Welbeck, where for much of the time she and her mother had been obliged to live with her half-brother, the sixth Duke of Portland, had sapped her confidence so irrevocably that she had developed an alarmingly extravagant appearance and manner to compensate. Six feet tall, she added to her stature with enormous hats and high heels, becoming, in Osbert

Sitwell's phrase, 'an animated public monument'.[12] Even late in life, when disfigured by an operation on her jaw and encrusted with face powder, she commanded attention; legend has it that when she dined in restaurants, waiters climbed on tables to get a better view.

The business of looking after Ottoline at Wissett fell mostly on Vanessa, as Duncan and Bunny were out working during the day. Neverthless when Monday morning arrived and she was due to depart there was general relief. She staggered them all at breakfast by appearing in a costume – red boots, silk tunic, white kaftan, ropes of pearls and tall Astrakhan fez – that made her look like a figure from a Russian ballet. When the horse and cart arrived to take her to the station, all went outside to see her off. In the raking sunlight it became apparent that in her dark little bedroom she had applied her make-up with a certain amount of guesswork. 'Why have you got all that on?' asked Quentin, as she bent to kiss him. Bunny recounts what happened next:

> There was a moment's silence after this unanswerable question; then a deep gurgle, half-growl, half-whine, from Ottoline, which passed itself off as a laugh – a rush of farewells from Vanessa, Duncan handed Ottoline up beside Cutts, she seated herself and waved and off they drove looking exactly like the advertisement for a circus.[13]

Twenty-two years later, at the memorial service that followed Lady Ottoline's death, her friend Lady Oxford quizzed members of Bloomsbury as to why so many of Ottoline's friends had quarrelled with her. There followed a pause, Virginia Woolf noted in her diary: 'She was *exigeante*, Duncan volunteered at last.'[14]

In September 1916 Duncan and Bunny learnt that, though the Central Tribunal had awarded them non-combatant service, the Pelham Committee had not given their work at Wissett the stamp of approval and they could no longer remain self-employed. Vanessa was elsewhere when Duncan heard this news. 'We think the best thing is to try and get work near here,' he told her. 'I miss you very much and wish you would come back soon. You mustn't be upset about this news. I don't want to leave Wissett otherwise I don't care much.' He ended, as always, with the nickname Adrian had first given him – 'Yr. loving Bear.'[15]

Vanessa took the matter in hand. She returned to Lewes, to that part of Sussex they knew well from their visits to Asheham and which offered the advantages of the countryside as well as easy access to London. There she went to see a farmer called Gunn, who told her that he had been in need of labour but only a few days before had given the work to a conscientious objector. Depressed by this news and feeling that fate was against her, Vanessa stumbled on, questioning the farmer further, and gradually got out of him that there was a young farmer called Hecks short of labour. He looked after New House Farm, which was situated near Charleston, a house that Virginia had urged Vanessa to consider taking in May and which would be vacant again at the end of the following fortnight. Before leaving, Vanessa agreed to meet Gunn the next day at Lewes market so that he could put her in touch with Mr Hecks and also with a Mr Stacey, who held the lease on Charleston.

That night she slept alone at Asheham and was again overcome with the peace and beauty of the area. Wide, open spaces led to the bare, austere Downs, their large outlines releasing the mind from petty concerns. The next day she made contact at the market with Mr Hecks, who agreed to take Duncan and Bunny on as farm labourers. She also bicycled out in the direction of Firle to find Charleston, a farmhouse surrounded by barns and pasture at the end of a track, about a mile east of Firle Park. She cast a somewhat cursory eye over the house and garden and left, unimpressed, for London.

House and garden, however, did not let her go. A couple of days later she caught the nine o'clock train from London, then took another connection and arrived at Glynde, the nearest station to Firle. Presently Mr Stacey drove up in a small motor and whisked her off to Charleston. She admitted to Duncan:

This time to my great surprise I saw something quite different. A large lake, an orchard, trees all round the back of the house and farm buildings, an old house – two hundred years old Mr Stacey said and he may be right for all I know – a walled garden quite as big or bigger than the Asheham one and a wall nearly as high, fruit trees trained against it all round – a bee hive! – everything much bigger and completely changed – on the whole improved. We went all over it. The rooms (according to today's impression) are very large and light and numerous – there are huge cupboards, innumerable larders – a dairy-cellar – all sorts of outhouses – lots of room for hens . . . I think the house could be made quite lovely. The rooms are very light and good proportions not low but not very high. There is also a tennis lawn! It has been so neglected that it's more like a bit of a field.

With her mind full of Charleston she went back with Mr Stacey to his home for lunch. There she was reminded afresh of the wartime circumstances that had brought her to the area. 'They live at Firle,' she ended her letter to Duncan, 'in a large house with an incredibly neat garden and the house like a glorified lodging house with the character taken from it. Mrs Stacey and I hated each other instinctively and she revealed to me the present state of mind of the British nation and why we want to go on with the war and why mothers like their sons to be killed.'[16]

In the meantime Duncan had written to the Pelham Committee asking to be allowed to stay on at Wissett until October. The fruit trees had to be harvested and the produce sent to Covent Garden. Vanessa, Julian and Quentin all helped, Duncan and Bunny now working twelve hours a day. The cockerels and rabbits had to be sold and numerous other small tasks remained. However, as Mr Hecks needed labour urgently, Bunny went on ahead to Sussex, arranging to stay, until Charleston was habitable, at the Ram Inn at Firle. *En route* he met Carrington and Barbara Hiles in London and persuaded them to accompany him on a jaunt to Sussex. They took bicycles on the train and rode out from Lewes to Firle, leaving their cycles at the inn. Then they walked across the shoulder of the Downs to Asheham, where they noticed that an upstairs window was open. Bunny climbed up a drainpipe and let himself in. Once all were inside the house, they found some apples and a bed made up with blankets. On this all three slept. The next morning they set off to find Charleston, this time inspecting house and garden without breaking in. Finally they walked back across Firle Park and had tea at the Ram Inn. In the evening the two girls bicycled back to Lewes from where they caught the train to London, and in the morning Bunny began pulling mangolds for Mr Hecks.

Though they had to face severe disapproval when Virginia found out they had broken in to Asheham, they freely admitted to snooping round Charleston. Carrington wrote to Vanessa:

> I must . . . tell you that we went and saw Charleston on Thursday. Never, never have I seen quite such a wonderful place! We sat round the pond and marvelled at it all, the house and the orchard, and the great downs behind . . . What excellent things there will be to paint in that garden with the pond and the buildings. We are telling nobody about the glories of Charleston. So you will not mind us having seen it will you?[17]

At the same time Bunny (his meaning clear, though his comparisons were muddled) told Duncan:

> Asheham is to Charleston what the Brontës were to the Elizabethans. It is open, spacious . . . I am fond of Wissett - but it is so cramped. I

realise that the rooms were wretched little rooms, that it was shadowy and overhung and that there were too many little things to attend to. Charleston is splendid. Easy, roomy. I am quite sure my temper will be infinitely better.[18]

In the meantime he had supper, bed and breakfast at the Ram Inn and lunch and tea with the Hecks family. Mr Hecks was keen to make a farmer of Bunny, in whom he recognised an able worker.

Left behind at Wissett, packing up books, paints, canvases, collecting chickens and ducks, Duncan found that everything reminded him of Bunny. 'I'm sitting at your table,' he wrote. 'Somehow the whole of life here is being cut off slowly with an axe. It's silly to mind so much when perhaps I shall see you again in a fortnight. But anyhow whatever may happen, this *has* come to an end.' He apologised for the emotional state he had got into a few days before Bunny left, for his tears and his weaknesses; 'but to whom may one reveal oneself in all one's horror if it isn't to those who love one? It's no good being told one's selfish and silly when one knows one is; what one wants is forgiveness and a prayer for the human race.'[19] Despite his melancholy and nostalgia, Duncan, too, was eager for their new life. 'It is splendid about Charleston,' he agreed with Vanessa, after receiving her description of it. 'It sounds a heavenly place.'[20] Then came a reassuring note from Bunny: 'the longer I am away from you the more I feel that even temporary absence from you is intolerable.'[21] So he wrote to Duncan, before turning his hand to a love sonnet that he was composing for Carrington.

Charleston stands alone, a house of outward sobriety. A substantial, rather austere two-storeyed building with an attic floor, dating back in part to the seventeenth century, it is situated at the foot of Firle Beacon, the highest in a run of downs from Newhaven to Cuckmere, and is remote, even from the nearby villages of Firle and Glynde. The house is reached by means of a lengthy farm track off the Lewes to Eastbourne road and is linked, by means of a footpath, to the old road between Alfriston and Firle, which remains a rough track for farm vehicles. On the south side of the house, in 1916, were barns, a pig-sty and wooden granary sheltering old Sussex wagons. In those days a gabled porch (later removed) framed the front door in the main façade, which overlooks a pond (Vanessa's 'large lake'). There are broad sash windows on this side of the house at both ground and first-floor levels, their generous proportions allowing light to spread into rooms that have relatively low ceilings. The proportions within each room are satisfying but not elegant, the house having a natural dignity, a stillness and peace.

In the Edwardian period it had been used as a lodging house, and to this day porcelain number plates can be seen on the bedroom doors. When Vanessa, Duncan and Bunny moved in, it was bare and unfurnished, the two men at first having to sleep on the floor. For a long time several of the rooms remained empty and unused. It was also very cold: inadequate heating made it sometimes necessary in winter to break the ice on a bowl of water before one's face could be washed. However, the relatively cheap cost of live-in help meant that Vanessa, who had some money of her own as well as an allowance from Clive, could afford to employ two or three servants. But limited funds, wartime circumstances and a willingness to respond to the needs of the moment caused Vanessa and Duncan to adopt an *ad hoc* attitude to furnishings and decoration. Pieces of furniture that had belonged to Vanessa's parents and were a part of her childhood at Hyde Park Gate were sent down from 46 Gordon Square. They mixed with Omega chairs, as well as some hideous items picked up cheaply in markets or second-hand furniture shops in Lewes. The decoration of each room likewise followed no standard of elegance or set of rules. Instead, there was a sympathetic mingling of colours, pictures and objects. In time motifs began to expand beyond the picture frame and to animate door panels, fireplaces and overmantels. Duncan ornamented a linen chest with the athletic shape of a swimmer, a simple wooden log-box with angels, wittily squeezing their proportions so that each fits into the space available. The decorations contrasted with the walls in the passages and other rooms, which were painted a pale, warm grey and, though hung with pictures, were otherwise left bare. Nevertheless, as it was painted, decorated and furnished, the house gradually took on the appearance of a continually changing work of art, without ever losing a certain shabbiness that become part of its nature.

Duncan, forced immediately into farm work, had little time to give to his new surroundings: it was Vanessa who painted the first decorations in a bedroom that eventually became known as Duncan's room. Though Charleston was free from the likelihood of air raids, the noise of gunfire occasionally echoed across the Channel. Zeppelins had begun to attack London and, when visiting his parents at Dartford, Duncan noticed that as soon as a raid began, his father ran out on to the lawn to watch, while his mother was inclined to be rather short with the maids if they showed any sign of fear. The war encouraged hasty weddings. Saxon Sydney-

Turner was to be bitterly disappointed in 1918 when Barbara Hiles suddenly married Nicholas Bagenal, who was about to go to war.

Of all Duncan's friends, the one who had the most insight into government policy on the war was Maynard, who continued to work at the Treasury. He was crucial to Charleston in its early years, for he not only oversaw Vanessa's finances and advised her on investments, but also gave practical help, sending down a sofa from Cambridge, a Chinese carpet from London and ordering new mattresses for beds. A welcome guest, he regarded Charleston as a place to recuperate from the excitements and frustrations of his work. He was very much at the centre of things, in contact with politicians and mixing socially with powerful figures such as Lord Beaverbrook, with whom he dined at the Ritz in Paris, afterwards fascinating Duncan with his insights into this man's character and influence. One weekend Maynard would be staying at the home of the Prime Minister, Asquith, the next with Reginald McKenna, Chancellor of the Exchequer, after which he would arrive at Charleston, where he immediately took an interest in the life of its inhabitants. Bunny thought him 'the most gentle and harmonious of our visitors'.[22] He loved weeding and would work his way, snail-like, along the paths at Charleston, having spent the morning in his room getting through a mass of work. He tore up papers after he had dealt with them and prided himself on having filled his waste-paper basket before lunch. In relation to his pacifist friends he was, however, in a difficult position: his work at the Treasury gave rise to their criticism that he was in effect helping to finance the war.

There had been an awkward moment in February 1916 at a dinner at 46 Gordon Square, when Lytton took Maynard to task on this matter, supported by the silence of the others, which implied unspoken criticism. Certainly, given such friends, Maynard, instead of being drunk with power, had constantly to question the integrity of his actions and recognise now and then a conflict between his beliefs and the policy of the coalition government. By January 1917 he was seriously dissatisfied with his job, as he told Duncan: 'The Treasury depresses me just now. I am badly overworked, need a holiday, and am filled with perpetual contempt and detestation of the new government ... I pray for the most absolute financial crash (and yet strive to prevent it – so that all I do is a contradiction with all I feel), but we always seem able to struggle on these months more.'[23]

Bunny, living and working alongside Duncan throughout these early years at Charleston, never heard him criticise Maynard. Like Vanessa, Duncan placed his trust in Maynard's grasp of money matters. Needing to invest the legacy left him by Aunt Hennie, he had placed the task in Maynard's hands and his £528 brought him an income of forty-seven pounds in 1917. More importantly, their long-standing friendship rested on a bond untouched by the ructions of daily life. While Maynard hobnobbed with political leaders, Duncan worked alongside the ill-assorted individuals left behind as farm labourers. He pulled turnips by hand in bitter north-east winds, amid sleet and snow, spattered with frozen mud. Hecks paid him and Bunny twelve shillings and sixpence a week. They worked seven and a half hours on weekdays and a half-day on Saturday. Overtime was paid at fivepence an hour. In May 1917 Duncan and Bunny spent an entire month hoeing a field of beans, happily telling each other stories as they worked side by side. In summer, during the hay season, they harvested hay eleven hours a day. At the same time, with fat and sugar rationed, they were living on a diet that was inadequate for hard manual labour. As the war progressed Bunny found that, though he had developed enormous physical stamina, he came increasingly to feel emotional and nervous strain and by the end of the war found his temper very difficult to control, while Duncan began to lose weight alarmingly and had a severe attack of rheumatism.

'There is another life,' Bunny wrote to his mother, ' – but I am too tired to attend to it.'[24] Nor could Duncan paint as much in the first eighteen months at Charleston as he had done at Wissett where, after their initial labours to restore the fruit farm, he had taken an afternoon or morning to paint when he felt like it. But there was more to the lives of both men than farmwork. In January 1917 Barbara Hiles, Dora Carrington and Saxon Sydney-Turner turned up at nearby Asheham and invited them to tea. Adrian and Karin Stephen, who were staying at Charleston, walked over with Duncan and Bunny and ate a tremendous amount, reminding Carrington of starving stags. A few days later they held a dinner party and on this occasion gave Vanessa, Duncan, Maynard and Bunny soup, beef sausages and leeks, plum pudding, lemon jelly and punch. If luxuries during the war were in short supply, they were not unheard of: when Clive visited Charleston he arrived bearing chocolate, magazines, Manila cheroots and bottles of wine.

Clive's continued concern for Vanessa's health and well-being was welcome: his companion, Mary Hutchinson, was not. Distantly related to the Stracheys, she irritated Vanessa, who took it out on Duncan by saying, 'Of course, she's *your* cousin, Duncan.' Mary knew that she was not welcome because she had read a passage in one of Vanessa's letters to Roger, which admitted that she 'dreaded' Mary's visits. It was not so much her fashionable manner that Vanessa disliked as that characteristic which her portrait of Mary conveys: a slyness that made Mary, in Violet Hammersley's opinion, 'unscrupulous but amusing'. She also seemed incapable of a disinterested emotion and adopted an extravagant, gushing manner to make up for her lack of generosity.

One positive move on Mary's part was to commission from Duncan and Vanessa painted decorations for the house at Hammersmith where she lived with her husband Jack. 'I can't get over the perfection in River House,'[25] Virginia wrote to Vanessa, after seeing these decorations, which, like so many other commissions by Grant and Bell, no longer exist. If their work helped smooth a difficult relationship, it had the opposite effect on Roger Fry, who thought that Vanessa and Duncan were undercutting the Omega by working independently and charging too little. Though the distance between London and Sussex meant that they now had little to do with the Workshops, both sent work to the 'Copies and Translations' exhibition, which Fry mounted at the Omega in May 1917. Copying from Old Masters was then a fairly standard art-school practice, but Fry was interested in it for more than pedagogical reasons. He believed that each generation has to remake its Old Masters. ('If we did not go on continually revaluing and remaking them they would be not merely old, but dead.')[26] He also thought that contemporary copies were interesting because they revealed what elements in the work of previous ages had relevance to a modern sense of design. Vanessa, when copying a Giotto the year before, had found herself thinking of Matisse. At Wissett she and Duncan had executed decorations on the walls of one bedroom based on postcard reproductions of Fra Angelico frescos. However, it is likely that copying Old Masters led away from experimentation and fostered Duncan's desire for a more solid method of representation.

He sent four copies to the Omega show, two of which (one based on a detail from Piero della Francesca's *Nativity* and the other on an Antonio Pollaiuolo) were bought by Maynard. Though farm work had impeded his career, Duncan still painted when he could and exhibited whenever possible. Both he and Vanessa showed in the 'The New Movement in Art' exhibition that Fry sent to Birmingham in July 1917.

That same year Jacques Copeau was planning a performance of Maeterlinck's *Pelléas et Mélisande* and wondered if Duncan could take on the task of designing clothes and scenery. If not, he wrote, would Vanessa do it? They decided to work together on screens and costumes for the play during the summer. Fry supplied a copy of the text and Barbara Hiles, who was camping in a field close by, agreed to help cut out and dye the material used. Each costume was dyed a different colour by hand on the kitchen table at Charleston in a most unprofessional manner, creating a blotchy, marbled effect. The costumes were then roughly tacked together so that they could be easily adjusted to fit. Realising that Copeau was about to transport the Vieux Colombier company to New York, Duncan asked for a description of the new theatre, which Copeau could not provide, knowing only at this point that he wanted to suppress all the existing decorations. Though he begged Duncan to have the costumes ready by early November, the play was not staged until early 1919. The *New York Times* of 11 February 1919 gave it a scathing review, remarking that the stage setting was 'conspicuous by its absence' and saying nothing at all about the costumes.

Whenever possible Duncan refreshed himself with a change of scene. He had escaped to London in February 1917, where he attended an 'Art Circle' evening at the Omega, sitting like others on sacks of straw. The highlight of this visit, however, was a trip to the National Gallery in Fry's company to see paintings on loan from the Hugh Lane collection. Duncan was much struck by Renoir's *Les Parapluies* and by a Rembrandt lent by the Duke of Buccleuch. On another occasion when Hecks gave him a day off Duncan went to see his parents, a visit he found depressing as his father had framed a lot of his old paintings and hung them, perhaps in protest at his son's more advanced style, all over the house.

At Charleston that year Vanessa had the idea of starting a small school. As an initial experiment she elevated the nurse, Mabel Selwood, to the position of governess and invited Amber Blanco-White, a young blue-stocking who had two daughters, one by H. G. Wells, to send them to Charleston so that they could share in this educational experiment. It was not a success. The nine-year-old Julian Bell resented this female intrusion and, losing control one day, pelted Anna-Jane and Justine with loose earth and dry sheep dung. Though the girls soon left, Vanessa persisted with the idea of educating her children at home and eventually found a reliable governess in a Mrs Brereton, who began work in January 1918. Her charges, Julian and Quentin, remained at the heart of Charleston life. During their first Christmas in the house Maynard overheard them discussing every morning for a week whether Father Christmas was really Duncan. They thought the evidence in his favour almost conclusive, this being an advance on the previous year, when Julian had been found looking up Father Christmas in the tradesmen's directory.

Duncan and Vanessa agreed that flamingos would add a wonderful dash of colour to the pond. To Duncan's delight, Vanessa found a letter in *The Field* from a gentleman who wrote in to say that his flamingos had weathered the severe winter without shelter and were admirable birds to keep in England on small ponds. They instantly wrote off to find out where to obtain some. Though nothing ever came of the idea, Duncan for a while hoped to rival the peacocks at Garsington.

'I often wonder how you come to be so infinitely preferable to everyone else in the world,' Vanessa wrote to Duncan, while staying with Roger in July 1917, 'and I meditate upon your character – also upon your extraordinary intelligence! What do you think about that? Don't you think it very astonishing?'[27] To outsiders it might have seemed surprising that the daughter of Sir Leslie Stephen, herself a quick reasoner and able to join in the conversation of men, should have given her affections to a painter who often blinked nervously when he spoke and was far less assertive in character than Clive, who animated any social occasion with his knowledge and airy, quick-witted talk; nor did Duncan have a mind as vigorous or as questioning as Roger's. But what made Duncan sympathetic to Vanessa was his creativity, his quick, vital response to whatever circumstances or people he encountered. Instead of any vehement character traits, he contained in his person a mingling of expressions; his often unpredictable but always precise comments were occasionally touched with cynicism or even malice; but this, combined with his ineffable gentleness, merely reinforced his inscrutability and elusiveness. He could not walk down a street without noticing some detail, action or human drama that interested or amused him and made the simple journey rich with excitement. David Garnett claimed that Duncan was 'the most entertaining companion I have ever known'; his lively mind never struck upon the obvious, and his sensibility made him acutely responsive to the mood of his companion.[28]

For Vanessa there was also his attraction as a painter. She had been repeatedly surprised by how differently Duncan saw things, and the solutions that he found always intrigued. He was a pure artist, his motivation springing not from desire for money, success or social prestige but from inner necessity. As a result his work, despite false starts and constant change, had a telling clarity of effect. His example stimulated others, both Vanessa and Bunny, the latter insisting, 'In Duncan's company I learned how an artist approaches his work and, when I came to write, I approached my subject as a conscious artist.'[29]

There were moments when Duncan aroused Vanessa's maternal feelings. She worried about his tiredness and whether he had enough to eat. He was also her lover, in his early thirties and exceptionally attractive. Virginia Woolf noticed his sensuality when she encountered him in London in March 1917. 'You were like a beautiful but rather faded moth, the other day,' she teased him, 'after your nights debauch among the red hot pokers and passion flowers of Hampstead.'[30] Bound to

Duncan by ties of need and love, Vanessa sometimes found it hard to leave him at Charleston, exhausted by farmwork, in order that she might fulfil an obligation in London. 'I wonder if you know how strong-minded it was of me to tear myself away from you today,' she wrote.[31]

Aware of conflicting loyalties, Duncan resorted in 1918 to keeping a diary, perhaps hoping that by writing down his feelings he could untangle them. He was sharing a bedroom with Bunny, who, when the opportunity arose, was still taking advantage of an earlier affair with Barbara Hiles. In the autumn of 1917 he had also begun an affair with Alix Sargant-Florence, who was simultaneously being courted by James Strachey. Bunny attempted to keep his affair with Alix secret from Duncan, knowing how jealous he could be. Two years before both men had visited Lady Ottoline, who had taken Duncan aside so that Bunny could talk with the young governess, Maria Nys. Bunny stayed on for an hour after Duncan left, and once outside Ottoline's house was very surprised to see a white-faced Duncan rush up, so full of emotion that he was scarcely able to speak. They got into a cab, Duncan giving way to howls and tears. The cause of this tantrum was his assumption that Ottoline had been plotting a union between Maria and Bunny. But Bunny's decision not to tell Duncan about his affair with Alix proved a mistake, as it enhanced Duncan's jealousy when he did find out. He begged Bunny not to see Alix, accused him of perfidy and even at one point threatened to commit suicide if Bunny went to London to see Alix. Angry scenes took place. On one occasion Bunny snatched the pipe out of Duncan's mouth, broke it and hit him repeatedly. He suffered great confusion, longed to see Alix but when he did so found her unimportant and wished himself back with Duncan.

This hysterical behaviour was caused partly by the claustrophobic conditions imposed on them by wartime restrictions. Their relationship, severely tested during the first three months of 1918, lurched unhappily from one crisis to another. Vanessa, herself ill and depressed in January, was privy to their agony but it remained hidden from the children. The eight-year-old Quentin, when quizzed by a maid about 'Uncle Bunny', corrected her: Bunny was not his uncle, he announced solemnly, but his bosom friend. That winter Julian was being taught manners. Bunny found it a trial, but less of a trial than when Julian had been allowed to throw food about, upset his chair, read history at the table and snitch sugar. He watched the young boy trying to bring an argument to a close without loss of dignity, perpetually interrupting the adults' conversation in order to give his opinion before he even knew what it was, and suffering continuously. Bunny could not help reflecting that Julian's agonised state mirrored his own, only in a more juvenile form.

On a visit to London Bunny poured out his woes to Maynard and was astonished by how well he knew and understood Duncan. 'It was a new experience,' Bunny afterwards wrote in his diary, 'talking to someone who knows Duncan – so different from Nessa . . . I daresay women don't understand and can't understand the relation of two men. They either read it in terms of advantage (Alix) or sentiment (Nessa).'[32] However, a discussion at Charleston on the topic of jealousy enhanced Duncan's affection and respect for Vanessa. She remarked that jealousy was rather like toothache – not entirely physical, utterly ungovernable and, however disastrous its effect on conduct, irresponsive to moral disapprobation as this only aggravated it. Vanessa's talk helped Duncan move away from the appalling jealousy he felt whenever he reflected on Bunny's dealings with Alix. He was further released from self-torturing thoughts by a good morning's painting.

In fact, as Duncan recorded in his diary he had never been so interested in his painting as he was now, in the first few months of 1918. In February he began a large picture, *Interior*,[33] showing Vanessa painting a still-life and Bunny writing at the table. 'I began my big interior of the dining-room this morning and couldn't bear anyone being in the room even Nessa, the tension is so enormous starting a thing of that sort.' In terms of compositional arrangement, it was one of the most complex pictures he had attempted. In painterly terms, it is one of his most laboured, his modelling now so dense that it had perhaps become an unconscious expression of the emotional claustrophobia in which he was living.

When visitors arrived, the conversation at Charleston could take any turn. Duncan himself might begin it by asking Saxon Sydney-Turner how he thought the ancient world compared with the modern and they would then touch on art, literature, the Greek way of life, present-day mores. Here was another source of comfort, for Duncan took great pleasure in his friends, even though, as he was to discover, these free-wheeling discussions could sometimes lead to painful conclusions.

Ever since Bunny had become intimate with Duncan it had been privately understood that Duncan and Vanessa wanted to have a child. Some years before, Adrian Stephen had observed to Ka Cox, 'Duncan wants children, but then of course he is rather like a woman in certain of his tendencies. Why don't you come to an arrangement with him?'[34] This throwaway suggestion had been disregarded by Ka, but the possibility of a child by Vanessa was a reality and it complicated Duncan's feelings towards her. At one level he felt a simple dependence on her. 'Goodbye,' he once ended a letter to her, 'and come back soon with your brats where you're badly needed.'[35] Sexual involvement, however, altered the nature of the responsibilities between them and left him uncomfortable. One night at Charleston, after their lengthy discussion concerning jealousy, Duncan wrote in his diary:

> I was hurt slightly by her [Vanessa] saying she got no more from me than a brotherly affection. I was paralysed by this as I always am. I am so uncertain of my real feeling to V that I am utterly unable to feign more than I feel when called upon to feel much, with the consequence that I seem to feel less than I do. I suppose the only thing lacking in my feelings to her is passion. What of that there might be seems crushed out of me, by a bewildering suffering expectation of it (hardly conscious) by her. I think I feel that if I showed any, it would be met by such an avalanche that I should be crushed. All I feel I can do in this case is to build slowly for her a completely strong affection on which she can lean her weary self.[36]

At times, however, his obsession with Bunny occluded his awareness of Vanessa's feelings. On one occasion when Clive and Roger were staying at Charleston, a conversation arose that forced Duncan to be aware of her pain. They began discussing whether one should go to bed with a person one loved if that person did not return this love. Various views were expressed, Clive stating that in such a situation he would rather not, as the favour would be too humiliating. After this remark Vanessa dropped out of the conversation and remained silent, lost in her own thoughts. When Duncan accompanied her upstairs later that evening he found, as he had suspected, that Clive's remark had made her bitterly aware of what she had lost through loving him. He did what he could to comfort her, but was unable to do so wholeheartedly, as he was depressed by the fact that Bunny had not returned to Charleston that evening as he had promised.

Soon after this Duncan found, to his surprise, that a weekend that he and Vanessa spent alone together at Charleston passed quietly and pleasantly. He wrote in his diary, 'I copulated on Saturday with her with great satisfaction to myself physically. It is a convenient way the females have of letting off one's spunk – and comfortable. Also the pleasure it gives is reassuring. You don't get this dumb misunderstanding body of a person who isn't a bugger. That's one for you Bunny. Not that my god I don't enjoy the excitement of it myself.'[37] He had, however, wept on Vanessa's shoulder on the Friday evening and felt angry that, though the

James-Alix-Bunny tangle seemed woolly and unreal, he was the one to feel wrong-footed because of his intense jealousy. There seemed, that month, no solution to his fraught relationships. 'Perhaps I'm too wicked to be happy,' he wrote in his diary, 'or to make anyone else happy. Certainly I don't succeed with Nessa. Although left alone with her I should be quiet and *she* might be happier.'[38]

Meanwhile, emotional scenes between Duncan and Bunny continued; worn down by farmwork, both men were now very much on each other's nerves. Duncan could be surly, distant and morose. At other moments he abandoned himself to black moods, hiding in tears in the bicycle-shed and saying that he was going mad. An hour or two later he would arrive for tea in a quite different state of mind, to everyone's relief. There were days of simple pleasure when the two men worked in the garden at Charleston, sowing onions, Brussels sprouts and lettuces. But there were also mornings when merely the sight of a letter from Alix for Bunny stung Duncan into uncontrollable misery. One day he showed Bunny a letter he had written to Alix but not sent. Bunny wrote in his diary, 'It was a queer document in eighteenth century language and put on her the business of deciding whether I was to live with her entirely and give him up or whether she should give me up.'[39] Illogical and inconsistent, Duncan hated Bunny to be absent on Sundays, their day off, but often spent all Sunday painting with Vanessa, exchanging no more than ten words with his friend. There were times when the emotional tension was so great that fights broke out, in which shelves came off walls and paraffin lamps were overturned. They were followed by copious tears and complete exhaustion, the two men finally sleeping deeply with their limbs entwined.

Vanessa neither intervened in these rows nor ignored them. 'I wonder how you'll think Duncan,' she wrote to Maynard in February 1918:

> There have been such storms within the last month or two. I was really rather worried a week or two ago . . . because I don't think one can go on indefinitely with such constantly recurring crises. Perhaps they'll get less. But I have also come to the conclusion that in spite of the horrors of them these storms perhaps do relieve Duncan more than anything else would and that he couldn't indulge in them unless he realised subconsciously that he could do so safely. I mean Bunny is too dependent on him really to give him up whatever he does. He certainly is a Turk . . .[40]

She did, however, advise Bunny to take rooms after the war separate from Duncan. She also made the curious remark that Duncan's jealousy was stirred partly by the fact that, whereas Bunny was having an affair, he was not. In this equation she played no part, neither in her mind nor in Bunny's, for afterwards he wrote in his diary, 'He would be happier with affairs of his own – but she probably prevented him.'[41]

By March Bunny had begun to hate farmwork like poison. He could no longer endure the stench of dung or rotting afterbirths and, feeling like a slave, he looked back incredulously to the untroubled freedom and happiness he had enjoyed in 1914 and 1915. He had let the Quakers know that he was looking for alternative employment and heard in March that Robert Tatlock, who was about to depart for Russia, had recommended him to look after the office work in London on behalf of the Russian Mission. When Duncan learnt this he announced that if Bunny left him working alone on the farm, he would either commit suicide or go to prison, and that Bunny's cruelty amounted to a desire to kill him. Duncan's attitude seemed to Bunny so completely selfish that he let rip, pouring out bitter and fierce condemnation of Duncan's behaviour, finally losing all semblance of control and collapsing in tears and hysterics. This scene appears to have marked a turning point. There were still turbulent times ahead, but Bunny's excoriating remarks had hit home and Duncan's attitude towards him gradually changed. If, however, in the months to come there was a lessening of antagonism, there remained a residue of pain. That spring Bunny, in a mood of great distress, groaned aloud as he walked round and round a room looking for onion seed. 'Come – we must go and sow onions,' he told Duncan and found himself adding, 'sow tears for ourselves', this offhand remark presaging a bitter legacy that was to surface in years to come.

THIRTEEN

Butter for the Baby

At his most miserable, Bunny realised that he had lost not only Duncan's trust but also Vanessa's. Attempts to restore a more cordial exchange failed. 'She works entirely by intuition and is quite unreliable,' he complained in his diary.[1] Duncan, meanwhile, could be equally unpredictable. When Bunny returned from one of his jaunts to London, Duncan, who had been fairly happy and contented in his absence, expressed his anger by speaking scarcely to anyone for two days, and everything Bunny said he contradicted with short, sharp remarks. His behaviour, Vanessa told Maynard, kept them all in a state of misery. Bunny wrote a poem ('Trouble'), which began 'What is the matter with this house?' and ended:

> 'What is the matter?' I cry out again.
> The thick old tiles protect our heads from rain
> But yet I swear more tears fall in these walls
> From your dear eyes, than from the whole sky falls.
> What is the matter? If we so ill together
> Within its walls can live, let us walk out
> And find in the hoarfrost and rough weather
> A fireside for our hearts, – the wind a clout
> Warmer than the cloak of love we tatter
> And better than this house, where what's the matter?[2]

Fortunately, the arrival of spring brought a lightening of mood. Duncan's diary records that he was less unhappy, greatly interested in his painting, often ravenously hungry and fairly indifferent to Alix or any other of Bunny's affairs. Severe weight loss and an attack of rheumatism caused him to have a medical examination, as a result of which he was permitted to cut down his working hours so that from now on he laboured only half of each day. He began to develop a more robust, less dependent attitude towards Bunny. Two things in particular gave him fresh zest: seeing Blake's illustrations to Dante, in an auction at Christie's in London, and, in Roger's studio, a catalogue of the forthcoming sale in Paris of Degas's collection. 'The illustrations in this last moved me to enormous enthusiasm,' his diary records, 'and at dinner before Barbara's party, I suggested to Maynard that he should get the money out of the Treasury to buy some of these pictures for the National Gallery.'[3]

Both sales were major events, attracting the attention of museum officials. At a personal level, the Degas sale was advantageous to Maynard as the action he now took, at Duncan's urging, regained him what he had recently lost – the respect of his friends. Word had gone round Bloomsbury that Maynard had gone to the dogs. In company he contradicted others and scorned discussion. He was perpetually tired and overworked, wanting in his spare moments to give only one-tenth of his mind to any issue that arose. Once, while Vanessa was staying at 46 Gordon Square, she, Norton and Sheppard began discussing whether or not they could have any respect for their country now that England had turned down the Austrian peace move. Maynard entered the room and, having much greater knowledge about the diplomatic manoeuvres involved, listened to the discussion with evident contempt. Angered by this, Sheppard told him that it was a mistake to despise his friends. Afterwards it was decided that Duncan should be asked to give Maynard a lecture. (Bunny, reporting this in his diary, added, 'Note – Duncan's lectures are damned serious and you've just had one Bunny.')[4]

Maynard acted immediately on Duncan's suggestion regarding the Degas sale. He first ensured that one particularly influential Treasury official would agree to the venture, then alerted Charles Holmes, Director of the National Gallery, presenting him with a pre-drafted letter to sign, which Maynard then took to the Chancellor of the Exchequer, Bonar Law. It amused Law to find this Treasury official, normally very resistant to expenditure, requesting a draft, but he officially approved one for 550,000 francs. By coincidence Maynard had to be in Paris during the week of the sale in order to attend an inter-Allied conference on finance and therefore accompanied the official party sent to view it, Holmes having shaved off his moustache and donned a pair of spectacles so that he would not be recognised by Paris dealers. With the art dealers Knoedlers acting on their behalf, the National Gallery succeeded in outbidding the Louvre for Delacroix's *Baron de Schwiter*, also obtaining works by Manet, Corot and Ingres. Holmes refused to buy a Cézanne and came home with £5,000 unspent, sufficient to have bought two El Grecos that were in the sale. Nevertheless it was an exciting event and Bunny, writing to Maynard before he left for France, passed on Vanessa and Duncan's advice regarding the need to obtain professional advice on the pictures. He added, 'They are very proud of you and eager to know how you did it. You have been given complete absolution and future crimes also forgiven.'[5]

On the evening of his return, Maynard, travelling by car with Austen Chamberlain from Folkestone, was dropped on the main road at the top of the mile-long farm track leading to Charleston. Presumably tired and overburdened, he left in the hedge in the lane a suitcase with a Cézanne inside it. On hearing this, Duncan and Bunny flew down the farm track in the clear moonlight and carried back in triumph the painting of seven apples that now hangs in the Fitzwilliam Museum, Cambridge. Its saturated colour and compact handling were endlessly discussed and analysed. It perfectly demonstrated how movement over a surface can be described as a progression of separate colours rather than variations in tone, a lesson that Duncan well understood. Its example would have enhanced his desire for a fuller, more solid method of representation. That evening, however, he was excited still further by a gift from Maynard, in recognition of his part in the venture, of a Delacroix sketch for the Galerie d'Appollon decorations in the Louvre.

That spring there was a move afoot to get Duncan registered as the gardener at Charleston. The Pelham Committee, however, refused to allow Vanessa to become his employer, as she was neither a farmer nor a market gardener, and he was obliged to stay on in the employment of Mr Hecks, unloading dung in the open fields, ramming chalk into the floor of the new cow stalls and in general turning his hand to whatever tasks needed doing. Once the gardener scheme was squashed, Bunny felt unable to leave: difficulties between Duncan and Mr Hecks made Bunny an essential go-between. 'Duncan is absolutely defenceless in the hands of these avaricious beasts,' Bunny told his mother. '. . . Duncan cannot bring himself to ask for days off, to alarm Mr Hecks, as I am always doing by showing evident annoyance, or to flatter him by a pretended interest. Duncan would rather be a slave all his life than do these things . . . he cannot help it. It's being a lineal descendant of John of Gaunt I suppose and a Highlander.'[6]

There was another possible route out of farmwork. Lady Ottoline, hearing that the Ministry of Information had begun employing artists, wrote to Robert Ross on Duncan's behalf. When Ross brought Duncan's name to the relevant committee, it was received with enthusiasm. As a result Duncan, at Ross's invitation, went to London to see him and was privately offered a commission as a war artist, on the condition that he enter the army and become a Major, the ranking automatically given to war artists. Duncan felt he had no choice but to refuse, as he had no intention of donning uniform and acting the part of Major. The matter did not end there. Towards the end of May the Ministry of Information wrote to the Chairman of the Pelham Committee requesting that Duncan Grant be placed at their disposal under the scheme for employing artistic talent for propaganda and record purposes. Ross's new idea was that Duncan could be employed on a picture of German prisoners of war working in the fields. Duncan asked Ross if instead a subject might be found in an aircraft factory. If officially appointed to this task, he would be released from farmwork and able, in his spare time, to do his own work.

In June the Ministry of Information took his case to the Central Tribunal stating, among other things, that Grant was physically unfit for more than half a day's work at agriculture; his employer had also written to the Pelham Comittee saying that, though prepared to continue employing Grant, he did not think him suited to the kind of heavy work he had now been doing for two years. This time Duncan's case reached the desk of Lord Beaverbrook, who replied by personal letter to Viscount Hambledon. A hand-written annotation on the Ministry of Information's letter of application reports the conclusion: 'Release of Grant not possible.'[7]

Though attempts to obtain him release from farmwork had failed, Duncan was appreciative of his friends' concern. Maynard, especially, kept Duncan in mind, involving him – even when he came straight from work with straw in his hair – in high society luncheons on his visits to London. 'I, for one,' Maynard wrote to Vanessa, 'am at Cambridge and have taken the opportunity to look out two suits of clothes for Duncan which will reach him before very long. I am afraid that neither is quite what he wants and that he won't be grateful – so I've looked out two instead of one in order to placate him.'[8] Duncan also received cigarettes and chocolates from Virginia. They were not entirely disinterested gifts for they brought her, in reply, letters and therefore Charleston news. This may not always have lived up to her expectations, for she imagined Duncan and Vanessa to be like 'the young women at the telephone exchange with the wires ringing little bells round them, as lovers, divorces, and copulations and insanities blaze out in London'.[9] In fact, though Clive and Mary Hutchinson, when they visited, seemed to Duncan 'very exquisite and gay', other visitors supplied little in the way of scandal. 'I came in from the garden,' Duncan told Virginia, 'and heard Saxon quietly saying "yes, there are times Vanessa, when I think it would be certainly better to be dead than alive". Nessa made no comment and went on sewing. It seemed very characteristic of both, and of course I had interrupted a heart to heart conversation which was a pity.'[10]

By June 1918 Vanessa realised that she was pregnant by Duncan. This news further improved the atmosphere at Charleston, where Duncan and Bunny now gave their small rations of butter to Vanessa for the baby's sake. Before this there had been an awful moment in April when Alix Sargant-Florence had ended her affair with Bunny and he had turned on Duncan in uncontrollable rage. Bunny suffered further when one of his friends let drop that he had expected Bunny to be in a suicidal state after listening to gossip concerning him and Alix. Again Bunny lost control and found himself walking the streets in a state of collapse and hysteria, poisonous feelings invading his whole being. That summer, however, he returned to sanity and, as he watched Vanessa eating his butter, consoled himself with the thought that he had not become completely horrible.

As his obsession with Alix faded, his admiration for Duncan revived. He also noticed the way in which the house was steadily being transformed – 'decorated and altered almost out of recognition as the bodies of the saved are said to be glorified after the resurrection'.[11] On Sundays he was familiar with the sight of Duncan, dressed in old blue cotton overalls, a piece of pale blue shirt hanging out of a tear in the seat of his trousers, busy with the latest project, whether it was a painted decoration or an attempt to ornament the walled garden with plaster casts mounted on rusting milk churns. 'Duncan, like a sailor, was always quietly occupied with some task of his own invention.'[12] He and Vanessa were both interested at this time in doing woodcuts, for there had been talk of publishing a book of woodcuts soon after the Woolfs bought a printing press in 1917. Some early Hogarth Press pamphlets bore woodcuts, two by Vanessa ornamenting Virginia's story 'Kew Gardens'. But the idea for a book of them was dropped when Vanessa realised that Leonard insisted on having the final word on the layout.[13] Instead, their interest in woodcuts was fostered by the Omega, Duncan designing and cutting a woodcut for the cover of an Omega exhibition catalogue in 1918. That year Roger Fry also decided that Omega artists should produce a book of woodcuts. Duncan and Vanessa fell to work eagerly. Duncan produced three for this venture, only two of which – *Hat Shop* and *The Tub* – appeared in *Original Woodcuts by Various Artists*, printed by Richard Madley on behalf of the Omega in an edition of seventy-five copies.[14]

Duncan's *Hat Shop* gave Fry an insight into his temperament and needs. He wrote to Vanessa:

I think I'd felt, going about London with Duncan, more than ever how wonderful his visual life is, how infinitely quick he is in his reaction to sight, how he misses the point of nothing. He can look at every face in the street and never miss one that has something in it, and all the time be seeing the whole effect and all with such a curious imaginative intensity. I think his *Hat Shop* is wonderful and typical of what's best and most characteristic in him . . . There's a point not exactly of wit but of delicate and half-humorous fantasy about it. It's splendid as coherence of form, but that's not all the point. He ought to *flâner* in London or Paris for at least two hours every day. He ought never to shut himself up in the country. He ought always to watch for a subject . . . with a definite point . . . only such a subject inspires him to the best of his purely formal sensibility.[15]

At Charleston aesthetic concerns inevitably mingled with practical matters. A house without electricity or central heating requires considerable labour to make it habitable and it is unlikely that without the advantage of cheap domestic labour Charleston would have become such a significant Bloomsbury outpost. Carrington, though she did once find a dead rat in the house, admired Charleston greatly. She spent only one day there in the summer of 1918, but it was enough to inspire her for some time to come. 'I have been so excited ever since I saw those artists at Charleston, and their work,' she told Virginia. 'I would not have missed that one day for any attractions you literary people can offer me!'[16]

Perennially there arose what both Virginia and Vanessa called 'the servant problem'. It was not easy to find staff willing to live in such a remote spot. Though Mrs Brereton, who lived at Charleston for the better part of 1918 with her daughter, proved a competent governess, she took a dislike to a maid called Emily who came from the slums of Glasgow. She, too, brought a child with her, a baby who crawled round the kitchen at Charleston in a filthy state. Mrs Brereton thought Emily lazy and slack and let her know it. Emily, hot-tempered and clumsy, responded by creating hysterical scenes. She also stole sugar (then rationed) and had finally to be sacked. The situation grew calmer when in September a temporary cook-housekeeper was found in a Mrs Hammond, who produced delicious meals and kept the house in apple-pie order. But periods of domestic harmony were, during the war years, few and far between.

That autumn Vanessa, while coming downstairs, lost the heel on one of her shoes and fell heavily on her side. She was now six months pregnant and a couple of days later, while staying at Durbins with Roger, she began to bleed. Over the next few weeks she took great precautions. She stayed longer with Roger than she intended, delaying her arrival at

Gordon Square, for she had planned on having one last visit to London, free of household cares, before the baby was born. 'Otherwise,' she told Maynard, 'I'm sure the baby will turn out to be Martha. Duncan takes it very seriously and says embryos can hear and that I must go to a lot of good music!'[17]

Duncan, meanwhile, was hoping to take over the lease on Sickert's studio at 21 Fitzroy Street. He gained access and there, with Nina Hamnett and a young South African artist who had recently joined the Omega, Edward Wolfe, made an elaborate nude pastel of Bunny. He had also lunched with Lady Cunard and as a result vowed never again to move in high society. 'The Duchess of Westminster, Lady Essex, etc., etc. The stupidity and ugliness but above all the bad taste were appalling.'[18] But such occasions had their advantages and Duncan walked away with an introduction to a dealer who had in his gallery a Gauguin more superb than any other picture by this artist that Duncan had ever seen.

The chief delight that autumn, however, was the Diaghilev Ballet. 'There is no genius in it this year,' Maynard had warned Duncan, referring to the absence of Nijinsky, who had parted company with Diaghilev, 'but all the same it is most enjoyable. The leading lady, Lopokova, is poor. But the new Nijinski [sic] – Mr Idzikovsky . . . has a charm or two.'[19] When Duncan arrived in London in September it was to find that Maynard had booked the Royal Box at Covent Garden for just themselves; at least, they would have sat in solitary splendour had they not met Lady Ottoline beforehand, with Dorothy Brett and a Huxley in tow, all of whom joined them in the box. The most popular item that year on the programme was *The Good Humoured Ladies*, based on a Goldoni comedy and choreographed by Massine to music by Scarlatti, in which the star was Lydia Lopokova, a dancer who may at first have failed to impress the man who was to become her second husband, but who in this ballet proved her ability to convey a variety of emotions, from pathos to comic gaiety, using her hands and arms in a way that no other dancer had attempted.

After the programme ended Lady Ottoline insisted on introducing Duncan and Maynard to Diaghilev. Duncan was amused to observe that, despite all her attempts to attach Diaghilev to her court (she was taking him to see the pictures at Hampton Court next day), Ottoline was no match for the wife of the Belgian Ambassador, Mme Lalla Vandervelde, who suddenly appeared, bore down on Diaghilev, embraced him and, holding the lapels of his coat, forcibly led him away. There were, however, other pleasures in store. With the rest of the party Duncan went backstage, where they were ushered into a small dressing-room to be introduced in turn to 'a little creature in a kimono ... Madame Lapohkova [sic] – the principal ballerina. She was absolutely charming without any sort of sham feelings and perfect manners and very pretty and intelligent looking, painted still with blue eyebrows.'[20] So Duncan's account to Vanessa ran on, mentioning also that he had taken quite a fancy to Massine, who invited Duncan to see those of his pictures that he had brought with him from Rome. In turn Massine accepted an invitation to see the paintings hanging at 46 Gordon Square.

After the excitement of this visit to the ballet, Duncan spent a slightly gloomy weekend alone at Gordon Square, its vast rooms heated only by small wood fires. 'I suffered intensely from the cold,' he wrote to Bunny, 'but amused myself with *Mansfield Park* which is *frightfully* good.'[21] He was also looking forward to beginning work on decorations for the first-floor sitting-room, which Maynard had commissioned from him and Vanessa. As it turned out Vanessa, when she arrived in London, thought it wiser to confine her contributions to advice from the sofa, and it was the young Edward Wolfe who assisted Duncan with the decoration of the doors, fireplace and shutters. Not a whisper of these decorations remains *in situ* today, but four cupboard doors were later removed from the room, kept by Keynes and today hang in King's College, Cambridge. Each of these is embellished with a decoration representative of a country – England, France, Italy and Turkey. In the upper panel two figures stand either side of a cartouche, behind which can be glimpsed an architectural scene. Below, in the lower panels, are still-lifes based on the breakfasts particular to each country.

While Vanessa was present, Maynard, with typical generosity, ordered a landau and horse so that she could get out and about. Molly MacCarthy, who was present when it arrived, joined Vanessa, Duncan and Maynard in the landau. They bowled round Regent's Park, down Baker Street, through Hyde Park and back through the great squares of Mayfair and those north of Oxford Street. Duncan adored it – 'a most curious sensation,' he afterwards told Bunny, 'everything looked totally different from usual, and the little boys laughed at us'.[22]

Before he left for a brief visit to Dartford to see his parents, Duncan attended the season's first night of *Scheherazade* and a party given by the Sitwells in honour of the Diaghilev Ballet, afterwards admitting to Lytton that because of the cakes filled with melting pears and cherries, it had been for him principally an affair of the stomach. Lopokova was the principal guest. Maynard, who was also present, began to appreciate her more. A few days later he went again to the ballet, this time taking

Edward Wolfe, both men visiting Lopokova in her dressing-room afterwards. She made them pinch her legs to see how strong she was, which they did shyly. Maynard regretted that Clive was not present to enjoy the situation. His own interest, as well as Wolfe's, was principally in Idzikovsky. When they enquired after him, Lydia, hearing Idzikovsky's voice in the corridor, told them to call him and in came a tiny figure with a pasty face and peaked features. Maynard noticed that no one took him seriously, and after he left Lydia said that she did not like dancing with him: 'It is not nice to dance with something only up to your breasts and I am always afraid he will drop me!'[23]

With the collapse that autumn of the peace proposals, Duncan and Bunny grimly braced themselves for another winter of farmwork. However, Maynard, who spent the last weekend of October at Charleston, remained optimistic about peace, believing the Germans more beaten than was apparent and therefore ready to accept almost any terms. The other guest that weekend was Duncan's mother who, though now in her mid-fifties, had no trace of grey in her hair and carried herself magnificently. To his own mother, Bunny wrote, 'Mrs Grant is such a lovely creature and is extremely like Duncan but her mind! At the South Pole . . . that is to say *concrete*.'[24] Later, when writing his autobiography, he forgot his irritation and remembered only her impressive presence:

> About her was that indescribable quality which women only have who have been greatly loved all their lives, and who have always known that they were beautiful. She was not in the least intellectual, but had that rich warmth which comes to women who have created the world they wanted around them, in face of all sorts of difficulties. She was very straightforward, not subtle, but with humour.[25]

Much of the talk that weekend concerned Lytton who, after years of straitened living (his annual income – one hundred pounds – had been supplemented by another hundred from Harry Norton), had become the toast of the season owing to the success of *Eminent Victorians*. Had farmwork not left Duncan in an exhausted state, he would have been prepared for this turn of events, but when Lytton had offered his friends a glimpse into the book he was writing – by reading passages aloud at Charleston – Duncan had fallen asleep.

In November the war tumbled suddenly to an end. When the Armistice was announced on 11 November Duncan and Bunny grabbed their bicycles and headed off for the first train to London, to join in the street celebrations. Reaching Gordon Square they learnt of an open house party at Monty Shearman's flat in the Adelphi, which had begun that morning and continued throughout the day. There they found many familiar faces. The heady excitement brought by the return to peace left neither Duncan nor Bunny inclined to work when they returned to the farm the next day, though officially they could not be released from farm labour until demobilised.

In fact, at Vanessa's request, Bunny stayed at Charleston until the start of the following year. She was anxious, as the arrival of her baby and Christmas drew near, to have him at hand, to help with the cutting of logs and so on, should Duncan go away and Clive be unable to visit.

There was no shortage of males in Vanessa's vicinity, but to the outsider, perhaps, no obvious father of the expected child. As she was married and already a mother, her social position protected her from gossip and allowed those who were not intimate with her to assume that the father was Clive. 'By the way Vanessa is going to have another child,' Bunny wrote to his mother. 'It will have an auspicious birth – born to be loved by a great many people.'[26] Not least by Clive, who had shown no resentment at the idea of Vanessa having Duncan's baby. Moreover he took steps to secure for the forthcoming child the same financial advantages that his own two children enjoyed, by keeping its illegitimacy a secret from his wealthy parents. 'It's worth taking some trouble to preserve our lien on the Bell millions,' he commented.[27] As soon as the baby was born, he suggested, a telegram should be sent to his mother from Charleston by Duncan, signed with Clive's name. He, too, he presumed, would receive a telegram, after which he would write to his parents with the news. Until then he would remain in London where he was working on a book, but he promised to spend a week at Charleston after the baby was born in order to 'write letters, impress the nurse and doctor, and generally make things respectable'.[28] In the meantime Vanessa, as if needing still more assurance, wrote to Maynard, 'I shan't see you I suppose, shall I, before the creature arrives probably? But you'll come as soon as you possibly can to give us both your blessing won't you? Oh lord, how sulky I shall feel if it's a girl!'[29]

The silence cast over the child's paternity extended even to Duncan. He duly informed Clive of the baby's arrival in a letter that gives no hint that he himself was the father. Perhaps he was wary of offending Clive's sensitivity by exulting in parenthood. Whatever the reason, he refers neither to 'my child' nor 'our child', terms that might have indicated a possessive instinct:

My dear Clive, Nessa's daughter was born on Christmas Day about 2

a.m. Nessa is remarkably well and so is the baby who weighed 7½ lbs.
I am occasionally allowed to see Nessa as you are not here and the
nurse is very strict. V. wishes me to give you her love and ask you to
put the fact in the *Times* newspaper, as she wishes to get congratulations and advertisement samples of Nestle's milk, etc. Also she has not
let your parents know, because she did not know where they thought
you were. Will you see to that?

Maynard has been here and goes this morning. We walked over to
Asheham yesterday. Virginia of course is delighted it is a girl and so I
think is Vanessa really.[30]

It had in fact been a more agitating experience than Duncan's letter
conveyed. He and Bunny had spent most of Christmas Eve afternoon and
evening sitting in Charleston's garden room, which had doors opening on
to the walled garden. When the big, coarse local doctor came down to
announce that Mrs Bell had been delivered of a daughter, Duncan had
gone up to see both mother and child. Bunny did not see the baby till the
next day and was rather shocked by how small she was. Over the next few
days there was much bicycling into Lewes for a breast pump and other
items from the chemist, for it soon became evident that the baby was
ailing. Orange juice had given her green motions. The doctor now
displayed his ignorance by prescribing dilute carbolic and the baby
shrank visibly, mewing pitifully, though stopping abruptly on one
occasion when Duncan began whistling a tune by Beethoven. With
Vanessa's permission, Bunny telephoned Noel Olivier, who was now a
fully qualified doctor. Unable to come herself, she sent a friend, a tall,
strapping, breezy young woman called Dr Marie Moralt, who instantly
inspired confidence and realised what was the matter. She altered the
baby's diet and after two days, during which matters seemed to be
stationary, the baby began to gain weight. Horror and despair receded as
normality returned.

Duncan's instinctive way of paying homage to his daughter was to
draw her. He did so, his agile line catching the jerking movement of the
child's naked limbs. Vanessa initially registered her as Helen Vanessa, but
after a month paid a fee to have the name officially changed to Angelica
Vanessa. Twenty-one years later Angelica asked Bunny for an account of
the first few days of her life. After recounting the problems, he wrote:

then you began to put on weight wonderfully and Duncan from being
some sort of ghost became himself again and Vanessa began to feel
happy and strong. I had to talk to Moralt in the evenings which as we
didn't like each other was difficult. She had asthma, felt injured by life,

and had an old mother. She attached herself for ever to Vanessa. For it was the one great action of her life. A heavy tiresome woman, she achieved greatness by saving your life. Vanessa could never be unkind to her after that.[31]

Bunny had known Angelica for less than twenty-four hours when he conceived the idea of marrying her. As he watched her being weighed in a shoe box on the kitchen scales on Christmas Day he marvelled at her perfection, detecting already signs of intelligence and an independent will. Still more a product than a person in his mind, she caught his imagination. 'Its beauty is the remarkable thing about it,' he told Lytton. 'I think of marrying it; when she is twenty I shall be 46 – will it be scandalous?'[32] Whether or not he mentioned this idea to Duncan at the time is not known. Its light-heartedness would anyway soon have been forgotten in the anxieties that followed over Angelica's weight loss. While the crisis lasted, Julian and Quentin were banished, first to their aunt and uncle at Richmond and then to Clive at Gordon Square. While they remained with the Woolfs, Duncan sent news and practical advice ('If you blow out the children's night light when you go to bed it will last some days . . .').[33] Meanwhile *The Times* Births section announced on 31 December 1918, in the conventional wording of the day, 'On Christmas Day at Charleston, Firle, Sussex, the wife of Clive Bell, of a daughter.'

'Such pandemonium as has reigned here for the last month must I think have equalled that at the Peace Conference,' Vanessa wrote to Maynard in January 1919; '. . . both the baby and I almost met our deaths at the hands of the Lewes doctor. After a fearful struggle with his ignorance, obstinacy and incredible rashness, she is now on the high road to recovery and I am practically well, thanks to the nurse's careful and pessimistic disposition and finally to the appearance on the scenes of Noel's friend Miss Moralt.' But the 'servant problem' had still to be resolved: Vanessa discovered that the maid and cook, Nellie Boxall, who had been lent to her by the Woolfs during this time of crisis, had written a letter in which Charleston was described as a 'wash-out'; Emily had left without warning or asking for a reference, taking her small child with her (Duncan found it a relief to have only one baby in the house). Given all the complications and expense of servants, Vanessa had good reason to value Maynard's friendship and his contribution towards Charleston's running costs. 'I have no room to thank you,' her letter ended, 'for all your financial strokes of genius but I see I shall be devoutly thankful for them.'[34]

In early January Clive paid his first visit to Charleston since the arrival of the baby. He could not endure illness and absented himself from sick-rooms, even those of his nearest and dearest. Fortunately, with the nurse and Marie Moralt living in the house, little was expected of him and he became slightly bored, as he admitted to Mary Hutchinson: 'What news should I have to send from a house where I sit in doors all day only faring forth to help Duncan chop up wood; I read some books, and get no work done.'[35] While Clive remained at Charleston, Duncan made a visit to his parents. He also took Julian and Quentin, who left Richmond on 9 January to spend about a week at Gordon Square, to the Tower of London, where the armour, guns and crowns were a great success.

Clive's second visit to Charleston, towards the end of January, was made festive by some cakes which he brought with him as a gift from Ka Cox. A delicious tea was eaten in Vanessa's bedroom, the gossip ending when the nurse brought in a much healthier baby for her bath. Duncan drew her, while Clive made an excellent impression on the nurse, who remarked of him that it was rare to see a father take such an interest in a baby. Duncan reported this conversation to Bunny verbatim, as if unaware of any irony. His own feelings towards Angelica were acute, and if she had a bad night or showed any sign of illness he was upset, surprising himself with instincts that he had not previously known were there. From the close intimacy of Vanessa's bedroom he went out into the fields with Clive for a walk. 'It was very still,' he told Bunny, 'and dripping and the sheep's bells were very varied in their notes.'[36]

His affair with Bunny had not ended but it was drawing to a close. Its final stages were recorded by Bunny in his diary. 'Duncan's feelings for me have altered very considerably since Christmas. It is not that he is not fond of me but that he feels I am in some way a weight – a drag, a bore, and that he feels his path is not mine.'[37] Bunny was himself looking elsewhere for emotional involvement. While visiting his parents he began an affair with a cousin, a young woman called Rayne, who worked as a professional gardener for the Duchess of Marlborough. When Bunny returned to Charleston it was with Rayne in tow. She helped with the garden, but at mealtimes, when seated beside Duncan, seemed suddenly coarse and uninteresting to Bunny. Vanessa thought her 'exactly like a wooden figure out of Noah's Ark or an over-sized doll who has been on a farm too'.[38] Bunny nevertheless clung to this affair, for, as he wrote in his diary, 'without her I should be in an almost suicidal condition of misery and despair, feeling myself outside everything which I have been inside of for so long'.[39] He suddenly felt that the only person in Bloomsbury on whom he could count as a real friend was Duncan. He trusted still in

Duncan's loyalty and love, yet it was the failure of their relationship that was driving him out.

There were occasional *rapprochements*, sudden emotional scenes that ended with Bunny once again lying in Duncan's arms. Even when he left Charleston at the end of January to work in a bookshop in Museum Street and live with his father at Pond Place, he continued to make return visits, often in Rayne's company. Much serious work was done in the garden that spring, but indoors a near-farcical situation arose, owing to the uncertainty as to who was with whom in which room, Bunny taking advantage of Rayne on the sofa in the drawing-room while Duncan talked with Vanessa upstairs. Duncan still cared enough about Bunny to enter Rayne's bedroom one evening pretending to look for a bag, but wanting to know if Bunny was with her. When Rayne disarmed him by publicly announcing at breakfast one morning that she and Bunny were in love, Duncan wrote an angry letter to Bunny warning him that he might soon tire of a woman who seemed to be about Julian's age in ripeness of intellect and experience, and that what seemed attractive to Bunny now would surely bore him as she became more dependent on him.

Towards the end of May Bunny turned up at Charleston unexpectedly, his mother having read a telegram for him inaccurately and leading him to think he would be welcome, when the house was in fact full of visitors, including Clive, Mary Hutchinson, Osbert Sitwell and the small, dark-haired painter Edward Wolfe, whom Bunny found in bed with Duncan, a situation that may have arisen for practical rather than sexual reasons.[40] Bunny, shocked by this discovery, announced that he would sleep in his tent in the paddock. Wolfe followed him downstairs, troubled by Bunny's wounded manner. Soon afterwards Duncan appeared and a scene occurred in which he vented his irritation with Bunny for turning up without warning. Feeling furiously jealous of Wolfe, Bunny lost all control and told Duncan that he never wanted to see him, or Charleston, again. For two nights he slept in the paddock and during the day spent much of his time walking alone on the Downs. But by the end of the weekend this emotional storm had passed. On Monday, after Vanessa, Clive and Mary Hutchinson left for London, Bunny forgot his anger, as his diary records: 'Duncan and I spent a happy day together in the orchard and a siesta in the afternoon . . . we completely made up for our quarrel and separation.' In this happier state of mind, Bunny saw his situation differently: 'In point of fact the only person I want to live with and to see continually is Duncan. Why then am I so sore about being an outcast from Bloomsbury? I have got Duncan to some extent much more than Bloomsbury has.'[41]

Now that Duncan was no longer confined to Charleston as a farm labourer, he often joined Bloomsbury gatherings in London. Virginia began to form an image of him. After visiting a Sickert exhibition in February 1919, she went with Clive and Mary Hutchinson to Verreys, a café in Regent Street. 'Duncan passed through – a strange shaggy interlude, but always and inevitably harmonious.'[42] He blinked, crumbled his brioche, gulped down his coffee, 'hoisted himself into an astonishing long black coat, like a non-conformist minister, hitched down his red waistcoat, and started off in a vague determined way to Victoria Station'.[43] A day later this picture of Duncan was re-created, slightly elaborated and possibly less exact, in a letter to Vanessa. It ends with Duncan joining Virginia's menagerie of friends. 'He is more and more like a white owl perched upon a branch and blinking at the light, and shuffling his soft furry feet in the snow – a wonderful creature, you must admit, though how he ever gets through life – but as a matter of fact he gets through it better than any of us.'[44]

Various plans were in the air now that peace had returned. The Omega was enjoying a revival, owing to a demand for more furniture than the shops could supply, as very little had been produced during the war. Fry had the idea of buying up second-hand furniture in country sales, much of it simple and basic, but which could be adapted to chic, modern sitting-rooms by the addition of paint. There was also a demand for hats, some of which Duncan designed, others which he decorated with paint. Roger hung an exhibition of Mikhail Larionov's marionette designs at the Omega and published an article in the *Burlington Magazine* on Natalia Goncharova and Larionov's work for the Russian Ballet. But his chief ambition was to disappear to France and paint, which partly explains why in June 1919 he decided to hold a clearance sale and close the Workshops down. One who benefited from this sale was Bunny. Roger sold him several Omega tables at a very cheap rate for use in the bookshop that he and Francis Birrell had started in Taviton Street, on the ground floor of a house owned by Roger's friend, Margaret Bulley. A venture had now ended which Duncan, many years later, likened to a party. 'One was often on one's own. And then the crowds would come in on one. It was tremendously encouraging. I think it was the best period of my life.'[45]

Though it was not immediately apparent, a wave of conservatism followed the return to peace. In April 1919 Roger admitted to Vanessa that 'the only picture of yours which has gone thin on my hands is that big abstract business which I have in my studio and which doesn't mean anything to me now'.[46] Neither Duncan nor Vanessa showed any interest at this time in pursuing their earlier experiments with abstraction.

Instead there was in Duncan's work a return to figurative subjects which, whether seen or half-invented, religious or mythological, displayed that 'delicate and half-humorous fantasy' that Roger admired.[47] Key works in this vein were *Juggler and Tightrope Walker*, *The Baptism* and *Venus and Adonis*,[48] all of which made adroit use of distortion and imaginative colour. Duncan painted with great urgency during the summer of 1919, feeling a need to make up for lost time. Charleston in June, he discovered, was an oasis of calm, comfort, light and leisure, and he worked hard, as the Paterson-Carfax Gallery in London had offered to give him his first solo exhibition. In August he turned again to Delacroix's *Journals* and would have re-encountered this artist's belief that in a painter it is the imagination that speaks before all else.

He still turned his hand readily to decorative schemes, that year enlivening a gramophone trumpet at Charleston with myriad colours. According to David Garnett, Duncan was always buying and playing gramophone records, Mozart especially, and if there was a piano in a house he was always attracted to it, though shy of playing in front of others. Almost certainly his love of music stimulated him as a painter, quickening his sense of rhythm, phrasing and interval. He was also an excellent dancer. A certain histrionic streak revealed itself at parties, not only when he danced but also when he improvised a character or when, fearless of all ridicule, he became a ballet dancer and partnered Lydia Lopokova in an entertainment for his friends.

Vanessa now arranged to take over Alix Sargant-Florence's flat at 36 Regent Square as her London *pied-à-terre*, the lease on 46 Gordon Square having been transferred to Maynard. It still remained Duncan's base on his visits to London, but under Maynard's stewardship it no longer suited Clive, who now took rooms in 50 Gordon Square. While this reshuffling went on, Vanessa, planning to spend the next winter in London, took pains to ensure that Charleston could be maintained as their country home. She was glad to find a young gardener called Daniel Johnson, who not only cleaned out the yards and outhouses, pumped water for the house and cut wood for the fires, but also produced a mother willing to clean the house and live in during the winter. The source of such good fortune was a young cook called Jenny. She had insisted that her young man should be installed as gardener, and after her wish came true the kitchen was always spotless and the cooking delicious. 'I think it's worth while getting this house and garden into good order,' Vanessa told Maynard, 'and having good servants. Life is too intolerable without.'[49] An added satisfaction was that Angelica's limbs were now decidedly plump. Vanessa's purse, however, was empty and, owing to some disagreement between Clive and his family, no Bell settlement on Angelica had yet come through. Duncan, now painting hard, offered Vanessa huge sums of money as soon as his fortune was made. Of more practical help, however, was the cheque for £200 that fell out of her next letter from Maynard. As usual it was cunningly presented in a way that could not be refused. 'I felt I oughtn't to take it but Duncan says I can't refuse money given to my daughter and I suppose he knows about such things.'[50]

Gradually, during the course of the year, Duncan regained a sense of his position and direction as an artist. In December 1918 Roger had published in the *Burlington Magazine* the article 'Line as a Means of Expression in Modern Art'. Among its illustrations was a pencil study that Duncan had made for the standing figure of the right-hand side of *The Kitchen*.[51] It reveals a thinking eye, for outlines are pursued only in so far as they provide the information he needs. He then abruptly breaks off, abandons outline, and uses areas of hatching to define the shapes that interest him. Perception is translated into graphic marks with great directness, speed and vitality, and without any attempt to prettify, impress or seduce. The quality that Fry admired in the Matisse drawings shown at the Second Post-Impressionist Exhibition – 'a tremulous intensity of life and a rhythmic harmony which fascinates by its daring'[52] – is also found here. Carrington, after seeing this drawing, wrote to Bunny, 'Give Duncan my love. Tell him I liked his drawing in the *Burlington Magazine* very much indeed. And reverence him for drawing it.'[53]

Matisse was still very much in Duncan's mind at this time: Carrington spotted Duncan at the Leicester Galleries that year, trying to persuade Maynard to buy a Matisse. He also went with Vanessa to the home of the collector, Monty Shearman, specifically to see a Matisse; and in November of that year he saw his own work exhibited alongside that of Matisse and Picasso as well as other French and English artists in Cambridge, in the premises of the *Cambridge Magazine*, at 6 King's Parade.

For Bunny, Duncan willingly designed a cover for his and Francis Birrell's first catalogue of second-hand books. 'My dear, I often think of you,' he wrote to Bunny in August 1919; 'I hope you do sometimes of me. I'm rather depressed about my painting but otherwise content enough.'[54] Bunny remembered all too well how, whenever Duncan began work on a big picture, there was always a period of strain and anguish when it was about two-thirds finished.

If relations between the two men remained uneasily familiar, those between Bunny and Vanessa broke down entirely that summer. Vanessa, tired by the practical difficulties that grew apace at Charleston and the responsibilities imposed on her by her family, and longing for a change of scene, lost her temper with Bunny on one of his visits to Charleston, afterwards apologising to him for her want of self-control: 'There is really no reason now as far as I'm concerned why we should be at daggers drawn when we meet but once one begins such a course it's very hard to get out of it. But I think I can simply be on ordinary friendly terms with you. It is absurd and painful not to be.'[55]

She was not alone in her need of a holiday. In the spring of 1919 Keynes had been a part of the British delegation during the peace negotiations in Paris. Convinced that the terms concerning German indemnity were outrageous and would only lead to more disorder and unrest, he returned home determined to alleviate the feelings that the peace conference had inspired in him by writing *The Economic Consequences of the Peace*. He enjoyed a period at Cambridge and by July had written almost eight chapters of the book. 'But writing is very difficult, and I feel more and more admiration for those who can bring it off successfully.'[56] He continued to work on this book during his visits to Charleston and that summer, like Duncan, grew alarmed at the extent to which the brunt of all hardships and responsibility fell on Vanessa. He even proposed taking over responsibility for the housekeeping, the ordering of food and paying of bills, leaving Vanessa to deal only with day-to-day problems as they arose.

Though Vanessa did get to see Diaghilev's *La Boutique Fantasque* with designs by Derain that summer, she missed the famous dinner party that Maynard and Clive held in July at 46 Gordon Square to which came Picasso, his wife Olga, and other figures associated with the Diaghilev Ballet. Duncan attended the dinner and would have had other opportunities to renew his friendship with Picasso, as the Spaniard stayed three months in London, visited the Omega, where he admired the pottery, and with Derain accepted informal hospitality from Roger. At the Gordon Square dinner party there had been a deliberate policy to exclude any too dominating personality. As a result, Duncan was aware of Lady Ottoline's injured air when he met her at the preview to an exhibition that Osbert and Sacheverell Sitwell had organised at Heal's Mansard Gallery. This was the first major post-war exhibition of modern French art in London and it made a considerable impact. Duncan found himself admiring two Matisses, a couple of Picassos, some Derains and discovering much interest in the work of other young painters. But his interest in the modern never crowded out his need for the Old Masters and he was equally excited that summer to see at the Sackville Gallery, London, Poussin's great painting showing the Israelites sacrificing to the Golden Calf (now in the National Gallery, London), the foreground frieze of dancing figures satisfying his love of patterned movement. In addition in the same gallery were some early Sienese panel paintings which, he told Vanessa, 'gave me more pleasure than anything I've seen for a long time'.[57]

Earlier that year Roger Fry sold Durbins and moved back to London, to a house in Dalmeny Avenue in Holloway. It had a vast garden and a substantial greenhouse with a grotto inside. Duncan, on his first visit, was instantly envious. 'There are subjects galore for the brush,' he told Vanessa, 'only I rather wish it wouldn't all be Roger's.'[58] This tiny aside confirms what Roger felt: that he had somehow fallen away and was no longer a part of Bloomsbury's central core.

Hopes were now pinned not on London but Paris as the source of new ideas. Clive's letters from the French capital did much to promote this view. 'The activity and excitement of the painters here is unheard of: here seems to be no end of pictures and picture-dealers. It all impresses me a good deal – even their passions and jealousies. I imagine Florence in the fifteenth century must have been something like it.'[59] He urged Vanessa and Duncan to plan a spring visit to Paris, assuring them that Duncan would find that he had more friends there than he realised. 'Everyone who saw *Twelfth Night* remembers it with pleasure; and I have got it firmly into the heads of the French artists that he is the interesting man in England – how furious the others will be when they find out.'[60]

In Paris, Clive frequented the Deux Magots and regularly saw Picasso, Derain, Marchand and Segonzac, as well as the poet and dealer Charles Vildrac and André Gide. Through Picasso he met Cocteau and Satie, and was delighted to find that he himself had a slight reputation in this city. His letters glow with satisfaction. 'My life here is so fantastically successful that I blush to tell of it,' he wrote to Vanessa. 'The *Nouvelle Revue* and *Le Temps* have asked me to write for them. Gide says the translation of my book [*Art*] will be an "*événement littéraire et artistique*". I am invited to lunch and dine every day; and, naturally, enjoyed [*sic*] myself. Bloomsbury is altogether to the fore – the name of Grant is pronounced with respect amongst the artists, that of Keynes amongst the intellectuals, that of Lytton Strachey among the *lettres* . . .'[61]

If this news was encouraging, it did not distract from the burst of productivity that Duncan enjoyed that autumn. He stayed on at Charleston in October after Vanessa and the children had moved back to London, as he was anxious to finish certain pictures. He seemed momentarily unable to abandon the past, reluctant to exchange the tranquillity of rural Sussex for London's noisy bustle. In his art he had reached a parting of the ways. Even in his imaginative works, such as *Juggler and Tightrope Walker*, he was now painting with great solidity, as if wanting to bring his fantasies down to earth. His work shared in the widespread 'return to order' that characterised the post-war period. Even the former Futurist, C. R. W. Nevinson, in the December 1919 issue of *Studio*, was quoted saying, 'The immediate need of the art today is a Cézanne, a reactionary, to lead art back to the academic traditions of the Old Masters, and save contemporary art from abstractions, as Cézanne saved Impressionism from "effects".'[62]

But for Duncan a more immediate concern that autumn was the state of his teeth. Before leaving Charleston he bicycled into Eastbourne with Bunny, had three teeth filled and the rest polished with a new electric circular brush. Afterwards he warned Vanessa that he would be arriving in London with a smile like that of the actress Zena Dare.

FOURTEEN

A Question of Labels

Duncan's first solo exhibition in February 1920, at the Paterson-Carfax Gallery in Old Bond Street, marked a turning point in his career. He already had admirers among museum officials, critics and collectors, and the year before he had begun exhibiting with the London Group; but so far his work had only been seen spasmodically, in rather esoteric shows and at the Omega. The Paterson-Carfax exhibition was the first opportunity that the public had to get a just measure of his talent. There were thirty-one pictures on show, among them farm scenes, still-lifes, portraits, mythological and imaginative subjects. No one was more pleased by this event than Duncan's mother. 'I was a proud woman yesterday,' she wrote the day after the private view. 'Your show is going to be a big success I am convinced. You will know that five pictures were sold when we got there ... I think the pictures are so well hung and when I went in the morning, with a bright sun and an empty room, the whole place seemed full of colour and joy. I felt exhilarated. Dear darling boy I am so pleased and hope you are going to make your mark at once.'[1]

Her hopes were fulfilled, though the exhibition was a mixed success. Where Duncan had treated the human body as a malleable vehicle for witty and expressive effects, as in *Juggler and Tightrope Walker* and in *Venus and Adonis*, others saw only a want of decorum. Sir Claude Phillips declared the distortions 'wilfully grotesque and absurd'. He warned readers of the *Daily Telegraph* that Duncan Grant, 'one of the most audacious and, it must be owned, one of the most brilliant of the post-impressionists, or extremists ... has challenged the unhappy citizen to face a show of the most defiant modernity'.[2] His article became a threnody on the misuse of talent. His accusations of perversity were countered by Roger Fry in the *New Statesman*. Fry admitted that some artists, in their desire for notoriety, do try to shock or astonish, but that this accusation was refuted in Grant's case by the 'transparent sincerity and simplicity' of his work. The inventive distortion in the painting called *Venus*, which so upset Sir Claude Phillips's desire for the noble and consoling, pleased Fry most for it gave new meaning to a well-worn subject. 'Whatever influences he has submitted to are all fused here into something that belongs entirely to our own age and country, and, indeed, just to one intensely individual outlook on life.'

Fry's review was not entirely favourable. He had spotted a desire on Grant's part to push his work further – 'to amplify, solidify, and deepen the expression of his vision'. In order to do this, Fry argued, he had abandoned the former brilliance of his palette, his ability 'to relate colours in such a way that each constituent colour of the chord has its full resonance and purity'; instead, his use of colour was now linked to the careful representation of density, mass and relief ('there is to be no evasion anywhere, no retiring into general or vague statements, the paint must be everywhere of the same uncompromising, flat unsuggestiveness'). Fry could not help noticing that the result, as in *Juggler and Tightrope Walker*, was a certain deadness and lack of resonance.[3]

Despite an uncertainty among the critics as to whether Duncan, as an artist, was in retreat or advance, the sales upheld his mother's prediction: twenty-four paintings sold for £855, the gallery charging 25 per cent commission and taking £213 15s from the total amount. Lytton Strachey, now flush with the money he was making from *Eminent Victorians*, paid sixty pounds for *Juggler and Tightrope Walker*, a picture that Sir Claude Phillips, disagreeing with Fry, praised for its 'delicate, brilliantly scintillating hues'. The most spirited encomium came from Clive Bell, who felt no embarrassment or moral scruple about using the press to promote the work of his closest friends. 'Duncan Grant is, in my opinion, the best English painter alive,' he boomed; '. . . Duncan Grant's ancestors are Piero della Francesca, Gainsborough and the Elizabethan poets . . . In Duncan Grant there is, I agree, something that reminds one unmistakeably of the Elizabethan poets, something fantastic and whimsical and at the same time intensely lyrical.'[4]

Virginia Woolf went to see the exhibition and found there Mrs Grant, with Colonel Young at her side. It astonished her that two people who figured so prominently in stories of Duncan's childhood and youth could suddenly be present in the flesh. She had for some time been an admirer of Duncan's work, as he was of her writing. 'What wonderful things you will be able to do with your pen loosed from all public responsibilities,' he had concluded after the Woolfs bought their own printing press.[5] In turn she had praised paintings by him that she had seen at the Omega. Now she underlined his success by reference to others. 'Ottoline yesterday was in fine feather about your show,' she remarked to Duncan, ' – the poor old thing undulated and eulogised till it really was like talking to some poor fowl in delirium – her neck became longer and longer and you know how she always hangs on to "wonderful" as if it were a rope dangling in her vacuum."[6]

In recognition of their friendship, Duncan gave Virginia a watercolour, a medium with which he was much occupied that year, for in November he exhibited twenty-one watercolours alongside sixteen by Vanessa at the Independent Gallery at 7a Grafton Street, which simultaneously displayed work by the French artist Robert Lotiron. Among Duncan's watercolours were three studies after Renoir. (He had greatly admired *Les Parapluies* when it went on show at the National Gallery in 1917.) But it was the influence of Matisse that the critics noticed in the work of both artists. A more telling observation, however, was that Duncan had virtually suppressed the use of outline, preferring to imply form by an infinite variety of lights. The Independent Gallery remained Duncan's chief outlet for the next few years. Its owner, Percy Moore Turner, had formerly run a gallery in Paris and took an active interest in contemporary art, holding mixed shows of French artists as well as solo exhibitions representing, for example, Friesz in 1921, Marchand in 1922 and Segonzac in 1923. He also devoted shows to Roger, Duncan and Keith Baynes, a young painter who had joined the London Group in 1919. His interest in French art aligned him with the Bloomsbury painters, with whom he soon established friendship.

No longer hidden in the countryside, Duncan and Vanessa had returned to London as a couple. Though the exact nature of their relationship was hard to define – Duncan later told Paul Roche that its sexual aspect ended soon after Angelica's birth – the fact of this partnership was now widely recognised. The ambiguities attached to it amused Clive. 'I shall have to hurry home to dress for the opera,' he wrote to Mary Hutchinson in March 1920, 'whither I am going with Vanessa – rather scandalous as Duncan will be out of town for the night. However I assure you he has nothing to fear.'[7] If Duncan and Vanessa were not lovers in a physical sense, they nevertheless shared a strong emotional dependence. When, in mid-March, Duncan found himself one night in London listening with Vanessa to a memoir by Virginia and the next night dining with Maynard at La Pérouse in Paris, he could not help writing afterwards to Vanessa, 'I do wish you could come before Friday night.'[8]

All three had decided to spend a month in Rome, Maynard banking correctly on the fall in value of the lire, which made life in Italy very cheap. In the autumn of 1919 he had begun speculating on currencies and in January 1920 had started a syndicate that included £4,500 of Duncan's and Vanessa's money. It was still realising considerable profits when they

left for Rome and, as the value of the pound more than doubled in
relation to the lire while they were in Italy, Maynard gaily told his
companions that they had a duty to spend. Some £300 duly went on
furniture, picture frames, fabrics, gloves and crockery, all of which were
packed up and shipped back to England.

Coming so soon after wartime constrictions, this holiday took on a
greater than usual glow. Vanessa, temporarily released from household
responsibilities and the need to look after her children, found it a
welcome experience. 'Oh it was nice in Italy with you two,' she
afterwards wrote to Maynard, ' – in spite of all my ill behaviour. I don't
think I've ever enjoyed anything so much for a long time, and it still
makes me very happy to think of it.'⁹ They had taken a studio in the Via
Margutta, in an old quarter that Baedeker described as a 'haunt of artists'.
Initially a certain difficulty was presented by the landlady, who thought
that an ingenuous use of curtains would enable her still to receive her
lovers in one corner of the studio. Maynard soon addressed the problem
and matters were put on a different footing. Meanwhile the Hotel Russie,
which though comfortable Duncan disliked, gave them rooms and
provided dinner. Duncan, if lost to the world when painting a still-life in
the studio, was at other times acutely conscious of what went on around
him. 'Rome is absolutely packed,' he told Bunny who, in Duncan's
absence, was using his room at 46 Gordon Square, 'and we have great
luck in having rooms at all . . . it is packed with the Italian aristocrats who
simply love living in hotels and leaving their estates to bolsheviks in the
country. Our hotel is cram full of contessas, marchesas, principessas and
duchesses. They don't get up till lunch at one, have a siesta till about
four, eat ices and drink coffee till five when they take a drive on the
Pincio, home to dinner at 9.30. Jazz till two, even the old ladies receive till
four or five in the morning.' He was equally amazed by the flowers in
Rome. 'One can buy masses of arum lilies irises roses pansies and
marigolds for a few francs on the steps of the Piazza di Spagna.'¹⁰

Though the front door of their hotel faced the Piazza del Popolo, its
back door opened on to the winding paths and terraces that divided the
slopes of the Pincio. As he wandered here and elsewhere in this city, as
yet uncluttered with tourists, Duncan appreciated its richly seamed
historical associations. The three friends began to abandon the excellent,
if rather dull, table d'hôte at the hotel and went in search of small
restaurants. The only cloud on the horizon was that Maynard, now a
celebrity, had accepted an invitation addressed to himself and his
companions to visit Bernard Berenson at his Villa I Tatti at Settignano,
outside Florence. Though the painters suggested that it might be possible

for Maynard to go without them, he would not hear of it, so towards the end of April all three boarded a train for Florence.

When Duncan had first visited I Tatti in 1907 it had been at the invitation of Berenson's step-daughters, Ray and Karin Costello. The two girls had involved him in youthful, high-spirited, mostly outdoor activities, which meant that he saw the great man himself only at meals. Duncan had been intrigued to meet the man whose books he had read. Even then, however, he had noticed that Berenson's remarks on art and artists were in the nature of *pronunciamentos* and not to be questioned. 'I was not used to Papal etiquette, and it impressed me unfavourably.'[11] Moving down the corridors hung with early Renaissance works of art, through rooms furnished with Louis XV furniture and into the garden which, unlike most Italian gardens, offered closely shaved lawns, Duncan, as a young man, would have spent his whole visit in a state of wonder and excitement, had not certain small shocks awoken him to the suspicion that underneath this settled wealth lay dissimulation and intrigue. He had paused in front of a painting labelled 'Amico di Sandro': 'How romantic, how charming I thought – the friend was able to draw so near his master!' In time, when he saw how slippery this label could be, he began to wonder about the motivations behind Berenson's creation of an artistic identity that was to dissolve under the weight of subsequent scholarship. Still more perturbing in 1907 was the fact that when Duncan asked Berenson about an early Renaissance painting showing animals fleeing from a forest fire, Berenson at first denied that any such picture was in the house and then, when Duncan told him he had seen it, angrily declared that the young man should not have gone into that particular room.

These troubled memories make it understandable that Duncan was a little unwilling to accompany Maynard to Settignano. To complain further seemed churlish, for the weather was halycon and each day at I Tatti delicious breakfasts were brought to their extremely comfortable rooms. Then, too, there was the pleasure of living again among works of art, which, even in the entrance hall, as Kenneth Clark observed five years later, were arranged 'with an air of finality'.[12] However, they had not been long at I Tatti before Duncan felt acutely aware that something was wrong. He assumed that their friendship with Roger Fry had stirred Berenson's antipathy, for soon after the *Burlington Magazine* was founded in 1903, Berenson and Fry fell out over matters of scholarship. Everything about the connoisseur expressed his exquisite taste; he was always beautifully dressed and often wore a carnation in his button-hole. Small, neat, with impeccable manners, he must have made Duncan and

Vanessa feel shabby and disorganised. The atmosphere was such that freedom of speech was impossible, there was little spontaneity and, according to Duncan, 'the moral atmosphere was shifty, or so I felt'.[13] When Vanessa announced a liking for Raphael, Berenson conveyed astonished disapproval. Whenever possible Duncan and Vanessa escaped into Florence for the morning to look at works of art, sometimes with another guest, the poet Robert Trevelyan. Only then, while lunching in a restaurant, could they talk freely and enthusiastically about what they had seen.

One day it was announced that a party was to be given in Maynard's honour by an American collector living outside Florence, Charles Loeser. For many years he and Berenson had indulged in a collectors' feud and the party was in part an *entente cordiale*. Duncan looked forward to it, as he knew that Loeser had some ten very fine Cézannes, and he realised *en route*, as he surveyed the results of the attention that the ladies had paid to their attire, that it was an event of some significance. It was a glorious afternoon and Loeser's handsome villa gleamed with beautiful objects. Sipping ice-cold Marsala and eating cakes, Duncan marvelled at how friendly the Italians seemed, as one introduction followed another and prevented him from joining Maynard and Vanessa, who were being shown the Cézannes. When the time came to leave Duncan was in so benign a mood that he decided to forego transport and walk across the countryside to I Tatti. Just as he was crossing the terrace, Loeser came up behind him and, addressing him as 'Mr Keynes', asked if he might make one more introduction and presented the Countess Serristori. Duncan, realising that all afternoon Loeser had mistaken his identity, had only seconds in which to decide what to do. Not wanting to disappoint, hurt or make a fool of his generous host, he chose what at that moment seemed the most expedient solution. In the same way that a painting in Berenson's possession was one day labelled 'Amico di Sandro' and the next day 'Botticelli', so Duncan momentarily bore the attribution of Maynard Keynes.

Thinking it quite possible that he would never see Loeser again, Duncan kept this mistaken identity to himself, an exhilarating secret, until later that day, by which time it had become an awful burden. At dinner it had been announced that the following night a return party for the Loesers would be given at I Tatti. Duncan, though he had acted for the best, now had to confess to a mistake, not of his making but with which he had colluded. Opprobrium descended not only on himself but also, for no apparent reason except that she too was a painter, on Vanessa. The next day Duncan found himself apologising to Loeser, at the same time hating and resenting the position in which he had been placed. At this second party the urbane, wealthy guests seemed much less friendly than before. When the time came to leave Duncan noticed, as he walked down one of I Tatti's corridors, that his favourite little painting by Botticelli had been demoted and once again bore the label 'Amico di Sandro'.

Before returning to London, Duncan and Vanessa spent some time in Paris, where, earlier that year, some of their paintings had been exhibited in Charles Vildrac's Rue de Seine gallery. A lively exchange with several French artists attended their involvement with the Parisian art scene and they had no hesitation in calling on Picasso, who readily showed them his latest works. His fame had not yet become an obstacle to ordinary human intercourse and Vanessa found him likeable and very easy. It was for him a transitional period. The language of Cubism was still evident in the abstracts he showed them, but at the same time he had embarked on a neo-classical phase and Vanessa was astonished to be shown 'two nudes most elaborately finished and rounded and more definite than any Ingres'.[14] This experience would have further encouraged an inclination already visible in their work: towards greater solidity in the modelling of form. On both sides of the Channel artists were experiencing a 'return to order', putting aside the iconoclastic experimentalism of the pre-war years in favour of an attempt to reinterpret older traditions in modern terms.

After Vanessa left for England, Duncan lingered on for a few days on his own in Paris. He lunched again at La Pérouse, this time in the company of André Gide and an attractive young man, Marc Allegret. Two years before Gide had arrived in England at a critical moment in his life, in the company of Allegret. He had left his wife in France with a letter in which he had stated that he was 'rotting away' while living with her at Cuverville, and that in order to renew his creative power he needed to escape and break new ground. He left France in a state of great agony, but with an introduction from Auguste Bréal to Lady Strachey, who had taken a house in Cambridge for the summer. Her daughter, Dorothy Bussy, then aged fifty-three, was also present and when Gide mentioned that he was looking for someone to teach him English, Dorothy proposed herself as his tutor. Gide had appeared for his first lesson the very next morning and before long Dorothy fell hopelessly in love with her brilliant, sensitive pupil. She became the translator of his work into English, his correspondent and loyal friend. But she was not the only person in England to be affected by his presence that summer. Roger

Fry, too, began to look on the French writer as an old friend. 'How I should like to talk endlessly with you,' he ended one letter to Gide.[15]

Duncan, occupied with farmwork during the summer of 1918, did not get to know Gide well until his visit to Paris in 1920. The French writer invited Duncan to return to Paris in February of the following year to work with him and Copeau on a production of *Saül*. Duncan did so, and on this occasion stayed in the house where Gide was then living, the Villa Montmorency, 18 bis Avenue des Sycamores in the Auteuil district. Marc Allegret arrived every morning and the conversation between the three men became more and more open. Duncan admitted to Vanessa that he had become slightly *épris* with Marc, but that she need not worry as Allegret, he thought, preferred women and asked very tenderly after Roger's daughter, Pam. Though the *Saül* project never got off the ground, this episode allowed Duncan a further glimpse into Gide's incisive, uncompromising, subtle and egotistical mind. And it gave him further opportunity to become *au courant* with the latest developments in French art, with Picasso, Derain and the hunchback, Marie Blanchard, whose work he admired. He greatly enjoyed a visit to the Cirque Medrano in Gide's company, but when he made another visit to Paris a couple of months later, Gide sent word that owing to nerves and melancholia he was unable to see anyone.

But in the summer of 1920, when he first got to know Gide, Duncan's attention was largely given to another author, Stendhal. 'I am ravished by Beyle's correspondence in four volumes,' he told Bunny. 'Do get it for your shop if you can.'[16] He arrived back in London with two case-loads of paintings executed by Roger in France. Later that month these formed an exhibition at the Independent Gallery. Duncan and others arranged a lunch at 46 Gordon Square on the occasion of Roger's private view. Eighty-one paintings were exhibited at low prices, but very few sold. Roger reckoned he was simply not fashionable enough. He was a serious painter, sensitive and intelligent; but because he had written on Picasso and Matisse, the public were baffled to find in his pictures allusions to the classical landscape tradition.

Duncan's own painting was becoming heavier in style. That year he completed a large composition based on the three figures in the right-hand-side of his painting *The Lemon Gatherers*. It was not only the increase in scale that helped give this picture a rather ponderous grandeur, but also the weighty rhythms created by the loops and curves in the landscape and figures. He had further opportunity that summer to uncover the rhythmic potential of the human figure when he and Vanessa designed eight allegorical figures for Maynard's sitting-room in Webb's

Court, King's College, Cambridge. These covered Duncan's earlier decoration and extended further down the room, the eight panels filling most of one side wall. The figures represent Science, Political Economy, Music, Classics, Law, Mathematics, Philosophy and History. Draped female figures alternate with male nudes, each holding an object associated with one of the eight subjects. The figures, like statuary in a niche, fill the entire panel, their heads touching the upper border. The ground behind each is mottled and the border framed with a band of gold paint. But the artists' decorative concern did not stop there: in order to make this line of figures merge with the room as a whole, Duncan and Vanessa advised on its colour scheme and on the choice of curtains.

Duncan worked on these figures at Charleston during August 1920. He momentarily worried that they seemed dull. 'Life here is very quiet,' he wrote to Bunny.[17] Julian and Quentin had begun collecting moths and butterflies, and Vanessa, who was an adept, gave them a lesson in setting. The only thing that had disturbed the peace was Julian's air gun, which he had brought into the house loaded and it went off by mistake under the table at lunchtime, the bullet fortunately lodging itself in a chair rather than in someone's leg.

When Duncan visited his parents that August he discovered that one of Aunt Daisy's patients, Miss Elwes, had joined the household as a paying guest. Aunt Daisy had trained as a nurse and ran a small private nursing-home in Eastbourne for members of well-to-do families who, either for mental or physical reasons, were incapable of coping with life on their own. She had sometimes taken Miss Elwes with her when she travelled abroad, and in this way Lytton had met her in Stockholm in 1909. He noted her 'hatchet nose and slate-pencil voice' and was fascinated by her conversation. ('Never have I met a more absolutely sterile mind – and yet how wonderfully cultivated! It's like a piece of flannel with watercress growing on it.')[18] Though tinged with madness, she was very sweet-natured and restrained in manner. It was difficult to learn much about her, but once when she was away, Duncan slept in her room at Wilmington House amid her family relics, including photographs of her dead sister, a prie-dieu with a crucifix over it, many devotional pictures and three shelves of religious books, the whole room breathing refinement and old-fashioned distinction.

Another addition to the Grant household resulted from the wartime marriage of Colonel Young to a woman considerably younger than himself. They had a child and were expecting another, and, presumably for reasons of economy, agreed to share Wilmington House at Dartford with Duncan's parents. This arrangement had a depressing effect on

Duncan's father. That summer Duncan found Bartle spending most of his time alone and hardly ever speaking at meals. 'I feel very sorry for him and must try to get Virginia to give him employment,' he wrote to Vanessa, hoping that a project could emerge that would involve his father with the Hogarth Press. At the same time he was aware that the rest of the household seemed to get along without much outward trouble and was amazed at his mother's proficiency in keeping the whole thing going.

Worried by his father's unhappy state, Duncan arranged for him to spend some time in London in October so that, among other things, he could meet the Woolfs. But in December, on his Christmas visit to his parents, Duncan found that the situation at Wilmington House had reached a sorry pass, as he told Vanessa. 'I think I must seriously try and get my father a job somewhere. I had a talk with my mother this morning and I see that things are pretty desperate here. Apparently he has taken the most violent dislike to Col. Young! and wants the whole family to decamp which I think would be suicidal as all they have to live on is my father's pension of £200 and Miss Elwes's contribution of £300 a year. The present idea is to send him to Cintra for a month or so and meanwhile I shall try and get him a job as an assistant librarian or something of the sort. He only wants £100.'[19]

In January Duncan designed the cover for a small book published by Bunny and Francis Birrell under the auspices of their Birrell and Garnett bookshop, *Some Contemporary English Artists*. Among its reproductions was Duncan's *Snow in London*, a view through a balconied window with bare trees beyond. As the Birrell and Garnett bookshop records (now in the British Library) show, Duncan was a loyal customer, for he still regarded Bunny as one of his most intimate friends. Tall, upright, his prominent lips adding to his striking appearance, Bunny had gained not only a livelihood through the bookshop but also greater maturity and new friends. Margaret Bulley, the owner of 19 Taviton Street, the shop's premises, let the rest of the house to those willing to experiment with communal living. One resident was Cecily Hey, Sickert's pupil and model, who in time married Robert Tatlock, another of Miss Bulley's tenants and an editor of the *Burlington Magazine*. A third tenant was a young woman of medium height who dressed sensibly and unobtrusively. She was emphatically silent but not unexpressive: set within her broad, dark-skinned face were brown eyes that could shine with delight or glimmer with unspoken criticism. She wore her hair cut in a bob and this, combined with her fringe, heightened the impression of child-like honesty and vulnerability. Whereas some found her painfully shy, Bunny saw that, as in a wild animal, the shyness was natural and allied to a spirited awareness of others.

Ray Marshall, as she was called, had studied book illustration under Noel Rooke at the Central School of Art. She came from a large upper-middle-class professional family and already had a distant connection to Bloomsbury, her elder sister having married Lytton Strachey's nephew, Dick Rendel. Her younger sister, Frances, soon after she left Newnham College, Cambridge, in the summer of 1921, became an assistant at the Birrell and Garnett bookshop, her prettiness and habit of laughing aloud to herself making her very agreeable. What initially impressed Bunny most about Ray, however, was the fact that in 1913 she had accompanied a Russian friend to the Caucasus and travelled up the Volga to Nijni Novgorod. On numerous occasions at 19 Taviton Street Bunny tried to involve Ray in conversation in order to break through her shyness. One day he paused on the staircase with his hand resting on the banister, intending to speak to Ray as she passed. She too stopped, but the noise of footsteps coming down from above put an end to Bunny's intention. He was about to move on when Ray suddenly stroked his open palm with her finger. Bunny, walking slowly downstairs back to the bookshop, realised that he was seriously in love with her and she with him.

They married suddenly, at St Pancras Register Office on 31 March 1921, travelling there on the tram with Cecily Hey and Robert Tatlock. Whereas when Adrian Stephen had married on 21 October 1914, Duncan had put aside his prejudice against Karin and acted as witness, he was not present at Bunny's wedding and may not even have known about it until afterwards.

As with Mallory's engagement, Duncan felt as if a door had been shut in his face. Bunny's attempts to suggest that nothing had fundamentally altered only angered him. 'It is a ridiculous argument that there is no difference between a liaison and a legal marriage,' Duncan wrote in April:

> A liaison is a relation between two individuals with no contract and no reality in the eyes of the world. A legal marriage is at once a reality in the eyes of the world of the most odious sort (in my opinion) and it is impossible I should say to escape the pyramid that the world builds up every day round a personal relationship and which it is humanly impossible for your instincts to square.

He could not now see Bunny alone, he went on, without being aware that Ray had superior claims on his attention, nor could he any longer feel at liberty to express his feelings or opinions confidentially:

After all this *is* an event in your life however much you pretend it isn't, and ... there must be no pretentions or reserves if our relation is to remain anything at all. You needn't mind hurting my feelings any more – that's done with and it only remains for me to settle down which I assuredly shall and very soon I could see you once or twice alone and at our ease. You are perfectly right to say that I don't want to see you necessarily very often. I have quite a full and interesting life. But ... a good deal of my happiness depends on something you can give me. But it must be alive and not dead. I would rather have the memory than a corpse and to keep it alive you *must* understand my feelings even if you disapprove of them.[20]

After this outburst Duncan was further upset to learn that Bunny and Ray wanted to begin having a family. 'I cannot in future have any confidence that you will discuss anything with me before it is too late,' he bitterly concluded.[21]

Despite his anger he managed over the next two months to initiate and complete a portrait of Ray that was his wedding present to them both. It is dark, mournful and airless, and very thoroughly painted. The sitter's large brown eyes stare out with disturbing intensity. Far from celebrating the happiness of a young woman about to be married, the portrait suggests a melancholy acceptance of her fate. With the knowledge of hindsight her watchful, reserved, almost accusatory passivity seems to carry a premonition of her early death. Duncan, himself, may have intended an expression of fatality, as he made the ambiguous remark to Bunny that Ray had sat 'like cream cheese on a plate'.[22]

Bunny hoped that Duncan would get to know and like Ray during the sittings for this portrait. Certainly by the autumn the two friends were once again on apparently easy terms, and when in October Ray's first child was still-born, Duncan was very sympathetic and much concerned on her behalf. When finally she gave birth successfully to a son in 1923 he was called Richard after his great-grandfather, who had been Keeper of Printed Books at the British Museum and wrote *The Twilight of the Gods*. His second name is Duncan.

Returning to Charleston in August 1921, it astonished Vanessa to realise that it was 'much the nicest place in England'. Moving from one room to another, she marvelled at how much effort had gone into the decoration of the house, how many tables, chairs and door panels bore painted patterns and motifs, and how many colour schemes they had invented. 'Considering what a struggle it was to exist here at all I can't think how we had so much surplus energy.' All the difficulties they had lived through during the first three years at Charleston rapidly passed through her mind, and when she opened some drawers belonging to Duncan and found sketches of Angelica as a baby looking like a skeleton, it seemed incredible 'that here one should be sane and sound with Angelica running about and talking sense'.[23]

That summer Duncan counted fifty-two peaches on the peach tree. There also promised to be an abundance of apples and pears. He designed a cover for a new musical magazine, *Fanfare*, edited by Leigh Henry, and enjoyed the visitors who came and went. 'Lytton is here and very benign,' he wrote to Bunny, mentioning also Maynard's young Cambridge friend, Sebastian Sprott, who that year briefly acted as tutor to Julian and Quentin. Sprott left Charleston with 'an exquisite young man called Davidson',[24] according to Duncan, both heading for Munich where they intended studying German. When Davidson returned to London in September, Duncan cancelled a meeting with Bunny in order to see more of this new friend, who was now heading for America. 'Douglas left this afternoon,' Duncan afterwards reported to Vanessa: 'You need not worry about the state of my heart, it is not desperate. I like D. and find him rather interesting but it's a pity I see that he has not a little more training of the mind. He's got a good deal of real feeling for pictures – you'll think I'm like Roger – and I very much enjoyed going to the Wallace [Collection] yesterday with him and to the National Gallery this morning.'[25] They afterwards had tea at Gunters, walked in Kensington Gardens and ended the day at the Palladium enjoying Little Tich and some French clowns.

Duncan was not misled about the young man's feeling for art: Davidson later turned to painting, his style owing much to Duncan's example, as can be seen in his decorations for George ('Dadie') Rylands's sitting-room in King's College, Cambridge. But he nevertheless troubled Vanessa: like other young men, he drew Duncan away and caused him to cut short his time at Charleston, leaving her uncertain as to when he would return. She admitted her feelings to Duncan, and realised that now he had ease of movement, an active social life and a growing circle of friends, she would have to accommodate his need of male friendship.

By 1922, however, Duncan had transferred his attention to Douglas's brother, Angus – a tall, handsome, magnificent figure of a man who inwardly wanted to be a tiny little woman. When Duncan told him that he thought he loved him in a way more than he had ever loved anyone before, Angus, after searching his feelings, declared that he had found a good deal of affection for Duncan, enough to want to see him occasionally. With that Duncan had to be content. But in fact Angus

Davidson was to prove one of his most loyal and lasting friends. Rather sheepish and unambitious, he applied for a job at the National Gallery in 1919, which he did not get, and later hoped, again unsuccessfully, that Agnew's would take him on. Like his brother, he had graduated from Magdalene College, Cambridge and was to write occasional art criticism for the *Nation & Athenaeum*. He also succeeded Dadie Rylands as assistant at the Hogarth Press, his kindness and intelligence charming his employers, but his slowness and inertia irritating Leonard. He eventually found his niche as a translator, of Alberto Moravia and Mario Praz, among others, and wrote a pioneering biography of Edward Lear in which the emphasis lay very much on his work as an artist. He posed naked for Duncan, for one of his most sensual paintings, and on many other occasions was either drawn or painted. He appeared at Charleston every summer, causing no strain, as he was easily overlooked but impossible to dislike. 'I'm sure he [Angus] has the correct graveside manner,' Quentin, as a young man, wrote to his brother, 'a kind of gentlemanly tragic urbanity, and a sorrowful but consoling way of screwing up his eyes as if he were getting a fleeting but blinding glimpse of kingdom come.'[26]

It had been arranged in the summer of 1921 that Vanessa, Duncan, the children and two maids would spend the autumn and winter at St-Tropez. They rented La Maison Blanche, a small villa on a hillside about a mile out of town overlooking the bay. Roger welcomed them on their arrival, as he was already installed in the town and painting hard. The house, which according to Vanessa, was 'a marvel of practical French arrangement',[27] was clean and well furnished. An additional advantage came in the form of a French *bonne*, Louise, who arrived each day to shop, cook and assist with the washing. Her fierce practicality rather terrified Nellie Brittain and Grace Germany, the two English maids, but Grace, who had only recently entered Vanessa's employment, showed great spirit, picking up a few essential French words and resorting to the dictionary when in need. She also improvised with her clothes to take account of the Mediterranean heat and generally displayed a readiness to adapt, which won her employer's admiration. She traipsed around, Vanessa observed, 'with a handkerchief tied round her head, very lovely and quite incompetent'.[28] The affection behind this remark was repaid: for the next forty years Grace continued to work for Vanessa and, after Vanessa's death, stayed on at Charleston as Duncan's housekeeper.

With domestic matters satisfactorily taken care of and lessons arranged for Julian and Quentin in town each day, the two painters quickly settled down to work. The various small rooms in the villa allowed Duncan and

Vanessa each to have a room of their own to paint in, with north light, and this suited Vanessa, as she was anxious not to fall too much under Duncan's influence, a worry that was exacerbated in St-Tropez by the news that a portrait of Sebastian Sprott by Vanessa had been mistakenly exhibited at the Independent Gallery under Duncan's name. It was therefore agreed that they would not look at each other's pictures during the first month. With Roger near at hand and plenty of other painters working in and around St-Tropez, there was no shortage of talk about art. Having picked up the latest copy of Proust in Paris, Duncan was also deeply absorbed in the reflections on homosexuality that follow Jupien's meeting with M. de Charlus at the start of *Sodome et Gomorrhe*.

Meanwhile life at St-Tropez offered many sensual satisfactions. Duncan wrote to Bunny:

> I have been here a week and have become completely *animalisé* by this existence and it will take several weeks to regain any sort of northern self-respect. To begin with the sea is like the bay of Naples and as warm as toast and the sun never gives up baking so that I simply become a sun soaker and tumble into the sea which is always as calm as a pond in the afternoon. The children are as happy as crickets and we all feed out of doors on the terrace – in two parties. Roger is a good deal on the *tapis* and more energetic than ever . . . There is hardly any food which is a trouble but any quantity of the most delicious red wine – sold for 1 franc 50 a bottle, about sixpence which makes up for the lack of marmalade for which I hanker from time to time.[29]

The food shortage was solved by a letter to Maynard, who instructed the Army and Navy Stores to send out a hamper of groceries. Vanessa was amused to discover that Duncan thought most problems could be solved by sending to England for what was needed, regardless of time and expense, and it was in this way that he obtained his paints. In the evenings they often dined with Roger in town, though his habit of searching out the most indigenous haunt used by the working population led him to favour what Vanessa thought a horrid little restaurant. After dinner one evening Roger took them to a café where sailors danced. One partnered Vanessa but she apparently fared here no better than she had done in Mayfair, where her half-brother George Duckworth had tried to introduce her into polite society. Afterwards the sailor gallantly remarked that though both French and English dance perfectly, they do not do so well together. Vanessa may have been distracted: Duncan, in one corner, was flirting with a house-painter from Toulon who, she observed, 'made the deadest set at him I've ever seen'.[30]

As the weather turned colder, other painters gradually left the town. The food hamper arrived, causing the greatest excitement, a large tin of golden syrup producing whoops of joy. Towards the end of November Roger returned to London. 'We are alone here now,' Vanessa wrote to Maynard: 'Roger having gone. It's rather a relief . . . as his painting gets on one's nerves and also makes him now out of sympathy with both Duncan's and mine – although he gave out criticisms at every point not withstanding. I think Duncan found it depressing and is happier without it. We are going (separately as the family can't be left alone) to visit the Raverats and the Bussys soon.'[31] Before taking herself off to Vence, where the Raverats were now living, she allowed herself to look at Duncan's paintings. 'Many of his are perfectly lovely. They'll sell like anything and I'm not sure he couldn't now put up his prices. Most of his things here are sketches done in one or a few sittings. I think coming to this climate has been very good for him as a painter.'[32]

She shared her views with Maynard, knowing that he took a particular interest. To coincide with the London Group exhibition of October 1921, Maynard had written a leaflet suggesting ways in which art could be put on better commercial terms with the public, and recommending investment in work by those associated with the London Group which, he said, included some of the most promising young English artists of the day. 'We thought your London Group letter very good,' Vanessa wrote.[33] It gave the critics an obvious line to take in their reviews. The *Observer* recommended Duncan Grant's *Notre Dame* for 'investment' ('it has massiveness, weight, a grand silhouette, and personal vision'), but trounced 'the dreary competition in bashed crockery and semi-caricature portraiture' and 'the uninspired borrowing of the Cézanne, Roger Fry, Matisse, Picasso recipes' found elsewhere.[34] According to the *Daily News*,[35] the most striking picture in the show was Duncan's *Cymon and Iphigenia*, a near-monochromatic study of a recumbent nude on classical drapery. Frank Rutter, writing in *The Sunday Times*, called it a *tour-de-force*,[36] and the *Manchester Guardian* critic declared it 'the most important work Duncan Grant has shown for some years . . . suggesting Jacques David in Gauguin's island'.[37] Such praise continued throughout the 1920s, Duncan's name regularly being singled out in group shows.

The knowledge that his work was selling well added to the confidence with which Duncan painted at St-Tropez. 'Duncan heard today that Turner [at the Independent Gallery] has sold two pictures . . . so with his London Group ones too I think he'll have made about £150 this month,' Vanessa reported to Maynard in November. 'He thinks of taking me to Monte Carlo and giving each of us £5 to gamble with . . . Your preface

239

has evidently been a huge success and has given it [the London Group] a great boon.'[38] But, as neither had much real interest in money, they continued to lead a cheap, hard-working existence, the expenses for the whole household amounting to just six pounds a week or less and Duncan falling asleep each evening at nine o'clock. He found St-Tropez and its environs so attractive to paint ('the country is superb in the Roman Campagna style and the port of St-Tropez rather like a Sicilian town'[39]) that he continued painting outdoors even when the Mistral blew and rain fell. Vanessa returned from the Bussys and the Raverats, having been surprised on this, her first visit to Roquebrune, to find an entire zoo in Simon Bussy's studio, for he had taken to making portraits of animals. A more melancholy situation prevailed at Vence, for Jacques Raverat was now crippled with multiple sclerosis and had to be carried everywhere by Gwen and a servant. Though he could no longer write, he could still paint and, as if in defiance of their difficulties, the couple were producing between them a quantity of wood engravings and oil paintings.

It was then Duncan's turn to travel the coastline to Roquebrune, where he too marvelled at Bussy's pictures. He stopped *en route* at Toulon, enjoying its seventeenth-century air and the thrill of seeing battleships in the harbour. At Marseilles he called on Auguste Bréal, now living at 14 Avenue Viton, and gained familiarity with the old part of the town, which he thought a sublime mixture of fallen grandeur, savagery and squalor. The more lurid details he sent to Bunny; to Vanessa he wrote about the landscape. 'I had a most wonderful journey in the train . . . the bit of coast between Cavaliere and Toulon is superb, especially round Hyères.'[40]

By early January 1922 they had begun to anticipate their return home. They were eager to discover how things stood with their friends, for they had caught glimpses in the letters they had received of Maynard's growing fascination with Lydia Lopokova and of Clive's sudden fling with an heiress, Juana de Gandarillas. With Mary Hutchinson temporarily in abeyance, Clive had fallen in love with Juana and was ready, if she asked, to abandon everything and enter her rich, floating, cosmopolitan world; but then he realised that a woman who did not read and had no life of the mind would deprive him of some fundamental ingredient. 'No,' he told Vanessa, 'I will not disappear to Andalusia. I don't suppose I shall disappear at all. I see more clearly that I am eternally committed to this pathetic life of the intellect: and that I can't really get on without reading books and looking at pictures and arguing with Roger and Maynard . . .'[41] Before Vanessa and Duncan had returned to London, Clive's wild dreams of a new life had dwindled to the prospect of being taken by Juana on a motoring tour of Spain, and to the attendant worry that he and Juana would be hard pushed to find things to talk about.

FIFTEEN

Qui Me Neglige Me Perd

The need to spring-clean La Maison Blanche and pack up broke what had been for Duncan a long and productive spell of work. Looking at his paintings he realised how much time he had needed to adjust to the colours and character of the landscape around St-Tropez. 'It takes several months to get over the extreme beauty of the place,' he told Bunny, 'and even now it occasionally obtrudes itself – a fatal thing for a landscape painter I feel sure.'[1] After a brief return to London he intended, with Vanessa, to spend some weeks in Paris, where he hoped to produce more landscapes, with the aid of sketches made at St-Tropez but without the seduction of the actual setting.

They returned to London on 12 January 1922. Vanessa immediately set about buying clothes for Julian and Quentin, preparing Julian for his first term as a boarder at the Quaker school, Leighton Park. Quentin, still at preparatory school, was to remain, while Vanessa was in Paris, with Angelica in the care of Grace Germany and others at 50 Gordon Square. In this interim period Duncan revisited the studio he had taken the previous year and had sub-let, while he was in St-Tropez, to a Polish painter called Popovitch. But even with his tenant gone, Duncan still slept at 46 Gordon Square, which remained his London base for a while yet.

Duncan's was one of two studios, each a mirror-image of the other and placed back to back, which had been built out behind 8 Fitzroy Street, itself a rather ordinary, largeish London house, in line with the mews that ran behind. Both studios were reached by means of a complicated route, part of which included 'a metal staircase and corridor apparently suspended in space, which clanked under our footsteps, and on which one or two amorous couples would be standing enlaced'. So Frances Partridge recalls, remembering also that in Duncan's studio 'Chinese or Spanish pottery, draped stuffs and dusty still-lifes stood about on tables, leaving a large central space for dancing or performance'.[2] This impressive studio, some forty foot long, twenty foot wide and twenty high, also comprised a small kitchen area, an entrance hall, lobby and model's dressing-room. Whistler had painted here in March 1896; for a while Augustus John had used the studio; and its most recent tenant had been Sickert.

The decision taken that January, to abandon London quickly in favour of Paris, largely reflected Vanessa's needs. At La Maison Blanche adults and children had all lived at close quarters and Vanessa had spent two hours each morning giving Julian and Quentin lessons before sending them off for another two hours with a French governess. In the evening she had taken the children in hand for a further two hours, in an attempt to instil in them a little Latin and French. What she now needed more than anything was a short time away from her family in order to do nothing but paint.

As it turned out Vanessa found herself busy nursing three invalids when the time came to depart and Duncan set off alone. He took a room in the Hôtel de Londres in the Rue Bonaparte, which had become their familiar Parisian haunt, and then found a small studio to rent in the Rue de Verneuil. Next door was a room to let, which he thought would suit Vanessa. Edward Wolfe, who was also in Paris, helped find all the things that Duncan needed, and he also saw something of Keith Baynes, whom he liked. But the painter who charmed him most in Paris was Matthew Smith, an exuberant colourist with an extremely diffident, nervous temperament. By the time Vanessa arrived in early February she found Duncan humming with life, looking young and happy. He now gave up his room at the Hôtel de Londres to Vanessa and slept in his studio at the Rue de Verneuil.

In Paris he began to assimilate news that had first reached them at St-Tropez. 'Have you heard about Maynard's affair with Loppy [Lydia Lopokova]?' Duncan asked Bunny. 'Perhaps it's a secret so don't let it out if it is. It's apparently very serious. I suppose they'll marry – like everyone else. It seems the chic thing to do.'[3] Vanessa had been the first to scent this danger and had lost no time in warning Maynard what an expensive wife Lopokova would make, how she would give up dancing and was far preferable as a mistress. On his brief return to London Duncan had insufficient time to assess this new turn of events in Maynard's love life, which continued alongside his homosexual relationships with two others.[4] Maynard himself was rather bewildered by his feelings and hoped that a prearranged visit to India – he had agreed to sit on a Royal Commission to advise on Indian fiscal policy – would save him from falling still more heavily in love. In the end he cancelled this visit and failed to respond to Duncan's wish that he might join him and Vanessa in Paris. Duncan, who was reading *La Cousine Bette*, hoped that

Maynard would not imitate Baron Hulot and spend the rest of his life with ballet dancers. Meanwhile Vanessa and Duncan's letters jittered with anxiety over Maynard's altered state. Duncan at first resisted any conclusions. 'As for Maynard until I can see him carrying on with L. I must give up imagining what happens . . . Do you think it's a lapse in his character or its saving?'[5] Three days later he had decided 'to decamp to the studio when I get back – 46 [Gordon Square] sounds too much like Petticoat Lane'.[6] It would, he reflected, also be cheaper. What money he had would have gone by the time he returned to London and, now that the post-war boom had ended, Maynard's speculations on his behalf were losing, rather than gaining, him money.

When Vanessa arrived in Paris she found Duncan still unwilling to offer opinions on Maynard and Lydia; he remained sphinx-like, she told Maynard. 'He says he cannot write or say anything until he has seen for himself but will only remark academically that (as you ought to know) he disapproves of marriage.'[7] She discerned, however, that Duncan was suspicious of the affair and unable to visualise the situation, as Maynard had become almost a new character to him.

'It'll be a bore if Loppy turns out to be another Mary in disguise,' he had offered at one moment.[8] This suggests that he had as yet very little idea of her character. Whereas Mary Hutchinson always presented to the world a very carefully prepared, stylish façade, Lydia wiped off her make-up the moment she came off-stage and, changing into the simplest of clothes, would skip home – as the ballet critic Cyril Beaumont has described – like a schoolgirl let out of school.[9] Moreover, while Mary was imbued with perceptions and prejudices particular to her class, Lydia, who had been born in St Petersburg, had danced with the Imperial Ballet and for seven years had performed in all manner of ways on stages in America, looked at English habits and customs with the fresh eyes of a foreigner. She had an artist's intuitive intelligence and, despite her imperfect English, could be extremely funny with what Maynard called her 'most knowing and judicious use of English words'.[10] She once wrote to Duncan, 'Dear Duncan, A thought descends on me after your and M's conversation. The high brows lack temperament and only irritate but not stimulate the lower brows, hence no progress. Lydia.'[11] As her vehicle for artistic expression was her body, she was intensely physical in her exuberant response to life. Though her face could at times take on an expression of grave sincerity, she had a gift for merriment, bringing a sense of glee to any occasion.

Clive hated it. Though himself a deeply sensual and convivial man, he approached company through his intellect, enjoying the play of one mind against another in conversation. During the spring and early summer of 1922, when it became clear that Lydia had become a permanent feature in Maynard's life, much talk within Bloomsbury focused on the problem of how they were to accommodate her within their intimate circle. She had danced in *The Sleeping Princess* in the winter of 1921–2 and when, a few days before it closed, Diaghilev fled London and his creditors, Lydia was left, like the rest of his company, stranded and penniless, no longer able to afford her room at the Waldorf Hotel. Maynard stepped in, took charge of her finances, persuading her to open a bank account instead of leaving her earnings with the Waldorf's head porter, and installed her in Vanessa's flat in 50 Gordon Square while its tenant remained in Paris. She then joined Massine's company in a programme of *divertissements* at Covent Garden. In one of these she danced a Scottish reel in a costume designed by Duncan. As passionate about dance as the Bloomsbury artists were about painting, she practised at all hours, even late at night, and Adrian and Karin Stephen who lived below sometimes had to restrain her. When in April Keynes disappeared to report on the Genoa Economic Conference for the *Manchester Guardian*, Vanessa, now back in London, looked after her lodger on Maynard's behalf. 'Lydia seems very well,' she reported, 'and in good spirits. Her new work is evidently much lighter. In fact I don't think she does enough to work off her energies really . . . She is perfectly charming in the Scotch dance, though she has got into some trouble with Duncan because she treated the kilt as a skirt at one moment.'[12]

The houses in Gordon Square are substantial five-storey buildings. Even so, the arrangement at 50 Gordon Square was now a little strained. Clive threatened to leave the house if Lydia or any other new person became a permanent resident. Vanessa considered moving herself and Angelica back to 46 Gordon Square, thereby leaving more room for Clive, but then realised that this would mean her children lived in two different houses. She also saw that if Lydia moved to 46, which Maynard was still sharing with Duncan, difficulties could arise. 'Don't you think the most satisfactory solution,' she wrote to Maynard, 'might be to find her rooms quite near – perhaps James [Strachey]'s at 41. She could then be quite independent and there'd be no scandal.'[13]

This still left unsolved the summer arrangements. For the past three years Maynard had spent part of each summer at Charleston. It was to him a kind of family home, to which he contributed sixty pounds a year, roughly one-third of its running costs. That summer he proposed renting Tilton Cottage on the neighbouring farm for himself and Lydia. Vanessa, foreseeing that Lydia would find housekeeping in the country laden with problems, envisaged them appearing each day at Charleston, which she knew would irritate Clive. He made his views clear to Vanessa on the understanding that it was her task to make them known to Maynard. Clive would not spend the summer at Charleston if Lydia was nearby, because in her presence he would only lose his temper and quarrel.

Clive's prejudice momentarily held sway and Vanessa, following his lead, attempted to close the ranks:

> Clive says he thinks it impossible for anyone of us, you, he, I or Duncan, to introduce a new wife or husband into the existing circle for more than a week at a time . . . Don't think however that . . . is any kind of criticism of Lydia for it isn't. We feel that *no one* can come into the sort of intimate society we have without altering it . . . I can't offer any solution to the summer problem. We would much rather you were at Charleston of course, but I'm afraid you may be forced to choose between us and Lydia. It all seems horribly complicated and I wish it weren't.[14]

As it turned out, Tilton Cottage was unavailable and Lydia's dancing commitments kept her busy in Manchester and Harrogate for part of August. By then Vanessa's attitude to Lydia had changed. 'Please give my love to Lydia and tell her I hope very much she'll come here,' she wrote to Maynard from Charleston, 'and not put us off vaguely at the last moment – English households can't be treated like that.'[15] Perhaps because other arrangements had already been made, five days later Lydia went to stay with her friends Harold and Vera Bowen, Maynard therefore arriving on his own at Charleston for the first week in September. He had surrendered his staff at 46 Gordon Square to Vanessa for the summer and as a result Charleston was blooming. The garden was bright with flowers. Fresh curtains and covers furnished every room and Mrs Harland's cooking obliged Clive to work in the garden each day to keep down his weight. Duncan took to doing exercises in the nude every day before dinner. And Vanessa was greatly pleased that the advent of a large airy motor bus, which conveniently stopped on the main road beside the end of the track leading to Charleston, took shoppers into Lewes after lunch and brought them back in time for tea. Grace Germany was also in high feather, having been elevated to the position of principal house-parlourmaid, and each morning a very competent Mrs Willard came to assist with the cleaning.

One complication in the Maynard–Lydia scenario was that she was still married to Randolfo Barocchi, Diaghilev's business manager. Compared with her turbulent background and the many talented and complex personalities with whom she had worked, Bloomsbury presented her with new but not insurmountable difficulties. She withstood their criticisms and by October 1922 it seemed to Vanessa that she and Maynard had, in all but name, settled into married life. Duncan, enchanted by her movements, drew and painted this short, compact, humorous, bird-like ballerina. She returned his interest: when his parents moved to Twickenham in 1923, Lydia found for Bartle a copy of R. S. Cobbett's *Memorials of Twickenham: Parochial and Topographical*, first published in 1872.

Though Matisse and Picasso never ceased to interest Duncan, the artists with whom he found affinity in the early 1920s were Derain, Segonzac and Jean Marchand, all of whom he knew personally and whose work he saw in exhibitions in both Paris and London. Marchand's love of severe, near-geometric treatment of form appealed strongly also to Fry, who owned two of his still-lifes. Segonzac's earthy colours were widely admired at this time and in April 1921 Duncan, who had considerable influence on Maynard's collecting,[16] urged him to buy a painting by this artist from the Independent Gallery. But it was Derain who seemed to dominate this period. Duncan, writing from Paris in May 1921, told Lytton, 'his [Derain's] success is so great that he has simply become a bouncing and benign giant. The things he is doing now are really very sublime.'[17]

In keeping with a widespread return to traditional motifs and methods of working, Duncan abandoned for a short period the imaginative playfulness he had formerly brought to figurative subjects, and concentrated instead on a careful pursuit of formal values. In certain still-lifes from this period a painstaking rendering of the fall of light and shade on solid shapes can be found. Every object is treated with the same thoroughness, the dark tones and sombre colours adding to the gravity of the whole. In these quiet, compelling paintings Duncan's customary use of calligraphic brushwork is entirely suppressed. As a result the best of them have a profound stillness, an absolute fixity and silence that, by contrast, incites awareness of transience and mortality. One of these still-lifes was bought by Lytton in June, when Duncan had a one-artist show at the Independent Gallery. In this painting the exact positioning of a small pot, a tight cluster of dim-coloured flowers and a bust by the French sculptor Marcel Gimond are offset by the bare architecture of the surroundings. (The painting hung at Ham Spray for many years, and afterwards in Frances Partridge's London flat.)

Duncan and Vanessa had stayed with Lytton at Tidmarsh, near

Pangbourne, early in May 1922. Though he enjoyed the visit, Duncan afterwards reprimanded Lytton for telling Virginia that he and Vanessa were bored with Lydia. This, Duncan insisted, was not only untrue, but would be awkward for everyone if it reached Maynard's ears. Such storms-in-a-teacup were a regular part of Bloomsbury life, personal relationships continuing to invite much analysis and speculation. And despite his protest, Duncan did in fact complain at times to Vanessa about the paralysing effect of Lydia's chatter.

The other side of the coin to Bloomsbury's love of gossip was their loyalty to each other. When Roger Fry, the subject of many jibes, delivered a public lecture, Bloomsbury turned out in force. In June 1922 he gave three lectures at Lower Mortimer Hall, not on contemporary French art but on the seventeenth-century artists, Rubens, Rembrandt and Poussin. Fry too had reverted as an artist to more traditional methods of representation, and as a critic seemed less forward-looking than anxious to evaluate keenly the lessons of the past.

Duncan was again in the audience when in the winter of 1922–3 Roger delivered a series of lectures tracing the history of design and 'significant form' in painting. These were not only well received but also, judging from a letter that Dora Carrington wrote to Gerald Brenan, major social events: 'He has amazing slides, Giotto and the Sienese school. He always shows one a great many that one has never seen before. The last lecture brought one up to Uccello. *Tout le monde* is at these lectures. The females are characterised by their plainness and serious countenances, and males by their long hair and pasty spotty faces. Everyone knows everybody so before the lecture begins, the babble of conversation is not to be described in words. Chelsea meets Bloomsbury, Hampstead bows to Richmond and even the ladies from Mayfair talk graciously to Logan Pearsall-Smith and Mr Tatlock.'[18] Although Duncan did not always agree with Roger's views on art, he would have been affected by the climate of thought which these lectures helped foster. Roger's insistence that an artist had to grapple with his or her vision in order to make form significant encouraged Duncan at times to overwork his oils. But if Duncan's paintings were effortfully sober, his studio made an excellent venue for parties. Carrington described one that followed Fry's lecture: 'It was rather a classical party, with an air of a French studio in 1889. Arthur Waley's mistress Miss De Z[oete] played Bach on a harpsichord; the room was lit by candles, young earnest Cambridge men twisted and twirled on their toes and shrieked in high nasal voices. Vanessa drooped like a flower with a too heavy head over some coffee boiling on a stove.

Duncan moved about with sprightly step with trays of biscuits and beer in glasses.'[19]

Frances Partridge claims that she first experienced Bloomsbury *en masse* at a party in Duncan's studio. It was given by Bunny and Ray Garnett on 9 March 1923 and was made memorable by the Negro songs sung in a husky voice by a young American woman, Henrietta Bingham. She had come to England to be with her friend, Mina Kirstein, whose portrait Duncan painted in August that year, Henrietta sitting, meanwhile, to the sculptor Stephen Tomlin and revealing, like him, an inexhaustible capacity for conversation. After Henrietta sang that evening, Lydia arrived straight from a performance at Covent Garden and proceeded to dance again for those present.

Living in Fitzroy Street in close proximity to the restaurants in Charlotte Street, Duncan often saw Sickert dining with his second wife Thérèse Lessore in the Etoile. Sickert gave Duncan prints of his recent etchings and talked, as Duncan observed to Vanessa, 'of nothing but painting now'.[20] Once Duncan was dining at the Etoile with Virginia when Sickert and his wife joined them. Virginia used the opportunity to suggest that Sickert should review a biography of the Victorian painter, Hubert Herkomer, for the *Nation*, Leonard having recently become its literary editor.

Duncan also knew Sickert's brother, Oswald, who offered him hospitality during his trip to Spain in June 1923. The brevity of the holiday may have made this impossible. Duncan and Vanessa visited Madrid, where they saw a bullfight, the Escorial, Segovia, Calatayud, where they enjoyed the market, and Toledo. But the main event for both painters, neither of whom had been to Spain before, was almost certainly their visit to the Prado.

Shortly before Duncan left for Spain an exhibition of his recent work opened at the Independent Gallery. Among the twenty-six oils and thirteen drawings and watercolours were portraits of Lydia Lopokova and Angus Davidson, a male nude for which Angus had posed, and *The Hammock*.[21] Duncan had worked on this last picture for some three years, making many sketches for it as well as a full-size study in oils. Vanessa lies in a hammock that Quentin, seated with his back to the viewer, rocks, while Julian sits in a boat on the pond at Charleston. Down a path on the right-hand side comes the small Angelica pulling a toy lamb, while Sebastian Sprott lies reading in the foreground. The composition, like the hammock itself, rocks between two perspectives, which attract the eye into the distance on either side of the central motif, the ropes of the hammock echoing this directional tug-of-war. Every shape found within the landscape adds to the network of relationships that binds this elaborate composition into a celebration of Charleston life. It contributed to the sensation that the show as a whole gave Vanessa, of 'solidity and richness, rather severe, but very much alive'.[22]

By the time Duncan reached Paris, *en route* to Spain, he had already sold £650 worth of pictures. 'I am rather alarmed at the sales in my exhibition,' he wrote to Vanessa. 'What does it mean? That I am a very bad painter? I expect Roger will come to that conclusion. But on the other hand when one thinks of it it is about three years work or more, £200 a year is a not unreasonable amount to make out of people, do you think?'[23] He was a success not only in financial terms but also with the press; the by-line in *Vogue* read, 'Notes on the Admirable and Stimulating Work of a Young English Artist Whose Painting is Yearly Increasing in Richness'. The one dissenting voice was that of Simon Bussy in the pages of the *Nation & Athenaeum*. 'Him I would exhort to more boldness, to more of science, to greater severity of choice and, may I add, to less exuberance of production,'[24] Bussy had written. Duncan first heard of this through Vanessa. 'It sounds rather like the lecture you gave me some years ago,' he commented,[25] refusing to worry about it in Paris, where in a very short space of time he had visited Segonzac, dined with Marchand, lunched with Jane Harrison and her friend Hope Mirlees, seen Maria Blanchard and attended an exhibition of bust portraits by Marcel Gimond. He admired them but rated Gimond less good than Frank Dobson.

But Bussy's opinions mattered and were not forgotten. Soon after he returned from Spain, Duncan thanked Bussy for his 'severe review'. Severity from a person one respected, he admitted, merited more attention than facile praise. He invited Simon and Dorothy, while they were in London, to dine with himself, Sickert and his wife. But he rebutted Bussy's warning that his art would be spoilt by success. 'I am afraid that you think a little success will stop me from working. But no, I am pleased to have collected enough money to enable me to work as I like for a while, but really it is the opinions of a small group of people like yourself which are worthwhile.'[26]

This small group included Roger Fry. In 1923 Leonard Woolf wanted to start a series of monographs entitled 'Living Painters', which he hoped Roger would edit. He proposed, as the first, one on Duncan's art, with twenty-four plates and an introduction by Fry. At the same time, however, Duncan was approached by the publisher Ernest Benn, who wanted him to be part of their Contemporary British Artists series. There followed a year's deliberation and negotiation between Woolf and Victor

Gollancz, then a director of Benn's, before the Hogarth Press went ahead with their idea and *Duncan Grant* appeared in February 1924. Though it bore the phrase 'Living Painters' on its half-title, this was the first and last in the series, the Woolfs presumably feeling it unwise to compete in the already well-developed field of art publishing.

Roger's appreciative essay contained one major point of contention: that the leaning towards a decorative conception in Grant's work hampered his attempts at more solidly realised constructions in a logically coherent space. Nowhere was the post-war agenda more evident than in this remark. As a result Fry is often blamed for a certain stodginess that enters some of Duncan's more laborious paintings of this period, even though his interest in a more solidly realised style had many sources. Elsewhere in Roger's essay, such phrases as 'lyrical joyousness of mood', 'charming poetic invention', 'infallible tact in colour oppositions' and 'melodious rhythm' indicated characteristics in Duncan's art that critics were to praise repeatedly. But growing appreciation of his work did not silence Duncan's self-criticism. September 1923 found him painting alone at Charleston, in a low state of mind about his work. A letter from Vanessa cheered him, as she sent Segonzac's encouraging remarks. Duncan wrote his reply sitting one evening in Vanessa's room. Looking up, his eye dwelt on two of her pictures, a small landscape of the pond at Charleston and a portrait of her two boys. He thought that the French adjective that best described them both was *sage*. Mindful that she too needed appreciation, he sent her his opinion, humbly, gratefully, adding, 'but I daresay you won't like it and anyhow it's not everything I think'.[27]

In the summer of 1923 Duncan's parents, Aunt Violet and Miss Elwes moved to Twickenham, to the three-storey Grosvenor House in Grosvenor Road, which had once belonged to Queen Anne's apothecary. A side extension had been added in Victorian times, which contained a drawing-room with tall sash windows looking out on to the walled garden. Its ancient pear and apple trees have since vanished to make way for parking lots and tall flats. But in 1923, while workmen were busy with alterations and repairs, Ethel Grant took Aunt Daisy to see the house and they came away laden with pears and flowers. On moving in, they filled the house with mementoes of their days in India and Burma – ceremonial swords, carved elephants, Oriental curtains that glittered with pieces of mirror, wall hangings – as well as paintings, mostly by Duncan.

For him, the close proximity of the house to the river meant an array of new subjects, some of them, as he knew, painted by Turner. On one of his first visits to the area he walked from Twickenham to Richmond,

coming back on the other side of the river through Petersham, then a
small village with seventeenth- and eighteenth-century houses and many
ornamental grilles and gates, which filled him with nostalgia for earlier
times. Everywhere he looked, Duncan found paintable subjects. 'You
must come here in the autumn,' he told Vanessa.[28]

Out of fondness for his parents, Duncan went regularly to Twickenham and from now on he usually spent Christmas there. In winter he
would enjoy walks in Richmond Park, returning to Twickenham
alongside the river and by means of a ferry. Duncan's father had been ill
at the time of the move and his health was still poor. But when Aunt
Daisy was present, as she often was, she could strike up a conversation
with him about yachts that left Bartle visibly cheered. It was presumably
for Aunt Daisy, who always took a camera on her many travels, that a
small dark room was made at Grosvenor House, which was stacked with
heavy glass photographic plates imprinted with ghostly negatives of
colonial life. The house was full of curiosities and evocative of another
era. The inhabitants depended on paid help, as all three sisters had only a
distant acquaintance with the art of cooking, though Aunt Violet, as
Duncan observed, was always tactful and busy. When Christmas 1923
arrived, Duncan found yet another female relative installed, Angie Willis.
She had a withered arm and sat all day, silently crocheting, a sensible,
equable creature who seemed to Duncan entirely unchanged since his
childhood days. Very little happened at Grosvenor House in winter.
Duncan drew in his father's sitting-room in the mornings and took walks
in the afternoon, and at empty moments he missed Vanessa and the
children and worried that Angelica on her new scooter might scoot
straight into the pond.

That year Angie Willis gave him a seal imprinted with a bird flying out
of a cage and the motto *Qui me neglige me perd* – 'which I think a good
one, so don't,' he told Vanessa.[29] There was little danger of that, as earlier
that year Vanessa had confessed to him, 'I feel isolated in the world when
I can't talk or even write to you.'[30] If bound together by mutual affection
and need, their relationship also rested on an acknowledgement of
separateness and difference. Vanessa, her children, the ambience of
Charleston, their friends and their shared interest in painting greatly
satisfied Duncan, but his sexuality was not appeased. Vanessa's sustaining
love necessarily had to remain a three-walled cage that allowed him ease
of escape.

At the Independent Gallery in 1923 Vanessa had admired the male
nude for which Angus Davidson had posed, knowing full well that he had
also been Duncan's lover. She may also have seen the more overtly

sensual nude of Angus that Duncan painted but did not exhibit. Angus hung about in Duncan's life at this time, never perhaps as central to it as he could have been, had he not been thwarted by his own diffidence and expectancy of failure. He was the cause of a slight argument between Duncan and Bunny in September 1922. 'I was naturally rather alarmed,' Duncan wrote to Bunny, when he learnt that Bunny and Angus had dined together and talked about him. 'Knowing your character rather better than A. and yr. delight in any sort of emotional complications, I rather wished to hear a few more details . . . P.S. I am glad to hear A. loves me. That is the first I've heard of it.'[31] Bunny replied that it was no good Duncan getting in a rage because talk had gone on behind his back. 'You would spend your life in a frenzy because so many people love you and sometimes speak of their love to each other.'[32]

At some point both Duncan and Angus found themselves attracted to Stephen Tomlin, a bright young sculptor who had been educated at Harrow and Oxford and was the son of a High Court judge. The combination of his stimulating conversation and striking face gave him considerable personal charm. He had trained for a year under the sculptor Frank Dobson and had set up a studio in Fulham, and went on to produce portrait heads, including fine likenesses of Lytton Strachey and Virginia Woolf. He also went through a succession of more or less unhappy love affairs, with men and women, which undermined his sense of self-respect. Then, in 1927, he married Lytton's niece, Julia Strachey, and went to live at Swallowcliffe in Wiltshire. The marriage ended after five years, owing partly to Tomlin's bouts of manic depression.

Known affectionately as Tommy, he had been at school with the Davidson brothers and it was probably through them that Duncan first met him. In 1924 Duncan was persuaded, by Maynard and Bunny who paid the cost, to sit to Tomlin for a bust portrait. 'What they call being immortalised in bronze,' Duncan remarked wryly to Mina Kirstein.[33] In October of that year when Bunny and Tomlin started the Cranium Club, a society of friends who met to dine together each month, named after Mr Cranium in Peacock's *Headlong Hall*, Duncan was a founder member. But the high tide of his affection for Tommy had come in April 1923. That month, because Mr Stacey was temporarily lodging some of his relatives at Charleston, Vanessa and her two boys spent Easter at the Woolfs' home, Monk's House, Rodmell, while Leonard and Virginia were abroad and Angelica remained in Grace's care in London. From Sussex Vanessa wrote, 'You are at the moment no doubt sitting in the arms of Tommy – at least feeling quite happy, I hope, also I hope not staying up too late.' But she was less detached than these words suggest and her letter continues, 'But please my Bear write and tell me what you do, for at this distance it won't matter and I feel very remote from you and want very much to know how the affairs of your heart progress. You seemed to me rather *distrait* and impenetrable. Are you keeping a great deal back from me? I cannot help wondering.'[34]

The fact that Duncan was conducting more than one affair at this time suggests that none filled the place that Bunny had formerly occupied. Realising this, Vanessa could treat Duncan's boyfriends lightheartedly. 'I wonder which arms are round you now. A's or D's or T's or XYZ's. Not B's or *are* they B's? It's quite possible another B is with you and if so there's no doubt where his arms are. But when you really make up your mind to leave them all in the lurch perhaps you'll come to the country with me. There's a great deal to be said for it.'[35] From Monk's House she made a brief trip to Paris, sending Duncan a list of places where he could reach her poste restante. She still needed more news than she had been given. 'I want very much to know about you and who you've been seeing – especially what happened with Tommy. On mature consideration I think perhaps he's too young for my tastes, but then the flesh isn't as important to me as to you, is it? not that beauty isn't. If you like you can give my love to Angus. Perhaps I shall write to him one day.'[36]

Vanessa spent six weeks apart from Angelica that spring, missing her horribly, as she admitted to Duncan, but nevertheless confident that her four-year-old would be well looked after at Gordon Square. For reasons of expediency Vanessa still allowed it to be assumed that Angelica was Clive's daughter, and the young girl was growing up believing the same. Even in the privacy of their letters Duncan and Vanessa never spoke of 'our' daughter. While they were apart in the spring of 1923 Vanessa wrote to Duncan in London, 'My dear, I really hope you are contented. You have my daughter at least so please be cheerful.'[37] When Christmas arrived and Angelica turned five, Duncan added a postscript to a letter sent from Twickenham, 'Dearest Nessa, I too thought about Christmas Day five years ago, and am perhaps almost as pleased as you at the result. But what makes me even more happy is that you should be.'[38] These moments of recognition remained private, hidden. In public Duncan's paternal relationship to Angelica was repressed, and a child thereby denied recognition of her real father.

Yet if his love for Vanessa and respect for Clive drew Duncan into this charade, he kept other relationships in good repair, remaining a loyal son, a devoted companion and true friend to many, without, however, losing an ability to float free of all commitments if need be. Painting continued to be the chief focus of his life. If he could not spend at least two or three hours each day with a brush in his hand he became irritable and ill at ease. He sustained long periods of time quite happily painting on his own, as he did at Charleston in the autumn of 1923. 'Bunny asked me who was with you and would hardly believe you were alone,' Vanessa wrote.[39] It was a particularly fine autumn and Duncan rejoiced in its colours – the russet hedges, red berries and rich harvest yellows. He read *Le Rouge et Le Noir* and thought Mme de Rénal in some ways like Vanessa. And when it poured with rain he took himself off to the cinema in Brighton. 'It was very black by the sea,' he told Vanessa.[40]

Throughout the second half of that year Bartle Grant's health had been in decline. At Christmas his temperature had to be taken each day and he was evidently depressed by the lack of any alteration or improvement. On 16 April 1924 he died. At his request his ashes were interred in the Rothiemurchus kirkyard, Duncan arranging for a stone to be made commemorating his name. Bartle's last undertaking, which Duncan had done much to encourage, had been preparation for the press of his great-grandmother's recipe book, written between 1756 and 1770 and never before printed. Though Duncan had hoped to interest the Woolfs in this project, *The Receipt Book of Elizabeth Raper* was published by the Nonesuch Press in September 1924, with decorations and a portrait of the author by Duncan. Bunny had a hand in its making, as the year previously he had given up the Birrell and Garnett bookshop and become a partner in Francis Meynell's Nonesuch Press, in the capacity of literary adviser. Ethel Grant wrote to thank him for her copy: 'Will you please tell Mr Meynell how much I like it. My only regret is that my husband should never have seen it. He was so much interested in it and I think the writing gave him real pleasure.'[41]

Sitting in the garden at Twickenham, a few days after his father died, Duncan painted a decorative pattern for his mother to work in tent-stitch. From then on it was an activity that was to absorb her greatly, and between 1924 and 1943 she kept a list of all the needlework she did, making a note of who created the design, by whom the work was commissioned and where, if need be, it was exhibited.[42] One of her many expert embroideries followed a design by Duncan based on musical instruments. It covers the large square stool that is today found in Duncan Grant's bedroom at Charleston. She also worked a more conventional design by Roger Fry for a footstool, now in the Victoria and Albert Museum. Many other commissions followed, including a fire screen for Virginia Woolf and five chair seats for Ethel Sands. In the spring of 1936 she undertook a small carpet for Charleston based on another of Duncan's designs.

Twickenham enhanced his love of river scenery. Gloriously fine weather followed his father's death and Duncan, after a rather good breakfast one morning at Euston station, sought out Douglas Davidson and with him went down to Hammersmith Mall, where they sat painting at the water's edge until almost cut off by the tide. The Hutchinsons were away, but the two men nevertheless left their wet paintings to dry at their home, River House, so that they could explore Chiswick, which Duncan found 'more lovely than you can imagine'.[43] He ended the day at the Coliseum listening to an abbreviated performance of *Don Giovanni*.

His love of the theatre, opera, music and ballet continued unabated. He appears always to have gone with fresh ears and eyes, remarking after a performance of *Twelfth Night* that it seemed 'like the dreams of a very complicated person'.[44] The year before he had willingly turned his hand to designs for *The Cyclops*, a play by Euripides that J. T. Sheppard had freely translated and adapted for a performance in the Fellows' Garden at King's College, Cambridge. Duncan's costumes, including the tubular head with its single eye, which he had made for Cyclops, were so much praised that Sheppard asked Duncan to design costumes for his next production, Aristophanes' *The Birds*. This was to be the Triennial Greek Play for 1924, a tradition originally begun in 1883, suspended during the First World War and begun again in 1921 with Sheppard's production of the *Oresteia*. Given the time available, Duncan felt unable to accept and suggested that Sheppard should approach Douglas Davidson. Davidson accepted the invitation to do the costumes, but hoped that Duncan could be persuaded to take responsibility for all the designs, which in the end he did.

Though Duncan wrote to Sheppard, 'if you mention the clothes etc at all in public please give *all* the credit to Douglas who deserves it all and me none',[45] his request was rightly ignored. The programme read, 'The costumes and scenery designed and painted by Mr Douglas Davidson, with the assistance of A. F. Clutton-Brock, King's, R. P. Hinks, Trinity, and W. D. A. Williams, Pembroke, from drawings by Mr Duncan Grant.'

As the press realised, Duncan had played a vital part in making this performance an outstanding success. His vivid, picturesque and imaginative designs were praised in every review. 'Red clouds float in a sky of green,' enthused the *Yorkshire Post* (27 February 1924), adding, 'The costumes exhibited every colour that birds can wear in any clime, and many other colours that have not yet been worn. But, of course, the birds of Aristophanes were such birds as fly only through the purple heavens of the fairyland of comedy.' The *Westminster Gazette* also commented on the riot of colour, while the *Morning Post* thought Duncan's costumes explained themselves so well that no commentary on the play was needed. Cambridge took these Greek plays very seriously, every Cambridge periodical discussing them at length and a series of public lectures preceding the performance. On the first night the audience rippled and sometimes shouted with laughter. *The Times* declared (28 February 1924), 'It is excellently mounted . . . the eye is engaged with innumerable whimsicalities and delicious absurdities . . . The costumes are a triumph of ingenuity, from the long-necked, red-legged flamingo to the sweet seductive nightingale.' Still more authoritative, perhaps, was the voice of a young man writing in *Vogue* in March 1924 – Raymond Mortimer: 'No sensitive person who saw the show could fail to realise that we have in England an artist in stage decoration of the first order; and the final impression left by the play was of a *tableau* as rich and subtle as anything that the Russian Ballet has given us.'

In the spring of 1924 there were two crises involving Angelica. She and the maid, Louie Dunnet, were knocked down by a car and taken to Middlesex Hospital, where Vanessa and Duncan rushed to her side. Because she had been violently sick after the accident the young doctor dealing with her had assumed that her belly had been crushed. Thinking her case hopeless, he had put her to one side while he investigated Louie's injured ankle. It was some time before it was realised that Angelica was unhurt and during that interval Duncan and Vanessa almost collapsed. Clive joined them at the hospital. As it was thought they might have to operate, blood samples were taken, with the ironic result that of all three, Clive alone was of the same blood group as Angelica. A second crisis involved a suspected abscess on her neck; there were several days of acute anxiety. Duncan, unable to rush to Angelica's bedside at Clive's parents' house, Seend, went instead alone to Charleston and there received news of her recovery.

'Well it's very nice after all this sordid town life to be here again,' he wrote to Vanessa. 'The quiet and peace and beauty are unbelievable.'[46] He found that the garden had been very well tilled by Mr Stephen, a local man who did occasional work for them for many years. Already lettuces and peas were springing up and success in the vegetable patch only made Duncan determined that more attention should now be paid to the flower garden. He himself dug and planted, discussed the choice of flowers with Vanessa and treated the garden as creatively as the house.

He was looked after by Grace Germany, who happily shuttled between Gordon Square and Charleston or wherever her services were needed.

When she had first entered Vanessa's employment in 1920 as a sixteen-year-old girl from Norfolk, she had been taken on as a junior maid. Quentin Bell recalls that she was 'a lively, innocent, forgetful and easily startled girl, coping in the most amicable manner with the eccentricities and vagaries of artists and their friends'.[47] She adapted willingly to any task – parlourmaid, nurse, cook, housekeeper – becoming more and more invaluable. In the kitchen at 50 Gordon Square she had listened with delight while Lydia entertained her and Quentin with tales of Old Russia, of samovars, *droshkis* and boyars. But wherever she found herself, Grace was amused and interested in the life which went on around her. When Louie Dunnet came to take over as Angelica's nurse, Vanessa remarked that though she seemed sensible and cheerful, 'she isn't half as aristocratic as Grace'.[48]

Tall and good-looking, Grace turned Duncan's head on more than one occasion. 'Grace looks more exquisite every day. She wore a red handkerchief with white spots on her head yesterday and I think I may make a sketch of her to put into a picture.'[49] He was still more *bouleversé* when she donned his large Spanish straw hat and a pair of Julian's breeches and went striding down the lane with Quentin at her side.

In June 1924 Duncan departed for Berlin to see his friend Franzi von Haas, a Viennese aristocrat married to a very wealthy Belgian lady whose ambition far exceeded his own. Franzi was eight years younger than Duncan and had come to London in 1923, possibly in connection with a commission because, at his wife's behest, he was attempting to establish himself as a portrait painter. He led a cosmopolitan life, keeping a studio in Paris and later one in London, where he was to paint a portrait of Angelica. His gentleness, aristocratic charm and perfect manners made him acceptable to Vanessa, who was less fearful of Duncan's boyfriends if she found she could befriend them. 'As for Franzi,' Duncan joked, 'I've no doubt you could cut me out if you cared to – that is why it was so very kind of me to introduce him to you.'[50]

Periodically Franzi revolted against portrait painting and settled down happily to still-life. But in Berlin in 1924 Duncan found him harnessed to a portrait of a female member of the Rothschild family. If he succeeded, friends had advised him, he would receive commissions from the richest people in Berlin and would be able to make money as and when he felt like it. This carrot kept him at the easel, while other members of the family stood round making comments and the portrait got worse and worse. Duncan, called in to comment, was appalled by what he saw but felt he had no alternative but to praise.

Franzi, knowing it would amuse Duncan, took him to some of the famous homosexual cafés in Berlin, as Duncan recounted to Vanessa. 'It was interesting to see but as you might imagine extremely proper and rather slow not unlike a Cambridge party at a rather shabby undergraduate's rooms. The only thing that was a little bolder was that the pictures on the walls were sometimes photos of nude young men with horses – very teutonic.'[51] Other aspects of German life repulsed him and he concluded that the Germans must have a different ideal of beauty from his own, though he quite liked the small, discreet hotel at which he stayed, close to Unter den Linden. He talked a great deal about painting with Franzi and dined with him most evenings on his return from the Rothschild portrait ordeal. 'I see the poor creature is really a hopeless case,' Duncan wrote to Vanessa, ' – until he can get rid of that awful wife. But I also see he is the sort of creature that never will, because she has somehow learned to prey upon him and appeal to his sense of pity. I think if it goes on any longer he will really be driven off his head.'[52] The more he saw of Franzi, the more desperately sorry Duncan felt for him. Nor had he misjudged his friend, for though Franzi managed to arrange matters so that he often spent periods painting in a different city from his wife, he never left her. In 1927 a breakdown in his health obliged him to recuperate in a clinic, from where he wrote to Duncan, 'You can't know how often I thank the fate that let me meet you – you are one of the events in my life that made me feel that life really was nice.'[53] For some fifty years Franzi, though aware that in some ways he irritated Duncan, sent him occasional letters in which he remained affectionate, grateful, wistfully aware that Duncan had occupied a place no other could fill.

During the daytime in Berlin Duncan was mostly alone. He went daily to the Kaiser Friedrich Museum where he made small watercolour copies of its masterpieces, marvelling at certain Italians, especially Signorelli, at Rembrandt and Holbein. 'Everything is shown with the most correct taste, beautiful frames etc. In fact there is no doubt that it is extremely well done. But *à la fin* one does feel rather profoundly that making a museum is a very different affair from making even the most minor work of art.'[54] He moved on to Dresden, which enchanted him. He stayed at the Hotel Palatz Weber and began his next letter to Vanessa, 'I have seen the Sistine Madonna.'[55] Finding it in a room by itself with a crowd of onlookers blocking his view, he sat down and waited for Raphael's picture to speak. He found himself likening its quiet mood and subdued colour to the *Madonna della Perla* in Madrid. Finally its perfection thrilled him, and, looking at the rough-and-tumble Sunday crowd that surrounded it, Duncan marvelled that a picture that depended so entirely on its formal beauty should have such wide appeal.

With nervous excitement he then went in search of Giorgione's *Venus*. This time he did not need to acclimatise himself to the work of art, for he came across it suddenly and was immediately overcome by its beauty, his eyes brimming with tears. The sensations this picture gave him exceeded any that he had experienced for a long time. He returned to England re-invigorated and inspired, if also regretful that Giorgione's early death had deprived the world of more beautiful things.

SIXTEEN

Humming with Heat and Happiness

At the general election in October 1924, which marked the end of the first Labour government, after only nine months in office, Maynard predicted a Liberal victory. He persuaded Vanessa and Duncan to join him in a gamble and they pledged themselves to seventy pounds each. He kindly overlooked these debts when the Conservatives romped home to another term of office. 'Well,' Clive wrote gleefully to Vanessa, 'in spite of Duncan's vote and your apathy, my Mr Baldwin will be prime-minister again.'[1]

Duncan knew little about money and was not greatly interested in it. Painting, however, continued to absorb him deeply. He could afford to trust in Maynard's speculative sense because the sale of his paintings had just brought him a cheque for £514 7s 4d from the Independent Gallery. Some of his recent pictures had been painted with the palette knife, possibly with Segonzac's example in mind. This tool offered none of the seductions associated with the brush, but it obliged him to keep the general composition always in mind and to use less detail. This, Duncan remarked, was to the good so long as the painting did not become empty. But it was a passing phase: for the rest of his career he used the palette knife only sparingly. Brushes, by comparison, were more pliable and expressive. He now began to give more attention to the act of painting than to the thing being painted. In 1926 he admitted to a friend, 'I always hold perhaps quite wrongly that subject to an artist is no more than a scapegoat or safety valve and that any subject will do equally well.'[2]

In his dealings with people, however, he remained alert to the ingredients in any situation. For instance, on the day that Quentin left Charleston for Leighton Park School, as a first-time boarder, Duncan travelled with him to Paddington. Aware that Vanessa regarded her son's departure as the end of an era, he sent her a reassuring report. Quentin, he remarked, was the kind of person who would 'grow old very slowly . . . always in an interesting way'.[3] Though Duncan could be acerbic ('prim and acid as ever,' Virginia noted in her diary),[4] his sympathy with others made him highly receptive, especially to his mother and aunts, whose foibles – such as Aunt Daisy's refusal to compromise or adapt – he simply accepted. 'It's quite true that she's completely unreasonable,' Lytton had once remarked of Daisy McNeil to Duncan, 'but I don't know whether she thinks she isn't, or whether she simply moves forward under the full sail of her instinct, which certainly *is* astonishingly vigorous.'[5]

In December 1924 Duncan and his mother travelled on Aunt Daisy's Dutch barge along certain canals and rivers in France. They set off from Dijon and by New Year's Eve had reached Verdun, where Duncan bought sparkling white Burgundy for the mate and his engineer, and everyone in the town, from the Mayor to the local prostitutes, danced in the Salle de la Renaissance. At Beaune, which Duncan thought 'full of things to paint, a perfect place'[6] he took his leave of the others and returned home via Paris.

While abroad he was glad to receive news of Angelica. 'Please give her best love and tell her I love her very much indeed,' he wrote to Vanessa.[7] She replied that he need not feel obliged to return until he was ready to do so, 'as of course I can get on without you, half baked though I feel in my solitary state'.[8] Duncan, who respected feelings – his own and other people's – knew that he was bound to Vanessa, not by any legal, religious or social convention, but by invisible ties that went deep. He was profoundly aware of the importance of personal attachments, and when Jacques Raverat died on 7 March 1925 Duncan immediately regretted that he had neither corresponded with Jacques nor gone to see him at Vence during his 1921 visit to St-Tropez. He admitted the same to Gwen Raverat, in a letter that touched her greatly, as Virginia told Vanessa,[9] for it was motivated not by conventional sentiment but by a frank and realistic appraisal of loss:

I have always felt you and Jacques to be the most ill fated of our generation and the most heroic. When I first heard the news of Jacques' death my feeling was that it was the end of a tragedy. Please do not think by this I mean that I am not feeling sorry for you now – I do not see how you should not feel battered and unhappy but perhaps your unhappy feelings will be about the past rather than the present. When I think of all the gifts Jacques had and of so many kinds and of what he might have done with them but for this wretched illness – I feel his life has been abominable bad luck for all of us. Please forgive me if I have said anything that does not sympathise with your own feelings – it is only that I somehow feel bound to express something of my own to you.[10]

He was more circumspect about Maynard's desire to marry Lydia as soon as a divorce had been obtained from her first husband. It was, Duncan admitted to Vanessa, a 'grim fact' to face. Nevertheless he went along, somewhat unwillingly, to St Pancras Central Registry Office on 4 August 1925 to act as best man. He knew from experience that marriage, a publicly recognised state bringing with it expectations and commitments, could often turn a harmonious union into a ghastly trap. He had dined with Matthew Smith and witnessed the tirade that his wife unleashed when Duncan let drop the seemingly innocuous detail that Matthew had eaten no lunch. ('He winced like a naughty child and was immediately blown up by the vixen.'[11]) At Maynard's wedding Duncan, who dealt admirably with the photographers, arrived with his boots impeccably polished but without the ring, which fortunately Maynard had remembered. It was Lydia who provided the only awkward moment, for she was inexplicably vexed and embarrassed when asked her father's profession. Relations between her and Duncan continued to be affectionate. He painted two three-quarter-length portraits of her and designed the décor for the pas de deux, *The Postman*, which she danced with Stanislas Idzikovsky at the Coliseum for three weeks in 1925. But he still became irritated with her conversation whenever there was a gathering of friends.

There were further distractions that August. It had been decided to fill in a courtyard at Charleston with a studio, which became a part of the house. Roger had drawn up plans and that month workmen of all kinds – painters, plumbers and carpenters – hammered away, dislodging the swallows from the eaves and creating a great deal of rubble, much of which went into the paths in the garden. Duncan had the idea for a fishpond in the small courtyard to one side of the new studio. These additions helped keep Charleston alive: it was now very familiar to its inhabitants yet constantly changing, its atmosphere thick with nostalgia yet at the same time conducive to experiment. No decoration was conceived as a fixed and final statement, but merely as a response to the needs of the moment. No single style directed the arrangement of the house, the beauty of which was informal, a means to no end other than enjoyment.

House and garden generated contentment. 'I never saw two people humming with heat and happiness like sunflowers on a hot day more than those two,'[12] Virginia wrote of Duncan and Vanessa that summer, during which they accompanied her to a school at Hayes Common in Kent where she delivered a lecture. Afterwards Virginia described how she 'drove home in the dark with Nessa and Duncan, who pour out pure gaiety and pleasure in life, not brilliantly or sparklingly, but freely quietly luminously'.[13] Their shared happiness set a standard against which Duncan could measure other experiences, such as his visit in August 1925 to Adrian and Karin Stephen's new home, the King's Head; an old wood-slatted house and formerly an inn, dating back in part to the early seventeenth century, it hung over the bank of an estuary, part of the Walton Backwaters at Landermere in Essex. Apart from a nearby row of cottages, the house was, and remains, very isolated. At low tide mudflats appear in the estuary, on the other side of which stretches saltmarsh as far as the eye can see. The setting reminded Duncan of certain Constable paintings, but he also saw that in winter it would be appallingly desolate. As well as Adrian and Karin and their two daughters, Ann and Judith, there lived in the house an elderly couple, a cook and a young German woman who looked after the children and did odd jobs. 'The noise and turmoil are terrific during the day,' Duncan told Vanessa. This peep into the Stephen ménage, their ragamuffin children and the general want of domestic comfort made him still more appreciative of Charleston, and he found himself wondering whether Vanessa had begun planting his lily bulbs. Then Adrian and Karin took him sailing down the estuary and his spirits rose. He was about to accept the gin Karin offered but changed his mind when she lifted her skirt and wiped the drinking cup on her drawers.

When Duncan admitted to Simon Bussy that he cared only for the opinions of a small group of people, he revealed both a strength and a limitation in his attitude to his work. Coterie approval freed him from any slavish following of the latest fashion, but it also discouraged comparison of his own work with that of artists from a different milieu. As a result, in the course of these inter-war years he became gradually less familiar with contemporary French art and artists, and more involved with decorative schemes commissioned by friends. One example, in the summer of 1925, was the clothes and scenery he designed for Lytton's play *A Son of Heaven*, a *jeu d'esprit* written some twelve years before. Set in the Imperial Palace, Peking, it concerned the affairs of the Empress Dowager and a Chinese Duke at the time of the Boxer Rebellion (of 1909). Two charity performances were held at the Scala Theatre to raise funds for the London and National Society for Women's Service, a voluntary organisation for women's rights, which later became the Fawcett Society and whose secretary was Lytton's sister, Pippa. Duncan, though immersed in a Japanese book (the first volume of Arthur Waley's translation of Lady Murasaki's *The Tale of Genji*), managed to produce fresh and original chinoiserie, possibly based less on his knowledge of Chinese culture than on D'Oyly Carte performances of *The Mikado*. The painter Robert Medley (roped in to play the silent part of a eunuch) remembered the colours used: clear ochres and greys, offset by pinks, oranges and emerald greens.[14] The decorative patterns on the costumes were all hand-painted by Duncan and Vanessa with a boldness reminiscent of the Omega. The leading lady, Miss Gertrude Kingston, when shown her costume on the night of the performance, refused to wear it and a taxi had to be sent hurriedly to 51 Gordon Square to fetch a Manchu robe belonging to Lady Strachey, its heavy embroidery and black brocade quite out of keeping with the rest of the costumes.

Shortly after this performance, one of the props, a screen with horses painted on it, caught the eye of Mina Kirstein, who asked to buy it. She had returned to London that summer as Mrs Henry Tomlinson (and under the name Minna Curtis later became an author, editor and teacher at Smith College). A portrait of Mina by Duncan already hung in her parents' home in Boston. Now her husband, wanting a smaller version, commissioned another, giving Mina the opportunity to see Duncan again and to view his recent portrait of Henrietta Bingham. In Mina's absence Henrietta, undergoing analysis and struggling with family disputes, had taken refuge at intervals in Duncan's studio, grateful for his sympathetic company.

He never lacked work, for in addition to his painting there was often some decorative project in hand. When the Woolfs moved from Hogarth House, Richmond, to 52 Tavistock Square in the spring of 1924, Virginia invited Duncan and Vanessa to undertake the decorations for a fee of twenty-five pounds. They produced three panels for her sitting-room, in each of which a cluster of objects creates a roundel motif, offset by freely drawn cross-hatching around the edges of the frame.[15] More decorations were made for her bedroom. 'My rooms are all vast panels of moonrises and prima donna's bouquets,' she contentedly told a friend.[16] When the Stracheys had their entrance hall and staircase repainted at 51 Gordon Square, Duncan prescribed the exact mixture of powder colours (ultramarine, raw umber, a touch of ochre) necessary to obtain a French grey. Robert Medley brewed the distemper, whitening and size over a gas ring in the dining-room.[17] Next door, at 50 Gordon Square, Clive Bell's flat had been transformed by Duncan and Vanessa's decorations on the door panels and around the fireplace. They inspired his friend, the literary critic Raymond Mortimer, to commission a wall decoration for his flat at 6 Gordon Place,[18] which kept Duncan busy during December 1925. Angus Davidson also lived in decorative splendour, owing to his friendship with Duncan. Certain staple ingredients recur in these decorations: jugs, flowers, musical instruments, curtain swags, simple ornamental patterns and loose imitation marbling. One particularly loyal client was Mary Hutchinson, who moved that year to Albert Gate in Regent's Park, and again asked Vanessa and Duncan to enliven her rooms. In addition to large schemes, Duncan turned his hand to individual items, designing chair covers for his mother to embroider and going to great lengths to find the right coloured wools for her. Unlike Vanessa, he did relatively little work for the Hogarth Press, but both of them worked on illustrations for Clive's *The Legend of Monte Della Sibilla*, published by the Press in 1923. Subtitled *Le paradis de la Reine Sibille*, it tells a rollicking story involving wine, women and song, and is enhanced by Duncan's frontispiece, showing two lovers embracing under a tree, and by his tailpiece of a sprawling buxom nude.

Consuming productivity made it necessary for Duncan to relax. At Twickenham during the Christmas of 1925 he found the tranquillity and comfort in which his mother and aunts lived entirely sympathetic. While there he came across some old family photographs, which allayed suspicions about Colonel Young. 'One of them of my father I think proves my parentage to be of wedlock as I think I see certain likenesses to myself.'[19] He found scant likeness to Rupert Brooke in Edward Marsh's memoir, which he was reading, and instead a mawkish symbol of heroism and loss. 'Hurry up living and don't die young or the same thing will happen to you,' Duncan wrote to Bunny.[20] Awareness of mortality led him the next day to pen a short note: 'To all whom it may concern I wish to be cremated when I die.'[21] (Fifty-three years later this note had become buried among the mass of papers that accumulated during his lifetime, and those responsible for his funeral were unaware of it.)

From Twickenham Duncan travelled to Hilton Hall in the village of Hilton, Huntingdonshire, which Bunny had bought in 1924. He was impressed by the romantic beauty of this house, by its Queen Anne façade, its large open fireplaces, oak beams, elm staircase, stone floors and eighteenth-century panelling in the wide central hall. Meanwhile, Vanessa stayed at Charleston while visitors came and went. She listened to Roger talk about his new-found love for Helen Anrep, their desire to live together and the difficulties this presented to Boris, Helen's husband, and Margery, Roger's sister. When Roger paused for breath, he began to take an interest in Duncan's sketch for a large composition based on male bathers. In the finished oil,[22] the various figures stand, sit, lean, bathe or wrestle, their various poses creating a complex net of directional forces. But in addition to purely formal considerations, the painting offered Duncan an outlet for his enjoyment of the male physique. He had found willing models in Robert Medley and his partner, the dancer Rupert Doone, one of Duncan's former pick-ups.

Because of the intimacy she shared with Duncan, Vanessa could frankly admit that she was glad that year when the Woolfs' Christmas visit to Charleston ended. 'I get very tired of the perpetual personal conversation that goes on. Yesterday Vita [Sackville-West] came to lunch . . . Virginia held forth in her usual style . . . Very amusing but also most uneasy, at least to my mind . . . It is brilliant of course . . . but one simply gets exhausted and longs for some quiet talk that will lead nowhere for a change. I even think how refreshing some of the pure male speculations to which as you know I cannot attend would be . . . Did you know that Eddie [sic] Sackville-West is desperately in love with Tommy like everyone else?'[23]

Gossip concerning Edward Sackville-West, who was in time to inherit Knole, mattered to Duncan: for some time he had silently adored this arrogant, quirky young aristocrat (sixteen years his junior), whose family had come to prominence in the reign of Elizabeth I. Eddy, as he was familiarly known, had an array of mannerisms, the most notable of which was his habit, caught by Graham Sutherland in a memorable portrait, of holding his head slightly tilted back. His drooping upper eyelids conveyed a world-weariness and hauteur, even though his thoughts were often occupied with the prosaic details of his minor ailments. A pale face and mournful eyes gave him the appearance of an El Greco saint, while his high voice and effeminate manner betrayed his sexual ambivalence: though he preferred the company of women, and on occasion proposed marriage, he was sexually drawn to men with temperaments very different from his own.

His tastes were musical and literary. He led a rather feverish literary life, holding vehement opinions on the work of D. H. Lawrence and T. S. Eliot, and writing novels, publishing his first, *Piano Quintet*, at the age of twenty-four. In 1927 his essay, *The Apology for Arthur Rimbaud*, appeared under the imprint of the Hogarth Press, for which he also translated Rilke's *Duino Elegies* with his cousin Vita Sackville-West. He was also to produce a book on De Quincey and later still to compile with the music critic Desmond Shawe-Taylor *The Record Guide*. Such cleverness impressed Duncan, who in the spring of 1926 managed to oust Stephen Tomlin in Eddy's affections. 'By the way I think I ought to tell you I have never received any proper education,' he warned Eddy. 'You may be shocked by my writing, spelling, lack of knowledge, etc. etc.'[24] That spring Duncan, often with half his buttons missing, braces too long and with pieces of his shirt sticking out, ordered a new suit, ostensibly for his forthcoming trip abroad, but more likely with visits to Knole in mind.

He shared his excitement over Eddy with no one except Bunny. Much else was happening at this time. Among other things the Keyneses had arrived in Sussex, having leased the nearby Tilton Farmhouse from the Firle estate, and in April they came and went in a large motor car without calling in at Charleston. 'It dawns on me', Vanessa remarked to Duncan, 'that they are no more anxious to see us than we to see them.'[25] Nevertheless, their association with Maynard had led to the formation of the London Artists' Association (LAA) which, underwritten by three business sponsors, was to guarantee to a select number of artists, including Duncan and Vanessa, an income. This would be offset by sales from regular LAA exhibitions. The first of these was to be held at the Leicester Galleries in June. Meanwhile that April Duncan was working hard at a large picture, possibly his *Bathers*, as he was drawing Rupert Doone and getting to know the young Robert Medley better. At the Slade, Medley's best friend had been one of Lady Strachey's grandchildren, John Strachey, and for a period he had more or less lived in the Strachey household, hearing a great deal about Duncan and Vanessa. At the age of twenty, like many of his generation, Medley looked on Duncan as something of a demi-god. Duncan showed no sign of letting such admiration bloat his self-esteem. In his spare moments that spring he read Chekhov's letters in Constance Garnett's translation. Writing to Bunny, he asked him to thank his mother for all the pleasure she had given him.

'Well do not tell a soul that I am in love,' his letter to Bunny ended. 'I think it very doubtful and haven't the least clue whether I am or not, and according to my new theories, it does not make the slightest difference whether I am or not. My best love to Ray and to my godchild and to the other.'[26]

His affair with Eddy appears to have begun shortly before his holiday in Venice with Vanessa and Angus Davidson in the spring of 1926. He set off in advance of the other two at the end of April, stopping *en route* in Paris, where he met by chance Franzi von Haas, with whom he dined, and toured the galleries on the Rue de Seine, where he was chiefly excited by two paintings by Derain. In Venice he booked into the Hotel Manin, toured the Zattere, looking for rooms in which to live when Vanessa and Angus arrived, and wrote a long letter to Eddy. There were aspects of his new friend that he found difficult to accept: his puzzling moods, his dislike of wine. ('No I don't mean that I do not admire your severity –

but I should like you to be a little more sympathetic to those who love wine.')[27]

Alone in Venice, Duncan wandered for hour after hour through the narrow alleys, often losing all sense of time and direction. The light, reflected off the water, danced on the coloured walls, and everywhere he looked there was something to catch the eye. He realised that his pleasure in these surroundings was entirely sensual, his critical faculty remaining in complete abeyance ('the beauty of everything is somehow so immediate and successful that I think it foolish to think at all').[28] Venice itself seemed remarkably empty and the tourists mostly Italian. He made little effort to do the sights but did wander into the Ducal Palace, where he studied a great many paintings by Tintoretto and Veronese. He ate well and cheaply at the Capello Nero and at a restaurant recommended by Sickert, the Giorgione, but admitted to Vanessa that his teatime chocolate and ices at Florian's cost almost as much as his dinner. He often returned to the Piazza after dinner, to listen to the Viennese waltzes, which in Venice kept ragtime firmly at bay.

By the time Vanessa and Angus arrived, Duncan had found rooms for them all at 234 San Gregorio on the Zattere. Though Virginia noted in her diary that Duncan was fined ten lire while in Venice for having 'committed a nuisance',[29] the holiday was an unmitigated success. Arrangements, such as their decision to meet at St Mark's in time for the evening service, were always a little vague owing to what Virginia termed Duncan and Vanessa's 'sublime ineptitude',[30] for neither had a watch and instead lived entirely by the sun and the great gun of St Mark's, which went off at midday. They visited Torcello by gondola on the hottest day and took a barouche to Padua to see, among other things, the Giottos in the Scrovegni Chapel. 'I had seen them before,' Duncan wrote to Eddy, 'but they are even finer than I had remembered and rather bracing after the art of Venice.'[31]

His relationship with Eddy was probably at its happiest while Duncan was in Venice, excited by this new affair and carrying in his head only an incomplete knowledge of the younger man's character. Though he could be a winning companion, there was also a negative streak in Eddy's nature, which made him peevish, melancholy, certain that things would not work out well. In return for a visit to Knole, Duncan invited Eddy to Charleston in September, but his stay was unhappy and seems to have soured their relationship. Eddy became very critical of Duncan's character and behaviour. 'You mustn't attack me so vigorously,' Duncan protested, 'because I know you have every right to think me bad, indifferent and neglectful. But of course this is far from true.'[32] His protests failed to quell Eddy's prickly dissatisfaction. Earlier, when Eddy had been offended by something Vita had done, Duncan had suggested that it would be better not to 'blow her up' but to keep silent. ('The best thing is, as is generally, complete silence.')[33] The same principle now helped gently to deflate their own relationship.

It had become Duncan and Vanessa's habit to return to Charleston for short periods at Christmas and Easter and for a long stretch during the summer. This pattern of existence offered changes of rhythm, the move from London's Fitzrovia to the depths of rural Sussex requiring an inner adjustment before the routine of painting could recommence. The new studio at Charleston proved a great advantage: even when children and guests filled the house, it provided a haven from the bustle elsewhere. 'I have begun to work and to think a little,' Duncan wrote to Eddy in August 1926; 'to have a low opinion of myself as a painter but to [have] come to the conclusion that if one is allowed to continue to paint by the world one is very lucky.'[34]

It is hard to reconcile this self-deprecating modesty with the fact that only two months beforehand Duncan had been the star of the London Artists' Association first exhibition, his name singled out for praise in almost every review. Younger artists imitated his manner of painting and he was widely celebrated. The Contemporary Art Society records show that they were prepared to pay as much for a Grant at this time as for a Sickert. None of this forestalled the renewed self-criticism that he brought to every picture he painted. His work varies in quality, but it is never unthinkingly repetitious or slick. An informal still-life of an ornate teapot, some mugs, a bottle and a large upright brown paper bag that once held provisions would be translated by Duncan into a tapestry of unexpected harmonies, irresistibly seductive and life-affirming. Owing to the intensity with which he looked at things ('intensity of regard,' he once scribbled on the back of a letter, 'reveals *character* of form'), he had coined a personal vision, and in order to keep it alive he doubted himself constantly, thereby keeping his responses on edge.

As a member of the LAA, he was one of seven artists guaranteed a salary of £150 a year, plus any sum in excess of that received from sales, less the commission, originally fixed at a percentage well below the commercial rate, but which in time had to be raised. Maynard masterminded the venture in order to help his friends. It must have seemed a rather blatant piece of favouritism, as the seven artists were all in some way connected with Bloomsbury: Duncan, Vanessa, Roger, Keith Baynes, Frank Dobson – the sculptor much admired by Fry and Clive

Bell – and Frederick Porter, whose presidency of the London Group had reflected his sympathy with Roger Fry's ideas, as did the work of Bernard Adeney, who also joined. Like his fellow artists, Duncan retained his membership of the London Group and continued to send to its twice-yearly exhibitions.

Though the LAA's exhibition had opened at the Leicester Galleries shortly after one of its two partners had committed suicide, it was a great success, some £1,600 worth of paintings selling within the first three weeks. The *Evening Standard* declared it Duncan Grant's show. *The Sunday Times*, relieved that abstraction and abnormality belonged to the past, noticed a 'leaning towards impressionism rather than post-impressionism . . . a general tendency to pay increased attention to illumination'.[35] Duncan was the leader of the group, announced the *Observer* critic, who noted the overriding influence of Cézanne, but thought Segonzac responsible for the 'unctuous quality of paint and the mellow loveliness of the browns and greys in such pictures as Mr Grant's *The Circus*'.[36] *The Times*'s critic praised Duncan's fluency and singled out a picture of game, *The Kitchen Table*, as 'very lovely in its combination of golden brown and mauve'.[37] When in September Duncan received his quarterly cheque from the LAA it far exceeded his guaranteed income and amounted to £395 7s 7d. Meanwhile the growing reputation of the LAA had attracted new names: by April 1927 Paul Nash, Douglas Davidson, William Roberts, Sydney Shepherd, Edward Wolfe and Christopher Wood had all accepted membership, though Wood resigned after six months. Matthew Smith had exhibited with the LAA but declined full membership.

Obligatory gratitude is often distasteful and the financial advantages brought by the LAA failed to mitigate the uneasy relations that existed between Charleston and the Tiltonians, as the Keyneses were called, when resident a couple of fields away at Tilton. On one occasion Duncan and Vanessa were made to feel ill-mannered when they refused to dine at Tilton in order to meet Mrs Courtauld, whose husband Samuel had agreed to underwrite the LAA. No longer did Maynard sit at ease in a rhorkee chair in the garden at Charleston while children clambered all over him. Instead it was agreed that summer that the two households should motor together to Birling Gap for a picnic. It was a somewhat forced occasion, made worse by the stormy weather and the fact that Lydia's little black dog was sick in the car and had to be deposited with a cottager. Afterwards they all sat by the stormy sea while the children gathered shells and Lydia poured out tea. The time of departure was carefully judged so that they could all be whisked home again by seven o'clock. To Duncan, it all seemed odd and unreal.

Though Charleston's visitors came and went, their presence caused very little adjustment to the routine of the house. 'Very plain living and high thinking,' remarked Vita Sackville-West a little tartly after her first visit in 1925.[38] She and others had to take things as they found them, or feel discomforted and out of place. Duncan's mother arrived for tea one day with two relatives, one of whom used her ear trumpet to advertise her deafness but not to hear what others had to say. This left her in a position of undeniable superiority. Duncan struggled valiantly with the situation, afterwards complaining to Eddy, 'Mixing one's relations with one's friends is always a very ticklish business and most exhausting.'[39] How much easier it was to host Roger Fry, who pursued ideas energetically, painted, read or wrote at the drop of a hat. 'One seems to work along at a greater pace when he's about,' Duncan observed.[40] He was enthralled when that summer Roger read aloud passages from a book he was writing on Cézanne, for in his analysis of the artist's development Fry seemed to make the artist's intention transparent.

Like Vanessa, Duncan involved himself with the work that enhanced Charleston each year. That summer he pounded and gravelled the garden paths and terrace, sweating profusely and afterwards falling asleep in his chair before dinner from sheer exhaustion. He looked forward to the arrival of Lytton, who intended staying a week, and to a shorter visit from Stephen Tomlin, even though both friends engendered an orgy of talk that left him befuddled. In the gaps between visitors he bicycled with Vanessa to see the Woolfs at Rodmell, where he had the unexpected treat of hearing Virginia read aloud a letter from Eddy. But it was painting that occupied the greater part of each day – to what purpose, he wondered, when he found an old picture of his that seemed to have merits far beyond anything he could see in his recent work? 'You will realise how depressing this is but I daresay it won't last for long . . .'[41]

In need of a change of scene, he crossed the Channel with Vanessa to Normandy in October, to stay with Ethel Sands. The visit was timely, as the approach of winter always made Duncan melancholy for he suffered from colds and, as a painter, dreaded the reduction in the number of daylight hours.

Château d'Auppegard, at Offranville near Dieppe, is a small, elegant seventeenth-century château, which the two painters Ethel Sands and Nan Hudson restored lovingly. They had stripped off the plaster on the south side, which had concealed the original black timber and cow-pat façade, repaired the eighteenth-century wood-panelling in certain rooms and had brought to bear on every detail of the furnishing their exquisite good taste. The fact that the château is only one room deep, each room having windows on two sides, adds to its lightness and grace. Vanessa and Duncan did not stay long on this visit, but it was probably then that they discussed the decoration of the loggia at one end of the house, a task they undertook the following year. On this second and more extended visit they found Nan and Ethel's impeccable lifestyle rather trying. The house and garden were both so neat and exquisite that in both Duncan had difficulty throwing away his cigarette butts. Nevertheless the murals, which cover all three walls of the loggia with rustic scenes, were a great success. They were painted in a style intended to be in keeping with the age of the château, but which reinvents the pastoral in modern terms, Duncan's exuberant brushwork adding to the bucolic charm of the imagery. Vita Sackville-West, who had thoroughly disliked their panels for the Woolfs' sitting-room in Tavistock Square, thought these murals 'absolutely enchanting'.[42]

After his first visit to the Château d'Auppegard, Duncan intended making a short tour of Normandy while Vanessa went to Paris to see Julian. He was spending an intermediary year there between school and Cambridge, attending lectures at the Sorbonne and, among other things, developing an interest in Chinese history. Now six foot tall, shaggy and large, he was out of place in Paris and wandered the streets with his mind full of Charleston and the birds that could be seen at Cuckmere Haven on a winter's day.

Duncan, too, ended his trip in Paris, Vanessa by now having returned to London. There he met the twenty-year-old Robert Medley, who had gained the right to visit Paris by asking Duncan to write a letter on his behalf to his parents. Together they made small watercolour sketches in the Louvre. With Medley in Paris was Rupert Doone, the dancer with choreographic ideas very much in advance of his time. Doone had hoped that Duncan would collaborate with him on theatrical projects, but though Duncan designed some costumes for a comic 'nigger-minstrel' duet and entered into long discussions with Doone for a ballet to be choreographed to music by Bach, nothing further came of this relationship.

Soon after Duncan returned to London plans were afoot for another trip to France, this time with his mother, Miss Elwes and Aunt Daisy; Aunt Violet, not being a traveller, had arranged to winter in Torquay. Aunt Daisy had arranged with Roland Penrose, a wealthy young man descended from successful East Anglian bankers, to rent Les Mimosas, the house Penrose had bought at Cassis on the advice of the artist Yanko

Varda. Duncan was to join the ladies there in the first week of January 1927.

Shortly before leaving for Cassis, Duncan began an affair with a tall, diffident, wealthy painter called Peter Morris, who lived at 25 Wilton Street in Belgravia with his sister Dora, to whom he was devoted. He had many friends in common with Duncan, including the Davidson brothers and the 'Tidcombe' boys, Paul Cross and Angus Wilson. Duncan fell heavily in love with this glamorous, gentle, sensitive, cultured dilettante, who had striking blue-green eyes. Less affected than Eddy, he was extremely shy and as a result could at first meeting appear haughtily aloof. Duncan warned Vanessa of this in a letter written from Paris, in which he expressed the hope that she would make the effort to meet Morris and therefore suffer less. 'I have told him nothing about you and me,' Duncan wrote to Vanessa, his remark exposing his divided loyalties. 'But of course I don't know what others have said. If I was there it would be perhaps easier . . . If you cannot face it, I shall understand.'[43]

Duncan's affair with Peter Morris was the first since Bunny seriously to alarm Vanessa. Though the affair with Angus Davidson had lingered on for some years, it was impossible to take offence at a creature so incapable of doing harm and Davidson had become an accepted part of Duncan's life and one of Charleston's perennial visitors. With Eddy, however, Duncan had felt a need for discretion and had asked him not to tell others about their feelings for each other. But if he was aware of the need to protect Vanessa, he was unaware until now of the extent of his own power to hurt. With his mother abroad, he had spent Christmas at Charleston and then gone to London, presumably to see Morris before leaving for Cassis. Vanessa, in a fraught state, had handed Duncan before he left a note that she afterwards regretted:

Duncan dearest I have felt so ashamed of myself for writing as I did just when you were leaving. Oh I wish I hadn't . . . I sometimes feel as if I'd really almost been insane for a time. I can't understand why one gets so miserable for nothing is really different and one knows it. In fact I think I know always that as far as anything can be permanent my relationship with you is, for it seems to me to depend on things that aren't likely to change in either of us till one gets old and doddering and then perhaps it won't matter if we both are.[44]

Duncan spent just under a week in London before leaving for Paris. He passed one afternoon looking at the Raphael cartoons in the Victoria and Albert Museum – 'am wildly excited about them,' he told Vanessa.[45] As he was a bad sailor, he dosed himself with Somnifene before crossing the

Channel and was so doped that on arriving by train in Paris he had to be prodded awake by a shocked French lady. He was pleased to find himself seated once again in the Deux Magots, but he carried with him on this trip an ineradicable memory of Vanessa's suffering.

It had been agreed that Angus would follow him to Cassis for a winter holiday and that Vanessa, too, would later join him for another long spell of painting, in a climate more sympathetic than wintry London. Soon after arriving at Les Mimosas Duncan admitted to Vanessa in the course of one letter that he had a temperature, mild flu and had gone deaf. Soon afterwards he collapsed in a feverish state. A Corsican doctor, and friend of Roger Fry, diagnosed bronchitis, which subsequently turned into pneumonia. When Angus arrived he was so alarmed by Duncan's state that he sent a report to Vanessa. On 21 January Virginia called on Vanessa and found her white-faced on the telephone, listening to the conclusions that Lytton's niece, Dr Elinor Rendel, was drawing from Angus's report, one of which was that Duncan might have typhoid. Vanessa immediately went into action: she had already let Duncan's studio and now she arranged to let her own; she also packed, sent cables and the following day left London with Angelica and Grace, planning a brief stop in Paris *en route* to Cassis.

Either just before she left or in Paris she received news that Duncan was over the worst, his condition no longer critical. She therefore spent a couple of nights in the Hôtel Londres and saw Julian at her leisure. Meanwhile Quentin was writing to Julian: 'I suppose you have seen Nessa plus fourteen cases of crockery, Grace, Angelica, nineteen canvases, rugs, paint boxes, etc ... I left Nessa sending scores of telegrams to Cassis and other places, trying to get all Duncan's clothes into three chests of drawers, a feat impossible ... with about nineteen Indians demanding admittance and wandering vaguely about the place.'[46] Her studio had successfully been let, but if Vanessa was free of racial prejudice, Duncan was not. 'My mother and I are both rather shocked you have let to Indians. But perhaps that's our Anglo–Indian prejudices. She says in spite of baths they smell. Also they are getting it very cheap. But I suppose if the agents think it's all right it is.'[47]

He was still very ill, scarcely able to eat as his digestion was very weak. Fortunately the cook who came in every day was also a good nurse, familiar with the practice of 'cupping' – clamping little glass jars on his back just after a piece of lighted cotton wool in each had gone out – which brought relief to his bronchial chest. High temperatures had kept him awake at night and by the time Vanessa arrived he was still too weak to do more than sit in the sun. She was frustrated in her desire to care for this thin, bearded convalescent by the presence of his relatives and Miss Elwes, who watched over him with a concern that was not always practical. In addition Mrs Grant, as Duncan admitted to Eddy, 'is slightly volcanic sometimes'.[48] Meanwhile Aunt Daisy, who had returned from one fancy-dress ball at three in the morning wearing a gold crown with coloured feathers in it, was *au mieux* with everyone in the town and had struck up a friendship with the painter Georges Braque, who was staying nearby, at La Ciotat. As the ladies did not plan to leave Cassis until the end of February, Vanessa, after lodging herself, Angelica and Grace in the Hôtel Cendrillon, discovered that she could rent the upstairs part of the recently built small villa owned by the Corsican doctor and named by him after his country. They had not been long installed in the Villa Corsica before Angelica and Grace, both now taking French lessons, announced that they were so happy they wanted to stay in Cassis for ever.

The unpretentious gaiety of this small port attracted Italian sailing ships, fishermen, local youth and bohemian painters. Penrose and Varda had built a studio with their own hands among the vines and the turning point for Duncan came in mid-February when he and Vanessa began to make use of it. 'He has begun to paint which is a great thing,' Vanessa told Maynard.[49] Returning to everyday life, after the curious unanchored existence brought on by severe illness, Duncan once again became aware how double-edged his relationship with Vanessa was. 'As for me,' he wrote to Eddy:

> I feel as if I had a very queer experience without quite knowing what it was. Almost I imagine like a loss of memory . . . all the same I feel different, not exactly indifferent, but I have a horror of meeting new people, a perfect horror of the pain that people can inflict on each other. My one object at the moment is neither to get nor to give pain to others and the only possible way out of the difficulty would be to become a trappist on a high promontory. Well, there are promontories and sea and a good deal of silence here, and I seriously think of giving up my studio in London and settling down somewhere in these parts. Do you think it cowardly?[50]

While ill, he had made the acquaintance of another English painter living in Cassis, Wyndham Tryon, and before many weeks had passed no lunch party in the area was thought complete without Duncan's presence: he could no more be a Trappist here than elsewhere, for his sympathy with humans was too great. Cassis in the spring captivated him. At the same time he learnt that one of his Plowden relatives had died intestate and that he was likely to receive a legacy of around £400. With this in mind, he began thinking of building a studio in the area. He was seized with the idea that Cassis should from now on become an annual refuge from the darkness and gloom which, like a metal dish-cover, descended every winter over cold, grey London.

SEVENTEEN

Cassis

'You would hardly recognise me here,' grumbled Clive, writing to Leonard from the cramped quarters of the Villa Corsica in Cassis, into which he had moved with Vanessa, Angelica and Grace. 'I live in a state of the highest spiritual exaltation and intense physical discomfort.'[1] He was hard at work on his book *Civilization*, in an attempt to recover from a sudden break in his relations with Mary Hutchinson. A month earlier he had told Vanessa, 'I am very unhappy, and you and Duncan are the only people in the world with whom I can ever imagine feeling better.'[2]

Clive soon abandoned Vanessa for a room in the town but continued to work at the Villa Corsica, which had two large balconies, one above the other, looking out over the two small harbours. He wrote while the artists painted. Duncan, by now dressed like a local in cotton clothes and espadrilles, had become, Clive thought, the man about Cassis. The painter John Howard met him in Wyndham Tryon's studio, where Duncan painted a portrait of Tryon playing the guitar. Howard recollected that Duncan and Tryon did portraits of Tryon's *femme de ménage*, who suddenly alarmed them by saying that her lover was '*très jaloux*', would not want her to be painted and was in the French colonial army. Tryon, himself, was an interesting painter whose career was terminated by mental illness and wiped out by the Blitz, one bomb landing on his studio and another on the depository where many of his paintings were stored.

Both Vanessa and Clive felt rather edgy about Cassis society, wanting for the purposes of work a similar isolation to that which they enjoyed at Charleston. In the same way that Duncan acted as a magnet for the Keyneses at Charleston, so at Cassis, Clive feared, he would attract all and sundry. But though Duncan saw something of his friend, the writer Peter Murphy, who lived at Nice, he had by April decided to drop out of local society. One exception was Colonel Teed ('the most attractive figure here'),[3] a former Bengal Lancer who had abandoned a wife in India in order to co-habit with an ex-nurse, Jean Campbell, who was a close friend of the New Zealand artist, Frances Hodgkins. The couple lived about a mile outside town on the Fontcreuse estate in a small seventeenth-century château, its nearby cypresses and orderly array of ponds in which frogs croaked giving way to an open expanse of vineyards.

Not far from their house, and looking down across fields towards Cassis, was an uninhabited workman's cottage. It was exactly what Duncan had hoped for. 'I have taken a cottage on his [Teed's] estate to be turned into a studio,' he told Eddy. 'It is in a most heavenly position. In a "classical" landscape some way from the town or village.'[4]

Though it was Duncan who found La Bergère, as it was called, all correspondence concerning its purchase was conducted between Colonel Teed and Vanessa and the lease was eventually in her name. Teed had not agreed to let immediately, and for a time Duncan went on looking elsewhere, even making a day trip to investigate the area around Toulon – 'a charming place with every inducement for one of my tastes'.[5] Then Teed fell in with the plan and negotiations, with all their necessary minutiae, continued over the summer. Teed was tough but sensible, pleased that Vanessa understood 'my indifferent grammar and involved explanations' and perfectly willing that they should have the right to sub-let.[6]

While at the Villa Corsica, Vanessa and Duncan attracted as many visitors as they did at Charleston: by April Leonard and Virginia, Stephen Tomlin, Julia Strachey and Douglas Davidson ('as spruce as ever with his silk dressing gown,'[7] Duncan observed to Eddy) had visited. Duncan, Clive and Vanessa in turn became visitors when they lunched with Auguste Bréal at his house, Lamardeto, at Ste-Marguerite outside Marseilles. Though Duncan found his Spanish wife almost unintelligible, he liked her greatly and was as impressed as always by Bréal, whom he continued to think one of the wittiest and cleverest of men. Duncan then moved on to Roquebrune and was equally smitten with the Bussys: 'They have been away six months in Egypt and are a fascinating trio. One lives in the greatest luxury, delicious food, divine weather. Gide had just been staying with them leaving a good deal of disarray I imagine behind in the female hearts . . . [Janie] is charming and intelligent as a needle and much more human. Simon is one of the wonders of the age and as good a riddle as the sphinx.'[8]

Duncan himself puzzled Virginia that spring. After her visit to Cassis, she remarked that, 'though some appearances are against it', Vanessa and Duncan seemed 'marmoreally chaste'.[9] In Duncan's case this was fairly accurate. His affair with Peter Morris, who was travelling somewhere near the Sahara, was in abeyance. Illness and the memory of Vanessa's pained outburst had left Duncan wary, uncertain of his feelings, of which he now tried to take stock. 'As for love,' he wrote to Bunny, 'in my case it hangs or lies suspended. Little by little I get used to or forget [that] my little heart flutters and miseries cannot last long if they are mute. If I don't get what I want amour propre comes into play a good deal which if it does not kill real love provides a corselet which deceives oneself, if not others.'[10]

This passivity also affected his work. He noted with a certain anxiety that his illness had left him 'incapable of doing anything except to lie still rather like a hand mirror and simply reflect life as it passed'; and he felt a need to pull himself together in order to prove that he still had a little will-power of his own.[11] While he was in this uncertain state a small exhibition of his work in London, at 163 New Bond Street, under the auspices of the LAA, reaffirmed his success. Seven out of the eleven paintings on show sold immediately and Fred Mayor, now acting as secretary to the LAA, told his mother that he could have sold Duncan's painting of Venice five times over. Prices ranged from forty-two guineas for *The Orange Jacket* to 140 guineas for a Provençal landscape. The detailed catalogue entries reminded viewers how widespread Duncan's reputation now was, for most of these works had been exhibited elsewhere, in Pittsburgh, New York, Berlin or at other London venues – the Chenil Gallery, St George's Gallery, the Claridge Gallery. They had also often been reproduced; for instance, in *Drawing and Design* earlier that year; in the Hogarth Press monograph on Duncan's art; or in the small Curwen Press book, containing seventeen illustrations and a two-page preface by W. G. Constable, which appeared that year in their 'British Artists of To-Day' series.

This select show was an important event. Carrington again urged Lytton to buy a painting. The press also took notice, *The Times* praising a 'characteristic purple-brown and apple-green', noting also how his orchestration of colours obtained the utmost value from every tint. 'His surface quality is as honest as needlework,'[12] the same critic remarked, a simile possibly suggested by a footstool, also exhibited, embroidered by Mrs Grant to Duncan's design, which caused a furore of interest. 'How horrid that you still have that mistral,' Ethel Grant wrote to her son meanwhile, 'but I hope you are able to paint some lovely things all the same. More are wanted my dear, more and more. Everyone is calling out for a "Duncan" . . . I cannot tell you my dear darling Dunk how much pleasure not to say pride your show is giving me. Bless you dear boy. Please send me the design for back of chair and wool as soon as you can. I have finished the seat.'[13]

Duncan, in turn, took pride in his daughter, noticing at Cassis that

Angelica got ever livelier and more remarkable. Vanessa thought the young girl must have inherited something from the Pattles, the family from which her mother was descended, which had produced strong-minded and beautiful women. No other child she had met seemed so masterful and terrific in character. 'She simply dominates everyone when she's there, but does it with great tact and charm so that one is simply fascinated and delighted to obey.'[14] When Julian and Quentin joined the party during the Easter vacation they brought with them the nurse, Louie Dunnett, who now took charge of Angelica, leaving Grace more time for other tasks.

Much excitement was caused by the arrival of Virginia's *To the Lighthouse*. Duncan took it with him when he went to Toulon for a night, reading it in train, tram, boat and café in a state of considerable excitement:

> I think it is a most moving and beautiful performance . . . I was so much astonished when that amazing creature Mrs Ramsay disappears that after reading the interlude I couldn't help wondering how you were going to invent another 'psychological volume' as they say to balance the first part. But Mr Ramsay does it in a most surprising way. I think by the way that the dinner party is an absolute chef d'oeuvre. If I was writing a review I should say I know 'nothing like it in English literature'. However unfortunately you know how little I know of English literature . . .
>
> Nessa is I suppose too much moved by it as a piece of portraiture to be able to take an entirely outside view of the book, and it has led to many fascinating discussions of your family. Its effect on Adrian (if he reads it) may affect a cure, I should think. Roger is reading it and is full of admiration. Poor Nessa has been forced to play chess with him at this moment in order among other things to prevent him reading out aloud to us either Shakespeare or *Claudine à Paris* both equally unintelligible. I cannot help thinking that either there are many likenesses in common or that you have occasionally used Nessa for getting into your mother [Mrs Ramsay]'s states of feeling. Well this is all absurd but I must tell you how much of an event the *Lighthouse* has been for me.[15]

They returned to London via Paris. In order that Vanessa could enjoy a few days there with Duncan, Angelica was sent back to London with Grace and began school with a Miss Rose Paul, in Mecklenburgh Square. She soon settled down, lunching two days a week with a fellow pupil, Gwen Raverat's daughter, Sophie, who in turn took lunch two days a week with Angelica. On her return to London, Vanessa was relieved to find her daughter chattering gaily, looking ravishing in her new clothes and with endless tea engagements and no lack of company. She went to inspect the studios at 8 Fitzroy Street (both tenants having left), arranged for them to be cleaned, and in the corridor she bumped into the painter Matthew Smith. He apologised profusely for the fact that he had rented one of the studios in the house for a trial period, with a view to taking it permanently. Vanessa said that she hoped he would. Then, hoping to calm his agitated, nervous manner, she added that they need not see each other, a remark that led to Smith's anxious insistence that she and Duncan should tell him if they found his presence intolerable. They shook hands three times and parted.

It may also have been in 1927 that Duncan became mildly embroiled with the actress Valerie Taylor, who had a knack for creating amorous situations. Duncan took her to the cinema and, it is rumoured, to bed, though perhaps it was the other way round. Among his papers is a sad letter from Valerie admitting how silly she had been in London, how blind to the hopelessness of the situation. 'All the same,' she added, 'I wish everything did not always seem to conspire together to keep you quite out of reach – even as one's most correct friend.'[16]

That summer Stephen Tomlin married Julia Strachey. Both were present at the nautical fancy-dress party given in July by the fashion journalist Madge Garland, at which Duncan appeared 'very exquisite as a commadore'[17] and Lytton as an admiral. The gaiety of the period helped improve relations between Charleston and Tilton. A dinner party given by the Keyneses in September was followed by an entertainment in which Lydia danced the character of Queen Victoria and Duncan, aided by a gramophone, mimicked Caruso. Music continued to be an important part of their life at Charleston that summer, Duncan having introduced a new gramophone on which he played Mozart and other of his favourite composers. He also took driving lessons from Louie Dunnet's husband Fred, and in time began to drive alone, as it was still possible to obtain a licence without passing a test.

He and Vanessa were making preparations for the Château d'Auppegard decorations when Roger Fry visited. Always their most stimulating guest, Roger arrived in time for tea and before it had ended had explained why the quantum theory had to be abandoned in favour of classical physics; had read aloud from proofs a large part of Robert Bridges's *The Testament of Beauty*; and had sketched out for them the decorations he was executing in his sister's rooms at Oxford. The appalling weather gave him the opportunity to demonstrate, with the aid of *The Times* weather map, why it was raining and would inevitably go on raining. The next morning he was found at breakfast scribbling an article while having his coffee and eggs, and he was as ready as ever to enter into a discussion of aesthetics should the mere hint of one arise.

That autumn work began on La Bergère, the cost of which Duncan and Vanessa shared between them. In October Duncan journeyed to Cassis to inspect the repairs, agree to innovations and decide on such details as the size of the pergola and the colour of each room. He stopped *en route* in Paris, where he saw Peter Morris and Franzi von Haas and then caught a train to Limoges, where Bunny met him at the station in a car. Thence they drove to Cassis. The terrace outside the house had been broadened and an extra room and bathroom built on one side. 'The whole effect,' Duncan told Vanessa, 'goes beautifully with the landscape which is extraordinary now with all the vines orange red and yellow.'[18] Jean Campbell took a particular interest in the renovation of the cottage and was anxious that it should be in complete order when Vanessa next visited. Through Duncan, Teed offered the use of his donkey to Angelica.

Everything seemed to bode well for the future: Elise Anghilanti, who had cooked for them at the Villa Corsica, wanted to work for them at La Bergère; their former maid, Gabrielle, helped Duncan choose all the cooking implements, bargaining in Provençal style over every pot; Jean drove him to Marseilles, where they shopped for the house and she also promised to get second-hand mattresses with good provenances; and Roland Penrose took Duncan and Bunny to a pottery at Aubagne that made use of eighteenth-century moulds and where Duncan got everything they needed for £2 10s. Afterwards they all lunched at the Penroses' with Roland's wife Valentine Boué, a poet, whose conversational habit of suddenly irrupting with vituperation against banality or convention terrified Duncan. Soon afterwards Bunny left in order to proceed with the next stage of his tour.

Left on his own in Cassis, Duncan was dragged back momentarily into another world when he spent an evening with the former Vorticist, the painter Jessica Dismorr, who chattered fascinatingly about Wyndham Lewis and Duncan's former friend, Frederick Etchells. But above all this visit confirmed him in his love of Cassis and he was overcome once more with the beauty of La Bergère's setting. When the time came to leave, he chose to catch a train to Paris, not from Marseilles but from Toulon, another place which, for more complicated reasons, he also loved.

No one was more surprised than Duncan at the success he enjoyed. To others it seemed enviable. When in 1928 an assistant at the Tate Gallery,

J. B. Manson, considered giving up his job in order to return to painting, he sought advice on what his earnings might be from Roger Fry. 'The position of the honest artist here is so desperate,' Fry warned, adding that it might be possible to hope for some £200–300 a year, but not more than that 'without some extraordinary piece of luck such as D. Grant has always had'.[19]

That autumn Duncan received an invitation to exhibit in Paris from the dealer Zborowski, almost as soon as he alighted in the city. He also ran into Derain in the Rue Bonaparte and lunched with H. S. Ede. Like Manson, Ede was an assistant at the Tate under the Director, Charles Aitken, who, despite newly opened galleries paid for by Sir Joseph Duveen and a generous fund for the acquisition of French pictures from Samuel Courtauld, had so far failed to correct the impression that the Tate was largely a dumping ground for sentimental Victorian pictures. 'Yesterday I had lunch with Eed [Ede],' Duncan told Vanessa, 'and we went picture hunting in the R. de la Boëtie. He really is very nice and very keen and quite intelligent about pictures. I cannot make out how he manages to keep so alive at the Tait [sic]. Perhaps he goads on Aitken.'[20] Ede's career proves Duncan's insight: while at the Tate he quelled frustration by simultaneously acting as secretary to the more go-ahead Contemporary Art Society until ill health caused him to retire, still a relatively young man. Thereafter he thrived, creating the house and collection that together make up Kettle's Yard in Cambridge, and lived happily into his nineties.

Because Duncan cared little for worldly success, he kept the centre of his life, his dedication to painting, uncorrupted. The critics lauded him again in November, the *Morning Post* praising his sure grasp of pictorial architecture and distinguishing him from others in the London Group as 'the one painter who really counts among the sheep-like fellows of the Cézannesque school'.[21] Duncan did, however, share in the increased prosperity that Bloomsbury enjoyed at this time, which was made noticeable by the appearance of motor cars. The Woolfs now journeyed the short distance from Rodmell to Charleston, not by bicycle but in 'the Old Umbrella', as Vita Sackville-West nicknamed their car. Duncan, seeing Vanessa set off for her parents-in-law's house Seend in her own car that Christmas, was reminded of a photograph he had seen in the *Daily Mirror* of the King and Queen making a similar grand departure. He himself went as usual to Twickenham where he painted a snowscape through one window, which he concluded must be rather bad as Colonel Young praised it. That year Duncan took his mother to the circus at Olympia.

In London he rarely lacked entertainment. One evening at 46 Gordon Square *divertissements* were performed to music by Chopin. Stephen Tomlin and the art critic and painter Alan Clutton-Brock were among the performers. Duncan found himself attracted to Clutton-Brock, though it was Rachel MacCarthy, who danced with Lydia, with whom he fell momentarily in love. Another entertainment that winter was the short play written by Beatrice Mayor, which Angelica and her friends performed in Duncan's studio. A different kind of excitement was provided nearby in Fitzrovia by the painter Cedric Morris, who held regular, largely homosexual, parties. Duncan attended one of these but did not greatly enjoy it, perhaps because he had to watch Bunny flirting with a ravishing young man whom Duncan instinctively distrusted. Though he crossed paths with Cedric Morris on several occasions, there was little sympathy between them, perhaps because Duncan felt ill at ease in certain homosexual quarters. If so, then the appeal of Vanessa's 'otherness' was that it allowed recognition of difference. She neither reinforced nor challenged his sexuality but accepted it, thereby releasing him from anxiety.

Duncan began 1928 by making plans to leave London. He let his studio to the painter James Holland while Vanessa, also preparing for a visit to Cassis, responded to questions from the Bedford estate concerning the number of residents at 37 Gordon Square. As it had become a *pied-à-terre* for many, including Lytton, Bunny, Douglas Davidson and Dadie Rylands, it was hard to know what the correct answer was. 'Your mysterious wife haunts the basement,' Vanessa wrote to Bunny in November of that year, 'and I sometimes see her flitting like a bat round the square.'[22] In January in addition to practicalities, Vanessa had also to cope with the nine-year-old Angelica's spiritual leanings. 'Angelica is very happy,' she told Leonard, 'but is suffering from a religious phase. I encourage it as far as I can and sent her to mass this morning with Duncan. She asks the most unanswerable (by me) questions about the Holy Ghost.'[23]

That year Julian embarked on his second term at Cambridge, where he was reading history at King's College. Quentin, owing to a contact provided by Franzi von Haas, had taken up lodgings with a Baroness von Massenbach in Munich, where his discovery that she spoke excellent French thwarted any hope of him learning German. Meanwhile Angelica had again been removed from school so that she could accompany Vanessa, Duncan and Grace to Cassis for their first visit to the newly restored La Bergère. On arrival they found wood fires lit, flowers in every room and a meal prepared, owing to the good services of Elise Anghilanti, who played no small part in making this small house a painter's paradise. Grace learnt much about cooking from Elise and, with Angelica, went off every morning to Cassis in the donkey cart for French lessons.

At Cassis Duncan made the mistake of ending one letter to his mother 'no news is good news'. She retorted, 'I think it both lazy and unkind, considering the sort of life you are leading.'[24] He did not need reprimanding again: at Easter he sent flowers to Lady Strachey, who wrote to Ethel, 'Dear Duncan never forgets anyone. Of course he would not forget *you*, but he remembers me too!' Ethel was so pleased by this remark that she reported it to Duncan, adding, 'Dear Aunt Janie, we shall never see her like again.'[25] In December 1928 Lady Strachey died and both Duncan and his mother were present at her funeral.

In Cassis they benefited greatly from the acquisition of a second-hand Renault car. In this Duncan travelled to Marseilles in March to meet Barbara Bagenal and her daughter Judith, who stayed on as a companion for Angelica after Barbara left. With a car they could explore the surrounding countryside, travel to La Ciotat for tea or have picnics beside one of the Calanques that cut into the shore between La Ciotat and Cassis. When Leonard and Virginia arrived they drove for two days without mishap on a tour to Tarascon, enjoying especially the country-side around Aix and visiting the Roman monuments at St-Rémy and the asylum in an old monastery where Van Gogh had stayed. 'The most peaceful beautiful garden,' Duncan recounted to his mother. 'We made a detour and saw Les Baux, an extraordinary and very ancient town built into very strange rocks high up in the Alpilles – really rather lovely.'[26] Duncan also spent some time alone in Toulon, where he sketched from the balcony of an hotel room that overlooked the port. Back at Cassis he was visited by Angus Davidson. It was decided that, when the time came to leave, Duncan, Vanessa and Angus should travel home by car, and Duncan looked forward to driving through the Périgord, famous for its culinary delights.

He complained that year that none of his paintings was finished; but that, Vanessa observed, was nothing new. Some days he was thwarted by the weather, which was poor and changeable. He also worried about Lady Ottoline, who had twice been operated on for necrosis of the jaw without any anaesthetic. He sent her a letter, which meant so much to her that, according to Virginia, 'she keeps it by her side, under a kind of chamber pot beneath [the bed]. Teeth are drawn daily, but she seems in the best of spirits and reads nothing but Shakespeare . . . Now it's a very odd thing how spirited the old thing is, how beautiful, with her jaw in a nosebag like an old horse, and yet so idiotic.'[27]

In Vanessa's opinion they led a relatively cheap, simple, sane, hard-working existence at La Bergère. When Julian visited in April, however, he found it impossible to get anything done and, writing to his brother, hinted at the clash of personalities that filled the small house:

> Everybody was more caracteristic [*sic*] than ever. Nessa bought masses of Provençal crockery, Provençal chairs and red Provençal petticoats for covering the latter, which set my teeth on edge so that I shrieked. Duncan was always late, quarrelsome and unable to understand a word of the conversation. Clive gave his blue silk pyjamas to a young lady and bought a nightshirt. Leonard had continual quarrels with Nessa and Duncan as to the exact shares each should pay for a litre of petrol. Virginia was quite dotty and asked perpetual questions ... As for Roger, he was unshakeably sane ... Angelica ruled the house with a rod of iron. I read practically the whole of English poetry to her. Grace mistook a bottle of brandy for water and drank a tumblerful ... I heard lurid tales about you.[28]

Duncan sent some of the product of this sojourn to the LAA group exhibition held at the Cooling Galleries, 92 Bond Street, in July. Whether he was in London or Cassis, he adjusted quickly to his surroundings and always found new things to paint. In June he spent a few days at Twickenham where, rocked by passing steamers, he sketched in a punt on the river. That summer he and Vanessa painted the noble façade of the Foundling Hospital which, with its two flanking wings, was pulled down in the autumn of 1928, despite protest mounted by the Foundling Estate Protection Lobby, to which Duncan sent a cheque for £55 2s 6d.

He had missed seeing the London Group Retrospective at the new Burlington Galleries in May but had been well represented by six paintings, three of them lent by Roger. Clive thought that Duncan's *Adam and Eve* (subsequently lost or destroyed while stored in the Tate Gallery) dominated one end of the gallery, while three paintings by Sickert dominated the other. Roger's introduction to the catalogue argued that in recent years construction in depth had replaced decorative surface organisation. He noted 'a feeling for a more rigorously planned construction, for a more close-knit unity and coherence in pictorial design, and perhaps a new freedom in the interpretation of natural colour'.[29] His analysis accurately described Duncan's development during the 1920s.

There were moments that summer when Duncan thought Charleston too full of people. By October he was in Paris again, seeing Clive and Quentin, who was now studying painting under Jean Marchand at the

Académie Moderne. As usual, Duncan made good use of his time. He saw a great many pictures, copied a Corot in the Louvre, visited Picasso and dined with Segonzac, also with Franzi von Haas. He had brought with him a copy of Virginia's latest book, her spoof biography, *Orlando*. Hearing that she was about to deliver a talk in Cambridge, he could not help wondering what effect her teasing, effervescent, brilliant mind would have on the male undergraduates.

Partly because of the doubts she was having about *Orlando*, Virginia was in an edgy state when she visited Charleston in August 1928. She thought Duncan 'a little too aloof and supercilious seeming',[30] an impression that runs counter to many others that he had inspired. To most of his friends Duncan appeared wholly unaffected by his growing fame. He became even more a celebrity in February 1929 when the Paul Guillaume, Brandon Davis Gallery in Grosvenor Street mounted a retrospective exhibition of thirty-four of his paintings. Journalists, with an eye to his success and still-youthful appearance, began referring to him as 'a darling of the gods'. *The Times* found in his work 'nameless hues of extraordinary subtlety' and noticed how in his landscapes 'all the elements of the scene, solid, aerial, and luminous, are brought into the same category of painting values'.[31] But his playfulness was still distrusted in the pages of the conservative *Morning Post*: 'He has not yet ceased to play fantastic tricks, as we see by the distorted *Venus and Adonis* and the cleverly droll *Pierrot Lunaire*.'[32]

Like other members of Bloomsbury, he was in the curious position of having joined the establishment (the Tate that year accepted his *South of France* offered by the Contemporary Art Society) whilst remaining in many ways a renegade. Even Clive, in some ways the most conventional of them all, led an unorthodox life, refusing in Paris to go out with Quentin because he thought Quentin looked like his son, and thus gave his age away, or like his lover and thus damaged his chances with potential mistresses. Few men of his huntin'-and-shootin' background could, as Clive did at a dinner that he gave for Marchand and his paramour, Sonia Lewitska, quote line after line of Mallarmé.

Of all Bloomsbury, it was Clive who pursued most vigorously friendship with Picasso. 'He was most affectionate about you both,' Clive reported to Vanessa, ' – said that if he had one atom of fashion about him he should think he was in love with Duncan – begged him to come and see him soon.'[33] If Duncan could have spent more time than he did in Picasso's company, he perhaps resisted doing so out of a need to protect his own artistic identity, which Picasso's ferocious creativity might have endangered. In addition Duncan's inclination to experiment had faltered, and he perhaps felt disinclined to subject himself to stimulus that was unsympathetic. His intermittent contact with Picasso remained friendly but it was no longer a source of creative inspiration.

Instead his eye alighted with interest on a host of different situations, his paintings reflecting his delight in the sight of a haystack or aspen trees rustling beside a pond, a hat shop in Bond Street or the congeries of boats found on the river at Twickenham. When travelling abroad Duncan responded with pleasure to every new experience that came his way. In January 1929 he, Vanessa and Quentin joined the Woolfs in Berlin, where Virginia was visiting Vita Sackville-West, whose husband Harold Nicolson was Counsellor at the British Embassy. They led what Vanessa described as 'a very rackety' week in the company of the Woolfs and the Nicolsons, with Eddy Sackville-West adding to the various tensions within the party, though not a hint of these tensions entered Duncan's letters to his mother. He especially enjoyed a day trip to Potsdam, where all the palaces were deserted and the parks full of temples and Chinese pagodas, white with snow. Afterwards he and Leonard drove back to Berlin in a sledge. On another occasion he sat drinking coffee with the rest at tables round the edge of an enormous swimming pool, and watched with amazement as the Berliners disported themselves amid the enormous waves, which were made to run the whole length of the bath. Later that year, when staying at Twickenham, he took a similar interest in the ice-skating rink at Richmond, to which he went as a spectator with his mother and Aunt Violet.

From Berlin he travelled with Vanessa to Dresden, Munich, Prague and Vienna, where they met Roger and enjoyed looking at paintings in his company. Even when abroad Duncan kept his mother firmly in mind and from Dresden sent her the name of a doctor, recommended by Adrian Stephen, to whom she could go for 'a course of suggestion against undue worries'.[34] It was not something he himself needed, in Virginia's opinion. 'And Duncan, whom I adore,' she wrote to Vanessa in spring 1929, 'is cased in oil silk from the assault of all elements. The two of you swim seal like through the waves.'[35]

Duncan knew that much of the ease he enjoyed was due to Vanessa. 'Owing to Vanessa's amazing arrangements everything goes like clock-work,' he noticed at La Bergère in June. 'I admire that woman's gifts more and more. They are unrivalled. Anyhow there is precious little for any of us others left to do – but paint, eat, drink, sleep and bathe – and with the heat I tend to become idler and idler.'[36] So many of Vanessa's family descended on Cassis that spring that they formed a small colony.

Clive and Julian put up at Fontcreuse with Colonel Teed, while Quentin had a room at the Hôtel Cendrillon. Virginia, when she arrived with Leonard, became an acute observer of life at La Bergère, her diary catching surface details such as Duncan's blue shirt, or the sight of Angelica and Judith doing their lessons on the terrace, as well as subtle, fleeting impressions such as the 'odd intimate, yet edgy, happy, free yet somehow restrained intercourse' between Vanessa and Duncan.[37] In a relationship where emotional loyalty was not accompanied by sexual commitment, restraint was perhaps inevitable. Both needed and depended on the other, yet silently acknowledged the gulf that lay between them. Each held the other in great respect, which strengthened their union but also kept familiarity at bay. And while Duncan found an outlet for his affections through his affairs with other men, Vanessa obtained intense richness of feeling through her relations with her children, especially her elder son.

Now in his second year at Cambridge, Julian was both popular with his fellow undergraduates and highly regarded by the Fellows and dons. Owing to his physical charisma, as he was soon to discover, he made female conquests easily. He beagled, spoke at the Union and at an Apostles dinner, wrote poetry and occasionally reviews for the *Nation & Athenaeum*, which had become a platform for Bloomsbury opinion ever since Maynard had taken over as Chairman of its Board in 1923. Julian's friends at Cambridge were mostly intellectuals – Anthony Blunt, Alister Watson, Harry Lintott and John Lehmann, among others, all of whom contributed to the shaping of his mind. But it was Vanessa with whom he remained most intimate. A transparent soul, he hid nothing, living his private life publicly and telling Vanessa, without any sense of shame, when he began sleeping with Blunt. Vanessa, far from being shocked by this revelation, perceived that the affair was not very serious and was instead delighted by the realisation that her son meant to keep nothing from her.

His Cambridge friends now added to the visitors that filled Charleston each summer. It was also probably owing to Julian that Bunny Garnett once again turned up at the house. After the exertion of beagling, Julian had on several occasions accepted Bunny's offer of a hot bath and hospitality at Hilton, where the two men had reminisced about Charleston and its history, talk that may have awoken in Bunny a desire to return. Others who called or stayed at Charleston during the summer of 1929 included Eddy Sackville-West ('alert and peevish as ever and more conceited,' Clive thought),[38] Raymond Mortimer, Francis Birrell, Carrington's husband Ralph Partridge and the woman with whom he was in love and would eventually marry, Frances Marshall. On 18 August Quentin's birthday was celebrated with a firework party, which from then on became an annual institution.

That autumn Angelica embarked on her first term at the boarding school, Langford Grove. 'Angelica has gone up to London with Nessa to be sent to school today – unbearable I find it,' Duncan told Bunny. 'But she seems to know her destiny.'[39] He was still worried about her when he went to France in October, though his immediate responsibilities lay with his fellow travellers, his mother and her companion, Miss Elwes. It had been suggested that they might enjoy a holiday at La Bergère, but such an adventure was not possible without practical help. Duncan willingly provided it. Nowhere in his letters describing their trip is there even a momentary hint of irritation with his elders, who depended completely on him. He knew exactly what would please and, after meeting them in Paris, took them for dinner at Laborde's and afterwards gave them ices at the Café de la Régence.

Paris was at its most beautiful, he thought, and the following morning he took the ladies to the Louvre to see the new Impressionist rooms, where there was also a whole wall of Corot landscapes. After lunching agreeably at the Café de Médicis, they walked in the Luxembourg Gardens. Twenty minutes before they were due to board the train for Marseilles, Aunt Daisy arrived from Copenhagen, still however unable to say whether she could join the party, as was hoped, for her affairs were in disarray; so they set off without her, Duncan sleeping profoundly throughout much of the journey. Arriving at Marseilles, they had time to breakfast and take baths before Colonel Teed arrived in a new Citroën. At La Bergère everything had been left ready for them by Elise Anghilanti and they passed an easy day settling in. Duncan's mother was delighted with the house, which she said was prettier and better arranged than anything she had expected. Miss Elwes immediately began weeding the terrace and developed plans for herbaceous borders, which Duncan forestalled, buying roses and honeysuckle to plant round the house. Each day Elise cooked an admirable lunch, washed up and left a soup prepared for the evening meal. Duncan took the ladies for drives in the surrounding countryside, where the *vendange* was everywhere in progress. The Fontcreuse wine had an excellent effect on the visitors, both Ethel Grant and Miss Elwes becoming very brilliant, so Duncan thought, and amusing under its influence. Before long he had also instituted Vermouth before dinner and Cointreau after lunch, which added further to the ladies' spirits. It was a holiday they did not forget.

While relieved that Angelica had not gone to Bedales, a hearty and more progressive public school, his concern for her well-being appeared to be his only anxiety while in Cassis. Through Vanessa and Angelica he was rooted to a family, and to a way of life and a past that meant much to him. 'I was very pleased to get your long letter yesterday for nice as it is here I was beginning to feel that a slicer had cut me off from any previous existence.'[40] When he caught up with one of Roger's wireless talks in the pages of *The Listener*, he not only thought it a masterpiece of concise expression but noticed that Fry's aesthetic ideas had reverted to a concern with subject matter, a development that amused Duncan, as he knew it would make Vanessa furious.

The demand for his paintings can only have added to his serenity. That year the Contemporary Art Society paid £650, not to Duncan but to a dealer, for the large interior painted in the dining-room at Charleston in 1918 (now in the Ulster Museum, Belfast). Together with Sickert's *Suspense*, it was the most expensive painting the CAS bought that year. *The Sunday Times* also affirmed that Duncan was on a par with Sickert when, in a review of the London Group exhibition that autumn, it declared Sickert, Grant and Harold Gilman the three main influences on the show. What further enriched his inner life was the sense that he belonged to a tradition of painting that stretched back through the centuries. This awareness gave a particular purpose to his looking at paintings when, for instance, at Christmas he stepped inside a deserted Hampton Court and took pleasure in a portrait by Bassano, a possible Titian and a Zurbarán bought by Queen Victoria.

'One shouldn't be staying in London so long,' Peter Morris wrote of himself to Duncan at around this time, 'it affects the nerves. I envy you your life which seems to me still and serene like a river under great trees, but I daresay it isn't really so at all.'[41]

George Bergen irrupted suddenly into Duncan's life in 1929. Wyndham Tryon introduced them and soon afterwards told Duncan things about Bergen that Duncan chose to ignore. By the first week of January 1930 they had become close. They went painting on Hampstead Heath together and were so much in each other's company that Vanessa grew alarmed. 'Do not worry my dear about me and my goings on,' Duncan assured her. 'They really can be of no importance to you. As for giving me anything that you could give that is all nonsense. It is all quite different. George is addicted to all the sexes so why should you bother more than I do? Which isn't much.'[42]

If Duncan had difficulty at first in recognising the extent of his feelings for George, this was not surprising: Bergen was a complex, difficult character with a reinvented past. He was born in 1903 in Minsk, but his father, a cabinet maker, left for America, his family joining him there when George was about six years old. Not until he was sixteen did he become a naturalised American, by which time he had decided that to succeed he had to get away from Brooklyn and bury his Jewish origins. The family name had been changed from Bogin-Beigin soon after they settled in America. As a youth George began to invent a new life for his father, pretending that he was a Dutch engineer. He also hated the fact that his family always talked Yiddish at home.

At a young age he got a scholarship to Yale School of Art and took with him talent, great charm, a strong personality and good looks as well as slanting Slav eyes. At eighteen he won a Prix de Rome and took off for Europe, meeting Lord Howard de Walden, who encouraged Bergen to come to London, where his chameleon-like character enabled him to adapt easily to the mores of English society. He found a loyal friend in the Hon. Gerald ('Timmy') Chichester, son of Alice, Lady Templemore, and one of Queen Mary's secretaries: he was said to have given Bergen an allowance on the condition that he went on painting. It was probably through Bergen that Duncan also made friends with Timmy Chichester, though for a while Bergen played off one man against the other. In time paintings by Duncan and Bergen filled Chichester's walls and a flower painting, framed with mirror, was specially executed for one of his rooms by Duncan and George together.

Bergen had begun to enjoy a degree of success before he met Duncan. His first solo exhibition was held at the Goupil Gallery in December 1929. Two years later Duncan held a show of Bergen's work in his studio, offering tea and cocktails to those invited. This was followed by a solo exhibition at the Lefevre Gallery in 1932, for which Bunny wrote the catalogue introduction. Then, in 1934, at the invitation of Constance Collier, Bergen went to Hollywood to paint her portrait and that of Lillian Hellman, Charlie Chaplin and Tillie Losch. (The day before his portrait of Chaplin was supposed to be finished it was stolen from the studio, a misfortune that smacks of a publicity stunt.) Back in England Bergen continued to enjoy a certain success (Lord Duveen bought his *Helmet, Hat and Hatchet*), and it was perhaps a mistake on his part to return to America a few months before war broke out. He lived in New York almost uninterruptedly for the next forty-six years until his death. Though he remained alert to changes in artistic fashion, becoming an abstract painter, he never, as far as is known, exhibited again. If one aspect of his Russian inheritance was an expansive exuberance, another was a self-destructive vein that led him to shun commissions even when he was badly in need of money.

In England he slithered to the top or bottom of society with ease. He greatly enjoyed painting the East End docks and specialised in what one critic called 'Limehouse types'. Equally, he was no stranger at country house parties and later astonished his brothers and sisters with the photographs he produced, including some of Queen Mary. In New York he liked to pretend that he was English and could fool most of his compatriots with a pseudo-English accent. If in England he had practised a convenient bisexuality, in America he had affairs with the wife of Franco's Spanish ambassador and with Lillian Hellman. He began to behave as if shocked by homosexuality, but the woman he married in 1951, Helen Gordon, was never entirely convinced by this. A very insecure, uneducated person who had at some point been deeply hurt, Bergen needed desperately to have power over others. He achieved it by adopting an intensity of manner that made the person to whom he was talking feel they were the only person in the world who mattered to him. Calculating and manipulative, he advised his wife to remain largely silent with people more intelligent than herself and to be inordinately flattering to others.

For some eighteen months Duncan's emotional life hinged on this man's existence and for many years to come he held him in affectionate regard. When Quentin first met Bergen in January 1930 in Duncan's studio, he commented afterwards, 'that was a strange young man'.[43] Later on he actively resented the pass that Bergen made at him in Duncan's presence. Though the agony that George caused Vanessa was kept from Virginia for many months, she eventually caught up with the disapproval. 'Duncan is as mellifluous as ever,' she wrote in January 1931, 'but how he can spend three months alone with his Russian who by all accounts is sheep headed, bird witted, and not nice into the bargain, we in Bloomsbury can't imagine. Or do you think each of us in proportion to our virtue requires some outlet? Then Duncan's virtue,' she concluded, 'must be very great.'[44]

EIGHTEEN

Love, Anxiety, Terror, Sadness

At the start of the new decade there appeared to be nothing amiss with Duncan's life. He visited the exhibition of Italian art at the Royal Academy and attended the supporting lectures delivered by Roger Fry. These were gala performances in a crowded Queen's Hall. Microphones were in use, as the seating capacity amounted to some 2,000, and a sense of occasion was generated by the organ prelude played at the start and the Italian ambassador brought on at the finale. At one lecture Duncan sat alongside Helen Anrep, her two children, Igor and Baba, and Pippa Strachey. None was shocked when Fry suddenly shot a Matisse on to the screen which, in this Italian context, Duncan thought, looked like a Simone Martini.

January 1930 also brought Matisse's daughter and son-in-law, the Georges Duthuits, to London. Duncan dined with them at the Gargoyle and felt, as he had done before, a slight flirtation in his exchange with Georges. 'It may very well be all on my side,' he admitted to Vanessa. 'He is a very sly character.'[1] Four days later he attended a Cranium Club dinner where he sat between a Cambridge mind, Goldsworthy Lowes Dickinson, and one of Lytton's former flames, Henry Lamb. Inevitably Duncan talked a great deal about painting with Lamb, but with more interest than warmth. 'He's always rather interesting but I don't somehow feel he trusts one or perhaps one doesn't quite trust him.'[2] Also present were many of his friends, Eddy Sackville-West, Raymond Mortimer, Bunny, Stephen Tomlin, as well as a new member whom Duncan thought 'nice and intelligent' – Roy Harrod.

Yet alongside the easy gossip ran anxiety and guilt, for Duncan was undergoing emotions that taxed his loyalty to Vanessa. All the delicacy that he habitually brought to his relations with others seemed inadequate in the current situation. 'I have had a terrible bout of crises this week,' he wrote to Bunny. 'When I say crises do not think that I am unhappy – only a madman has entered my life and tried to wreck it. I will perhaps tell you when I see you. This madman is not George.'[3] This new person was a man so violently in love that a former way of life was threatened. It was George Bergen he loved: the madman was an aspect of himself.

In these fraught circumstances it was agreed that Duncan should bring George to Charleston so that they could spend time alone together. In this way Duncan hoped that, away from the whirligig of London, he would get to know George a little better and gain more control of his feelings. Vanessa not only agreed to this plan but, before leaving Charleston for London, made sure that enough fuel, food and everything for their comfort was provided. Duncan and George arrived at Charleston during a gale ('the wind was terrific and burst open the doors right and left beating the rain in gusts against the windows')[4] but they found a roaring fire in the dining-room and soon had the lamp lit and tea made. In the morning a Mrs Stephens arrived, who proved a willing cook and housekeeper. Once the studio stove was alight, the two men began to establish their own *modus vivendi*.

Various feelings coursed through Duncan's mind during the next few days. 'My principal feeling at the moment is one of deep shame,' he wrote to Vanessa the day after he arrived, for he disliked the thought of her coping with wintry London while he enjoyed the peace that had returned to Charleston. He thought a great deal about her and, while familiarising himself with George's habits and character, realised that he loved Vanessa more than ever. Partly because George needed to recover from his hectic social life, he and Duncan led a rather mute existence, sitting for hours without talking, playing the gramophone and occasionally dancing. The notion of reading a book seemed novel to Bergen, and Duncan wondered if it was something he had ever learnt to do, but once he began reading he did it, like much else, to excess. In London Duncan had suffered from Bergen's constant change of plans. Now that he was at Charleston it was a relief not to have to worry whether he would turn up or not. After only three days Duncan wrote to Bunny suggesting that he might visit, without however telling others. 'For although Nessa knows George and I are here she might not like other people to know.'[5]

On 5 February Duncan went up to London in order to give a small lunch party in Vanessa's honour and to attend the private view of her show, opening that day at the Cooling Galleries in Bond Street. The whole performance was so convincing that Virginia, who attended the lunch and the private view, having written a preface for the catalogue, was wholly unaware of the agony and insecurity that Vanessa was suffering. As they walked from the Gargoyle in Soho towards Bond Street, Virginia told Clive the following day, Duncan became 'inextricably involved telling a story about a – about a – oh I can't remember, if indeed I ever knew what Duncan's story was about, and so we went on, until the afternoon light was waning, and Duncan and I walked to Bond Street, and were so elated by every incident, – for one thing the discovery of Blake's house . . .'[6]

Duncan's day must have ended less happily than Virginia here suggests, as that evening Vanessa wrote to him, 'I am sorry I was so stupid today. I think I was too tired to be sensible. I went to sleep in a chair after you had gone. I think – I know – we care too much for each other for things not to come right in the end.'[7] After receiving her letter the next day, Duncan replied, 'You are really my only touch with the outside world as the *Daily Mirror* does not carry one very far . . . I have no intention of going away for long or deserting you in any way. Do not for a moment think I am concocting any plans. I only feel I should like to wait a little doing nothing.'[8]

This protest suggests that in Vanessa's mind, if not in Duncan's, the notion had arisen that he now wanted something more than the slight and inconsequent affairs that had characterised his love life for a decade. If Bergen was to become Duncan's partner in a more complete sense, then the focus of his life would shift. There was talk at one point of George settling in Hampstead or Highgate, close enough to draw Duncan away from Fitzroy Street, where Vanessa now had the studio next to Duncan's and where they always began the day together over morning tea. While having the satisfaction of knowing that two days after her show opened she had earnt 330 guineas from the sale of twelve pictures, Vanessa simultaneously confronted a personal dilemma and arrived at an ultimatum: 'I feel all future life with you must be put aside at the moment for I can't think of it with any definiteness . . . Duncan dear, I don't want you to come back, as far as I'm concerned, until you come back altogether.'[9]

At Charleston one morning Duncan woke to find that the world had turned white. He promptly went in to Lewes, the snow making urgent his need for rubber boots. Six days after Vanessa's ultimatum he wanted to return to the studio: George had invited a friend for the weekend and though Duncan had agreed to this, he did not relish the prospect. Could he return for Saturday and Sunday, he asked Vanessa, or would she find it too painful? Either after this or another visit to London, the return to Charleston and the Downs relieved his spirits. 'I've never seen the country quite so lovely as yesterday afternoon driving out in the bus from Lewes,' he wrote to Vanessa. 'Floods of clear sunlight and very beautiful cumulus clouds above the downs and miraculous beautiful colour.'[10]

The business of waiting had worn Vanessa down. 'My dear I don't quite know what to do. I sometimes feel I can't stand this vagueness much longer. Is it necessary?'[11] At other moments she felt calmer, as if some kind of insanity had passed. The fear that Duncan might set up home with George subsided. 'Duncan my dearest please forgive me for all the horrors I have made you go through,' she wrote. '. . . The fact that I don't know George at all and don't know if he's the kind of person who ever can live quietly near you and see us both and work and be happy with you makes it much harder for me. The chance of getting to know him is put off and that has been one of the things that has made it so difficult for me to do anything but wait.'[12]

Duncan capitulated. By the beginning of March both George and Vanessa were painting a portrait of him in the studio at Charleston. One evening he retired to his room to write a letter to Bunny, whom he still relied on as a confidant.

I have left George and Nessa in the studio. It is after supper and seems to me the first time I have been alone for weeks. That is alone and able to think and reflect a little – my life for the last two months has been simply turmoil. Turmoil of love, anxiety, terror and sadness and happiness, but all at such a rate I have no particular memory of time or night as being different from day . . . Doubts about love – others love to oneself – are terrible. Why can't one just love and expect that others will too . . . I know perfectly well that George loves me . . . But why do I get into a state when he is tired and I am tired and therefore think that he has no feeling for me? And why does Nessa not believe that I love her as much as ever I did? When she is unhappy I am unhappy too . . . Why does she not realise that my love for George gives me *more* power to love her instead of less. And when she is not here I feel too that something is wanting in my life however happy I am alone with George.

The truth is I want them both. I want too much I suppose. Sometimes I find the tears rolling down my cheeks simply because I love them both so much. That is a detestable form of self-pity. But at the same time I cannot help thinking that if Nessa could see into my soul at such moments she would see that everything is all right . . . I sometimes see myself in a detestable light as one who deliberately makes other people unhappy because I cannot control myself. But it is better not to take too close a moral view. As I am made as I am I must do the best with myself and best I can do with others . . . Only I know that sometimes Nessa suddenly feels that I give something to George that I don't give to her . . . Thank the lord though that she is sensible. But it hurts me terribly to realise when one loves there must be pain and pain of that particular sort that almost seems to menace love itself.[13]

Though Bergen caused rocky passages in the months to come, the immediate crisis evaporated with the arrival of spring. In the Easter vacation Charleston once again became the gathering place for family life, while across the fields the Keyneses took up residence at Tilton. That April there was little or no communication between the two houses. Duncan felt that the Keyneses blamed the Charlestonians, but admitted it was more soothing to conclude that their neighbours were just too busy to see them. Vanessa, meeting Maynard and Lydia in Lewes, noticed how stiff and cold Lydia was and departed from them hurriedly, feeling that she was to blame for the various small rows they had had with Maynard. He continued to mastermind the London Artists' Association, but since the 1929 Wall Street Crash it had become much more difficult to sell pictures. By January 1931 Duncan's finances, always fluctuating and mysterious, were in such a poor state that he tried to extract an advance from the LAA via Maynard, only to have his request refused. It has also to be said that the appointment of the good-natured, vague and leisurely Angus Davidson as the LAA's Secretary had not helped its affairs.

It was Angus who declared that Duncan had a double in Buster Keaton when they went to see one of his films together. 'I can't very well tell about appearance,' Duncan afterwards told Vanessa, 'but he stepped back at one moment into a folly as once I did.'[14]

In his working relations with Vanessa, Duncan sometimes affected a strict note. 'Do you realise that in a month or so you must have two or three *important* landscapes ready? Which are they to be pray? You don't seem to be doing any . . . That wretch George has not written yet again. Isn't [that] monstrous. He is not even punctual.'[15] Duncan had in mind the LAA June exhibition at the Cooling Galleries, 'English Landscape Painting, 1750–1930', which, in an attempt to show continuity, mingled work by Gainsborough, Richard Wilson, Peter de Wint, Steer and others with paintings by Fry, Bell and Grant. 'Nothing among the works by living artists makes a more solid impression than *Sussex Weald* by Duncan Grant,' wrote *The Times*'s critic, 'with the principles of Cézanne completely domesticated in English painting.'[16]

Charleston played no small part in binding Duncan to Vanessa. Visitors to it felt they had entered another world – one complete unto itself, satisfying, apart. Angelica, recalling these days in Christopher Mason's film, *Duncan Grant at Charleston*, conjured up memories of voices, laughter, the smell of cigars and the sound of music flowing out of the French windows into the garden. There were dramatic moments, as when Bunny arrived by aeroplane, landing in the field behind the house and causing Roger, arriving simultaneously by car, to hit the gatepost in astonishment. But these apart, the appeal of the house, though indelible in the minds of visitors, was largely undramatic. It remained shabby but civilised, grew steadily in charm and comfort but was never luxurious. Once, when Clive was in Paris, seeing fewer friends than usual and resisting the dissipating effects of the social round, he boasted to Vanessa, 'Here I lead a life of almost Charlestonian virtue and economy.'[17] After Duncan left the house in April 1930, he wrote to Vanessa: 'I enjoyed my family life at Charleston. I hope you have no more of that distressing migraine. You must be careful of yourself. So much always depends upon you – it is terrible.'[18]

Like Vanessa, Duncan found it impossible to ignore Angelica's beauty, which was becoming more and more pronounced. It was a constant delight to Vanessa, who also took great pleasure in her sons. To Bunny she admitted that 'one gets more actual enjoyable pleasure from one's children than from any other relationships – at least at times'.[19]

Inevitably Duncan's obsession with George still caused her pain. His sudden changes of mood, his doubts about his painting and gloom over his character in relation to Vanessa were exacerbated by the pall of uncertainty that George cast over everything. One positive outcome was that Duncan's involvement had re-awoken his friendship with Bunny. 'It does me the greatest good in the world to see you from time to time,' he told Bunny in April.[20] In July he asked if he could bring George to Hilton Hall, in the course of a trip that they made to Cambridge and Ely, Duncan meanwhile admitting to Vanessa that he felt the most selfish person alive. He left Hilton impressed by Bunny's way of life, by his wife Ray, his two sons, his pigeons and peaches. He was no more able to see the imperfections in this marriage than Virginia, in September, was able to spot the tension between Vanessa and Duncan. 'As for Nessa and Duncan,' she wrote in her diary, 'I am persuaded that nothing can be now destructive of that easy relationship because it is based on Bohemianism.'[21] In the long term she was proved right.

Duncan left Hilton for Twickenham, while George went on a spree with his friends in the East End. 'I have to remember he told me we are now part of each other and also that he is fonder of me than he dare tell me,' he wrote to Bunny. 'Both of which he told me at Hilton. When I paint by the river and the sun is out it's all right. But there are moments when I should like to hear these things said again. How beastly self-centred one gets.'[22]

In October Duncan attempted to resolve the split in his life by taking George with him to La Bergère, Vanessa having gone ahead with Quentin. It was not a success. Though on first meeting Vanessa, George had treated her with politeness and charm, his manner could now be insolent and rude. He may have intuited her dislike, for, if she so wished, Vanessa could be 'as cold as ice and as withering as gall'.[23] This was the first time Vanessa had travelled to Cassis without Grace. ('Everyone of course asks a great deal after you,' she wrote to Grace, 'and I have to invent messages from you. I hope you trust me to do so.')[24] They were also without the benefit of help from Elise Anghilanti, whose son was seriously ill with tuberculosis. News that the doctor had said there was no hope cast a sadness over all who knew Elise. It had also been agreed that after just over a fortnight Vanessa would depart, leaving Duncan and George alone together.

This short holiday was interrupted by a visit from Roger Fry and Helen Anrep, who persuaded Vanessa and Quentin to accompany them on a journey around Provence. Vanessa was irritated by Fry's excessive use of the hooter, even when *she* was driving. Despite this there were moments when La Bergère seemed a hive of industry, with Vanessa, Duncan, Quentin and George all painting hard. Duncan returned to a subject that he had first painted in 1928,[25] of a view through a window of the fields leading down to the sea. Like Matisse, he liked the contrast of the brightly lit exterior scene with the dark interior. At La Bergère, this contrast was enhanced by the baroque roses in the wallpaper surrounding the window. After Vanessa left Cassis, it worried Duncan to think of her wandering round Paris on her own. ('Perhaps you will come round to my view that Paris *can* be very *triste*.')[26] He and George meanwhile gave a party at La Bergère, with musicians playing on the terrace all afternoon.

Duncan had little inclination to return to London. 'I don't know why but I really am beginning to have rather a horror of seeing most of my friends. Not because I do not like them but they seem to become more and more different in their tastes as they grow older. Is it because they are mostly literary folk?'[27] Though, as he admitted to Bunny, George occasionally gave him a bad time, Duncan was at other moments rapturously happy. 'But I know one can't ever be so happy for long so I am as much as I can be – is it very wrong?'[28] When George disappeared to Marseilles to meet Colin Davidson (a well-connected business man and one of his former lovers), Duncan felt very little jealousy and enjoyed being on his own for a while. He told Vanessa: 'The local people here are simply like children and *never* can be alone. I think them perfectly charming, but it means they live simply from moment to moment – which is what you say I always do. Well I think I do more than most of one's friends, but I sometimes have a bout of wanting to think things over. Perhaps think is rather a strong word but to dream things over . . . The terrace at Fontcreuse is like the most marvellous setting for *Twelfth Night* – real and marvellous at the same time.'[29]

George decided to stay at Marseilles and Duncan prepared his return to London, on the understanding that he would not see his friend for some time. Nor would he expect many letters, for Bergen found the business of putting pen to paper, even for people he was fond of, impossibly difficult. Though Duncan felt some new stage in their relationship had been achieved, his letters betray a sense that, temporarily at least, his need for George had been satiated.

He returned home in December and spent Christmas as usual with his mother. 'I loved being at Twick. and enjoyed my walk in Richmond Park,' he wrote from Charleston as the year ended. Vanessa had met him at Lewes station in her car, and they had gone straight to dine with the Keyneses. During the New Year there were no limitations on their time together, no agitations: George was out of the country and – momentarily – Duncan was undistracted.

In the year that Duncan was born the Labouchère Criminal Law Amendment Act had modified an existing law that made homosexuality a capital offence, but in so doing, Parliament redefined the crime in much wider terms, this greater scope making it possible to sentence Oscar Wilde to two years' hard labour. There was no alteration to this law for the next eighty-two years. Throughout the greater part of his adult life Duncan, as a practising homosexual, lived outside the law, a fact that may at times have sharpened his innate nervousness. But there is little evidence that this illegality troubled him, and it could be argued that – because, like many of his lovers, he belonged to the educated middle-class – he was fairly well protected by his social position. Moreover, the domestic security and depth of feeling that he shared with Vanessa may have weighed against promiscuous inclinations. Yet there were opportunities that he certainly took. One of his male models, the handsome Charles ('Tony') Assirati, became the subject of some of his most sensual paintings. Two others, Jack Moore and Charles Boyle, were coloured. As a painter, Duncan was fascinated by the colouristic possibilities of dark skin tones, but it also had for him an erotic attraction, that of the forbidden other. During his 1926 trip to Venice he found himself in a *gabinetto* that had glass doors decorated with blackamoors and their female inamorati – some black, some Caucasian. 'How charming for the Turks,' he observed to Eddy Sackville-West, to 'have such a choice so much a matter of course it appears. For in Europe always it occasioned a certain scandal to unite oneself with a black.'[30]

What differentiates this remark from those found in Duncan's letters to Vanessa is the tone rather than the detail. Writing to another homosexual, Duncan could play upon assumptions that he did not share with her. He hid little from her, but when telling her of his adventures he left them deliberately unspiced. For instance, while staying with his mother at Twickenham over Christmas in 1930 he decided to look up a policeman called Harry Daley who was stationed as a constable at Hammersmith. This working-class man, whose father had died at sea when Harry was ten, had met J. R. Ackerley in the street one day and in conversation let Ackerley know that he had seen his play, *The Prisoners of War*, which had a homosexual theme, at the Lyric Theatre, Hammersmith. A friendship between the two men had been established and, through Ackerley, Daley met Raymond Mortimer and E. M. Forster. Sociable and easy, Daley had never tried to disguise his homosexuality, even within the ranks of the Metropolitan Police. He liked nothing better than 'a good sexy romp' and later wrote a rare record of working-class homosexual experience of the period entitled *This Small Cloud*.

At Twickenham that Christmas the dismal weather made it impossible to paint. So Duncan's letter to Vanessa began:

> My great relief has been an outing last night with the cultivated policeman who is a friend of Raymond and Morgan. He's really a very nice fellow. As he lives at Hammersmith I thought it a good opportunity of going to see him and he invited me to go the 'rounds' last night and he showed me all the little village streets by the river. I must say it is a lovely place – the other side of the bridge to Mary's old house. We then went to a series of parties at his friends' houses and drank a great deal of beer and danced hilariously. The very poor are a sympathetic race – but I suppose hopeless. But they are a great relief and nicer than a great many of one's friends. I missed my train home and had to sleep in the Police Section Home.[31]

In 1931 Duncan painted a half-length portrait of Daley wearing his helmet and with a row of gleaming brass buttons down his chest.

Daley's unfussed acceptance of his homosexuality seemed to Duncan infinitely preferable to the self-regarding world of some inverts. Virginia Woolf notes in her diary that Leonard went to see Forster one day and 'found him with the usual bugger crew; which,' she adds, 'Duncan dislikes when it's self-conscious, as at Raymond's'.[32] Nevertheless, Duncan usually fell in love with precisely the kind of men whom Mortimer cultivated. One of these was the thirty-one-year-old Jimmy Sheean, who in January rented Clive's flat at 50 Gordon Square for two months while Clive was in an eye-clinic near Zurich, suffering temporarily from blindness in one eye.

Sheean was an Irish-American who came to Europe in 1922 from the American Midwest, fluent in several languages and with a rare erudition. As a foreign correspondent, he initially signed his articles 'J. V. Sheean' but was advised against this and ordered to use his second name 'Vincent'. In this way he acquired, as he said, 'a name like a mask', from behind which he continued to work. He had an uncanny knack of being on the spot at important events; and his work for the *Chicago Tribune* and other newspapers provided him with experiences which in 1935 he put into a political autobiography that set the style for a whole genre of journalistic memoirs.[33] Despite his strong left-wing sympathies, he could not help enjoying what another part of him felt needed to be destroyed: the aristocracy and the pleasures and material seductions of bourgeois life. A brilliant, very funny but somewhat difficult man, he later married twice, and twice divorced, the woman he first met in 1935 – Dinah Forbes-Robertson, daughter of the great Shakespearean actor Sir Johnston Forbes-Robertson.

This cosmopolitan intellectual arrived one afternoon in February 1931 at 50 Gordon Square, still a bachelor, and sang for Duncan, he afterwards boasted, forty complete operas, with emphasis on *Tristan* and *Tosca*. 'Everything I say or do or see or hear, wherever I go, makes me think of you,' he swore a few days later. 'And long for you – and love you – more and more. How do you explain this? What am I to do about it? I think I am definitely in what is called a state.'[34] Unfortunately, someone else was also in a state: Eddy Sackville-West. To Duncan he wrote:

> You knew . . . that for nearly two years now Jimmy and I have cared for no one else and all the time my one hope was that he would gain time and money enough for us to be together abroad for a time. Now that time has come and you have shoved your nose in and [destroyed?] my happiness and the best dream of my life. The moment J. came to Gordon Square you have sat on his doorstep and pushed and poked at him, trying to get him for yourself, without the slightest regard for either of us. At last you have succeeded and have caused me unspeakable grief and pain . . . it is incredible that you, who once

Maynard Keynes, 1908, The Provost and Scholars
of King's College, Cambridge

ABOVE: *Lemon Gatherers*, 1910, Tate Gallery
BELOW: *South of France*, 1922, Tate Gallery

Football, 1911, Tate Gallery

ABOVE: *Portrait of Katherine Cox*, 1915, National
Museum of Wales, Cardiff
OPPOSITE: *The Baptism*, c.1919, Collection
Wolfgang Kuhle

ABOVE: *Les Femmes Savantes*,
c. 1930s, The Britten–Pears
Foundation
RIGHT: *Portrait of Ethel Grant* by
Vanessa Bell, Private Collection,

ABOVE: *St Paul's Cathedral*, 1941, Imperial War Museum
OVERLEAF: *Vanessa Bell*, 1942, Tate Gallery

pretended (for a short time) to care for me, could have done such a thing.

I will never forgive you or speak to you again.[35]

Duncan must have told Vanessa of this, as he also reported to her the embarrassment he felt on meeting Eddy at a Cranium Club dinner in April. ('I forgot about Eddie [*sic*] and there he was ... we were at opposite ends of the table and I didn't have to say a word to him, but I felt a bit silly.')[36] Encouraged by Sheean, Duncan did not take Eddy's feelings too seriously: there were many reasons for his unhappiness and his affair with Sheean was largely phantasy.

Duncan's attention might not have wandered had Bergen not prolonged his stay in the South of France throughout January. Duncan was still very bound up with him and in early April held a *vernissage* in his studio in an attempt to sell George's pictures, for Bergen began threatening to return to America if he failed to make some money. Vanessa, aware of another potential crisis, not only made her studio available for the party but also helped arrange the pictures.

Meanwhile letters flew back and forth between London and Rome, where Sheean was now working. Sheean was 'both fickle and obstinate', Raymond Mortimer warned Duncan, suggesting that he too had been in love with the American, something that Sheean denied. 'It simply paralyses me with joy to think that you may come here,' he wrote to Duncan,[37] reiterating his feelings in subsequent communications. 'One thing would make me happier than I have been for years upon years: to be with you *altogether* – that is, without stopping. Couldn't we do that "for a bit" ... I want to *live* with you – even though I know it can't be for long – really *live* with you, for once.'[38]

In anticipation of this possibility Sheean arranged to move from the Grand Hôtel de Russie into an apartment in the Palazzo Locatelli. Meanwhile Duncan, in one of his replies, must have stressed his attachment to Vanessa, as Sheean insisted that she was the last person in the world whom he would wish to cause a moment's annoyance or embarrassment. It was a reassurance that, after the difficulties with Bergen, Duncan must have welcomed.

Before he left the Grand Hôtel de Russie, Sheean fell into conversation in the bar one night with an Englishman who, on hearing that Sheean had recently been living in Gordon Square, began talking about Bloomsbury and Duncan in particular. At Sheean's encouragement, the man went on to say that he had been at school with Duncan whom, though they had not met for years, he thought unforgettable, one of the greatest charmers in the world. When Sheean enthusiastically agreed, the man looked at him keenly and said, 'Forgive me if this question displeases you, but tell me: are you to any degree homosexual?'[39] When Sheean assented that he was, the man went on to admit that he was eternally grateful to Duncan, as he had been his first experience of love and had removed his innocence at school some twenty-five years ago. Sheean, mellowed by cocktails and greatly amused, admitted that he was more in love with Duncan than anyone in the world. Over dinner Sheean discovered that this former correspondent for the *Daily Telegraph* in the Ruhrgebiet now worked for the League of Nations. His name was Leigh Farnell and as a result of this meeting he renewed his schoolboy acquaintance, becoming a loyal friend in Duncan's later years.

Duncan set off for Rome, stopping *en route* in Paris where, with Clive, whose eyesight was now restored, and his new girlfriend, the American heiress Mary Baker, he visited the banker-collector Alphonse Kahn. He was the owner not only of a couple of major Picassos but also three early Cézannes, two large ones that had come direct from the walls of the Jas de Bouffan, and a small *Temptation of St Anthony*, which Duncan thought one of the most exciting pictures he had ever seen. Furthermore, unframed Matisses hung among works by Chardin and Rubens. Kahn himself, however, made less impression on Duncan than Larionov and Goncharova, whom he re-encountered. 'They won my heart as only Russians can do by their extraordinary charm.'[40] Duncan also saw Derain, Stravinsky and Ernest Ansermet, all of whom involved him in interesting talk about ballet.

By the time Duncan reached Rome, Jimmy Sheean was in a nervy state. He had gravitated towards the kind of society he loathed for political reasons and found himself giving cocktail parties for various royals and aristocrats. For financial reasons he had agreed to 'ghost-write' for the Princess of San Faustino who, though an outrageous scandal-monger in life, wanted only to shower *boniments* on her friends in her memoirs, which were dull as a result. Sheean also felt he had to pay court to the Contessa Locatelli, having taken an apartment in her palazzo. After one of her gatherings, he apologised to Duncan for having subjected him to such insufferable company.

Though Duncan had come to Rome primarily to see Sheean, this cosmopolitan city offered many delights. Quentin had been living in the Via Margutta for about six months and Duncan painted from the model in his studio. Timmy Chichester was currently working in Rome and Lady Ottoline was visiting. Despite the ghastly operations on her jaw, she had lost none of her regal manner: when it threatened to rain while she was lunching al fresco with Quentin in a restaurant near the Spanish Steps, she had raised a masterly hand to the heavens and commanded, 'Desist'. Another familiar figure shortly to arrive was the elegant Peter Morris. He wanted to visit the city while Duncan was there, as did Vanessa. But in the meantime Duncan settled into the Palazzo Locatelli apartment with Jimmy.

Sheean, far from spending every moment with Duncan as suggested, often left him to his own devices. As a result, Duncan met by chance Lady Ottoline in St Peter's. 'I saw I must go in to St Peter's for a moment,' she wrote in her journal: 'It is always disappointing, for it is so like a huge drawing room and the proportions are so balanced as not to surprise or thrill – only leaving one rather dully gaping . . . I was hunting round alone in this great building when Duncan Grant appeared – which was a great surprise and joy, for I felt he was not so prejudiced – even though he might not like Bernini he would see that he is rather fine.' Later that day they bumped into each other again in the Medici Gardens. 'He was full of appreciation and loved it all,' Ottoline noted.[41]

Thereafter they saw much of each other. Duncan rang and invited Ottoline to go for a drive. His intrepid Aunt Daisy had arrived in Rome for a few days before leaving for Tripoli to write a guide book. Now a Fellow of the Royal Geographical Society, she had acquired a degree of fame as a writer and explorer, to such an extent that her arrival in Tripoli was noticed in the press. Lady Ottoline thought her a 'dear eccentric woman', talkative and fun, and took to her immediately, especially when Miss McNeil proved to be the only one in the party able to direct the chauffeur to the Villa Madama. After whirling round Rome they set off through the Porto Pio and sailed up to the Villa where Ottoline, employing her sweetest Italian, obtained them entrance. As she recorded in her journal, 'We all enjoyed it and Duncan is always charming and makes everyone good tempered and happy for he is natural and has so few complex[es] and antagonisms.'[42]

Sheean accompanied Duncan on this outing, and another day lunched with him and Lady Ottoline at her hotel. Afterwards they visited the Farnesina and Santa Maria in Trastevere, where Duncan admired the mosaics. Lady Ottoline noted that Duncan left after this alone in order to do some painting, saying that he became 'captious' if he did not paint. An easier guest it was hard to imagine, yet the situation between Duncan and Sheean had deteriorated badly. After less than two weeks Sheean's passion for Duncan, all flame and smoke at the start, had ended in cinders. He left a note for Duncan inside a copy of *Guido of Verona*:

I've got something to tell you . . . I simply *cannot endure* living with anybody – sharing the same bathroom, getting toothbrushes mixed up, being conscious of somebody else even in the tiniest details of getting up in the morning, and all that. I can't stand it, and never could, and I was a fool to think I could now. It throws me into an utterly abnormal state of irritation . . .

It only took me about one week to see that I had been a fool to force you to come here. It was a terrible mistake – and I am terribly sorry – but honestly, my dear, if you do not go away I shall have to.[43]

After writing this note, Sheean had his hair shampooed and began to feel remorse at having brought Duncan to Rome and then disrupted his plans. As a result he suddenly packed his bags and departed for Naples. 'It was impossible for me to remain in the house another day,' he wrote to Duncan. 'I don't expect you to understand that – you systematically refuse to understand anything I do or say . . . You always have made me feel like a coarse and unreasonable brute during the last fortnight. I daresay I have been one, but it's not a feeling that can be endured for long. And whenever I tried, as gently as possible, to explain to you, you always cried – which stops any explanation automatically. When I didn't see you I felt like a brute, and when I *did* see you it was worse. In the circumstances I simply had to get out – to be alone for a few days, and write . . .'[44] In years to come his future wife Dinah was to witness several occasions when Sheean made friends, only to turn suddenly against them. This happened not only with Duncan but also Quentin, to whom Sheean admitted that he could only feel affection for those who felt no affection for him.

If Sheean's rejection left him downhearted, Duncan did not show it. His *amour propre* recovered fairly swiftly. 'It was a great joy to get your letter,' he wrote to Bunny, 'and it has made me feel less cut off from my friends and my past . . . in spite of all your ill-natured remarks about first class sleepers and duchesses. I have given up *all* social life and I travelled here second class. Moreover I've quarrelled with Jimmy and am living in a second class hotel . . . So you see I am beyond any of your reproaches and feel inclined to be dignified and proud.' He was painting morning and evening on the Palatine, among the ruins, and had been pleased to hear from Bunny news of George. 'He never writes but I suppose by now I ought to know he can't.'[45]

The arrival of Vanessa was a great source of comfort. In order to be near Quentin she settled into a hotel near the Via Margutta and Duncan joined her there. In her wake, Roger arrived. Vanessa wrote home to Grace, 'Mr Fry has been here with his new car, so we have had some lovely drives. I wish you could see Rome. I'm sure you'd be fascinated by the people and the place and some of the country round is most beautiful. You won't be surprised to hear that I have bought a lot of pots.'[46] Meanwhile Duncan began to find Rome enervating and for a few days took himself off to Frascati. Whilst there he visited the Villa Falconieri, which Mussolini had given up to the League of Nations. He wanted to paint in its gardens and hoped that Leigh Farnell could help him obtain the necessary permission.

Owing to a landslide, he and Vanessa had to alter their plans for the journey home and eventually caught a train from Pisa to Paris. There they found a telegram from Angus Davidson saying that the preview to Duncan's LAA exhibition of recent work was the next day. They travelled back on the night boat, breakfasted on the train and had a hectic day, giving lunch to Mrs Grant and Virginia before the private view, which began at three in the afternoon. Fifty-one paintings by Duncan were on show at the Cooling Galleries, several priced at over a hundred guineas, and among them were portraits of Jimmy Sheean, the policeman Harry Daley, Peter Morris's sister Dora and a full-length of Vanessa in fancy dress. Lady Ottoline, having rehearsed it nervously for several days beforehand, gave the opening speech, based on notes jotted down in her journal: 'He beckons one on to see the old world . . . with New Vision . . . gay . . . poetical. What an enchanting Guide he is leading and beckoning one to see.'[47] Further praise, written by Bunny, formed the preface to the catalogue: 'Grandeur, restraint, and rigid observance of the rules are not his line at all . . . Almost all of the paintings here are marked by this new mood of his latest painting: a reckless mastery, a deliberate audacity . . . The painting is as solid as ever, but he has attacked his subjects with new gusto.'

Virginia expressed mock horror at the thought that all of art and society would be present at the opening. There was certainly much interest in the show and by the end of the third week some £1,600 worth of paintings had sold. The *Observer* noted that the same finesse of feeling could be found in Duncan's realistic paintings as in his more decorative items. 'He grows lighter and freer every year,' *Time and Tide* blithely remarked.[48] 'There was Duncan's show,' Virginia noted in her diary; '& considerable content, indeed a kind of bubbling rapture I think, in Fitzroy Street.'[49] After the show closed Duncan and George Bergen held a cocktail party at 8 Fitzroy Street. Lady Ottoline thought it ghastly: 'Duncan was flitting in and out and these extraordinary beings were flushed, silly and excited with cocktails, looking most offensive . . . artificial and terrible altogether. I fled very soon, and went in to see

Vanessa – next door ... who seemed absurdly matronly and old compared to them. She looks so staid – like an Old Aunt. Duncan is very fond of her and it is nice of him to be so.'[50] Vanessa's attitude was less patronising and more robust. 'I fear Duncan is in danger of too much celebrity,' she told Roger. 'We had a terrific cocktail party to wind up his show at the gallery. However, I tease him about it, but it makes no difference and most of his ladies have to walk over my corpse first – not knowing his telephone number.'[51]

Those ladies brazen enough to reach Duncan included two painters, Ethel Walker and Frances Hodgkins. Duncan delighted the first by asking her to tea with himself and Vanessa to meet Virginia. He visited Frances Hodgkins in her studio, taking an art critic with him to look at her paintings. More demanding were his female relatives at Twickenham whom he visited regularly, his attention quickening with interest lives that might otherwise have become humdrum. Typically, the Christmas card he designed for 1931 conveyed nothing except affection. 'A Big Squeeze for Christmas' it read, under an image of two clasped hands.

He extended small kindnesses to many, his homosexuality perhaps giving him an innate sympathy with those who, for some reason, lived outside or on the edge of society, like Roland Lee Warner. Nicknamed 'Tut', as he believed himself to be Tutankhamun reincarnated, Warner spent his life in and out of asylums and had persistent money problems owing to his love of gambling and the fact that he regularly 'blew' his allowance. He exhausted Duncan's patience with his rambling letters and ceaseless talk. Once, when 'Tut' turned up at Charleston early one morning, Lottie, the cook, went upstairs to tell Duncan of his arrival. Still half-asleep, Duncan flung out, 'Oh, for heaven's sake, say I'm dead.' Lottie repeated this message to the unfortunate Tut, who left the house rather madder than usual.

Another impecunious young man was the cockney known as 'H', who became a lover of Stephen Tomlin. A likeable, gregarious, smallish fellow with not entirely natural blond hair, he became a loyal friend of Duncan and over the years gave him warnings when it was known that the police had targeted certain homosexual meeting places. At one time 'H' worked in a draper's shop in the Holloway Road, at other moments he picked up work as a gentlemen's helper. He turned up at intervals like an unsinkable cork bobbing on life's surface and, whenever he could, repaid the money that Duncan had given him. Duncan continued to send him small amounts at intervals until the early 1970s, when he was greatly upset to learn that 'H' had died.

Duncan's sympathy with very different kinds of people left him free of rigid prejudices or any fixed moral standard. In old age he told Richard Shone that G. E. Moore's *Principia Ethica* remained 'the source of all my moral philosophy which possibly does not amount to much'. At the root of this philosophy lay the belief in good and bad states of mind. Judgement, Duncan believed, lay not with any external authority but with the individual. 'In fact it all depends on oneself.'[52] In practice, this meant applying humanity and common sense to the problem in hand. It was a moral code that did not impose standards of behaviour on others, but allowed them leeway to struggle with their own choices. Duncan's kindness, compassion and creativity attracted the passing thought that Virginia logged in her diary in May 1930: that she might one day write his life.

NINETEEN

Exuberance of Fancy

At Duncan's 1931 Cooling Galleries exhibition one of the paintings had been of Penns-in-the-Rocks, a late-seventeenth-century house at one time owned by William Penn, the founder of Pennsylvania, and situated at Withyham in Sussex near a fantastic outcrop of rocks and boulders that contributed to its name. It now belonged to Lady Dorothy Wellesley, who in 1928 commissioned Duncan and Vanessa to decorate her dining-room. Though the main body of work had been done by November 1929, in time for a champagne party to celebrate the commission, the room was not finished in every detail until 1931.

It was the most elaborate and expensive of all their decorative jobs. Duncan and Vanessa were given responsibility for the entire room, and the total cost, including the lighting and furnishings, came to £775 16s 7d. The artists took £350 of this, for Vanessa decided that, having for years accepted too low a fee for the sake of friendship or advertisement, they should now be recompensed properly.

The commission involved them in many visits to Withyham, some twenty miles from Charleston and a pleasant drive across Ashdown Forest. Though the dining-room was a mid-Victorian extension, the William and Mary house also boasted a fine collection of Italian baroque paintings. These seem to have determined Duncan and Vanessa's choice of style, for the figurative panels, which were fixed flush with the walls at intervals around the room, offered a light-hearted, modern pastiche of an Italianate style, the decoration of the room as a whole upholding a notion of gracious living, which the Grand Tour had done much to inspire.

When seen in certain lights, the figurative panels took on the appearance of statuary in arched niches. The overall colour scheme was restrained. The fireplace, painted a dull pink, was ornamented with a row of green circles. On either side were semi-illusionistic niches, in beige and white, similar to those Duncan had painted on the fireplace in the Garden Room at Charleston. Over the fireplace at Penns-in-the-Rocks hung a large octagonal mirror, its shape echoed in the dining table and in the two smaller mirrors that hung on the opposite wall above the ground-glass wall lights. Beneath these were two grey panels (one a serving hatch), which were outlined with white circles. This motif was picked up again in the grey ceiling, which had a border of pale blue, green and purple circles. The carpet was also grey and the walls grey-green. Most of the warm colours in the room came from the figurative panels, which had been painted in places with a sponge, the dappling allowing the brown-pink underpaint to show through. When seen at night multiplied in the mirror reflections and softened by diffuse light, the decorations gave to the room a gentle iridescence.

In the course of their work Duncan admitted to his mother that much had been the result of guesswork, as there were so many details to consider and not until the workmen had put everything in place could they judge the effects. After the house changed hands, the room was dismantled and today five of the six figurative panels, together with the fireplace, belong to Southampton City Art Gallery. Seen out of context the panels can seem vapid and sentimental. Yet as vehicles for warmth, colour, movement and sensuous charm they contributed significantly to the success of the room. If in terms of modernism they seem a wilful throw-back to another age, they take on a different value in a post-modern climate, their stylistic playfulness offering an alternative to the more autocratic International Style. Dorothy Todd and Raymond Mortimer spotted this aspect of Duncan and Vanessa's decorative work as early as 1929, the year that they published *The New Interior Decoration*, a book that boldly contrasts the work of these two Bloomsbury artists with that of Le Corbusier, Mies van der Rohe, Marcel Breuer, Marion Dorn and McKnight Kauffer. A further accolade came in the form of Madge Garland's article on the dining-room in *Vogue*. What pleased Duncan most, however, was the knowledge that Yeats admired the room, as did many other of Lady Dorothy's friends. Several were present at the inauguration party held in November 1929. 'Dottie's weekend was a great success, I think,' Duncan reported to his mother. 'Vanessa and I went down on Friday before the other guests arrived on Saturday to get the rooms finished and had to work hard all that day and Saturday . . . the room looks rather lovely. The mirrors make it look much larger and brighter and Vanessa's curtains are really lovely I think. The guests when they did arrive expressed great admiration so all was well. Ethel Sands was there. Hugh Walpole the novelist and your friend Leigh Ashton, and also Mrs Nicholson [*sic*] . . . Food delicious, plenty of champagne and fires in one's bedroom.'[1]

One feature in the dining-room at Penns had been the tiled side-tables.

Duncan and Vanessa had found in Greenwich a man called Mr James, who made and fired tiles which they decorated. These tiles had then formed surfaces for the side-tables which, like all the furniture in the dining-room at Penns, had been made by Kallenborn, the craftsman who had earlier executed marquetry work for the Omega. The two artists had found a further outlet for their tiled tables at LAA exhibitions.

Whether stirred by the success of the dining-room or the reminder of Omega days that Kallenborn represented, Vanessa persuaded Maynard that there should be an independent sale of decorative items at 46 Gordon Square in November 1930. A great variety of items was on offer – screens, lampshades, cushions, sofa-covers, trays, tiles, chairs, tables and artificial flowers – by herself, Duncan, Roger, Keith Baynes and Frederick Porter. Pre-sale publicity must have been good, for within an hour all the items had sold and orders for replicas were being taken. This event had a precedent, for Vanessa and Duncan had mounted a show of their decorative work at 46 Gordon Square in January 1924. It had been heralded in *Vogue* with the by-line 'Some Vigorous Modern Work in Refreshing Contrast to Hackneyed "Period" style' and the artists, whom *Vogue* claimed were the best-known British artists on the Continent, were praised for taking 'a pride in the design of the present'.[2]

Under the knowing editorship of Dorothy Todd, an early admirer of Virginia Woolf, and her assistant Madge Garland, *Vogue* in the 1920s had led the way not only in fashion but as a guide to the modern movement in the arts. Its readers were introduced not only to permanent waves and electric slimming devices but also to Picasso and Matisse. Bloomsbury featured both in its gossip columns and in its 'Hall of Fame'. Clive Bell and Raymond Mortimer became regular contributors, and even Virginia was seduced into 'sweeping guineas off the *Vogue* counter'.[3] Duncan's reputation, and to a lesser degree Vanessa's, owed much to *Vogue*. It discussed his art twice in 1923 and thereafter regularly promoted his work, to such an extent that in 1925 he appeared in nine articles. 'Vogue this week is full of us,'[4] he told Vanessa in April 1925, referring to the double-page spread on their decorations for Clive Bell's rooms and the article by him ('Spring Shows in and off Bond Street') that illustrated one of Duncan's paintings.

Bloomsbury designs had also figured largely in an article on 'Modern Embroidery' in October 1923 and photographs of almost all Duncan and Vanessa's major decorative projects appeared in *Vogue*, which also paid considerable attention to Duncan's designs for the theatre. 'Houses, like women, are very well dressed,' it remarked pertly in late August 1926, before praising Duncan and Vanessa's decorations for Mary Hutchinson's new house overlooking Regent's Park. 'Few people know what brains are confined within a radius of a hundred yards or so,' it said of Bloomsbury in further adulation of this group, which included, it claimed, 'the best of contemporary painters, Duncan Grant'.[5]

But if Duncan had become a household name, he did not reach a mass market as a decorative artist until he and Vanessa began an association with Allan Walton. All three met, with Keith Baynes, at the Café Royal in January 1931 to discuss the possibility of fabric designs. Walton had begun to train as an architect before studying painting at La Grande Chaumière in Paris. After the First World War he had returned to art, working under Sickert at the Westminster School of Art. In 1925 he achieved success as an interior decorator when he designed Marcel Boulestin's first restaurant in Leicester Square. His family owned a bleach and dye works at Collyhurst, Manchester, where his brother saw to the practical side of a business that was to produce fabrics by Duncan, Vanessa, Baynes, Frank Dobson, Cedric Morris and Bernard Adeney, which sold through the Waltons' shop in the Fulham Road, at Fortnum & Mason and at shops specialising in interior decoration. They were also exhibited at the Cooling Galleries in 1931 and the following year at Zwemmer's in Charing Cross Road, in an exhibition entitled 'Room and Book'. It coincided with the publication of Paul Nash's book of the same title and allowed Nash and Robert Wellington, the gallery curator, to turn the gallery into a domestic environment displaying fine and applied art. The *Observer* thought it 'a very good opportunity to test personal reactions to what may be called the twentieth-century style in useful and decorative items'.[6]

Duncan's interest in fabric design had not ended with the Omega. From Paris in 1922 he had written to Vanessa, 'I am rather excited about doing designs for stuffs. I've seen some brocades designed by [Raoul] Dufy and woven at Lyons by machine. They really are very lovely things ... They are wonderful colours and charming designs but I think one might invent a rather newer sort of treatment – they are very much in the tradition.'[7] Walton, likewise, wanted to abandon the traditional as well as vulgar imitations of Cubist patterning. In his fabric designs for Walton, Duncan, while turning away from the abstract patterning that had made Omega fabrics so innovative, retained a modern airiness. He also demonstrated a preference for more fluent, less spare handling of pattern. As in his other decorative work of this period, he looked to classical mythology for motifs, his use of them 'slyly allusive', as Raymond Mortimer observed.[8] In keeping with his gentle, lyrical vocabulary he chose colours muted to a pastel shade by the addition of white. Most characteristic of all is the buoyant movement that stirs the foliage in his 'West Wind' design and creates emphatic loops of shadow in 'The Little Urn'. Other popular designs by him were 'Grapes' and 'Apollo and Daphne', the latter winning a medal at the 1937 Paris International Exhibition.

There were further attempts at this time to create a liaison between industry and artists. One of the most successful ventures was Jack Beddington's work for Shell-Mex Ltd. Put in charge of publicity in 1929, he commissioned a long list of artists to produce pictures of the English countryside, which were translated by colour lithography into lorry bills. Vanessa found her motif close to Charleston, in the church at Alfriston. Duncan chose the bridge at St Ives in Huntingdonshire, which would have been familiar to him from his visits to Bunny at Hilton. In 1934, when a selection of posters made for Shell-Mex and BP formed the 'Pictures in Advertising' exhibition at the New Burlington Galleries, Duncan's poster was among the exhibits. At the time there seemed no irony in linking the delights of the English countryside with an increase in the sale of petroleum and the scheme was approved by the Council for the Preservation of Rural England.

Working on this poster in August 1931, Duncan found his mind much occupied with George Bergen, who was still insisting that for financial reasons he ought to return to America. 'I've persuaded him to be reasonable', Duncan told Bunny, 'and he is *not* going. Thank God – I should be desperately unhappy if he did. We had an amusing time with some of his East End police friends. A regular beano – lasting from Saturday to Monday.'[9] Three weeks later, however, George's plans were once again in disarray and Duncan felt sickened by the uncertainty. 'Nessa has been a perfect darling about it and decided to go and have a talk with George in London but it would be better here,' he wrote again to Bunny from Charleston.[10]

Duncan's renewed need of his friendship was now so marked that Bunny felt no hesitation in asking Duncan to design the jacket for his next book. Since the collapse of the fine-book market in 1929–30, Bunny had terminated his association with the Nonesuch Press and now devoted his time to writing, for a period also acting as literary editor to the *New Statesman* and, like his father, literary adviser to Jonathan Cape. 'I would feel it a great honour to do your jacket,' Duncan replied. 'Only I think I ought to warn you that Hatchards said he would tear off the one I did for Julian [Bell's *Winter Movement*, 1930] from every copy that entered his shop.'[11] Leonard Woolf recorded a similar reaction to Vanessa Bell's dustjacket for *Jacob's Room*, which he described as 'almost universally condemned'.[12] Nevertheless, whereas Vanessa went on to design every single jacket for her sister's books, Duncan produced relatively few in the inter-war years. Though Frances Marshall told Clive Bell that she thought Duncan's dustjacket for Julia Strachey's novel *Cheerful Weather for the Wedding* (1932) entirely appropriate, Duncan had taken it round to the press convinced that it was vulgar and poorly lettered. 'I badly needed your advice as to choice of colours,' he told Vanessa.[13]

In November 1931 Duncan exhibited for the first time at Agnew's in Bond Street in an exhibition of contemporary British art. 'Mr Duncan Grant sends only slight works,' Fry wrote in the *New Statesman and Nation*, 'but some of them of his freshest, most spontaneous quality.'[14] The shift of venue represented a change of allegiance: in July Duncan, Vanessa and Keith Baynes had resigned from the LAA and established a joint agreement with Agnew's and the Lefevre Gallery, which gave them a guaranteed salary, paid in quarterly instalments offset against sales. Maynard was furious and in a letter to Duncan pointed out that over the last six years the Association had sold £10,587 worth of his pictures. But this incontrovertible proof of financial success did not alter the fact that as the Association had grown in size, Duncan and Vanessa had increasingly found themselves in disagreement with Maynard on artistic matters. In his attempt to manage the Association fairly, a justifiable concern from the management point of view, he had sometimes let in work of uneven quality. In addition, during the difficult economic climate after the Wall Street Crash, he had in January 1931 at first refused Duncan a £100 advance on his one-artist show booked for that June. Next he agreed to the advance but on the condition that if the LAA's funds were low in April, Duncan would forego his guaranteed salary. As the Association's best-selling artist whose presence had done much to make it viable, Duncan was understandably offended and had promptly withdrawn his agreement for a show in June. As a result Maynard immediately gave him his advance unconditionally and for a little longer an uneasy peace had reigned.

One cause of sadness that year was the news, sent by Clive from Cassis in June, that Elise Anghilanti's boy had died. A few months later Lytton's health was a cause for concern. At the end of November he took to his bed with what was thought to be gastric influenza. At times he appeared to be making a recovery, but the speed with which he had deteriorated became evident when he could no longer read. Three nurses, two doctors and four specialists deliberated and various diagnoses were put forward, none discerning what a post-mortem later revealed, that a cancerous growth was blocking his intestine. Duncan joined Lytton's brothers and

sisters at the nearby Bear Hotel in Hungerford, and while there told
Bunny that Lytton seemed a little better. 'Pippa is practically always with
him and seems to make him content and he is perfectly clear in the
head.'[15] But the illness dragged on and more specialists were brought in,
to no avail. On 21 January 1932 Lytton died, at the age of just fifty-two.
'How queer it was last night at the party,' Virginia wrote the following
day, 'the tightness round everyone's lips – ours I mean. Duncan Nessa
and I sobbing together in the studio – the man looking out of the mews
window – a sense of something spent, gone: that is to me so intolerable:
the impoverishment: then the sudden vividness. Duncan said "One
misses people more and more. It comes over one suddenly that one will
tell them something. Then the pang comes over one, after years." '[16]

Five days after Lytton died, Duncan wrote to Dorothy Bussy: 'I never
knew one could miss anyone as I miss Lytton. I know that one will grow
less unhappy about it, but I think one will miss him always. I always
thought too that he would live to be very old – and not suffer for it and
that whatever happened he would always be there. And to my thinking he
was always advancing to something better and more increasing. It's
devastating.'[17]

The anxiety caused by Lytton's final illness had waxed and waned. On
Christmas Eve it had seemed certain that he would die, but a few days
later hopes for his recovery had returned. At this point Duncan, noticing
that Bergen, who had been suffering a cold, looked run down, took him
off to Brighton to the Royal Albion Hotel. He told Bunny that he hoped
to pay for the trip by doing some sketches of Brighton. 'I sold one at
Agnew's last month and was told I might sell any number of pictures of
Brighton and as I adore Brighton and find plenty of subjects, I hope I
may succeed.'[18] The following day he received an account from Agnew's,
together with a cheque for £125, and wrote to Vanessa, 'It's a mercy to
have prompt business relations signed yrs faithfully Thos. Agnew & Sons
instead of begging letters from Maynard. I hope you have had yours too.'
On other matters, however, he was less confident. 'I'm beginning to think
that I agree with you about Brighton *au fond*, especially at this time of
year. It's a bit grim and so are the people who come here . . . But I still
hold to it that it's a very paintable place. I've begun a sketch on the
pier . . .'[19] When the weather turned stormy and painting became
impossible, there seemed little else to do but return to London.

George Bergen continued to disturb the rhythm of his life. It upset
Vanessa not to know when he would arrive at Charleston, or for how

long. Duncan, aware of her unhappiness, felt wretchedly incapable of alleviating the situation. He absconded again with George in August 1932, to the Globe Hotel at King's Lynn, Duncan painting an interior there one day when it poured with rain. Wherever he went Duncan delighted in what he found, whether it was the bread and beer he tasted at Boston, its magnificent church tower called the Stump, or the countryside through which they had travelled to get there. His breadth of interest left him critical of others. Once, when listening to Virginia's remark that Raymond Mortimer could make a story out of life while Stephen Tomlin, though he sat in pubs, could not, Duncan felt bound to interject, as Virginia recorded. 'Raymond only sits in drawing rooms, says D. testy.'[20]

The holiday in King's Lynn ended suddenly: George had rheumatism, Duncan toothache, but the final straw was a letter from Lefevre's saying that George had to sign his paintings before the end of that week. It agitated Vanessa, at Charleston, to learn that they were suddenly back in London and their plans for the immediate future vague. George talked of going to Gravesend to paint boats, of an inn whose name he could not remember in the heart of Epping Forest, but finally they telegraphed Hilton Young, asking if they could stay with him at Wroxham, near Norwich, for a day or two before looking for an inn somewhere on or near the Broads. No sooner had they arrived at Wroxham than George announced that, owing to bad news from America, he had to return immediately to London so that cables could reach him. It was all very unsatisfactory and made more so owing to the fact that, following his solo exhibition at the Lefevre Gallery in July, Bergen's long-term intention was to live and work in Paris for six months. 'As he has made a little money out of his show,' Duncan told Bunny, 'there is no reason he should not, but I shall feel a bit lost.'[21] When September arrived he thought wistfully of Charleston. 'I feel very envious of you being at Charleston with Angelica in the hot sunshine without any crises anywhere about,' he admitted to Vanessa. 'I feel I should like to go to sleep under a tree for one month.'[22]

If Duncan's relationship with George remained turbulent, his work had never been more successful. In March 1932 his costumes and scenery had enlivened *The Enchanted Grove*, a ballet choreographed by Rupert Doone and set to music transcribed from Ravel's 'Le Tombeau de Couperin'. It was performed by Anton Dolin, Ninette de Valois and the Vic-Wells Ballet at the Sadler's Wells Theatre and showed a group of court ladies and gentlemen enacting the tale of Eros and Psyche. 'It is a delightful, if inconsequent piece,' enthused *The Times*, 'full of beauty and of half-whimsical, half-satirical humour. The beauty comes chiefly from Mr Grant's clear washes of colour and his costumes which owe something to Picasso.'[23] The following year he and Vanessa did designs for the recently founded Camargo Society, Duncan working for Frederick Ashton on Act II of *Swan Lake*, for which he produced sets and costumes based on designs by Inigo Jones.

Still more successful was Agnew's display of recent work by himself, Vanessa and Keith Baynes in June 1932. With twenty paintings to his name, twice as many as Keith Baynes and six more than Vanessa, Duncan dominated the show, though *The Times* did observe that Vanessa, who exhibited among other things a large work called *The Nursery*, was emphatically not his understudy and that with her more direct and deliberate response to nature she achieved 'a quieter apprehension of beauty'. The same critic extolled Duncan's 'spectacular virtuosity' and thought that in his firm and elegant *Head of a Girl* it was as if Derain and Gainsborough had compared notes. 'His natural gift of making a seductive pattern with his brush strokes, much in the manner of Gainsborough, has now developed into a rhythmical and rapid mode of construction.'[24] The *Manchester Guardian* admired his 'very sure and brilliant sense of colour'[25] and unequivocal praise appeared in *The Scotsman*:

> Though still loosely classed with the 'young', Duncan Grant is now nearer fifty than forty years of age, and past the anguished experimental phases of his career . . . his style is now formed, his handling vehement, his colour exceedingly lovely and personal . . . the landscapes are the most satisfying . . . There he is most himself, most happy, and English, and forgetful of the cackle of advanced coteries. His brush, charged with juicy greens, browns and yellows, simply ripples over the canvas.[26]

Less positive was the young Kenneth Clark's reaction to Duncan's work on his first visit to his studio. Looking back on this time when he was Keeper of Fine Art at the Ashmolean Museum, Oxford, Clark recollected finding at 8 Fitzroy Street groups of rustic pottery gathering dust and fading mimosa. 'On these unappetising themes both Duncan and Vanessa concentrated their talents . . . our hearts sank at the sight of their brown and purple canvases.'[27] He was relieved to discover some richly colourful pastels where, in his opinion, the medium had saved Duncan from 'Bloomsbury mud'. Clark brought to this description an element of hindsight. Duncan's tendency to 'muddy' his colours was a later phenomenon, noticeable especially in certain paintings that he reworked during the 1940s. Moreover, if Clark's first impression had been so dispiriting, it is unlikely that he would have commissioned a portrait of his wife, as he did – the first of two that Duncan painted of Jane Clark. Further evidence that the observations Clark put into his autobiography do not do justice to his early appreciation of Duncan can be found in their exchange of correspondence. From this it can be ascertained that Kenneth Clark was, for at least a decade, one of Duncan's most loyal and influential supporters.

When Agnew's mounted an exhibition of Duncan's drawings in June 1933, Clark was asked to write the catalogue introduction. 'If you think this is too bad,' he told Duncan, 'ring up Agnew's and tell them not to print it. I should be very relieved. And of course alter anything that you or Vanessa dislike.'[28] Such was Clark's enthusiasm for this show that, in addition to the preface, he reviewed the exhibition in the *New Statesman and Nation*. His strongest praise was reserved for a series of pastels of the nude model: 'They are drawn with magnificent breadth . . . have almost the quality of a late Degas . . . Duncan Grant's vision is so instinctively chromatic that he can build up a passage of modelling with strokes of pure colour, each one of which falls perfectly into its place.'[29] He bought two pastel studies of the nude (*The Orange Bandeau* and *Stooping Nude*), the first of several pictures by Duncan to enter his impressive collection.

In 1933, soon after Clark first met Duncan, he was appointed Director of the National Gallery. This marked the onset of the 'Clark Boom', as he termed it, a period in which he and his wife lived in great style. Duncan found himself frequently invited to drinks, dinner or cocktail parties at the Clarks', and sometimes Vanessa was persuaded to accompany him. The portrait Clark had commissioned of his wife took some years to produce but helped seal their friendship, as did Clark's request that Duncan and Vanessa decorate an entire dinner service for him. In his autobiography Clark states that the dinner service was an attempt 'to revive' Duncan's interest in decorative art. But, as Richard Shone has commented, 'Never, in fact, had the artists [Vanessa and Duncan] been so fully or interestingly employed as when they squeezed in this commission to oblige new friends.'[30]

The person most excited about this venture was W. W. Winkworth, known to his friends as Billy. An occasional painter, collector and great expert on Far Eastern ceramics, he wrote to Vanessa immediately he caught wind of the project:

I have just seen the Clarks, and of course, being a great enthusiast not only about your work and that of Mr Grant, but about dinner-sets, I was much moved to think what an addition to ceramic achievement might be made if you designed one.

I felt in fact an irresistible desire to interfere.

The Clarks told me that you are now contemplating the idea of enlisting the services of Wedgwood and I am delighted to hear it! ... Designing original pottery is of course an activity in which some of the greatest artists have interested themselves; your own work and Mr Grant's is well known to everybody, in this connection.

But a dinner service is a different thing. Faced with the problem of producing a multiplicity of domestic objects, the painter has a function quite distinct from that of the artist-potter and should adopt a different attitude.

He envisaged Duncan and Vanessa reviving the 'hausmaler's' art, and his imagination flirted with all kinds of possibilities:

It is an art where the traditional symbolism of allusion may justifiably appear in full panoply, and the vast repertoires of traditional art be ransacked for every emblem that may enliven dinner table discussion; and where even mottoes and proverbs need not be out of place. One is pleased at meals by the familiar, the friendly even the facetious ... : in fact, I find I am expecting a literary element ... The names of innumerable novels and mineral waters are appearing in my imagination and becoming entwined with the mottoes of Railway companies, and it's time I ceased to think of the borders of dinner plates. I am yours sincerely ... [31]

Such insistent enthusiasm was hard to resist. Kenneth Clark, who had since boyhood had a mania for china and had taken especial delight in New York, when dining at Lord Duveen's, in eating off the Sèvres service made for the Empress Catherine of Russia, was surprised at the result of his commission. Instead of the gay cascade of decoration he had expected, he received forty-eight plates portraying famous women: twelve queens, twelve famous beauties, twelve writers and twelve actresses. In addition there was a set of period women and two portraits of the artists, Duncan painting Vanessa and vice versa. They had taken Billy Winkworth's advice and employed 'the familiar, the friendly even the facetious' so that the diner, on clearing his or her plate, encountered Queen Victoria or Greta Garbo, Simonetta Vespucci or Miss 1933.

Though this dinner service is unique, both artists also produced designs for china for the mass market. In 1933 Brain & Co., of Stoke-on-Trent, makers of Foley China, approached various artists with the opportunity to decorate blanks for mass production. Ben Nicholson,

Graham Sutherland and Paul Nash were among those who took part in this scheme, as did Duncan, Vanessa and, at their suggestion, the fourteen-year-old Angelica. Duncan's 'Old English Rose' design showed a blown pink rose on a green field. At much the same time the Burslem firm, Susie Cooper Pottery and Arthur J. Wilkinson & Co., makers of Clarice Cliff's 'Bizarre' range, decided to expand its products by making use of artists' designs. Again Duncan worked with floral motifs, a loose posy of flowers and simple rhythmic borders for his 'Lustre' tea service. This and his 'Old English Rose' service went on show in 1934 at Harrods in 'Modern Art for the Table', a display of china, pottery and glass designed or decorated by artists. Raymond Mortimer, writing on the exhibition for the *New Statesman and Nation*, found both Duncan and Vanessa's work 'ravishing in colour and sensitive in design'.[32]

More characteristic of Duncan's ceramic decoration is the work he did with the potter Phyllis Keyes. They first met in 1931, when Duncan and Vanessa accompanied Miss Keyes to a kiln in Lambeth, where they experimented with colours and glazes. Her simple, heavy shapes – she often made casts from traditional Italian and Spanish pottery – suited the ebullience of their decoration. The immediate success of their partnership encouraged Phyllis Keyes to set up her own workshop in 1933 in Warren Street. Three years later she had moved to Clipstone Street, off Great Portland Street. Throughout the 1930s Duncan and Vanessa had fairly regular contact with her, despite the fact that in 1935 Duncan had to make it clear that he had no feelings for her except friendship, whereas by then she doted on him. Their unequal feelings led to misunderstandings and on one occasion Miss Keyes had to be led to see reason, with the aid of a letter composed by Vanessa on Duncan's behalf.

At Duncan's request she made a copy of a two-handled jug that he had brought back from Tunis in 1914. This he decorated and included in the Music Room, another entire interior decorated by himself and Vanessa, shown in an upstairs room at the Lefevre Galleries in King Street, St James's, in December 1932. This event had been made possible by Virginia Woolf's willingness to put up £100 against items that she promised to buy. On the strength of this sponsorship, Duncan and Vanessa went to town, painting with freedom and frivolity a series of five-by-seven-foot wall panels with semi-illusionistic drapery looped above and below octagonally framed vases of flowers. Mirrors were again a significant feature. A large mirror, with small circular ones set into its frame, hung over the fireplace, while still larger circular mirrors formed the top part of the wall panels. A low screen showed figures playing musical instruments; the gramophone cabinet was ornamented with neat patterning; and semi-abstract floral shapes floated their way across the sides and lid of a baby grand piano. Chairs with embroidered decorations set into their cane backs stood around the room, while elsewhere Duncan's 'Grape' fabric provided curtains, sofa and chair covers.

Exuberant yet relaxed, this controlled riot of pattern and colour became the setting for a glamorous cocktail party at which young men in white jackets served blue and green cocktails with what looked like gold-leaf floating on the surface. 'You must come to a quite ghastly party that Nessa and I are giving on Wednesday,' Virginia told Lady Ottoline. 'It's a purely commercial (don't whisper) affair, to induce the rich to buy furniture, and so employ a swarm of poor scarecrows who are languishing in Fitzroy street.'[33] Even after the event Virginia still could not quite believe, as she put it, 'us two hussies entertaining the peerage'. Yet its success produced a eulogy from Cyril Connolly: 'At the inauguration the room vibrated to a Debussy solo on the harp, and the music, with its seasonal elegiac, seemed to blend with the surrounding patterns of the flowers and falling leaves in a rare union of intellect and imagination, colour and sound, which produced in the listener a momentary apprehension of the life of the spirit, that lonely and un-English credo.'[34]

Virginia had her eye on the screen, and eventually bought it (now in Portsmouth Museum and Art Gallery), even though earlier that year Duncan had sold her a firescreen embroidered by his mother to his design. Virginia also acquired other items, including a carpet woven by Wilton Royal. This was not the one made for the Music Room, the pattern of which was echoed in a smaller rug, but one designed specially for her by Duncan, in which compartmentalised abstract, floral and vase motifs were drawn with Matissean economy. It aroused her to flights of fancy in a letter of thanks ('a triumphant and superb work of art, and produces in me the sensation of being a tropical fish afloat in warm waves over submerged forests of emerald and ruby').[35] Even in her diary she confessed that it made her feel as if she had risen socially to the rank of younger sons of baronets – 'it is like being real gentry, sitting with our feet embedded in pile'.[36]

At Lefevre's the fanciful exuberance of the Music Room had been combined with an exhibition of paintings by the East London Group. As *The Times* nicely observed, 'Elegant sophistication and sober realism are neatly contrasted.' Its critic was also astute about the Music Room. 'It is emphatically a painter's room, and we cannot but feel that the work is most satisfying when it consists in painting, as in panels and some of the furniture, and not in "design".'[37] Nevertheless the room represented another landmark in Duncan and Vanessa's output as decorative artists. Though the various items within it were dispersed, they reappear from time to time in private homes, dealers' galleries or the salerooms, and if matched in the viewer's mind with the two black and white photographs of the original room, it is still possible to taste the 'romantic splendour', which in Connolly's opinion had been 'the one element lacking in their former distinction'.

Given the number of exhibitions and decorative commissions that punctuate the early 1930s, it can be reckoned as one of the most productive periods in Duncan's life. He achieved a great deal while coping, privately, with a period of turbulence and stress. He had constantly to reassure Vanessa. 'My dear when I think of all the things we have in common and how much I depend on you for all sorts of the most valuable things in life – it seems absurd of you to think I want to do without them that it really must be possible to arrange our lives so that we can enjoy all these things. I express myself stupidly but perhaps you understand.'[38]

In these circumstances Charleston took on an additional use, Vanessa staying on after Christmas in order that Duncan might see George Bergen freely in London. It had become noticeable, when friends and family gathered at Charleston, that at mealtimes Vanessa was often the most silent. Owing to an innate refinement, she could not pass a dish without a certain elegance of movement and, though very much part of the proceedings, she yet seemed to those who did not know her well a rather glacial and subterranean figure. Even her sister, who could be so brilliantly perceptive, had little intimation of the agony of uncertainty that Vanessa was enduring. It was Carrington who, some twelve years before, had seen that 'Vanessa lives in terror of a second Bunny settling himself upon her ménage.'[39]

Sitting on the sidelines at this time was Timmy Chichester, a gentle, hesitant character, as prone to anxiety as Lewis Carroll's White Rabbit. When the King and Queen attended a film première of J. B. Priestley's *Good Companions*, Timmy gave George three complimentary tickets. He and Duncan made use of them, giving the third to Grace, whom Duncan thought looked far smarter than most of the ladies present. Duncan found the Royal Family no less fascinating than anyone else and would relay to Vanessa Timmy's stories about his employer, Queen Mary. 'I saw Timmy yesterday who was throroughly upset because the Queen never asked him what he had been up to all the seven weeks of his absence but merely said "It is a long time since we met" and then continued her conversation with Lady Desborough who is her lady-in-waiting. It's rather like Nellie [Boxall, the maid] and Leonard.'[40] When summer arrived and Cowes week approached, Timmy turned ill at the thought of being trapped on the royal yacht, never able to have a moment to himself. 'I rather pity him,' Duncan remarked.[41]

Grace was delighted when Timmy Chichester gave a party in Duncan's studio in March 1933, as Princess Patricia Ramsay, Queen Victoria's granddaughter, was among the guests. Timmy and Duncan appear to have avoided any show of jealousy in their mutual concern for Bergen. Chichester was also the kind of homosexual whom Vanessa could assimilate, and he in turn expressed his sympathy with her in gifts, Vanessa at one point receiving a haunch of venison from Balmoral, with the explanation from Timmy that he and his mother, Lady Templemore, did not like it. Such was her self-abnegation at this time that Duncan had to assure Vanessa that he wanted her to come to London whenever she wished. This uneasy period continued until Bergen left for Spain. A more significant departure, however, occurred in September, when Bergen made a return visit to America. Duncan motored over to Southampton from Charleston to see him off. He arrived just before the boat sailed, to find Timmy Chichester also waving from the quay.

In April 1933 a London art dealer, Tooth's, mounted a loan exhibition entitled simply 'Important Landscapes'. Among the thirty-one paintings were two by Duncan, *Barn by the Pond* and *A Sunny Day* and, though *The Sunday Times* was relieved to find them 'unhampered by the mannerisms which disturb several of his paintings',[42] most critics agreed that both showed Duncan's work at its best. In the view of one critic:

> Grant's real talents do not lie in the field of intellectual invention in painting. He is not a heavyweight of the Picasso and Derain class. Indeed, all his best things have been in pure rococo decoration and in direct landscape painting. These two great landscapes are incomparably fresh and juicy in pigment, and convey the loveliness of spring sunshine in the English countryside, with a lyrical intensity . . . Here is great landscape in the direct tradition of Constable, but absolutely individual, with a lusciousness in the colour, and an excitement in the handling that are peculiar to this great contemporary painter.[43]

Different aspects of his painting satisfied different critics. Roger Fry, though he appreciated the vein of fantasy and lyricism in Duncan's work, had done much to encourage a more laborious manner, for in both his writing and conversation he repeatedly praised austerity and solidity of construction, the two qualities he admired in the work of Cézanne and Poussin. Duncan owed much to French art while being, as Kenneth

Clark once remarked, 'as English as Hogarth and Gainsborough'.[44] His graphic work betrayed this most. At the start of 1933 he had sent two works to the Pastel Society at the Royal Institute Galleries, where they drew notice from *The Times*'s critic. By the following year Duncan's habit of using pastel was so ingrained that he told Harold Sawkins, who wrote an article on him for the 'Famous Artists' series published in *The Artist* in August 1934, that he solved many of his problems with pastel. Certainly it contributed to the success of his 1933 drawings exhibition at Agnew's, which sold out. 'His drawings are tense with vitality; the rhythms of life and fancy, the potential force of young men and women, and the lyric colour harmonies of alluring designs all testify,' the *Morning Post* applauded, 'to the superb qualities of his art.'[45]

In 1933, the year that Hitler rose to power, the Artists' International Association was founded in England under the banner 'Unity of Artists for Peace, Democracy and Cultural Development'. Both Duncan and Vanessa joined, their membership making them more acutely aware of the growing threat of Fascism. When the artist Arthur Lett-Haines organised an exhibition of contemporary British art at the Anglo-German Club in December 1933, and announced in his letter requesting loans that it was hoped that an exhibition of German art would follow, Duncan and Jacob Epstein refused to exhibit on political grounds. The previous month, on Armistice Day, Julian Bell had taken part in an anti-war demonstration in Cambridge, driving a car armoured with mattresses through the streets, with Anthony Blunt as his navigator. There were now times when Julian and Quentin clashed with Clive on politics, the young men finding their father's views embarrassing and wrong-headed. As had become apparent in 1928 when he published *Civilization*, Clive had reneged on his earlier radicalism and now favoured autocracy over democracy, as he doubted that the latter could protect the things he valued. By the mid-1930s, with dictators looming on the European scene, such views had difficult implications; as Quentin Bell has remarked, 'the Fascists seemed rather a long way from the Medici'.[46] But even Clive, who since his break with Mary Hutchinson had become rather desperate in his pursuit of the opposite sex, could not ignore the worsening political climate. Conversation with Jimmy Sheean, who still remained friends with Duncan and occasionally visited Charleston, kept him in touch with left-wing views. In his autobiography Sheean, while admitting the 'moderating influence' that Bloomsbury had on his 'mutinous impulses', tells of the frustration he felt at the belief held by his English friends that orderly democratic processes, rather than revolutionary ideals, would bring about social rearrangement.[47]

In this more political era different questions were being asked, as Duncan discovered when in May 1934 John Rowdon wrote a short book on his art, the first in a series entitled 'Revaluations' published by Hayward J. W. Marks. Rowdon spent more time castigating the bourgeois practices associated with art (exhibitions in private galleries, sales to private owners) than on Duncan's art. He was overly prescriptive as to what art should do and be, and urged Duncan to return to abstract art. His essay contains some insight into the influence of Cézanne and an intelligent analysis of Duncan's *The Bathers*, but his adverse remarks are ham-fisted. 'For much that is wrong with Duncan Grant blame should be laid at the door of the Omega Workshops. It was the Omega . . . that taught him to throw paint about indiscriminately, to cut down his angulated compositions to a bare curvilinear minimum, and to turn his interest towards painting women (made up of repetitive curves) holding fans (semi-circles).'[48] To add insult to injury, Rowdon asked Duncan to write a preface to the book. Duncan refused. Rowdon instead printed Duncan's letter of refusal. Whether or not he had Duncan's permission, it makes an interesting preface:

As I am used as a mere peg on which to hang your theories I do not feel so personally involved that I cannot enjoy your attacks on my work. And I can admire in your book the boldness with which you tackle and dismiss so many problems that seem to me still to remain riddles. I must certainly make it clear that I admire the book, most of all because it is a vigorous statement of an attitude which is new and important.

You have practical ideas about the whole value of aesthetic effort and exactly what place it ought to take in a properly organised society.

I have had the dangerous luck to live in a period which has on the whole assumed that the artist is allowed complete liberty of expression and I cannot help wondering with trembling interest what the future you envisage might mean for these curious, mad and undesirable folk.

My advice to them would be to give way seemingly in all points as most artists in the past have done. You may drive the wretched creatures to paint slaughter houses, corpses or The Alps, but tell them how they must paint them and they are apt to become conscientious objectors.

It is as a conscientious objector then that I think it would be safest to sign myself for in certain possible and very terrifying circumstances I think I should prefer Death to Dishonour.[49]

An artist's success or failure was of less importance to Duncan than whether or not he or she was true to his or her self. 'By the way,' he once wrote sternly to Vanessa, 'I'm horrified to hear from Quentin that you contemplated painting over an old work. *Do not do this.*'[50] But he always doubted his own perception of his work, and after a trip to Cornwall in March 1934 he had to wait for Duncan Macdonald's visit to his studio to find out with any certainty whether his Cornish pictures were any good.

George Bergen had returned to London in March, after a difficult time in New York, where he had attempted to produce a portrait of Lord Duveen. Duncan, determined to save Bergen from becoming a fashionable portrait painter, persuaded him to put in for a Guggenheim Scholarship and asked Clive to supply a reference. Bergen settled back into his London life, taking a studio in Adelaide Street and beginning an affair with Sonia Cubitt (Alice Keppel's daughter). After a few months he disappeared to America again, to paint portraits in Hollywood: Timmy Chichester gave him a farewell party in his cerulean blue room at Bryanston Square.

In May 1934 Grace Germany, after working fourteen years for Vanessa, married a Sussex man called Walter Higgens. As she could no longer follow Vanessa to London, it was assumed that her employment would end, but when it was discovered that the cottage Walter had found for her was a gloomy hovel, it was suggested that the couple should live at Charleston, Grace becoming its resident housekeeper. 'My dear Grace, I am sending you two cheques, one for your wages – the other a wedding present from Mr Bell, Mr Grant and myself. I am so glad that I need not write to say goodbye, but only to send you every affectionate good wish from us all and hopes that you will be very very happy and make yourselves a lovely home. Yours affectionately, Vanessa Bell.'[51] At the same time Grace wrote to Clive Bell, 'I am so glad that although I am married, I am still living at Charleston, it is very kind of Mrs Bell and yourself . . . I hope some day to be able to repay the many kindnesses to which I am indebted to you both.'[52]

That same month Duncan exhibited forty-eight new paintings in a solo exhibition at Lefevre's, Kenneth Clark again writing the preface to the catalogue.[53] Because in his introduction he referred to Duncan's 'freshness and lyrical grace', *The Times* countered with appreciation of Grant's 'masculine control of the colour architecture into which he translates his impressions of Nature', claiming also that the best paintings in the show were of riverside and harbour subjects.[54] Although the exhibition was another huge success, in terms of sales and critical attention, there was some adverse criticism. The *Morning Post* observed 'a tendency to congestion' in Duncan's pictures.[55] And Frank Rutter, in *The Sunday Times*, continued to resent the flattery that Clive Bell and Raymond Mortimer poured in Duncan's direction. 'If he is far from being "England's greatest living painter", as we have so tiresomely been told, he is a painter who, despite his inequality [*sic*] and occasional wilfulness, has great powers of design and his own very beautiful sense of colour . . . There is something exotic, almost artificial, in his colour. His *Regent's Canal* recalls not Regent's Canal but Debussy's *"L'Après Midi d'un Faune"* . . . The truth is that Mr Duncan Grant is incurably romantic.'[56] This show heightened Grant's stature in the eyes of another artist, Stanley Spencer: 'As surely as Epstein is the greatest sculptor this country possesses, so surely in my opinion is Duncan Grant the greatest painter.'[57] Not surprisingly, when Harold Sawkins interviewed Duncan for *The Artist* he found Grant's studio empty of all finished canvases and drawings.

One of Roger Fry's theories, which helped give rise to the nickname 'Old Credulous', was that the wearing of a saffron-coloured vest prevented tuberculosis. No theory of Fry's, however, helped Duncan that summer while he suffered from piles. After two operations, which placed him in the care of Maynard's brother, the surgeon Geoffrey Keynes, he recovered quickly and, to his relief, was soon able to return to his work.

He had been much occupied that year with thoughts about Gainsborough. In January he had been bowled over by this artist's work at the Royal Academy's winter exhibition of English art. He had also attended one of Roger's lectures at Queen's Hall, timed to coincide with this exhibition, and had found the second half entirely given over to a moving panegyric to this artist. Gainsborough's passion for landscape painting, sharpened and frustrated by his dependence on portraiture, would have made him sympathetic to Duncan, but it is his painterly handwriting that offers the most obvious link between the two artists. When in November 1934 Agnew's mounted 'Gainsborough to Grant,' *The Times* argued, 'Much has happened since Gainsborough, but . . . a return to statement in terms of the brush is evident.'[58]

'Oh Lord oh Lord what am I to say,' Fry had written to Duncan of the English show. Owing to his dislike of story-telling art, he damned much English painting as social documentation and not art. 'But really you know our particular lot you Nessa even Porter and a few others are much more like real painting than most of the stuff there.'[59] After he vented his anti-English prejudice on the radio, many people sent back their tickets for the Queen's Hall lectures. Later that month Duncan dined with

Georges Duthuit and Roger, who at midnight was quite prepared to begin a lengthy discussion on the works of Rembrandt, had not his fellow diners quickly steered the conversation to more frivolous topics. Roger's eccentricities delighted Duncan, as they did other members of Bloomsbury, and stories about his doings or remarks often filled their letters.

Though Fry was now in his late sixties, his interests and energy showed no sign of lessening. Having been made Slade Professor at Cambridge, he had decided not to follow custom and confine himself to a specialist subject, but to apply certain aesthetic ideas to the entire history of art. After ten lectures he had reached as far as the later Greeks, and throughout the summer of 1934 was preparing to embark on the rest when in September, the day after he had returned from France, he slipped and broke his hip bone. He was taken into the Royal Free Hospital on the night of 6 September, Helen Anrep sending Vanessa a note to this effect, and three days later, on the morning of Sunday 9 September, he died suddenly of heart failure.

'It seemed such an unnecessary accident,' Duncan wrote to his mother, 'and then we heard he was getting on as well as could be expected and it was a great shock to hear of his sudden death. I am afraid he will leave a real blank in a great many people's lives. I feel myself lucky to have known him so long.'[60] The funeral service took place the following Thursday. 'Dignified and honest and large – "large sweet soul" – something ripe and musical about him – and then the fun and the fact that he had lived with such variety and generosity and curiosity,' wrote Virginia in her diary. 'I thought of this.'[61] The following month a memorial service was held at King's College, Cambridge, after which his ashes were placed in the vault in a casket decorated by Vanessa. The day after his sister Margery wrote to the Provost, J. T. Sheppard: 'The reading of the Song of Solomon with its frank delight in the world as given by the senses fitted perfectly with Roger's philosophy of living . . . One can accept his going as in the course of nature, and even be happy for him in its timing, he would have hated decay. But it's like the setting of the sun on a landscape for us of his own generation, there's beauty left and interest but all the brilliance is gone.'[62]

TWENTY

Inside the Queen Mary

The Bloomsburies were a watchful, somewhat high-minded group. Their respect for work meant that whenever one of these friends published a book or held an exhibition, it received the attention of a testing inner circle. An exception was Clive Bell's art criticism for the *New Statesman and Nation*, in which he let loose a spate of injudicious praise of Duncan Grant and, as John Rothenstein has argued, wearied a whole generation with Duncan's name. Clive's friend Raymond Mortimer also erred in this direction, but the more usual coin of exchange among these friends was analytical severity. Virginia Woolf's observation of Duncan's 'flickering adder's tongue a-playing around my verbiage' is affectionate but also very sharp.[1] Elsewhere she noted, 'Duncan when he's angry snaps. Nessa is terrifically monolithic and impervious – a terrifying woman in her way.'[2]

The couple most frequently exposed at this time to the glare of Bloomsbury analysis were the Keyneses. Duncan had never reconciled himself to their marriage and continued to believe that such different personalities could not co-habit without cancelling out aspects of each other's character. Yet he was very fond of Lydia and followed her career with interest. When she turned from dancing to acting, with unexpected results owing to her fluent but odd English and thick Russian accent, Duncan made sure he caught her performances. In September 1933 she had appeared as Olivia in *Twelfth Night* at the Old Vic. 'We must go and see her,' he wrote to his mother. 'It sounds a very good cast. I only hope she will be intelligible.'[3] The following year she had her first real success as Nora in Ibsen's *A Doll's House*, in which her accent well served her portrayal of a Norwegian to an English audience. Vanessa admired the way she conveyed great agitation at one point by dancing a tarantella without, however, becoming a professional dancer. Duncan was so moved by her performance that he sent her a note comparing her with the great 'Réjane', who had turned the tables in the last scene in the grand French magisterial style; this, even at the age of eighteen, Duncan had thought 'silly, if impressive'. He added, 'Yours is the only version I've seen which blends the earlier and the later scenes into a possible whole. I enjoyed yr. performance and thought it *lovely*.'[4]

Between Maynard and Lydia there was a running joke about Duncan's sweetness of character and practical incompetence. 'Duncan has done a record even for him!' Maynard told her after Duncan, invited to a dinner at King's College, Cambridge, rang from Peterborough station to say that he would not arrive until 9.30 p.m. as he had caught the wrong train.[5] When Maynard advised dining on the train as the food would be eaten by the time he reached Cambridge, Duncan confessed that he had lost all his money at King's Cross and had already borrowed from the station master in order to make the telephone call. A few months later, in February 1934, Duncan, who had been invited to read a paper to the Cambridge Art Society, astonished Maynard: not only did he arrive on time ('an incredible miracle') but he also delivered a very interesting and learned paper ('I went in order to be sure that it actually happened').[6]

Though Keynes was to settle an annuity on Duncan in 1937, his financial largesse did not mend his relationship with the Charlestonians. Robert Skidelsky has written of Vanessa's 'constant maliciousness' towards 'the Keynes',[7] without acknowledging the habits of mind and character that gave rise to her condemnatory remarks, with most of which Duncan concurred. Both felt that Keynes was no longer the person they had loved and admired and who had been such an important figure in their lives. In Vanessa's eyes he had lost all his quickness and charm. She realised this most clearly in August 1935:

> We went to tea with the Woolves today. When we arrived I saw through the window that someone was there, an elderly man with grey hair and very stout, looking rather like a Duckworth I thought, but I couldn't be sure – and when we got in it was Maynard! Really he has changed with the last few months it seemed to me – Lydia also I thought looking very plain and middle-aged. No doubt they returned the compliment, but Maynard surely needn't look so much older and coarser than Clive, Leonard or you – I think it's owing to his greed which is really colossal and slightly revolting, for it's not a really discriminating greed. He simply likes masses of cake as far as I could see . . . I feel miles away from the Keynes now. I think Lydia doesn't like one to have any reference to the past with Maynard . . . Sometimes he looks as though he still has moments when he remembered another state of things but it is always swamped by Lydia.[8]

'Your account of Lydia-Maynard quite appals me,' Duncan replied. 'Is it all Lydia's doing? I expect so because on the rare occasions I've seen

Maynard alone at Cambridge, he's quite different though I agree rather bloated – but even there more high-minded and less greedy than with Lydia. I think she must dispirit him. After all they are *utterly* unsuited.'[9]

The distance between Duncan and Maynard owed much to the busyness of their respective lives. When the GPO approached Duncan over the design of posters in January 1935 he was simultaneously preparing for two spring shows: Lefevre's 'Work of Thirty British Painters' and 'An Exhibition of Paraphrases' at the Storran Gallery. 'These free copies,' Raymond Mortimer wrote in the catalogue to the latter, 'have a life rarely found in the mechanical products of the professional copyist.' Duncan had chosen to paraphrase Delacroix's *The Bride of Abydos* and Gainsborough's *The Baillie Family*, both in the National Gallery. Because he had been so highly praised, critics were now quick to pounce on work that did not match his high reputation. And his lack of interest in innovation had caused him instead to place much emphasis on vigorous handling, which sometimes betrayed a factitious liveliness. *The Times*'s critic, reviewing the Lefevre show, found in his *Farm in Sussex* (now in the Walker Art Gallery, Liverpool) 'a hardness, a sense of strain . . . a rather laborious Cézanne',[10] which is an apposite comment on the over-insistent thoroughness with which the chopped brushstrokes, rendering sunlight and shade, cover the entire canvas. Later that year, at an exhibition at the Leicester Galleries of Country Seats and Manor Houses, the same critic took offence at Duncan's *Ham House, Petersham* – 'the acid green of his lawns, intensified by the dark red of the house . . . almost makes you hiccup'.[11]

To some extent Duncan's critical rigour may have been weakened by the loss of Roger Fry. His absence affected many ('How curious my dear you should remember that you had never written to me since Roger's death,' Duncan wrote to Vanessa in January 1935),[12] and agitated discussion went on concerning by whom, and how, his life should be written. Fry had shared a house at St-Rémy-de-Provence with two French intellectuals, Charles and Marie Mauron, and Marie especially was worried that Margery Fry wanted interesting things left out. Though Margery would have liked to write the book herself, the task was given to Virginia Woolf. Vanessa now realised that she would have to tell Virginia of her affair with Roger. Helen Anrep, aware that Vanessa dreaded the shock it would cause, urged disclosure, arguing that Fry would have wished to be represented as completely and as truly as possible.

Since Fry's death, discussion at Charleston would nowadays turn less often to aesthetics than to politics. Quentin had become an active member of the Labour Party and that spring spoke at election meetings. An argument, largely conducted by Quentin and Julian, as to whether or not the BBC was politically biased, could last almost an entire meal. In the summer, when a sham air raid was mounted on Lewes, Vanessa watched with fearful fascination as vast beams raked the sky. 'The trees looked like great feathers with the rays coming up behind them like a fan.'[13]

With Vanessa, Duncan attended a dinner in March given in honour of the painter Ethel Walker at the Belgrave Hotel: they arrived late and had to sit at a table apart from the rest. Better organised was Duncan's attendance with his mother at the Silver Jubilee on 6 May celebrating the twenty-fifth anniversary of King George V and Queen Mary's accession to the throne. Armed with shooting sticks, sandwiches and a bottle of wine, Duncan made sure that he and his mother reached the Mall in time for a good view of the constant excitements – the sight of the two princesses at a window in the Palace, and the procession – 'marvellous soldiers in pre-war uniforms, powdered footmen, admirals and Royals'. The King and Queen, he thought, looked like 'painted dolls' in a brilliantly coloured carriage. 'The Queen you may tell Angelica looked like a pale pink rose very much painted and powdered ... The great moment after they came back was when the whole family came out onto the balcony and waved to us for ten minutes. I was able to watch them closely and will tell you all about them one day.'[14] According to Timmy Chichester, God's gift to the occasion had been the blessing of good weather.

Duncan's delight in life made him responsive to society at every level. He dined as willingly with Kenneth and Jane Clark, or the debonair and well-connected Mrs Violet Hammersley, whose portrait he had been working on for a year, as he did with Harry Daley and his working-class friends. 'Duncan still hob-nobs with the police,' Vanessa remarked to Quentin, '... I long to meet them all but am not allowed to – yet.'[15] Daley proved helpful when Duncan wanted to reach a young boy he had befriended, Sam Gentzler, or Tony Glen as he renamed himself, who had been arrested. Daley advised writing via the Borstal Society in Trafalgar Square, marking his letter with the instruction that it should be forwarded to the correct institution. Glen's reply, from Wormwood Scrubs, was the first of several letters Duncan received on prison notepaper, for his liking for young men, and his sympathy with them, did not end when, as sometimes happened, they fell foul of the law.

In order to leave for Italy in April, Vanessa had ended Angelica's schooling before she sat her School Certificate. This did not matter greatly, as Angelica had already been allowed to give up the subjects that bored her, such as Maths and Science. So instead of sitting examinations she travelled in style with her mother across France in a chauffeur-driven car, which Harold and Vita Nicolson had need of in Rome. At Roquebrune they picked up Quentin, who had been staying with the Bussys. Once in Rome, Vanessa quickly found a large studio room at 33 Via Margutta, with a small kichen and bathroom attached. Quentin took a room nearby and before long everyone had settled down to work, Angelica taking Italian lessons with a Signorina Boschetti. From Rome Vanessa wrote to Grace Higgens at Charleston, having received news of the birth of Grace's son, John, and wanting to hear all the details. The house had been let. 'I hope Mr and Mrs Read like being at Charleston and that everything is in good order.'[16] It would seem that Herbert Read, the critic who espoused the modernist cause and was soon to become a spokesman for Surrealism in England, did not take to Charleston: after that summer he never visited the house again.

Duncan, meanwhile, was also letting his studio so that he too could set out for Rome. His most pressing concern, however, was a commission from Cunard White Star Limited, which had been under discussion for some months, a contract finally arriving at the end of May. Three months earlier he had, at Cunard's request, submitted designs for three decorations for the main salon in the new liner, the RMS *Queen Mary*. Two were to be overmantel paintings and the third a twenty-foot-high centre line painting. He had received visits from the American architect, Benjamin Morris, who had been appointed to serve as joint architect of the main public rooms with the British firm of Mears & Davis, and from a Mr Leach who worked for the contractors, the Bath Cabinet Makers Company Limited. Both men had admired and approved Duncan's initial designs. In the course of discussion, Duncan had also secured work for Vanessa, a wall painting for a small ante-room to the Roman Catholic chapel, for a fee of £200. It was further agreed that both artists would produce carpet and fabric designs for both rooms.

Duncan's contract seemed exceptionally good. Work had to be completed by 30 November 1935 and he was to be paid £650 for the large panel and £300 for each of the two overmantel pictures. 'This seems to me to be very substantial,' he wrote to Vanessa, 'what do you think? It seems to me to make me colossally rich. But of course I will have to give a third to Lefevre which seems very unfair as Tooth got me the job ... I get £900 I suppose.'[17] Inevitably he spent much of the next three months in Italy working on his cartoons for these decorative panels.

He had arrived in Rome to find Vanessa fully installed in her cool rooms in the Via Margutta which, he told Bunny, 'is absurdly the counterpart in Italian of Fitzroy Street'.[18] Moving into the large studio on the top floor above, he settled down to work. The room opened on to a large, wide roof terrace where Angelica, draped in sheets, posed for him. He and Vanessa did not escape society entirely (they were seen occasionally at parties given by people from the Embassy and by Roman aristocrats), but they preferred taking drinks at the Café Greco, eating at an unpretentious *trattoria* and then wandering round the fountains at their ease. For the most part their working hours were interrupted only by the occasional expedition, as when they rented a small Fiat and drove to Pompeii. Then, towards the end of July, Vanessa left suddenly for England on hearing that Julian had been offered a job in China. Duncan stayed on alone in Rome, taking sulphur baths in the afternoon at the Bagni di Tivoli, painting in the garden of the Villa Medicis in the early evening, and one night watching from his balcony the fireworks marking the last day of the Trastevere Festa. To Vanessa he wrote, 'Do you know I discovered that the little house at the end of the Villa Medicis wall which I can see from my studio and have always envied was where Ingres spent five years of his life? There is a little notice to that effect which one can see from the garden. He must have been very happy there.'[19] Duncan also made another trip south, to visit the museum at Naples. 'I have a passion for Pre-Christian art, however bad, especially the painting . . . it is very suggestive to me.'[20] As September approached he grew melancholy at the prospect of leaving, a habit of mind that engulfed him wherever he went.

In London he was alarmed to discover that the English architect overseeing progress on the *Queen Mary* had cancelled his carpet designs. He wrote immediately to Mr Leach for an explanation. Leach's reply brought the devastating news that his cartoons had not met with the Directors' approval, 'who felt that too high a proportion of the murals would appeal to a limited coterie interested in the development of modern painting, and that this condition must be changed to provide these pictures with wider general appeal'. As Leach explained, a good deal of apprehension had been expressed concerning the scale of Duncan's figures and his choice of subject. Given that Maurice Lambert's metal reliefs over the proscenium arch and the four entrance doors had already filled the salon with some two dozen female figures, it was felt that Duncan's large-limbed creatures, which had been arrived at by means of paper cut-outs and owed something to Matisse in their decorative simplification, were too much. 'There appears to be a case for some change in the paintings,' Leach's letter concluded.[21]

Duncan replied:

I am surprised that at this date there should be any question of asking me to modify my scheme for the salon of the Queen Mary to the extent you suggest. According to my contract I was to work with the architects and Mr Morris with whom I talked over the whole plan of the salon, never mentioned the possibility of interference by any other persons. Again according to my contract my designs were to be submitted to the architects for approval. This I did more than three months ago and have a letter from Mr Morris with suggestions which I have since adopted. Also on Mr Morris's advice I have from the beginning consulted Mr Lambert, shown him my designs and have been sent by him in return tracings of his own. I presume that both sets of designs have been seen by the architects, so that I consider it rather late in the day to criticise my choice of subject. If the subject of my panels or Mr Lambert's are likely to cause offence, it might have been taken into consideration in the first instance. I have been working since the end of May on my designs, given up all other work, and put myself at considerable expense in consequence.[22]

This letter brought Mr Leach and an architect hurrying to his studio. The outcome was that Duncan agreed to modify the size of his figures, and he and Vanessa, who had also been subject to contractual interference, made a visit to Liverpool in order to see work in progress on the ship. It was a pleasant visit, as they were well treated and relations between artists and patron were restored, Duncan receiving assurance that his contract still held good. He now collected the 15 per cent of his fee to which he was entitled, and in November 1935, when the work was half-complete, was paid another 25 per cent, leaving £812 10s to be paid thirty days after the panels had been completed.

In connection with the *Queen Mary*, Cunard had showered commissions on a great many artists and designers, wanting the cachet of modernity but not the difficulty that sometimes accompanies reception of the new. As a result, aesthetic considerations were severely compromised by commercial instincts, for Cunard had many important links with businesses in America and had no wish to perpetrate anything that might trouble or offend their passengers.[23] Cunard had also realised that they had to take into account the taste of the Royal Family, for this shining example of British enterprise, named after the current Queen, had inevitably attracted royal interest. This growing nervousness on their part soon proved an insurmountable obstacle. In February 1936 two of Duncan's three panels, complete except for the necessary alterations to be done *in situ*, were positioned in the ship and instantly rejected by Cunard's Chairman, Sir Percy Bates, whose dislike of them was shared by the majority of the directors, including Lord Essendon, Chairman of twenty-seven shipping and insurance companies and a person of great influence in the shipping world. 'I am tremendously relieved at your decision about the pictures in the Lounge,' he wrote. 'I thought the one I saw simply appalling.'[24] Mr Leach, it was decided, should inform the artist that the Chairman had felt such large areas of mural painting ill-suited a room that would be used for a variety of functions. Leach reported back to Cunard that Grant had been 'dumbfounded', wanted to discuss the matter with his agent (Agnew's) and begged that the canvases should not be destroyed. News that his final cheque was *en route* did little to console him.

Duncan's first action, on the advice of Kenneth Clark, was to write a formal letter of complaint suggesting that he was entitled to substantial compensation for the damage to his reputation resulting from 'cancellation of contract'. He also asked if the paintings could be returned to him. Cunard, in reply, argued that they had done no more than they were legally entitled to do and therefore could not discuss compensation. Meanwhile the paintings would remain the Company's property until mutual agreements were reached regarding their disposal. They had in fact been hurriedly put in store at Clydebank.

The rejection of these panels at the eleventh hour, after the designs had been seen and approved and laborious alterations had been made to the final paintings, was shabby behaviour that Cunard perhaps thought they could get away with. They had not bargained with the tremendous following that Duncan Grant's reputation now commanded. Before the month was out, a letter of protest reached them signed by the Viscount D'Abernon, a former Chairman of the Tate Trustees and of the Standing Commission on Museums and Galleries; Lord Balniel, a Tate Trustee; the Hon. Sir Evan Charteris, Chairman of the Tate Trustees; Samuel Courtauld, Chairman of the National Gallery Trustees; as well as the directors of the Tate, National Gallery, Victoria and Albert Museum and the Courtauld Institute of Art, among other dignitaries.[25] The *Evening Standard* rang Cunard, telling them that there was a good deal of indignation in London about Grant's rejected panels and would the company like to make a statement? Cunard remained silent, though a flurry of memoranda went on behind the scenes and Sir Percy Bates wrote hurriedly to Major Hardinge at Buckingham Palace, 'You may remember last year giving me a warning on the subject of a certain Artist and the suitability of his work for the *Queen Mary*. You are now fully entitled to say "I told you so", as I found when I saw the work in position that it was most unsuitable.' He informed Major Hardinge that something on this matter might appear in the *Evening Standard* and that he was writing simply to assure him 'that though there may be some damage to the artist's pride, there is none to his pocket, as our Contract has been carried out in full'.[26]

The controversy reached the Earl of Crawford and Balcarres, whose wheat Cunard transported. He wrote urging Sir Percy Bates to give friendly consideration to the letter of protest on Grant's behalf and warning him 'how vexatious this kind of dispute could become, especially at a moment when everybody looks forward to an occasion of rejoicing'.[27] 'I hope you will be ready to believe that I am not entirely a monster of unfairness or depravity,' Bates replied,[28] but he nevertheless refused to alter his decision about the panels. Meanwhile Duncan and Kenneth Clark had wired the American architect for help. Morris, having had no invitation to do so, had not followed the regular procedure of inspecting the artist's work while in progress. Though it was his recommendation that had brought Grant the commission in the first place, he was aware that his expression of deep regret was unlikely to reverse Cunard's decision.

Duncan now sought legal help, putting the matter into the hands of Messrs Field Roscoe & Co., who began to act on his behalf. Meanwhile the Earl of Crawford and Balcarres, aware that the conditions of the contract were at issue, warned Bates, 'Pray . . . remember that the *Queen Mary* is looked upon by the country as a whole, perhaps by Parliament too, as something of very national concern – shall I say in the nature and status of a Crown Colony? – and as such, of interest in all her ways and manifestations and waywardnesses too!'[29] Cunard still baulked at the notion of paying compensation, but they began to relent about the question of ownership of the panels. They suggested that if Duncan completed them they could then become a joint gift from the artist and Cunard to the Tate Gallery, on the assumption that what was not good enough for the *Queen Mary* could easily be off-loaded into a national collection.

At this point Duncan went to Spain for a month, leaving Field Roscoe unable to reply until he returned. By some quirk of fate, his attempt to escape the *Queen Mary* fiasco landed him in a lounge very similar to the one he was trying to forget, for he travelled by ship to Gibraltar and observed how stratified floating society was, though theoretically every part of the ship was open to all. When he got off, a cockney family, *en route* to Australia, announced that he would be greatly missed.

He had decided to follow in the footsteps of Lytton, Carrington and the Woolfs and visit Gerald Brenan, who as a young man had emigrated to Spain with 2,000 books. Since then he had settled into a house at Málaga, married an American and acquired two children – one adopted, the other his illegitimate daughter by their resident cook. Duncan arrived to find them all managing to live like grand seigneurs on only £350 a year, in an eighteenth-century house, simply furnished but full of fine examples of native pottery and furniture. From Málaga he set out on a tour, travelling first to Algeciras and Cádiz. Brenan had advised a private car, but Duncan thought a seat on a bus was as good and sat up front alongside the driver. Cádiz fascinated him, and as he walked round the town a large yellow moon rose over the Atlantic. After looking at Cádiz's Zurburáns, Murillos and an El Greco, Duncan went on to Seville where, again with guide book in hand, he radically revised his view of Murillo, for one of his works in the cathedral reminded him of late Titian. But it was Zurburán who most impressed him. 'It's a very extraordinary experience to meet a new artist who is so definite especially as there seems to me yards and yards of Spanish painting in all the museums and churches . . . of a fourth-rateness which is really below Romney or the worst of English painting.'[30]

Seville itself seemed to Duncan more cut off from the rest of Europe than he had imagined; despite the animated life of this great southern capital, he felt as if he had arrived at the end of the world. When Holy Week began, its streets filled with elaborate processions in which enormous Madonnas with glass tears and scarlet and gold robes were carried slowly through the town accompanied by mournful trumpet music. On Easter Sunday of 1936 he stood outside the cathedral and watched as five bishops, all in mitres, said mass while young men holding candles lined the altar steps. 'They really were a magnificent sight, rather like a Greco – it would be fun to paint them.'[31] His eye took delight not only in the pageantry of a mass or a bullfight but also in the gentle pastel colours, the pale yellows and pinks, that coloured the old buildings in certain quarters of these Spanish towns.

He longed for news of the *Queen Mary*, but still felt the notion that his panels should be presented to the Tate a ridiculous proposition. 'I don't see why I should be forced into being generous at my own expense, when my feelings make me feel the reverse as far as the Cunard Co. are concerned.'[32] But his tour of Spain was not yet over. He visited Granada, a grander and more beautiful place than anyone had led him to expect, and thought the Alhambra a dream. He noticed how extensively coloured tiles were used in the gardens and had notions of doing the same at Charleston. He developed a keenness for Moorish architecture, and when travelling to Valencia went via Almería so that he could make a day trip to

Nijar, where he bought a great deal of pottery. Aware that Quentin was talking of becoming a potter, Duncan conceived the idea of starting a small pottery collection at Charleston. 'We shall soon have enough for a small museum and potters always ought to have examples before them.'[33] Duncan was also hoping that George Bergen would join him at some point on this holiday. But George's dilatory arrangements and passport problems left this hope unfulfilled. Instead Duncan ended his holiday with his mother in Mallorca, where his Aunt Daisy had taken a villa. Unfortunately, one of his aunt's guests was Phyllis Keyes who, on a visit to the monastery at Valledemosa, where George Sand had lived with Chopin, made out that she saw a likeness between Chopin and Duncan. When he tried to return home, Duncan found all the boats cancelled due to a workers' strike. 'It's a bore,' he told Vanessa, 'and I dare say you will laugh at my situation vis-à-vis Phyllis on a desert island – but . . . so far I have managed to avoid all tête-à-têtes.'[34] He spoke too soon, for the next day he received a declaration of love on the garden path. He hurried the poor woman inside and, until the time came to depart, made it his single object never to be left alone in her company.

While he was away, the row over his *Queen Mary* decorations had been made public, first by William Hickey in the *Daily Express*. In addition Clive had written a cutting article, 'Inside the *Queen Mary*', for the *Listener*, in which he referred to 'titterings in paint, wood, glass, plaster and metal'. He explained, 'What the management wants, and gets, is the humoristic-artistic. That is the prevailing note: the Teddy Bear style. Nothing is suffered to be merely good-looking, it must be funny as well; which means hardly anything is good-looking and that almost everything is vulgar . . . the decoration of the *Queen Mary* is facetious.'[35] This was so violently dismissive that Kenneth Clark used it as an excuse to abandon the idea of a letter to *The Times*, arguing that few would now be willing to put their names to further protest. His decision was not uninfluenced by a three-hour conversation with Christabel Aberconway, wife of the Chairman of John Brown, the firm that had built the *Queen Mary*, and formerly one of Clive's mistresses.

Field Roscoe assured Cunard that their client knew nothing of the *Daily Express* article and that the photograph of him in it had shown him standing by a painting that had nothing to do with the *Queen Mary*. However, Cunard, badly rattled by such adverse publicity, were now keen to reach an agreement. They not only now agreed to pay compensation, but also returned his panels to Duncan on the condition that he signed an undertaking to make no further claims and not to 'exhibit copy dispose of or use them [the panels] without first communicating with you [Cunard] for your consideration whether such use will prejudicially affect your interests'.[36] This Duncan duly signed on 29 May 1936. The same month he sent in a bill for designs he had done for carpets, textiles and panel borders, which Cunard honoured.

Eighteen months later Agnew's invited Duncan to hold an exhibition of his recent work. Very properly, Duncan wrote to Cunard asking if they had any objection to him now showing his *Queen Mary* paintings. No objection was raised and Sir Percy Bates was invited to the private view, held on 9 November 1937. Again, Cunard underestimated Duncan Grant's éclat, for the exhibition caused a buzz of comment, several critics expressing astonishment that these gay, vivid pictures, with their masterly handling of large-scale figures, had been rejected by the shipping company. The twenty-two-foot high *Seguidilla*, with its six figures either dancing or playing musical instruments, looked particularly impressive, its title alluding to a Spanish flamenco rhythm using an irregular five-four time, melancholy and ironic in character. Duncan told a *News Chronicle* reporter that he had worked on this and the other two panels, *The Flower Gatherers* and *The Sheaf*, for some eighteen months. As if to underline the hard work that had gone into their making, he also exhibited many studies for them, in paint, pastel and pencil. The effect of the total ensemble on Agnew's magnificent but rather sombre galleries was to transform them into a joyous riot of colour.

Even critics who felt reservations about Duncan's art were won over. Eric Newton began his *Sunday Times* review by arguing that, despite all its good qualities, Grant's work in the final distillation lacked bite and personality ('A little more fanaticism, a little more blind love or acidulated hatred and Duncan Grant would be a memorable as well as an admirable painter'). But he went on to praise the *Queen Mary* decorations wholeheartedly, for having 'a light-hearted swing and a freshness in spite of their size and their seriousness'.[37] The *Manchester Guardian* likewise found the paintings bright and cheerful. 'The *Queen Mary* must be filled with masterpieces if these had to be discarded as unworthy,' it concluded sarcastically.[38] *Country Life* went still further: 'this glorious song of colour', it declared, was far too good for the decoration of a luxury liner and ought to find a permament home in the magnificent new sculpture galleries opened earlier that year at the Tate or in the foyer of the new National Theatre.[39] Duncan, likewise, hoped that a public patron would come forward and buy his panels, which were being offered as a group for £1,100. None appeared and the paintings remained unsold for some thirty-five years.[40]

Suitably chastised by the critical acclaim, Cunard refused to run the gauntlet again in 1939 when the British Council asked permission to send the two smaller *Queen Mary* panels to the United Kingdom Pavilion at the New York World's Fair. Cunard's General Manager, S. J. Lister, advised Lord Essendon that as both Grant's paintings and the Cunard White Star presentation would be shown in the same pavilion, there was a danger that the old controversy would be revived: 'If anything should appear on the pictures that they had been done in the first place by Duncan Grant for the *Queen Mary*, the whole fat would be in the fire.'[41] Though their initial reply to the British Council stated that Grant himself should request permission to exhibit the panels, this was a mere formality *en route* to a flat refusal. Even when the British Council wrote a second time, promising that no mention of the *Queen Mary* would be made in the catalogue, Cunard still withheld permission, knowing full well that a critic might recognise the paintings and reawaken the controversy over their rejection.

In the same month that the British Council received Cunard's final refusal, the GPO began distributing the posters that Duncan had designed, advertising its service and illustrating various types of worker: postman, telegraph messenger, telephonist, engineering workman. 'They are so "like",' wrote a *Daily Express* reporter, 'that they would surely please even Sir Percy Bates, who turned down Grant's decorative designs for the *Queen Mary*.'[42] Slight though this mention was, it was noticed by Cunard and the cutting added to a file already prickling with embarrassment.

Duncan, though he wrote a fierce letter of abuse to his MP in the wake of Mussolini's invasion of Abyssinia and the British government's equivocation, let no reflection of the growing international crisis enter his art. 'The expanding fear, the savaging disaster,' as Auden termed it, seemed only to enhance Duncan's need to take pleasure in the near at hand. As the titles of his pictures confirm, he remained largely content within the traditional genres of portraits, still-lifes and landscapes, though he played occasionally with mythological subjects and classical allusions. Now in his early fifties, he still enjoyed a high reputation. At the Goupil Winter Salon in December 1936 *The Times*'s critic announced that the two most outstanding works were Duncan's *Parlour of Crown Inn, King's Lynn* and Stanley Spencer's *The Fireplace*.[43] That same month Duncan showed in an exhibition of gouaches and small oils at the Mayor Gallery. 'Duncan Grant is here at his happiest, lyrical, spontaneous and poetic,' declared the *New Statesman*, adding that his *Venus* seemed one of the best paintings he had ever exhibited.[44]

Yet Duncan also had his critics, among them his painter-friend Peter Morris, who accused him and his circle of living and painting in a way similar to that in which Cézanne, Renoir and Manet were living and painting in the 1870s: 'But as I see it an absolutely fundamental change has been coming about life during the last fifteen years or so – a new rhythm which will not be satisfied by the modifications and compromises which ... has always been the English way of success till now.'[45]

Certainly Duncan stepped willingly into the rôle of a Victorian artist when asked to play G. F. Watts in *Freshwater*, a rumbustious satire, written by Virginia Woolf to entertain friends and first performed in Vanessa's studio on 18 January 1935. Duncan felt less at ease at the Private View of the International Surrealist Exhibition held in London in June 1936. Finding a ten-shilling note on the floor, he tried to attach it to a statue in an attempt to give it meaning, but when asked by Paul Nash to remove the stinking herring that William Walton had attached to a Miró painting, he refused. He and Vanessa took little notice of this avant-garde movement: the jarring effect on the imagination of unexpected juxtapositions was something that happened unintentionally in their Fitzroy Street studios. Had they become Surrealists, they wondered, without realising it?

They remained loyal to the London Group and became embroiled with others, during the winter of 1935–6, in an attempt to defeat a dissentient clique who were plotting to remove the President and Treasurer, the sculptor Rupert Lee and his wife Diana Brinton-Lee. Despite various tea parties and artists' gatherings held at 8 Fitzroy Street, Duncan and Vanessa were on the losing side and resigned from the London Group, not rejoining until the war years.

Their sense of comradeship with other artists extended not only to group affiliations but also to individuals. Like other members of Bloomsbury, they innocently gave support to an attractive, vivacious painter called Patricia Preece. Her real name was Ruby Preece. As a young woman she and a female friend had been invited by Sir William Gilbert, of Gilbert and Sullivan, to bathe in his private lake at Harrow. There Ruby, finding herself out of her depth, called for help. The seventy-four-year-old Sir William gallantly dived in, had a heart attack and sank like a stone. At the inquest, Ruby was obliged to admit that she could swim 'a little'. Afterwards she thought it wise to change her name and became Patricia. Her love of manipulating others, however, remained unaltered. In 1922, a year after leaving the Slade, she had secured an introduction to Roger Fry, who gained her entry to the Dorothy Warren Gallery. There her work caught the attention of Augustus John who praised it in *Vogue*. Owing largely to Fry's support, Preece, by 1929, had become an accredited artist and a probationary member of the select London Artists' Association, one whose work, Fry said, 'is serious and really counts'.[46]

Little did Fry realise that in fact she rarely lifted a brush. The first to notice it was Stanley Spencer, who began courting her in 1932 and in 1937 made her his second wife. The failure of this marriage was implicit at the start, when Preece insisted that her friend Dorothy Hepworth should share the honeymoon. What had tipped her into marriage was the need for money to help her bankrupt father. Spencer, when he remarked that he never saw her hold a brush, may have guessed at her duplicity. Ever since leaving the Slade, Preece had shared her life with Hepworth, a shadowy figure, blunt-featured and awkward but a skilful, sensitive painter, with a Stanley Spencerish interest in human idiosyncrasies. At some point, perhaps because she herself disliked coping with dealers, exhibitions and private views, Hepworth had agreed to the arrangement whereby her paintings and drawings carried Preece's signature.

This hoax caused occasional difficulties. After Fry died, his sister Margery provided financial assistance for Preece. Helen Anrep and Vanessa also helped, the latter suggesting that Preece should do a portrait of Dame Ethel Smyth and offering her the use of her studio. This put Preece in a terrible flutter and she managed to dodge the task without alienating Vanessa who in 1936 secured for Preece a solo exhibition at the Lefevre Gallery. When it was due to open, Preece pleaded illness and took to her bed. In her place Vanessa helped hang the show and took responsibility for all the decisions that had to be made. Duncan was persuaded to write the preface to the catalogue, a copy of which he sent to the collector Sir Edward Marsh, and he also persuaded friends to buy Preece's drawings, thereby adding to her patrons, who included Kenneth Clark and Virginia Woolf. Two years later, in the catalogue to her second solo show at Lefevre's, Clive Bell praised 'the ardour and energy of her feelings' and pronounced her art 'obstinately sincere'.

Small wonder that Duncan and Vanessa became recipients of the home-made toffee that Preece and Hepworth made each year for Christmas presents. Preece was one of the artists selected by Duncan and Vanessa for an exhibition of contemporary British art held at Agnew's in 1937. Relations between her and Vanessa, however, began to cool after this, perhaps because Preece had obviously fallen in love with Vanessa and may have become too demanding. In 1947 Vanessa assured Preece that she had not lost interest in her work, and that same year Duncan bought one of her drawings for King's College, Cambridge, the library having allocated him £100 to start a loan collection of drawings for undergraduates. Both he and Vanessa thought Hepworth's rather Spencerish drawings so remarkable that they could not understand why the name Preece was not among the list of London Group members. Duncan therefore offered in 1949 to show a folder of these drawings to the jury when it next met. Unfortunately this folder, which had been left with him at Charleston, went missing. Preece and Hepworth interpreted its disappearance in the worst possible light and its eventual reappearance two years later did little to revive their trust. Meanwhile, despite all the help and encouragement, their existence was dogged by poverty, Preece also suffering, as a result of pernicious anaemia, from persistent health problems. Though duplicitous in their art, they were loyal to each other. Lifelong companions, they were finally buried in the same grave.

Throughout most of the winter months Charleston, cold, damp and silent, remained unused, even though the Higgens family – Grace, Walter and their small son, John – lived in a part of it, Grace acting as caretaker. In February 1936 Vanessa hoped that Patricia Preece might go there and paint. 'I never bother about people I don't know or like,' she wrote, 'that's why I object to your calling me kind . . . But I wish you could go to Charleston.'

> It's a very shabby old house which we have been to for twenty years now and gradually got more or less furnished – only as soon as one room gets in order another seems to fall to pieces. I have painted lots of walls myself and made all the curtains and covers and everyone has had a hand in it. So it's pleasant for artists if for no one else, as it has at least very little mechanical quality.[47]

Though Preece never came, for others the house had magnetic powers of attraction that drew them back each year. 'I believe we shall all be back at Charleston in September,' Julian Bell wrote to Grace Higgens in the summer of 1935, while Vanessa and Duncan were in Rome, 'but I never know what my mother means to do.'[48]

Julian's hope that September 1935 would find them all at Charleston was scuppered by his decision to accept the post of Professor of English at the University of Wuhan, in the ancient capital of Hupei Province. He set off for China in August, less anxious about the girlfriends he left behind than the fact that he would not see his mother for three years. From China he began sending long, weekly letters, which Vanessa would read aloud or show to Duncan and others. At Wuhan it became apparent to the wife of his Dean, Ling Su-Hua (Mrs Chen), that Julian needed a family environment, as he developed the habit of turning up at their house in between classes and sometimes in the evenings. Though elsewhere he encountered a wariness of foreigners, he felt at home with the Chens, for his Dean was a critic and translator of Turgenev, and Su-Hua wrote short stories and edited a literary page in one of Hankow's newspapers. She was also the daughter of the fourth concubine of a highly cultured scholar and ex-mayor of Peking and was therefore able to talk to Julian not just about Westernised Chinese culture but also about the ancient traditions of Imperial China. He furnished his house with her help, took her sailing and spent much time in her company, yet still felt homesick. 'Alas, dearest, I've found out more than ever how much our relationship matters to me,'[49] he wrote to Vanessa. He had always been open with her about his affairs with women and she was the first to learn when he and Su-Hua became lovers.

What he could not admit to Vanessa was his sense of having been thwarted again, that the move to China had failed to satisfy his longing for some testing climax that would resolve his purpose and character. He was further aggravated by the fact that world events now took a turn for the worse. When Hitler sent troops into the Rhineland in March 1936, a move towards appeasement began. 'To show you how far the pro-German feeling in this country has gone,' Quentin wrote to Julian, 'Clive is now ardent for an alliance with Hitler "to keep the peace".'[50] While Quentin became more and more immersed in politics, using his bulk at one meeting to overturn a platform at a Fascist rally, Julian was developing political views in relative isolation. Before leaving for China he had edited a collection of essays by pacifists entitled *We Did Not Fight*, but in the face of the growing international crisis he began to feel that Fascism should be met with a loaded gun. The detached position of the free intellectual now irked him: increasingly he wanted involvement with people and action. When skirmishing broke out in China in June 1936 and the country seemed in danger of civil war, Julian momentarily considered offering his services to an English newspaper as war correspondent. A month later he learnt, while travelling in north China, of Franco's *coup d'état*. This, he realised immediately, was the cause left-wing intellectuals had been waiting for. He waited anxiously for news from England but, for the time being, did not consider himself free to join those prepared to fight.

That autumn his family gathered once again at Charleston and prepared for the arrival of the Bussys. Duncan had a deep affection for this family and in 1935 had helped Janie obtain an exhibition at Lefevre's by speaking to Duncan Macdonald on her behalf. Though Janie liked nothing better than a good political argument – an interest that brought her close to Quentin at this time – her most memorable performance that autumn was a brilliant rendering of 'La Vase brisée'. At the same party she also took on the rôle of a thoroughly objectionable French bourgeoise being shown round Charleston as a tourist a hundred years on by a guide (Christopher Strachey) in the company of a large American lady (Quentin), who wore a muff as a fur hat and a lot of lipstick. 'Very amusing and rather grim,' Duncan commented.[51] Still more sensational was Duncan's own appearance as dancer from a Spanish music hall, a cardboard body strapped to his person transforming him into a lady entirely naked except for her mantilla and the intermittent decency brought by a fluttering fan.

'Julian and Quentin inspire you and lighten you more perhaps than you know,' Bunny had once written to Duncan.[52] If family life cheered and enlivened him, he in turn gave much to others. Jacques Copeau made a return visit to London that summer, the first for many years, and afterwards wrote to Duncan, 'Meeting again a friend who is faithful both to himself and to the past – there is no more pure happiness nor anything more satisfying to the heart. Really my dear Duncan you did me a lot of good, you have given me courage.'[53] He had delighted also in Vanessa's company and in Angelica's beauty, and vowed not to lose touch with them again.

Even slight acquaintances were moved by Duncan's presence. In 1938 he made a brief visit to Fritton Hithe, a low-thatched house on Fritton Lake in Norfolk, which had been taken by Hilton Young and his wife, the sculptor Kathleen Scott. Her speciality as an artist lay in capturing the noble features of statesmen and men of action, like her first husband Captain Scott, and in the making of symbolic nudes with uplifting titles. Duncan fell short of her ideals. 'He is a sweet, attractive, nervous creature, his eyes very blue, his clothes deplorable, but infinitely endearing,' she afterwards wrote in her diary. But again he had reached further than most: Lady Scott, in his company, was prepared to attend to a matter normally beneath her dignity. 'I mended his coat for him' she recorded. 'I can scarcely believe it.'[54]

TWENTY-ONE

Fits and Starts

An offhand remark of Clive's early in 1937, that no one had died lately, proved the prelude to a period riven with tragedy. A few months earlier Duncan's mother had lost the faithful Colonel Young ('my dearest old friend is going,' she had told him in September 1936), but more shocking was the news in mid-January 1937 that Stephen Tomlin had died, aged only thirty-five. After many affairs with both sexes and marriage to Julia Strachey, his life had deteriorated suddenly into a psychological muddle, made worse by drink. His quick sensibility, his loquaciousness and lovable, warm character had somehow become twisted and unbearably egotistical. 'A tragic, wasted life,' Virginia Woolf wrote in her diary: 'something wrong in it; and wrong that we shouldn't feel it more. Yet one does, by fits and starts, this very fine spring morning.'[1]

The following month Vanessa heard from Charles Mauron: Julian had informed him by letter that he intended joining the International Brigade in Spain. Vanessa, though surprised to hear of her son's decision at second hand, was not unprepared; during the previous autumn the tone of Julian's letters had become increasingly bellicose. 'War ... is unavoidable,' he had written to Quentin in October 1936, 'the only real problem now is how to beat the Fascists cheaply ... The only real choices now are to submit or to fight, and if we're going to fight to do so effectively.'[2] While he havered as to what line of action to take, his position at Wuhan suddenly became untenable when his lover's husband caught them *in flagrante delicto*. 'You've probably heard from Nessa about our catastrophe and my resignation,' Julian told Quentin in November.[3] Apparently less concerned about Su-Hua's reputation than about his own future, he decided that if a victory was won in Spain before he returned home, he would ask his uncle Leonard to help him obtain a job either as private secretary or in the central office of the Labour Party. Much solitary thought had left him convinced that 'a national-socialist defence campaign' was needed; 'an alternative army, police and administration so that we can follow the Hitlerian model and follow up an electoral victory with a *coup d'état*'. He estimated, correctly, that in three years' time

Europe would have to face Fascism or war. 'As to pacificism; we must abandon it.'[4]

As he had arranged with the Maurons, he went straight to their house at St-Rémy, after landing at Marseilles. He wanted to say goodbye to Vanessa in Cassis, not in England, where he would have to face views contrary to his own, for the reaction of his elders was still to fight intellectually rather than physically. In February, Duncan wrote to him with the utmost delicacy, much exercised on Vanessa's behalf. In a long letter he asked Julian to realise that Vanessa's reasonableness made her anxious *not* to impose her views on him. 'From talking things over with her today I think that what she would mind most is the possibility of not being able to agree with you about your reasons for going, quite apart from her personal fears for you.' So the letter proceeds, objective argument overlaying fraught emotions. 'Obviously I am not the person to argue with you on the Spanish question . . . No-one can think that those volunteers who in the beginning of the war rushed out to fight for the government had any motives which were not disinterested and unselfish. But things are still far from being clear and I cannot help thinking personally that it is still doubtful whether Spain is going to be the battlefield of all *our* hopes and fears. In fact I agree with Charles that you might be of far more use to the world as a free agent than as part of a machine.' This 'plea for consideration', as Duncan termed this letter, ended with the suggestion that if Julian's mind was not definitely made up, a telegram to Vanessa informing her of this would 'be the greatest relief'.[5]

Prevailed upon to return home, Julian arrived in England in March, thinner and more serious, and frequently at odds with his elders. He was persuaded to abandon his idea of enrolling with the International Brigade and applied instead for work with Spanish Medical Aid. Outwardly, calm returned. Julian made preparations for his departure in June. Vanessa and Duncan, meanwhile, had been asked by Agnew's to help organise an exhibition of contemporary British art to mark the coronation of George V. They were also planning a spring visit to Paris.

Though his work had sold well for almost two decades, Duncan was not a wealthy man. He paid little attention to money because it was a by-product of his life, not his means of expression. If he had money, he spent it, with the result that there were often periods when he was left with an absence of funds and anxiety as to how to manage. In April 1937, after overhearing two friends grumbling together about their lack of funds at a meeting of the Memoir Club, Maynard made two deeds of covenant, one to settle an annuity on Duncan and the other to help

Bunny pay his sons' school fees. 'The idea of having a settled income is having more effect on me already than I imagined such a thing could have,' Duncan wrote to Maynard:

> My first idea was to have breakfast in bed every day and do no work ever again and retire to the country. My second to build a gazebo by the pond at Charleston and my third to settle in a Levantine palace and live like a Prince . . . But honestly it is the greatest blessing that I need no longer worry about old age and decrepitude making me a burden to the rates, quite apart from all the pleasure it will give me to have a little extra money now. It will also I am sure be a great comfort to my mother to think that I am provided for. I have never been able to save any money and this seems an odd sort of punishment for my thriftlessness.[6]

If it eased him mentally, it had no effect on his working habits, painting having become as necessary to his life as breathing.

Still in many ways a renegade, Duncan had also become part of the establishment, taking his place in Westminster Abbey on Coronation Day. Because his Card of Admission had given instructions as to where he should be dropped and what his chauffeur should do, he had employed one of his male models to act as chauffeur, only to discover when they set off that the young man had no idea how to manage a car. Duncan ended up driving himself to the Kenneth Clarks' for a breakfast of kidneys and bacon and then parked at a distance from the Abbey and walked through the streets in his finery in order to arrive, as instructed, by eight o'clock. Once installed in his seat in the front rank of the gallery, he feasted his eye on the theatre of events, noticing that behind him sat the ruling family of Nepal, one gentleman in this party wearing a hat trimmed with pearls, and with emeralds the size of a thumb hanging from the brim.

Lord Gage was amused to see Duncan at the Abbey. In turn, Duncan noticed that his Sussex landlord seemed very much at his ease, nudging his neighbours and munching sandwiches. Relations between the Charlestonians and Lord Gage had improved ever since his marriage in 1930 to Imogen Grenfell, or 'Moggie' as she was affectionately known. She had an especial fondness for Duncan, whose company she enjoyed, and occasional invitations brought the Charlestonians to Firle Place, the seat of the Gage family since the fifteenth century. Because Lord Gage left the management of the estate to his agents, he had little need to meet his tenants. Once, when he had turned up unexpectedly at Charleston, he had immediately been directed to the bathroom by Roger Fry, who mistook him for the plumber.

Duncan cut short his time at Charleston that April because George Bergen was again in London. Bergen, however, had become an intermittent figure in his life and the five days that Duncan spent in Paris in May were in Vanessa's company. Quentin was also there, painting and working in archives on a history of Monaco. Duncan thought him much occupied with politics and living in a nest of conspirators: he had just persuaded Picasso to agree to sit on a platform in the Albert Hall in London at an event to raise funds for the children of Bilbao. Quentin accompanied Duncan and Vanessa on a visit to Picasso, who had taken two floors with vast rooms in a seventeenth-century hotel. They found him in a room almost completely bare except for an immense allegorical picture, on which he had begun work soon after the bombing of the Basque town of Guernica in April 1937 and which, as he intended, was shown later that year in the Spanish Pavilion at the International Paris Exhibition. In *Guernica*, as well as in the paintings and studies related to it, Picasso employed a method of paraphrasing appearances for expressive effect that was far removed from Duncan's current style. As a result, Duncan was impressed by Picasso's painting but uninvolved with it. In a letter to Bunny he admitted that he thought it very fine, but he wrote far more about the dancers at the Bal Tabarin, where they went in the company of Segonzac. Afterwards Vanessa returned to London while Duncan spent a fortnight in the South of France.

He took a room in the Hôtel de la Rade at Toulon and there painted a still-life of roses. Welcoming the peace that London could not provide, he visited Cagnes, in an unsuccessful attempt to see the painter Roderic O'Conor, and also went to look at Renoir's house. He also felt obliged to call on Eddy Sackville-West, who was staying nearby at Aldous Huxley's villa. In turn Duncan was visited by Colonel Teed and Jean Campbell, who insisted that he should stay at Fontcreuse for a few days. This he did, partly because he had to attend to their furniture now that their lease on La Bergère had run out. He found the small house occupied by a French couple, who had filled it with ornaments and furniture and had knocked an arch through from the sitting-room into Vanessa's studio. Duncan regretted that they had not spent more time at La Bergère. He arranged for certain pieces of furniture to be sent home and left some at Fontcreuse, where Jean Campbell had offered them the use of two floors in the tower. As always when he was in this area, Duncan went to see Auguste Bréal at Marseilles. He found him looking like a Daumier drawing, bedridden and covered in sticking plaster as a result of a bad fall, but well enough to stumble downstairs and show Duncan a full-length portrait of a mistress whom he had pinched many years ago from Bussy. Duncan had to give his word that no mention of this portrait would reach Bussy's ears.

While in the South, Duncan hoped to persuade Matthew Smith, at nearby Aix, to send to their Contemporary British Artists show at Agnew's. Back in London, he and Vanessa spent a strenuous few days gathering further items and hanging them, in time for the exhibition to open at the end of June. Duncan was pleased with the result: 'Many people think it the best show of modern English painting as yet. The whole room looks inviting and the individual pictures do not often let one down.'[7] So he told Maynard, who was unable to see the show as he was ill in Cambridge with heart disease. He had resigned as buyer for the Contemporary Art Society, his place having been taken by Sir Edward Marsh, who visited the exhibition but bought nothing, even though Vanessa and Duncan had cast their net fairly wide, bringing in an old brigade – Sickert, Gertler, Augustus John, Lucien Pissarro, Frances Hodgkins, Sir William Rothenstein, Dobson – as well as George Bergen, Patricia Preece, the late Stephen Tomlin, Keith Baynes, Frederick Porter, Edward Wolfe, H. E. du Plessis and Allan Walton. Among the younger artists represented were Ivon Hitchens – who considered it a great honour to be invited by Duncan – Roger Hilton and three artists shortly to be associated with a new school of painting – William Coldstream, Victor Pasmore and Claude Rogers. Henry Moore, though invited to send and initially willing to do so, was not listed in the catalogue, and Jacob Epstein had declined to exhibit because of a show that he was having elsewhere. Duncan hung four of his own paintings, including a weighty portrait of Mrs Hammersley playing his square piano. 'Incisive and full of dignity,' pronounced *The Times*.[8] However, Raymond Mortimer, writing in the *Nation*, thought Duncan's pictures disappointing, and his Mrs Hammersley 'a *tour de force*, but . . . rather a cumbrous one'.[9] Typical of the disaffection with Bloomsbury painting now prevalent among younger artists was the comment William Townsend put in his journal: 'there is a strong family resemblance . . . a real school of that kind of painting that Grant leads in; but it is not very good . . . Feel they are almost all amateurs whose aim is status and the pleasures of the artist's life and pleasant things around.'[10]

Soon after the show opened, Duncan paid his first visit to Mrs Hammersley's home at Wilmington on the Isle of Wight, perceiving the island's charm through sea drizzle when she took him on a drive. Meanwhile at Charleston a kiln had been installed, Quentin having abandoned his history of Monaco in favour of potting. That same month Matisse visited London, reminding Duncan, at a cocktail party given by the Bussys, of a benign, tame owl. Picasso, however, did not appear at the Albert Hall, as Quentin had hoped, though the fund-raising event was a success. The war in Spain continued, Vanessa following developments with Julian in mind, for she was aware that he was now close to Madrid, doing ambulance work on the Brunete front. Then on 20 July 1937, at around seven in the evening, she answered a telephone call: Julian had died two days earlier, after being wounded in the chest by flying shrapnel. Duncan was present in the studio when she received the call and witnessed her immense grief. 'I don't think that anything keeps her going at the moment except that she must not give up entirely because of Angelica and Quentin,' he wrote to Bunny later that evening. 'Do come and see her soon the more friends old friends she can see the better. O Lord. Yr. loving Duncan.'[11]

The following day, in a slightly calmer state of mind, he wrote to Maynard:

I don't know whether you will have heard yet that Julian has been killed in Spain. Nessa was telephoned the news yesterday about 7 p.m. Luckily I was in. She seems utterly knocked out physically, but is perfectly sensible. Leonard drove down at once to Charleston and fetched up Quentin. She seemed to want to be with her children more than anything and Angelica is here. Virginia is also here. She had a quiet night after a sleeping drug. But it is very hard for her to bear. I hope she will want to go to Charleston soon . . .[12]

Nine days passed before she could be moved to Charleston. Letters of condolence poured in. Violet Hammersley, who had herself experienced the death of a son, visited and though Vanessa lay prostrate, the two women talked together of their sons. A constant vigil was kept in Vanessa's studio by Quentin, Angelica, Duncan and Virginia. Despite her discipline of writing, Virginia found that she could record nothing until almost three weeks after Julian's death. 'That was a complete break; almost a blank; like a blow on the head: a shrivelling up. Going round to 8 Fitzroy Street that night; and then all the other times, and sitting there . . . there was no relief. An incredible suffering – to watch it – an accident, and someone bleeding. Then I thought the death of a child is childbirth again; sitting there listening.'[13]

On 29 July Leonard and Virginia drove Vanessa to Charleston. The weather was good and she sat all day either just inside the studio door or outside, on the patio. She was too exhausted at first to paint, though

Duncan encouraged her to try. 'She is still pretty weak on her legs,' he informed Bunny, 'but can walk round the garden and she eats and sleeps fairly well.'[14]

Occasionally she broke down, afterwards explaining to Duncan that he was the only person in whose company she felt able to do so. Though all shared in the responsibility of caring for Vanessa, it was ironically the elusive Duncan on whom her future depended. It was he who, through example and encouragement, restored her life-giving interest in painting; whose odd and unaccountable ways amused her; and whose essential simplicity of character, sincerity and honesty invited her trust. He, too, had a sensible streak; he hoped that the completeness of her present grief would dispense with the likelihood of return shocks, which might set her back again in the future. 'Of course it will be a long long business but I think it will be a natural process,' he wrote to Dorothy Bussy. 'Quentin is a perfect angel and seems to think of nobody but Nessa though he is very much feeling Julian's loss. Angelica too is almost too sensible. I do hope she is not controlling herself too much.'[15]

At Charleston that summer Duncan tried to galvanise Grace's husband, Walter Higgens, whose laziness was having a disastrous effect on the garden. Partly to inspire a more vigorous atmosphere, he brought with him from London a twenty-two-year-old Irish man, one of his artist's models, who had agreed to help build a greenhouse, as Duncan reported to Bunny: 'He works very hard and I really like him very much. He started life as a horse smuggler in N. Ireland, and now simply picks up a living as he may. He at one time took drugs and I am trying to break him of it. But he may disappear any day if the urge becomes too great. But I like a completely uneducated intelligent person as a companion with absolutely no prejudices.'[16] His proletarian lovers became the topic of conversation one day when Duncan was absent, either in London or elsewhere, and talk moved on to the fact that many of them had 'done time'. Vanessa remarked wryly that it always turned out they had somehow been wronged. She then smiled. Clive, who was present, observed this with delight, for it was one of the first times she had smiled since Julian's death.[17]

Vanessa chose not to attend Julian's memorial service, held at King's College, Cambridge, on 17 October 1937. To her old friend, the Provost, J. T. Sheppard, she explained, 'I cannot help these things meaning either too little or too much for me and I feel that I am better away.'[18] But she was well enough that month to spend a few days in Paris looking at paintings, with Duncan, Quentin and Angelica. Back in London she and Duncan were closely involved with the setting up of a new art school, originally called The School of Drawing and Painting, but renamed the Euston Road School when it moved premises early the next year, from 12 Fitzroy Street to 316 Euston Road. Run by four artists, Victor Pasmore, Claude Rogers, William Coldstream and Graham Bell, it ended its first term, in December 1937, with some twenty students and six pounds in hand, after paying heating, models, rent and the initial expense caused by the cost of easels and donkeys. Not a penny had so far been paid to the teachers, for the school had been run without profit and had funded a secretary with difficulty. Duncan outlined the situation to Maynard Keynes and asked him to guarantee the rent on the two large rooms at Euston Road so that more students could be accommodated and more fees earnt. 'I think it is rather important to keep the school going because it is about the only one in London where painting and drawing for their own sake are being taught. Nearly all the new schools are for teaching commercial art, and I honestly think it might be made a great success.'[19] Though Maynard refused to guarantee the rent, he undertook to meet actual loss, the amount needed when expenses exceeded income. He was not the only person tapped for funds: Margery Fry promised thirty pounds a year, and Virginia twenty-five. In an attempt to attract further benefactors, Duncan let Helen Anrep throw a party in his studio. In reply to a letter from Vanessa, Augustus John wrote, 'I am not familiar with Claude Rogers or Victor Pasmore – it is enough that you and Duncan support them and my name is at their disposal accordingly.'[20] One memorable event was the lecture Sickert gave at the school in the summer of 1938. He did so at Duncan's request. Though his memory was faulty and at moments he seemed befuddled, he was still provocative and entertaining, still a complete egoist if also now rather pathetically dependent. But his eyes, Duncan noted, were still wonderful, sympathetic and quick to take in impressions of human character.

Owing to the support that the school received from Duncan, Vanessa and Helen Anrep, it was regarded by some as an offshoot of Bloomsbury; Douglas Cooper, for instance, later dismissed two of the Trustees at the Tate, William Coldstream and Lawrence Gowing, a former pupil of the Euston Road School, as purveyors of the 'Bloomsbury smudge'. Yet one aim of the school was a return to objective realism, measured observation and unemphatic treatment, to a style and method that opposed the heightened colour and calligraphic brushwork that had been such a feature of Duncan's work over the last ten years. Victor Pasmore, while acknowledging Duncan as 'one of the principal leaders of the London avant-garde in my young days', admits to having had little interest in his art: 'Although I owe a lot to the support which I received from the

Bloomsbury Group I never liked their work except one painting by Duncan – a very large and free abstract collage which hung, in a rather dilapidated condition, over the fireplace in his studio.'[21] Duncan was right, however, in thinking that the school would be a success: though the war terminated its existence after only two years, Euston Road School methods became disseminated through various art schools during the post-war period and had a far-reaching influence on art teaching in England.

It is possible that Vanessa attended Duncan's private view at Agnew's in November, but Virginia's diary merely mentions that she met there 'the bugger boys', as she referred to Joe Ackerley, E. M. Forster and William Plomer, and 'savoured the usual queer scent'.[22] Meanwhile another homosexual, Raymond Mortimer, writing in the *Listener*, came to the conclusion after seeing the *Queen Mary* panels at Agnew's that Grant was 'the finest decorative artist that this country has produced'.[23] Such hyperbole did Duncan little good, for it reinforced an impression Clive Bell had already created, that his real achievement was obscured by such intemperate praise.

What interested Duncan far more than his reputation was the picture or project on which he was at work. He enjoyed writing for the Memoir Club that year a subtly comic account of the visit to Berenson's Villa I Tatti in 1920, when his identity was confused with that of Maynard Keynes.[24] He readily agreed to draw on lithographic stone at the Curwen Press for the Contemporary Lithographs scheme begun by Robert Wellington, of the Zwemmer Gallery, and the artist John Piper, who acted as technical adviser. The 1937 prospectus announcing the first ten prints, stated that the intention was to produce original works by living artists suitable for the decoration of schools. The second series, published in 1938, was aimed at 'households with small incomes', though the purpose of both series was the same – to disabuse the public of the notion that good pictures are exclusively museum objects. The prints, limited to editions of 400, sold at the modest price of 31s 6d or 25s, according to size, and there was a discount for schools. Duncan's print, one of the second series, plays on the contrast, in colour and movement, between audience and stage, with brilliantly lit ballet dancers flitting like birds above the serried rows of seated figures. As with other prints in the series, the choice of subject pandered to the English love of the familiar and anecdotal.

As the first Christmas since Julian's death approached, Duncan encouraged Vanessa to spend it at Cassis and sent warning of this to Jean Campbell. 'Any time you feel like coming we can fit you in,' she replied to Vanessa. 'Peter and I long to do something for you, and grieve for you, will do so all our lives. I did appreciate Duncan writing to me.'[25] Because La Bergère was still let, Vanessa and Angelica settled into the tower at Fontcreuse and were soon joined by Quentin. Duncan also arrived after a few days in Paris with his seventy-five-year-old mother, who was still game for a visit in his company to the Cirque Medrano. When the others returned to England, he moved to Villefranche to paint, taking a room for a fortnight in the Hôtel Welcome. Though he felt he was painting badly, it pleased him greatly to wake up on a January morning with the sun blazing into his room and the noises and cries of port life coming through the window. One Sunday he took a bus along the coast to Mentone. 'It was a lovely afternoon and Mentone is full of memories for me. It also gave me a *nostalgie* for Italy. It is somehow very Italian and quiet and seems hardly to belong to this age. It had hardly changed at all and people still drive about in open horse carriages. It has a heartrending touch of the 1820s of Milords and leisure. Perhaps I shall end my days there.'[26]

One evening at dinner Duncan fell into conversation with a man from Aix whose grandfather had been an intimate friend of Cézanne. He took further pleasure in a visit to Nice, where the Bussy family were now living in an apartment, rather isolated (they knew no one except for Matisse) and poor, eating, Duncan thought, scrappy meals. He talked family history for hours with his cousin Dorothy who, at the time of Julian's death, had told Duncan, 'Your brotherliness is and has always been one of the comforts of my life.'[27]

Another person whom he comforted that spring of 1938 was a thin and exhausted Lady Ottoline. Duncan is said to have visited her regularly during the last weeks of her life. She died on 20 April in a Tunbridge Wells clinic, aged sixty-four. Six days later Duncan attended her funeral at St Martin-in-the-Fields. It was possibly on this occasion that he accepted the commission to paint Lady Ottoline's daughter, Julian. A month later he had to employ a professional model to pose for her figure, as Julian sat badly. Julian then angrily accused Angelica of having acted as her substitute, and Angelica's denial only made matters worse, as Duncan had to admit that he had used a model. For once his charm failed him and he was roundly told off. The portrait was abandoned and a painting of St Paul's Cathedral accepted in lieu.

After her son's death, Vanessa agreed that a compilation should be made of Julian's poems, essays and letters. She wrote to several of his friends requesting material, which Quentin then edited. Charles Mauron was invited to write an introduction and Bunny was asked to produce a personal memoir. Whilst acting as literary editor to the *New Statesman*, Bunny had given Julian books to review and had made him welcome at Hilton. Though an obvious candidate for the task, he was inordinately pleased to be asked, for it seemed to signal his return to the fold. 'I belong to you in some way,' he wrote to Vanessa.[28]

Outward appearances suggested that Bunny was firmly ensconced at Hilton with Ray and their two sons. Yet his marriage had been weakened by his affairs and by Ray's own affair, partly out of desperation, with Stephen Tomlin's brother, Garrow. This had hurt Bunny, despite the fact that he was simultaneously involved with a married woman. In addition, their first child, born some six or seven months after they married, had been still-born, and grossly deformed. This had upset and disturbed them both deeply, Bunny afterwards making urgent medical enquiries as to the likelihood of it happening again. Their eventual family life and the pleasures of living in the country had failed to cure Ray of a neurosis that made her compulsively silent, unable to recover the vitality that she had earlier poured into her illustrated children's books and her account of her trip to Russia. Another blow was the discovery of breast cancer which made necessary a mastectomy.

In 1936 Bunny invited the seventeen-year-old Angelica to dinner. She had just returned from four months in France and had begun living semi-independently in a room at 64 Charlotte Street, near her mother, with whom she had breakfast before dashing off each morning to Michel Saint-Denis's drama school, the London Theatre Studio. In the autumn of 1936 she moved back to 8 Fitzroy Street, and the following year began to perform in some of the London Theatre Studio's productions. She was gaining in confidence and independence when Julian's death caused a hiatus, the life of her family then turning inwards in order to focus protectively on Vanessa. An awkwardness had already begun to develop between mother and daughter, partly because underneath Vanessa's verbal concessions to freedom and initiative lay a paralysing possessiveness. Out of mistaken love, Vanessa had not shared with Angelica her fears about Julian's attitude to Spain. A further silence had been caused unintentionally: Julian had said he would himself inform Angelica of his decision to go to Spain but failed to do so, leaving Vanessa to tell her at the last moment. After his death the intensity of Vanessa's grief must have left Angelica feeling further shut out. Duncan's anxiety that she was 'controlling herself too much' was a shrewd insight, hinting at the repression that blocked her relations with her mother.

Angelica was also the victim of gross misjudgement: not until the summer of 1937, when she was eighteen, did her mother reveal that

Duncan was her father. As a schoolfriend had already suggested this to her, the information confirmed inchoate knowledge and did not seem to upset her. Nor did it initially make much obvious difference. She did not confront Duncan with her new-found knowledge; nor did he speak to her about it. Vanessa also warned Angelica that Clive liked to think of her as his own daughter and would be upset if he learnt she now knew otherwise. In this way the deception continued, fed by protective motives, which simultaneously denied Angelica her right to identify with and be recognised by her father. 'Any strength and resilience that might have accrued from a warmer relation to Duncan was simply not there, and as a result my sexuality, nourished by romanticism, was of an unbelievable fragility . . .' So Angelica wrote in her memoir *Deceived with Kindness*, in which she also remarked that it is 'the conventionality of the deception that is surprising'.[29] In years to come the bitter legacy of this deception was to leave her, in relation to Duncan, at times rigid with suppressed love and at others aware of unsatisfied desires.

Only gradually did Bunny, now forty-six, realise that Angelica was no longer a young girl, but an adult. Julian's death brought them closer together and before long he discovered that his attraction to her was returned. Vanessa and Duncan had often remarked on Angelica's affection for Bunny and made jokes about the number of letters she received from him. One evening early in April 1938 Bunny suddenly asked Duncan how he would feel if he became '*too* fond' of Angelica. Duncan took the question lightly; but when Vanessa pointed out that Angelica's refusal to open Bunny's letters until after breakfast was indicative of a certain excitement, he began to consider the matter more seriously. Angelica must fall in love with someone soon, Vanessa argued, and perhaps Bunny was not such a bad person to start with. Duncan, trying to be objective and disinterested, worried about the possibility of it leading to unhappiness; thought someone of her own age might be more suitable; but finally admitted that falling in love with Bunny might be acceptable if it did not become too serious.

Soon after this an avalanche of letters arrived for Angelica from Bunny. Vanessa suggested to Duncan that he ought to ask Bunny what his 'intentions' were with regard to his daughter. The word 'intentions' amused them both with its old-fashioned, Victorian overtones, but it was the word Duncan eventually used in the letter he wrote to Bunny.

Next Bunny came down to Charleston on a visit. Nothing at first was said about his relations with Angelica, though Vanessa found them the first evening in each other's arms in the studio and again asked Duncan to speak with him. On the third day of Bunny's visit and the evening before he left, a conversation took place between Bunny and Duncan in the room in which Angelica had been born nineteen years before. Duncan afterwards recorded their exchange in a large diary-notebook. Some twenty years before, he had used this book as an outlet for his troubled feelings towards Bunny, but since 1919 it had been left untouched. It quickly emerged that evening that Bunny was angered by Duncan's use of the word 'intentions':

> ... his excessively emotional condition upset and at the same time annoyed me. I thought that if he was in such a disintegrated state somehow it would be very unfair to Angelica to have to deal with him. After all he was the one who had all the previous experience and should I thought be more capable of seeing things calmly and discussing them calmly instead of entering blindfold on an adventure with a mere child. So instead of speaking calmly I said that I did want to know what the state of affairs was. He said he would rather talk about it another time. This angered me and I said that now was a good opportunity and I thought he ought to do so. He then said it was absurd was it not for me to talk about seduction and morals like a Victorian father. This I'm afraid enraged me and I told him I thought it would be a great mistake for him to start a serious affair with A just now when she was just entering on life and that of course she would have to have a love affair soon but that I had hoped it would be with a person to some degree inexperienced and not with someone of his age. This I think touched him to the quick and he shortly left the room saying goodnight to which I did not answer.
>
> I was much agitated by the whole affair because all sorts of unnecessary emotions had suddenly welled up inside me, which I do not rightly understand even now. My heart beat very fast and I could not get to sleep for a long time. In the night I woke up from a dream when Quentin came into my room his throat encircled with blood saying 'I met Angelica coming out of B's room'.
>
> The whole thing may be of course jealousy on my part, mixed up with some curious complex/taboo about sex.[30]

Bunny left Charleston vexed by Duncan's outburst. Prior to his visit he had pleaded his cause to Vanessa. 'I have a lot of good qualities – one of which is my unalterable love for him [Duncan] and of you.' Surely it would be better for Angelica to fall in love with him rather than 'someone who feels ill at ease with all of you and profoundly hates and despises all the things you care about'.[31] Now he returned to this theme, hoping that if he gained Vanessa's approval, Duncan's objections would fall away. 'My love for Angelica is made up of every sort of love; it is mixed up with my love of you and Duncan and the past; but it is extremely strong and sincere, and I think unselfish.'[32]

In turn Vanessa told Bunny about the importance Duncan had for Angelica. In her view, there was nothing lacking in Duncan's relationship with his daughter: he had given her many opportunities for delight; as a teenager and young adult she had found in him a male figure with whom she could talk about most things, even though a certain quality of heterosexuality was absent. Mindful of her own pleasure in Duncan's company and in his unusual powers of observation, Vanessa insisted, 'No one could have helped her more than he has done to grow up and be, as she certainly is, remarkably free and independent.'[33] But, as Bunny knew, there was also an adverse side to Duncan, a crusty, obstinate, contradictory streak, which was one reason why he had been nicknamed 'the Bear'. Equally, Duncan knew Bunny's weaknesses and was 'frightened of the uncontrolled self-ignorance of B when he falls in love. There is something unreal, unstable in it.'[34]

In the summer of 1938 Angelica and other students from Saint-Denis's school formed the London Village Players and toured with a performance of *Gammer Gurton's Needle* around the Sussex villages. Momentarily Bunny suffered pangs of jealousy, as he suspected she was in love with somebody else. At the end of that summer Angelica abandoned the stage and enrolled instead at the Euston Road School, a move welcomed by Vanessa, who felt that she understood what was going on inside the heads of painters far better than she did those of actors. Up till now Bunny, mindful of Duncan's feelings, had held back from sexual relations with Angelica, but in August they became lovers. Directed more by his heart than his head, Bunny wrote a letter to Angelica which exposed his confused loyalties. 'Darling, darling Jelly Cat, I love you so much. I wish I hadn't made love to you but you are so adorable . . . I can't help it. All the same I don't love you physically as much as you suppose – but because you are the child of two people I love most, and I see them both in you. Knowing you intimately is like starting life again.'[35]

When John Rothenstein took over the directorship of the Tate in 1938, he rehung the collection. Whereas his predecessor, J. B. Manson had, in Clive's opinion, 'done nothing but harm to modern painting',[36] Rothenstein had considerable interest in those artists who had first made their mark in the pre-1914 period. On visiting the Tate in October 1938 Clive was pleased to see, alongside a very poor exhibition of Canadian art, a room devoted to Duncan and Vanessa's generation – 'it looks very well and reflects great credit on our age,' he remarked.[37] British art was also recognised that year in Paris, the Salon d'Automne inviting independent British artists, including Duncan, to exhibit.

Duncan still had a supporter in Kenneth Clark, who in 1938 bought *Figures in a Glass*, a still-life in which a painting by Bergen can be glimpsed on the background wall, for Birmingham Art Gallery. And it was Clark who selected the art exhibited in the British Pavilion at the New York World Fair in the spring of 1939. In the catalogue introduction he linked Duncan Grant with Matthew Smith, as artists who had 'created their own world ... through the joy of the senses'. More paintings by Duncan and Vanessa hung that summer at Osterley Park, where Lord Jersey had given up five rooms to contemporary English painters and sculptors. Then, in November 1939, the Queen, visiting Agnew's, bought two of Duncan's paintings, a small picture of Newhaven Pier and a large canvas of St Paul's Cathedral.

He and Vanessa suffered a setback that month when somewhere between Cassis and Saulieu a roll of recently painted canvases dropped off their car. They had travelled out at the time of the Munich crisis, and at Paris had found trenches being dug and people leaving in their thousands in cars. Duncan had thought Chamberlain's plan to go and see Hitler 'a very courageous and good step to take', though in the outcome he felt sorry for the Czechs.[38] But it was a relief when the horror of immediate catastrophe receded and they arrived at Cassis in time to find the black grapes covered with bloom and the *vendange* about to begin. They were able once more to make use of La Bergère and reckoned the arch knocked through into Vanessa's studio an improvement. Elise Anghilanti once again came daily to cook their meals, helping to foster the illusion that the old times had been restored. That year a sudden passion for boules took Quentin, Angelica and Duncan regularly into town.

Yet for Duncan it was a melancholy visit, and not just because Auguste Bréal, no longer able to talk, was dying at Marseilles. The darkening situation in Europe, his feelings of apprehension towards Bunny, anxiety over Angelica, his beached emotions over George Bergen and the fact that Vanessa, in coming to terms with her grief, had become rather stern and set in her ways – all these may have left him feeling snared with unhappiness. One day when he was sitting in a café in the town, the painter Yanko Varda, who was passing, introduced him to the young publisher James MacGibbon, who took away a strong impression that Duncan was horribly depressed. He made a similar impression on the young Scottish painter, Robert Frame, who met Duncan in the early 1940s in a pub in Fitzrovia. Frame was startled at how nervous and ill-at-ease Duncan seemed, for he scarcely talked to anyone and emanated depression.[39]

In 1938 they could have stayed longer at La Bergère, but they returned home in November because Quentin had already left and, as Vanessa admitted to Bunny, she needed to be near him. 'Not that he isn't perfectly contented to be alone at Charleston – but I know I can't stand nowadays being separated from him very long.'[40] London, for Duncan, offered more complex society and diverting conversation, which he loved. One current topic was Bunny's edited collection of T. E. Lawrence's letters. 'Dinner at Clive's,' reads Virginia Woolf's diary for 28 November 1938. 'An English Turkey. Duncan flown; argumentative, persistent; chattering against T. E. Lawrence etc. amusing.'[41]

One mystery in his life resolved itself in February 1939 at the Whitechapel Art Gallery. He and Vanessa sat on the jury for a painting competition and, while having tea afterwards with Graham Sutherland, William Coldstream and Percy Horton, were astonished to hear Horton describe how he had bought a Delacroix drawing at Hammond's in Lewes for one shilling. From his description Duncan realised that it was the one Maynard had acquired for him at the Degas sale in 1918 and which in recent years had gone missing: suspicion had fallen chiefly, and quite unjustifiably, on their erstwhile tenant Herbert Read. Now Duncan remembered that he had taken the Delacroix into Hammond's for new glass and never collected it. In due time, and after some rather delicate negotiations, the drawing was returned to him.

Charleston in the spring restored his spirits, even if world politics cast a shadow on all their lives. 'I hope you are enjoying as lovely weather as we have here,' Duncan wrote to his mother. 'If it wasn't for the deplorable doings of the dictators it would be very peaceful.'[42] Owing to the likelihood of war and therefore the fact that Charleston might again become their permanent home, major alterations were under way. An attic room was converted into a studio with a large north-facing window and, at Bunny's suggestion, the larder next to the downstairs studio was given French windows and converted into a bedroom for Vanessa. That April a telephone was installed – 'but you mustn't breathe a word of it to anyone,' Angelica warned Bunny, 'our great object is not to be rung up!'[43] The same month Duncan painted a large and elaborately detailed picture of Angelica playing the piano in the sitting room.

One visitor who stirred things up was Virginia. Her conversation was sometimes very one-sided, but always stimulating. She was intrigued as to what was happening to Angelica at this time, for she guessed more than she was told. While shopping in Lewes that spring Angelica suddenly heard loud and prolonged yelps, which turned out not to be some animal run over but her aunt, 'looking more utterly wild and angular and strange than ever'. Writing to Bunny, she continued, 'We walked up and down the street talking, and she was very curious as to why I had gone to London, asking me whether it was some wild love affair to which I replied that I had gone only to fetch my paintbox . . . She is a queer bird and so fearfully indiscreet.'[44]

Their love affair had been made easier when Bunny took a room in Charlotte Street in 1939. His work required him to be much in London, as he was reader for Jonathan Cape and was also writing the 'Books in General' page for the *New Statesman*. His personal loyalties, meanwhile, were torn in three directions. He and Angelica sometimes dodged having to see Duncan when they went in and out of 8 Fitzroy Street, Bunny not wanting to face the fact that he was hurting his old friend. In addition, Bunny had also to face his responsibilities towards Ray. In the spring of that year evidence of her cancer returned. Seeing her in March exhausted by X-rays but with her courage and composure returned, Bunny suddenly felt overwhelmed with emotions – tender love for his wife mingling with despair. 'Could not talk,' he wrote in his diary. 'Yet I shall have to, as I cannot live without seeing Angelica.'[45]

Left alone much of the time at Hilton while her sons were at school and Bunny was in London, Ray struggled with fear and depression. In his torn emotional state, Bunny opted for openness and honesty and told Ray of his love for Angelica. She thought him cruel and cold-hearted, and the harrowing letters she afterwards wrote to one of her brothers caused him never to speak to Bunny again. In May 1939 Bunny took a holiday in France with Angelica and Quentin, his happiness riven with guilt. 'I cannot separate my life from yours,' he wrote to Ray. 'It is unthinkable and impossible: I love you . . . want to spend half my life with you, and to share my interests and yours . . . But you must allow me to see and love Angelica.'[46]

When Angelica had to go into a nursing home in June with stomach pains, Bunny told Duncan the news. The shock it caused momentarily brought the two men close. Duncan asked Bunny for his help in telling Vanessa, who was down at Charleston.

The next morning Bunny, with Duncan, drove Angelica to the nursing home. (A day or so later, seeing Vanessa sit in the place where his mother-in-law had once sat, Bunny suddenly realised that it was the same nursing home where Ray had been delivered of her still-born child.) Afterwards he dropped Duncan back at Fitzroy Street. About an hour later he saw Vanessa's car in the street, rang the bell to her studio and

Duncan answered. Inside he found Vanessa in a state of complete collapse. Bunny stayed for some time, repeating all the doctor's diagnoses that Angelica was probably suffering from a kidney infection. On leaving, he returned to the nursing home and was chatting to Angelica when Vanessa and Duncan arrived. Vanessa had completely regained her composure and showed no trace of emotion. She talked of Charleston news and begged Bunny to come to dinner.

Just before dinner, when Bunny was alone with Vanessa, she asked him if Angelica was pregnant. Relieved to learn that this was not the case, she asked Bunny to promise to tell her if ever such a situation arose, as abortions were much less dangerous at an early stage in pregnancy. Bunny, who had recently been delighted to hear Angelica say that she wanted to have a child by him, felt his blood freeze. Later that evening, when Vanessa wondered aloud why Angelica had let her go off to Charleston without telling her something was wrong, Bunny blurted out that she did not tell Vanessa because she did not want her to know. Aware that he had hurt Vanessa and infuriated Duncan, he left. From now on Bunny was unable to disguise from Vanessa the fact that he felt she often mishandled her relations with her daughter.

This small episode left a bitter aftermath. Vanessa objected to Bunny saying that she treated Angelica like a child. 'Any human relationship but especially those of mothers and children are perpetually changing, developing and growing,' she retorted.[47] While attempting to justify Duncan's antagonism towards Bunny, she also began to share his distrust and anxiety. Bunny's diary of July 1939 reads: 'It is clear she is rather alarmed about Duncan's being so upset about my relationship with Angelica, though he has said nothing. Angelica is his biggest emotional interest now, she feels sure, as George never writes.'[48] But Duncan's emotional interests were not so selfless. Bunny's conquest of Angelica may have left him feeling usurped on both sides. Duncan refuted Bunny's suggestion that he 'hated' him, saying it was an example of Bunny's method of 'over-sentimentalising the emotions'. 'As long as Angelica is happy I really don't care anything else as regards her,' he remarked.[49] Looking back, Angelica has asked what lay behind the barrier of simplicity and kindness that stood between her and her father. Was there anything further to see? 'Assuredly there was, but it was too nebulous, private and self-centred to respond to the demands of a daughter. As a result our relationship, though in many ways delightful, was a mere simulacrum.'[50]

With the approach of war Vanessa and Duncan agreed to let their

London studios and arranged to transfer a large number of canvases to Sussex, together with furniture, books and Duncan's square piano. Two large vans eventually arrived at Charleston. The first, Vanessa recounted to Duncan, 'began to give forth paintings at an alarming rate which we stacked in the yard. Quentin nearly collapsed and I had to rub in your command not to give way to terror . . . nude followed nude of every sex and colour.'[51] A month later another van brought Clive's books and furniture. His large bookcase fitted very neatly into Vanessa's former bedroom, which now became a library. It was a time of change and endings. Duncan attended Mark Gertler's funeral after he took his own life in July, and keenly felt Gertler's loss. Three months later another friend, Timmy Chichester, aged fifty-three, died in his sleep of heart failure.

That summer Quentin volunteered for anti-aircraft work but was rejected because of having had tuberculosis. Instead, he accepted Maynard's offer of a full-time job on his farm. This greatly relieved Vanessa, as it meant that Quentin could continue to live at Charleston and she could keep an eye on his health. Meanwhile, Bunny, in the event of war, was invited to join the Air Ministry Intelligence. At the same time Ray discovered a small lump beneath her collar bone, the first sign that disseminated cancer had set in.

The announcement of war caused panic and anxiety. Duncan's mother and Aunt Violet arrived at Charleston certain that if they remained in Twickenham (not an area that had been scheduled for evacuation) they would be murdered in their beds. One evening a motor car drove up at Charleston and dumped five evacuated children on the house. All eventually went elsewhere, even Ethel Grant and Aunt Violet realising, as the Phoney War continued, that Twickenham was not suffering too badly. Victor Pasmore moved into Duncan's studio and Bunny, as he had agreed, enlisted for service as an Intelligence Officer in the Air Ministry.

That autumn Ray grew rapidly worse and by November a nurse was permanently installed at Hilton. In March 1940 Bunny was granted compassionate leave. On 24 March, after much suffering, the end came. The nurse called Bunny from his lunch and a moment or two after he entered Ray's bedroom she died. 'Thank God. Oh thank God,' he cried.[52]

TWENTY-TWO

Under Siege

During the winter of 1939–40 the inhabitants of Charleston settled down to the restrictions of wartime existence. The life of the house, which had so delighted Frances Partridge on her first visit ('the impression I got on first entering the hall . . . of life being intensely and purposefully lived, of animated talk, laughter, brilliant colour everywhere, youth')[1] had not greatly altered, though a melancholy sadness clung to Vanessa's silences and there were no longer any children ready to entertain the adults with plays or skits. And, despite the radiators that had been installed in the sitting-room and in the bedrooms belonging to Clive and Quentin, the house remained very cold. One factor that impressed many was the regularity with which excellent meals were produced, Grace having gained the assistance of Lottie, formerly Clive's cook in London. Nor had the love of conversational argument diminished. Clive and Quentin differed in their political convictions; but it was only after 1945 that their disagreements became acute and unpleasant.

Charleston owed much to Vanessa's love of domestic order. She took great pleasure in the details of daily life, in the furnishing of a room, as well as the weather-proofing of the tool shed and the tidy arrangement of its tools. Though her manner with those she employed never invited intimacy, she had a very real affection for Grace, with whom she co-operated on the management of the house.

She and Duncan would plan the garden together, looking through seed catalogues in the winter months and selecting flowers and plants for their colour. They favoured old-fashioned plants – German irises and single hollyhocks – as well as those that had grey, silky leaves, as they complained that England in the summer was too green. Prior to their tenancy, the garden at Charleston had been used chiefly for growing vegetables and fruit, the soil having been well cultivated for many years. In addition ten-foot-high walls effectively transported the garden several degrees south, while the great elms that used to grow outside the garden walls protected it from winds that travelled along the north face of the Downs and were severe in winter. Within this sheltered quarter of an acre Duncan and Vanessa created a 'painter's garden', favouring the kind of 'sweet disorder' which is an aspect of the English cottage garden. One summer, roses mingled with Canterbury bells and sweet-williams down one side of the garden, while a sea of blue anchusa grew in the middle mixed with white pinks, deep red roses and irises. From July onwards they harvested beans for themselves and sunflower seeds for the chickens, while Clive obtained pheasant, rabbit, hare or partridge by means of his gun. In many ways Charleston offered a very satisfactory wartime retreat: 'Everything here is calm and luxurious,' Angelica wrote to Bunny in July 1940.²

One regular visitor during the war was the painter Keith Baynes, who had moved to Iden, near Rye, and was prepared to use the last ounce of his rationed petrol on visits. 'Thank you so much for what you say of Vanessa's pictures and mine,' Duncan wrote after one of his appearances. 'It is a great pleasure to show one's work to you especially as one feels rather isolated in the country and seldom has outside impressions.'³ This wartime isolation served to intensify their Sussex life.

On Christmas Day 1939 Duncan set off on foot for Firle village with a tie for Eric Stephens, a local man who occasionally helped Vanessa in the garden. In the afternoon the Keyneses with their guest, the economist Richard Kahn, came for tea and a magnificent cake was produced, decorated by Vanessa with twenty-one candles in celebration of Angelica's birthday. After they left, the Woolfs arrived for dinner, Virginia bringing Angelica an edition of Mme du Deffand's letters to Walpole. 'We had wonderful turkey, wonderful champagne, wonderful conversation,' Angelica reported to Bunny. 'Virginia got absolutely drunk in about five minutes, and shrieked and waved her arms. Everyone made speeches – Leonard's and Duncan's were the funniest.'⁴ On the twelfth day of Christmas a party was held in Angelica's honour. Duncan, wearing a dress kilt, danced with Lydia and with Angelica's friend from drama school, Chattie Salaman, also performing an eightsome reel under Marjorie Strachey's orders. Clive behaved less well, owing to an excess of drink and the attractions of the female guests. A musical entertainment followed the next day, with the pianist Michal Hambourg, who lived at Firle, performing, after which some of Angelica's friends sang and played the flute.

Mostly, however, the inhabitants of the house entertained themselves. January 1940 found them reading *Mansfield Park* aloud every evening and discussing avidly the characters of Miss Crawford, Edmund, Fanny, Mrs Norris and the rest. But underneath these pleasures lay tensions. Angelica at this time found that she could not paint in the same room as Vanessa without a continuous dread as to what her mother would say next. 'Whatever it is it's sure to break in on one's world and shatter it to bits. I feel so relieved when she goes out of the room.'[5] At times an obscure but powerful melancholy overwhelmed her. 'I don't know what's the matter with me,' she admitted to Bunny, ' – I can't stop crying, all the afternoon. It doesn't mean I'm unhappy only that it's something deeper than one can immediately know about. I want something but what is it? What do I want? Why is this happening? I feel bewildered and tired.'[6]

After Ray Garnett's death in March, it became possible for Bunny and Angelica to talk of living together. Duncan and Vanessa worried that Angelica, at a young and adventurous stage, would suddenly find herself saddled with the responsibility of looking after two schoolboys. Bunny retorted that the boys now did most things for themselves and that his elder son Richard would soon be leaving school and going to Cambridge. But Duncan was still concerned: would living with Bunny have the same effect on Angelica as it had had on Ray, who had given up painting? Despite Bunny's reassurances it angered Duncan, somewhat irrationally, when in May Bunny took Angelica to Butts Intake, a stone cottage that he owned in North Yorkshire. Partly in order to distance himself from his immediate past, Bunny decided that spring to let Hilton. When he and Angelica began looking for a house, Vanessa, hoping that it would be near Charleston, offered to help find one. This offended Angelica, who felt they should discover a house themselves. She was also very aware that Vanessa and Duncan were at some level still opposed to the idea of her making a life with Bunny. In April his two sons had stayed at Charleston and won the admiration of all the adults present. Bunny had said he wanted his sons to know Charleston, the place and its people; but he may also have wanted the Charlestonians to know more about himself.

In this awkward period filled with anxieties over separation and loss, Angelica found herself admiring Duncan's instinct for self-preservation. 'I was so envious of Duncan yesterday,' she wrote to Bunny, 'as he said that if ever [he] got fits of depression he thought he was silly and soon got out of it.'[7] Occasionally he heard tiny scraps of news of George Bergen from his friend Bill Bayly, who ran a gallery in Wardour Street, but nothing to alleviate his stagnant emotions. He turned to others for distraction and made friends with a young black Jamaican, Patrick Nelson, the son of the famous wicket-keeper Leopold Nelson. They may have met through the painter Edward le Bas, who liked to cruise the East End from time to time and who, after Duncan let his studio in Fitzroy Street, would put him and Patrick up occasionally. Patrick made a strikingly good-looking model and posed for one portrait wearing a white cocktail jacket. He missed Duncan, who was now mostly in Sussex, met a girl called Olive and began to think of marriage, while telling Duncan, 'if you were still in London there would be no need for me to be fond of the girl, nor anyone else, it is only because we can't see each other as we use[d] to at the old studio. O Duncan I wish we could again be intimate and once more enjoy life – do you think the days gone by will ever come again? We must hope?'[8]

One unconscious fear surfaced in a dream that Bunny had in February 1940. He dreamt that George Bergen appeared and came between him and Angelica. Bunny grew angry with Bergen and shook him until he turned into withered leaves. 'You are one for having queer dreams,' Angelica remarked, ' – I'm sure it is a very significant one according to Freudian doctrines. George, thank goodness, has turned to nothing but withered leaves in our lives – at any rate for the moment.'[9]

In 1939 Duncan was invited with five others – Frank Dobson, Glyn Philpot, Frances Hodgkins, Alfred Munnings and Edward Wadsworth – to represent Britain at the Venice Biennale in 1940. Told that he would be allocated a room to himself, he decided on a retrospective display and in January 1940 began sifting through photographs of his early work. Many of these Post-Impressionist paintings were new to Angelica and excited her greatly. She marvelled at how much he had done and in so many different ways – 'experimenting and always fresh and sincerely gone through'.[10] Four months later the British Council withdrew from the Biennale, officially because it could not risk sending some £30,000 worth of art abroad in wartime circumstances. French participation was cancelled for the same reason. Instead the British selection was shown in London, the Trustees of the Wallace Collection reopening Hertford House for three weeks in May. Clive was responsible for hanging the show. When Vanessa arrived to inspect Duncan's room she disguised her horror at Clive's arrangement and very tactfully changed it little by little until the final result was greatly improved.

On 21 May they heard at Charleston that the Germans had reached Amiens. This news, and the increased number of aircraft passing overhead, left them gloomy and on edge. In Quentin's memory they were at their most demoralised in early June. He came home from the hay field one day to find a tea party in progress in the garden. Vanessa, Clive and Duncan were there, as well as Lord Gage, Dora Romilly (Peter Morris's sister) and Jimmy Sheean. The American journalist described the devastating strength and efficiency of the German army. Gage discussed what he would do under German rule and everyone seemed to take defeat for granted. 'They will be in Paris next week,' said Dora, her prediction proving accurate and confirming everyone in their worst expectations.

Flying gaily like a banner in this grim period was Duncan's still-buoyant reputation. In May, with the Venice Biennale selection showing at Hertford House, he was also said to 'dominate' the 'Nine Painters at the Lefevre' exhibition and had a solo show of forty-one drawings and sketches at the Calman Gallery in 42 St James's Place. One critic called it 'Grant's week', causing Vanessa to protest, 'I think you're really getting too famous.'[11] As with his Hertford House display, Duncan had incorporated into his solo show some early work, including two drawings done in 1903. In the *New Statesman and Nation* Raymond Mortimer argued that Duncan's elegance as an artist, his ability, for instance, to bring a spontaneous grace to his rendering of a mother and child, resulted from intensive study of the Old Masters. 'A gay artist born out of his time into a distressed age: he should have been a contemporary of Fragonard or Tiepolo or Correggio or the fifteenth-century Sienese ... The whole show makes for happiness – even the prices are inviting.'[12]

At Lefevre's, the painting that caught most attention was his nearly four-by-five-foot oil *Girl at Piano*, begun in the spring of 1939. Painted in the sitting-room at Charleston, it shows Angelica, her back to the viewer, playing the piano, a cat asleep in an armchair on her left and an empty armchair and a light-filled window on her right. Small diagonals offset and buttress the composition, which offers a sonorous chord of vertical shapes. The most acute perception of the strengths and weaknesses in this painting appeared in the *New Statesman and Nation*:

> Every inch of the canvas is loaded, and one could cut a dozen lovely little pictures out of it. Look at the handkerchief on the girl's head, the bowl, the two pots, the music lying on the piano top. But the picture does not flow, the tones fail to carry the rhythm through, the objects are too separately realised. This surprises in Grant, a master of decorative painting with a natural, as it were Italian, grace, who had so often carried a melody *legato* right through a picture. But the picture is far more remarkable than it may seem to the careless visitor, and rewards long study.[13]

Still more pleasing was the letter Duncan received from the Tate's director, John Rothenstein, who saw the picture at Lefevre's a couple of hours after returning to London from a lecture tour of America. 'It impressed me more than any work of yours I have seen in recent years. It seems to me to express so completely what you stand for that I feel it should represent you here.'[14] Rothenstein had no difficulty in convincing his Trustees and certain Royal Academicians, and *Girl at Piano* was duly bought with their combined authority as a Chantrey Bequest purchase. In keeping with the terms of that bequest, it had to be shown at the 1941 Royal Academy Summer Exhibition before it entered the Tate collection. It attracted considerable attention at the Academy and again the following spring, when a display of the Tate's recent acquisitions went on show at the National Gallery. *Girl at Piano* hung in a place of honour in the first room.

Much of his success in May 1940 Duncan learnt about second hand, for at the request of the War Artists' Advisory Committee (WAAC), set up in November 1939 and chaired by Kenneth Clark, he had exchanged Charleston for Plymouth. He had first been approached by E. M. O'R. Dickey, secretary of the WAAC, in March. After a visit to the Ministry of Information, where he talked with Dickey and Leigh Ashton, Clark's assistant, Duncan agreed to undertake naval subjects in return for one pound a day, plus travelling expenses, on the condition that he would submit all sketches and finished work for censorship. He would also show all his work to the Ministry of Information so that, under the auspices of the WAAC, it could either buy drawings he had done on the spot or commission a large painting.

Though he intended spending a month at Plymouth, Duncan stayed only two weeks, lodging first at the Duke of Cornwall Hotel, then in a room on The Hoe at 3 Windsor Place. He bumped into John Nash, now an official war artist and wearing uniform, who warned Duncan that spy mania was rife in the dockyards and he would be subjected to constant interruption if he tried to paint there. Duncan settled instead on the safe and rather uninspiring subject of sailors having a gunnery lesson in the naval barracks. Sketches for this scene, together with the final picture (Imperial War Museum) and the study for it (National Art Gallery, Wellington, New Zealand) suggest that the WAAC's emphasis on the need for factual accuracy was allowed to override aesthetic interest.

He was, however, grateful for a glimpse into naval life, high and low. He hurriedly threw away his cigarette when a Captain Dent indicated that they were about to enter the presence of the Commander-in-Chief ('a magnificent gentleman who was a cross between Macaulay of King's and the Duke of Wellington,' Duncan told Vanessa).[15] The Admiral invited him to lunch and as a result Duncan found himself the next day discussing tiger shooting with him as they paced the terrace. At Plymouth he was struck by the apparently universal belief in Churchill and was filled with respect for the efficiency and charm of the navy. Even so, it was, he told Vanessa, 'a great comfort getting a whiff of home life in your letter in this extraordinary place,'[16] for the news regarding the war worsened daily and during his last few days at Plymouth the whole of the barracks was in a state of turmoil.

Inevitably Duncan made friends at Plymouth, among them a young man called Mark Rodier whose portrait he painted, and who soon renewed contact when he found himself stationed at Hove. He and Duncan met a couple of times in Brighton and then lost touch. In 1945, while preparing for an exhibition at the Leicester Galleries, Duncan sent Rodier a letter telling him he was thinking of including his portrait in this show. His letter was returned, with a note from Rodier's sister: the young man had been killed in the raid on St-Nazaire on 28 March 1942. Duncan gave the portrait to his family.

'The war has become sheer nightmare,' he wrote to Vanessa at the end of May. 'My landlord turns on the news at breakfast. I generally hear it at one [o'clock] at the barracks, buy an evening paper and hear it at nine. I really think this is too much.'[17] Appalled by what was happening in France, Vanessa tried turning her mind elsewhere and, in Duncan's absence, began sorting his drawings, which filled studio and outhouse and ranged in date over some thirty-five years. She also prepared for the Graham Sutherlands, whom she had invited for a weekend. When they cancelled, she experienced such relief that she vowed never again to invite anyone.

In early June she reported to Janie Bussy in France that though butter and sugar were now rationed, they still had good beef and mutton and felt they lacked none of the luxuries of life. Because they were some six miles from the shops and had on occasion to take paintings to London, they were allowed extra petrol and so were able to pay weekly visits to the Woolfs at Rodmell. Clive, who sat on various committees, went regularly to London while Quentin sat on a red tractor making, Vanessa thought, with his mahogany-coloured skin and flaming hair, a wonderful sight. But despite a relatively quiet life, composed of painting, gardening, keeping chickens and seeing few people, Duncan and Vanessa could not escape the war. They were particularly disturbed by Jimmy Sheean's visit in early June, for he warned them that France was on the point of collapse and that the bombing of England would soon begin. With this news, Vanessa could bear Angelica's absence no longer. She wrote angrily to Bunny, 'You tell me of the delight of being with her, but I have known that very much longer than you have and this complete separation has been sometimes almost unbearable.'[18] When France capitulated, she momentarily panicked and asked Bunny to take Angelica to America: Jimmy Sheean had told them people were still leaving on Canadian boats and there was no need to fear submarines, as they were unlikely to waste their torpedoes on passenger ships. 'I spend my days arranging books', she concluded one letter, ' – what else can one do?'[19]

The changes in daily life caused by war began to have their effect. The Gages moved into a farmhouse on their estate and allowed a girls' school in Lewes to take over Firle Place. Lefevre's threatened to stop trading, leaving Duncan wondering where he could dispose of yet more pictures. He, Clive and Quentin joined the Home Guard, donned khaki and tin helmets and went on night watches, Duncan proudly holding an extinct species of rifle that would accept no known form of ammunition. They attended a local meeting to discuss how to defend Firle against attack. It soon became evident there were not enough men to protect both ends of the village. Which, therefore, was most exposed to danger? This question provoked such heated debate that no decision was reached.

Though the Blitz did not begin in earnest until the spring of 1941, an early victim of the enemy was Duncan's slightly feeble-minded, sweet-natured and completely harmless Aunt Violet. She stepped outside the front door at Grosvenor House one evening in September 1940 to call in the cat and received a sharp blow on her head from what was afterwards thought to have been part of an incendiary bomb. Putting up her hands to shield her face, she discovered that her hair was on fire. She rushed up to her room and buried her face in a rug to put out the flames. Afterwards she was unable to open her eyelids for two days and, with scabs forming on her face, feared that she would be permanently disfigured. 'I do not want people to look at me,' she was heard to remark, 'but I don't want them to turn from me.'[20]

Later that month Duncan's Fitzroy Street studio was gutted by fire when an incendiary bomb fell on the workshop next door. No one was hurt, even though Ferro, the master wood-carver who occupied a workshop underneath the studios, was still living on the premises. Duncan's loss was mitigated by his earlier decision to move a great deal of his belongings to Charleston or Grosvenor House so that he could let the studio to Victor Pasmore, who was one of the first to inspect the damage: 'Both studios are just a heap of charred wood. The rickety iron passage . . . is still intact and from there through the windows you can see the funeral pyre of this time-honoured chamber of genius.'[21] Though Vanessa's studio was less badly damaged, she too lost everything in it except for a Sickert drawing. She took it philosophically, saying that she could always paint more pictures. There was also the likelihood that both painters would in time receive compensation. In Duncan's case it amounted to £1,700.

When another incendiary bomb was dropped almost on the doorstep of Grosvenor House and the cornice in the drawing-room came down with a loud crash, Ethel Grant announced that she could take no more. She took down paintings, put away china, consigned the Benin bronzes to the cellar and rang Lady de Salis, a cousin of Miss Elwes, who lived in the country, and offered herself and Aunt Vi as paying guests. Duncan, meanwhile, investigated the environs of Cambridge in the hope of finding a more permanent home for them. However, the ladies had friends in Twickenham, among them a very devoted retired Professor of Architecture from Liverpool University, Charles Reilly, and were easily persuaded to return there when Aunt Daisy urged them to take a flat in Meadowside, a large modern development arranged like an Oxbridge college in Cambridge Park, close to the Thames. 'I'm rather drawn to a flat at Meadowside,' Ethel wrote to her son. 'Aunt Daisy says they are built of concrete and steel, firewatchers are on the roof at night and Air Wardens in the building, and that you are as safe in a ground floor flat as you would be in a cellar or an Anderson shelter.'[22] Daisy was herself living in one of these flats looking after another of her patients, most of whom came to her via Adrian Stephen. There was also a restaurant in the complex, which removed the need for a cook. Early in March 1941 Ethel Grant and Aunt Violet settled at 13 Meadowside, later moving to number 58. From there they could keep an eye on Grosvenor House, which had been let. Miss Elwes moved into their guest room, continuing an arrangement that lasted in all some forty years.

Meanwhile Angelica found a job teaching at her old school, Langford Grove, which had moved to Herefordshire. She found school life strained, and a few months later obtained further exemption from National Service by taking a job in London with the Cotton Board. In order to release Angelica from war work, Bunny began talking of marriage. Vanessa and Duncan disliked the idea, fearing her loss of freedom. Vanessa remained silent on the subject but seemed to Angelica to exert a mood of emotional blackmail. Duncan managed to talk to Angelica but, because he did so before she herself had thought seriously of marrying, it had little effect.

For some two years Duncan had seemed hostile towards Bunny; privately he referred to him as a 'snake in the grass'. Even when Angelica began living with Bunny in a nearby part of Sussex, Duncan still could not accept the situation. He more or less cut Bunny dead one day in London, when Bunny greeted him on walking into the York Minster pub in Dean Street with his *New Statesman* colleague, George Stonier. Bunny retaliated by turning his back on Charleston. 'I suppose he [Bunny] is very hurt by Duncan's enduring hostility,' Helen Anrep remarked to Vanessa; '. . . it is more or less natural that since Charleston will have none of him that he should go his own way with bravado.'[23] But one reason why he now wanted to marry Angelica was, as he admitted to her, to put an end 'to Vanessa and Duncan's refusal to accept that you love me' and 'their hope of separating us'.[24]

The suggestion of marriage, as Angelica had already discovered, met intense opposition. 'They are very nearly fanatical about marriage,' she told Bunny, ' – they think it the first step in the descent to hell. And not only Duncan and Vanessa but Clive and possibly Quentin as well.'[25] 'My views on marriage . . . are and always have been very definite,' Duncan stated, in forthright manner:

> I see that as a last resort marriage may seem the only way out of being made to join the ATS or WACS or something frightful of that sort, but marriage itself seems to me to be a thing to be avoided if possible. Unless it is to set up a family I see no point in marriage at all, and for a female it is a loss of freedom and nothing more, and for you at a time of life when you may want it very much. Indeed if it wasn't for this hellish war, I doubt if the idea would have entered your head – and the war whatever happens cannot go on for ever.[26]

Angelica protested that marriage seemed less of a bogey to her than a practical measure, which would make things easier for everyone. The controversy left her miserable. 'I spend nearly all my time thinking of it and it is not very delightful thinking when I know how much against it you all are.'[27] Duncan, remorsefully, suggested that if she had made up her mind, she should worry no more. 'After all it is your affair more than anyone else's. The only worry was whether it was for your happiness and . . . you are probably the best judge of that. Anyhow I shall now accept the fact and will not talk about it unless you want me to.'[28]

When the wedding took place in May 1942 Vanessa and Duncan were not invited. Neither of them took pleasure in the marriage, as Duncan admitted to his mother, but they concluded that the only sanity was to try and forget the painful months of difficulty and estrangement that had led up to it. If reconciliation felt a little forced in the months that followed, it was immeasurably strengthened by the arrival of their first grandchild, Amaryllis, who, as a small baby, paid her first visit to Charleston in November 1943.

'But I don't think you can realise how terribly it matters to us, more than ever now, that Angelica should live within reach.'[29] So Vanessa wrote to

Bunny in May 1941, a month after her sister's body had been found in the River Ouse. Virginia's suicide, which had followed signs of ill health and the fear that she was again losing her reason, affected many. 'My dearest precious Vanessa,' wrote Pippa Strachey, '*The Times* this morning has taken away all my courage and I can do nothing but weep and think of the joy that has departed.'[30] Clive expected Vanessa to suffer the most, as he told Mary Hutchinson: 'Vanessa has stood the shock much better than Duncan or Quentin or I expected. We feared some utter physical collapse – something comparable with what happened after Julian was killed. So far at any rate, she seems only sadder and more silent than ever. For the rest of us, for you and for me, Duncan, the children, Vita, Desmond, it's an appalling loss which, it seems to me, one won't be able to measure for a while.'[31]

Vanessa's ability to assimilate this new tragedy increased Duncan's respect for her. The following year he painted a full-length portrait of her, using a pose and setting that gives her an aristocratic, almost royal, mien. In *Portrait of Vanessa Bell* (Tate Gallery) she sits in a high-backed Victorian chair beneath purple swags, dressed in a long cape, its rose lining framing her black dress. Though the thick paint and relatively free handling are modern, the portrait looks back to the eighteenth century, and, as Robert MacPherson has said, the black-shoed foot pointing downwards may contain an echo of one of Duncan's favourite Gainsboroughs, *Countess Howe* at Kenwood.[32] At first sight pose and setting give the picture a rather chilling formality; but with increased familiarity the portrait conveys a subtle intimacy, as well as the sad dignity that pervades this haunting work.

It may have been while sitting for this portrait that Vanessa discussed with Duncan every character in *War and Peace*, for he spent two of the war years reading it. Equally readily he gossiped about his friends and felt nostalgia for the past, especially in April 1942 when he took a short holiday in Lyme Regis with his elderly mother. She sat in a glass-fronted shelter reading *Persuasion* aloud while her son attempted to paint her. '*Persuasion*,' he wrote to Vanessa, 'is really remarkably good. I'd forgotten how amusing it is. The description of Lyme is very accurate, I think Jane must have been very happy here. It's impossible alas now to walk along the Cobb and settle where Julia Musgrave slipped and fell, but I have found Jane's house – uninhabited with the walls cracked and almost tumbling down. There is a good deal of local feeling I gather against the owner who lives in Bournemouth and will do nothing about it.'[33] At the Alexandra Hotel, where they lodged, the food, Duncan thought, was good but skimpy compared with what he was used to at Charleston.

He was kept busy during these relatively secluded years by a number of projects. In May 1941 the WAAC had asked if he would be interested in painting a picture of the thirteenth-century Chapter House at Salisbury Cathedral, which was currently housing bombed-out refugees. Duncan was away when the letter from E. M. O'R. Dickey arrived, but on his return he accepted the task, on the understanding that this time he would do drawings and not a painting. 'Making a painting from drawings always involves one in endless difficulties and work if I cannot refer to the subject from time to time.'[34] However, by the time he reached Salisbury in June the refugees had been moved to better quarters and the Chapter House was empty. A month later Sir Kenneth Clark offered him another WAAC commission – a view of St Paul's Cathedral seen from Queen Victoria Street across ruins. Duncan investigated the location, but then saw a photograph of St Paul's in *The Times*, taken from a high-up window, which gave a magnificent view of the building as a whole. He wrote to the photographer and was given the address of a solicitor's office. The final work, now in the Imperial War Museum, celebrates in dense, rich colour Wren's magnificent classical rhetoric.

Owing to an administrative muddle, John Rothenstein had to admit that year that Duncan's *Adam and Eve*, stored by the Contemporary Art Society in the Tate, had gone missing. Perhaps because it was wartime Duncan made little fuss. He was also perhaps too busy. In December 1942, among other things, he agreed to sit on the CEMA (Council for the Encouragement of Music and the Arts) art panel. CEMA, having at first limited itself to subsidising the British Institute of Adult Education, had recently bought a small collection of inexpensive pictures out of a grant from the Pilgrim Trust, and in 1942 it had begun to circulate exhibitions. Duncan was one of three artist advisers, the others being Tom Monnington and Henry Moore.

Often the post in wartime brought bad news. In October 1941 Duncan had learnt that Patrick Nelson had become a prisoner of war in Germany. As his father, Leopold Nelson, was unable to send parcels from Jamaica, he asked if Duncan would act as his son's next-of-kin in England and send parcels through the Red Cross, which Duncan did. After three years' imprisonment, Nelson suffered a nervous breakdown and was diagnosed schizophrenic. He was repatriated in 1944, his hopes of becoming a lawyer dashed by ill health, one temporary job giving way to another in an increasing struggle to survive. On a visit to London in 1962 he wrote to Duncan from Arlington House, a hostel for the homeless in Camden Town. He died a year later, of heart disease.

Duncan's main project during 1941–2 was the decoration of Berwick church. The man responsible for initiating this commission was Ethel Grant's friend Charles Reilly, Emeritus Professor of Architecture from Liverpool University, who wrote in the autumn of 1940 to George Bell, the Bishop of Chichester, proposing that Duncan Grant should decorate a Sussex church. A month later Duncan met Bishop Bell in Brighton and suggested that as he lived in a house with three other artists – Vanessa, Quentin and Angelica – all might have a hand in the decoration, with Duncan acting as Director of Works. It was agreed that a scheme should be drawn up for the Bishop's approval.

The notion that painting could extend beyond the bounds of a picture frame and enhance the environment had interested Duncan ever since he had set eyes on Piero della Francesca's murals at Arezzo. It had stimulated his many decorations at Charleston and elsewhere, and even the wretched disappointment caused by the *Queen Mary* panels had not dented his enthusiasm. In 1939 he had been a founder member of the Society of British Mural Painters, which had supported the photographic exhibition 'Mural paintings in Great Britain, 1919–1939' shown at the Tate Gallery in May 1939. At this he and Vanessa had been represented by illustrations of murals they had done for Lady Wellesley's dining-room and for Raymond Mortimer's library, commissions which, being secular and unconstrained by anything other than an individual's taste, had given them a fairly free rein. Now they were to turn their hands to the more codified imagery associated with sacred art and to experience the more cumbersome procedures that Church patronage entailed.

The church belonged to the neighbouring village of Berwick. Small and unadorned, it dates back in part to the twelfth century. A tower had been added in 1603 and the interior altered and enlarged in 1856. Even at that date the parish was still poor and largely illiterate, for over the centuries it had served just the kind of farm labourers whom Vanessa was to portray in her *Nativity* on one of the side walls of the nave. When its spire had been destroyed by lightning in 1779, three of the church's four bells had to be sold to pay for its repair. Its plainness and simplicity invited an absence of mannerism in the design of the murals, and an avoidance of clever conceits in the decorations around the screen and the pulpit. The need to be legible made necessary a naturalistic style, Duncan having earlier demonstrated in his GPO posters how demotic and accessible use of this language could be.

While Professor Reilly and Bishop Bell found patrons for this project, the artists at Charleston began making sketches and studies and gradually a scheme evolved. At this stage it was confined to the chancel arch, on which Duncan was to produce a *Christ in Glory*, and the nave walls, for which Vanessa prepared an *Annunciation* and a *Nativity*. At the same time Quentin devised a plan whereby wise and foolish virgins could be cleverly squeezed into the awkward space provided by the far side of the chancel arch, as seen from the choir, and it was suggested that a *Madonna and Child* by Angelica could ornament the north wall, opposite the entrance door.

The project had to pass through various ecclesiastical hoops before it was fully approved. Berwick's Parish Church Council voted by seven to one in May 1941 to apply for a Faculty to allow for the execution of wall paintings. By July the scheme had passed the Church Advisory Committee, and in the first week of August the Bishop rang to tell Duncan that the Chancellor of the Diocese had granted a Faculty. This meant that they could begin work in earnest. Duncan's former friend, Frederick Etchells, now an eminent architect, was asked to advise. He argued that the rather amateurish 1856 reconstruction had left few of the church's old features in their original position and therefore decorations would not interfere with the authenticity of the building. He also recommended the artists to paint not directly on the walls of the church but on plaster-board panels. These were erected in September in a barn at Charleston, Maynard having taken over responsibility for the nearby farm in an attempt to stop its buildings falling into decay. Models were found among local people – George Mitchell, the parson at Berwick, sitting for his own portrait in the right-hand corner of Duncan's *Christ in Glory* and bringing a young soldier, the son of the Berwick station master, to pose as one of the representatives of the armed forces in the left-hand corner. The shepherd on the Firle estate proudly stood in for his counterpart in Vanessa's *Nativity* and Angelica modelled as the Virgin for the *Annunciation*. Her friend, Chattie Salaman, twisting this way and that, draped in a sheet and kneeling on a garden dictionary, became an ascending angel. Before long an agnostic, if not atheistic, household found itself plunged into religious drama. 'The house is chaotic,' Vanessa wrote in November 1941, 'and all a dither with Christianity.'[35]

For the artists this work represented less a contradiction of their beliefs than an affirmative continuation of an artistic tradition that looked back to Giotto, Masaccio, Piero della Francesca and many others. In England, and especially in Sussex, there lingered evidence of medieval wall paintings, which had once made churches colourful and visually instructive. This, however, had been forgotten by those parishioners at Berwick (there were thirty-seven on the electoral roll) who began to listen to the Hon. Mrs Sandilands, who ran a jam-making circle and was against the idea of the plain walls of their church being transformed with decorations. When Duncan produced a model of the church showing the decorations in place, it caused an emergency meeting of the Parochial Church Council on 4 September 1941, for it was objected that the model differed substantially from the scheme that had earlier been approved. Although the objection was overruled, again by seven votes to one, Mrs Sandilands, who had crossed swords with the vicar on several occasions, now grew more determined in her opposition to the scheme. An attempt to get up a petition failed, but the Revd. Mitchell had good reason to complain of 'the fifth column activities of the jam kitchen'.[36] Finally Mrs Sandilands entered an Act of Petition against the Faculty and as a result the decorations had to be tried before a Consistory Court.

Sir Kenneth Clark, who had earlier donated twenty-five pounds to the scheme, acted willingly as a nominated representative, for, as he told Bishop Bell, 'If the scheme falls through, I would consider it a very serious blow to British art.'[37] The other representatives on the artists' behalf were Etchells, Bertram Nicholls (a local artist with archaeological interests) and T. A. Fennemore, Director of the Central Institute of Art and Design and former secretary of the Society of Mural Painters. Two days before the court met, Bishop Bell called a meeting in Berwick School at which villagers were invited to inspect sketches and plans for the decorations and have them explained by the Bishop himself. It was a cunning move, as much hostility to the decorations was here voiced and removed. But, it was rumoured, there were also personal objections to the artists.

This greatly alarmed Vanessa and the whole situation seemed fraught with drama. The artists could have been hard hit, but Mrs Sandilands chose to aim her largest gun at a false target: she publicly denounced Quentin as a conscientious objector, an accusation that was untrue and easily refuted. Bentham Stevens, who acted as the solicitor for the Diocese of Chichester, reported to the Bishop, 'Everything went off extremely well. All our witnesses turned up, and except that poor Mr Grant was somewhat nervous, everyone gave evidence very well indeed.'[38] The fact that only one of Mrs Sandilands's eight witnesses was on the electoral role had further weakened her case.

Writing to Kenneth Clark about this matter, Duncan admitted that it had a Trollopian touch of humour. But he also quoted Bishop Bell's remark that 'the case is important in all sorts of ways and may be regarded as a test case'.[39] It represented a triumph against the kind of conservative philistinism that often stymies innovation, and its success owed much to Bishop Bell, a modest and seemingly simple man who proved in this and other ways his independent mind and fighting spirit.

He was not a pacifist, but he did not think total warfare compatible with Christian belief and in the House of Lords in February 1944 was to challenge the War Cabinet's policy of obliteration bombing of German towns. He was also the person who commissioned T. S. Eliot's *Murder in the Cathedral*. To Duncan he proved a most obliging sitter, going down on his knees so that Duncan could draw him in the position he wanted and lending his elaborate crosier, robes and mitre in order that work could continue in his absence. Bishop Bell's experience at Berwick further confirmed his desire to overcome the estrangement between the Church and modern movements in the arts. In 1942 he founded the Sussex Churches Art Council, its purpose being to commission works of art for various churches in his diocese and to bring artists of every kind into direct connection with the needs of the Church. Duncan agreed to sit on this council.

Though Angelica failed to contribute as Duncan had hoped, the main decorations were largely finished by January 1943 and put into position that spring. In June *Country Life* published a spread of photographs alongside an article on the decorations by Clive, who praised them for being 'contemporary, gay and regional'. He also noted that Duncan possessed 'the power of setting up a rhythm at once fluent and full', which, he argued, was the *sine qua non* of a designer.[40] Duncan himself was not entirely happy with the end result and a couple of months later arranged for a house painter to add coloured bands to the arches and chancel. 'I think the effect of more colour in the church enormously improves the pictures,' he told his mother.[41] A formal dedication service took place on 10 October at which Bishop Bell presided, and two days later *The Times* carried a photograph of Vanessa's *Nativity* alongside a notice of the event.

Though the original commission was now complete, the marriage between these artists and Berwick Church had not ended. In April 1944 a new Faculty was granted, permitting decorations on the chancel screen and pulpit, a crucifixion on the west wall and an altar-picture. Edward le Bas posed (tied to an easel) for the large *Crucifixion* painted by Duncan, who also did roundels based on the four seasons for the outside panels of the chancel screen. On the inside Quentin painted six panels representing the various sacraments. He also produced *Supper at Emmaeus* for the altar, setting the scene against a view of Firle Beacon. Three panels filled with archangels by Vanessa decorated the pulpit (destroyed by vandalism in 1962 and replaced soon afterwards with designs based on fruit and flowers by Duncan).

Duncan's involvement with this church now extended to ritualistic needs. At his suggestion Ethel Grant, assisted by Miss Elwes, embroidered an altar frontal, while his mother's cousin Elinor Ewbank, who delighted in Duncan's tiles and cross-stitch designs, worked a bible cover. Finally, again at Duncan's suggestion, a ceramic cross and candlesticks were commissioned from Phyllis Keyes. When in December 1944 Duncan went to deliver all these items as Christmas gifts to the church and to finish painting the chancel screen, he thought the total ensemble made a splendid show. It pleased him greatly when the gravedigger, a fine old Sussex man, came in and complimented him on the beauty of the colour. Though extensive damage had been done to the church windows by bombs in October 1944, the decorations remained unharmed. In the spring of the following year the Annual Parochial Church Meeting put on record 'its gratitude to Mr Duncan Grant and his friends for their generous use of their great talents for Berwick and to express the deep appreciation of all they have done to beautify the Church'.[42]

Since that date Berwick Church has surprised and delighted many, but one of those whom it most pleased at the time was Charles Reilly. After being met at Lewes station by Duncan, given a large glass of whisky and lunch at Charleston, he was taken to see the church. 'It's like stepping out of foggy England into Italy,' he remarked.[43] Two years earlier he had travelled from Twickenham to inspect the scheme in its early stage and had returned home much set up by his visit. So he told Ethel Grant, who proudly boasted to her son, 'You took him into another world.'[44]

While the Berwick Church murals were in progress, two sisters decided that Lewes should become a wartime cultural centre. At first sight Mrs Frances Byng Stamper and Miss Caroline Lucas were an unlikely duo for this task. The elder, Mrs Byng Stamper (known as 'Bay'), spoke with a grand voice but so slowly it was as if she had a speech impediment. Her sister (called 'Mouie' because she had at one time bred Jersey cows) had become an animal sculptor after training under John Skeaping, and also painted in a rather fey, nervous style that matched her character. She was small, slightly affected and often ill. But it was Mouie's idea that they should build a gallery at the back of their house, 'Miller's' in Lewes High Street, and hold exhibitions there. Among the artists they helped were two abrasive young Scots, Robert Colquhoun and Robert MacBryde, whose begging letters arrived regularly. But the person who inspired in them unmitigated devotion was Duncan. They felt unthreatened by him and liked his charm and good looks.

'I went last Monday to see a certain Mrs Byng-Stamper and her sister a sculptress who have bought a house in Lewes and have built behind it a little pleasant gallery,' Duncan wrote to Keith Baynes in April 1941. 'They intend to have a series of exhibitions there. If it is well run I think it has possibilities. It is only one hour by train from London and I think people would be glad of a day at Lewes in the summer if there is something to see.'[45] The sisters began with an exhibition of French and English paintings drawn from nearby private collections. Duncan tapped his friends for suitable loans and was delighted in July with the end result. 'I'm sending you a catalogue and some literature about the strange venture at Miller's in Lewes,' he wrote to Pippa Strachey. 'I call it strange because the ladies who are responsible are more than strange to look at anyway.'[46] He proudly added that more than eighty people a day from all over Sussex were visiting the exhibition, including soldiers, sailors and school children. He was particularly grateful to Pippa for the loan of Simon Bussy's portrait of Lady Strachey.

This was the first of several successful exhibitions. On the sisters' instruction, Duncan again collected items, from Tilton, Charleston and from his friends, for an exhibition of French and English drawings, which Sir Kenneth Clark opened in September 1942. Clark was also persuaded to lend five small bronzes by Rodin, Maillol, Degas and Henry Moore to an exhibition of modern sculpture held in July 1942. The catalogue preface was written by Duncan, and Bishop Bell gave the opening speech. He told his audience that the artist was a most important member of the community, especially in wartime, and should be employed in every sort of way for the public good, in halls, hospitals and pubs. Duncan thoroughly agreed. The following February Miller's showed three generations of Pissarros – Camille, Lucien and Orovida – in an exhibition opened by John Rothenstein.

The ladies of Miller's knew how to extract useful contacts, through Charleston especially. As a result Raymond Mortimer hurried down from London to review exhibitions, E. M. Forster read a paper at Miller's, Clive gave a talk on modern art and when Julian Bell's Chinese mistress, Ling Su-Hua, came to England, she addressed an audience at Miller's on Chinese painting and calligraphy. 'Those ladies are indefatigable,' Duncan commented to his mother.[47] If Vanessa sometimes declined their invitations, preferring to hear the reports brought back by Duncan, she could not help becoming involved in their various projects, including their attempt to redirect the design and decoration of theatres. They collected and arranged an exhibition for CEMA called 'Designs by Various Artists for Decoration in the Theatre'. It went on tour in 1943, opening at the British Drama League in Fitzroy Square in January. Duncan wrote the preface:

The idea behind this exhibition is a very simple one. It is that it might be possible to build, after the war, in a town the size of Lewes, a small theatre holding about 300 people. That included in the same building should be a picture gallery, space for the inclusion of a theatrical library and for the exhibition of prints and drawings of costume and production, as well as kitchens, a restaurant and café.

The painters, sculptors and weavers involved – among them Ethel Mairet, Ivon Hitchens, John Piper, Du Plessis, MacBryde and Colquhoun, John Tunnard, Graham Sutherland and Keith Baynes – showed, either in model form or full scale, the kind of items that might enhance such a theatre. All the exhibitors, Duncan wrote, supported 'a proper collaboration between the artist and the architect, a state of things which, either from parsimony or from architectural theory, has latterly become very rare'. Gaiety and colour, he continued, had a long tradition in theatre decoration. 'Lately, there has been a movement to dignify the Theatre, to make it severe and even rather grim. But it is to be hoped that severity will not become the permanent decorative feature of the playhouse.'[48] Duncan's point of view was so contrary to current trends that Philip James, the Art Director at CEMA, requested alterations to the preface because Lewis Casson, the recently appointed Drama Director, felt that the kind of theatre it put across was not in line with any official view. Duncan politely but firmly replied that no alteration was necessary if they inserted a note saying that his piece in no way represented their official view as to theatre planning. No such note appeared.

Duncan and Vanessa exhibited a model theatre for which they had planned, according to *The Times*, 'a very pretty little auditorium with yellow seats and grey and white walls festooned with silver and gold disks'.[49] They also designed its proscenium arch and drop-curtain. Quentin had decorated its foyer and first-floor passages and Angelica the box offices and ground floor. Also included were Duncan and Vanessa's enlargements of four portraits of famous actresses (Duse, Siddons, Lloyd and Bernhardt), which, in miniature, ornamented this theatre. Still more elaborate, however, was the small theatre which the ladies of Miller's had made themselves. Sir Kenneth Clark was so impressed by the total ensemble that he asked if the entire show could join the Planning Exhibition at the National Gallery later that month.

The success of this venture left the sisters aflutter with new ideas: a bookshop was mooted, and a children's theatre and art school. Just at that moment, however, the Ministry of Agriculture requisitioned their house and they were only able to proceed with the art school, which opened in

May 1943. Duncan, as he told his mother, was asked, with Vanessa, to teach there. 'The Ladies have really made a very nice studio out of stables with a drawing room for the model and an anteroom for the students. It leads out of a queer little yard with a door on to the street and on the other side is a large garden which will be delightful in the summer to go into during the rests. I am rather nervous about teaching.'[50] But there was never any hesitation in his mind as to whether he should give his time and energy to this small, *ad hoc* school, for he approved of any venture that promoted painting – except the Royal Academy: when William Coldstream was elected ARA that year, Duncan and Vanessa were deeply shocked and she voiced the fear that before they knew it Pasmore would be producing chocolate-box pictures.

In 1944 the ladies of Miller's became interested in lithography and before long decided to publish a portfolio of lithographs – two each by Duncan, Vanessa, Mouie and Enslin Du Plessis, the collection of eight selling for five pounds when it finally appeared in January 1945. 'I am amazed at their energy and persistence in pushing it through in these difficult times,' Duncan remarked to his mother.[51] He sent one lithograph – an experiment that was not included in the Miller's portfolio – to his mother as a Christmas card. Duncan had gone several times to Miller's to work with a printer whom the sisters had invited down from London. The intention had been to follow in the tradition of the French *peintres-graveurs*. The sisters quickly discovered that artists need no longer work on stone but could draw on prepared lithographic paper, which was afterwards sent either to the well-known lithographic printer, Louis Ravel, in Paris, or to the Chiswick Press. The aim was, through the conjunction of good-quality paper and inks, to eliminate a certain deadness and flatness inherent in the lithographic process and replace it with a velvety depth and richness of colouring often lacking in English lithography. To promote this idea Miller's founded the Society of London Painters-Printers in 1948 in association with the Redfern Gallery, which held regular exhibitions of the society's work. Most of Duncan's lithographs were produced for these shows.

He wrote to Boris Anrep, Keith Baynes, Hans Feibusch and others on Miller's behalf in the summer of 1944, in connection with a religious art exhibition that July. It was too big for the gallery and overflowed into a nearby Norman church. On show were paintings, sculpture, stained-glass designs, pottery, embroidery and textiles. It was hoped that the Sussex Churches Art Council would help tour the exhibition to various Sussex churches. 'It created more interest than most of the shows, I think,' Duncan told Keith Baynes, 'and may have repercussions. Several parsons

in the neighbourhood want to *borrow* things for their churches which may
lead to people *buying* them. Anyway it was interesting to see the reactions
among church-goers . . . many violently objected, were reasoned with by
an old-fashioned parson, and when the things were taken away at the end
of the show, expressed themselves sorry to see them go!'[52]

The many projects generated by Miller's enlivened Duncan's war.
Other opportunities were few and far between. He was briefly involved
with the Manchester Cotton Manufacturers, and had difficulty in
extracting payment for fabric designs, which it seems they did not like.
He exhibited in an Artists' International Association exhibition, which
was sent round factory canteens and also had work shown in certain
British restaurants. There was talk of him and Vanessa painting
decorative panels for the canteen in the National Gallery but nothing
came of this, though Duncan's *Queen Mary* panels hung there for a
period. Stanley Unwin invited him to design a book jacket for Arthur
Waley's translation of *Monkey* (1942), a sixteenth-century novel strangely
compounded of adventure, popular folklore, Buddhist mysticism and
pure poetry – a kind of Chinese *Pilgrim's Progress*, religious but not
pietistic. Duncan, using a South American monkey, designed the jacket
so that his body wound round the entire book, and David Unwin, the
publisher's son, suggested that in keeping with the back-to-front nature
of Chinese books, all written information giving title and author's name
should be put on the back. When the books were placed in piles in
bookshops, all people saw on the cover was the front half of a monkey.

An invitation from Allan Walton, now Director of Glasgow School of
Art, to address his students took Duncan to Glasgow in the spring of
1944. After he had offered his reactions to slides of the students' work, he
visited his friend Dr Honeyman, Director of the City Art Gallery, and
then spent a week in Edinburgh. Back home at Charleston, he was
gladdened by the arrival of visitors and even sent Bunny a warm
invitation, urging him to stay for a few days, which he did in March. The
following month Desmond MacCarthy spent ten days there and sat for
his portrait to Vanessa and Duncan.[53] In July 1943 Desmond had
entertained Bloomsbury, at a meeting in London of the Memoir Club,
with an animated account of his early days at Eton. Normally only two
papers were read, but this time three were heard, Molly MacCarthy
recounting her experience of the Blitz and Quentin describing his
schoolboy visit to Paris. Afterwards everybody adjourned to a nearby
restaurant for an excellent dinner and four flagons of Chianti, 'which was
most delicious', Duncan recounted to his mother, 'and much appreciated
by all these days. It was a delightful evening.'[54]

For three days in September 1944 he attended a conference for artists and writers held by Bishop Bell in his palace at Chichester. Duncan, dodging the rather overpowering Dorothy Sayers, lodged very happily in the same inn as Henry Moore and Hans Feibusch. The conference as a whole was well organised and a great success. So Duncan informed his mother: 'My admiration for the Bishop rose higher than ever. It was not at all a formal affair and everyone felt able to say what they felt without constraint. Every sort of thing was discussed that had any bearing on art and the church and we were made to feel there was no necessity to go to church on Sunday if we did not wish to. As a matter of fact I was curious to go to the morning service which was plainsong, as the choir was having its annual holiday. It was very impressive and the ritual different from anything I had seen. The clergy had on their best robes and the Bishop appeared in robes and mitre. The Palace where we held our meetings is really a large lovely old house with a vast fifteenth-century kitchen where we sometimes sat.'[55]

Duncan's mother fared less well during the war years. Her eyesight was failing, which made embroidery increasingly difficult. One of the last pieces she worked was the deliberately simple design that Vanessa drew for her, in white, grey, brown and black, for a Dutch sofa that still furnishes Duncan's bedroom at Charleston. Even in the best of health, as she often was, Ethel was soothed by Duncan's visits and he remained a great joy to her. They shared a tremendous responsiveness to life, to places, people, flowers, new-laid eggs or bundles of asparagus, cross-stitch designs, boxes of chocolates, the gramophone and the many records that Duncan brought her. In between his visits their easy familiarity with the daily minutiae of each other's lives continued in an unending exchange of letters. When Duncan came across examples of Ethel's work, such as the cushion in the book room at Miller's, he always took pleasure in it and conveyed his delight to his mother. Though Clive once dismissed Ethel Grant as fundamentally self-complacent, a memsahib preoccupied with trivialities, noting also how on her infrequent visits to Charleston she obliged Angelica to play four-handed piano duets introduced by a laboured 'one, two, three, four', she in fact hid an underlying nervousness beneath a calm manner. Nor did her carefully reined-in conversation convey the extent of her feelings.

In February 1944 Duncan arranged for a car to take his mother and Miss Elwes from Durrant's Hotel to Tottenham and back, so that they could attend the ceremony at which his and Vanessa's *Cinderella* decorations for a children's dining-room at Devonshire Hill School were unveiled. He himself was absent, owing to a bad cold, and Maynard – or

Lord Keynes as he now was – speaking on behalf of CEMA, made a presentation address and announced that Mrs Grant should be looked on that afternoon as Duncan's representative. She was deeply flattered, still more so when the Mayor of Tottenham was brought over to her to be introduced. The murals, done under the auspices of CEMA and the British Institute of Adult Education, were rather humorous, deliberately light, pleasing and anecdotal (though destroyed by a later regime.) After the opening, tea was served in a nearby British Restaurant. The *New Statesman and Nation* opined, 'It is fitting that the borough celebrated for its Hotspur should display such enterprise and dash.'[56]

The arrival of the 'doodlebugs' in June 1944 caused a fresh outbreak of wartime terror. In an attempt to calm his female relatives, Duncan brought them to Tilton for safety, while Maynard and Lydia were away in America, but the ladies did not stay long. September saw the sudden exodus of the soldiers who had arrived a few months previously to camp in a field and to erect a searchlight, which ran off a noisy dynamo. Duncan and others waved a friendly goodbye as they departed, standing up in a truck filled with all their paraphernalia. That same month Duncan kept an anxious eye on Vanessa as she convalesced at Charleston, after the discovery of a malignant tumour caused a mastectomy. The house must have seemed full of invalids, for Quentin had his appendix removed and Bunny hobbled around after an operation for a ruptured cartilage.

That Christmas Duncan heard from Ethel Sands and Nan Hudson that a bomb had fallen in the farmyard next door to the Château d'Auppegard, shattering all its glass but leaving the loggia decorated by Duncan and Vanessa unharmed. Fortunately, before evacuating the house they had stored all their pictures and drawings in a barn belonging to Jacques-Emile Blanche. Since then the house had been looted and reduced to havoc by the Germans. 'Everything has been taken, every stick of furniture,' Ethel wrote.[57] Mindful of the love and care that the two women had bestowed on Auppegard, Duncan searched for a watercolour to send them. 'Your lovely and heart-breaking little sketch of the church at Auppegard has given me infinite pleasure,' Nan Hudson wrote in January 1945, 'in spite of the ache that must accompany any thought or memory of the poor little place.'[58]

The end of the war in Europe came suddenly in May, one armistice after another being signed over a period of just four days. 'One has a deep feeling,' Duncan wrote to his mother, '. . . that something wonderful has happened.'[59] There was also an atmosphere of anticipation at Charleston as two arrivals were expected – Angelica's second child and the Bussys from France.

TWENTY-THREE

Narcissus

Duncan emerged from the war ready for change. He acquired two new suits, began preparing for a forthcoming show and threw himself into post-war festivities. During Victory Week those at Charleston dined at Tilton with Maynard, Lydia and Logan Thompson, the farm manager, after which all the retainers were ushered in to listen to the broadcast of the King's speech and to drink his health. This rather feudal behaviour shocked Vanessa, for the atmosphere generated by this erstwhile member of Bloomsbury-turned-peer seemed to her perilously close to that which her parents-in-law had created at Seend. Duncan, gladdened by a liberal amount of port, did not seem to mind. The following evening the two households met again at Tilton, together with local farmhands and their families, for beer, biscuits and cheese, songs, recitations and dancing. Quentin had made a large figure of Hitler out of straw and the evening ended with his trial, Maynard acting as judge and Quentin as prosecutor. Duncan spoke in Hitler's defence. 'He made such peculiar faces and talked such broken English,' Vanessa reported to Angelica, 'that I saw Roma [a former employee of Mrs Grant, now working for Lydia] looking at him in astonishment and hardly able to keep her seat for laughing.' Afterwards Hitler was carried off by torchlight procession to the top of a nearby hill and burnt on a huge bonfire. 'It was,' Vanessa concluded, 'the most lovely sight.'[1]

Since January 1942 when he had taken over as Chairman of CEMA, Keynes had given much thought to its future and to the role of state subsidy in the nation's cultural life: in June 1945 he supported the announcement that CEMA was to be incorporated into the Arts Council of Great Britain. Through his conversations with Keynes, Duncan had exerted some influence on this development. He also maintained the artist's way of life, the value of which Keynes recognised and respected. A sign of this were the invitations he gave Duncan and Vanessa, involving them, for instance, in a lunch at the Savoy with the French Ambassador, Anton Zwemmer, Sir Kenneth Clark, Sir Colin Anderson and others, before the opening of 'French Book Illustration 1895–1945' at the National Gallery in April 1945.

The following month the same institution held a party to celebrate the return from store of some of its pictures. Duncan and Vanessa were among the guests watching as Kenneth Clark led the Royal Family around the room. Vanessa cast an astute eye over the procession, noticing the Queen's perpetual smile and animated manner. 'No doubt she asked intelligent questions, but her blue eye has a slightly glassy look and I am sure she must long sometimes to lie by the fire smoking a cigarette and let herself go.' George VI impressed her far less ('a coarse creature and quite uninteresting and must be appalling to live with') and the total ensemble stirred in her a mix of pity and astonishment. 'But how we have managed to get Royalties to be Royalties I can't think. The Queen's clothes were unlike anything seen outside a pantomime – no human being could possibly dress like that, all in exactly one colour, feathers, veil, coat, all – really more like a Principal Boy than anything else.'[2]

When an exhibition of the Tate Gallery's wartime acquisitions went on show at the National Gallery in June, Duncan's 1942 portrait of Vanessa caught the attention of the young art critic John Russell, who praised its 'cadaverous grandeur'.[3] However, Duncan's work was soon to appear out of kilter with the post-war era. A more austere mood, underlined by the continuation of rationing, made his visually seductive art seem old-fashioned. A shift had occurred in the values by which painting was appreciated and a Duncan Grant, however pleasurable, claimed less attention in a period troubled by the atrocities uncovered within the concentration camps and the implications of the atom bomb. In a climate more sympathetic to the tenets of French Existentialism than those underpinning G. E. Moore's *Principia Ethica*, Duncan could only beat with light wing against the ivory gate, a singer born out of his due time, like the narrator of the enchanted tales in Morris's *The Earthly Paradise*.

He did not, however, lose his public immediately. When his one-artist show opened at the Leicester Galleries in June 1945, the critics mustered only cool praise,[4] but all the large paintings sold, earning him in all some £700 after commission. A certain nervousness is reflected in Duncan's remark to an *Evening News* reporter that the show represented the fruit of six years' seclusion in the country. On the day of the preview he chose not to appear until late afternoon when the crowd had thinned out.

He rated the opinions of artists more highly than critics' remarks, and many younger painters still revered him for the skill and understanding that he brought to his art. Allan Gwynne-Jones, one of the luminaries at the Slade and a Trustee of the Tate Gallery, insisted on including examples of Duncan's work in a portrait exhibition that he organised for the Arts Council in June 1945. He also illustrated Duncan's *Pour Vous* (otherwise known as *Miss Holland*) and the Tate's *Vanessa Bell* in his book, *Portrait Painters*, published in 1950.

Nor was Duncan as yet out of the running for commissions. He and Vanessa painted decorative murals for the celebratory exhibition 'Britain Can Make It', which opened at the Victoria and Albert Museum in the summer of 1946. He also turned his hand to illustrations, designing a cover for a catalogue issued by the Socialist Book Centre in December 1945 and, in August that year, four designs for Coleridge's 'Ancient Mariner', which Allen Lane published in a private edition of 700 copies. Lane stipulated that he wanted a vignette of the becalmed ship as the frontispiece, but then left Charles Prentice in charge of the book's production. Restricted to four colours plus black owing to the use of line block, Duncan chose hues that were bright and keen. His becalmed ship has an unearthly quality and its barred design may also carry an echo of the ghost-like ship that appears with the sun peering through her ribs as through a grate. Though the text was set and printed in Edinburgh, the plates were printed by the Baynard Press in London.

Duncan had emerged from the war with the letters RDI (Royal Designer for Industry) after his name. He had been presented with this honour at the Society of Arts, along with a magnificent diploma in a leather case, in June 1941. But the benefits that he hoped would accompany it, namely more commissions for fabric designs, did not materialise. Attempts to sell both his and Vanessa's designs in the post-1945 period met with no success, despite a brief revival of interest in the Omega Workshops caused by an exhibition at Miller's in May 1946. Duncan's love of decoration, however, showed no loss of impetus and, if exiled from the annals of design history, he nevertheless continued to turn out decorative items, such as tiles and screens, for friends, and to ornament pottery. While Quentin remained at Charleston, Duncan was fortunate in having a resident potter in the house.

The potter Phyllis Keyes still figured in his life, now largely as a loyal friend to his mother and Aunt Violet. Having looked after 'the ladies', as he referred to his mother and her entourage, all through the war, sending them vegetables and fresh eggs from Charleston, as well as cigarettes for Aunt Violet, Duncan now resumed his regular visits to Twickenham. The death of Miss Elwes in August 1945 distressed Ethel Grant considerably ('I miss her more than I could have imagined . . . she was so always true and faithful')[5] and she was greatly touched when Vanessa sent her some lavender in commiseration. Unlike Duncan's cousin Ailie

Grant, who raged perpetually at a hostile world, Ethel adopted a benign and accepting point of view, her letters constantly expressing appreciation of others. But she was cast down by illness and after the war suffered a painful attack of shingles. In such situations Aunt Violet, nicknamed 'the little aunt' owing to her slight build, proved an excellent nurse, with her unending store of patience and warmth. Now and then came to her aid Frances Todd, who had been at school with a member of the Grant family and during the war began visiting 'the ladies' regularly. Occasionally Miss Todd drove them to Kew, where she lived with her parents opposite the gardens, round which her very elderly father would escort visitors. His middle-aged daughter had a child-like enthusiasm for life (over the years she sent Duncan endless newspaper cuttings on subjects that touched, however remotely, on Bloomsbury), combined with an invaluable vein of unremitting good sense. When illness lowered the ladies' spirits, it was Miss Todd who turned up on their doorstep with some delicacy or an excellent bottle of port.

Duncan first met Miss Todd in the course of a Scandinavian holiday in the early summer of 1946. He and his mother had set out alone, taking a boat from Harwich on the last day of May, arriving in Copenhagen the following morning. 'It has all the things I consider essential to a capital city,' he wrote to Vanessa that evening. 'Prancing equestrian bronze horses is on[e] of them and great open spaces and really lovely eighteenth-century architecture. There is nothing medieval left which is perhaps a good thing. It was all burned down about 1680 and Nelson finally set alight to the cathedral with a bomb. Now it is all built in the finest Greek style with a Christ-like Jupiter over the altar by Thorvaldsen. This artist . . . is a more considerable figure than I'd imagined, I think better than Canova who had the sense to call him "il divino" . . .' As his mother had gone to bed early, Duncan had ventured alone up a gloomy staircase in search of a restaurant bearing the title 'Café Royal'. By the end of the evening he found himself seated amid a group of regulars, talking French to the artist whose Ecole de Paris paintings ornamented the room and plying his mistress with cigarettes, in surroundings that had proved to be agreeably bohemian.

From Copenhagen they moved on to Tyringe, Miss Todd by now having joined the party with Aunt Daisy. The latter was behaving inconsequently owing to her loss of memory, her near-blindness and a misery that made her cantankerous. 'I am very sorry for her but really she is a great anxiety,' Duncan wrote to Vanessa, 'as she will not realise that she cannot behave like a woman of thirty-five.'[6] Miss Todd, on the other hand, intrigued him with her respect-worthy life, her gratitude for small mercies and her refusal to be put out by Aunt Daisy's habit of brow-beating her for being dull. 'I very much admire these simple English ladies,' he wrote of Miss Todd to Vanessa, 'she made no complaint and seemed [to] be enjoying herself immeasurably.'[7]

When they reached Stockholm the ladies went to stay with friends of Ethel Grant's in the country while Duncan put up, first at the Grand Hotel, then with the Countess Hamilton. What he saw and experienced of Swedish life filled him with mixed feelings. He admired the public services and hoped England, under a Labour government, could enjoy the same, but he disliked the notion of equality. 'I rather hanker after the poor – the English poor seem to me to get more fun out of life than the excellent bourgeois.'[8] He finally concluded that despite its many virtues, its good taste and democratic government, Sweden was not a country for which he felt any predilection. 'There is a side rather like the grimmer parts of Hans Andersen underneath the surface of Frenchified civilisation . . . the stories I hear of life here in winter give one the shudder.'[9] Despite the splendour of Stockholm's streets and shops, he experienced relief at finding himself back again in war-impoverished Copenhagen, where he saw a Van Gogh exhibition and visited the National Gallery. When rain prevented him working out of doors, he bought a small bouquet and painted it in his hotel room.

He had been saddened earlier that year by the loss of his oldest friend, when Maynard, after eight years of heart trouble, died suddenly on Easter Day. His last contribution had been to the Anglo-American financial negotiations that had followed the Bretton Woods Conference. Duncan felt proud to have known him and went willingly with Vanessa the evening after his death to dine with Lydia, at her request. In September a letter from one of Maynard's trustees, his brother Geoffrey, informed Duncan that the annuity settled on him would continue during his lifetime, and that even if he survived Lydia the ultimate beneficiaries of Maynard's estate, King's College, Cambridge, would still honour it. He also received a legacy of £1,000 and the assurance that as King's was the ultimate resting place for all Maynard's paintings, he would be well represented there.

There was talk that summer of Vanessa and Duncan using rooms in 51 Gordon Square, the home of the Stracheys, as a pied-à-terre, but despite Vanessa's promises ('we'll do our best to be clean and quiet, two virtues essential in tenants'),[10] the arrangement did not last. Instead Vanessa rented a room in Marjorie Strachey's flat in Taviton Street, while Duncan continued to make use of Edward le Bas's hospitality. Le Bas, who owned an array of properties, had several empty rooms in his house,

53 Bedford Square, and since 1943 had set one aside for Duncan's use. 'I look forward to your visits,' he told Duncan, 'and it is really rare to find anyone with whom one can feel at home right away which I do with you.'[11]

The loss of Maynard made Edward le Bas's friendship especially welcome, for this talented painter and discerning collector was also a witty and generous host. As the only son of a Jersey iron and steel magnate, he had struggled to reconcile a passionate desire to paint with his obligations towards the family firm. This dual life paralleled his sexuality, for though homosexual by disposition, he had at the age of twenty-one fallen in love with a married woman, Miyadera Unwin, a violinist who was half-Japanese, and for the next ten years, until she died in his arms, had eyes for no one else. Through her he met Charles Ginner, an artist whose friendship helped imbue le Bas's painting with a Camden Town flavour. Though he inherited a considerable legacy following the death of his father in 1935, he had earlier resigned from the family business in order to travel and paint. The administration of the various companies that came under the Le Bas Investment Trust passed into the hands of his brothers-in-law, but when they entered the forces with the onset of war, Edward once again had to accept responsibilities that caused him an unusual degree of nervous strain. Eventually, on doctors' advice, he did little more than turn up at the firm's annual meeting at Claridge's to sign the necessary papers.

In 1943 Duncan's acquaintance with Edward le Bas turned into friendship. That year le Bas made his first visit to Charleston. 'I did enjoy the weekend,' he wrote afterwards, 'you've no idea how much: to see again how life can really be lived ... The church paintings grow in my mind in calmness and power.'[12] He had already formed a considerable part of his collection, which included works by Delacroix, Cézanne, Braque, Bonnard, Matisse, Picasso, Sickert and Klee. A fluent, cultivated painter, elected ARA in 1943, he helped organise exhibitions and represented the Royal Academy on the committee for the Chantrey Bequest. Capable of complex loyalties, he could acknowledge his commitment to the Royal Academy and appease Duncan at the same time: 'You've no idea what an anchor I feel you to be when I venture into the savage (but fascinating) world of the R.A. which is a thousand miles away. You may not like being an anchor but you are.'[13] As a source of gossip about art and artists, the evil or benign practices of the Royal Academy, he proved excellent company and was also a renowned party-giver, his shy charm and gently fizzing humour arising out of a need not to negate but to counterbalance suffering. 'You may be glad to hear,' he told Duncan in 1944, 'that the new bombs have cut down the Royal Academy attendances to almost nil.'[14]

Le Bas's homosexuality allowed for confidences that Duncan could not now share easily with Vanessa. Aware of this, she needed reassurance that le Bas would not take Duncan away from her. Le Bas was quick to supply it and their friendship was sealed by a particularly successful holiday in Dieppe in the autumn of 1946. All three lodged in the Hôtel du Rhin, one of the few hotels along the badly bombed front that had managed to keep going. At the top of the hotel was a series of empty, unused rooms in which they painted on wet days. They entertained Ethel Sands and Nan Hudson with oysters and white wine and in turn visited them at Auppegard. The small château was bare and in need of repair, the floor in one room having completely collapsed, but the two women had recouped a couple of bedrooms and the dining-room, in which they lived. When they sat down to lunch Duncan was pleased to see a great pat of Normandy butter and a large jug of thick cream and to be given vegetables cooked in cream and butter. Afterwards he and Vanessa worked in the loggia, touching up their murals, which time and the Germans had made necessary, while Edward le Bas painted two little sketches of the château.

Two subsequent trips abroad, to Paris in 1947 and Venice in 1948, were also made with le Bas, the second also with Angelica. Edward le Bas had the impression, perhaps mistakenly, that Vanessa and Duncan would have liked her to fall for him, even though she was now a wife and mother. Certainly Duncan had hoped that Phyllis Keyes might shift the focus of her affections to le Bas.

Duncan sought his advice in October 1946 on the confused feelings stirred in him by a letter he had received from a man he had first met that July. While crossing the road at Piccadilly Circus, an area that would have been associated in Duncan's mind with male prostitution, he noticed a lithe, attractive young man holding a bicycle and waiting to cross. In turn, the young man noticed Duncan, his hand-tailored, comfortable, chequered suit and his black-and-white spotted bow tie. He saw Duncan glance at him with a friendly, quizzical look, which compelled the young man once they had completed the hazardous crossing to draw him into conversation with a casual remark about the traffic. Duncan responded and, with an innocent yet slightly mischievous look, enquired if he had far to go. After further exchange, Duncan asked if the young man liked pictures. 'Yes,' said the young man, thinking he meant the movies. Duncan then hailed a taxi and the next minute the two men and the bicycle sailed off up Shaftesbury Avenue towards Bedford Square, stopping *en route* to pick up a bottle of rum. Inside Edward le Bas's house, and with a large tumbler of rum in his hand, the young man found himself confronted with dozens of paintings. He collapsed with laughter in front of a Sickert, saying that the woman portrayed looked like a monkey dressed up. Duncan himself was by then rather merry and not too nonplussed by the young man's lack of understanding. As Paul Roche recalls, 'When he asked me if I would come again the next day and sit for him, vanity and curiosity made me say yes.'[15]

So began a friendship that lasted thirty-two years, until Duncan's death. It was based at the start on certain misconceptions. Paul Roche told Duncan that his name was Don and encouraged him to believe that he was as young as he looked, for though thirty, he could be mistaken for eighteen. He was also dressed as a sailor. This was a disguise often used by so-called 'Bond Street sailors' out for adventure, and Duncan may have suspected as much. However, not wanting to reveal his true job, Roche maintained the appearance of a sailor by obtaining further outfits, posing in these for Duncan over the next few weeks. By the autumn, unwilling to sustain the deception any longer, Paul admitted in a letter to Duncan that he was in fact a Catholic priest.

'I liked Don's letter but can well understand your feelings about the priesthood,' Edward le Bas wrote.[16] But if Duncan had qualms about his new friend's subterfuges, he had fallen deeply in love. Having been sexually frustrated during the greater part of the war ('You can't tell me anything about the agonies of a sexless life,' one of his male friends had commiserated in 1940),[17] he had found in Paul an outlet for his intense adoration of male beauty. He drew and painted him repeatedly, making no attempt to disguise his ravished emotions, as is evident in the first oil that he made of Paul, for which the young man sprawled naked on the carpet at Bedford Square.

Behind Paul Roche's carefree appearance lay a complex personal history. His great-grandfather, Antonin Roche de la Baume, came to England around 1837, taught French, married the daughter of Ignaz Moscheles (composer and friend of Beethoven), became a naturalised Englishman and shortened his surname to Roche. One of his daughters married Charles Dickens's son Harry, while his son, Henri, had an undistinguished career. Henri's son, Robert, joined the Royal Engineers and became part of the British army in India, before working for the Great India Peninsula Railways as an engineer. He married Roberta Arathoon, daughter of an Armenian aristocrat. Their three children – Paul was the second child and the younger of two boys – were brought up in India but returned to England on leave and, in Paul's case, to attend preparatory school at St Leonard's-on-Sea.

In 1927, when Paul was eleven, his mother died in Poona of smallpox, and his strict, rather puritanical father sent the two boys to Ushaw College, near Durham, an ancient Catholic institution. Paul spent four years there, mainly reading the classics. He also became attacked by scruples that left him prey to every aspect of the Catholic discipline and reduced him to such a state of terror that he was moved to a Benedictine day school, Ealing Priory School, near Hanwell where his father, now remarried, had bought a house. The parish priest at Hanwell thought he discerned in Paul the material for a priest. After two years at St Edmund's College, Ware, he moved to the English College in Rome, the Jesuit-run Gregorian University, where he studied Aristotelian and Thomist philosophy and developed a new madness, the belief that he had to solve all the metaphysical problems. He acquired two degrees, in philosophy and theology and, with the outbreak of war, returned to Stoneyhurst until 1943 when he was ordained. It was while serving at St Mary's, Cadogan Gardens, as one of three curates that he met Duncan.

It took just three days, Paul Roche claims, for Duncan to fall in love with him. Duncan told the young man that he had been looking for him for a long time, that all his previous male lovers had something about them he disliked, but that Paul was perfect in every detail, right down to his toes. Roche claims that when he first posed naked, Duncan kissed each garment he took off, an act that must have seemed to Paul like a de-initiation process, for he was more familiar with the priest's habit of kissing each vestment as it is put on. What attracted Paul was the admiration that Duncan poured over him like balm. 'You must never change,' Duncan would say, over and over again. 'Please don't change, stay as you are.' Coming after the loss of his mother at an early age, the rigours of boarding school, immersion in a religion which, with its promise of unconditional love, had short-circuited his need to establish relationships in other ways, this repeated affirmation of himself by another proved irresistible. Seeing himself in Duncan's eyes, Roche fell in love, with a reflection of himself.

He did not immediately lose his Catholic faith and for some three years continued to perform his duties as a priest, troubled though he was by a conviction that he was leading a diabolical life. (Eventually he obtained a doctor's letter saying that he was suffering from nervous strain and was granted leave of absence, but did not return to the job.) During this period he made use of the room that Duncan had taken over from Vanessa, in Marjorie Strachey's flat at 1 Taviton Street. This Duncan paid for and used as a *pied-à-terre* for two or three days most weeks, but it was in fact Paul's home for eight years. There he lived with some degree of independence, for in addition to his job he had been left a little money by his mother and this, plus money from the occasional sale of one of Duncan's pictures, helped to support him after he gave up the Church.

Paul quickly discovered that Bloomsbury, famed for its tolerance, was at its most intolerant when it came to religion. It amused Marjorie Strachey hugely when on a couple of occasions someone called asking for the Reverend Paul Roche, though Duncan doubted that she knew what this appellation meant. He himself was perturbed by Paul's religion. Coming from the Highlands, traditionally more full of folk traditions and superstitions than religious feeling, and an area of the Grampians untouched by the Catholic faith, he had inherited a Protestant morality, which he had, in turn, reacted against. The sceptical, Voltairean influence of the Stracheys had further imbued him with a distrust of dogmatic religion. The puzzle represented by his attraction to Paul led him in 1950 to write a novella about Patroclas and Narcissus, two characters clearly based on himself and Paul. Patroclas, the narrator, claims he holds no dogma against love of any sort and argues that his bias towards freedom comes from Protestantism, in the wide sense:

> And he put the moral right he had for this freedom down to his ancestors' fight for it against Reactionary Forces. And now he was face to face with a Reactionary Force in full plumage. A beautiful young creature he had met by accident in the street. Here was a being he instinctively loved . . . a creature Pagan to the bottom of his soul. Yet he talked to Patroclas as a Christian – or to be more precise as a Catholic.
>
> But after hours of talk throughout long nights, in bed, out of bed, during which Patroclas was often reduced to tears, through sheer argumentation, Patroclas realised there was no point whatever as far as argument was concerned – the whole thing resolved itself into the fact that he Patroclas had no belief whatsoever – and that Narcissus for all his so-called beliefs was the most thorough-going immoralist that Patroclas had ever met. This really was the basis of their love for one another. When this became somehow clear to their minds arguments ceased.[18]

In time Paul himself accepted a compromise between his faith and his instincts. Later still, he abandoned Catholicism entirely and came to see Duncan as a gift from heaven that had released him from the arms of an oppressive Church. The older man completed his education by taking him to the ballet, theatre, opera, round the galleries and, in general, awakening his senses, which all those years spent reading philosophy and theology had left undeveloped. It seemed to Paul that Duncan was the exact opposite of his Jansenistic father, who had permitted wine, but only on special occasions, his puritanical attitude negating any pleasure it might give.

Paul found Duncan an easy companion, for the sixty-year-old Duncan seemed to take on the age of the person he was with. He was always interested to hear about people whom Paul had met, his question 'What did you talk about?' betraying his fascination with life. Occasionally they went to films, but avoided spy thrillers because they found them too confusing. Often they ate lunch in the upstairs restaurant at the York Minster pub in Dean Street. Duncan gave Paul his ticket to the YMCA in Great Russell Street where he had, in the past, picked up models, and there Paul began exercising daily.

During the two or three days that Duncan spent each week in London, a routine developed at the heart of which was his need to draw and paint. Roche posed willingly, but charged the going rate. His obsession with his own body made him an easy, confident sitter and he was willing to adopt any pose the artist fancied. Duncan expressed his feelings for Paul on canvas and paper. Soon after he met Paul, he asked courteously if he might have his permission to love him. Astonished by this humility, Paul allowed Duncan to kiss every part of his body, but recoiled when he tried to kiss him on the lips. Willing to be an object of love, he could not return it and sexual relations remained unilateral. Paul's interests were heterosexual and after he broke with the Church he became eager for intercourse, as he recalls: 'Unfortunately, my years in the seminary had ruined my confidence in approaching the opposite sex and blunted my understanding of women . . . When Duncan came on the scene, he was for me a godsent "pis aller". My appetite for sex was insatiable. He could suck or jerk me off and save me from the sheer tedium of girl hunting; though the girl hunting resumed the moment he left for Charleston . . . There was never any love-making in the ordinary sense between Duncan and me. And as for buggery – which is what he really wanted – it was out of the question.'[19]

One one occasion the two men bumped into Clive at the opera. A brief, rather formal exchange took place between Duncan and Clive, and it afterwards surprised Paul to learn that this was the man with whom Duncan shared a house in Sussex. At such moments Duncan would have been acutely aware that he was leading a double life, dividing his loyalties between two people, two domestic settings. 'If only other people would understand . . .' he would at times complain to Paul, who eventually understood 'other people' to mean Vanessa. She had, however, in part contributed to the vacuum that Paul had filled, for the intensity of her grief over Julian's death had for a while left her in a petrified state. In addition Bergen had gone and Maynard had died. Duncan needed to go to London for diversion and to Paul for emotional replenishment. Yet there was never any likelihood that he would, or could, leave Vanessa and Charleston:

> It was hard for Patroclas to part from Narcissus. But there was no way out of it. Patroclas had other ties, of long standing and deep roots; he could not cut adrift without wounding too deeply those that loved him and whom he loved.[20]

Though Duncan's alliance with Paul was not hidden from Vanessa, its clandestine nature tightened the bond between the two men. For the most part Duncan's thoughts about Paul were what he experienced alone, just as Vanessa had depths of grief that Duncan, for all his tenderness towards her, could not reach. Yet Duncan may have come to understand Vanessa better at this time, owing to the fact that he was now experiencing a love that must have been as frustrating as hers was for him. It was a surprising reversal of role. 'Even if not loved your loving Duncan,' he ended one letter to Roche, or 'Don' as he always called him.[21]

Duncan's friendship with him was not built on the kind of complex undertow of feeling that made his relations with Vanessa so intense, and he may have turned with relief to this easier kind of intimacy. Attempts were made to break down the division between his two lives. Once Vanessa accompanied Duncan, at his request, to Taviton Street, to use Paul as a model, and in 1950 she invited Paul to visit Charleston. Afterwards Duncan wrote to her, 'I was so much relieved that at last there seemed to be a possibility that what you call my double life might come to an end. I felt that whether you liked Don or not was of very secondary importance and that a load was taken off my back by the fact that you were able to deal with him yourself.'[22] But Vanessa was not able to cope with the situation. Paul made scant attempt to charm her, as Edward le Bas and others had done, for he regarded her as little more than a grandmother figure. She in turn had been distressed in London to see evidence of the domestic life that the young man shared with Duncan. The wild hope that Duncan had at one time conceived – that Roche might live with them at Charleston – vanished. The difficulties that had arisen left behind a gloom; at times the house seemed laden with the weight of unspoken feeling.

In May 1947 the Tate Gallery bought from Duncan two of his portraits, of Lytton and James Strachey, for the sum of £150 and £100 respectively. The fact that his early work was now respected and bought (as a result of which likenesses of his two cousins would remain in perpetuity in a national collection), showed that he had become an historic figure. Then in 1948 Raymond Mortimer's monograph on his work appeared, as one of the 'Penguin Modern Painters' series edited by Sir Kenneth Clark. One detail on which he had insisted was a reference to Simon Bussy who, he told Mortimer, was the first person to have had any direct influence on him.

Aware of the vagaries of fortune that affect an artist's life, Duncan responded immediately to a letter from his old friend Constance Lloyd containing a bitter allusion to dealers. This sent him to Lefevre's which promised to include examples of Constance Lloyd's work in mixed shows. When nothing further happened, Duncan removed her pictures from Lefevre's and took them round to the Adams Gallery, which was run by two brothers who readily agreed to give her and Janie Bussy a joint show in 1947. Two years later he persuaded the Leicester Galleries to put on a show of Simon Bussy's pastels. There were many small ways in which Duncan helped other artists, including the part he played in persuading King's College, Cambridge, to set up a loan collection of drawings.

It pleased the young A. L. Barker to discover a few days before the publication of her first book, *Innocents*, in 1947 that Duncan Grant had designed the dustjacket. The image he used, of a boy diving, drew on an incident in 'Submerged', one of the short stories in this collection, published by Leonard Woolf at the Hogarth Press.[23] That summer Leonard was the only member of the Memoir Club whose expression showed no sign of amusement when Duncan read a paper based on the Apostles – 'Where angels fear to tread'. In spite of the fact that the pages of the manuscript were read in a rather unconventional order, it made E. M. Forster giggle, induced an orgy of indiscretion from Desmond MacCarthy and was generally judged a success.

Vanessa now mostly made only day trips to London. She and Duncan visited the recently restored Tate Gallery in September 1947, where they looked in particular at the Turners and Constables and afterwards lunched with Simon and Janie Bussy. Social life had resumed with the return of peace and visitors came readily to Charleston, Kenneth and Jane Clark, for instance, calling for tea on their way to Glyndebourne.

Children had once again become an ingredient in the life of the house. In May 1945 Angelica had a second daughter, Henrietta. She and her elder sister Amaryllis caught chickenpox in March 1947, four months after the birth of their twin sisters, Frances (Fanny) and Nerissa, and were promptly sent to Charleston. 'Yesterday evening the objects of all this solicitude appeared,' Quentin wrote to Janie Bussy. 'Henrietta, a radiantly pretty child she is, at once remarked, with pleasant complacency, that she had been sick in the car twice. Amaryllis fired by the spirit of emulation declared, between dripping mouthfuls of cake and jam, that *she* had been sick three times all over the seat. You may imagine how the conversation developed.'[24]

Duncan's chief worry at this time was his mother's ill health, for she had been stricken by cancer and, quite by coincidence, was seeing a Mr Alex E. Roche, a Harley Street doctor who was also Paul's uncle. The situation was aggravated by the fact that earlier that year Aunt Daisy had suffered two strokes. Ethel and Aunt Violet had done their best to keep her at home, but she was a most difficult patient and by mid-May, when Aunt Violet was near breaking point, Frances Todd found a nursing home at Hampton Hill: Aunt Daisy died there in July. By then Ethel herself was so ill that it hurt her to walk. When Duncan cancelled a visit in October it disappointed her greatly and a rare note of complaint entered her letters. 'I am very old now Duncan and unfortunately really ill . . . Can't you give me a day a week without too much upset to your life?'[25]

Over the Christmas period he travelled every day to Twickenham to see his now bedridden mother and in the first week of January 1948 she died, having lost her great interest in life only a few days before. 'There was no one whom it was easier to love and admire,' wrote Pernel Strachey, 'and from my earliest days I have connected her with everything that was good and lovely.'[26] 'You always seemed to be thinking of things to please her and to help her,' wrote Mary Hutchinson, '. . . that long friendship between you must be a lasting possession and happiness to you.'[27] But it was Dorothy Bussy who provoked Duncan to reflect that his mother, whose opinions had once shocked him with their conventionality, had developed considerably in her sympathies and understanding and in her desire to know the truth. 'I feel dreadfully her loss,' he admitted. 'She remained beautiful, even more beautiful in a very heartrending way . . .'[28] He also knew that it would now be very lonely for

Aunt Violet, who had nursed Ethel to the end, but he trusted in her good sense and capacity to make her own life.

Another person in poor health was Adrian Stephen. Having worked during the Second World War as a psychiatric doctor in the army, he had since returned to private practice. He had, however, never recovered his full strength after a near-fatal attack of pneumonia in 1941. Karin decided, for the sake of his health, that they should go on a cruise, but when they reached Portugal he suddenly became much worse and they had to be put ashore and return home. He died in May 1948. Duncan and Vanessa attended the cremation, at which they found Karin in a state of collapse. From then on she suffered alternately from depression and euphoria. She underwent electric-shock treatment, which seemed to have little or no effect, withdrew more and more from family and friends and began over-prescribing morphine for her own use. She was to die of an overdose in 1953.[29]

It must have been some consolation to Duncan to find himself in the autumn of 1948 in Venice, with Vanessa, Angelica and Edward. Angelica noticed that le Bas was often the butt of their gentle humour for he was very impressionable, nervous, excitable and easily taken in. They all put up at the Pensione Seguso on the Zattere and followed a routine that began with sketching before breakfast and ended with coffee, ices and grappa at Florian's in the Piazza San Marco. From Venice they travelled to Padua, to revisit the Scrovegni Chapel, to Castelfranco to see the Giorgione, to Asolo to see Freya Stark's colony of silk weavers and to the Villa Maser. In November, after two months away, Duncan and Vanessa returned to Charleston with 139 oils.

In February 1949 Agnew's mounted 'Six Painters', in which Duncan and Vanessa's work hung alongside paintings by Winifred Nicholson, Keith Baynes, Rodrigo Moynihan and Charles Ginner. Both artists also showed in the 1950 Pittsburgh International Exhibition, visited by 146,107 people, but took more interest in the parochial machinations of the London Group. They attended its meetings, usually after a very good lunch with le Bas, and each year found that its members, looking older and shabbier, were determined to get rid of those members who had not paid their subscription for some twenty years. When it got to that point, they were always unable to carry out their intent.

In the late summer of 1948 Duncan had tried to persuade Paul to give up the priesthood. He had also grown suspicious of Paul's friendship with a boy he had met at the swimming bath. Paul reassured him that the boy meant nothing to him and that 'no one comes near the place I have for you'. When Paul finally took sick-leave and somersaulted away from the Church, he felt free to pursue his heterosexual inclinations, as Duncan learnt in Italy, in the summer of 1949.

He and Vanessa had joined Edward le Bas and his friend Eardley Knollys in Paris and all four had travelled the rest of the journey by car. It was a harmonious holiday, the walled town of Lucca offering many subjects to paint, though Eardley Knollys noticed that Duncan was prepared to put up his easel anywhere, almost without thought as to choice of motif. They travelled on to Siena and Pisa, where the extent of the war damage depressed their spirits, but this apart, the only other upsetting ingredient, from Duncan's point of view, was a parcel from Paul, containing the diary he had kept on holiday in France and Italy. He had slipped into Greek whenever mentioning his affairs with girls, thinking that Duncan would be unable to read those passages. Unfortunately Duncan retained enough of his schoolboy Greek to decipher them and was bitterly jealous.

That November he waited at Taviton Street for Paul's return in a frenzy of emotion. To Vanessa, he made light of what happened:

> I'm afraid I was rather horrid and accused him of staying away too long and carrying on with girlfriends. I suppose this is quite natural for him and perhaps he had better not tell me. But on the whole I feel I had rather not be kept in the dark ... Anyhow we have made it up and are now quite happy and content and I do not think we do anything that ought to distress you. A good deal of time is taken up with cooking a meal for Marjorie too. The rest of the time is taken up with talking about his travels and adventures and drawing ... I feel sorry for Don – that is part of my affection for him – because I think he has very few friends that he feels quite at ease with, and I think he dreads going back to his priest's hole. But I don't know what he can do.[30]

In Paul's memory the first three nights after his return to Taviton Street were terrible. Duncan tried to drown his jealousy in neat whisky, which made him incapable of sleep. Since they shared the same bed, Paul recalls, 'my third-degree torture was inescapable'.[31]

This episode unleashed in Duncan feelings to which he had rarely, if ever, before given voice. When he realised that Paul's need for women was now obsessive, he developed the habit of making nagging, short, cutting remarks. 'I suppose I'm only a pis aller for you ... you come home all squeezed out ... tout épuisé.' But these moods were infrequent and most of his references to Paul's sexuality, though petulant, also carried wistful affection. One evening at Charleston, after listening to Clive and his ex-army brother Cory hold forth like two old fogeys, he retired to his bedroom and lay on the floor by the fire wishing that Paul were there, waiting for him. 'But that I'm afraid is a thing of the past . . . Why oh why is it worthwhile to go on loving you?'[32]

One characteristic that Paul appreciated in Duncan was his enormous tolerance towards all forms of existence. He never heard Duncan utter a critical remark about Clive, though the two men were very different in character, Duncan simply accepting Clive as a creature to be appreciated in his own right. Once, when Paul was complaining about his father's meanness with money and he flung out, 'How can one love a miser?', Duncan quietly contradicted him. 'Especially a miser,' he replied.

Paul, noticing also how well-read Duncan was, detected all sorts of inspiration from literature and poetry in his work. In turn, Duncan thought he discerned the makings of a poet in Paul. As a result of Duncan's encouragement Paul began writing poetry. An urge to succeed in the literary world replaced his involvement with the Church, and he expressed a desire to meet Stephen Spender. Duncan agreed to introduce him ('I think he is very nice indeed, but perhaps a bit of a goose').[33] However, before any introduction took place, Paul had a poem accepted by John Lehmann for his radio programme *New Soundings* and he met Spender at the BBC.

Spender took to calling on Paul at Taviton Street, where he would sit on his bed murmuring, 'So beautiful! So beautiful!' Paul was relieved that no advances were made, for Spender gave the impression that he wanted an affair. Meanwhile Paul completed a collection of fables, *The Rat and the Convent Dove*, published in 1952 by Erica Marx under the imprint of the Hand and Flower Press, with illustrations by Anne Scott. Paul fully expected Spender, a regular contributor to the *Listener*, to give it a puff, but no word appeared. Nevertheless he sent Spender the manuscript of his next book, *O Pale Galilean*, a novel based on his own experience of the need to compromise Christian belief with a more humanist philosophy. Originally titled 'Gisco', after its satyr-hero, it was Duncan who drew Paul's attention to Swinburne's lines 'O pale Galilean, thou hast conquered./The world has grown grey with thy breath.'

Spender's initial reaction to the manuscript was encouraging, but when he heard that the Harvill Press had agreed to publish it, which they did in 1954, with a dustjacket and designs by Duncan, he turned against it, sending Paul a letter criticising its combination of emotional innocence and philosophical sophistication. Spender later admitted that he had suddenly taken against Paul ('I daresay I over-reacted against him when I had first over-reacted for him'),[34] after Paul sent him a letter listing six things he had expected Spender to do for him, but which he had failed to do. This, combined with Paul's lecturing voice and the loss of what Spender called his 'Medici' looks, stirred in Spender an antipathy equal in strength to the sympathy he felt.

Spender remembered vividly the huge mirror that hung opposite the bed in Taviton Street and the tame mice that Paul allowed to roam round the room. He also noticed that Paul was genuinely fond of Duncan and regarded him as the best living English artist. Though he later claimed that he had never liked Roche's work, finding it pretentious, Spender seemed in two minds about his talent when in 1954 Paul took off for America. 'You'll come back famous, and I shall be furious,' he remarked.[35]

Duncan could also look quizzically at Paul. 'It was [a] jolly sight to see you on Friday in your shorts at your table,' he wrote, 'surrounded by such bizarre objects as the mouse cage and all your drolleries. What a strange creature you are.'[36] Spender's impression of Paul ('he used one to the utmost') differed from that held by Duncan, who merely expressed surprise when Paul announced that he had sold one of Duncan's pictures. ('It was clever of you to sell a picture to Miss Browse [of the Roland, Browse and Delbanco gallery]. I think they are rather sharks.')[37] He continued to encourage Paul and to share enthusiasms with him: when Leonard Woolf published selections from Virginia's diaries under the title *A Writer's Diary* in 1953, Duncan urged Paul to read it. 'It's a wonderful book – one walks step by step with genius – painful sometimes but encouraging ... as a writer you ought to possess it.'[38]

Duncan's own creative output showed no sign of faltering. Angelica accompanied him and Vanessa to France in the summer of 1950. They painted at Cézy and on their way home were so taken with Auxerre that they booked themselves into a commercial travellers' hotel and began painting river scenes. 'Duncan and Nessa are turning out sketch after sketch,' Angelica reported to Bunny. 'I can't adjust myself so quickly to new surroundings.'[39]

Back home Duncan began painting the cement factory and quarry just outside Lewes, and, in one of several paintings of this subject, chose to adopt a pre-Impressionist style. In 1950 he had turned his hand to religious subjects, sending a *Resurrection, Deposition* and *Last Supper* to the first exhibition since its founding in 1939 of the Society of Mural Painters, of which he was Vice-President. At the invitation of the Arts Council, he also began work on a seven-by-six-foot canvas for the exhibition '60 Paintings for '51', planned to coincide with the Festival of Britain celebrations held in 1951. Vanessa told Angelica that Duncan was 'going to use a very rakish affair he did a long time ago, meant for a theatrical scene, with lots of fantastic figures, a knight upon a prancing horse in the middle and architecture [all] around, all extremely gay and lively and the sort of thing no-one else could do.'[40] Perhaps because it was a rehash of an old idea, Duncan failed to animate this stilted scene and *The Arrival of the Italian Players*, though reproduced in the *Illustrated London News* and noticed by many, remained unbought. It was later admired by Peter Pears, who wanted to buy it for the library at the Red House, Aldeburgh, which he shared with Benjamin Britten; but either because he liked it too much or too little, Duncan refused to sell.

Peter Pears sat for his portrait at Taviton Street on several occasions, Roche recalls, but a good beginning was spoilt by persistent reworkings, a pitfall that Duncan avoided in his portrait drawing of the history don G. S. R. Kitson Clark. This had been commissioned by Trinity College, Cambridge in 1951, for a fee of £33 4s. Clark was a jovial, rubicund Yorkshireman, full of rumbustious banter. Duncan kept the drawing simple and direct and, by not taking the likeness too far, was able to suggest the sitter's reflectiveness and moodiness. Another of his portrait drawings, of Mrs Violet Hammersley, was bought that year by Southampton Art Gallery for twenty-five guineas, while the Arts Council paid £100 for his oil, *Artificial Flowers*. He welcomed commissions, rarely turning them down. He executed for John Lehmann a dustjacket for Paul Valéry's *The Dance* and, with Vanessa and Quentin, undertook some tile pictures for the Garden Hostel, the new annexe to King's College, Cambridge.

The architect of the Garden Hostel was Geddes ('Paul') Hyslop, who was shortly to set up house with Raymond Mortimer in Canonbury. His brick-and-metal frame building had a central stairwell, one side of which was filled with a continuous window. To alleviate the air of austerity, it was agreed that tile pictures should ornament the entrance hall, stairwell and corridors. The artists accepted invitations to submit designs, only to find that the Provost and a number of worthy dons who comprised the building committee would not tolerate nudity, even in an allegorical representation of the seasons. Only Quentin's designs, based on wild flowers, for panels intended to punctuate the long corridors, were accepted. 'Quentin's are all right,' Vanessa told Angelica, 'but ours are refused on the grounds that being figures the undergraduates will scribble over them. It's absurd for one can't scribble over tiles, or if one does it's easy to wash off. However we shall have to try some others of such unexciting subjects as flowers and landscapes.'[41] In the final solution Duncan, who undertook the largest tile painting in the entrance hall, got away with a male nude who sits beside a fountain, earnestly reading an enormous volume, which discreetly relieves his nudity. As if to mock this prudery, Duncan's signature rests on the book's open page.

John Rothenstein, who was writing a book of essays on modern English painters, wanted to make Duncan one of his subjects and wrote in August 1951, asking if he could discuss with Duncan certain aspects of his work. Duncan obliged. A sense of responsibility towards his work also motivated his attempt, with Vanessa's help, to put the paintings at Charleston into some kind of order. Several days had been spent making lists of stretched and unstretched canvases. At the final count Duncan had some 700 paintings at Charleston, as well as thousands of drawings. It now seemed to Vanessa that the incendiary bomb in the war, which had destroyed many of her early paintings, had been to their advantage: without it, the storage problem at Charleston would have left them unable to turn round.

Duncan no longer wrote to George Bergen because he said it was like writing to a wall. But suddenly, in April 1951, Bergen telegrammed him with the news that he was getting married the next day. A further shock came in December when Pernel Strachey died. Leonard, in a letter of condolence to her sister Pippa, remarked, 'I have never known anyone who gave out such a feeling of immediate and complete intellectual integrity.'[42] The news left Duncan much saddened, but it was Pippa Strachey who was the most distraught. 'Darling Duncan,' she wrote. 'One clings to the treasures one has left and you are one of those few most precious treasures of my heart. Your loving Pippa.'[43]

One event in Duncan's social calendar during the early 1950s was his annual invitation to a Buckingham Palace garden party. He did not always enjoy these occasions, often glimpsed little more than the Queen's nose and once found nobody he knew, except Claude Rogers and his wife, Elsie, who were glued to the refreshment tent, more interested in iced coffee and cakes than any passing royalty. After one of these events it was a relief to escape to a small drinks party at the Kenneth Clarks', where Duncan was shown a Turner and a Constable, two of their latest acquisitions. Occasionally he went to dinner at the Royal Academy as Edward le Bas's guest, having borrowed the necessary attire from Clive. At one of these dinners, given in honour of the Royal Family, he was introduced by the President, Sir Gerald Kelly, to the Queen. Having been coached beforehand, he bowed from the waist and called her 'Ma'am' and was charmed by her amiable remarks about his pictures, two of which she owned, as she reminded him. Afterwards the Academicians tried to persuade Duncan to join the Royal Academy, but Edward helped him to remain evasive and non-committal. More purely enjoyable were the parties given by Mrs Gilbert Russell, otherwise known as Maud, in her Mayfair house, 39 Upper Grosvenor Street. Here champagne flowed and a great many old friends appeared from the worlds of music, literature, society and the ballet – the choreographer Frederick Ashton flinging his arms around Vanessa.

To wake up in the country, after the mêlée of London, sometimes left Duncan wanting to do nothing except revel in the silence. If it was October he would go down into the garden to see if the medlars were fat enough to pick and whether the quinces were ripe. In August he delighted in the sight of the red-hot pokers, the dahlias and a hedge of morning glory, which one year he visited every morning after breakfast.

Because the conversation at Charleston ran over a bedrock of familiarity, it was often quick, like shorthand, with more understood than was actually stated. It mostly avoided the rut of prejudice and was often masterminded by Clive. Vanessa's remarks were short but well timed, whereas Duncan would bubble up at odd moments and at others would fall silent. There was always some project afoot. In the spring of 1949 Duncan, Vanessa, Quentin and Janie Bussy decorated the piazza in one corner of the garden with bricks and broken crockery embedded in cement, turning domestic disasters into formal patterns. That summer the dining-room was painted black and stencilled with a simple, light grey and yellow motif. ('They can't keep their brushes off anything, those two,' the policeman Harry Daley reported Raymond Mortimer saying.)[44] The same method was used to enliven the walls of the garden room with a comma-like motif on a pale grey ground. In the summer of 1953, Vanessa, proud of the result, made the newly decorated garden room the setting for a large painting, showing Clive and Duncan talking together by lamplight.[45]

It had pleased her when early in 1952 Quentin had announced that he was going to marry Olivier Popham, daughter of the Keeper of Prints and Drawings at the British Museum. She had trained as an art historian and was then working for the Arts Council. They married in February and that autumn Quentin began work as a lecturer in Art Education at King's College, Newcastle-upon-Tyne. Habitually they returned to Charleston for the greater part of the summer holidays. In July 1953 they brought their small son, Julian, and Duncan set to work on a large family portrait. It was an elaborate composition, Duncan even making notes in his diary as to when Quentin or Olivier would be able to sit. He was also pleased when Quentin spent many hours cutting down the bulrushes that had overtaken the pond, making visible again the water and reflections. Yet amidst all this activity he ended one letter to Paul, 'I sometimes feel very deserted without you.'[46]

The novella 'Narcissus', which Duncan had written in 1950, for himself and Paul, had given him the opportunity to explore the imbalance in their relationship and to look at the nature of their love. The first part of the tale draws on actual experience, including a clandestine meeting with Paul in Paris that Duncan managed to arrange in 1949, the day before he left with Vanessa, Edward and Eardley Knollys for Italy. In the novella Patroclas slips away from his friends to meet Narcissus:

> There was Narcissus on his bicycle, orange-coloured like an apricot, in little shorts and vest among the hubbub of the workers returning home, up and down the Rue de Seine. He might have been one of them. To escape notice from any friends they went inside the little corner café on the quay, given over mainly to students of the Beaux Arts and ordered two Pernods and then two more. They were very happy – Patroclas to be in a place he knew well with someone he loved and who had never been there before. Outside blazing sun was sinking low over the Louvre, the river was reflecting every change of sky.[47]

'Narcissus', as it proceeds, touches very acutely on many aspects of Duncan's relationship with Paul and on its subtle and particular blend of dependence and need. In Duncan's summary, Patroclas sees no faults in the young man he loves, or if he sees them, he forgives them 'because his picture of Narcissus had something of a poetic unity, which he felt unable to pull to pieces. This picture was a joy to Narcissus, if he could feel he was really able to live, without much effort on his part, this poem he would be happy, and he could live and perhaps even return some of the love that went to the creation of this picture.'[48]

One thing Duncan did fear was that Paul might become a playboy. On two occasions he disappeared, to Cornwall and to Jersey, in the company of some wealthy homosexuals. He had a knack for picking up rich friends and was not averse to accepting the benefits this brought. 'I must say,' Duncan retaliated, 'however good the food and drink is, to me there is something lurid and vulgar about a hotel in a beautiful place, run for nothing but smart rich people.'[49]

Duncan himself got away from time to time, visiting Perugia, Arezzo and Florence in June and returning to Venice with Vanessa and Edward in October 1952. In April 1953 he and Vanessa stayed with Quentin and Olivier in Newcastle, Quentin driving them one day to Durham, where Duncan made a few drawings. He was pleased to see his cousin, Julia Strachey, now married to one of Quentin's colleagues Lawrence Gowing

– 'a remarkable character and a good painter,' Duncan told Paul.[50] Now that he and Vanessa had taken over Olivier's former flat in Islington, 26a Canonbury Square, Duncan came less frequently to Taviton Street and Paul thought of moving to Sydenham, as he wanted somewhere he could sunbathe nude. Duncan suggested that it would not be such a good thing for his writing to be so far from the centre of life. Gently he protected and guided Paul; and gradually he came to terms with aspects of their relationship that he could no longer ignore. 'If I do not expect what is obviously impossible,' he admitted to Paul, 'I can be reasonably happy. What I do not want is to have to go back to an habitual state of resigned melancholy, which before I met you – and in spite of periodical adventures – was my lot.'[51] But circumstances were against him. Though he had often flung out to Paul the remark that he should get himself a good wench and have a beautiful child, he was taken aback when Paul got not one, but two women pregnant. The first was Mary Blundell, a physicist studying at the University of London, whose son Tobit (Toby) was born in December 1953. She brought him to see Paul the following February. At this stage Duncan did not seem too worried. 'Dearest, I hope Mary's visit will go off all right. It will be fun for you to see the baby. I wonder very much what your paternal feelings are like. I'm afraid I shall be dead when he can take your place as a model.'[52] Though according to Paul, Mary had initially tried to insist on marriage, she later decided he was not good material for a husband, finished her training and became Head of the Physics Department at Hong Kong University, where she married a Canadian economist. Only a couple of months after he first set eyes on Toby, Paul learnt that an American woman, Clarissa Tanner, whom he had first met in Paris, was also pregnant with his child. Rather taken aback to have made the same mistake twice, Paul now thought that he should marry. This decision was to take him away from Duncan and to cause his removal to America, where he and Clarissa, whose father ran an advertising agency, could benefit from the support of her parents. There, in October, his daughter Pandora was born.

Paul left for America with a Savile Row suit, a gift from Duncan, who had also given him over the years quite a collection of his own work. Paul paid for his ticket to America by selling one of Duncan's paintings to Heal's. He also made off without asking with a trunk belonging to Marjorie Strachey, who was furious. Paul said farewell to Duncan in Regent Street and jumped on a bus, leaving Duncan angry and distraught. In Paul's memory the first few letters he received from Duncan in America, which have not survived, were extremely bitter. After a couple of months Duncan's more usual manner returned, and he sent quizzical, amusing descriptions of his comings and goings. These letters also made it plain that, though he had come to accept their separation as inevitable, his feelings towards Paul had in no way diminished.

TWENTY-FOUR

Time's Thievish Progress

'I'm sick to death of Bloomsbury, or rather of hearing people talk about it every evening on the radio.'[1] So Duncan complained to Bunny in 1951, shortly after the appearance of Roy Harrod's biography of Maynard Keynes. Harrod had been brave enough to visit Charleston in 1949 to listen to criticisms of his manuscript, but, even so, the final book caused offence, Leonard Woolf giving it a hostile review.

Duncan, like Vanessa, did not much like the idea of having his personal life aired in books. He neither hid nor advertised his homosexuality, managing his private affairs with discretion but not deceit. Nevertheless, he shared in the sense of outrage felt by homosexuals in 1954 towards the outcome of the famous Montagu trial. Following the decision of the Home Secretary, Sir David Maxwell Fyfe, to make a drive against 'male vice', the police had stepped up the number of arrests for homosexual offences. One of those convicted was Lord Montagu of Beaulieu, along with four others. Two gained their freedom by turning Queen's evidence against the other three, who went to prison. 'I feel disgusted and disgraced to belong to a country that sends three young men to prison for having been to bed with someone two or three years ago and then only because of the Judas-like blackmailing of the tarts they picked up,' he wrote to Paul. 'I don't believe even the Catholic Church would think prison were the penalty. Then there's the super atom bomb – but that depresses me less. If one is going to be blown up, the more thoroughly it's done the better. I'm thinking of writing . . . a dialogue about buggery between Socrates and the Archbishop. It will have to be delicately ironical, will shock Christians I suppose no end – but it might make people pause. I wonder if Stephen [Spender] would publish it.'[2]

In 1953 he enjoyed the first volume of David Garnett's memoirs, *The Golden Echo*, but dreaded the next, knowing that it would cover the years he had spent with Bunny at Wissett and Charleston. The steady transformation of their private world into a public terrain had already begun and 1954 saw the publication of the first serious study of

Bloomsbury by an academic, J. K. Johnstone. As interest in Bloomsbury grew, so extreme reactions set in, including both fanatical admiration and the intense antipathy that Angelica noticed after Garnett's second volume of memoirs, *The Flowers of the Forest*, appeared. To Bunny she wrote, 'the animosity which exists against Bloomsbury is extraordinary because it is so strong, and the desire to belittle it in all its aspects and all its members is almost pathological.'[3] Duncan, meanwhile, wriggled out of any objective judgement of Bunny's book by seizing on the details he admired, such as the description of Francis Birrell: 'How glad I am that a real portrait has been done of him. It brings out all his charm as well as the queernesses and dirty habits – altogether a loveable figure.'[4] But to Janie Bussy he admitted, 'I have just finished *The Flowers of the Forest*. Rather gruesome for one of the victims. But I believe the book is selling well, and therefore I hope bringing in some cash.'[5]

He was at this time adjusting to Paul's absence. Shortly before leaving for America, Paul had written: 'I cannot bear it if you think that this is the end of all. I know myself that it is the end of nothing and that only external circumstances will interfere a little with the outside of things; but my love of you has never been deeper or more enduring. If only you could see this. My relationship with Clarissa cannot interfere with my feelings for you, for it is something quite different . . . at least it means for me that sex cannot spoil our love.'[6]

So Duncan had and had not lost his heart's desire. But for how long would Paul be gone? He lived happily for a while at his father-in-law's house in Michigan, but when their second child Martin (known familiarly as 'Potie') was born, Clarissa's aunt obtained for Paul a job in the English Department at Smith College, Northampton. There Paul and Clarissa enjoyed the life of the faculty and made friends with Ted Hughes and Sylvia Plath. As Plath's journals record, she was both repelled and fascinated by Paul. She noticed that when he wore an absinthe-green suit it made 'his eyes the clear unearthly and slightly unpleasant acid green of a churned winter ocean full of ice cakes', a view that chimes with Clarissa Roche's gradual discovery that Paul had 'implacable detachment'.[7]

One important development in Paul's life had come about almost by chance. Wanting one day to read *Antigone* aloud to Clarissa, he had picked up a translation and had been appalled at the overloaded, pseudo-Swinburnian prose. He decided to do his own translation and had it accepted by the New American Library, the editor Victor Weybright commissioning further translations of the other two plays in the Theban cycle, *Oedipus the King* and *Oedipus at Colonna*. Roche's translations were admired by William Carlos Williams, who attended one of his readings, and also brought him friendship with the poet Marianne Moore, who gave him a briefcase with his initials on it. When Bunny Garnett, travelling in America in 1957, looked Paul up at Smith College, at Duncan's request, he completely lost his heart to him, on account of Paul's charm, beauty and the fact that his living-room was completely hung with Duncan's paintings.

Meanwhile, among Duncan's memories of Paul were those of their visit to Lincoln, shortly before he had left for the States. The Edwin Austin Abbey Memorial Fund, set up in 1952 by the widow of the illustrator and historical painter to promote murals in public places, had placed a notice in *The Times* on 2 May 1952 inviting proposals. One of these had come Duncan's way, helped no doubt by Vanessa's presence on the Fund's committee, and he was to decorate the chapel dedicated to St Blaize, patron saint of the wool industry, in the Russell Chantry at Lincoln Cathedral. He and Paul had taken a train to Lincoln, once a centre of the wool trade, so that Duncan might view the chapel, the town and also visit Wells-next-the-Sea, the port from which wool had been shipped to the Continent. Climbing the hill that leads up to the cathedral, they had paused at a curiosity shop and Duncan had bought his companion a long, medieval wooden spoon. Paul had teased him with the adage 'When one sups with the devil one needs a long spoon.' Back in London, Duncan had begun to draw Paul in some of the poses that he needed: for the men shearing sheep and for the full-length figure that dominates the altar wall, the Good Shepherd, carrying a sheep on his shoulders. On the wall opposite he was to paint a view of medieval Lincoln, with a busy harbour scene in the foreground. On the right-hand side men heave bales of wool, their balletic poses echoing the curves found in the ships' prows, while on the left three statuesque figures – Angelica, Vanessa and Olivier – are linked with the men by the small boy pulling at Olivier's hand. Simon Watney has suggested that the contrast between these still, watchful women and the exuberant, sensual animation of the dockers is a subconscious representation of a division in Duncan's own life that he had long tried to reconcile.[8]

If thoughts about Paul occasionally made him glum, he found a fellow sufferer in Violet Hammersley, who was exceedingly gloomy, but always in such a way that made others laugh. She had been the second wife of a wealthy bank director and in the past had entertained grandly, in Cadogan Square and at Marlow, by the Thames, where they had kept a Venetian *sandalo*, complete with a gondolier called Giulio. Widowed young, she had been left with three children, all sons, and saw much of her fortune disappear when her late husband's bank went bankrupt.

Though still very comfortably off, she felt she had been plunged into ruin and became a prey to all sorts of anxieties, fearing destitution and wrapping herself in shawls even on hot days to protect her health. One phobia she developed was an inability to travel alone in taxis, even though her adventurous spirit still took her on travels to India and Africa. A strange and fascinating creature, she had a love of high gossip and an immense curiosity about life.

When Duncan first met her in the 1930s she was living in an artist's house in Tite Street, Chelsea. Ethel Sands painted a portrait of the living-room in this house, with Violet seated in one corner. Though Mrs Hammersley was very fond of the room portrayed, she hated the likeness of herself ('I have . . . the startled look as of someone who has received a severe shock in childhood')[9] and near the end of her life, when it was unlikely that Ethel Sands would ever see the painting again, she asked Duncan to paint her out, which he did. During the war she had retired to her house, Wilmington, at Totland Bay on the Isle of Wight, and was thereafter dependent on others for hospitality on her trips to London.

She had suffered greatly over her sons, one of whom had died young. When in 1950 another decided to go and live in the Virgin Islands, she was desolate. She found consolation in Catholicism, once delighting Duncan, who took a slightly malicious interest in her habit of attending retreats, by telling him of a nun's remark: 'Dear, dear Mrs Hammersley – you're on your last lap. Isn't that *glorious*. Hosannah.' She also found inspiration in literature. She made a selection and translation of Mme de Sévigné's letters, which she published in 1955. Eventually, however, she decided that Sévigné was soulless and, when depression left her at her lowest ebb, turned instead to Jane Carlyle's letters or those of Katherine Mansfield.

She had a great fear of getting lost. Duncan began to perform for her the role of Universal Aunt; he would fetch her from the heart of Mayfair or far-flung Hampstead in order to lead her by the hand into the depths of Islington, to have lunch with Raymond Mortimer. It was in this role that he first met Andrew and Deborah ('Debo'), the Marquis and Marchioness of Hartington, who became the Duke and Duchess of Devonshire in 1950 and inherited Chatsworth. They lived at Edensor, less than a mile from Chatsworth, but spent part of each year in Ireland at Lismore Castle, and Duncan acted as Mrs Ham's chaperone on a visit there in May 1954. The Devonshires recollect that they did not know who or what to expect, but took immediately to their new guest. Despite the fact that his appearance was slightly scruffy and the cigarette that perpetually hung on his lip dropped ash all over his clothes, Duncan fitted in so easily that it was almost possible to forget he was there. He was so gentle and enthusiastic about everything that it made it easy to see when he was displeased. On this and subsequent visits to Edensor and later Chatsworth, Duncan continued to retain their affection. The Duke thought 'benign' was the word that was the key to Duncan. 'Impishly benign,' his wife added.[10]

Duncan enjoyed Lismore hugely, though he had to battle for time to paint. He loved the odd, dug-in characters he met in Ireland. Surrounded by dukes, duchesses, a dowager and by a Mr Ogilvie Grant, who claimed distant clanship, he adjusted to his new surroundings, grateful to Mrs Ham, 'who really keeps the table in a roar and whose support is the greatest value to me'.[11] There was no end of conversation that amused him, even when it referred to characters unknown to him called 'Boosie' or 'Wife'. 'Woman' turned out to be another Mitford, Pamela Jackson, Debo's sister, who had been left by her husband in a nearby castle and was living with a lady called 'Husband'. But there were moments when Duncan hankered for the tranquillity of Charleston, and he had been deeply alarmed *en route* to Lismore, during their forty-mile drive from Limerick, when Mrs Ham suddenly leaned forward groaning, as if struck by a heart attack. Duncan, not knowing what else to do, had passed her his brandy, thankful that it was too dark for her to see that the flask was an old Dettol bottle. It proved to be the cure.

But the person who impressed him most on this trip was his hostess, Debo. Her wild theories and aspersions rather shocked her mother-in-law. 'Not that Debo is in the least malicious but totally without reserve of any kind which is perhaps her great charm. She is I've discovered a superbly capable housewife and runs this huge place very well without turning a hair.'[12]

'Don't become *too* ducal,' Vanessa had written to Duncan from Roquebrune, where she was staying with the Bussys, ' – it's rather alarming.'[13] She had cut short her visit to France owing to Simon's sudden illness and soon after returning to England learnt that the man whom Duncan always claimed first taught him the habit of work had died. 'When I was young,' he once reminisced to Paul, 'I used to hear Simon Bussy say that he and his painter friends . . . used to say that every picture had its "clou". I think they meant something like a nail in the right place.'[14] Duncan was as relieved as Vanessa to find himself once again at Charleston. 'We came here a week ago,' she wrote to Angelica, ' – rather glad to get back to one's own surroundings and have no more long journeyings in prospect. Duncan and I each had a lot to tell of our days in Ireland and France and spent a great deal of time chatting.'[15]

They also agreed on a new method of heating the large studio, and that year a large Pither stove was installed.

In October 1955 Duncan, while painting his Lincoln murals, jumped off a high stand on to a stool that overturned, and cut his head on an electric fire. The accident was minor, but the murals he was painting played a large part in helping him through a low period, for the public at this time showed little interest in his work. His contract with Agnew's and Lefevre's had not been renewed and though he occasionally sold pictures through Freddie Mayor at the Mayor Gallery, through the Zwemmer Gallery and the Leicester Galleries, he belonged to no dealer's stable and had no regular outlet, other than the London Group and the annual exhibition mounted by the Royal West of England Academy at Bristol. He had begun sending to the RWEA in 1952, becoming a member in 1953 and the following year his five paintings included two Irish scenes. His career continued to tick over, but his unfashionableness became apparent when in 1957, the year after the death of Dorothy Wellesley (by then the Duchess of Wellington), Penns-in-the-Rocks was sold. The auctioneer at first offered the contents of the dining-room – the furniture, decorations, curtains and carpets – as a single lot. There were no takers and the contents of the room were split into twelve separate lots, the six mural panels painted by Duncan and Vanessa selling for seventeen pounds. According to one journalist, the dealers were much more interested in the eighteenth-century pictures and furniture for sale and had little time for 'that sort of stuff', as one blithely described the work of these two Bloomsbury painters.[16]

In March 1956 John Piper informed Duncan that the English Opera Group was performing John Blow's short opera *Venus and Adonis* along with Holst's *Savitri* at the Aldeburgh Festival. Would Duncan consider designing the 'Venus and Adonis'? It would not, he assured Duncan, involve him in a great deal of work as the artistic director, Michael Northern, would be on hand to interpret his drawings and designs. It was an opportunity that brought Duncan into closer contact with Peter Pears and Benjamin Britten, and on the day of the first night he and Vanessa lunched with the two men at the Red House, their home in Aldeburgh. Amongst their collection of paintings were several by Duncan, as well as others by their friend and neighbour Mary Potter, whom Duncan and Vanessa met. On a subsequent visit to Aldeburgh in 1959, Duncan and Vanessa visited her studio in order to see more of her paintings and she in turn, accompanied Britten and Pears on a visit to Charleston in 1960.

Still more welcome at Charleston were the grandchildren. Duncan shared Vanessa's delight in their different characters and unexpected behaviour. Bribes were offered, after which Amaryllis and Henrietta posed willingly, adopting what they called 'graceful poses' in the studio. They were no trouble to look after, as they spent much of the day reading and were often taken for a walk by Clive after tea. Later on it pleased Duncan that one of the twins, Nerissa, showed a talent for painting. Because her grandchildren now occupied a large place in her thoughts, Vanessa welcomed the arrival of Quentin and Olivier's two daughters, Virginia and Cressida, in 1955 and 1957. Of all these children, the one who seemed to invite the most comment from her elders was Amaryllis, who from an early age had shown a rare combination of character, imagination and sympathy. Clive thought her a mixture of the best of the Stephen and Garnett intellects. There was, however, a melancholy in her nature, and an acute awareness of the weight of her family inheritance, which left her, when she read Bunny's *The Flowers of the Forest* at the age of twelve, feeling 'so very small . . . like a bit of old moth-eaten brocade'.[17]

If the routine of life at Charleston had become a little fixed, it was alleviated by periodic trips abroad. In 1955 after a visit to Charleston from Diana Uhlman, who was preparing an exhibition for the Artists' International Association called 'The Fitzroy Street Retrospective' – one of the first shows to take a historical look at the period – Vanessa and Duncan, together with Edward and Eardley, set off for Asolo in Italy, having been fired by Diana's account of this old, walled town. They also travelled in Edward's grand Bentley to Venice for the day and to the Villa Maser to see again the Veronese decorations. Towards the end of that year they acquired a *pied-à-terre* at 28 Percy Street and were to move to another in this same street, five years later, when Saxon Sydney-Turner entered a nursing home and his flat became vacant.

One noticeable difference between Duncan and Bunny in late middle age was that whereas Bunny was still mastered by his emotions, Duncan, though aware of his feelings and their intensity, became more detached. He had such extraordinary sweetness of character that Stephen Keynes, visiting him at Charleston in the company of his aunt, Lydia, found himself kissing him, realising with surprise that Duncan was the first man he had kissed since his father. 'You keep your end up and never appear to hedge your opinions,' Charles Reilly had once observed to Duncan, 'and yet leave one perfectly happy.'[18] What Duncan brought to others was sympathy and patience. As a result, advice, when he gave it, seemed worth having. His appearance, too, had a certain distinction, though everything about him seemed an attempt to deny it: increasingly he wore good clothes badly and often used a tie in place of a belt. As a result his trousers once fell down when he was judging the children's fancy-dress competition at a Firle fête.

Bloomsbury loyalty kept friendships alive even when, by force of circumstance, contact was infrequent or slight. What was looked for was not riches or social prestige, but an independent mind and genuine values.

When Vanessa and Duncan agreed to visit Ham Spray in February 1956, Frances Partridge, preparing to receive them, found herself in a state of near-panic owing to the intense cold. 'Our two Bloomsbury birds put us to shame by being the nicest guests and best company we have had for ages,' Frances's diary records:

> They can and will talk about anything and everything with unfailing interest and gaiety. I must admit that Vanessa seems physically an old lady as one hears her bumping slowly downstairs, but mentally and spiritually she is ageless; while having Duncan in the house is like having a young irresponsible undergraduate to stay, and I even felt a slight surprise at seeing him reading a solid history book. His hair is quite black still and there is nothing to remind one that he is seventy. Both Ralph and I were charmed by them. The only entertainment we provided was to take them to lunch with the Moynes at Biddesden . . . Bryan [Lord Moyne] took us upstairs to show us a painting by Duncan, and didn't appear to mind when Duncan peered at it closely and said, 'I have absolutely no recollection of ever seeing it in my life before.'[19]

Other homes they visited included Raymond Mortimer and Paul Hyslop's large, dignified house in Canonbury, Islington, where Duncan painted in the garden. Soon after the war Mortimer, with Edward Sackville-West, the music critic Desmond Shawe-Taylor and Eardley Knollys, had taken a share in Long Crichel, a Victorian rectory in Dorset. Duncan and Vanessa had paid their first visit in October 1951 and enjoyed the good cooking, warmth and music; again they fitted in easily, though Vanessa could not share Eddy Sackville-West's enthusiasm for Graham Sutherland's paintings.

Like Virginia Woolf, Duncan had little interest in official honours and in 1953 he had turned down the offer of an OBE. That year he earned £534 6s 8d, a reasonable income, but, like most artists, his income fluctuated and by 1956 he was glad to receive his share from the sale of a Vlaminck that hung at Charleston. Towards the end of his life, he admitted that as an artist he had never felt secure. When his art sold he had felt 'more secure and more encouraged', but the underlying feeling had always been of insecurity.[20]

The solo exhibition given by the Leicester Galleries in May 1957 was the first he had held for twelve years. 'What a delight to see someone who paints and can hold the whole, wonderful complexity of a subject – and yet have such endless variety,' wrote Helen Anrep, ' – and your colour is so strange and beautiful and unique. I keep thinking of Casals playing the 'cello.'[21] Even if the critics paid little attention, Duncan still had a loyal following. 'Up early and to London for the day for Duncan's private view,' reads Frances Partridge's diary:

> Many old friends were collected under the hot light beating down from the glass roof; very old they seemed, and dusty too, with the flash of false teeth and the glitter of spectacles. Vanessa stood beaming seraphically from under a huge inverted wicker basket. Marjorie Strachey like a swollen spider all in black. I came away feeling saddened.[22]

At least once Duncan was made acutely aware that his painting had failed to please. In 1956 he agreed to paint a portrait of Sir Alexander Cadogan, whose wife offered criticisms, while the painting was in progress, first aloud and then, more tactfully, inscribed in a notebook in which Duncan would write replies, such as 'I will try to do better with the left eye'. After her husband died, Lady Cadogan continued to worry about the accuracy of the portrait and in 1969 returned it to Duncan for further alteration. In despair Duncan passed the painting to Angelica. Quentin also had a hand in it, as did Henrietta. When finally Duncan took it back to the widow, her reponse was 'My God, how awful!' Duncan thought she spoke the truth.

Though G. L. Kennedy, in 1924, had praised 'the roominess which is so magical a quality in the colour of Duncan Grant',[23] that same quality did not impress Claude Rogers when in 1958 he began to help select a Duncan Grant retrospective. This had first been mooted by a former pupil of the Euston Road School and Trustee of the Tate Gallery, Lawrence Gowing. Claude Rogers, though he had been brought in at Duncan's suggestion, was at this time moving away from the traditions that Duncan upheld. He enjoyed writing doggerel and, after a strenuous afternoon in the Tate's basement with Duncan's pictures, composed the following:

Dear Duncan, I've looked at your pictures

I'm not much concerned with the style
But the Colours you choose
And the Mixtures you use
Are indescribably vile.[24]

The Tate retrospective opened to the public on 12 May 1959. Though the selection, which numbered eighty-four oils and fifty-three drawings and watercolours, was good, the perplexing shifts of idiom made it difficult for the critics to discover a distinctive style. Moreover, in the eyes of the critics, Duncan belonged to a period that was then in disfavour – and no one falls as far from favour as a favourite. Alan Clutton-Brock, art critic for *The Times* and a friend of both Duncan and Clive, wrote the catalogue introduction. He argued that in Grant's art, as in Bloomsbury conversation, there was recurrent grace and wit. 'Both cubist and *fauve* painting contributed much to his style but he used their discoveries and conventions with almost as light a hand as Dufy.' Because he had not been involved in the selection, Clutton-Brock felt free also to extol the show in the *Listener*:

Fashion . . . has passed him by and few will have suspected that his talent was as many-sided and as highly original as the exhibition of his work at the Tate Gallery now shows him to be. The organisers of this exhibition have dug away, unearthed and often cleaned and reframed – for whatever else they may have been the Bloomsbury intellectuals were not expert in museography – a most impressive and unexpected variety of paintings and other work.[25]

One visitor to the show was Aunt Violet, now in her nineties and in a wheelchair. After Ethel Grant's death she had stayed at Twickenham with Duncan's help, for he visited her regularly, looked after her affairs, and now and then sent her small cheques. Increasingly frail, she had occasionally to tell him of a fall or some other disaster, but in doing so expressed almost more concern at having to give him bad news. She ended one letter, 'I can hardly believe it is myself who am so disabled.' In 1957, no longer able to manage alone, she had moved into a home for the elderly at 31 Queen's Gate Terrace (where, a few years later, Mrs Hammersley also spent the last years of her life). Duncan had arranged Aunt Violet's move with the help of the loyal Frances Todd, who was startled one day to hear Violet say, 'Ethel is here: you will be very glad to see her.' A few days later Violet died. Duncan arranged for her funeral to be held at Holy Trinity Church, Prince Consort Road, on 21 December 1959, and rather touchingly kept a list of those who came to pay respect.

Out of gratitude to Mrs Gurney, who ran the home at Queen's Gate Terrace, and to her staff, he donated one of his paintings of St Paul's in remembrance of his aunt.

He was aware that Miss Todd's loyalty was not entirely disinterested. But her love for Duncan and her gift of sympathy won him over and he sent her tickets to the London Group, took her to concerts, met her at exhibitions and gave her an oil of the Royal Square in Copenhagen, which was where they had first met. 'My one special prayer is to know how to love you,' she wrote,[26] sending him more letters than he replied to, for some of the feelings she aroused were akin to those he felt for Phyllis Keyes.

He and Vanessa were pleased to learn that Bloomsbury art could be seen at the new Courtauld Institute Galleries in Woburn Square. This part of the display was based largely on a collection of paintings, objects and furniture, which Margery Fry had given to the Courtauld in memory of her brother. Duncan now added to it two Omega chairs and a turquoise Omega vase, for which he received a letter of thanks from Anthony Blunt. But what would have been for Vanessa one of the year's high points – Duncan's opening at the Tate – she had to miss, because of another bout of bronchial pleurisy which had left her much frailer earlier that year. (In March, at Charleston, she had also been pulled over and dragged a little way when Duncan started to drive off, without realising that her dress was caught in the door. She was more shocked than wounded, but the expression on Duncan's face when he realised what had happened, and the speed at which he dashed inside for brandy, was something Grace, who was present, never forgot.)

Mrs Hammersley had suggested that they should visit Chatsworth together soon after his Tate show opened. Duncan agreed, but then cancelled the arrangement because of Vanessa's illness. Mrs Ham was scathing: could not Vanessa, who was surrounded by people, be left for a week, whereas she, Mrs Hammersley, who lived alone for months at a time, had to be denied? She got her way and during the last week of May Duncan found himself staying with Mrs Ham at Edensor House, Bakewell, near to the great house, and preparing himself to paint a portrait of his hostess, seated informally in an armchair with her arms folded and legs crossed. Among the other guests were Barbirolli, whom they heard conduct the Hallé Orchestra at Buxton, and the Princess Royal. One of the joys of Chatsworth for Duncan were the hundred or so Solander cases in the library, which had the outward appearance of large books with lettered spines but contained in them an outstanding collection of Old Master drawings.

At home, entertaining company was near at hand when Cyril Connolly and his young wife Deirdre took over the lease on Bushey Lodge, another farmhouse on the Firle estate, in 1958. Though Cyril, twenty-eight years older than his wife, had known Clive for many years, both Connollys felt nervous when the Charlestonians, Clive, Vanessa and Duncan, first came to dinner. Cyril, with *To the Lighthouse* in mind, insisted that they should serve *boeuf en daube*, and Deirdre had found a recipe that tested the endurance not only of their Calor gas stove but their own, since they had to get up in the night in order to stir the stew. It proved the making of the evening, for their jokes about it broke the ice, and Cyril went on to deliver an amusing account of Firle's Madame Bovary, also their char, who was having an affair with a farmworker and brought up their breakfast tray with straw sticking to her person. The fact that she had also posed for the Virgin Mary at Berwick Church made the Charlestonians laugh still more. Deirdre Connolly was surprised to see a woman of Vanessa's age and distinction smoke Gauloises. When she was taken upstairs to see Deidre's daughter asleep in a crib, Vanessa remarked with pleasure at the sight of the baby and the cat curled up on the floor beneath. It touched Deirdre still more, at the end of the evening, to see Clive and Duncan standing either side of Vanessa and both helping her on with her coat.

After this, the two households met regularly, for drinks or meals. Invitations and messages were sent via the postman, for the Connollys knew that on reaching Charleston in the mornings he paused, usually to have tea with Grace.

In 1958 Duncan completed the Lincoln murals, which had for so long dominated the studio at Charleston. In order to see them installed, he and Vanessa travelled north and booked in at the White Hart. (While staying there the year before, Duncan had seen television for the first time. 'I really think it is the end of civilisation as we know it,' he wrote to Vanessa, 'but of course one can't help glancing in its direction from time to time.')[27] He had put a great deal of thought and labour into this decorative scheme, and at one point had used paper cut-outs to help him decide on the exact positioning of the sheep on either side of the Good Shepherd. Paul had modelled for the young beardless Christ. Consciously or unconsciously, Duncan had drawn on an early Christian tradition which, to ease the transition from paganism to Christianity, depicted Christ in a manner reminiscent of Mercury. Duncan's Good Shepherd, surrounded by a mandorla of light, fills the centre of the altar wall and faces the view of medieval Lincoln on the wall opposite. Skilful design, animated movement, joyous, warm colour and a lightness of mood make these decorations if anything more successful than those he had earlier done for Berwick. But the cathedral authorities thought otherwise, and not long after the public unveiling (performed by B. L. Hallward, Vice-Chancellor of Nottingham University, on 6 June 1959) the chapel was usually locked and for twenty years effectively turned into a broom cupboard. Legend has it that a certain Dean thought, wrongly, that Duncan had used his own likeness for the head of St Blaize, who leans out of a roundel over the entrance door, and that his rapt gaze, directed towards the Good Shepherd on the altar wall, expressed not contemplation of Christ but an elderly painter's obsessive lust for his model. But if homoeroticism is an ingredient in the Lincoln murals (as it is in the Sistine ceiling) it does not alter the iconography, which continues to offer the visitor to this chapel a clear, simple Christian message.

As 1959 drew to a close, Duncan and Vanessa decided to escape the cold and go to Roquebrune. In January 1960 they therefore set out for La Souco, left empty while Dorothy and Janie Bussy wintered in London. Grace went too, to do the cooking, and had the help of a local woman who came every day to do shopping and housework. A little further along the coast, Clive was staying at Menton-Garavan with the painter and gardener Humphrey Waterfield, at the Clos du Perronet. With Clive was Barbara Bagenal, now separated from her husband, a willing traveller, companion and helpmate. She and Clive took to arriving every Sunday at La Souco for lunch. The house, perched on the hillside, overlooked the Mediterranean, its garden falling away in terraces in which lemons shone like lamps. By March the garden was full of little white periwinkles, jonquils and other flowers. When Angelica joined them she found Duncan was grumpy and cantankerous because of his anxiety over Vanessa, who was often abstracted and silent. The house itself was in a bad state of repair and this added to the air of desolation.

Angelica's arrival improved matters; having inherited her mother's efficiency in practical matters, she hired a car and took the painters out in search of motifs. The arrival of Edward le Bas further enlivened the party, as did Peter Morris, who, on a return visit from Mexico, lodged in Vanessa and Duncan's London flat before joining them at Roquebrune. Afterwards Peter wrote to Vanessa, 'Thank you dearest Vanessa for those gentle weeks spent with you, I shall never forget them.'[28] Before they all left Roquebrune a case, packed with oranges and lemons, was sent to Janie and Dorothy Bussy in London. Duncan threw in a sprig of mimosa, which showed Janie that a tree she had planted the year previously was still alive.

If Duncan found La Souco blighted with neglect, he witnessed far worse on a short holiday in Scotland in July. He havered over James Strachey's invitation to join him and his sister Pippa at Rothiemurchus but, at the last moment, accepted and arrived by train, wearing a beret. He was met by Angelica who drove him to Coyhun House, Rothiemurchus, where Pippa greeted him with shrieks of joy. Angelica noticed, when she drove them to Loch an Eilan, that her elders seemed to know every cottage and tree. But they were saddened by the sight of the Doune which, unlived in since the First World War, had become derelict and a near-ruin, huge fungi growing in the drawing-room, where the ceiling had half fallen down.

That year Duncan's loyal friend Angus Davidson moved to Brighton, whence he could visit Charleston regularly. Vanessa still enjoyed visitors, but that winter she refused to leave the house. She wrote affectionately to Frances Partridge after hearing of Ralph's death in December, and in March 1961 felt great concern for Clive who, having recently undergone an operation for cancer, had fallen and broken his leg while recuperating at Menton. He was flown home and went straight into the London Clinic, where Barbara Bagenal visited him daily.

In 1956 the Adams Gallery had given Vanessa a solo exhibition. At Edward le Bas's suggestion, the two brothers in charge now offered her another. She responded somewhat hesitantly, but began putting her paintings in order for a show in October 1961. 'I have been reading *Mansfield Park* aloud to Duncan,' she wrote to Angelica in February, ' – we're both absolutely fascinated. It's wonderful when one can leave Jane alone long enough to be able to enjoy it again.'[29] At the end of March Duncan, while taking tea with the ladies of Miller's, realised he had a cold. He spent most of the following day in bed and felt much better the day after that. But two days later Vanessa fell ill with bronchitis. After only three days her condition was so critical that Quentin, who had arrived on a prearranged visit with his son, took Julian back to London, where his grandfather Hugh Popham received him at the National Gallery. Quentin returned to Sussex by train and spent the afternoon with Vanessa. Towards early evening she slept. Duncan and Quentin sat in the studio, with the door between studio and bedroom open so that they could hear her breathing. At around six o'clock her breathing stopped and she died.

Later that evening Angelica arrived, and though strengthened by her presence and that of Quentin, Duncan wept unconsolably, grief mingling with guilt over the hurt he had caused the person who had shared his life for some forty years. Five months later Peter Morris still had to beg him not to reproach himself – 'everyone knows the comfort and devotion you gave – one cannot live in this world without causing sometimes some suffering. Please let it go at that.'[30]

In the immediate aftermath of Vanessa's death he managed to resume an appearance of normality. 'Duncan is evidently better and a good deal more cheerful,' Angelica wrote to Bunny on 9 April 1961. 'We talk about Delacroix and Wilkie Collins whose life he is reading with a great deal of interest.'[31] Grace, who said it helped to keep busy, cooked them all excellent meals and there was also the comfort of quietness. On 12 April Vanessa was buried in Firle churchyard. 'There is to be no ceremony, as she would not have wished for one,' Duncan informed Lydia, 'and Quentin and Angelica think it would be best for no one to be there but ourselves.'[32] The following day Clive left the London Clinic and went to Barbara Bagenal's house at Iden, whence he announced that he could not at the moment do without Barbara and would be bringing her with him to Charleston the following Monday. Duncan worried that Clive wanted to install Barbara permanently at Charleston and was relieved when he learnt this was not the case. Then a letter arrived from Edward in the Canary Islands inviting Duncan to join him at Tenerife. It seemed too far to go for only a short visit and Duncan replied that he would prefer to travel later in the year with Edward to France. Only after all this did he suddenly, during the first week of May, begin to recover: 'This is the first day I have felt at all myself since April 7,' he noted in his appointment diary.[33]

Inundated with consolation letters, he replied to them diligently, even those that insisted no answer was needed. To Raymond Mortimer he admitted, 'It's a very good thing that I have such a long period of happiness to look back to, but I dread the emptiness ahead.'[34] One of the first things discussed when Clive returned was the future of the house, and it relieved Duncan to learn that Clive, too, did not wish to leave it.

Among the letters Duncan received was one from Kenneth Clark. 'When writing,' he claimed, 'I always used to say to myself "What would Vanessa think of this?" It saved me from a good deal of humbug and vulgarity.'[35] It was a sentiment with which Duncan would have agreed. On 3 June he wrote the following note:

After lunch I suddenly became aware that I am now 'on my own', for better or for worse. Exactly what [do] I mean? I can only guess by using the word 'deference' – that is what I always felt with V. I do not mean the suggestion of flattery which the word has, but I did always defer to her opinions and feelings. Now henceforth I think I shall always defer to her *opinions*, I know or can guess so often what they could be – but her feelings no longer exist so in that prospect I feel I am alone.[36]

He seemed momentarily to have forgotten the eloquence of her paintings. 'I am glad that you have two of Vanessa's pictures,' he had earlier written to Keith Baynes. 'It is extraordinary how much of a painter can continue to exist in his pictures.'[37]

TWENTY-FIVE

Les Femmes Savantes

On 11 May 1961 Duncan dined at Edward le Bas's in London. Also present was Frances, wife of the novelist and translator, Basil Creighton. She observed that Duncan was so distraught with grief when talking about Vanessa that at one point his face almost touched the table. Le Bas, seeing how miserable Duncan was, made immediate arrangements for a holiday in France. Thus, on 4 June, Duncan boarded an aeroplane for the first time and flew the short hop between Lydd and le Touquet. Thereafter he and le Bas toured the region between Abbeville and Auxerre, taking in, among other places, the Chantilly Forest, Beauvais and Senlis, and stopping for a week at Allerey in order to paint. On a day trip to Vergelles, they found Copeau's house in the Rue Jacques Copeau and were shown round by two women. Copeau's study had not been touched since his death in 1949 and Duncan was pleased to find a marionette that he had given Copeau as well as some drawings for *Nuit des Rois*.

Emotionally he must have felt in some kind of limbo, severed from his past and facing an uncertain future. Yet there was one thread in his life which, for the past seven years, he had held on to by writing twice-weekly letters to Paul in America. In 1958 Roche had been awarded a Bollingen Foundation Grant to assist his translation work and, in order to accept the grant of $4,000, had to resign from Smith. Someone had told him that the cheapest place to live was the Island of Nevis in the West Indies, and for a few months he, Clarissa and their two children, Pandora and Potie, made a home there. After four or five months there they moved to Taxco, in Mexico, where their third child, Vanessa, was born.

In March 1961 Paul, desperately short of money, made a trip to New York in the hope of picking up another contract and some readings. Duncan wrote to the New York address that Paul had given him soon after Vanessa died and on 11 April Paul replied, 'My poor dearest Duncan, I am ready to fly out if you say the word. There are not many who could console you or distract you so well as I. Please let me come for a few weeks.' Paul promised to telephone George Bergen and suggested

432

that he and Duncan might now travel together or that Duncan could visit him in Taxco. 'I think of Vanessa with fondness and admiration, even if with great regrets that she could never accept me . . . If you think I can help you now, I am prepared to at any time of the day or night.'[1] After hearing this, Duncan asked Paul to come, offering him the use of the flat at 28 Percy Street. On 28 June Paul boarded a Greek ship called the *Arkadia* at Montreal, working his passage as a student adviser. He landed at Tilbury on 8 July at five in the morning to find Duncan waiting for him with a taxi.

To Paul, Duncan seemed, after a gap of seven years, 'a little wistful but not pessimistic, overjoyed at my return, but apprehensive, hoping but not daring to presume to expect that things could be the same as before'.[2] The relationship between the two men was still vital but less intense. Greater freedom ('all that business of hiding me had gone')[3] made it easier, but in addition the terms on which it rested had changed. Duncan now felt that the continuation of sexual relations would be disloyal to Clarissa, and this made possible greater detachment. When he first arrived, Paul did not plan to stay more than a couple of months and had much that he wanted to do. Duncan helped him to give readings, hosting one himself at Percy Street. Together they went to some familiar haunts, dining at Edward's and visiting the Victoria and Albert Museum. But for much of the time Duncan left Paul to his own devices and got on with life at Charleston.

His appointment diary suggests that he in fact saw more in the next few weeks of Lindy Guinness, who, in the course of a weekend party at Firle Place, stepped suddenly into Duncan's life. She had wandered off into a field and noticed an old man leaning against a tree, making drawings of a bonfire. They began talking and discovered an immediate liking for each other. He said that he lived nearby and invited her to visit Charleston. Lindy went the next day and met Duncan properly. She was jumpy, energetic, vibrantly responsive and wildly unhappy. In her background lay huge wealth, considerable glamour (she was the granddaughter of the Duchess of Rutland and the great-niece of the famous beauty Lady Diana Cooper) and understanding that was more worldly than humane. When she was eight her parents had divorced, both soon remarrying, her father leading an exotic life in Palm Beach, Mexico and places all round the world and her mother, by marrying Sir Robert Throckmorton, entering the aristocracy and the oldest Catholic family in England. As a child, Lindy had led a fragmented, cosmopolitan life that left her on edge and confused. She was living with her grandmother in London when she first met Duncan. She was also in a depressed state of mind, while he, just three months earlier, had lost Vanessa.

At first no one could understand their relationship, which flared up with the intensity of a love affair. Lindy became fascinated by Duncan's character and understanding, and by something deeper still – a rhythm of life that approximated to a religion and with which she felt in harmony. He seemed exactly the person she needed and she adored him unreservedly. He fired her with his love of painting and soon she began working alongside him in the studio, for a while becoming the most frequent visitor to the house. 'He became my guiding force,' she recalls. 'He totally formed my way of thinking about what happiness was about. He taught me a rhythm of living – the central fireplace was painting and everything else was around it. Everything went back to painting. You got up, ate, flirted, loved and enjoyed and painted. It was very peaceful ... To have this emotional tie-up with painting was ideal at this stage.'[4]

She noticed that Duncan was disinclined to talk about the past and instead lived very much in the present. She also thought that he was possibly relieved by their unintellectual chat. Yet he was linked very directly with the outside world and loved hearing about her life. He always listened uncritically, without questioning things. She felt instinctively that he had a fundamental goodness and that he taught by osmosis: simply by being with him one picked up his way of looking at things, a lilting vision, full, and truly felt.

Lindy gave Duncan a taste for young friends. So he told her after he became acquainted with the Bridge family, who lived at Firle. He painted a subtle and delicate portrait of Mrs Bridge's daughter by her first marriage, Phyllis Fox, who soon afterwards developed schizophrenia; and he became a friend of her brother James Fox, later famous for his book *White Mischief*.

When Vanessa's paintings went on show at the Adams Gallery in October 1961 Duncan was pleased that Kenneth Clark bought a late self-portrait (now part of the collection at Charleston), but was more curious about a young, unknown buyer, Richard Morphet, who bought Vanessa's *Iris Tree*: 'I wonder who he is?'[5] Richard Morphet, shortly to join the British Council and then to move to the Tate, was to become a major supporter, a key figure in the rehabilitation of Duncan's career.

After giving a reading at the home of Lindy's grandmother, the Duchess of Rutland, Paul was offered £1,000 by his former publisher, Erica Marx, if he settled in England. Soon afterwards Clarissa Roche arrived in London with their three children and spent two nights at Duncan's Percy Street flat, before moving to Paul's father's house at

Hanwell. The eldest child, Pandora, noticed the look of curiosity on Duncan's face as he sat on the edge of a low, tiled table, smoking a cigarette and watching the children eat boiled eggs. She also remembers trying to instill some kind of order into the litter on the mantelpiece and suddenly realising, without anything being said, that she had incurred Duncan's displeasure.

The Roche family stayed at Hanwell, then at Hythe, within easy driving distance of Charleston. Duncan would come over for the day or stay a night. He was always welcomed by Clarissa, who recognised and accepted the important place he had in Paul's life. The children also found him a delightful guest and enjoyed occasional visits to the strange and exciting world of Charleston. The situation altered after Paul bought a house at Aldermaston, for thereafter it was he who did the travelling in order to see Duncan, either in London or at Charleston. The birth of his fifth child (the fourth by Clarissa), Cordelia, in 1962, and the need to keep his family going soon obliged Paul to take on temporary teaching posts and residencies at American colleges for three or four months at a time. Every time Paul left for the States, Duncan became very agitated. Though their relationship was now largely one of companionship, there were episodes lasting a few seconds when they were alone and Duncan, looking at Paul with tremendous yearning, would say, 'I wish you knew how much I love you.'[6]

Still of the greatest importance to Duncan, Paul was not quite as central to the older man's life as he had once been. Duncan was now often alone at Charleston. Clive's health was failing and, after two further operations, his dependency on Barbara Bagenal increased. Though he still regarded Charleston as his home, he spent more time in the London flat he shared with her in Percy Street. Later, when Barbara bought a little house at Hucksteps Row, Rye, which she converted in order to accommodate him, Clive moved in, with the bed that Vanessa had decorated for him.

Grace, though approaching retirement, continued to produce delicious meals, to bottle fruit and make jams, jellies and marmalade. Under her rule, the kitchen was always warm, the Aga well stoked and a smell of fresh coffee in the air; the concrete floor was mopped daily and the walls and ceiling regularly whitewashed, a task she undertook herself. Duncan's dependence on her is reflected in the letters he sent her when abroad, which in tone and detail were identical to those he had sent Vanessa. He also dreaded her brief disappearances. For the most part Grace was a constant yet unobtrusive presence. Her respect for Duncan's privacy left him able to invite whom he liked to Charleston.

One new friend whom he met on Lewes station was Iain MacLeod, who had just come out of Lewes prison. He agreed to pose naked for Duncan with his boyfriend John. The interest and help that Duncan gave Iain at a rocky period in his life left him profoundly grateful, though he had also to admit that he did not much like being fondled and kissed by Duncan. Once his life gained a more even course, he settled down as a hairdresser.

Now, too, Duncan could continue his interest in erotic art without any inhibition. He drew male figures involved in athletic acts of buggery or fellatio, on the backs of envelopes, the covers of financial reports to shareholders or any paper that came to hand, often using a ballpoint pen, or 'the odious biro' as Clive called it, afterwards adding a swift watercolour wash to indicate different-coloured skins, for his white men often copulate with black. Frequently two or more figures are combined in a ballet-like formation, with elegant results. These drawings, a collection of which belonged to Edward le Bas, became a significant outlet in old age for his sensual, amatory imagination and were drawn with great zest. They also betray a playfulness similar to that which led him to draw genitalia over the *cache-sexe* worn by models in *Physique Pictorial*, published by the Athletic Model's Guild, copies of which Paul sent him from America. Duncan never exhibited any erotica, regarding it purely as a form of private entertainment for himself and his friends. However, Douglas Turnbaugh published a collection in 1989 with the Gay Men's Press, entitled *Private: The Erotic Art of Duncan Grant*, claiming in his introduction that Duncan gave him the drawings on the condition that they would eventually be published. (In fact all the drawings in the book had been lent to him by Paul Roche, to whom they still belong.)

Duncan witnessed Edward le Bas's unsuccessful attempt to turn a former boyfriend, Alan Till, into his major-domo. Till, uncertain of his rôle, became an alcoholic, but remained in le Bas's service. In December 1961 Edward took Till and Duncan to San Roque, Cadiz. It was the wettest season since the year of the Civil War and amid the deluge Frances Partridge arrived *en route* to Malaga to stay with Brenan. She brought with her Eardley Knollys, who remained behind with le Bas's party, which now also included Basil and Frances Creighton and Lindy Guinness. At Lindy's suggestion, Duncan painted a back view of the Creightons seated on the terrace on Christmas Day.

Edward often, and very happily, did the cooking. 'Everyone lit up when they came into his ambiance,' Frances Creighton recalled.[7] They sat round a log fire in the *salone* in the evenings with plenty to drink, for there was a choice of good local wine, an innocuous Spanish gin or a strong Spanish brandy. On New Year's Eve the local youth serenaded the house with songs that Duncan thought dated back to pagan times. Greatly moved, he went on to the roof terrace at midnight to see the New Year in, listening to a mêlée of sounds – frogs, owls, church bells in San Roque, sirens from the fleet at Gibraltar and music from nearby houses.

From San Roque he travelled to Tangier, which disappointed him ('the modern town is too chic and out of place'),[8] returning to Madrid, where he spent a day alone in the Prado. 'I cannot tell you what a wonderful experience my visit to the Prado was,' he wrote to Lindy. 'It was odd to have such a very vivid experience, when otherwise I found myself alone in an unsympathetic enormous city, without a friend or a word of Spanish. But after I had that experience I felt I must get away and home the sooner the better.'[9]

One disturbing event during his holiday in Spain had been the arrival of Diana Holman-Hunt, whose book *My Grandmothers and I* had made Duncan laugh out loud. She was a tall, witty, glamorous woman with large, pale blue eyes, seldom seen without a cigarette, and who spoke, moved and dressed with mesmerising elegance. Her second husband had died of cancer in his forties and she had moved to London where Edward le Bas, who was intensely moved by both male and female beauty, fell in love with her at first sight. When Edward confided to Duncan that he was thinking of marrying her, Duncan was horrified, dreading the effect she would have on their regular gatherings at Edward's house and studio in Glebe Place. Diana laughed a lot, cracked jokes like a youth and was fond of wearing gleaming brocades, none of which Duncan objected to, but which cumulatively increased her powerful presence. However, she was to remain le Bas's intimate companion until his death in 1966. They did not marry, both preferring freedom and independence. Moreover, each said the other was unmarriageable, she claiming he drank too much, and he protesting she talked too much, and neither disputing the other's claim.

At San Roque Edward had insisted on taking Diana into Duncan's bedroom to say goodnight. They found him cocooned in dressing-gowns. She was very put off by the chamber pot left in the middle of the floor, while he continued to regard her with suspicion. In times to come Diana often amused him but could not entirely disarm him. It was perhaps a deliberate policy on Edward's part that he never again combined Diana and Duncan on the same trip. And he was to organise many more, for in the course of this holiday he and his friends visited Brenan in Málaga and on their return stopped at Marbella, where le Bas was seduced into buying a magnificently situated house.

After a bout of Spanish cooking, Duncan was glad to be back at Charleston with Grace. Lord Gage's elder son, Sammy, who was living nearby and managing farmland, liked to drop in on Duncan, finished off Grace's scones in a twinkling and agreed to sit for his portrait. 'I find life here alone rather peaceful,' Duncan told Lindy. 'It gives one time to think over all the things that have happened to one, and I do not mind being alone, in fact I like it.'[10] News of others reached him by letter. The concert pianist Harriet Cohen, whom he had first met in the early 1930s and who had doted on his pictures since first seeing some as a teenager at the Mansard Gallery, was a friend of George Bergen and on a visit to New York in 1961 she wrote to Duncan: 'George here talks of you incessantly: he says he *can't* write to you because he has so much to say, *too* much! But he thinks of you all the time.'[11] Despite his wife's sweetness of character, George seemed trapped, a fact not helped, Harriet Cohen thought, by their small daughter, Margaret, who tended to play each parent off against the other. Not long after this she wrote again to inform Duncan that George and Helen Bergen had separated.

'Here I am mostly alone, quite content,' ran the refrain in Duncan's letters to Lindy, 'though I sometimes wish you were painting the same still life.'[12] After failing to win a place at the Slade, Lindy had driven with Angelica to Florence, where she stayed on to paint. Duncan was keen to hear what she was painting and whether she had been to see the Fra Angelicos. He wanted also to know how she got on in Austria, where in August she went to take lessons with Kokoschka. It was as if suddenly he could admit an interest he might have pursued more fully in connection with his own daughter, had his relationship with her not been compromised by pretence. With Lindy he was openly paternal: he urged her to get a house of her own so that she would feel more solidly established. When she found 24 Holland Park Road, she asked him to help her make it homely and 'Duncanish'. She had already bought three of his paintings and a screen and over the years acquired an important collection of his work. She continued to drop into his life *en route* to Ireland, New York or somewhere else, her *mouvementé* existence grounded by her love of painting.

Duncan himself turned up in a variety of places. He went to Glyndebourne, as a guest of Lady Birley, widow of the portrait painter Sir Oswald Birley, who lived at Charleston Manor; he appeared at the Connollys' cocktail parties and at Bunny's seventieth birthday party in London, where he was charmed by the sight of Bunny's now teenage daughters. He visited Mrs Hammersley in the Isle of Wight and was entertained by her imitation of 'Lucian Fraud', as she called the painter whom she met occasionally at the Devonshires'. Then 'Gumbo', as Marjorie Strachey was affectionately nicknamed, invited Duncan to the opera, to hear Handel's *Alcina*, on the slightly alarming condition that he should support her on the stairs.

In the summer of 1962 Duncan took Paul to Lady Aberconway's yearly cocktail party. As a hostess, Christabel Aberconway had been on the crest of her wave during the interwar period; but if now something of a relic, she remained a buoyant one, with considerable intelligence beneath her artificial manners. She had moved to 12 North Audley Street, to a house tucked between shops and picture galleries. As Duncan hoped, the party was useful to Paul, Lady Bridget Parsons and Lady Bonham-Carter both agreeing to host salons at which he would read aloud his poems. When Duncan sat at table to eat cakes and chocolate-covered strawberries, he found he was next to one of the richest men in the world, Paul Getty, who seemed to Duncan, on this slight meeting, also one of the saddest.

Roche continued to join Duncan on his regular two-day visits to London. Owing to a demolition order, Duncan had to move flat in September 1961 and was offered the top floor of 24 Victoria Square, a house owned by Leonard Woolf and occupied by various tenants. His nephew, Cecil Woolf, and his wife Malya had the basement and ground floor, a communal sitting-room took up most of the first floor while the two bedrooms on the second floor were used by the publisher Ian Parsons and his wife Trekkie, Ian staying at his club and ceding his rights to Leonard when their visits overlapped. This was the first move Duncan undertook without the benefit of Vanessa's calm practicality and it completely undid him. Paul found him sitting among his unsorted belongings and furniture at 24 Victoria Square in a state of emotional collapse, unable to focus on the mess. 'I think it's simpler just to die,' he told Paul.

His tenancy at 24 Victoria Square was at best a mixed success. Clarissa Roche helped brighten his rooms by renewing curtains and covers, and it was pleasant to discover that his neighbour was Mrs Constance Sitwell, author of several short autobiographical books with a strong spiritualist bent. She was a year younger than Duncan but crippled by a fall and he rarely turned up at the square without bringing her flowers from Charleston. But his habit of giving keys to the house not only to the Roche family but also to Iain MacLeod and other young friends, who clattered up and down the stairs late at night, angered Leonard, who also remarked on the appalling state of Duncan's living-room.

'Duncan doesn't make one think of age at all,' Frances Partridge wrote in her diary that year.[13] She did, however, wonder if Vanessa's death might affect the silence that still clouded Angelica's parentage. At one party, after Duncan had gone to get Angelica a drink, Christabel Aberconway turned to her and said, 'I *have* sometimes thought that *that* man was your father.' Angelica changed the subject to Clive, hoping that Christabel would take the hint, but she returned to the attack a little later with other remarks, which again Angelica squashed. 'The same sort of thing has happened to me several times lately,' Angelica complained to Duncan, 'and can be embarrassing as though I would love to acknowledge myself openly as your daughter I suppose Clive might mind, and no-one ever seems to think of that. However, I only tell you all this because I think it would be sensible to let the children know of this fact . . . this sort of ambiguousness about the whole thing *en famille* seems to me a little ridiculous.'[14] At around this time David Cecil, quite unconsciously, transgressed the silence surrounding this subject by referring in conversation with Duncan to 'your grand-daughter'. Those present at the dinner table froze with interest at what Duncan's reaction might be. He blinked and paused, but showed no visible surprise, though this was probably the first time he publicly acknowledged his grandchildren and, by implication, Angelica.

From Angelica he learnt in May that his granddaughter, Henrietta, had fallen in love with Frances Partridge's son, Burgo, a fascinating, slightly nervy character who in 1956 had published a book called *A History of Orgies*. Amaryllis, meanwhile, had opted for the acting profession. With her in mind, Bunny and Angelica bought a London *pied-à-terre*, a houseboat called *Moby Dick* moored at Battersea Bridge. The two youngest sisters, Fanny and Nerissa, were now fourteen, 'take eight-and-a-half shoes and will be terrifying young women if they continue to practise judo,' observed their mother.[15] Because Henrietta, of all four sisters, had the greatest gift for home-making, Angelica did not oppose her marriage to Burgo that year, though Henrietta was only seventeen. The wedding took place at Chelsea Town Hall on 22 December 1962, with Duncan acting as a witness along with Burgo's best man, David Gillies. Frances Partridge and Amaryllis were also present. Afterwards they went back to their flat in Cadogan Square for lobster mayonnaise and cherry tart, Duncan having provided the champagne and Angelica a professionally made cake ornamented with two partridges designed by her. That Christmas Duncan chose to stay at Hilton Hall instead of Chatsworth, turning down an invitation from the Devonshires in favour of his daughter, who was greatly pleased.

Soon after Duncan's 1959 retrospective, the Tate bought one of his earliest extant paintings, *The Kitchen*, and he gave a drawing to the Cecil Higgins Art Gallery in Bedford. Further works entered public collections when, in 1963, the National Portrait Gallery acquired one of his portraits of Vanessa and the curator Carol Hogben began preparations for an exhibition at the Victoria and Albert Museum to celebrate the fiftieth anniversary of the founding of the Omega Workshops. Duncan agreed to sell his Omega signboard to this museum for forty pounds, negotiations also beginning for the eventual acquisition of his *Blue Sheep Screen*. In addition, it was pleasing to be made an honorary member of the London Group, to be visited at Charleston by a young artist eager to meet him, Philip Sutton, and to be invited (though he did not accept) by Arthur Lett-Haines to visit the East Anglian School of Painting, which he and Cedric Morris ran at Benton End in Hadleigh, Suffolk.

John Nash, with whom Duncan renewed his acquaintance, learnt that Duncan wanted a show at the Minories in Colchester. Nash, who lived nearby, liaised with the curator J. Wood Palmer and helped make possible the exhibition, which took place in April 1963. Though it attracted scant critical attention, it earned Duncan almost £1,000. Grateful for this proof that his worst period of neglect was now over, he was as pleased to hear in February 1962 that Angelica was exhibiting some of her paintings in a Cambridgeshire pub with Gwen Raverat's daughter, Sophie Pryor. Meanwhile Lindy's career as a painter, he now realised, would always have to battle against the circumstances that swept her along. 'I went to a very pleasant gathering of young people at Lindy's in London,' he wrote to Clive in June. 'She had come to the conclusion that bathing in the lagoons of Florida, meeting the Kennedys, and dancing with princes, was [a] waste of time. But in spite of that I think she got some fun.'[16] Clive, too, had fallen for Lindy who, learning of his favourite tipple, sent him a half-dozen bottles of Nuits St Georges.

When Duncan lunched with Edward le Bas at Brighton in July 1963, he found him very low, partly because his doctor had ordered him not to drink spirits. 'I am afraid that Holman Hunt has seized the opportunity of his being ill to take every liberty of being kind and helpful,' he wrote to Lindy.[17] Owing to complex emotional problems, le Bas had succumbed to bouts of debilitating depression. Meanwhile Humphrey Brooke, the Secretary at the Royal Acadamy, asked Diana Holman-Hunt to persuade le Bas to let the RA mount an exhibition of his collection. The interest that this aroused in him was timely and in Diana Holman-Hunt's opinion this show, entitled 'A Painter's Collection' – le Bas refusing to have his name used in the title – added another three years to his life.

In July 1963 Alan Bowness of the Courtauld Institute of Art wrote to

Duncan, asking if one of his final-year students, Sarah Oppenheim, could question him about his early work. She came that summer, to find both Duncan and Clive at Charleston, though the latter seemed grumpy, old and unwilling to involve himself much with the young visitor. Feeling on this first visit a little out of her depth, she nevertheless remarked that the painting hanging over the fireplace in Clive's book room, which Duncan had bought in Paris in 1921 thinking it might be by Dughet, looked like a Poussin. She asked if she might bring it to the attention of the Courtauld lecturer and Poussin expert, Anthony Blunt. Duncan agreed, and in return sought her advice on the merits of a television. (Lindy had offered to give Duncan one of these, in addition to paying for a new downstairs lavatory to be installed at Charleston.) 'P.S.,' Sarah's letter of thanks ended, 'I strongly recommend a television.'[18]

Blunt came to look at the painting with his colleague John Shearman, a specialist in Poussin's landscapes. They took it back to London to have it X-rayed and investigated under infra-red light, after which it sat for a while in Blunt's room at the Courtauld Institute. He had thought that the snake, from which a man appears to be fleeing, might be a later addition, but it proved genuine. He therefore concluded that, in its study of fear, the picture was a trial run for the painting in the National Gallery, in which a man has been killed by a snake. According to Blunt, the picture had once belonged to the celebrated Italian patron, Cassiano dal Pozzo. To Duncan, Blunt wrote saying that he would sell everything he could in order to buy it, should Duncan ever consider selling the painting. The financial situation at Charleston was such that Blunt's offer could not be ignored. Only the year previously Clive had had to sell his Picasso still-life, Quentin painting a copy of it which, like Vanessa's copy of the Vlaminck, now hangs in the garden room. As soon as Blunt heard that Duncan would sell, he obtained estimates from Colnaghi's, Christie's, the National Gallery and Tommas Harris. These ranged between £10,000 and £12,000 and Blunt offered Duncan the top price, in three lump sums of £4,000 each.[19]

During this period Duncan struggled valiantly with a portrait of Peter Pears, first mooted in September 1962, when Duncan met Pears by chance during a fortnight's holiday in Venice. A month later Duncan wrote to Pears, pursuing the idea and also suggesting that sittings should take place in Holland Park Road, in Lindy's large studio. Duncan had heard Pears sing on several occasions and was present at the performance of Britten's *War Requiem* at the Albert Hall on 9 January 1963. This was not the first performance, for the piece had been commissioned to celebrate the opening of the new Coventry Cathedral, but it was the first at which Galina Vishnevskaya finally sang the part that had been written for her. 'I was immensely moved and electrified by the beauty of the music,' Duncan wrote afterwards, 'and by the performance – every word you sang was clear and I need not say beautiful . . . Ben must have been happy at the way that enormous audience rose to their feet to show what I thought was an absolutely sincere enthusiasm for his work.'[20] After listening to Britten's setting of Wilfred Owen's eerie poem 'Strange Meeting', Duncan had a not unsimilar experience, for there in the foyer was Charlotte Bonham-Carter, grasping his hand in greeting though only a week before he had read that she had died. Concluding that she must be a ghost, he escaped her grasp as quickly as he could and fled. (A tenacious lover of the arts, she in fact outlived him.)

According to Paul Roche, the portrait of Pears began well. In September 1963 Duncan decided more work needed doing to it, especially the face and hands. A year later, at a time when Pears began negotiations for Duncan's *Les Femmes Savantes*, a richly colourful oil based on the *commedia dell'arte*, Duncan was working on a larger version of his original study. Six years later, however, he confessed, 'I must tell you that my portrait of you turned out to be a complete failure. I worked on the head a good deal, but only to bad effect.' In compensation, Duncan offered Pears as a birthday present a drawing he had done of Pears's head and hands during one sitting at Victoria Square. This proved acceptable and the drawing, together with *Les Femmes Savantes* and other works by Duncan, remains part of the Red House collection at Aldeburgh.

Whereas formal and commissioned portraits often proved difficult, when Duncan worked casually, during a couple of sittings, at a likeness of a friend, he generally had happier results. On one of his visits to Long Crichel he painted a lively sketch of Desmond Shawe-Taylor sitting at his writing desk. Shawe-Taylor did not pretend to pose, but got on with his work, which involved darting round the room in search of facts and references for *The Record Guide*, on which he collaborated with Eddy Sackville-West. Equally observant was the portrait of Duncan that his fellow guest, Frances Partridge, composed in her diary:

> In his stained ill-fitting suit he looks rather like a Jewish pawnbroker, standing a little apologetically and as if about to shuffle or rub his hands together; rather hunched, looking up and blinking anxiously at us from his still forget-me-not-blue eyes in a crumpled rose-petal face. Yet his air of apology, seeming to say, 'I don't really know how to behave. I'm not concerned with the world and its values'. This

childlike innocence wouldn't take in anyone, nor does it take in Duncan himself. He has an excellent opinion of himself and quite right too, is probably well aware of his terrific power to charm, and certainly confident that his values are the right ones, and that what he excludes and doesn't know about isn't worth knowing. I think this self-confidence and lack of self-criticism (which could also be called unselfconsciousness) is the salient thing about his character, and derives from the fact that so many people have loved him and been in love with him, and Bloomsbury always spoiled him and laughed delightedly at his half-conscious wit. Buoyed up by which, he's been able to dedicate himself simply and directly to what he wanted to do. He must be ranked, along with Bunny, among the happiest men alive.[21]

Duncan rang up Frances Partridge in the summer of 1963, concerned that there had been no news about Burgo and Henrietta's baby, which was overdue. Eventually, on 9 August, after a dangerously long period of labour, Henrietta underwent a Caesarean and Sophie was born, Duncan becoming a great-grandfather. He arrived at the hospital clutching flowers from Charleston and a picture by Janie Bussy, which, with the aid of a nail and a hammer that he had brought with him, he hung on the wall. He brought messages from Grace and Clive, kissed Henrietta and wept when he saw the baby.

Angelica and Bunny had been in France at the time of Sophie's birth, staying in a house they had bought in an ancient village, St-Martin de Vers, a stronghold of the Knights Templar in the twelfth century, some twenty miles from Cahors in the Lot. Duncan joined them in September and there they heard the shocking news about Burgo who had, at the age of twenty-eight, died suddenly and wholly unexpectedly of a heart attack, leaving Henrietta, at the age of eighteen, a widow. Bunny immediately flew back to England and then brought Henrietta and Sophie back with him to France. Henrietta recalls that Duncan's presence was 'of incalculable comfort to me. We seldom, he and I, referred directly to the terrible inescapable tragedy of Burgo's death but we were very close to one another and, in his feline way, he lent me courage. I shall never forget his kindness to me when we sat on the old town wall at St Cirque la Popie and examined the toad flax and saxifrages and he gave me his handkerchief.'[22]

After Henrietta returned to London, Duncan recounted what had happened to Lindy:

Angelica has had a heartrending tragedy in her family. Henrietta's
husband Burgo Partridge to whom she was only married for a little

over [under] a year, died suddenly, from some sort of heart trouble. He was telephoning to a friend when it happened. I was terribly sorry for his mother whose only child he was, and for poor little Henrietta who still seems a child to me. However enough of these horrors. Henrietta has taken it all in a wonderful way, not at all hysterical, and thank goodness has a little baby, who must have her attention. She came here for a complete change and flew back to London yesterday from Bordeaux.[23]

The following spring, after Henrietta had moved with Sophie to Spain, Duncan saw her several times during the course of another visit to Edward le Bas's house at Marbella. He was glad that Frances Partridge's friend, Janetta Jackson, was staying nearby and could keep an eye on his granddaughter. When Lindy joined him, he marvelled at the way in which she left her other life behind and painted with great intensity. Once before at Marbella, Duncan had found himself embroiled in a great many cocktail parties by Edward's sister and brother-in-law, Brocas and Molly Burrows. That year they were again present, but cocktail parties were out, as Molly was convinced that an operation to improve her nose had left her disfigured. When the matter was brought to his attention, Duncan confessed that he had not noticed any difference.

Early in 1964 Barbara Bagenal spread the rumour that Duncan was often lonely at Charleston. Angelica resolved to make more regular visits, something she could more easily do if she was based in London. That spring her two youngest daughters were away and Bunny was teaching at Southern Illinois University. Angelica was therefore able to rent a studio at 404 Fulham Road from Derry Moore, a young man whom Lindy had introduced. It was, in effect, a bid for independence. For some time now Angelica had resented the demands Bunny made on her, partly because, as she told Bunny, she had reached a stage in her life when the demands of her own nature seemed imperative. 'Also there are a good many demands to answer; the children, then I think probably more and more Duncan, who I must go and see as often as I can, because I think he is lonelier now than he will admit, also his memory is rapidly becoming worse.'[24]

Behind her dissatisfaction lay a complex history and the inchoate recognition that at the start of her marriage, having never enjoyed a full parental relationship with her real father, she had looked for a father substitute. Visiting Charleston in February, Angelica found herself suddenly overwhelmed by the past and she succumbed to depression. 'Duncan was of course charming,' she told Bunny; '. . . I had hoped to paint a picture as a neighbour's daughter was coming to sit, but what is so exasparating is that once I am there [at Charleston] I no longer feel my own identity; my eyes get full of all the colours and patterns I see there, which I long to dissociate myself from – the result is a ghastly constipation and absolute misery – nothing I do is right and at the same time I pretend that all is well or Duncan gets distressed.'[25]

A more detached visitor, Frances Partridge, experienced Charleston very differently. 'Yesterday I drove Henrietta and Sophie to Charleston to stay with Duncan,' she wrote in her diary, 'and here we all are.'

As we approached the smooth couchant, enormously high shapes of the downs a pervasive calm and contentment enveloped us – Henrietta and me, at any rate, for Sophie was by now asleep. It has been with me ever since. Plunged in this Old Bloomsbury civilisation (for all we may have laughed at its 'croquet hoops', and the paint peeling here and there) I am over-powered with pleasure and emotion at the sense that all round me *real* values have been aimed at and achieved, and that the house, garden and all it contains is a unique work of art, something lovingly created and kept alive . . . One thing I am absolutely convinced of is that the lasting value of what Old Bloomsbury stood for and did will go on being recognised – indeed it *is* being recognised. Duncan says that with his pictures it is people between thirty-five and fifty who find them too old-fashioned, and the young are beginning to like them again . . . I have been so emotionally stirred all the time I was here by the first-rateness of this Bloomsbury world, the charm of Duncan, the calm and peace which gently lapped us round from the beautiful downs which have been all weekend swathed in tepid mist . . . it's like the repeated reassertion of something one believes to be true and is glad is true. Last night, very gay, delightful talk, and some television-watching in the studio for the three of us, Duncan, Henrietta and me. Sophie has all day padded happily about crooning in a sweet, high voice . . . and occasionally pointing at the pictures with a little cry.[26]

In March 1964, at the opening of Vanessa Bell's memorial exhibition organised by Ronald Pickvance for the Arts Council, Duncan met Richard Morphet, who three years before had bought Vanessa's *Iris Tree*. He was invited to visit Charleston, arrived in May, and between lunch and tea was given a tour of the house and its paintings. His exuberant response acted like a tonic on Duncan, who was pleased when in the summer Richard asked to come again. 'He's very charming,' Duncan afterwards wrote to Angelica, 'and wildly enthusiastic about the 1914 period!'[27] On later visits – with Sally Richmond, whom he married in 1965, and eventually with his two daughters – Richard occasionally purchased one of Duncan's paintings, taking meticulous care that Duncan should not, as was his habit, charge too low a price. 'We should greatly love to live with more of your work,' he wrote, 'but we should hate to do so at your expense.'[28]

In September 1964 Richard Morphet sent a sympathetic message to Duncan after Clive died in a London nursing home. One unexpected visitor, during his last days, had been his old flame, Mary Hutchinson. He took pleasure also in Frances Partridge's visits, while loyal Barbara Bagenal went in every day at four in the afternoon, to read to him and to give him tea and supper. When the end came, she was exhausted and went down to Charleston for a week's rest. Duncan now showed her greater friendliness and occasionally visited her at Rye, where her small house on Hucksteps Row looked out over Romney Marsh. There she sat by her window, a little bored, depressed and rheumatic, but always enlivened by talk of Bloomsbury. In the last months of Clive's life she had slept with her bedroom door open so that she could hear if he called, and for a while after his death she woke regularly in the night, thinking that she had heard his voice.

Earlier that year Duncan had lost his friend Mrs Hammersley, but Clive's death hit him far harder, for it removed a source of humour, shared memory and benign understanding. 'His company and wit and sympathy were like wine and food of the best and most invigorating sort,' John Betjeman wrote to Duncan.[29] 'You must feel,' Raymond Mortimer commented, 'that a whole vast area of your life has now ceased to exist except in your memory.'[30]

A month after Clive died, Lindy Guinness married Sheridan, the Marquess of Dufferin and Ava. It was a tremendous affair, the ceremony taking place in Westminster Abbey and mustering a hundred members of the Guinness family, as well as the Queen and Princess Margaret and a bevy of bridesmaids. Edward le Bas refused to go, but Grace Higgens was thrilled to be invited and enjoyed it hugely. Duncan also climbed willingly into morning dress and sent Lindy a note, which reached her on the morning of her wedding. 'Darling Duncan, I loved your letter this morning – I'm also thinking of you getting into all those fancy clothes!! – how terrifying it all is. Kisses, Lindy.'[31]

The other event that occupied him this month was his forthcoming retrospective at the Wildenstein Gallery in Bond Street. There had been a terrible two days in August when, helped by Paul, he had sorted through all his pictures in both the big studio and the outer studio, which was largely used as a store. Some 200 paintings had been sent to Wildenstein for the art historian Denys Sutton to look at and select what he needed for the show. 'It is very harrowing looking over the work of years,' Duncan admitted to Angelica, 'and I have no critical powers left.'[32] In fact, he took more care than usual over this show, spending a lot of time altering, varnishing, signing and occasionally dating paintings, not always accurately.

The exhibition, entitled 'Duncan Grant and His World', opened in early November, partly in celebration of Duncan's eightieth birthday the following January. There were ninety-one of his pictures on show, as well as a wall of thirteen paintings by artists whom Duncan had either known or admired – Cézanne, Matisse, Sickert, Fry, Bussy, Derain, Marchand, Vlaminck, Segonzac, Matthew Smith, Vanessa Bell and Edward le Bas. The selection paid scant tribute to Duncan's pre-1910 work but gave the impression, overall, of a more complete representation than the Tate Gallery retrospective of 1959. Yet although this exhibition acknowledged his return to favour, it was an awkward moment for his art to be reviewed: recent exhibitions had introduced a British audience to the American avant-garde and the resulting trend towards large-scale abstract art made Bloomsbury painting seem very English, dilettantish and old-fashioned. In addition, Bloomsbury's critical reputation was at its lowest ebb. 'Their comfortable, moneyed indulgence of life and of *beautiful things* seems to us now to belong more to the twilight of old England than to the dawn which they believed they were heralding,' wrote Edward Mullins in the *Sunday Telegraph*.[33] The *Daily Mail* referred to Duncan as 'the most illustrious "unknown" living British painter',[34] while Terence Mullaly, in the *Daily Telegraph*, denounced him with the remark that there had been no development in his art since 1939, other than 'a descent into trivial decoration'. 'Duncan Grant', he concluded, 'is a minor artist capable of perceptive portraits and decorative charm. Where this exhibition does his reputation a disservice is in its inclusion of a wallful of pictures by Cézanne, Matisse, Matthew Smith and others.'[35]

Fortunately the public ignored the critics: Duncan was much fêted and the paintings sold well. In all he earnt almost £5,000 – Wildenstein, for tax reasons, spreading payment over the next two or three years.

The success of this show also revived interest in him as a personality. Nevile Wallis wrote a profile of Duncan for the *Sunday Telegraph Magazine*, which was accompanied by a large colour photograph of him, eating fried eggs and bacon and drinking Harvey's beer (which he bought by the crate) in the dining-room at Charleston. Those who had known him in earlier days were astonished that at seventy-nine his hair was still dark. Another photograph, taken in the studio, showed his painting bench, on which sat the television that Lindy had bought, surrounded by brushes, paints and jam jars. The article's by-line read: 'A past that lingers.'[36]

That winter, in the wake of Clive's death and despite the success of his Wildenstein show, Duncan felt out of fashion. So he told Franzi von Haas, with whom he still kept in touch. 'Do you think that Matisse or Cézanne will ever growe [sic] out of fashion,' Franzi upbraided him. 'I don't, and in any way I feel your work is more complete than theirs.'[37] As if in support of Franzi's words, a letter arrived out of the blue from Richard Shone, a fifteen-year-old schoolboy at Wrekin College, Shropshire, who had read William Gaunt's review in The Times of Duncan's show and had sent to Wildenstein's for a catalogue. Duncan replied and a correspondence developed. In time Shone visited Charleston and, as he was a great admirer of Virginia Woolf, Duncan took him to tea with Leonard. Thereafter he soon became one of Duncan's close friends.

Two of Duncan's friends died in 1965, Helen Anrep and Eddy Sackville-West. Perhaps because the familiar faces were fewer in number, Duncan welcomed visitors of all kinds to Charleston. Leonard used to bring the actress Peggy Ashcroft, Eardley Knollys, his friend, the frame-maker Mattei Radev. The artist and teacher George Hooper became a friend and painted in the garden, while another who swam into Duncan's ken at this time was the novelist Francis King, who had recently settled in Brighton. Whenever he came to Charleston he noticed the cold terribly and had to get up from the table in the dining-room in the middle of lunch or tea, pleading need of the bathroom, in order to keep warm. 'Are you unwell?' Duncan would ask solicitously. A temporary coldness affected King's friendship with Duncan after the novelist put a likeness of the painter into his character Maurice Rhodes in A Domestic Animal. For the dustjacket King persuaded the publishers to use a watercolour by Duncan of a male nude. They agreed, but were worried by the male member and deliberately placed the 'K' in the author's name over it. 'This prissy action aroused Duncan's scorn,' King recalls.[38]

Through Francis King, Duncan met the writer John Haylock, who never forgot how the spry, eighty-year-old painter showed him and King round the house without demur or apparent effort. 'His quiet voice, his modest, courteous manner were the first things that impressed me. Gently, he would, if asked, disclose information about a picture, a decorated door, a panel.'[39] Haylock also recalled that on this occasion he bought two drawings, and Francis King an oil, from Duncan, who seemed almost apologetic about asking them to pay for what they had chosen. After the visit Haylock, who had a house in Cyprus where he

449

spent the better part of the year, rang Ripe 265 whenever he was in Brighton, in the hope of hearing Duncan's soft, diffident 'Hello?', and was often invited to lunch or tea.

In 1965 Duncan heard again from the Courtauld student Sarah Oppenheim, who had recently married an art dealer, Clovis Whitfield. She had now begun her research into Bloomsbury painters and writers, with particular reference to Roger Fry, partly because she had been asked to help Ronald Pickvance with an exhibition, 'Vision and Design', dealing with Fry's work as both painter and critic, and which was to be held at the University of Nottingham in 1966. 'In view of both jobs,' Sarah Whitfield wrote to Duncan, 'I wondered if I might catalogue the contents of your studio (but only if this is in accordance with your wishes) sometime during July.'[40]

Her visit to Charleston that summer lasted five days. Perhaps because she was there, Duncan did less painting than usual. Certainly she received the impression that he was pottering in his studio rather than painting. She found him very companionable, happy to talk about Roger Fry or Lady Ottoline Morrell, but the numbers of unsold paintings struck her as tragic. At one moment she picked up his *Self-Portrait in a Turban* and put it on the mantelpiece. Duncan looked at it for a long time and then asked her if she liked it and was pleased when she said yes. It seemed to give him pleasure to look at one of his paintings with someone who had never seen it before. When she left he asked her to choose a painting as a gift, which she did: a side-view portrait of David Garnett painted during the First World War. 'Wouldn't you like something more recent?' Duncan asked.[41]

Feeling rather rich after the success of his Wildenstein show, Duncan bid thirty pounds in December 1964 and obtained at auction a portfolio of Simon Bussy pastels of animals, among them a snake and a monkey, which he had framed and then hung in the studio at Charleston. The following year his own work helped to form the beginning of an art collection that Dr Malcolm Easton was buying for the University of Hull. That year, too, Quentin, together with a Victoria and Albert Museum purchase grant, helped the University of Leeds acquire fifteen Duncan Grant drawings. Duncan himself donated some watercolours by his mother's protector, Colonel Alfred Harcourt, to the India Office Library, and a year later, in 1966, lodged some of his papers with King's College, Cambridge. The Librarian, A. N. L. Munby, thanked Duncan for allowing 'the box of your correspondence and papers to be added to those deposited in the College Library by Quentin Bell ... It is splendid to have so much of the material for the history of "Bloomsbury" in one place.'[42] Duncan's awareness of the past was further stirred that year by the Roger Fry exhibition 'Vision and Design', at which he re-met his fellow assistant at the Omega, Winifred Gill. The meeting aroused such memories that afterwards she sent him a series of letters containing many details and anecdotes about the Workshops.

One side-effect of this interest in the past was that Angelica now urged Duncan to hold back Vanessa's increasingly valuable pre-1914 work. When two young men, Dick Chapman and Ben Duncan, moved into a recently built house outside Cambridge – very pure, austere and deliberately curtainless – they decided that one or two paintings by Vanessa Bell would help to warm and enhance their new environment. At the suggestion of a friend, Chapman wrote to Angelica, who replied enthusiastically and advised him to approach Duncan. The result was an invitation to lunch at Charleston, after which Duncan took Chapman up to the attic studio to look through piles of Vanessa's canvases. He put to one side those that interested Chapman and was pleased with the two paintings he eventually bought, though a portrait of Lytton Strachey and an early painting of Studland Bay were vetoed by Angelica.

Occasional commissions still came Duncan's way. He received twenty pounds for an illustration to Virginia Woolf's short story 'Nurse Lugton's Golden Thimble', first published in *The Times Literary Supplement* on 17 June 1965. While the nurse sleeps over her sewing, the animals on the fabric underneath her hands come to life. The story, which Virginia had written for her niece Ann Stephen, had been found by Wallace Hildick in the manuscript of *Mrs Dalloway* in the British Museum. Leonard liked it enough to reprint it in 1966, in the form of a cloth-bound quarto volume with six illustrations by Duncan in black, white and grey. A more significant commission came via his old friend Arthur Waley: in February 1965 the Folio Society decided to publish an edition of *Monkey* in Waley's translation with either eight or twelve illustrations. Duncan opted for twelve, making vibrant use of only two colours, but also sometimes using the white of the paper to create positive shapes. He gained ideas from a book that Cyril Connolly lent him on monkeys, and in some illustrations deliberately employed a Chinese style. In his initial letter Waley had told Duncan that the publisher would even accept abstract illustrations, if he felt that way inclined. He did, but only for the outer boards of the book, on which a line takes a walk with great freedom, meets a few black dots and finds the shapes it creates reinforced by an orange-red opaque wash. This unfussed design has a sumptuous effect.

In order to discuss this project, Duncan had gone to see Waley at his home in Southwood Lane, Highgate. There he met the New Zealander Alison Grant Robertson, who had for many years been a background figure in Waley's life and had shared it openly since the death of Beryl de Zoete, with whom Waley had always been associated. Waley, who was to die of cancer of the spine, was already ill when in 1966 he and Alison had a car crash that broke his spine. A message reached Duncan from Gerald Brenan, telling him that Waley was now paralysed from his armpits down, was often doped or in pain, but had one or two lucid hours a day when he liked to see old friends and felt abandoned if they did not visit. He was not expected to live much longer. A note from Alison also warned Duncan that Waley might not recognise him or be able to speak. 'I went to see Arthur Waley last week,' Duncan wrote to Bunny, ' – he looked like a corpse, but was made comfortable by that admirable character Alison, whom he married as it were on his deathbed, and he seemed to enjoy her conversation with me. She drove me back to the station so wrecklessly [*sic*] that I wondered if she had been the cause of the accident, but did not dare to ask.'[43]

What shocked him more in February 1966 was to learn that Angelica and Bunny were thinking of getting a divorce. Angelica explained that she felt her whole self had suffered from her attempt to be what Bunny wanted, at a time when she was developing very differently. Duncan admitted that he had been ignorant of any difficulties and had thought that she had taken the house in London with Bunny's approval, in order to have some leisure to paint, now that her children were out in the world. His response was gentle, kind, sympathetic and detached. Partly because Angelica's children were now independent, he did not try to influence her decision. However, three months later the couple decided to get together again – 'Bunny has been most marvellously generous and unreproachful,' Angelica told Duncan.[44] But in the course of the previous months there had been revelations that altered the basis of their marriage and the reunion was not to last, though separation rather than divorce was the final outcome.

'*Toujours la peinture*,' Duncan flung out at Charleston as Donald Milner, the Honorary Secretary of the Royal West of England Academy, and its President, Lord Methuen, took their leave. They had been making preparations with Duncan for an exhibition of his and Vanessa's work, which the RWEA mounted in Bristol in 1966, alongside a display of designs by Phyllis Barron and Dorothy Larcher, whose work had carried further the modernist emphasis begun at the Omega. Duncan showed fifty-four paintings to Vanessa's fifty-eight and earnt £1,395. Milner passed on the many tributes that the show received. His own opinion was that some of the most recent pictures, painted a few months before, while Duncan was staying with the art dealer Rex Nan Kivell at Tangier, made the freest use of colour. Milner was in effect registering the repercussions on Duncan's art of a major Bonnard exhibition held in February 1966, at the Royal Academy. Duncan had been so moved by it that he came to the conclusion, as he told Derry Moore, that Bonnard was the greatest painter after Cézanne.

John Betjeman opened the Bristol show, in return for which he was invited to Charleston in July. He was entranced by it and afterwards wrote a thank-you letter which, as he admitted, made him sound 'like a gushing actress writing a Collins but – but I mean what I say'.[45] The following month Duncan went to the Garnetts' house at St-Martin de Vers, but before leaving made a visit to the Tate in order to see his recently restored Borough Polytechnic decoration, *The Bathers*, a picture he had not seen for fifty-five years. 'I am rather agitated at the idea of seeing my picture hung between a Matisse and a Picasso,' he told Richard Morphet.[46] He was agreeably surprised to see how much had been achieved at the Tate under its new director, Norman Reid, and resolved to visit it more frequently.

A further plan that he and Paul had hatched took them to New York in October. They flew out on 4 October and were met at Kennedy airport by George Bergen, whom Duncan had not seen since the 1930s, and by Derry Moore and Mrs Pat Gilbert-Read, with whom Paul stayed while Duncan accepted George's hospitality at 38 Central Park South. Derry Moore was running a travel agency in New York and willingly acted as their chauffeur in the evenings. Each morning he arrived to take Duncan to breakfast at Rumpelmeyer's, which was suitably pink and old-fashioned, and afterwards Duncan followed a packed itinerary, visiting the Frick, the Museum of Modern Art, the Metropolitan, the Whitney and the Guggenheim Museum, which, with its spiralling ramp, as his diary notes record, made him feel dizzy. He attended a reading of Paul's, called on Betty Parsons at her gallery, with an introduction from Lindy, and met artists in Greenwich Village. He was also present at a party given by the collector Ben Sonnenberg, in Grammercy Square, and dined with the lawyer Millaird Bloomer. Derry took him inside the Lincoln Opera House to see decorations by Chagall and Dufy and to the United Nations building, where Duncan admired a Chagall window, a Picasso tapestry and a Barbara Hepworth sculpture.

He accompanied Paul to hear him read from his *Agamemnon* translation at Yale. Over drinks a member of the faculty offered to drive Duncan to Boston the next day to see its art museum and the Isabella

453

Stewart Gardner collection. Other trips included a visit to Philadelphia and to Washington, where Duncan and Paul were joined by Derry, who noticed, during their return to New York, that Duncan fell asleep the moment he sat down in the aeroplane, and in general appeared self-contained and unfettered by anxiety or guilt. He always seemed pleased to see people but, Derry noticed, never played on his age or vulnerability in order to make them feel wrong-footed when they left. It also startled Derry one day, in the course of a discussion about pornography, to learn that Duncan was for it. 'Why?' Derry asked. 'Because it gives pleasure,' came the reply.[47]

'It was a great joy your being in New York,' Derry afterwards wrote to Duncan, 'and added very considerable poetry to all the places we went to.'[48] Another person who never forgot meeting Duncan in New York was the biographer Bill McBrien, who was astonished that this painter, whose art seemed to him to celebrate a lazy domesticity, took such pleasure in the tense outlines of the steel and glass skyscrapers. 'He simply and unapologetically delighted in New York City.'[49]

Back at Charleston, Duncan slept on and off for a week. He was exhausted, not so much by his travels as by George Bergen who, hungry for art talk, had frequently kept him up till three in the morning. Soon after, he was telephoned by Paul with the news that Edward le Bas had died, and cried, alone, at the loss of so close a friend. 'Edward le Bas' death was a great blow to me,' he told Richard Morphet.[50] At the memorial service, however, Duncan chatted and laughed, his seemingly irreverent behaviour shocking Basil and Frances Creighton, whereas in fact it betrayed an irrepressible love of life, of which Edward would certainly have approved.

TWENTY-SIX

Toujours la Peinture

Once, when travelling with Duncan on a London bus, Paul, noticing that a certain building had been pulled down and others spoiled by redevelopment, began to grieve at the changes he saw. 'If you go on like that,' Duncan retorted, 'you won't be able to enjoy what's left.'[1] This attitude helped him keep the depressing aspects of life in proportion. He had been aware that, for some months before his death, Edward le Bas had been miserable, had found painting difficult and, despite his bad heart and high blood pressure, had ignored the doctor's advice and begun drinking – as he had confessed to Duncan – a bottle of whisky a day. It saddened Duncan further to learn that another of his intimate friends, Peter Morris, had cancer in his pelvis and spinal column. He wrote to Peter suggesting that he should give up Mexico and come and live at Charleston. Morris, however, felt that ill health and Vail Morford, his now severely alcoholic partner, made this impossible. 'Nothing less than these obstacles would have kept me away from you for so long ... O dear, to live with you at Charleston what a heavenly thought – how I wish it could be, there are few places which pull me so and I am seldom as happy and never as amused as when I am with you.'[2] Morris died the following year, in 1967.

Living on his own at Charleston, with Grace and Walter Higgens in their separate quarters, Duncan now tended to confine himself on the ground floor to the studio and dining-room. The house had begun to decline and Grace grumbled at the torn and ragged state of the curtains. Duncan was to benefit from Quentin's appointment to the Chair of Art History at the University of Sussex which enabled him to return to the area, with his wife and three children, in the summer of 1967. Once settled at Cobbe Place, Beddingham, they were only three miles from Charleston. There Quentin was to continue work on his life of Virginia Woolf. He also began visiting Charleston at least once a week, partly in order to use the kiln and partly to 'keep an eye' on Duncan and see that things were well managed.

In the company of old and new friends, Duncan began to sparkle again.

At Richard and Sally Morphet's house in Durand Gardens he dined that November with the painter Howard Hodgkin and his wife Julia. 'I am gradually feeling my way back to normal life after New York,' he wrote to Michael Holroyd.[3]

Holroyd had first approached Duncan by letter in December 1962, in connection with his study of Lytton Strachey. 'I am *not* going to make a lot of "revelations" about him,' he told Duncan, 'but I do feel that any impressions and memories I can collect from his friends will undermine the false but popular gingerbread figure which the reading public has, of a character wholly flippant, superficial and remote, and make possible my task of revaluating [*sic*] his work.'[4] Duncan agreed to help, and Holroyd visited Charleston early the following year. Nervous and apprehensive, for he was in possession of copies of all Duncan's letters to Lytton Strachey, Holroyd knew by then that 'revelations' would in fact be a major aspect of his book. In Duncan he was confronting a man fifty years older than himself, whose private life during the first decade of this century he was proposing to make public. As they talked, Holroyd found himself diverted by the deceptive simplicity of Duncan's answers to his questions. But a few minutes later he would discover a second meaning in something Duncan had said, and would wonder if it had been intended. 'Duncan was a master of these beguiling *double entendres*,' Holroyd recalls.[5]

This was Holroyd's sole contact with Duncan during his research. Duncan heard no more until May 1966, when Holroyd wrote to inform him that the book was nearing completion and to ask if he might check the accuracy of certain pages and consult with Duncan on illustrations. Invited to lunch at Charleston, Holroyd arrived on 10 June with the manuscript of his first volume for Duncan to read.

What Duncan encountered as he turned the pages was a book that, in its detail, ambition and depth, far exceeded the method of biography that stylish writers like David Cecil and Harold Nicolson, following in the footsteps of Lytton Strachey, had made popular. Holroyd's monumental, massively documented book gave space to the cultural milieu and minor characters. It also exposed the homosexuality of Strachey, Keynes and Grant and was full of 'revelations'. If the nature of the beast surprised Duncan, he was aghast to find his private life laid bare. 'To be frank,' he wrote to Holroyd, 'on reading the part of your book dealing with my affair with Lytton I received rather a severe shock ... I cannot help feeling very averse to having my most private feelings of so long ago openly described.' He suggested that the feelings of the living should be taken into consideration and expressed particular concern for Lydia

Keynes, Geoffrey Keynes and for Arthur Hobhouse, should he still be alive and, if not, for his widow. 'But I then pulled myself together,' his letter continued, 'and realised that I must take a more objective view and that your account of Lytton's feelings at that time was an important part of his development, and that you would not wish to leave it out.'[6] Uncertain as to what recommendations he should make, he sought advice from others, and asked Frances Partridge and Bunny Garnett to read relevant passages. This action stirred a hornet's nest of opinion and during the next few weeks various figures associated with, or descended from, Bloomsbury found themselves debating surprisingly unliberal action, namely whether or not Holroyd's book should be suppressed.

This discussion took place before the law regarding homosexual acts was reformed in 1967. 'Shall I be arrested?' Duncan asked at one point, in connection with Holroyd's revelations. Holroyd attempted to assure Duncan that the public attitude to homosexuality had everywhere changed. Bunny said this was not true and that if Holroyd's book were published, weak and wavering minds might react by reaching for safety to the conventional standards of the past. Angelica upheld Bunny's point of view and told Frances Partridge that she thought Holroyd's book would shock Duncan's conventional friends. When Frances asked Bunny who these were, he mentioned some friends of his own – a colonel and his wife – who would be shocked. Should books be judged by colonels, Frances replied? 'There was always that foot fumblingly advanced by Bloomsbury towards the conventional and aristocratic enclave,' she wrote drily in her diary, 'their Victorian childhoods perhaps coming to the surface in a way totally inconsistent with their defiance of *idées reçues*'.[7]

Bunny was the most vigorously opposed: he disparaged Holroyd's judgement; thought the book likely to cause pain and embarrassment to most of the people mentioned in it; and favoured wholesale suppression. Frances Partridge did not agree with this, but suggested that Duncan could ask for cuts or omissions in the passages concerning himself, if there were things he found objectionable. Quentin supported this idea and wrote to Holroyd on Duncan's behalf: 'He is certainly not an enemy of historical truth or, I think, at all ashamed of his erotic adventures . . . he is very much torn between a desire not to be unfair and obstructive and a natural reluctance to see one's private emotions made so very public.'[8] The final outcome was that Holroyd agreed to receive all their notes and suggestions and to look carefully at the passages that Duncan marked. But on one general point he held his ground. 'I do not agree with David Garnett's view that my book will harden people's reaction against homosexuality – any more than Phyllis Grosskurth's biography of John Addington Symonds did a year or so back,' his letter to Duncan reads.

> It seemed to me that, if Lytton's homosexual loves were treated not slyly or sensationally, but with openness and truth, using what was emotionally significant just as one would in describing a heterosexual love, then this could only have the effect of increasing tolerance, of getting the public to take things for granted. I feel sure that this is the right line – but . . . I did not wish to agitate you and do not now wish to be at all unreasonable. I agree with you that there's sure to be a way out of any difficulties.[9]

Perhaps as a result of this letter, Duncan's requests were not onerous: a reference to 'copulation' was removed; Hobhouse was given a pseudonym, an alteration that had also been legally advised; and Duncan's feelings towards Maynard were described as those of great friendship rather than love, to avoid giving offence to Maynard's widow and brother. By the middle of September 1966 Holroyd was able to assure Duncan that he had altered everything he had marked, as well as other items, along the principles Duncan had outlined. The homosexual nature of the friendship between Lytton and Duncan was neither veiled nor suppressed; but a statement by Holroyd, made in 1994, that 'Duncan finally decided to ask for no excisions',[10] should, he admits, be interpreted as an expression of his relief and gratitude that the cuts were relatively minor.[11]

Another year was to pass before Holroyd's first volume was published and in the interval Duncan, though he made a drawing from a photograph for the dustjacket, managed to put it out of his mind. Much was to happen in the course of that year. In January 1967 Angelica flew to New York. This was the first leg of a journey that was to take her to Texas, where she joined Bunny, who had been on a lecturing tour, but in New York she became increasingly close to George Bergen. ('The person who is infinitely kind,' she told Duncan, 'is George who rang up immediately from the country, took me out to supper and I see him constantly.')[12]

Duncan, meanwhile, made a two-day visit to Paris in February 1967. Before setting out he visited the Royal Academy's Millais exhibition ('What a gifted youth he was').[13] In Paris he was persuaded to stand in the cold in a queue, in order to get into the Picasso exhibition. He was afterwards glad he had done so, as he gained an idea of the immensity of Picasso's production, but he took more actual pleasure in the Bonnard show at the Orangerie, where the late paintings especially enchanted him.

In May he went abroad again, flying to Athens with Paul Roche, where they spent a couple of days before travelling by rickety taxi to Ioannina, where *Oedipus the King*, in Paul's translation, was to be filmed with Orson Welles in the star rôle. Duncan found living among a troupe of actors, managers, producers and cameramen a complicated matter and was glad to see Clarissa when she arrived with her son Potie, with whom Duncan shared a room. The excitement caused by the impending arrival of Orson Welles astonished Duncan, as did the continuous gossip and backchat. Each day they were driven by taxi to the old theatre of Dodona, where Duncan became something of a mascot among the cast, as he wandered around with his paints and board. Once he strayed into the scene with Oedipus (Christopher Plummer) and Jocasta (Lili Palmer) as it was being shot. Lili gently indicated that he should get out of the way, but, thinking she was beckoning to him, Duncan walked towards her, right into the limelight. Small wonder that at other moments he found relief in the fourth volume of Leonard Woolf's five-volume autobiography, *Downhill All the Way*.

Money seemed to flow like water. Paul was given fifty pounds a week just for being on hand as the author of the translation. Duncan's own finances were bolstered by another £1,000 payment from Wildenstein, left over from his 1964 show. He also sold an oil of a sleeping nude to Francis King for £200 and a portrait of a woman for £100 to Swindon Art Gallery, which was advised on its purchases by Richard Morphet. A further £200 arrived in April from the screenplay writer William Rose, who, in 1964, had commissioned a portrait of his wife Tania. The sittings had been interrupted soon after they began, and when they recontinued Tania was recovering from a breakdown as well as going through marital difficulties. Duncan's watchful and considerate manner made Tania aware that he knew more than he had been told, and she welcomed the peacefulness of the sittings. In the course of their conversations, he discovered that her daughter was at school in Shropshire and asked her to look up Richard Shone on her next visit. Whereas all previous contact with Duncan had involved Richard in a move from his own world into another, Tania seemed to him an emissary moving in the opposite direction, bringing welcome recognition of Duncan's affection and interest.

News that Tania and William Rose had finally split up reached Duncan in 1967. He summoned Tania to his flat in Victoria Square and, when she arrived, told her that he simply wanted to satisfy himself that she was all right. More characteristic of his relations with others was an apparent vagueness, which enabled him to get what he wanted without causing offence. Sometimes this allowed him to disguise confused feelings, such as those which he felt towards Angelica. She, on her return to England from America, went to Charleston in March in order to look after Duncan while Grace and Walter Higgens were away. There she shopped, cooked, did not bother much about housework, painted and played the violin. 'I suffer less from ghosts and the past than usual,' she told Bunny,[14] perhaps helped by the arrival of her daughter Fanny with her boyfriend, the musician Graham Treacher.

Angelica did not mention to Duncan at that time that she had fallen in love with George Bergen, though he had guessed as much from her letters from New York. When her hopes that George would come to England proved unfounded, she broke her silence. 'Dearest Angelica,' Duncan wrote from Greece, 'of course I am deeply interested to hear of your feelings for George. I only hope that his complete inability to write letters may not make things difficult for you, because he is sometimes a difficult person to understand as you probably know. And then he is unaccountable in some ways. He could easily make money but the mere mention of it prevents him taking steps.'[15]

Did it worry Duncan that Angelica had again fallen in love with one of his own ex-lovers? Henrietta recollects that it did, and that he discussed the matter with her in the studio at Charleston. But there is no evidence in his letters that he had any interest in the psychology of the situation. He was more mindful of Angelica's long-term happiness. Having spent many hours in George's company in New York, Duncan concluded that Bergen had become a gentler and more mature person. Angelica, now in her fiftieth year, had her own needs and rights, which Duncan respected. Whatever doubts and anxieties lingered, he managed to push them to the periphery of his mind, where they joined his worry about Holroyd's forthcoming book and, perhaps, concern over his grandchildren. '*Surely she ought to get a job* and get on with her profession,' thundered Bunny that spring, when he learnt that Amaryllis was about to disappear to Morocco with a boyfriend.[16] But Duncan, though touched by others' problems, remained detached and continued to welcome his grandchildren whenever they alighted at Charleston. He also took particular interest in the painting that Nerissa was producing at the Slade.

On his visits to London, Duncan often lunched with Ava, Viscountess Waverley in Lord North Street. There, in April 1967, he met the future Prime Minister, Edward Heath. They got on so well that Duncan suggested that when Heath next went to Glyndebourne he should visit Charleston, which he did later that year. In Heath's presence, Duncan must have remarked that he had never seen Canterbury Cathedral

(Richard Shone remembers him mentioning this fact with boastful astonishment and a twinkle in his eye – 'I've *never* been to Canterbury, I suppose you've all been?'), for Heath afterwards wrote offering to show him the cathedral and entertain him at Broadstairs, an invitation that Duncan never pursued. There were times now when he opted for the familiar, instead of the excitement offered by grand people and houses. That year he also turned down an invitation from the Devonshires to spend Christmas at Chatsworth, in favour of Aldermaston and the Roche family. 'I am going for a few days to stay with Paul Roche where there are four children,' he told Richard Morphet. 'I consider these essential at feast times.'[17]

Duncan and his world were rapidly becoming history. In the summer of 1967 Rye Art Gallery, stirred into action by Barbara Bagenal, brought together 101 paintings, pottery and furniture in what proved to be a landmark exhibition entitled 'Artists of Bloomsbury'. Richard Morphet was concurrently working on an article entitled 'The Significance of Charleston' for the October issue of *Apollo*, which conveyed the historical and aesthetic importance of the house and its decorations. Both exhibition and article provided evidence of a new critical interest in Bloomsbury. Quentin Bell was especially grateful, because the very qualities that Morphet praised were in danger of being destroyed. That year the Firle Estate had said that the tenancy of Charleston could not continue in Quentin's name after Duncan died. Instead, the intention was to strip down the walls, repaper, repaint and turn it once again into a farmhouse or into a stockbroker's country cottage.

But the event that firmly reinstated Bloomsbury in the public mind was the appearance in September 1967 of Michael Holroyd's *Lytton Strachey. Volume I. The Unknown Years 1880–1910*, rapidly followed by volume two, in February 1968. If in 1964 Duncan had seemed 'forgotten', now he suddenly felt too well known. When he heard that review copies were available in July, he wrote to Desmond Shawe-Taylor, 'I'm horrified to hear that *Lytton Strachey* is published. I cannot bear my very private feelings served up to the public. I put a stop to some of the worst but the author, a well meaning young man, blackmailed me by saying that it was necessary to Lytton's story, so for art's sake I gave way.'[18] Come October, he still felt unable to look at what Holroyd had written, as he admitted to Raymond Mortimer, 'How I hate having my personal feelings made publick [*sic*]. I have not read the book and shall put off doing so but the reviews make me squirm.'[19] When he did pluck up courage to open the book, he was chiefly concerned with what he felt to be a distorted account of life at 69 Lancaster Gate. In February 1968 he sent Holroyd a long letter, 'purely for my own satisfaction', in which he tried to set the record straight.[20] The following month he wrote again, admitting absolute fascination with Holroyd's second volume of Strachey's life.

Only when extracts from it appeared in *The Sunday Times*, heralding publication of the first volume, did Richard Shone learn that Duncan was homosexual. Though Duncan had never hidden this fact from his friends, it now became public knowledge and his life acquired greater transparency. 'I think it's *splendid* of you to let Holroyd write so candidly,' Raymond Mortimer had replied in October 1967, 'and that you are not put out by the anti-bugger frenzy of some reviews, which was to be expected alas.'[21] The discomfort Holroyd had caused Duncan lessened in time. And one benefit arising from the book was an increase in understanding. He received out of the blue a letter from a complete stranger, a retired colonel in Barbados, who, having learnt that Duncan's birthday was within three days of his own, wrote to say that he would be opening a bottle of champagne and hoped Duncan would do the same, as he was by far his favourite character in Holroyd's book. Such a well-disposed missive suggested that colonels could, after all, judge good books.

In September 1967, after the diagnosis of a tumour in her breast, Angelica went into St Mary's Hospital, Paddington, for an operation. Duncan, at Angelica's request, told George Bergen and was himself alarmed to learn that a second operation – the removal of the ovaries – was performed a week later, to reduce the likelihood of the tumour recurring. Afterwards Angelica recuperated at Charleston, where she luxuriated in the television that Lindy had given Duncan. (It had become embedded in the clutter of the studio and a part of Duncan's working life, for he liked drawing the newscaster or people being interviewed and loved watching sport with the sound switched off. For entertainment he watched *Dad's Army*, and also *Dr Finlay's Casebook*, because it was Scottish.)

Angelica convalesced that autumn at St-Martin de Vers, where she and Duncan were looked after by Nerissa. Much of that year she had busied herself with making mosaics, an interest that in 1964 had led to her writing a small book on the subject, but by October she could no longer bear the unresolved nature of her relationship with George and decided to return to New York. The day before she left for America, she lunched with Frances Partridge. 'Some bubbles are all the better for bursting,' Frances afterwards wrote to Bunny.[22]

That winter Duncan seldom went to London and was often alone at Charleston. He had become very fond of Deirdre Connolly, who would drop round with potted geraniums, magazines and books, and he now accepted a commission from Cyril to paint her portrait. Things were difficult for the Connollys, who were shortly to move to Eastbourne as their lease on Bushey Lodge had run out. But though unhappy with Cyril, Deidre was loyal to him, and she did not talk about her love for the Jesuit poet Peter Levi, whom she was to marry after Connolly's death. She also deflected the conversation when Duncan tried to tell her about some young man or other, heading off intimate topics with a giggle. She thought Duncan one of the most enchanting people she had ever met; also very selfish, but in a nice, self-contained way.[23]

The bird of paradise in Duncan's life, however, remained Lindy. He continued to be flattered by her attention and, when she arrived for a couple of nights in November 1967, he fell under her spell immediately. In turn he continued to encourage her painting. On her visits to Charleston she painted like a tornado. That November she produced three pictures in one day, including a large outdoor scene. 'She has a real talent wasting in a deplorable life,' Duncan grumbled after she left.[24]

News of Angelica reached him by letter. Now living with George, she had gone with him and Derry to Starhill Farm, a house built by George before the war in neo-Georgian style, which looked across the Hudson River to the Catskill mountains. George blamed his inability to leave America on his failure to sell this house, which he loved almost more than anything else. But back in his Manhattan apartment, Angelica experienced afresh his divided, self-destructive nature and the paralysis that left him unable to act or co-operate. She realised that a part of him resented her presence: he feared that she would give his wife, Helen, from whom he was legally separated, a handle for divorce and that he would lose custody of his daughter, Margaret.

'It is obvious that the girl's future is more important than Angelica's and my convenience,' Bunny sourly observed, having begun divorce proceedings at Angelica's request, but now cancelling them again.[25] Duncan expressed sympathy, for one curious effect of Angelica's affair with Bergen was that it restored the affection between Duncan and Bunny, reviving in both a need for the other's company. Though Bunny was occasionally gloomily aware that he had been abandoned, he was surprisingly free of resentment or jealousy. Both men felt anxiety for Angelica, for they perceived from her letters that she was experiencing at best a confused happiness.

After seven months in America, she suddenly returned home. 'It was a

strange delight to see you about the house again after so many months,'
Duncan told her: 'I have been thinking a great deal about you and George
since our long conversation on Saturday and of course I got a much
clearer idea of your feelings than I could from letters. I must admit that I
was rather horrified by some of the things you told me of George's
outbursts of cruel temper ... But of course I know that when one is
deeply in love one can take things that one cannot swallow in ordinary
life.'[26] While in New York, Angelica had reached the conclusion that
George had at some point been hurt so deeply that he could no longer
believe in anyone else's integrity. 'The only way I can bear it is to
remember that a large proportion of this spirit of destruction is directed
in reality against himself and that while it may appear he is destroying me
he is suffering infinitely more himself.'[27]

Pippa Strachey's death in 1968 was another poignant alteration in
Duncan's social kaleidoscope. With every new twist, the pattern altered.
That same year Derry Moore married Eliza Lloyd, the daughter of Mrs
Paul Mellon by her first marriage. Duncan designed the decorative
border of sheaves of corn for the invitation to their wedding dinner. The
person who appeared to benefit most from the turning of fortune's wheel
was Paul Roche. In 1967 he had inaugurated at the Purcell Room, and
later at the Wigmore Hall, a series of readings called 'The Poet and
Actor', at which his poems and translations were read by himself and a
changing roster of famous names, among them Sybil Thorndike, Diana
Rigg, Janet Suzman and Vivien Merchant. Christabel Aberconway
invited Duncan to be her guest at the first of these readings and she may
have had a hand in their instigation. On these occasions Paul would
appear looking immensely dapper in a velvet dinner jacket, sharply
creased trousers, shiny black shoes and a fur coat. He continued to pick
up fellowships and awards in America and in 1972 became poet-in-
residence at the Californian Institute of Arts, where he grew his hair long,
adopted Californian mannerisms and began marketing himself like a pop
star. In London he made a record with Mercury Records – 'Paul Roche –
A Poet. A Man. A Mind.' – with a psychedelic cover. Meanwhile his
translation of *Oedipus* was being used in high schools all over America.
  Duncan himself was far from inactive. In March 1968 he received
£100 for the book jacket, endpapers and six illustrations that he designed
for *In an Eighteenth-Century Kitchen*, published by Leonard Woolf's
nephew Cecil and his wife in an edition of 2,000 copies, from a
manuscript that had belonged to Beverley Nichols for over thirty years.[28]
Duncan also enjoyed himself greatly as a guest of the 'Crichel Boys'

ABOVE LEFT AND RIGHT:
The Flower Gatherers and *Seguidilla*,
decorations for the Queen Mary,
1935
LEFT: Duncan Grant finishing
Seguidilla at Agnew's, 1937

TOP: *The Bathers*, *c.*1926, National Gallery of Victoria
ABOVE: *Granada*, 1936, Govenment Art Collection

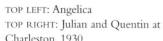

TOP LEFT: Angelica
TOP RIGHT: Julian and Quentin at
Charleston, 1930
ABOVE: Patrick Nelson
RIGHT: Paul (Don) Roche

TOP LEFT: Vanessa, Duncan and Virginia Bell
TOP RIGHT: Duncan and Vanessa at La Souco, Roquebrune
RIGHT: Grace and Walter Higgens
BELOW: Edward La Bas, Barbara Bagenal, Clive Bell, Vanessa,
Peter Morris, Duncan outside the Hotel Britannia, Menton

TOP LEFT: Deirdre Connolly and Duncan
TOP RIGHT: Amaryllis Garnett
ABOVE: Mark Lancaster and Angelica Garnett
RIGHT: Duncan and Lindy Guinness

LEFT: Duncan
ABOVE: Duncan painting Gilbert and George
BELOW: Duncan at Rye Art Gallery, with Paul Roche (showing him a picture), Russell Scott kneeling beside, and Richard Shone talking to Barbara Bagenal
OPPOSITE: Duncan and Henrietta Garnett

Duncan's ninetieth-birthday dinner party at 9 Dering Street,
with (clockwise around Duncan from lower left) Richard
Shone, Anthony d'Offay, Angelica Garnett, Jennifer Brook,
Derry Moore, Caroline Cuthbert and Paul Roche.
(Photograph: Derry Moore)

during the last weekend in July, staying with Raymond Mortimer in Dorset. He wrote afterwards to Desmond Shawe-Taylor, 'It was delightful and the weather perfect and for one who mainly lives alone the conversation exhilarating. And what a pleasure it was for me to renew my acquaintance with Cousin Julia [Strachey], whom I had not seen for many years.'[29] But immediately on his return to London Duncan lunched with Paul, his daughter Pandora – now studying ballet at Mme Rambert's school – and Richard Shone, for he needed young friends as much as, if not more than, the solace of established customs and manners.

Earlier that year a hiatus had occurred when Grace threatened to leave Charleston. In 1959 she had bought her parents' house in Banham, Norfolk, and over the years had spent a fair amount of money modernising it. But set against the attractions of retirement was the enormous responsibility she felt towards Charleston. She had battled bravely, in the house and garden, against the encroaching decay, but that year admitted to Duncan that it was more than she could cope with. She was persuaded to stay on but, partly in order to give her a rest, Duncan arranged to spend almost three months of 1968 abroad.

He went first to stay with Rex Nan Kivell in his house El Farah at Tangier. Now retired from the Redfern Gallery, which he had founded, Nan Kivell had restored this large, rambling house (formerly an hotel), which sat on the side of a steep hill looking down over Jews Bay, and had filled it with fine paintings and elegant furniture. Though lame and dependent on crutches, he was a pleasant and undemanding host. He had devised the house so that others could enjoy it and he entertained a flow of guests, among them Patrick Proctor, who remembers Duncan sitting on the terrace making drawings of a roaming cat. Visitors to El Farah soon became aware that the Moroccan housekeeper had been nicknamed Kiffi because he smoked kiff almost continuously. He was also notorious for making love with either sex with equal appetite. But it was not until a later visit that Duncan discovered the extent to which Nan Kivell's staff abused his trust and generosity.

John Haylock, who was staying in Tangier, visited Duncan at El Farah. Its terrace made an excellent place to sunbathe but also looked east and so faced the *levante*, the prevailing wind. 'Sometimes you can't stand upright out here,' Duncan told Haylock.[30] In October he moved to Fez, where Angelica joined him. The Moroccan government, through the auspices of the Inspection des Monuments Historiques, gave them each a studio rent-free. Though somewhat primitive, these large rooms were next door to each other in an old school and had marble floors. Duncan settled down happily enough and for a short while enjoyed the companionship of a young friend who had joined him in Tangier, James Rushton, a former Barnardo's boy who had been placed with foster parents near Lewes and now made a living buying and selling antiques. It was apparent to all who saw them together that Duncan was besotted with this lively, blond youth and so when a young Moroccan arrived at his studio one day, offering his services as a model, Duncan sent him through to Angelica. But Abdel-Ali Taïtaï became an important part of their Moroccan visit. A few weeks later John Haylock drove down to Fez from Tangier and found a head-and-shoulders portrait of the young Moroccan on Duncan's easel and several studies of him littering the floor. After giving Haylock wine in a paint-spattered glass, Duncan announced, 'Let's go and see Vanessa,' for he quite often made the mistake of calling Angelica by her mother's name.

Duncan returned to England on his own, Haylock and Logan driving him to Tangier airport. Though the weather was mild, he chose to wear the thick brown *djellaba* he had bought. With the cowl over his head he looked, Haylock thought, like a reprobate monk. Angelica stayed on at Fez for another five months. She became very fond of Taïtaï and promised to help him acquire a passport so that he could come to London to study mathematics. 'My relationship with him,' Angelica wrote to Bunny, 'is half lover, half filial-maternal – he is full of imagination and sensibility and has warmed me up so I feel gratitude – and we enjoy each other's company.'[31] The following spring Taïtaï followed her to London and lived in her Islington house while attending the Lycée. His presence helped Angelica forget George Bergen. When eventually Taïtaï left London to continue his education in Paris, he made return visits, the filial-maternal aspect of their relationship permitting a lasting friendship.

Back at Charleston Duncan found a letter from Richard Morphet informing him that Mark Lancaster, whom he had met at the Bloomsbury exhibition in Rye, had become artist-in-residence at King's College, Cambridge, where his interest had been aroused by Duncan and Vanessa's decorations in Keynes's former sitting-room in Webb's Court. Lancaster had abandoned a career in a family textile business to become an artist. In 1964 he had gone to New York with an introduction to Andy Warhol from his art-school tutor, Richard Hamilton. He had spent much of the summer helping in the Warhol 'factory', and from this had sprung crucial friendships with Warhol, Jasper Johns and others, later including John Cage and Merce Cunningham, with whom he was to work as a designer. Though Lancaster made his reputation chiefly as a painter, his creativity also found an outlet through collecting and the making of domestic environments. Wherever he lived, his surroundings became a work of art.

At King's, Lancaster became concerned that the wall paintings by Duncan and Vanessa in Webb's Court should be properly looked after. He was also anxious to persuade the college authorities that a similar care should apply to the decoration of the room as a whole. As a result, Duncan was invited to visit Cambridge during the first weekend in December 1968, to advise on the curtains, the colour of the walls and the furnishing of the room. Mark met him at the station, looked after him and gave a drinks party in his honour on Sunday morning. The day before, Duncan had searched out Richard Shone, who had gone up to Clare College, Cambridge, in October and had hung his rooms with Duncan Grant paintings borrowed from Paul Roche. At Duncan's request, Richard came to the party and was introduced not only to Mark but also to Dadie Rylands.

Duncan had difficulty in remembering Keynes's room as it used to be. On his return to Charleston he found an old photograph of the room, which he sent to Mark with the admission that it proved how very much at fault his memory had been. Not until February 1969, when he learnt that the row of painted figures which today still dignify the room were to be taken down for cleaning, did he inform Mark of the earlier mural hidden underneath. At that time the College was unaware of the mural, abandoned by Duncan some sixty years before, after it had reduced him to tears. Its temporary re-exposure caused him to make another visit to Cambridge. On this occasion he posed proudly for a photograph in front of the mural and was pleased to learn that Richard Morphet admired it.

Owing to Mark's easy and gregarious nature Duncan greatly enjoyed his visits to Cambridge. He was taken punting on the river, dined in the hall at King's and met various young men. He saw again his old friend Morgan Forster, and drew him as he slept after lunch in King's Combination Room. On another occasion he watched with Mark from his window as Morgan made one of his slow crossings of the Master's grass. Mark found Duncan 'invariably amusing, absolutely charming', his interest in what others were doing and or what was in a room 'so astute and a source of the enormous pleasure'.[32] Having been given fine rooms in the centre of the Gibbs Building, Mark hung them with a mixture of artifacts; a Vanessa Bell design for a rug; a stark oil painting of a bowl on a chair by Roger Fry (borrowed from the college); an Alfred Wallis borrowed from Kettle's Yard; an Andy Warhol's silkscreen of Elizabeth Taylor; a lithograph by Frank Stella and a light-bulb sculpture by Jasper Johns; as well as his own paintings in progress. 'It was a great relief to sit in your beautiful room and look at pictures painted by a different person than oneself.'³³ So Duncan wrote after a party that Lancaster held to celebrate the opening of 'Portraits by Duncan Grant', an Arts Council touring exhibition, which opened in Cambridge in November 1969. This had been selected by Richard Shone, a job that had given him the chance to look through all the canvases – stretched and unstretched – in the damp outer studio at Charleston. He also wrote the catalogue introduction. 'He has written a pleasant preface,' Duncan told Paul, 'no technology.'³⁴ When hung chronologically, as it was at the University of Nottingham Art Gallery, the exhibition provided a telling insight into the various shifts of style and method that had animated Duncan's career.

Shone, Lancaster and Morphet all helped Duncan keep in touch with the changing artistic climate. So did Lindy Dufferin, whose husband, Sheridan, was a partner in the Bond Street gallery run by John Kasmin, who did much to promote an interest in contemporary American art. Kasmin had discovered David Hockney, whose *A Bigger Splash* hung in the Dufferins' London house among other pictures by young artists. Shone introduced Duncan to Hockney in the Dufferins' garden in the summer of 1968, and both artists drew the dancer Wayne Sleep who posed for them at Holland Villas Road.

The astonishment Duncan expressed at all that Lindy did for him had a degree of boastfulness, for despite her disarming spontaneity she was far richer and better connected than most of his friends. He was aware that Sheridan's dry comments and common-sense attitude to life offered a rock against Lindy's turbulence, but he also saw that her marriage had brought the additional burden of managing Clandeboye, a vast treasure-filled house built by the first Marquis of Dufferin and Ava, one of the great Viceroys of India, on a large estate in Ulster.

Duncan's imagination was caught by the house. He instructed Lindy on her first visit to Clandeboye to keep an illustrated account of all that happened to her. He himself made two visits, in June 1964 and at Easter the following year, and on the second of these found himself alone for part of the time with Lindy's mother-in-law, Maureen, Lady Dufferin – Sheridan and Lindy having missed their plane. From that time on he took a rather gloomy view of Clandeboye, finding it too grand and the weather too grey. He was aware that during the summer months Lindy kept up an incessant flow of weekend parties. Guests were given bedrooms named after places that had been important to the first Marquis. Duncan, on one of his visits, found himself in 'Paris', which overlooked the lake that had been dug in the shape of a shamrock. He afterwards claimed that while drawing from his window he had seen a ghost, the White Lady of the Lake, as he called her. She had walked up out of the lake, only to be enveloped once more in the mist.

In January 1969 Lindy gave a memorable birthday party for Duncan at Holland Villas Road, to which came the Connollys, Michael Holroyd, the Bells, Lord Moyne, Raymond Mortimer, Frances Partridge, the Morphets, Richard Shone and others. Duncan, though terrified in advance, enjoyed it hugely and was seated at dinner between Peggy Ashcroft and Mary Hutchinson. Afterwards he told Angelica, 'Amaryllis and Henrietta looked lovely and were much admired by Cyril Connolly.'[35] He was often more interested in the young than the old: the novelist Anthony Powell made no profound impression on him when they met at a dinner given by Denys Sutton, though the evening had been enlivened, for Duncan, by Sutton's interesting talk about Roger Fry, whose letters he was editing; but Simon Watney, one of Quentin's students at Sussex University, who was willing to help make lists of all the paintings at Charleston, became yet another new friend.

That year Julian Jebb made a BBC documentary on Virginia Woolf's life and fiction. *A Night's Darkness, A Day's Sail* incorporated many tightly edited and often humorous interviews with those who had known her, including Duncan, who told of Virginia's amusement at hearing that one of his forebears had been eaten by a bear. Jebb thought it 'glorious'. A month later Duncan again sat under under the eye of the camera for the film *Duncan Grant at Charleston*, made by Christopher Mason, who was married to Joanna, the niece of Dora Carrington. Duncan supplied Mason with some autobiographical notes and also agreed to a filmed interview with Quentin. Further clips showed him ornamenting a plate and painting the garden while Vanessa's granddaughters, Virginia and Cressida, while they played shuttlecock and battledore. Mason made good use of the house, taking the camera into various rooms and afterwards obtaining a taped commentary from Duncan, to explain the various shots. When Quentin suggested that mention should be made of the fact that Maynard Keynes had written part of his *Economic Consequences of the Peace* in one bedroom, Duncan, apparently unaware of this piece of literary history, was taken up to the room and, with a microphone stuck in front of him, was asked to mention this fact. 'ThisistheroominwhichMaynardKeyneswrotethe*EconomicConsequencesof-thePeace*isthatallright?' he asked, knowing full well it wasn't.[36]

Leonard had tried to rid Angelica of nervousness before her interview for the first of these two films: despise the BBC, he had advised, despise Julian Jebb, despise the programme and give it not a moment's thought beforehand, for the whole point is to be spontaneous and nothing else matters. When a month later Leonard died, he was sorely missed. 'So dear old Leonard has left us! How the ranks are thinning!' Christabel Aberconway wrote to Duncan, two months after the death of Boris Anrep. 'I suppose we all "owe god a death" as the little tailor said to Falstaff. But I deplore this habit of dying . . . people seem to be doing it, nowadays, all the time. We must *check* this bad habit. I hope you agree.'[37]

One person with a very ambivalent attitude to Bloomsbury's past was Amaryllis Garnett. She and her sisters had grown up at Hilton aware that they had exceptional family connections. The house had a special atmosphere because of the importance given to painting, music and books, and in this environment all four sisters had shown themselves to be talented, artistic and articulate. Of all four girls, Amaryllis seemed the one most likely to make a name for herself. For Julian Jebb's film she had done the voice-over, reading Virginia Woolf's words with keenness and sensitivity. As an actress, she had attracted attention among her contemporaries. 'You must work with Amaryllis,' the young Max Stafford-Clark was told, and, recognising in her a strong, 'character' actress with class, he duly invited her to join the Traverse Workshop, a touring company based in Edinburgh. It gave her the structure she needed, for she had in effect once again joined a large family. She performed memorably as Helena in *A Midsummer Night's Dream* and got her name in lights at the Royal Court in a play called *Amryllis*. But when not acting, she got into muddles, especially with money, for she was recklessly extravagant. She had given up living on the houseboat, *Moby Dick*, and had bought a house in Islington with money from the sale of the Cearne, her grandparents' house, which Bunny had given her.

In December 1969 Amaryllis went one evening with Duncan and Richard Shone to dinner at the Bells', as her diary records:

I sat on the drawing-room floor feeling uncomfortable, a draft down my back, muzzy headed with the thin trickle of drink steadily poured down my throat through the evening, and bored; reminiscences, investigations of Bloomsbury. It's envy as well I know; of their gifts, friends etc. but I want to leap up and dance a farrango: we're living here and now, what about *our* gifts; fuck their inner circle. Quentin read aloud from his biography [of Virginia Woolf], it was fascinating, but you'd think they were living under the shadow of the Pyramids, and I prefer a live flea to a dead butterfly. Aren't they ever bored of celebrating their ancestors? Outside the fields wave across the window like a pea green sea met by the misty watery sky.

The following day she and Quentin talked alone. 'Quentin and I, moving nearer to each other with the kind of tender respect one gives ill people, both frightened of touching a painful place, or of demanding movement, unwrapping each other's bandages, and frightened of being hurt ourselves.'[38]

In the autumn of 1969 Grace, tired out by the labour needed to keep Charleston going and wanting to retire, issued a second ultimatum. Barbara Bagenal was present at the time and, foreseeing that things would be very difficult for Duncan if Grace left, made her promise to stay on. She did so, but from now on Duncan tried not to have too many visitors staying at once.

He went to Amsterdam that autumn with Leigh Farnell to see a Rembrandt exhibition. Advised beforehand by Simon Watney on the attractions of the city, they spent one evening agreeably surrounded by some nice boys at the Palace Hotel. Nor were their cultural expectations disappointed: the Rembrandt exhibition was 'of the first importance, the drawings too are without parallel', Duncan afterwards told Simon.[39]

Recognition of his own work continued to grow apace. The Towner Art Gallery in Eastbourne mounted an exhibition in September of Duncan's and Vanessa's sketches and studies for Berwick Church. The Tate considered buying two of his pictures, *Interior at Gordon Square* and *The White Jug* and, though it only bought the first of these, it acquired *The Mantelpiece* in 1971 and *Venus and Adonis* in 1972. Richard Morphet, cataloguing these works, found Duncan very willing to answer questions about them. When discussing his *Venus and Adonis*, he revealed that his Adonis pursues his own concerns in the protective shadow of Venus' female presence, as Duncan had done in relation to Vanessa. 'I can remember being faced with the rather mountainous figure of Venus calm and unpreoccupied,' he wrote, ' – in the distance Adonis it appears hunting safely. This was the whole of my inspiration.'[40]

Until the late 1960s twentieth-century British art was generally considered to be little more than a pale reflection of more vigorous movements elsewhere. One event that helped change this climate of opinion was the 'Abstract Art in England 1913–1915' exhibition mounted by the Anthony d'Offay Gallery in Dering Street in November– December 1969. Because it was the first real survey of the Vorticist movement since 1919, the exhibition received critical acclaim, so much that the Arts Council took over the show and toured it outside London. It successfully renewed interest in the pre-1914 English avant-garde.

Anthony d'Offay brought a catalogue with him when he made his first visit to Duncan at Charleston in December 1969. 'I liked d'Offay and thought him intelligent and nice,' Duncan afterwards told Angelica. 'He chose some drawings of mine which he would like to show and wants to know if you will sell him Nessa's yellow abstract work and also a pile of small canvases . . . He also wants to buy a large picture of mine which I am not sure I did! of Virginia Stephen and Leonard on the roof of Brunswick Square.'[41]

With no dealer to manage the sale of his work, Duncan had allowed many visitors to Charleston to buy pictures direct from him. The procedure often seemed like an auction in reverse, for his diffidence meant that every time he mentioned a price in the course of conversation with prospective buyers, it was lower than what it had been a few moments before. Anthony d'Offay was to offer Duncan a contract that changed this, and during the 1970s he was to create a new market and price range for Bloomsbury art. As he entered his eighty-sixth year Duncan found himself in the hands of a highly professional, ambitious young man who, within little more than a decade, was to become, not just within London but on an international level, one of the most powerful 'gallerists' in the field of contemporary art.

TWENTY-SEVEN

A Veteran of Glorious Battles

Although he sometimes felt a little exhausted by his visits to London, Duncan still welcomed the stimuli they provided. It had been his habit regularly to tour certain West End galleries. In his eighties he went more often to exhibitions of contemporary art. He discussed Francis Bacon's paintings with Richard Shone, viewed the Richard Hamilton retrospective organised by Richard Morphet at the Tate Gallery in March 1970, and the following month enjoyed a David Hockney exhibition at the Whitechapel Art Gallery. This last, he told Morphet, 'was crowded like the Hamilton show with marvellous young people in brilliant colours. In some cases they became part of a picture.'[1] When taken to see 'A New Art' at the Hayward Gallery in 1972, a seminal exhibition of minimal and conceptual work, Duncan's attention was arrested by one of Richard Long's elemental stone circles.

Duncan's eagerness to participate in any new experience made him an inspiriting companion. In April 1970 he journeyed to Cyprus, to stay with John Haylock, who had made a house out of an old police station that sat on the outskirts of the village of Myrtou. On his arrival Duncan obtained some trousers and a straw hat, and then sat in the garden (formerly the prison yard) painting the view of Mount Kornos. Haylock arranged matters so that sight-seeing trips, to a castle, a ruin or a painted church, were interspersed with days at home. He noticed that Duncan got much more pleasure from a trip to Kyrenia to see some Greek sailors dance than he did from a cocktail party or tea with the British High Commissioner. At Nicosia, at a ballet performed by a German troupe, the President, Archbishop Makarios, was in the audience. 'In the foyer during the interval,' Haylock recalled, 'the Archbishop passed by. Duncan bowed, Makarios paused and inclined his head, their eyes meeting as if in recognition of each other's distinction.'[2]

Haylock's other guest, the short-story writer Frank Tuohy, had moved out to make room for Duncan, but he returned to the old police station for his meals. A copy of his recent collection, *Fingers in the Door*, came Duncan's way. 'Rather brilliant I think – a bitter sort of Katherine

Mansfield perhaps,' he observed to Simon Watney, adding, 'I gather that what is called love in this island is on a commercial basis, not so agreeable to me after Amsterdam.'[3] But he made no complaints and seemed to Haylock 'the most rewarding of guests . . . undemanding, appreciative, interesting and above all interested in everyone and everything'.[4] Duncan painted, as a present, a portrait of his host. 'Having you here was a great joy,' Haylock wrote, after he left.[5]

One result of Leonard Woolf's death was that Trekkie Parsons, his executor, had to sell the lease on 24 Victoria Square in order to pay death duties and legacies. Duncan was given six months' notice that he would have to vacate his flat by 1 July 1970. That same month he attended a Convocation at the Royal College of Art, where he was awarded an honorary degree, Sir Colin Anderson making the presentation speech. There followed an alcoholic lunch, after which Duncan had to be helped up the stairs at Victoria Square, where he spent the rest of the day lying on his bed, smiling blissfully.

Meanwhile, with the help of Eardley Knollys, he found a new *pied-à-terre* in the basement of 3 Park Square West. This large Regency house belonged to an eminent eye surgeon with an interest in art, Pat Trevor-Roper, who had recently taken a share in Long Crichel House. Eardley Knollys had insisted that Duncan would be willing to pay rent, but Trevor-Roper suggested instead that Duncan might give him a painting or drawing each year in lieu of rent, an arrangement that Duncan happily accepted. His large and well-proportioned basement room had no outlook, but its ample skylight filled the room on fine days with a beautiful light. In a recess was a small kitchen and a bathroom and lavatory. Paul and Clarissa Roche did a great deal to make the room look attractive, to avoid a repetition of the despair that had overcome Duncan in the course of moving to Victoria Square.

Though he had abandoned his habit, when in the country, of taking afternoon walks, Duncan had surprising reserves of energy. After a long session at the Tate Gallery's Hogarth exhibition in December 1971, he joined Frances Partridge at the Coliseum in St Martin's Lane for a performance of *Carmen*. 'Last week I had two delightful meetings with Duncan,' she afterwards wrote in her diary:

He came to *Carmen* with me at the Coliseum, arriving with wild hair and somewhat tremuloso, having walked all the way in haste from the Embankment (he belongs to the generation that almost never takes a taxi). He was thereafter absolutely alert and interested and remained the best possible companion, eating cold supper in my flat until midnight. Next day I went to have a drink with him in the basement of Pat Trevor-Roper's house where he is now lodged. He has made it very attractive with lovely pictures, painted screens and books. Beside Pat, we only had the unprepossessing 'Don' (poet Paul Roche) and 'my new friend David Pape', a dark intelligent Canadian. I asked Eardley what was supposed to be the point of Don? 'He has the most beautiful figure in the world.'[6]

Almost irresponsibly youthful in his enjoyment of life, Duncan continued to fall in love. A young Frenchman, Pierre Herreweg from Entrecastoux, turned up at Charleston two summers in succession (leaving his saxophone in France on his second visit, to Duncan's relief), posed willingly and, though heterosexual and shortly to marry, was greatly stirred by Duncan's affection. Flirtations such as these did not alter Duncan's need of Paul. Richard Shone marvelled at the contentment of daily life when Paul was at Charleston, for there was laughter, teasing and an animated atmosphere that could be exhilarating. When Paul went abroad, Duncan poured his daily news into letters, one of which ended, 'Good night it's a comfort that you are in the world.'[7]

It surprised Paul to discover after one of his visits to the States that Duncan and Charleston had more or less been taken over by the young Canadian, David Pape, who had come to England in order to write a thesis on Thomas Hardy. He was intelligent, sensitive, had an impressive physical presence and was first introduced to Duncan at Lindy's party after the preview of *Duncan Grant at Charleston*.

Duncan made a pastel portrait of Pape, which the young man took home to his parents in Toronto. Later, when his parents visited England, Pape brought them to Charleston to meet Duncan, a visit that was not a success. But David was genuinely touched by Duncan, took up painting at the older man's suggestion and briefly attended art school. Once, while drawing in the studio, he began groaning aloud that he was making a hopeless mess. 'That's what painting is all about,' Duncan replied. For a time Pape moved into Charleston. When the painter John Hubbard visited the house in the company of Kenneth Clark's daughter, Colette, he thought that Pape's jealousy and possessiveness poisoned the atmosphere.

Pape, though often callow towards Duncan, appears to have been impressed by the wisdom of Duncan's passivity. Writing to him in 1973, he recollected that Duncan had once said that he had come to an end of trying to understand things. Pape himself suddenly reverted to the religion that his parents had let lapse and began writing to Duncan in his Hebrew name, David Sholom. He embraced the Torah and now felt certain that everything about him mattered to the House of Jacob and that all his ancestors took joy in everything he did. He once arrived at Charleston intoxicated with notions of God. 'I wonder if I can manage to go on seeing him,' Duncan wrote to Paul. 'Luckily for me the Jews never try to convert a non Jew.'[8] But what finally tested his tolerance was Pape's sudden insistence on a kosher diet, which caused culinary problems and arguments at Charleston. Pape left suddenly, with the announcement that he was going to New York to convert millions of lapsed Jews to the orthodox faith – the only way, as he saw it, to prevent another Hitler.[9]

Pape was one of the first to notice a change in Duncan's art. This followed a decision finally to abandon a large figurative work based on a gymnasium, which he had worked at, on and off, for years. What had begun well, in a lively fashion, had, like a rotting pear, begun to look bruised and mouldy. Once he turned his back on this large picture, Duncan began to use a lighter touch and more transparent colour, both of which enabled him to bring fresh sensations of light and energy to his painting of material objects. Various influences came together at this time; these pictures were inspired in part by the Bonnards that Duncan had seen at the Royal Academy in 1966 and in Paris in February 1967, and also by his interest in late Titian, stirred at this time by the public subscription (to which he sent eighty pounds) that helped save Titian's *Death of Actaeon* from export to California. The focus on this painting had drawn attention to the loose, feathery brushwork that is such a seductive feature of Titian's late style. This was the context in which Duncan began to register still-lifes in terms of a subtly changing flow of coloured light, which translates mass into shifting, energised form.

Some of these late paintings, such as Duncan's reworking of mantelpiece still-lifes, offer a reprise on earlier themes. They revived his love of unexpected juxtapositions and the blending of everyday objects with his own painted decorations, art reproductions – such as Matisse's cut-out, the *Blue Nude* – or photographs of Nijinsky. When John Haylock returned from a visit to Tokyo in 1971 he gave Duncan a few pieces of cotton cloth on which were printed replicas of nineteenth-century woodblock prints. One of these, by Toshusai Sharaku, portrayed the actor Idikawa Ebizo as Takemura Saadanoshin in the play *The Loved Wife's Particoloured Halter*. Duncan was so taken with the image that he incorporated it into several studio still-lifes. He was probably unaware that the actor was portrayed showing his feelings before committing *seppuku*, suicide by disembowelling.

Richard Morphet admired what he called the 'rich interdependence' of form and fantasy in Duncan's work. This was one of the points that he wanted to make in an interview with Duncan at the ICA in November 1971. The event, arranged by Lindy, included a showing of *Duncan Grant at Charleston*, followed by a discussion during which Duncan, seated on the platform with Claude Rogers, Richard Shone, Richard Morphet, and his granddaughter Henrietta Garnett, was supposed to answer questions about his life and work. He had looked on this event as a form of torture, may have had a little too much to drink beforehand and entertained the audience by behaving like a complete owl. He got entangled with the microphone wire, spilt his wine, and produced a cigarette to be lighted just as the mike was pushed his way. To Richard Morphet's earnest art-historical questions, he answered obliquely, blinking at the slides of his paintings thrown up on the screen and at one moment asking, 'Did I paint that?' 'I was horrified by the whole business,' he later wrote to Paul, 'but my behaviour made people laugh and it was not too serious.'[10]

Duncan was a little sceptical about the fresh attention that his late work was attracting – 'I suppose you'll all say I've changed my style,' he flung out in protest. But he did not resent the increased demand for his work. In March 1970 Angelica had outlined to Duncan the terms on which Anthony d'Offay wanted to manage both Duncan's work and Vanessa Bell's estate. But, either because the terms were still being negotiated or because he did not understand the agreement, Duncan did not consider himself bound to d'Offay. When Jacob Rothschild visited Charleston that month, he took away five paintings by Duncan and one by Vanessa for £1,000. Two months later the dealer, Andras Kalman, met Duncan in London and was invited to visit Charleston. He did so in July, and was astonished at the sheer number of unstretched canvases, piled like rugs one on top of the other. He expressed the desire to mount a retrospective of Duncan's work and arranged to buy some thirty canvases. 'I'm very glad to hear such a very good account of Kalman,' Duncan wrote to Paul in October. '. . . I think I do well to have him and d'Offay as my dealers don't you.'[11]

What Duncan failed to realise was that d'Offay had asked for exclusive rights, and the following year began paying him a retainer of £500 every quarter. No mention of this had been made to Kalman, who was shocked to receive a letter from d'Offay's solicitor, demanding the return of all the paintings and stating that the purchase price would be refunded by Duncan. After this, Duncan was under no illusion as to his commitment to d'Offay. He respected d'Offay's decision to include work by himself and Vanessa in a mixed exhibition of English art from 1910 to 1920 and also agreed to an exhibition of his own watercolours and drawings. But the working methods of the two men were too disparate to make for a happy business relationship. d'Offay's ambition was to reverse neglect, to set right wrongs and to tell a story that had not been properly told – not only in relation to Duncan but to a whole forgotten period of British art. He would spend an entire morning selecting very carefully a small number of works for a choice exhibition, only to learn that Duncan had suddenly remembered that some of them belonged to Paul. As a result, certain exhibitions that might have happened did not materialise. Like many others, d'Offay enjoyed Duncan's company but was distressed and occasionally infuriated by Duncan's vagueness and by an unworldliness that made his attitude to the sale of his work seem amateurish. d'Offay was also aware that some of those around Duncan regarded him as a shark. The atmosphere was thick with moral enquiry. 'One felt emotionally bruised by it,' d'Offay recalls, to this day remaining disappointed with the work he did on Duncan's behalf, which he feels was incomplete.[12] With Duncan's agreement, d'Offay made a flat for himself at Charleston, but made little use of it, and the arrangement soon lapsed.

The professionalism on which d'Offay insisted was evident in the careful selection and presentation of the exhibition 'Duncan Grant. Watercolours and Drawings' in April 1972. Some fifty exhibits, ranging in date from 1910 to the late 1960s, gave the art critic Fenella Crichton the impression that Duncan Grant 'must be an unusually happy man, or at least he is truly gifted in communicating a pleasurable and sunny happiness in visual terms'. She added, 'A communicable euphoria in the work's execution is the outstanding merit of this collection.'[13] While the portraits in the show displayed Duncan's alertness to particular observation, the various mythological creatures, sporting in meadows, embracing or reclining, hinted at the richness of his imagination. In the finely printed catalogue Stephen Spender likened Duncan in old age to the two Chinamen carved in lapis lazuli in Yeats's poem 'Lapis Lazuli'. Yeats's observation – 'Their ancient glittering eyes, are gay' – applied, Spender argued, to Duncan's attitude to his work: 'The refusal even in the midst of tragedy, private and public, to be heavy, self-pitying or doom-laden and the insistence on lightness, quickness and gaiety, characterises it.' He could call to mind, he went on, no landscape, nude, still-life or mythological scene by Duncan that was not also joyful and light in execution. To which might be added a remark made by Richard Shone in *Arts Review*, that 'wit and clarity save him from sweetness'.[14]

*

478

During Vanessa's lifetime, Duncan usually sat at the dining-room table at Charleston with his back to the fire. After her death he more often than not sat in her place, with his back to the small window that overlooked the farmyard. But, if he had assumed her position, he could not run the house as she had done. To James Fox, who interviewed Duncan for an article in *Vogue*, he admitted, 'The whole life of the place changed after Vanessa died. The whole steerage of the house suffered.'[15] Its seediness now sometimes shocked visitors. Even old familiars, like Frances Partridge, were puzzled by the twenty-year-old newspapers wrapped round the bathroom pipes and were never quite prepared for the cascade of water that fell outside the cistern each time the lavatory plug was pulled. Matters became worse after February 1971 when Grace finally left. It was a melancholy departure, despite the champagne that Duncan drank with her and Walter in the dining-room as a toast to their future. Grace had sold her parents' home in Norfolk and had bought a bungalow in nearby Ringmer. There she quickly became an active member of the local Evergreen Club and a familiar figure at coffee mornings, jumble sales and garden parties. It was arranged that two young artists would live in and take over her job. But as there was a gap of almost three months before they arrived, the Garnett twins, Fanny and Nerissa, did a great deal to help. Fanny stayed on afterwards, having obtained a job helping in the wings at Glyndebourne. 'Her energy is terrifically rampant,' Duncan wrote to Bunny, 'no tree is safe.'[16]

At times the house seemed a place for ghosts; at others it swelled with visitors. But no longer were they woken by Grace bringing jugs of hot water to their bedrooms to wash in. In her absence a different, less regular regime began. Grace's replacements, John and Angela Greenland, arrived in May bringing their small daughter, Naomi, with them. 'All seems to be well here,' Duncan wrote to Bunny, ' – my new young couple seem very happy.' Nevertheless, he felt puzzled as to 'what should I be doing with a young couple who have never possessed a servant in my life – I cannot regard Grace as anything but a family appendage'.[17] If the new situation left him slightly incredulous, the Greenlands were wholly unprepared for the role they had to fulfil. They were an amiable couple but out of their depth. John, who painted occasionally and proved handy at mending cars, spent much of his time tinkering with motorbikes. The burden of running the house was left to Angela, who cooked well but always looked exhausted. In addition, she was already pregnant with her second child, Thaddeus, born in April 1972.

From now on long-established customs at Charleston began to unravel. A long-standing order with an Algerian coffee shop in London, which every month sent coffee to 'Mrs Bell', was cancelled by Paul in an attempt to save money. The house became even more remote, owing to the refusal of tradesmen and even, for a period, the Lewes taxi-men to drive up the lane full of pot-holes. Duncan could not bring himself to ring the Firle Estate and request repairs which the house now needed. What seemed to some a charmed paradise felt more like Wuthering Heights to others. When Matthew and Maro Spender visited, they found themselves sleeping in the attic under damp sheets. The house was very cold, some of the curtains were in tatters and Duncan hardly spoke.

But Duncan went on painting and appeared serene and happy. The garden began to look neglected, but it still put forth an abundance of flowers. And the Bells were nearby. Ever since January 1970 when Bunny had moved to Montcuq, in France, Angelica and her daughters often gathered at Charleston at Easter and Christmas and combined with the Bells at Cobbe Place for some festivity. To entertain the assembled company Quentin's son, Julian, on one occasion read aloud Ella Wheeler Wilcox in an Eton voice; on another Quentin became a *douanier* while Duncan took off an Australian trying to smuggle through customs a baby kangaroo, which emitted touching noises from his breast-pocket.

On a return visit to England in 1971 Bunny stayed at Charleston and was astonished at the social whirl in which Duncan lived. He could be glimpsed that year at a 'Whitebait's Dinner', a Royal Academicians' dining-club, as a guest of John Nash. He attended Barbara Bagenal's eightieth birthday party at the University Women's Club in South Audley Street and went along to the Fine Art Society in Bond Street to a ninetieth-birthday exhibition held in honour of Maxwell Armfield, whom Duncan had not seen since their last meeting in Paris sixty-five years earlier. At Lady Birley's invitation, he exhibited at the annual festival at Charleston Manor, where a concert conducted by Graham Treacher was performed in Duncan's honour. He suffered occasional setbacks, as when he was knocked down by a car near Victoria Station and found himself in Westminster Hospital in the care of some charming nurses; more serious was the pneumonia he suffered in May 1971, but it was soon cured by drugs and he continued to dine with the Morphets and, as he told Leigh Farnell, to 'see a lot of my young friends which keeps me going.'[18]

Young and old came to Duncan's eighty-sixth birthday, which he celebrated a day early, on 20 January 1971, at 3 Park Square West by holding an informal supper party for eighteen people. There was an abundance of food and drink, and among the guests were several Garnetts and Roches, the Bells, the Morphets, Simon Watney, Richard Shone and Julia Strachey. Rosamond Lehmann, the guest of honour, arrived looking enormous in a green and gold dress. Eardley Knollys was so taken by her appearance that he persuaded her, in the forthcoming months, to sit for her portrait to him and Duncan in his London studio. Also present was Angus Davidson, bemoaning his personal ills and remarking rather smugly that it was wonderful the way Duncan never worried. So Frances Partridge recorded in her diary, adding, 'A cloistered world, but very lively.'[19]

Towards the end of 1971 Duncan began planning a holiday in Portugal. Not wanting to travel alone and in order to avoid lonely evenings, he decided he needed a companion. As a result Richard Shone, now living in London, set out with Duncan for Lisbon the following February. They were met by Keith Baynes, who spoke Portuguese and was already settled at their destination, a small fishing and holiday resort called Cascais, just along the coast from Lisbon. Here they stayed, leading a relatively quiet existence until Lindy Dufferin arrived in a whirlwind of gossip and *Tatler* magazines, with Anthony d'Offay. Despite Keith Baynes's gift for discussing trivial matters in tedious detail, frayed tempers, complaints about hard beds and the lack of entertainment, their visit, Duncan thought, was a success. He himself produced a lot of drawings and pastels and enjoyed a visit to the Gulbenkian Foundation in Lisbon.

On his return he declined an invitation from Richard Sanders to become artist-in-residence at Duke University, North Carolina. The idea for this had come from Paul, who taught at Duke in April and the following September left again for America, this time on a year's residency at the California Institute of Arts. Though he returned to England during the Christmas vacation, such a lengthy absence distressed Duncan, and to prevent it happening again he made financial arrangements to help Paul with school fees and to 'allow you to lead a reasonable life instead of going to that in many ways deplorable America'.[20]

In March 1972 Duncan attended a performance of Walton's *Façade* with Clarissa Roche, who often suggested outings when Paul was abroad. He spent many solitary days at Charleston, seeing no one apart from the Greenlands, and did not mind this, but when scholars wrote, asking to see him, he readily assented. In this way began his friendship with Paul Levy, who was writing a book on G. E. Moore and the Apostles. E. M. Forster's biographer, P. N. Furbank, also spent a day at Charleston, noticed the damp, the peeling wallpaper and that Duncan seemed a little stiff in his joints. John Woodeson, a student from the Courtauld Institute, wrote asking for help with his bold plan to write on Duncan as one of a series of histories of British painters. (Only one of these, a biography of Mark Gertler, appeared, though Woodeson signed a contract for a book on Duncan Grant and managed to scoop documents connected with Sickert and Roger Fry.) Duncan may have been relieved when Woodeson fell by the wayside, as he discovered that he had upset Richard Shone by agreeing to Ben Duncan's idea for a book on Charleston and the people associated with it: as a result, he asked Ben Duncan not to proceed. On leaving Cambridge in 1971, Richard had been commissioned by Phaidon Press to write *Bloomsbury Portraits* which, when it appeared in 1976, was primarily an art-historical account of Duncan and Vanessa's careers up to the Second World War. But not for nothing had Grace nicknamed Richard 'Mr Boswell', for part of the attraction of the book was its biographical seasoning.

Duncan himself contributed to the history of Bloomsbury by writing with Richard Shone a chapter on Maynard Keynes's picture-collecting for a volume of essays edited by his nephew Milo Keynes. He also admitted having a hand in Betty Askwith's description of his uncles, Richard Strachey and Trevor Grant, in *Two Victorian Families*, which he enjoyed reading. The historical significance of his own work, however, was less clear to him than to others. Simon Watney was the first to rediscover at Charleston, mouldering in an old cardboard box, Duncan's *Abstract Kinetic Scroll* of 1914. But the person who drew it to the attention of the Tate was a black-bearded veterinary surgeon who visited Charleston in August 1972. Whilst working as a vet in Africa, David Brown had become passionately interested in art and eventually abandoned his career in order to train as an art historian at the University of East Anglia. He had chosen to write his thesis on Duncan and Vanessa's work during the 1908–20 period. 'I am engaged on this work as . . . part of the course,' he wrote, with great directness, 'but this is secondary – primarily I like looking at your and Vanessa Bell's paintings.'[21]

Though Duncan made a visit to the Tate Gallery in September to see the Caspar David Friedrich exhibition, he admitted to his old friend Leigh Farnell that he did not much enjoy London nowadays. His mental alertness and freshness of response impressed many, but his physical frame was failing. His voice, Frances Partridge noticed when she visited Charleston in May 1972, was softer and gentler, even though his replies were still paradoxically witty. In October he lost his balance when a train, just before coming to a standstill at Lewes, shunted forward, causing him to crack three ribs. When Christmas arrived he seemed to Angelica perceptibly older, 'tottering in his mole's trousers always on the point of coming down in spite of a new belt, and with a small red knitted cap on his head and his wisps of fine grey hair sticking out beneath – looking a trifle uncertain, like an impossibly trustful little grizzly bear walking the plank, unaware of the dangers.'[22] When the Bells, Garnetts and Anthony d'Offay gathered round the dining-table at Charleston, Duncan regarded the assembled company with pleasure. 'I'm sorry you were not here at Christmas to see the rows of beautiful profiles,' Duncan wrote to Bunny. 'They really were superb – I sat in the inglenook and could see without talking. I think the modern English are very beautiful of all classes and I put it down to after war milk.'[23] He and Angelica went to see Grace and Walter Higgens at Ringmer, and the following day they broached Lydia in her lair at Tilton, as Angelica told Bunny: 'The light was on, and Lydia came out at once peering out of the door exactly like Mrs Mole – tiny and round, with an extraordinary knitted helmet on her head of a tawny orange colour. As soon as she saw Duncan making his way towards her she was delighted, and warmly embraced him – a couple of lamp-lit old moles hugging each other.'[24]

Family and friends congregated again at Angelica's house in Islington for a Twelfth-Night party. Two days later Duncan took a train to King's Lynn in Norfolk, for the opening of an exhibition at the Fermoy Gallery. It was to contain twenty-one new pictures by Duncan, ranging in price from £70 to £350, as well as two paintings lent by the Queen Mother. One of the attractions of the event was that the Queen Mother was expected to visit from nearby Sandringham. She was interested to see more of Duncan's work and it was the Dowager Lady Fermoy, one of her ladies-in-waiting, who had launched the gallery in 1963.

The combination of Duncan's advancing decrepitude and Paul's fondness for Bloody Marys made this a perilous expedition. It began badly, with Duncan falling on the stairs at Park Square West while Paul carried their bags out to the taxi. He seemed unhurt, but once in the taxi had no idea where they were going. Paul steered him into the train and produced his flask of specially blended Bloody Mary, after three of which Duncan fell asleep. They were met at King's Lynn station and taken to the gallery, where a full glass of wine was thrust into Duncan's hand and soon refilled. A stylishness in his speech and behaviour meant that, even at his most shambolic, he always looked distinguished. On this occasion Paul's influence was apparent, for Duncan's C & A suit had been bought at Paul's direction and his brightly coloured tie was a gift from California. A little after eight Lady Fermoy drove them to her house at Uphall, where they were to dine with Derry Moore and the conductor Raymond Leppard. Here Duncan was given a strong gin, the effect of which was disastrous for, once seated at the elegant round table in the small dining-room, it soon became evident that he was beyond food. Lady Fermoy smiled and the conversation flowed until the dessert had been served, by which time Duncan had long since left the shores of consciousness. Derry and Paul carried him to his bedroom, mindful of Lady Fermoy's reminder that at eleven the following morning the Queen Mother was to visit the gallery.

In Paul's account of this visit, Duncan woke blissfully free of a hangover and in a debonair mood.[25] But Helen Luckett, the exhibition organiser, remembers him shuffling around in carpet-slippers and looking extremely ill. When the Queen Mother arrived he paid his obeisances and they began to move slowly round the room. Paul, following at a distance, noticed that every time the Queen Mother expressed enthusiasm for a picture, Duncan responded with extreme diffidence. Paul stepped in and told her how a printer's strike had prevented his essay, 'The Education of an Eye', from reaching the catalogue (a falsehood, since it had in fact been vetoed for being less about Duncan's art than Paul's own vision). The Queen Mother asked him to send her a copy, and when finally she decided to buy Duncan's *Still-Life with Matisse*, Paul murmured, 'Your Majesty has chosen well.'[26]

In celebration of Duncan's eighty-eighth birthday the *Guardian*, in January 1973, ran a full-page interview with him by Janet Watts. Fetched from the station by John Greenland, she found Duncan dressed in a straw hat, unzipped-up carpet-slippers and wearing a dark-red dressing-gown over his clothes as protection against Charleston's cold corridors. One question she asked was whether he resented the public exposure of private lives brought about by Holroyd's life of Strachey and also by Quentin Bell's recent biography of Virginia Woolf. 'I've come to the conclusion that it's better,' Duncan replied. 'Everyone's past has been revealed now, and I'm rather in favour of it. It makes the lives much easier to understand; and otherwise things would be questioned without people knowing the answer, and I think that's a bad thing.'[27]

The interview succeeded in conveying the wistful melancholy that underlay his situation. 'Lately, I've wondered if I might not be turned out, living alone in this big house,' he remarked, in mild concern. 'I thought perhaps I shall be made to move by Public Opinion.' When Janet Watts wondered if his dead friends were irreplaceable, he said, 'I make great new friends . . . But of course they can't take the same place – because they're newly there.'[28] Disinclined to wallow in the past, he then moved the conversation on to talk about Fellini, hitch-hiking and Andy Warhol.

He enjoyed talking about painting with his granddaughter, Nerissa, who, on arriving at the Slade, had impressed her fellow students with her confidence. She flirted with various techniques and with photography, though not at this time with pottery, which later became a major interest. Despite the promise that she showed, she did not take off at the Slade, though on leaving there was never any idea that she should be anything but an artist. She never had a job and had hardly any money. For almost a year she lived alone in her parents' house in France. Later she made use of *Moby Dick*, the small houseboat moored at Cheyne Walk.

During the summer of 1971 there were times when Nerissa, clearly suffering from intense depression, was frightening to be with. She dealt with this alone, but occasionally submitted herself and others to dramatic scenes. One took place at the Sadler's Wells Theatre, at an evening of Martha Graham's work, which Nerissa attended in the company of Duncan and Angelica. She was in a manic state until Angelica made an offhand common-sensical remark, which suddenly pricked the balloon of Nerissa's madness, and twenty-four hours later her crisis seemed a thing of the past. But earlier that summer at Charleston her state of mind had been so alarming that Quentin rang John Greenland and asked him to hide the guns. Duncan, throughout this tense period, accepted Nerissa's oddness and replied even to her maddest remarks.

The following year Amaryllis became the focus of concern. She had apparently been doing well: praised for her part in John Spurling's *In the Heart of the British Museum* at the Royal Court, she had also caught Harold Pinter's attention when performing in one of his plays. He had got her a part in Joe Losey's film *The Go-Between*, for which Pinter had written the script. Then there had been a performance of *The Duchess of Malfi* by the Traverse Workshop in Edinburgh, made memorable partly by the fact that the casting had ignored gender considerations. Amaryllis had played Ferdinand, an unstable character whom she saw as trying to frighten, startle, shock and bribe people so as to feel his power over them. It took her to extremes, and it is probable that the unremitting ferocity of the play left her utterly drained. After a final tour to Stockholm, the Traverse Workshop disbanded at the end of 1972. Just at a time when, as Peggy Ashcroft later said, Amaryllis seemed on the brink of making her reputation, she experienced difficulty in getting work and became depressed. When she visited Bunny in France in January 1973, he had the impression that she was confident about her acting ability. He was baffled to learn soon afterwards that she had decided to give up acting altogether.

In the months that followed Amaryllis continued to disturb her elders.

One cause of her unhappiness was her hopeless love for the painter Tim Behrens, her affair with him remaining the central one around which others grew. She poured melancholy, introverted, acutely analytical thoughts into her diary, which reveals the underside to her flamboyance. While in Stockholm she had met a man with spiritual leanings inspired by the teachings of Gurdjieff. She subsequently went to Amsterdam and returned full of talk about 'transcendentalism', Ouspensky, Gurdjieff and Krishnamurti. Having sold her house in Prebend Street, she moved into a friend's flat in Lonsdale Square and embraced an Oriental way of thinking and feeling that was impressive, if not completely convincing. The glimpses of her that people caught at this time compose an image of someone searching for a way out of a situation to which other solutions had failed. She tried to join a Gurdjieff commune in the Cotswolds, but did not fit in with the regime and was asked to leave almost immediately.

After her body was found in the Thames, some of her friends tried to argue that her lack of bodily co-ordination, the wobbly gangplank to *Moby Dick*, in which she was staying, strong tides and the possibility that she was drunk or drugged all pointed to the likelihood of an accident. The inquest brought in an open verdict, allowing it to be assumed that she had slipped off the gangplank, but it was also noted that there was no evidence of alcohol or drugs. Though she left no suicide note, her diary was full of negative introspection. It convinced Bunny that the world had lost a great writer in Amaryllis, as it was 'the most tragic, heartrending, sensitive document I have read, with touches of genius in it'.[29] In Angelica's opinion, Amaryllis's death was consciously chosen, 'a step to which she had felt magnetised for some time'.[30]

Duncan was not present at her cremation, which Nicky Loutit, one of Amaryllis's friends, remembers as unbearably grim. But a few weeks afterwards he invited himself to dinner at Ellington Street, a visit that Angelica and her daughters found well timed and consoling. 'Duncan is very sad but is continuing to work,' Angelica told Bunny.[31] 'It is wretched not having any idea as to a possible motive for Amaryllis to end her life,' Duncan admitted to Deidre Connolly, whose brief note of condolence had touched him greatly. It had convinced him, he said, that 'love and sympathy are the only things that do good in bad times'.[32]

On 18 July 1973, dressed in mustard-gold robes, red ribbons and a black mortar board, Duncan received his second honorary degree, this time from the University of Sussex. In his rôle as Professor of Art History, Quentin gave the address in which he referred to Duncan as 'a veteran of glorious battles'.

It seemed appropriate that he should have a part-time secretary to help answer his mail. Quentin found a woman who came one morning a week and typed admirable letters. Admittedly, Duncan afterwards had to do a lot of telephoning to explain that his replies came out a little terse through this medium, but on the whole the arrangement suited him well. But it alarmed him when she began to tell stories about an unbelievably iniquitous husband, and still more so when she suddenly appeared at the dead of night in his bedroom. There followed wildly deluded letters, after which she took an overdose and was hospitalised. From her hospital window she could see the Downs in the far distance, and these, she told Duncan, combined with her sense of his continuing presence, brought her hopes of happier times.

The dramatic impact made by Vanessa's extremely radical post-impressionist work at the Anthony d'Offay's in November 1973 excited Duncan. Richard Morphet wrote the catalogue introduction. 'The qualities of seriousness, of beauty and sometimes of joy in her painting are made vivid to me in your writing,' Duncan wrote to Morphet, adding news of his own: 'I have been back a few days from a wonderfully happy holiday in Turkey. The country on the Mediterranean coast is magnificent, the ruins grand and the weather perfect, sometimes *too* hot. But I like the heat.'[33]

The holiday had been Paul's idea. He had tried to lure Duncan to Mexico and the Caribbean, but he had resisted the idea of long plane journeys. ('One leaves one's soul behind' was one objection.)[34] But he did agree in his eighty-ninth year to fly with Paul to Istanbul and on to Antalya by air freight. Their itinerary was far from smooth and Paul's management of the trip haphazard. Hotel rooms were hard to find and their rented car broke down; Duncan was now unable to walk far and tired easily. But it had become Paul's habit to fuel their journeys with a liberal supply of alcohol, and his lethal Bloody Marys took the edge off any disaster.

After Antalya they moved to a small hotel at Side, making short expeditions by car along the coast and to nearby ruins, on one occasion driving up a mountain to find the Roman theatre at Aspendus still in perfect condition. Whereas Duncan's automatic reaction to his new surroundings was to sketch or paint, Paul's recurrent desire was to run, walk, swim and remove all his clothes in a pagan embrace of the sun and the ancient landscape. Duncan, grumbling aloud at Paul's desertion, nevertheless painted contentedly when left wedged crab-like into a gap in the rocks or marooned on a park bench. Enticed into the sea in his underpants, he clung to Paul like a monkey and was swirled back and forth. Certain that he could still swim, he begged to be unknotted and silently dipped out of sight.

They made such a curious couple that they caught the attention of many. One young Turkish couple gave a small party in their honour, for they had been impressed by Duncan's habit of painting in the mornings and late afternoons and by the air of courtesy that surrounded him. Paul pretended that Duncan was his father, a lie that in fact came very close to the nub of their relationship. But he had also begun referring to himself as 'Nanny', thereby casting Duncan in an infantile role. 'I hope Nanny knows what she's doing,' Duncan riposted after Paul admonished, arranged, promised and bribed him into doing something he didn't want to do. When asked to take a photograph, Duncan was baffled by the camera, despite being instructed which hole to look through and which trigger to press. Roche, holding an epic pose, did what he could to explain, hector and entreat, but only when his face gave way to angry impatience did he hear the camera click. But, as Roche's account makes clear, they enjoyed an easy companionship and this, combined with Duncan's perennial delight in the world around him, made their holiday memorable. 'How Delacroix would have loved him,' Duncan remarked of a praying Turk, and when Roche despaired at the ugliness and pollution of Istanbul's suburbs, Duncan replied, 'Think of Santa Sophia.'

Before leaving Istanbul, Paul noticed that Duncan had grazed his shin. Despite ointment and plaster, the wound became infected and after a few days back in England it was discovered that Duncan had a poisoned leg. It was soon cured but it left him tired, shaky and liable to fall over. Angelica installed him in Vanessa's bedroom at Charleston, on the ground floor next to the studio. She and Paul now realised that he needed more care and initially an uneasy arrangement was formed in which the two of them would alternate at Charleston roughly every ten days. Though Paul had been sexually estranged from Clarissa for some years, he was happy with their home at Aldermaston and whenever he got in the car to make the three-hour journey to Sussex he felt an enormous wrench. Clarissa did not wish for his departure but saw, with insight, its necessity. 'You must be with Duncan, or you'll regret it all your life,' she told Paul.[35] He conceived a solution: Clarissa and the children should come and live at Charleston and take over the house. Duncan was enthusiastic, but, daunted by Charleston's damp and dereliction, Clarissa was not to be persuaded.

Others helped. Henrietta occasionally cooked when Angela Greenland needed a break. Angelica gardened, finding some ease from a constant grief over Amaryllis in the joy she obtained from her other daughters and her granddaughter Sophie. Nerissa brought her new boyfriend, the actor Toby Salaman, and, on one visit, painted Duncan's portrait. Duncan liked company and remained mentally as alert as ever. For Richard Shone's friend Peter Ackroyd, he designed a cover for his second book of poems, *London Lickpenny*. And he pottered on with his attempts at a double portrait of two young artists, Gilbert Proesch and George Passmore, who had successfully merged their two personalities into the dual-headed persona of Gilbert and George.

This artistic duo had decided while at St Martin's School of Art to turn themselves into 'living sculptures'. At a time when student dress was avowedly casual, they had adopted a quaint formality of dress and behaviour that at first seemed a humorous satire on English behaviour. But as their work progressed a darker aspect emerged, their spectatorial rôle often charging their surroundings with deliberate unease. At the time that they contacted Duncan, through Anthony d'Offay, with a request for a portrait of themselves, they had embarked on some 'drinking sculptures'. In 1972 they had shown two huge charcoal drawings on artificially aged paper, entitled *The Bar*, at Anthony d'Offay's gallery and simultaneously, at Nigel Greenwood's in Sloane Gardens, they had exhibited 'photo-pieces', which captured them drinking in pubs. They both posed to Duncan in London, at Lindy Dufferin's studio, and visited Charleston. He produced an extensive body of work based on this pair – single as well as double full-length portraits, as well as many studies – but it is far from his best work; much of the drawing is tentative and indeterminate, and the fact that he inscribed 'Gilbert' under a drawing of George suggests a confusion in his mind. But the notion of a double portrait intrigued him and he went on with the task in the sitters' absence, working from photographs of the duo.

Running parallel with this commission was another from the *Observer* which, in an attempt to attract more readers, had hit on the idea of offering limited editions of original prints. Once it was ascertained that Duncan was keen to be involved, Carol Catley, who was in charge of commissioning the artists, and Stanley Jones, the master lithographer at the Curwen Press, went down to Charleston in 1973 to discuss the project. They were astonished to find the house completely open and no one around, except Duncan, who was working in the studio. Stanley Jones recollects that the studio was inches thick in dust and that Duncan seemed quite isolated. But a meal was produced by the Greenlands and it was agreed that the following spring he would visit the Curwen Press studio in Midford Place, off the Tottenham Court Road, and work on two lithographs.

In keeping with Curwen Press practice, Duncan was encouraged to draw on the grained zinc plate. Several of his previous lithographs, done for the Miller's Press, had been executed on paper coated with gum arabic and gelatine. The image had been transferred from this paper on to a plate and then printed, with the result that the image appeared, not in reverse, but as it was originally drawn. At the Curwen Press, in order that Duncan did not have to draw in reverse, Stanley Jones used offset printing. He noticed that Duncan was pleased to be once again in this part of London and that after lunch he would take himself off to look at Fitzroy Square. He readily accepted Stanley Jones's help with the intricacies of colour separation and, with his undemanding manner, got on well with the printers. When his 'Washerwoman' and 'Standing Woman' went on offer in the paper, each in an edition of 350 and selling for fifty-five pounds each or ninety-nine pounds for the pair, the offer was accompanied by a photograph of Duncan taken by Lucinda Lambton. Sent down by the *Observer*, she had established an immediate rapport, with the result that many of the photographs she took show him beaming with pleasure. The one selected for the newspaper made a wide audience aware that this artist, more usually associated with a vanished era, was still very much alive and still working.

TWENTY-EIGHT

'Their ancient glittering eyes, are gay'

In 1971 the Southover Gallery opened in Lewes, run by Deirdre Bland. She and her husband had decided to turn two rooms in the 1830 house into a gallery. Access was through the front door and at private views the crowd spilled over into the downstairs room on the other side of the hall. So successful were these openings that Deirdre Bland began holding them on Sunday mornings as well as Saturday evenings. The first that Duncan attended was an exhibition of Trekkie Parsons's paintings held in March 1974. On arriving at the doorstep, his trousers fell down. Asked if he would like to take his coat off when seated in a chair, he replied, 'Better not.'[1]

'It was simply Mayfair in Lewes,' he afterwards told Paul. 'The noise was so terrific I could hardly bear it. I had a few words with Lady Birley but I cannot remember what she said.'[2] Soon afterwards Deirdre rang to ask if she could exhibit his work in her gallery. He agreed, but later sent her a note saying it would be better if she discussed it first with Anthony d'Offay. This she did and an agreement was reached whereby she obtained paintings and drawings from d'Offay for sale at her gallery. She first showed Duncan's work in a mixed exhibition in July 1974. Solo exhibitions followed in February 1975 and October 1976. Everything seemed to conspire to make the gallery a success. Its home-like atmosphere was much admired and Deirdre Bland, who accepted payment by instalments, had a gift for selling; her technique was to leave her visitors entirely alone until they began to dither, whereupon she bore down on them, vigorously confirming their interest in a certain picture. Such was her success that at Duncan's 1976 show she sold forty-four works for a sum of £5,380.

Perhaps when some gypsies mended the cane in the dining-room chairs at Charleston in the summer of 1974 Duncan crossed their palms with silver, for luck, grace, tact and charm continued to protect him. On the advice of Lady Freyberg, who became a close friend after an introduction from Charlotte Bonham-Carter, he went that year to see Ed Fricker, who called himself a nature healer. Duncan had for some time been suffering from lumbago and pain in his back. Fricker merely ran his hands up and down Duncan's back, found what he said was the trouble spot, massaged it slightly and told him he would have no more pain. Nor did he in his back, but Fricker's gift for healing did not extend to Duncan's legs, which sometimes failed to move when he wanted them to. Yet he remained very independent and tried to do everything for himself. 'You must not . . . feel bound to come here when you are free,' he wrote to Paul in March 1974. 'I know you have all sorts of other arrangements. But you know that I am happy when you can be here.'[3]

That year he and Paul decided to go to Scotland for their holiday. On 27 August they put on the night-sleeper to Edinburgh Duncan's blue Mini, which Paul, who had never managed to pass his test, drove on a provisional licence. After dinner in the Great Northern Hotel, Duncan took to his bunk and they arrived in Edinburgh the next morning. The Festival was in full swing and they saw *Tartuffe* and *The Bacchae* and made several visits to the National Gallery, where they bumped into Sheridan and Lindy Dufferin. David Brown, now qualified as an art historian and employed at the Scottish National Gallery of Modern Art, gave them haggis and neeps one evening in his lodgings. In preparation for their tour of the Highlands, Paul turned the boot of the car into a mobile cellar, buying enough wine, brandy and gin to see them through any eventuality.

They headed first for Aviemore, Paul wanting to visit Duncan's birthplace at nearby Rothiemurchus. On arrival they were unable to get in touch with the Laird, who was away, but made contact with his son and daughter-in-law, John and Philippa Grant, and called on them at Boat House. It was a bad year to visit the Doune as the Laird, ashamed of its condition, discouraged visitors and had agreed that his son, whose ambition was to restore the house, should take over responsibility the next year. John Grant's mother, Lady Catherine, arrived while they were having drinks and invited them to meet the Laird on his return in a couple of days' time. Paul then drove Duncan to within half a mile of the Doune and they had a picnic lunch. Afterwards, while Duncan dozed on a grassy bank, Paul set off, realising that in order to see the Doune he would have to trespass.

Paul had no difficulty, as the house was in such a state of dereliction that a window was open on the ground floor. Everything lay smashed and fallen; books lay strewn on the library floor and torn canvases hung out of their frames; display cases lay overturned and the remains of a stuffed flamingo stood forlornly at the foot of the stairs. Bemused and entranced by the forlorn chaos, Paul walked back slowly to the spot where Duncan was sleeping. Later that afternoon Paul saw a farmer get out of his car and unlock the gate to the drive. He accosted him, explained that his ninety-year-old companion had been born in the Doune and asked if the following day they could drive up to the house. The farmer reacted pleasantly and, while locking the gate, told them he would leave it unlocked as the man in charge was away. True to his word, the next day the gate was not only unlocked but wide open and they drove right up to the house.

Duncan would not go inside. He gazed at the Doune in silence, got out his sketchbook and observed ruefully the ragwort and thistles growing where once he and the Stracheys had played cricket. Paul went inside again, foraging for some memento and bringing back with him a chamber pot. Afterwards Duncan told Simon Watney that the house had the atmosphere of a Chekhov play, minus the conversation. On the drive back to their hotel, he spoke not a word.

In their absence the Laird had telephoned and the following day he took them in his Land Rover on a tour of the estate. While Paul bombarded Sir John Peter Grant with questions, Duncan remained largely silent. He may have been a little uneasy, for he was aware that the Grants of Rothiemurchus had broken off relations with him after he had become a conscientious objector in the First World War, and the present Laird, a former colonel, had not forgotten this fact. Back at Dromontale Lodge, the Laird's home, the situation was greatly helped by the trolley-full of drinks that Lady Catherine had prepared, together with pâté on toast and a large plum cake.

Still more pleasant was the hospitality they received at Kyle House on Skye, from Colin and Clodagh Mackenzie, whom Duncan had previously visited in Edinburgh. They were not only long-standing admirers of his work – their Skye house boasting three very fine paintings by him – but also excellent cooks and considerate hosts, whose fine garden was permanently open to the public. From his bedroom window, which looked across the sea to the mainland, Duncan painted some water-colours. After a few days he and Paul moved to another part of the island, Ardvasar, to a guest house run by a Miss Isabelle Moore, before continuing with their Highland tour.

Back at Charleston, however, domestic matters did not run smoothly. The Greenlands resented Paul's tendency to treat them like servants, and things became so bad that in 1976 both Paul and Angelica asked Henrietta to intervene and sack the Greenlands. Rather against her will, she did so, but the following day Angelica re-employed them, as Duncan was genuinely fond of the Greenlands and they of him. As a result nothing changed, and the tensions involved in running Charleston continued to exacerbate the psychological warfare between Angelica and Paul over the care of Duncan.

When Pandora Roche went down to Charleston, she noticed that Duncan read a great deal. Even while painting he either listened to Radio 3 or enjoyed having a book read aloud. Pandora read him Angus Davidson's new biography of Edward Lear. She interested Duncan, partly because she had given up ballet for painting. With Paul he went to see her diploma exhibition at the Ruskin School of Art. On the day the show opened she had become engaged to a fellow student, but soon afterwards broke off the engagement and went down to Charleston. While there she found a note from Duncan: 'I think that T[oby Roche] has gone to make some tea. I believe that you have already found the rhym [rhythm] of your working life. This is the most important thing in existence I feel sure. So please do not get married. I hope you will see the two ends and how they join together. Love, Duncan.'[4]

Because Duncan was so unaffected and free of self-importance, his young friends felt able to bring to Charleston their own concerns, their positive feelings as well as their anxieties and griefs. Soon after he first began coming to Charleston, Simon Watney felt 'validated' by Duncan, for he had previously felt unhappy with the realisation that he was gay. In Duncan's company, he found he could gossip freely, talk about his love life and introduce his boyfriend, Mark Rowlands. He persuaded Duncan to accompany him to a meeting of the Gay Liberation Front soon after it came into existence. Duncan, always keen to hear Simon's news, was later saddened to learn that he and Mark had split up. The break caused Simon deep psychic distress, which required him to spend short periods in hospital. Duncan saw that he needed help and in 1974 arranged for him to spend a month in Cyprus with John Haylock. Afterwards Duncan told Haylock that he thought the visit had saved Simon's life.

Another person who had gained in confidence through knowing Duncan was James Rushton. For a period he had worked as assistant to Brian Epstein, the Beatles' manager, but after Epstein's death Rushton had come back to live in Lewes. Dealing in antiques and old cars, he also had a flair for making picture frames and would occasionally do work for Duncan. James was at Charleston when Nerissa, in a disturbed state, and obsessed with certain religious ideas, declared she had been 'born again'. An announcement of this fact, combined with an invitation to tea, was sent to the Bells, who decided to dress for the occasion, Quentin sporting a clergyman's collar, and twelve-year-old Cressida his academic gown on top of her nightdress. The Greenlands produced a cake laced with alcohol and Nerissa insisted on reading aloud from her diary and announced wild, sexually promiscuous plans for her future. Embarrassed and disturbed, her guests felt that the safest course was to allow her mood to run its course. But Quentin was so alarmed by the situation that on leaving he took with him Clive's gun.

Duncan's habit of camouflaging his feelings with vagueness makes it difficult to know the extent to which he understood what was going on. He allowed a muddle to develop over the writing of his will until, on Quentin and Angelica's advice, the solicitor, Mungo McFarlane, was brought in. Duncan had always been generous with money, especially to his young male friends, but on occasion he had been taken advantage of. When James Rushton was had up for speeding, it was discovered that he not only had silver stolen from Glynde Place in the car, but that the house where he was living contained sixty to seventy paintings and drawings by Duncan. It was concluded that when framing six works, he had only returned five and that his knowledge of Charleston had made it easy for him when leaving to pop round to the studio door and help himself from the racks. Duncan was interviewed by the CID, after which a large van arrived at Charleston. One picture after another was shown to him in order to ascertain whether it had been stolen or given to James. Duncan's vagueness on this occasion was extreme. This, combined with a letter Duncan subsequently wrote, removed the charge of theft in relation to the paintings, but other charges took Rushton to Arundel Prison, whence he observed in a letter to Duncan that prisons were factories producing sadness.

With the approach of Duncan's ninetieth birthday, various plans were afoot. Anthony d'Offay, now determined to mount a major showing of his work, began making regular visits to Charleston. He pushed and bullied Duncan until he began to see what d'Offay was after – something professional, interesting and up-to-date. d'Offay was sometimes so angered by Duncan's waywardness that he wanted to wring his neck, but at the same time Duncan's ineffable charm meant that conversations always ended in laughter and jokes. While d'Offay went ahead with plans for an exhibition of recent work, to be followed by another of early paintings, David Brown, in Edinburgh, began sending out loan forms for a Duncan Grant retrospective. This was to open at the Scottish National Gallery of Modern Art in June 1975 and afterwards travel to the Museum of Modern Art in Oxford. Meanwhile the Tate Gallery decided to mount a ninetieth-birthday display of all the works by Duncan in its own collection. Though it had been steadily acquiring his paintings over the last few years, it was not so long since the mere mention of Duncan's name at the Tate had been equivalent to that of Lenin at a Conservative Party conference. The moving spirit for the exhibition had been Richard Morphet, who had sent a long memorandum to Norman Reid, the Tate's Director. The go-ahead allowed Morphet to arrange for Duncan's *Abstract Kinetic Scroll*, which the Tate had acquired in 1973, to be filmed by Christopher Mason so that it could be experienced as the artist originally intended it – in movement and with musical accompaniment. Duncan chose the Adagio to Bach's first Brandenburg Concerto. Though Morphet had intended the Tate's display to open on 21 January, Duncan's birthday, major structural repairs to the assigned gallery delayed the opening until the following month.

Another place that had begun showing Bloomsbury art was the Edward Harvane Gallery in Bourne Street, near Sloane Square. 'It's a pleasant little gallery and they take pains over their shows,' Duncan wrote to Keith Baynes, whom Edward Harvane had asked to exhibit.[5] Lindy Dufferin, exhibiting under her maiden name of Guinness, held her first show there in January 1975. It contained paintings and watercolours produced over the previous ten years and the catalogue bore a foreword by Duncan. In this he managed to summarise both his relationship with Lindy and the various emotions that her work and life, and the conflict between them, had aroused in him. He described how they first met, visits they had made together to galleries, and the astonishment he had felt on first seeing her oils, watercolours, gouaches and sketches. His worries that she would be torn in two between her glittering social life and the demands of art had been unnecessary: she had done the impossible, he concluded, forging a way through the many demands on her and becoming a painter in her own right.

Lindy had given a party for Duncan's eighty-ninth birthday and she gave another for his ninetieth on 21 January, the day after the opening at the Anthony d'Offay Gallery of his recent work. 'Sometimes I forget my age and it's quite a shock when I remember,' Duncan told a reporter from the *Evening Standard*. He had arrived at the gallery at around half-past three in the afternoon in the company of Angelica, Richard Shone, Paul and his son Martin. Although it was a grey, rainy day, the galleries were brightly lit and a host of people were already gathered, among them Raymond Mortimer, William Coldstream, Barbara Bagenal and Richard Morphet. Patrick Proctor, wearing a Victorian tail-coat and orange tie, decided to attribute all Duncan's paintings to Richard Shone and told him, 'I think, my dear, you're keeping your colour very clear.'[6] Duncan, smiling hugely and seated on a gallery chair, which was a copy of the throne Arthur Evans had discovered at Knossos, was photographed for the newspapers. In the downstairs gallery he became involved in conversation with Lucian Freud who, he had always supposed, either did not like him or was unsympathetic to his work, but with whom he now talked easily and with interest. That evening Anthony d'Offay, with the help of his assistant Caroline Cuthbert and another member of the gallery staff, gave a dinner party for Duncan, Angelica, Paul, Richard Shone and Derry Moore.

Congratulatory compliments flowed in. A telegram arrived from the Queen Mother. The *Sunday Telegraph* praised his 'sparkling preface' to Lindy's show. *The Sunday Times* printed an encomium to his d'Offay show: 'It is a glowing exhibition, the paintings fluid, fluent and delightfully conveying a feeling of affection for the souvenirs of human activity, things given and shared with friends.'[7] The following month another exhibition of his work opened at the Southover Gallery in Lewes and a private gathering was held at the Tate to celebrate his ninetieth-birthday display. Richard Morphet had arranged for the evening to begin with a preview of the film that had been made of the *Abstract Kinetic Scroll* and was deeply embarrassed when, perhaps because the projector had not been warmed up, the music, slurred and distorted, was not at first synchronised with the image.

In March Duncan went to hear Richard Morphet lecture on Bloomsbury art at the Tate and afterwards gave him a painting of an Italian piazza, wrapped up in polythene, which Morphet opened in the lamplight outside the gallery, discovering 'a most lovely warmth of hue and judgement of tone that make it a joy to explore'.[8] It was around this time that the Morphets invited Duncan to dinner with Alan Bennett, who at one point asked Duncan if there was any painter he would have liked to have been. 'Titian,' he replied, after a moment's thought, and then added, ' – sometimes.'[9]

A similar playfulness emerged in the course of Roy Plumley's interview with Duncan on the radio programme *Desert Island Discs*, broadcast on 15 and 17 March. What did Duncan think of painters today, Plumley asked: did he feel they were outrageous? 'I never feel they're outrageous,' Duncan replied, 'but perhaps wrongly directed. I hope they are [outrageous].' Meanwhile his own reputation continued to blossom. When the Duke of Devonshire mounted an exhibition of modern paintings in his collection this year, he put on the cover of the catalogue Duncan's painting of the Gold Drawing Room at Chatsworth. By August the Scottish National Gallery of Modern Art retrospective had reached Oxford, where the museum's Director, Nicholas Serota (later to become Director of the Tate Gallery) arranged for the addition of several more paintings and objects from the Omega period. As a result, the exhibition now represented the largest assemblage of radical Bloomsbury art of the 1914–15 period that had so far been mounted.

During these busy months Duncan was at one point reduced to gloomy exhaustion. A belligerent American sculptress, Fredda Brilliant, whom Paul had met ten years before, wanted to make a bust of Duncan, as she had done of Gandhi and other famous people. Paul agreed, and she took up residence at Shelley's Hotel in Lewes, whence she had to be ferried to Charleston daily. She not only looked bizarre, but contained in her person a whirlwind of egotism, vulgarity, strange jokes and a desperate need for affection. Demanding to the point of cruelty, she insisted that Duncan should pose standing, for such long periods that at one point he nearly fainted. After the first few days John Greenland gave up on her and sent a taxi to fetch her. When it arrived at Charleston she refused to pay the driver and a furious row between her and John took place in front of Duncan, while her bust of him wobbled on the plinth. The agreement had been that Fredda would be given a painting by Duncan in return for the bust. It annoyed Paul that she not only walked away with a major work – *The Baptism* (c.1919) – but insisted that the bust had to appear in one of her exhibitions, after which it went missing.

Increasingly troubled by a lack of co-operation in his legs, Duncan accepted the wheelchair that Angelica brought to Charleston in September and in this he propelled himself from the downstairs bedroom into the studio. At the end of that month his doctor visited Charleston to see if he was well enough to take an autumn holiday in Tangier. According to Paul, Dr Blake pronounced Duncan as fit as a fiddle and said he would return to inject him against smallpox and cholera. 'That will be the end of me,' Duncan said. 'I doubt it,' Paul answered, having no premonition of the crisis that lay ahead.

On 17 October 1975 Duncan and Paul caught a late afternoon flight from Heathrow. The wheelchair, which had now become a necessity, removed all formalities and Duncan was hoisted on high and into the flanks of the Boeing, along with the packed dinners. They arrived at Tangier about nine in the evening and made their way to Rex Nan Kivell's house, El Farah, three miles outside Tangier, which Duncan had visited twice before, in 1966 and 1968. Formerly an hotel, it had twenty-eight bedrooms, none of which they actually used, as Paul decided they would sleep downstairs in a narrow oblong room with beds at either end, off one side of the dining-room, which opened on to the terrace. From there they could look down on to the town, out across the sea or along the hillside towards the distant mountains. Though Duncan had earlier doubted the wisdom of the trip, everything seemed to bode well for their three-week holiday.

A local doctor, Fraser Anderson, made available a wheelchair and in this Paul wheeled Duncan round the sub-tropical garden filled with cacti, hibiscus and bougainvillaea. Invitations began to arrive from the English community, including David Herbert, the youngest son of the Earl of Pembroke, and the painter Marguerite McBey, who had been married to the famous etcher James McBey. Hot sun during the day left them ill-prepared for the sudden drop in temperature in the evenings, and on their return from other people's houses they began to notice how cold and damp El Farah was. Paul asked for the central heating to be turned on, but his request was ignored. Only after he had sent a wire to Rex Nan Kivell in London did they achieve more than one hot bath a week. Moreover an increase in heating and hot water had come too late: at a lunch party given by Lady Tweedsdale, Duncan's unhinged remarks ('How do you know that donkeys like strawberries?') suggested that he was far from well. That night he tossed feverishly. The following afternoon Dr Anderson came to see him and wrote out a prescription. The day after he diagnosed pneumonia.

Furious with the staff at El Farah, Paul was determined to keep Duncan warm by whatever means were available to him. Finding some eucalyptus logs in the garden, he began hauling them across the Persian carpets into the dining-room, where he kept a fire going night and day. Smoke darkened the ceiling, the rare blue tiles around the fireplace turned grey and a rosewood table buckled owing to the heat. But Paul never lost his determination to restore Duncan to health, even when the doctor's prognosis turned grave and he suggested to Paul that they should discuss funeral arrangements.

An alteration in Duncan's breathing was the first indication that the crisis had passed. Within remarkably few days he was well enough to be wheeled into the studio, where he began working again. He was, however, very weak and at times confused. Paul found him on one occasion cutting up his sheets and blankets with a pair of nail scissors, in preparation, he said, for an exhibition of designs in Japan.

The dealer, Bernard Jacobson, arrived, with a metal plate on which he asked Duncan to etch a tribute to Constable, to be hung, along with similar homages by other contemporary artists, at the Tate in 1976 at the time of a major Constable exhibition. Duncan set to work on an image of Salisbury Cathedral, his inability to co-ordinate fully the wavering lines and intermittent hatching giving the print an affecting delicacy and transparency. Meanwhile his conversation with Jacobson, Paul and others showed him to be hovering between dream and reality. Waking from sleep, he would insist that Frederick the Great was coming to tea or that some cushions in the corner of the room were ladies of quality, as Paul describes in his memoir of this period.[10] Duncan's mercurial imagination had always responded to Paul's make-believe games of rape and pillage; in order to get the older man out of bed, Paul would swoop down on him playing the role of a lecherous Turk, while Duncan – blinking in mock-terror and clutching the sheets – became the damsel in distress. Recuperating in Tangier, Duncan could be completely transported by Paul's nightly pretence, after wheeling him several times round the rosewood table, that they were dining at some restaurant in Charlotte Street or elsewhere. After eating the meal that Paul had cooked, and having drunk a passable Algerian *rioja*, Duncan would sleepily murmur, 'Don, see that you give the waiter a good tip.'[11]

By mid-December it was apparent that though Duncan had triumphed over pneumonia he was still not well. In fact he was feeling so ill that he asked Dr Anderson to provide him with the means of committing suicide. This was so out of character that Paul realised immediately something else was wrong and he soon determined that it was Duncan's bowels. After an enema, Duncan rallied. When Christmas arrived he was still very weak but his former self. 'Dearest Lindy,' he wrote on 31 December. 'I have decided to return to life. But that does not mean I can write letters. What I can say is God Bless You.'[12] For the next few weeks he sat on the terrace, where he drew, drank and dozed. In the evenings Paul read aloud to him, getting through book after book. When Rex Nan Kivell came out, he could not believe that his beautifully furnished house could have suffered so much havoc and destruction. Paul and Duncan finally left in April 1976, having stayed not three weeks but seven months. Nan Kivell forgave them the damage, for he realised that the crisis had been very real and he was greatly moved by the body of work Duncan had achieved, some of it when he had been close to death.

Duncan returned to Charleston to find that the Greenlands had been getting on Angelica's nerves. In order to ease the situation and reduce Angela's burden, Angelica had turned Clive's book room into another kitchen so that she and others could cater for themselves.

Paul had realised, on his return from Tangier, that he must now move to Charleston, as Duncan could no longer be left on his own. Once there, Paul often grew angry with the Greenlands's housekeeping. The fraught situation was eased by Paul's illegitimate son, Toby, who had been in contact with Paul's family by Clarissa since he was nine, and now helped with the business of looking after Duncan. Aged twenty-three, Toby wanted to become a painter and was about to take up a place at Camberwell School of Art and Crafts in the autumn. During the hot summer he often painted alongside Duncan in the studio. He also carried Duncan, slung over his shoulder, from chair to bed or wherever, managing physical difficulties, including the catheter attachments that were now necessary, with a nice mixture of kindness and gaiety. It was, however, Simon Watney who arranged with Lewes Social Services for a wheelchair with a commode to be delivered.

Often with Toby at Charleston was his friend Russell Scott and Potie, Paul's son by Clarissa. An all-male, slightly madcap household hastened Charleston's drift towards squalor and decay, and cannabis now grew in the vegetable garden. Simon Watney, distressed by the circumstances in which Duncan was living, began to stay away. The set-up at Charleston agitated Quentin, but Duncan made no complaints and went on painting. He also kept in touch with his old friend Leigh Farnell, though owing to their shaky, infirm handwriting, both had difficulty in reading what the other wrote. Failing strength meant that Duncan now sometimes drifted off to sleep in the middle of a meal, or suddenly made remarks that suggested he had entered a dream world. The next moment, however, he would emerge from his torpor with a remark that showed he was completely on the ball. 'I don't think Emma would approve,' he once interjected and everyone present knew instantly that he meant Jane Austen's Emma. At other moments the fantastic ingredient in his stories or talk turned out to be true, so that to be in his company was to have no clear sense of the boundary between truth and imagination.

A Bloomsbury revival was meanwhile gathering steam. Jane Beckett, from the University of East Anglia, organised a lively exhibition called 'A Terrific Thing – British Art 1910–1916', which opened at the Castle Museum, Norwich, in October 1976. The catalogue took the form of a newspaper, and among the exhibits was not only the 'Morpheus' bedhead from Charleston that Duncan had made around 1916, shaping the God of Sleep's nose and brow out of two pieces of wood, but also a huge Omega banner, which the organisers had unearthed in the Victoria and Albert Museum. The previous month 'Portraits by Roger Fry' had opened at the Courtauld Institute Galleries. Duncan turned up at the preview in his now familiar straw hat, with pheasant feather, and with his beard, which he had begun growing during his illness in Tangier, now reaching halfway down his chest. Toby Roche, who wheeled him round, afterwards took him to a small supper party at the home of Fry's daughter, Pamela Diamand, in Holland Park. Soon after this he had another bout of pneumonia but recovered quickly and within a week was sitting in a chair at the Southover Gallery in Lewes, practically mobbed by the crush of people wanting to congratulate him on his new show. Some of the best things in it were paintings he had done at Tangier, when his life had been despaired of. In December he did not make the preview of 'Bloomsbury Portraits', at the Fine Art Society in Bond Street, to celebrate the publication of Richard Shone's book, the first to bring a historical perspective to bear on Duncan and Vanessa's art. A day or two later Duncan was taken to the show. He was also wheeled up the road to the Anthony d'Offay Gallery where, as it was mid-morning, Caroline Cuthbert offered him coffee or tea. With impeccable manners and his usual gentleness, Duncan obtained a strong gin.

Since his return from Tangier in a somewhat emaciated state, the planes of his face had acquired a new fineness and his hands, formerly rather square and practical though also expressive of his personality, had become thin and elegant. Having taken to his wheelchair, his persona changed, for with his sage-like beard and his array of straw hats, he had somehow acquired an aura of venerability. At the Southover Gallery in October 1976 he had definitely held court and he did so again at the party, held on midsummer's day 1977, to celebrate Paul Levy's marriage to Penny Marcus. This was an immense affair, to which came the Bloomsbury friends that Levy had made while writing his book on G. E. Moore, as well as many artists, among them Howard Hodgkin, Barry Flanagan and David Hockney, who brought the American curator Henry Geldzahler, the guests numbering in all close to 500. Large marquees had been erected in an Oxfordshire garden but Duncan, after being wheeled round for a while by Paul, asked if he might go inside the house and rest. He lay down on a Second Empire *chaise-longue*, his face looking, Paul Levy thought, like a death-mask of William Morris. But gradually other guests got to hear where he was and for the rest of the party, which went on until the early hours of the morning, a regular stream of people came to see him and pay homage.

Sometimes he revealed a child-like vulnerability. While listening to Beethoven and painting in the studio with Simon Watney one afternoon in November 1976, he admitted he felt 'homesick'. It was a curious remark, Simon afterwards noted in his diary, 'but I think I have an idea what he meant.'[13] At other moments Duncan seemed isolated. Richard Shone recalls a meal at Charleston when everyone was chattering loudly except Duncan, who was silent. 'Do you know that Mary's died?' he asked suddenly, referring to Mary Hutchinson, who died in January 1977. Her name meant little to the assembled company and Shone saw how poignantly alone Duncan was with his thoughts. Like others, Richard read aloud to Duncan, happily taking him through *Northanger Abbey* and *Mrs Dalloway*, which Duncan thought Virginia's masterpiece. When the first volume of her diary appeared in 1977, edited by Olivier Bell, it bore an abstract design by Duncan on the dustjacket. Richard read large chunks aloud, pausing to ask, 'Are you asleep, Duncan?' To which came the reply, 'No! I'm riveted. Do go on.'

He continued working. Clarissa bought him a box of pastels, a medium to which he gladly resorted. He also produced a spirited drawing for the programme of *Don Giovanni*, one of the six operas performed at Glyndebourne during the summer of 1977. His interest in abstract art revived further. When shown a postcard reproduction of a hard-edged abstract painting by the American artist Frank Stella, which Paul Levy and Penny Marcus had bought, he so admired its exuberance that, as a wedding present for the young couple, he made them a design based on it. This capacity to respond and create was one reason why it angered Simon Watney to see Duncan treated offhandedly at Charleston, spoken for, talked down to or left out of consideration. From the studio he overheard a brisk district nurse asking Duncan what it felt like, after such a long life, to live in a world that was getting worse and worse.

Certainly the running of Charleston did not improve, for in February 1977 Paul sacked the Greenlands and was full of mad schemes as to how to manage the house. There was talk of charging fifty pounds for 'Bloomsbury' weekends, and a plan was afoot to take Duncan to Barbados. One project that Paul did achieve that year was an exhibition at Rye Art Gallery of Duncan's work, much of it produced at El Farah. He also succeeded in sub-letting Charleston to two Americans, Mr and Mrs Robert Soderberg, who, Paul heard, had been disappointed in their hope of renting Monk's House from the University of Sussex. They arrived expecting to take over an empty house, but it was some days before Duncan and Paul left, and then not for Barbados but for Aldermaston, where it had been decided Duncan should spend the winter.

He continued to have extraordinary dreams. 'Quick, you fool, they're abducting the Queen,' he would shout, at other times waking up convinced that Maynard was coming to tea. Duncan enjoyed telling his dreams when he woke, either to Paul or to Simon Watney, who helped out when Paul needed to be elsewhere. But on his first visit to Aldermaston in late October 1977, Simon was appalled to see Duncan being spoon-fed and treated in other ways like an infant. Paul had turned his downstairs study, which had a conservatory on one side, into a bedroom for Duncan. Elsewhere the house was hung like a shrine to him, his paintings on every wall.

In January 1978 Richard Morphet wrote to Paul telling him of an exhibition of Cézanne's late work that was to open at the Grand Palais, Paris, in April. He also reminded Paul that George and Sarah Walden, whom Duncan had met at Paul Levy's wedding, were both working in Paris, Sarah as a restorer for the Réunion des Musées Nationaux, and George at the British Embassy with the Ambassador, Sir Nicholas Henderson, who had known Duncan since he was a schoolboy. Paul acted on this information and on 18 April the *Financial Times* carried the following report: 'A fragile but alert passenger at Heathrow yesterday afternoon was the ninety-three-year-old artist Duncan Grant . . . He was off to Paris for a special preview of the momentous Cézanne exhibition opening later this week at the Grand Palais. "Cézanne was my painterly grandfather," explains Grant, who will be staying for three days with the British ambassador, Sir Nicholas Henderson.'[14]

Perhaps because Duncan's infirmities were now a familiar part of their daily life, Paul had failed to give Sir Nicholas any inkling of his companion's parlous condition. To Henderson, Duncan seemed scarcely in a state to be moved from room to room, let alone taken abroad on a sight-seeing trip. But he and Paul arrived safely, were given connecting bedrooms, and found that they had a well-stocked bar in their rooms. Henderson, however, soon noted that though Paul treated Duncan like a child, he did not pay adequate attention to his lavatorial needs, which caused recurrent problems. Duncan's occasional rude abruptness was indicative of his physical frustrations and discontent. During pre-dinner drinks one evening, having addressed one woman as Lady Ottoline, Duncan suddenly asked Henderson to stop the guests making such a noise. When Henderson protested that he could not, as his guests were there to meet each other, Duncan retorted that this only proved he was not much good as an ambassador.

Quentin was present when Duncan and Paul visited the exhibition, as were two of Paul's daughters, Cordelia and Pandora. They stayed almost two hours. Back at the Embassy, Duncan continued to capture certain hearts, including that of the maid, who spent an hour cleaning up the Burgundy that Duncan had dropped on his bedroom carpet. Two footmen, who brought him and Paul breakfast each morning, were equally enchanted by Duncan. On what was to have been their last night at the Embassy, Duncan dreamt he was trying to catch a train to Cambridge to keep a rendezvous with Maynard and fell out of bed. Paul found him at eight in the morning huddled in a ball on the floor.

Paul insisted that Duncan needed twenty-four hours to recover. The flight was postponed and a doctor called to certify that Duncan was fit to travel. The following day when they were all set for departure, Paul, who had greatly enjoyed the princely style in which he had been living for the past four days, remarked half-jokingly to Henderson, 'I wish it were pneumonia, then we could stay on here a long time.'[15]

Both Paul and Duncan had colds that day. Back at Aldermaston, Duncan, pronouncing himself 'inspired' by his recent experience, began work on a small flower piece, but his cold got worse. Paul teased Duncan about his new, deep, sexy voice. 'Laugh if you will,' Duncan answered, 'it's only because you're jealous.'[16] A few days later he began breathing with difficulty. Bronchial pneumonia had once again set in, and in addition bedsores began to appear. His condition was now so grave that Paul rang Angelica, who had spent the winter at Charleston. She drove to Aldermaston with Quentin and they arrived after lunch. Duncan's extreme frailty reminded Angelica of a skeleton leaf. He was obviously lucid but unable to talk and they had the awkward experience of making a conversation in which the answers had to be taken for granted. Quentin did most of the talking. Paul tried to raise the matter of Duncan's biography and suggested that he and Quentin should collaborate on it. Quentin tactfully avoided any straight answer. They stayed about an hour, during which Duncan, wearing a multi-coloured, knitted cap, reminded Angelica of a cross between a mandarin and gnome. But he also seemed to her 'as usual perfectly self-possessed, alive to what was going on round him, gentle and remote, and incredibly touching'.[17]

At some point during the winter at Aldermaston Clarissa had remarked, 'Duncan and I are agnostics.' Quite sharply, Duncan had replied, 'Speak for yourself.'[18] A few days after Quentin and Angelica's visit, in the early hours of 9 May, Paul bent low and whispered in Duncan's ear words that assured him of forgiveness. Returning to the habits of a priest, he told Duncan, 'you are of such a mind that if you knew God's will there is nothing else you'd want.'[19] He then kissed him and went to bed, returning a little before eight, when he was immediately aware that the laboured breathing had ceased. Momentarily he wondered if Duncan had foxed them all again. But on drawing the curtains Paul saw that Duncan had died.

Like the breaking of a light bulb, the protective membrane around Duncan, which his buoyant, mercurial nature, his courtesy, tact, charm and lightness of spirit had kept in place, instantly shattered. Jealousies and distrust now came to the fore to increase the muddle and confusion, for in the immediate aftermath of his death it was not quite clear who was to take responsibility for the necessary arrangements. There were angry telephone conversations about Paul's refusal to let the body leave the house. Clarissa, ordering a coffin at the undertakers, had to assess the size needed against a passing man in the street. When it arrived at Aldermaston, its hideousness caused a wail of protest, and before long the brass was stripped off and garlands of flowers painted on it by Pandora. Duncan's body was then taken to a Chapel of Rest in Lewes while the funeral arrangements were made. At Paul's suggestion, Quentin had arranged for Duncan to be buried at Berwick, but when Olivier Bell pointed out that it made more sense for him to be buried in his own parish beside Vanessa, these plans were changed in favour of Firle.

The funeral was short and simple. At the right moment Lord Gage, in a dark suit, appeared through the door in the wall that linked the churchyard with Firle Place, to pay his respects. Among the small crowd of people were Grace and Walter Higgens. Angus Davidson remained the most dignified and unemotional, his calm presence a welcome antidote to Paul's hysteria, for he could not walk more than a few steps without collapsing with grief. Angelica was aware that while others were in tears, she remained dry-eyed and apparently frigid. Richard Shone remembers primarily his self-consciousness about his hair, which had been cut very short. The only creature who seemed at ease on this grey day as Duncan's coffin, with his straw hat on top, was lowered into the grave, was Beasty, the Roches' ancient black labrador, which lolloped around. Afterwards a small group of people, including Lindy, Richard Shone and Simon Watney, the twins and Henrietta went back to Charleston for tea. 'We sat round the round table,' Angelica wrote in her diary, 'feeling purged and purified: all in rather the same state of mind, we all got on well together.'[20]

A month later a memorial service was held in the crypt of St Paul's Cathedral. About sixty people came, among them Stephen Spender, Howard Hodgkin, Richard Morphet and Gilbert and George. Lord Clark delivered a tribute in which he praised Duncan but, rather insensitively, given the occasion and his audience, tried to separate Duncan from the ethos of Bloomsbury, whose critical sense, he claimed, was 'somewhat overdeveloped'.[21] Paul read his poem 'The Artist', modelled on Duncan, which ended with the words 'Visions within and without him / bundling and streaming' and had dignity; but the music merely reminded some of Duncan's friends how much he had disliked the organ.

Duncan had himself once been confused about the year of his birth, so it was perhaps in keeping that *The Times* got the date of his death wrong. The obituarist referred to his 'unassuming dignity' and his 'deeply held conviction that the best of human activities is painting'.[22]

In the aftermath of his death, Charleston seemed a shadow of its former self, its atmosphere thin and wasted. Later, after the Charleston Trust had been set up, to acquire the house from the Firle estate, to restore and preserve it for posthumous generations, something of his presence returned. Now that the house is open to the public, the visitor encounters, through the various sensory markers in every room – paintings, objects and mementoes – a strong intimation of the personalities associated with Charleston and the life that went on within it. The vision shared by Duncan Grant and Vanessa Bell can be experienced in their pictures and, more generally, in the house itself, with its unexpected conjunction of objects, colours and patterns, for it is a vision that finds spiritual significance and sensual logic in the fabric of the everyday world. Moving outside, through the garden and past the pond, the visitor eventually reaches the point where John Haylock liked to remember Duncan, 'leaning on the gate at Charleston, his wise old pale grey eyes watching me drive away and at the same time, it seemed, gazing wonderingly into the unknown'.[23]

SOURCE NOTES AND ABBREVIATIONS

After his death, all Duncan Grant's papers passed to his granddaughter and literary executor Henrietta Garnett. These include certain memoirs he wrote, a diary, appointment diaries, memorabilia and a mass of letters, dating back over a long period of time, from a vast range of correspondents. I have referred to this archive as the Duncan Grant Papers. In addition, some of his personal papers, books, sketchbooks and memorabilia belong to Paul Roche and to Clarissa Roche. In many instances, Duncan Grant's letters remain in the possession of those to whom they were written. Others can be found in the following public collections: the Tate Gallery Archives; the archives of King's College, Cambridge; Cambridge University Library; the British Library Manuscript Department; Lambeth Palace Library; the National Art Library, Victoria & Albert Museum; the Britten-Pears Library, The Red House, Aldeburgh; the University of Sussex Library; the Sussex Archaeological Society, Lewes; the Berg Collection, New York Public Library; the Harry Ransom Humanities Research Center, University of Texas at Austin, and Chiba University of Commerce. Letters written by his father and mother, and by himself as a child, can be found among the Strachey Papers in the India Office Library. The whereabouts of other unpublished documents, drawn on for the purposes of this book, is indicated in the footnotes.

The following abbreviations have been used in the notes:

AVG	Angelica Garnett
Berg	Berg Collection, New York Public Library
BL	British Library
CP, LUA	Cunard Papers, Liverpool University Archives
CUL	Cambridge University Library
DG	Duncan Grant
DGP	Duncan Grant Papers
HG	Henrietta Garnett
HRHRC	Harry Ransom Humanities Research Centre
IOL	India Office Library
KCC	King's College, Cambridge
NAL	National Art Library, Victoria & Albert Museum
RG	Richard Garnett
RS	Richard Shone
TGA	Tate Gallery Archives
UCL	University College Library

References to Virginia Woolf's collected letters, edited by Nigel Nicolson and Joanne Trautman and published between 1975 and 1980 by the Hogarth Press, have been abbreviated to *Letters*, followed by volume and page numbers. Likewise her diaries, edited by Anne Olivier Bell and published by the Hogarth Press between 1977 and 1984, have been similarly abbreviated to *Diaries*, followed by volume and page numbers.

NOTES

CHAPTER 1: OF SCOTTISH DESCENT

1 Osbert Sitwell (ed.), *Free House. The Writings of Richard Walter Sickert* (London: Macmillan, 1947), p.292.

2 Elizabeth Grant, *Memoirs of a Highland Lady* (1898), new and unabridged edition (Canongate Classics, 1988), p.3; also quoted in Walter Scott Seton-Kerr, *Grant of Rothiemurchus: A Memoir of the Services of Sir John Peter Grant, GCMG, KCB* (London: John Murray, 1899), unpaginated.

3 DG, 'Memoir 2', unpublished manuscript: DGP.

4 In its abridged form, edited by Lady Strachey, *Memoirs of a Highland Lady* was reprinted four times in one year when first published in 1898. In 1911 a shorter version was published and it was from this text that Duncan Grant's friend, Angus Davidson, prepared the 1950 edition. The original manuscript, now on loan to the National Library of Scotland, was returned to for the unexpurgated edition published by Canongate Classics in 1988, edited by Andrew Tod. This new edition reveals how much Lady Strachey toned down or left out; there was 'a steelier and racier side to her reminiscences', as Andrew Tod comments in his introduction.

5 Sent to Bombay by the Crown to act as one of the 'King's judges', independent of the East India Company, the first John Peter Grant became known as the 'wild elephant' of Lord Ellenborough's despatch, who had to be put 'between two tame ones'. Unpopular with the Bombay government, he was loved by the natives. When in 1830 he resigned and was recalled home, some 7,000 Indians gathered to show their respect and witness his departure. Until recently one of Bombay's main thoroughfares bore his name.

6 Sir John Peter's dislike of being exiled from Rothiemurchus is clear from a letter written by Lady Grant from Norwood to her solicitor in June 1892. 'Sir John informed me this evening that he had determined to proceed at once to Rothiemurchus for a few weeks as he wished to speak to you about two or three things. I said there was no house [available] at present and he said he could probably get one in the neighbourhood. I am really quite powerless to contend with his crazes. I have no money whatever to pay for his journey and his going North and coming back will take a whole month's pay or more . . . If you can in any way prevent this journey I shall be most grateful. It is coming to this, that I cannot go on managing. If I cannot control the outgoings I must be allowed to give up . . . Not only can I not influence Sir John in *any* way, but I have no one to help me . . .', Lady Grant to Donald Grant, solicitor, 30 June 1892: Grant Archives, the Doune, Rothiemurchus.

7 The Chichele Plowdens traced their lineage back through a fifteenth-century Sheriff of London, whose brother was the Archbishop of Canterbury and a founder of All Souls College, Oxford, to Roger the Crusader of 1190.

8 'Record of Family Faculties', Strachey Papers: IOL.

9 *The Receipt Book of Elizabeth Raper*, introduced by Bartle Grant (London: The Nonesuch Press, 1924), p.37.

10 Lady Grant to Sir J. P. Grant, 28 February 1868: IOL.
11 Lady Grant to Sir J. P. Grant, 24 August 1868: IOL.
12 In an undated letter from Ethel Grant's cousin, Tilly Anderson, to Duncan Grant (DGP) it is claimed that the McNeils were descended from the lairds of Ayrshire and not from Kircubrightshire, as Raymond Mortimer inaccurately states in his *Duncan Grant* (Harmondsworth: Penguin Modern Painters, 1948).
13 Examples of Colonel Harcourt's paintings can be found as illustrations to his book *The Himalayan Districts of Kooloo, Lahoul and Spitti* (London: W. H. Allan, 1871).
14 Ethel McNeil to Jane Strachey, 30 May 1883: IOL.
15 Bartle Grant to Jane Strachey, 1 June 1883: IOL.
16 Ethel McNeil to Jane Strachey, 30 May 1883: IOL.
17 In the course of recent renovations, the Victorian additions to the Doune, including this room, have been pulled down.
18 Recounted to the author by Paul Roche, who heard it from DG.
19 DG, memoir note, dated 5 January 1960, quoted in Simon Watney, *The Art of Duncan Grant* (London: John Murray, 1990), p.17.
20 DG to Lady Grant [20 May 1894]: IOL.
21 'Professor Quentin Bell in Conversation with Duncan Grant', taped interview, 1969, quoted in Watney, *The Art of Duncan Grant*, p.81.
22 Carl Hillerus to David Garnett, 8 February 1950: DGP.
23 Watney, *The Art of Duncan Grant*, p.81.
24 Ethel Grant to Duncan Grant, 9 October 1897: DGP.
25 Watney, *The Art of Duncan Grant*, p.81.
26 Transcript of *Desert Island Discs*, transmitted 15 and 17 March 1975, Radio 4.
27 Ethel Grant to Lady Strachey, 3 June 1898: IOL.
28 See note 31.
29 DG to Lindy Guinness, 24 February 1962: Lady Dufferin.
30 Louise Jopling's memoirs, *Twenty Years of My Life 1876–1887* (London: John Lane, 1925) gradually dwell less on the practice of art and more on her many invitations to balls, dinners and country-house parties. She had no difficulty in persuading Sir Frederic Leighton to look in at the National Gallery when her pupils were copying there.
31 Ethel Grant to Lady Strachey, 10 November 1901: IOL.
32 Watney, *The Art of Duncan Grant*, p.81.
33 Ethel Grant to Lady Strachey, 24 November 1901: IOL.
34 Ethel Grant to Lady Strachey, 14 December 1907: IOL.
35 Bartle Grant to Lady Strachey, 15 December 1901: IOL.
36 Robert Cholmely to Lady Strachey, 16 December 1901: IOL.

CHAPTER 2: AN INHABITANT OF THE ATTICS

1 DG, 'Where Angels Fear to Tread', unpublished manuscript: DGP. For further description of this 'crammed, high, hideous edifice' see Michael Holroyd, *Lytton Strachey* (London: Chatto & Windus, 1994), p.1.
2 DG, 'Where Angels Fear to Tread'.
3 Clive Bell, *Old Friends. Personal Recollections* (London: Chatto & Windus, 1956), p.38.
4 Lady Strachey to Bartle Grant, 11 February 1902: Charleston Trust.
5 Virginia Woolf, 'Lady Strachey', *Nation & Athenaeum*, 27 December 1928.
6 Lisa Tickner, in *The Spectacle of Women: Imagery of the Suffrage Campaign 1907–14* (London: Chatto & Windus, 1987), pp.16–18, points out that certain differences between the preparatory sketches and the final print suggest that it may have been

redrawn on the lithographic stone by a commercial lithographer.

7 DG to Michael Holroyd, 9 February 1968: Michael Holroyd.

8 Ibid.

9 DG, 'Paris Memoir', unpublished manuscript: TGA.

10 Peter Quennell, *The Marble Foot: An Autobiography* 1905–1938 (London: Collins, 1976), p.88. Quennell's mother was a friend of Marius Forestier's sister, Nelly.

11 DG, 'Paris Memoir': TGA.

12 Ibid.

13 See Richard Shone, *Bloomsbury Portraits* (London: Phaidon Press, 1993), p.37, caption to illustration. Duncan Grant's memory for dates in the latter part of his life was notoriously inaccurate, but as this painting must have been painted in a particular place, possibly Streatley-on-Thames, where he spent the summers of 1902 and 1903, it is possible that, recognising the interior, he was able to date it fairly accurately. It is difficult from a stylistic point of view to establish its precise date because very few oils remain from this period.

14 DG to Diana Holman Hunt, quoted in 'Painters and Patronesses', *Harper's & Queen*, July 1978.

15 Holroyd, *Lytton Strachey*, p.13.

16 DG to Michael Holroyd, 9 February 1968: Michael Holroyd.

17 The Guieysse family connection with the Stracheys began when Louise's brother, Georges, met Lady Strachey on a Channel crossing and offered to carry her rug. Auguste Bréal had many English friends, having studied at Cambridge, where he met Roger Fry, before turning to painting. Also studying with him, Bussy and Matisse at Gustave Moreau's was Eugène Martel. After Bussy's death, Duncan Grant acquired at auction a small oil portrait by Bussy of Martel (Collection Clarissa Roche).

18 See the letter from Pernel to Pippa Strachey quoted in Betty Askwith, *Two Victorian Families* (London: Chatto & Windus, 1971), p.61.

19 'The chief amusement at present is the visit of Bussy ... We have long conversations on every subject and I find that the obscurity of a foreign language is a great help to freedom of speech.' Dorothy Strachey to Pippa Strachey, 21 November [1901]: British Library, Department of Manuscripts.

20 For an appreciation of Bussy's art, see Lucy Norton, 'Simon Bussy, Channel Painter', *Apollo*, September 1970. The first full account of this artist's life and art – Philippe Loisel, *Simon Bussy (1870–1954): L'Esprit du Trait: Du Zoo à la Gentry* (Paris: Editions Somogy Editions d'Art, 1966) – was published to coincide with a major Simon Bussy retrospective held at Beauvais, Dole and Roubaix between June and November 1996.

21 DG, manuscript notes for a speech occasioned by the opening of the Simon Bussy exhibition at Miller's, Lewes, in the 1940s: DGP.

22 Ibid.

23 This animal painter had become particularly associated with polar bears after a painting of this subject had been bought by the Chantrey Bequest. As part of the Chantrey Collection, it was shown at the Tate Gallery when it opened in 1897. The *Sunday Times Short Guide to the Tate Gallery of Contemporary Art* (1897), on the lookout for nationalistic sentiment, observed that its white bear, red sunset and blue ice were 'painted in the colours of the Union Jack'.

24 DG, Notes on Lady Strachey: Monk's House Papers, University of Sussex.

25 Quoted in Watney, *The Art of Duncan Grant*, p.81.

26 Bartle Grant to Lady Strachey, n.d. [April 1903]: IOL.

27 Leigh Farnell to DG, n.d. [22 September 1903]: DGP.

28 DG, unpublished memoir notes on his earliest sexual experiences: Clarissa Roche.

29 Then called Mentone, as at that date it was just inside the Italian border.

30 DG, 'Mentone 1902', unpublished memoir: Clarissa Roche.

31 DG, 'A Curious Incident', an expanded version of the above essay, written for the Memoir Club, unpublished: DGP.

32 See note 27.

33 Ibid.

34 This painting, formerly in the collection of Maynard Keynes, now belongs to King's College, Cambridge. For further discussion of this and other DG copies of Piero della Francesca see Luciano Cheles, 'Copie ed echi di Piero in Inghilterra', in R. Varese (ed.), *La Conoscenza di Piero* (Ancona-Bologna: Il Lavoro Editoriale, 1997).

CHAPTER 3: LYTTON AND PARIS

1 Pernel Strachey to DG, 26 February 1905: DGP. The Whistler memorial exhibition at the New Gallery opened just as a massive Watts memorial exhibition at the Royal Academy closed and went on tour to Newcastle, Manchester and Edinburgh.

2 Marius Forestier to DG, undated fragment [1905]: DGP.

3 G. E. Moore, *Principia Ethica*, Cambridge University Press, 1903, revised edition 1993, introduced by Thomas Baldwin, p.234.

4 See J. M. Keynes, 'My Early Beliefs', in *Two Memoirs* (London: Macmillan, 1949) and Leonard Woolf, *Sowing: An Autobiography of the Years 1880–1904* (London: Hogarth Press, 1967), pp.148–9.

5 An instance of this is Strachey's description of the doughty Cambridge matron, Henry Sidgwick's widow – 'a faded monolith of ugly beauty, with a nervous laugh and an infinitely remote mind, which, mysteriously realises all'. Quoted in Holroyd, *Lytton Strachey* (1994), p.157.

6 Recounted to the author by Paul Roche, who heard it from DG.

7 Quoted in Holroyd, *Lytton Strachey* (1994), p.261.

8 Michael Holroyd (ed.), *Lytton Strachey by Himself. A Self-Portrait*, (London: Heinemann, 1971), pp.114–15.

9 Quoted in Holroyd, *Lytton Strachey* (1994), p.284.

10 Quoted in Holroyd, *Lytton Strachey* (1994), p.126.

11 Lytton Strachey to J. M. Keynes, 11 October 1905: KCC.

12 Lytton Strachey to J. M. Keynes, 13 October 1905: KCC.

13 J. M. Keynes to Lytton Strachey, 18 October 1905: KCC.

14 Lytton Strachey to J. M. Keynes, 23 October 1905: KCC.

15 Lytton Strachey to J. M. Keynes, 26 October 1905: KCC.

16 Lytton Strachey to J. M. Keynes, 30 October 1905: KCC.

17 J. M. Keynes to Lytton Strachey, 15 November 1905: KCC.

18 Lytton Strachey to J. M. Keynes, 17 November 1905: KCC.

19 Lytton Strachey to J. M. Keynes, 24 November 1905: KCC.

20 Lytton Strachey to J. M. Keynes, 9 December 1905: KCC.

21 J. M. Keynes to Lytton Strachey, 10 December 1905: KCC.

22 Lytton Strachey to J. M. Keynes, 19 December 1905: KCC.

23 Lytton Strachey to J. M. Keynes, 9 January 1906: KCC.

24 J. M. Keynes to Lytton Strachey, 10 January 1906: KCC.

25 Lytton Strachey to J. M. Keynes, 21 January 1906: KCC.

26 J. M. Keynes to Lytton Strachey, 20 January 1906: KCC.

27 Lytton Strachey to J. M. Keynes, 10 January 1906: KCC.

28 Lytton Strachey to J. M. Keynes, 5 February 1906: KCC.

29 Lytton Strachey to J. M. Keynes, 4, 5 February 1906: KCC.

30 For an account of the formation and exhibiting history of this club see Richard Shone, 'The Friday Club', *Burlington Magazine*, May 1979,

pp.279–84; reprinted in the catalogue to a Friday Club exhibition held at the Michael Parkin Gallery, London in 1996.

31 DG, 'Paris Memoir': TGA.

32 Ibid.

33 Ibid. The statement, drawn from this memoir, that Grant was too shy to show his Chardin copy to Blanche conflicts with Richard Shone's mention of this copy in *Bloomsbury Portraits* (1993), p.42.

34 Dorothy Bussy to Lady Strachey, 18 February 1906: IOL.

35 DG to Lytton Strachey, 1 March [1906]: BL.

CHAPTER 4: *SIC TRANSIT*

1 Quoted in Michael Holroyd, *Augustus John. Volume I. The Years of Innocence* (London: Heinemann, 1974), pp.265–6.

2 J. M. Keynes to Lytton Strachey, 20 January 1906: KCC.

3 DG to Paul Roche, quoted in Robert Skidelsky, *John Maynard Keynes. Volume I. Hopes Betrayed, 1883–1920* (London: Macmillan, 1983), p.191.

4 Lytton Strachey to DG, 5 March 1906: BL.

5 Ibid.

6 DG to Lytton Strachey, 8 March [April] 1906: BL.

7 Skidelsky, *John Maynard Keynes*, I:172.

8 Lytton Strachey to DG, 10 April 1906: DGP.

9 DG to Arthur Hobhouse, 10 July [1906]: copy, Robert Skidelsky, of original belonging to Richard Shone.

10 James Strachey to Lytton Strachey, 18 December 1906: BL.

11 DG to James Strachey, 18 December 1906: BL.

12 Maxwell Armfield to DG, 21 March 1906: KCC.

13 Ethel Grant to DG, n.d. [February 1906]: DGP.

14 Ethel Grant to Lytton Strachey, 23 February 1906: BL.

15 DG to James Strachey, 6 March [April] 1906: BL.

16 DG to Lytton Strachey, 20 May 1906: BL.

17 DG to Lytton Strachey, 5 July 1906: BL.

18 DG's 'Paris Memoir' suggests that he returned to Paris in October 1906: the Slade School of Art's registers in their Archives prove otherwise.

19 Quoted in Paul Roche, *With Duncan Grant in Southern Turkey* (Renfrew: Honeyglen, 1982), pp.74–5.

20 Lytton Strachey to J. M. Keynes, 21 November 1906: KCC.

21 DG to James Strachey, 16 January 1907: BL.

22 DG to Lytton Strachey, 21 January 1907: BL.

23 DG to Lytton Strachey, 20 February 1907: BL.

24 DG to Lytton Strachey, 20 February 1907: BL.

25 DG to Lytton Strachey, [10] March 1907: BL.

26 Degas's *Interior* is in the Henry P. McIlhenny Collection, Philadelphia. The picture has been exhaustively discussed by various scholars, including Theodore Reff. See his *Degas. The Artist's Mind* (London: Thames & Hudson, 1976), pp.200–38.

27 DG to Lytton Strachey, [10] March 1907: BL.

28 In the Tate Gallery collection.

29 Anrep later married Helen Maitland, but only after the birth of their second child. Having first produced a daughter, Helen had a boy the second time round. Boris disapproved of illegitimate sons and so tied the knot.

30 Lytton Strachey to DG, 1 April 1907: BL.

31 Lytton Strachey to Clive Bell, 25 March 1907: BL.

32 Clive Bell to DG, 5 April 1907: KCC.

33 DG to Lytton Strachey, 9 April 1907: BL.

34 DG to Lytton Strachey, 7 April 1907: BL.

35 Maxwell Armfield, 'My Approach to Art', *Maxwell Armfield 1881–1972*,

exhibition catalogue, Southampton Art Gallery, Birnmingham Art Gallery and the Fine Art Society, London, 1978.

CHAPTER 5: MAYNARD

1 DG to Lytton Strachey [30 June 1907]: BL.
2 Ethel Grant to DG, 10 May 1907: DGP.
3 DG to James Strachey [8 December 1907]: BL.
4 DG to Lytton Strachey, 8 November 1907: BL.
5 Lytton Strachey to DG, 20 January 1907: BL.
6 Lytton Strachey to Clive Bell, 17 January 1906: BL.
7 J. M. Keynes to Lytton Strachey, 11 March 1906: KCC.
8 Quoted in Holroyd, *Lytton Strachey*, p.292.
9 DG to J. M. Keynes, 3 June 1908: RS.
10 Paul Roche to Robert Skidelsky, 14 November 1981: R. Skidelsky.
11 J. M. Keynes to DG, 28 July 1908: KCC.
12 DG to J. M. Keynes, 27 June 1908: RS.
13 Lytton Strachey to James Strachey, 17 July 1908: BL.
14 DG to J. M. Keynes, 25 July 1908: RS.
15 DG to J. M. Keynes, 29 July 1908: RS.
16 Ibid.
17 DG to J. M. Keynes [2 August] 1908: RS.
18 DG to J. M. Keynes, 6 August 1908: RS.
19 J. M. Keynes to DG, 31 August 1908: BL.
20 J. M. Keynes to DG, 13 August 1908: BL.
21 In the collection of King's College, Cambridge.
22 DG to J. M. Keynes, [?] October 1908: RS.
23 J. M. Keynes to DG, 24 October 1908: BL.
24 J. M. Keynes to DG, 25 October 1908: BL.
25 James Strachey to Lytton Strachey, 2 November 1908: BL.
26 DG to J. M. Keynes, 29 December 1908: RS.
27 DG to J. M. Keynes, 21 January 1909: BL.
28 Ibid.
29 Arthur Cole was to found and endow the Rowe Music Library at King's College, Cambridge, where DG's portrait of him still hangs.
30 DG to J. M. Keynes, 24 January 1909: BL.
31 DG to J. M. Keynes, 1 February 1909: BL.
32 Lytton Strachey to DG, 6 February 1909: BL.
33 Vanessa Bell to DG, 3 November [1909]: DGP.
34 DG to J. M. Keynes, 31 July 1909: RS.
35 Vanessa Bell, untitled, unpublished two-page autobiographical memoir: KCC.
36 Lytton Strachey to DG, 2 June 1907: BL.
37 DG to Lytton Strachey, 15 January 1908: BL.
38 J. M. Keynes to DG, 16 February 1909: BL.
39 J. M. Keynes to DG, 14 February 1909: BL.
40 DG to J. M. Keynes, 25 February [1909]: BL.
41 'M. Simon Bussy's Pastels', *Spectator*, 6 March 1906.
42 'Mr Wilson Steer's pictures', *Spectator*, 15 May 1909.
43 'The New English Art Club at Suffolk Street', *Spectator*, 19 June 1909.
44 S. P. Rosenbaum, *Edwardian Bloomsbury. The Early Literary History of the Bloomsbury Group*, (London: Macmillan, 1994), p.287.
45 'The New Victoria and Albert Museum', *Spectator*, 26 June 1909.
46 DG to J. M. Keynes, 30 March 1909: BL.
47 DG to J. M. Keynes, 5 April 1909: BL.

48 DG to James Strachey, 22 April 1909: BL.
49 DG to J. M. Keynes, 26 April 1909: BL.
50 DG to Lytton Strachey, 7 May 1909: BL.
51 DG to J. M. Keynes, 25 May 1909: BL.
52 *Horizon*, 7 June 1914.
53 DG to J. M. Keynes, [July 1909]: BL.
54 Formerly in the collection of J. M. Keynes and now on loan to the Fitzwilliam Museum from King's College, Cambridge.
55 Lytton Strachey to J. M. Keynes, 13 August 1909: KC.

CHAPTER 6: A CEREMONIAL BIRCHING

1 So Richard Shone states in *Bloomsbury Portraits* (1993), p.255. Reference to Vera Waddington's involvement with this mural can be found in her diaries. I am grateful to Dr Christina Roaf, Vera Waddington's daughter, for sending me extracts from these.
2 Richard Shone, 'The Friday Club', *Burlington Magazine*, May 1975, p.280.
3 DG. Transcript of a conversation held at Charleston with Quentin Bell, 3 April 1967: University of Sussex.
4 See William Rothenstein, *Men and Memories, Vol. II* (London: Faber & Faber (1934), pp.180–1.
5 Virginia Woolf, *Letters*, I: p.377
6 DG, *Desert Island Discs*, transmitted 15 and 17 March 1975, Radio 4.
7 Adrian Stephen, *The Dreadnought Hoax* (London: Hogarth Press, 1936), p.10.
8 Not as Emperor Menelik and his suite, as has been stated.
9 Not 10 February, as has been stated.
10 See note 7.
11 DG to J. M. Keynes, 9 February 1910: BL.
12 Ibid.
13 Adrian Stephen, *The Dreadnought Hoax*, pp.40–1.

14 DG, 'Early Memories of Virginia Woolf', MS in the possession of Paul Roche. First published in *Horizon*, June 1941, Vol.III, No.18; reprinted in Joan Russell Noble (ed.), *Recollections of Virginia Woolf* (London: Peter Owen, 1972).
15 Ibid.
16 Ibid.
17 Ibid.
18 DG to J. M. Keynes, 25 January 1910: BL.
19 Now in the Metropolitan Museum of Art, New York.
20 See note 14.
21 DG to J. M. Keynes [12 January 1910]: BL.
22 D. W. J. A. Barber to J. M. Keynes, 12 January 1910: BL.
23 DG to J. M. Keynes [28 February 1910]: BL.
24 Roger Fry, *Vision and Design* (London: Chatto & Windus, 1920), p.25.
25 DG to Lytton Strachey, 15 April 1910: BL.
26 J. M. Keynes to DG, 30 May 1910: DGP.
27 J. M. Keynes to DG, 10 June 1910: BL.
28 DG to J. M. Keynes, 2 June 1910: BL.
29 DG to J. M. Keynes, 18 August 1910: BL.
30 DG to J. M. Keynes, 1 September 1910: BL.
31 J. M. Keynes to DG, 17 December 1910, quoted in Robert Skidelsky, *John Maynard Keynes: Hopes Betrayed 1883–1920* (London: Macmillan, 1983), p.256.
32 DG to J. M. Keynes, 13 October 1910: BL.
33 R. Fry to DG, 30 October 1910: KCC.

CHAPTER 7: THE ART-QUAKE OF 1910

1 Then owned by the Yorkshire Penny Bank.
2 Quoted in Hugh and Mirabel Cecil,

Clever Hearts: Desmond and Molly MacCarthy – A Biography (London: Gollancz, 1990), p.107.

3 Ibid., p.102.

4 Quoted in Desmond MacCarthy, 'The Art-Quake of 1910', *Listener*, 1 February 1945.

5 See Ian Dunlop, *The Shock of the New: Seven Historic Exhibitions of Modern Art* (London: Weidenfeld & Nicolson, 1972); J. H. Bullen (ed.), *Post-Impressionism in England* (London: Routledge, 1988); and S.K. Tillyard, *Impact of Modernism, 1900–1920* (London: Routledge, 1988).

6 *Morning Post*, 7 November 1910; reprinted in Bullen (ed.), *Post-Impressionism in England*, p.101.

7 See T. B. Hyslop, 'Post-Illusionism and the Art of the Insane', *Nineteenth Century*, February 1911; reprinted in Bullen (ed.), *Post-Impressionism in England*, pp.220–81.

8 For an excellent discussion of Roger Fry's 'desire to persuade his readers to change the way they see' and the political implications of Post-Impressionism, see *A Roger Fry Reader*, edited and introduced by Christopher Reed (University of Chicago Press, 1996), pp.48–58.

9 Quentin Bell, *Roger Fry. An Inaugural Lecture* (Leeds University Press, 1964), p.13.

10 In Richard Shone's possession.

11 In the Tate Gallery collection.

12 Roger Fry to DG, 9 November 1910: KCC.

13 Quoted in Ysanne Holt, *Philip Wilson Steer* (Mid-Glamorgan: Seren Books, 1992), p.110.

14 DG to J. M. Keynes, 14 November 1910: BL.

15 When the Tate Gallery bought *The Lemon Gatherers* in 1922 it acknowledged Clive Bell as its original owner. DG confirmed this in *The Artist* (August 1934), where he is quoted as saying that his first sale of a painting was to Clive Bell at a Friday Club exhibition and that the picture he bought was in the Tate Gallery. This can only refer to the *The Lemon Gatherers*.

16 Vanessa Bell to Clive Bell [23 June 1910]: TGA.

17 In the Tate Gallery collection.

18 The wriggling brushstrokes in the treatment of the grass are likened by Simon Watney in *The Art of Duncan Grant* (p.28) to the Italian use of decorative scribble to create imitative marbling.

19 Private collection, London.

20 DG to J. M. Keynes, 29 November 1910: BL.

21 'The Grafton Gallery – I', *Nation*, 19 November 1910; 'The Post-Impressionists – II', *Nation*, 3 December 1910; 'A Postscript on Post-Impressionism', *Nation*, 24 December 1910; and 'Post-Impressionism', *Fortnightly Review*, 95, May 1911, pp.856–67.

22 Now in Southampton Art Gallery.

23 Roger Fry to Clive Bell, n.d. [*c*. March 1911]: Denys Sutton (ed.), *The Letters of Roger Fry* (London: Chatto & Windus, 1972), Vol. I, p.344.

24 Quoted in Barbara Strachey, *Remarkable Relations. The Story of the Pearsall Smith Family* (London: Gollancz, 1980), pp.250–1.

25 Lytton Strachey to James Strachey, 20 March 1911: BL.

26 DG to J. M. Keynes, 3 March 1911: BL.

27 Jacques Raverat to DG, 19 July 1911: DGP.

28 DG to J. M. Keynes, 29 April 1911: DGP.

29 DG, typescript of interview with Sarah Whitfield: TGA.

30 Private collection, Northern Ireland.

31 Vanessa Bell to Virginia Stephen, 24 June [1910]: Berg.

32 Vanessa Bell to Roger Fry [6 July 1911]: TGA.

33 *Pall Mall Gazette*, 11 April 1913.

34 Both presented by DG to the Tate Gallery in 1943.

35 *Morning Post*, 19 July 1911.

36 Quoted in Miranda Seymour, *Ottoline Morrell: Life on a Grand Scale*

(London: Hodder & Stoughton, 1992), p.80.

37 Adrian Stephen to DG, 19 August 1911: DGP.

38 James Strachey to Lytton Strachey, 3 August 1911: BL.

39 J. M. Keynes to Francis Birrell, 8 August 1911: courtesy of R. A. Gekowski.

40 Vanessa Bell to DG, 7 September 1911: DGP.

41 Vera Waddington's diary, 6 June 1912: Dr Christine Roaf.

42 Karin Stephen's diary, MSS: Lilly Library, Indiana University, Bloomington, Indiana.

43 Ibid.

CHAPTER 8: 'THE COMING GENIUS'

1 DG to Lytton Strachey, 4 January 1912: BL.

2 DG to J. M. Keynes, 13 February 1909: RS.

3 Lytton Strachey to Clive Bell, 21 May 1909: BL. Quoted in Holroyd, *Lytton Strachey* (1994), pp.205–6.

4 Quoted in Frederick Spotts (ed.), *The Letters of Leonard Woolf* (London: Weidenfeld & Nicolson, 1989), p.149.

5 George Mallory to Ruth Turner [23 May 1914]; Mallory Papers, Magdalene College, Cambridge.

6 George Mallory to DG, 1 November 1910: DGP.

7 DG to George Mallory, 7 November 1910: Copy, DGP.

8 David Pye, *George Leigh Mallory* (Oxford University Press, 1927), p.67.

9 DG to George Mallory, n.d.: Copy, DGP.

10 DG to George Mallory, n.d. [1914]: Copy, DGP.

11 Virginia Woolf, *Letters* I: 431.

12 Ka Cox to DG, 26 March 1912: DGP.

13 One of these two portraits is in a private collection in London, the other in the National Museum of Wales, Cardiff.

14 Ka Cox to James Strachey, 23 July 1912: BL.

15 Ka Cox to James Strachey, 12 August 1909: BL.

16 Rupert Brooke to J. M. Keynes, 22 August 1911: KCC.

17 Michael Hastings, *The Handsomest Young Man in England. Rupert Brooke* (London: Michael Joseph, 1967), p.58.

18 Vanessa Bell to Clive Bell, n.d. [16 January 1912]: TGA.

19 G. H. Luce to J. M. Keynes, 2 December 1912: KCC.

20 G. H. Luce to J. M. Keynes, n.d.: KCC.

21 G. H. Luce to J. M. Keynes, 27 April 1913: KCC.

22 Private collection, Somerset.

23 Anthony d'Offay, London.

24 Now in the collection of King's College, Cambridge.

25 H. M. Plowden to Lady Strachey, 31 March 1911: IOL.

26 Jane Harrison to J. M. Keynes, n.d. [February 1912]: BL.

27 Jane Harrison to DG, 22 February 1912: DGP.

28 Robert Gathorne-Hardy (ed.), *The Early Memoirs of Lady Ottoline Morrell* (London: Faber & Faber, 1963), p.228.

29 See Richard Buckle, *Nijinsky* (London: Weidenfeld & Nicolson, 1971), pp.258–9.

30 Quoted in Miranda Seymour, *Ottoline Morrell: Life on the Grand Scale* (London: Hodder, 1992), p.167.

31 DG to J. M. Keynes, 28 September 1912: BL.

32 One of DG's designs for the Crosby Hall exhibition was included in a Sotheby's sale in London on 28 September 1994 (lot 65). The catalogue entry stated that it had been withdrawn from the Crosby Hall exhibition because it was earmarked by the Contemporary Art Society, which did not, in the final outcome, acquire it. This statement conflicts with the observation in one of Vanessa Bell's letters that none of their designs had been hung at Crosby Hall.

33 Now in the Ferens Art Gallery, Hull.
34 Neither the mural nor the house itself still exists, but contemporary photographs of the mural suggest that its size must have been about 9 × 30 inches.
35 Denys Sutton (ed.), *Letters of Roger Fry*, Vol.I, p.356.
36 Vanessa Bell to DG, 2 May 1912: DGP.
37 Some sixty-three years later, on the radio programme *Desert Island Discs*, DG was asked which picture of his he would choose if only one of his paintings were to survive. He replied that he could not answer that question with any conviction, but that *The Tub* had seemed to him 'satisfactory' at the time it was painted and still seemed so. He was then aged ninety.
38 DG to Virginia Woolf, 23 September 1912: Monk's House Papers, University of Sussex.
39 Rupert Brooke, 'The Post-Impressionist Exhibition at the Grafton Galleries', *Cambridge Magazine*, 23 November 1912.
40 *Observer*, 27 October 1912.
41 'The Post-Impressionists – II', *Cambridge Magazine*, 30 November 1912.
42 Hilton Young, 'In and Out', The Life and Opinions of Lord Kennet (Hilton Young) MS: CUL.
43 Vanessa Bell to Hilton Young, 13 January [1913]: CUL.

CHAPTER 9: IMMORAL FURNITURE

1 Recounted by Osbert Sitwell in his introduction to *A Free House: The Writings of Walter Richard Sickert* (London: Macmillan, 1947), p.xvii.
2 Adrian Stephen to Ka Cox, n.d. [January 1913]: Mrs Arnold Forster.
3 DG interview with Sarah Whitfield, *c.* 1970–1: Tape and typescript in TGA.
4 Ibid.
5 In the collection of the Victoria & Albert Museum.
6 Regina Marler (ed.), *Selected Letters of Vanessa Bell* (London: Blooms-

bury, 1993), p.137.
7 Ibid., p.121.
8 Vanessa Bell to Hilton Young, 13 January [1914]: Cambridge University Library.
9 *Selected Letters of Vanessa Bell*, p.112.
10 Duncan Grant to Virginia Stephen, July 1911: University of Sussex Library.
11 *Selected Letters of Vanessa Bell*, p.100.
12 Ibid., p.131.
13 DG, 'Jacques Copeau', unpublished manuscript: DGP.
14 When questioned about this production in his later years Duncan Grant was under the impression that it was never performed. There is no record of any Granville-Barker production, but Lillah MacCarthy, in her autobiography, refers to the success of Grant's *Macbeth* designs in Paris. No record of any Parisian production has so far been found. MacCarthy may have been confusing *Macbeth* with *Twelfth Night*, which was performed in Paris with designs by Duncan.
15 *Selected Letters of Vanessa Bell*, p.139.
16 Vanessa Bell to DG, 19 May [1912]: TGA.
17 Virginia Woolf, *Letters* II: p.25.
18 *Selected Letters of Vanessa Bell*, p.139. A footnote to this letter states that Vanessa is here referring to Duncan Grant. This is questionable.
19 Ibid., p.156.
20 Quoted in Judith Collins, *The Omega Workshops* (London: Secker & Warburg, 1984), p.42.
21 In the collection of the Victoria and Albert Museum.
22 The design is in the Victoria and Albert Museum and the rug itself in the Courtauld Institute Galleries.
23 Roger Fry to DG, 28 November 1913: KCC.
24 Quoted in Winifred Gill to DG, June 1966: NAL. This is one of a series of letters that Gill wrote to Grant on the Omega and the source of several of the anecdotes in this chapter.
25 Winifred Gill to DG, 10 March 1970: DGP.
26 Winifred Gill to Agnes Fry, 27 Sep-

tember 1934: KCC.

27 Quoted in Winifred Gill to DG, 4 July 1966: NAL.

28 Vanessa Bell to DG, 28 September 1913: DGP.

29 Ibid.

30 J. M. Keynes to DG, 14 October 1913: BL.

31 *Letters of Roger Fry*, II: 373.

32 For this and other documents connected with the Ideal Home rumpus see S. P. Rosenbaum (ed.), *The Bloomsbury Group* (London: Croom Helm, 1975), p.337ff.

33 *Daily Sketch*, 20 December 1913.

34 In the Ferens Art Gallery, Hull.

35 George Mallory to DG, 8 February 1914: DGP.

36 DG to Lytton Strachey, 6 January [1914]: BL.

37 *Daily Telegraph*, 5 January 1914.

38 *Selected Letters of Vanessa Bell*, p.154.

39 DG to J. M. Keynes [24 January 1914]: BL.

40 DG to Lytton Strachey, 26 January [1914]: BL.

41 Lytton Strachey to DG, 6 February 1914: BL.

42 *Selected Letters of Vanessa Bell*, p.160, where this letter is incorrectly dated 25 March 1914. Its correct date is 29 January 1914.

43 Ibid., p.155.

44 DG to Clive Bell, 26 February 1914: TGA.

45 Ibid.

46 *Selected Letters of Vanessa Bell*, p.158.

47 Jacques Copeau to DG, n.d. [1913], translated by DG for his unpublished essay 'Jacques Copeau': DGP.

48 DG, 'Jacques Copeau', unpublished manuscript: DGP.

49 Michel Saint-Denis, *Training for the Theatre* (London: Heinemann, 1982), p.34.

50 Jacques Copeau to DG, 27 May 1915: DGP.

51 DG, 'Jacques Copeau', unpublished manuscript: DGP.

CHAPTER 10: CROQUET AND CUCK-OLDS

1 Roger Fry to DG, 5 March 1914: KCC.

2 Vanessa Bell to DG, 25 February [1914]: DGP.

3 Vanessa Bell to DG, 17 February [1914]: DGP.

4 Roger Fry, 'Representation in Art', unpublished lecture notes: KCC.

5 In the Sir Michael Sadler Collection, University of Leeds.

6 Private collection, Sussex.

7 National Portrait Gallery.

8 *Daily Herald*, undated press-cutting: TGA.

9 Quoted in William Rothenstein, *Men and Memories. Volume I*, p. 181.

10 Both paintings are now in the Tate Gallery collection.

11 Richard Morphet, introduction to *Vanessa Bell*, catalogue to exhibition held at the Anthony d'Offay Gallery, London, 1973.

12 Vanessa Bell to J. M. Keynes, 16 April [1914]: KCC.

13 DG to Lytton Strachey [30 April 1914]: BL.

14 Winifred Gill to DG, 12 September 1966: NAL.

15 Adila d'Aranyi to DG, 24 July 1914: DGP.

16 Ferenc Békassy to DG, July 1914: DGP.

17 DG to Ferenc Békassy, n.d. [late July/early August 1914]: DGP.

18 Manuscript notes on the *Abstract Kinetic Scroll*, on back of receipt: DGP.

19 See Shone, *Bloomsbury Portraits* (revised edition 1993), p. 141; and Watney, *The Art of Duncan Grant*, pp. 39–41.

20 Karin Stephen's Diary, MS: Lilly Library, Indiana University, Bloomington, Indiana.

21 Typescript notes based on DG's comments, in conversation with Quentin and Olivier Bell, 5 April 1967: University of Sussex Library.

22 Virginia Woolf, *Diary*, I: p.87.

23 Karin Stephen's Diary, MS: Lilly Library, Indiana University.

24 Karin Stephen's Diary, quoted in

Barbara Strachey, *Remarkable Relations: The Story of the Pearsall Smith Family*, p. 271.

25 See note 22.
26 DG to Lytton Strachey [8 September 1914]: BL.
27 Maresco Pearce to DG, n.d. [1914?]: DGP.
28 Francis Birrell to J. T. Sheppard, n.d. [1914?]: KCC.
29 DG to George Mallory, 4 October 1914: Copy, DGP.
30 J. M. Keynes to DG, 4 November 1914: BL.
31 J. M. Keynes to DG, 18 November 1914: KCC.
32 Clive Bell, Minutes of the Play-Reading Society: KCC.
33 Vanessa Bell to DG, n.d. [September 1914]: DGP.
34 David Garnett, *The Golden Echo* (London: Chatto & Windus, 1954), p. 253.
35 DG to David Garnett, 15 January 1913, with Garnett's inscription on the back: Henrietta Garnett.
36 Garnett *The Golden Echo*, p.18.
37 Ibid., p.85.
38 Ibid., pp.210–11.
39 Ibid., p.211.
40 Lady Ottoline Morrell, quoted in Miranda Seymour, *Ottoline Morrell. Life on the Grand Scale*, pp.205–6.

CHAPTER 11: AN INTRICATE DANCE

1 David Garnett, Diary, MS: RG.
2 DG to David Garnett, n.d. [January 1915]: HG.
3 See note 1.
4 Ibid.
5 Clive Bell to Mary Hutchinson, 7 January 1915: HRHRC.
6 See note 1.
7 Ibid.
8 DG to David Garnett [25 January 1915]: HG.
9 Clive Bell to Mary Hutchinson, 17 February 1915: HRHRC.
10 See note 1.
11 Vanessa Bell to DG [6 May 1915]: DGP.

12 J. M. Keynes to DG, 25 April 1915: KCC.
13 Lytton Strachey to DG, 25 April 1915: BL.
14 David Garnett, in *D.H. Lawrence: A Composite Biography. Volume One, 1885–1919*, gathered, arranged and edited by Edward Nehls (University of Wisconsin Press, 1957), pp.266–7. This passage is based on the account given in David Garnett, *The Flowers in the Forest* (London: Chatto & Windus, 1955), pp.34–5.
15 Ibid., p.267.
16 DG to Edward Nehls [27 November 1953], quoted in *D. H. Lawrence; A Composite Biography*, Vol. I, p.269.
17 George J. Zytarck and James T. Boulton (eds), *The Letters of D. H. Lawrence: Volume II June 1913–October 1916*, (Cambridge University Press, 1981), p.263.
18 *The Letters of D. H. Lawrence*, Vol. II, pp.320–1.
19 Ibid., p.319.
20 Ibid., pp.320–1.
21 See Quentin Bell, *Bloomsbury* (London: Weidenfeld & Nicolson, 1968), p.52; and S. P. Rosenbaum, 'Keynes; Lawrence, and Cambridge Revisited', *Cambridge Quarterly*, 1982, Vol. XI, No. 1, pp.252–64.
22 David Garnett's 1915 diary, unpublished: RG.
23 Vanessa Bell to Clive Bell [?25 March 1915]: TGA.
24 Clive Bell to Mary Hutchinson, 30 March 1915: HRHRC.
25 DG to David Garnett, n.d.: HG.
26 DG to Hilton Young, n.d. [April 1915]: UCL.
27 Vanessa Bell to David Garnett [12 April 1915]: HG.
28 DG to David Garnett [12 April 1915]: HG.
29 Vanessa Bell to Clive Bell [28 April 1915]: TGA.
30 Roger Fry to Vanessa Bell, 16 September 1917: TGA.
31 Roger Fry to DG, 25 April 1915: DGP.
32 *Letters of Roger Fry* II: 385.
33 Roger Fry to Clive Bell, 28 May 1915:

TGA.

34 DG to David Garnett, 22 July 1915: HG.

35 DG to David Garnett [6 May 1915]: HG.

36 DG to David Garnett [13 June 1915]: HG.

37 DG to David Garnett, n.d. [July 1915]: HG.

38 Vanessa Bell to David Garnett, 12 July 1915: RG.

39 DG to David Garnett, 12 July [1915]: HG.

40 Vanessa Bell to DG [6 August 1915]: DGP.

41 Vanessa Bell to David Garnett, 22 September [1915]: RG.

42 Vanessa Bell to DG, n.d. [September 1915]: DGP.

43 DG to David Garnett [11 October 1915]: HG.

44 DG to George Mallory, 27 October 1915: Copies, DGP.

45 DG to David Garnett [11 October 1915]: HG.

46 DG to George Mallory, 27 October 1915: Copies, DGP.

47 H. C. Wallis to Daisy McNeil, 9 November 1915: HG.

48 DG to David Garnett, 6 November 1915: HG.

49 Now in Leicester Museum and Art Gallery.

50 DG to Mark Gertler, n.d. [December 1915]: Luke Gertler.

51 DG to David Garnett, 19 November 1915: HG.

52 DG to David Garnett, n.d. [November 1915]: HG.

53 David Garnett (ed.), *Carrington. Letters and Extracts from Her Diaries* (Oxford University Press, 1970), p.55.

CHAPTER 12: FROM WISSETT TO CHARLESTON

1 David Garnett to DG, n.d. [early 1916]: DGP.

2 DG to David Garnett, 3 March 1916: HG.

3 Now in the collection of King's College, Cambridge.

4 DG to David Garnett [7 March 1916]: HG.

5 DG to David Garnett, n.d. [March 1916]: HG.

6 Vanessa Bell to DG [15 March 1916]: DGP.

7 Vanessa Bell to DG, 14 March 1916: DGP.

8 Clive Bell to Mary Hutchinson, 6 February 1916: HRHRC.

9 DG to Vanessa Bell, n.d. [1916]: TGA.

10 *Selected Letters of Vanessa Bell*, p.195.

11 Ibid., p.198.

12 Quoted in Miranda Seymour, *Ottoline Morrell: Life on the Grand Scale*, p.323.

13 David Garnett, *The Flowers of the Forest*, p.117.

14 Virginia Woolf, *Diary*, V: 136.

15 DG to Vanessa Bell, 1 September 1916: TGA.

16 Vanessa Bell to DG, n.d. [late September 1916]: DGP.

17 Dora Carrington to Vanessa Bell, n.d. [September 1916]: KCC.

18 David Garnett to DG, n.d. [September/October 1916]: DGP.

19 DG to David Garnett, 3 October 1916: HG.

20 DG to Vanessa Bell, 28 September 1916: TGA.

21 David Garnett to DG [9 October 1916]: DGP.

22 Garnett, *The Flowers of the Forest*, p.145.

23 J. M. Keynes to DG, 14 January 1917: BL.

24 Garnett, *The Flowers of the Forest*, p.140.

25 Virginia Woolf, *Letters*, II: 171.

26 'Copies and Translations', catalogue, Omega Workshops, May 1917.

27 Vanessa Bell to DG, 11 July 1917: DGP.

28 Garnett, *The Flowers of the Forest*, pp.29–30.

29 Ibid., p.28.

30 Woolf, *Letters*, I, p.144.

31 Vanessa Bell to DG, n.d. [spring 1917]: DGP.

32 David Garnett, Diary: unpublished

manuscript, RG.

33 Ulster Museum, Belfast.

34 Adrian Stephen to Ka Cox, 16 March [1913/14]: Mrs Mark Arnold-Forster. Further proof of DG's desire for a child appears in a letter from Clive Bell to Mary Hutchinson (16 June 1918): 'I have heard from Vanessa: she and Duncan have been trying to get a baby these two years; no precautions or anything of that sort; they had quite given up hope.' (HRHRC).

35 DG to Vanessa Bell, n.d. [1917–18]: TGA.

36 DG, Diary: unpublished manuscript, HG.

37 Ibid.

38 Ibid.

39 David Garnett, Diary: RG.

40 Vanessa Bell to J. M. Keynes, 18 February [1918]: KCC.

41 David Garnett, Diary: RG.

CHAPTER 13: BUTTER FOR THE BABY

1 David Garnett, unpublished diary: RG.

2 David Garnett, unpublished poem: RG.

3 DG, unpublished diary: HG.

4 See note 1.

5 David Garnett to J. M. Keynes, n.d. [March 1918]: KCC.

6 David Garnett to Constance Garnett, 22 April [1918]: HRHRC.

7 Ministry of Information to the Chairman, Central Tribunal, 13 June 1918: Imperial War Museum.

8 J. M. Keynes to Vanessa Bell, 25 August 1918: KCC.

9 Virginia Woolf to DG, n.d [1916/17]: DGP.

10 DG to Virginia Woolf [June 1918]: Monk's House Papers, University of Sussex.

11 Garnett, *The Flowers of the Forest*, p.175.

12 Ibid., p.175.

13 The only book of woodcuts published by the Hogarth Press was Roger Fry's *Twelve Original Woodcuts* in 1921.

14 *Original Woodcuts by Various Artists* was compiled in 1918 and bears this date on its title page, but it was not in fact available to the public until early the following year.

15 *Letters of Roger Fry*, Vol. II, p.438.

16 *Carrington. Letters and Extracts from Her Diaries*, p.104.

17 Vanessa Bell to J. M. Keynes, 11 September [1918]: KCC.

18 DG to Vanessa Bell [25 September 1918]: TGA.

19 J. M. Keynes to DG, 17 September 1918: BL.

20 DG to Vanessa Bell [23 September 1918]: TGA.

21 DG to David Garnett [30 September 1918]: HG.

22 DG to David Garnett [8 October 1918]: HG.

23 Lydia Lopokova, quoted in J. M. Keynes to DG, 20 October 1918: BL.

24 David Garnett to Constance Garnett, 27 October [1918]: HRHRC.

25 Garnett, *The Flowers of the Forest*, p.27.

26 David Garnett to Constance Garnett, 27 October [1918]: HRHRC.

27 Clive Bell to Vanessa Bell, n.d. [1918]: TGA.

28 Clive Bell to Vanessa Bell, n.d. [1918]: TGA.

29 Vanessa Bell to J. M. Keynes, n.d. [December 1918]: KCC.

30 DG to Clive Bell, n.d. [?26 December 1918]: TGA.

31 David Garnett to Angelica Bell, n.d. [1939]: KCC.

32 David Garnett to Lytton Strachey, 25 December 1918: BL.

33 DG to Virginia Woolf [?28 December 1918]: Monk's House Papers, University of Sussex.

34 Vanessa Bell to J. M. Keynes, 30 January [1919]: KCC.

35 Clive Bell to Mary Hutchinson, 8 January 1919: HRHRC.

36 DG to David Garnett, 27 January [1919]: HG.

37 See note 1.

38 Vanessa Bell to J. M. Keynes, 9 March [1919]: KCC.

39 See note 1.

40 In conversation with the author,

Wolfe, in his eighties, though an outspoken homosexual, had no recollection of any affair with Duncan Grant, when asked specifically about this visit to Charleston.

41 See note 1.
42 Virginia Woolf, *Diary*, I: 240.
43 Ibid.
44 Virginia Woolf, *Letters* II: 331.
45 DG in conversation with Simon Watney.
46 *Letters of Roger Fry*, II: 449.
47 See note 15.
48 The first two are in private collections; *Venus and Adonis* in the Tate Gallery.
49 Vanessa Bell to J. M. Keynes, 17 March [1919]: KCC.
50 Vanessa Bell to J. M. Keynes, 19 March [1919]: KCC.
51 Reproduced in Watney, *The Art of Duncan Grant*, p.44.
52 Roger Fry, 'Line as a Means of Expression in Modern Art', *Burlington Magazine*, December 1918, p.202.
53 *Carrington. Letters and Extracts from Her Diaries*, p.126.
54 DG to David Garnett [13 August 1919]: HG.
55 Vanessa Bell to David Garnett [28 July 1919]: HG.
56 J. M. Keynes to DG, 17 July 1919: BL.
57 DG to Vanessa Bell [26 July 1919]: TGA.
58 DG to Vanessa Bell, n.d. [1919]: TGA.
59 Clive Bell to Vanessa Bell, 20 November 1919: TGA.
60 Clive Bell to Vanessa Bell, 27 November 1919: TGA.
61 Clive Bell to Vanessa Bell, n.d. [November 1919]: TGA.
62 *The Studio*, December 1919, Vol.78, No.321, p.95.

CHAPTER 14: A QUESTION OF LABELS

1 Ethel Grant to DG, 6 February 1920: DGP.
2 *Daily Telegraph*, 16 February 1920.
3 *New Statesman*, 21 February 1920.
4 *Athenaeum*, 6 February 1920.
5 DG to Virginia Woolf, 31 July 1917: University of Sussex.
6 Woolf, *Letters*, II, p.422.
7 Clive Bell to Mary Hutchinson, 11 March 1920: HRHRC.
8 DG to Vanessa Bell, 16 March [1920]: TGA.
9 Vanessa Bell to J. M. Keynes, 15 May [1920]: KCC.
10 DG to David Garnett, 29 March 1930: HG.
11 DG, 'I Tatti: A Question of Labels', *Charleston Magazine*, Issue 10, Autumn/Winter 1994.
12 Kenneth Clark, *Another Part of the Wood. A Self-Portrait* (London: John Murray, 1974), p.127.
13 DG, 'Afternoon in Florence', MS fragment: DGP.
14 Vanessa Bell to Roger Fry, 17 May 1920: TGA.
15 Quoted in David Steel's 'Escape and Aftermath: Gide in Cambridge 1918', *The Yearbook of English Studies*, Vol.15, 1985, p.147.
16 DG to David Garnett, 29 September 1920: HG.
17 DG to David Garnett, 23 August [1920]: HG.
18 Lytton Strachey to DG, 1 August 1909: BL.
19 DG to Vanessa Bell [27 December 1920]: TGA.
20 DG to David Garnett, 17 April 1921: HG.
21 DG to David Garnett [22 April 1921]: HG.
22 Quoted in Garnett, *The Flowers of the Forest*, p.233.
23 Vanessa Bell to DG, 3 August [1921]: DGP.
24 DG to David Garnett, 4 September 1921: HG.
25 DG to Vanessa Bell, 22 September 1921: TGA.
26 Quentin Bell to Julian Bell, n.d. [*c.* 1935]: KCC.
27 *Selected Letters of Vanessa Bell*, p.258.
28 Vanessa Bell to Clive Bell [?23 October 1921]: TGA.

29 DG to David Garnett, 20 October 1921: HG.

30 Vanessa Bell to J. M. Keynes, 23 October [1921]: KCC.

31 Vanessa Bell to J. M. Keynes, 22 November [1921]: KCC.

32 Vanessa Bell to J. M. Keynes, 6 December [1921]: KCC.

33 Vanessa Bell to J. M. Keynes, 23 October [1921]: KCC.

34 *Observer*, 6 November 1921.

35 *Daily News*, 25 October 1921.

36 *The Sunday Times*, 23 October 1921.

37 *Manchester Guardian*, 25 October 1921.

38 Vanessa Bell to J. M. Keynes, 1 November [1921]: KCC.

39 DG to Sebastian Sprott, 19 November 1921: KCC.

40 DG to Vanessa Bell [17 December 1921]: TGA.

41 Clive Bell to Vanessa Bell, n.d. [1921]: TGA.

CHAPTER 15: QUI ME NEGLIGE ME PERD

1 DG to David Garnett, 4 January 1922: HG.

2 Frances Partridge, *Memories* (London: Victor Gollancz, 1981), p.91.

3 DG to David Garnett, 26 [January] 1922: HG.

4 Sebastian Sprott and Gabriel Atkin.

5 DG to Vanessa Bell [25 January 1922]: TGA.

6 DG to Vanessa Bell, 28 January 1922: TGA.

7 Vanessa Bell to J. M. Keynes, 4 February [1922]: KCC.

8 DG to Vanessa Bell, 28 January 1922: TGA.

9 Cyril Beaumont, *The Art of Lydia Lopokova* (1920), quoted in Milo Keynes (ed.), *Lydia Lopokova* (London: Weidenfeld & Nicolson, 1983), p.74.

10 J. M. Keynes to Vanessa Bell, 22 December 1921: TGA.

11 Lydia Lopokova to DG, n.d. [*c.* 1923]: BL.

12 Vanessa Bell to J. M. Keynes, 12 April [1922]: KCC.

13 Vanessa Bell to J. M. Keynes, n.d. [early May 1922]: KCC.

14 Vanessa Bell to J. M. Keynes, n.d. [early May 1922]: KCC.

15 Vanessa Bell to J. M. Keynes, 22 August [1922]: KCC.

16 For details concerning Maynard's activities as a picture collector and DG's influence, see Richard Shone with Duncan Grant, 'The Picture Collector' in Milo Keynes (ed.), *Essays on John Maynard Keynes* (Cambridge University Press, 1975), pp.280-9.

17 DG to Lytton Strachey [18 May 1921]: BL.

18 *Carrington: Letters and Extracts from Her Diaries*, pp.236-7.

19 Ibid.

20 DG to Vanessa Bell, 11 May 1923: TGA.

21 Now in the Laing Art Gallery, Newcastle-upon-Tyne.

22 Vanessa Bell to DG, 11 June [1923]: DGP.

23 DG to Vanessa Bell, 13 June 1923: TGA.

24 *Nation & Athenaeum*, 9 June 1923.

25 DG to Vanessa Bell, 13 June 1923: TGA

26 DG to Simon Bussy, 27 June 1923 (author's translation): Copy, DGP.

27 DG to Vanessa Bell [26 September 1923]: TGA.

28 DG to Vanessa Bell 31 July 1923: TGA

29 DG to Vanessa Bell, 26 December 1923: TGA.

30 Vanessa Bell to DG, 11 June [1923]: DGP.

31 DG to David Garnett [15 September 1922]: HG.

32 David Garnett to DG, n.d. [September 1922]: DGP.

33 DG to Mina Kirstein, 18 November 1924: Berg.

34 Vanessa Bell to DG [April 1923]: TGA.

35 Vanessa Bell to DG [April 1923]: TGA.

36 Vanessa Bell to DG, n.d. [1923]: TGA.

37 Vanessa Bell to DG [April 1923]: TGA.

38 DG to Vanessa Bell, 28 December 1923: TGA.

39 Vanessa Bell to DG, 8 October [1923]: DGP.

40 DG to Vanessa Bell [11 October 1923]: TGA.

41 Ethel Grant to David Garnett, 22 September 1924: RG.

42 Ethel Grant's list of her embroideries: TGA.

43 DG to Vanessa Bell [22 April 1924]: TGA.

44 DG to Vanessa Bell, 1 January 1924: TGA.

45 DG to J. T. Sheppard, n.d. [early 1924]: KCC.

46 DG to Vanessa Bell [25 April 1924]: TGA.

47 Foreword to *Grace at Charleston: Memories and Recipes*, printed by the Charleston Trust, p.5.

48 Vanessa Bell to DG, 8 October [1923]: DGP.

49 DG to Vanessa Bell [28 September 1923]: TGA.

50 Ibid.

51 DG to Vanessa Bell [16 June 1924]: TGA.

52 DG to Vanessa Bell, 24 June [1924]: TGA.

53 Franzi von Haas to DG, 22 June 1927: AVG.

54 DG to Vanessa Bell [16 June 1924]: TGA.

55 DG to Vanessa Bell [22 June 1924]: TGA.

CHAPTER 16: HUMMING WITH HEAT AND HAPPINESS

1 Clive Bell to Vanessa Bell, 1 November 1924: TGA.

2 DG to Edward Sackville-West, 10 August [1926]: RS.

3 DG to Vanessa Bell [19 September 1924]: TGA.

4 Woolf, *Diary*, III, p.91.

5 Lytton Strachey to DG, 23 August 1909: BL.

6 DG to Vanessa Bell, 3 January 1925: TGA.

7 DG to Vanessa Bell, 15 June 1924: TGA.

8 Vanessa Bell to DG [14 June 1923]: DGP.

9 Woolf, *Letters*, III, p.176.

10 DG to Gwen Raverat, 24 March 1925: National Art Library, Victoria and Albert Museum.

11 DG to Vanessa Bell [4 January 1924]: TGA.

12 Woolf, *Letters*, III, p.209.

13 Ibid, III, p.237.

14 Robert Medley, *Drawn from the Life* (London: Faber & Faber, 1983), pp.54–5.

15 Reproduced in Hermione Lee, *Virginia Woolf* (London: Chatto & Windus, 1996), plate 44.

16 Woolf, *Letters*, III, p.209.

17 Medley, *Drawn from the Life*, p.53.

18 Reproduced in Shone, *Bloomsbury Portraits* (1993) p.225, plate 155.

19 DG to Vanessa Bell, 25 December 1925: TGA.

20 DG to David Garnett, 26 December 1925: HG.

21 DGP.

22 In the National Gallery of Victoria, Melbourne.

23 Vanessa Bell to DG, 27 December [1925]: DGP.

24 DG to Edward Sackville-West, n.d. [1926?]: Private Collection.

25 Vanessa Bell to DG [? April 1926]: DGP.

26 DG to David Garnett, 6 April 1926: HG.

27 DG to Edward Sackville-West, n.d. [April/May 1926]: Private Collection.

28 DG to Vanessa Bell, 30 April [1926]: TGA.

29 Woolf, *Diary*, III, p.87.

30 Ibid., III, p.306.

31 DG to Edward Sackville-West, n.d. [1926]: Private Collection.

32 DG to Edward Sackville-West, 1 January 1927: Private Collection.

33 DG to Edward Sackville-West, n.d.: Private Collection.

34 DG to Edward Sackville-West, 2 August 1926: Private Collection.
35 *The Sunday Times*, 23 May 1926.
36 *Observer*, 23 May 1926. *The Circus* is now in the Government Art Collection.
37 *The Times*, 4 June 1926.
38 Nigel Nicolson (ed.), *Vita and Harold. The Letters of Vita Sackville-West and Harold Nicolson* (London: Weidenfeld & Nicolson, 1992, p.135.
39 DG to Edward Sackville-West, 13 August 1926: Private Collection.
40 Ibid.
41 DG to Edward Sackville-West, 17 September 1926: Private Collection.
42 *Vita and Harold*, p.204.
43 DG to Vanessa Bell, 7 January 1927: TGA.
44 Vanessa Bell to DG, n.d. [January 1927]: AVG.
45 DG to Vanessa Bell, 1 January 1927: TGA.
46 Quentin Bell to Julian Bell, 22 January [1927]: KCC.
47 DG to Vanessa Bell, n.d. [late January 1927]: TGA.
48 DG to Edward Sackville-West, 10 February 1927: Private Collection.
49 Vanessa Bell to J. M. Keynes, 13 February [1927]: KCC.
50 DG to Edward Sackville-West, 10 February 1927: Private Collection.

CHAPTER 17: CASSIS

1 Clive Bell to Leonard Woolf, 10 March 1927: Monks' House Papers, University of Sussex.
2 Clive Bell to Vanessa Bell, 28 [January] 1927: TGA.
3 DG to Edward Sackville-West, 3 April [1927]: RS.
4 Ibid.
5 DG to David Garnett, 6 May 1927: HG.
6 Colonel Teed to Vanessa Bell, 2 August 1927: KCC.
7 DG to Edward Sackville-West, April [1927]: RS.
8 DG to David Garnett, 24 May 1927: HG.

9 Woolf, *Letters*, III, p.363.
10 DG to David Garnett, 6 May 1927: HG.
11 Ibid.
12 *The Times*, 22 April 1927.
13 Ethel Grant to DG, 29 April [1927]: DGP.
14 Vanessa Bell to DG, 28 April [1926]: DGP.
15 DG to Virginia Woolf, May 1927: University of Sussex Library.
16 Valerie Taylor to DG, n.d.: DGP.
17 *Carrington. Letters and Extracts from Her Diaries*, p.368.
18 DG to Vanessa Bell, 17 October 1927: TGA.
19 Roger Fry to J. B. Manson, 21 August 1928: TGA, Manson Papers, 806.1.331.
20 DG to Vanessa Bell, 26 October 1927: TGA.
21 *Morning Post*, 9 November 1927.
22 Vanessa Bell to David Garnett, 11 November [1928]: RG.
23 Vanessa Bell to Leonard Woolf, 29 January [1928]: Monk's House Papers, University of Sussex.
24 Ethel Grant to DG, 18 February 1928: DGP.
25 Ethel Grant to DG, 12 April 1928: DGP.
26 DG to Ethel Grant, 15 April [1928]: DGP.
27 Virginia Woolf to DG [? May 1928]: DGP.
28 Julian Bell to Quentin Bell, 22 April [1928]: KCC.
29 Roger Fry, introduction to *London Group Retrospective* (catalogue), New Burlington Galleries, 1928.
30 Woolf, *Letters*, IV, p.191.
31 *The Times*, 21 February 1929.
32 *Morning Post*, 12 February 1929.
33 Clive Bell to Vanessa Bell, n.d. [spring 1929]: TGA.
34 DG to Ethel Grant, n.d. [January 1929]: DGP.
35 Woolf, *Letters*, IV, p.40.
36 DG to David Garnett, 2 June 1929: HG.
37 Woolf, *Diary*, III, p.232.
38 Clive Bell to Vanessa Bell, 30 June 1929: TGA.

39 DG to David Garnett, 2 October 1929: HG.

40 DG to Vanessa Bell, 2 October 1929: TGA.

41 Peter Morris to DG, n.d. [*c*. 1930]: DGP.

42 DG to Vanessa Bell, 2 October 1929: TGA.

43 Quoted in DG to Vanessa Bell, 6 January 1931: TGA.

44 Woolf, *Letters*, IV, p.276.

CHAPTER 18: LOVE, ANXIETY, TERROR, SADNESS

1 DG to Vanessa Bell, 6 January 1930: TGA.

2 DG to Vanessa Bell, 10 January 1930: TGA.

3 DG to David Garnett, 12 January 1930: HG.

4 DG to Vanessa Bell, 1 February 1930: TGA.

5 DG to David Garnett, 3 February 1930: HG.

6 Woolf, *Letters*, IV, p.134.

7 Vanessa Bell to DG [5 February 1930]: DGP.

8 DG to Vanessa Bell, 6 February 1930: TGA.

9 Vanessa Bell to DG, 7 February [1930]: DGP.

10 DG to Vanessa Bell, 18 February 1930: TGA.

11 Vanessa Bell to DG, 10 February [1930]: DGP.

12 Vanessa Bell to DG, 13 February [1930]: DGP.

13 DG to David Garnett, 3 March 1930: HG.

14 DG to Vanessa Bell [24 April 1930]: TGA.

15 DG to Vanessa Bell, 9 April 1930: TGA.

16 *The Times*, 9 June 1930.

17 Clive Bell to Vanessa Bell, 20 May 1930: TGA.

18 DG to Vanessa Bell, 23 April 1930: TGA.

19 Vanessa Bell to David Garnett, 12 June [1929]: HG.

20 DG to David Garnett [5 April 1930]: HG.

21 Woolf, *Diary*, III, p.316.

22 DG to David Garnett, 1 August 1930: HG.

23 Angelica Garnett, notes to the author, June 1996.

24 Vanessa Bell to Grace Higgens, 28 October [1930]: John Higgens.

25 Manchester City Art Galleries. Reproduced in Shone, *Bloomsbury Portraits* (1993), p.235, plate 167.

26 DG to Vanessa Bell [14 November 1930]: TGA.

27 DG to Vanessa Bell [27 November 1930]: TGA.

28 DG to David Garnett [26 November 1930]: HG.

29 DG to Vanessa Bell, 5 December [1930]: TGA.

30 DG to Edward Sackville–West, n.d. [1926]: RS.

31 DG to Vanessa Bell, 27 December 1930: TGA.

32 Woolf, *Diary*, V, p.6.

33 Entitled *Personal History* (*In Search of History* in the English edition), it was banned in both Russia and Nazi Germany. Heinrich Himmler, head of the Gestapo, made it a crime against the Third Reich to circulate, sell or buy anything by Vincent Sheean. Churchill also thought Sheean's political autobiography subversive, but he nevertheless became a personal friend of the author. Among Sheean's later books were ones on Gandhi and Nehru.

34 Jimmy Sheean to DG, 4 March 1931: DGP

35 Edward Sackville–West to DG, 26 February [1931]: DGP.

36 DG to Vanessa Bell, 10 April 1931: TGA

37 Jimmy Sheean to DG, n.d. [1931]: DGP

37 Jimmy Sheean to DG, n.d. [1931]: DGP

39 Quoted in Jimmy Sheean to DG [6 March 1931]: DGP

40 DG to Vanessa Bell [15 April 1931: DGP.

41 Lady Ottoline Morrell's journal, 15

April–10 May 1931, MS: Adrian Goodman.
42 Ibid.
43 Jimmy Sheean to DG, n.d. [1931]: DGP.
44 Ibid.
45 DG to David Garnett, 21 May 1931: HG.
46 Vanessa Bell to Grace Higgens, 2 June [1931]: John Higgens.
47 Lady Ottoline Morrell's journal, 1931.
48 *Time and Tide*, 27 June 1931.
49 Woolf, *Diary*, IV, p.30.
50 Lady Ottoline Morrell's journal, 23 July 1931: MS, Adrian Goodman.
51 Vanessa Bell to Roger Fry [?] July 1931: TGA.
52 DG to Richard Shone, 8 May 1972; quoted in Shone, *Bloomsbury Portraits* (1993), p.254.

CHAPTER 19: EXUBERANCE OF FANCY

1 DG to Ethel Grant, n.d. [November 1929]: DGP.
2 *Vogue*, January 1924, Vol.63, Issue 1, pp.50–51, 74.
3 Woolf, *Diary* (16 June 1925).
4 DG to Vanessa Bell, 22 April 1925: TGA.
5 'Early Autumn Days in Town', *Vogue*, October 1925, Vol.66, Issue 7, p.55.
6 *Observer*, 17 April 1932.
7 DG to Vanessa Bell [28 January 1922]: TGA.
8 Raymond Mortimer and Dorothy Todd, *The New Interior Decoration* (London: Batsford, 1929) p.?
9 DG to David Garnett [15 August 1931]: HG.
10 DG to David Garnett [7 September 1931]: HG.
11 DG to David Garnett [28 October 1931]: HG.
12 Leonard Woolf, *Downhill All the Way. An Autobiography of the Years 1919 to 1939* (London: Hogarth Press, 1967), p.76.
13 DG to Vanessa Bell [4 August 1932]: TGA.
14 *New Statesman and Nation*, 20 November 1931.
15 DG to David Garnett [4 January 1932]: HG.
16 Woolf, *Diary*, IV, p.378.
17 DG to Dorothy Bussy, 26 January 1932: McFarlanes, Solicitors.
18 DG to David Garnett [4 January 1932]: HG.
19 DG to Vanessa Bell [5 August 1932]: TGA.
20 Woolf, *Diary*, IV, p.109.
21 DG to David Garnett [24 August 1932]: HG.
22 DG to Vanessa Bell [20 September 1932]: TGA.
23 *The Times*, 12 March 1932.
24 *The Times*, 21 June 1932.
25 *Manchester Guardian*, 20 June 1932.
26 *The Scotsman*, 20 June 1932.
27 Kenneth Clark, *Another Part of the Wood. A Self-Portrait* (London: John Murray, 1974), p.247.
28 Kenneth Clark, to DG, 30 May 1933: DGP.
29 *New Statesman and Nation*, 17 June 1933.
30 Shone, *Bloomsbury Portraits* (1993), p.231. See also *Duncan Grant designer* Bluecoat Gallery, Liverpool, 1980
31 W. W. Winkworth to Vanessa Bell [3 March 1932]: KCC.
32 *New Statesman and Nation*, 27 October 1934.
33 Woolf, *Letters*, IV, p.130.
34 *Architectural Review*, February 1933; see also Shone, *Bloomsbury Portraits* (1993), pp.227–78.
35 Woolf, *Letters*, IV, p.129.
36 Woolf, *Letters*, IV, p.131.
37 *The Times*, 5 March 1932.
38 DG to Vanessa Bell [26 January 1933]: TGA.
39 Dora Carrington to Alix Strachey, 15 April 1921: HRHRC
40 DG to Vanessa Bell [8 February 1933]: TGA.
41 DG to Vanessa Bell [25 February 1933]: TGA.
42 *The Sunday Times*, 23 April 1933.
43 *New Scotsman*, 24 April 1933.
44 *New Statesman and Nation*, 17 June 1933.
45 *Morning Post*, 10 June 1933.

46 Quentin Bell, *Elders and Betters* (London: John Murray, 1995), p.36.
47 Vincent Sheean, *Personal History* (1935; Secaucus, N.J.: Citadel Press, 1986), pp.275–6.
48 John Rowdon, *Duncan Grant* (London: Hayward J. W. Marks, 1934), unpaginated.
49 DG, preface to the above.
50 DG to Vanessa Bell [27 April 1934]: TGA.
51 Vanessa Bell to Grace Higgens, 23 May 1934: John Higgens.
52 Grace Higgens to Clive Bell [May 1934]: KCC.
53 Duncan Macdonald had initially invited Roger Fry to write this preface. Fry had declined, as he was aware of criticism that suggested Bloomsbury tended to boost each other. Rebecca West had been mooted, but sudden appendicitis prevented her from accepting the task.
54 *The Times*, 15 May 1934.
55 *Morning Post*, 9 May 1934.
56 *The Sunday Times*, 20 May 1934.
57 Stanley Spencer, quoted in Keith Bell, *Stanley Spencer. A Complete Catalogue of the Paintings* (London: Phaidon, 1992), p.366. TGA 733.3.32.
58 *The Times*, 8 November 1934: DGP.
59 Roger Fry to DG, 30 December 1934: DGP.
60 DG to Ethel Grant [13 September 1934]: DGP.
61 Woolf, *Diary*, IV, p.243.
62 Margery Fry to J. T. Sheppard, 20 October 1934: KCC.

CHAPTER 20: INSIDE THE *QUEEN MARY*

1 Woolf, *Letters*, III, p.490.
2 Woolf, *Diary*, IV, p.297.
3 DG to Ethel Grant, 3 September [1933]: DGP.
4 DG to Lydia Keynes, n.d. [1934]: KCC.
5 J. M. Keynes to Lydia Keynes, 15 November 1934: KCC.
6 J. M. Keynes to Lydia Keynes, 24 February 1935: KCC.
7 Robert Skidelsky, *John Maynard Keynes. The Economist as Saviour, 1920–1937* (London: Macmillan, 1992), p.217.
8 Vanessa Bell to DG, 6 August [1935]: DGP.
9 DG to Vanessa Bell, 10 August [1935]: TGA.
10 *The Times*, 12 March 1935.
11 *The Times*, 8 October 1935.
12 DG to Vanessa Bell [11 January 1935]: TGA.
13 Vanessa Bell to DG, 6 August [1935]: DGP.
14 DG to Vanessa Bell, 23 May 1935: DGP.
15 *Selected Letters of Vanessa Bell*, p.380.
16 Vanessa Bell to Grace Higgens, 24 May [1935]: John Higgens.
17 DG to Vanessa Bell, 23 May 1935: DGP.
18 DG to David Garnett, 4 July 1935: HG.
19 DG to Vanessa Bell, 30 July 1935: TGA.
20 DG to Vanessa Bell, 31 July 1935: TGA.
21 Mr Leach to DG, 21 September 1935: CP, LUA, Duncan Grant file, D42/C3.430.
22 DG to Mr Leach, 23 September 1935: CP, LUA.
23 When the *New York Herald Tribune* ran an article on the ship on 1 December 1935, while work was still in progress, the by-line read: 'Modern but restrained decoration to prevail aboard the *Queen Mary*'.
24 Lord Essendon to Sir Percy Bates, 10 February 1936: CP, LUA.
25 Lord Balniel and others to Sir Percy Bates, 26 February 1936: CP, LUA.
26 Sir Percy Bates to Major Hardinge, 26 February 1936: CP, LUA.
27 The Rt Hon. Earl of Crawford and Balcarres to Sir Percy Bates, 3 March 1936: CP, LUA.
28 Sir Percy Bates to the Rt Hon. Earl of Crawford and Balcarres, 29 February 1936: CP, LUA.
29 The Rt Hon. Earl of Crawford and

Balcarres to Sir Percy Bates, 3 March 1936: CP, LUA.

30 DG to Vanessa Bell, 8 April [1936]: TGA.

31 DG to Vanessa Bell, 12 April 1936: TGA.

32 DG to Vanessa Bell, 8 April 1936: TGA.

33 DG to Vanessa Bell, 22 April [1936]: TGA.

34 DG to Vanessa Bell [1 May 1936]: TGA.

35 *The Listener*, 8 April 1936.

36 DG's signed agreement in Duncan Grant file: CP, LUA.

37 *The Sunday Times*, 14 November 1937.

38 *Manchester Guardian*, 8 November 1937.

39 *Country Life*, 20 November 1937.

40 They were eventually bought from Agnew's by Kenneth Clark's son the Hon. Alan Clark, MP.

41 S. J. Lister to Lord Essendon, 19 January 1939: CP, LUA.

42 *Daily Express*, 10 March 1939.

43 *The Times*, 12 December 1936.

44 *New Statesman*, 12 December 1936.

45 Peter Morris to DG, n.d.: DGP.

46 Quoted in Frances Spalding, 'The Patricia Preece Hoax', *Charleston Magazine*, Issue 5, Summer/ Autumn 1992.

47 Vanessa Bell to Patricia Preece, 17 February [1936]: Christine Hepworth.

48 Julian Bell to Grace Higgens, 2 July [1935]: John Higgens.

49 Quentin Bell (ed.), *Julian Bell. Essays, Poems and Letters* (London: Hogarth Press, 1938), p.44.

50 Quentin Bell to Julian Bell, 6 April 1936: KCC.

51 DG to David Garnett [10 September 1936]: HG.

52 David Garnett to DG, n.d. [1930s]: HG.

53 Jacques Copeau to DG, 6 June 1936: DGP.

54 Quoted in Louisa Young, *A Great Task of Happiness. The Life of Kathleen Scott* (London: Macmillan, 1995), p.239.

CHAPTER 21: FITS AND STARTS

1 Woolf, *Diary*, V, p.48.

2 Julian Bell to Quentin Bell, 21 October [1936]: KCC.

3 Julian Bell to Quentin Bell, 3 November [1936]: KCC.

4 Ibid.

5 DG to Julian Bell, 2 February 1937: KCC.

6 DG to J. M. Keynes, 21 April 1937: KCC.

7 DG to J. M. Keynes, n.d. [July 1937]: KCC.

8 *The Times*, 2 July 1937.

9 *Nation*, 3 July 1937.

10 William Townsend in Andrew Forge (ed.), *The Townsend Journals. An Artist's Record of His Times 1928–1951* (London: Tate Gallery, 1976), p.42.

11 DG to David Garnett [20 July 1937]: HG.

12 DG to J. M. Keynes, 21 July 1937: KCC.

13 Woolf, *Diary*, V, p.104.

14 DG to David Garnett [13 August 1937]: HG.

15 DG to Dorothy Busssy, n.d. [July 1937]: MacFarlanes, Solicitors.

16 DG to David Garnett [13 August 1937]: HG.

17 See Quentin Bell, *Elders and Betters*, p.57.

18 Vanessa Bell to J. T. Sheppard, 17 October [1937]: KCC.

19 DG to J. M. Keynes, 6 December 1937: KCC.

20 Augustus John to Vanessa Bell, 22 June [1937]: TGA.

21 Victor Pasmore to the author, 11 April 1993.

22 Woolf, *Diary*, V, p.120.

23 *Listener*, 24 November 1937.

24 For this memoir see the *Charleston Magazine*, Issue 10, Autumn/Winter 1994, where it is incorrectly dated *c.* 1950.

25 Jean Campbell to Vanessa Bell, 28 September 1937: KCC.

26 DG to Vanessa Bell, 28 January [1938]: TGA.

27 Dorothy Bussy to DG, 22 July [1937]: DGP.

28 David Garnett to Vanessa Bell [23 September 1937]: HG.

29 Angelica Garnett, *Deceived with Kindness* (London: Chatto & Windus, 1984); Pimlico reprint, 1995, p.123 and p.37.

30 DG, unpublished diary: HG.

31 David Garnett to Vanessa Bell, 9 March 1938: HG.

32 David Garnett to Vanessa Bell [16 April 1938]: HG.

33 Vanessa Bell to David Garnett, 20 April [1938]: RG.

34 DG, unpublished diary: HG.

35 David Garnett to Angelica Bell, 24 August 1938: KCC.

36 Clive Bell to Vanessa Bell [6 March 1938]: TGA.

37 Clive Bell to Vanessa Bell, 27 October [1938]: TGA.

38 DG to Ethel Grant, n.d. [September 1938]: DGP.

39 Both James MacGibbon and Robert Frame, in conversation with the author.

40 Vanessa Bell to David Garnett, 16 October [1938]: RG.

41 Woolf, *Diary*, V, p.190.

42 DG to Ethel Grant, 9 April 1939: DGP.

43 Angelica Bell to David Garnett [19 April 1939]: KCC.

44 Angelica Bell to David Garnett [? March 1939]: KCC.

45 David Garnett, unpublished diary, March 1939: HG.

46 David Garnett to Ray Garnett, n.d. [May 1939]: HG.

47 Vanessa Bell to David Garnett, 1 July [1939]: RG.

48 David Garnett, unpublished diary, July 1939: HG.

49 DG to David Garnett, 2 September 1939: Angelica Garnett.

50 A. Garnett, *Deceived with Kindness*, p.125.

51 Vanessa Bell to DG, 23 July [1939]: DGP.

52 David Garnett, *The Familiar Faces* (London: Chatto & Windus, 1962), p.218.

CHAPTER 22: UNDER SIEGE

1 Frances Partridge, 'Bloomsbury Houses', *Charleston Newsletter*, No.11, June 1985.

2 Angelica Bell to David Garnett, 27 July [1940]: KCC.

3 DG to Keith Baynes, 20 [March?] 1940: Lt-Col Sir John Baynes.

4 Angelica Bell to David Garnett [25 December 1939]: KCC.

5 Angelica Bell to David Garnett [2 February 1940]: KCC.

6 Ibid.

7 Angelica Bell to David Garnett, 30 October [1940]: KCC.

8 Patrick Nelson to DG, n.d. [c. 1939–40]: DGP.

9 Angelica Bell to David Garnett, 15 February [1940]: KCC.

10 Angelica Bell to David Garnett, 5 January 1940: KCC.

11 Vanessa Bell to DG [20 May 1940]: DGP.

12 *New Statesman and Nation*, 11 May 1940.

13 Ibid.

14 John Rothenstein to DG, 8 May 1940: DGP.

15 DG to Vanessa Bell, 15 May 1940: TGA.

16 DG to Vanessa Bell, 18 May 1940: TGA.

17 DG to Vanessa Bell, n.d. [late May 1940]: TGA.

18 Vanessa Bell to David Garnett, 15 June [1940]: RG.

19 Vanessa Bell to David Garnett, 17 June [1940]: RG.

20 Reported in Ethel Grant to DG, 10 September 1940: DGP.

21 Victor Pasmore to DG, 24 September 1940: DGP.

22 Ethel Grant to DG, 9 February 1941: DGP.

23 Helen Anrep to Vanessa Bell, n.d. [1941]: KCC.

24 David Garnett to Angelica Bell, 18 November 1941: KCC.

25 Angelica Bell to David Garnett, 21 November 1941: KCC.

26 DG to Angelica Bell, 23 April 1942: AVG.

27 Angelica Bell to DG, 2 May 1942: DGP.

28 DG to Angelica Bell, 5 May 1942: AVG.

29 Vanessa Bell to David Garnett, 23 May [1941]: RG.

30 Pippa Strachey to Vanessa Bell, n.d. [April 1941]: Fawcett Library.

31 Clive Bell to Mary Hutchinson, 31 March 1941: HRHRC.

32 *Independent*, 24 May 1994.

33 DG to Vanessa Bell, 3 April 1942: TGA.

34 DG to E. M. O'R. Dickey, n.d. [received 31 May 1941]: Imperial War Museum.

35 Vanessa Bell to Angelica Bell [24 November 1941]: AVG.

36 Revd George Mitchell to the Hon. Mrs Sandilands, 5 September 1941: Sussex Archaeological Society, Lewes.

37 Kenneth Clark to Bishop Bell, 26 September 1941: Sussex Archaeological Society, Lewes.

38 Bentham Stevens to Bishop Bell, 2 October 1941: Sussex Archaeological Society, Lewes.

39 Bishop Bell, quoted in DG to Kenneth Clark, 25 September 1941: TGA.

40 *Country Life*, 4 June 1943.

41 DG to Ethel Grant, 19 August 1943: DGP.

42 Minutes of Berwick's Annual Parochial Church Metting, 3 April 1945: Courtesy the Revd Peter Smith.

43 Quoted in Richard Shone, *The Berwick Church Paintings* (The Towner Art Gallery, Eastbourne, 1969; revised 1986), unpaginated.

44 Ethel Grant to DG, n.d. [1941]: DGP.

45 DG to Keith Baynes, 5 April 1941: Lt-Col Sir John Baynes.

46 DG to Pippa Strachey, 25 July 1941: Fawcett Library.

47 DG to Ethel Grant, 27 July 1942: DGP.

48 Catalogue introduction to 'Designs by Various Artists for Decoration in the Theatre', CEMA, 1943.

49 *The Times*, 14 January 1943.

50 DG to Ethel Grant, 9 May 1943: DGP.

51 DG to Ethel Grant, 1 November 1944: DGP.

52 DG to Keith Baynes, 23 August 1944: Lt-Col Sir John Baynes.

53 DG's portrait of Desmond MacCarthy is in the National Portrait Gallery.

54 DG to Ethel Grant, 7 July 1943: DGP.

55 DG to Ethel Grant, 18 September 1944: DGP.

56 *New Statesman and Nation*, 14 March 1944.

57 Ethel Sands to DG, 26 December [1944]: DGP.

58 Nan Hudson to DG, 20 January [1944]: DGP.

59 DG to Ethel Grant, n.d. [May 1944]: DGP.

CHAPTER 23: NARCISSUS

1 *Selected Letters of Vanessa Bell*, p.497.

2 Ibid., p.499.

3 Typical of the critical response was Eric Newton's review in *The Listener* (21 June 1945): 'His pictures don't smile . . . They are alive, yet they lack liveliness.'

4 *Sunday Times*, 24 June 1945.

5 Ethel Grant to DG, 17 August 1945: DGP.

6 DG to Vanessa Bell, 12 June 1946: TGA.

7 DG to Vanessa, Bell, 14 June 1946: TGA.

8 Ibid.

9 DG to Vanessa Bell, 12 June 1946: TGA.

10 Vanessa Bell to Pippa Strachey, 26 July 1946: Fawcett Library.

11 Edward le Bas to DG, 23 April 1946: DGP.

12 Edward le Bas to DG, 2 July 1943: DGP.

13 Edward le Bas to DG, 24 April 1944: DGP.

14 Edward le Bas to DG, 1 July 1944: DGP.

15 Paul Roche, in conversation with the author.

16 Edward le Bas to DG, 11 October [1946]: DGP.

17 Robert [?] to DG, 27 November 1940: DGP.

18 DG, 'Narcissus', unpublished MS: Simon Watney.

19 Paul Roche, 'Duncan, Love and Sex', unpublished notes written for the author's use.

20 See note 18.

21 DG to Paul Roche [8 November 1953: Clarissa Roche.

22 DG to Vanessa Bell, 11 October 1950: AVG.

23 Previously rejected by Jonathan Cape, *Innocents* won the Somerset Maugham Award for fiction in 1947 and marked the start of A.L. Barker's distinguished career as a short-story writer.

24 Quentin Bell to Janie Bussy, 27 March 1947: MacFarlanes, Solicitors.

25 Ethel Grant to DG, 17 October 1947: DGP.

26 Pernel Strachey to DG, 8 January 1948: DGP.

27 Mary Hutchinson to DG, 12 January 1948: DGP.

28 DG to Dorothy Bussy, 5 April 1948: MacFarlanes, Solicitors.

29 During the last years of her life, Karin Stephen worked on two books: one on the life and importance of Freud, the other on human misery. Though she is said to have made good progress with both, neither manuscript was ever discovered.

30 DG to Vanessa Bell, 23 November 1949: DGP

31 Paul Roche in conversation with the author, 23 March 1992.

32 DG to Paul Roche, nd [*c.* 1953]: Clarissa Roche.

33 DG to Paul Roche, New Year's Eve 1952: Clarissa Roche.

34 Stephen Spender to the author, 20 September 1992.

35 Reported by Paul Roche, in conversation with the author.

36 DG to Paul Roche, 31 January 1953: Clarissa Roche.

37 DG to Paul Roche, 31 January 1953: Clarissa Roche.

38 Two undated letters, DG to Paul Roche: Clarissa Roche.

39 Angelica Garnett to David Garnett, 12 July 1950 KCC.

40 Vanessa Bell to Angelica Garnett, 26 March [1950]: AVG.

41 Ibid.

42 Leonard Woolf to Pippa Strachey, 25 December 1951: Fawcett Library.

43 Pippa Strachey to DG, 20 December 1951: DGP.

44 From notes made by P. N. Furbank, in conversation with Harry Daley: P. N. Furbank.

45 In the collection of Birkbeck College, London.

46 DG to Paul Roche, 9 August 1951: DGP.

47 See note 18.

48 Ibid.

49 DG to Paul Roche, 29 July 1953: Clarissa Roche.

50 DG to Paul Roche, 26 April 1953: Clarissa Roche.

51 DG to Paul Roche, [?] June 1953: Clarissa Roche.

52 DG to Paul Roche, 22 February 1954: Clarissa Roche.

CHAPTER 24: TIME'S THIEVISH PROGRESS

1 DG to David Garnett, 11 February 1957: HG.

2 DG to Paul Roche, 25 March 1954: Clarissa Roche.

3 Angelica Garnett to David Garnett, 10 October 1955: KCC.

4 DG to David Garnett, 1 November 1955: HG.

5 DG to Janie Bussy, 31 October 1955: MacFarlanes, Solicitors.

6 Paul Roche to DG, 30 January 1954: Paul Roche.

7 Clarissa Roche to the author, 2 April 1994.

8 Watney, *The Art of Duncan Grant*, p.76.

9 Violet Hammersley to DG, 17 March 1961: DGP.

10 The Duke and Duchess of Devonshire, in conversation with the author.

11 DG to Paul Roche, 5 May 1954: Paul Roche.

12 DG to Paul Roche, 8 May 1954: Paul Roche.

13 Vanessa Bell to DG, 10 May [1954]: DGP.

14 DG to Paul Roche, 4 October 1953: Clarissa Roche.

15 Vanessa Bell to Angelica Garnett, 25 May [1954]: AVG.

16 Reported in *The Lady*, 28 February 1957.

17 Amaryllis Garnett to David Garnett, n.d. [October 1955]: KCC.

18 Charles Reilly to DG, 26 March 1942: DGP.

19 Frances Partridge, *Everything to Lose. Diaries 1945–1960*. (London: Gollancz, 1985), p.246.

20 Transcript of *Desert Island Discs*, transmitted 15 and 17 March 1975, Radio 4.

21 Helen Anrep to DG, 7 May 1957: AVG.

22 Partridge, *Everything to Lose*, pp.278–9.

23 G. L. Kennedy, *Henry Lamb* (London: Ernest Benn, 1924), p.28.

24 Quoted in Jenny Pery, *The Affectionate Eye: The Life of Claude Rogers* (Bristol: Sansom & Co., 1995), p.158.

25 *Listener*, 21 May 1959.

26 Frances Todd to DG, 14 April 1956: DGP.

27 DG to Vanessa Bell, 16 April 1960: KGG.

28 Peter Morris to Vanessa Bell, 16 April 1960: AVG.

29 Vanessa Bell to Angelica Garnett, 7 February [1961]: AVG.

30 Peter Morris to DG [8 September 1961]: DGP.

31 Angelica Garnett to David Garnett, 9 April [1961]: KCC.

32 DG to Lydia Lopokova, 10 April 1961: KCC.

33 DG's 1961 appointment diary: DGP.

34 DG to Raymond Mortimer, 13 April 1961: Rare Books and Special Collections, Princeton University.

35 Kenneth Clark to DG, 12 April 1961: DGP.

36 DG, note dated 3 June 1961: AVG.

37 DG to Keith Baynes, 16 April 1961: Lt-Col Sir John Baynes.

CHAPTER 25: *LES FEMMES SAVANTES*

1 Paul Roche to DG, 11 April 1961: Paul Roche.

2 Paul Roche, in conversation with the author.

3 Ibid.

4 Lady Dufferin (Lindy Guinness), in conversation with the author.

5 DG to Angelica Garnett, 18 October 1961: AVG.

6 Recounted by Paul Roche, in conversation with the author.

7 Frances Creighton, in conversation with the author.

8 DG to Clive Bell, 24 February 1962: DGP.

9 DG to Lindy Guinness, 27 February 1962: DGP.

10 DG to Lindy Guinness, 28 February 1962: Lady Dufferin.

11 Harriet Cohen to DG, [?] December 1961: DGP.

12 DG to Lindy Guinness, 12 March 1962: Lady Dufferin.

13 Frances Partridge, *Hanging On: Diaries 1960–63* (London: Collins, 1990), p.102.

14 Angelica Garnett to Duncan Grant, n.d. [*c*. 1962]: DGP.

15 Angelica Garnett to Clive Bell and Barbara Bagenal, 26 January 1962: KCC.

16 DG to Clive Bell, 21 June 1963: DGP.

17 DG to Lindy Guinness, 26 July 1963: Lady Dufferin.

18 Sarah Oppenheim (later Whitfield) to DG, n.d. [summer 1963]: DGP.

19 When in 1974 Blunt retired from the Courtauld Institute of Art, losing the upstairs flat that had come with the job, he had no capital and, in order to pay for the lease on a Bayswater flat, sold this Poussin to Montreal Museum of Arts. The large sum he

received for it, far in excess of what he had paid for it, did not affect the satisfactory nature of the original agreement, which served Duncan well at the time.

20 DG to Peter Pears, 11 January 1963: The Britten-Pears Library, Aldeburgh.

21 Partridge, *Hanging On*, p.73.

22 Henrietta Garnett to the author, 9 January 1992.

23 DG to Lindy Guinness, 28 September 1963: Lady Dufferin.

24 Angelica Garnett to David Garnett, 25 November [1964]: KCC.

25 Angelica Garnett to David Garnett, 9 February [1964]: KCC.

26 Frances Partridge, *Other People: Diaries 1963–66* (London: HarperCollins, 1993), pp. 89–91.

27 DG to Angelica Garnett, 24 August 1964: AVG.

28 Richard Morphet to DG, n.d. [late 1960s]: DGP.

29 John Betjeman to DG, 29 September 1964: DGP.

30 Raymond Mortimer to DG, 29 September 1964: DGP.

31 Lindy Guinness to DG [21 October 1964]: DGP.

32 DG to Angelica Garnett, 24 August 1964: AVG.

33 *Sunday Telegraph*, 8 November 1964.

34 *Daily Mail*, 4 November 1964.

35 *Daily Telegraph*, 6 November 1964.

36 *Sunday Telegraph Magazine*, 20 November 1964.

37 Franzi von Haas to DG, 12 December 1964: DGP.

38 *Charleston Newsletter*, no.11, June 1985.

39 Ibid.

40 Sarah Whitfield to DG [June 1965]: DGP.

41 Recounted by Sarah Whitfield, in conversation with the author.

42 A. N. L. Munby to DG, 17 January 1966: DGP.

43 DG to David Garnett, 1 July 1966: AVG.

44 Angelica Garnett to DG [19 May 1966]: DGP.

45 John Betjeman to DG, n.d. [July 1966]: DGP.

46 DG to Richard Morphet, 27 August 1966: Richard Morphet.

47 Recounted by Lord Drogheda (Derry Moore), in conversation with the author.

48 Derry Moore to DG, 7 November [1966]: DGP.

49 Bill McBrien to the author [20 June 1995].

50 DG to Richard Morphet, 29 November 1966: Richard Morphet.

CHAPTER 26: *TOUJOURS LA PEINTURE*

1 Recollected by Paul Roche, in conversation with the author.

2 Paul Morris to DG, 7 September 1966: DG.

3 DG to Michael Holroyd, 15 November 1966: Michael Holroyd.

4 Michael Holroyd to DG, 5 December 1962: DGP.

5 Michael Holroyd, 'A Visit with Duncan Grant', *South-West Review*, Spring 1985, Vol.70, No.2, p.148.

6 DG to Michael Holroyd, 4 July 1966: Michael Holroyd.

7 Partridge, *Other People: Diaries 1963–66*, p.248.

8 Quentin Bell to Michael Holroyd [1966]: copy, TGA.

9 Michael Holroyd to DG, 6 July 1966: DGP.

10 See 'Double Preface' in Holroyd, *Lytton Strachey* (1994), p.xxvii.

11 Michael Holroyd to the author, 13 March 1996 ('. . .generally I was very much relieved by Duncan's modest and reasonable requests. That relief translated itself into the sentence I wrote in my Double Preface'.).

12 Angelica Garnett to DG, 8 January [1967]: DGP.

13 DG to Richard Morphet, 14 February 1967: Richard Morphet.

14 Angelica Garnett to David Garnett, 24 March [1967]: KCC.

15 DG to Angelica Garnett, 20 May 1967: AVG.

16 David Garnett to Angelica Garnett, 13 April 1967: KCC.

17 DG to Richard Morphet, 18 December 1967: Richard Morphet.

18 DG to Desmond Shawe-Taylor, 11 July 1967: Estate of Desmond Shawe-Taylor.

19 DG to Raymond Mortimer, 13 October 1967: Rare Books and Special Collections, Princeton University.

20 DG's letter to Michael Holroyd was published in full in the *South-West Review*, Spring 1985, Vol.70, No.2, pp.150–3.

21 Raymond Mortimer to DG, 12 October 1967: DGP.

22 Frances Partridge to David Garnett, 18 October 1967: KCC.

23 Deirdre Levi, in conversation with the author.

24 Duncan Grant to David Garnett, 23 November 1967: KCC.

25 David Garnett to DG, 17 November 1966: DGP.

26 DG to Angelica Garnett, 28 May 1968: KCC.

27 Angelica Garnett to David Garnett, 26 April 1968: KCC.

28 Beverley Nichols describes the finding of this manuscript in *A Thatched Roof*, as mentioned in his preface to *In an Eighteenth-Century Kitchen*, edited by Dennis Rhodes (London: Cecil and Amelia Woolf, 1968).

29 DG to Desmond Shawe-Taylor, 4 July 1968: Estate of Desmond Shawe-Taylor.

30 John Haylock, 'Some Recollections of Duncan Grant', *Charleston Newsletter*, June 1985, No.11.

31 Angelica Garnett to David Garnett, 7 December [1968]: KCC.

32 Mark Lancaster to the author, 28 February 1994.

33 DG to Mark Lancaster, 16 November 1969: Mark Lancaster.

34 DG to Paul Roche, 18 November 1969: Clarissa Roche.

35 DG to Angelica Garnett, 26 January 1969: AVG.

36 Recounted by Christopher Mason, in conversation with the author.

37 Christabel Aberconway to DG, 18 August 1969: DGP.

38 Amaryllis Garnett, unpublished diary: AVG.

39 DG to Simon Watney, 4 November 1969: Simon Watney.

40 DG, quoted in *Tate Gallery 1970–72* in the catalogue entry for T1514 *Venus and Adonis*.

41 DG to Angelica Garnett, 20 December 1969: AVG.

CHAPTER 27: A VETERAN OF GLORIOUS BATTLES

1 DG to Richard Morphet, 12 April 1970: Richard Morphet.

2 *Charleston Newsletter*, June 1985, no. 11.

3 DG to Simon Watney, 24 April 1970: Simon Watney.

4 See note 2.

5 John Haylock to DG, 12 May 1970: DGP.

6 Frances Partridge, unpublished diary, ? December 1971.

7 DG to Paul Roche, 10 October 1971: Clarissa Roche.

8 DG to Paul Roche, 26 May 1973: Clarissa Roche.

9 Reported by DG to Paul Roche in the above-mentioned letter.

10 DG to Paul Roche, 30 November 1971: Clarissa Roche.

11 DG to Paul Roche, 20 October 1970: Clarissa Roche.

12 Anthony d'Offay, in conversation with the author.

13 *Connoisseur*, May 1972.

14 *Arts Review*, 22 April 1972.

15 *Vogue*, 15 March 1972.

16 DG to David Garnett, 9 May 1971: AVG.

17 DG to David Garnett, 13 October 1971: HG.

18 DG to Leigh Farnell, 30 November 1971: DGP.

19 Frances Partridge, unpublished diary, 21 January 1971.

20 DG to Paul Roche [16 March 1974]: Clarissa Roche.

21 David Brown to DG, 21 July 1972: DGP.

22 Angelica Garnett to David Garnett, 4 January 1972: KCC.

23 DG to David Garnett, 18 January 1972: HG.

24 See note 22.

25 See Roche, *With Duncan Grant in Southern Turkey*, p.14.

26 Ibid., p.15. *Still-Life with Matisse* is reproduced in Shone, *Bloomsbury Portraits* (1993), p.251, plate 185.

27 *Guardian*, 22 January 1973.

28 Ibid.

29 David Garnett to Angelica Garnett, 5 May 1973: KCC.

30 Angelica Garnett to David Garnett, 5 May 1973: KCC.

31 Ibid.

32 DG to Deidre Connolly, 21 May 1973: Deidre Levi.

33 DG to Richard Morphet, n.d. [October 1973]: Richard Morphet.

34 Roche, *With Duncan Grant in Southern Turkey*, p.7.

35 Recounted by Paul Roche in 'With Duncan Grant in the Highlands', unpublished memoir: Paul Roche.

CHAPTER 28: 'THEIR ANCIENT GLITTERING EYES, ARE GAY'

1 Deidre Bland, in conversation with the author.

2 DG to Paul Roche [27 March 1974]: Clarissa Roche.

3 Ibid.

4 DG to Pandora Roche, n.d. [October 1976]: Pandora Roche.

5 DG to Keith Baynes, 9 May 1972: Lt-Col Sir John Baynes.

6 Richard Shone, unpublished diary, 20 January 1975: Richard Shone.

7 *The Sunday Times*, 26 January 1975.

8 Richard Morphet to DG, 18 March 1975: DGP.

9 Recounted by Alan Bennett, in conversation with the author.

10 See Paul Roche, 'With Duncan Grant in Tangier', *Charleston Magazine*, Issue 8, Winter/Spring 1993/4.

11 Ibid.

12 DG to Lindy Dufferin, 31 December 1975: Lindy Dufferin.

13 Simon Watney, unpublished diary, 8 November 1976.

14 *Financial Times*, 18 April 1978.

15 Quoted by Nicholas Henderson in *Mandarin: The Diaries of an Ambassador 1969–1982* (London: Weidenfeld & Nicolson, 1994), p.162. Roche does not now remember what he said on this occasion, but questions the callousness of this remark, as reported by Henderson.

16 Recollected by Paul Roche, in conversation with the author.

17 Angelica Garnett, unpublished diary, writen three years after the event, on 20 March 1981.

18 Recounted by Paul Roche, in conversation with the author.

19 Recounted by Paul Roche, in conversation with the author.

20 See note 17. After Duncan died, Angelica tried for a period to live at Charleston, suffered severe depression and, after she recovered, wrote a cathartic account of her childhood and relations with her elders, *Deceived with Kindness*. Paul and Clarissa eventually set up separate homes, Paul moving to Mallorca and Clarissa to Somerset. Tobit (Toby) Roche became a painter exhibiting in various places, including the Maas Gallery, London, in 1996. In the course of time Henrietta eventually settled in France with Mark Divall. Richard Morphet became Keeper of the Modern Collection at the Tate Gallery, and is now its Emeritus Keeper. Richard Shone became an associate editor of the *Burlington Magazine* and an authoritative commentator publishing books, articles and reviews on historical and contemporary artists. Simon Watney also published books and articles on British art, including his *The Art of Duncan Grant*, and began working for the Terence Higgins Trust and other AIDS organisations. Quentin Bell, whose move to Sussex had 'made sense of the past', as Duncan told Richard Shone, died in December 1996.

21 Clark's memorial speech was reprinted in Douglas Blair Turnbaugh, *Duncan Grant and the Bloomsbury Group* (Secausus, New Jersey: Lyle Stuart, Inc., A Mario Sartori Book, 1987), pp.107–8.

22 *The Times*, 10 May 1978.

23 *Charleston Newsletter*, June 1985, no.11.

INDEX

539

Heaven 264–5; decorates houses
with VB 265–6; impressed by
Hilton Hall 266; his affair with
Eddy Sackville-West (*q.v.*)
267–70; in Venice 268–9; the
star of LAA exhibition 270–1;
and life at Charleston 271–2;
first visit to Château
d'Auppegard 272–3; further trips
to France 273–5; his affair with
Peter Morris 274, 279; illness
275, 280; at Cassis (*q.v.*) 273–4,
275–9; finds La Bergère 279;
sells well in London 280; excited
by VW's *To the Lighthouse* 281;
embroiled with an actress 282; a
new gramophone and driving
lessons 282; his artistic success
283, 284, 288; and London
parties 285; explores the French
countryside 286; in Germany
with the Woolfs 289; Cassis,
Charleston and Cassis again
289–91; his affair with Bergen
(*q.v.*) 292–4, 295–6, 301–2; other
homosexual acquaintances 302–4,
310; his affair with Sheean
304–8; in Rome 306–9; another
successful show 309–10;
decorates Lady Wellesley's
dining-room 312–14, 421; his
fabrics 315–16, posters 316, and
dustjackets 316–17; exhibits at
Agnew's 317, 318, 320, 321; and
Lytton's death 318; a holiday
with Bergen 318–19; costumes
and set designs 319–20;
decorates Clark's dinner-service
321–3, and the Music Room
323–5; joins Artists' International
Association 327; and Rowdon's
'Revaluations' 328; exhibits at
Lefevre's 329–30, 334; has a
piles operation 330; and Fry's
death 331, 334; and the
Keyneses 332–4; at George V's
Silver Jubilee 335; and society at
every level 335; in Rome 336–7;
his *Queen Mary* decorations
rejected 336, 337–40, 341,
342–4; in Spain 340–2; his
reputation and his critics 344–5;
acts in VW's *Freshwater* 345;

resigns from the London Group
345; and Preece 346–7; and the
Bussys at Charleston 348–9; as a
Spanish dancer 349; Lady Scott
mends his coat 349

1937–48
accepts an annuity from Keynes
351–2; at the Coronation 352;
sees friends in France 353–4;
exhibits at 'Contemporary British
Artists' show 354; and Violet
Hammersley (*q.v.*) 354; and
Julian Bell's death 355, 356; sets
up Euston Road School with VB
356–8; his lithographs for
Curwen Press 358; in Cassis
358–9; and Lady Ottoline's
death 359; and Bunny and
Angelica's relationship 361–3,
366–7; finds France depressing
364–5; recovers his Delacroix
drawing 365; and Angelica's
illness 366–7; and the outbreak
of war 367–8; plans the garden
with VB 369–70; at Angelica's
21st 370; worried over Angelica
and Bunny 371; his instinct for
self-preservation 371; in the
Venice Biennale show 372, 373;
his buoyant reputation 373–4; as
a war artist in Plymouth 374–5;
joins the Home Guard 376;
against Angelica and Garnett's
marriage 377–8; with his mother
in Lyme Regis 379; WAAC
commissions 380; decorates
Berwick Church 380–5; and
Miller's Gallery, Lewes 385–9;
designs jacket for Waley's
Monkey 389; addresses Glasgow
School of Art 389; and Bishop
Bell 390; his *Cinderella*
decorations 390–1; speaks in
Hitler's defence! 392; his
reputation declines 393–4; takes
his mother to Scandinavia
395–6; and Keynes' death 396;
and Le Bas (*q.v.*) 396–7; meets
Paul Roche (*q.v.*) 398–9, 400;
helps other artists 404; reads a
paper at the Memoir Club 404;
and his mother's death 405–6

212; her pride in DG 224, 280; meets VW 225; her *ménage à quatre* 232, 233; moves to Twickenham 251, 252; takes up embroidery 255; with DG on a barge 262; at Twickenham 266, Charleston 272, and Cassis 273–4, 276; her Anglo-Indian prejudices 275; her footstool exhibited 280; reprimands DG 286; DG recommends a doctor for her 'undue worries' 289; delighted with La Bergère 291; in Mallorca 342; and Colonel Young's death 350; in Paris with DG 359; and the war 368, 377; in Lyme Regis with DG 379; embroiders altar frontal for Berwick Church 385; as DG's representative 390–1; and Miss Elwes's death 394; a Scandinavian holiday 395–6; illness and death 405–6; mentioned 27, 34, 35, 65, 83, 185, 284, 289, 302, 309

DG to 286, 313, 331, 332, 365, 388, 391

Grant, George (uncle) 4
Grant, Henrietta (aunt) 5, 171, 195
Grant, Lady Henrietta (*née* Plowden) (grandmother) 1, 2, 3–4, 7, 11; *DG to* 11
Grant, John 492
Grant, John Peter (great-grandfather) 3
Grant, Sir John Peter (grandfather) 1, 2, 3, 4; Watts portrait 57
Grant, Sir John Peter (uncle) 4, 5
Grant, Sir John Peter (cousin) 56–7, 65, 492, 493
Grant, Lady Marjorie (*née* Stewart) (great-grandmother) 3
Grant, Ogilvie 420
Grant, Philippa 492
Grant, Trevor (uncle) 4, 15, 19, 30, 31, 51, 482
Grant, William (great-great-grandfather) 6
Granville Barker, Harley 122, 133–4, 146
Graves, Robert 117
Greco, El 205
Greece 91, 94, 95
Greenland, Angela 479, 481, 488, 489,

493, 494, 500, 503
Greenland, John 479, 481, 484, 485, 489, 493, 494, 498, 500, 503
Greenwood, Nigel: Gallery 489
Guardian 484
Guieysse, Emma 26
Guilbert, Yvette 49
Guinness, Lindy *see* Dufferin, Lady Lindy
Gunn, Mr (farmer) 189, 190
Gwynne-Jones, Allan 393–4; *Portrait Painters* 394

Haas, Franzi von 258–9, 268, 283, 285, 288, 449
Hallward, B. L. 428
Hambledon, Viscount 207
Hambourg, Michael 370
Hamilton, Cuthbert J. 139, 141
Hamilton, Lady 140, 149, 396
Hamilton, Richard 466, 473
Hammersley, Violet 196, 335, 355, 418–19, 420, 425, 426, 438, 447; DG's portrait 354, 410
Hammond, Mrs (cook) 209
Hamnett, Nina 139, 210
Hampstead, London: Fellows Road 27, 65, 83
Hampton Court 210, 292; Mantegna cycle 109, 111
Harcourt, Colonel Alfred 7, 450
Harcourt, Georgina (*née* Willis) 7
Hardinge, Sir Charles 87, 88
Hardinge, Major: *Sir Percy Bates to* 339
Hardman, Freddie 158
Hardy, Dudley 14
Harland, Mrs 246
Harrison, Jane 69, 121, 129, 250
Harrod, Roy 295, 416
Harvane, Edward: Gallery 496
Harvill Press 408
Haylock, John 449–50, 465, 466, 473, 474, 476, 494, 507
Heath, Edward 460–1
Heath, Ellen 47
Hecks, Mr (farmer) 190, 192, 191, 195, 197, 206
Hellman, Lillian 293, 294
Henderson, Sir Nicholas 504, 505
Henry, Leigh 236
Hepworth, Dorothy 346, 347
Herbert, David 499
Herbin, Auguste 99

John, Ida (neé Nettleship) 50, 61
Johns, Jasper 466; light-bulb sculpture
467
Johnson, Daniel 219
Johnstone, J. K. 416–17
Jones, Stanley 489, 490
Jopling, Joe 14
Jopling, Louise 14
Jouvet (actor) 146

Kahn, Alphonse 306
Kahn, Richard 370
Kahnweiler (dealer) 123, 144
Kallenborn, John Joseph 137, 138, 314
Kalman, Andras 477
Karsavina, Tamara 108, 139
Kasmin, John 468
Kelly, Sir Gerald 411
Kennet, Lord see Young, Hilton
Keyes, Phyllis 323, 342, 385, 394, 398,
426
Keynes, Geoffrey 330, 396, 457
Keynes, John Maynard: at Cambridge
36, 37; his 'typewriter intellect'
37; and Hobhouse 37–8, 50–1,
52, 53; and Lytton's affair with
DG 38–42; enjoys economics 39;
ruins the romance of Versailles
62; on Bloomsbury 35; at
Cambridge 66–7; his
'cocksureness' 67; relationship
with DG 66–71, 73–4; no
musical interest 75; and women
students 77; entertains at King's
77; DG's portrait 79; at Versaille
with DG 79–80; his triangular
relationship with Lytton and
DG 80–2; recommends DG for
teaching post 91; in Greece and
Turkey with him 91, 94, 95;
their friendship 95, 96, 97; rents
house at Burford 96; gives DG
money 102; in Sicily and
Morocco with DG 105, 106–7;
summer visitors 118; and Luce
119, 120; at the Russian Ballet
129; defends Fry 141; camping
140; has diphtheria 144;
supports Omega 149; like a
Chinese Buddha 153; helps
Békassy 154; hosts a Café Royal
party 163, 164; mourns Brooke
166; rouses feelings of revulsion

in Lawrence 168–9; in Sussex
with DG and the Bells 171, 177;
more financial help 185; at the
centre of things 194; a 'gentle
and harmonious' visitor 194;
criticised by his friends 194; and
DG 194–5; buys his pictures
196; and Garnett 200; buys
Degas pictures for National
Gallery 205–6; abandons a
Cézanne 206; sents suits to DG
207; introduced to Lydia
Lopokova 210, 211–12; orders a
landau 211; optimistic about
peace 212; sends money to VB;
at Paris peace negotiations 221;
writes The Economic Consequences
of the Peace 221; hosts famous
dinner party 221; in Italy with
DG and VB 226–30; DG
decorates his rooms 231–2; sends
hamper to DG in St-Tropez
238; writes London Group letter
239; and Lydia 240, 243–7;
gambles on a Liberal victory
261; his wedding 263; leases
Tilton 268; and LAA 268, 270,
299; and uneasy relations
between Tilton and Charleston
271–2, 282, 299; and Nation &
Athenaeum 290; angry with DG
and VB 317; and Bloomsbury
analysis 332; VB on 333;
distance between him and DG
334; settles annuity on DG 333,
351–2, 396; heart disease 354;
funds Euston Road School 357;
offers Quentin Bell a job 368; at
Angelica's 21st 370; and CEMA
390–1, 392; his feudal behaviour
392; death 396; and Holroyd's
Lytton Strachey 456–7, 458; DG
writes on 482; mentioned 83,
114, 118, 121, 141, 181, 184,
187, 197, 219, 253, 302, 314,
365, 391
The Economic Consequences of the Peace
221, 469
VB to 202, 204, 213, 215, 219, 227,
239–40, 245, 246, 276; Brooke to
119; DG to 76, 87, 92, 102, 103,
144, 352, 354, 355; Garnett to
205–6; Jane Harrison to 121; LS